Encyclopedia of Canadian Fishes

Limited edition

Number _____ of 2,000

Brian W. Coad has worked on fishes in the field and laboratory for over 25 years. He received his B.Sc. from the University of Manchester, England in 1970, his M.Sc. from the University of Waterloo, Ontario in 1972 and his Ph.D. from the University of Ottawa in 1975. He has led and participated in expeditions in Asia, Europe and North America, collecting fishes from both fresh and marine habitats. His current interests centre on the systematics and zoogeography of the freshwater fishes of Southwest Asia, in particular Iran, and the ecology and systematics of fishes from unusual environments. Dr. Coad works as a Research Scientist in the Canadian Museum of Nature, Ottawa and was the Curator of Fishes for the National Collection there. Formerly he was an Associate Professor in the Department of Biology at Shiraz University, Iran where he taught Ichthyology, Vertebrate Zoology and General Zoology. He serves on the editorial boards of two scientific societies. Dr. Coad has published over 160 popular and scientific works on fishes including the recent *Guide to the Marine Sport Fishes of Atlantic Canada and New England* from the University of Toronto Press and Canadian Museum of Nature.

Henry Waszczuk and **Italo Labignan**, founders of Canadian Sportfishing Productions Inc., are two of North America's foremost angling educators. Their work in television, books, magazines and seminars has promoted angling as a family outdoor activity, emphasizing sportsmanship and conservation of Canada's outstanding fishing resource.

Encyclopedia
of Canadian Fishes

Brian W. Coad

Brian W. Coad

with
Henry Waszczuk and Italo Labignan

© 1995, Canadian Museum of Nature and
           Canadian Sportfishing Productions Inc.
Printed in Singapore

ISBN 0-9692391-7-3

Canadian Cataloguing in Publication Data

Coad, Brian W.
           Encyclopedia of Canadian Fishes

Co-published by Canadian Museum of Nature.
Includes bibliographical references and index.
ISBN 0-9692391-7-3

        1. Fishes—Canada—Encyclopedias. I. Waszczuk, Henry, 1950- II. Labignan, Italo,
1955- III. Canadian Museum of Nature IV. Title.

QL626.C63 1995   597.0971   C95-900735-0

Publication assistance was provided by these sponsors:

BASF Canada Inc.

C A N A D I A N   M I S T   W H I S K Y
THE LARGEST SELLING RYE IN THE WORLD

DURACELL®

EXPORT "A" INC.

Ford Motor Company of Canada, Limited

Contents

Foreword

I am twice pleased for the opportunity to recommend the *Encyclopedia of Canadian Fishes* to readers here and abroad.

First, it is an important and valuable addition to world literature concerning fish species and the sport of angling. Aquatic resources, both freshwater and marine, provide considerable enjoyment for Canadians and visitors, as well as opportunities to create wealth and work.

Second, it is a model of partnership between private sector and government.

This alliance has spawned an information product of a quality that neither could have managed alone. Dr. Coad and the Canadian Museum of Nature ensured that the Encyclopedia is comprehensive and scientifically exact. Messrs. Waszczuk and Labignan contributed vivid and colourful illustrations that they assembled while producing the Canadian Sportfishing series, as well as statistics on record catches and information on contemporary angling techniques.

Both explicitly in its text, and implicitly in its vivid depictions of aquatic life, the *Encyclopedia* delivers a powerful message of support for species conservation and habitat preservation. This is more imperative than ever as we learn more about the limits of exploitation and the need for renewal.

The *Encyclopedia of Canadian Fishes* will be of value to researchers and to sportsmen.

It looks to me to be that publishing rarity, an instant classic.

Brian Tobin
Minister of Fisheries and Oceans
Canada

Introduction

by Henry Waszczuk and Italo Labignan

Humans have always had an affinity with water. After all, water sustains our planet's life, and throughout the ages it has been associated with rejuvenation, refreshment, peacefulness and life. In addition, water provides the opportunity for myriad recreational activities enjoyed throughout the world. In our opinion, the earth's waters are the single most important global resource, and as Canadians, we can be proud of having over a million freshwater lakes, rivers, and streams within our boundaries and three oceans on our borders.

Canada is the second largest country in the world, encompassing nearly 10 million square kilometres. The coastline is 243,816 kilometres long, over six times around the world or over half way to the moon. Our inland waters comprise about 16 percent of the world's fresh water — more than 755,000 square kilometres in surface area. They range in size from Lake Superior, the largest freshwater lake in the world, to innumerable bogs and marshes. Our rivers range from many thousands of unnamed streams to such monarchs as the Mackenzie which flows for 4,240 kilometres.

The sport fishing available in Canada varies from the well-known and eagerly sought sport and food fishes to rare, deep-sea fishes only likely to be seen by scientists using special equipment. These descriptions of Canada's fishes reflect our current state of knowledge and each species' relative importance to us. Familiar sport fish have longer accounts in this book because more is known and interest is greater. However, the rarer, and often unusual, species also warrant inclusion, both for general interest and for the lack of other readily available informa-

tion on them. It will soon become apparent to any reader that very few species have been well studied and many aspects of their biology remain to be discovered.

Fishes are an important part of the Canadian economy. The commercial fishing industry is worth $4 billion and 120,000 jobs (1989 figures). The Atlantic fisheries accounted for about 85 percent of the annual catch of almost 1.6 million tonnes and about 70 percent of the market value. British Columbia takes up much of the rest. Canada has been the world's leading exporter of fish since 1978.

Sport fishing is a major recreational activity and attraction for tourists and is an industry in its own right. Only about 75 species are of primary importance to anglers, but those fish are pursued by over 6.5 million anglers annually, and an estimated 330 million fish are caught. In 1990 anglers spent almost $2.9 billion on goods and services directly related to fishing and over $5.3 billion for boats, motors, camping gear and other goods.

Consider our freshwater species. Canada's southern ranges hold enough warm water to sustain thriving populations of largemouth and smallmouth bass, walleye, pike, muskie, and a generous mix of warm water coarse fish and panfish. The central and northern ranges of our country support the world's largest populations of char, which include the Arctic char, the lake trout, the Dolly Varden, and the brook trout. These same waters contain large populations of important forage fish in the form of freshwater herring and many whitefish species. On top of all these, there are numerous species of minnows and other fish that have been introduced from other parts of the world, such as the common carp and the majestic brown trout. And that's just a quick overview!

In western Canada, the cold waters of the Pacific have intermixed with the rocky coastal shorelines to create a unique environment that sustains both a diversity of ocean mammals and a multitude of Pacific fish species and aquatic organisms including the world's largest Pacific salmon populations. In Canada's frigid Arctic Ocean, fish and organisms flourish in a delicate ecosystem that is found predominantly under a polar ice cap. In eastern Canada, the rich waters of the Atlantic Ocean have harboured some of the world's largest commercial fish stocks near the Grand Banks of the ocean's floor, not to mention a diversity of other fish species and North America's most prolific lobster grounds.

We have traveled the world and experienced sportfishing in over 12 countries. From our perspective, Canada has the greatest fishery by far. Canada not only has plentiful gamefish species, but a volume of other species as well. Given this magnitude and the vastness of Canadian waters, we are pleased to work with the Canadian Museum

of Nature in producing Canada's most comprehensive book on fish, the *Encyclopedia of Canadian Fishes.*

Dr. Brian Coad of the Canadian Museum of Nature has provided detailed information on over 1,150 fish species, each supported by an illustration. We are proud to add a sportfishing flavour to this authoritative book. When you read about some of Canada's popular gamefish, panfish, and coarse fish, you will find our recommendations on:

• the best time of year to catch each species
   • the best spots
   • the best tackle and equipment
   • the best bait.

Many "exotic" saltwater gamefish species are detailed in this book that have been captured from time to time in our coastal waters, but because these are "rare" catches we have not included sportfishing information on them.

Most importantly, as you read and learn about Canada's resident fish, we hope you will gain a greater respect for the vastness, the diversity, and the value of this resource. Enjoy fishing as it should be, and, as always, conserve our waters.

Using the Encyclopedia

A. *Layout*

The Encyclopedia is alphabetical by common name and every fish species, fish family and fish order reported from Canada is listed. Fishes in Canada have a standard common name given in Don E. McAllister's "A List of the Fishes of Canada / Liste des poissons du Canada" (1990) which is followed here with a few additions and modifications.

Each account follows a standard format described below:

Common name

This is the heading for each account. Common names are used for species, for families and for other groups of fishes which combine species of similar appearance or relationship. Common names are more accessible than scientific names, which often require specialist knowledge.

For example, under the letter "A" there are distinct species listed as **abyssal skate, abyssal snailfish, Acadian redfish, Acadian whitefish**, and so on. However all skates are related and form a family of fishes which share characters and biology. It would be redundant to repeat these features for every skate, and so they are dealt with under the heading **Skate Family.** There is also a **Snailfish Family.** The family account lists all the species found in Canada but each species account is found in its alphabetical place. Redfishes and whitefishes, however, do not form families of their own but are only parts of larger families containing fishes with a variety of names. A reader may know a fish as a "whitefish" but not know its full common name. The heading **whitefishes** will lead to the family which includes white-

fishes and to all the species in the family. A general index also serves to locate information by other common, scientific and French common names.

This arrangement is necessary because some fish names are popular and have been applied to a number of unrelated species. The term "bass" is a good (or rather bad!) example. There is a **Sea Bass Family,** a **Temperate Ocean Bass Family** and a **Temperate Bass Family** and several species called bass related to none of these. Those fish familiar to anglers, the **smallmouth bass** and the **largemouth bass** are actually members of the **Sunfish Family**! Here then the heading **basses** serves to direct the reader to a number of headings to find out about all those fishes afflicted with the name bass. Occasionally, the same name has been given or used for more than one species. The **yellow walleye**, *Stizostedion vitreum,* a member of the **Perch Family**, is often called a pickerel by anglers yet pickerel is more accurately used for members of the unrelated and very distinctive **Pike Family**. And of course the blue pike is not a pike, but a relative of the **yellow walleye**! Account headings in the plural, such as **whitefishes** and **basses,** are an indication that the term is neither a unique species of fish nor a family of fishes.

Scientific name

This heading gives the scientific name. If you know only the scientific name of a species, its account can be found by using the index.

Common names, as must be evident from the above comments, do not always indicate relationships and quite unrelated fish can have similar names. Scientific names and the classification system that goes with them do indicate relationships of fishes. But a scientific classification of fishes is not static and names change. Many fishes are poorly studied and much remains to be learned. New knowledge is continually being published and the classification system modified. For this book, we have followed the overall classification used by Nelson (1994) and the names used by McAllister (1990) and by Robins et al. (1991) with some minor changes and additions. These works should be consulted by any serious students of the scientific names of fishes.

The scientific name is unique to a single species and is used the world over, even in languages with different characters like Russian and Japanese. The scientific name comprises two words, the first of which is the genus (plural genera) and the second the species or trivial name. The genus is always spelt with a capital first letter, the species name with a lower case first letter and the name should be printed in italics or underlined. Thus, *Salmo salar* is the scientific name of the **Atlantic salmon**. The **brown trout**, *Salmo trutta*, is a close relative of the **Atlantic salmon** and is placed in the same genus *Salmo,* but this is uniquely combined with the trivial name *trutta* to show that we are dealing with a fish which is distinct anatomically and does not normally interbreed with other, related species. Other members of the **Salmon Family** are more distantly related to the Atlantic salmon and some are placed, for example, in a distinct genus *Coregonus* which includes **whitefishes** and **ciscoes**. The scientific name is followed by the name of the person who first described it scientifically, and the year of the published description; hence *Salmo salar* Linnaeus, 1758. When the describer and date are in parentheses, this species was originally described in another genus, but it has since been re-classified.

Family name

Related fishes are grouped together into families. Once the family name of a species is known, reference may be made to the family account where general information can be found and where all the relatives of a species are listed. All scientific family names end in -idae.

Other common names

Some fishes have more than one name and this section includes the more common ones. The index should be used if a fish name cannot be located in its alphabetical place in the text.

French name

The French common name from McAllister (1990) is listed under this heading.

Distribution

This section summarises the distribution of each family or species in Canada and elsewhere.

Characters

Characters describe the fish's appearance, its colour and its size. Family descriptions will contain anatomical information found in all the species, e.g. all **Bullhead Catfish Family** members lack scales and have barbels, and this is not repeated under each species.

A detailed description of a fish's characters can run to several pages. The characters listed here are selected to distinguish between related species and to emphasise features not obvious in the illustration such as internal structures and structures which show a range of variation like scale and fin ray counts. The family account may also give a summary of characters used in distinguishing species.

A brief series of characters may serve to distinguish between species in a family but some families have numerous species and their distinguishing characters are too many or too subtle and complex to summarise in a few lines.

Identification of fishes depends on a number of characters which must be taken into account. Distribution is often useful, eliminating many species and even families of fishes from consideration. The position, size, number and shape of fins are often one of the more obvious clues to identity. Many of the lower fishes (**soft-rayed fishes**) have no spines in their fins while the higher fishes (**spiny-rayed fishes**) do. The number of rays in the fins may be used with counts separated into spines and soft rays or into unbranched and branched rays. Scales may be absent or present, on the body but not the head or on both, extending onto fins, and of a particular kind — cycloid (smooth and often easily detached), ctenoid (with tiny teeth on their edge and often firmly attached), or placoid (rough as in **sharks**). The size of scales is often critically important in identification and this is usually presented as scale counts along the side of the body or in other configurations. Counts of scales and fin rays are given as ranges, but the extremes at each end of the range are seldom encountered. The head may have barbels around the mouth in particular patterns, cirri (fleshy flaps of skin) and spines in various arrangements. The body may carry photophores (light emitting organs) arranged in complex and unique patterns. Colour and colour patterns may be distinctive with spots, blotches, bars (vertical), stripes (horizontal), vermiculations (worm tracks), reticulations, ocelli (spots resembling an eye with a contrasting ring of colour around the central spot), and so on. Colour however is often variable within a species and young, males and females may be quite different. Individuals may change colour to match their environment, when spawning or in reaction to some stimulus such as fright.

Many very useful characters are internal and require dissection to examine. Others are small and require a microscope to see clearly. Yet others are relative (how large is a large mouth?) and require experience to assess properly. Such body proportions may be expressed as proportions; head length in standard length or eye diameter in head length. Fish lengths may be given as total length (from snout tip to the end of the spread tail), standard length (to the end of the vertebral column, the tail flexure), or fork length (to the centre of the fork in the tail fin). And finally some fish are most easily identified by what they are not, i.e. they have no obvious, unique, external characters by which they can be recognised but are defined mostly on internal characters.

Nevertheless Canadian fishes can be identified with care and patience. This Encyclopedia can serve as an introduction to their diversity in characters and most species could be identified from the descriptions given. Here the illustrations are a major help but for really accurate identification of unusual, rare or difficult species the reader should refer to the technical books listed in the Bibliography or, if they prefer the fish can be preserved or frozen and sent for identification to a local museum or to :

Canadian Museum of Nature,
P.O. Box 3443, Station D,
Ottawa, Ontario K1P 6P4

Biology

This section deals with a variety of topics including habitat, food, predators, behaviour, reproduction, age and growth, economic importance, and so on. The availability of this information varies greatly between species, some being exceptionally well-known with several books written on them while virtually nothing is known about other species.

B. Sources

A book of this kind depends on the wealth of information built up over centuries and recorded in the scientific literature. Canada is fortunate to have several synoptic works on the fish faunas of the Pacific and Atlantic coasts and of fresh waters. We have also used the extensive files of the Ichthyology Section in the Canadian Museum of Nature which comprise over 30,000 reprints of scientific articles, many books and computer data bases. Last, and most importantly, we have examined specimens of most of the species of fish found in Canada and preserved in the Canadian Museum of Nature and in other museums in North America and Europe. This preserved material, the scientific collections, is an invaluable data base accessible for many studies on biology, ecology, environment, biodiversity, zoogeography, systematics and taxonomy and is a permanent record of the fishes of Canada.

C. Classification

Classification places **fishes** and their relatives in a hierarchical scheme, each level of which has a name and a series of shared characters. The **vertebrates** (having vertebrae and a skull) are divided into four "Classes," one each for amphibians, reptiles, birds and mammals, but also includes "fishes" (and their relatives) which alone encompass another five classes (four in Canada). "Fishes" are therefore a very diverse group. Within each class are "Orders" which comprise a set of related "Families." Some classes, like the Myxini or **hagfishes,** have only a single family while the **ray-finned fishes** has 435 families world-wide and are by far the most numerous and diverse of the **fishes.**

Below are two tables covering the scientific classification of Canadian fishes. The first table is a partial scientific classification to show the hierarchical arrangement and relationships of the higher groups and the second table is a simplified list of all the classes, orders and families. All words in bold have entries under them in the body of the Encyclopedia.

The classification is arranged in order of relationships roughly from the most "primitive" to the most "advanced." This progression does not imply that some fishes are better than others — **sharks** are early in the list but are a very successful group. An evolutionary tree cannot be accurately represented by a linear arrangement, the arrangement is continually being changed as more research reveals new relationships, and even the same set of facts may be interpreted differently.

Table 1.
Higher, Scientific Classification of Canadian Fishes

Phylum Chordata (**chordates**)
  Subphylum Vertebrata (**vertebrates**)

i) Superclass Agnatha (**jawless fishes**)
  1. Class Myxini (**hagfishes**)
  2. Class Cephalaspidomorphi (**lampreys**)
ii) Superclass Gnathostomata (**jawed fishes**)
  3. Class Chondrichthyes (**cartilaginous fishes**)
    Subclass Holocephali (**chimaeras**)
    Subclass Elasmobranchii (**sharks and rays**)
  4. Class Actinopterygii (**ray-finned fishes**)
    Subclass Chondrostei (**sturgeons and paddlefishes**)
    Subclass Neopterygii (**gars, bowfins, and true bony fishes**)
      Division Teleostei (**true bony fishes**)
        Subdivision Osteoglossomorpha (**bony tongues**)
        Subdivision Elopomorpha (**tarpons, bonefishes, eels, gulper eels**)
        Subdivision Clupeomorpha (**herrings**)
        Subdivision Euteleostei (the rest: **Carps** and below in Table 2.)

Table 2.
Classes, Orders and Families of Canadian Fishes

The figure after each class, order and family is the number of species.
1. CLASS MYXINI (**hagfishes**) (3)
  1. Order Myxiniformes (**hagfishes**) (3)
    1. Family Myxinidae (**hagfishes**)......3
2. CLASS CEPHALASPIDOMORPHI (**lampreys**) (11)
  2. Order Petromyzontiformes (**lampreys**) (11)
    2. Family Petromyzontidae (**lampreys**) 11
3. CLASS CHONDRICHTHYES

	Canada	World	Canada/ World percent
Classes	4	5	80
Orders	46	55	84
Families	199	482	41
Species	1150	>24,618	4.7

D. Introduced Species

The exotic species listed in Table 3 have been introduced to Canadian waters by accident or design. Those marked with an asterisk (*) do not have accounts in this book since they have not established reproducing populations or were recorded for Canada after this book was being completed. They are, for the most part, tropical fishes requiring warmer conditions than exist in Canada. The remaining species do have accounts as they are well established; recent immigrants reported more than once and probably capable of establishing themselves; exotic species already established in U.S. waters adjacent to Canada; are continually being stocked or farmed; or are tropical species established in a hot spring.

Many native Canadian fishes have been moved within the country and reference to these introductions may be found in the species accounts.

Table 3.
Exotic Species in Canada

A. **Gar Family** (Lepisosteidae)
1. Florida gar * / ? / *Lepisosteus platyrhincus* DeKay, 1842 / Ontario

B. **Carp Family** (Cyprinidae)
1. bitterling * / bouvière / *Rhodeus sericeus* (Pallas, 1776) / Ontario
2. **common carp** / carpe / *Cyprinus carpio* Linnaeus, 1758 / Across Canada
3. **goldfish** / cyprin doré / *Carassius auratus* (Linnaeus, 1758) / Across Canada
4. **grass carp** / carpe de roseau / *Ctenopharyngodon idella* (Valenciennes in Cuvier and Valenciennes, 1844) / Alberta; Ontario
5. **rudd** / gardon rouge / *Scardinius ery-*

throphthalmus (Linnaeus, 1758) / Ontario
6. **tench** / tanche / *Tinca tinca* (Linnaeus, 1758) / British Columbia; Alberta

C. Characin Family * (Characidae)
1. pacu * / ? / *Colossoma bidens* (Spix in Agassiz, 1829) / Ontario

D. Suckermouth Catfish Family * (Loricariidae)
1. royal panaque * / ? / *Panaque nigrolineatus* (Peters, 1877) / Ontario

E. **Mudminnow Family** (Umbridae)
1. Alaska blackfish * / dallia / *Dallia pectoralis* Bean, 1880 / Ontario

F. **Salmon Family** (Salmonidae)
1. **brown trout** / truite brune / *Salmo trutta* Linnaeus, 1758 / Across Canada
2. cherry salmon * / ? / *Oncorhynchus masou* (Brevoort, 1856) / Ontario
3. **golden trout** / truite dorée / *Oncorhynchus aguabonito* (Jordan, 1892) / Alberta; British Columbia
4. houting * / lavaret / *Coregonus lavaretus* (Linnaeus, 1758) / Québec
5. huchen * / huchon / *Hucho hucho* (Linnaeus, 1758) / Québec

G. **Livebearer Family** (Poeciliidae)
1. green swordtail * / queue d'épée / *Xiphophorus helleri* Heckel, 1848 / Alberta
2. guppy * / queue de voile / *Poecilia reticulata* Peters, 1859 / Alberta
3. **mosquitofish** / gambusie / *Gambusia affinis* (Baird and Girard, 1853) / Alberta
4. **sailfin molly** / molliénésie à voilure / *Poecilia latipinna* (Le Sueur, 1821) / Alberta

H. **Perch Family** (Percidae)
1. **ruffe** / grémille / *Gymnocephalus cernuus* (Linnaeus, 1758) / Ontario

I. **Cichlid Family** (Cichlidae)
1. convict cichlid * / cichlide à bande noire / *Cichlasoma nigrofasciatum* (Günther, 1867) / Alberta
2. freshwater angelfish * / scalaire / *Pterophyllum scalare* (Lichtenstein, 1823) /

Alberta

3. jaguar guapote * / ? / *Cichlasoma managuense* (Günther, 1867) / Ontario

4. **jewelfish** / cichlide à deux taches / *Hemichromis bimaculatus* Gill, 1862 / Alberta

5. oscar * / astronotus / *Astronotus ocellatus* (Agassiz, 1831) / Ontario

J. **Goby Family** (Gobiidae)

1. **tubenose goby** / gobie à nez tubulaire / *Proterorhinus marmoratus* (Pallas, 1814) / Ontario

2. *round goby* * / gobie arrondie /

Neogobius melanostomus (Pallas, 1811) / Ontario

K. Gourami Family (Anabantidae)

1. Siamese fightingfish * / combattant / *Betta splendens* Regan, 1909 / Alberta

2. threespot gourami * / gourami bleu / *Trichogaster trichopterus* (Pallas, 1770) / Alberta

L. Righteye Flounder Family (Pleuronectidae)

1. **European flounder** / flet d'Europe / *Platichthys flesus* (Linnaeus, 1758) / Ontario

Fish Structures

The anatomy of fishes can be quite complex. The accompanying illustrations give some details of structures used in identifying and describing Canadian fishes. Scientists have worked out a system of abbreviations for certain characters, like the photophores, to simplify their description.

External structures of a shark

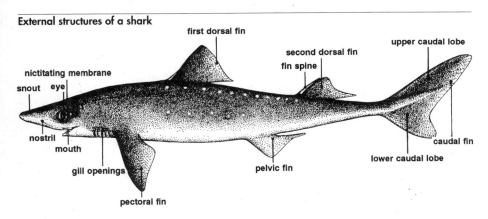

Internal anatomy of a shark

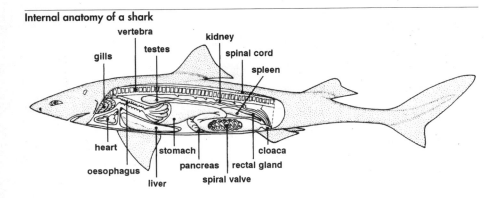

External structure of a skate

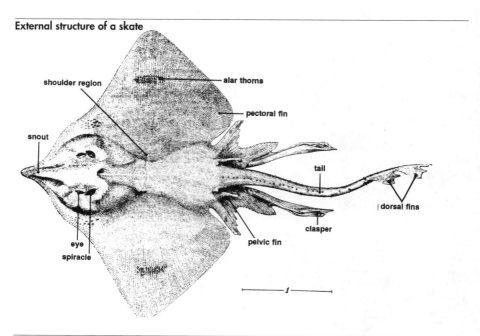

shoulder region

alar thorns

pectoral fin

snout

tail

eye

spiracle

clasper

pelvic fin

dorsal fins

1

Skate ventral view

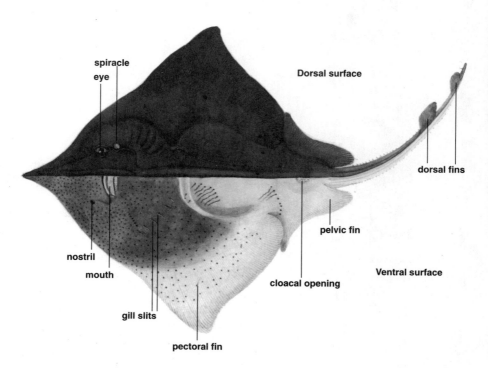

spiracle

eye

Dorsal surface

dorsal fins

pelvic fin

nostril

mouth

Ventral surface

gill slits

cloacal opening

pectoral fin

External structures of a soft-rayed bony fish

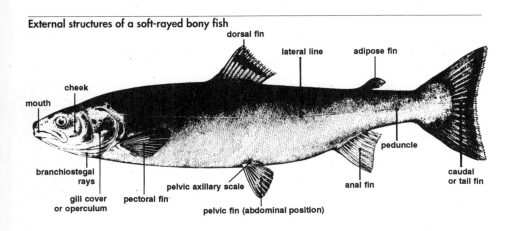

dorsal fin

lateral line

adipose fin

mouth

cheek

peduncle

branchiostegal rays

caudal or tail fin

gill cover or operculum

pectoral fin

pelvic axillary scale

anal fin

pelvic fin (abdominal position)

External structures of a spiny-rayed bony fish

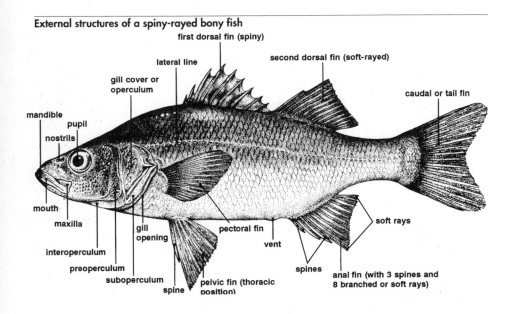

first dorsal fin (spiny)

lateral line

second dorsal fin (soft-rayed)

gill cover or operculum

caudal or tail fin

mandible

pupil

nostrils

mouth

maxilla

gill opening

pectoral fin

soft rays

interoperculum

vent

preoperculum

suboperculum

spines

spine

pelvic fin (thoracic position)

anal fin (with 3 spines and 8 branched or soft rays)

Internal anatomy of a bony fish

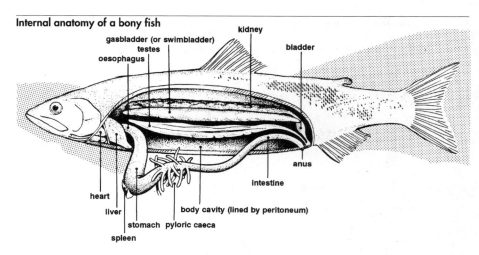

Skeleton of a bony fish

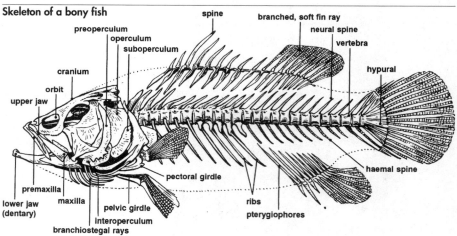

Skull of a bony fish

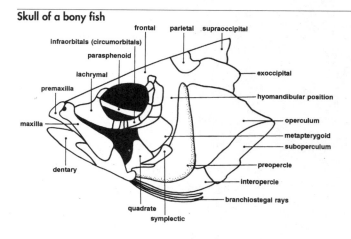

Cross section through a bony fish

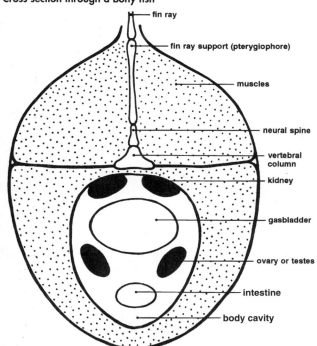

fin ray

fin ray support (pterygiophore)

muscles

neural spine

vertebral column

kidney

gasbladder

ovary or testes

intestine

body cavity

Gill of a bony fish

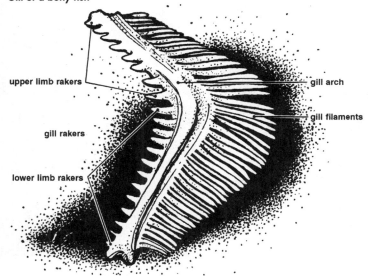

upper limb rakers

gill arch

gill filaments

gill rakers

lower limb rakers

Mouth of a bony fish

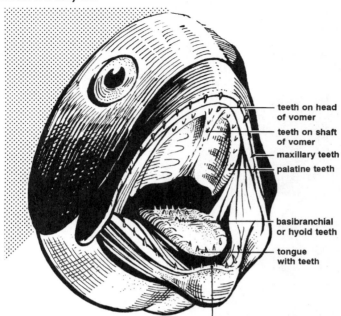

teeth on head
of vomer

teeth on shaft
of vomer

maxillary teeth

palatine teeth

basibranchial
or hyoid teeth

tongue
with teeth

lower jaw or mandible with teeth

Herring otoliths

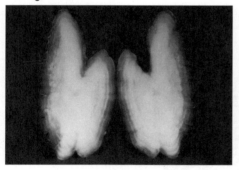

Cycloid scale   Ctenoid scale   Placoid scale

Bristlemouth Family

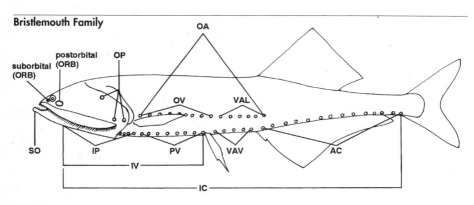

Lanternfish Family

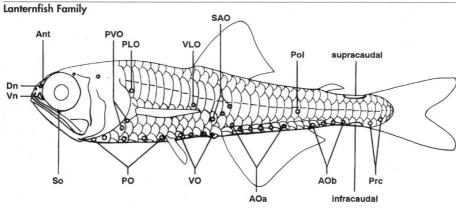

Lamprey Family

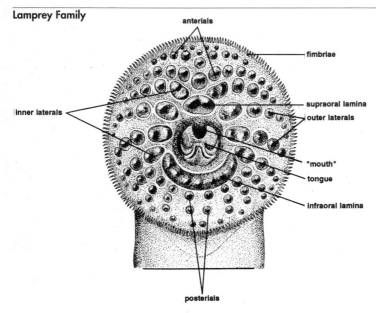

Silver Hatchetfish Family

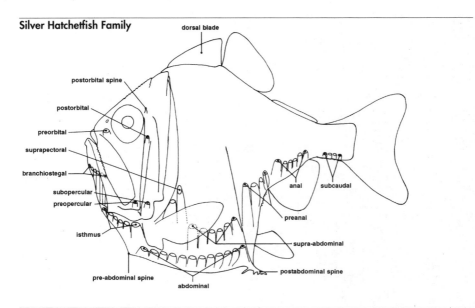

Scorpionfish Family

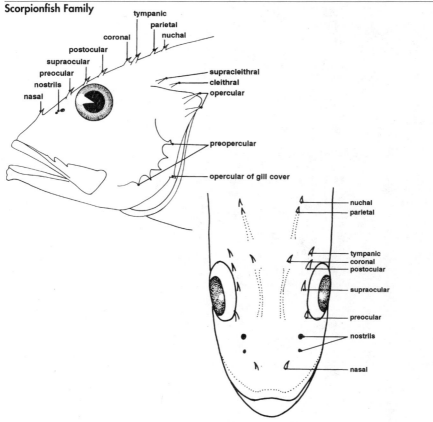

A

abyssal skate

Scientific name: *Bathyraja abyssicola*
  (Gilbert, 1895)
Family: **Skate**
Other common names: deepsea skate, raie de
  profondeur
French name: raie abyssale

Distribution: Found from Japan to Baja
California including British Columbia.

Characters: This species is separated
from its Canadian Pacific relatives by having
a soft and flabby snout with its cartilaginous

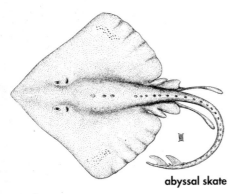

abyssal skate

support thin and flexible, cartilaginous supports of the pectoral fins almost reaching the
snout tip, no scapular thorns (large shoulder
spines) but 3–5 nuchal thorns present, and
underside of disc and tail covered with prickles. There are 1–5 median nuchal thorns separated from 21–33 median tail thorns. Males
have stout alar thorns in 24–26 longitudinal
and 7 transverse rows. There are 27–36 parallel rows of pointed, recurved teeth in the
upper jaw. The upper and lower disc surfaces
are light to dark brown with small, faint dots.
Nuchal and tail thorns are creamy against the
brown body in preserved fish. The anterior
margins of the spiracles are whitish. The
underside of the tail is dark. The mouth,
cloaca, anterior gill slit and nostril margins,
and clasper tips are whitish. Reaches 1.35 m.

Biology: This species is the deepest of
any skate with a range of 362–2903 m, the
depth record being off the Queen Charlotte

Islands. Males are mature at about 110 cm. It
is rarely caught.

abyssal snailfish

Scientific name: *Careproctus ovigerum*
  (Gilbert, 1895)
Family: **Snailfish**
Other common names: abyssal liparid
French name: limace de profondeur

Distribution: Found from British Columbia
to Oregon.

Characters: This snailfish is distinguished
from its Canadian Pacific relatives by having
a fleshy adhesive disc with its posterior margin anterior to the level of the gill opening, a
single nostril, dorsal fin rays 43–46, and
16–19 pyloric caeca. Anal fin rays 34–37,
pectoral rays 31–34 with a lower lobe of 4–6
rays, and caudal fin rays 11. Teeth are simple
and in broad bands. The adhesive disc is very
large. The gill slit extends from above the
pectoral fin downward to about the eighth
pectoral fin ray. Body colour is pale pink
with some light brown mottling. Fin margins
are black. Gill and mouth cavities are pale.
The peritoneum is black or mottled, the stomach pale. Reaches 43.1 cm standard length.

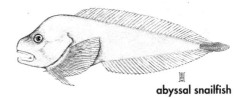

abyssal snailfish

Biology: Capture depths are in the range
2510–2904 m from the Queen Charlotte
Islands southward. This species was first discovered and described from a British
Columbia specimen. Food is probably caught
by a sudden dart. Eggs are very large, over
7.7 mm in diameter, yet number an estimated
756. Spawning may occur at long intervals.
A male was caught with eggs in his mouth,
and this was assumed to be parental care —
but it is now thought that the male may have
been eating them.

academy eel

Scientific name: *Apterichtus ansp*
(Böhlke, 1968)
Family: **Snake Eel**
Other common names: none
French names: serpenton de l'Académie

Distribution: Found in the Caribbean Sea and the Bahamas and on the Atlantic coast of Canada.

Characters: The species is named for the *Academy of Natural Sciences Philadelphia.* Larvae have 127–136 myomeres (muscle

academy eel

blocks) with a strongly looped gut with up to 9 strongly pigmented loops or peaks, dorsal fin restricted to the tail tip and 3 spots below the tail midline. It lacks fins as an adult. The tail is longer than the head and body. There are 123–131 readily visible lateral line pores. Eyes are very small. The supratemporal canal has 4–6, usually 5, distinct pores. The body is pale and there may be a pale band across the head behind the eyes and along the lower jaw. Larvae are 45–50 mm long in Canada. Adults attain 54 cm.

Biology: Known only as stray larvae (or leptocephali) in Canadian waters taken at 128–200 m. Adults burrow in sand in surfy regions, and in water depths to 38 m.

Acadian redfish

Scientific name: *Sebastes fasciatus*
Storer, 1854
Family: **Scorpionfish**
Other common names: Labrador redfish, rosefish, ocean perch, redfish, beaked redfish, sharp-beaked redfish
French name: sébaste d'Acadie

Distribution: Found only in the western North Atlantic Ocean from the Labrador Shelf south to the Gulf of Maine and perhaps Virginia. Found rarely off Iceland and Greenland.

Characters: This species is distinguished from other Atlantic coast scorpionfishes by having 14 dorsal fin spines, and from its clos-

est relatives, the **deepwater** and **golden redfishes** by a combination of overlapping characters, some of which are internal and require dissection to see. Easily misidentified. This is a less robust redfish with a larger eye than the **golden redfish**. Anal fin soft rays 6–8, usually 7 or fewer. Total vertebrae 29–31, usually 30. The knob at the tip of the chin is long and sharp. A key internal character is the muscles attaching to the gas bladder. In this species there are 1 or 2 muscle heads with tendons passing mostly between ribs 3 and 4, more rarely (5%) between ribs 4 and 5, the muscle is narrow and the posterior tendon has 3 branches attached to vertebrae 8, 9 and 10. Larvae have 26–42 ventral row melanophores. Overall colour is orange-red with green-black blotches on the upper flank and side of head and green, iridescent markings. The pelvic and anal fins are a deep red. Reaches 45.7 cm and 1.36 kg but usually up to 30 cm.

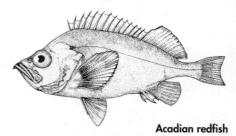

Acadian redfish

Biology: A shallower water species than its two relatives and found further south. This is the most numerous of the redfish species on Georges Bank and in the Bay of Fundy. It is found as shallow as a few metres and as deep as 592 m. The biology of redfishes has not yet been fully worked out because of the difficulties in separating the species. Food is crustaceans and, when larger, fishes which are taken at night when this redfish rises in the water column to capture pelagic prey. This is a slow-growing and long-lived species reaching about 20 years of age. Acadian redfish populations have half the individuals mature at 18.5 cm for males and 29.5 cm for females. Spawning occurs in March–July. About 15–20,000 live young are produced. An important commercial species making up the bulk of the catch in the Georges Bank-Gulf of

Maine area. The commercial fishery is a recent development with a maximum catch of 389,000 tonnes in 1959. Catches since then have been less as quotas were imposed to prevent overfishing. In 1979 the catch was worth 15.5 million dollars and weighed 81,587 tonnes. All three redfish species are managed as a single unit and often appear on the market, fresh or frozen, as "ocean perch."

Acadian whitefish

Scientific name: *Coregonus huntsmani*
  Scott, 1987
Family: **Salmon**
Other common names: Atlantic whitefish,
  Sault whitefish
French name: corégone d'Acadie

Distribution: Known only from the Tusket River system, including the Annis River, from Hebb, Milipsigate, and Minamkeak lakes in the Petite Rivière system and in the sea at Yarmouth Harbour, Hall's Harbour and off Wedgeport, Nova Scotia.

Characters: This member of the **Salmon Family** is distinguished from its relatives by having large scales (110 or less), no parr marks, teeth absent from the jaws and roof of the mouth, forked tail fin, 2 flaps of skin between the nostrils, the mouth is almost at the tip of the head, premaxilla bone of the upper jaw curves backward, the adjacent maxilla bone is two times or more longer

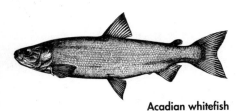

Acadian whitefish

than wide, lower fins are clear but sometimes with dark spots, gill rakers 23–29, 64–67 vertebrae, and lateral line scales 88–100. The adipose fin is smaller than in **lake whitefish**, the pelvic axillary process is longer, and the adipose fin to caudal fin distance is shorter. Dorsal fin rays 10–12, anal rays 9–12, pectoral rays 15–16 and pelvic rays 11–12. Small teeth are present on the jaws, tongue and roof of the mouth. Nuptial tubercles in males are

present on the flank scales and top and sides of the head. The back is dark blue to dark green, flanks are silvery and the belly silvery-white. The dorsal and caudal fins are dusky. Reaches 50.8 cm and 3.63 kg.

Biology: Reported from marine and fresh waters, the Petite Rivière fishes being land-locked and the others anadromous. In lakes it is found down to 11 m. The Tusket River population was anadromous with a spawning run in September–November before dams blocked its migration. Marine specimens contained amphipods, periwinkle snails, worms and **Atlantic herring**. Freshwater food includes aquatic insects. There was a minor sport fishery up to the early 1950s on the Tusket River and at Yarmouth and Wedgeport but poaching, overfishing on the spawning run, incidental catches in the **gaspereau** fishery, pollution such as acid rain, and ineffective fish ladders connected with dam construction leading to turbine blade mortality, have decimated this species. It was reputed to be a tasty fish. These fish were caught on a baited hook or a fly and would leap once hooked. This fish appeared on a Canadian postage stamp in 1983 as an endangered species, a status given in that year by the Committee on the Status of Endangered Wildlife in Canada. It is probably doomed to become extinct.

Adolf's eelpout

Scientific name: *Lycodes adolfi*
  Nielsen and Fosså, 1993
Family: **Eelpout**
Other common names: none
French name: lycode d'Adolf

Distribution: Found off east and west Greenland and the Davis Strait.

Characters: This species differs from all other Atlantic members of the genus *Lycodes* by the absence of scales on the front half of the body (completely absent in young) and by the pointed posterior tip to the gill cover. There is 1 lateral line running near the anal fin posteriorly, preanal length is less than 45% standard length, there are 25–30 scale rows between the dorsal and anal fins, no distinctive colour pattern and body depth at the anus is less than 10% standard length. Dorsal fin rays 90–99. The lower jaw has a well-developed crest and there are no distinct head pores. All gill rakers are knob-like. Overall colour is light brown with fins and head darker. The peritoneum is blackish-brown.

Adolf's eelpout

Biology: Recently discovered and described from the Davis Strait about half way between Baffin Island and Greenland, this species may well occur in Canadian waters. It is reported from depths of 527–1380 m at –0.4 to 3.7°C. Food is crustaceans. Spawning probably occurs in summer and eggs are about 2 mm in diameter.

Agassiz' cusk-eel

Scientific name: *Monomitopus agassizi*
   (Goode and Bean, 1896)
Family: **Cusk-eel**
Other common names: none
French name: donzelle d'Agassiz

Distribution: Found in the Atlantic Ocean including off Atlantic Canada.
Characters: This species is characterised by an elongate body, 2–3 spines at the lower corner of the preoperculum and a strong

Agassiz' cusk-eel

operculum spine, an eye about equal to snout length, and a single, central basibranchial tooth patch. The mouth is large. The lateral line is indistinct. Overall colour is brownish. Maximum size unknown.
Biology: First reported for Canada in 1988 from the upper continental slope off Nova Scotia between 790 and 797 m. A poorly known species.

Alaska eelpout

Scientific name: *Bothrocara pusillum*
   (Bean, 1890)
Family: **Eelpout**

Other common names: none
French name: lycode à oeil ovale

Distribution: From the eastern Bering Sea to southern British Columbia.
Characters: This species is separated from its Canadian Pacific relatives by lacking pelvic fins, having a large gill opening, minute scales

Alaska eelpout

present, eyes oval, no lateral line and eye diameter greater than snout length. There are no nape scales. The flesh is delicate and transparent, especially in the head region. Dorsal fin rays 108–116, anal rays 95–102, and pectoral rays 14–17. Overall colour is light brown with dorsal and anal fin margins black. Attains 15.5 cm standard length.
Biology: Reported off southern Vancouver Island at 2189 m and in Gardiner Inlet at 425 m, elsewhere depth range is 221–2189 m.

Alaskan lamprey

Scientific name: *Lampetra alaskense*
   (Vladykov and Kott, 1978)
Family: **Lamprey**
Other common names: darktail lamprey
French name: lamproie d'Alaska

Distribution: Found in Alaska and the Mackenzie River basin of the Northwest Territories.
Characters: Trunk myomeres number 66–72. There are 2 cusps on the bar above the mouth, 3 bicuspid teeth on each side of

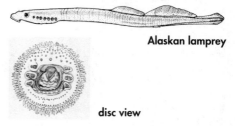

Alaskan lamprey

disc view

the mouth and 6–11 cusps on the bar below the mouth. This species is distinguished from other Canadian lampreys by its distribution, small size, small disc, weak dentition and non-functional gut. Preserved adults are grey-brown with a white belly. The first dorsal fin is unpigmented but the second dorsal fin has an anterior, dark blotch. The tail is dark. Attains 18.8 cm.

Biology: This is a non-parasitic species found in fresh water. Its biology has been little studied. Spawning in Alaska occurs in May–July at temperatures above 12°C. Egg numbers are 2200–3500 with a maximum diameter of 0.9 mm. A nest is built by both sexes in the shallows of lakes and rivers. Each nest is 15–25 cm in diameter and up to 7.6 cm deep. Nests have 5–6 spawners at a time. Ammocoetes transform to adults at about 4 years of age in the fall and move downstream into lakes to overwinter. The Committee on the Status of Endangered Wildlife in Canada considered in 1990 that there was insufficient scientific information on which to base a status designation for this species.

albacore

Scientific name: *Thunnus alalunga*
 (Bonnaterre, 1788)
Family: **Mackerel**
Other common names: long-finned tuna
French name: germon

Distribution: Found world-wide in warmer waters entering those off British Columbia and Alaska and off Nova Scotia.

Characters: This species is separated from its relatives on both coasts by the extremely long pectoral fins which extend beyond the second dorsal fin. Greatest body depth is below or slightly ahead of the second dorsal fin. The ventral surface of the liver is striated. First dorsal fin spines 12–14, second dorsal fin with 2 spines and 13–16 rays followed by 7–9 finlets. Anal fin with 2 spines and 12–13 rays followed by 7–9 finlets. Pectoral rays 31–36. Cycloid scales on body but corselet weakly developed. Gill rakers 25–31. The back is metallic blue to brown or bronze and the flank silvery. There is an iridescent bluish lateral stripe. The first dorsal fin is a deep yellow, the second dorsal and anal fins are light yellow and anal finlets are dark or silvery. The caudal fin has a narrow white edge. Reaches 1.5 m and 43 kg. The world, all-tackle angling record is a 40 kg specimen caught at the

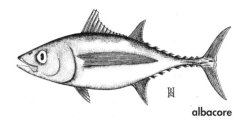

albacore

Canary Islands in 1977. "Albacore" is derived from an Arabic word for tuna.

Biology: This is an offshore tuna found swimming in surface to deeper waters in schools at a temperature range of 12.2–25.2°C, with excursions into water as cold as 9.5°C. Up to 90% of Pacific coast albacore are in water at 15.6–19.4°C. Schools may be associated with floating weed or debris. It is a summer visitor to Canadian waters. There is a northward migration along the Pacific coast with recorded speeds of 11 km/day with spurts to 24 km/day off Oregon when cold upwellings cause them to move rapidly offshore. There are northern and southern stocks in both the Atlantic and Pacific oceans each having distinct spawning areas and seasons. Albacore may descend to 600 m. Food includes **herrings, anchovies, sauries, lanternfishes, rockfishes,** squid and euphausiid crustaceans. They are eaten by **marlins**. Maturity is attained at 94 cm fork length in both sexes in the Atlantic and at 90 cm for females and 97 cm for males in the Pacific Ocean. Life span is up to 10 years. Spawning takes place in January–June between Hawaii and Japan. Up to 3 million, reddish-brown eggs are released in at least 2 batches. Anglers catch 230,000 albacore annually in a June-September fishing season on the U.S. Pacific coast. Commercial catches are made by longlines, trolling and purse seining. Albacore are caught by British Columbia fishermen sporadically in Canadian waters and more regularly off Washington and Oregon. As much as 1010 tonnes in 1949 has been caught by fishermen based in British Columbia. The total Canadian catch in 1988 was 47 tonnes. The main fisheries for this species are in the Pacific Ocean by Japanese fleets although some are taken in the Atlantic Ocean. Albacore are frozen for canning or eaten fresh. It is "white meat tuna" while other species are "light meat." The world catch has been declining from a peak of about 245,000 tonnes in 1974. It is possibly the most important tuna commercially.

Alfonsino Family

Scientific name: Berycidae
French name: béryx

Alfonsinos are deepwater marine fishes of the Atlantic, Pacific and Indian oceans. There are about 9 species with 2 reported from Canada's Atlantic coast.

They are relatives of the **Slimehead**, **Spinyfin** and **Ogrefish** families which, with other families not found in Canada, form a group of fishes (**Alfonsino Order**) intermediate between "lower" fishes with few or no spines in their fins and the "higher" fishes which are typically spiny-rayed. Alfonsinos resemble higher fishes in possession of spines and ctenoid scales but the pelvic fin is thoracic to abdominal and has more than 5 soft rays. The head and body have strong, rough scales and there are obvious ridges bearing spines on the head. The soft rays of the dorsal, anal and pelvic fins may be elongated, particularly in smaller specimens. The dorsal fin lacks a notch and has 4–7 spines increasing in length posteriorly.

They are found at depths of about 200–700 m near the bottom, occasionally in shallower water.

Little is known of the biology of alfonsinos but they are excellent food fish, appearing on markets in Madeira and Japan.

See **narrowside alfonsin**
wideside alfonsin

Alfonsino Order

Alfonsinos, pinecones, lanterneyes, flashlight fishes, squirrelfishes, soldierfishes, fangtooths, **spinyfins, ogrefishes, slimeheads** or roughies and their relatives (or Beryciformes) comprise 7 families and about 123 species mostly in shallow warmer seas but also in the deep sea. In Canada there are 4 families with 6 species on the Atlantic coast.

This order is characterised by varying body forms, usually with large heads, and varying sizes usually less than 30 cm, fin spines usually well-developed, 16–17 branched caudal fin rays, usually more than 5 soft rays in the abdominal or thoracic pelvic fins, ctenoid scales, 2 supramaxillae present in some, spines on various parts of the body in some species, a swimbladder connected to the gut in some species but usually ductless, the orbitosphenoid skull bone is present, subocular shelf present, unpaired, procurrent caudal fin spines, 3 epural bones and a low crest on the second preural vertebra in the tail skeleton, the nasal bone turns laterally at its anterior part to contact the lachrymal and has a unique innervation, and in particular mucous cavities on the head are well-developed in varying degrees among the families.

The **flabby whalefish, redmouth whalefish, ridgehead** and **whalefish** families now in the **Pricklefish Order** were once placed here. The Alfonsino Order is often regarded as one representing the stock which gave rise to the vast diversity of species in the **Perch Order**. The order has a mix of characters found in both higher and lower fishes. Spines and ctenoid scales are characteristic of higher fishes while the orbitosphenoid bone is lost. The relationships and placement of families within the order remain uncertain. Alfonsinos may be related to the **Dory Order** based on the shape of the otoliths or "ear-stones." Fossil records date back to the Cretaceous period, 120 million years ago.

See **Alfonsino Family**
Ogrefish Family
Slimehead Family
Spinyfin Family

American brook lamprey

Scientific name: *Lampetra lamotteni*
(Le Sueur, 1827)
Family: **Lamprey**
Other common names: brook lamprey, small black brook lamprey
French name: lamproie de l'est

Distribution: Found from the Great Lakes basin of Ontario to the Upper St. Lawrence River basin in Québec and south to Virginia, Tennessee and Missouri.

Characters: Trunk myomeres number 63–74. The bar below the mouth has 6–10 cusps. This species is distinguished from other Canadian lampreys by having 2 dorsal fins, the bar above the mouth with 2–3 pointed cusps, teeth along each side of the mouth bicuspid and pointed, and by distribution. Adults are blue-grey when spawning with

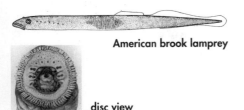

American brook lamprey

disc view

orange tinges on the head, back, tail and fins. Otherwise brown is the overall colour, the belly is white to light grey and fins are yellowish. Ammocoetes are pale brown. Often called *Lampetra appendix* (DeKay, 1842), the correct name may be *Lampetra wilderi* Gage, 1896. Attains 31.7 cm (perhaps 35 cm) but these were "giants" which may have fed parasitically. Usually up to about 21.7 cm.

Biology: This is a non-parasitic species found in cooler (9–12°C) small streams and rivers than the **northern brook lamprey**. At Ottawa in the large Ottawa River it is found unusually in sandy areas at 13–25°C. It does not migrate. Spawning occurs in mid-May to early June in Québec at 17°C. In Delaware spawning occurs in March–April at 6.8–12.0°C and in Ontario in April–May. Nests up to 30 cm long are built. The male begins construction and the oval to circular nests are in gravel between larger rocks. Up to 25 lampreys may spawn in one nest with 5 times as many males present as females. Up to 5185 pale yellow to light green eggs about 1.2 mm in diameter are produced by each female. Ammocoetes live 5–6 years (perhaps 7.5 years) and transformation begins in the fall and over winter. Ammocoetes have been sold as bait for sport fish in Québec.

American eel

Scientific name: *Anguilla rostrata*
(Le Sueur, 1817)
Family: **Freshwater Eel**
Other common names: common eel, Atlantic eel, Boston eel, snakefish, silver, yellow-bellied, bronze, black or green eel, anguille argentée

French name: anguille d'Amérique

Distribution: Found in the western North Atlantic from central Labrador south to Brazil. Also in freshwater drainages of the Mississippi and Great Lakes basins, the Hudson Bay drainage of Alberta and Saskatchewan (by introduction) and throughout Maritime Canada.

Characters: The American eel is distinguished by its shape, by having 103–112 vertebrae (110–119 in the European eel), larger size than the European eel and a 1 year span of life as a leptocephalus larva versus 3 years in the European eel. The dorsal fin has about 60 rays. Branchiostegal rays 8–14. The lower jaw projects and the mouth extends to the rear, or beyond, of the eye. The larvae are transparent, the transformed elvers or glass eels are also transparent (with black eyes) but soon become grey-green to black while freshwater adults are overall yellow, greenish, muddy or olive-brown with a dark back, sometimes yellow, green, orange or pink flank tinges and a creamy or yellowish-white belly. Such adults are called yellow eels. Adults migrating to the sea have a bronze to black back, a metallic sheen and a light to silvery belly. They are then known as silver, bronze or black eels. Colour will also change gradually to match the substrate. Reaches 1.5 m and 7.5 kg in females and 50.3 cm in males. The world, all-tackle angling record weighed 3.88 kg and was caught at Cliff Pond, Massachusetts in 1992.

American eel

Biology: Eels are found in mud-bottomed rivers, streams and lakes. They can be seen looped over weeds in rivers but are usually nocturnal and lie buried in mud during the day. In winter they bury themselves in mud and are torpid. They can travel overland to reach isolated water bodies, using snake-like movements when the ground is wet. Elvers can climb short vertical, wet walls such as those at canal locks. The Moses-Saunders Hydroelectric Power Dam on the St. Lawrence River at Cornwall was a barrier to young eels migrating into Lake Ontario. An eel ladder (a trough and baffle system with rest pools crisscrossing an ice chute through the dam) was built and over 3 million eels used it in 4 years. There is some evidence of a homing ability to their river of origin if they are displaced. In Lake Ainslie, Nova Scotia, eels have been observed in clumps or eel balls of up to 30 fish found on the bottom or even breaking the surface. Eels can be heard making chirping or sucking noises in warm summer weather on Cape Breton Island.

Life span is at least 43 years. Males mature at about 28–30 cm and females at 46 cm. Females grow larger than males, as much as twice the length.

In the sea larvae eat plankton but in freshwater food is any bottom invertebrates, frogs and fishes. Smaller eels favour insects but large eels eat fish and crayfish. In New Brunswick eels are important predators of **Atlantic salmon** in nets or traps. Elvers are cannibals. A wide variety of fishes and birds eat eels at various life stages.

Silver eels in Newfoundland migrate to sea at age 9–18 years. They leave Nova Scotian waters in late August to mid-November. Adults in Passamaquoddy Bay, N.B. are active by day and night in contrast to freshwater eels, and made frequent surface to bottom dives perhaps to sample geoelectric fields as orientation cues for migration. Spawning in the Sargasso Sea is believed to occur from February to July but has not been observed. Egg numbers have been estimated as up to 20 million per female but the number released is guesswork as none have been found. The adults take 2–3 months to reach the Sargasso. The Sargasso spawning grounds of the American eel are to the southwest of the European eel grounds although there is evidence for a more southern spawning ground.

Leptocephali take 1 (perhaps more) year to drift to Canadian shores and transformation to a young eel or elver occurs at 60–65 mm during winter while drifting to or in nearshore waters. Glass eels near Saint John's, Newfoundland have been observed about 2 m below the surface drifting heads up and tails down. This may be done as camouflage from predators which swim horizontally, to counteract sinking, to escape vertically from predators

and to facilitate vertical migration. The elvers enter estuaries in April and are 65–90 mm long. They are found in coastal rivers from May to July. The run lasts from a few days to several weeks depending on the river. In the northern Gulf of St. Lawrence young eels only move upstream in their second summer of stream residence. Temperature may be a factor in successful elver arrival. Males tend to stay near the coast in estuaries while females move up rivers sometimes as much as thousands of kilometres. All 356 eels sexed in Lake Champlain were female for example. Males also appear to be much rarer than females in northern waters. Males may have this distribution to ensure rapid maturation and return to the spawning ground. They do not need to be large to produce adequate amounts of sperm and estuaries are good feeding areas. Females require a delayed maturation as a larger body size results in more eggs. Cold northern and inland waters favour this.

There are different stocks of eels in Canadian waters. Lake Ontario eels can be distinguished from those in St. Lawrence River tributaries and the Maritimes by the presence of mirex, a chemical used in insecticides. Pollutants are now a convenient method for stock identification but a sad reflection on the state of the environment. Eels in Québec are heavily contaminated with PCBs. Eels can be a nuisance to fishermen as they eat other fish caught in nets. They are used in physiological and other studies in laboratories and are easy to keep, surviving without food for up to 22 months.

Adult eels are caught in Canada for export, particularly along the Gulf of St. Lawrence, using weirs, baited setlines, and pots, fyke nets, eel traps and hoop nets. Some are speared during winter when they are buried in mud. The catch in Lake Ontario reached 221,940 kg in 1978 and the total Quebec fishery for the same year was 527.9 tonnes and for the Maritimes about 320 tonnes. The total Canadian catch in 1988 was 1016 tonnes, worth about $2.3 million. Increased fishing pressure in Lake Ontario resulted in a decrease in average eel size. Elvers have been caught in Canada for raising in ponds in the U.S.A. and the Far East.

Efforts to start such aquaculture in Canada have not met with extensive success but are potentially viable. Eels are exported live, on ice, or frozen. Live eels are used in making jellied eels which are popular in England. Smoked eel is an important, tasty and highly priced product. Eels should be cleaned with care as the blood has a neurotoxin which can affect humans but is destroyed in cooking.

Most accessible from early June to the end of July.

- St. Lawrence River and the Great Lakes.
- Medium action spinning and baitcasting outfits used with 12– to 20–pound test monofilament.
- Worms and pieces of cut, dead bait such as **smelt, (= gaspereau)** and **minnows** fished on the bottom.

American shad

Scientific name: *Alosa sapidissima*
(Wilson, 1811)
Family: **Herring**
Other common names: shad, Atlantic shad, white shad, common shad, gatte
French name: alose savoureuse

Distribution: Found on the Atlantic coast of Canada from northern Labrador and the Gulf of St. Lawrence south to Florida. Enters coastal rivers and streams but does not penetrate further inland than the lower Ottawa River and formerly Lake Ontario. Introduced to the Sacramento River on the Pacific coast in 1871 and first caught near Vancouver Island in 1876. Now found from Kamchatka to Baja California.

Characters: This species is distinguished from its Pacific coast relatives by having enlarged scales on the caudal fin, a row or rows of 4 or more dark spots on the upper flank, and a strong keel of enlarged scales (or scutes) on the belly. In Atlantic drainage freshwaters it is separated from related species by having fewer than 26 anal fin rays, the last dorsal fin ray the shortest, more than 56 lower arch gill rakers and 4 or more flank spots. In marine waters on the Atlantic coast it is separated from related species by the sharp, saw-toothed scutes on the belly, rounded and crenulate exposed scale mar-

gins, high gill raker count and the lower jaw fitting into a notch in the upper jaw. Dorsal fin rays 15–20, anal rays 17–25, pectoral rays 14–18 and pelvic rays 9. Scales along flank 50–64, lateral line not apparent. Gill rakers 56–76. Pre-pelvic scutes 18–24, post-pelvic scutes 12–19. The overall colour is silvery with lustrous blue to blue-green on the back, silvery sides and silvery to white belly. Fins are clear, light green or dusky and the caudal fin has a black margin. The spots number up to 28 with first the largest in the dorsal row. A second row of 1–16 spots and a third row of 2–9 spots are variably present. Peritoneum pale grey to silvery. Reaches 76.2 cm and 6.8 kg. The world, all-tackle angling record weighed 5.1 kg and was caught in 1986 in the Connecticut River, Massachusetts.

American shad

Biology: The biology of Pacific coast populations is not as well known as that of Atlantic populations on which this account is based. The American shad is anadromous and enters rivers in the tens of thousands to spawn in slow-flowing water each spring from May-June, sometimes into July. The migration is not as extensive as the **gaspereau** which ascends much further up rivers although American shad migrate 370 km up the St. Johns River in Florida. Timing of the migration and of spawning depends on temperature and so varies between rivers. Spawning begins at 12°C and peaks at 18.3°C. Most spawning occurs in the evening and at night but does continue throughout the day. Males arrive first on the spawning ground. Each female has several courting males and the fish disturb the water surface by their energetic movements. Eggs are shed and fertilised above the bottom in the evening and at night. They sink slowly and are carried downstream by the current before settling. Fertilised eggs are pink, amber or transparent, non-adhesive, have a diameter up to 3.5 mm, and number up to 659,000. The larvae drift downstream and by autumn have entered the sea.

Spent adults return to the sea but may return as many as 5 times to spawn in the same river in subsequent years. The proportion of repeat spawners is a particular river increases with latitude but fecundity decreases. Energy is put into migration in northern rivers rather than egg production to increase survival after spawning. This is an adaptation to the harsher conditions of Canadian rivers.

Most spawning fish are 4–5 years old and life span is 13 years. Many spawning runs have been blocked by dams or estuarine pollution. The St. John River, N.B. has a late summer and early fall "run" of shad after the spawning migration, probably strays from adjacent sea feeding grounds. Most of the life span is spent at sea but they remain close to the coast. There is a northward migration in spring to enter not only the river in which they were spawned, but even the particular tributary. Each Canadian river has its own stock therefore. The ocean migration rate is 21 km/ day. In October to November the shad move southward to winter off the U.S. coast. Migrations of up to 3800 km have been recorded. In the sea the fish are distributed where temperatures are about 13–18°C, usually in surface waters. Also recorded down to 221 m and at temperatures of 3–13°C. There is a vertical migration pattern which follows the movement of their plankton food. Food is various small crustaceans, insects and small fishes filtered from the water. Fish entering rivers to spawn do not feed extensively but resume feeding on the downstream migration.

Accurate catch statistics are not available as they are lumped together in reports with **gaspereau** and **blueback herring**. Anglers alone caught over 20 tonnes in the Annapolis River in 1981. The inner Bay of Fundy has had a shad fishery using weirs since 1750. Up to 100,000 shad can be caught on a single tide. They are mainly caught on the spawning run in gill nets, weirs, trap nets and scoop nets. Proposed tidal power projects in the inner Bay of Fundy would have a serious effect on the

shad. A large part of the total western Atlantic coast stock (Florida to Québec), numbering 35 million fish, may enter the Bay each summer. Habitat alterations, altered migratory routes and mortality during passage through turbines would severely deplete this species. The total Canadian catch in 1988 was 120 tonnes. This is a good game fish on a fly rod or lure and is excellent eating when smoked. Caviar can be made from the roe.

American straptail grenadier

Scientific name: *Ventrifossa occidentalis*
    Goode and Bean, 1885
Family: **Grenadier**
Other common names: western softhead
    grenadier, grenadier scie
French name: queue-de-rat d'Amérique

Distribution: Found in the Atlantic Ocean including from the Scotian Shelf south to Argentina in the western Atlantic Ocean.

Characters: This species is distinguished from its Canadian Atlantic coast relatives by having second dorsal fin rays shorter than

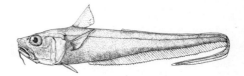

American straptail grenadier

anal rays, 7 branchiostegal rays, a large mouth which is only slightly inferior, and 8 pelvic fin rays without the first ray being elongated. The first dorsal fin has 2 spines and 11–14 rays, the pectoral fin 21–27 rays. Scales have small spines numbering about 20–40 per scale. The branchiostegal rays bear scales. Colour is a light brown to grey above, silvery below, with the abdominal area dark from the peritoneum being visible through the body wall. The upper and anterior edges of the snout, around the eye, lips and gular membrane are black. Reaches about 45 cm.

Biology: Reported from a single specimen off Banquereau Bank at 243 m in 1896. Its depth range is 150–585 m. Food is small crustaceans. It is taken in by-catches and used for fish meal and for oil.

Anchovy Family

Scientific name: Engraulidae
French name: anchois

Anchovies are found world-wide in warmer seas and occasionally in fresh water. There are about 139 species with 2 species on Canada's Atlantic coast and 1 on the Pacific coast.

Anchovies are small fishes which have a characteristic, pig-like snout protruding over the mouth and the upper jaw extending back to the rear of the head in most species. Teeth are present or absent, small or large. Gill rakers are usually short and not very numerous although in some species they are long and number over 100. A pelvic scute or modified scale with lateral arms is always present but a row of scutes before and behind the pelvic fin is present in most Indo-Pacific species and absent in New World species. Most anchovies have a blue-green back and silvery sides often with a silver flank stripe.

Anchovies are relatives of the **Herring Family** and share with the herrings the character of the lateral line canal system being restricted to the head. They are members of the **Herring Order.** "Anchovy" is derived from the Spanish for these fishes.

These fishes are feeders on zooplankton although some of the larger species eat fish. The mouth gapes at an angle greater than 90° when chasing food and the red gills can be seen as the gill covers flare out, giving the impression that the head is coming apart. The mouth is closed every few seconds and the food swallowed. Larger food items are caught by "biting" or "pecking" each individual prey but also these fishes can filter smaller food from the water. It is supposed that larger, and more nutritionally valuable, food items are fast enough to escape passive filter-feeding and the sudden seizure of larger items by a bite prevents their escape.

Anchovies are found in large schools in coastal waters but some live permanently in fresh water, such as the upper Amazon River. Anchovies produce large numbers of eggs which hatch into planktonic larvae. Larvae and adults are an important food for many other fishes in the ocean. The Peruvian anchoveta, a close relative of the **northern anchovy**, was the most heavily exploited fish in the world, with a catch exceeding 13 million tonnes in 1971, but with a great decline in catches since then. Millions of sea birds, along with dolphins, sea lions and numerous fish species, depend on this anchoveta for food. The decline in the fishery, because of overfishing, has severely affected the bird populations. The immense numbers of birds produced enough faeces to support a guano or fertiliser industry. The fish are caught at 8–10 cm standard length in immense schools. The 1971 catch must have numbered over 500 billion fish. These huge catches are usually made into fish meal. Other anchovies are sold fresh, canned or turned into paste. They are important bait fishes for sport fishermen.

See **northern anchovy**
silver anchovy
striped anchovy

Angel Shark Family

Scientific name: Squatinidae
French name: anges de mer

The angel sharks or sand devils are found in cool-temperate to tropical waters and comprise 13 species. Only one species is likely to occur in Canada on the coast of British Columbia where it has not yet been collected. This shark is known from southeast Alaska and California so it may eventually be caught in Canadian waters.

Angel sharks are easily recognised since they lack an anal fin and have a flattened body reminiscent of a skate or ray but with free anterior pectoral fin lobes where skates and rays have their pectoral fins united with the head. The mouth is at the tip of the head. Angel sharks are members of the **Angel Shark Order.**

Most angel sharks are small, less than 1.6 m in length and feed on small fishes, crustaceans, squids and molluscs using their strong protrusible jaws and sharp teeth to grab prey suddenly. They have been caught from the intertidal zone down to over 1300 m and often lie buried in sand or mud during the day, becoming active free-swimmers at night. They should be handled with care since they snap quickly when touched and these sharp teeth can inflict a nasty wound. Some species are heavily fished for food, oil and fish meal.

See **Pacific angel shark**

Angel Shark Order

Angel sharks and sand devils of the Order Squatiniformes comprise a single family with 13 species, 1 of which probably occurs along Canada's Pacific coast.

These **sharks** are recognised by the absence of an anal fin, the flattened body (= depressed), 2 dorsal fins without spines positioned on the tail, 5 gill slits mostly on each side of the head, and the terminal mouth. The anterior pectoral lobes are not attached to the body and the nostrils are just above the mouth, each with a barbel (unlike the superficially similar **rays**). The lower lobe of the caudal fin is longer than the upper. Spiracles are large.

Angel sharks are sometimes placed within the **Dogfish Shark Order**.

Biology is summarised in the family account.

See **Angel Shark Family**

anglefin whiff

Scientific name: *Citharichthys gymnorhinus*
Gutherz and Blackman, 1970
Family: **Lefteye Flounder**
Other common names: none
French name: plie carrelée

Distribution: Found from Nova Scotia south to the Caribbean Sea and Guyana.

Characters: This species is distinguished from its Canadian Atlantic adult relatives by having short pelvic fin bases with that of the eyed side being on the midline of the belly, no bony snout protuberance, no snout scales and 33–37 lateral line scales. The eyed side of the pelvic fin has 5 rays. Males have strong head spines, 2 on the snout and 1 on the chin in addition to large and small spines in front of the eyes. Dorsal fin rays 70–77, anal rays 51–61, blind side pectoral rays 5–7, usually 6, eyed side pectoral rays 8–11. Dorsal and anal fins are highest and sharply angled at midbody. Total gill rakers 15–20.

Scales are ctenoid on the eyed side, cycloid on the blind side. Larvae have 3 elongate, dorsal fin rays known as tentacles. Overall

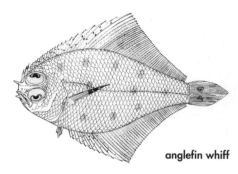

anglefin whiff

body colour on both sides in preserved fish is straw-coloured to brown, covered with small dark pigment spots in males but only on the eyed side in females. The body is also blotched dark in 2 rows of 4 following the dorsal and ventral body contours and faintly along the lateral line. The eyed-side pectoral fin has 4–5 bars. Both the dorsal and anal fins in males have a large black spot opposite the middle of the body. The caudal fin has 2 spots, one above the other on the upper half of the fin. Reaches 7.5 cm.

Biology: Known only from a stray larval specimen caught on Georges Bank in 1982. Adults only occur as far north as Florida and are at 35–201 m. Food is crustaceans. Females may mature at only 2.1 cm. Spawning is in spring to summer.

Anglerfish Order

Anglerfishes are marine and found worldwide usually in the deep sea from the tropics to temperate waters. Some are found drifting with floating seaweed and some are found inshore and are large enough to be used as food although most species are small. There are about 297 species in 16 families in the world and 34 of these in 12 families have been reported from Canada. They belong to the Order Lophiiformes.

Their name is derived from the fishing apparatus which is developed from the first ray of the spiny dorsal fin. The illicium or fishing rod has an esca or bait on the end and this is used to attract other fishes close enough to be gulped down by the anglerfish's mouth, which acts quickly to suck in the unsuspecting prey. This motion is so rapid as to be invisible to the naked eye. The bait may be luminous or have fleshy filaments to enhance its enticement qualities. Light is produced by luminescent bacteria in the esca. The pectoral fins may be modified to enable the fish to move slowly along the bottom. Anglerfishes are almost motionless and let their food come to them rather than actively seeking it. There are no scales but the body may carry small spines. The pelvic fins are often absent. Most have an ugly or threatening appearance to humans and so have received a variety of unusual names. Some species are only known from a few specimens.

In some species, the males are minute and parasitic on the female, serving only as a source of sperm and receiving all their nourishment directly from the blood supply of the female. The male becomes little more than a sperm-producer as many organs degenerate. Release of sperm is controlled by hormones in the blood of the female. One female may have several small males attached to her. Many more males are produced than females to increase the chances of at least one male finding a mate in the dark ocean depths. Should a male fail to locate a female, his thick gelatinous food layer stored while feeding as a larva is soon exhausted and he dies. While this curious arrangement is interesting it would seem to have little relevance to humans since these deepsea anglerfishes are only seen by scientists using special equipment. Nevertheless, since the male(s) becomes physically attached to the female this arrangement may be important in understanding tissue rejection in humans. Males of other species are also minute, compared to females, but are non-parasitic. They do attach to the female by means of pincer-like denticular teeth, but there is no fusion of the blood supply.

The males locate the female in the vast and dark ocean depths by detecting a chemical known as a pheromone emitted by the female. Males have large olfactory organs. At close quarters, the shape of, and light pattern given out by, the esca may also be used in identification. There is only one recorded case

of a male attaching to a female of the wrong species, so this location system works well.

The differences in structure between males, females and larvae are so marked that they were often described as separate species.

Other characters of this order include a small, tube-shaped gill opening usually at, above or behind the pectoral fin base, 5–6 branchiostegal rays, 2–4 pectoral radials, no ribs, eggs produced in a mucous sheath, skin spiny or naked and often covered in fleshy outgrowths and pelvic fins when present with 1 spine and 4–5, usually 5, soft rays placed in front of the pectoral fins.

See **Batfish Family**
Dreamer Family
Fanfin Family
Footballfish Family
Frogfish Family
Goosefish Family
Leftvent Family
Sea Toad Family
Seadevil Family
Werewolf Family
Wolftrap Family
Whipnose Family

archer eelpout

Scientific name: *Lycodes sagittarius*
   McAllister, 1975
Family: **Eelpout**
Other common names: none
French name: lycode à arc

Distribution: Found at Cape Bathurst, N.W.T. and in the Kara Sea.

Characters: This species is separated from its Canadian Arctic-Atlantic relatives by having small pelvic fins, a mouth under the

archer eelpout

snout, no large nostril-like, pores around the mouth, crests on the chin, scales on the body and dorsal and anal fins, lateral line single and low on the anterior flank but midlateral above the anal fin, tail long (preanal length 37–43% total length), peritoneum sooty to black, pectoral fin rays 16–18, and 20–27 scales across the body at anal fin origin level. Dorsal fin rays 95–107, anal rays 81–92, and vertebrae 96–109. Overall colour a grey-brown or dark brown, sometimes uniform but in Canada usually with 7–9 oblique light bars on the dorsal fin and upper back. Bars extend below the midflank in young fish. Scales are lighter than the background. Mouth and gill cavities dusky. Reaches 27.8 cm.

Biology: Depth range is 335–600 m on mud and clay bottoms at temperatures below 0°C. Food is worms, clams, snails and crustaceans. Spawning is probably in late summer or early autumn.

Arctic alligatorfish

Scientific name: *Aspidophoroides olriki*
  Lütken, 1876
Family: **Poacher**
Other common names: armed bullhead,
  Arctic sea poacher
French name: poisson-alligator arctique

Distribution: Found from the Alaskan border along the Arctic coast to Hudson Bay and Baffin Island to Labrador. Also off northern Europe and Alaska.

Characters: This alligatorfish is 1 of 3 species in the Canadian Atlantic and Arctic oceans. It is distinguished from its relatives the **Atlantic alligatorfish** and the **Atlantic poacher** by having a stout body with 1 dorsal fin, 1 pair of barbels at the corner of the

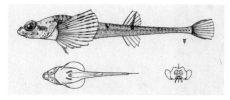

Arctic alligatorfish

mouth, and 33–40 plates in the dorsal row. The dorsal and anal fins both have 5–7 soft rays. The pectoral fin has 14–15 rays, without finger-like modification of the lower rays although lower membranes are more incised than upper membranes. There is 1 cirrus at the rear of the upper jaw. Gill membranes are not joined to the isthmus. The dorsal part of the body is dark grey, brownish-grey, or greenish and the flanks have several vague bars. The operculum, pectoral fin and caudal fin have a dark spot. There is a bar from the eye running back and downwards. Males develop milky-white areas on the dorsal and anal fins. Attains 8.6 cm total length.

Biology: Found on the bottom over sand, mud or rock at 15–400 m, sometimes down to 520 m. They live in temperatures below 3°C. Food is often small crustaceans and worms. A major food item in the Canadian Arctic was found to be siphons of the clam, *Macoma calcarea*, nipped off as they protrude. Up to 260 eggs of 1.7 diameter are laid and sink to the bottom. Little else is known of the biology.

Arctic char

Scientific name: *Salvelinus alpinus*
  (Linnaeus, 1758)
Family: **Salmon**
Other common names: alpine char, silver
  char, Hearne's salmon, sea trout,
  Coppermine River salmon, European
  char, Hudson Bay salmon, mountain char,
  Arctic salmon, blueback trout, Greenland
  char, Québec red trout, ekaluk, ilkalupik,
  kaloarpok, ivatarak, iloraq, aniaq, nutidi-
  lik, and many others
French name: omble chevalier

Distribution: Found around the Northern Hemisphere including the Arctic coast and islands of Canada, Labrador, and northern Québec, Newfoundland, the Québec north shore and in lakes of southwestern Québec and New Brunswick. Introduced to Alberta. Also in lakes of Maine and New Hampshire in North America.

Characters: This species is characterised by having small scales (123–152 in the lateral line), few major anal fin rays (8–11, total 11–15), teeth only on the anterior or head end of the vomer bone in the roof of the mouth, a truncate or square-cut caudal fin, and colour pattern. Teeth are present on the jaws, tongue and the palatine and basibranchial bones. Major dorsal fin rays 10–12 (total 12–16), pectoral rays 14–16 and pelvic rays 9–11. Pyloric caeca 20–75, upper arch gill rakers 7–13, lower arch rakers 12–19. Males develop a kype or hooked lower jaw during spawning in anadromous populations. Anadromous males also develop a dorsal ridge anterior to the dorsal fin and enlarged teeth, characters not found or only poorly-developed in land-locked males.

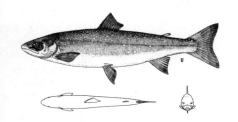

Arctic char

Colour varies between landlocked, migratory and spawning fish and between individuals by sex. However the pectoral, pelvic and anal fins have a white leading edge, followed by contrasting black and red bands, with the rest of these fins and other fins dusky. Generally non-spawners are an overall silvery colour. A spawning male has a brown, dark green to blue-green or steel blue back, flanks are silvery-blue with white to cream, orange to pink or red spots larger than the pupil and the belly is white or golden to a bright orange-red. Some populations lack spots while in others the spots have a blue halo. This bright spawning colour may be retained year-round in some freshwater populations. Residual males (non-migrating fish, part of an anadromous population) retain parr marks, have yellow flank spots and are nearly black dorsally. Isolated, stream-resident males are similar in colour to residual males. Young fish have 8–17 oval parr marks along the flank.

There is considerable variation in characters of Arctic char around the Northern Hemisphere and even within one lake. A lake may have a dwarf form with a large head and a pelagic form with a small head. In Matamek Lake, Québec there is a large, robust, red-bellied char and a thinner white-bellied char. There are also well-defined eastern and western Arctic char in the western Arctic, the former only in lakes and the latter with stream resident, anadromous and isolated populations. The species is known as the Arctic char

"complex" as an acknowledgement that more than one species or subspecies may exist. Landlocked forms in eastern North America are known as the blueback or Oquassa trout of Maine, Québec red trout or Marston trout and Sunapee or golden trout of Maine and New Hampshire and have been given scientific names (*oquassa*, *marstoni* and *aureolus* respectively). They are generally recognised now as relict Arctic char, descendants of an older, anadromous form of char which became landlocked and isolated from later char forms invading eastern North America. An alternative view is that char forms are the result of generalist or specialist life history styles, the former in perturbed environments and the latter in unperturbed environments. Quebec red trout have been introduced to Alberta. Natural hybrids with **lake trout** are reported from northern Labrador.

Reaches 101.6 cm and 16.0 kg. The world, all-tackle angling record from the Tree River, N.W.T. weighed 14.77 kg and was caught on 30 July 1981 by Jeffrey L. Ward. This catch is also recognized as the Canadian record.

Biology: This char is found in inshore marine waters migrating into coastal rivers and lakes and is also landlocked in lakes and in streams by impassable falls. Anadromous char enter the sea in spring (except when spawning) and return to fresh water in fall to overwinter. During a single summer at sea, char can travel 300 km or more while remaining close to shore, although many char stay close to river mouths. Some char, almost all males, are part of the anadromous population but mature in rivers and streams without migrating.

Arctic char are predators on various crustaceans, insects, snails, clams and fishes, feeding in both salt and fresh water on whatever is available. Amphipods are an important food when at sea near Baffin Island. In a Newfoundland lake **rainbow smelt** were the predominant food. Diet shifts occur depending on which, if any, fish species the char is sympatric with. They are cannibals and are eaten by some birds and seals.

Life span exceeds 40 years and growth varies between localities. Isolated stream resident fish seldom live longer than 10 years however. Landlocked fish tend to be smaller than sea run fish of the same age, as do northern compared to southern sea run fish. Anadromous char caught in the commercial fishery of Cambridge Bay and Rankin Inlet, N.W.T. are 5–25 years old and 38–85 cm fork length. Growth is more rapid in the sea where food is more abundant. In Candlestick Pond, Newfoundland landlocked char have slow growth, a short life span of 7 years, small size (to 16.4 cm fork length), maturity at age 3 and low fecundity (104 ova per fish maximum). Maturity can be attained at 1 year for landlocked females in Newfoundland but anadromous fish can mature as late as 10–25 years with ages in between for various populations. Tree River, N.W.T. char, for example, begin to mature at 8–9 years and all are mature by 11 years.

Spawning occurs in August to October in the far north or as late as December in southern Québec. Char which spawn do not migrate to the sea but may go downriver as far as estuaries. Females spawn only every 2–3 years in the north but may do so annually in the south. The absence of a sea migration in northern populations which spawn is a major energy drain and prevents fish from spawning 2 years in succession. In the central Canadian Arctic and Arctic islands spawning takes place in lakes as the rivers are completely frozen in winter. Females clear a nest area by turning on their sides and flapping the caudal fin on stream gravel or rocky lake shoals. Pair spawning takes place at about 4°C during the day. Males guard territories and may spawn with more than 1 female. The male circles the female on the redd, quivering as he passes along her flank. The female and male quiver and release the sex products during one of the passes by the male. The female undulates over the eggs to force them into the gravel and dislodges upstream gravel to cover the eggs but only after several spawning acts. A female may construct 10 or more redds but is eventually abandoned by the male when she is spawned out after 4 hours to 3 days. The male will court a new female. Eggs are up to 5.5 mm in diameter when deposited and number up to 9245. The eggs hatch at ice break-up in the following spring. Temperatures over 7.8°C will kill the eggs. Young char of

Frobisher Bay remain in streams or lakes until 5–7 years old when they migrate to the sea, elsewhere at 1–9 years.

Arctic char have long been used as food for humans and dogs in the north and are caught in nets, traps and by spearing. They are eaten fresh, smoked, salted or dried. The English char pie, weighing up to 28 kg, is now but a memory. The flesh is red, pink or white. Some char are shipped south as a delicacy for restaurants with red flesh being the most expensive. An export fishery for char in Labrador, dating back to 1860, produced over 200 tonnes a year valued at over $180,000. The 1988 Canadian catch was 88 tonnes valued at $486,000. The char are caught at sea or in estuaries using gill nets from July to September. There are also small Arctic fisheries, e.g. in the Cambridge Bay and Rankin Inlet area of the N.W.T.

There are some sport fisheries for this far northern fish but they are expensive because of the travel costs. The Tree River, N.W.T. trophy sport fishery produces 0.4 char/angler hour. The fishery showed a gradual decline because of high exploitation but limits on take and number of anglers were reflected in increasing size of catches. Possession and catch limit is 2 fish per angler, the annual quota is 700 fish and only 70 anglers a week are allowed. They are strong fighters and smaller fish may leap though large ones seldom do so. Char are caught on streamers, spoons and dry flies, which they may follow for long distances before striking. Char populations grow slowly and have a low fecundity so they can easily be fished out. However some char are now being farmed in fresh and salt waters.

Char are important research tools for biologists, being the only fish species present in some undisturbed northern lakes. They can be used to test conceptual models since the ecosystem is much less complex than the multi-species lakes of southern Canada.

• Most accessible in July and August.

• In freshwater rivers, September is best for coloured fish. The Arctic drainage system in both the Northwest Territories and Ungava Bay in northern Quebec.

- Medium action, seven-foot spinning rods and reels outfitted with 10– to 17–pound test line. Fly fishermen should use nine-and-a-half-foot, nine-weight fly rods loaded with 200– to 300–grain shooting tapers.

- For saltwater fishing, use bright flashy spoons between 1/4 and 1/2 ounce, and saltwater streamer fly patterns in hook size 2 to 2/0.

- For freshwater lakes and river fishing, use 1/4– to 3/8–ounce spoons in fluorescent colours, an assortment of spinners, jigs and a variety of steelhead flies, streamers and nymph patterns.

Arctic cisco

Scientific name: *Coregonus autumnalis*
(Pallas, 1776)
Family: **Salmon**
Other common names: salmon-herring, kaktak, kraaktak, kapisilik
French name: cisco arctique

Distribution: Found from Alaska to Queen Maud Gulf, N.W.T. and in Eurasia.

Characters: This species is distinguished from other **salmons** by having 82–111 lateral line scales, a strongly forked tail, no parr

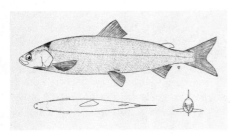

Arctic cisco

marks, 2 skin flaps between the nostrils, mouth terminal and 35–51 slender gill rakers. Characters among **ciscoes** (q.v.) overlap and so the species cannot be easily separated. Dorsal fin rays 9–12, anal rays 9–14 (12–14 major rays), pectoral rays 14–17 and pelvic rays 11–12. Males develop breeding tubercles on the flank scales. Overall colour is silvery with the back brown to light green.

Dorsal and caudal fins are dusky. Reaches 64 cm and up to 7 kg.

Biology: This cisco is widely distributed in coastal waters and river estuaries and it has a wide tolerance range for salinity and temperature. It spends more time in the sea than other **whitefishes**. All Arctic cisco from the Canadian and Alaskan Beaufort Sea coast are derived from spawning grounds in the Mackenzie River. Apparently cisco migrate westward from the Mackenzie along the coast to the Colville River of Alaska as young fish. There they stay for several years until mature when they return to the Mackenzie to spawn, moving through the delta as early as May and being abundant there throughout summer. The journey from the Colville to the Mackenzie River can take as little as 7 days under favourable wind and current conditions but usually takes 35 days at a speed of 10.5–17.2 km/day.

Food is crustaceans, and worms, clams, insect larvae, plant material, and small fishes such as **sculpins**. Life span is 21 years and fish mature at 5–10 years.

Spawning follows a migration up rivers from the sea or estuaries in spring or summer, sometimes for as far as 1000 km. Spawning takes place in August and September and is completed by early October. Spent fish move down to the delta. Spawners may stay close to the Mackenzie delta while non-spawners disperse farther. A group of cisco that disperses along the Beaufort coast from the Mackenzie Delta overwintering site is made up of juveniles, mature non-spawners and mature spawners. Eggs are shed over gravel in fast current in the fall and may number up to 90,000 per female with a diameter of 1.1 mm. Females do not spawn every year but there is repeat spawning. The young are believed to hatch in spring and descend to estuaries. Adults and juveniles overwinter in bays and lagoons at a salinity range of less than 1 to 20 parts per thousand.

Arctic cisco have been used by native people as human and dog food on the lower Mackenzie River. There is a small commercial fishery in Alaska. It is tasty when smoked since it is a fatty fish on the migration.

Arctic cod

Scientific name: *Boreogadus saida*
(Lepechin, 1774)
Family: **Cod**
Other common names: Arctic tomcod, polar
cod, ogaq, equaluaq, itok, ôgark, ovac
French name: saïda franc

Distribution: Circumpolar including
throughout Arctic Canada and south to the
Gulf of St. Lawrence and the Grand Bank in
Atlantic Canada.

Characters: This species is distinguished
from other Arctic-Atlantic **cods** by having 3
dorsal and 2 anal fins, lower jaw projecting,

Arctic cod

barbel small, anal fin origin below second dorsal fin, scales small, embedded and non-overlapping, sensory head canals poreless or with
few, very small pores, the lateral line not continuous before the second dorsal fin and wavy
behind the middle of this fin, caudal fin
forked, and palatine bones in the roof of the
mouth toothless. There are minute bony, spiny
plates on the side of the head, body and fins.
First dorsal fin rays 10–16, second dorsal rays
12–18, and third dorsal rays 16–24. First anal
rays 13–22 and second anal rays 17–24. Pectoral rays 18–21. Gill rakers 37–46. Overall
colour dark brown to black fading to silvery
below. The upper flank may have violet or yellowish tinges. The back and flank may have
dark spots. Fins are dusky to dark with a
lighter margin. Reaches 34 cm standard length.

Biology: Arctic cod are found near the surface and down to below 900 m offshore but
also entering river mouths. They are mostly
near the surface. Large schools are found in
ice-free water, a defensive measure against
predators. They are often caught under drifting ice, favouring ice with a rough undersurface where they concentrate in crevices.
Arctic cod are also found under landfast ice.
Fish taken offshore tended to be smaller than
those inshore at Pond Inlet. Arctic cod may

also be found under jellyfish in Resolute Bay.
Immense schools form and numbers fluctuate
with such environmental variables as temperature and plankton supplies. Their preferred
temperature range is 0 to 4°C.

Food is plankton taken pelagically. Large
Arctic cod are cannibals. They are an important food resource for **Atlantic salmon,
Arctic char, Atlantic cod, ogac, Greenland
halibut**, numerous sea birds, seals, whales,
polar bears and Arctic foxes.

In the Arctic this species lives 10 years and
off Labrador only 6 years but growth in the
south is faster. Off Newfoundland fish are
about 10–18 cm but in northern waters, such as
off northern Labrador, they are larger, 25–30
cm. Arctic cod is an r-selected species characterised by early maturity, rapid growth, larger
numbers of offspring at a given parental body
size, small body size, most young produced at
an early age, high mortality and short life
span. Such fish are best adapted to an environment liable to unpredictable, catastrophic
changes. It is of no advantage to invest reproduction in large, long-lived fish if adults are as
liable as young to sudden disaster. Large numbers of these cod have been observed cast onto
beaches after storms (which is when Arctic fox
and polar bears eat them).

Maturity is attained at 2–3 years for males
and 3 years for females. Spawning under ice
near the sea bed occurs from October to
March peaking in January to February in the
Arctic. Females produce up to 21,000 buoyant
eggs of 1.9 mm diameter.

This cod is not used as human food but its
abundance in the Arctic makes it a critical
component of the food chain there. Former
Soviet trawlers take this species off Labrador
in the capelin by-catch.

Arctic eelpout

Scientific name: *Lycodes reticulatus*
Reinhardt, 1835
Family: **Eelpout**
Other common names: sulupavak
French name: lycode arctique

Distribution: Almost circumpolar, across
the Canadian Arctic and south to the Grand
Bank and Gulf of St. Lawrence, and to
Massachusetts.

Characters: This species is separated from its Canadian Arctic-Atlantic relatives by having small pelvic fins, a mouth under the snout, no large pores around the mouth, crests on the chin, lateral line single and on midflank, tail short (preanal distance in the range 44–52% of total length), scales present as far forward as dorsal fin, pale peritoneum, gill opening not below the pectoral fin base, pectoral fin rays 19–21, vertebrae 93–96, and 7–10 bands on the body becoming reticulate in large fish. Dorsal fin rays 81–96, anal rays 71–78 (each including half of the continuous caudal fin rays). Colour varies with age and locality. Usually a brown background with bands darker. Reaches 76 cm.

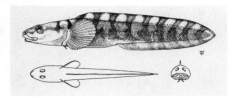

Arctic eelpout

Biology: Common in trawls in Atlantic Canadian waters at depths of 55–229 m and temperatures between –0.9 and 3.5°C. Also reported down to 750 m. Found at temperatures below 0°C in the Arctic. Food is assumed to be various bottom invertebrates. Bearded seals are known to eat this eelpout in Ungava.

Arctic flounder

Scientific name: *Pleuronectes glacialis* Pallas, 1776
Family: **Righteye Flounder**
Other common names: none
French name: plie arctique

Distribution: From the White Sea east to the Bering Sea and the Sea of Okhotsk. In Canada in the Beaufort Sea east to the Dease Strait, N.W.T. Distribution may well be circumpolar.

Characters: This Arctic species is characterised by a small, asymmetrical mouth and an almost straight lateral line. There is a distinct dorsal branch to the lateral line. Dorsal fin rays 48–62, anal rays 33–46, and pectoral rays 8–12. Gill rakers number 9–15 and lat-

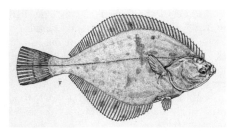

Arctic flounder

eral line scales 73–100. Eyed side dark brown or olive with dark spots which may form wide bands. Fins have small and large spots. Some specimens lack spots. Blind side white, rarely spotted. Attains 44 cm.

Biology: This species is found in shallow, mud-bottomed coastal waters and may enter rivers. Food includes clams, crustaceans, sea squirts and worms, and it is reported to bury itself in mud to ambush fishes. Arctic flounders are mature at 5 years for males and 8 years for females in the Beaufort Sea. Up to 200,000 eggs of 1.6 mm diameter are laid under ice in January–June at depths of 5–10 m. Life span is at least 26 years and females grow faster than males

Arctic grayling

Scientific name: *Thymallus arcticus* (Pallas, 1776)
Family: **Salmon**
Other common names:American grayling, bluefish, Back's grayling, arctic trout, sailfin arctic grayling, tittimeg, poisson bleu, tchulupa, kewlook powak, sulukpaugaq, sulukpauvak
French name: ombre arctique

Distribution: Found from Siberia south almost to North Korea and in all Alaska, Yukon, most of the N.W.T., northern British Columbia, Alberta, Saskatchewan and Manitoba. Also in the Flathead River of southeastern B.C. and the Belly River of southwestern Alberta adjacent to natural Montana populations. Formerly in Michigan rivers tributary to lakes Michigan, Huron and Superior. Introduced populations to rivers of northwestern Ontario did not survive but Saskatchewan introductions to lakes and Lac la Ronge apparently did survive. Also introduced in Utah, Colorado and Vermont.

Characters: This species is distinguished from other members of the **Salmon Family** by having 75–103 lateral line scales, a forked caudal fin and a long-based dorsal fin (longer than the head) with 14–25 total rays. Gill rakers 14–23 and pyloric caeca 13–21. Anal fin rays 10–15, pectoral rays 14–16 and pelvic rays 10–11. Males have a very large dorsal fin reaching back to or beyond the adipose fin when pressed flat against the body. Pelvic fins are also longer in males than in females.

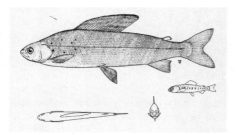

Arctic grayling

Nuptial tubercles are found on the scales at the rear of the body. In males they are placed anteriorly on each scale and are knob-like. In females they are diffuse and cover most of the scale. Tubercles on the posterior part of the body help to maintain contact during mating. In females the tubercles extend ventrally to protect the belly against abrasion and to maintain contact with the substrate during spawning. The back is dark or light blue, or dark purple to mauve, the flanks are dark blue or green-grey to grey and the belly is grey or white. The flanks may be tinged with iridescent pink or violet-grey cast and have small, blue-black spots concentrated anteriorly but extending back beyond the pelvics in some fish. Flank scales are outlined in light brown. There is a dark, dusky or brown stripe running from the pectoral to the pelvic fins. The inner edge of the lower jaw has a black stripe. The eye is dark green to light brown or gold. The branchiostegal rays are black. The margin of the dorsal fin is mauve with a blue band below and rows of orange-red, mauve, or bright, dark green spots. The spots are largest and more elongate posteriorly. The background colour is blue to grey. Pelvic fins are black and have wavy mauve or orange stripes edged in black.

Other fins are dusky to bronze. Males are more brightly coloured than females. Young have 10–20 parr marks with 2–3 rows of black spots or broken lines above them. Grayling are reputed to smell like wild thyme when fresh. Reaches 76 cm. The world, all-tackle angling record weighed 2.69 kg and was caught in the Katseyedie River, N.W.T. on 16 August 1967 by Jeanne P. Branson. This catch is also recognized as the Canadian record.

Biology: Grayling prefer clear, cold rivers, streams and lake shallows. Food is insects, particularly terrestrial insects such as beetles, ants, bees, wasps, grasshoppers, etc. which fall on the water surface, and also aquatic insects, small fishes and fish eggs, crustaceans, molluscs and even lemmings, shrews and voles. They are cannibals.

Life span is about 22 years with maturity attained as early as 2–4 years. Most spawning fish are 5–9 years old. Longevity varies from population to population. Otoliths or earstones give a better reading of age than scales which are usually used, being more accessible, and are better than fin ray sections. Maximum scale age was 7 years as opposed to 12 years for otoliths in one study.

Spawning takes place primarily in small, gravelly streams just after ice break-up in May–July when lakes are still frozen over. Water temperatures are 5–10°C. Males defend territories, 2.5–3.0 m wide and 3.5–4.5 m long, with a threat display to other males using a raised dorsal fin, extended pelvic fins and gaping mouth. The black branchiostegal rays and heightened colour of the enlarged dorsal fin are readily apparent. Persistent intruders were nipped, shoved and chased off the territory. Such smaller cruising males can reduce the reproductive success of males who must expend energy to defend their territory. Rarely, homosexual spawning attempts have been observed. Females adopt a submissive display with a depressed dorsal fin and tail region and the body resting on the stream bed. Spawning takes place during the day particularly in mid-afternoon and evening. The male wraps his dorsal fin over the female, both sexes quiver and gape, the male places his caudal peduncle over the female's, the female arches downwards and the vent is pushed into the substrate and eggs and sperm are shed. Gaping is usually associated with release of eggs and sperm in the **Salmon Family**. Eggs are partially covered by sediment disturbed by the quivering. Spawning acts last 9–25 seconds. Both sexes spawn with other mates. The adults return to a lake or large river after spawning although females may spawn again elsewhere. Spawning lasts about 1–3 weeks. The amber eggs are 2.5 mm in diameter before fertilisation and a female may contain up to 15,905. Young grayling remain in the stream until freeze-up.

Grayling are good sport fishes which readily take a fly because of their preference for insects fallen on the water surface. They may also be taken on small lures and salmon eggs. The large, erected dorsal fin increases the resistance against the water and hence the fighting ability of the hooked fish. This is an important species attracting sport fishermen to remote northern areas of Canada. They are little used as food in modern times but have been caught by native peoples when other, preferred species were scarce. They are good eating. Grayling are particularly susceptible to pollution, and environmental disturbance whether from alterations to turbidity and stream temperature or from introduced, competing species. They are easily fished out of an area; even a 7–year sport fishery in the immense Great Slave Lake caused a reduction of average population length, weight and age. Only 175 anglers visited the fishing camp each year, catching 1.11 to 1.73 grayling per rod hour.

- Most accessible end of June to the end of August.
- The Northwest Territories and the northern regions of Alberta, Saskatchewan and Manitoba.
- Ultralight to light action spinning outfits with four- to six-pound test line. Flyfishermen should use seven- to nine-foot, four- to seven-weight fly rods loaded with weight-forward floating lines and regular sinking lines.
- Good assortment of small, 1/8– to 1/4–ounce spinners, spoons and jigs. Top flies include a good assortment of Wulffs and Bombers for surface fishing, and a variety of dark, wet fly patterns such as gnats, woolly buggers and nymphs.
- Use a 1/4– to 1/8–ounce hair jig and add a tippet one to three feet above the line, rigged with a wet fly. The jig enables the angler to cast farther and acts as an attractor. Arctic grayling normally hit the fly. Having two fish on at once is quite common.

Arctic lamprey

Scientific name: *Lampetra japonica* (von Martens, 1868)
Family: **Lamprey**
Other common names: northern lamprey, Pacific river lamprey
French name: lamproie arctique

Distribution: From Norway across the Arctic Ocean to the Bering Sea, Alaska and south to Korea. In Canada found in the Yukon River, parts of the Mackenzie River basin including Great Slave Lake and northernmost Alberta and along the shore of the Beaufort Sea.

Characters: There are 59–74 myomeres. The bar above the mouth has 2 (rarely 3) cusps and the bar below the mouth has 5–10 cusps. This lamprey is distinguished from Canadian relatives by having 2 dorsal fins, the bar above the mouth with 2 cusps, inner teeth near the mouth 3, at least one or all bicuspid, and by its distribution. Adults are dark brown to blue-black or grey on the body, lighter below, with clear brown fins in

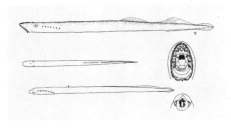

Arctic lamprey

disc view

fresh water and steel-blue with a pale to silvery belly in the sea. Ammocoetes are brown to grey. Attains 62.5 cm when anadromous.

Biology: Anadromous and landlocked populations are known for this species. Spawning occurs in late May to early July at 12–15°C in slower currents than the main rivers. Nests are up to 25 cm across and are built by males and females. Up to 8 fish spawn and each female produces up to 107,000 eggs of 1 mm diameter. Ammocoetes transform at 15–21 cm and move downriver to a lake or the sea in August to November. Immature adults disperse in lakes or the sea in late spring and early summer and maturation probably occurs over winter. Adults return to spawn the following year. In Great Slave Lake ammocoetes live 4 years and adults 1 year for a 5 year life span. Adults parasitise **salmon**, **trout**, **inconnu**, **suckers**, **whitefish** and even the small **threespine stickleback** at 6 cm. **Burbot**, **northern pike**, **walleye** and **inconnu** eat Arctic lampreys and gulls may take some in confined situations near water reservoir intakes. These lampreys have been used in times of food scarcity by humans in Canada and for dog food. Ammocoetes are used as bait. Smoked Arctic lamprey are sold in Japan.

Arctic lumpsucker

Scientific name: *Cyclopteropsis macalpini* (Fowler, 1914)
Family: **Lumpfish**
Other common names: none
French name: petite poule de mer de MacAlpine

Distribution: Known only from Ulrisk Bay in northwestern Greenland and the Barents Sea but probably enters Canadian waters.

Characters: This species is distinguished from its Arctic-Atlantic relatives by having the gill opening above the pectoral fin, about 5–6 large, blunt tubercles restricted to the anterior half of the body, compressed anterior body, usually no supplemental pores above the lateral line, first dorsal fin rectangular with rays equal, and postorbital tubercle row absent. The head is pointed and the mouth strongly oblique. Dorsal fin spines 7, soft rays 11, anal rays 12, and pectoral rays 26. Tubercles are blunt with many, minute

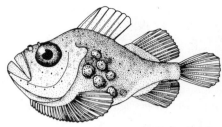

Arctic lumpsucker

prickles. There is no record of life colour. Reaches 7.5 cm.

Biology: This species is benthic over mud at 174 m or more. About 60–70 eggs, about 5 mm in diameter, are laid in shells or protected areas and guarded by the male.

Arctic sculpin

Scientific name: *Myoxocephalus scorpioides* (Fabricius, 1780)
Family: **Sculpin**
Other common names: false seascorpion, northern sculpin, kanayuk, tivaqiq
French name: chaboisseau arctique

Distribution: Found across the Canadian Arctic north to Ellesmere Island and south to James Bay and the Gulf of St. Lawrence. Also in Greenland and the northern Bering Sea.

Characters: This species and its Arctic-Atlantic relatives are distinguished from other sculpins by the upper preopercular spine being a simple straight point, the vomer bone in the roof of the mouth bears

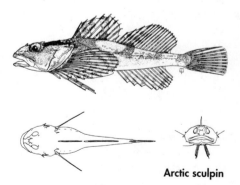

Arctic sculpin

teeth but palatine teeth are absent, there are no oblique folds on the lower flank, and the lateral line lacks plates. It is separated from its relatives by having 3 preopercular spines (1 pointing forward to downward, 2 pointing backward), the uppermost preopercular spine is less than twice as long as the one below, the spiny dorsal fin origin is not obviously in front of the rear operculum edge, pectoral rays are usually 14–16 (range 14–18) and there are tabs or cirri over the eyes. First dorsal fin spines 8–10, second dorsal rays 13–17 anal fin rays 10–14. Colour is a dark olive to blackish-brown with darker mottles or bands. The second dorsal and anal fins are dusky with light spots. The caudal fin base has a pale blotch. The pectoral fin has broad, dark bands in females or 4–5 rows of clear spots in males. Other fins have bands or white blotches. Males have white or silvery spots with dark borders on the flank under the pectoral fin and above the anal fin. The breast and belly have dark spots in males and there is a broad white stripe on the reddish-orange belly running from the pelvic fins to the anal fin. Males have spots on the lower lip. Reaches 30 cm standard length.

Biology: This sculpin is found in shallow coastal waters most commonly between tides on rocky bottoms among algae. Spawning takes place in the fall and eggs are demersal and up to 1.3 mm in diameter. It survives under ice cover at −1.4°C because its blood contains an anti-freeze protein which blocks ice formation in the tissues at temperatures down to −2°C. The protein concentration in the fish increases as temperatures in the sea fall. Food is known to be crustaceans, but other aspects of its biology have not been studied.

Arctic shanny

Scientific name: *Stichaeus punctatus*
  (Fabricius, 1780)
Family: **Shanny**
Other common names: spotted snakeblenny
French name: stichée arctique

Distribution: A circumpolar species found on all three coasts of Canada as far south as Massachusetts in the western Atlantic Ocean and to British Columbia in the eastern Pacific Ocean.

Characters: This species has a relatively deep body like its relatives the **radiated**

shanny and the **fourline snakeblenny** but is distinguished by its incomplete lateral line ending near midbody. There are 46–51 dorsal fin spines, 1–2 anal fin spines followed by variable counts of soft rays (32–35 in the Atlantic, 36–38 in Hudson Bay). The mouth is terminal. There are 15–16 rays in the large pectoral fin. The overall colour is brown to scarlet fading to paler or white on the belly. The flanks are mottled. The cheek and ventral surface of the head have 6–7 bars. The anal, pectoral and caudal fins are banded. The dorsal fin has 4–9 large dark spots pos-

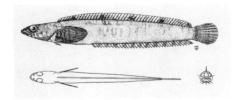

Arctic shanny

teriorly edged in white with the last 2 near the rear of the fin. The pelvic fins are yellow. Reaches 22 cm.

Biology: Found in shallow waters down to 35 m, over hard bottoms and sometimes sandy areas, hiding in crevices and under rocks in storms. A territory is defended as soon as young settle from the plankton in Newfoundland. A threat action involves erecting the dorsal fin, arching the body and inclining the head upwards. Shaking the body, gaping and slow tail wagging are also involved. Nipping and chasing follow if threats are unsuccessful. Dorsal fin spots darken and chin bars blanch in a dominant fish, the reverse in a subordinate. Food includes crustaceans and worms. Arctic shannies are eaten by various other fishes and seabirds such as the black guillemot. They may live 6 years or more. Spawning occurs in February to March in Newfoundland and eggs may number up to 2475 and be 1.7 mm in diameter. Eggs are deposited in ovoid masses, later than those of **rock gunnels** and earlier than those of the **radiated shanny**. Larvae are planktonic and settle to the bottom in Newfoundland waters in mid-July and early August after appearing in the plankton in mid-June.

Arctic staghorn sculpin

Scientific name: *Gymnocanthus tricuspis*
(Reinhardt, 1831)
Family: **Sculpin**
Other common names: none
French name: tricorne arctique

Distribution: Found throughout Arctic Canada, and south to Maine in the eastern Atlantic Ocean. Also in Greenland and on the Arctic coast of Eurasia.

Characters: This species is characterised by the upper preopercular spine being broad at the tip or with 2–3 spinules and the vomer

Arctic staghorn sculpin

and palatine bones in the roof of the mouth lacking teeth. First dorsal fin spines 10–12, second dorsal rays 14–17, anal rays 15–19 and pectoral rays 17–21. There are no scales except under the pectoral fins. The top of the head has prickles or warts. Males have a large genital papilla. The back is dark brown to grey and is clearly separated from the yellowish belly. The flanks have blackish brown bands formed from dark blotches. Dorsal and pectoral fins have brown or black bands and the pectoral fin has a yellow tip. The anal and pelvic fins have yellow rays. Colouration is brightest in adult males which have roundish white spots on the belly. Reaches 30 cm standard length.

Biology: This species is common in Arctic and Labrador waters, rare to the south. It has been caught as shallow as 1.8 m but is usually below 18 m down to 240 m on rock, sand or sand-mud bottoms at temperatures of -1.8 to 12.5°C, usually at or below 0°C. It may burrow into sand bottoms and enter brackish water. Food includes small fishes like **sand lances** and invertebrates. Amphipods, cumaceans and worms are important diet items in the Canadian Arctic. It is eaten by harp seals and black guillemots. Spawning occurs in October at Newfoundland. Eggs are up to 2 mm diameter and number 35,000 in large females.

Arctic telescope

Scientific name: *Protomyctophum arcticum*
. (Lütken, 1892)
Family: **Lanternfish**
Other common names: none
French name: télescope arctique

Distribution: Found in the North Atlantic Ocean from 70°N on the west coast of Greenland south to about 40°N in the western Atlantic Ocean off Canada.

Characters: This species is separated from its Atlantic coast relatives by lacking photophores near the dorsal body edge, the PLO photophore is well below the upper base of the pectoral fin and is in front of and usually slightly higher than the first PVO photophore, mouth terminal, and the PLO, first and second PVO photophores do not form a triangle shape. The eyes are semi-telescopic. Dorsal fin rays 10–13, usually 12, anal rays 21–24 and pectoral rays 14–17. Total gill rakers 18–21. AO photophores 14–16. Adult males have a single, supracaudal luminous gland, edged in black, and first appearing at 2.1 cm. Females have a single infracaudal patch at 2.5–2.6 cm, a second patch develops later and at 3.2 cm the two patches coalesce. Reaches 4.5 cm.

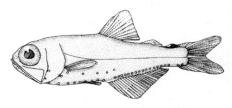

Arctic telescope

Biology: This is the second most common lanternfish in the Newfoundland Basin after the **glacier lanternfish**. First caught in Canadian waters in 1910 northeast of the Flemish Cap but not reported until 1959. Depth distribution generally is 250–850 m by day and 90–325 m by night. The largest catches are taken at 350 m by day and 250 m by night. Food is probably crustaceans. This lanternfish is food for ivory gulls in the southwest Davis Strait which indicates a shallower occurrence at this latitude.

Argentine Family

Scientific name: Argentinidae
French name: argentines

Argentines are found in all oceans but only on the Atlantic coast of Canada. There are about 20 species world-wide with 2 reported from Canada.

Argentines (also known as herring smelts) are silvery (hence "argentine") fishes of normal body shape and fin arrangement. The Canadian species have an adipose fin, normal eyes and a small mouth. The dorsal fin origin is in front of the pelvic fins. The pectoral fins are low on the body. Easily detached scales are present and the fin rays are not spiny. There are no light organs. The swimbladder often has a silvery layer.

Argentines are related to the **Pencil Smelt**, **Deepsea Smelt**, **Spookfish**, **Slickhead**, **Tubeshoulder** and **Smelt** families of the **Smelt Order**, and were formerly placed in the **Salmon Order**.

These fishes are found on the continental shelf and upper slope and are benthopelagic. The **Atlantic argentine** is economically important and the former U.S.S.R. started a fishery on Canada's coast in 1963 and was joined by Japan in 1968. About 15,000–20,000 tonnes is probably the sustainable yield. Argentines have pelagic eggs and larvae.

The silver pigment from scales and the swimbladder is used to produce "pearl essence" from which artificial pearls are made.

See **Atlantic argentine**
     striated argentine

armored searobin

Scientific name: *Peristedion miniatum*
    Goode, 1880
Family: **Searobin**
Other common names: none
French name: malarmat à dix aiguillons

Distribution: Found from Nova Scotia south to Brazil.

Characters: This species is distinguished from its Canadian relatives by the 4 rows of plates on the body, 2 long, lower, finger-like pectoral rays and 2 projections making a forked snout. The snout spines are narrow

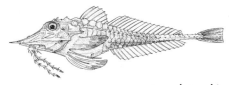

armored searobin

and usually shorter than the eye length. There are 9–11 barbels on the lower jaw, 2 very elongate at the mouth corner and bearing branches. First dorsal fin spines 7–8, second dorsal fin with 17–18 rays. Anal fin rays 17–19. Overall colour is pink, red or bright crimson, with the dorsal fins edged with red-black. There are 4–5 dark saddles across the back. A black bar crosses the upper half of the pectoral fin base and the outer two-thirds of the fin is black. Reaches 35.5 cm.

Biology: Occasionally caught on the Scotian Shelf by commercial trawlers. The northern limit is off Sable Island. This species can be found at 64–910 m, a range greater than the unarmored searobins. Food is almost wholly small crustaceans.

Armorhead Family

Scientific name: Pentacerotidae
French name: têtes casquées

Armorheads or boarfishes are found in the Indo-Pacific and southwestern Atlantic oceans. There are about 12 species with 1 reported off the Pacific coast of Canada.

The head of these fishes is encased in bone which is visible (no skin) and roughly striated. In young fish the head is covered with small spines and knobs. The body is compressed. Fin spines are strong and thick. The pelvic fin has 1 spine and 5 soft rays. There are 2–5 spines in the anal fin. There is no supramaxilla. Scales are small and ctenoid and there is a complete lateral line.

Armorheads are related to the **Sea Chub** and **Butterflyfish** families in the **Perch Order**.

These are fishes of cooler waters and many were poorly known until recently. They have been used commercially in Japan.

See **longfin armorhead**

armorhead sculpin

Scientific name: *Gymnocanthus galeatus* Bean, 1881
Family: **Sculpin**
Other common names: none
French name: chabot casqué

Distribution: Found from Japan through the Bering Sea to the Alaska-British Columbia border.

Characters: This sculpin is distinguished from its Pacific relatives by having an upper preopercular spine with 2 or more spinules or barbs on its upper edge, no scales above the lateral line, and the top of the head and nape have bony granulations, sometimes extending onto the sides of the head. Palatine and prevomerine teeth are present in the roof of the mouth. First dorsal fin spines 10–12, second dorsal rays 14–17, anal rays 16–20 and pectoral rays 18–21. T-shaped scales are present in the axil of the pectoral fin, and the lateral line pores number 40–48. The back and upper flank are dark brown, the lower flank posteriorly light brown to orange, with the belly white. There are several blotches and spots on the flank. Fins are barred except

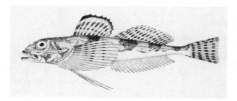

armorhead sculpin

the anal and pelvic fins. The pectoral and caudal fins have yellowish areas between the dark bars. Reaches 36 cm.

Biology: Rare in Canadian waters. First reported from Canada in 1976 based on 3 specimens. Depth range is the shallows to 420 m, possibly 625 m, with older fish commonly deeper than 50 m. Usually on soft bottoms but has been taken on a gravel-cobble beach and shell bottoms.

arrow goby

Scientific name: *Clevelandia ios* (Jordan and Gilbert, 1882)
Family: **Goby**
Other common names: none
French name: gobie-flèche

Distribution: From Baja California to southern British Columbia.

Characters: This goby is distinguished from its relatives, the **bay goby** and the **blackeye goby**, by its small scales, lack of a

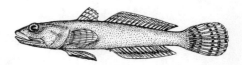

arrow goby

crest and 4–6 dorsal fin spines. There are about 70 cycloid scales along the flank. The second dorsal fin has 0–1 spines and 14–17 soft rays. The anal fin has 14–17 soft rays preceded by 0–1 spines. Gill rakers 7–9. There is a fleshy ridge in a depression running from the pelvic fins to the anus on the belly. Mouth large extending beyond the eye. Pale grey to olive-green or tan and almost transparent. Speckled with orange and black and with green and iridescent white flank spots. Fins are striped, the anal fin conspicuously so in males. Attains 6.4 cm.

Biology: Found in bays and estuaries, burrowing in sand or mud, or occupying burrows built by ghost and mud shrimps, clams or worms such as the fat innkeeper worm. The burrows are used to hide from predators and to prevent desiccation at low tides. These fish can be found by digging at low tide. They are very tolerant of temperature and salinity changes. Food includes diatoms, green algae, and shrimp eggs and young. Adult shrimps do retaliate by nipping the goby. Large food items are deposited near crabs which tear them up and thus the goby can seize the smaller pieces. Many larger fish and birds feed on these gobies. The main spawning season is March to June. Eggs are 0.7–0.9 mm in diameter and are laid in groups of up to 1100. They do not care for the young unlike other goby species. Larvae are pelagic. Used as live-bait by anglers.

arrowtail

Scientific name: *Melanonus zugmayeri*
  Norman, 1930
Family: **Arrowtail**
Other common names: coalfish
French name: more noir

Distribution: Pacific, Atlantic and Indian oceans including off the coast of British Columbia.

Characters: There is a single obvious dorsal fin, raised at the front. A second dorsal fin and a second anal fin are joined to the caudal fin to form an arrow-shaped tail (hence the name). There are 67–73 first dorsal fin rays, 51–59 first anal fin rays. The second dorsal fin has 22–24 rays and the second anal fin has 20–21 rays respectively in the tail. Pectoral fin rays 12–14, 7 pelvic fin rays, 9 caudal fin rays and 6–11 gill rakers on the lower arch. The body tapers to a characteristic, narrow caudal peduncle. The teeth

arrowtail

vary in size and some are needle-like. There is no chin barbel. The body is an overall dark brown or black. Attains 28 cm.

Biology: This species is uncommon and is caught by scientists using midwater trawls at 475–530 m over depths down to 2377 m off British Columbia. Nothing is known of its biology.

Arrowtail Family

Scientific name: Melanonidae
French name: mores noirs

This family contains only 2 species worldwide in tropical and temperate oceans with 1 species off the British Columbia coast.

The **arrowtails**, coalfishes or pelagic cods, are similar to the **Mora Family** and were included within it. The family is a member of the **Cod Order**. The body has a characteristic, narrow caudal peduncle and the head bears parallel ridges with neuromasts.

Arrowtails are uncommon, meso- to bathypelagic fishes and almost nothing is known of their biology.

See **arrowtail**

arrowtooth flounder

Scientific name: *Atheresthes stomias*
  (Jordan and Gilbert, 1880)
Family: **Righteye Flounder**
Other common names: long-jaw flounder, turbot, arrowtooth halibut, needle-tooth halibut, bastard halibut, French sole
French name: plie à grande bouche

Distribution: Found from the Chukchi and Bering seas to California including British Columbia.

Characters: This species is distinguished from Canadian Pacific relatives by having 2 rows of arrow-shaped teeth in the jaws and a high lateral line scale count. The mouth is large and extends beyond the lower eye. The upper eye is on the margin of the head and can be seen from the blind side. The caudal fin is lunate. There is no spine in front of the anal fin. The preopercular bone on the side of the head has a round lower corner. Dorsal fin rays 92–115, anal rays 72–99. Gill rakers on the lower arch 10–16. Lateral line scales about 135. Coarse scales on the eyed side are ctenoid, on the blind side cycloid. The eyed side is brown to olive brown with scale margins darkened, the blind side white with fine black dots. Reaches 84 cm.

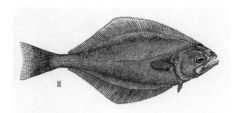

arrowtooth flounder

Biology: Common in British Columbia with larvae in surface waters and adults on soft bottoms down to 900 m, usually deeper than 20 m. The greatest age for females is 20 years and for males 10 years. Food is various crustaceans, **flatfishes** including other **arrowtooths** and fishes such as **herring, walleye pollock** and **shiner perch**. **Walleye pollock** are the principal food in the eastern Bering Sea, up to 86% of the diet by weight. Not used commercially as food for humans, but important as food on mink farms. The 1988 Canadian catch weighed 140 tonnes.

Asiatic arrowtooth flounder

Scientific name: *Atheresthes evermanni*
　　Jordan and Starks, 1904
Family: **Righteye Flounder**
Other common names: Kamchatka flounder
French name: plie asiatique à dents crochues

Distribution: Found from Japan to British Columbia.

Characters: This species is recognised among Canadian Pacific **flatfishes** by the arrow-shaped teeth in 2 rows and the low lateral line scale count. The upper eye is lateral and not on the head margin. Dorsal fin rays 98–116, anal rays 76–94. Lateral line scales 86–109. Scales are weakly ctenoid on the eyed side and cycloid on the blind side. Lower arch gill rakers slender, 9–12. Caudal fin lunate. The mouth is large and extends beyond the lower eye. Eyed side brown, blind side pale. Fin margins dusky. Attains 1 m or more.

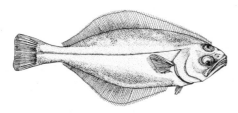

Asiatic arrowtooth flounder

Biology: Reported from a single specimen off southern Vancouver Island at 550 m. This fish was caught by a Russian vessel in 1965 and was a mature female. It may be a stray from northern waters. Depth range is 60–900 m.

Atka mackerel

Scientific name: *Pleurogrammus monopterygius* (Pallas, 1810)
Family: **Greenling**
Other common names: forktail greenling
French name: maquereau d'Atka

Distribution: From the Queen Charlotte Islands around the North Pacific Ocean to the Sea of Japan. Also reported from California, but rare south of Alaska.

Characters: There are 20–29 spines and 24–29 soft rays in the dorsal fin. Total anal rays are 24–28 and pectoral rays 24–26. Total gill rakers 22–26. Lateral line pored scales are 139–166. This species is distinguished from other Canadian greenlings by having 5 lateral lines, no notch in the dorsal fin and a forked caudal fin. Overall body colour is olive with a few broad dark flank bars. Attains 50 cm.

Atka mackerel

Biology: First reported from British Columbia in 1977 where it was caught between 12.2 and 36.6 m. Elsewhere descends to 122 m. It appears to be mostly pelagic. Food is plankton and it is a cannibal. Life span is at least 8 years. In Alaska it is found among kelp in early spring and summer. It is caught by trawl, gill net and on hook-and-line, and is a good food fish. There is a fishery by former Soviet vessels in the Gulf of Alaska.

Atlantic alligatorfish

Scientific name: *Aspidophoroides monopterygius* (Bloch, 1786)
Family: **Poacher**
Other common names: sea poacher, aspidophore
French name: poisson-alligator atlantique

Distribution: From the Labrador coast south to Massachusetts, and rarely New Jersey.

Characters: This alligatorfish is 1 of 3 species in the Canadian Atlantic and Arctic oceans. It is distinguished from its relatives, the **Arctic alligatorfish** and the **Atlantic poacher**, by having a slender body with 1 dorsal fin, no barbels, and 45–50 plates in the dorsal row. The dorsal fin has 5–6 soft rays and the anal fin 4–6 soft rays. The pectoral fin has 9–11 rays. Body colour is a dark brown with 4–5 dark bars along the flank. There are bars on the dorsal and pectoral fins. The caudal fin is dusky. The dorsal, pelvic and lower pectoral fins develop white pigmentation, probably at spawning. Reaches 17.8 cm.

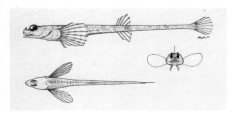

Atlantic alligatorfish

Biology: Found over sand and mud at 18–332 m and temperatures below 3°C. Larvae may enter the brackish water of estuaries. This species rests with the pectorals splayed and braced on the bottom. It is eaten by **cod**, **haddock** and **halibut**.

Atlantic argentine

Scientific name: *Argentina silus*
  Ascanius, 1775
Family: **Argentine**
Other common names: greater argentine,
  herring smelt, greater silver smelt
French name: grande argentine

Distribution: Found in temperate to Arctic waters on both sides of the North Atlantic Ocean including Davis Strait, off southern Labrador, the Grand Banks and Georges Bank.

Characters: The pectoral fins are low on the side of the body and lateral line scales do not extend onto the tail fin. The eye is large and scales are easily lost on capture. The Atlantic argentine is distinguished from the **striated argentine** by having 64–69 lateral line scales, scales with minute spines, 11–17 lower arm gill rakers and a dorsal fin origin above the tip of the pectoral fins. There are 6 branchiostegal rays. In colour this fish is a pale green-yellow, brown or olive with silvery flanks and a white belly. The flanks have golden tints. The adipose fin is yellow-

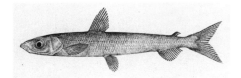

Atlantic argentine

ish. The swimbladder is silvery. Reaches 60 cm, although most are under 50 cm.

Biology: Found in schools at 55–550 m near the ocean bottom but has been caught down to 1400 m. They are abundant off southwestern Nova Scotia. On the Scotian Shelf they are found at a temperature range of 4–13°C. Young are found in shallower water than adults. Food includes crustaceans, squids, arrow worms, comb jellies and small fish. Atlantic argentines may mature as early as 4 years of age and live for 29 years. Males and females mature at similar lengths but males are almost a year older than females. Growth is rapid up to 7–8 years of age. Spawning occurs in March–April on the Scotian Shelf and the oily eggs float in midwater. Eggs are 3.0–3.5 mm in diameter and may number up to 38,599. The flesh is white and flaky and this species has been marketed in Europe. Catches in Canadian waters are by Japanese and former U.S.S.R. fleets but catch limits have decreased the take from 49,040 tonnes in 1966.

Atlantic batfish

Scientific name: *Dibranchus atlanticus*
  Peters, 1875
Family: **Batfish**
Other common names: chauve-souris
  atlantique
French name: malthe atlantique

Distribution: Found in the North Atlantic Ocean including the southwest Grand Bank south to the Caribbean Sea.

Characters: The depressed, oval or disc-shaped head and the stalked, arm-like pectoral fins are characteristic. The head margin has about 28 triangular projections tipped with sharp spines. The dorsal fin has 6–7 rays, the anal fin 5 rays and the pectoral fin 13–15 rays. There are only 2 gills on each side. Scales

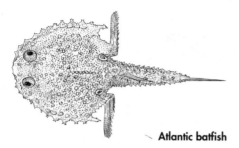

Atlantic batfish

have a star-shaped base and a conical spine. The fishing apparatus is short in this **anglerfish** and may be retracted. The gill openings are in the posterior half of the body above the pectoral fin bases. Overall colour is reddish-grey to grey-brown with pink tinges. Fins may be white or a brilliant rose-red and the iris black, blue or green depending on the light. The dorsal surface can glow a bright yellow with bioluminescence. Attains 39.4 cm.

Biology: Usually found between 274 and 1300 m but sometimes as shallow as 40 m in Canada. Food includes worms, crustaceans, molluscs and other benthic organisms such as brittle stars and sea spiders. Spawning may occur in spring and summer and it has been suggested that females lay eggs in a veil as in some other **anglerfishes**. Specimens are sometimes dried and sold as curios.

Atlantic bonito

Scientific name: *Sarda sarda* (Bloch, 1793)
Family: **Mackerel**
Other common names: common bonito,
    belted bonito, horse mackerel, bloater,
    bone jack, Boston mackerel, skipjack,
    pélamide
French name: bonite à dos rayé

Distribution: Found in the Atlantic Ocean and the Mediterranean and Black seas. In the west from the southern Gulf of St. Lawrence to Argentina.

Characters: This species is separated from its Atlantic coast relatives by the dorsal fins being very close together, almost confluent, a high dorsal fin spine count, and 5–20 dark

bluish, oblique stripes on the upper flank which extend below the lateral line. The mouth is large, extending back to the rear eye margin. There is no swimbladder. There is a large median keel with a small one above and below. First dorsal fin spines 20–23, second dorsal rays 13–18. Anal fin rays 14–17. Pectoral fin rays 23–26. Dorsal finlets 7–10, usually 8, anal finlets 6–8, usually 7. Scales are small and cover the whole body except the caudal keels distally. There is a corselet of larger scales in the region of the pectoral fin with a wing of these scales extending to the first dorsal fin origin. The back and upper flank are steel blue and the lower flank and belly silvery. The dorsal fin is black. Young have faint vertical bars. Attains 91.4 cm. The world, all-tackle angling record is a 8.3 kg fish caught in the Canary Islands in 1953.

Atlantic bonito

Biology: This bonito is a relatively common late summer stray to Canadian waters from August to October. It is usually found in offshore surface schools or brackish waters at 12–27°C and 14–39% salinity. In Canada it occasionally enters the Miramichi River estuary. Food is other schooling fishes such as **herring** and **mackerel** and occasionally squids and shrimps. This bonito jumps a lot when pursuing prey. It is a cannibal. Maturity is attained at about 40 cm. Spawning occurs in June–July in the northwestern Atlantic and at varying times elsewhere. Spawning does not take place in Canadian waters. This bonito is an excellent sport fish which will strike at a surface trolled bait or lure. There are commercial fisheries in the Gulf of Mexico and Caribbean Sea where this fish is caught by purse seines, gill nets, seines, trap nets and on hook and line. The main fisheries are in the Mediterranean and Black seas and in the south Atlantic Ocean. The flesh is firm, light in colour, tasty and is usually canned.

Atlantic cod

Scientific name: *Gadus morhua*
   Linnaeus, 1758
Family: **Cod**
Other common names: cod, codfish, rock
   cod, scrod, northern cod, "fish", morue
   commune, morue de l'Atlantique, ogac,
   ovak, uugak
French name: morue franche

Distribution: Found in the North Atlantic
Ocean in Europe in the east and from southern Baffin Island to North Carolina in the
west. There is a brackish water population in
Ogac Lake, Baffin Island.

Characters: This species and its relative,
the **ogac**, are separated from other Canadian
Arctic-Atlantic cods by having 3 dorsal and
2 anal fins, the first dorsal fin being rounded,
a projecting snout, the upper jaw extends
back beyond the front of the eye, a slender,
well-developed chin barbel about twice the
pupil diameter, no large, black blotch on the
flank, a light lateral line lighter than the surrounding flank pigmentation, and a large eye
entering 4.0–5.5 times in head length. The
Atlantic cod is distinguished from its relative
by the spotted body and a silvery-grey peritoneum with small black spots. First dorsal
fin rays 13–16, second dorsal rays 18–24 and
third dorsal rays 17–22. First anal fin rays
19–27, second anal rays 17–22. Adults have
numerous, median length, horn-shaped
tubercles on the back, flank and belly scales.
There are at least 14 cod stocks which can be
distinguished by vertebral numbers but
stocks do mix. For example, the Labrador-
Newfoundland stocks have high vertebral

Atlantic cod

counts while those on the Grand Bank have a
low count. Overall colour is very variable
depending on the background, usually brown
to dark red or grey to green. Flanks have
many brown to reddish spots. The belly is
whitish, grey or red tinged. Some fish can be
almost black and occasional marbled individuals are caught. The iris is dark. Attains
possibly 200 cm and 95.9 kg but most fish
caught are much smaller. The world record,
all-tackle, rod-caught cod was 44.79 kg and
was taken off New Hampshire in 1969.

Biology: Cod are extremely numerous
near the bottom from low tide to the edge of
the continental shelf. They may be found at
the surface and down to over 2000 m.
Temperature is a limiting distributional factor,
cod usually favouring waters below 10°C, but
differing stocks have differing preferences.
Seasonal preferences also occur. Schools
move inshore in summer and offshore in winter in Canada, although some fish overwinter
in nearshore waters of Newfoundland. Off
Labrador and eastern Newfoundland, for
example, cod are in deep, warm areas of the
continental slope and shelf in winter and early
spring. This supports an offshore fishery by
otter trawlers which at times has exceeded
537 million fish.

In spring the cod migrate inshore to warming surface waters. This supports an inshore
fishery using cod traps, line gear and gill nets
with a maximum catch of over 79 million
fish. Cod may move as fast as 25.7 km/day
over a period of nearly a month. Schools may
be several kilometres long and 8–10 km wide.
A mass of cod 55 km long and 35 km wide at
a depth of 150 m has been observed off the
northeast coast of Newfoundland. This mass
was about one-third the size of P.E.I.
Intermingling of stocks occurs throughout the
Canadian range. For example, the northern
Gulf of St. Lawrence stock migrates southwards to winter on the northern side of Cabot
Strait where it mixes with the Burgeo Bank
(off the south coast of Newfoundland) stock.
Long distance movements have been reported
from the North Sea of Europe to the Grand
Bank, a distance of at least 3228 km over 4.5
years. In Newfoundland, young cod are associated with large algae which are used as
cover from predators and to a lesser extent as
a feeding area. Small food is located on or in
the seabed using the chin barbel and pelvic fin
rays which have touch and taste cells. Gravel

is carried away from buried food in the mouth and stones rolled away with the head. Midwater foods, as small as 2 mm, are captured by sight as are the larger bottom foods. Groups of cod feed more effectively than individuals since groups can uncover deeply buried items or tear apart larger items. Crustaceans are the principal food of small cod but cod longer than 50 cm eat mostly fish such as **capelin, sand lances, herring** and **redfishes**, as well as many other fish species. Commercially important snow crabs are eaten in spring off Cape Breton Island. The snow crab fishery in the Gulf of St. Lawrence in 1983 was worth $29.1 million while the cod fishery was valued at $17.4 million. A wide variety of other organisms have been extracted from cod stomachs including clams, squids, mussels, echinoderms, comb jellies, sea squirts, worms and even unwary seabirds. Cod are cannibals and are eaten at various life stages by various other fishes, seals and whales.

Cod, like many other groundfishes, are susceptible to sealworm infestations. Inspection of fillets for sealworm in Atlantic fishes costs $60–70 million. The grey seal is the primary host of the parasite and seal numbers have increased in recent years. A programme of seal deworming and reproductive control using contraceptives has been advocated.

Growth varies with the stock. Northern stocks tend to grow more slowly and live longer than those in the south. Age of commercial catches has declined to 5–6 years, a sign of overfishing. Over 90% of the eastern Georges Bank cod landed by Canadian otter trawlers are age 5 or younger. In the southern Gulf of St. Lawrence size at maturity of males fell from 50 to 36 cm and of females from 60 to 36 cm from 1959 to 1979. On the Scotian Shelf both length and age at maturity declined by about half between 1959 and 1979. Cod are no longer "so great a quantity … that at times they even stayed the passage of his (i.e. John Cabot's) ships" (Peter Martyr, ca. 1516). Maximum age is 29 years.

In the Saguenay Fjord, cod become sexually mature at 4 years and live 15 years. Spawning occurs from November to March and fecundity was 261,122–2,242,822 eggs.

The flesh had a high mercury content in fish caught from 1975–1977 and could not be safely consumed by humans. Spawning in Labrador begins in February–March while on Georges Bank it begins in December and runs to April. Intermediate areas tend to spawn at progressively later dates with decreasing latitude. Up to 12 million, 1.9 mm diameter, pelagic eggs are produced usually at about 100 m depth. North Atlantic cod off Labrador and eastern Newfoundland spawn in March–June below 250 m near bottom temperatures of 3°C. The eggs develop as they drift in the Labrador Current as far as 1000 km to the south to nursery areas. Adults also home southwards after spawning, perhaps to their growing areas. Adults and new spawners begin to return northward in fall to the spawning grounds.

Cod is the most valuable Canadian fish and many other countries fish for this species in Canadian waters. So important is the cod to the Maritime economy that fishermen use "fish" as a synonym for cod, especially in Newfoundland. Catches landed in Canada may exceed half a million tonnes with a value over $187 million. The Canadian catch in 1988 was 466,400 tonnes, about twice the weight of the second most important species, the **Atlantic herring**. About three-quarters of the northwest Atlantic Ocean cod are caught by Canadians using trawls, Danish seines, handlines, jiggers, gill nets and cod traps. Anglers also pursue this species and the tourist industry runs party boats to catch cod. Cod are caught by bait fishing on the bottom, by jigging and by deep trolling. Cod is sold fresh, frozen, salted and smoked. Some are turned into sticks, blocks and fillets. Cod cheeks and cod tongues are delicacies. Cod are also used in fish meal, glue production and for cod-liver oil.

Efforts were made to farm cod in Newfoundland. Live fish are taken from cod traps, held in pens and fed **capelin** from June to September and harvested in October to January when prices are most favourable. Product quality was high.

The major commercial fishing areas were off Labrador, the Grand Bank and the northern Gulf of St. Lawrence. These, and various other stocks were classed as depressed, rebuilding or stable and the total allowable catch (TAC) was modified accordingly. However, in the 1990s, the stocks of northern cod collapsed and a fishing moratorium was declared. Various reasons have been advocated for this catastrophic collapse and its devastating effects on the economy. Reasons include trawlers harvesting fish before they can spawn or destroying the spawning beds, increased cod-eating seal numbers since the European ban on seal products, stock mismanagement, improved fishing gear, increased numbers of fishermen, and adverse environmental conditions.

Atlantic constellation fish

Scientific name: *Valenciennellus tripunctulatus*
(Esmark, 1871)
Family: **Silver Hatchetfish**
Other common names: none
French name: poisson constellation atlantique

Distribution: Found in all oceans from tropical to temperate waters including off southern Nova Scotia where first reported in 1973.

Characters: The body shape is elongate, not hatchet-shaped. There are no light organs at the chin. The dorsal fin is situated at midbody over the origin of the anal fin and the adipose fin is shorter than eye diameter. The colour darkens at night. There is a series of 15–18 black spots between the head and tail. The head and belly are brown while the back and tail are whitish or translucent. Light organs on the side of the head are purple. A small species, reaching 7.5 cm in total length.

Atlantic constellation fish

Biology: It is found at 300 m and deeper. This species is responsible for much of the sonic scattering at 400–600 m off Bermuda. Feeding occurs during the day and no vertical migration occurs. Spawning can occur year round with individuals spawning 2–3 times in a life span of 1 year. Mature females are about 2–3 cm long and mature males 1.9–2.5 cm. Eggs are up to 0.7 mm in diameter.

Atlantic eelpout

Scientific name: *Lycodes atlanticus*
Jensen, 1902
Family: **Eelpout**
Other common names: none
French name: lycode atlantique

Distribution: Found from the Gulf of St. Lawrence and Grand Bank south to off Virginia.

Characters: This species is separated from its Canadian Atlantic relatives by having small pelvic fins, a mouth under the

Atlantic eelpout

snout, no large pores around the mouth, crests on the chin, a single lateral line running down towards the anal fin origin or paralleling the anal fin base, a long tail (preanal length 37.6% of total length), and uniform brown colour. Dorsal fin rays 111–113 and anal rays 94–98 (including half the continuous caudal fin rays in each count). Pectoral fin rays 21–24. Reaches about 40 cm. The Atlantic eelpout may be the same species as the **Newfoundland eelpout**.

Biology: This species is found on mud bottoms or nearly vertical canyon walls from 1704 to 2452 m off the U.S. coast. Food includes organisms found within the mud.

Atlantic fanfish

Scientific name: *Pterycombus brama*
Fries, 1837
Family: **Pomfret**
Other common names: none
French name: poisson-éventail atlantique

Distribution: Found in the North Atlantic Ocean including the Grand Bank, Flemish Cap and near Halifax, Nova Scotia.

Characters: This species is distinguished from its Canadian relatives by lacking scales on the dorsal and anal fins and these fins fold down into a sheath formed by elongate scales at their bases, by scales covering the back in front of the dorsal fin, and usually there are 51 dorsal fin rays. The fan-like dorsal and anal fins are also characteristic. Dorsal fin rays 48–53, anal rays 40–43, and pectoral rays 19–23. Scales in longitudinal series 48–53, bearing small spines even in adults. Juveniles have a lateral line but this is absent in adults. Body silvery in life with dorsal, anal, caudal and pelvic fins black except posteriorly. The snout and lower jaw are dark. The tongue, roof of the mouth and lips are dusky. Reaches 46 cm.

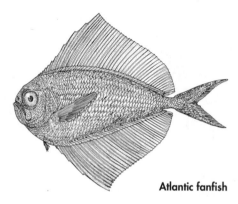

Atlantic fanfish

Biology: Several specimens have been reported from Atlantic Canada. Usually found offshore. Spawning is thought to occur year round off the east coast of Florida and in the Caribbean. Eaten by **swordfish** in Canadian waters.

Atlantic flyingfish

Scientific name: *Cypselurus melanurus*
(Valenciennes in Cuvier and Valenciennes, 1846)
Family: **Flyingfish**
Other common names: none
French name: exocet atlantique

Distribution: Found from Newfoundland south to Brazil and in the eastern Atlantic Ocean.

Characters: This species is distinguished from its Canadian relatives by having 2–5 more dorsal fin rays than anal fin rays, the

anal fin origin lies under ray 3 or higher of the dorsal fin, by fin colour, and by having about 56–60 lateral line scales and the dorsal

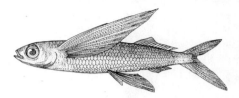

Atlantic flyingfish

fin lower than long. Dorsal fin rays 12–14, usually 13–14, anal rays 8–10, usually 9. The second pectoral fin ray is branched, and there are 15–16 rays. The young have 2 barbels. The back and upper flank is a dark blue-grey to greenish, silvery on the lower flank and belly. The dorsal fin is transparent except in young where it is banded. The pectoral fin is black with a central transparent area which becomes wider at the rear of the fin and does not extend to the front margin of the fin. The caudal fin is dusky. Young have dark bands on the belly, narrower than spaces between them. Reaches 40 cm.

Biology: Nineteenth century records without details report this species from banks off Newfoundland. Also recorded from Sable Island in 1859 and Prospect Harbour, Nova Scotia in 1970. The few records are strays from the south. This species is found both offshore and entering bays. Females apparently spawn in June–August in the western Atlantic. Eggs are 1.8–1.9 mm in diameter and are covered in filaments.

Atlantic gymnast

Scientific name: *Xenodermichthys copei*
(Gill, 1884)
Family: **Slickhead**
Other common names: bluntsnout smooth-head
French name: gymnaste atlantique

Distribution: Found in all oceans and at the southeastern Grand Bank off Newfoundland.

Characters: This species is unique among Canadian slickheads, because the body is completely scaleless. Light organs are found as small nodules on the thick skin. The forehead over the eye is strongly rounded and leads to a blunt snout. There are 27–31 dorsal fin rays, 26–30 anal fin rays and 7–8 pectoral fin rays. The colour is black overall. It reaches 20 cm in length. The common name is taken from the Greek for naked and refers to the absence of scales.

Atlantic gymnast

Biology: First caught in Canada in 1950 but quite rare. The Atlantic gymnast is a mid-water species of the continental slope found at about 100–1230 m. In some areas it can be quite abundant but is not utilised commercially since the flesh is watery. It feeds on small crustaceans and squids. Spawning occurs from September to November near the bottom. Eggs are large (2.7 mm in diameter) and only a few are laid (about 150).

Atlantic hagfish

Scientific name: *Myxine limosa* Girard, 1858
Family: **Hagfish**
Other common names: northern hagfish, slime eel
French name: myxine du nord

Distribution: North Atlantic Ocean and Mediterranean Sea, including Greenland, Baffin Island, Labrador, and south to Florida and the Gulf of Mexico.

Characters: The only hagfish on our Atlantic coast, it is distinguished by a single gill opening in the form of a pore in front of

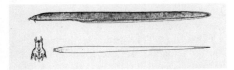

Atlantic hagfish

the ventral fin fold. There is a single nostril (or nasohypophysial opening) at the tip of the snout, and 6 pairs of gill pouches internally. Three pairs of mouth barbels are present. Slime pores number 24–33 in front of the gill

pore, 51–70 between the pore and anus, and 10–13 posterior to the anus (total 88–102). Teeth have 32–36 cusps. Red-brown or blackish-purple on the back fading to pale grey or whitish below. Midline of back with a narrow pale streak extending forward from the tail variable distances. Occasionally piebald mottled. Tongue teeth are orange. Formerly called *Myxine glutinosa* Attains 79.0 cm.

Biology: Found from 20–1006 m and deeper on mud bottom avoiding brackish water and temperatures above 12°C. The body may be completely buried in the mud, or the head may protrude. Most active at night. Very numerous in suitable habitats. Food is dead or moribund fishes, located by smell, and also various invertebrates. Their peculiar feeding method is described under **Hagfish Family**. Up to 30 large, white, oval eggs are released at any time of year. Eggs have anchor-shaped filaments at each end. A considerable nuisance to commercial fishermen, eating fish in nets and coating nets with slime. Used in research to investigate heart function (it has several hearts with diffused pacemakers), immunology (wounds heal very slowly but do not become infected) and endocrinology.

Atlantic halibut

Scientific name: *Hippoglossus hippoglossus* (Linnaeus, 1758)
Family: **Righteye Flounder**
Other common names: greys, cherry bellies, giant halibut, common halibut
French name: flétan atlantique

Distribution: Found from the northern tip of Labrador and western Greenland south through Atlantic Canada to Virginia. Also in Europe.

Characters: This Atlantic species is characterised by a large, almost symmetrical mouth, an arched lateral line over the pectoral fin, white blind side and a high dorsal fin ray count. The upper eye projects a little above the head margin. The caudal fin is concave. Dorsal fin rays 92–110, anal rays 69–85. There is a strong, forward directed spine at the anal fin origin, which may be hidden by skin in older fish. Lateral line scales about 160. The body is slimy with mucus. The eyed side is greenish to dark brown or black, the blind side white. There is usually some mottling on the eyed side. The blind side may have grey mottles (hence "greys") or red mottles ("cherries"). Young have spots or marbling. Attains 4.7 m and 330 kg, one of the largest Canadian fishes. The largest, all-tackle, rod-caught specimen weighed 115.78 kg and was caught off Gloucester, Massachusetts in 1989. Atlantic halibut are genetically distinct from **Pacific halibut** and biochemical studies indicate that isolation occurred in the Pliocene between 1.7 and 4.5 million years ago.

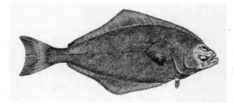

Atlantic halibut

Biology: Halibut are found at 37–2000 m, usually at 160–230 m when adult but in shallower water when young. They are caught above the sea bed also and can actively pursue prey fish. They prefer temperatures above 2.5°C, entering shallow water in summer and retreating to deeper water in winter. On the Scotian Shelf they are found at 1–13°C and 27–366 m, mostly at 55–108 m. They do not migrate extensively but one fish moved from Anticosti Island to Iceland over a 7 year period.

Food is restricted to a wide variety of fishes when halibut are over 80 cm long. Halibut are reputed to stun cod with their tail. Smaller halibut feed on worms and crustaceans, gradually adding fish to their diet as they grow. **Greenland sharks** are known to eat halibut. Females grow much faster than males and both sexes grow faster than other Atlantic coast flatfishes. There are also differences in growth rates between stocks within Canada and between stocks in the western and eastern Atlantic Ocean. Maximum age is about 35 years. Size at maturity has declined from 84 cm for males and 98 cm for females in 1959–1969 to 66 cm and 70 cm in 1970–1979, a result of heavy fishing.

Halibut spawn mostly in November–December in Canadian waters at depths of 183 m or deeper. Over 2 million eggs is the estimated production by larger females of about 90 kg. Egg diameter is 3 mm. The eggs sink slowly as they develop but are neutrally buoyant at first, floating at 54 m or as deep as 800 m on shedding.

The fishery describes halibut by name and weight as snapper (2.3–3.6 kg), chicken (3.6–6.8 kg), small medium (6.8–20.4 kg), medium (20.4–36.3 kg), large medium (36.3–56.7 kg) and whale (over 56.7 kg). The fishery is important in Canada and the flaky, white flesh of halibut fetches a high price. Halibut are caught on longlines when large and by otter trawl when smaller. They may be a by-catch or a directed fishery. As much as 5909 tonnes was landed in 1950 but recent catches are between 1684 and 3936 tonnes with values in the 3–5 million dollar range, in some years higher to about $15 million for eastern Canada.

This is an excellent fighting fish for anglers but is not too common inshore. It is caught by drift fishing on the bottom using fish, crab, squid and clam baits. Large diamond jigs will catch very large halibut.

Atlantic herring

Scientific name: *Clupea harengus*
 Linnaeus, 1758
Family: **Herring**
Other common names: sea herring, Labrador
 herring, sardine, Digby chick, bloater,
 kipper, skadlin, sperling, brit, yawling,
 mattie, sid
French name: hareng atlantique

Distribution: Found in the North Atlantic Ocean and from Baffin Island south to North Carolina in the west.

Characters: This species is distinguished from its Canadian Atlantic coast relatives by the sharp edge to the belly scales (but not a saw-toothed edge) and teeth on the roof of the mouth. Dorsal fin rays 16–22, anal rays 12–21 and pectoral rays 14–22. Scales before the pelvic fin on the belly 26–33, behind 11–17. Gill rakers 40–49 (and less in fish smaller than 10 cm). The back and upper flank are green to green-blue or blue and the lower flank and belly are iridescent silver or tinged violet. The operculum may be tinted golden, brown or brassy and this may extend along

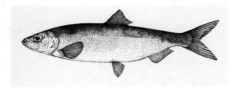

Atlantic herring

the flanks. Peritoneum dusky. Atlantic herring are now recognised as a species distinct from **Pacific herring**. Reaches 45 cm.

Biology: This herring is found in large schools in inshore waters and offshore down to 364 m. On the Scotian Shelf, the preferred depths are 55–90 m and 146–163 m at temperatures of 1°C and 7–9°C. Total temperature range was 0–11°C. There are distinct stocks in Atlantic Canada, each with particular feeding, spawning and wintering areas. There is a migratory pattern between these areas and also some mixing of stocks. Recruitment to stocks in the Gulf of Maine varies by as much as 20 to 1, depending on temperature and food availability.

Herring feed on phyto- and zooplankton by selecting items visually during daylight. The size of items consumed increases with size of the herring. Larval fish are an important item of the diet as well as various planktonic crustaceans and molluscs. Blooms of toxic dinoflagellates, which cause paralytic shellfish poisoning in humans, also kill herring. Such a kill occurred in the Bay of Fundy in 1976. Herrings and their eggs are eaten by many other fishes, birds and marine mammals.

Most herring mature by age 5 although some are mature at 3 years. Life span is at least 19 years. Spawning time varies between stocks from April to November in Canada. Spring spawning stocks may be genetically distinct from fall spawners. Earlier spawning occurs in northern coastal waters, later spawning offshore in southern deep water. The timing of herring arrival on spawning grounds in the southern Gulf of St. Lawrence depends on temperature but temperature at spawning ranges from 0°C in spring to 20°C in the fall in high latitudes. Eggs settle and

adhere to the bottom in ribbons, are 1.4 mm in diameter and number up to 261,000. Spawning concentrations of fish on Georges Bank are up to 80 km long and 13 km wide. Males are said to release ribbons of milt 1–2 cm long over the eggs which are 1–15 layers deep. Layers deeper than 4 eggs have high mortality. Females select spawning sites visually in shallow water, preferring rougher surfaces. Most spawning occurs in areas of mixing where high levels of primary production, and hence food, occur for larval growth. Spring spawners have fewer but larger eggs than fall spawners. There are also differences in length and age composition of the stocks, year-class strengths, growth rates, counts of fin rays and gill rakers, and ear-stone structure. While they spawn separately they mix on feeding and wintering grounds.

Herring have long been used by man as food, at least 5000 years in Europe. Much economic development has depended on herring stocks and wars have been fought over access to the fishing grounds. There was a Battle of Herrings in 1429. In Canada herring are caught in weirs, traps, gill nets and purse seines. Young herring are caught in weirs and sold canned as "sardines." The fishery here probably pre-dates Columbus. The world catch of Atlantic herring usually exceeds that of Pacific herring by a factor of 2–8. In the mid-1960s the world catch of the two species was 4.5 million tonnes (about 11.5% of the world marine fin fish catch) and second only to the Peruvian anchoveta. The names bloater and kipper are used for smoked herring and skadlin and variations for salted and smoked herring. They may be vinegar-cured as rollmops or soused herring and marinated as "Solomon Gundy." Fresh and frozen herring are also sold and some herring become canned pet food, or processed for fish meal and oil. They have also been used as fertiliser and the scales for pearl essence. Herring roe is exported to Japan. Stocks have decreased in recent years and the fish are now used mainly as human food rather than for oil or fish meal. Herring has a high nutritional value, surpassed only by **eels**. Canadian landings have been as high as 528,000 tonnes in 1968 but were 242,340 tonnes in 1988, second in weight to **Atlantic cod**.

Atlantic hookear

Scientific name: *Artediellus atlanticus*
  Jordan and Evermann, 1898
Family: **Sculpin**
Other common names: hookear
French name: hameçon atlantique

Distribution: Found from southeastern Baffin Island south to Cape Cod. Also in Greenland and across the northern coast of Eurasia.

Characters: This fish and its relatives, the **rough** and **snowflake hookears**, are distinguished from other Arctic-Atlantic sculpins

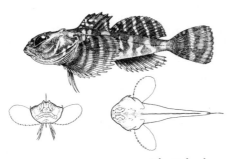

Atlantic hookear

by having the upper preopercular spine pointed and strongly hooked upwards, the margin of the first dorsal fin is often dark and both dorsal fins in males are spotted or barred. This species has 24–28 caudal fin rays, no parietal cirri, 13–24 teeth on the vomer bone and 16–39 teeth on the palatine bone, both in the roof of the mouth. First dorsal fin spines 7–9, second dorsal rays 12–16, anal rays 9–13 and pectoral rays 18–24. Lateral line pores 17–28. The overall colour is a light green-brown with dark brown to black or reddish blotches. The caudal peduncle has a dark band. The dorsal fins are dark with whitish streaks and broad bars. Other fins are thinly barred with dark pigment. Males have a higher first dorsal fin than females and the white streaks on it are prominent. Reaches 16.8 cm standard length.

Biology: This species is usually found on soft bottoms from shallows down to 875 m, usually deeper than 183 m but in shallower water in the Saguenay Fjord. Temperatures preferred are 0–3°C. Food is bottom inverte-brates such as worms, molluscs and rarely crustaceans. Males are larger than females. Mature females are 6.0 cm total length. Spawning is from May to November, perhaps as early as March–April in the Gulf of St. Lawrence, with each female having up to 150 eggs of 4.2 mm diameter.

Atlantic mackerel

Scientific name: *Scomber scombrus*
  Linnaeus, 1758
Family: **Mackerel**
Other common names: common mackerel, tinker, tacks, Boston mackerel
French name: maquereau bleu

Distribution: Found in Europe and in the western Atlantic Ocean from southern Labrador, Newfoundland and the southern Gulf of St. Lawrence south to North Carolina.

Characters: This species is distinguished from its Atlantic coast relatives by the widely separated dorsal fins (distance between greater than snout length), a low dorsal fin spine count, usually 5 dorsal and anal finlets, and no median but 2 short keels on the caudal peduncle. There is no swimbladder. An adipose eyelid is present. First dorsal fin spines 10–14, second dorsal rays 9–15 followed by 4–6 finlets. Anal fin with 1 spine, 10–14 soft rays and 4–6 finlets. Pectoral fin rays 18–21. Scales are small, cycloid and cover the whole body. The back is dark greenish-blue or blue-black with 20–33 wavy, dark bars on the upper flank. The bars become deep blue in dead fish. The lower flank and belly are white with silvery or copper tinges and may have some iridescent red or pink tinges. Jaws

Atlantic mackerel

and gill covers are silvery. Fins are dusky and the pectorals may have a black base. Attains 56 cm fork length and 3.4 kg. The world, all-tackle angling record weighed 1.2 kg and was caught in 1992 in Norway.

Biology: Large surface schools of mackerel are found in Canada in summer and fall, retreating to 70–200 m depths from Sable Island Bank southward in winter at temperatures above 7°C. Adults prefer 9–12°C temperatures but may be common up to 20°C and first appear in spring at 7–8°C, sometimes at temperatures as low as 2.8°C in the Cabot Strait. They are usually found in cooler water only as young fish ("tinkers"). Schools are made up of fish of the same size and age, since larger fish swim faster than smaller fish. They are rapid swimmers which move constantly in warmer weather to keep water flowing over the gills to satisfy a heavy oxygen demand. There are 2 populations in the northwestern Atlantic, one of which migrates to coastal U.S. waters in spring while the other migrates to the Gulf of St. Lawrence, a spawning ground. After spawning the Canadian fish move to feeding grounds off Newfoundland and Nova Scotia, and later to the Sable Island wintering area.

Mackerel filter feed on plankton but also pick individual crustaceans, arrow worms, squid and young fishes. They are food for such diverse fishes as **bluefish, Atlantic cod, threshers, bluefin tuna, striped bass, spiny dogfish, porbeagles, swordfish**, and squid, seabirds, porpoises and seals. Absence of a swimbladder facilitates rapid dives to evade their predators.

Growth is rapid in the short Canadian summer after spawning. Females grow bigger than males. Life span is about 18 years. Recruitment of age 1 fish to the stock varies greatly. For example from 428 million fish in 1962–63 to 7791 million fish in 1969. Sexual maturity is reached by some fish at 2 years and most are mature at 4 years and 32–34 cm.

Spawning in the Magdalen Shallows in Canada takes place principally from mid-June to mid-July. Larger fish arrive first at the spawning site. Spawning time coincides with maximum abundance of summer plankton which are smallest at this time and provide suitable food for larval mackerel. The larval mackerel grow in size with increasing plankton size as the summer progresses. Eggs are released in open water near the surface at 9–13.5°C and float in the upper 18 m of the water column. The average fecundity is about 400,000 eggs of 1.4 mm diameter. As the summer progresses, egg size decreases being only 1.1 mm in fish spawning in mid-August.

Mackerel are important sport fish in the U.S. caught from boats or in harbours by trolling or bait fishing. They are commercial fish in Canada with a 19,972 tonne catch in 1983 worth about $5 million. The catch in 1985 reached 29,862 tonnes. Mackerel are caught by purse and bar seines, gill nets, weirs and trap nets. They are sold fresh, frozen, canned, smoked or as fish meal. Mackerel are used as bait for snow crab and in the longline fishery for **tuna** and **swordfish**.

Occasionally some mackerel may have an odour reminiscent of a petroleum refinery. This is not caused by pollution but by the presence of the harmless chemical dimethyl sulphide which comes from eating pteropods, a pelagic snail. Paralytic shellfish toxins have been found in mackerel from the southwest Bay of Fundy.

Atlantic menhaden

Scientific name: *Brevoortia tyrannus*
　　(Latrobe, 1802)
Family: **Herring**
Other common names: pogy, mossbunker,
　　old wife, fat back, bugfish, bughead,
　　menhaden tyran
French name: alose tyran

Distribution: Found from the Gulf of St. Lawrence south to Florida.

Characters: This species is distinguished from its Atlantic coast relatives by a sharp, saw-toothed belly, dorsal fin not obviously anterior to the pelvic fins, and scale margins vertical with fine, fringing teeth. Dorsal fin rays 19–20, anal rays 20–24, pectoral rays 16–17 and pelvic rays 7. Lateral line scales

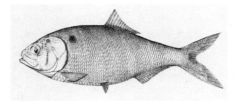

Atlantic menhaden

40–58. Gill rakers about 100–150. Pre-pelvic scutes 19–21, post-pelvic scutes 11–13. The overall colour is silvery, back with dark blue, green or brown tints, sides with some yellow to brassy tints. The upper flank behind the head bears a large black spot followed by several smaller ones in about 6 lines. Fins are yellowish. The caudal fin may be dusky at the edge and base. Peritoneum black. Reaches 51.0 cm.

Biology: This species is not common in Canadian waters and captures are usually regarded as strays from the south. Occasionally large schools enter Canadian waters. Resident populations are known from the Saint John River in New Brunswick, to 24 km upstream. Usually found in bays and tidal areas in Canada, elsewhere in coastal waters in large schools numbering many hundreds of thousands of fish which break the surface with their snouts and fins in a distinctive fashion.

Food is plankton such as diatoms, crustaceans and worms filtered with the numerous gill rakers. An estimated 28 litres/minute of seawater is filtered for its food content. The use of phytoplankton such as diatoms is rare in Canadian fishes. Numerous fish species as well as marine mammals and birds feed on menhaden.

Sexual maturity is attained at ages 2–3 and life span is up to 12 years. Spawning occurs May–October at night off the northern U.S.A. and requires a monthly mean maximum over 20°C. The Saint John River population is assumed to spawn there. Eggs are up to 1.9 mm in diameter and are buoyant. Up to 630,000 eggs are shed by each female. Menhaden are susceptible to mass mortality because of lowered temperatures or oxygen levels.

Menhaden are caught commercially by purse seines and over 420,000 tons may be taken annually on the American coast. This is the most important U.S. fishery in pounds landed on the Atlantic coast. The concentrated schools are spotted from the air using small aircraft. The pilots direct fishermen to the schools. Stocks have declined rapidly because of overfishing as evidenced by the fact that most of the catch prior to the mid-1960s was over 3 years old but now most is under 3 years. The menhaden are used in oil production and for fish meal and fertiliser. The flesh is too oily for human consumption. They are also important bait fish. Menhaden have been used to culture bacteria for antibiotic production and their oil is used in the manufacture of paints, linoleum, cosmetics and steel.

Atlantic moonfish

Scientific name: *Selene setapinnis*
    (Mitchill, 1815)
Family: **Jack**
Other common names: shiner, horsefish,
    bluntnose, dollarfish, musso atlantique
French name: assiette atlantique

Distribution: From Nova Scotia to Uruguay and in the eastern Atlantic Ocean.

Characters: This species is distinguished from its Canadian Atlantic coast relatives by the very compressed, deep body with an almost vertical but concave head margin, and by the anterior soft dorsal and anal fin rays being short. First dorsal fin spines 8, very short. The second dorsal fin has 1 spine and 21–24 soft rays, the anal fin 3–4 spines and 16–19 soft rays. Anal fin spines are not easily detected in adults. Overall colour is an iridescent silver with a metallic blue or bluish-green back. The second dorsal fin is greyish, with light yellow at its base. The caudal fin is greenish-yellow. Pectoral fins are light yellow to dusky green. Young fish have an elongate, black spot on midflank. Reaches 38 cm.

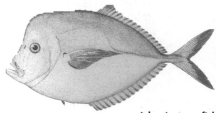

Atlantic moonfish

Biology: Strays from southern waters occur in Nova Scotia in most years, from late summer to fall. It is reported as not uncommon in St. Margarets Bay from September to October. The northern range limits are Halifax Harbour and off Sable Island Bank. A common species around docks and piers and down to at least 54 m. Young fish are found near the surface up to 180 km from shore while juveniles may enter bays and river mouths. Food is other fishes and crustaceans, often taken at night. It is eaten in Venezuela but is rarely used as food in North America.

Atlantic poacher

Scientific name: *Leptagonus decagonus*
   (Bloch and Schneider, 1801)
Family: **Poacher**
Other common names: Atlantic sea poacher,
   northern alligatorfish
French name: agone atlantique

   Distribution: Found from the Alaskan border along the Arctic coast to Baffin Island and south to the Grand Bank and rarely Sable Island and also in northern Europe and the Okhotsk and Bering seas.

   Characters: This poacher is 1 of 3 species in the Canadian Atlantic and Arctic oceans. It is distinguished from its relatives, the

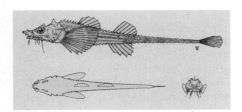

Atlantic poacher

Atlantic alligatorfish and the **Arctic alligatorfish**, by having 2 dorsal fins and 5 pairs of barbels around the mouth. The barbel at the rear of the jaw is branched. There are 41–48 keeled or spiny plates in the dorsal row. There are 5–8 first dorsal fin spines and 5–8 second dorsal fin soft rays. The anal fin has 5–8 soft rays. The pectoral fins have 13–17 rays. There are strong spines on the head and back. The overall colour is a yellowish-grey to brownish-grey with 2–3 darker bars along the flank. The pectoral and caudal fins are brown-black near their tips. A black band runs from the tip of the snout through the eye and fades posteriorly on the head. Attains 22.6 cm.

   Biology: Usually found over mud, clay and sand in colder waters down to –1.7°C but as warm as 5°C from 27–930 m, with deepest

records in Baffin Bay. Food is various crustaceans, molluscs, worms and other bottom organisms. There are some records of pelagic crustaceans in the diet so it may well swim off the bottom too. Spawning is suspected to occur in spring and summer. Eggs are pink, number up to 1750, and may be 2 mm in diameter. Fry are pelagic.

Atlantic pomfret

Scientific name: *Brama brama*
   (Bonnaterre, 1788)
Family: **Pomfret**
Other common names: Ray's bream
French name: grande castagnole

   Distribution: Found on both sides of the North Atlantic Ocean including, in the west, the Grand Bank south to northern South America. Also found in the South Atlantic and South Pacific oceans and the Indian Ocean.

   Characters: This species is distinguished from its Canadian relatives by the adults having scales on the dorsal and anal fins, a rounded head profile, a strongly compressed head such that the lower jaw bones touch each other at the ventral midline, caudal peduncle scales not abruptly larger than those on the caudal fin base, and more dorsal and anal fin rays on average than the **Pacific pomfret**. Dorsal fin rays 35–38, anal rays 29–32, pectoral rays 20–23. Scales in lateral series about 70–80. Body scales lack spines. All fins except the pectoral are scaly, with scales reaching almost to the edge of the fin. There is no caudal peduncle keel. Overall colour is a mottled silvery-black. The snout

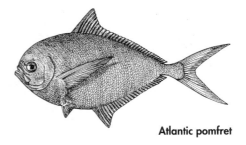

Atlantic pomfret

tip is black. Fins are generally black where not covered by scales. The innermost pectoral fin rays are clear and only the first 2 pelvic rays are black. The edge of the caudal fin is light. The mouth cavity is black. Reaches 70 cm standard length, but this was probably a northern expatriate.

Biology: First reported for Canada in 1881 or earlier but still a rare species. Found at 219.5–246.8 m in Canada, elsewhere to 1000 m. A pelagic, offshore species in waters at 12–24°C. Spawning may occur year round. Food includes crustaceans, fishes and squids. There is a longline commercial fishery off Spain for this species where most fish are 40–55 cm long. Fish are sold fresh or canned. Some are heavily parasitised.

Atlantic salmon

Scientific name: *Salmo salar*
  Linnaeus, 1758
Family: **Salmon**
Other common names:ouananiche, landlocked
  salmon, lake Atlantic salmon, sebago,
  Kennebec salmon, black salmon,
  grayling, bratan, saumon d'eau douce,
  sâma, saama, saamakutaak, kavisilik
French name: saumon de l'Atlantique

Distribution: Found from Ungava Bay south to the Gulf of Maine throughout Atlantic Canada including the Grand Bank and over deep ocean east of the Grand Bank, and up the St. Lawrence River, once to Lake Ontario. Rare specimens enter eastern Hudson Bay. Across the Atlantic to Greenland, Iceland and in western Europe. Introduced unsuccessfully to British Columbia and Alberta but may become established by farming operations. A successful introduction occurred in a lake near North Bay, Ontario. There are a number of naturally landlocked populations, known as ouananiche.

Characters: This species is characterised by having 109–124 lateral line scales, 10–12 principal dorsal fin rays, 8–11 principal anal rays, vomer bone in the roof of the mouth with teeth on its head and shaft, no spots or rows of spots on the caudal fin, 2–3 large spots on the gill cover, upper jaw not usually extending beyond the eye, no red on the flank or adipose fin in adults. Pectoral rays 14–15 and pelvic rays 9–10. Pyloric caeca 40–74. Spawning males develop a kype, or hooked lower jaw. The back is brown, green or blue,

flanks are silvery, and the belly is white. Black spots, often x- or y-shaped are found on the upper flank and back and sometimes on the caudal fin. Spawning males have bronze to dark brown colour and may have red,

Atlantic salmon

orange or rust-brown spots on the head and body. The pectoral and caudal fins may darken. Spawning females are grey to purple-blue and may become blackish. After spawning they become very dark and are known as kelts, slinks or black salmon. Young fish have a red spot between each of 8–11 narrow, parr marks. Young fish migrating to sea, known as smolts, racers, grilts or fiddlers, become silvery. Ouananiche have dark brown, bronze or bluish flanks with larger spots than sea run fish and sometimes light halos around the spots. Anadromous and non-anadromous salmon in the Gambo River, Newfoundland are reproductively isolated and genetically distinct. Reaches 150 cm and 35.9 kg. The world, all-tackle angling record from Norway in 1928 weighed 35.89 kg. The Canadian record was taken in 1982 by Donal C. O'Brien Jr. from the Cascapedia River, Quebec. His Atlantic salmon weighed 21.34 kg.

Biology: Atlantic salmon adults are found in coastal waters and some travel as far as Greenland, a migration of about 2400 km, or even Norway. They home to their birth river to reproduce after 1 or more years at sea. The ability of salmon to home to their birth stream over thousands of kilometres has not been fully explained. The earth's magnetic field, ocean currents or stars may be used to navigate to coastal waters where smell directs them to their stream of birth.

Fish returning to fresh water after 1 year are known as grilse and weigh 1.4–2.7 kg. Fish with 2 sea years weigh 2.7–6.8 kg and are known as salmon. Salmon in the sea grow much more rapidly than those in fresh water because of the year-round access to a wide range of foods compared to a 4–month feeding period restricted to smaller, less varied and sparse aquatic insect supplies. Maximum life span is 11 years as some fish survive spawning and run to sea more than once. Although some fish spawn twice, very few survive the arduous migrations and spawning acts to reproduce for a third time. Rarely some fish spawn 8 times. Repeat spawners may comprise as much as 34% of the Grand Cascapedia River, Québec population while in other rivers repeat spawners are as low as 5%.

Ouananiche are generally smaller than fish which have access to the rich food in the sea. Ouananiche in Gros Morne National Park, Newfoundland have slow growth, a small maximum fork length of 25 cm, low fecundity at a maximum of 268 eggs, and retain juvenile characters.

Young salmon or parr spend 2–4 years in fresh water in cool streams and rivers until 12–15 cm long when they run to sea as smolts. In Ungava this is delayed until 4–8 years of age and 18 cm. They may spend 6 or more years in the sea. Landlocked salmon remain in a lake and run into tributaries to spawn. Some ouananiche may have access to the sea but do not migrate while others are truly landlocked by physical barriers. Males grow faster and are larger than females.

Food of young salmon in fresh water is aquatic and terrestrial insects and of adults in the sea various crustaceans and a wide variety of fishes such as **capelin, smelt, gaspereau, herring, Atlantic cod, sand lance** and **mackerel**. Salmon on the spawning run do not feed and why they readily strike at wet and dry flies is something of a mystery. **American eels, sharks, swordfish, pollock, tuna**, birds and seals all eat salmon as young or adults.

Salmon spawn in October and November after entering estuaries from spring to autumn. The time of entry to each river is the same each year. The timing of entry depends in part on distance to travel. Spring runners often run to distant headwater streams and fall runners to lower reaches. The migration is not blocked by rapids or low waterfalls which the salmon leaps spectacularly, sometimes over 3.5 m.

The female excavates a redd in gravel bars and riffles by turning on her side and lashing her tail. Redds are up to 5.9 m long and 0.9 m wide and are found in water about 25 cm deep. Non-anadromous salmon in Newfoundland scatter their eggs among boulders while the anadromous salmon in the same stream construct redds. The male drives away competitors particularly grilse. Large male reproductive success depends on successful competition for access to a female as the large male rarely survives spawning. The female enters the redd by backing in and tests it with her anal fin for spawning suitability. She is joined by the male and eggs and sperm are shed as the pair quiver and gape. The male may nudge the female and glide across her. The female uses her tail at the upstream end of the redd to dislodge gravel and bury the eggs as deep as 25.4 cm. Small male parr, only 10–15 cm length, rush in to fertilise eggs during the spawning act. These are known as "sneaky males."

In some Canadian waters, such as the Matamek River, Québec, the proportion of grilse has increased from about 70% to about 85–90% and precocious parr (sneaky males) are much more numerous. The capture of large adults at sea by commercial fishermen has shifted reproduction to earlier life history stages. The shift is genetic as grilse matings result in offspring which return to spawn as grilse rather than salmon.

The large adults repeat the redd excavation and spawning for a week or more. Eggs are up to 7 mm in diameter, orange to amber and number up to 629 per kilogram of female body weight (and some females have over 20,000 eggs). Spawned out fish or kelts may rest in a pool for a few weeks or over winter or run to sea immediately. Eggs hatch in April after overwintering and the young fish, known as alevins, emerge from the gravel in May and June. Small salmon are called fingerlings or underyearlings and parr once the characteristic flank marks develop. Parr retreat into the gravel and under large rocks in the fall when temperatures drop to 9–10°C and re-appear only in spring and early summer when waters warm up. During the summer, most parr are found above the stream bed holding station over a stone.

Atlantic salmon are the quintessential sport fish as well as having great commercial importance. Comments on the lore and techniques of catching salmon are almost superfluous as numerous books have been written. They are easy to catch on the spawning migration using flies. Salmon rivers are a valuable commercial resource, access being controlled by public and private clubs. Their concentration in rivers for spawning make them susceptible to environmental changes and their high seas life to commercial exploitation by nations without an interest in conserving freshwater runs. The coastal fishery in Newfoundland and Labrador for example includes some fish from other Canadian provinces and from Maine. The West Greenland area is very important for maintaining Canadian stocks which are dependent on limitations on this fishery. About 40% of Canadian fish visit the Greenland feeding grounds and some travel as far as the Faroes. The annual North Atlantic catch is about 10,000 tons or 3 million fish. The Canadian catch in 1988 was 3847 tonnes and landings were worth about $4 million. Lake Ontario salmon were fished to extinction by 1890, compounded by construction of dams which blocked spawning streams. In addition to dams throughout its range, various pollutants and acid rain are just a few of many threats to this species.

The species is now being farmed in Canada with cage-reared fish in the Bay of Fundy being worth an estimated $16 million in 1987, with figures for more recent years expected to reach about $100 million. Attempts are being made to incorporate the "anti-freeze genes" from **winter flounder** into salmon to facilitate winter survival in inshore waters and so make cage-culture more effective.

- Most accessible from the middle of June to the middle of September depending on the individual river runs and seasonal variables.
- The drainage system of the north and south shores of the St. Lawrence River near Gaspe Bay as well as the drainage systems of the Maritime provinces and the northern rivers of Quebec emptying into Ungava Bay.
- Medium action spinning outfits loaded with 10– to 14–pound test line. The best

flyfishing equipment includes eight-and-a-half to nine-and-a-half-foot, eight-weight and nine-weight fly rods loaded with weight-forward floating fly lines.
- Wide assortment of 1/4– to 1/2–ounce casting spoons, spinners and minnow-imitating baits. Traditional patterns of Atlantic salmon flies in both dry and wet patterns are the standard.

Atlantic saury

Scientific name: *Scomberesox saurus*
  (Walbaum, 1792)
Family: **Saury**
Other common names: billfish, saury, saurel,
  skipjack, needlefish, skipper, aiguille de
  mer
French name: balaou

Distribution: Found in the temperate North Atlantic Ocean, in the west from the southern Gulf of St. Lawrence south to North Carolina, and in all southern oceans.

Characters: The only saury in Atlantic Canada with both jaws elongated into slender beaks and with 5–7 finlets behind the

Atlantic saury

posteriorly placed dorsal and anal fins. The lower beak is slightly longer than the upper beak. Teeth are in 2 rows on the upper and lower beaks and in 1 row behind the beaks. Scales number 107–128 in midline. Gill rakers number 34–45. Dorsal fin rays 15–18 and anal rays 17–21 (counts include finlets). Pectoral rays 12–15. The body is green or blue-green above, silvery below with golden tinges. The flanks have a silvery stripe. The flank has a dark green spot above the pectoral fin. The dorsal fin is greenish. Reaches 50 cm.

Biology: Found in the southern Gulf from Gaspé to central Newfoundland and the Grand Bank, and southward. It is an open ocean species at temperatures between 8.2

and 24.8°C. Schools can be abundant. This saury migrates north in summer and south in fall, and from surface waters to a maximum of 50 m deep and back each day. Food is zooplankton and occasionally small fishes. Spawning occurs in winter and early spring in the south when fish are 2–3 years old and at least 26 cm long. Eggs lack the filaments for attachment found in related species and are up to 3.2 mm in diameter. Life span may only be 4 years. Atlantic sauries are important food for other fishes such as **Atlantic cod, hakes, pollock, swordfish, marlins, tunas** and **mackerel**, marine mammals and sea birds. Sauries skip along the water surface when pursued by predators. They are fished for food and often canned but not in Canada where occurrence in commercial quantities is too irregular. Foreign ships, mostly Russian, took 3429 tonnes in 1972 but only 490 tonnes in 1975 in the northwest Atlantic.

Atlantic sharpnose shark

Scientific name: *Rhizoprionodon terraenovae*
  (Richardson, 1836)
Family: **Requiem Shark**
Other common names: sharpnosed shark,
  requin aiguille gussi
French name: requin à nez pointu

Distribution: From the Bay of Fundy, Nova Scotia south to the Caribbean Sea.

Characters: This requiem shark is distinguished by prominent labial furrows not extending in front of the eyes, no lateral keels on the caudal peduncle, teeth in both jaws without obvious serrations, triangular, oblique and notched on their outer edge, and anal fin origin obviously anterior to the origin of the second dorsal fin. The second dorsal fin is much smaller than the first, the

Atlantic sharpnose shark

snout is rounded and longer than mouth width, there are no posterior eye notches, and the rear tip of the first dorsal fin is ante-

rior to the pelvic fin origin. Grey or grey-brown to bluish grey fading to white below. Large fish have light spots on the upper body. The pectoral fins have white margins and dorsal and tail fins have dusky tips. Up to 1.2 m. The world, all-tackle angling record weighed 6.01 kg and was caught at Galveston, Texas in 1989.

Biology: There is only a single Canadian record taken at Grand Manan Island, N.B., in 1857 and preserved at the Museum of Comparative Zoology, Harvard University. Elsewhere from the intertidal zone down to perhaps 280 m. This shark is rare in Canada but to the south it is common in water shallower than 10 m, being found on sandy beaches in the surf, in enclosed bays, harbours and estuaries. There is some migration to deeper water offshore in winter with a return to shallow waters in spring. Food is small fishes such as **menhaden, silversides, jacks,** and others, and shrimps, crabs, worms and the feet of snails. The sharpnose shark is viviparous with a yolk-sac placenta. Unlike other requiem sharks, only the left ovary develops. There are 1–7 young per litter with larger females carrying more young. Gestation lasts 10–11 months and young are born in early summer. Females drop their young in shallow water and young measure 28–41 cm at birth. Males are mature at about 80–85 cm and 2–3 years and females at about 85–90 cm and 2–4 years. Maximum age is 7 years, rarely longer. This shark is fished for food in Mexico. The flesh is excellent. It is harmless to man but a nuisance in that it will take bait meant for larger fishes. Anglers do not usually fish for it because of its small size but it will take shrimp baited hooks on light tackle.

Atlantic silverside

Scientific name: *Menidia menidia*
  (Linnaeus, 1766)
Family: **Silverside**
Other common names: sand smelt, whitebait,
  shiner, sperling, capelin, green smelt
French name: capucette

Distribution: Found from the southern Gulf of St. Lawrence to Florida.

Characters: The long anal fin with 1 spine and 20–26 soft rays and a nearly straight edge characterises this species, the only Canadian Atlantic coast species in its family. First dorsal fin spines 3–7, second dorsal rays 7–10 with the fin origin over the middle of the anal fin. Scales 44–50 in lateral series with definite

Atlantic silverside

tubes on each scale for the lateral line. The back is translucent green, the flank has a silver stripe bordered above by a narrow black stripe and the belly is white. The top of the head and the chin are dusky. Scales are outlined by green or brown pigment spots. Fins are translucent. Apart from the head, gut and backbone, the whole body may be transparent. The peritoneum is black. Attains 15 cm.

Biology: Large schools of this silverside are found in bays, estuaries and salt marshes, often following the tides. They favour sandy or gravelly areas. However they have been found up to 170 km offshore and down to 126 m. Most fish were caught in one study at 2–6°C but the range was 1–22°C. Silversides move offshore during winter to avoid stressful or lethal low temperatures and mortality is high (90–99%). They are important in transferring energy from tidal areas to open water. Reported from the Saint John River, N.B. and from under ice in Malpeque Bay, P.E.I.

Food is plankton seized visually. It includes crustaceans, worms, squids and fish eggs, including their own, and small fishes. Insects are food in the Bay of Fundy in late summer when other foods are less abundant. Food is taken on the ebb tide since a rising tide creates extreme turbidity. However the rising tide disturbs bottom organisms which are eaten after high tide. **Striped bass, weakfish** and **bluefish** are important predators on silversides.

Females are larger than males. Life span in Canada can exceed 2 years since growth is slower, and stops in winter, than in southern U.S. waters where fish die after spawning at 1 year of age. However in P.E.I. age 1 and older

fish represent less than 3% of samples. Sexual maturity in Canada is attained at 1 year.

Spawning occurs from April to July in northern latitudes, earlier depending on temperature and latitude elsewhere. There is an inshore migration to vegetated areas. Spawning occurs only on filamentous algae. The time of spawning is at high tides during mid-morning at new and full moons. Preferred temperatures in Massachusetts are 9–21°C from late April to June and the silversides have 5, fortnightly spawnings. Eggs are up to 1.2 mm in diameter and become attached to the underside of algal mats by adhesive threads which are 5 times longer than the egg. The eggs may be spawned on a vertical algal mat such as those encrusting floating docks. A female may contain up to 5103 eggs. The eggs can be exposed to air for up to 10 hours a day as the tide recedes. Up to 10 males pursue a female and nudge or nip her vent region. Eventually the female quivers and releases eggs in the vegetation to be fertilised by the males. Water hardened eggs can pass unharmed through the gut of **mummichogs** and embryos pass through ruddy turnstones intact.

This silverside has temperature-dependent sex determination (TSD) in southern waters. At lower temperatures mostly females develop but males predominate at higher temperatures. The females are spawned in spring with a whole summer's growth ahead and the food to build up energy rich eggs. Males develop later in the summer when it is warmer but when there is less opportunity for growth. Males do not need to be as large as females which have to accommodate eggs, since sperm require much less space and energy. There is no TSD in Nova Scotia and sex is determined genetically, not environmentally. Here there is no advantage to being an early female because the growing season is short. Also northern areas have, perhaps, more variable temperature regimes between years and TSD would be too erratic.

Silversides are most important as food for commercial species but are edible particularly when fried as "whitebait." Some were canned in World War II. In 1979 316 tonnes valued at $91,000 were exported to Japan from P.E.I. as a food fish but the market in Japan failed in 1980. The catch was made with traps and dip-nets because seines are too efficient and contact with the bottom sediments caused a quality loss. The 1988 Canadian catch was 50 tonnes.

Atlantic snailfish

Scientific name: *Liparis atlanticus*
　(Jordan and Evermann, 1898)
Family: **Snailfish**
Other common names: seasnail
French name: limace atlantique

Distribution: Found from Ungava Bay along the Labrador coast to the estuary and Gulf of St. Lawrence, Newfoundland and south to the Bay of Fundy and on to New Jersey.

Characters: This snailfish is distinguished from its Arctic-Atlantic relatives in Canada by having an adhesive disc, 2 pairs of nostrils, a dorsal fin with an anterior notch in males and 31–35 rays, anal rays 25–29, pec-

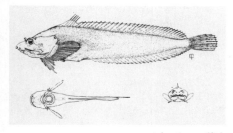

Atlantic snailfish

toral rays 26–31 and pyloric caeca 19–45. The lower pectoral lobe has finger-like rays. Teeth are trilobed and in bands. Males have thumb-tack shaped prickles on the body. Colour varies with the habitat, from black, grey and olive to reddish-brown. Fins are often barred with white, blue or pink. There may be light bars on the flank. The caudal fin is faintly barred. Peritoneum pale with faint brown dots. Reaches 14.4 cm. This species was first described from Godbout, Québec.

Biology: This snailfish is common in weedy tidepools, attached by the disc to the underside of rocks or to kelp. Favoured temperatures are 7–14.6°C. It may descend to 91 m. Food is taken mostly in the early morning and evening and is principally amphipods

and worms. Males tend to be larger than females. Most fish are mature at 6–7 cm and 2 years of age. Adults move into shallow water in October, retreating to deeper water only in very cold weather. Spawning occurs from March to June in Canada judging by females with large eggs. A large female has about 700 eggs which are laid in small egg masses, and then gathered into a single, large, attached mass by the male. Fertilised eggs are up to 1.4 mm in diameter.

Atlantic soft pout

Scientific name: *Melanostigma atlanticum*
　Koefoed, 1952
Family: **Eelpout**
Other common names: none
French name: mollasse atlantique

Distribution: Found from off central Labrador, the Gulf of St. Lawrence, the south coast of Newfoundland and the Grand Bank south to Cape Hatteras. Also off Europe and West Africa.

Characters: This species is distinguished from its Canadian Atlantic relatives by the lack of pelvic fins, terminal mouth, loose scaleless skin, gelatinous flesh, pore-like gill opening and 6–9, usually 6–8, pectoral fin rays. Dorsal fin rays 92–99 and anal rays 77–84 (includes caudal fin rays — without caudal rays 87–96 and 73–81 respectively). Vertebrae 93–99. Males usually have canine teeth in both jaws. The head and anterior body are a brilliant silvery-blue and the rest of the body is translucent. May be purplish-grey above becoming black near the tail. Peritoneum and anus black. The snout, nostril and chin are dark and the gill opening is dark brown. The gill and mouth cavities are black. The caudal fin may be bright red to brown and black. Reaches 15 cm.

Atlantic soft pout

Biology: Occasionally found in shallow water or down to 1853 m but usually at 276–366 m in Canada. This is a pelagic species.

Food is small crustaceans such as copepods. It is eaten by **redfish** in Canadian waters. Spawning occurs in summer and few (up to 56) large (3.9 mm) eggs are produced and guarded. Unusually, this pelagic species is found at 15–32 cm in burrows in silty clay, probably a reproductive behaviour. Eggs and juveniles have been found in subsurface anoxic sediments in early May, suggesting development over winter.

Atlantic Spanish mackerel

Scientific name: *Scomberomorus maculatus* (Mitchill, 1815)
Family: **Mackerel**
Other common names: thazard tacheté
French name: thazard atlantique

Distribution: Found from Nova Scotia south to Yucatan.

Characters: This species is distinguished from its Atlantic coast relatives by having the dorsal fins close together (separated by a dis-

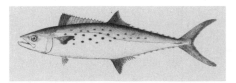

Atlantic Spanish mackerel

tance less than snout length), 17–19 first dorsal fin spines, 7–16, usually 10–16, gill rakers, the first dorsal fin black anteriorly and flanks with 2–3 rows of yellow to orange or bronze spots (dark in preserved fish). The lateral line is gently decurved under the second dorsal fin. Second dorsal fin rays 17–20 followed by 7–9 finlets. Anal fin rays 17–20 followed by 7–10 finlets. Pectoral rays 20–23. There is no corselet. Back dark blue and flanks silvery. The first dorsal fin margin is black but the basal, posterior membranes are white. Reaches 120 cm and 9 kg but usually to 77 cm. The world angling record weighed 5.98 kg, a fish caught at Ocracoke Inlet, North Carolina in 1987.

Biology: This mackerel was first caught in Canadian waters in 1985 off Sauls Island, Nova Scotia, a northern range limit. It is a schooling species of surface waters. There is a northward migration of some fish along the Atlantic coast in spring as waters warm and a retreat to overwinter off Florida in the fall. Food is such schooling fishes as **gaspereau, menhaden** and **anchovies** as well as crustaceans and squid. Most fish are mature at 3 years but some mature as early as 1–2 years. In Florida females mature at 25–32 cm fork length and males at 28–34 cm. Spawning off Florida occurs from July to September. Eggs measure 1.0 mm in diameter and are released in batches. This is a valuable sport and commercial species in the southern U.S. and Mexico. Airplane spotter pilots help to locate the schools. Annual production in Mexico is about 4900 tonnes in the Gulf of Mexico. Anglers catch this fish by trolling or drifting using boats or from shore by live bait fishing, jigging and drift fishing. The catch is sold fresh, frozen or smoked.

Atlantic spiny lumpsucker

Scientific name: *Eumicrotremus spinosus* (Fabricius in Müller, 1776)
Family: **Lumpfish**
Other common names: pimpled lumpsucker, man-iktoe
French name: petite poule de mer atlantique

Distribution: Found in the Arctic Ocean, including across the Canadian Arctic, and in the North Atlantic Ocean south to Cape Cod in the east.

Characters: This species is separated from its Arctic-Atlantic relatives by having the gill opening above the pectoral fin, many large, pointed tubercles each with many spines on the head, body and tail, supplemental pores above the lateral line, rounded anterior body, first dorsal fin spines not covered by a thickened layer of skin, pectoral fin base with tubercles, 4–5 tubercle rows between the eyes, and caudal area tubercles larger dorsally. Dorsal fin spines 6–7, soft rays 10–13, anal rays 9–13, and pectoral rays 21–26. Lateral line pores 13–14. Tubercles large and rough. There are 1–4 rows of tubercles under the lower jaw. Three pairs of tubercles are along the base of the first dorsal fin. Olive in young, darker in adults. There may be stripes or bands posteriorly. Tubercles sometimes fringed with a dark ring. Reaches 13.2 cm.

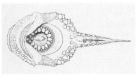

Atlantic spiny lumpsucker

ventral view

Biology: This species lives on stone, gravel or mud bottoms at 5–100 m and down to 930 m with young in shallow waters. Temperature range is –1.8 to 3°C. Food is crustaceans, oikopleura and fish. This lumpfish is eaten by **Atlantic cod** and thick-billed murres. Spawning occurs in March and/or early fall at 20–30 m. Eggs are orange or golden-yellow and 4–5 mm in diameter. It is common in Atlantic Canada.

Atlantic sturgeon

Scientific name: *Acipenser oxyrinchus*
    Mitchill, 1814
Family: **Sturgeon**
Other common names: sea sturgeon, common sturgeon; and when young — sharpnose sturgeon, pelican, escargot or escaille
French name: esturgeon noir

Distribution: Found from Hamilton Inlet, Labrador south throughout Atlantic Canada to Florida. Possibly as far north as Ungava Bay.

Characters: This sturgeon is distinguished from its eastern Canadian relatives by usually

Atlantic sturgeon

having 4 small plates between the anal fin and the caudal fulcrum. The snout is long and pointed. Dorsal fin rays 38–46, anal rays

26–28. Dorsal row plates 7–16, lateral plates 24–35 and ventral plates 8–14. Gill rakers 15–27. The back is blue-black to olive-green fading to a white belly. The dorsal fin tip is white as is the posterior margin. The rest of the fin is grey to blue-black. The leading edge of the pectoral and pelvic fins, the lower lobe of the caudal fin and the anal fin are white. The rest of the pectoral, pelvic and anal fins is grey. The eye is pale golden. The body cavity organs and the peritoneum are nearly white. The spiny keel of the dorsal and lateral plates is white. Ventral plates are wholly white. The specific epithet is also spelt *oxyrhynchus*. Reaches 5.49 m and reputedly, 364.9 kg, although most are much smaller.

Biology: This species is anadromous, living in the sea and moving into fresh water in May to July in Canada to spawn but as early as February in the southern U.S.A. The upstream migration is slow and spawning occurs in summer. Tagging in Canadian waters has shown a distance of at least 1448 km may be travelled in the sea over a period of 1 year.

Food is molluscs, aquatic insects and crustaceans in fresh water and worms, snails, crustaceans and such fish as **sand lances** in the sea. They do not feed during the spawning migration. **Sea lampreys** may kill Atlantic sturgeon and these sturgeon are known to jump in an apparent effort to rid themselves of this parasite.

Life span is over 60 years. In the St. Lawrence River sexual maturity is attained at 22–24 years and 165 cm for males and 27–28 years and 190 cm for females but much earlier in Florida. Spawning takes place at 13–18°C and is presumed to occur in deep pools below waterfalls in rivers. There is a 3–7 year interval between spawnings. Eggs are light to dark brown and adhere to the bottom. Each egg is up to 3.0 mm in diameter and a female may have up to an estimated 3,755,745 eggs. The young remain in fresh water for 3–6 years before migrating to the sea.

Both the flesh and the eggs of this species have been used. The flesh is best when smoked and was known as "Albany beef" in New York. It is not as good as the flesh of lake sturgeon. The scutes were used in Colonial times as nutmeg graters. Catches in Canadian waters have declined and are usually incidental to other fisheries. Sturgeon are caught with gill nets, pound nets and weirs. A New Brunswick catch of 23 tonnes in 1980 was worth $50,860. Canadian landings are at about 3.4% of former levels, i.e. 120,000 kg annually in the 1980s compared to 3.5 million kg in the 1880s. The decline is owing to dams obstructing the spawning migration, pollution, and fishing pressure when easily accessible on the migration. This sturgeon has been exploited by man for over 4000 years based on excavations of native sites.

Atlantic tomcod

Scientific name: *Microgadus tomcod*
　(Walbaum, 1792)
Family: **Cod**
Other common names: tommycod, winter cod, snig, frostfish, poisson de Noël, loche, petite morue, poisson des chenaux
French name: poulamon atlantique

Distribution: Found from southern Labrador and the Gulf of St. Lawrence to North Carolina and in fresh water at various localities in Atlantic Canada.

Characters: This species is separated from other Canadian Arctic-Atlantic cods by having 3 dorsal and 2 anal fins, the first dorsal fin being rounded, a projecting snout, a short, broad barbel about as long as pupil diameter, no large black blotch on the flank, a white lateral line and a small eye entering about 6.2 times in head length. The second pelvic fin ray is elongated and the tail is rounded. Teeth in the jaws and roof of the mouth are fine and

Atlantic tomcod

numerous. First dorsal fin rays 11–15, second dorsal rays 15–20 and third dorsal rays 16–21. First anal fin rays 12–25 and second anal rays 16–22. Pectoral fin rays 16–19. Gill rakers 16–21. Overall colour greenish-brown, olive-brown to brown tinged green or yellow, with pale blotches and marbling on the body and fins. The belly is grey to yellowish. Attains 42.1 cm and 570 g.

Biology: The tomcod favours shallow, inshore waters and enters brackish or fresh waters to spawn. Spawning migrations are not extensive although some fish move up to 240 km from salt water. Landlocked populations have a life cycle confined to fresh water such as in Lake St. John, Québec and Deer Lake, Newfoundland.

Tomcod feed on crustaceans primarily but also take worms, molluscs, squids and a variety of smaller fishes. Food concealed in the seabed can be sensed by the barbel and pelvic fin tips. In the Bay of Fundy 75% of the food is a single species of amphipod crustacean. Chironomid larvae and fish eggs are important food in brackish water populations in addition to amphipods. Life span is short, less than 7 years and fish can be mature at 1 year. Spawning occurs from November to February as adults enter inshore waters to lay eggs in estuaries and rivers, often under the ice. Some eggs develop in frasil ice, up to 115 eggs/l, being reported. Each female may deposit up to 65,780, 1.9 mm diameter, adhesive eggs over sand, gravel or rocks. Development requires fresh or brackish water and does not take place when eggs are in water saltier than 30‰. Temperatures at spawning are about 0–4°C. Young drift downstream into estuarine areas. Males have testes with a small number of lobes, characteristic of brackish and freshwater **Cod Family** members.

Tomcod are caught by anglers in summer along the coast but the main sport fishery is in winter using baited hooks through the ice in estuaries after the spawning run. They are also caught with dip-nets in streams during the spawning run. Pollution of spawning rivers has eliminated many of the Québec winter ice fisheries. The most famous fishery is at Sainte-Anne-de-la-Pérade where 500–600 tomcod can be caught by an angler overnight during the Christmas period. Here the tomcod spawn under the ice at depths of only 1–3 m. Anglers erect as many as 1000 cabins, supplying them with heat and electricity. Cabins are also rented to tourists. A long rectangular hole is cut in the ice and covered with a board to prevent freezing when not fishing. Baited hooks are used to catch the fish. Commercial quantities of tomcod are taken in **smelt** trap nets in the Miramichi River estuary of New Brunswick but this only amounts to about 200 tonnes annually with a value of about $25,000. This catch is turned into animal food. The total Canadian catch in 1988 was only 10 tonnes.

Atlantic torpedo

Scientific name: *Torpedo nobiliana*
   Bonaparte, 1835
Family: **Electric Ray**
Other common names: Atlantic electric ray, numbfish, crampfish
French name: torpille noire

   Distribution: Found in the North Atlantic Ocean and Mediterranean Sea. In the western Atlantic from Nova Scotia south possibly as far as Florida.

   Characters: This is the only electric ray in Atlantic Canada and it is recognised by the rounded, thick, smooth, spineless disc, short,

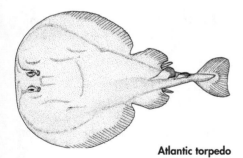

Atlantic torpedo

thick tail and 2 dorsal fins, the anterior one the larger. Spiracles have smooth margins. Teeth are small with sharp, curved cusps and up to 7 rows functioning at any time. Dark chocolate to purplish brown, black or slate-grey above, white to cream below. The lower disc margins and pelvic fin edges are often dusky. The tail has irregular, dark markings. Reaches at least 180 cm and 65 kg, possibly to 90 kg.

   Biology: This electric ray strays into Canadian waters in the summer months as far north as LaHave Bank, St. Margarets Bay and

the neighbouring coast, and into the lower Bay of Fundy at depths down to 110 m. Elsewhere reported from 10 to 350 m, and so not likely to be encountered by bathers. Adults migrate long distances and are frequently pelagic. Food is mostly large fishes which are captured by a sudden spring, envelopment by the pectoral fins and a discharge of the electric organs. Each female may have up to 60 embryos. Young are born alive offshore in summer after a year-long gestation. They are then 25 cm long. This electric ray can deliver 220 volts, a shock powerful enough to floor a man and dangerous to those with a heart condition. Most shocks cause only a slight numbing sensation.

Atlantic warbonnet

Scientific name: *Chirolophis ascanii*
   (Walbaum, 1792)
Family: **Shanny**
Other common names: Yarrell's blenny
French name: toupet marbré

   Distribution: From Baffin Island to the Gulf of St. Lawrence and off southeastern Newfoundland. Also in the eastern North Atlantic Ocean.

   Characters: This is the only Atlantic member of a related group of 5 shanny species which includes the **warbonnets** and the **pearly prickleback**. It is the only Atlantic shanny with obvious cirri. It has 50–54 dorsal fin spines, 35–40 anal fin rays and a large cirrus over each eye with a smaller one in front. There are various other small cirri on the head and anterior dorsal fin spines. The body is yellowish-brown, has bright red-brown lines and is darkly blotched or banded. A dark ring around the eye continues ventrally as a cheek bar. Attains 25 cm standard length.

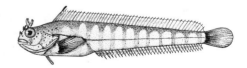

Atlantic warbonnet

   Biology: Canadian Atlantic records are all of small, young fish. Found in rocky areas among seaweed from 20 to 400 m. It is not intertidal. Food is worms, molluscs, hydroids, sponges and algae. In Europe spawning occurs in October and November and eggs (2.3–2.8 mm in diameter) are deposited in small flattened masses on stones. The young are pelagic.

Atlantic wolffish

Scientific name: *Anarhichas lupus*
  Linnaeus, 1758
Family: **Wolffish**
Other common names: striped wolffish, ocean wolffish, catfish, ocean whitefish, seacat, rock salmon
French name: loup atlantique

Distribution: Found in the North Atlantic Ocean. In the western Atlantic from Davis Strait and Labrador through maritime Canada including the Gulf of St. Lawrence to New Jersey.

Characters: This species is distinguished from its Arctic/ Atlantic relatives in Canada by the colour pattern and by having the teeth

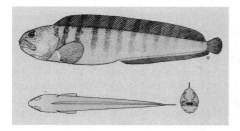

Atlantic wolffish

on the vomer bone in the centre of the roof of the mouth extending back beyond the palatine teeth at the sides. Dorsal fin spines 69–79, anal rays 42–48, pectoral rays 18–20, and vertebrae 72–78. Caudal fin rays 22–26, usually 24–25. Mean vertebral counts increase from north to south, the reverse of the usual pattern in other fish species with pelagic eggs. Colour is variable from blue-grey or slate, to yellowish, olive-green and purplish-brown. The flank and dorsal fin have 9–13 dark brownish and irregular bars. The belly is a dirty white. Reaches about 152 cm. The world, all-tackle angling record weighed 23.58 kg in 1986 and was caught on Georges Bank, Massachusetts.

Biology: This wolffish is more common in southern waters than its relatives. It is found close to shore in the north but around Newfoundland and on the Scotian Shelf it is usually at 22–366 m and in water temperatures as low as –1°C and up to 13°C. It does not form schools. Young Atlantic wolffish are not found in inshore Newfoundland waters and probably live in deep water until they become sexually mature. Large wolffish on Georges Bank migrate to shallow waters in spring and return to deep waters in fall. They tend to stay in one area for many years; some tagged in the Newfoundland area were within 3.2–8.0 km of their capture site 5–7 years later. One fish, however, moved 853 km from the Flemish Cap to Labrador.

Food is mainly sea urchins and starfish, molluscs and crustaceans with the occasional unwary **redfish**. Anterior teeth are used for grasping prey and the molariform lateral and posterior teeth for crushing. Green sea urchins are 75% of the diet in eastern Newfoundland. **Atlantic cod** are known to eat young wolffish.

Adults are mature at 8–10 years when 50–60 cm long although some females are mature at 31 cm and some males only at 69 cm. They live about 22 years.

Spawning is preceded by an inshore migration in spring but only takes place in August–September. Fertilisation is internal, copulation taking place during a 3–6 hour period when the male and female are close together. Eggs are released over the 7–15 hours following as the female lies on her side. The eggs are very large, up to 6.5 mm in diameter, and are yellow. A large spawning area has been reported south of LaHave Bank based on egg masses dredged up in March. Larvae are pelagic until 5–6 cm long. Males do not feed while guarding egg clusters.

Atlantic wolffish are incidental catches in trawl fisheries for groundfish and are sold as "catfish." The flesh is excellent. About 3109 tonnes were caught in 1984 in Atlantic Canada and the northwest Atlantic catch for this species and the **spotted wolffish** was 10,200 tonnes in 1981. The 1989 catch in Canada was worth about $439,000. This wolffish has been reported to make "furious" attacks on waders in tidal pools in Maine.

aurora rockfish

Scientific name: *Sebastes aurora*
(Gilbert, 1890)
Family: **Scorpionfish**
Other common names: none
French name: sébaste aurore

Distribution: Found from northern British Columbia to Baja California.

Characters: This species is recognised by a small toothed knob at the tip of each upper jaw. Dorsal fin spines 13, soft rays 12–14, usually 13. Anal fin soft rays 5–7, usually 6, the second anal spine is twice as thick as the third and curved posteriorly in Canadian specimens. The second spine is equal or longer in length than the third spine. Pectoral fin rays 16–19, usually 17, with 0–6 rays unbranched. Gill rakers 24–28. Vertebrae 26. Lateral line pores 27–31, scale rows below the lateral line 41–50. Head spines are strong and only the coronals may be absent. Rose-red, pink, peach or orange-red on the back, silvery on the sides and belly. The mouth and gill cavities are red. The peritoneum is black, or silver-grey with black dots. When caught by trawlers, the scales are lost, leaving white pockets rimmed with red. Reaches 39 cm.

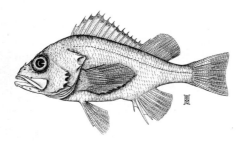

aurora rockfish

Biology: A common offshore species at 183–768 m on soft bottoms, but first reported from off Vancouver Island in 1968. It is caught by trawlers and in traps meant for **sablefish**. Young are born in June or later in British Columbia and have an extended midwater life. They have strong dark bars alternating with practically transparent body areas. This pattern serves as a concealing mechanism in the open ocean.

aurora trout

Scientific name: *Salvelinus fontinalis timagamiensis* Henn and Rinckenbach, 1925
Family: **Salmon**
Other common names: aurora char
French name: omble de fontaine aurora

Distribution: Found in White Pine, Whirligig, Wilderness and Aurora lakes of northeastern Ontario in the Ottawa River basin.

Characters: The aurora trout is a sub-species of the **brook trout** according to some authors, merely a distinctively coloured stock

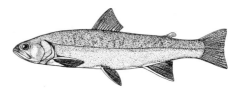

aurora trout

according to others. It was originally described as a distinct species. The attention paid to this fish as a symbol of loss from the effects of acid rain warrants a separate account. Aurora trout lack the yellow spots and vermiculations found in **brook trout**, have fewer red spots on the flank (0–6, mean 1.4 compared to a mean of 11.2), more caudal vertebrae (29–31, mean 30.6 compared to 26–29, mean 27.8), more total single neural spines (27–32, mean 28.5 compared to 20–29, mean 26.3), and more ribs with bifid heads (33–36, mean 34.5 compared to 31–36, mean 33.2). Other countable characters like scales and fin rays are similar to **brook trout**. Aurora trout are a brilliant vermilion red on the flanks when spawning. The back is a deep, purple-black and males have a jet-black, hooked lower jaw and a humped back. The flanks are usually silvery, sometimes with a purplish sheen and the back olive-brown. The belly is white. Pectoral, pelvic and anal fins have a white leading edge, followed by a black bar and orange or reddish on the rest of the fin. Juvenile aurora trout do show vermic-ulations as in **brook trout** but these fade with growth (over 19.0 cm total length). Reaches 60.0 cm total length and 3.5 kg. The largest recorded catch of an aurora trout was made by Geoff Bernardo in September 1993. It weighed 1.76 kg. and was taken out of Carol Lake in northern Ontario. This species is not being promoted as a viable sportfish due to its extreme sensitivity to changes in environmental conditions, and to the fact that only very small numbers are naturally reproducing in the wild.

Biology: The natural populations became extinct by 1971 because of acid rain which lowered the pH to 4.5–4.8 by the mid-1980s. **Trout** have trouble reproducing below pH 5.5 and are eliminated below pH 5.0. The aurora trout survives only as hatchery stock which have been introduced into various northern Ontario lakes which are designated fish sanctuaries. Some lakes were opened to anglers in 1986 for the month of August with a limit of one aurora trout per angler. However there has not been significant spawning success in lakes and survival depends on hatchery stocks. The trout are also being re-introduced into Whirligig Lake after limestone has been added to reduce acidity. Sulphur dioxide emissions from nickel smelting plants in nearby Sudbury, the cause of acid rain, has decreased enough in recent years to give the trout a chance of survival. Food was mostly water boatmen and whirligig beetles. Some other aquatic insects, crustaceans including crayfish, and **brook sticklebacks** were also eaten. Growth was similar to **brook trout**. Life span was 6 years with maturity attained at 2–3 years. This trout spawned on lake shoals in late October and early November at 4–6°C while **brook trout** favour stream spawning. Spawning time is later than that of **brook trout**. Fecundity reached 7000 eggs. The Committee on the Status of Endangered Wildlife in Canada gave this fish a status of "endangered" in 1987. The few anglers who have caught this fish report that it had twice the fight of **brook trout** and jumped more.

aurora unernak

Scientific name: *Gymnelus retrodorsalis* Le Danois, 1913
Family: **Eelpout**
Other common names: aurora pout
French name: unernak aurore

Distribution: Found from Bathurst Inlet in the Canadian Arctic east to Greenland and the Barents and Kara seas. Also recorded from Bonavista Bay, Newfoundland.

Characters: This species is distinguished from its Canadian Arctic-Atlantic relatives by lacking pelvic fins, having a terminal mouth,

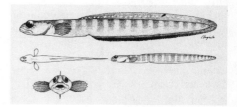

aurora unernak

gill opening extending to middle of pectoral fin base, firm skin, no scales, 13–20 brown bars on the body and tail running to the anal fin base, usually 10–11 pectoral rays, 90–105 vertebrae, and dorsal fin origin at or behind the pectoral fin margin. There are 3–14 pterygiophores (internal fin ray supports) without rays at the front of the dorsal fin. Dorsal fin rays 76–99, anal rays 71–85 and pectoral rays 9–12. Overall colour is light tan to translucent cream. There may be several blue-black eye spots on the dorsal fin. Males have a black anal fin. The pectoral fin is whitish. Young fish may have 11–14 white spots along the base of the dorsal fin. Reaches 14 cm.

Biology: Reported on mud, sand, clay and gravel bottoms at 5–481 m and –1.8 to 4.0°C. Life span is about 5 years. Females mature at 9–10 cm standard length and spawning is in late summer to fall. Eggs number up to 28 and are 4.8 mm in diameter.

B

backfin tapirfish

Scientific name: *Lipogenys gilli*
  Goode and Bean, 1894
Family: **Tapirfish**
Other common names: none
French name: tapir à dorsale

Distribution: Found off Nova Scotia to the southwestern Grand Bank, south to the Hudson Canyon off Maryland. Also from Japan.

Characters: Most of the characters are summarised in the family account. The underside of the snout has many fine barbels, particularly close to the mouth. Light brown

backfin tapirfish

overall with the ventral part of the gill covers and the gill cavity dark brown. Fins are blackish-brown. Mouth lining a light yellowish tan. Attains 43 cm.

Biology: An uncommon species with only about 14 specimens preserved in museums, 9 from Canadian waters. Found at depths of 350–1582 m in cool waters (4–5°C). Food is obtained from the muddy bottom by sucking up large quantities of oozy material. The very long intestine extracts any food items embedded in the mud. They may feed continuously to obtain enough nutrition.

bald halosaur

Scientific name: *Aldrovandia phalacra*
  (Vaillant, 1888)
Family: **Halosaur**
Other common names: none
French name: halosaure chauve

Distribution: Found in the Atlantic, Indian and Pacific oceans including off Atlantic Canada.

Characters: This species is distinguished from its relative, the **longfin halosaur**, by having an unpigmented lateral line and black pyloric caeca. Dorsal fin with 10–12 rays, pectoral fin with 1 spine and 11–13 soft rays and pelvic fin with 1 spine and 8 soft rays. The pectoral fin is short, not reaching the

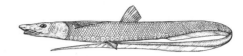

bald halosaur

dorsal fin. There are 24–28 scales anterior to the anus. The snout upper surface, head and opercle are scaleless. Pyloric caeca 5–8. The body is light grey, the head silvery-blue on the top and sides and dark below, and the gill cover margin is black. Mature males have enlarged nostrils with the anterior nostril a black tube. Attains 50 cm.

Biology: First reported from Canada on the upper continental slope off Nova Scotia in 1988 between 933 and 1125 m. Elsewhere it is found swimming just above the mud or ooze sea floor at 500–2300 m, usually above the 4°C isotherm. Food is small crustaceans such as amphipods and copepods. Females are caught 4 times more often than males.

balloonfish

Scientific name: *Diodon holocanthus*
  Linnaeus, 1758
Family: **Porcupinefish**
Other common names: spiny puffer
French name: diodon tacheté

Distribution: Found from Nova Scotia south to Brazil in the western Atlantic Ocean but world-wide in warmer waters.

Characters: The beak-like jaws and body covered with double-rooted, moveable spines are characteristic. Spines are folded back when

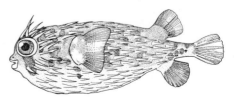

balloonfish

the fish is not inflated. The spines on top of the head are longer than those on the body. The dorsal and anal rays number 13–15. Adults are brownish-yellow with dark brown to black spots and blotches on the flanks. There are 4 dark saddles across the back and a broad, dark bar runs vertically through the eye. The belly is a pale yellow. Reputed to attain 56 cm.

Biology: Found in Canada only as larval or postlarval strays at depths of 100–200 m. Adults are found in shallow water on reefs and soft bottoms. Food is sea urchins, molluscs, and crabs crushed by the beak. Eggs are pelagic and measure 1.7–1.8 mm in diameter. The skin has a poison distasteful to most predators. Balloonfish are often dried and sold as curios.

ballyhoo

Scientific name: *Hemiramphus brasiliensis*
  (Linnaeus, 1758)
Family: **Halfbeak**
Other common names: balourou
French name: demi-bec brésilien

Distribution: Found from Nova Scotia south to Brazil and in the eastern Atlantic Ocean.

Characters: Distinguished from its only Canadian relative, the **silverstripe halfbeak**, by having 11–15, usually 12–13, anal fin rays, the pelvic fin is long reaching back beyond the dorsal fin origin, and by colour. Dorsal fin rays 12–15. Dorsal and anal fins are unscaled. Lower caudal fin lobe long. Dark green to bluish above, silvery on the flanks and whitish below. The lower jaw tip

ballyhoo

is red and upper caudal fin lobe is orange-red to yellow-orange. Young have weak bars. Reaches 40.5 cm.

Biology: Known from a single specimen caught southeast of Halifax in 1978 as a stray from the south. This is a northern range record. Adults are found in bays and near reefs in very large schools in southern waters.

Young are pelagic. Food is small fishes and manatee grass in southern U.S.A. A popular bait species for fishermen chasing sailfishes and **marlins**, ballyhoo can be caught under lights at night or in seines.

banded gunnel

Scientific name: *Pholis fasciata*
  (Bloch and Schneider, 1801)
Family: **Gunnel**
Other common names: mottled gunnel, tissy, tansy, kugsaunak
French name: sigouine rubanée

Distribution: North Pacific Ocean, but not British Columbia, North Atlantic and Arctic oceans including Coronation Gulf, Hudson Bay, Labrador, Newfoundland and rarely Passamaquoddy Bay.

Characters: There are 83–91 dorsal fin spines (usually more than in the related **rock gunnel**) and 2 spines with 41–48 soft rays in the anal fin. The pectorals are present with

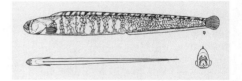

banded gunnel

11–13 rays, but the pelvics may be present or absent. Yellow-grey overall. A dark band over the head, through and below the eye posteriorly, is offset by a light band with a posterior dark margin. This light band is absent in the related **rock gunnel**. The dorsal fin and upper back have 10–12 triangular light areas often with darker areas between forming saddles, and speckled with darker spots. Flanks have light bars and may become scarlet. Attains 30.3 cm total length. The French common name is a variant of scie égohine or égoïne, a compass saw, in reference to the sharp dorsal spines which can easily cut the hand.

Biology: Found intertidally or below the tide level down to at least 28 m, usually associated with rocks. Food is small crustaceans and worms. Eaten by various sea birds and by inshore fishes such as **Arctic cod** and **Sculpin Family** members.

banded killifish

Scientific name: *Fundulus diaphanus*
  (Le Sueur, 1817)
Family: **Killifish**
Other common names: freshwater mummi-
  chog, freshwater killy, grayback, topmin-
  now, eastern and western banded killifish,
  menona killifish, barred minnow, hardhead
French name: fondule barré

Distribution: Found in Arctic and Atlantic
drainages of Canada including brackish waters
of the Atlantic coast. It is found from southwestern and southeastern Newfoundland,
Anticosti Island, rarely on the north shore of
the Gulf of St. Lawrence, and from the southern Gulf of St. Lawrence south to South
Carolina. It extends up the St. Lawrence valley, across southern Ontario and in the southern Great Lakes basin but not north of Lake
Superior, and is in Lake of the Woods and
southern Manitoba and as far west as eastern
Montana.

Characters: This species is distinguished
from its relatives, the **mummichog** and the
blackstripe topminnow by lacking a strong,
dark lateral stripe, gill rakers are 4–7 and the
dorsal fin origin lies in advance of the anal
fin origin. Dorsal fin rays 10–15, anal rays
9–13 and pectoral rays 14–19. Scales in lateral series 35–51, no lateral line pores.

Back brown to olive-green or olive-yellow, silvery on the flanks and white or yellow

banded killifish

on the belly. There are 8–20 green-brown
bars along the flank. Males have more and
wider bars than females (8–15 bars).
Breeding males develop a green-gold dorsal
fin with faint black bars, stronger, wide,
green flank bars, a yellow throat and have an
intense blue-green back. Males have larger
dorsal and anal fins than females.

Hybrids with **mummichog** are reported
from 2 localities in Canada. There are 2 subspecies in Canada: *F. d. diaphanus* found from
the Atlantic coast to east of Lake Ontario and
the upper St. Lawrence River and *F. d.
menona* Jordan and Copeland, 1877 in the
rest of Canada. They are distinguished by the
western subspecies having fewer lateral
scales, fewer dorsal, anal and pectoral fin
rays, and a stripe through the bars on the
caudal peduncle. Attains 11.4 cm.

Biology: This killifish is primarily a
freshwater species but was first reported
from Newfoundland in 1952 and the Québec
North Shore in 1977 and can presumably tolerate saline conditions long enough to cross
the Gulf of St. Lawrence. In fresh waters
banded killifish are found in schools in quieter parts of lakes and slow rivers over sand,
gravel or detritus near aquatic plants. It tolerates low oxygen and high temperatures
(above 38°C). When disturbed this fish will
dive into the substrate at an angle of 45°,
burying itself by vigorous lateral body
movements. It may remain wholly or partially buried for less than a minute to more
than 2 hours. This behaviour can be learned.

Food is taken at all levels in the water column and includes insect larvae, crustaceans,
molluscs, flatworms, and flying insects at the
surface. Feeding occurs mainly in the afternoon with a shorter period starting just before
dawn. It is eaten by various fishes and birds.

Life span is up to 4 years. Spawning
occurs in spring and summer. In Québec
spawning occurs in mid-July to August when
fish are 2 years old and water temperatures
are 21–25°C. Elsewhere maturity at 1 year
has been recorded. Males establish territories
in weedy areas and fight off other males. The
male pursues a female until she extrudes an
egg which hangs from her body by a filament. The male redoubles his pursuit and
drives the female into vegetation, presses
against the female using his dorsal and anal
fins, and the female extrudes 5–10 more
eggs. The male quivers, bends his body and
fertilises the eggs. The eggs separate from
the main thread and each other and become
tangled in weeds by their own threads. This
mating takes only 15–30 seconds and is

repeated several times over 5 minutes until about 50 eggs are deposited. Egg diameters are up to 2.0 mm and a female can contain 426 yellow-orange to orange eggs.

This killifish has been used as bait in the Maritimes since it is easily transported, reputedly for days packed only in leaves in a can.

The Committee on the Status of Endangered Wildlife in Canada approved a status of "vulnerable" for populations of this species from Newfoundland in 1989.

banded rudderfish

Scientific name: *Seriola zonata*
　(Mitchill, 1815)
Family: **Jack**
Other common names: amber jack, pilotfish,
　seriole guaimeque
French name: sériole à ceintures

Distribution: Found from Prince Edward Island and Nova Scotia south to Brazil.

Characters: This species is distinguished from its Canadian Atlantic coast relatives by the moderately deep but not highly com-

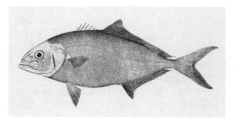

banded rudderfish

pressed body, a lateral line without enlarged scales (scutes), a fleshy lateral caudal peduncle keel, a long upper jaw extending to the rear eye margin or beyond and 8 first dorsal fin spines. The second dorsal fin has 1 spine and 33–40 soft rays. The anal fin has 3 spines and 20–21 soft rays. Gill rakers number 20–25 when fish are under 10 cm fork length and 14–17 when over 40 cm fork length. Young fish up to 30 cm have 5–6 broad, blackish bands on the flank, extending onto the dorsal and anal fins. Adults lose these bands but retain one which runs from the eye to the first dorsal fin origin. Overall colour is blue to blue-brown or silver-brown.

The dorsal fin is greenish with the margin white. Reaches 69 cm fork length and 5.2 kg.

Biology: This jack is caught occasionally from June to October in Nova Scotian waters and as a rare stray near Prince Edward Island. The first record is from 1928. It is caught in most years in St. Margarets Bay, N.S. on rod and line, in trap nets and in gill nets. This species frequents buoys or other floating objects in coastal areas where it is easily observed. Young are found under jellyfish or drifting seaweed. In Louisbourg Harbour one banded rudderfish accompanied a diver for about one hour, orienting itself to stay at the same level as the diver's face mask. Food is fish and shrimps. It is reported to be very good eating.

bandtooth conger

Scientific name: *Ariosoma balearicum*
　(Delaroche, 1809)
Family: **Conger**
Other common names: Balearic conger
French name: congre des Baléares

Distribution: Found in the tropical Atlantic Ocean, Mediterranean Sea, Red Sea and western Indian Ocean. Also reported from off Nova Scotia.

Characters: This species is distinguished as an adult from other Canadian congers by having the dorsal and anal fin rays unsegmented and the posterior nostril is below the mideye level. The adult has 43–53 preanal lateral line pores, 9 prepectoral pores, 3 supratemporal pores, 3 postorbital and 6 supraorbital pores.

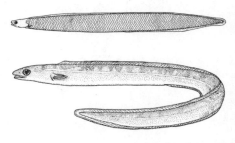

bandtooth conger

The dorsal fin origin lies over the pectoral fin base. The upper edge of the gill opening is in front of the middle part of the pectoral fin and the opening is crescent-shaped. Adult colour is yellowish or brownish with small yellow-red patches. The dorsal and anal fins have a black edge. The pectoral fin is reddish. The eye is orange dorsally. A dusky mark runs between the eye and corner of the mouth. Larvae have pigment in oblique lines below the midlateral line, a long gut, the dorsal fin begins over the anus and 121–136 myomeres (muscle blocks). A larva from Canadian waters was 82.5 mm long. Adults attain 50 cm.

Biology: First reported from Canada in 1988 at a depth of 50 m as a larval stray. Adults are benthic on sand and mud bottoms at 1–732 m where they burrow. Larvae live for about 20–22 months and metamorphose into adults at about 20 cm.

Banff longnose dace

Scientific name: *Rhinichthys cataractae smithi* Nichols, 1916
Family: **Carp**
Other common names: none
French name: naseux de rapides de Banff

Distribution: Found only in the vicinity of the Cave and Basin Hotsprings, Banff National Park, Alberta.

Characters: This subspecies was distinguished by having 48–59 lateral line scales, on average fewer than the 55–76 (often more

Banff longnose dace

than 60) found in typical **longnose dace**. Branched dorsal fin rays 6–7. Nuptial colouration is unknown. The back was olive fading to a silvery-white belly. Young had a dark flank stripe from snout to tail. This subspecies was named for the collector, Harlan I. Smith of what is now the Canadian Museum of Nature. Reached 5.5 cm standard length.

Biology: Descriptions of the environment of this now extinct subspecies are found in the tropical fish accounts (see below). Food probably included various aquatic insects and crustaceans. Little else is known about their biology. The introduction of competing tropical fishes (see **mosquitofish, sailfin molly** and **jewelfish**), introgression or mixing with **longnose dace** from the nearby Bow River, and draining of the habitat have all contributed to eliminate this unique Canadian subspecies. The Committee on the Status of Endangered Wildlife in Canada listed this subspecies as extinct in 1987.

Barbeled Dragonfish Family

Scientific name: Stomiidae
French name: dragons à barbillon

This deepsea family of moderate-sized fishes is found in all oceans. There are 228 species with 30 reported from the Atlantic, Pacific and Arctic coasts of Canada.

Barbeled, scaled or scaly dragonfishes, **viperfishes, snaggletooths, scaleless** or scaleless black dragonfishes, **loosejaws,** and **sawtailfishes** or black dragonfishes are characterised by various internal characters such as lacking gill rakers in adults, reduced or absent mesopterygoid, only 1 infraorbital bone (related families have 2–6), 0–1 supramaxillae, light organs without a lumen or ducts, and most have a chin barbel. Fangs are present on the jaws of some. When scales are present, they are easily lost or dissolved in preservative, leaving only a typical hexagonal pattern along the flank. There are light organs on the lower part of the body in rows, behind the eye and, in some species, on the hexagonal areas in various patterns.

They are members of the **Widemouth Order.** The **viperfishes** (Chauliodontidae), **snaggletooths** (Astronesthidae), **scaleless dragonfishes** (Melanostomiidae), **loosejaws** (Malacosteidae) and **sawtailfishes** (Idiacanthidae) are now included within the Stomiidae but were once separate families.

These fishes are quite common in mesopelagic waters down to about 4000 m. They are only rarely seen alive and, like most deepsea fishes, their delicate bodies are damaged in the long haul to the surface in nets. They have a leptocephalus larva and the intestine lies outside the body until the larva develops into a young fish.

The red-emitting light organs of some species of loosejaws are matched by a red-sensitive retina. This arrangement has been likened to a "snooperscope", enabling these loosejaws to see and catch prey which are sensitive only to the more usual blue-green light of deepsea organisms.

The larvae of sawtailfishes are unusual in having immensely long stalked eyes, a thin transparent body, pectoral fins and the posterior part of the digestive tract outside the body! With growth, the eyes become shorter and normal and the guts become enclosed by the body. So distinctive are these larvae, that they were thought to be a distinct species and were named *Stylophthalmus paradoxus*, the paradoxical stalkeye. The strange males exist only to reproduce, probably an adaptation to deepsea life where food is hard to come by. The anterior rays of the anal fin are modified as an intromittent organ, a delivery mechanism for the sperm-filled body. Males have a large light organ behind the eye and it has been suggested that the faster swimming females pursue the smaller males through the ocean depths, guided by the flashes of this light organ.

In living viperfishes, the body is covered by a gelatinous membrane which has nerves and a blood supply. In addition there are light organs in two rows on the lower flank and the hexagonal areas have small light organs arranged in patterns. A small tooth projecting laterally protects a light organ near the eye. This light organ shines into the eye, apparently to sensitise it to light. The light organs along the lower flank can adjust their intensity to match illumination from the ocean surface and so blank out the viperfish to predators from below. Many light organs around the mouth may serve to attract small crustaceans and fish towards, or even into, the mouth. The elongate dorsal fin with its fleshy tip (which may be luminous) could also be used to attract prey if dangled in front of the mouth.

Viperfishes are common in deep water of the mesopelagic and bathypelagic zones, although they may migrate near to the surface at night. These fish are rarely seen alive because of the depths from which they are hauled to the surface. Their feeding mecha-nism is unusual since some food items are larger than the viperfish, and damage to delicate organs near the mouth, such as gills and the heart, would seem to be inevitable. However a series of adaptations prevent this. The most anterior vertebrae are not bony in viperfish. Instead of becoming hard and inflexible, these vertebrae remain as a cartilaginous rod which enables the head to hinge backward, bringing the stabbing fangs into play by pushing both upper and lower jaws forward. The vertebrae may also act as shock absorbers against the struggles of impaled and wriggling prey. As the mouth opens, the shoulder girdle and the attached heart are pulled back and down out of the way of the large food item. Other muscles pull the gills down and away. The prey is forced through the throat by moveable teeth and the various organs return to their normal position.

See **bearded dragonfish**
    bigmouth loosejaw
    black snaggletooth
    bluenose rearfin
    boa dragonfish
    bronze-green flagfin
    crescent loosejaw
    Dana viperfish
    flatbarbel rearfin
    flexfin dragonfish
    gem snaggletooth
    highfin dragonfish
    largeye
    large-eye snaggletooth
    longfin dragonfish
    manylight viperfish
    Pacific viperfish
    pitgum lanternfish
    Pleiades loosejaw
    ribbon sawtailfish
    shining loosejaw
    shortbarbel dragonfish
    shortnose loosejaw
    sooty dragonfish
    stoplight loosejaw
    tenrayed loosejaw
    Tittmann's loosejaw
    triangle-light dragon
    tripletwig smoothgill
    whitebearded snaggletooth

barndoor skate

Scientific name: *Raja laevis* Mitchill, 1817
Family: **Skate**
Other common names: sharpnosed skate
French name: grande raie

Distribution: Found from the Gulf of St. Lawrence and the Grand Bank south to North Carolina.

Characters: This species is separated from its Canadian Atlantic relatives by having a rigid snout with its cartilaginous sup-

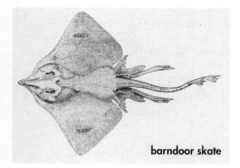

barndoor skate

port thick and stiff, cartilaginous supports of the pectoral fin do not reach the snout tip, dorsal fins separate at the base, mucous pores on ventral surface pigmented black, and no large thorns on the back but 3 rows of large spines on the tail. Teeth number 30–40 in the upper jaw and 28–38 in the lower jaw. Males have pointed teeth in rows, females flat teeth in a quincunx. There are small spines on the snout and the front margin of the pectoral fins. There are spines around the eyes. Males have erectile alar spines towards the edge of the pectoral fin. The underside has prickles on the snout. Egg cases are yellowish and 12.4–13.2 cm by 6.8–7.4 cm. Horns are very short at 2.5 cm. The upper disc is brown with a reddish hue with darker dots. Mucous pores are black. There is a dark blotch on the inner part of each pectoral fin. The underside is white with grey blotches and mucous pores outlined in black or black streaks. Attains 152 cm and 18 kg.

Biology: This is the largest Canadian skate found from shallow water down to 750 m and at temperatures of 1.2 to 20°C. There is an offshore migration if shallow waters become too warm. This skate has a broad diet including clams, worms, squid, crabs, lobsters and shrimps. Various fishes are also taken such as **spiny dogfish, gaspereau, cunners, tautogs, herring, hakes, flatfishes** and others. It may use its snout to dislodge clams from the sediment, since adult snout spines are worn smooth. Spawning occurs in winter. This skate is often caught on hook and line. Only an incidental catch in trawls and weirs, but may be used as fish meal and pet food.

Barracuda Family

Scientific name: Sphyraenidae
French name: barracudas

Barracudas or arrow-pikes are found usually in subtropical to tropical seas worldwide. There are 18 species with 1 species on the Atlantic coast and 1 on the Pacific coast of Canada.

The body is elongate and stream-lined. The jaws are large and have impressive canine and shearing teeth. The lower jaw protrudes. There is a spiny dorsal fin with 5 rays well-separated from the second dorsal fin which has 1 spine and 9–10 soft rays. The anal fin has 2 spines and 8–9 soft rays. The caudal fin is large and forked. The pelvic fins are on the abdomen and have 1 spine and 5 soft rays. Gill rakers are poorly developed. The lateral line is well-developed and scales are small and cycloid.

Barracudas have been related to the **Mullet Family** and are members of the **Perch Order**. Barracuda is a Spanish-American word for these fishes.

Barracudas are found in coastal areas and sometimes enter estuaries. These fishes will attack humans and in some areas are regarded as much more dangerous than sharks. Barracudas are curious and will follow divers around. They are very fast swimmers and as young hunt other fishes in packs. Larger fish tend to be solitary and lie in wait for prey which is attacked in a sudden rush, triggered by movement.

They are a popular food but can cause ciguatera, a form of food poisoning. Commercial trawlers catch these fishes.

See **northern sennet**
     Pacific barracuda

Barracudina Family

Scientific name: Paralepidae
French name: lussions

Barracudinas are found in all oceans including the Arctic and Antarctic oceans. There are about 50 species and in Canada there are 2 on the Atlantic coast, 1 on the Arctic-Atlantic coast, 1 on the Pacific coast, 1 on the Atlantic and Pacific coasts, and 1 on the Atlantic, Arctic and Pacific coasts. This latter species is divided into 2 sub-species, 1 on the Pacific and 1 on the Arctic-Atlantic coast.

Barracudinas have a resemblance to the **Barracuda Family** members, hence their name, but are not related. They have a fragile skeleton as an adaptation to midwater life where food sources are sparse. The mouth is large and carries sharp fang-like teeth. On the lower jaw and the palatine bone in the upper mouth fangs are alternately fixed and depressible. The dorsal fin is at the midbody and there is an adipose fin behind it. Some species have an adipose fin in front of the anal fin. The anus is usually near the pelvic fins, well separated from the anal fin. Dorsal fin rays 7–16, anal rays 20–50, pectoral rays 11–17, and pelvic rays 8–13. Cycloid scales are present or absent. There is no swimbladder. There may be 1–2 luminous ducts in the belly muscles in some species.

Barracudinas are members of the **Flagfin Order** and are related to the **Lizardfish, Daggertooth** and **Sabertooth Fish** families.

These fishes are very numerous in midwater, sometimes reaching the surface. They are thought to be very agile swimmers as few adults have been caught in nets. Observers in submersibles have seen some species swimming vertically with the head up. Others are reported to swim head down. Food is fishes, crustaceans and cephalopods. They are an important food for **salmons, tunas, cods, sharks, albacores** and whales and seals. Barracudinas bite at mooring cables, causing a stress which eventually results in the cables breaking. They may be attracted to light emitted by luminous animals fouling the cable. Some barracudinas undergo a diurnal vertical migration, follow-ing their crustacean food. They may then be caught at night using bright lights to attract them close to the surface. This is a popular method in the Philippines.

See **duckbill barracudina**
    pale lathfish
    ribbon barracudina
    sharpchin barracudina
    slender barracudina
    white barracudina
    winged barracudina

barreleye

Scientific name: *Macropinna microstoma*
    Chapman, 1939
Family: **Spookfish**
Other common names: none
French name: vise-en-l'air

Distribution: Found from the Bering Sea to Baja California including off the Queen Charlotte Islands and at Ocean Station Papa (50°N, 145°W).

Characters: This species is distinguished from other spookfish by a laterally compressed and short body, no sole-shaped light organ on the belly and the pelvic fins lie closer to the pectoral fins than the dorsal fin. The eyes are tubular and stick above the head

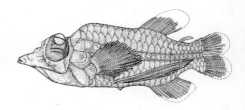

barreleye

outline. The brain is clearly visible through the thin, transparent bone of the skull. There are 11–12 dorsal fin rays, 14 anal fin rays, 17–19 pectoral fin rays and 9–10 pelvic fin rays. Lateral line scales number 23–26. Colour is dark brown in adults, with dark bars on a light brown background in young fish. Reaches 16 cm.

Biology: Caught from less than 100 m to over 900 m. Biology is unknown in detail.

barrelfish

Scientific name: *Hyperoglyphe perciformis*
  (Mitchill, 1818)
Family: **Ruff**
Other common names: logfish, rudderfish,
  black pilot
French name: pompile d'Amérique

Distribution: Found from the Grand Bank
and off southern Nova Scotia south to Florida
and the eastern Gulf of Mexico. Also in
Europe.

Characters: This ruff is distinguished by
the strong dorsal spines which are shorter
than the soft rays. Dorsal fin spines 6–8, soft

barrelfish

rays 19–22. Anal fin spines 3, soft rays
15–18. Pectoral fin rays 18–22. The lateral
line is arched anteriorly but straightens out
over the anal fin. There are 83–96 scales in
the lateral line. The overall colour is dark
green to dark brown, lighter ventrally. There
may be iridescent green flecks over the
lower flanks. Young fish are blackish with
some mottling. Attains 91 cm and 12.3 kg.

Biology: Young fish are found as strays
from June to November in drifting seaweed
in Canada, more rarely inshore. They have
been reported to follow drifting logs across
the Atlantic to the British Isles. The name
"barrelfish" comes from this habit of hiding
under debris such as barrels, boxes and
boards. Some have even been found trapped
inside boxes, having entered when young
and outgrown the exit! Adults form shoals in
deeper water. Food is crustaceans, squid,
hydroids, molluscs, barnacles, and young of
other fishes. They do not associate with jellyfish. Adults have been caught by anglers
using powered reels at 60–121 m. They are
sold as food in Japan.

bartail sculpin

Scientific name: *Malacocottus zonurus*
  Bean, 1890
Family: **Soft Sculpin**
Other common names: darkfin sculpin
French name: chabot à queue barrée

Distribution: Found from the Bering Sea
to Washington including British Columbia.

Characters: This soft sculpin is distinguished from its Pacific coast relatives by
having the spiny rays and soft rays in the
dorsal fin the same height and clearly separated, no spines on top of the head, no free
fold to the gill membranes ventrally, and the
primary preopercular spine is without an
accessory spine at its base. There are 4 well-
developed, preopercular spines. Cirri are present, particularly on the anterior nostril and
behind the eye on top of the head. Dorsal fin
spines 8–9, soft rays 12–15. Anal fin rays
9–12, pectoral rays 19–23. Overall colour is
a dark brown to black and the fins have
broad light and dark bands. Exceeds 20 cm.

bartail sculpin

Biology: Found from 27 to 275 m and not
uncommon in Canada, but little is known of
its biology.

basking shark

Scientific name: *Cetorhinus maximus*
  (Gunnerus, 1765)
Family: **Basking Shark**
Other common names: bone shark, nurse
  fish, sailfish
French name: pèlerin

Distribution: From Newfoundland and
the Gulf of St. Lawrence to Florida and from
Alaska to Mexico. Also in Europe, the southern hemisphere and the Far East.

Characters: The immense gill slits
extending from the top to the bottom of the
head are unique to this shark. The great size
is only exceeded by the **whale shark**, the

largest fish. The caudal peduncle has well-developed keels and the tail fin is lunate. The minute teeth are hook-like and number over 200 in each jaw. The snout in young basking sharks is protuberant.

basking shark

Overall colour is grey-brown, grey, blue-grey or black fading to white below. There may be darker patches arranged as vague longitudinal streaks. Snout and belly sometimes with white bars or patches. The belly may be dark not white.

Reported to reach 15.2 m but most are 10 m or less. A 9.2 m specimen weighed 3900 kg and weights up to 4476 kg have been reported. A 12.27 m specimen was trapped in a herring gill net in Musquash Harbour, New Brunswick in 1851, a 12.19 m basking shark was stranded in a herring weir on Grand Manan Island, New Brunswick in 1958 and another 12.19 m specimen was taken at Burgeo, Newfoundland in 1962.

Biology: These sharks, despite their size, can be found near the surf line and in enclosed bays as well as offshore. They may be encountered singly or in schools of more than a hundred. Several basking sharks in a row may well have been the origin of sea-serpent legends. Stranded and decomposed basking sharks have also been taken as evidence of sea-serpents since the vertebrae are partly calcified and not like the cartilage of other sharks. The massive jaws and gill arches are soon washed away. The vertebrae and box-like cranium are all that remain and give a curious appearance. A sea monster was reported from Henry Island on 19 November 1934 by a fishermen, Hugo Sandstrom, to the Prince Rupert Pacific Fisheries Experimental Station. It became known as the "Prince Rupert Sea Serpent" and attracted world-wide attention until it was identified as the remains of a basking shark. As their name suggests

they swim at the surface with dorsal fins out of the water or even belly up, although they probably don't bask in the true sense. Basking may be associated with feeding, courtship and mating. These sharks are often hit by ships.

Food includes copepods, barnacles, crab larvae, and fish eggs and is said to resemble a tomato-red thick soup. Half a ton of plankton may be in the stomach at any one time. An adult passively filters an estimated 2000 tons of water each hour at a cruising speed of 2 knots. The mouth is held open for 30–60 seconds then closed and the gill arches constricted to swallow the food with as little water as possible.

Basking sharks have been reported to leap from the water, a remarkable feat when their usual maximum speed is probably only 6–7 km/hour. Leaping, if it occurs which some authors doubt, may be an attempt to dislodge irritating parasites such as copepods and lampreys or commensals like remoras. In the Bay of Fundy, basking sharks have been seen swimming in a circle nose to tail. These sharks are migratory and segregated by sex and size. Pregnant females and newborn young are very rarely caught at the surface for example. Adults appear off the Atlantic coast of Canada in summer and off the Pacific coast in spring and summer. Capture temperatures off Newfoundland are 8–12°C. Some overwinter in the deep waters of the Gulf of St. Lawrence.

Males are mature at 4–5 m and females at 8.1–9.8 m. Maximum age has been estimated at 20 years but this is not accurately known. Females have up to an estimated 6 million minute eggs in their right ovary only and this species is assumed to be ovoviviparous and to show uterine cannibalism. At birth young may be about 1.5–1.8 m long but this is not known for certain. Gestation may last 3.5 years. Basking sharks have been the subject of a harpoon fishery in such places as California, Ireland, Scotland, Norway, Peru, China and Japan among other places. However they are very vulnerable to overfishing because of the long gestation period, a probable low fecundity, slow growth and maturation, and small population sizes. They are also caught in nets and are a nuisance to salmon gillnetters on the Pacific coast. At one point Pacific coast

Department of Fisheries patrol vessels were equipped with sharpened prows to kill basking sharks and some hundreds were destroyed. Damage to gear and loss of fish in Newfoundland amounted to 2–3% of the total value of the inshore fishery. The body mucus is heavy and smelly and is said to rot nets rapidly.

Their flesh can be eaten fresh or dried and salted. Fins have been made into soup, the skin into leather, the carcass into fish meal, and the liver into lamp oil. Up to 600 gallons of oil were taken from each fish. The chemicals pristane and squalene were also extracted from liver oil and used in cosmetics and as a lubricants for delicate machines. In 1981 a market developed in Newfoundland for basking shark livers and fins. In the period 1980–1983, 371 basking sharks were caught incidentally, mostly from mid–June to mid–July. Only 61 are recorded for the period 1876–1962.

This large shark can be easily approached by boats and by swimmers in the water. It is not dangerous to man in an aggressive sense but its huge size make it dangerous when harpooned or when a fin hits a swimmer. The scales are sharp with hooked crowns and can inflict serious lacerations.

Basking Shark Family

Scientific name: Cetorhinidae
French name: pèlerins

This family contains only one species with a wide distribution in colder, coastal waters. The basking shark is very large, pelagic, and uniquely characterised by the enormous gill slits which extend onto the top and bottom of the head. Only the **whale shark** is larger.

The **Basking Shark Family** belongs to the **Mackerel Shark Order** and is related to the **Mackerel Shark, Thresher Shark** and **Sand Tiger Shark** families.

The mouth is huge and has many, small, hooked teeth. The denticles in the skin in some specimens point in all directions so that, unlike in most sharks, the skin feels rough even when stroked posteriorly. Unique, hard, bristle-like, gill rakers, formed from modified hair-like dermal denticles, filter-feed planktonic organisms from the water aided by mucus secreted in the pharynx. The basking shark merely swims along with its huge mouth open and its gills distended. The mouth has to be closed to swallow the accumulated plankton. The bristly gill rakers number 1000–1300 on each side of all five arches. The rakers are modified placoid scales up to 15 cm long. The liver is extremely large and is contained in a long body cavity serving as a "hepatic float" to give the shark near neutral buoyancy. Curiously, the basking shark sheds its hundreds of gill rakers in early winter and may take 4–5 months to fully replace them. At this time, plankton densities fall and there is probably insufficient food to maintain the normal cruising activity of this huge shark. Some workers have suggested, without proof, that basking sharks hibernate on the bottom at the edge of the continental shelf during this rakerless period. Possibly the shark feeds on benthic organisms, or survives on the stored food in its oil-rich liver while swimming slowly in cold, deep water.

See **basking shark**

basses

The term bass has been applied to a number of unrelated species of **spiny-rayed fishes** with thick, muscular bodies which are usually food or sport fishes in the sea and fresh water. There is a **Sea Bass Family** (including the **yellowfin bass** and the **black sea bass**), a **Temperate Bass Family** (including the **white bass** and the **striped bass**), a **Temperate Ocean Bass Family**, and such species as the **smallmouth bass**, **largemouth bass** and **rock bass**, which are members of the **Sunfish Family**. "Bass" is derived from an Old English word.

Batfish Family

Scientific name: Ogcocephalidae
French name: malthes

Batfishes or seabats are found principally in subtropical to tropical waters with a few in temperate waters. There are 57 species and Atlantic Canada has 1 species.

The body of batfishes is depressed or flattened and is oval or triangular in shape. The snout may have a beak. These are **anglerfishes** with a short fishing apparatus which can be retracted into a cavity. The esca or bait may emit a chemical to attract prey. The fishing apparatus is rotated across the mouth and some species favour vibrating to the right, others to the left. The mouth is almost horizontal. The gill opening is in the posterior half of the body. There are two or two and a half gills since the first arch is reduced and lacks filaments and the fourth may be absent or incomplete. Scales are in the form of tubercles topped by a spine and lateral line scales are distinctive. There may also be cirri on the back.

Batfishes are relatives of the **Sea Toad Family** and members of the **Anglerfish Order**.

They use the large, stalked pectoral fins and small pelvic fins to walk along the sea bed and are poor swimmers. They remain motionless when approached by a diver and may need a strong prod to show signs of life. They may be found in both shallow areas around rocks and in deep water on mud and clay. Food is fishes, crustaceans, worms and molluscs.

Batfishes have been used in the Far East as a baby's rattle. The guts are removed, the fish dried and small pebbles inserted through a hole which is then sewn up. The skin spines are rubbed flat. They are also sold as curios.

See **Atlantic batfish**

bay goby

Scientific name: *Lepidogobius lepidus*
  (Girard, 1858)
Family: **Goby**
Other common names: finescale goby
French name: gobie de baie

Distribution: From Baja California to northern British Columbia.

Characters: This goby is distinguished from its relatives, the **arrow goby** and the **blackeye goby**, by its small scales, lack of a

bay goby

crest and 7–8 dorsal fin spines. About 86 scales along the flank. Soft dorsal fin rays 14–18 after 0–1 spines. Anal fin rays 13–16 after 0–1 spines. A deep groove runs from the pelvic fins to the anus. The mouth is small and ends below the eye. Head pores are prominent. Almost transparent, colour is tan to olive-green or reddish-brown overall, mottled with black on the back and fins. Tip of the spiny dorsal fin is black. Attains 10 cm.

Biology: Found on mud bottoms from the intertidal zone down to 201 m. It lives in shrimp, geoduck clam or *Urechis* worm tubes. The gobies fight each other for burrows and food resources, larger fish and/or those with a prior residence claim usually win. Large schools have been detected on echo-sounders but are not caught by trawlers or seines because they retreat into burrows. Food is worms, crustaceans and molluscs taken at any time when young and mostly at night when adult. These gobies feed by "substrate biting", taking in mouthfuls of bottom sediment along with food items and expelling the inedible bits through the gill opening. Probe-feeding shorebirds and **Pacific staghorn sculpins** feed on bay gobies. Life span is 7 years but growth is rapid with fish reaching half their final length by the end of the second year of life. In California, ripe females are found from September to March and spawning takes place mostly in January to March. Northern populations spawn later than this as larvae are common in Oregon waters from April to September.

bay pipefish

Scientific name: *Syngnathus leptorhynchus*
  Girard, 1854
Family: **Pipefish**
Other common names: none
French name: syngnathe à lignes grises

Distribution: From Baja California to southcentral Alaska including the coast of British Columbia.

Characters: This is the only Pacific coast pipefish in Canada. Dorsal fin with 28–44 rays. Pectoral fin with 11–13 rays. There are no pelvic fins. The anal fin is only present in the female where it is minute and has 2–5 rays. The bony plates are in 6 rows anteriorly

(2 on each flank, 1 dorsally and 1 ventrally) and in 4 rows posteriorly (1 on each flank instead of 2). Trunk rings number 16–21, tail

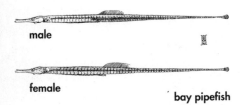

male

female
· bay pipefish

rings 36–46, for a total of 53–63. Northern populations tend to have more tail rings and dorsal rays than southern populations. Colour varies with habitat, from various shades of green to brown or purple. Narrow lines present on flank. Variously mottled or spotted. Attains 38.5 cm.

Biology: Found in shallow water in eel-grass beds and around jetties and wharves. Males mature at about 8 cm standard length although the smallest male with a brood pouch in another study was 11.0 cm. Females are larger than males. Males with eggs and young are found from February to August and in some areas year round. Canadian populations have egg-carrying males only in May to August. Eggs are 1.3–1.5 mm in diameter. Food is small crustaceans such as copepods, amphipods and crab larvae.

bearded dragonfish

Scientific name: *Echiostoma barbatum*
   Lowe, 1843
Family: **Barbeled Dragonfish**
Other common names: none
French name: dragon barbu

Distribution: Found in the Atlantic, Indian and Pacific oceans including off the southern Scotian Shelf of Atlantic Canada south to the Caribbean Sea.

Characters: This dragonfish is separated from its Canadian Atlantic relatives by having the dorsal and anal fin bases about the same length, pelvic fins are low on the flank, no luminous organs (the preorbital and suborbital) before and below the eye, the lower jaw not projecting or strongly curved upwards, pectoral fin with 1 long ray separated from 3–4 short ones, and 25–28 photophores

between the pectoral and pelvic fin insertions. The barbel is about three-quarters of head length. The barbel tip changes form with age from complex to simple. Young fish have a large and small bulb with filaments at the tip. Older fish have a tapering tip, no bulbs, and filaments along the sides as well as at the tip. Dorsal fin rays 12–15, anal rays 14–18, and pelvic rays 5–9, usually 8. Overall colour is purplish-black to brown-black. Fin rays are black, brown to reddish, the latter perhaps because of blood vessels showing through the skin. The chin barbel is black with the bulb grey-brown, green or pinkish and the filaments pink or purple. The eye is yellow. The body gives a greenish-white glow from the scattered light organs. The light organ behind the eye appears to be

bearded dragonfish

under some control giving off pink or greenish-white light. The photophores along the lower belly direct a rosy to red light downwards. Reaches about 37 cm.

Biology: Occasional captures have been made off the Scotian Shelf at 100–500 m. This species has been taken from near surface waters at night down to nearly 2000 m. It has the distinction of being one of very few deepsea fishes which have been kept alive in an aquarium, albeit for only 6 hours. It swam strongly and made vigorous snaps, especially when its barbel was touched. The red bioluminescence may be used to search for food or avoid predators since most deepsea fishes are insensitive to red light. The yellow eye lens and two banks of rods in the retina help detect red light reflected from a prey or predator.

bearded rattail

Scientific name: *Coryphaenoides liocephalus*
   (Günther, 1887)
Family: **Grenadier**
Other common names: none
French name: grenadier barbu

Distribution: Known from Japan, the mid-Pacific Ocean and possibly in British Columbian waters.

Characters: This grenadier may be the same species as the **ghostly grenadier**. The only difference appears to be in overall colour

bearded rattail

which is blackish in this species and whitish in the **ghostly grenadier**.

Biology: A single specimen was identified as this species from off Queen Charlotte Sound at a depth of 2760 m, caught in 1965. However it has been re-identified as a **pop-eye**. The mid-Pacific bearded rattails were caught at 3750 m.

Beardfish Family

Scientific name: Polymixiidae
French name: barbudos

Beardfishes are found in warmer waters of the Atlantic, Indian and western Pacific oceans. There are 6 species with 2 reported from the Atlantic coast of Canada.

These fishes have a distinctive pair of hyoid or throat barbels. The dorsal fin is single with 4–6 spines and 26–38 soft rays. The anal fin has 3–4 spines and 13–18 soft rays. The pelvic fins have 1 unbranched and 6 soft rays, no spine. Pectoral fins with 15–18 soft rays. Scales are ctenoid and cover the body, cheeks, opercles and lower jaw. Gill rakers number 11–21. Jaw teeth are fine.

The French name "barbudos" is from the Cuban name for these fishes (long-bearded). This family is a member of the **Beardfish Order**.

Beardfishes are usually caught on the bottom between 180 and 770 m but may be found as shallow as 90 m. Food includes fishes, crustaceans and worms. These are good food fishes but are not commercially exploited.

See **Caribbean beardfish**
 stout beardfish

Beardfish Order

The beardfishes or Polymixiiformes comprise a single family of the same name, once included in the **Alfonsino Order**. The characters are described under the family account. They were once considered to be a primitive member of the **spiny-rayed fishes** but were removed into a group of orders of similar evolutionary level but which lacked some of the characters used to define typical **spiny-rayed fishes**.

See **Beardfish Family**

Bering cisco

Scientific name: *Coregonus laurettae*
 Bean, 1881
Family: **Salmon**
Other common names: lauretta, freshwater
 or lake herring, tullibee
French name: cisco de Béring

Distribution: Found from the Pacific coast of Alaska to the Beaufort Sea including Canadian waters and in the upper Yukon River of the Yukon. Also in the eastern Arctic drainages of Siberia.

Characters: This species is distinguished from other **salmons** by having 76–95 lateral line scales, a strongly forked tail, no parr

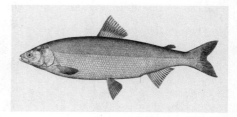

Bering cisco

marks, 2 skin flaps between the nostrils, mouth terminal and 31–40 gill rakers. Characters among **ciscoes** (q.v.) overlap and so the species cannot be easily separated. Dorsal fin rays 10–13, anal rays 10–14 (12–14 major rays), pectoral rays 14–17 and pelvic rays 10–12. Overall colour silvery with a brown to green back and silver-white belly. The dorsal and caudal fins are dusky. The iris is yellowish. May be a subspecies of the **Arctic cisco**. Reaches 48 cm fork length.

Biology: First reported from Canada in 1981 at Dawson in the Yukon based on a single specimen. This species lives in coastal waters and mouths of rivers although in Alaska it has been reported 840 km from the ocean. Life span is 8 years with maturity attained at 3–4 years. It migrates up rivers in late summer to spawn in early fall and then returns to the sea. Some fish may overwinter in the middle Yukon River. Eggs hatch in the spring. Food is probably crustaceans such as amphipods and small fish. It is utilised to some extent in native fisheries but most Bering cisco are too small to be caught in **salmon** and **whitefish** nets. The Committee on the Status of Endangered Wildlife in Canada found in 1990 that there was insufficient scientific information on which to base a status designation for this species.

Bering flounder

Scientific name: *Hippoglossoides robustus*
  Gill and Townsend, 1897
Family: **Righteye Flounder**
Other common names: none
French name: plie de Béring

Distribution: Found in the Bering and Chukchi seas and Bathurst Inlet, N.W.T.

Characters: This Arctic flounder is characterised by the large, almost symmetrical mouth, ctenoid scales and the straight lateral line with a gentle bend over the pectoral fin. The middle rays of the caudal fin are the longest and the tail is round. The upper eye is lateral, not on the head margin. There are 7 branchiostegal rays. Dorsal fin rays 67–80,

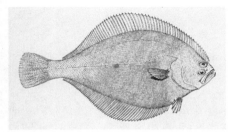

Bering flounder

anal rays 51–62 and pectoral rays 8–12. Gill rakers on the lower arch 9–13. There are 87–94 lateral line scales. Eyed side a light,

brownish yellow with brownish speckles and large dark spots along the dorsal and anal fins and on midbody. The blind side is white with a silvery sheen mainly below the lateral line. Attains 30 cm. This flounder has been placed as a subspecies of the **flathead sole**, but genetic and anatomical evidence warrant its place as a distinct species.

Biology: The Bering flounder favours deep, cold water in the depth range 18–425 m. Growth is slow in such waters taking 11 years to reach 23 cm. Spawning occurs in summer in shallow water. This species is too small to be commercially important.

Bering wolffish

Scientific name: *Anarhichas orientalis*
  Pallas, 1814
Family: **Wolffish**
Other common names: aaqaksaaq
French name: loup de Béring

Distribution: Found in the northwest Pacific Ocean, but not on the British Columbia coast, and on the coast of the Northwest Territories in Canada.

Characters: This wolffish is distinguished from other Canadian species by colour, teeth on the vomer bone in the centre of the roof of

Bering wolffish

the mouth extending back beyond the palatine teeth at the sides, and by fin ray counts. Dorsal fin spines 81–86, anal rays 50–54 and pectoral rays 21. Overall colour is a dark brown with marbling and blotching. Young have spots on the head and 3–5 interrupted flank stripes. Reaches 112 cm and 15 kg.

Biology: Known only from Bathurst Inlet, N.W.T. (and Camden Bay of the Alaskan Beaufort Sea near the Canadian border), this species is classed as "vulnerable" by the Committee on the Status of Endangered Wildlife in Canada. It is known to live in very shallow water among algae covered stones or over gravel and sand. It moves offshore when ice forms along the coast. Life span is at least 17 years. Crabs and mussels are important foods. Spawning may occur in spring and summer and egg diameters are up to 4.5 mm.

Bermuda chub

Scientific name: *Kyphosus sectatrix*
  (Linnaeus, 1758)
Family: **Sea Chub**
Other common names: calicagère blanche
French name: kyphose des Bermudes

Distribution: Found from the Grand Bank south to Brazil. Also in the eastern Atlantic Ocean.

Characters: This species is the only member of its family on the Atlantic coast of Canada and is identified by its incisor-like teeth, fin ray counts and internal anatomy. Dorsal fin with 10–13, thick spines and 11–13, usually 12, soft rays; anal fin with 3–4 spines and 9–12, usually 11, soft rays. Total gill rakers 22–27. Lateral line scales 51–58.

The body is dusky to bluish with straw yellow lines along the margins of the scale rows. A yellow stripe runs from the corner of the mouth to the preopercle edge. There is a white line across the nape and a yellow spot behind the eye. The opercle margin is black. Young fish between 30–75 mm are covered with eye-sized pale blotches.

Reaches 76 cm. The all-tackle, world record from Bermuda was caught in 1993 and weighed 5.04 kg.

Bermuda chub

Biology: Found off the Scotian Shelf in 1965, off Browns Bank in 1966 and from the stomach of a **bigeye tuna** caught on the southwest Grand Bank in 1982. Common in turtle grass beds and around rocks and reefs in the Caribbean. Young are found among floating sargassum weed. Food is mostly plant material but small invertebrates such as crabs and molluscs have also been found as stomach contents, whether as accidental inclusions while feeding on plants or deliberately selected is unclear. Reputedly a good fighter as a game fish. It has been used for food but is not a popular fish in this respect.

big skate

Scientific name: *Raja binoculata*
  Girard, 1854
Family: **Skate**
Other common names: Pacific great skate,
  Pacific barndoor skate
French name: raie biocellée

Distribution: Found from Alaska to Baja California including British Columbia.

Characters: This species is distinguished from Canadian Pacific relatives by having a rigid snout with its cartilaginous support thick

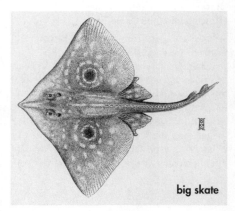

big skate

and stiff, cartilaginous supports of the pectoral fin do not reach the snout tip, no enlarged snout tip thornlets or scapular (= shoulder) spines, pelvic fins with a very shallow notch and no lateral tail thornlets. There is a single middorsal spine behind the eyes and about 33 median spines on the posterior body and tail. There are spines near the eye but these are buried in the skin of larger fish. Egg cases may be 30 cm in length and have 1–7 embryos. There are 2 curved ridges on the upper egg case surface, 2 keels on each side, and short horns. Overall disc colour is olive-brown, or reddish-brown to grey or black. There is a large eye spot on each pectoral fin surrounded by interrupted rings of light and dark. Light rings have some red. The under-surface is white. Attains 2.4 m and at least 91 kg. The world, all-tackle angling record from California caught in 1993 weighed 41.27 kg.

Biology: A common Canadian skate. Depth range is 3–800 m. Food includes crustaceans and such fishes as **great sculpins**. Life span is at least 12 years with age at maturity being 8–11 years. The pectoral fins are sold fresh as "wings." Big skates are caught occasionally by sport fishermen.

Bigelow's skate

Scientific name: *Raja bigelowi* Stehmann, 1978
Family: **Skate**
Other common names: none
French name: raie de Bigelow

Distribution: Found from the Newfoundland Basin and south to the Gulf of Mexico. Also in the eastern North Atlantic Ocean.

Characters: This species is separated from its Canadian Atlantic relatives by having a rigid snout with its cartilaginous support thick and stiff, cartilaginous supports of the pectoral fin do not reach the snout tip, the underside of the disc is dark brown and darker than the upper side, 26–33 (usually less than 30) thorns

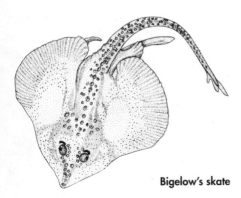

Bigelow's skate

on the midline of the back and tail, and 3–15 thorns on the snout tip. Dorsal fins joined at the base. Upper jaw teeth rows 34–44, 34–41

in the lower jaw. The upper surface of the disc is prickly except that males have a bare patch in the centre of the pectoral fins. There are thorns around the eyes, 10–18 thorns on the nape and shoulder and 2–4 irregular rows of up to 30 thorns on each side of the midline posteriorly. The underside is smooth except for bands along the edge of the tail. The upper disc is dusky grey with the back and tail lighter. The underside is always dark brown with the tail lighter. Reaches 50 cm.

Biology: Reported at 650–2500 m, usually below 1500 m. This species is only recently distinguished from the **chocolate skate** and its biology is unknown.

bigeye

Scientific name: *Priacanthus arenatus* Cuvier, 1829
Family: **Bigeye**
Other common names: Atlantic bigeye, beauclaire soleil, catalufa
French name: priacanthe sablé

Distribution: Found on both sides of the Atlantic Ocean and from Nova Scotia to Argentina in the west. Also in the Indo-Pacific Ocean.

Characters: This species is separated from its relatives, the **bulleye** and the **short bigeye**, by having pelvic fins shorter than the head, the

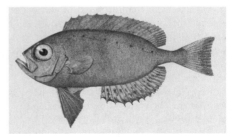

bigeye

second and tenth dorsal fin spines about equal in length, and by scale and fin ray counts. Dorsal fin spines 10, rarely 11, soft rays 13–15, usually 14. Anal fin soft rays 14–16, usually 15. Pored lateral line scales 61–73, midlateral scale row 71–86. The overall colour is a bright scarlet to orange-red, sometimes blotched. Pelvic fin membranes are dusky to blackish and there is a black spot at the pelvic base. The anal and caudal fin margins are dusky to black. Reaches 41 cm. The world, all-tackle record weighted 1.13 kg and was caught at Ocracoke, North Carolina in 1988.

Biology: A Canadian specimen was extracted from the stomach of a **pollock** in 1972. The **pollock** was caught on hook and line off Hopson Island, Nova Scotia. This is the northern range limit for the bigeye in the western Atlantic Ocean and only the 14th specimen reported from this area. It may be found in water less than 2 m deep in the Bahamas, but is usually an inhabitant of deeper waters down to over 200 m, found in small schools over reefs, feeding nocturnally on small fishes, crustaceans and worms. Sometime sold in the U.S.A. as "red snapper."

Bigeye Family

Scientific name: Priacanthidae
French name: priacanthes

Bigeyes or catalufas are mostly tropical to subtropical fishes of the Atlantic, Indian and Pacific oceans. There are about 18 species with 3 reported from Atlantic Canada.

As their name indicates, these fishes have very large eyes. The mouth is also large and very oblique with the lower jaw projecting. Scales are small and strongly ctenoid making bigeyes rough to the touch. Scales cover the body, head, the maxilla bone of the upper jaw and the lower jaw. The dorsal fin usually has 10 spines followed by 10–15 soft rays without a strong notch between spines and soft rays. The anal fin has 3 spines and 9–16 soft rays. The pelvic fin has 1 spine and 5 soft rays and is connected to the body by a membrane. There are 14 branched caudal fin rays. Bigeyes are usually bright red.

This family is related to other spiny-rayed fishes such as the **Perch Family** and the **Cardinalfish Family**, among many others in the **Perch Order**.

Bigeyes are usually nocturnal and are common on coral reefs and around rocky areas. They hide in crevices during the day. They may be found deeper than 400 m. Young are associated with floating debris near the surface in the open ocean; as a result bigeyes are widely dispersed by ocean cur-

rents. They are carnivores, eating small fishes, crustaceans and worms.

See **bigeye**
 bulleye
 short bigeye

bigeye flashlightfish

Scientific name: *Protomyctophum thompsoni* (Chapman, 1944)
Family: **Lanternfish**
Other common names: bigeye lanternfish
French name: télescope à grands yeux

Distribution: Found across the North Pacific Ocean from Japan to British Columbia and southward to Baja California. Also reported from Ocean Station Papa (50°N, 145°W).

Characters: This lanternfish and its relative, the **penlight fish**, are distinguished from other Pacific coast species by having 2 Prc photophores and the PLO photophore at about the level of the lowest pectoral fin ray. This species is separated from its relative by the SAO photophore series being angulate, the first SAO photophore over the third VO photophore and the AO series numbers 15–17. There are no lateral line pores. Dorsal fin rays 11–13, anal rays 21–25, pectoral rays 14–17 and total vertebrae 37–39. Total gill rakers 16–20. Supracaudal luminous glands develop in males as early as a length of 2.5 cm or as late as 3.6 cm. The telescopic eyes of young develop into a more normal shape with growth. Reaches 7.0 cm.

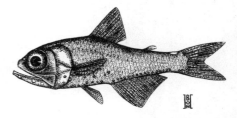

bigeye flashlightfish

Biology: At night this species can be caught at the surface and as deep as 693 m in Canada. Elsewhere reported down to 1370 m. In the eastern subarctic Pacific Ocean it remains below 200 m by day and night, feeding during the day.

bigeye scad

Scientific name: *Selar crumenophthalmus*
(Bloch, 1793)
Family: **Jack**
Other common names: goggle eye jack,
google-eyed scad, selar coulisou
French name: sélar à grandes paupières

Distribution: From Nova Scotia south to Brazil and world-wide in warmer waters.

Characters: This species is distinguished from its Canadian Atlantic coast relatives by having a moderately compressed and deep body, a gently arched lateral line anteriorly and enlarged scutes in the lateral line posteriorly, the upper jaw extends back only to

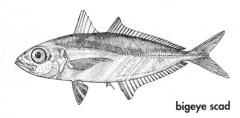

bigeye scad

below the eye pupil, and the pelvic fins almost reach the anus. The eye is much larger than snout length. There are no finlets behind the dorsal and anal fins. The inside rear edge of the gill cavity has 2 fleshy tabs. There is an adipose eyelid covering the eye except for the central oval slit (hence goggle-eye). The first dorsal fin has 8 spines, the second 1 spine and 23–27 soft rays. The anal fin has 3 spines and 20–23 soft rays. The overall colour is silvery to yellowish, metallic blue to bluish-green on the back. A faint spot is usually present on the gill cover. There may be a yellow stripe along the flank. The fins, snout and lower jaw tip have dusky marks. Reaches a reputed 61 cm, although most are smaller.

Biology: Strays from the south are not uncommon off Nova Scotia in late summer and fall and the first record, for Canso, is in 1907. The northern range limit is St. Georges Bay on the Gulf of St. Lawrence coast of Nova Scotia. It forms schools in inshore, cloudy waters down to 170 m. Food is planktonic and benthic invertebrates, and fish. Spawning takes place in July in the Caribbean area. This species is a good food and sport fish and is also used for bait. In the Indo-Pacific area it is a commercial species.

bigeye sculpin

Scientific name: *Triglops nybelini*
Jensen, 1944
Family: **Sculpin**
Other common names: mailed sculpin,
Nybelin's sculpin, ribbed sculpin
French name: faux-trigle aux grands yeux

Distribution: Found from Baffin Island and Davis Strait south to Ungava Bay and northern Labrador and across the Arctic to Alaska. Also around Greenland and the northern coast of Eurasia.

Characters: This species is distinguished from its eastern Arctic and Atlantic relatives by having the upper preopercular spine a simple point, the vomer is toothed, the lateral line plates have backward pointing spines, the lower flank has oblique skin folds with serrated edges, 20–22 pectoral fin rays, and colour pattern. The eye diameter is large, about equal to or longer than postorbital distance. First dorsal fin spines 9–11, second dorsal rays 24–28 and anal rays 23–28. The middle pelvic ray is the longest. Plate-like lateral line scales about 45–50. The body has 4–5 oblique lines. The head is dusky. Fins are clear except for thin bars on the lower pectoral rays. In males the flank lines merge into 2 stripes and the pectoral fin has black markings. Peritoneum densely spotted and black. Reaches 17.0 cm standard length.

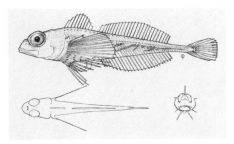

bigeye sculpin

Biology: Sometimes found inshore but usually below 135 m down to 930 m at temperatures below 0°C. Food is crustaceans. It is eaten by thick-billed murres in Hudson Bay. Females grow larger than males. Spawning takes place in summer and females may have up to 1000 eggs of 3.0 mm diameter.

bigeye smoothhead

Scientific name: *Bajacalifornia megalops*
(Lütken, 1898)
Family: **Slickhead**
Other common names: none
French name: alépocéphale à grands yeux

Distribution: Found in all oceans including off Baffin Island and off the Scotian Shelf in Arctic and Atlantic Canada.

Characters: This species is distinguished by having teeth on the maxilla bone of the upper jaw, having the dorsal fin origin in

bigeye smoothhead

front of the anal fin origin, and the lower jaw has a conical knob pointing downwards. Overall colour is brownish. Attains at least 28 cm.

Biology: Known from only 2 specimens in Canadian waters. Adults have been reported from 820 to 1425 m and larvae and young from 250 to 3182 m. A poorly-known species.

bigeye squaretail

Scientific name: *Tetragonurus atlanticus*
Lowe, 1839
Family: **Squaretail**
Other common names: none
French name: tétragonure gris

Distribution: Found in temperate to tropical waters of the Atlantic, Pacific and Indian oceans, including Atlantic Canada from off the Scotian Shelf and off northern Georges Bank, and south to Panama.

Characters: This species is distinguished from the related **smalleye squaretail** by a lower scale count, 73–95 from the head to the origin of the caudal peduncle keels. Scales are keeled and spiny so the skin feels rough and has a frosty appearance. First dorsal fin with

14–17 spines, second dorsal fin with 10–13 soft rays. Anal fin with 1 spine and 9–12 soft rays. The overall colour is a uniform dark brown to almost black. Reaches 50 cm.

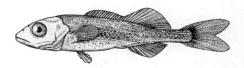

bigeye squaretail

Biology: Canadian adult specimens have been taken from a **swordfish** stomach and from the sea as adults and larvae, but only 4 specimens were recorded from 1933–1980. Found mostly in the upper 100 m of the open ocean although adults probably go deeper. Young fish may associate with jellyfish and with such salps or tunicates as *Salpa* and *Pyrosoma*, and feed on them and ctenophores (comb jellies) using their slicing teeth and scoop-like lower jaw. Spawning occurs in winter and spring in the western Atlantic Ocean.

bigeye starsnout

Scientific name: *Bathyagonus pentacanthus*
(Gilbert, 1890)
Family: **Poacher**
Other common names: bigeye poacher
French name: astérothèque à cinq épines

Distribution: Found from the Bering Sea through British Columbia to southern California.

Characters: This poacher is one of 4 related species called starsnouts (**bigeye, blackfin, gray** and **spinycheek starsnouts**) for an

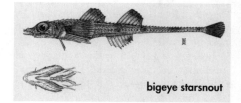

bigeye starsnout

arrangement of 5 or more small spines at the tip of the snout on a moveable plate which form, supposedly, a star. Three spines point vertically and 2 laterally. The bigeye starsnout is identified by having a pit on the back of the head, 2 pairs of plates in front of the pelvic fins, no spines on the bones beneath the eye and 41–44 dorsal plates. The eye is large. The anal fin origin is under the space between the dorsal fins. The first dorsal fin has 5–8 spines, the second dorsal fin 6–8 soft rays. The anal fin has 6–8 soft rays and the pectoral about 15 rays with the lower 4–5 obviously finger-like. There are 2 cirri at the rear of the upper jaw and 1 to several on each lower jaw. Gill membranes are joined to the isthmus. The body is olive-brown fading ventrally. There are 5–6 dark brown saddles on the back and flanks. The anal and pelvic fins are pale but the other fins are dark brown or dusky. Reaches 23 cm.

Biology: The habitat is soft bottoms at 110–910 m.

bigeye tuna

Scientific name: *Thunnus obesus*
  (Lowe, 1839)
Family: **Mackerel**
Other common names: thon obèse, patudo
French name: thon ventru

Distribution: Found world-wide in warmer waters including off the Scotian Shelf in Canada.

Characters: This species is distinguished from its Atlantic coast relatives by having the dorsal fins close together (separated by a

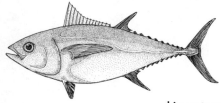

bigeye tuna

distance less than snout length), first dorsal fin spines 11–15, 23–31 gill rakers, second dorsal and anal fins not greatly elongated, no white border to the caudal fin and the pectoral fin not reaching beyond the rear of the second dorsal fin. The greatest body depth is near the middle of the first dorsal fin. The ventral surface of the liver is striated. Second dorsal fin rays 14–16 followed by 8–10 finlets. Anal fin rays 11–15 followed by 7–10

finlets. Pectoral rays 31–35. The back is dark blue, the flanks are light blue and the belly white. The flank has an iridescent blue to brown stripe. The dorsal fins are yellow, finlets are bright yellow with black margins, and pectoral and caudal fins are reddish black. Reaches 239 cm. The world, all-tackle angling record weighed 197.31 kg and was caught off Peru in 1957.

Biology: First caught east of Browns Bank in 1957 with other catches to the north since then. Found in oceanic waters from the surface to 250 m in schools at 13–29°C, optimally at 17–22°C. Schools may be associated with floating weeds or debris. Food is various fishes, squid and crustaceans. Spawning is year round in the tropics and up to 6.3 million eggs of 1.1 mm diameter are released. Mature fish spawn at least twice. Bigeyes become mature at the end of their third year of life at about 100–130 cm. Life span exceeds 9 years. This is a commercially important species caught by Japanese and Korean ships using longlines, pole-fishing and sometimes purse seines. Longlines may be over 130 km long and are monitored using radar. The world catch in 1980 reached 214,000 tonnes. The Canadian catch in 1988 was 95 tonnes. The flesh is sold fresh, frozen or canned and is used in *sashimi* as a substitute for **bluefin tuna**.

bigeye unernak

Scientific name: *Gymnelus hemifasciatus*
  Andriashev, 1937
Family: **Eelpout**
Other common names: halfbarred pout
French name: unernak à grands yeux

Distribution: Found from Dease Strait south of Victoria Island in the Canadian Arctic westward to the Barents Sea and south to the Bering and Okhotsk seas.

Characters: This species is distinguished from its Canadian Arctic-Atlantic relatives by lacking pelvic fins, having a terminal mouth, gill opening extending to middle of pectoral fin base, firm skin, no scales, body and tail with 12–16 dark bands, tail bands only as low as lateral line, or rarely a reticulate pattern with tail bars running below lateral line, vertebrae 85–95, usually 10–11 pectoral rays, and dorsal fin origin over the pectoral fin. Dorsal fin rays 80–94, anal rays 68–77 and pectoral rays 10–12. Overall body

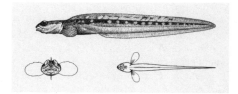

bigeye unernak

colour is pale. There may be several eye spots on the dorsal fin. Males have black anal fins. Reaches 14.0 cm standard length.

Biology: Reported on mud and gravel bottoms from intertidal areas to 200 m at –1.8 to 2°C. Food includes clams, worms and crustaceans. Females are mature at 7–8 cm and spawning occurs in late summer or early autumn. Large females have up to 26 eggs with a maximum diameter of 4.4 mm.

bigfin eelpout

Scientific name: *Lycodes cortezianus*
(Gilbert, 1890)
Family: **Eelpout**
Other common names: big-finned eel-pout
French name: lycode à grandes nageoires

Distribution: Found from Alaska to California including British Columbia.

Characters: This species is distinguished from its Pacific coast relatives by having prominent ridges on the ventral surface of the lower jaw known as "mental crests", and teeth are absent from the vomer bone (centre of the mouth roof) but present on the palatine bone in the side of the mouth roof. There is a carti-

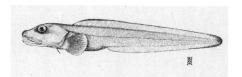

bigfin eelpout

laginous stay on the under surface of the head, parallel to the lower jaw. Pelvic fins are present and there are no mucous pores on the

jaws. The flesh is firm. Dorsal fin rays 105–109, anal rays 89–93 and pectoral rays 18–21. Vertebrae number 112–115. Overall colour is brown to blue-black, lighter on the belly. Scale pockets are white. Dorsal and caudal fin margins are black, as is the posterior anal fin margin. There is a black blotch on the anterior margin of the dorsal fin. There is a blue-black area above the base of the pectoral fin and the margin is light yellow (sometimes pale in small specimens). Gill cavity dusky and peritoneum black. Reaches 50 cm.

Biology: Reported in the depth range 73–800 m, and relatively common in British Columbia in trawl catches and **sablefish** traps.

bigfin lanternfish

Scientific name: *Symbolophorus californiensis*
(Eigenmann and Eigenmann, 1889)
Family: **Lanternfish**
Other common names: none
French name: lanterne à grandes nageoires

Distribution: Found from Alaska and British Columbia to Baja California and at Ocean Station Papa (50°N, 145°W).

Characters: This species is distinguished from other Pacific coast lanternfishes by having 2 Prc photophores close together and

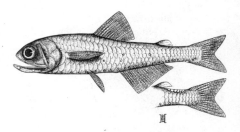

bigfin lanternfish

well below the lateral line, the PLO photophore above the pectoral fin origin, and a terminal mouth. Dorsal fin rays 13–15, anal rays 19–22, pectoral rays 15–20 and total vertebrae 37–40. Total gill rakers 21–25. Total AO photophores 14–17. Lateral line scales 42–46. Male supracaudal glands have 3–7 small, round to oval luminous scales which do not overlap. Female infracaudal glands have 3–8 small, round, non-overlapping spots. These glands develop at 5.5–6.0

cm in males and 6.5–7.0 cm in females. Larvae of this species are large and have elliptical eyes on short stalks. In adults the back is black, flanks silvery and fin bases dusky. Photophores emit a pale green light. Attains about 13 cm.

Biology: This species has been captured at the surface at night, attracted by lights, and down to 1560 m. It is one of the commonest Pacific lanternfishes and is food for many fishes, squid, birds and marine mammals. Life span is estimated to reach 7 years. Food is small crustaceans. Spawning occurs in spring and summer.

bigmouth buffalo

Scientific name: *Ictiobus cyprinellus*
 (Valenciennes in Cuvier and
 Valenciennes, 1844)
Family: **Sucker**
Other common names: redmouth buffalo,
 common buffalofish; gourdhead, gourdseed, roundhead, bullhead, stubnose,
 brown, bullmouth, bullnose, pugnose,
 mud, white, lake, blue, slough, or
 trumpet buffalo
French name: buffalo à grande bouche

Distribution: Found in Lake Erie, Lake St. Clair, the St. Clair River, Lake of the Woods and possibly Lake Ontario (the latter may be an introduction), the Red and Assiniboine rivers and Lake Manitoba of Manitoba and in the Qu'Appelle River of Saskatchewan. In the U.S.A. distribution is centred on the Mississippi River basin with introductions elsewhere.

Characters: This species is distinguished by having 23–32 dorsal fin rays, the anterior rays in a sickle-shape but not very elongate and filamentous (longest ray about 3 times as long as shortest ray in the fin), the subopercle bone on the side of the head broadest at the middle, the anterior fontanelle (an opening in the skull between the nostrils) is reduced or absent, lower fins are dark, the gut has elongate loops, the mouth is large, terminal and very oblique, and the lips are thin, without papillae, only weakly striated, and have shallow grooves. The upper lip is level with the lower eye margin. Pharyngeal teeth numerous, short, thin and fragile, twice

as high as wide. Gill rakers number nearly 100. Anal fin rays 7–10, pectoral rays 14–15, and pelvic rays 10–11. Lateral line scales 32–43. Breeding males have nuptial tubercles over most of the head, body before the dorsal fin, midflank caudal peduncle and leading edges of the dorsal, anal, upper pectoral and upper and lower pelvic rays and the whole caudal fin. The tubercles are best developed on caudal peduncle scales where there are up to 20 per scale with 6–12 tiny ones lining the scale margin and a few larger ones near the scale centre.

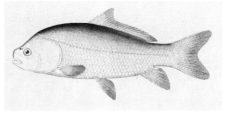

bigmouth buffalo

Overall colour brown to olive-brown fading to a white, orange-yellow or yellowish belly. Fins are dusky to grey or brown. Breeding males have an olive-green to greenish upper head, back and upper caudal peduncle. The flanks are copper, pale green or bluish. The dorsal and caudal fins are grey to black, the anal and pectoral fins are olive. The pectoral and pelvic fins may have white margins, the pelvics are lighter and the pectorals become dull white. Peritoneum black.

Reaches 157.0 cm and 36.3 kg. The world, all-tackle angling record weighed 31.89 kg and was caught in Bussey Brake, Louisiana in 1980.

Biology: This buffalo is a midwater to bottom schooling species found in still to slow waters of shallow lakes, impoundments and large rivers often over mud, silt and sand. It is tolerant of turbidity, low oxygen and temperatures up to 31.7°C. Distribution may be limited by a requirement of warm summer temperatures, the 22.5°C July isotherm. Individuals have been seen resting at a lake surface on calm days with the dorsal fin sticking out of the water. Motor boats may injure them at this time.

Planktonic and benthic crustaceans, insect larvae and diatoms are eaten by young. Adults take mouthfuls of mud and debris seized by "skipping" up and down at an angle to the bottom of about 55°. The numerous gill rakers filter out small food items. Some plankton is also taken by adults which feed as opportunity permits.

Males in Saskatchewan begin to mature at 30.5–32.8 cm and the majority are mature at 35.6–37.9 cm. Females only mature at about 50.0 cm or larger. Females live longer than males. Life span exceeds 20 years. Growth is slower in Canadian populations than southern U.S. ones.

Spawning takes place from April to June at temperatures generally over 15°C in Canada but as low as 8°C in Illinois. There is a migration into shallow, small streams, marshes or flooded areas. A female and 2–8 males will make rapid (2–3 second) rushes of up to 6.0 m through the water, with males pushing the female to the water surface and then sinking to the bottom. They may do this vertically with their tails sticking out of the water. Adhesive eggs are scattered onto vegetation with much splashing which foams up the water and can be heard almost half a kilometre away. Preserved eggs are 1.8 mm in diameter, and each female may carry up to an estimated 750,322 in Saskatchewan.

The blood of this species and its relative, the **black buffalo**, has cells known as secretory granulocytes found in few other organisms. The function of these cells is unknown.

This species is commercially important in the U.S.A. and has been fished for in Saskatchewan but is not particularly tasty except when smoked. The Committee on the Status of Endangered Wildlife in Canada assigned the status of "vulnerable" to this species in 1989.

bigmouth loosejaw

Scientific name: *Photostomias guernei*
    Collett, 1889
Family: **Barbeled Dragonfish**
Other common names: none
French name: drague à grande gueule

Distribution: Found in subarctic to tropical waters world-wide including Atlantic Canada.

Characters: This species is unique in its family in Canada by its lack of pectoral fins, of a barbel and of a suborbital light organ.

bigmouth loosejaw

The light organs along the lower flank are evenly spaced and not in groups. Pelvic fins are very long, sometimes more than half the standard length. Overall colour is black. The postorbital light organ is pink or reddish and the flank rows of light organs are white to bluish in preservative. Reaches 16 cm.

Biology: Found south of the Grand Bank at 50–600 m at the northern range limit in the western North Atlantic. First collected in 1979.

bigmouth sculpin

Scientific name: *Hemitripterus bolini*
    (Myers, 1934)
Family: **Sculpin**
Other common names: none
French name: hémitriptère à grande bouche

Distribution: Found from the Bering Sea to California including British Columbia.

Characters: This sculpin is distinguished from its Pacific coast relatives by the very large mouth and protruding lower jaw and the first dorsal fin rays are incised between the spines and the spines have flaps at their tips.

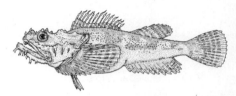

bigmouth sculpin

Nasal spines small but sharp. A ridge runs over the eye. The suborbital, tympanic and cleithral spines are blunt. There are 2 blunt spines under the eye. The preopercle has 4 spines, the upper 2 being long and pointed and the lower 2 blunt. First dorsal fin spines 11–15, mostly 14, second dorsal rays 11–14. Anal fin rays 12–14, pectoral rays 20–23 and pelvic fin with 1 spine and 3 soft rays. Scales are in the form of prickles and tubercles embedded in the skin and at fin bases. Lateral line with 40–42 pores. Cirri are large and found on the jaws, eyeball, top and sides of the head and pectoral fin. The lower jaw has 10 or more complex, branching cirri.

The back is brown to grey and mottled with 4–5 dark saddles. The head has 2 brownish bars. The area below the spiny dorsal fin is red. The spiny dorsal fin is red-brown on the membranes and barred, the soft dorsal fin is brown with grey blotches. The caudal fin is dark red-brown with grey-brown bars. The anal fin is light grey with orange blotches and black dots. The pectoral fin has bands of yellow-brown, grey and dark brown. The liver is bright orange. Reaches 73 cm total length and 8.5 kg.

Biology: Reported down to 208 m in Canadian waters and has a depth range of 25–925 m but is not very common at the shallower depths. Food includes **scorpionfish** and whelks.

bigmouth shiner

Scientific name: *Notropis dorsalis*
(Agassiz, 1854)
Family: **Carp**
Other common names: Gilbert's minnow
French name: méné à grande bouche

Distribution: Found in southern Manitoba in the Pembina, Assiniboine and Woody rivers. In the U.S.A. from New York west to Wyoming and south to Missouri with the main distribution west and south of lakes Superior and Michigan.

Characters: This species and its relatives in the genus *Notropis* (typical **shiners**) are separated from other family members by usually having 7 branched dorsal fin rays following thin unbranched rays, protractile premaxillaries (upper lip separated from the snout by a groove), no barbels, large lateral line scales (fewer than 50), and a simple, s-shaped gut. It is distinguished from its relatives by having usually 7 (range 6–8) branched anal rays, a large, horizontal and ventral mouth with the upper jaw longer than the eye, and a wide middorsal stripe on the back which passes on each side of the dorsal fin. Predorsal scales are irregularly arranged. Dorsal fin branched rays 7, pectoral rays 14–15 and pelvic rays 8. Lateral line scales 32–39. Pharyngeal teeth 1,4–4,1, 1,4–4,0 or 0,4–4,1 with a slightly hooked tip. Breeding males have minute tubercles on the top and sides of the head, the largest under the eye, on the nape, and on pectoral rays 2–10 in 6 or more rows.

The back is pale brown to yellowish with silvery flanks and a white to silvery belly. Upper flank scales are weakly to clearly outlined with pigment. Fins are clear. Peritoneum silvery. Reaches 7.6 cm.

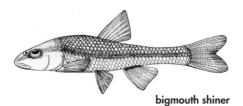

bigmouth shiner

Biology: This species was first recorded for Canada in 1970. Bigmouth shiners are a schooling species and have been caught in both clear and turbid waters over gravel and sand usually in open parts of streams and rivers. They may also be found in lakes. Food is principally benthic aquatic insects, with some mites and algae. They may take in mouthfuls of sand, separating and swallowing the food content, and ejecting sand from the mouth and gills. This species is more active at night. Life span is 4 years with maturity attained at 1–2 years. Spawning may extend from late May to August in Wisconsin. Spawning habits are unknown but it probably occurs in midwater with eggs drifting downstream. Females can contain up to 1275 yellow eggs of 1.0 mm diameter. The Committee on the Status of Endangered Wildlife in Canada assigned a status of "rare" to this species in 1985. In the U.S.A. it has been used as a bait fish for **crappies** and **yellow perch**.

bigpored snailfish

Scientific name: *Paraliparis latifrons*
Garman, 1899
Family: **Snailfish**

Other common names: none
French name: limace à front large

Distribution: Found from Alaska to Panama including British Columbia.

Characters: This snailfish is identified among its Canadian Pacific relatives by the lack of pelvic fins and an adhesive disc, by

bigpored snailfish

having 6 branchiostegal rays, no barbels or papillae on the snout and no laterally directed opercular spine, horizontal mouth, teeth in bands, gill slit running from above the pectoral fin downward in front of at least 10 pectoral rays, and a pale stomach with a black peritoneum. Dorsal fin rays 54–57, anal rays 48–50. Pectoral fin rays 21–24 with a notch dividing the fin into an upper lobe of about 13–17 rays and a lower lobe of about 4–5 rays. Lower lobe rays are almost completely free of the membrane and are elongate. Skin colour is dark brown, particularly on the head. Gill and mouth cavities and peritoneum are black. Reaches 14.5 cm.

Biology: Canadian records are from off southern Vancouver Island. Reported from depths of 2030–3279 m over the whole range. Eggs are up to 4.5 mm in diameter and number 2–8 per female. Females mature at about 6.1 cm and spawning probably occurs year round.

bigscale pomfret

Scientific name: *Taractichthys longipinnis*
(Lowe, 1843)
Family: **Pomfret**
Other common names: long-finned bream
French name: castagnole fauchoir

Distribution: Found from Nova Scotia south to Puerto Rico. Also in the eastern and southern Atlantic Ocean.

Characters: This species is distinguished from its Canadian relatives by the adults having scales on the dorsal and anal fins, a rounded head profile, scales on the caudal peduncle abruptly larger than those on the

caudal fin base and no scaleless area over and behind the eye. The anterior lobes of the dorsal and anal fins are high with a sickle-shape. Dorsal fin rays 33–38, anal rays 27–30, and pectoral rays 20–22. Scales in lateral series 39–45. There is no lateral line in adults. Scales have a strong central spine (except in the largest adults) forming lines along the body. There is no caudal peduncle keel. Overall colour is grey or silver with coppery tints. Preserved fish are black with the pectoral fins and the outer part of the pelvic fins whitish and edges of the dorsal, anal and caudal pale. The mouth cavity is not pigmented. Reaches over 100 cm standard length with northern expatriates largest.

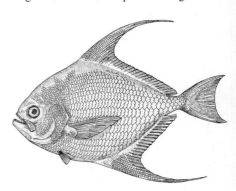

bigscale pomfret

Biology: Rare in Canada, with 1 specimen from Browns Bank in 1928, 1 specimen from Georges Bank in 1968 and a third from Lange's Cove, Nova Scotia in 1985. The latter is a northern range record in the western Atlantic Ocean and was collected with the aid of a shotgun. These are pelagic fishes found offshore in warmer waters. Spawning may occur year-round. They are eaten by **tunas**. May live at least 8 years.

bigtail snailfish

Scientific name: *Osteodiscus cascadiae*
Stein, 1978
Family: **Snailfish**
Other common names: none
French name: limace à tête trouée

Distribution: Found from British Columbia to Oregon.

Characters: This species is characterised by an adhesive disc covered only by thin skin, mostly skeletal and lacking a fleshy

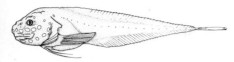

bigtail snailfish

margin. Six supporting fin rays around the disc are webbed and form a concave disc when erected. Nostrils are single. Head pores are very large. There are 6 branchiostegal rays. Teeth are in narrow bands. The skin is covered in prickles. Dorsal fin rays 47–52, anal rays 40–44, and pectoral rays 20–25. The pectoral fin has a moderate notch. Overall colour is black to dark brown. Mouth and gill cavities and the peritoneum are black. The stomach is pale with black streaks. Reaches 8.5 cm standard length.

Biology: Reported from off Queen Charlotte Sound and southern Vancouver Island. The functions of the unusual adhesive disc and the prickles are unknown. The disc is not suited to attachment but may serve to adjust the body angle relative to the sea bed. Prickles are too small to ward off predators and they occur on both young and adults of both sexes and so are probably not involved in reproduction. Calcium for prickle production is difficult to obtain nutritionally in the deep ocean so they must have some significance. This species is found at 1900–3000 m. Egg numbers are 1–7 per female with a diameter up to 5.3 mm. Females mature at about 6.5 cm and spawning probably occurs year round.

billfishes

This is a general term for those fishes which have a "bill" or rostrum formed from the premaxillae. The term includes the sailfishes, spearfishes and marlins and these are dealt with under **Swordfish Family**. There are 2 species in Canadian waters in addition to the **swordfish** itself.

See **blue marlin**
     white marlin

binocular spookfish

Scientific name: *Dolichopteryx binocularis*
   Beebe, 1932
Family: **Spookfish**
Other common names: none
French name: revenant à yeux télescopiques

Distribution: Found near Bermuda and southeast of Sable Island in Atlantic Canada.

Characters: This is the only spookfish from Atlantic Canada and is distinguished from related species by its elongate pectoral fin, by having about 5 luminous bodies along the middle of the belly and the pelvic fin base closer to the caudal fin than to the pectoral fin base. There are 15 dorsal fin rays, 11 anal fin rays, 14 pectoral fin rays and 9 pelvic fin rays. There are about 58 lateral line scales. The tubular eye has a posteroventrally directed light organ in a black sac. Overall colour is transparent white with a dark snout and black along the belly midline. Reaches 12 cm.

binocular spookfish

Biology: Reported from only a single specimen in Canada and few other specimens are known. Found possibly from as shallow as 350 m and as deep as 2700 m.

black buffalo

Scientific name: *Ictiobus niger*
   (Rafinesque, 1819)
Family: **Sucker**
Other common names: mongrel, round, blue, prairie, pumpkinseed, deepwater, bastard and current buffalo; chopper, buglemouth, bugler, router, blue rooter, reefer, kicker, chucklehead, buoy tender
French name: buffalo noir

Distribution: Found in the Mississippi River basin south to the Gulf states and Mexico, and marginally in lakes Michigan, Huron and Erie. In Canada found in Lake

Erie and some tributary streams and in the Niagara River.

Characters: This species is distinguished by having 27–31 dorsal fin rays, the anterior fontanelle (skull opening between nostrils)

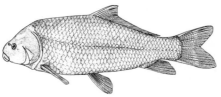

black buffalo

reduced to absent, the subopercle bone on the gill cover is broadest at the middle, the anterior lobe of the dorsal fin is sickle-shaped and its longest ray is about 3 times longer than the shortest dorsal ray, lower fins are dark, and the mouth is subterminal and almost horizontal. Lips are thick, coarsely striated and have deeply separated plicae. The upper jaw is shorter than the snout. The upper lip is below the eye level. Anal fin rays 8–9 and pelvic rays 9–11. Lateral line scales 36–39. Gill rakers on the rear face of the first arch number less than 60. The gut is very long with numerous, elongate loops parallel to the body. Pharyngeal teeth are short, strong, narrow and very numerous on each arch, about as wide as high. Males have 10–15 nuptial tubercles on each scale, and minute tubercles on the sides of the head and on the anterior pelvic fin rays. The back is grey-green to bronze or black fading through brownish flanks to a lighter white or yellowish belly. Fins are grey to dark olive. Breeding males may be black. Reaches 104.1 cm and 31.8 kg. The world, all-tackle angling record weighed 25.17 kg and was caught in Cherokee Lake, Tennessee in 1984.

Biology: Black buffalos are found in lakes and large rivers with strong current over a wide variety of bottoms. They may also be found in backwaters and impoundments. Food is primarily molluscs and aquatic insects, with some crustaceans such as crayfish. Algae scraped off rocks and duckweed are also eaten. Black buffalos snuffle through sediments and turn over stones and debris looking for food. Life span is reported to be

as high as 24 years with maturity in southern waters attained as early as 2 years. Spawning occurs in April-June. Details are uncertain but large, excited aggregations may develop but pairs separate for spawning. Over 400,000 eggs may be found in each female. The Committee on the Status of Endangered Wildlife in Canada assigned the status of "vulnerable" to this species in 1989.

black bullhead

Scientific name: *Ameiurus melas*
(Rafinesque, 1820)
Family: **Bullhead Catfish**
Other common names: black catfish, yellow belly bullhead, horned pout, brown catfish, stinger, lowbelly bullhead, river snapper, mudcat, slick, polliwog, chucklehead
French name: barbotte noire

Distribution: Found from New York tributaries of the St. Lawrence River south to the Gulf coast west of the mountains, mainly in the Mississippi River basin. In Canada found in southern Saskatchewan and Manitoba and extreme southwestern Ontario. Introductions to the Columbia River in Washington have spread into British Columbia in the Okanagan and Kootenay river systems.

Characters: This species is identified by the posterior tip of the adipose fin being free of the back, the caudal fin is not deeply forked, mouth corner barbels are about twice as long as nostril barbels, there is no bony

black bullhead

ridge between the head and the dorsal fin, the anal fin does not touch the caudal fin when pressed to the body, all barbels are dark brown to black, caudal fin base lightened, pectoral spine teeth are absent or weak, gill rakers 15–24, usually 17–19, anal rays are usually 19–21 (range 17–25) and the dorsal fin membranes are dark. The dorsal fin has 5–6, usually 6, soft rays. The pelvic and pectoral fins usually have 8 soft rays. Barbs on the dorsal fin spine are weak to absent.

The back and upper flank are dark brown, black or olive, the flanks yellowish-olive, greenish or golden without mottles, and the belly bright yellow, in breeding males, to white. The caudal fin base has a whitish bar. Barbels are grey to black and may be spotted on the chin. The fins are dusky with black margins and dark membranes in contrast to light rays. The anal fin has a light bar at the base and a dark bar at the margin. Breeding males and young are dark black above.

Formerly in the genus *Ictalurus*. Reaches 61.0 cm and 3.62 kg, the world, all-tackle sport record taken at Lake Waccabuc, New York in 1951.

Biology: This bullhead is quite rare in Canada but to the south is a common, schooling fish. Generally found in small streams, ponds, backwaters of larger rivers and in lakes over silt and mud. It is tolerant of pollution, turbidity, and high temperatures (up to 35°C) and replaces **brown** and **yellow bullheads** when conditions deteriorate.

Black bullheads are active at night, feeding on crustaceans, insects, molluscs, leeches, plant material and fishes such as **common shiners** and **yellow perch**. In British Columbia a wide variety of birds prey on this bullhead. Young fish tend to be most active around dusk and dawn and do not feed at night. They school during the day while adults are inactive in dense vegetation.

Life span is 10 years. Population numbers may be high so that individuals are stunted. Growth tends to be faster in clear water than in turbid water and in ponds than in streams. They mature at 2–4 years depending on food availability and population numbers.

Spawning takes place in May and June, perhaps as late as August, at a temperature of 21°C or higher. Females excavate a saucer-shaped nest in gravel or sand beneath weeds amongst wood debris, under overhanging banks or even in muskrat burrows. The female pushes pebbles aside with her snout and fans debris away with her fins. A male

and female pair will nudge each other and when the male wraps his caudal fin over the head of the female, eggs are laid. There may be up to 5 spawnings an hour with the female fanning eggs already laid. Both sexes guard and fan the egg mass which contains about 200 cream, adhesive eggs. However a female may contain up to 6820 eggs. Eggs are 3 mm in diameter. On hatching, the young remain in a school, or "ball", guarded by one of the parents until they are 25 mm long.

An important sport and farm pond species in the United States. Its flesh is said to be more flavourful than that of a **brown bullhead**. This bullhead has been used as an experimental animal to test toxic chemicals.

black crappie

Scientific name: *Pomoxis nigromaculatus* (Le Sueur in Cuvier and Valenciennes, 1829)

Family: **Sunfish**

Other common names: calico, strawberry, speckled, silver, banklick, butter, straw, grass or Oswego bass; shiner, moonfish, lamplighter, papermouth, bitterhead, razorback, bachelor perch, tinmouth, barfish, specks, slab, Mason perch

French name: marigane noire

Distribution: Found from extreme southwestern Québec in the St. Lawrence, Richelieu and Ottawa river basins, southern Ontario including all the Great Lakes, and southern Manitoba. Also introduced to the lower Fraser River in British Columbia. In the U.S.A. south to Florida and Texas and west to Montana but widely introduced.

Characters: This species is characterised by usually 7–8 (range 6–9) dorsal fin spines, an anal fin base slightly longer than that of the dorsal fins, and flanks irregularly blotched with black. Second dorsal fin soft rays 14–16, anal fin with 6–7 spines and 16–19 soft rays and pectoral rays 13–15. Lateral line scales 31–44. Gill rakers 22–23 on the lower arch.

The overall colour is silvery with some iridescent green, the back is olive, brown or dark green, the flanks silvery green with dense black blotching, and the belly is silvery-white. Eye yellow-brown. The dorsal, anal and caudal fins have black vermiculations or "worm tracks" surrounding yellow to pale green spots or ocelli. Pectoral fins are dusky. Pelvic fins have black tips and white leading edges and are generally opaque. Breeding males become much darker and more iridescent on the head and breast. Peritoneum silvery.

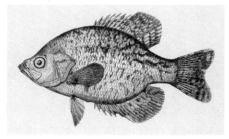

black crappie

Hybrids with **white crappie** are known. Reaches 48.9 cm and 2.3 kg. The world, all-tackle angling record from Kerr Lake, Virginia was caught in 1981 and weighed 2.05 kg. The Canadian record from Hillman Marsh, Lake Erie was caught in 1984 by Charles Serril and weighed 1.72 kg.

Biology: This schooling **crappie** is found in still waters of lakes and ponds or slow flowing, large rivers where there is abundant plant material or other cover. It prefers cooler and deeper water than the **white crappie** and is less tolerant of turbid conditions, growing more slowly there than in clear waters. It may enter brackish waters in the St. Lawrence River.

Food includes plankton, aquatic insects and fish fry when young. In the Ottawa River copepods and water fleas are the main diet of young-of-the-year, switching to amphipods in the fall. Even adults may rely principally on water fleas for food, taken by filter feeding in midwater using the numerous gill rakers, but fish become increasingly important as black crappies grow. Stunting is not uncommon where forage fish are rare. Feeding continues through winter, an unusual habit in a **sunfish**. The black crappie is a predator on the young of sport fishes and may affect population numbers significantly. Peak feeding is

between early evening and the early morning hours and in the morning around dawn. Young are diurnal and feed mostly on zooplankton in littoral midwater.

Life span is 13 years with maturity attained at 1–3 years. Growth varies with the habitat and with latitude to some degree. However an Ottawa River population at the northern range limit had growth comparable to other populations.

Spawning occurs in May to June at 13–23°C in Ontario. Males clean a rounded area in vegetated shallows or under banks. Each nest can be up to 38.1 cm across and nests occur in colonies, about 2 m apart. Each male guards his nest, fans the eggs and protects newly hatched young. Each female spawns with more than 1 male, depositing white adhesive eggs about 0.9 mm in diameter. A female can carry up to 188,000 eggs.

This species enters into commercial catches. The flesh is white and flaky. Sport fishermen catch them on baited hooks in both summer and winter.

- Most accessible in the spring right after ice-out when water temperatures rise over 42°F.

- The bays and shorelines of the Great Lakes and their watersheds.

- Ultralight to light action spinning outfits used with four- to six-pound test monofilament line.

- Good assortment of 1/16– to 1/8–ounce hair jigs and plastic grubs. Small live **minnows** and worms are the best bait, fished below a float.

black dogfish

Scientific name: *Centroscyllium fabricii*
  (Reinhardt, 1825)
Family: **Sleeper Shark**
Other common names: none
French name: aiguillat noir

Distribution: From southern Baffin Island and Greenland south to Virginia and possibly the Gulf of Mexico. Also in Europe and South Africa.

Characters: The absence of an anal fin, presence of dorsal fin spines in grooves, teeth in both jaws alike with 3–5 triangular cusps, and a dark brown to black body distinguish this shark. The abdomen is long and the caudal peduncle is short. The conical,

black dogfish

hooked denticles are widely separated, leaving most of the skin bare. The second dorsal fin is larger than the first dorsal fin. There is a spiracle behind the eye. Dark chocolate brown to black above and below, no other markings. Up to 1.07 m.

Biology: This is a deepwater, schooling species, abundant at temperatures of 3.5–4.5°C or even as low as 1°C, usually below 256 m and down to 1600 m. Black dogfish may approach the surface, especially at night and in the winter. They have been caught through the ice at the surface. They approach shallow waters in the Arctic. They are ovoviviparous and the embryos reach at least 14 cm. Food includes pelagic crustaceans, cephalopods, small redfish and jellyfish. Populations may be segregated by sex and size. Schools move into shallower water in winter and spring. Adult females are 58–70 cm long. This shark has luminescent organs scattered through its skin. This is the most abundant species in deep water off Atlantic Canada and is often caught by bottom trawls and line gear but is little used.

black drum

Scientific name: *Pogonias cromis*
  (Linnaeus, 1766)
Family: **Drum**
Other common names: sea drum, common
  drum
French name: grand tambour

Distribution: From Nova Scotia to Argentina in the western Atlantic Ocean.

Characters: This drum is separated from its Canadian Atlantic relative, the **weakfish**, by dorsal and anal fin ray counts. First dorsal fin with 10 spines, second dorsal fin with 1 spine and 19–23 soft rays. The anal fin has a short

spine followed by a long, stout spine and 5–7 soft rays. The lateral line has 41–47 scales. The snout has 5 upper pores and 5 marginal pores. The lower jaw has 5 pores and 10–13 pairs of small but obvious barbels. Colour is silvery-grey to brassy or dark with 4–5 broad, black, flank bars. Bars fade with age. The fins are all dusky to blackish. Both greyish and reddish forms of this drum are found. Reaches 1.8 m and 66.28 kg. The world, all-tackle angling record weighed 51.28 kg and was caught in 1975 at Lewes, Delaware.

black drum

Biology: First caught in 1947 at Halls Harbour in the Minas Channel. Also known from single specimens in southwestern Nova Scotia at Lockeport Harbour and Petpeswick Inlet. These are strays from the south. This drum favours coastal waters with sand or sand-mud bottoms near large river estuaries. There is a northward and inshore migration each spring and the reverse occurs in the fall. Food is heavy-shelled items like mussels, which are crushed by the pharyngeal or throat teeth. Life span is 35 years or more. Drumming noises are made with the swimbladder to attract and locate the opposite sex in the spawning season. In the U.S. this species is often caught from boats, piers, bridges and on beaches using clam or crab baits as well as jugs and spoons, but is said not to be good eating. The large, silvery scales are often sold as a form of jewellery curio.

black eelpout

Scientific name: *Lycodes diapterus*
  Gilbert, 1892
Family: **Eelpout**
Other common names: blackmouth eelpout,
  black-finned eelpout

French name: lycode noire

Distribution: Found from Japan to California including British Columbia.

Characters: This species is distinguished from its Pacific coast relatives by having prominent ridges on the ventral surface of the lower jaw known as "mental crests", teeth are present on the roof of the mouth, the pectoral fin outline is notched, the mouth and gill cavities and the peritoneum are black, and the eye diameter is greater than snout length. The skin is loose and translucent and the lateral line is indistinct. Pelvic fins are present and there are no mucous pores on the jaws. The flesh is firm. Dorsal fin rays 90–124, anal rays 92–107, pectoral rays 18–25. Vertebrae number 111–125. Overall colour pearly with fine black spots or dusky brown dorsally and blue-black ventrally. The pectoral, pelvic, dorsal and anal fins have blue-black on them, concentrated

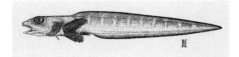

black eelpout

at the edge. There are light spots over the scales. There are 3–9 light flank bars extending onto the dorsal fin. Mouth and gill cavities jet black. Peritoneum dusky to black. Reaches 37.1 cm.

Biology: Depth range in Canada is 120–640 m, elsewhere at 13–2260 m over mud bottoms. This species is caught by shrimp trawlers.

black hagfish

Scientific name: *Eptatretus deani*
(Evermann and Goldsborough, 1907)
Family: **Hagfish**
Other common name: none
French name: myxine noire

Distribution: Found from Baja California to southeastern Alaska including British Columbia.

Characters: The black hagfish is distinguished from other Canadian species by having 10–12 gill pores, 4 pairs of barbels, a distinct eye spot and 4–10 (usually 6–8) slime pores before the branchial region. Total slime pores 67–80. The upper two tooth

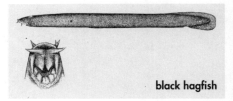

black hagfish

plates bear 11–13 teeth, the lower two 10–11 teeth. The ventral finfold is small. Prune or purplish-black coloured when alive, but becoming black when preserved in alcohol. White area on head reveals the eye position. Often spotted with lighter colour, and edge of the ventral finfold does not have a pale margin. Attains 63.5 cm.

Biology: A common species in deeper waters found from 155–373 m off the Canadian coast and in midwater over the deep ocean. Also reported in warmer latitudes down to 2743 m. Females contain a few (8–15) large (5.2 cm by 1.1 cm) mature eggs among hundreds of minute eggs. These mature eggs are curved in shape. Samples of this species are about three-quarters female and one-quarter male.

black prickleback

Scientific name: *Xiphister atropurpureus*
(Kittlitz, 1858)
Family: **Shanny**
Other common names: black blenny
French name: lompénie noire

Distribution: From Baja California to southeastern Alaska including British Columbia.

Characters: This species is related to the **ribbon** and **rock pricklebacks** and like them lacks pelvic fins and a head crest, has 4

black prickleback

lateral line canals and has the anal fin joined to the caudal fin. It is distinguished by having no anal fin spines, the dorsal fin origin well behind the head, and by colour. There are 65–73 dorsal fin spines and 1 spine and 40–55 soft anal fin rays. The pectoral fins are reduced to tiny flaps. Scales are indistinct. Colour is variable, from black or dark brown to a reddish brown. The caudal fin base often has a pale or white bar. 2–3 dark bars with white edges (black in the **rock prickleback**) radiate back and down from the eye. Reaches 30.5 cm.

Biology: Common under rocks and in gravelly areas in the intertidal zone and down to 7.6 m. They are also found under algae when the tide is out and can survive from several hours to a day without being covered by water. Food is worms, molluscs and crustaceans. Black pricklebacks are eaten by other fishes, garter snakes, mink and raccoons. Spawning occurs in winter and spring. Winter spawning takes place on rocky beaches protected from waves but during spring an increasing exposure to potential wave action in choice of rocks occurs, a response to ameliorating environmental conditions. Females lay eggs in masses of up to 1680 eggs under rocks which the male guards by wrapping his body around them. Males may look after 3 egg masses at once from different females. Used by anglers as bait for **scorpionfishes** and **greenlings**.

black redhorse

Scientific name: *Moxostoma duquesnei*
(Le Sueur, 1817)
Family: **Sucker**
Other common names: black mullet, finescale redhorse, finescale mullet, blue sucker, white sucker, bigjawed sucker, Pittsburgh sucker
French name: suceur noir

Distribution: Found in the Great Lakes and Mississippi River basin from New York west to Wisconsin and south to Mississippi. In Canada it is reported from tributaries of lakes Erie, St. Clair and Huron in southwestern Ontario.

Characters: This species is distinguished by a short dorsal fin, a swimbladder with 3 chambers, lateral line scales usually 44–47 (range 42–51), scales around caudal peduncle usually 12 or 13 (rarely 15–16), lower lip thick, its rear edge almost straight or broadly obtuse, no papillae and no cross lines on the plicae, pharyngeal teeth not molar-shaped but narrow and fragile, pelvic fin origin below the middle of the dorsal fin, eye diameter usually less than half the snout length and about half the lip width, and the nostrils are above the end of the maxilla of the upper jaw. The caudal peduncle is slender, its depth usually less than two-thirds of the length from the end of the anal fin base to the end of the body. The mouth is markedly overhung by the snout. Gill rakers 30–32. Dorsal fin rays 11–15, anal rays 6–7 and pectoral rays 15–20. Pelvic fin rays usually 10, range 8–11. The intestine has 4–5 rounded coils. Males have nuptial tubercles on the anal and caudal fins, largest on the lower lobe, and on the back, flank scales and anterior rays of the dorsal, pectoral and pelvic fins. Tubercles are lost completely within 2 weeks of spawning.

black redhorse

The back and upper flank are olive-brown, olive-green to grey or black, flanks silvery and belly silvery to white. There is often a silvery-blue sheen over much of the body. The flanks may have bronze reflections in larger fish. Young fish have an even dusky to black upper flank, rather than lighter central areas on each scale as in **golden redhorse**. Fins are generally grey to orange. Scales are outlined in black. Spawning males have a pink flank stripe bordered above and below by metallic green-black. The anal, pectoral and pelvic fins are dark pink. The tail is not pink but a light grey. Peritoneum silvery. Reaches 65.8 cm.

Biology: Black redhorses are in deeper pools of medium to larger streams with clear water and gravel, rock or sand beds. They are intolerant of siltation. Food is taken in with mouthfuls of bottom silt and is filtered out leaving a trailing cloud. It includes various crustaceans, molluscs, insects, mites and worms. Most feeding occurs in the evening in schools of 15–20 fish. Life span is at least 10 years. Sexual maturity is reached at 2–5 years, usually about 4 years for both sexes. Spawning occurs by day and night over gravel riffles at 15–61 cm depth in March to June, probably late May–early June in Canada. There is a spawning migration from pools to the riffles. Spawning lasts about 4 days. Males defend territories on riffles, chasing away other males, and have been seen to leap out of the water. Each female enters the male territory, is flanked and clasped on the posterior half of the body by 2 males and the trio vibrates while eggs and sperm are shed in a few seconds. A female may contain up to 17,252 eggs of 2.9 mm diameter. This species is caught on live baits, by spearing and by snagging in the U.S.A. It is said to be exceptionally tasty. The small bones in the flesh are softened by deep frying after the flesh has been scored. The Committee on the Status of Endangered Wildlife in Canada assigned the status of "threatened" to this species in 1988.

black remora

Scientific name: *Remora remora*
　(Linnaeus, 1758)
Family: **Remora**
Other common names: remora, common
　remora
French name: rémora noir

Distribution: Found world-wide in warmer waters including the Atlantic coast and probably the Pacific coast of Canada.

Characters: This remora is distinguished from its Canadian relatives by having a small disc with 16–20, usually 18, laminae, rounded pectoral fins, a stout body, no stripes and 20–27 soft dorsal fin rays. The anal fin has 20–25 rays. The pectoral fin is flexible and has 25–32 rays. There are 29–34 gill rakers. Blackish or dark brown on body and fins. Attains 86 cm.

black remora

Biology: The black remora has been caught only 19 km outside Canadian territorial waters southwest of British Columbia, probably as a result of the El Niño warming of 1982–1983, and is not uncommon as a stray from warmer waters in Nova Scotia and on the Grand and St. Pierre banks. This remora is found on large **sharks** and also **bony fishes** and may swim free of hosts when it is caught by fishermen. Parasitic copepods are an important food item for this species, particularly when young.

black rockfish

Scientific name: *Sebastes melanops*
　Girard, 1856
Family: **Scorpionfish**
Other common names: black bass, black
　rockcod, black snapper
French name: sébaste noir

Distribution: Found from the Aleutian Islands south to Baja California including British Columbia.

Characters: This species is identified by colour characters and body proportions. It lacks the 3 mandibular pores of the similar

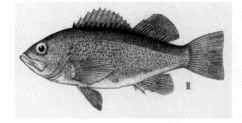

black rockfish

dusky rockfish. The space between the eyes on top of the head is convex. The caudal peduncle is deep. The upper jaw extends to or past the rear of the eye. Dorsal fin spines 13–14, usually 13, soft rays 13–16. Anal fin soft rays 7–9, usually 8, second anal spine only slightly thicker than the third and shorter. The posterior anal fin margin slopes forward. Pectoral fin rays 18–20, usually 19. Gill rakers 33–39. Vertebrae 26. Lateral line pores 46–55, scale rows below the lateral line 50–55. Head spines are mostly absent, nasals are weak and the preoculars can be present.

The back is black to blue-black with the flanks grey and mottled and blotched with black which extends onto the lower dorsal fin. The lateral line has a grey or white stripe. The belly is a dirty white. The rear of the spiny dorsal fin is dark and other fins are dark. The peritoneum is silvery-white, sometimes spotted. Young fish are grey with brown spots and mottles and an obvious black spot on the dorsal fin.

Reaches 63 cm and 4.8 kg. The world, all-tackle angling record weighed 4.56 kg and was caught in 1986 in Puget Sound, Washington.

Biology: Found in coastal areas among rocks and kelp from the surface down to 366 m. They are also found pelagically over 445 km from shore over depths of 4938 m. Common in British Columbia forming schools off and on the bottom but may occur singly. Young fish are in shallower water than adults. Schools feed near the sea surface and some fish jump out of the water while chasing such fishes as **sand lances**. Many other fishes and crustaceans are also eaten. The young are born in April in offshore Canadian waters after parents mated in September or October. At 6 months they enter nearshore waters and may be caught in tide pools. Life span is at least 36 years. Maturity is attained at 40–42 cm or 10–13 years for males and 38–42 cm or 9–12 years for females. An important incidental catch of the Washington sport fishery when anglers are trolling for salmon. This rockfish is excellent eating. Its rocky habitat prevents it being a common trawl catch.

black ruff

Scientific name: *Centrolophus niger*
  (Gmelin, 1788)
Family: **Ruff**
Other common names: blackfish, rudder fish, black pilotfish
French name: pompile noir

Distribution: Found from the Scotian Shelf, Grand Bank and St. Margarets Bay, Nova Scotia, south to New Jersey. Also known from South Africa, New Zealand, and Europe.

Characters: This species is distinct in having an elongate body, a small head with prominent pores, a lateral line scale count of 160–230, a continuous dorsal fin with very weak spines and no teeth on the roof of the mouth. There are 4–5 spines and 32–37 soft rays in the dorsal fin. The anal fin has 3 weak spines and 20–24 soft rays. There are 19–23 pectoral fin rays. The overall colour is brown of varying shades, sometimes approaching black, to dark bluish or blue-grey. The dorsal, anal and pelvic fins are darker than the body. Young fish have 2–4 bars on the flank. The peritoneum is light. Reaches 1.5 m.

black ruff

Biology: This species is a stray in Atlantic Canada. It was first caught in 1936. Reported from mackerel traps in St. Margarets Bay and down to 430 m offshore, and to at least 805 m. It is a temperate water species usually found in the open ocean. The black ruff has been found associated with jellyfish and with the **ocean sunfish** (hence the name black pilotfish). Food is fish, crustaceans and jellyfish. One specimen was found with an onion and pieces of potato in its stomach! Growth is very rapid. Spawning occurs from October to December. Eggs are 1.2 mm diameter. The flesh is said to be quite unpleasant by some authors and tasty by other authors!

black scabbardfish

Scientific name: *Aphanopus carbo*
  Lowe, 1839
Family: **Cutlassfish**
Other common names: sabre noir

French name: aphanope charbon

Distribution: Found world-wide including the eastern Arctic, Atlantic and Pacific coasts of Canada.

Characters: This cutlassfish is distinguished from its Canadian relatives by having the spiny and soft parts of the dorsal fin

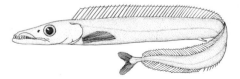

black scabbardfish

about equal, and a total dorsal fin ray count of 90–98. Dorsal fin spines are 38–42, soft rays 53–57. Anal fin with 2 spines, the second enlarged and dagger-shaped, and 44–50 soft rays. Pectoral rays about 12. There is a pelvic fin composed of a single spine in young fish but this is lost in adults. Live fish are coppery to coppery-black, with an iridescent sheen, but this fades to black when dead. Fishes caught by trawlers often have their delicate skin scraped off and appear white. Oral and gill cavities are black. Reaches 129 cm and larger.

Biology: First found in Canada on the northeast Newfoundland Shelf in 1959 and on the southwestern Sable Island Bank in 1960. First captured in 1972 off Cape Flattery on the Pacific coast with a second specimen recorded in 1986 west of Sydney Inlet, Vancouver Island. Usually found swimming above the sea bed but may approach the surface at night. Canadian specimens have been caught at 550–840 m in the Atlantic, about 292–500 m on the Pacific coast and at 640 m in the Davis Strait. Reported elsewhere at 146–1600 m. Food includes squids, fishes and crustaceans. Black scabbardfish chase squid and a modification of the swimbladder may allow rapid pursuit into shallow water without expansion of the swimbladder gases. The swimbladder has a thick wall and is enclosed in a cage of ribs and muscle masses. Life span exceeds 40 years. An important food fish off Madeira where it is caught on baited longlines at 600–1460 m.

black sea bass

Scientific name: *Centropristis striata* (Linnaeus, 1758)
Family: **Sea Bass**
Other common names: blackfish, tally-wag, black bass, hannahill, black-will, black-Harry, black perch, bluefish, rock bass, humpback, fanfre noir
French name: mérou noir

Distribution: Found from Florida to the Bay of Fundy and the outer coast of Nova Scotia.

Characters: This species is distinguished by scale and fin ray counts from other sea basses. Scale rows number 48–50. Dorsal fin spines 10, soft rays 11. Anal soft rays are 7. There are small fleshy tabs on the dorsal fin spines. The upper caudal lobe has a short filamentous extension, particularly developed in adult males. Overall colour is blue-black to dark brown with blotches. Scales have paler centres which line up to form narrow flank stripes. The dorsal fins have vague white lines. The dorsal and anal fin margins are white. The upper and lower edges of the

black sea bass

caudal fin are white. Males have large white patches on the head and a pronounced central lobe to the caudal fin. A blue hump develops behind the head in the spawning season. Young fish have a dark band along the flank. Attains 61 cm. The world, all-tackle record weighed 4.3 kg and was caught at Virginia Beach, Virginia in 1987.

Biology: A rare and sporadic visitor to Canadian waters. Adults are found over hard bottoms or around wrecks and harbours. There is a winter migration offshore to deeper water at 73–165 m. Food is crustaceans, fishes, molluscs, echinoderms and plants. Spawning occurs from spring to summer at

18–45 m. Eggs are pelagic. Yearlings enter estuaries which are used as nurseries. Females mature at 2 years of age and, since these fish are hermaphrodites, male tissue develops at 3 years of age. Each individual fish passes through a female phase before becoming a male. Nearly all fish larger than 25 cm are male. The largest females are about 34 cm and 8 years, while males are about 45 cm and at least 12 years old and up to 20 years. This species is important in the U.S.A. mainly as a sport fish but also as a commercial species caught in pots and by trawls. The flesh is firm and white. The catch in the U.S.A. in 1988 was 2190 tonnes. Anglers catch this hard fighting fish on light tackle year round using fish, shrimp, crabs, squid, clams, worms or mackerel jigs. It may be caught from shore or drifting boats, fishing on the bottom.

black seasnail

Scientific name: *Paraliparis bathybius*
    (Collett, 1879)
Family: **Snailfish**
Other common names: none
French name: limace noire

   Distribution: Found in the North Atlantic Ocean including West Greenland and Baffin Bay.
   Characters: This snailfish is separated from other Canadian Atlantic species by the lack of an adhesive disc and pelvic fins, by having 1 pair of nostrils, and a black body. The mouth is horizontal and teeth are in broad bands. Dorsal fin rays 57–60, anal rays 49–55. Pectoral rays about 19. The lower pectoral fin lobe is made up of 3–4 separate rays. The pectoral fin is above the level of the eye centre. The gill opening is above the pectoral fin level. The tail is dusky to black. Reaches 25.3 cm standard length.

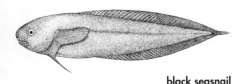

black seasnail

   Biology: This snailfish is found in cold waters on or above the bottom at 600–4009 m. It may be found in groups. Food includes pelagic amphipods and benthic snails and crustaceans. Spawning occurs in the summer and possibly at other times. Females have over 400 eggs up to 4.5 mm in diameter.

black snaggletooth

Scientific name: *Astronesthes niger*
    Richardson, 1844
Family: **Barbeled Dragonfish**
Other common names: black star-eater
French name: dragon-saumon noir

   Distribution: In all major oceans and off the Atlantic coast of Canada.
   Characters: The black snaggletooth is separated from related Canadian species by teeth on the maxilla bone of the upper jaw being

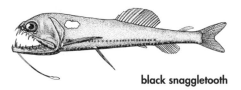

black snaggletooth

comb-like, close together and slanted rearward, a ventral adipose fin, 50–56 light organs in the ventral row, the lower row of light organs forming a u-shaped bend at the pectoral fin level, 15–17 anal fin rays and a barbel with an elongate swelling at the tip. There are fang-like teeth in the jaws. The head and body are velvety black. The barbel is pale in small, preserved fish. Large fish have pale luminous patches in front and above the eye, on the upper jaw and on the body above the pectoral fin and below the dorsal fin. Small, preserved fish have the sides and lower surface of the head, lower flanks and belly profusely covered with white photophores, each distinctly edged in black. Attains 16 cm.
   Biology: Found off or on the Scotian Shelf in Canada. This species is taken in surface nets at night and is the commonest snaggletooth. May descend to over 1000 m. It needs moonlight for vertical migrations either to initiate or direct the movement, but is most concentrated at the surface when the sun and moon are below the horizon. It is known to eat lanternfishes. When caught its light organs produce a violet-white flash.

black snake mackerel

Scientific name: *Nealotus tripes*
　　Johnson, 1865
Family: **Snake Mackerel**
Other common names: none
French name: coelho tripode

Distribution: Found world-wide in temperate to tropical oceans, including Atlantic Canada.

Characters: The body form somewhat resembles a **tuna** but is more elongate. The soft dorsal fin has 15–18 rays. There are 2 spines, the first large and sharp, in front of the anal fin which has 16–18 soft rays, and is followed by 2 finlets. This species is distinguished from other Canadian snake mackerels by having 20–21 dorsal fin spines, no caudal peduncle keel, and the pelvic fins consisting of only 1 small spine. Most of the body is scaleless. Overall colour is brownish. Attains 30 cm.

black snake mackerel

Biology: Known in Canada from a stray caught off Sable Island in 1966 and from off the Grand Bank. It may be found at the surface and down to 550 m. This snake mackerel is eaten by **swordfish** and **longnose lancetfish**.

black swallower

Scientific name: *Chiasmodon niger*
　　Johnson, 1863
Family: **Black Swallower**
Other common names: none
French name: grand avaleur

Distribution: Found from the Caribbean Sea to the Flemish Cap in Atlantic Canada.

Characters: The distensible mouth and stomach and colour are characteristic. The dorsal fin has 11–13 spines and 26–29 soft rays. The anal fin has 1 spine and 26–29 rays. The pectoral fin has 12–15 rays and the pelvic fin 1 spine and 5 soft rays. Some teeth are depressible at the front of the mouth and teeth generally overlap the lips when the mouth is closed. There is a small spine at the lower corner of the preopercle. Overall black to brownish. Attains at least 25 cm.

black swallower

Biology: Specimens from Canadian waters have been caught as deep as 1000 m and floating at the surface. The usual range is 550–2745 m.

Black Swallower Family

Scientific name: Chiasmodontidae
French name: grands avaleurs

Found in the temperate to tropical waters of the Atlantic, Pacific and Indian oceans with about 15 species, 1 of which enters Atlantic Canada. Other species may occur there but have yet to be identified.

Black swallowers have a very distensible mouth and stomach and an overall black colour which gives them their name. Even the internal supporting skeleton of the anal fin is not attached to the body muscles, allowing the stomach to distend further. The upper jaw bones are long, slender and joined at the rear. The halves of the lower jaw can separate to enlarge the mouth. Teeth in both jaws are long and sharp. There are no gill rakers. Scales may be absent or present, small and rough. There are 6–7 branchiostegal rays.

This family is a relative of the **Sandfish Family** which is found on the Pacific coast. It is a member of the **Perch Order**.

These are deepsea, meso- or bathypelagic fishes which often catch and eat fish larger than themselves.

See **black swallower**

blackbelly eelpout

Scientific name: *Lycodopsis pacifica*
　　(Collett, 1879)
Family: **Eelpout**

Other common names: black-bellied eel-pout
French name: lycode à ventre noir

Distribution: Found from Alaska to Baja California including British Columbia.

Characters: This species is distinguished from its Pacific coast relatives by having prominent ridges on the ventral surface of the lower jaw known as "mental crests", and both the vomer and palatine bones in the roof of the mouth lack teeth. There is a cartilaginous stay along the bottom of the head. Pelvic fins are present and there are no mucous pores on the jaws. Flesh is firm. Dorsal fin rays 90–107, anal rays 70–90, and pectoral rays 16–19. Overall colour is light grey to reddish-brown or pink, almost transparent. The scales have a light spot. Pale bars margined in black on the flank are most evident in young. The dorsal and posterior anal fins have a black margin with the rest of the fins grey and semi-transparent. Dorsal fin rays may appear to be white because they transmit light better then the fin membranes. Anterior edge of the dorsal fin with an elongate blotch. Pelvic fins pale. Peritoneum black. Reaches 46 cm.

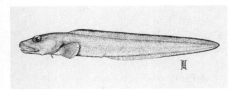

blackbelly eelpout

Biology: The commonest Canadian Pacific eelpout found on mud bottoms at 18–220 m, elsewhere 9–400 m. Food is worms, amphipods, crabs, clams and brittle stars. It is a food item for **sablefish** and **rockfishes**. Most males mature at 17 cm and females at 16 cm. Life span is about 5 years. Each female has 7–52 eggs and spawning occurs from September to January, mostly November and December. Mature eggs average 5 mm in diameter. Few, large eggs suggest parental care and submersible observations off California indicate burrows may be constructed. This species is common in shrimp trawls.

blackbelly pearleye

Scientific name: *Scopelarchus analis*
    (Brauer, 1902)
Family: **Pearleye**
Other common names: none
French name: oeil-perlé à ventre noir

Distribution: Found in all warmer oceans and off Nova Scotia.

Characters: This species is separated from other Canadian pearleyes by having obvious stripes above and below the lateral line on the

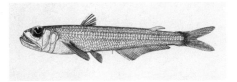

blackbelly pearleye

posterior part of the body. In addition the pectoral fins are longer than the pelvic fins. Dorsal fin rays 7–9, usually 8, anal rays 21–26 and pectoral rays 18–22. Lateral line scales 45–50. Scale pockets are marked by pigment above the lateral line. There is no heavy pigment on the anal and adipose fins but the other fins are usually pigmented on the membranes and rays in varying degrees. Peritoneum black. Reaches 12.6 cm.

Biology: First caught in Canadian waters in 1978 at about 220 m. This and other larvae off Nova Scotia are range extensions for the northwest Atlantic Ocean first reported in 1988. Larvae have been caught elsewhere at 30–50 m and adults down to 800 m. Adults feed on other midwater fishes.

blackbelly rosefish

Scientific name: *Helicolenus dactylopterus
    maderensis* Goode and Bean, 1896
Family: **Scorpionfish**
Other common names: red bream, blue
    mouth, sébaste chèvre
French name: chèvre impériale

Distribution: Found from Argentina to Nova Scotia. Also in the eastern Atlantic Ocean and Mediterranean Sea.

Characters: This species is distinguished by fin ray counts. Dorsal fin spines 11–13, usually 12, soft rays 10–13. The anal fin has 3–6, usually 5, soft rays. The pectoral fin has 16–21, usually 19, rays. The lower 7–9 pectoral rays are free from the membrane and the posterior margin of the upper part of the pectoral fin is straight. Lateral line pores usually 28–29, transverse scale rows 42–48. The head lacks fleshy tabs and cirri.

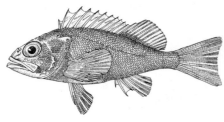

blackbelly rosefish

The body is pale red, with some darker scarlet blotches, particularly evident in adults. The back may have green or brown and the upper flank has scale margins dusky. The gill cover has a dusky blotch. The dorsal fin base between spines 7 or 8 to 11 is dark but large adults lose this. The gill cavity and mouth are purplish-black. The soft dorsal, anal and pelvic fins have white margins. The spiny dorsal fin is mottled white. The peritoneum is black and this is visible externally (hence "blackbelly"). Reaches 39 cm in Canada, but usually smaller.

Biology: This species is usually found offshore at 110–735 m over rocky bottoms or perched on worm mounds as a viewing platform on soft bottoms. It may occur in water as shallow as 2 m and as deep as 1000 m. It is not common in Canada and its biology is poorly known. Food in the Mediterranean Sea is pelagic sea squirts, benthic crustaceans, worms, squids and fishes. It is not a commercial species since most individuals are quite small although some are caught with bottom trawls and sold fresh.

Blackchin Family

Scientific name: Neoscopelidae
French name: mentons noirs

Blackchins are known from all tropical to temperate oceans. There are six species of which only one has been reported from the Pacific coast of Canada.

Blackchins are small, deepsea fishes having a dorsal fin in front of the middle of the body and the anal fin behind it. There is an adipose fin. Scales are large and easily lost.

They are close relatives of the **Lanternfish Family** but the eyes are smaller and light organs are few or lacking. This family is a member of the **Lanternfish Order**.

See **glowingfish**

blackchin shiner

Scientific name: *Notropis heterodon*
(Cope, 1865)
Family: **Carp**
Other common names: black-striped minnow
French name: menton noir

Distribution: Found in the Great Lakes basin except northern Lake Superior, including southwestern Québec, southern Ontario, the Quetico region west of Lake Superior, and also southern Manitoba. Also in the upper Mississippi River basin.

Characters: This species and its relatives in the genus *Notropis* (typical **shiners**) are separated from other family members by usually having 7 branched dorsal fin rays following thin unbranched rays, protractile premaxillaries (upper lip separated from the snout by a groove), no barbels, large lateral line scales (fewer than 50), and a simple, s-shaped gut. It is separated by having 6–7

blackchin shiner

branched anal fin rays, and a strong, black, zig-zag, midflank stripe extending onto the head including the upper lip and chin. Dorsal fin branched rays 6–7, usually 7, pectoral rays 12–14, and pelvic rays 7–8. Lateral line scales 31–38, the lateral line interrupted or incomplete in some fish. Pharyngeal teeth hooked with a cutting edge, 1,4–4,1, 1,4–4,0, 1,3–4,1 or 4–4. Breeding males have minute nuptial tubercles on the top of the head and pectoral fin rays.

The back is yellowish, the flanks silvery and the belly white to yellowish. Upper flank scales are outlined with black but there is a gap or light stripe of unmarked scales between them and the flank stripe. Fins are transparent. Breeding males are a bright golden yellow. Peritoneum silvery to dusky. Reaches 7.1 cm.

Biology: Blackchin shiners prefer clear, weedy water of pools in rivers and streams or lakes inshore. It is intolerant of turbidity and weed loss. This **shiner** is a schooling species found over dense vegetation. Food is planktonic crustaceans, small aquatic insects, terrestrial insects such as flies taken at the water surface, and diatoms from bottom ooze. Food is also taken off vegetation. Peak feeding occurs at dawn and dusk. Life span is 3 years with maturity attained at 1 year. Spawning occurs in May to July, and as late as August in Wisconsin. Eggs are up to 1.2 mm in diameter and number up to 1800.

blackeye goby

Scientific name: *Coryphopterus nicholsi*
  (Bean, 1882)
Family: **Goby**
Other common names: crested goby,
  bluespot goby
French name: gobie aux yeux noirs

Distribution: From Baja California to the Queen Charlotte Islands in British Columbia.

Characters: This goby is distinguished from its relatives, the **arrow goby** and the **bay goby**, by its large scales and the crest running from the eyes to the dorsal fin. There are about 21–28 scales along the flank. There are 4–7 first dorsal fin spines and 12–16 soft dorsal fin rays. Anal fin rays 11–14. The eyes are dark. The body is a pale, orange-tinged olive, pale tan or light yellow, which may be mottled with purple-brown and green streaks, mottles and speckles. The fish may be pink to red. The first dorsal fin is tipped with black. The pelvic fins are dark black in adult males, grey in females. Fin margins are light, bluish

in some. Iridescent but faint stripe or a blue spot under the eye. Dorsal and anal fins pale yellow with orange lines. A mottled, dark colour pattern is assumed by subordinate fish. Attains 15.2 cm.

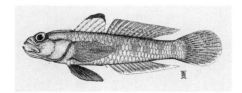

blackeye goby

Biology: Found near the bottom in shallow water down to 126 m where they maintain territories near rocks, holes or reefs. Often seen by scuba divers in southern British Columbia, they hide in crevices when approached. There is some overlap in territories which dominant fish use freely but subordinate fish can use only when dominants are absent. They live about 5 years. Food is principally small crustaceans with some molluscs, worms, bryozoans and starfish taken on rapid forays from crevices or holes under rocks. This goby is a protogynous hermaphrodite, a female which later changes to a male. Males mature at 3 years and females at 2 years of age. Males clean a nest site under a rock in April to October. Females are attracted by displays of the black pelvic fins. The male guards the pink eggs which number about 1700 and are stuck to the underside of the rock. Ripe eggs number up to 4788 per female and spawning may occur more than once each year in southern California. Young are pelagic near river outlets.

blackfin cisco

Scientific name: *Coregonus nigripinnis*
  (Gill in Hoy, 1872)
Family: **Salmon**
Other common names: black-fin tullibee,
  black-back tullibee, mooneye cisco, bluefin
French name: cisco à nageoires noires

Distribution: Found in lakes Huron, Michigan and Nipigon.

Characters: This member of the **Salmon Family** is distinguished from its relatives by having large scales (110 or less), no parr marks, teeth absent from the jaws and roof of the mouth, forked tail fin, 2 flaps of skin between the nostrils, the upper and lower jaws are about equal, giving the front of the

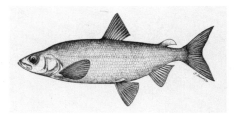

blackfin cisco

head a pointed appearance, the premaxilla bone of the upper jaw curves backwards, gill rakers 36–54, and lateral line scales 74–89. Characters among **ciscoes** (q.v.) overlap and so the species cannot be easily separated. The lower jaw may be equal to, or project beyond, the upper jaw, usually the former. The rear end of the upper jaw usually reaches the anterior pupil edge. The body is broad and deepest anteriorly. Dorsal fin rays 9–11, anal rays 10–13, pectoral rays 15–18 and pelvic rays 11–12.

Overall colour silvery with pink or purple iridescences. The lower flank is a pale blue-green. The back is dark green to blackish and the belly silvery-white. The jaws are whitish but have some dark pigment. Fins are blue-black, a distinctive feature among Great Lakes populations of **ciscoes** but not among **ciscoes** from other lakes in Canada.

The separation of this species from the widespread **lake cisco** is unclear, and distribution records outside the Great Lakes are probably misidentifications. Records for Lake Superior are large **shortjaw cisco**. Early records for Lake Ontario are in error. Some others consider this species to be a variant of the **shortjaw cisco** in the Great Lakes. Reaches 51.0 cm total length.

Biology: This **cisco** is commonly caught from depths as shallow as 37 m but is also reported below 183 m. Some fish have been taken in riverine areas in the summer and fall, on a spawning migration. In the Great Lakes it was usually caught deeper than other **cis-**coes. Food is mostly opossum shrimps, with some aquatic insects. **Lake trout** were a major predator. **Sea lampreys** parasitised this **cisco** because of its large size. Life span reported as 11 years with maturity attained at 4–5 years but this is probably based on misidentified fish. Spawning probably occurred in October to January in the Great Lakes. It is probably extirpated in Lake Ontario and only Lake Nipigon fish may survive. Blackfin ciscoes were once very important in the "chub" or **cisco** fishery of the Great Lakes. They were excellent eating when smoked. They have been extirpated from the Great Lakes. The last blackfin was caught in Lake Huron in 1923. The Committee on the Status of Endangered Wildlife in Canada gave this species the status of "threatened" in 1988.

blackfin sculpin

Scientific name: *Malacocottus kincaidi*
 Gilbert and Thompson, 1905
Family: **Soft Sculpin**
Other common names: bullhead
French name: chabot à nageoires noires

Distribution: Found from Japan to Washington including British Columbia.

Characters: This soft sculpin is distinguished from its Pacific coast relatives by having the spiny rays and soft rays in the dor-

blackfin sculpin

sal fin the same height and clearly separated, no spines on top of the head, no free fold to the gill membranes ventrally, and the primary preopercular spine has an accessory spine at its base. There are 4 preopercular spines. There are large, branched cirri on the anterior nostril and small cirri on the ends of the dorsal spines, the upper eyeball, the upper jaw and 2 widely-separated pairs on the back between the eye and the dorsal fin origin.

Dorsal fin spines 8–10, soft rays 13–15. Anal fin rays 10–13, pectoral rays 19–21. Lateral line pores 14–15. Overall colour is grey to light brown, with darker blotches, spots and speckles. Some light spots are present. Fins are barred alternately dark and light and the pectorals may have bright blue on the lighter parts. Males have golden margins to the dorsal fins when breeding. Reaches 20 cm.

Biology: Found from 27–275 m and not uncommon in Canada. Captures at these depths may be on soft bottoms, around rocks or in midwaters over deep ocean down to 2000 m. Food is primarily crustaceans, both from the bottom and higher in the water column, with some hydrozoans and worms. These fish may be a nuisance to shrimp trawlers as they contaminate the catch with a non-commercial species.

blackfin starsnout

Scientific name: *Bathyagonus nigripinnis*
   Gilbert, 1890
Family: **Poacher**
Other common names: blackfin poacher
French name: astérothèque à nageoires noires

Distribution: From the Bering Sea to northern California, including British Columbia.

Characters: This poacher is one of 4 related species called starsnouts (**bigeye, blackfin, gray** and **spinycheek starsnouts**) for an arrangement of 5 or more small spines at the tip of the snout on a moveable plate which form, supposedly, a star. Three spines point vertically and 2 laterally. The blackfin starsnout is distinguished by its lack of a pit at the back of the head, the projecting lower jaw and the deep blue-black fins. Spines are present or absent on the eyeballs. The first

blackfin starsnout

dorsal fin has 6–8 spines and the second dorsal fin 5–8 soft rays. The anal fin has 6–9 rays and the pectoral fin 14–16 rays with the lower 4–5 rays free of the membrane near their tips but not finger-like. Lateral line pores number 40–44. There is a large and a small cirrus at the rear end of the upper jaw. Gill membranes are joined to the isthmus. The body is brown overall with the lower head surface bluish. All fins are a deep blue-black, other poachers have clearer fins particularly the anal and pelvic fins. Attains 21 cm.

Biology: Found from 92–1250 m on a soft bottom. Shrimp nets often haul up this species.

blackfin waryfish

Scientific name: *Scopelosaurus lepidus*
   (Krefft and Maul, 1955)
Family: **Waryfish**
Other common names: none
French name: guetteur à nageoire noire

Distribution: On both sides of the North Atlantic Ocean including the Labrador coast, Grand Banks and off Nova Scotia.

Characters: Distinguished from other waryfishes in Canada by having 17–20 gill rakers on the lower arch, long pectoral fins

blackfin waryfish

with 13–15 rays and numerous (16–30) pyloric caeca (finger-like extensions of the digestive tract). There are 60–64 lateral line scales. Dorsal fin rays 10–12, anal rays 16–19 and pelvic rays 9. The body is light to dark brown with scale pockets outlined in black. In larger specimens, the pectoral fins have a large black patch at their base with a white band at the tip. Reaches 36.4 cm standard length.

Biology: Young blackfin waryfish are found at 70–200 m while adults live deeper at 500–995 m. This waryfish is very active and can easily dodge trawls. Food is crustaceans and small fishes. Spawning occurs in midwater far from shore and there is known to be a concentration in the Sargasso Sea. This waryfish is eaten by **Atlantic cod** and other large fishes.

blackgut tendrilfin

Scientific name: *Dicrolene intronigra*
(Goode and Bean, 1883)
Family: **Cusk-eel**
Other common names: none
French name: nageoire-frangée

Distribution: Found in the western North Atlantic and Gulf of Mexico and off northwest Africa and South Africa.

Characters: This species is distinguished from its Atlantic coast relatives by the long, lower rays in the pectoral fin. Dorsal fin rays

blackgut tendrilfin

100–114, anal rays 85–95. Pectoral fin rays 25–29, with the 6–9 lower rays free and longer than the upper rays. Developed gill rakers 11–17. There are about 110–120 scales along the flank. The rear margin of the preopercle has 3 spines and there is a strong, straight opercular spine. The head bears obvious pores and is scaled. Colour is a fleshy, rosy grey. The mouth and gill cavity are black. The margins of the dorsal and anal fins are black. The free pectoral rays are darkly pigmented. Reaches about 30 cm standard length.

Biology: First recorded from Atlantic Canada without further details in 1988. Reported from depths between 200 and 1700 m off the Middle Atlantic U.S. coast at 3.7–5.0°C and with a mean density up to 68.3/ha, the most abundant member of its family. Smaller fish tend to be in shallower water than large fish. Food is principally worms and crustaceans living in the bottom sediments. Spawning occurs from June to September and females then were larger than males. A female can contain up to an estimated 45,400 eggs.

blackline prickleback

Scientific name: *Acantholumpenus mackayi*
(Gilbert, 1896)

Family: **Shanny**
Other common names: pighead prickleback, spiny eelblenny
French name: terrassier à six lignes

Distribution: Arctic Coast of Canada in the Beaufort Sea, south to the Bering Sea and Japan.

Characters: This species is 1 of 8 related Canadian shannies which have very elongate bodies, large pectoral fins and pelvic fins with 1 spine and 2–4 soft rays. It is distinguished by distribution, 59 dorsal fin spines, 2 anal fin spines and 41 soft rays. The pointed snout projects beyond the upper lip. The body is yellowish to yellowish-brown. There is a solid black line along the base of the dorsal fin and 2 other dashed lines or blotches on the flank. The upper of these 2 lines may form a reticulate pattern. The top of the head has a fine reticulate pattern. Pectoral fins are orange. The roof of the mouth is black. The lower flank is unmarked as are the caudal and anal fins. Attains 70 cm total length.

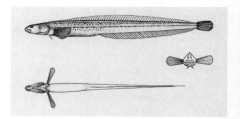

blackline prickleback

Biology: They may live as long as 16 years, but almost nothing is known of their life history in Canada. The species was listed as "vulnerable" in 1989 by the Committee on the Status of Endangered Wildlife in Canada. Depth range is from the shoreline to 60 m on mud and sand bottoms. Food is principally worms, crustaceans, young sea urchins, clams and snails, all minute species which the small mouth can accommodate. Females taken in Tuktoyaktuk Harbour in August were nearly ripe.

blackmouth slipskin

Scientific name: *Lycodapus fierasfer*
Gilbert, 1891

Family: **Eelpout**
Other common names: none
French name: lycode nacrée

Distribution: Found from the Bering Sea to Peru including British Columbia.

Characters: This species is distinguished from its Pacific coast relatives by having the branchiostegal membranes free of the isthmus posteriorly, gill slit extending above the upper base of the pectoral fin, and gill rakers long, slender and pointed reaching past the adjacent raker when depressed. Scales and

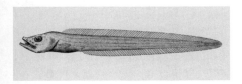

blackmouth slipskin

pelvic fins are absent. The flesh is gelatinous. Dorsal fin rays 78–85, anal rays 68–74, and pectoral rays 6–8. Total vertebrae 83–91. The skin is transparent in life with body underneath mottled light grey to grey-pink. Peritoneum, cheeks and gill cover iridescent blue-green or black depending on light. Mouth and gill cavities and stomach black. Lips are black. Attains 14.1 cm.

Biology: Depth range 102–2189 m, living on the bottom and in midwaters. Reported from off Vancouver Island and the Queen Charlotte Islands.

blackmouth widejaw

Scientific name: *Synagrops bellus*
(Goode and Bean, 1896)
Family: **Temperate Ocean Bass**
Other common names: blackmouth bass
French name: beau gueulard

Distribution: Found off Nova Scotia and south to the Gulf of Mexico.

Characters: This species is distinguished from its Atlantic coast relatives by having separate dorsal fins, by scale and fin ray counts, and by the anterior edge of the pelvic spines being smooth. First dorsal fin spines 9, second dorsal fin with 1 spine and 9 soft rays. Anal fin with 2 spines and 7 soft rays.

Pectoral rays 16–19. Scales in lateral line about 29–32. Gill rakers 17–20. The back and head are purplish-brown. The spiny dorsal fin has a dark, triangular blotch near the margin

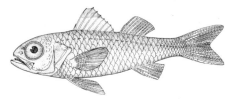

blackmouth widejaw

between spines 2 and 6. Reaches 9 cm.

Biology: Young specimens have been caught in 1979 off the Scotian Shelf at about 50–300 m. Maximum reported depth is 512 m. Biology is unknown.

blacknose dace

Scientific name: *Rhinichthys atratulus*
(Hermann, 1804)
Family: **Carp**
Other common names: eastern blacknose dace, striped dace, redfin dace, brook minnow, potbelly, pottlebelly, slicker
French name: naseux noir

Distribution: Found from western Nova Scotia through New Brunswick, Québec and Ontario, in Lake of the Woods but not northeast of Lake Superior, and in southern and central Manitoba. In the U.S.A. south to Georgia and Mississippi.

Characters: This species is distinguished by the premaxillaries not being protractile (no

blacknose dace

groove between the upper lip and snout), a barbel at each mouth corner and the snout not projecting markedly beyond the mouth.

Dorsal fin branched rays 6–7, usually 7, anal fin branched fins 5–7, pectoral rays 12–16, and pelvic rays 8. Lateral line scales 46–75. Pharyngeal teeth hooked, 2,4–4,2. Males have nuptial tubercles on the head, scales and fins, particularly the pelvic fins. The membranes of pectoral rays 2–5 are swollen at the tip to form breeding pads.

Overall colour is olive-green or bluish-olive to dark brown or blackish with various mottles and blotches on the flanks, or only finely speckled, fading to a whitish belly. Usually a light stripe separates a dusky mid-lateral stripe from the dark back. The iris is brassy. Breeding males have a rusty-red, brick red, orange or cinnamon brown flank stripe and orange to red pectoral, pelvic and anal fins. Dorsal and anal fins are tinged orange. Young fish have a broad, flank and head stripe ending in a basal, caudal spot. Peritoneum dusky brown to silvery. Reaches 9.5 cm total length.

Western and eastern subspecies of this **dace** are sometimes recognised as distinct species. The western blacknose dace (*Rhinichthys meleagris* Agassiz, 1854) is found from Manitoba and Lake of the Woods to western Lake Ontario and south to Nebraska. Western blacknose dace males have large blotches and patches of dark scales on the back and flank, the rusty flank stripe is present all year round, breeding males have little orange on their pectoral fins and are more a pale yellow, the back is more humped and the caudal peduncle is deeper compared to the eastern blacknose dace. Young and females are difficult to distinguish.

Biology: This dace is found in small, clear, gravel-bottomed streams with moderate to rapid flow. In November in southern Ontario, these **dace** retreat into crevices beneath rubble when water temperatures fall below 5°C. The fish are torpid and can be picked up by hand. They reappear in open water in late March, when water temperatures reach 4°C.

Feeding almost ceases during winter and body reserves are depleted. Food is mostly aquatic insects but also includes diatoms and desmids, and their own eggs. **Brook trout** eat this dace as do a variety of birds.

Life span is about 4 years with maturity attained at age 2. Spawning occurs in May and June at temperatures over 12°C in shallow riffles. Males may defend a territory and clear silt away, perhaps incidental to defensive movements. Territories are up to 60 cm across. Defensive actions include chases and darting movements. A pair of males swim rapidly in tight circles head to tail, and are swept downstream. They regain station by swimming upstream side by side, bumping each other as they do so. Males court females with a "dance." Females move gravel with the snout to indicate spawning readiness. A female is accompanied by several males once she leaves deeper pools and approaches the spawning territory. One male comes to lie by her side, maintaining contact with his tubercles, after driving away his rivals. Eggs and sperm are shed as the fish vibrate strongly for up to 2 seconds. The female may push eggs into sand or gravel with her anal papilla and the male defends the eggs against other **dace** which rush in to eat them. Eggs are amber, 1.0 mm in diameter, and number up to 1360 mature eggs.

Blacknose dace have a cleaning symbiosis with wood turtles (*Clemmys insculpta*), 3–6 fish nipping at the skin presumably to remove algae and parasites. Turtles extend neck and legs to facilitate the process and on one occasion a turtle was seen to pick a food item off the bottom which the dace nibbled at as the turtle held it.

The English common name "potbelly" derives from a parasitic worm infestation which distends the belly. This dace has been used as a bait fish in Canada.

blacknose shiner

Scientific name: *Notropis heterolepis* Eigenmann and Eigenmann, 1893
Family: **Carp**
Other common names: northern blacknose shiner, blacknose dace, black-sided minnow, Muskoka minnow, Cayuga minnow, blunt-nosed minnow
French name: museau noir

Distribution: Found from Nova Scotia and southern New Brunswick through southwestern Québec and Ontario, to southern Manitoba and Saskatchewan. In the U.S.A.

southward in a narrowing distribution to Missouri and Tennessee.

Characters: This species and its relatives in the genus *Notropis* (typical **shiners**) are separated from other family members by usually having 7 branched dorsal fin rays following thin unbranched rays, protractile premaxillaries (upper lip separated from the snout by a groove), no barbels, large lateral line scales (fewer than 50), and a simple, s-shaped gut. It is separated from its relatives by having anal fin branched rays usually 7, often 6, 32–40 scales in a usually complete lateral line, a dark lateral stripe running onto the snout but not the chin (best seen in dead fish), and a dorsal fin origin over or behind the pelvic fin insertion level. Dorsal fin branched rays 6–8, pectoral rays 12–14 and pelvic rays 7–8. Pharyngeal teeth 4–4, slightly to strongly hooked at their tips. Breeding males have fine tubercles on top of the head. The back is yellowish to olive, flanks silvery and the belly silvery-white. Scales on the back are outlined with black pigment. The anterior flank stripe is made up of a series of crescent-shaped marks, the tips pointing rearward. The chin is white. Fins are mostly clear. Peritoneum silvery. Reaches 9.5 cm.

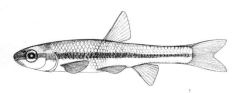

blacknose shiner

Biology: Blacknose shiners are found in small, quiet streams and lakes which are clear and weedy. They are intolerant of turbidity and are schooling fish over vegetation during the day. Food is aquatic insects, crustaceans, molluscs, sponges and algae, mostly taken from the bottom, peaking at dawn and dusk. Life span is about 2 years with most growth occurring in the first year. Spawning occurs in July in Ontario over sand bottoms. Yellow eggs may number up to 1420 per female with a diameter of 0.9 mm. This **minnow** has been sold as bait in Ontario.

blackside darter

Scientific name: *Percina maculata* (Girard, 1859)
Family: **Perch**
Other common names: none
French name: dard noir

Distribution: Found from western Lake Ontario south of Lake Superior to southern Manitoba and eastern Saskatchewan and south to Alabama and Texas. Canadian records in the Great Lakes are for Lake Erie tributaries and southern Lake Huron tributaries.

Characters: This darter is recognised by the small mouth not extending beyond the anterior eye margin, a smooth edge to the pre-

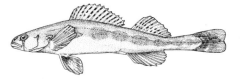

blackside darter

opercle bone on the side of the head, a large anal fin at least as large as the soft dorsal fin, belly midline with 7–13 enlarged scales in males, naked in females, 2 anal fin spines, no groove between the snout and lip (premaxillaries not protractile), snout not strongly protruding, lateral line scales 53–81, and 12–17 (usually 13–14) dorsal fin spines. Dorsal fin soft rays 10–16, usually 12–13. Anal fin rays 7–13. Pectoral fin rays 11–16. The breast is not scaled.

Overall colour is yellowish, olive or olive-brown. The back has 6–11 saddles. The flank has 5–9, blue-black, elongate blotches which tend to merge into a band extending onto the snout and to the tail base where it may form a spot. There is a black bar beneath the eye. Belly white to cream. The upper opercle is black. Lower fins are yellowish white or transparent. The soft dorsal and caudal fins are barred. Spawning males have darkened black pigments which contrast markedly with yellow and white areas on the body. Only during the spawning act are any bright colours seen when green or gold tints may briefly appear. Reaches 11.4 cm.

Biology: Blackside darters are found in streams of moderate current with gravel and sand bottoms, in pools and raceways. Food is aquatic insects, crustaceans and fish. It is an unusual darter in favouring midwaters at least when young and has even been seen leaping out of the water to catch flying insects! A well-developed swimbladder enables it to use the midwaters. Males and females grow at about the same rate and live up to 4 years. Maturity is attained at 1–2 years. Spawning occurs probably in May-June in Canada in pools with gravel bottoms. Water temperatures are usually 16°C or more. It may take place on **hornyhead chub** nests. There is an upstream spawning migration. A female partially buries herself in the gravel, the male lies over her clasping with his pelvic fins and with his tail region alongside hers, both fish vibrate, and 10 or more eggs are laid and fertilised in the gravel. Eggs are at depths of 30–60 cm in the gravel. Females spawn with several different males and each female can have up to 1758, 2 mm diameter eggs. There is some fighting between males, but no clear territory is defended except around a courted female. Eggs are deserted. This species is easily maintained in aquaria.

blacksmelts

Blacksmelts are members of the **Deepsea Smelt Family** with 6 species in Canada. Their name is taken from their colour and resemblance to the **Smelt Family**.

See **goitre blacksmelt**
popeye blacksmelt
slender blacksmelt
smalleye blacksmelt
starry blacksmelt
stout blacksmelt

blacksnout snailfish

Scientific name: *Paraliparis copei*
Goode and Bean, 1896
Family: **Snailfish**
Other common names: none
French names: limace à museau noir

Distribution: Found from the Davis Strait south to Cape Hatteras and throughout Atlantic Canada.

Characters: This snailfish is separated from other Canadian Atlantic species by the lack of an adhesive disc and pelvic fins, by having 1 pair of nostrils, and weak teeth in a single row. Dorsal fin rays 59–68, anal rays 54–60, and upper pectoral fin lobe rays 13–17 (total 20–22). There are 8–9 caudal rays. There are 6 pyloric caeca. The body mostly lacks pigment and is a translucent or milky white. The horizontal mouth is darkly pigmented. The abdomen, gill cavity and snout are black. Peritoneum dark, stomach pale. Reaches 16.7 cm standard length.

blacksnout snailfish

Biology: This species occurs at 210–500 m in the Gulf of St. Lawrence within 2 m of the bottom, and elsewhere down to 1976 m. Food is apparently pelagic comb jellies, cnidaria and possibly salps. Spawning may occur in spring and summer in Canadian Atlantic waters but in the U.S. mature males and females are caught almost year round. Eggs are up to 3.5 mm in diameter and number up to 88.

blackspotted stickleback

Scientific name: *Gasterosteus wheatlandi*
Putnam, 1867
Family: **Stickleback**
Other common names: twospined stickleback
French name: épinoche tachetée

Distribution: Found from Newfoundland and the Gulf of St. Lawrence south to New York.

Characters: This species is distinguished from the related **threespine** and **white sticklebacks** by having usually 2 (range 1–3) soft pelvic rays with 2 obvious cusps at the pelvic spine base, no caudal peduncle keel, and colour. The flank has 4–10 bony plates in Canada but American populations, particularly south of Cape Cod, have some fish with plates all along the flank and a caudal peduncle keel. Dorsal fin spines 3, soft rays usually 7–12. Anal fin with 1 spine and 5–9 soft rays. Pectoral fin rays 9–10. Overall colour is yellow to greenish-yellow with dark flank spots and blotches. Breeding males have orange pelvic fins and are a

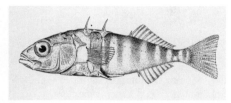

blackspotted stickleback

bright, lemon yellow, golden-yellow or greenish-yellow. Pelagic females in winter have dark backs and are silvery-white below. Reaches 7.6 cm.

Biology: Blackspotted sticklebacks are found principally in coastal marine and estuarine brackish waters but also rarely in fresh waters of river mouths. They may also be found among floating seaweed. Adults and larvae have been collected up to 100 km offshore in winter. Under experimental conditions resembling spring this stickleback preferred brackish water at 21‰ which fits with the breeding season field conditions.

Food is plankton and some benthic crustaceans, snails and aquatic insects. The blackspotted stickleback has the smallest mouth among Atlantic coast sticklebacks and thus consumes smaller prey than the other species. Females in salt marshes have been shown to feed exclusively in the early morning. Males cannibalise more eggs than females, perhaps as a source of energy so they can breed again although this may only be needed where food is limited.

Females grow larger than males but life span is only 1 year and a few months. Spawning takes place in May to June in Canada in brackish streams, tidal pools and marshes. The time of spawning is later than in sympatric **threespine sticklebacks** although the first nests to appear are those of blackspotted sticklebacks in early May at Isle Verte, Québec. Eggs are up to 1.5 mm in diameter and each female can contain up to 276. Nests can contain over 400 eggs suggesting that males spawn with 2 or more females. Young leave tidal pools in July–August.

The male leads the female to the nest he has constructed often near or in dense algal mats, by a zig-zag movement and leading in a head down (30°) position, the female apparently fixating on the orange pelvic fins. He indicates the nest position by poking his snout into it and then the female enters. The male runs his snout along the female's flank to stimulate egg laying. The female vacates the nest and the male swims through it to fertilise the eggs.

The male fans the eggs and may remove eggs with his mouth, masticate them and then discard some and return others to the nest. The male removes excess sand from the nest by opercular pumping, and repairs his nest. Nest construction involves such activities as digging sand in mouthfuls, collecting plant fragments, stems and roots, pushing and gluing these fragments together, boring and tunnelling to shape an entrance, and sand covering.

The male parental cycle is about 9–15 days and the female spawns at intervals of 17.5 days. However at Isle Verte, Québec males and females only stay at the spawning site to complete one spawning cycle.

blackstripe topminnow

Scientific name: *Fundulus notatus*
  (Rafinesque, 1820)
Family: **Killifish**
Other common names: blackback minnow
French name: fondule rayé

Distribution: Found in central North America in the Mississippi and southern Great Lakes basins. In Canada found only in the Sydenham River basin in southwestern Ontario.

Characters: This killifish is distinguished from its relative, the **banded killifish**, by the dorsal fin origin being well behind the anal fin origin and a broad, dark stripe on the midline of the head and body. Dorsal fin rays 7–10, anal rays 11–12. Scales in lateral series 29–36. Lateral line pores few. Males have larger dorsal and anal fins and females have a fleshy sheath at the anterior anal fin base. The back and upper flank are olive-brown and the lower flank and belly white to yellowish. The blue-black midflank stripe is straight-edged in females but breaks up into bars above and below in males. Scales are outlined with pigment. Dorsal, anal and pelvic fins bright yellow in males, white in females. The dorsal, caudal and anal fins are

blackstripe topminnow

finely spotted, most noticeably in males. Males have a blue chin and yellow branchiostegals. Females have white branchiostegals. There is an opalescent spot on top of the head in life. Attains 9.7 cm.

Biology: This species was first collected in Canada in 1972, perhaps expanding its range to take advantage of turbid waters. The blackstripe minnow is more tolerant of disturbed conditions than **banded killifish**. It is found in slow-moving streams and ditches and is rare in lakes. Most of the time it is in the top 2.5 cm of the water body and is usually in contact with the surface film. This topminnow orientates itself to surface waves, quickly turning head on to them. When disturbed it darts into vegetation. In winter it moves to deeper water among vegetation. Food comprises a large proportion of terrestrial insects taken at the water surface, with some snails, spiders and crustaceans. Life span is only 2 years although some may survive to 3 years. Spawning occurs from May to August. Eggs are up to 1.8 mm diameter and number several hundred. These topminnows form pairs and maintain a territory 6–12 m long and less than 4 m from shore. Both male and female will drive away other topminnows. The male follows the female below and behind within their territory until she approaches vegetation. The male folds his dorsal and anal fins over those of the female, his body bends in an s-shape, both fish quiver and expand their throats, and a single egg is produced and flipped into the plants by the male's caudal fin. Eggs may be spawned in batches of 20–30 at intervals of several days. Females may spawn as often as 30 times in 20 minutes

with 3 different males. The Committee on the Status of Endangered Wildlife in Canada approved a status of "rare" in 1985 for this species in Canada.

blacktail snailfish

Scientific name: *Careproctus melanurus*
    Gilbert, 1892
Family: **Snailfish**
Other common names: black-tailed liparid
French name: limace à queue noire

Distribution: Found from Alaska to California including British Columbia.

Characters: This snailfish is distinguished from its Canadian Pacific relatives by having a fleshy adhesive disc with its posterior margin anterior to the level of the gill opening, a single nostril, dorsal fin rays 53–58 and 20–31 pale pyloric caeca. The adhesive disc is small. Teeth are both simple and trilobed in bands in the jaws. Anal fin rays 37–51, pectoral rays 27–33, and caudal rays 9–11. The pectoral fin has upper and lower lobes which are indistinct in larger fish. The lower 6 rays are separate from their membrane, the next 5 are variably separated and longer than the rays above them. Body colour is pink to reddish or off-white with fins margined with black. The tail region is dusky. Mouth and gill cavities and peritoneum black. Stomach pale. Reaches 31.2 cm standard length.

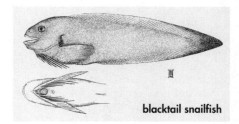

blacktail snailfish

Biology: This species is found at 90–2286 m and is often caught by commercial fishermen in bottom trawls and **sablefish** traps. It has been recorded off northern Vancouver Island. Some individuals reach at least 6–7 years of age. Females are mature at about 20–22 cm. This snailfish is a commensal with a lithoid boxcrab. As many as 424 snailfish eggs can be found in one gill cavity of the crab, where they are presumed to gain protection from predators. The crab's respiration is affected since the gills collapse. Maximum egg diameter is 4.6 mm and up to 534 eggs are found in each female. Spawning may be restricted to spring and summer.

blacktip poacher

Scientific name: *Xeneretmus latifrons*
(Gilbert, 1890)
Family: **Poacher**
Other common names: none
French name: agone à dorsale noire

Distribution: From British Columbia south to Baja California.

Characters: This poacher and the related **bluespotted** and **smootheye poachers** are distinguished by the absence of a pit on top

blacktip poacher

of the head and by an exposed snout plate having a single dorsally pointing spine. This species is identified by not having cheek plates (or only 1), 1 cirrus at the rear of the upper jaw, the anal fin origin before the second dorsal fin origin, and 3–6 spiny plates on the eyeball. First dorsal fin spines 6–8, second dorsal fin soft rays 6–8, anal fin rays 6–9 and pectoral fin rays 13–15, the lower 4–5 rays obviously finger-like. Lateral line pores 39–41. Gill membranes are joined to the isthmus. Brown or tan overall with 5–8 vague saddles on the back with bars on the flank. Both dorsal fins and the caudal fin have black margins. Reaches 19 cm.

Biology: Found on soft bottoms from 18–400 m. Food is small crustaceans. They live at least 6 years. Spawning occurs in the spring in the south of its range. Young are pelagic.

blackwing flyingfish

Scientific name: *Hirundichthys rondeleti*
(Valenciennes in Cuvier and
Valenciennes, 1846)

Family: **Flyingfish**
Other common names: exocet aile noire
French name: exocet à nageoires noires

Distribution: Found in the Atlantic and Pacific oceans. In the western Atlantic from Nova Scotia south to Brazil.

Characters: This species is distinguished by the dorsal and anal fin ray counts being about equal within 1–2 rays, and by pectoral

blackwing flyingfish

fin colour pattern. Dorsal fin rays 10–12, usually 11, anal rays 11–13, usually 12. Pectoral rays number 16–19, usually 17. The second pectoral fin ray is unbranched. Young lack barbels. The back and upper flank are iridescent blue or green, the lower flanks and belly silvery. The dorsal fin is dusky except in young where it is transparent with a dark area near the edge. The pectoral fin is bluish-black with a transparent, narrow band along the posterior margin. Reaches 30 cm.

Biology: A single specimen was caught in Prospect Harbour, Nova Scotia, in 1970, a northern range limit and a stray from southern waters. Found in both the open ocean and close inshore. Food is mostly planktonic animals. Eggs are 1.4–1.5 mm in diameter with 80–100 filaments.

blennies

Blennies are members of the marine **Combtooth Blenny Family**, which has only 1 species in Canada, the **feather blenny**. The name blenny is derived from the Greek word for slime and refers to the mucus covering of these fishes.

bloater

Scientific name: *Coregonus hoyi*
(Gill in Hoy, 1872)
Family: **Salmon**
Other common names: bloat, Hoy's cisco

French name: cisco de fumage

Distribution: Found in all the Great Lakes except Lake Erie, and in Lake Nipigon.

Characters: This member of the **Salmon Family** is distinguished from its relatives by having large scales (110 or less), no parr marks, teeth absent from the jaws and roof of the mouth, forked tail fin, 2 flaps of skin

bloater

between the nostrils, the upper and lower jaws are about equal, giving the front of the head a pointed appearance, the premaxilla bone of the upper jaw curves backwards, gill rakers 37–50, and lateral line scales 60–84. Characters among **ciscoes** (q.v.) overlap and so the species cannot be easily separated. The lower jaw is thin, protruding and has a knob at its tip. Gill rakers are longer than gill filaments, paired fins are long but pelvics do not usually reach the anus, the eye width is less than snout length, and the body is deepest at its middle. Dorsal fin rays 9–11, anal rays 10–13, pectoral rays 14–17 and pelvic rays 10–12. Males have 1–3 tubercles on the flank scales.

Overall colour is silvery with pink or purple iridescences and a green to grey tinge above the lateral line. The belly is silvery-white. Dorsal and caudal fins have dark edges, other fins weakly pigmented to clear except the pectoral fin has a broad, black margin. Bloaters are named for the body swelling which results from swimbladder expansion as the fish are hauled up rapidly from lake depths. Reaches 36.6 cm total length. It may be the same species as **lake cisco** according to one recent author, distinct according to others.

Biology: Bloater are found in shallower water than other deepwater Great Lakes cis-

coes. Depth range is from 13 m to 183 m, in Lake Ontario maximum abundance was recorded at 76–91 m.

Food is chiefly opossum shrimps and amphipods taken on or near the bottom with some crustacean zooplankton, fish eggs and molluscs. This species may also feed pelagically, particularly when young. Strongly swimming prey is taken with a dart and suck motion or by gulping several items at once. They can take buried prey. In Lake Michigan, the invasion of **gaspereau** and competition with them for zooplankton has apparently caused the bloater to shift to bottom habitats and prey 2 years earlier than usual. Gill raker number and length also changed, becoming less. In contrast, the abundant bloaters in Lake Huron showed an increase in gill raker number through hybridisation with the rare **lake herring** as man-induced environmental changes affected the natural balance of species (see **ciscoes**). **Lake trout** are probably a major predator and **burbot** also take some bloaters.

Females live longer and grow larger than males, to ages 11 and 9 respectively in Lake Ontario. Maturity is attained at age 2 and all fish 3 and older are mature. Spawning occurs principally in February and March in Lake Huron at 36–91 m, and November–March in Lake Ontario. However, spent bloaters have been caught in all months. A female may have up to 34,891 eggs of 1.95 mm diameter in her ovaries.

The Lake Nipigon population has been extirpated and probably the one in Lake Ontario also. This species has suffered in the Great Lakes through overfishing, competition with **rainbow smelt** and **gaspereau**, eutrophication and predatory attacks by **sea lampreys**. This species formed the bulk of the commercial catch of **ciscoes** in the U.S. Great Lakes fishery after other species were decimated but was not important in Canadian waters. There are commercial catch quotas in Canada and the U.S.A. and this species comprises 90–99% of the commercial catches of deepwater **ciscoes**. The Committee on the Status of Endangered Wildlife in Canada regarded this species as not being in jeopardy in 1988.

blob sculpin

Scientific name: *Psychrolutes phrictus*
    Stein and Bond, 1978
Family: **Soft Sculpin**
Other common names: none
French name: chabot maculé

Distribution: Found from the Bering Sea to California including British Columbia.

Characters: This soft sculpin is distinguished from its Pacific coast relatives by having a continuous spiny and soft dorsal fin with the spiny section buried in tissue, no preopercular spines, pectoral rays 22–26, usually 24–25, the upper jaw overhangs the lower, the anus is midway between the anal and pelvic fin bases, and 19–20 soft dorsal fin rays. Cirri are scattered on the head and body but there are no papillae. Dorsal fin spines 7–9. Anal fin rays 12–14. Lateral line pores 12–14. Overall colour is grey to black, paler ventrally and with some faint mottling on the head. Large fish have a white head anteriorly. Reaches 70 cm and 9.5 kg.

blob sculpin

Biology: Found between 480 and 2800 m. Caught in Canada for the first time in 1978 off the Queen Charlotte Islands at a depth of 1829 m. Also caught off Cape Cook in 1979 at 839 m. Apparently quite common in the Bering Sea. Larvae and juveniles are thought to be pelagic. Food is sea pens, crabs, snails and a variety of other items. A plastic bag was found in one stomach, an indication of how pervasive this form of pollution is, since the blob sculpin was only described by scientists in 1978. Octopus beaks in the stomachs and sucker marks on the skin show that cephalopods are successfully eaten.

blotched snake eel

Scientific name: *Callechelys muraena*
    Jordan and Evermann, 1887
Family: **Snake Eel**

Other common names: none
French name: serpenton couperosé

Distribution: Found from the Gulf of Mexico and Florida to the Atlantic coast of Canada.

Characters: Larvae are distinguished by having 7 strong gut loops, little pigment in the midline in front of the anus, spots in the body

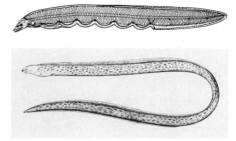

blotched snake eel

wall on the tail and lateral to the gut loops, 138–148 total myomeres (muscle blocks) and 81–88 nephric myomeres. In adults, the tail has a sharp point and no tail fin. There are no pectoral fins. The head is sharply pointed and the dorsal fin origin is on the nape. The anterior nostrils are obvious tubes projecting in front of the short lower jaw. Mouth small with weak teeth. The body and head are olive-green or tan, blotched with darker shades of the same colour, particularly anteriorly. The dorsal and anal fins have a pale edge and are dusky near the body. Larvae are 49–58 mm long in Canada. Adults attain 60 cm.

Biology: Known only as stray larvae (or leptocephali) in Canadian waters and first reported in 1988. Adults are burrowers found in seagrass beds and down to 115 m. They are quite rare.

blue antimora

Scientific name: *Antimora rostrata*
    Günther, 1878
Family: **Mora**
Other common names: blue hake, longfinned
    cod, flatnose cod, flatnose codling
French name: antimore bleu

Distribution: Found world-wide in all oceans. In Atlantic Canada it is reported from the Davis Strait, southern Baffin Island, Ungava Bay and southward, to North Carolina.

Characters: This species is separated from its Atlantic coast relatives by having a flattened snout forming a broad, pointed

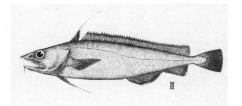

blue antimora

plate with a ridge on its side. Gill filaments on the first gill arch number 76–90. First dorsal fin with 4–7 rays, second dorsal fin with 48–56 rays. Anal fin rays 36–49, anal fin deeply indented and almost like 2 fins. There are about 115 scale rows along the side. A chin barbel is present. Overall colour is deep violet to blue-black, blue-grey or blackish-brown, even on the belly and in the mouth cavity and gill chamber. Reaches 75 cm or more.

Biology: Found as shallow as 229 m in colder Canadian waters, this species is caught down to 2933 m off Virginia where it lives close to mud bottoms and is the dominant member of the deepsea fish community. Juveniles and sexually mature specimens are rarely captured so the reproduction of this important deepwater fish remains to be determined. A maturing female had an estimated 1,351,300 eggs. Food is crustaceans and squids. Males are generally smaller than females and are found in shallower water.

They have been observed swimming at 39.2 cm per second at a depth of 2400 m, comparable in power and speed to a **rainbow trout**. The blue antimora may undertake a northerly migration to spawn in Canadian waters.

This mora has a thick, spongy, white or cream mass occupying the whole swimbladder. This "foam" is believed to serve as a diffusion barrier and maintains high gas and oxygen pressures in the swimbladder of this deepsea fish. This fish has been studied by scientists for its "foam" composition, lipid production and haemoglobin function, but occurs too deep for a commercial fishery. Samples collected in the 1880s and stored in museum collections were examined for mercury content and compared with recently collected fish. There has been no increase in mercury in the last century. High concentrations of mercury in deep-living marine fish are the product of natural events, not industrial pollution.

blue-eyed searcher

Scientific name: *Bathymaster signatus* Cope, 1873
Family: **Ronquil**
Other common names: searcher
French name: chercheur aux yeux bleus

Distribution: From the East Siberian Sea and the Bering Sea south to the Queen Charlotte Islands and northern British Columbia.

Characters: This species is distinguished from its relatives the **northern ronquil** and the **bluefin searcher** by having only the first 3–4 dorsal fin rays unbranched (the rest are branched), ctenoid scales but none on the cheek, a black patch at the front of the dorsal fin on rays 1–5, and an upper jaw reaching the posterior eye margin. Dorsal fin rays are about 47–49, anal fin rays 32–35 with tips free, and pectoral rays about 20–21. Scales extend about half-way along the dorsal and pectoral fin membranes. Gill rakers on the lower arm of the arch 15–18. The head bears numerous, raised pores with a collar. Light

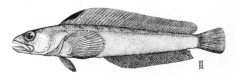

blue-eyed searcher

brown or olive-brown above or even dark green to black fading to a lighter shade below with yellow or orange streaks. The back may have dark brown patches. Flanks with broad, dark bars. The pelvic fin is dusky and the eyes are blue. Reaches 30.5 cm.

Biology: A soft bottom living species from inshore down to 825 m, mostly at 50–250 m. Spawning occurs in the spring and young are pelagic but are found close to shore.

blue lanternfish

Scientific name: *Tarletonbeania crenularis*
   (Jordan and Gilbert, 1880)
Family: **Lanternfish**
Other common names: none
French name: lanterne bleue

Distribution: Found at Ocean Station Papa (50°N, 145°W) and along the Pacific coast of North America including off British Columbia and south to Baja California.

Characters: This lanternfish is distinguished from its Pacific coast relatives by having only 1 Prc photophore and, in males, a

blue lanternfish

long, thin supracaudal gland with the infracaudal gland absent or short, weakly developed and hidden under the body scales. Females lack these glands and are difficult to distinguish from the related **tail-light lanternfish**. Identification is complicated further by hybridisation between the two species. In addition only the first 2–3 scales of the lateral line are perforated. Dorsal fin rays 11–14, anal rays 17–20, pectoral rays 11–15, total vertebrae 39–42. AO photophores 13–16 and total gill rakers 15–18. Photophores emit a bluish glow. The back is a bright metallic blue. Reaches about 12.7 cm.

Biology: Found at the surface where easily attracted by lights and, albeit confused with its relative, the commonest lanternfish at night off the British Columbia coast in the upper 20 m. It migrates from daytime depths of about 500–1000 m. Reported down to 1750 m at Ocean Station Papa. Food is crustaceans such as euphausiids. **Albacore** are reported to eat this lanternfish in British

Columbia. This lanternfish is able to match downwelling light with its ventral photophore luminescence production. This removes its shadow to predators approaching from below and the fish becomes "invisible" against the light streaming down from the surface of the ocean. The supraorbital photophores shine a diffuse spot of light into the eyes. By adjusting the output of these photophores, the spot will disappear from view when its strength equals that of light from the ocean's surface. The output of the ventral photophores can then be adjusted to match that of the supraorbital photophores and the surface light.

blue ling

Scientific name: *Molva dypterygia*
   (Pennant, 1784)
Family: **Cod**
Other common names: ling
French name: lingue bleue

Distribution: Found from southern Labrador to the southeast Grand Bank in Atlantic Canada. Also in Greenland, Iceland and northern Europe.

Characters: This species and its relative, the **European ling**, are distinguished from other **cods** by having 2 dorsal and 1 anal fin, no elongate dorsal fin ray, 6–7 pelvic fin rays, a well-developed barbel and over 54 anal rays. It is separated from its relative by having no marbling on the flanks, white edge to the median fins nor a black spot at the rear of the first dorsal fin, second dorsal fin rays 69–84, 62–81 anal rays and 18–21 pectoral rays. Vertebrae 72–79. First dorsal fin rays 11–15. The lower jaw projects. Overall colour is a uniform copper-brown which may

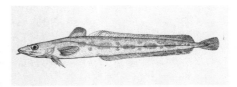

blue ling

fade to a grey-brown. The end of the dorsal and anal fins have a diffuse dark mark. Reaches 155 cm.

Biology: First caught in Hermitage Bay, Newfoundland in 1959 in 240 m with subsequent records on the southeast slope of the Grand Bank at 510–550 m in 1964, off southern Labrador in 1965 at 236–260 m and off Banquereau Bank at 430 m in 1990. Depth range in Europe is 200–1500 m, usually at 350–500 m, and – 0.2 to 6°C. There is a seasonal migration from deep water in summer to shallower water on the continental slope. Food is crustaceans and fishes. Maturity is attained at 80 cm and 5–6 years. Females grow faster and live longer (14 years) than males (10 years). In Europe spawning occurs from May to June at 500–1000 m. It is commercially important in Europe.

blue marlin

Scientific name: *Makaira nigricans*
    Lacepède, 1802
Family: **Swordfish**
Other common names: Atlantic blue marlin
French name: makaire bleu

Distribution: Found in the Atlantic Ocean including off Nova Scotia and southward.

Characters: The blue marlin is distinguished from its relative, the **white marlin**, by having a pointed first dorsal fin tip, first dorsal fin height less than body depth and a rounded body. The forehead or nape region

blue marlin

rises steeply from the eye to the dorsal fin. First dorsal fin rays 39–46, usually 40–44, second dorsal rays 6–7. First anal fin rays 13–16, second anal rays 6–7. Body scales are embedded and have 1–3 elongate, acute spines. The lateral line has a branched, chain-like or hexagon pattern often difficult to see in adults. Young have a sail-like dorsal fin and the chain-like lateral line is distinctive. Back blue to blue-grey or brownish, fading on the flanks to a silvery belly. Fins

are dark and the first dorsal has blue markings. There are about 15 vertical rows of pale blue spots and narrow bars on the flank. Attains 4.5 m and 818 kg. The world, all-tackle angling record weighed 636 kg and was caught in 1992 in Brazil.

Biology: Reported only twice from Browns Bank in 1930 and 1931 as a rare summer stray. Preferred temperatures in open, oceanic blue waters are in the range 22–31°C. Concentrations of this species appear in the western North Atlantic from June to October. It is not a schooling species. Food is many species of pelagic fishes but also includes crustaceans and cephalopods. The bill is used to stun and slash the prey, although some authors dispute that it plays an important role since marlin with broken bills are as healthy as normal fish. A 290 kg blue marlin is reported to have swallowed a 50 kg **bigeye tuna**. The ability to catch such fast swimmers as tunas indicates the speed of which the marlin are capable. Females grow larger than males and are mature at 50 kg compared to 40 kg. Eggs are about 1 mm in diameter. Larvae have been reported off Florida and southward but spawning season and grounds are unknown. The world catch in 1982, mostly on longlines, was 2448 tonnes. Rivalled only by the large **tunas** as a sport fish, it is caught by trolling natural or artificial baits on the surface at 4–8 knots. It is an excellent food fish as well as a trophy.

blue rockfish

Scientific name: *Sebastes mystinus*
    (Jordan and Gilbert, 1881)
Family: **Scorpionfish**
Other common names: priest-fish, bluefish, blue perch, black bass, black rockcod
French name: sébaste bleu

Distribution: Found from the Bering Sea south to Baja California including British Columbia. The northern limit is uncertain and may be only as far as Vancouver Island.

Characters: This species is recognised by its colour, convex space between the eyes on top of the head, head spines almost absent, the upper jaw ending below the middle of the eye, and the rear edge of the anal fin slanting posteriorly. Dorsal fin spines 13, soft rays 15–17, usually 16. Anal fin soft rays 8–10, usually 9, second spine only slightly thicker than third and shorter. Pectoral fin rays 16–19, usually 18. Gill rakers 32–38. Vertebrae 26–27, usually 26. Lateral line pores 47–56, scale rows below lateral line 50–56. Only nasal spine tops, and occasionally very small preocular spines, are present.

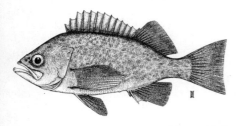

blue rockfish

The overall colour is bluish-black, with some paler mottling on the flanks, and a paler belly. All fins are dusky to blackish. The young under about 13 cm are grey or light blue with fine black dots and reddish streaks. The peritoneum is light in small and large fish but black in fish 23–33 cm long. Reaches 53 cm. The world, all-tackle angling record weighed 1.58 kg and was caught in 1993 in Neah Bay, Washington.

Biology: Found in schools off the bottom over reefs and around kelp from the surface down to 550 m. Not commonly found in British Columbia. Food is mostly krill but also includes jellyfish, salps, sea-squirts and fishes. Blue rockfish may leap clear of the water in pursuit of prey. A male has an active courtship display, drawing alongside a female, turning slowly to bring his vent region close to or in contact with the female's snout, fluttering his tail in her face and a repetition of this process. Females remain motionless during male displays. A female may give birth to 524,000 young in November to January in California. The males are mature at 3–4 years and females at 4–5 years of age. Life span is at least 13 years. Other fishes and marine mammals are important predators of this rockfish. An important commercial and sport species in California.

blue runner

Scientific name: *Caranx crysos*
(Mitchill, 1815)
Family: **Jack**
Other common names: hardtail, yellow jack, yellow mackerel, carangue coubali
French name: carangue jaune

Distribution: Found from Nova Scotia south to Brazil, and in the eastern Atlantic Ocean.

Characters: This species is distinguished from its Canadian Atlantic coast relatives by having a moderately deep body, greater than 28% of fork length, scutes (enlarged scales) in the lateral line posteriorly, an upper jaw not reaching the back of the eye and a short, strong arch to the lateral line anteriorly. The anus lies below the centre of the spiny dorsal fin. The first dorsal fin has 8 spines, the second 1 spine and 22–25 soft rays. Anal fin with 3 spines and 19–21 soft rays. The chest is covered in scales. There are 23–28 gill rakers on the lower limb of the gill arch. The adipose eyelid is poorly developed. The back is dark olive to bluish, the flanks and belly silvery to golden or brassy. The gill cover has a large black spot. Males become black when spawning. Young fish have flank bars. Reaches 54.7 cm total length. The world, all-tackle angling record weighed 3.18 kg and was caught at Bimini in the Bahamas in 1989.

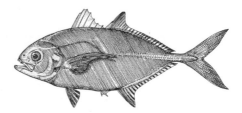

blue runner

Biology: Probably the commonest jack along the coast of Nova Scotia but still only a late summer and fall (August-October) visitor from southern waters. The northern limit is St. Georges Bay on the Gulf of St. Lawrence shore of Nova Scotia. Blue runners may form large schools offshore, perhaps a spawning aggregation. They form inshore schools down to at least 100 m. Young fish are found in sargassum weed. Food is mostly other fishes but also some invertebrates. Life span is up to 11 years and growth is fast. About 75% of maximum size is reached in 3–4 years. Spawning probably occurs from January to August off the southeastern U.S.A. Blue runners are fished commercially using beach seines in the northeastern Gulf of Mexico, where about 600 tonnes are landed annually.

blue shark

Scientific name: *Prionace glauca*
(Linnaeus, 1758)
Family: **Requiem Shark**
Other common names: blue dog, blue
    whaler, great blue shark, peau bleue
French name: requin bleu

Distribution: From St. John's, Newfoundland southwards in the Atlantic to Argentina and all along the B.C. coast north to Alaska. Also in the open ocean off the B.C. coast. In all warmer seas.

Characters: Distinguished by the slender, spindle-shaped body, very long and narrow pectoral fins, and dark blue colour. There is no spiracle and the first dorsal fin is nearer the pelvic than the pectoral fin. The caudal peduncle is short, with weak lateral keels and with well-marked pre-caudal pits. The papillose gill rakers are unique. The mouth is ventral with large, sharp, serrated teeth. The larger upper jaw teeth are sabre-shaped. The first dorsal fin is of moderate size and the second dorsal is small and above the anal.

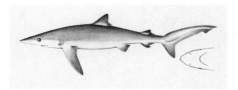

blue shark

Scales are minute and the skin is not noticeably rough. Back dark blue, almost indigo, sides a bright iridescent blue, belly white or grey-white. This typical bright colouration is lost after death and the fish becomes a dull grey. The tips of the pectoral and anal fins are dusky. Up to 3.96 m but reputedly reaching 7.6 m. The world rod-caught record weighed 198.22 kg and was caught at Catherine Bay, New South Wales, Australia in 1976.

Biology: Found at 7–27°C but not usually near to shore. This species has the greatest geographic range of any shark. Occurs from the surface down to at least 500 m. Blue sharks are pelagic and may occur in packs, singly or in pairs. They are found in Canadian waters particularly during the warmer summer months and may be plentiful. The longline catch of large sharks on both Georges Bank and the Grand Banks is about 88% blues. They are reported to travel long distances, e.g. 2764 km in 64 days or 43.2 km/day. Tagged fish have been shown to swim clock-wise around the north Atlantic Ocean from the U.S.A. and Canada to Europe, south to Spain and the Canary Islands and across to the Caribbean Sea.

Young are born alive at about 45–53 cm and each female may produce 4–135 young. Blue sharks are mature at about 5–6 years for females and 4–5 years for males at lengths over 2 m and may live 20 years or more. Females are more numerous than males in northern waters. Five-year-old females mate from late spring to early winter and store sperm in their shell glands, possibly for years. Fertilisation occurs the following spring and young are born in the female's seventh year after 9–12 months gestation. The female has thicker skin than the male as protection against his courtship bites.

Their diet includes a wide variety of small fishes such as **cod**, **haddock**, **pollock**, **herring**, **salmon**, and others. Even sea birds are taken while at rest on the water surface. These sharks may also scavenge and have been implicated in attacks on humans.

No major commercial fishery exists but this shark is sometimes a nuisance to fishermen because it destroys gear and catches. It has been caught on pelagic longlines, on hook and line, and in pelagic trawls. It may be caught by chumming with live or dead bait, or by trolling. Baits are squid, **eels**, **mackerel**, **herring** and other fishes, either cut or alive. A blue puts up a poor fight on rod and line but may put on bursts of speed or even jump and is considered a game fish by the International Game Fish Association. One 3 m long, blue shark was observed on 10 September 1980, within 15 m of the shore near Hall's Harbour, Bay of Fundy, leaping out of the water at the seagulls. Blues are edible but must be prepared quickly before decomposition of the urea in the circulatory system produces ammonia. They have been eaten fresh, smoked, dried and salted, and as shark fin soup. Fish meal and liver oil are also uses of this shark as well as leather from the skin.

blue walleye

Scientific name: *Stizostedion vitreum glaucum*
  Hubbs, 1926
Family: **Perch**
Other common names: walleye, blue pike
French name: doré bleu

  Distribution: Formerly found in Lake Erie, Lake Ontario and the Niagara River and rarely in Lake Huron.
  Characters: This is 1 of 2 subspecies of **walleye**. The **yellow walleye** is the other subspecies in Canada. The "blue pike" is not

blue walleye

related to true pikes of the **Pike Family**. It was distinguished from its close relative, the **yellow walleye**, by being bluish-grey on the back instead of a brassy-yellow colour, larger eyes and space between the eyes on top of the head narrower (1.4–2.0 times in orbit diameter). Pelvic fins were bluish-white. Flanks were a silver-bluish. There were 4–14 saddles across the back, most evident in young fish. Adults attained 50.8 cm and 3.3 kg.
  Biology: This subspecies is extinct. It should not be confused with blue-grey forms of the **yellow walleye** in Lake Nipissing and elsewhere. The causes of its extinction are not known in detail, but undoubtedly included

pollution, oxygen depletion, interbreeding with **yellow walleye**, commercial and sport overfishing and competition with exotic species such as **rainbow smelt**. Its habitat in lakes was open, clear and deep waters. Food included mayflies in summer, but mayflies disappeared from Lake Erie in the 1950s. The major food items were such fishes as **yellow perch**, **rainbow smelt**, **trout-perch** and **minnows** such as the **emerald shiner**. Growth was slower, and maximum size smaller, than the **yellow walleye**. Spawning time and place differed from that of the **yellow walleye**. Up to the 1950s, this subspecies was sought after as a sport fish and was a commercial fishery item. Landings in the 1950s were as high as 12 million kg, falling to less than 90 kg in 1964. The last fishery landings were in 1965.

blue whiting

Scientific name: *Micromesistius poutassou*
  (Risso, 1826)
Family: **Cod**
Other common names: Couch's whiting,
  merlan bleu
French name: poutassou

  Distribution: Found from Sable Island Bank south to Cape Cod in the western Atlantic Ocean Also off Greenland, Iceland and Europe including the western Mediterranean Sea.
  Characters: This species is distinguished from other Atlantic **cods** by having 3 dorsal and 2 anal fins, the lower jaw projects slightly, the chin barbel is absent, and the anal fin origin is below the first dorsal fin origin. First dorsal rays 11–15, second dorsal rays 9–14 and third dorsal rays 22–28. First anal fin rays 30–42 and second anal rays 22–30. Pectoral fin rays 18–23. Lateral line

blue whiting

scales 163–181. Gill rakers 26–34. The back is silvery blue to blue-grey, flanks silvery and the belly is white. The pectoral fin base has a vague dark spot in some fish. The peritoneum is black. Reaches 47 cm standard length.

Biology: This is a midwater, schooling species at depths of 30–400 m on the continental slope in spring and summer. Winter depths are probably greater. Temperature range is –0.3 to 15°C. Young fish may be found inshore. Life span is at least 6 years, perhaps up to 20 years. Food is euphausiid crustaceans and such **lanternfishes** as the **highvelo hugo** as well as **barracudinas**. There is a daily vertical migration in pursuit of prey. Males are mature at 19–20 cm, females at 20–25 cm. Spawning occurs in March to May probably at 180–360 m about 10–30 m above the sea floor. Eggs measure 1.3 mm in diameter. Young larvae live near the surface. This species is commercially exploited in Europe for fish meal and oil and in recent years as food for humans.

blueback herring

Scientific name: *Alosa aestivalis*
(Mitchill, 1814)
Family: **Herring**
Other common names: blueback shad,
    river herring, glut herring, gaspereau,
    summer herring, blueback mulhaden,
    black belly, kyack
French name: alose d'été

Distribution: Found from the southern Gulf of St. Lawrence south to Florida.

Characters: This herring is distinguished from its Canadian Atlantic coast relatives by the dorsal fin origin not being far forward of the pelvic fins, no enlarged scales before the dorsal fin on the back, back blue-green,

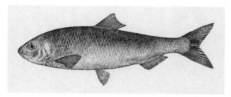

blueback herring

branched pelvic rays 8, the belly has a sharp, saw-tooth edge, there are no teeth on the roof of the mouth, lower limb gill rakers 41–52, lower jaw projecting and not fitting into the

upper jaw notch, black or sooty peritoneum, eye diameter shorter than snout length, and a diamond-shaped scale pattern. The scale base has an arch of pigment rather than a straight one as in the **gaspereau**, this gives the diamond-shape. The dorsal fin has 14–20 rays, anal rays 15–21 and pectoral rays 12–18. Scales along flank 41–54. Scutes on the belly 18–22 in front of the pelvic fins and 12–17 behind. The back is blue-green or dark blue, flanks and belly an iridescent silver, sometimes with bronze on the flank. The flanks may have longitudinal lines and there is a black spot just behind the head. Fins are pale yellowish or greenish. Reaches 38.1 cm.

Biology: Adults are found in the sea as much as 200 km offshore and run into fresh water in May in Nova Scotia to spawn. Marine populations are in shallower water than **gaspereau**, particularly at 27–55 m, overwintering near the bottom.

Food is the smaller zooplankton and some fish fry and eggs and there is a daily vertical migration to capture the zooplankton which are taken selectively.

Females are longer and weigh more than males of the same age. Life span is at least 11 years with maturity being reached usually at 3–4 years with some mature at 2 or as late as 5 years.

The spawning run occurs at temperatures of 13.3°C or higher, usually about 3–4 weeks later and at warmer temperatures than **gaspereau**. The migration does not ascend as far up rivers as **gaspereau**. Spawning also occurs in lakes and ponds but fast running water over a hard bottom is preferred at 21–24°C. Spawning groups consist of a female and several males which swim in circles with the males nudging the female's belly. Speed of swimming increases gradually and ends with a deep dive and release of eggs and sperm near the river bed. Spawned out adults leave the river within a few days. Eggs are yellowish, 1.1 mm in diameter and number up to 349,700. Eggs are released between dusk and 1 a.m. in the West River, P.E.I. and spawning in the Maritimes is mostly in June–July. Eggs become attached to the river bottom or to vegetation. Some fish spawn in 8 successive years.

Bluebacks are caught on the spawning run and sold along with **gaspereau**. Young fish descend to the sea in September–October in the Annapolis River, N.S. This movement is associated with increasing rainfall, rapid decrease in water temperature (below 12°C) and the moon phase (dark nights). These factors are the same for **American shad** and **gaspereau**. This species appears to have increased in abundance in Canadian waters in recent years and is not in jeopardy according to the Committee on the Status of Endangered Wildlife in Canada.

bluebarred prickleback

Scientific name: *Plectobranchus evides*
    Gilbert, 1890
Family: **Shanny**
Other common names: black-and-white prickleback
French name: lompénie à barres bleues

Distribution: From southern California to central British Columbia.

Characters: This species is most closely related to the **Y-prickleback**. It is distinguished by having 54–57 dorsal fin spines, 2 anal fin spines and 34–36 soft rays, and by colour. The pectoral fin has about 15 rays, the lower 4–6 elongated. The pelvic fins are long. Scales are found on the body and posterior part of the head. The lateral line canal is indistinct. Head pores are obvious. Olive-brown

bluebarred prickleback

overall, fading to lighter shades ventrally. There are about 25 narrow, light bluish bars along the flank and 3–4 oval blotches spaced at regular intervals overlying these bars. The dorsal fin is obliquely barred overall and has 2–3 dark spots on the posterior half. The pectoral, anal and caudal fins have a bar at midfin with fin margins pale. The caudal fin may have a dark spot on its top edge. The pelvic fins are unmarked. Attains 13.2 cm.

Biology: Found from 84–274 m over sand or mud, but little is known of its biology.

bluefin driftfish

Scientific name: *Psenes pellucidus*
    Lütken, 1880
Family: **Driftfish**
Other common names: blackrag, flotsamfish
French name: pompile à nageoires bleues

Distribution: Found in the temperate and subtropical Pacific, Indian and Atlantic oceans, and from southeast of Sable Island and east of Georges Bank in Atlantic Canada.

Characters: This species is distinguished from its relative, the **silver driftfish**, by more dorsal and anal fin rays and by colour. The

bluefin driftfish

body is very compressed, soft and flabby. There are long knife-like teeth in the lower jaw and finer teeth in the upper jaw, some with recurved tips. First dorsal fin spines 9–12. Second dorsal fin with 1–2 spines and 26–32 soft rays. Anal fin with 2–3 spines and 26–31 soft rays. Total number of scales in lateral series 143–152. The body is almost transparent, particularly near the dorsal and anal fins, but adults are dark-brown to blackish. The first dorsal fin is blue-black. The pectoral and caudal fins have a dark margin. The second dorsal fin and the anal fin have 2 blue-black stripes. Young fish have 6–8 blue blotches on the base of the anal fin, sometimes extending onto the flanks as bars. Reaches 80 cm standard length.

Biology: Canadian specimens are juvenile strays found at 50 m and captured in 1979. Young are found in surface waters associated with *Sargassum* weed and flotsam, but adults are bathypelagic and feed on **bristlemouths**, other fishes and crustaceans.

bluefin searcher

Scientific name: *Bathymaster caeruleofasciatus*
    Gilbert and Burke, 1912
Family: **Ronquil**
Other common names: Alaskan ronquil
French name: ronquille à nageoires bleues

Distribution: Found from the Bering Sea to the Queen Charlotte Islands.

Characters: The bluefin searcher is distinguished from its relatives, the **northern ronquil** and the **blue-eyed searcher**, by having

bluefin searcher

a long upper jaw which extends to the rear eye margin or beyond, no black patch at the front of the dorsal fin, strong ctenoid scales and no cheek scales. The dorsal fin has about 45–50 rays, the anal fin 32–36. Pectoral fin rays are 17–19. Lateral line pores number 90–100. The lower arm of the gill arch has 12–14 rakers, total 15–20. Overall colour is blue-black to brownish, tinged reddish in young fish, with evident blue-green bars on the flanks. These fade to a dull dark-blue on capture. The anal fin has some indistinct brownish markings. Young fish are paler and have a blotch near the margin of the operculum. Reaches about 30 cm.

Biology: This species is found in rocky areas down to about 30 m. It hides in crevices when disturbed.

bluefin tuna

Scientific name: *Thunnus thynnus*
    (Linnaeus, 1758)
Family: **Mackerel**
Other common names: northern bluefin tuna,
    tunny, common tunny, short-finned tuna,
    horse mackerel, great albacore, giant tuna
French name: thon rouge

Distribution: Found from southern Labrador southward in Atlantic Canada and off central and southern British Columbia. Also in the Gulf of Alaska. World-wide in temperate to tropical waters.

Characters: This species is separated from its Atlantic and Pacific coast relatives by large size, dorsal fin spine count, 32–43 gill rakers, absence of stripes, and a short pectoral fin (less than 80% of head length). There is a strong median keel on the caudal peduncle and smaller keels above and below. A swimbladder is present. First dorsal fin spines 12–14, second dorsal fin with 1 spine and 13–15 rays followed by 8–10 finlets. The anal fin has 1 spine and 12–16 rays followed by 7–9 finlets. Pectoral fin rays 30–36. Scales cover the body and there is a weak corselet of larger scales in the pectoral area.

The back is dark blue to black, light blue on the flanks and silver-grey on the belly. A golden stripe may separate the belly and back coloration. There may be faint white lines and white or silvery spots on the lower flank in fresh fish. The first dorsal fin is yellowish or bluish, the second dorsal fin and anal fin are silvery-grey, grey-yellow or red-brown. Finlets are bright yellow with black margins. The median caudal keel is black. Young have pale bars on the flank.

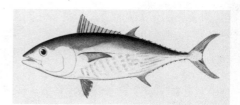

bluefin tuna

Attains 4.3 m and 910 kg. The world, all-tackle angling record was a 679 kg, 304 cm fork length fish landed in Aulds Cove, Cape Breton, N.S. on 26 October 1979 by Ken Fraser. The bluefin tuna on the Pacific coast are referred to a distinct subspecies *Thunnus thynnus orientalis* (Temminck and Schlegel in Siebold, 1844).

Biology: Tunas are oceanic fishes but come close to shore also. Adults enter Canadian Atlantic waters from June to October or later and weigh 136 kg or more ("giants"). Canadian fish move here from as far away as the Gulf of Mexico and some fish migrate across the Atlantic and back again. A journey of at least 6779 km from the Bahamas to Norway took 4 months. There are also trans-Pacific migrations between California and Japan. Smaller tuna, called "jumpers", weighing 68 kg or less are rarer and enter southern Atlantic Canada in late August or September. Tuna only enter British Columbia in the summer months of warmwater years. Adults are found in schools of less than 50 fish at 27–183 m. The counter-current heat exchange system enables tuna to maintain a body temperature 10–15C° warmer than the sea and so they can enter cold Canadian waters and feed on the abundant fish stocks. The warmer body increases digestion rate and rate of feeding. Stores of fat accumulate which can be used as energy sources for their long migrations.

Food includes such schooling species as **herring, sauries, capelin, lanternfishes, barracudinas, mackerel, hakes** and squid. Euphausiid crustaceans are also eaten. When feeding, tuna may break the surface with their backs and their prey scatters in all directions, jumping out of the water and attracting flocks of seabirds. Killer whales, pilot whales and **makos** eat large tuna and smaller tuna are food for a variety of fishes and seabirds.

Males tend to grow longer than females but females live longer. Maximum age is 38 years. They begin to mature at 4–5 years. Spawning does not occur in Canada. The major areas in the western Atlantic Ocean are the Straits of Florida and the Gulf of Mexico. A female can produce over 60 million, 1.3 mm, pelagic eggs which hatch in a few days in warm southern waters.

Large tuna may occur in numbers sufficient to support sport fisheries in Newfoundland, the Gulf of St. Lawrence, off Nova Scotia and in the mouth of the Bay of Fundy. There was an International Tuna Cup Match at Wedgeport, N.S. from 1937–1976. Variations in tuna numbers and concentrations in Canada mean that the sport fishery shifts localities. They can be caught by trolling live or dead fish or squid, and by trolling spoons, plugs or feathers.

In St. Margarets Bay, N.S. large tuna were caught in trap nets, held in pens and fattened. Cleaned, refrigerated tuna were sent by air to Japan for the *sashimi* and *sushi* market. The 1985 quota for Canada allowed by the International Commission for the Conservation of Atlantic Tunas was 573 tonnes or 1521 fish but only 329 fish were caught. The 1989 Canadian landings weighed 730 tonnes worth about $7.3 million.

There is a black market for bluefin tuna in Atlantic Canada. Understandable when a single fish weighing 325 kg was sold fresh in 1992 for U.S. $69,273.30! However prosecutions are difficult to obtain since the culprits are usually caught with dressed fish. Fishery officers in one case were unable to convince a judge that this dressed fish was a bluefin tuna and not another species to which regulations did not apply. DNA "fingerprinting" or genetic typing has been developed for tunas to combat the identification problem.

Pacific coast Indians have caught tuna in small numbers for thousands of years. Elsewhere tuna are caught in traps, purse seines and on longlines. They are eaten fresh or canned.

- Most accessible in June and July.
- The Atlantic waters off the Maritime coast.
- Penn International 50– to 80–pound test big game outfits.
- Large offshore trolling plugs, as well as large dead and live bait.

bluefish

Scientific name: *Pomatomus saltatrix*
(Linnaeus, 1766)
Family: **Bluefish**
Other common names: tailor, elf, snapper (young), rock salmon, snapper blue, Hatteras blue, roach, bream, sunfish, blue sunfish, snapping mackerel, chopper, balarin, marine piranha
French name: tassergal

Distribution: Found from Nova Scotia south to Argentina and in the Atlantic and Indian oceans generally. Absent from the eastern Pacific Ocean.

Characters: The bluefish is recognised by its low, short, first, dorsal fin with 6–8 spines which fold into a groove, followed by the second dorsal fin with 1 spine and 23–28 soft rays. The anal fin has 2 minute, embed-

bluefish

ded spines and 23–27 soft rays. The lateral line is almost straight and has about 90–106 scales. The mouth is large with very sharp, flattened, triangular teeth. The cheeks and opercles are scaled. There is a short spine on the opercle bone. Bluefish have an odour of cucumbers when fresh. Blue to blue-green or blue-grey above with silvery flanks and a white belly. There is a black blotch at the pectoral fin base. The caudal fin is dusky. Reaches 1.2 m and a reputed 23 kg but 14.4 kg is a more reliable figure based on the world, all-tackle record taken at Hatteras, North Carolina in 1972.

Biology: Canadian bluefish are strays from the south but are caught quite often in nets during a summer, northward movement. They may reach Passamaquoddy Bay, the Bay of Fundy and Cape Breton. Bluefish are found in very large schools in coastal waters from the surface down to 200 m. Schools as long as 8 km have been reported in the U.S.A. Young bluefish may enter bays and estuaries. Bluefish arrive inshore when the temperature reaches 12–15°C in late spring and summer in the U.S.A. and leave in early winter. The bluefish is a voracious predator, killing more fish than it eats, by slashing with its large jaws and formidable teeth. Crustaceans and squids are eaten but the principal food is **mackerel, herring, anchovies, shads** and **mullets**. Even seabirds have been attacked. Bluefish can eat twice their own body weight in a day. Bathers have been bitten, probably accidentally, as bluefish packs chase schools of fish into shallow water. One victim

required 55 stitches. Schools of **menhaden** have become stranded on beaches in piles in their attempt to escape the blue fish attacks.

Bluefish live at least 14 years. Spawning occurs in June to August and eggs are buoyant.

Bluefish are an important commercial and sport fish on the U.S.A. coast with a delicious taste fresh or smoked. The flesh does not keep well if frozen for long periods. They fight well on hook and line and jump repeatedly ("saltatrix" is Latin for dancing girl!). Some anglers can "sniff out" bluefish since these fish have a fresh cucumber odour. Bluefish are caught by casting, jigging, trolling and chumming using live bait preferably. Plugs and feathers can also be used. They can be caught from shore or boats. Bluefish should be handled with care as a large specimen can sever a finger. The northwest Atlantic catch in 1988 weighed 6234 tonnes.

Bluefish Family

Scientific name: Pomatomidae
French name: tassergals

Bluefish are found in the Atlantic, Indian and Pacific oceans. There is 1 species in the family and it is reported for Atlantic Canada.

Bluefish are recognised by a low first dorsal fin with 6–8 spines followed by a higher second dorsal fin. The soft dorsal and anal fins are covered with small scales. Scales are cycloid. The preoperculum bone on the side of the head has a membrane flap over the suboperculum.

Bluefish are related to the **Cobia Family** and are relatively primitive members of the **Perch Order**. In some classifications, the gnomefishes are included with the Bluefish Family. A gnomefish is reported from the Straits of Florida, but none have been recorded near Canadian waters.

Biology is summarised in the species account.

See **bluefish**

bluegill

Scientific name: *Lepomis macrochirus* Rafinesque, 1819
Family: **Sunfish**
Other common names: northern bluegill

sunfish, common bluegill, blue sunfish, sun perch, bream, blue bream, copper-nosed bream, pale sunfish, bluegill bream, bluemouth sunfish, roach, blackear bream, chain-sided sunfish, dollardee, strawberry bass
French name: crapet arlequin

Distribution: Found in southwestern Québec, southern Ontario including the Great Lakes but not northern and eastern Lake Superior, although appearing again in its western drainages. In the U.S.A. south to northeastern Mexico and Georgia west of the Appalachian Mountains and from Florida north to Virginia. Also widely introduced throughout North America as well as in Europe and South Africa.

Characters: This species is distinguished by having 9–12, usually 10, dorsal fin spines, 3 anal fin spines, 38–50 lateral line scales, a completely black opercular or "ear" flap which has about the same length as width and has an entire bony edge (not crenate or wavy), and a black blotch at the rear of the dorsal fin base. Second dorsal fin soft rays 9–13, soft anal rays 8–12, usually 11, and pectoral rays 12–15.

bluegill

The back and upper flank are green, olive or brownish to almost black with a bluish or purplish iridescence fading to a silver or white belly. The "ear" flap may have a blue anterior edge. Flanks have 5–9 vague, olive, double bands but these can be absent in large fish or fish living in turbid water. The breast is yellow. The sides of the head have a metallic green and blue sheen and the chin and lower operculum are blue. The pectoral fins are transparent and yellowish. The pelvic and

anal fins may have a white anterior edge. Young have 9–12 dark flank bars. Breeding males develop a yellowish to copper-orange breast and the pelvic and anal fins become black or dusky. A hump develops in front of the dorsal fin. Peritoneum silvery. Hybrids with **pumpkinseed** are common in Canada and the hybrids breed with either parental form giving a complete and continuous range of characters between the 2 species. This often makes identification difficult.

Reaches 41 cm. The world, all-tackle angling record from Ketona Lake, Alabama caught in 1950 weighed 2.15 kg. The Canadian angling record from Mississippi Lake, Ontario was caught by Jeff Buck in May 1994 and weighed 0.50 kg.

Biology: Bluegills are often found in ponds, lakes, streams and rivers where there is little current, shallow water and much vegetation. Bluegills are often in small schools of 10–20 fish. They retire to deeper water in winter, or in summer if the shallows are too hot. They are intolerant of high turbidity and siltation.

Food includes aquatic and flying insects, crustaceans, molluscs, worms, fish fry, bryozoans and algae. Growth is better when diet includes some algae. Feeding is greatest at dawn and dusk. Food may be taken in midwater, on the bottom or at the surface, often using sight to select items. Some bluegills have been found to contain the external fish louse in their guts. They are "cleaners," picking such parasites off other infected fish. Cleaning has been observed on **striped mullet, largemouth bass** and even manatees in Florida. Bluegills are commonly eaten by other fishes when small.

Life span is 11 years with older fish in the northern part of the range. Maturity is attained at 2–8 years for males and 3–4 years for females although some populations, especially in the south, mature at 1 year. Growth varies greatly between populations depending on various environmental factors. Stunting is not uncommon in ponds.

Spawning peaks in late June to early July in Canada but may extend from May to August in northern populations. Temperatures are usually in the range 19–27°C. Males excavate a shallow depression about 61 cm across on gravel, sand or mud bottoms using their caudal fins. These shallow water nests are colonial, with up to 50 in an area of radius 21 m at a traditional site. Males compete for access to central nest sites in the colonies, large ones usually winning, and females favour central sites because predation is less. Males defend their nests and eggs. Defense postures involve erected fins, butting and biting but usually stops with a rush at the intruder. A nesting colony of males, females and non-nesting males will mob a large turtle, perhaps to draw attention to its presence or to drive it away.

Females arrive on the spawning ground after the males. A spawning pair swims in circles around the nest and then comes to lie side by side with the male vertical and the female inclined so their genital openings touch. Some eggs are shed and fertilised and the circling is repeated. Males make grunting sounds during courtship perhaps to attract females.

A female can have up to 81,104 eggs. The eggs are amber, adhesive and up to 1.4 mm in diameter after water hardening. The eggs are guarded and fanned for 2–3 days, the fry for 3–4 days, after which they disperse as do the males to feed. Nests may be re-used by other males since the spawning season may extend into August. Several females lay eggs in one nest which can have about a quarter million eggs. Adults can have 2–5 brood cycles and reproduce for 2–3 years.

Small sneaker males rush in to steal fertilisations from adults and satellite males mimic females to also cuckold the large male. The large male looks after the eggs and young while females, sneakers and satellites leave. Large males are sexually inactive until age 7 in Lake Opinicon, Ontario when they are large enough to defend nests. Sneakers and satellites mature at age 2, first being sneakers and then satellites as they become large enough to mimic females. These cuckolders do not become large, parental males. Apparently selection is acting to maintain this stable system.

Bluegill are very important sport and commercial fishes in the U.S.A., less so in Canada.

In the U.S.A. it is stocked in farm ponds and reservoirs, yielding up to 330 kg/ ha/year. They may be caught on flies or live bait and are excellent sport, particularly for the younger angler. Bluegill fight strongly by swimming in circles with the body broadside to the angler giving a disproportionate pull for the size of the fish. There are small commercial catches in Ontario and Québec and the flesh is white, flaky and good eating. Some consider the bluegill as the tastiest freshwater fish.

bluenose rearfin

Scientific name: *Melanostomias bartonbeani* Parr, 1927
Family: **Barbeled Dragonfish**
Other common names: none
French name: nageoires-reculées nez-bleu

Distribution: Found in the Atlantic, Indian and Pacific oceans including Atlantic Canada.

Characters: This species is distinguished from its Canadian Atlantic relatives by having 4–5 equal length pectoral fin rays with unbranched tips and without luminous material, dorsal and anal fin bases about equal in length, pelvic fins low on the flank, no luminous organs before (preorbital) or below (suborbital) the eye, 22–26 photophores between the pectoral and pelvic fin insertions, and by the barbel tip being flattened and at least 5 times as long as wide. In addition, there is only 1 prominent bulb on each side of the barbel axis and the barbel ends in a tapering filament. Dorsal fin rays 12–16, usually 13–15, anal rays 16–20, pelvic rays 7. The barbel is shorter to longer than the head. Overall colour is black but there are obvious white spots on the snout, rear top of the head,

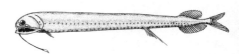

bluenose rearfin

between the eye and nostrils and on the front of the throat. The barbel stem is black but the tip is unpigmented. Reaches 26 cm.

Biology: Reported from the Newfoundland Basin and south of Browns Bank at depths of 500–512 m.

bluespotted cornetfish

Scientific name: *Fistularia tabacaria*
   Linnaeus, 1758
Family: **Cornetfish**
Other common names: tobacco pipefish
French name: fistulaire tabac

   Distribution: Found from Brazil to Nova
Scotia and Newfoundland and in the eastern
Atlantic Ocean.
   Characters: The very long snout, the rear
position of the dorsal and anal fins and the fil-
ament trailing from the caudal fin are distinc-

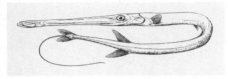

bluespotted cornetfish

tive. Dorsal and anal fin rays 14–16. Snout
ridges smooth, not serrate. Olive-brown on the
back with large, pale-blue spots on the back
and a row lateral to this. Two rows of blue
spots on the snout. The caudal filament is deep
blue. Approaches 2 m in length but weighs
only about 3 kg because it is so slender.
   Biology: Rare in Canadian waters but
first reported in 1863 from Halifax Harbour.
A pelagic species in coastal waters down to
200 m. Food is small crustaceans and fishes.
The body is bent into an s-curve for up to 5
seconds before striking at prey. About half
the strikes are unsuccessful. The sucking
action involved in the strike may send small
fish down the whole length of the snout. A
second fish may be struck while the first is
still in the snout. Often caught by anglers.

bluespotted poacher

Scientific name: *Xeneretmus triacanthus*
   (Gilbert, 1890)
Family: **Poacher**
Other common names: none
French name: agone à trois épines

   Distribution: From British Columbia south
to Baja California.
   Characters: This poacher and the related
blacktip and **smootheye poachers** are dis-

tinguished by the absence of a pit on top of
the head and by an exposed snout plate having a single dorsally pointing spine. This

bluespotted poacher

species is identified by having 1–4 bony
plates filling the cheek area, 2 cirri at the
rear of the upper jaw, the anal fin origin
below the second dorsal fin origin, and 2–6
spiny plates on the eyeball. First dorsal fin
with 5–7 spines, second dorsal fin with 6–7
soft rays. Anal fin rays 5–7, pectoral fin rays
12–14 with lower 4 rays finger-like. Gill rakers number 9–14. Gill membranes are joined
to the isthmus. Olive-brown dorsally with 6
dark blotches on the flank. The fin rays and
spines are dusky. There is no black edge to
the dorsal fin. There are frequently bright
blue spots behind the head. Reaches 18 cm.
   Biology: Found on soft bottoms from
73–373 m.

bluethroat argentine

Scientific name: *Nansenia candida*
   Cohen, 1958
Family: **Pencilsmelt**
Other common names: none
French name: argentine à gorge bleue

   Distribution: Found on the Pacific coast
between the Queen Charlotte Islands and
southern California.
   Characters: The bluethroat is distinguished
from the **large-eyed argentine** by having
25–31 gill rakers (instead of 37–45), and by

bluethroat argentine

the dorsal fin being further back, behind the
midpoint of the body. It is distinguished from
the **forgotten argentine** by having a low

number of branchiostegal rays (3) which also separates it from similar fishes in other families. Dorsal fin rays 7–10. Anal fin rays are 8–10, usually 9. Cycloid scales number 45–47 along the lateral line. Body colour in preservative is brown although in life it is probably a silvery fish. Reaches 22.2 cm.

Biology: Caught at depths between 100 and 825 m varying with time of day. Probably feeds on zooplankton.

blunthead puffer

Scientific name: *Sphoeroides pachygaster*
(Müller and Troschel in Schomburgk, 1848)
Family: **Puffer**
Other common names: none
French name: sphéroïde trogne

Distribution: Found in all warmer seas and from Nova Scotia south to Argentina in the western Atlantic Ocean.

Characters: This species has a four-toothed beak in the mouth and is distinguished from related species by fin ray counts and the absence of prickles. Dorsal fin rays are 8–10, anal fin rays 8–9, and pectoral fin rays 14–18. The skin on the belly and underside of the head is wrinkled. The

blunthead puffer

head is blunt and rounded when seen from the side. There is 1 lateral line. Overall colour of back and flanks is olive-grey to brownish peppered with small black spots, with the belly white. There may be dark spots and blotches on the flanks. The caudal fin of adults is dark with white lobes. Young are dark green without spots. Reaches 26 cm.

Biology: Only a single specimen has been caught in Canadian waters in 1974. It was found in a trap net. This is usually a relatively deepwater species (from 25–480 m) which feeds mainly on squid. Young are pelagic.

bluntnose bristlemouth

Scientific name: *Margrethia obtusirostrata*
Jespersen and Tåning, 1919
Family: **Bristlemouth**
Other common names: none
French name: cyclothone camuse

Distribution: Found in the warmer waters of the Atlantic Ocean including off Canada.

Characters: This species is distinguished from all other Atlantic coast bristlemouths by having 16 branchiostegal rays, lacking

bluntnose bristlemouth

isthmus photophores, 1 row of photophores on the body, SO and OA photophores absent and 21–26 anal rays. Dorsal fin rays 15–16. Photophores: ORB 1, OP 3, BR 10–13, IV 12–14 + 2, VAV 4, AC 16–17, IC 35–36. The back and the anterior dorsal and anal fin rays are dark, the flanks yellowish. The operculum is silvery. The caudal fin base and the caudal peduncle are dark brown. Reaches 8.3 cm standard length.

Biology: Caught on the northeast Georges Bank at 200–500 m in 1979 and first reported in 1988. Found usually at 100–600 m and does not undergo a daily vertical migration. Food is crustaceans and small fishes. Spawning occurs from summer to autumn.

bluntnose minnow

Scientific name: *Pimephales notatus*
(Rafinesque, 1820)
Family: **Carp**
Other common names: bluenosed chub, bullhead minnow, fat-head chub
French name: ventre-pourri

Distribution: Found in southwestern Québec, southern Ontario but not north of Lake Superior, Lake of the Woods and southern Manitoba. In the U.S.A. south to Virginia in the east and in the Mississippi River basin.

Characters: This species is identified by having premaxillaries protractile (lip separated from the snout by a groove), no barbel, the first, unbranched dorsal fin ray is short and separated by a membrane from the next, longer ray, scales in front of the dorsal fin are much smaller and more crowded than flank scales, the back is flattened, the lateral line is complete, the mouth is under the snout and there is a caudal fin base spot. Dorsal fin branched rays 7, anal branched rays 6–7, mostly 6, pectoral rays 14–17 and pelvic rays 8. Lateral line scales 37–50. Pharyngeal teeth are 4–4, hooked and serrated, and the gut is elongated with several coils. Males have 3 rows of 14–17 large tubercles over the snout anterior to the nostrils and small tubercles on the upper pectoral fin rays. Breeding males have a fleshy papilla at each mouth corner, rather like a barbel.

The back is olive-green to sandy-brown, the flanks silvery and the belly white. There is a dusky flank stripe from snout to tail. Scales are outlined in black. Fins are yellowish and the dorsal fin has a dusky blotch just above the anterior base. Breeding males become almost black to bluish-black overall with a whitish pad on the anterior back. Peritoneum black. Reaches 11.0 cm.

bluntnose minnow

Biology: Bluntnose minnows are found in lakes, ponds and streams over sand, gravel and mud. Food is detritus and includes organic matter, chironomid and other insect larvae, diatoms and algae. Algae may be taken particularly in winter. Some surface insects and plankton are also taken as well as its own eggs and fry and those of other fish species. Various other fishes are predators of this **minnow**.

Life span is at least 3 years for males. Males grow much larger than females.

Females mature at 1 year and males at 2 years of age. Spawning occurs in late May to August at 19°C water temperatures or warmer. Eggs are laid at intervals through the season, 5–547 at a time. Clutches laid varied between 7 to 26 per female. A spawning season at any one locality was about 7 weeks in one study to 3 months in another. Each female has up to 10,164 eggs in her ovaries in several stages of development, up to 1.5 mm in diameter.

This level of egg production exceeds that of other species like the "prolific" **common carp** in terms of body weight. Generally those fish species that build nests and guard eggs are supposed to produce fewer eggs which have a better chance of individual survival than the numerous eggs produced and abandoned by prolific species. The bluntnose and **fathead minnows** are exceptions to this general rule.

The male defends a nest in shallow waters. The nest is a space under a stone, log, clam shell or even a board or tin can, cleaned out with the aid of his tubercles and tail sweeps. The undersurface of the stone is cleaned with his mouth and spongy back pad and eggs are deposited there mostly at night but also during the day. The male and female turn on their sides under the nest stone with the male under the female, pressing against her. The male rapidly arches his caudal peduncle against the female's urogenital region, the female rapidly undulates through an s-shape and an egg is extruded. The egg is transferred to the upper side of the female and the undulation rolls it along between her side and the nest cavity roof. When the adhesive egg reaches the tail she presses it against the roof where it sticks. How the female transfers the egg from her papilla to her side is unknown and the question remains why this sideways process is used when other roof spawners simply turn upside down and deposit eggs directly. The process may serve to roll eggs into a vacant roof space, occupying the roof most efficiently. Eggs laid on top of others may not attach well or prevent proper development of the underlying eggs. Nest construction takes about 1–2 hours. Over 5000 eggs at various developmental stages from several females are found in a single nest. The male guards the eggs, removes dead ones, and keeps them free of silt and aerated until they hatch.

Bluntnose minnows are used as bait fish in Canada, and in the U.S.A. where they have been raised in ponds for distribution as a forage fish for game species.

boa dragonfish

Scientific name: *Stomias boa ferox*
  Reinhardt, 1843
Family: **Barbeled Dragonfish**
Other common names: none
French name: dragon-boa

Distribution: Found in the North Atlantic Ocean including Arctic and Atlantic waters off Canada. Also in the Indian and Pacific oceans.

Characters: Distinguished from the **shortbarbel dragonfish** by having 6 rows of hexagonal areas above the light organ rows. The barbel is about as long as the head and bears three short filaments on the bulb at its tip. Dorsal fin rays 17–21, anal rays 19–23 and pectoral rays 6. There are 82–91 light organs in the ventral series. Colour is iridescent silver on the sides but black on the belly and back. The hexagonal areas form a distinct pattern. Size attains 31.8 cm standard length. This subspecies may be a full species distinct from another subspecies in the Mediterranean Sea and off West Africa.

boa dragonfish

Biology: Descends below 1000 m but most are caught above 300 m. Feeds on fish and crustaceans and a vertical migration occurs. One Canadian specimen comes from the stomach of a **swordfish** harpooned on Browns Bank. Also eaten by **Atlantic cod**. Spawning occurs in the spring.

Boarfish Family

Scientific name: Caproidae
French name: sangliers

The boarfishes are found in the Atlantic, Indian and Pacific oceans. There are 6 species with 1 on the Atlantic coast of Canada.

These fishes have small ctenoid scales and resemble **Dory Family** members except they lack plates on the abdomen. The body is deep and compressed. An occipital crest is found on top of the head. The mouth is small and protractile, and its resemblance to a pig's snout gives the family its name. The body has small ctenoid scales, but lacks the plates, bucklers and basal fin spines of related families. Most boarfishes are red in colour.

Boarfishes are related to the **Eyefish**, **Diamond Dory**, **Dory** and **Oreo** families, members of the **Dory Order**.

Found mostly in deep water in schools, sometimes below 600 m or as shallow as 40 m. Adults are deeper than juveniles. They may be associated with deep rocky areas. Crustaceans are a main food item.

See **shortspine boarfish**

bocaccio

Scientific name: *Sebastes paucispinis*
  Ayres, 1854
Family: **Scorpionfish**
Other common names: salmon grouper,
  brown bomber, rock salmon
French name: bocaccio

Distribution: Found from Alaska to Baja California including British Columbia.

Characters: This species is recognised by its large mouth (= bocaccio) extending beyond the rear of the eye and the greatly projecting lower jaw, a concave head profile but with the space between the eyes on top of the head convex, and weak head spines. Dorsal fin spines 12–15, usually 13, soft rays 13–15, usually 14. Anal fin soft rays 8–10, usually 9, second anal spine shorter than third and not much thicker. Pectoral fin rays 14–16, usually 15. Gill rakers 27–32. Vertebrae 26. Lateral line pores 51–70, scale rows below lateral line 72–90. Head spines usually absent with only nasals and parietals sometimes present. The back is olive-brown to brick or dusky red, with flanks silvery-red or pink. Some fish may have abnormal black blotches or be bright red or golden-orange.

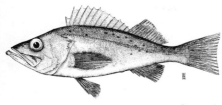

bocaccio

Young fishes have brown flank spots. Peritoneum silvery-white, sometimes dotted black. Reaches 91 cm. The world, all-tackle record weighed 9.63 kg and was caught in Neah Bay, Washington in 1986. "Bocaccio" is from the Italian for ugly mouth.

Biology: Adults are found over rocks or a clear bottom from the surface to 475 m with young fish in shallower water forming schools. Young may be caught in the surf zone. Food is other fishes including other rockfishes and this is a voracious predator. About half the population is mature at 42 cm or 4 years of age. They may live for 30 years. In California females give birth to as many as 2.3 million young in November followed by a second brood in March. In British Columbia spawning occurs before February. This is a popular sport fish but is not of great commercial importance in Canada as it is in California.

Bolin's lanternfish

Scientific name: *Notoscopelus bolini*
Nafpaktitis, 1975
Family: **Lanternfish**
Other common names: none
French name: lanterne de Bolin

Distribution: Found in the temperate to subtropical waters of the Atlantic Ocean and Mediterranean Sea including off Atlantic Canada.

Characters: This is 1 of 4 Atlantic coast species characterised by stiff, spine-like rays at the upper and lower caudal fin bases, no large glands on the upper and lower caudal peduncle outlined by heavy black pigment,

and a dorsal fin base longer than the anal fin base. It is distinguished from its relatives (**northern saillamp**, **patchwork lanternfish** and **spinetail lanternfish**) by having 26–29 gill rakers, 23–26, usually 25, dorsal fin rays, no gland on top of the caudal peduncle in males but large patches of luminous tissue on the cheek and above the eye. Anal fin rays 18–20 and pectoral rays 12–14, usually 13. Photophores: AO 7–9, usually 8, + 6–8, usually 7, total 14–17 in the Atlantic Ocean. Adult males have the luminous patches noted above. Reaches 10.2 cm.

Bolin's lanternfish

Biology: Known only from a single Canadian specimen taken southeast of Browns Bank in 1978. This is a relatively uncommon species found below 1000 m in the day and at the surface down to 125 m during the night in the Atlantic Ocean.

bonaparte

Scientific name: *Bonapartia pedaliota*
Goode and Bean, 1896
Family: **Bristlemouth**
Other common names: none
French name: bonaparte

Distribution: Found in the warmer waters of the North Atlantic Ocean including off Atlantic Canada. Also in the Indian Ocean.

Characters: This species is distinguished from other Atlantic coast bristlemouths by having 13–17 branchiostegal rays, lacking isthmus and OA photophores, 1 row of photophores on the body, SO photophores present and 27–32 anal fin rays. Dorsal fin rays 16–20. Photophores: SO 1, ORB 1, OP 3, BR 11–13, IV 14–15, VAV 5–6, AC 18–21, IC 37–41. The back is dark but the operculum and peritoneum are silvery. The cheeks and iris are silvery blue. The dorsal and caudal fin rays are pigmented. Becomes darker at night. Photophores have a light blue iridescence. The genus was named for the

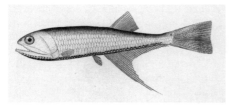

bonaparte

Italian naturalist, Prince Charles Lucien Bonaparte, nephew of the Emperor Napoleon Bonaparte. Reaches 7.5 cm.

Biology: Found off the Flemish Cap, and probably off the Scotian Shelf, but only 1 Canadian specimen has been collected, in 1968. Found usually at 100–700 m with the largest fish deepest. Some records are down to 2744 m. Larvae sink from surface waters as they develop. There may be a vertical migration.

bonefish

Scientific name: *Albula vulpes*
 (Linnaeus, 1758)
Family: **Bonefish**
Other common names: ladyfish, grubber,
 bananafish, phantom, silver ghost
French name: banane de mer

Distribution: Cosmopolitan in warm seas from New Brunswick south to Brazil in the western Atlantic Ocean.

Characters: The conical protruding snout and small mouth are obvious features. There

bonefish

are 65–73 small scales in the lateral line. There is no elongate ray in the dorsal fin. All these characters are distinct from the related **tarpon**.

Dorsal fin rays 15–19, anal rays 5–9, pelvic rays 9–10, pectoral rays 17. Leptocephali have 65–72 myomeres. Back blue-green with about 10 faint bars, especially in young, but overall silvery. There is a dark blotch at the upper pectoral fin base. Pelvic fin base may be yellow. The snout tip is black and the upper lip may be pinkish. Reaches 1.04 m and 8.6 kg.

Biology: Very rare in Canadian waters with only 1 specimen recorded in 1913, perhaps in error. Occurs in inshore waters on mud and sand flats moving in and out with the tide. Often found in schools except the largest fish which are solitary. Food includes worms, crustaceans, sea urchins and molluscs nosed out of sand and mud. Occasionally fish and squid are taken. The tail may stick out of the water in shallow areas when feeding. This behaviour is known as "trailing." Feeding by bonefish schools is called "muddling" because of the disturbed sediment clouds that result. Not a good food fish because of the many small bones, although quite tasty. Much sought after by anglers on light tackle because they fight and run hard. Anglers use plugs, flies or various dead and live baits cast from a small boat or fished while wading in tidal shallows.

Bonefish Family

Scientific name: Albulidae
French name: bananes de mer

Bonefishes or ladyfishes are found in most tropical seas, rarely entering brackish or fresh waters. There are at least 2 species with 1 species reaching Atlantic Canada.

These fishes are characterised by the infraorbital (under the eye) lateral line canal carrying onto the premaxilla, an upper jaw bone. As in the related **Tarpon Family**, there may be a gular plate on the throat although this is reduced to a thin splint, or is absent in some species. Branchiostegal rays 6–16 and the maxilla is toothless in contrast to the **Tarpon Family**. The swimbladder is joined to the gut by a duct.

This family is a member of the **Bonefish Order**.

The larva is a leptocephalus as in **eels** but has a forked tail fin.

See **bonefish**

Bonefish Order

Bonefishes or Albuliformes are tropical marine fishes with about 29 species in 3 families. Seven species are found on the Atlantic, Arctic and Pacific coasts of Canada.

These fishes are characterised by a mandibular sensory canal lying in an open groove in the dentary and angular bones.

They vary considerably in body form. The bonefishes have a herring-like body, abdominal pelvic fins, no fin spines, silvery, cycloid scales, a compressed body, wide gill openings, a deep fork in the caudal fin and a primitive caudal fin skeleton, paired fins having a long, axillary scale, an inferior mouth under a conical, cartilaginous snout, the mouth bordered mostly by the maxilla bone, a gular plate on the throat reduced or absent, branchiostegal rays 6–16, the swimbladder connected by a duct to the gut, mesocoracoid and postcleithral bones present in the pectoral girdle, and a lateral line canal on the premaxilla bone of the upper jaw. There is a ribbon-like or leptocephalus larva with a forked tail fin unlike that in eels.

The tapirfishes and halosaurs have an eel-like body, there is a retrorse spine, pointing backward, from the rear dorsal edge of the maxilla, the premaxilla and maxilla bones form the upper mouth border, the mouth is inferior, lying under a snout, the skin on the head is not interrupted over the eyes but is transparent there, gill openings are wide with an opercular flap, branchiostegal rays 5–23, fin spines are present in some species, pectoral fins are high on the flank but lack a strong connection to the skull, the pectoral girdle lacks a mesocoracoid arch, pelvic fins are abdominal and connected to each other by a membrane, the dorsal fin is short, the anal fin is long and confluent with the long tapering tail, the caudal skeleton is reduced or absent (usually no true caudal fin), a swimbladder is present but without a duct connecting it to the gut, and various skull bones are absent such as the basisphenoid, intercalar, orbitosphenoid and pterosphenoid. The tail can be broken off by accident but will regenerate and may then resemble a caudal fin. Some species have light organs. There are no oviducts and eggs are released into the abdominal cavity. They are laid through 2 abdominal pores near the anus. The larva is ribbon-like or leptocephalus and lacks a caudal fin although there is a filament at the end of the body. These larvae can be very large, up to 1.84 m, the largest larva in the Animal Kingdom, before metamorphosing into an adult. The popular press was very impressed by such a large larva when it was caught off South Africa in the late 1920s, calculating it would change into an adult eel over 30 m long — the mythical giant sea serpent. However another larva was later caught in the process of metamorphosis and was clearly a tapirfish. Tapirfish do not grow much after metamorphosis and an explanation for sea serpents was lost. Adults are found from relatively shallow depths down to over 5 km below the surface of the sea.

This order is closely related to the **Tarpon Order** and is sometimes included within it. The fishes of this order have also been classified within the **Eel Order,** with the **Tarpon Order** distinct. **Tapirfishes** and **halosaurs** are sometimes placed in a separate order, Notacanthiformes.

See **Bonefish Family**
Halosaur Family
Tapirfish Family

bonitos

Bonitos are members of the **Mackerel Family** and there are 2 species in Canada, the **Atlantic** and the **Pacific bonito.** Bonito is a Spanish word meaning pretty good or pretty and may well apply to the appearance of these streamlined, striped, metallic blue and silvery fishes and to their excellent flesh.

bony fishes

Bony fishes or Teleostomi is a general term which comprises most of those organisms known generally as **fishes**. It excludes the 3 classes of **cartilaginous fishes, hagfishes** and **lampreys**. Bony fishes used to comprise a Class, Osteichthyes, but this category is no longer used. Canadian fishes fall in the Class Actinopterygii (ray-finned fishes) which is almost equivalent to the Class Osteichthyes. By far the greatest number of **fishes** are bony fishes: about 45 orders, 435 families and over 23,000 species. Included are the lungfishes of tropical South America, Africa and Australia and the fringe- or tassel-finned fishes represented only by the living coelacanth of the Indian Ocean (Sarcopterygii or lobe-finned fishes), and the **ray-finned fishes** (Actinopterygii). The lungfishes and the coelacanth make up only 7 species so the vast majority of bony fishes belong in the **ray-finned** fishes.

Bony fishes are usually contrasted with the other **jawed fishes**, the **cartilaginous fishes**. They are characterised by the possession of true bone in their skeleton, including bony scales, the skull has sutures between separate bones, a true gill cover, teeth usually fused to the underlying bone and not replaced by rows of teeth from behind, a swimbladder or lung is present, 3 semicircular canals, spiral intestinal valves are rare and found only in lower bony fishes (e.g. in **sturgeons**), eggs are mostly fer- tilised externally, but if fertilisation is internal it is not by modified pelvic fins (with one unique exception), eggs are not enclosed in a case, the blood usually contains little urea or trimethylamine oxide and osmotic regulation is an active process requiring energy expendi- ture, pleural ribs are present, jaws are present and the upper biting jaw is usually formed by the premaxilla and maxilla dermal bones, the nostrils are double openings (or paired) on each side of the upper part of the head, paired pectoral and pelvic fins, and soft fin rays are usually segmented and their origin is dermal (they are known as lepidotrichia).

The origins of the bony fishes are uncer- tain. They are not simply more advanced descendants of the **cartilaginous fishes** as was once thought. Bone precedes the oldest fossil **cartilaginous fishes**. The fossil Acanthodii or spiny sharks of 440 million years ago (which are not **sharks**) probably share a common ancestry with the bony fishes since they had a bony skeleton, true bony scales, paired pectoral and pelvic fins and a heterocercal (upturned skeleton) cau- dal fin similar to that of early bony fishes. Spiny sharks are the first true **jawed fishes**. Bony fishes first appear in the fossil record in the Lower Silurian.

See **Alfonsino Order**

Anglerfish Order
Beardfish Order
Bonefish Order
Bony-tongue Order
Bowfin Order
Carp Order
Catfish Order
Cod Order
Cusk-eel Order
Dory Order
Eel Order
Flagfin Order
Flatfish Order
Gar Order
Gulper Eel Order
Herring Order
Killifish Order
Lanternfish Order
Mail-cheeked Order
Mullet Order
Needlefish Order
Opah Order
Perch Order
Pike Order
Pricklefish Order
Puffer Order
Salmon Order
Silverside Order
Smelt Order
Stickleback Order
Sturgeon Order
Tarpon Order
Toadfish Order
Trout-perch Order
Widemouth Order

Bony-tongue Order

The Bony-tongue Order or Osteoglossi- formes contains 6 families and about 206 species mostly in tropical fresh waters of South America, southeast Asia, Africa, Australia and New Guinea. There are 2 Canadian species. Tropical members include the freshwater butterflyfish, the featherbacks, knifefishes and elephantfishes, well-known in the aquarium trade, as well as the bony- tongues for which the order is named.

The order is characterised by a diversity in body form masking a series of relating internal features. The latter include the parasphenoid bone in the mouth roof and the tongue usually having well-developed teeth — hence the name of the order since these teeth are the ones used mainly in biting although there are jaw teeth; a gut coil which lies on the left of the oesophagus and stomach while in most other jawed **vertebrates** it lies on the right; paired, usually bony rods at the base of the second gill arch (not bony in the **Mooneye Family**); 1–2 pyloric caeca; 3–17 branchiostegal rays; a caudal fin with no more than 16 branched rays; a caudal fin skeleton usually with a large first ural centrum and no urodermal bones (the **Mooneye Family** is the exception); scales large, cycloid and with a complex, reticulate pattern of radii; epineural bones are present; no supramaxilla bone in the upper jaw; the nasal capsule is rigid without a mechanism to pump water over the odour-sensitive tissues; and no epipleural intermuscular bones.

Fossils date back to the Upper Jurassic.

Some tropical members of this order can transmit and detect weak electrical charges, enabling them to find each other and food at night in turbid waters. Most species are small but some are large and 1 species, the pirarucú of South America, is one of the largest freshwater fishes reaching 2.5 m. Some species are sport fishes and a number are used locally as food.

See **Mooneye Family**

bottlelight

Scientific name: *Danaphos oculatus*
    Garman, 1899
Family: **Silver Hatchetfish**
Other common names: none
French name: danaphe

Distribution: First reported from Canada in 1986 off the Pacific coast. Found in the Pacific and Indian oceans.

Characters: The body shape is elongate, not hatchet-shaped. There are no light organs at the chin. The eye is tubular and directed upwards. The dorsal fin is in front of the midpoint of the body and the adipose fin is poorly developed and can be absent. Dorsal fin rays 6, anal rays 24–25. Gill rakers 13–15. There are 9–10 branchiostegal rays. Preserved fish have darkly-edged, silvery photophores, a yellowish body and patches of radiating lines as

pigment spots in series along the upper flank. The rear half of the head and belly appears black from the gill cavity and photophore linings. Reaches 5.7 cm.

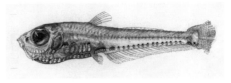

bottlelight

Biology: Very little is known. This species is usually found at 183–914 m.

bouncer headlightfish

Scientific name: *Diaphus metopoclampus*
    (Cocco, 1829)
Family: **Lanternfish**
Other common names: none
French name: lampe-de-tête de casseur

Distribution: Found in the Atlantic, Indian and Pacific oceans including off Nova Scotia.

Characters: This species and its relatives, the **flashlight**, **eventooth**, **square**, **straightcheek**, and **Taaning's headlightfishes** and the **doormat** and **slanteye parkinglightfishes**, are separated from other Atlantic

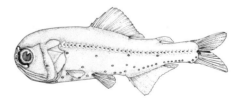

bouncer headlightfish

coast lanternfishes by not having photophores near the dorsal body edge, the PLO photophore is well above the upper pectoral fin base level while the second PVO photophore is at or below this level, there are 4 Prc photophores, the PO and two PVO photophores form a straight, ascending line as do the first 3 VO photophores, supracaudal luminous glands are absent, and there is more than 1 pair of luminous head organs. This species is separated from its relatives by having the So photophore absent, vomer with a small, round to oval patch of teeth on each side, Dn photophore well-developed in a deep cup, directed forward and equal to or larger than the nasal rosette, Vn photophore extending under eye to behind midpupil level, head depth is almost equal to head length and body photophores are small. Dorsal fin rays 14–16, anal rays 14–16 and pectoral rays 10–11. Total gill rakers 22–26. AO photophores 11–13. Lateral line organs 36–37. The "headlights" or Dn, Vn and Ant photophores are large and in contact and are distinguishable at 2.2 cm body length. Reaches 7.9 cm.

Biology: This is a temperate and partly subtropical species. Depth distribution in the Atlantic Ocean is 375–850 m by day with maximum abundance at about 500 m, and 90–850 m by night with maximum abundance at 200–250 m. Some fish of all sizes do not migrate. Life span is at least 2 years. Sexually mature at 4.8 cm with spawning occurring over a short period in spring or summer. This headlightfish is food for **swordfish** in the western North Atlantic Ocean.

bowfin

Scientific name: *Amia calva*
    Linnaeus, 1766
Family: **Bowfin**
Other common names: dogfish, mudfish, mud pike, grindle, grinnell, griddle, spot-tail, lawyer, cottonfish, blackfish, speckled cat, scaled ling, beaverfish, cypress trout, poisson de marais, choupique
French name: poisson-castor

Distribution: Found from the St. Lawrence and Lake Champlain drainage of southern Québec westward around the Great Lakes in southern Ontario as far as Minnesota. In the south it reaches Florida and Texas.

Characters: The gular plate, a large bony structure between the lower jaws on the underside of the head, identifies this freshwater fish. The dorsal fin has 42–53 soft rays, the anal fin 9–12 rays and the pectoral fin 16–18 rays. There are 62–70 scales in a complete lateral line. The anterior nostrils have a barbel-like flap.

The back is a dark-olive or brownish with the flanks mottled, marbled or reticulated with olive and yellow. The belly varies from white to light green. The dorsal fin is dark olive with 2 dark broken stripes, the anal, pelvic and pectoral fins are bright green. Males have an eye spot at the upper caudal fin base. The spot is dark and about twice as large as the eye and is surrounded by an orange or yellow halo. This spot is absent in females. Such eyespots are used to deflect the attack of predators from the eye to the less important tail, which may well give the predator a slap in the face! The anal, pectoral and pelvic fins have orange bases and tips in males. Young fish are lighter overall and have a black margin to the dorsal and caudal fins. There is a narrow stripe from the snout through the eye onto the opercle. Young smaller than 3–4 cm are black. Bowfin refers to the long, undulating dorsal fin.

bowfin

Attains 109 cm. The world, all-tackle record from Florence, South Carolina in 1980 weighed 9.75 kg. The Canadian record, 6.16 kg, was taken from Whitefish Lake, Ontario by Thomas Heinze in 1989.

Biology: Bowfins prefer warm quieter waters with a lot of vegetation. They can survive temperatures up to 35°C in stagnant waters which other predatory fish cannot utilise. Bowfins can aestivate for short periods in a moist chamber, 20 cm in diameter and 10 cm below the soil surface when flood waters recede.

Food is mainly other fishes, with some crayfishes and frogs, taken at night after moving into shallower water. The bowfin feeds by a rapid lunge, opening the mouth to suck in the prey. The opening and closing of the mouth takes about 0.075 seconds.

Life span may exceed 30 years. Males are smaller than females and probably do not live as long. Bowfins become sexually mature at 3–5 years of age when they are about 61 cm (females) and 45.7 cm (males). Growth is rapid with some fish exceeding 20 cm in the first year of life.

This species spawns from April to June depending on latitude. Nests are constructed by the male in shallow (usually less than 1.5 m), weedy areas of lakes and rivers. The nests are under logs or other objects, or are circular areas up to 76 cm across where all vegetation has been bitten off and removed. The male defends his nest against other males and during the spawning season torn fins are not unusual.

Spawning takes place at 16–19°C when the male entices a female into the nest, circles her for 10–15 minutes while she lies on the bottom of the nest, and nips her snout and flanks. The male then lies with the female, their fins vibrate rapidly and eggs and sperm are released within a minute. This may happen 4–5 times over 1–2 hours. Several females may spawn with one male and each female may deposit eggs in more than one nest. Eggs number up to 64,000 in females but number up to 5000 in nests. They stick to the plant roots or gravel in the bottom of the nest. The male guards the eggs and fans them with his pectoral fins. Eggs are 2.8 × 2.2 mm in dimensions. The eggs hatch in 8–10 days and the young use an adhesive snout organ to attach to vegetation for a further 7–9 days while the yolk-sac is absorbed. The male continues to guard and herd the young fry until they are about 10 cm long. The fry form into a ball which follows the male. So defensive are males, that one attempted to attack a human standing on the bank, coming 20 cm or so out of the water and repeating the attack several times.

The bowfin is a good sport fish on light tackle, but is seldom fished for. Some are taken by spearing while diving. It is edible, though not particularly tasty, and some commercial catches in Ontario have been sent to the United States where it is a more familiar food fish and better appreciated. "Cajun caviar" is made out of the roe in Louisiana. Small bowfins are excellent aquarium fish because of their "lung", colouration and predatory habits.

- Most accessible June through August.
- The shorelines and tributaries of the St. Lawrence River and the Great Lakes.
- Medium action spinning and baitcasting outfits used with 14– to 20–pound test line.
- Bowfin will strike most lures or bait.

Bowfin Family

Scientific name: Amiidae
French name: poissons-castors

The bowfin is found in fresh waters of eastern North America and is the only member of its family. Fossil amiids are known world-wide and the oldest are of Jurassic age, 135–195 million years ago. Eocene amiids have been described from British Columbia, Palaeocene and Cretaceous ones from Alberta and Palaeocene and Oligocene ones from Saskatchewan. The genus *Amia* has been extant for 70 million years; evolutionary change is very slow.

The general body form of a bowfin is unmistakeable. In addition there is a large bony structure on the underside of the head between the lower jaws known as a gular plate. Branchiostegal rays number 10–13. There are no pyloric caeca. The caudal fin is an abbreviate heterocercal one. Heterocercal tails have the vertebral column turned upwards into the upper lobe of the fin, which is longer than the lower lobe. In the bowfin, the lobes are not noticeably different in size. Scales are cycloid but are reinforced with ganoin. Some teeth are pointed canines while others are peg-like. Gill rakers are reduced to knobs but bear small spines.

The bowfin's relationships to other fishes have long been discussed and large monographs have been written on the details of its anatomy. It is, in a sense, a living fossil, since many related families and species were widespread in the Jurassic and Cretaceous periods, but the bowfin is the only surviving representative. Unlike **sturgeons**, the skeleton is bony but it has the heterocercal tail and a trace of a spiral valve. The gular plate, heavy bone plates on the head, and ganoin containing scales are also ancient characters. It is now considered to be related to the Teleostei or teleosts and with its fossil relatives is placed in the Halecomorphi which is equal in rank to the thousands of **teleost** species. It is the only living member of the **Bowfin Order**.

The bowfin swimbladder can be used as a lung since it has an opening to the gut and the internal surface is well-supplied with blood vessels. This fish can survive out of water for a day, and thrives in low oxygen waters such as stagnant swamps. Recent studies have shown that bowfins cannot aestivate like the tropical lungfishes because they cannot detoxify ammonia waste or reduce metabolism and they die after 3–5 days of air exposure.

See **bowfin**

Bowfin Order

Bowfins or Amiiformes are found in fresh waters of North America. There is only 1 living species but several families lived in the Jurassic and Cretaceous periods.

The characters of this order are summarised in the family account.

See **Bowfin Family**

Boxfish Family

Scientific name: Ostraciidae (= Ostraciontidae)
French name: coffres

Boxfishes are mainly subtropical and tropical and are found in all oceans. There are about 30 species of which 2 are rare visitors to Atlantic Canada. They are also known as cowfishes or **trunkfishes**.

This family is characterised by a body enclosed in a bony box or carapace with the mouth, nostrils, eyes, gill slits, anus, fins and tail protruding. The carapace is made of firmly linked hexagonal plates. The gill cover cannot move so to compensate and facilitate breathing, the floor of the mouth can be raised and lowered. The constant movement of the pectoral fins also helps remove oxygen-poor water from the gills. The gill slit is small. There are no pelvic fins and also no pelvic skeleton, unlike the related **Filefish Family**. There is no spiny dorsal fin and both the dorsal and anal fins have 9–13 rays. There is no lateral line. There are about 10 teeth in each jaw. The eyes can move independently.

Boxfishes are usually identified by the shape of the box and the position of spines. Colour tends to be very variable between males and females. The family is a member of the **Puffer Order**.

Some species emit a toxin from the mouth membranes called ostracitoxin, which can kill other fishes when in an enclosed space, like an aquarium, but is not as harmful to themselves.

Boxfishes are found swimming slowly by sculling with the dorsal, anal and caudal fins around rocks and coral reefs, in open areas and in seagrass beds. They can also swim in tight circles, hardly changing their body position. They feed on worms and other invertebrates by blowing water from their mouth to wash away concealing sand on the sea floor. They have been used as food and are considered a delicacy in the Caribbean area. Dried boxfishes are sold as ornaments. The carapace is often colourful.

See **rough trunkfish**
     smooth trunkfish

brassy minnow

Scientific name: *Hybognathus hankinsoni*
     Hubbs in Hubbs and Greene, 1929
Family: **Carp**
Other common names: grass minnow,
     Hankinson's minnow
French name: méné laiton

Distribution: Found in southwestern Québec, southern Ontario, western but not northern or eastern Lake Superior drainages, southwestern Manitoba, Milk River basin of southwestern Saskatchewan and southeastern Alberta, the Peace River basin in northwestern Alberta and the Athabasca River basin in northeastern Alberta, and in the lower and upper Fraser River and the upper Peace River in British Columbia. In the U.S.A. from New York to Montana and south to Kansas.

Characters: This species resembles the **shiners** (genus *Notropis*) but has an elongate intestine which has coils on the right, and a subterminal mouth. It is distinguished from its relatives, the **eastern** and **western silvery minnows**, by the rounded dorsal fin, brassy colour and 14–20 radii on scales in the adult. Dorsal fin branched rays 6–7, usually 7, anal branched rays 5–8, usually 7, pectoral rays 13–15 and pelvic rays 8. Lateral line scales 35–41. Pharyngeal teeth 4–4 with a flat, oblique grinding surface. Males have breeding tubercles on rays 2–8 of the pectoral fin in multiple rows (5 or more distally).

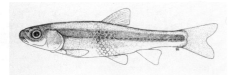

brassy minnow

The back is olive-green to brown with a brassy sheen, the flanks are brassy to dull silvery and the belly cream-white. There is a midflank stripe which is best developed from below the dorsal fin posteriorly. Scales above the stripe are darkly outlined and form 2 indistinct, zig-zag stripes. There is a middorsal stripe on the back. Dorsal, anal and caudal fins are yellowish and rays are outlined by dark pigment. The dorsal fin membranes are lightly spotted. The anterior pectoral and pelvic fin rays are outlined with dark pigment and the rest of these fins is clear. Breeding males become more brassy and fins take on a brassy tinge. Peritoneum jet black to dusky black. Reaches 9.7 cm total length.

Biology: Brassy minnows are found in dark, acidic ponds, shallow lakes and small, slow streams which have silt bottoms. Such areas have few or no predators. Food is bottom ooze for the algae, bacteria, protozoa and minute crustaceans, and some aquatic insects. Up to 94% of the food is the algae, such as diatoms and desmids. Plankton may also be taken. Feeding occurs in schools with a peak at 1–3 p.m. in one study. Maturity may be attained at 1–2 years with some fish reaching 5 years of age. Spawning probably takes place in May-July in Canada in marshy areas. Eggs are shed on silt bottoms at 10°C or higher. Eggs are up to 0.8 mm in diameter, yellow and number 2500. In Wyoming spawning occurred between 11 a.m. and 5 p.m., peaking at 2 p.m., in and over vegetation. Males and females aggregate in schools numbering in the thousands. One to 15 males approach a female at the edge of the school and she would respond in one of two ways. She may spiral up and leap out of the water, discouraging the males, or swim to vegetation which would stimulate one or more males to press against her, quiver and release eggs and sperm. The vibrations stir up sediment. This **minnow** is used as bait in the U.S.A.

bridgelip sucker

Scientific name: *Catostomus columbianus* (Eigenmann and Eigenmann, 1893)
Family: **Sucker**
Other common names: Columbia small-scaled sucker
French name: meunier de l'ouest

Distribution: Found in the Columbia and Fraser river basins of British Columbia, Washington, Oregon, Idaho and Nevada.

Characters: This sucker is identified by having 87–130 lateral line scales, an incompletely cleft lower lip and 2–5 rows of papillae on the upper lip. The mouth is overhung a little by the snout. Cartilaginous jaw edges can be seen in the open mouth. The lower lip has 2–5 rows of papillae between the cleft and the mouth. Pharyngeal teeth are flat and comb-like. Gill rakers 58 or more. The gut is long with 6–14 loops anteriorly. Breeding males have tubercles on the rear half of the body and on the anal and lower caudal fins. Dorsal fin rays 11–14, anal rays 7, pectoral rays about 17 and pelvic rays 10–11. The inner pelvic rays are connected to the body by fleshy stays. The back and top of the head

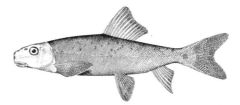

bridgelip sucker

are dark brown to olive-green, the flanks mottled pale brown fading to yellow or white on the belly. The lateral line is pale. Breeding males have an orange to red flank stripe. Females may also have this stripe. Young fish may have 3 flank blotches. The peritoneum is black. Reaches 38.1 cm.

Biology: This species is usually found in fast-flowing streams but also occurs in larger rivers and lakes. It lives in deeper, faster water than the **largescale sucker** during the day but occurs with that species in shallow waters at night. Food is probably algae and associated invertebrates scraped from rocks judging by the long gut, sharp jaw edges and black peritoneum. Maturity is attained at about 12–13 cm. Spawning occurs in June in Canada, April–May in Washington. Eggs reach 2.8 mm. It hybridises with the **largescale sucker**.

bridle shiner

Scientific name: *Notropis bifrenatus*
　(Cope, 1869)
Family: **Carp**
Other common names: none
French name: méné d'herbe

Distribution: Found only in Lake Ontario and the upper St. Lawrence River to Trois-Rivières in Canada, and south to South Carolina in the U.S.A.

Characters: This species and its relatives in the genus *Notropis* (typical **shiners**) are separated from other family members by usu-

bridle shiner

ally having 7 branched dorsal fin rays following thin unbranched rays, protractile premaxillaries (upper lip separated from the snout by a groove), no barbels, large lateral line scales (fewer than 50), and a simple, s-shaped gut. It is separated from its relatives by having 5–7, usually 6, branched anal fin rays, a flank stripe extending onto the snout but not the chin, and an incomplete lateral line with up to 17 scales pored. Dorsal fin branched rays 6–7, pectoral rays 11–14 and pelvic rays 7–8. Pharyngeal teeth 4–4. Scales in lateral series

31–37. Males have small nuptial tubercles on the head top and sides, nape and pectoral fin rays 1–6 in a shagreen-like layer. The back is yellowish, the flanks silvery and the belly silver-white. Upper flank scales are outlined with dark pigment. Fins are clear. Breeding males are yellow to gold below the black flank stripe and both sexes have yellowish dorsal, anal and caudal fin rays. Male pectoral fin rays and dorsal scale margins are a darker brown than in females. Peritoneum silvery and speckled. Reaches 5.0 cm.

Biology: Bridle shiners prefer weedy areas with silt and sand bottoms and clear, warm water. They occur in brackish waters in the U.S.A. Food is various aquatic insects and planktonic crustaceans taken by sight during the day. Some molluscs, mites and plant material are also eaten. Life span is about 2 years and maturity is attained at 1 year of age. Spawning occurs from May to August in groups of a few females and many males. Some authors report spawning near the surface after a pursuit. In still waters males nose the vent of a female. Several males will chase a single female and at the end of the pursuit the female is flanked by 1–2 males. Only a few eggs are laid at a time and there are many pursuits during each day. Water temperatures in New Hampshire were 14–27°C during the spawning season. Eggs mature through the long spawning season, reaching about 0.8 mm before being shed into dense weed beds. A female may have up to 2110 eggs.

brindled madtom

Scientific name: *Noturus miurus*
　Jordan, 1877
Family: **Bullhead Catfish**
Other common names: brindled stone cat
French name: chat-fou tacheté

Distribution: Found from southern Lake Ontario drainages of New York and southward west of the mountains in the Mississippi River basin. Only in southwestern Ontario in Canada in Lake St. Clair and Lake Erie tributaries and in the Niagara River.

Characters: This species is identified by the posterior tip of the adipose fin not being free but attached to the back, pectoral spine usually curved, scimitar-like with small anterior and large posterior teeth, posterior teeth recurved towards spine base, colour pattern of dark blotches or saddles on the back, caudal fin rays 54–65 (typically 57 or more), one internasal pore, dark blotch on adipose fin extending to margin, anterior of dorsal fin black-tipped, no dark midcaudal band, and eye diameter enters 1.1–1.8 times in snout length. Dorsal fin rays 5–7, usually 6, anal rays 13–17, pectoral rays 7–9, usually 8, and pelvic rays 8–10, usually 9. Spawning males develop bulging cheeks and head muscles, a broadened and flattened head, and the bases of the upper jaw barbels thicken.

brindled madtom

The body colour is whitish, yellow, brown, orange-red, or pinkish with 3–4 saddles across the back. The flanks are mottled and the belly white to yellowish. The upper flank is variously blotched. Barbels are lightly coloured or speckled. The dorsal fin has a dusky base and a blotch near the margin. The caudal fin margin and its junction with the caudal peduncle have a black ring internally lined with white. The anal, pelvic and pectoral fins have a blotch submarginally. Reaches 13.2 cm.

Biology: Found in clear, rapid-current streams over gravel but most common in pools over mud and sand bottoms with leaves and twigs. Also in lakes where the bottom is sand, stone and debris and wave action is light. Food is aquatic insects and crustaceans taken at night. Life span is 3 years and males are mature at 2 years, some females at 1 year. Spawning occurs at 24–27°C, in June to August and late at night. Large, amber eggs are deposited in a nest under flat rocks (or preferentially in pop-top beer cans!). The male guards the eggs which number up to 81 in each nest. Each female produces up to 143 eggs, each up to 3.8 mm in diameter. The pectoral fin spine has toxic tissue and can inflict a nasty sting. This madtom was classed as "rare" in 1985 by the Committee on the Status of Endangered Wildlife in Canada.

Bristlemouth Family

Scientific name: Gonostomatidae
French name: cyclothones

Bristlemouths, lightfishes or anglemouths are found in all seas including the Arctic and Antarctic oceans. There are about 26 species with 7 reported from Canada's Atlantic coast, 1 from the Arctic and Atlantic coasts, 4 from the Pacific coast and 1 from the Atlantic and Pacific coasts, for a total of 13.

These fishes have an elongate body with or without an adipose fin. Photophores, or light organs, are present in a regular row along the belly, on the branchiostegals and variably on the isthmus. These are black-rimmed. Photophores emit red or green light. The mouth is large, with long jaws reaching back behind the eye at an angle, and is armed with bristle-like teeth. There are no barbels. The black skin and cycloid scales are often rubbed off during capture. It is rare that a bristlemouth is captured in good condition because they are so fragile. Identification is often difficult as a result. Some bristlemouths are almost transparent. Males have larger olfactory organs than females.

Bristlemouths are related to the **Silver Hatchetfish Family**, with which they share photophores in a row with a lumen or duct, true gill rakers and small, mostly equal-sized jaw teeth. Photophore patterns are important in identification and scientists have worked out a system of abbreviations to simplify their description. This family is a member of the **Widemouth Order**.

Bristlemouths are probably the most abundant fishes in the world in terms of numbers of individuals. However they are deepsea fishes and are usually seen only by scientists. Adults and young are found between 200 and 300 m by day. Small fish are shallower than larger fish. Larvae are near the surface but sink as they develop. They are an important food for other fishes. Some bristlemouths do not migrate and their swimbladder is poorly developed. Others are partial or daily vertical migrants. They feed on various crustaceans and fry of other fishes and their own family members.

See **bluntnose bristlemouth**
bonaparte
longtooth anglemouth
ribbon bristlemouth
showy bristlemouth
slender bristlemouth
slender fangjaw
spark anglemouth
spottail anglemouth
tan bristlemouth
veiled anglemouth
white bristlemouth
yellow bristlemouth

broad skate

Scientific name: *Raja badia* Garman, 1899
Family: **Skate**
Other common names: grande raie
French name: raie large

Distribution: Found from British Columbia to Panama.

Characters: This species is distinguished from Canadian Pacific relatives by having a rigid snout with its cartilaginous support

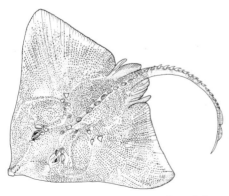

broad skate

thick and stiff, cartilaginous supports of the pectoral fin do not reach the snout tip, enlarged thornlets on the snout tip, 2–3 pairs of scapular (= shoulder) spines, and ventral surface smooth. There are 24–29 thorns along midline of body and tail. The upper

jaw has 37–42 rows of curved teeth. The upper disc is grey-brown to chocolate brown with dark spots and blotches. The lower surface of the disc is the same colour as the upper surface. There is a brown bar over the shoulder region. The snout, disc margins and pelvic fin tip are dark. The lower tail surface is dark. Mouth, gill slits, cloaca and nostrils are whitish. Reaches 98.5 cm.

Biology: This species is rarely caught with only 6 specimens known from the eastern Pacific Ocean. Depth range is 1280–2322 m. The Canadian record is from off southern Vancouver Island at 1920 m in a **sablefish** trap.

broad whitefish

Scientific name: *Coregonus nasus*
(Pallas, 1776)
Family: **Salmon**
Other common names: round-nosed whitefish, sheep-nosed whitefish, tezra, tizareh, anaklek, an-ark-hlirk, anah'lih', aanaaksiiq
French name: corégone tschir

Distribution: Found in Siberia and north-western North America from Bering and Beaufort sea coastal waters and tributary rivers including the Yukon River as far as extreme northern British Columbia, the Coppermine River and the Mackenzie River, and as far east as the Perry River on Queen Maud Gulf, N.W.T., not reaching as far south as the prairie provinces (i.e. below 60°N).

Characters: This member of the **Salmon Family** is distinguished from its relatives by having large scales (110 or less), no parr marks, teeth absent from the jaws and roof of the mouth, forked tail fin, 2 flaps of skin between the nostrils, the mouth is under the snout, the premaxilla bone of the upper jaw curves backward, the adjacent maxilla bone is less than twice as long as wide, the gill rakers are short and number 18–25, and lower fins are opaque and bluish. The snout is blunt, hence the various common names. There are weak teeth on the tongue. Dorsal fin rays 10–13, anal rays 11–14, pectoral rays 16–17 and pelvic rays 11–12. Lateral line scales 84–102. Pyloric caeca 148. Nuptial tubercles are best developed in males on the flanks.

The back is black, brown or olive-brown, the flanks silvery sometimes with grey or brown, and the belly silvery-white to yellowish. Scales are outlined in black. The sides of the head are brown with light spotting. Fins

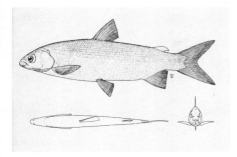

broad whitefish

are grey to dusky. The pectoral and anal fins may have blue to purple iridescences. Females develop a white first ray in the pectoral fin during the breeding season. Reaches 71 cm and 16 kg in Siberia, much smaller in Canada.

Biology: This **whitefish** is found principally in rivers but also occurs in lakes (as far south as Teslin Lake, B.C.) and enters brackish coastal waters. Populations on the Tuktoyaktuk Peninsula overwinter in lakes and the inshore zone of the Mackenzie River delta. Food is aquatic insect larvae, molluscs and crustaceans. Life span is up to 35 years and maturity is attained at about 7 years. Spawning occurs in October-November after a spawning migration and at water temperatures near 0°C. Some reports have spawning occurring in July and August. Repeat spawning occurs in subsequent years. Eggs are a pale yellow. Broad whitefish are caught locally by gill net for human and dog food. It may be eaten fresh, dried or smoked and is reputedly very good eating.

broadfin lanternfish

Scientific name: *Lampanyctus ritteri*
    Gilbert, 1915
Family: **Lanternfish**
Other common names: none
French name: lampe à grandes nageoires

Distribution: Found from off Vancouver Island south to Baja California and at Ocean Station Papa (50°N, 145°W).

Characters: This species is separated from other Pacific coast lanternfishes by having 4 Prc photophores, the fourth PO photophore is elevated above the others, 2 Pol photophores, the SAO series is angled, and there are scale-like, luminous caudal glands. It is distinguished from its relatives, the **brokenline** and **pinpoint lanternfishes** by the short, narrow-based pectoral fin, photophores not small, and the VLO photophore is on a line from SAO photophores 1 and 2. The third SAO photophore is well behind the anal fin origin. Dorsal fin rays 12–15, anal rays 16–19, pectoral rays 10–13, and vertebrae 35–38. Total gill rakers 13–15 and AO photophores 14–17. Lateral line scales 37–38. The mouth and gill cavities are black and the dusky fins bear wavy lines. Reaches about 19 cm.

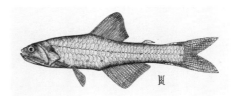

broadfin lanternfish

Biology: Caught only at night at 60 m from the Canadian weathership and off the British Columbia coast at various depths. Elsewhere as deep as 1375 m. Food is arrow worms, crustaceans and small fishes.

broadgill cat shark

Scientific name: *Apristurus riveri*
    Bigelow and Schroeder, 1944
Family: **Cat Shark**
Other common names: none
French name: holbiche grandes oreilles

Distribution: Found in the western North Atlantic Ocean including off Atlantic Canada.

Characters: This species is distinguished from its Atlantic coast relatives by lacking a crest over the eye, by the first dorsal fin being much smaller than the second and by up to 4 rows of pores along the undersurface of the snout. The caudal fin lacks a well-developed crest of denticles. Teeth number 24 to 29 on each side of the upper jaw and 19 to 22 on each side of the lower jaw. Female and young male teeth bear 3 smooth-edged cusps, the central cusp the longest. Adult males have a single, conical cusp. Flank denticles have slightly erect cusps so the skin is fuzzy to touch. Colour is an overall dark brown. The gill slits may have black skin without denticles. Egg cases are a translucent greenish with faint lighter or darker bands and measure about 5.5 cm by 1.3 cm. Attains 48 cm.

broadgill cat shark

Biology: This cat shark is found on or near the bottom of the continental slopes from 860 to 1098 m. Adult males are 43–46 cm and females 40–41 cm. Males have larger teeth than females. The mouth is longer and wider in males too. These are thought to be adaptations for grasping females during courtship. It is an oviparous species and one egg is laid at a time from each oviduct.

broadnose worm eel

Scientific name: *Myrophis platyrhynchus*
  Breder, 1927
Family: **Snake Eel**
Other common names: none
French name: serpenton à nez plat

Distribution: Found from Brazil and the Caribbean Sea north to the Atlantic coast of Canada.

Characters: Larvae have 140–149 total myomeres (muscle blocks) with 6 spots below the midline, with spots 2–6 on the tail, and a spot at the base of each anal ray. Nephric myomeres 49–54 and predorsal myomeres 21–27. In adults, the dorsal fin origin lies midway between the snout tip and anus, further forward than in the related **speckled worm eel**, and there are 2 postorbital pores. Also the body is more compressed and the snout is flatter. The tail tip is flexible and has fin rays and the pectoral fin is well developed. Adults are pale overall, with fine dark spots over the back and

flanks. The belly and lower flank anterior to the anus are not spotted. Adults attain 20.8 cm and larvae 85 mm.

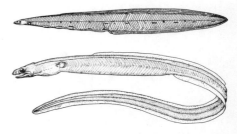

broadnose worm eel

Biology: Known only from a single stray larva (or leptocephalus), 66 mm long, taken at 186 m and first reported in 1988. Adults are found in shallow water in bays and creeks as well as down to 220 m.

brokenline lanternfish

Scientific name: *Lampanyctus jordani*
  Gilbert, 1913
Family: **Lanternfish**
Other common names: none
French name: lanterne à ligne brisée

Distribution: Found from Japan to California and at Ocean Station Papa (50°N, 145°W).

Characters: This species is separated from other Pacific coast lanternfishes by having 4 Prc photophores, the fourth PO photophore is elevated above the others, 2 Pol photophores, the SAO series is angled, and there are scalelike, luminous caudal glands. It is distinguished from its relatives, the **broadfin** and

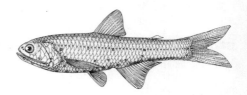

brokenline lanternfish

pinpoint lanternfishes by the long, broad-based pectoral fin. Dorsal fin rays 10–14, anal rays 16–20, pectoral rays 14–17, and vertebrae 37–40. Total gill rakers 20–25 and AO photophores 14–18. Reaches 14 cm.

Biology: First recorded in 1981 from the Canadian weathership Ocean Station Papa below about 500 m down to 1300 m. Elsewhere reported to rise to 200 m at night, and rarely the surface.

bronze-green flagfin

Scientific name: *Bathophilus vaillanti*
(Zugmayer, 1911)
Family: **Barbeled Dragonfish**
Other common names: none
French name: étendard vert-bronzé

Distribution: Found in the North Atlantic Ocean including from off the Scotian Shelf in the west and south to the Bahamas.

Characters: This species is distinguished from its Canadian Atlantic relatives by the dorsal and anal fin bases being about the same length and the pelvic fins are near the midline of the flank. Dorsal fin rays 13–16, anal rays

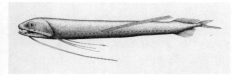

bronze-green flagfin

14–17. Pectoral fin rays are 3–5, usually 3. Pelvic fin rays are 4–6, usually 5. Photophores between the pectoral and pelvic fin insertions number 12–14. The barbel can be longer than the fish when unbroken. Overall colour is black with iridescent blue or green tinges.

Biology: Caught occasionally at 200–300 m off the Scotian Shelf over deep water. Known to eat **lanternfish**.

brook silverside

Scientific name: *Labidesthes sicculus*
(Cope, 1865)
Family: **Silverside**
Other common names: skipjack, topwater, friar, glassfish
French name: crayon d'argent

Distribution: Found from the Ottawa River and upper St. Lawrence River across southern Ontario to Georgian Bay and Lake Huron west to Minnesota, south to Gulf of Mexico drainages and Florida.

Characters: This is the only freshwater family member in Canada and is easily recognised by the short, spiny, centrally placed first

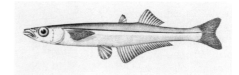

brook silverside

dorsal fin and longer soft second dorsal fin, both over a long anal fin. First dorsal fin spines 3–6, second dorsal fin with 1 spine and 9–13 soft rays. Anal fin with 1 spine and 20–27 soft rays and pectoral rays 12–13. There are 74–95 scales in lateral series, only a few of them pored. There are 24–29 long gill rakers. Overall translucent with some internal organs visible. Preserved fish are opaque. The back is pale green to olive or yellowish, the flank has an iridescent silvery stripe outlined by a black stripe above. The belly is white or silvery. Scales on the back are outlined with dark spots. Fins are translucent but breeding males have a black tip to the first dorsal fin. Attains 11.2 cm.

Biology: This silverside is found in surface waters in large schools in lakes and large rivers, but not brooks. The schools are not maintained through the night. Young fish avoid any solid objects perhaps as a mechanism to keep them out of shallow water where potential predators are found. The young swim with their heads touching the surface film of the water. Larger fish enter shallows. They are intolerant of turbidity.

Food is water fleas, midge larvae, other insects and plankton, and flying insects and spiders which land on the water. These items are taken with a snap and some flying insects are taken by a leap out of the water. Leaps may be up to 10 times body length. Silversides are food for many sport and other fishes.

Life span seldom reaches 2 years and most fish die after spawning a year after being born. Growth is extremely rapid, 0.4 mm per day, reaching adult size in only 3 months.

Spawning occurs in spring and summer (May–August) at 17–23°C over vegetation or gravel. Males may defend a territory against other males. Territories eventually break down. Females are pursued by 1 or more males and may leap from the water followed by the males to a height of 2–3 cm landing up to 10 cm away. When caught by a male, the 2 fish glide downward with their bellies in contact and eggs are thought to be extruded and fertilised. Orange eggs are up to 1.4 mm in diameter and have 1–3 greatly elongate, adhesive filaments to attach them to vegetation. Some are deposited on floats and anchor ropes. There are up to 785 mature eggs present in a female at any time. Silversides in Florida have internal fertilisation and sperm are transferred by a short, genital palp when ventral surfaces of a breeding pair are pressed together. Whether this occurs in northern populations is unknown.

This species has been used as bait by anglers.

brook stickleback

Scientific name: *Culaea inconstans*
   (Kirtland, 1841)
Family: **Stickleback**
Other common names: five-spined, black,
   variable, common, or six-spined stickle-
   back; pinfish
French name: épinoche à cinq épines

Distribution: Found from western Nova Scotia and New Brunswick west to northeastern British Columbia and the Mackenzie River basin. It is absent from northern Saskatchewan and Manitoba. In the U.S.A. south to Indiana and Nebraska and as a relict in New Mexico.

Characters: This species is distinguished by having 4–7 short dorsal fin spines, no obvious bony plates on the flank and all spines are smaller than the eye diameter. Soft dorsal fin rays 8–13, soft anal rays 7–12 after 1 spine, pectoral rays 9–12 and pelvic fin with 1 spine and 1 soft ray. There are 30–36 tiny plates along the midflank. Many populations in Alberta lack part or all of the pelvic girdle and fin, and various populations across

Canada show the occasional fish with reduced pelvic skeletons.

The back and flanks are olive-green, the flanks with lighter spots or short wavy lines. The belly is whitish-yellow or silvery-white. The dorsal and anal fin membranes are dusky. Breeding males are jet black, sometimes tinged with copper, and the pelvic fins have a red tinge. Females are a light green but develop a dark and light pattern when spawning. Peritoneum silvery with many melanophores. Albino brook sticklebacks are reported from artesian wells in Alberta. Reaches 8.7 cm fork length.

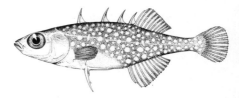

brook stickleback

Biology: Brook sticklebacks are found in small streams, bogs, ponds or lakes down to 55 m. They prefer heavy vegetation and are tolerant of low oxygen. Rare populations are reported from brackish water, for example in Hudson Bay, and they live in alkaline pothole lakes of Alberta. Tornados are reported to have picked up these sticklebacks from a stream and dropped them in a farmer's field in Alberta. However these fish do spawn in temporary steams which can dry up and this may be the origin of these stranded fish. Gas bubbles under ice in winter prolong survival of this fish since it can take advantage of a microlayer of water with higher oxygen next to the bubble. Brook sticklebacks may burrow into silt, remaining covered for more than half an hour. In some instances this behaviour is a search for food.

Food is aquatic insects, crustaceans, snails, worms, algae, sponges and fish eggs and fry including those of brook sticklebacks. In Manitoba vegetated stream margins, most feeding occurs between noon and 8:00 p.m. Feeding consists of five phases — swim, hover, aim, dart and handle. The hover or aim phases involve deciding whether to eat or reject the item seized. "Food fighting" occurs, especially under crowded conditions. Large food items are shaken apart and this causes up to 7 sticklebacks to compete for large food fragments. This process establishes a hierarchy among the fish.

These sticklebacks are eaten by a variety of other fishes, leeches, birds, shrews, muskrats, and large larvae of water beetles and dragonflies. Pelvic spines protect against fish predators by increasing the size of mouth which can handle them. However water beetles seem to favour eating those sticklebacks with pelvic spines and are less successful at grasping spineless fish. This may be due to the closer approaches to the predator made by spiny fish; those lacking spines are more wary. Fish without spines compensate by a changed behaviour, perhaps taking more advantage of vegetation as shelter.

Life span is 3 years at most and fish mature at 1 year. Most populations are annual fish which die after spawning in their second summer. Spawning takes place from April to August at 4.5–21°C, usually at 8°C or warmer. Spawning is later in the north than the south.

Males arrive on the spawning ground before females and build and defend nests. Ritualised displays against other males involve swimming parallel head to head or head to tail, fluttering their bodies and with spines erected. This is often followed by a quick attack. Males darken during this display and attack and develop black bands through their eyes.

The nest is built on stems of vegetation near, or more rarely on, the bottom using dead and living fragments of vegetation, glued together with the white kidney secretions. The nest is a round barrel, up to 5.0 cm in diameter with a single opening. The male courts a female with nips, nudges and butts. Once she enters the nest he stimulates egg laying by prodding her belly and caudal peduncle. Eggs are yellow, adhesive and about 1.3 mm in diameter. Females produce on average up to 1926 eggs in a season in Manitoba, spawning 214 eggs every 3 days for 28 days. The female leaves the nest by pushing out, creating an exit hole which the male tries to repair. The female is driven away by the male. As more females are induced to spawn he enlarges his nest. The male looks after the eggs by fanning them with his pectoral fins. The young are also defended until they leave the nest.

This species has occasionally been used for bait in Québec.

brook trout

Scientific name: *Salvelinus fontinalis* (Mitchill, 1814)
Family: **Salmon**
Other common names: speckled trout, brook char, eastern brook trout, brookie, square-tail, sea trout, salter, redspotted trout, mud trout, slob, coaster, harness trout, native trout, mountain trout, speck, whitefin, truite mouchetée, truite de mer, iqaluk tasirsiutik, anokik, anuk, aanak, anakleq, aanaatlik, a na, i ha luk, âna
French name: omble de fontaine

Distribution: Found from the shores of Hudson Bay and Labrador south in marine waters to Cape Cod in the east and Georgia in the Appalachian Mountains, west through all the Maritime provinces, Québec and Ontario (except the extreme west) to northeast Manitoba. Widely introduced to western Canadian provinces, the U.S.A., South America, Europe, Asia and Australasia.

Characters: This species is characterised by 109–132 lateral line scales, 8–13 anal fin principal rays, light-coloured spots on the body, teeth on the head of the vomer bone in

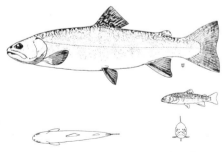

brook trout

the roof of the mouth, pectoral, pelvic and anal fins with a white leading edge followed by contrasting black, truncate caudal fin, dorsal and caudal fins have wavy, dark lines and blotches and the back has dark or light green or cream, worm-track markings (vermiculations). Dorsal fin principal rays 9–14, pectoral rays 10–15 and pelvic rays 7–10. Pyloric caeca 20–55. Spawning males develop a hooked lower jaw or kype.

The back is olive-green to dark brown or blackish fading to a silvery-white belly. Flanks have a red to yellow tint. Flank spots are pale but there are also small, red spots with blue halos. The pectoral, pelvic and anal fins are yellow, orange, or reddish behind the white and black leading edges. Sea run fish have a blue-green back and silvery flanks with a purplish tinge. Spots are obscured except for the red ones. Brook trout in large lakes are also more silvery than stream resident fish. The jaw tips and the roof of the mouth are blackish. Spawning males are much brighter in overall colour and have an orange-red lower flank and upper belly, bordered below by black on each side which delimits the white belly. Young have 6–12 brown parr marks, the widest equal to eye diameter, and small red, yellow or blue flank spots. The white leading edge to the lower fins is apparent.

Hybrids with **bull trout** are known from Alberta. Northern and southern populations within North America may be distinct subspecies based on genetic and biochemical studies. Attains a reputed 86.0 cm but most are smaller. The world, all-tackle angling record was caught in the Nipigon River, Ontario in July 1916 by W.J. Cook and weighed 6.57 kg. This catch is also recognized as the Canadian record.

Biology: Brook trout are found in cool waters of streams and lakes, usually less than 20°C. Pools, underneath banks, under overhanging bushes or behind rocks are favoured spots. During summer months they retreat to deeper water, to about 8 m, in lakes. Some populations (salters) run to sea in Hudson Bay and Atlantic Canada. They stay in coastal waters, not moving more than a few kilometres from their natal stream. Populations in the Great Lakes live and feed mostly in the lake and run up natal streams to spawn. They are known as "coasters."

Food includes aquatic and terrestrial insects, molluscs, various fishes, frogs, salamanders and even snakes, mice, voles and shrews. Stream-dwelling fish feed heavily on drifting aquatic organisms during spring run-off but in summer as drift decreases surface insects become important. Most feeding occurs in the early morning and late evening although some food is taken throughout the day. Diet shifts in response to competition with other species. Trout feed on large, bottom invertebrates in some Québec lakes but switch to zooplankton when found with **creek chub**. Brook trout are more aggressive in groups but chub forage successfully in groups. Sea run fish take various marine invertebrates and fishes. Sea run adults in spring and summer eat crustaceans and fish in lower estuarine areas while young are in the upper estuary eating crustaceans and insects. During the fall in the river adults eat little and during winter back in the estuary consumed mostly crustaceans. There is thus a division of food resources between young and adults. Brook trout are cannibals on their eggs and young and are eaten themselves by other fishes, water snakes, turtles, various birds and otters.

Maximum life span is over 20 years but most reach only 5 years. Maturity is attained at 2–3 years, some males at 1 year. Growth is often faster than other **trout**. Stunting is common in small streams while sea run fish grow faster than freshwater ones. Optimum growth temperatures are 10–19°C.

Spawning takes place from August to December, earlier in the north and later in the south. Sea run trout enter their natal stream in spring and summer even though spawning occurs in fall. Each year they spend 1.5–3 months feeding in the sea. The spawning ground is usually gravelly streams but may be lake shoals if there is some current or spring outflow to keep eggs oxygenated. Spring flows are preferred even in streams.

Males arrive on the spawning ground first and defend a territory. Both sexes will rush at other fish entering the redd area. The female cleans a redd of debris by turning on her side and lashing her tail. Redd depth between stones is tested by inserting the anal fin. Redd construction may take up to 2 days with work being carried out both by day and night.

Courtship involves gentle pushes, touches and strokes of the female by the male. The female is ready to spawn when she crouches in the redd with her genital area between the stones. The male arches his body and may press the female against the redd bottom, both fish vibrate and eggs and sperm are shed. Accessory or sneaky males may rush in to shed sperm. The female lashes her tail to push eggs into the gravel and then dislodges gravel with her anal fin to cover the eggs to depths as great as 20 cm. Yellow-orange eggs are up to 5.0 mm in diameter and number up to perhaps 17,000 per female although averages range from the low hundreds to a few thousand. Both sexes may spawn again with other fish. The eggs develop over winter, taking 165 days at 2.8°C but only 47 days at 10°C. Temperatures above 11°C will kill the eggs.

Brook trout are very popular sport fish in eastern Canada caught on lures, live baits and flies. These **trout** are easier to catch than **brown trout** and take a wider range of lures. They fight well but are often quite small and do not leap spectacularly like some **Salmon Family** members do. Brook trout taken on baited hooks and returned to the water show 14 times the death rate of those taken on flies. Anglers wishing to conserve stocks or in search only of trophy fish are best advised to use flies. Hatcheries stock various waters with this trout, sometimes dropping them into lakes from planes.

The ready availability of this salmonid has made it a useful experimental fish for various physiological, biochemical, toxicological and other studies. Some reared stocks however show deformed or lost fins and distorted mouths.

The possibility of "sea-ranching" brook trout in Atlantic Canada has been explored by releasing stream trout in estuarine areas to improve angling. In fresh water their preference for cool and clear water makes them susceptible to loss if waters are dammed, channelised and polluted or if banks are eroded deforested and overgrazed.

• Most accessible in May and June.

• Labrador and Quebec.

• Ultralight to light action spinning outfits used with four- to eight-pound test line. Flyfishing equipment includes six- to nine-and-a-half-foot, four- to eight-weight outfits loaded with weight-forward floating line or sinking lines.

• Assortment of small 1/8– to 1/4–ounce spoons, spinners and minnow-imitating plugs and jigs. Flies include streamers, wet flies and dry flies. Worms are the most common live bait.

brotulas

There is a single species, the **red brotula**, in Canadian waters on the Pacific coast of Canada. It is a member of the **Livebearing Brotula Family**, also known as viviparous brotulas. Brotula is an Spanish-American name for a related species.

brown bullhead

Scientific name: *Ameiurus nebulosus* (Le Sueur, 1819)
Family: **Bullhead Catfish**
Other common names: northern brown bullhead, mudcat, horned pout, brown catfish, marbled bullhead, common bullhead, speckled cat, bullpout, minister, mud cat, creek cat, red cat, wooly cat, Schuylkill cat, Sacramento cat
French name: barbotte brune

Distribution: Found in southern Nova Scotia, New Brunswick and Ontario, the extreme south of Québec, Lake of the Woods, southern Manitoba and southeastern Saskatchewan. Introduced to British Columbia in the lower Fraser River and southern Vancouver Island. In the U.S.A. south to Florida and Alabama. Widely introduced elsewhere in North America and Eurasia.

Characters: This species is identified by the posterior tip of the adipose fin being free of the back, the caudal fin is not deeply forked, mouth corner barbels are about twice as long as nostril barbels, there is no bony ridge between the head and the dorsal fin, the anal fin does not touch the caudal fin when pressed to the body, all barbels are dark brown to black, pectoral spine teeth strongly developed and numbering 4–9, total anal rays usually 20–24, gill rakers 12–16, caudal fin base dusky to dark, and the dorsal fin membranes are not particularly dark. Dorsal fin soft rays 6–7, and pelvic rays 8. The dorsal fin spine has weak to absent teeth on barbs.

brown bullhead

The head, back and upper flanks are blue-black to yellow-brown or olive. There may be a violet iridescence. The flanks are lighter and may be mottled brown. The belly is yellowish to white. Fins are similar in colour to the adjacent body with some membranes darker.

Formerly in the genus *Ictalurus*. Reaches 53.2 cm. The world, all-tackle angling record weighed 2.49 kg and was caught in 1975 in Veal Pond, Georgia. The Canadian record was caught by Jeff Sereda in July 1989. It weighed 1.08 kg. and was caught in Raleigh Township, Ontario.

Biology: This bullhead lives in the shallow, weedy, warm waters of ponds, bays in lakes and river backwaters. Bottoms are usually sand or mud down to about 12 m and this fish may burrow into mud to escape poor environmental conditions. However it is tolerant of pollution, low oxygen and high temperatures (over 36°C). Their numbers can be high. In the Ottawa River below Ottawa they comprise 86% of the fish catch.

Food is taken mostly at night aided by the sensitive barbels in an opportunistic manner. It includes crustaceans, insects, worms, molluscs, algae and fishes. Bullheads also scavenge for waste and dead organisms and eat the eggs of commercially important species such as **lake trout**, although their impact on **trout** populations is probably not highly significant.

Maturity is attained mostly at age 3 and about 20–33 cm and life span is 18 years. Some females mature as early as age 2. Males grow faster than females near Montréal and the population there includes both a slower and a more rapidly growing group. Stunted populations occur in poor environments where food is lacking and temperatures are low.

Spawning occurs in May to July in Canada at a water temperature over 20°C. Southern U.S. populations may spawn twice in a year. The male and/or female, usually the latter, excavates a nest in mud, sand, among plant roots or in a burrow in a bank. Pebbles may be carried away in the mouth. The spawning pair touch and caress each others barbels and come to lie head to tail. Pale cream, adhesive eggs are shed and fertilised at intervals. Up to 13,800 eggs are recorded from 1 female.

Both parents guard, fan and manipulate the ball of eggs. Manipulation includes stirring with the barbels or fin spines and even picking up with the mouth and spitting out. Manipulation is essential for hatching. The young bullheads travel in a school for several weeks until they are about 5 cm long when they disperse. Either or both parents guard the school. These schools or catfish balls can number in the many hundreds and a ball can by walked through, parting and reforming behind one.

The flesh is red to pink and is excellent eating. Bullheads are easy to catch on worms, **minnows**, shrimps and cut meat. In the U.S.A. they are used in pond culture. There are some minor commercial catches in Canada, mostly in Ontario. The brown bullhead has been used widely as an experimental animal to study uptake of pollutants and in physiological studies.

- Most accessible in May and June.

- Marshy bays and the watershed of the Great Lakes.

- Medium action spinning and baitcasting outfits used with 10– to 14–pound test.

- The best bait is lively night crawlers.

brown cat shark

Scientific name: *Apristurus brunneus*
(Gilbert, 1892)
Family: **Cat Shark**
Other common names: brown shark,
holbiche brune
French name: roussette

Distribution: Found from southeast Alaska and British Columbia to Mexico and probably Peru.

Characters: This species is distinguished by the first dorsal fin above or behind the pelvic fins, the space between the dorsal fins is longer than the first dorsal fin base, the anal fin twice as long as the second dorsal fin and reaching the tail fin, the distance between the pectoral and pelvic fin bases is longer than the snout tip to spiracle distance, and the dorsal axis of the tail in line with the body. There are no supraorbital crests on the skull. Gill slits are small. The head is flattened, the snout elongate and usually longer than the mouth width and the labial furrows are very long. Teeth are small, fine and pointed in 3 rows in each jaw. Each tooth has 5 cusps with the central cusp the largest. The scales are small but give the skin a fuzzy texture. Overall colour is dark to medium brown with dark margins on the fins. Reaches 69 cm.

brown cat shark

Biology: Found from 33 to 1189 m but mostly from 110–369 m in British Columbia where it is common usually on the bottom but is also reported in the water column. Food is mostly shrimps, squids and small fishes. Adult males are 49–57 cm while females are 42–49 cm or larger. It is oviparous laying one egg from each oviduct at a time. Egg cases are 5.2–5.6 cm by 1.9–2.5 cm with long, coiled tendrils and are translucent brown. Eggs may incubate for a year and females carry egg cases from February to August. Young hatch at about 7 cm. It may be caught in bottom trawls, sablefish traps or on longlines but occurs too deep to be of interest to anglers.

brown cutthroat eel

Scientific name: *Ilyophis brunneus*
Gilbert, 1891
Family: **Cutthroat Eel**
Other common names: muddy arrowtooth eel,
ooze eel
French name: anguille égorgée brune

Distribution: Found world-wide but in widely-separated areas including off Atlantic Canada.

Characters: This eel is distinguished from other family members in Canada by the pointed head, large mouth reaching back

brown cutthroat eel

beyond the eye and the dorsal fin origin over the pectoral fins. Gill openings are horizontal, ventral slits. Teeth are small, recurved, and sharp and in bands on the jaws. There is a single large row of teeth on the roof of the mouth. The anterior nostril is tubular and the posterior nostril is near the eye with a raised collar. The pectoral fin is present but very small. The lateral line has 35–38 preanal pores and 4–6 prepectoral pores. Scales are minute, elongate and arranged in a "basketwork" pattern. Body colour is dark brown with violet tinges on the snout. Fins are darker and the lateral line pores are white. Reaches 61.4 cm.

Biology: First recorded from Canada in 1982 off the Scotian Shelf based on a single larval specimen taken at 995 m. Elsewhere descends to 3120 m. Adults are said to swim over the bottom searching for food but may burrow into soft sediments. Food of adults is crustaceans and clams.

brown Irish lord

Scientific name: *Hemilepidotus spinosus*
    (Ayres, 1855)
Family: **Sculpin**
Other common names: none
French name: chabot trilobé brun

Distribution: Found from the Gulf of Alaska to California including British Columbia.

Characters: This species and its relative, the **red Irish lord**, are distinguished from other Pacific coast sculpins by having 4

brown Irish lord

pelvic fin soft rays and scales in 2 bands, one below the dorsal fin and one around the lateral line. It is separated from its relative by having 6–8 dorsal scale rows and 6–8 ventral rows and branchiostegal membranes fused to the isthmus without a fold or rarely a minute one. The nasal spine is rounded, blunt and skin covered. The upper 3 of 4 preopercular spines are close together and stout. There are 2 cleithral spines above the pectoral fin base. First dorsal fin spines 10–11, second dorsal soft rays 18–20. The spiny dorsal fin is notched behind the third spine and is joined to the second dorsal fin. Anal rays 14–16 with free tips, pectoral rays 14–16 with lower 7–8 rays finger-like at their tips. Lateral line pores 57–72. Pyloric caeca 4–5. There are small nasal cirri, a large, branched cirrus over the eye, 2 small cirri on top of the head, a large cirrus on the nape, a cirrus on the operculum and preoperculum, a flap-like cirrus at the rear end of the upper jaw, a cirrus on the lower jaw and small cirri below the suborbital ridge. There are many small cirri along the lateral line some being large and white including the one near the last

pore. Overall colour is light to dark brown with red tinges on the back and 4 dark saddles. Fins are barred. Reaches 29 cm.

Biology: This sculpin occurs from the intertidal zone down to 97 m. It is not as common as its relative. It favours rocky areas with cracks and crevices and it is well camouflaged among algae.

brown peeper

Scientific name: *Physiculus fulvus*
    Bean, 1884
Family: **Mora**
Other common names: metallic codling
French name: physicule fauve

Distribution: Off the Atlantic and Gulf of Mexico coasts of North America including Canadian waters.

Characters: This species is separated from its Canadian relatives by not having a flattened snout, by having a small, dark scaleless area over a light organ in front of the anus, and by having a chin barbel. There are no teeth on the vomer bone in the roof of the mouth. First dorsal fin with 9–10 rays, second with 49–54 rays. Anal fin rays 54–61, anal fin not indented. There are 5 pelvic fin rays. Scales in lateral line about 61–62. Overall colour is a light, yellowish-brown with the lips, lower head surface, belly, pectoral fin axil and the dorsal and anal fin margins very dark brown. The operculum has a dark brown blotch and the mouth and gill cavities are white. Reaches an unknown maximum size but the original description gives 8.9 cm.

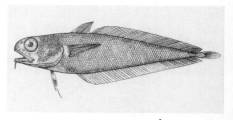

brown peeper

Biology: The only Canadian specimen was caught on Sable Island Bank in 1977, a northern record for the species. Originally described from Georges Bank in the U.S.A.

brown rockfish

Scientific name: *Sebastes auriculatus*
   Girard, 1854
Family: **Scorpionfish**
Other common names: bolina, brown rockcod
French name: sébaste brun

Distribution: Found from southeast Alaska to Baja California including British Columbia.

Characters: Body colour and the strong, prostrate coronal spine distinguish this species. Dorsal fin spines 13, soft rays 12–15,

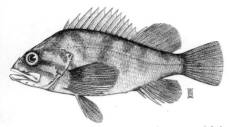

brown rockfish

usually 13. Anal fin soft rays 5–8, usually 7, second spine about twice as thick as third and about same length. Pectoral fin rays 15–19, usually 18. Gill rakers 25–30. Vertebrae 26–27, usually 26. Lateral line pores 42–50, scale rows below lateral line 45–52. All head spines except supraoculars are present, strong and lie flat. The coronals may be absent. The body is a light brown mottled with dark brown or orange-brown. Vague, dark bars may be apparent dorsally. There is an obvious brown blotch on the gill cover. The belly, anal fin and pectoral fin base are pink. The lower part of the head is pink or yellowish. Reaches 55 cm.

Biology: Found in shallow water around rocks covered in sea weed and sometimes on soft bottoms down to about 128 m. Females at 47.7 cm give birth to 339,000 young in June. It forms hybrids with the **copper rockfish**. Brown rockfish can be caught on light tackle from jetties and wharves and form a small part of the commercial catch.

brown trout

Scientific name: *Salmo trutta*
   Linnaeus, 1758

Family: **Salmon**
Other common names: German brown trout, European brown trout, sea trout, brownie, Loch Leven trout, Von Behr trout, spotted trout, liberty trout
French name: truite brune

Distribution: Found in all Canadian provinces, except P.E.I., Yukon and Northwest Territories, as an introduced species from Europe and western Asia. Most widely distributed in southern Ontario and Alberta, sporadically elsewhere.

Characters: This species is a relative of the **Atlantic salmon** and is distinguished from it by the upper jaw extending beyond the eye in adults (and below rear half of the eye in young rather than the centre in young), the gill cover has many spots, dorsal fin principal rays usually 10–14 and orange to rusty-red spots are often present on adult flanks. Principal anal fin rays 9–12, pectoral rays 13–14 and pelvic rays 9–10. Lateral line scales 110–136 and pyloric caeca 30–60. Males develop a hooked lower jaw when spawning and the brown colour becomes more intense and golden.

Overall colour is a light to golden brown with silvery flanks and a white to yellowish belly. The back, flanks, side of the head and dorsal and adipose fins bear black or dark brown spots, often with a lighter halo of orange, pink or red, and the flank has pink or red spots. Only brown trout have both light and black spots on the flanks. The caudal fin may have spots restricted to its upper lobe. The adipose fin is orange to orange-red. Sea run or lake fish are more silvery, obscuring

brown trout

some of the spots. Spots may be x- or y-shaped. The red flank spots usually have blue halos. Young have 7–14, narrow parr marks and a few red spots along the lateral line. The adipose fin is orange with a light margin.

Hybrids with **brook trout** are called tiger trout for their distinctive markings. Reaches 1.4 m and reputedly 50 kg. The world, all-tackle angling record from Arkansas in 1992 weighed 18.25 kg. The Canadian record is now held by Rick Matusiak. The fish was caught in Lake Ontario in September 1994 and weighed 15.61 kg.

Biology: Brown trout were first introduced to what is now Canada in 1884, to Newfoundland. They are mostly stream and river dwellers although some are in lakes and ponds or run to sea and thus spread through coastal waters. They can tolerate warmer and more turbid waters than **brook trout** and only the **rainbow trout** is more tolerant among salmonids. Brown trout may survive in areas no longer suitable for **brook trout** because deforestation has increased stream temperatures and agriculture and industry have increased pollution and turbidity.

Food is aquatic and terrestrial insects, crustaceans, molluscs, various fishes, frogs, salamanders and even small mammals. Most food is taken as drift, the trout positioned in slower water behind a rock and darting out into faster current to seize prey. Predators include other fishes, birds, water-snakes and otters.

Life span is over 18 years with maturity attained at 2–4 years. European fish may spend up to 9 years in the sea.

Spawning occurs from October to January depending on locality, usually at 7–9°C but as low as 2°C or as high as 14°C. It usually takes place in gravel stream riffles but may occur on rocky shores. The female excavates a redd into which the spawning pair deposit eggs and sperm while gaping and quivering over a 4 second period. The female covers the redd with gravel after spawning to protect the eggs. Subsequent spawning occurs, usually after a 10 hour interval. Occasionally a community redd is excavated by a number of fish spawning close together. Eggs are up to 5.0 mm in diameter and each female can contain 20,865. Young may spend about 2 years in their natal stream before going to a lake but some fish remain permanently in streams.

This **trout** is a valuable and popular sport fish in Europe, less so in Canada because of its localised introductions. There is an extensive European literature on angling methods and it is reputed to be a wilier fish than native **brook trout** in Canada. However studies in an Ontario stream compared catchability favourably with native species. They tend to bite best in the late evening or at dawn, especially when large. These **trout** are caught on worms, crayfish, lures and flies. Brown trout have white to pink flaky flesh and are excellent eating. Flesh colour changes with age, to pink, and is related to diet.

- Most accessible August through September.

- The Great Lakes and their watersheds.

- Light to medium action spinning outfits and specialized nine-and-a-half-foot steelhead outfits used with six- to 14–pound line.

- Lures for casting and trolling include a variety of 1/4– to 3/8–ounce spoons and minnow-imitating plugs. Lures for river fishing include 1/4– to 3/8–ounce spinners, spoons and small wobbling plugs. The top baits include fresh worms and spawn sacks.

buckler dory

Scientific name: *Zenopsis conchifera*
  (Lowe, 1852)
Family: **Dory**
Other common names: sailfin dory
French name: zée bouclé d'Amérique

Distribution: Found in the Atlantic Ocean including the Canadian coast at various localities in Nova Scotia and New Brunswick.

Characters: Scales are absent which distinguishes this species from the related **red dory**. Also there is only 1 spine and 5–6 soft rays in the pelvic fin. The body is deep and compressed. The lateral line has a large, sweeping arch anteriorly. There are 7 large bucklers along the dorsal fin base and 5–6 along the anal fin base. Keeled scutes number 7–8 in two rows between the pelvic fins and anus. Scutes also line the dorsal and anal fin bases. Dorsal fin spines are 8–10, the first

3–5 bearing filaments, soft rays 24–27. Anal fin spines are 3, soft rays 22–26. The pectoral fin has 12 rays. Overall colour is sil-

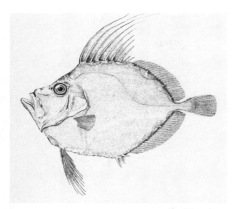

buckler dory

very-grey with a midflank spot just behind the pectoral fin. Pelvic fin membranes are black and the filaments of the dorsal fin are black. Juveniles have 12–14 black spots on the flank. Attains 80 cm.

Biology: Found from 55 to 400 m or deeper, sometimes in midwater or near the bottom in small schools. Some Canadian specimens have been caught in a weir and coastal trap net.

buffalo sculpin

Scientific name: *Enophrys bison*
(Girard, 1854)
Family: **Sculpin**
Other common names: none
French name: chabot-bison

Distribution: Found from the Gulf of Alaska to California including British Columbia.

Characters: This species is distinguished by the large preopercular spines, the uppermost being greatly elongated with an anteriorly serrated base but no barbs as in the related **leister sculpin**. The lower 3 spines are shorter and the lowest is flattened and directed ventrally. The operculum has 2 sharp spines at its edge. There is a supracleithral spine at the upper corner of the gill opening. The head top bears preorbital, supraocular, parietal and nuchal ridges.

The nasal spines are sharp in young but blunt in adults. First dorsal fin spines 7–9, second dorsal fin rays 9–13, usually 12. Anal rays 8–10, usually 9, pectoral rays 15–18 and pelvic fin with 1 spine and 3 soft rays. The lateral line has 30–35 body plates. Vertebral count low, 29–31. There are 1 to more cirri at the rear end of the upper jaw. The dorsal fin spines have simple cirri at their tips in young and tufts in adults. Overall colour brown, dark grey, green-black or black and white mottled. There are 3 dark saddles. The top of the head may be pink to purplish. The belly is white. Fins have dark brown to black spots forming bars, least developed on the anal fin and absent on the pelvic fin. The caudal and pectoral fins may have orange to red tinges. Reaches about 38 cm.

buffalo sculpin

Biology: This sculpin is common on beaches and around rocky areas in British Columbia down to about 20 m. If removed from the water it produces an annoyed hum. The heavy spines are flared when this fish is approached. Food is crustaceans, young fishes such as **herring, sand lance, seaperches** and **salmon**, and sea lettuce. Spawning occurs in shallow water in February-March when orange-brown eggs in clusters are deposited in areas subject to strong tidal currents. Egg clusters are up to 14 cm in diameter and 4 cm thick and are laid among encrusting invertebrates like mussels and barnacles or at crevice entrances. Fertilised eggs are about 2 mm in diameter and fecundity is estimated to reach 31,900 eggs. The male guards and fans the adhesive eggs but deserts them when less than 1 m of water covers them. **Striped seaperch** are predators on the eggs. Males spawn with more than 1 female in each breeding season and have up to 9 egg clusters under their care. Larvae have been found 2–28 km from shore.

Buffalo sculpins are occasionally caught by anglers.

bulbous dreamer

Scientific name: *Oneirodes bulbosus*
    Chapman, 1939
Family: **Dreamer**
Other common names: bulb-fish
French name: queue-de-rêve bulbeuse

    Distribution: Found in the North Pacific Ocean and the Bering Sea including off the Queen Charlotte Islands and at Ocean Station Papa (50°N, 145°W).

    Characters: This species of deepsea **anglerfish** is part of a group of dreamers including the **spiny dreamer** on the Pacific coast. The females of this group are distinguished by having sphenotic spines, a deeply notched operculum posteriorly, a short and broad pectoral fin lobe, the tip of the lower jaw with a spine, the illicium or fishing rod emerging from between the frontal bones on the head, the dorsal edge of these bones being strongly curved, usually 4 anal fin rays and the caudal fin not covered by skin beyond the base. Females of this species are distinguished from its relative on the Pacific coast by having an esca or bait with well-developed medial appendages. Dorsal fin rays 6–7 and pectoral fin rays 15–18. Overall colour black to dark brown with esca not pigmented in some areas and the mouth cavity unpigmented. Females reach 11 cm.

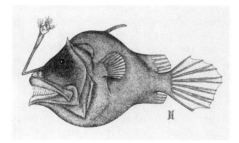

bulbous dreamer

    Biology: Found from less than 600 m to 1090 m off British Columbia. Females use the fishing apparatus to attract prey close enough to be gulped down.

bull pipefish

Scientific name: *Syngnathus springeri*
    Herald, 1942
Family: **Pipefish**
Other common names: none
French name: syngnathe bouledogue

    Distribution: Found from Panama to east of Georges Bank in Atlantic Canada.

    Characters: This species is distinguished from its straight-bodied relatives by having 22–24, usually 23, trunk rings and its dorsal

bull pipefish

fin ray count. A caudal fin is present. The snout is moderately long (length enters head length 1.7–2.3 times). Tail rings 34–37, usually 36. Dorsal fin rays 32–38, pectoral fin rays 12–14, usually 13. Overall colour is pale to brown. The body bears about 13 dark saddles over the back. The head has a lateral stripe. The caudal fin is brown to black with a clear margin. Attains 34.5 cm.

    Biology: Only encountered as strays in Atlantic Canada. This pipefish prefers deeper water than others along the Atlantic coast and is not found intertidally but offshore at 11–127 m. Young, and rarely adults, are found pelagically and in floating *Sargassum* weed. Up to 1390 eggs are carried in the brood pouch and males with eggs are taken almost year round.

bull rhinofish

Scientific name: *Poromitra capito*
    Goode and Bean, 1883
Family: **Ridgehead**
Other common names: none
French name: rhino boeuf

    Distribution: North Atlantic Ocean, including Atlantic Canada on the East Flemish Cap. Possibly in the South Pacific Ocean also.

    Characters: Distinguished from the related **largeye rhinofish** by having more than 28 gill rakers and a moderate-sized eye (diameter less than one-sixth head length) and from the related **crested ridgehead** by having a strong spine at the lower corner of the preopercle. Other opercular bones have spines on their rear and ventral margins. Scale rows 25–36.

bull rhinofish

Dorsal fin with 3 spines and 11–12 soft rays. Anal fin with 1 spine and 8–9 soft rays. Pectoral rays 13–14 and pelvic fin with 1 spine and 7 soft rays. There is a serrated crest on top of the head and a vertical spine between the nostrils. Overall colour is probably dark. Scale pockets are outlined in brown in preserved fish. Mouth and gill cavities are dark. Attains 10.2 cm standard length.

Biology: Known only from a single specimen in Canadian waters caught in 1968. Adults are usually found below 750 m off Bermuda while small juveniles migrate from 700–850 m to 150–250 m. A spawning peak occurs in November or December off Bermuda. Adults spawn at 3 years of age and then die. This species is often eaten by **black scabbardfish**.

bull trout

Scientific name: *Salvelinus confluentus* (Suckley, 1858)
Family: **Salmon**
Other common names: mountain char, western brook trout, inland char
French name: omble à tête plate

Distribution: Found from Alaska to California including the Yukon, British Columbia and Alberta.

Characters: The bull trout is very similar to the **Dolly Varden** but is distinguished by head length in standard length being 3.6–3.9 (4.0 or more in **Dolly Varden** but these are means and ranges overlap), the eye is closer to the dorsal head margin (distance from centre of eye to top of head shorter than distance from centre of eye to nostril), the upper jaw has a downward curve, the head is long and

broad, mandibular pores typically 7–9 as opposed to 6, branchiostegal rays 12–16 (compared to 10–13) and gill rakers (usually 14–20) are stout with strong teeth on the inner margin. Most other characters like fin ray and scale counts overlap. Pyloric caeca 22–34.

The back is olive-green to blue-grey. The flanks are grey to greenish with silvery overtones and with white to yellow, pink or red spots. The lower fins have a white leading edge but without a contrasting black band behind. Fins are mostly transparent. The mouth roof is whitish. Spawning males are orange to red on the belly. Young have 7–10 wide and oval parr marks.

Reaches 103 cm and 18.3 kg. The world, all-tackle angling record weighed 14.51 kg and was caught at Lake Pond Orielle, Idaho in 1949. The Canadian record was caught by Terry Iwamoto in March 1995. It weighed 10.44 kg and was caught in Kootenay Lake, British Columbia.

bull trout

Biology: This is mainly a freshwater species which has also been found in Puget Sound. It appears to favour cold waters fed by snow melt and the bottoms of deep pools. Fishes are a primary food item including various **whitefishes, yellow perch** and **sockeye salmon**. Aquatic insects, crustaceans, and molluscs are also eaten. Life span is 19 years with maturity attained at 4–6 years. Spawning occurs in a 2 m by 1 m redd in stream gravel after a migration from deep pools or a lake. The migration takes place in August in Alberta, or as early as April in the Flathead River basin of British Columbia since this involves a movement of 250 km from Montana. The female tests sites for a redd with her anal fin and may use her snout to loosen large stones in addition to the sideways tail thrashing. The pair settle to the bottom of the redd, gape, quiver violently and shed eggs and sperm. Eggs are pushed further into the gravel by an undulating motion and gravel is dislodged to cover the eggs to a depth over 20 cm. Each female sheds about 5500 eggs from late August to October at temperatures below 10°C. The male defends the redd. The young remain in the nursery streams for 1–3 years after emerging from the redds in spring. Not all adults spawn each year and the frequency of repeat spawning is thought to vary by age and sex. Bull trout are good fighters. The flesh is pink and flavourful. It has been extirpated from much of its range because of angling pressure on a slow growing and late maturing life cycle.

- Most accessible June through July.
- The northern portion of inland British Columbia.
- Medium action spinning outfits used with eight- to 14–pound test line.
- 1/4– to 3/8–ounce spoons, a variety of spinners and jigs.

bullet tuna

Scientific name: *Auxis rochei* (Risso, 1810)
Family: **Mackerel**
Other common names: bullet mackerel, auxide
French name: bonitou

Distribution: Found world-wide in warmer waters but only in the Caribbean Sea and off Atlantic Canada in the western Atlantic Ocean.

Characters: This species is distinguished from its Atlantic coast relatives by having widely separated dorsal fins (distance apart greater than snout length), 9–12 first dorsal fin spines, 6–9 dorsal finlets, 6–8 anal finlets and a median keel on the caudal peduncle. Second dorsal fin with 10–13 rays. Anal fin with 2 spines and 11–13 rays. Pectoral rays 23–25. Gill rakers 42–49. The corselet extends back from the pectoral area under the second dorsal fin origin where it is more than 6 scales wide, usually 10–15. There is a pointed flap of skin on the belly between the pelvic fins. The back is dark blue, bluish-green to brown, almost black or purplish on the head, with silvery flanks and a silvery to white belly. Pectoral and pelvic fins are pur-

ple with the inner surface black. There are 12 or more broad, dark bars on the upper flank. Reaches 50 cm fork length and about 2 kg.

bullet tuna

Biology: Only known from east of Georges Bank where 3 specimens were caught in 1955. Bullet tuna are found in both coastal and oceanic surface waters, their distribution limited by temperature. They form large schools by size. Food is principally fishes such as **anchovies** as well as crustaceans and squid. Bullet tuna are eaten by other **tunas, billfishes, barracudas**, and **sharks**. Bullet tuna are cannibals. Females are mature at 35 cm and males at 36.5 cm in the Mediterranean Sea. There is a large spawning ground in the Gulf of Mexico where young have been caught from March to August. Eggs are up to 1.0 mm in diameter and number up to perhaps a million, spawned in several batches of 31,000–103,000 eggs. It is not fished for specifically but is caught while fishing for **tunas**. Pole-and-line gear is commonly trolled by Japanese fishermen but a variety of other gear is used generally. They are sold fresh, frozen, canned, smoked or flake-dried. The world catch for this tuna (and its only relative which is not separated in statistics) was 137,043 tonnes in 1980.

bulleye

Scientific name: *Cookeolus japonicus* (Cuvier, 1829)
Family: **Bigeye**
Other common names: none
French name: priacanthe oeil-de-taureau

Distribution: Found on both sides of the Atlantic Ocean and much of the Pacific Ocean. In the western Atlantic found from Nova Scotia to Argentina.

Characters: The bulleye is separated from its relatives, the **bigeye** and the **short bigeye**, by having pelvic fins longer than the head, and the last dorsal fin spine more than twice the length of the second. Dorsal fin spines 9–10, soft rays 12–14. Anal fin soft rays 12–14. Pored lateral line scales 52–61, mid-lateral scale rows 58–73. Overall colour is coppery changing to red on freezing. The iris is mostly red-orange, but dusky on the dorsal and posterior margins. The edges of the pelvic and caudal fins are black and the pelvic membranes are black. The dorsal and anal fins are red, white or yellowish on spines and rays with membranes black to dusky, sometimes spotted. The caudal fin is red to yellowish with orange membranes. Pectoral fins are a light yellow. The inside of the mouth is red. Reaches 60 cm.

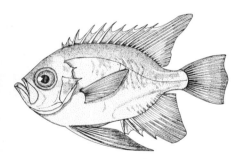

bulleye

Biology: A single Canadian specimen was caught in a mackerel trap net at St. Margarets Bay, Nova Scotia in 1971, the northern range limit in the western Atlantic Ocean. Off the United States, this species has been caught at 60–411 m. It may be more pelagic than benthic in habitat as reflected by food which is pelagic crabs. Life span may exceed 9 years. This species is eaten by **yellowfin tuna**.

Bullhead Catfish Family

Scientific name: Ictaluridae
French name: barbottes

Bullhead or North American freshwater catfishes are found from southern Canada to Guatemala. There are about 45 species with 10 recorded from Canada, 5 in the Atlantic drainage, 4 in the Atlantic and Arctic drainages and 1 in Atlantic, Arctic and Gulf of Mexico drainages. The **brown bullhead** of Arctic-Atlantic drainages has been introduced into the Pacific drainage where catfishes do not occur naturally. **Brown bullheads** have also been introduced to Europe, the former U.S.S.R. and New Zealand.

This is the only **catfish** family in Canada and is easily recognised by the scaleless skin, 8 barbels (2 on the nostrils, 2 at the upper jaw corners and 4 on the chin) and the dorsal and pectoral fins with a spine at the front. There are usually 6 dorsal fin soft rays. The palate lacks teeth. An adipose fin is present. In the United States some members of this family exceed 1.3 m and 45 kg.

Bullheads are members of the **Catfish Order**. They are related to the **Carp** and **Sucker** families which also have the chain of bones connecting the swimbladder to the ear. Important identification features are the nature of the pectoral spine and the number of anal rays. Ray counts include all rays, even rudimentary ones and a needle and some dissection may be required. Also important are pore numbers on the head and colour pattern.

Bullheads show a variety of interesting behaviours. All species construct nests and protect their young, although some smaller species take advantage of pollution by nesting in beer cans. Some species can recognise other fish individually by smell and even determine their social status. Chemical "strangers" are subject to aggression. Home sites are also recognised by substrate chemical marks applied by the fish. Territories may be marked chemically in this way. The nostrils are very sensitive to pheromones, hormones released into the water in urine, from the skin and from various glands. The barbels and skin are taste- and touch-sensitive and used to detect food. This is particularly useful in muddy water and at night. Many of these catfishes are nocturnal. "Taste" can also be used in breeding behaviour and in schooling.

A Weberian apparatus, modified vertebral bones connecting the brain and swimbladder, are used to transmit sound and bullhead hearing is excellent. Some species can be trained to respond to names!

Catfish lack scales and are aged by making cross sections of pectoral spines to read growth rings. The fin spines can be very toxic because of poisonous cell secretions on the sheath of the spine. Wounds can be painful and extremely swollen for days. **Madtoms** are named for their hyperactive, darting and dashing behaviour and perhaps stinging effect but even the bullheads (*Ameiurus* species) can inflict an uncomfortable, poisoned wound. The spines are an effective defense mechanism for these catfishes but are not fatal to humans. All catfishes should be handled with care. The spines in the dorsal and pectoral fins can be locked in an erect position by an unique arrangement of muscles attached to the spine and associated bones.

Bullhead catfishes are hardy and very tolerant of domestic pollution. Three American species are blind and live in artesian wells and nearby ditches in Texas and Mexico. Larger catfishes, such as the **channel catfish**, are commercially important in the U.S.A. and are cultured in ponds. Catfish restaurant dinners are a speciality in the southern U.S.A. and catfish figure prominently in fish and chips. These fishes are also sought after by anglers, being strong fighters and good eating. Smaller specimens and species have been used in the aquarium trade.

See **black bullhead**
     brindled madtom
     brown bullhead
     channel catfish
     flathead catfish
     margined madtom
     northern madtom
     stonecat
     tadpole madtom
     yellow bullhead

burbot

Scientific name: *Lota lota* (Linnaeus, 1758)
Family: **Cod**
Other common names: ling, sand ling, eelpout, American burbot, freshwater cod, mother-of-eels, gudgeon, maria, methy, freshwater cusk, spineless cat, dogfish, lawyer, lush, loche, freshwater eel, lotte de rivière, titaliq, nätarrnaq, tiktabek, shulukpaoluk, nettârnak

French name: lotte

Distribution: Found throughout Canada except coastal British Columbia, extreme northeastern N.W.T., the Arctic Islands, the outer coast of Québec and Labrador, Nova Scotia, P.E.I. and Newfoundland. Also in the northern U.S.A. and across all of northern Europe.

Characters: This is the only freshwater member of the **Cod Family** with 2 dorsal and 1 anal fins. There is a large chin barbel and large, tubular nostrils. First dorsal fin rays 7–16, second dorsal rays 60–94. Anal fin rays 52–86, pectoral rays 15–24 and pelvic rays 5–9. The embedded scales are very small. Pyloric caeca 31–150.

Overall colour varies from yellow-brown to brown or dark olive with black mottling and blotching. The belly is yellowish-white. Some fish may be uniform brown, purplish-black or black. The pelvic fins are pale and other fins are dark and mottled. The second dorsal, caudal and anal fins have a dark, submarginal band while the margin is bright yellow or orange. Young fish can have a white anal fin with a black edge and black rays in the pectoral fin.

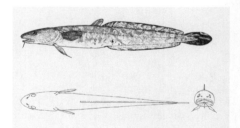

burbot

Reaches over 1.22 m and 34 kg. The name lawyer is said to be in allusion to its slipperiness. The word "burbot" is derived from the Middle French "bourbotte" from the verb bourbeter, to wallow in mud. The world, all-tackle, angling record weighed 8.27 kg and came from Pickford, Michigan in 1980. The Canadian angling record from Little Athapapuskow Lake, Manitoba, in April 1994 weighed 10.22 kg. and was caught by Vaughn Kshywiewcki.

Biology: Burbot are found in lakes down to 214 m and in large, cool rivers, preferring water colder than 18°C. They have been caught in brackish water. A preferred habitat is under rocks, among roots or in holes in banks. In the south, deeper water is preferred than in the north. They may move into shallow water at night in summer.

Food, taken at night, is aquatic insects, crayfish, molluscs and other invertebrates when young (up to 50 cm) but older burbot eat mostly fishes with some opossum shrimps and other crustaceans. The burbot is thus a competitor with many fishes for food, especially since it feeds indiscriminately and voraciously on whatever is available. The barbel and the pelvic fins are used to taste food before ingestion, even ejecting a food item from the mouth and passing it back to the pelvics several times before finally consuming it. Young burbot are eaten by various other fishes.

Females are larger than males and often mature later. Maturity is usually attained at 3–4 years and life span is up to 20 years. In Lake Simcoe, Ontario males mature at 34.3 cm and 255 g and females at 41.9 cm and 680 g, both at age 3.

Spawning takes place from January to March under ice. There is a movement into shallow water for spawning, usually at depths less than 3 m, over sand or gravel near the shore or on shoals. Males arrive first on the spawning grounds followed in 3–4 days by females. Water temperatures are 0.6–1.7°C. Up to 12 fish form a moving, wriggling ball over the bottom at night. Eggs are shed, fertilised and left unattended. Eggs are up to 1.9 mm in diameter and number as many as 1,362,077, perhaps up to 3 million. They are semipelagic and take up to 5 weeks to hatch. Young burbot can be common in lake shallows and streams.

Burbot have been used for fish meal, oil and food for animals raised for fur. It has white, flaky flesh and is good eating but has not found general acceptance as a food fish. Smoked burbot livers are a delicacy in Europe. Anglers often catch burbot when ice fishing for **lake trout**. The tough skin was once used in the windows of Siberia as a substitute for glass. Burbot can be a nuisance to commercial fisheries, eating other commercial fishes caught in gill nets or clogging gill nets and wasting time in removing them.

- Ice fishing during January to March.
- Cold water lakes normally fished in the winter for **lake trout** in Manitoba, Saskatchewan and Ontario.
- Ice fishing tip-ups used with 10- to 14-pound line.
- Live or dead **minnows** fished near the bottom.

butter sole

Scientific name: *Pleuronectes isolepis* (Lockington, 1880)
Family: **Righteye Flounder**
Other common names: scalyfin sole, Bellingham sole, Skidegate sole
French name: plie à écailles régulières

Distribution: Found from Alaska to California including British Columbia.

Characters: This species is characterised among Canadian Pacific **flatfishes** by bright yellow tips to the dorsal and anal fin rays. The mouth is small, asymmetrical and teeth are strongest on the blind side. Scales are large and strongly ctenoid on the eyed side, cycloid on the blind side body and ctenoid on the head. Ctenoid scales extend onto the fin rays. The lateral line has a slight arch anteriorly and has 78–90 scales. An accessory branch lateral line parallels the dorsal fin to end over the latter half of the pectoral

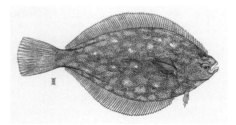

butter sole

fin. Dorsal fin rays 78–92, anal fin preceded by a sharp, exposed spine and with 58–69 rays. Caudal fin rounded. The eyed side is grey, light or dark brown and irregularly blotched, sometimes with yellow or green spots. Blind side white. Reaches 55 cm.

Biology: This is a shallow water species but also reported down to 425 m. Young are in shallower water than adults but there is a summer shallow and winter deep migratory pattern for adults. Food is worms, crustaceans, sand dollars, **sand lance** and young **herring**. Females live 11 years and males 10 years and females grow larger than males. Spawning occurs from February to April depending on locality. In Skidegate Inlet, eggs were found to be heavier than water and 1.1 mm in diameter. This is an excellent food fish but difficult to skin and fillet in bulk because of small size, thinness and rough scales. It is not favoured in the commercial fishery except as mink feed, but 590 tonnes have been caught in 1 year (1970).

butterfish

Scientific name: *Peprilus triacanthus*
  (Peck, 1804)
Family: **Butterfish**
Other common names: dollarfish, shiner,
  sheepshead, harvestfish, skipjack,
  starfish, pumpkinseed, lafayette, cryptous
  broad shiner
French name: stromatée à fossettes

Distribution: Found from eastern Newfoundland and the Gulf of St. Lawrence south to the Gulf of Mexico.

Characters: This species is distinguished from the related **Pacific pompano** by distribution, having 17–25 large pores below the anterior half of the dorsal fin and teeth at the front of the upper jaw with 3 small cusps. Dorsal fin with 2–4, usually 3, spines and 40–48 soft rays. Anal fin with 2–3, usually 3, spines and 37–44 soft rays. No pelvic fins. Colour varies from bluish to greenish to dark grey on the back. Flanks are silvery, usually with irregular dark spots. Reaches 30.5 cm.

Biology: Found inshore over sandy or mud bottoms during May to September, retreating offshore in winter down to 183 m. In the southern part of its range it descends to 420 m, and migrates inshore in winter. It can live in brackish water. The young are found with jellyfish, such as *Cyanea* and

butterfish

Chrysaora, weeds or swimming alone. Young feed on jellyfish, but also on other fishes, squid, arrow worms, crustaceans and worms. Spawning occurs from May to July and eggs measure 0.7–0.8 mm in diameter. They become mature at 2 years and live up to 6 years. Many commercially important fishes feed on butterfish. It is commercially-important itself in the northwestern Atlantic Ocean with over 460 million fish or 19,454 tonnes caught in 1973 by vessels from Japan, U.S.A., the former U.S.S.R. and Poland. Mean weight and age of butterfish declined in the period 1968–1976 as the fishery increased. The northwest Atlantic catch was 2016 tonnes in 1988. It is not commercially important in Canada. Anglers find it delicious eating when freshly caught.

Butterfish Family

Scientific name: Stromateidae
French name: stromatées

Butterfishes or harvestfishes are found in tropical to temperate seas world-wide. There are about 13 species. There are 2 species in Canada, 1 each on the Atlantic and Pacific coasts.

The body is very deep, oval and compressed and adults lack pelvic fins. The young of some species have pelvic fins. The dorsal fin is continuous and similar in size and shape to the anal fin with the anterior end higher. Some species have 5–10 small, blade-like spines in front of the dorsal fin. Pectoral fins are elongate and pointed. Scales are minute, easily detached and cycloid. The eye is surrounded by fatty tissue forming an adipose eyelid. The roof of the mouth is toothless.

This family is related to the **Ruff**, **Drift-fish**, **Sequinfish** and **Squaretail** families, all of which share toothed, sac-like outgrowths of the gut. If the gill cover is lifted, the sacs may be seen behind the last gill arch. Members of the **Driftfish** and **Squaretail** families are sometimes included in this family. These families are distinguished by number of dorsal fins, presence/absence of pelvic fins in adults, number and size of dorsal fin spines, presence/absence of keels on the caudal peduncle and whether there are teeth on the roof of the mouth.

This family is a member of the **Perch Order**.

These are pelagic fishes often found in large schools near the coast. Young fish are found under floating debris and seaweed or associated with jellyfish. These fish secrete large amounts of mucus from an extensive canal system which may protect against jellyfish stings by inhibiting discharge of stinging cells or by counteracting the toxins produced. Some species are commercially important.

See **butterfish**
> **Pacific pompano**

Butterflyfish Family

Scientific name: Chaetodontidae
French name: palhalas

Butterflyfishes or coralfishes are found in temperate to tropical waters of all oceans but are most diverse in the Indo-Pacific Ocean. There are about 120 species, but only 1 is reported from Atlantic Canada.

Butterflyfish are some of the most colourful and beautiful fishes in the sea. A frequent part of their colour pattern is a band through and obscuring the eye and an eyespot near the rear of the body. These serve to confuse predators since a strike at the eyespot will enable the fish to swim away more efficiently than a strike at the real eye. In fact, butterflyfish will swim slowly backwards and when attacked will dart quickly forwards, thoroughly confusing any predator.

They have a small, protrusible mouth with fine teeth in bristly bands on the jaws (*Chaetodon* means bristle tooth). Scales are ctenoid and extend onto the head and onto the dorsal and anal fins. The pelvic fin has 1 spine and 5 branched rays and an axillary process. The caudal fin is rounded or emarginate. There is no spine at the lower corner of the preopercle although it may be serrated. The gut is elaborately coiled. The larva is oceanic and known as a tholichthys stage and the head is covered in bony plates which extend backward.

Butterflyfish are related to the **Sea Chub** and **Armorhead** families. They are often identified by their distinctive colour patterns which are used in camouflage, contact between species members and to warn of territorial boundaries. This family is a member of the **Perch Order**.

They feed on small invertebrates, algae and coral polyps in shallow coral and rocky habitats and around man-made structures. Some are found as deep as 200 m. Some young and a few adults are cleaners, picking parasites off other fish species. They are easily seen fishes active in the day and chasing away intruders from their territory. They are sought after for marine aquaria although they are difficult to keep and the larger species have been used as food.

See **spotfin butterflyfish**

C

C-O sole

Scientific name: *Pleuronichthys coenosus*
Girard, 1854
Family: **Righteye Flounder**
Other common names: C-O turbot, spot
flounder, popeye sole, muddy flounder,
mottled turbot, stinker
French name: plie vaseuse

Distribution: Found from Alaska to Baja
California including British Columbia.

Characters: This species is distinguished
by a black, eye-size spot in the middle of the
body and a similar spot in the middle of the

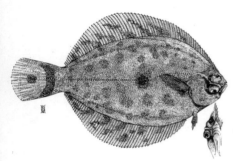

C-O sole

caudal fin with a curved bar at the fin base
(hence C-O). Cycloid scales are on both sides
of the body, are embedded and there are
77–92 in the lateral line. An accessory or
branch lateral line runs close to the dorsal fin
back to about midbody level. The mouth is
small and asymmetrical and teeth are mainly
on the blind side of the jaws. The first 4–6
dorsal fin rays are on the blind side of the
head. Dorsal fin rays 65–78, anal rays 46–56,
preceded by a small, hidden spine. Caudal fin
rounded. Total gill rakers 11–15. Eyed side
brownish-green, dark brown or black, with
many lighter speckles. All fins dark and blind
side creamy white, often with dusky blotches.
Specimens living near pink coralline algae
acquire pink blotches. Occasionally a brown
or yellow-brown blotch at midbody on the
eyed side. Reaches 36 cm.

Biology: Abundant in the Strait of Georgia
and off western Vancouver Island. Reported
generally at 18–350 m, young being in shallower water than adults. Found over sand bottoms often near rocks, and in algal beds. Food
includes worms, clam siphons, small **rockfish**
and crustaceans. Eggs are pelagic and 1.88
mm in diameter. Most spawning occurs from
May to September. This species is caught by
trawls and sold, but is difficult to fillet because
of the tough skin. SCUBA divers are said to be
able to pick it up by hand.

cabezon

Scientific name: *Scorpaenichthys marmoratus*
(Ayres, 1854)
Family: **Sculpin**
Other common names: giant marbled
sculpin, blue garnet
French name: chabot marbré

Distribution: Found from southeastern
Alaska to Baja California including British
Columbia.

Characters: This sculpin is recognised by
the single flap-like cirrus on the snout and the
marbled colour pattern. Nasal spines are
strong but blunt and skin-covered. There are
3 blunt, skin-covered preopercular spines, the
upper 2 being the strongest and directed posteriorly. First dorsal fin indented at spines
3–4 and with 8–12 spines total, second dorsal
fin with 15–19 soft rays. Anal rays 11–14, all
tips free, pectoral rays 14–16 with lower 6–8
finger-like at tips. Pelvic fin with 1 spine and
4–5 soft rays. Lateral line pores 71–88 with
4–8 on the tail. Scales deeply embedded and
difficult to see. There is a large, branched cir-

cabezon

rus above the rear eye margin and a fleshy
flap at the end of the upper jaw. Overall
colour is olive-green to brown or grey, or red-

dish in some young, with large pale mottles on the body and fins. The belly is white to greenish. Attains 99 cm and 14 kg. The world, all-tackle angling record from Port Townsend, Washington in 1988 weighed 8.16 kg. This species is regarded as the most primitive **sculpin**. "Cabezon" is derived from the Spanish and Latin for head.

Biology: Abundant in shallow water and found down to about 183 m. Food is crustaceans, fishes and molluscs when adult. Females grow faster than males and maximum life span is about 13 years. Spawning occurs in January-March in British Columbia. Eggs adhere to rocks in shallow water and are greenish, red or purple in colour but are toxic and are not eaten by birds and other predators at low tide. A large female may produce over 95,000 eggs. Males guard the eggs which are laid in community nest sites, used year after year. Young are pelagic. This large sculpin is often caught by anglers and scuba divers. It is an important sport fish in California. The flesh is bluegreen but good eating and turns white when cooked. However the eggs are toxic and may contaminate the flesh if the fish is not carefully cleaned, and humans can become very ill with alternating chills and fever and with diarrhoea and vomiting. Rats and guinea pigs have died after eating cabezon roe but a well-known ichthyologist and his wife proved to be of sterner constitution.

calico sculpin

Scientific name: *Clinocottus embryum*
    (Jordan and Starks, 1895)
Family: **Sculpin**
Other common names: mossy sculpin
French name: chabot calico

Distribution: Found from the Bering Sea to Baja California including British Columbia.

Characters: This species and its relatives, the **mosshead** and **sharpnose sculpins**, are separated from other Pacific coast sculpins by having 3 pelvic fin rays, branchiostegal membranes joined and forming a fold over the isthmus, largest preopercular spine not antler-like, no scales, and the anal fin origin is below the second dorsal fin. This species is separated from its relatives by lacking a pelvic fin membrane attached to the belly, no cirri on the end of the upper jaw, the upper lip groove has a small, fleshy tubercle in the middle and there are no cirri between the upper pectoral fin base and the lateral line. First dorsal fin spines 8–10, second dorsal fin rays 14–17, anal rays 9–12 and pectoral rays 12–15. The pectoral fin is very long and the lower 5 rays are finger-like. There are 34–38 lateral line pores with 1–2 on the tail. The snout is narrow. Males have a large, tubular anal papilla which curves anteriorly. There are large, branched cirri along the anterior third of the lateral line as far forward as the eye, a row of branched cirri on top of the head in the centre, on the nasal and preopercular spines and at the upper corner of the gill opening. Overall colour is olive-green, pink, red or maroon. There are 6 dark saddles over the back and dark vermiculations on the lower flank. Lips are black ante-

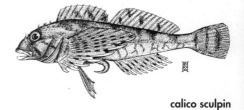

calico sculpin

riorly. Bars radiate back and down from the eye. Fins have brown to orange bars except for the dusky pelvics. Reaches 7 cm.

Biology: Relatively common in rocky inshore areas particularly in among coralline algae and in subtidal areas.

California headlightfish

Scientific name: *Diaphus theta*
    Eigenmann and Eigenmann, 1890
Family: **Lanternfish**
Other common names: Theta lanternfish, white-spotted lanternfish
French name: lampe-de-tête à taches blanches

Distribution: Found from the Gulf of Alaska south to Baja California and at Ocean Station Papa (50°N, 145°W). Also in the southern hemisphere.

Characters: This species is separated from its Pacific coast relatives by having 4 Prc photophores, the fourth PO photophore is elevated above the others, no caudal luminous glands and several luminous organs around

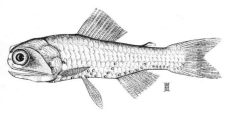

California headlightfish

the eye margin. Dorsal fin rays 11–15, usually 13, anal rays 12–14, pectoral rays 9–12, and vertebrae 34–36. Total gill rakers 19–23 and AO photophores 10–12. Lateral line scales 34–37. Reaches about 11.4 cm.

Biology: Reported from 10–450 m in daylight and down to 1690 m. There is a diel vertical migration of 250–350 m. Food is various crustaceans taken at night near the surface. This species is often caught inshore by shrimp trawlers in shallow water.

can-opener smoothdream

Scientific name: *Chaenophryne longiceps*
    Regan, 1925
Family: **Dreamer**
Other common names: none
French name: doux-rêve ouvre-boîte

Distribution: Found world-wide and in the North Atlantic Ocean from Iceland southward including Atlantic Canada.

Characters: This species of deepsea **anglerfish** and its relative, the **smooth dreamer**, are distinguished by the lack of

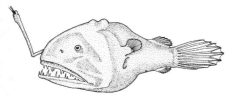

can-opener smoothdream

sphenotic spines, a slightly concave operculum posteriorly and high cancellous bones. The female can-opener smoothdream is sep-

arated from its relative by distribution, an esca or bait on the fishing apparatus with a pair of anterior appendages and a medial appendage or appendages, and pectoral fin rays 17–22, rarely less than 18. Males have 17–22 upper, and 23–27 lower, denticles on the jaws. Overall colour is dark brown to black. The mouth is unpigmented as are parts of the esca. Females attain 20.7 cm.

Biology: Only a single specimen has been found off Newfoundland, the largest known, collected in 1968. Mostly found below 850 m where females use their fishing apparatus to catch fishes, cephalopods and crustaceans as described under **anglerfishes**.

Canadian plaice

Scientific name: *Hippoglossoides platessoides*
    (Fabricius, 1780)
Family: **Righteye Flounder**
Other common names: American plaice (in
    U.S.A.!), sand dab, blackback, rough dab,
    long rough dab, flounder, sole, faux flétan
French name: plie canadienne

Distribution: Found from Frobisher Bay, Baffin Island and western Hudson Bay south throughout Atlantic Canada to Rhode Island. Also in Europe.

Characters: This species is found primarily in Atlantic waters with only 2 localities in Arctic waters as listed above. It is distin-

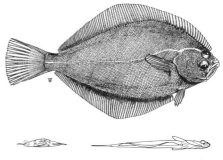

Canadian plaice

guished by the large, almost symmetrical mouth, a rounded caudal fin, almost straight lateral line and the dorsal fin ray count. Dorsal fin rays 76–101, anal rays 60–79 and pectoral rays 9–12. Scales are ctenoid on the eyed side and both ctenoid and cycloid on the blind side. There are 85–97 lateral line scales. Eyed side red or russet to grey-brown, blind side white. Dorsal and anal fin margins white. Young have 3–5 dark spots on each body margin. Some specimens are partly dark on the blind side. Reaches 82.6 cm and about 6.4 kg.

Biology: Plaice are found in a depth range of 18–713 m, on mud or sand, usually at temperatures close to 0°C but also as warm as 13°C. Some are caught in midwater so they are not confined to the sea bed. Plaice enter brackish areas of rivers. They retreat to deeper water in winter. Plaice are most abundant on the Grand Bank in the northwest Atlantic Ocean.

Food is worms, molluscs, echinoderms, sea squirts, crustaceans and, most importantly in most populations on a weight basis, fish. **Northern sand lance** are particularly important dietary items. Green sea urchins comprised 62% by weight in an eastern Newfoundland population living near bedrock. Many other fishes eat plaice including **Greenland sharks, cod, halibut, skates** and **sea ravens**.

Plaice are slow growing flatfish with females living longer than males, up to 26 years. Growth is slower in colder, northern waters than in the south. Males mature at 22–23 cm and 4–5 years and females at over 30 cm and over 8 years on the Scotian Shelf. Size and age at maturity have declined over a 20 year period, and this is usually indicative of overfishing. Up to 50% of females and 60% of males landed in the 1970s were 10 years old or less — particularly critical for females.

Spawning occurs in April–July at —1.3 to 3.5°C, with timing later in the north and in deeper water. Up to 1.5 million floating eggs of 2.8 mm diameter are released.

Plaice are important commercially in Canada and comprise about half of all flatfish landed. They are caught in otter trawls, Danish seines and gill nets and as much as 60,521 tonnes has been caught in 1985. The 1989 catch for Canada was estimated at 45,557 tonnes and was valued at over $18 million. However a sustainable catch of 5000 tonnes is more reasonable over the long term. The situation is complicated because plaice are taken as a by-catch with cod so catch limits for that species also affect the plaice stocks. They are sold as fresh or frozen fillets and have white, tasty flesh.

canary rockfish

Scientific name: *Sebastes pinniger*
  (Gill, 1864)
Family: **Scorpionfish**
Other common names: orange rockfish,
  yellow snapper, red snapper
French name: sébaste canari

Distribution: Found from southeast Alaska to Baja California including British Columbia.

Characters: This rockfish is distinguished by colour, head spines, smooth scales on the lower jaw and 1 sharp triangular spine on the lower edge of the bone below the eye. Dorsal fin spines 13, soft rays 13–15, usually 14. Anal

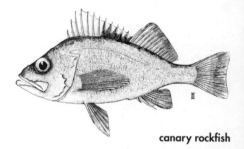

canary rockfish

fin soft rays 7, second anal spine only slightly thicker than third and shorter. Posterior edge of anal fin with an anterior slant. Pectoral fin rays 16–18, usually 17. Lateral line pores 39–47, scale rows below lateral line 43–50. Gill rakers 40–45. Vertebrae 26. Coronal and nuchal spines are absent, remaining spines small. The background colour is grey mottled with orange or may be orange mottled with yellow. The lateral line is grey or lighter than the rest of the flank. The belly is pale to bright orange. Fin membranes are bright orange. The spiny dorsal fin in smaller fish, under 36 cm, has a dusky or dark blotch posteriorly. The peritoneum is white and in young white with black dots. Reaches 76 cm. The world, all-tackle record weighed 4.53 kg and was caught in 1986 at Westport, Washington.

Biology: This species is common over rocky bottoms in Canada at 91–366 m, elsewhere to 425 m. Northern populations are in shallower water than those in the warm south. Young fish favour shallow waters. Food is krill and small fishes such as **anchovies** and **sanddabs**. Canary rockfish are eaten by **lingcod** and **yellow rockfish**. Spawning occurs in January to March in Canada and the largest females give birth to 1.9 million young. Half the male population is mature at 41 cm, females at 48 cm. Life span is estimated to be more than 70 years. This rockfish has been caught on hook and line and by commercial trawlers. It is sometimes sold as "red snapper."

Cape fathead

Scientific name: *Cubiceps capensis*
(Smith, 1849)
Family: **Ruff**
Other common names: Cape cigarfish
French name: pompile du Cap

Distribution: Found in temperate to subtropical waters from southeast of Browns Bank in Atlantic Canada and from off South Africa and in the Pacific Ocean.

Characters: This ruff is distinguished from the related **slender** and **fewray fatheads** by having teeth on the vomer bone in the roof of the mouth in one row, 11–12 upper procurrent (= inclined forward) caudal rays, the snout anteriorly lacks scales and tongue teeth are in 1 row. Dorsal fin with 10–11 spines followed by 1 spine and 19–26 soft rays. Anal fin with 3 spines and 19–23 soft rays. Pectoral fin rays 20–24. Lateral line scales 63–71. Preserved specimens are purplish-brown with brown to black fins. The head around the eyes, on the snout and

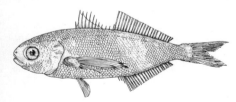

Cape fathead

on the jaws is blue-black to black. The mouth and gill cavities are black. Reaches 101 cm.

Biology: This species has been caught only once in Atlantic Canada by a Japanese tuna longliner at 65 m. This is the northern limit for the species and is one of the few western Atlantic records.

capelin

Scientific name: *Mallotus villosus*
(Müller, 1776)
Family: **Smelt**
Other common names: caplin, whitefish, Pacific capelin, moiva, lodde, amagiak, qulilirraq, nulilighuk, holili-gah, ko le le kuk
French name: capelan

Distribution: Circumpolar in the northern Atlantic and Pacific oceans. South to Juan de Fuca Strait on the British Columbia coast and south to Cape Cod in the western Atlantic Ocean. Across southern Arctic Canada including southern James Bay.

Characters: This species is distinguished by having 8–14 upper arch gill rakers, teeth on tongue small and brush-like, and a com-

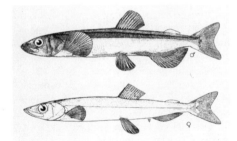

capelin

plete lateral line with 170–220 scales. Dorsal fin rays 10–18, anal rays 16–26, and pectoral rays 16–22. The last pelvic ray is reduced in size. Pyloric caeca 3–9. Gill rakers 33–48. Breeding males develop 4 rows of overlapping, elongated scales along the lateral line into a strong ridge. The ends of the scales give the ridge a hairy appearance. Development starts 4–5 weeks prior to the start of the spawning season. In addition the anal fin is enlarged with the first 10–12 rays thickened, and projects from a ridge on the belly, pectoral and dorsal fins are enlarged and tubercles develop on the head, lower pectoral and caudal fin rays and the belly. Overall translucent with olive-green to yellow-green back, silvery lower flanks and a white belly. The operculum is spotted. Scales are outlined with pigment. The peritoneum is silvery but has dense dark speckles and appears almost black. "Capelan" is from the Old Provençal for a codfish and literally means chaplain. Reaches 25.2 cm total length.

Biology: This is a pelagic species found from the surface down to 200 m, possibly as deep as 725 m, in coastal areas and on offshore banks. There are daily vertical migrations. Five stocks have been identified in the northwest Atlantic Ocean.

Food is plankton, particularly euphausiids and copepods, but also includes worms and small fishes. There are early morning and evening feeding peaks. Feeding is intense before spawning in late and early spring but stops during spawning. Capelin are extremely important as food for **Atlantic cod, haddock, Greenland halibut, Canadian plaice, yellowtail flounder** and **Atlantic salmon** and are probably the most important prey species in the northern Atlantic Ocean. Capelin may form up to 98% of the cod diet and are the principal food for **salmon. Winter flounder** eat capelin eggs with up to 25% of their annual growth coming from this food source. Minke whales, fin whales, harp seals and **Atlantic cod** annually consume 3 million tonnes of capelin in the northwest Atlantic Ocean.

The annual consumption of capelin by seabirds in Newfoundland waters is about 250,000 tonnes, about as much as that taken by seals and whales but only a tenth of that taken by **Atlantic cod**. Murres and puffins have few other acceptable prey in waters around Newfoundland. These birds and other animals are in a precarious situation because of their dependence on a single prey species. Decline in capelin stocks through exploitation by foreign fleets is a major concern in Atlantic Canada because of their role as fodder fish. Some argue capelin should not be fished at all.

Maximum life span is 10 years. Males grow faster than females until maturity when growth is about equal. Northern populations

grow more slowly and mature later than those in the south. For example Labrador capelin mature a year later than Grand Bank capelin.

Spawning involves a migration onto beaches (the capelin scull or roll) although there is evidence for a population which lives in deep water and spawns on the shallow (46–49 m) Southeast Shoal of the Grand Bank about 350 km from the nearest spawning beach. The timing of spawning depends on temperature, latitude, tides, daylight, salinities, turbidity and winds and can occur from April to August in Atlantic Canada and September to October in southern British Columbia. Temperatures range from 2.5–12.5°C and vary between localities, between years and between weeks. Mating is reported as most intense at intermediate tides or during ebbing tides at or near a time of greatest tides. Spawning takes place at night or on heavily overcast days and occasionally on sunny days. Large females spawn several weeks earlier than small females. Reddish eggs are laid on coarse sand, fine gravel and pebble beaches and certain areas are known as capelin-spawning beaches. The grain size of the beaches is 1–15 mm and on the Southeast Shoal 0.5–2.5 mm. The fish swim onto the beach on wave crests and up to 60,000, 1 mm diameter eggs are shed and fertilised.

A male presses against the side of a female and sometimes the female will be flanked by a male on each side. The spawning ridges and larger fins of the male help to hold the female. The female and accompanying males rush up the beach as far as possible and are stranded in one spot as the wave recedes. Vigorous movements of the fins and body audibly scoop out a small pool where eggs are shed and buried. Spawning takes less than 5 seconds and thrashing movements help the fish regain the water as the next wave rolls up the beach. The eggs can be buried more than 15 cm in the sand to which they adhere. Wave action buries the eggs and in this position they are protected from predators and dehydration. Spent fish can be stranded in large numbers on a beach and not all eggs are safely buried, neighbouring rocks being covered by a continuous layer. Those which are buried may exceed

800/sq cm. Most capelin die after spawning but repeat spawning by females may occur.

Males gather in schools near the beach prior to spawning while females are in deeper water. More males die after spawning, perhaps because of greater damage in their longer stay in turbid beach water. Larvae emerge from the beach gravel when onshore winds blow warm water into the shallows. This warm water is usually rich in the smaller zooplankton but has relatively few predators such as jellyfish and arrow worms, ideal conditions for larval growth and survival.

Capelin are scooped in large numbers from beaches on the spawning run with buckets, nets and hands. Sun dried or smoked they make a delicious snack. They have been so abundant that they were used as fertiliser, dog food and bait for use in the **cod** line fishery. Capelin are now processed into fish meal and oil and some are used for feeding **salmon** and **trout** reared in cages. Fat content prior to spawning can reach 23% of the fish mass. Some is exported to Japan, especially from an inshore Newfoundland fishery for a lucrative capelin roe market. The females are sold in sushi bars as skishamo, a fried delicacy. Landings in 1982 in Atlantic Canada weighed 31,893 tonnes with a value of $6,691,000. The Canadian catch in 1988 weighed 85,500 tonnes, making this the third largest catch by species, and was worth over $21.7 million. The peak offshore catch in 1976 was 370,000 tonnes by former Soviet midwater trawlers and Norwegian purse seiners. The offshore foreign fishery was closed in 1979 after starting in 1972, peaking in the mid-1970s and declining steeply. Capelin are not commercially important in British Columbia.

carapine grenadier

Scientific name: *Lionurus carapinus*
  (Goode and Bean, 1883)
Family: **Grenadier**
Other common names: none
French name: grenadier à barbillon court

Distribution: Found in the North Atlantic Ocean including from Nova Scotia south to North Carolina.

Characters: It is distinguished from other Canadian Atlantic coast grenadiers by having

second dorsal fin rays shorter than anal fin rays, 6 branchiostegal rays, 9–11 pelvic fin rays, serrated anterior edge to the first 1–2 rays of the first dorsal fin, origin of the second dorsal fin behind the anus level, scale-

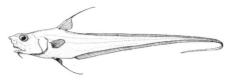

carapine grenadier

less areas on each side of the upper snout surface, and a short pectoral fin not reaching, or just touching, the anal fin. First dorsal fin with 10–11 rays, pectoral fin with 17–20 rays. There are no scales on the underside of the snout. Scales lack spines on the belly but have small spines in rows elsewhere on the body. Overall colour when preserved is pale-grey with scattered, small spots. The mouth and gill cavities, lower head surface, first dorsal and pectoral fins, peritoneum and the inner and outer pelvic fin rays are all brown. Reaches 35 cm at least.

Biology: Found near Sable Island Bank and Georges Bank, the latter at 2011–2422 m. It has been recorded off Sweden down to 5610 m. This species has been observed in the western Atlantic Ocean from a submersible at 1704–2507 m, swimming strongly against a current. When startled, a specimen stuck its head in the bottom sediment. It often hovers head down and feeds on such bottom foods as brittle stars, worms and crustaceans. Females are larger than males and spawning is thought to occur in winter.

Cardinalfish Family

Scientific name: Apogonidae
French name: apogons

Cardinalfishes are found world-wide in warmer marine waters. A few species enter fresh water in the tropics. There are about 207 species with 2 reported from Atlantic Canada.

These are small, colourful (often cardinal-red) large-eyed fishes with usually 2 dorsal fins. The first dorsal fin has 6–9 spines and the second dorsal fin 1 spine and 7–14 soft rays. Uniquely, the distal radial (fin support bone) of the last spine is short. The anal fin has 2 spines and 6–18 soft rays. Scales are usually ctenoid but may be cycloid or even absent. There are 7 branchiostegal rays. Some species are luminescent.

Cardinalfishes are related to the **Greateye Family** which is included within the cardinalfishes by some authors. Cardinal-fishes lack scales on the soft dorsal and anal fins and have fewer than 30 pored scales in the lateral line (or the lateral line is absent). This family is a member of the **Perch Order**.

These fishes are found abundantly around reefs, mangroves and in shallow water. A few species are found in deep water. They tend to be active at night and hide during the day. Some species will play dead if threatened. Some species live in the mantle cavity of a living conch and come out at night to feed, others associate with sponges and corals.

Many cardinalfishes are mouthbrooders with the males incubating an egg ball in some species, only females in others, and both sexes in some. In one species the eggs are picked up in the mouth only when danger threatens.

Cardinalfishes are often kept in marine aquaria.

See **flamefish**
twospot cardinalfish

Caribbean beardfish

Scientific name: *Polymixia lowei*
Günther, 1859
Family: **Beardfish**
Other common names: none
French name: barbudo des Caraïbes

Distribution: Found from the Grand Bank south to French Guiana.

Characters: This species is distinguished from its only Canadian relative, the **stout beardfish**, by lower dorsal fin soft ray counts and higher gill raker counts. Dorsal fin with 5–6 spines and 26–32 (usually 28–29) soft rays. Anal fin with 3–4 spines, soft rays 13–17. There are 31–36 lateral line pores and 50–62 scales. Gill rakers number 14–22 (usually 17–20). The back is a metallic blue with silvery flanks and belly. The dorsal and caudal fins have black tips. Males have black

tips to the anal rays, females are pale to slightly dusky. The peritoneum is black. Reaches 20 cm.

Caribbean beardfish

Biology: First caught on the southwest Grand Bank in 1954 (a northern range record) but also known from southwest Browns Bank in 1968 and off Sable Island in 1986. The latter was caught at 185 m depth. This species is eaten by **summer flounder**.

Caribbean divinglamp

Scientific name: *Lobianchia gemellari*
(Cocco, 1838)
Family: **Lanternfish**
Other common names: none
French name: lampe-de-plongée des Caraïbes

Distribution: Found in all temperate to tropical seas including off Atlantic Canada.

Characters: This species is distinguished from other Canadian species by having soft flexible rays at the caudal fin bases, the AO photophores in 2 series, a distinct Pol photophore, anal fin base about equal in length to the dorsal fin base, and by having luminous glands on the top and under the caudal peduncle. In contrast to its relative, the

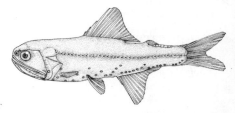

Caribbean divinglamp

Mediterranean divinglamp, this species has the Pol photophore midway between the lateral line and anal fin. Dorsal fin rays 16–18, usually 17, anal rays 13–15, usually 14, and pectoral rays 11–13, usually 12. Photophores: AO 4–6, usually 5, + 5–7, usually 6, total 10–12, usually 11. Males have a luminous gland on top of the caudal peduncle made up of 6 overlapping scale-like structures with 5 pairs of the smaller, triangular ones along the sides. Females have 2–4 heart-shaped glands under the caudal peduncle flanked by 1–2 pairs of smaller triangular ones. Reaches 10 cm, but these are abnormally large and 6 cm is a more usual maximum.

Biology: Found off the Scotian Shelf in Canada but not common. Large specimens in these waters may be expatriates, growing to a large size (10 cm), but not developing caudal luminous glands and not reproducing. Found at 300–800 m during the day and 25–350 m at night off Bermuda. Fish are found at different depths according to size as well as by time of day. Spawning near Bermuda takes place in late fall or in winter when fish measure 40–45 mm.

carinate snipe eel

Scientific name: *Labichthys carinatus*
Gill and Ryder, 1883
Family: **Snipe Eel**
Other common names: none
French name: avocette carênée

Distribution: Found world-wide in all oceans including off Atlantic Canada.

Characters: This species is distinguished from its Canadian relatives, the **closepine** and **slender snipe eels,** by its lack of a caudal filament, only 1 pore on each segment of the lateral line, the presence of short sensory ridges on the head behind the eyes, and the anus

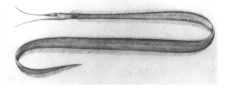

carinate snipe eel

below the pectoral fins. The upper jaw is longer than the lower jaw. Dorsal fin rays 239–361, anal fin rays 272–357. Lateral line pores 170–191. Overall colour a uniform dark

brown. The anterior, tubular nostril is dark. Reaches 80 cm.

Biology: First reported from Canadian waters in 1988 from off Georges Bank. This species makes vertical migrations and has been caught as deep as 1250–1500. The spawning season is prolonged.

Carp Family

Scientific name: Cyprinidae
French name: carpes

Carps, minnows, shiners, daces, chubs and their relatives comprise 53 species in fresh waters across Canada. Some species may enter brackish water but the family is primarily a freshwater one. Five species are exotics, introduced species from Europe and Asia. The family is also found in Africa but is absent from South America, Madagascar, New Guinea and Australia. There are over 2100 species, almost 10% of the world's fishes.

Carps are small (under 5 cm) to large (up to 3 m) fishes characterised by throat or pharyngeal teeth in 1–3 rows, with a maximum of 8 teeth in a row, there are no jaw teeth, lips are usually thin and not sucker-like, the upper jaw is bordered by the premaxillae bones, barbels are present in 0–3 pairs (mostly 1 pair or none in Canadian species), 3 branchiostegal rays, no true stomach, cycloid scales, and there are no true fin spines (some species have a hardened, unbranched ray in the dorsal and/or anal fin). The 4 anterior vertebrae are modified into Weberian ossicles which connect the swimbladder, in effect a sounding board, to the inner ear. Carps have extremely sensitive hearing and this is thought to account for their success. Carps produce an "alarm substance" when injured. This chemical stimulates other carps to flee and hide, another useful adaptation.

Carps are members of the **Carp Order**. The greatest diversity in form and species is found in southeast Asia. Fossils date back to the Palaeocene but are more recent in North America. Pharyngeal tooth counts are an important diagnostic feature. These teeth lie on a modified, fifth gill arch which can be seen or probed behind the shoulder girdle, just inside the gill opening. The arch has to be removed with dissecting equipment to count the teeth.

Tooth counts are presented as a formula such as 2,5–4,1 which indicates 2 teeth in the outer left row and 4 on the inner right row. Teeth may be lost from major or minor rows so variant formulae are given after the principal one. A horny pad on the underside of the basioccipital bone of the skull is used to masticate the food against. Tooth form varies with the food - molar-shaped teeth are used to crush molluscs, flat but grooved surfaces for grinding plant food and sharp edged teeth for slicing various invertebrate foods. Fin ray counts are also important in identification. The dorsal and anal fins have 3–4 unbranched rays followed by several branched rays. The first 2–3 unbranched rays are short or close together and may be difficult to see. The branched rays are usually well-separated and obvious. The last 2 branched rays are traditionally counted as 1 ray since they articulate with a single basal bone in the supporting skeleton. North American scientists give counts of dorsal and anal fin rays to include the *last* unbranched ray (i.e. as 1 ray) plus all branched rays with the last 2 counted as 1. In this book I have given only branched ray counts for dorsal and anal fins with the last 2 counted as 1.

Carps are remarkable for changes they undergo during the spawning season. Some fish, which are usually silvery, develop bright reds and yellows. Nuptial, pearl or breeding tubercles develop on the head, scales and fin rays often in distinct patterns, and there are in some species swellings of the head or fin rays. These changes are most apparent in males. Tubercles and swollen rays are used to clasp females during the spawning act. Tubercles are also used to fight other males and defend and clean nests. Colour attracts females for mating. Generally males have longer pectoral fins than females. Nest building males are larger than females, the reverse of the situation in most fishes where egg-bearing females are the largest. Not all species build nests and some simply broadcast eggs over weed, gravel or sand. Fractional spawning is common in carps. This is a prolonged spawning season which ensures no single batch of eggs is lost to unfavourable, temporary environmental changes such as floods. Carps are mostly

omnivores, feeding on small crustaceans, insects and some minute plants but some specialise in eating large plants, or other fishes. Diet is reflected in pharyngeal tooth shape as mentioned above. Gut length is important too. A long intestine indicates a reliance on plant material which takes longer to digest. A simple, s-shaped gut is found in insectivorous fish. A black peritoneum is thought to protect gut bacteria from damaging light. The bacteria aid in breaking down the strong cell walls of plants. Size and shape of the mouth are also indicative of diet. Carps are found in many diverse habitats from swift, cold streams to warm bogs. These are schooling fishes, especially when young.

Carps play an important role in fresh waters as food for other fishes and some species are commercially important as bait fish, as sport fish, or as food in Asian countries. Raising **minnows** as bait and as forage fish for sport fish is a big business in the U.S.A. They are an important element in the commercial aquarium trade and certain species are used in experimental studies by scientists.

See **Banff longnose dace**
    bigmouth shiner
    blackchin shiner
    blacknose dace
    blacknose shiner
    bluntnose minnow
    brassy minnow
    bridal shiner
    central stoneroller
    chiselmouth
    common carp
    common shiner
    creek chub
    cutlips minnow
    eastern silvery minnow
    emerald shiner
    fallfish
    fathead minnow
    finescale dace
    flathead chub
    ghost shiner
    golden shiner
    goldfish
    grass carp
    gravel chub
    hornyhead chub

lake chub
leopard dace
longnose dace
mimic shiner
northern redbelly dace
northern squawfish
peamouth
pearl dace
pugnose minnow
pugnose shiner
redfin shiner
redside dace
redside shiner
river chub
river shiner
rosyface shiner
rudd
sand shiner
silver chub
silver shiner
speckled dace
spotfin shiner
spottail shiner
striped shiner
tench
weed shiner
western silvery minnow
Umatilla dace

Carp Order

The **carps** or **minnows**, loaches, hill-stream loaches, algae eaters, **suckers** and their relatives form the Order Cypriniformes, found in fresh waters of North America, Eurasia and Africa. They vary from very small to large fishes and show a wide variety of body form. There are 5 families and over 2660 species with 2 families and 71 species in Canada.

The order is characterised by having 4 modified anterior vertebrae (the Weberian apparatus or ossicles) connecting the swimbladder to the inner ear as a mechanism for transmission of sound, a kinethmoid bone is present between the ascending processes of the premaxillae, the swimbladder is connected to the gut by a duct, the mouth is toothless and usually protractile, scales are cycloid and absent from the head, the adipose fin is usually absent, the fifth gill arch is modified and bears teeth ankylosed to the bone, the vomer is toothless, 3 branchiostegal rays, no true spines in the fins (although some species have hardened rays), the caudal fin is homocercal (no upturned vertebrae), and intermuscular bones are present.

The order is related to the **Catfish Order** and other orders not found in Canada such as the characins and knifefishes. These orders are related by a series of characters and are known as the Ostariophysi. The characters include the Weberian apparatus with its great importance in transmitting sound to the brain, a protractile upper jaw in many species, no true fin spines, pelvic fins abdominal in position when present and not attached to the pectoral girdle, basisphenoid bone of the skull absent, orbitosphenoid bone of the skull usually present, the parietal bone and the interorbital septum are greatly reduced in size, mesocoracoid bone of the pectoral girdle usually present, pectoral fins horizontal and low on the flank, postcleithrum bone(s) of the pectoral girdle present or absent, all anterior haemal spines are fused to the centra in the vertebrae, the anterior cervical vertebrae are modified including loss of the anteriormost supraneural bone, the first pleural rib is enlarged and mobile, expanded anterior neural arches thus roofing the neural canal, swimbladder present (absent or reduced in some) and comprising a small anterior chamber covered with a silvery peritoneal membrane and a large posterior chamber, the anterior chamber is attached to the 2 anterior pleural ribs, a duct connects the gut to the swimbladder near where the 2 chambers join, scales are cycloid, modified into bony plates or absent, minute, single-cell, horny projections known as unculi present, for example on the mouth, ventral surface of the paired fins, or breast, multicellular breeding or nuptial tubercles with a keratin cap present particularly in males, and a pheromone known as alarm substance or Schreckstoff produced from club cells of the epidermis which causes a predator-avoiding fright reaction, usually a scattering of the fish school and a dive into hiding on the bottom. Fossils date back to the Upper Cretaceous. Ostariophysi are the dominant freshwater fishes with about 6000 species.

Members of the order are used as food fishes in Asia, are popular sport fishes in Europe and form a significant part of the aquarium trade.

See **Carp Family**
Sucker Family

Carpet Shark Order

Carpet sharks, blind sharks, wobbegons, bamboosharks, zebra sharks, nurse sharks and **whale sharks** of the Order Orectolobiformes comprise 7 families and about 31 species found world-wide primarily in tropical, coastal waters. Most species are in the Indo-West Pacific region. They are small to extremely large and often benthic sharks as their name suggests. There is only 1 family and its single species in Canada.

The order is characterised by possession of an anal fin, 2 dorsal fins and no fin spines, a deep groove from the mouth to the nostril, 5 gill slits, and the short mouth is in front of the eyes. Some species are dramatically spotted or have highly developed lobes and tassels on the sides and front of the head. They are oviparous with eggs in oval cases or ovoviviparous. Most feed on molluscs and crustaceans which are crushed with specially adapted teeth although some are fish feeders. Most species have no commercial importance although some are used as food or their colourful skins are tanned as leather. Some colourful species have been kept in home aquaria. The nurse shark of the Atlantic and western Pacific oceans has been kept in large aquaria and used extensively in behavioural and physiological studies. They are quite hardy and show a ready learning ability.

See **Whale Shark Family**

cartilaginous fishes

The cartilaginous fishes or Class Chondrichthyes is one of the 5 classes which comprise those organisms known generally as **fishes**. The other 3 classes in Canada are the **ray-finned fishes, hagfishes** and **lampreys**. Cartilaginous fishes comprise 10 orders, 45 families and about 850 species. There are 2 subclasses of cartilaginous fishes, the **chimaeras** and one containing the **sharks** and **rays**. Both have Canadian representatives.

There are 8 orders, 18 families and 71 species of Canadian cartilaginous fishes.

Cartilaginous fishes are usually contrasted with that other group of **jawed fishes**, the **bony fishes**. They are characterised by a cartilage skeleton which may be hardened by calcification but is not bony, the skull has no sutures between separate bones, no true gill cover, teeth are not fused to underlying bone but are replaced by rows of teeth moving forward from behind on the jaw, swimbladder and lung absent, spiral intestinal valves present, eggs are fertilised internally by means of claspers (modified parts of the pelvic fins), the egg is enclosed in a horny case, the blood contains urea and trimethylamine oxide in high concentrations which allow passive transport of water into the body, jaws are present and the upper jaw's biting edge is formed by the palatoquadrate bone, the nostrils are single openings on each side of the lower part of the head, paired pectoral and pelvic fins are present and soft fin rays are unsegmented and their origin is epidermal (they are known as ceratotrichia).

See **Angel Shark Order**
Carpet Shark Order
Chimaera Order
Cow Shark Order
Dogfish Shark Order
Ground Shark Order
Mackerel Shark Order
Ray Order

Cat Shark Family

Scientific name: Scyliorhinidae
French name: roussettes

Cat sharks form the largest shark family with about 96, mostly small species found from arctic to tropical waters. There are 7 species in Canada, 1 on the Pacific coast and 6 on the Atlantic coast.

They are recognised by their anal fin and rudimentary nictitating eyelids, absence of fin spines, normal head, 5 gill slits, 2 dorsal fins, spiral intestinal valve, first dorsal fin base opposite or behind the pelvic fin base, and teeth small with several rows functional at once. Egg cases are broader at the posterior end. The eyes are slit or cat-like. The spiracle is well-developed. There are no precaudal pits.

Cat sharks are members of the **Ground Shark Order** and are relatives of the **Requiem Shark** and **Hound Shark** families.

Cat sharks are found from the intertidal zone down to depths over 2000 m generally on the bottom in coastal waters. In some species, individuals sleep together in rocky crevices during the day emerging at night to feed separately. Some produce tough egg cases with tendrils and the embryo may develop for almost a year attached to the substrate. Others hatch more readily, in less than a month, after a long internal development, to reduce the risks of being eaten. Still other species are ovoviviparous. Food is mainly invertebrates and small fishes. Deepwater catsharks are black but those in shallow waters have complex patterns on the body. Some species in the eastern Atlantic Ocean are used for human food, fish meal and oil. Canadian species are generally too rare or too deep to have a commercial importance.

See **broadgill cat shark**
brown cat shark
chain cat shark
deepsea cat shark
ghost cat shark
Iceland cat shark
smalleye cat shark

Catfish Order

Catfishes of the Order Siluriformes comprise 34 families and over 2400 species found world-wide mostly in benthic fresh waters although 2 families are mostly marine. South America has the greatest diversity in species. They range in size from under 10 cm to over 3 m. In Canada there is a single freshwater family with 10 species.

These fishes are characterised by a naked skin or are armoured with plates but typical scales are absent, 1 to 4 pairs of barbels are present around the mouth, the maxilla bone is reduced and toothless in many groups and becomes a support for a barbel, eyes are usually small since barbels are used to find food, the premaxillae bones of the upper jaw usually have teeth, a Weberian apparatus is present (fused and modified anterior 5 vertebrae for transmission of sound from the swimbladder, used as a sounding board to the inner ear), the symplectic, subopercular, basihyal and intermuscular bones are absent, the vomer bone in the roof of the mouth is toothed, teeth are on pterygoid and palatine bones, parietal bones are fused to the supraoccipital in the skull roof, mesopterygoid bone very reduced, preopercle and interopercle bones of the gill cover small, the posttemporal is probably fused to the supracleithrum in the pectoral girdle suspension, adipose fin usually present, serrated spines often present at the front of the dorsal and pectoral fins which can be locked erect, no pelvic fin spines, and some families (not in Canada) have an air-breathing apparatus.

The order is related to the **Carp Order**. Fossils date to the Palaeocene.

Catfishes are important food and sport fishes and the smaller species are well-known in the aquarium trade. The pectoral fin spines are venomous in some species, including Canadian ones, and certain tropical catfishes can cause death in humans. Catfishes may spawn in open water, build nests to protect young or brood eggs in the mouth. Some South American catfishes are parasitic on other fishes taking blood from the gills and skin. The candiru may enter the human urethra causing a unique and distracting pain. The electric catfishes of South America can deliver a numbing shock.

See **Bullhead Catfish Family**

catfishes

Canadian catfishes all belong to a single family, the **Bullhead Catfish Family**, or North American freshwater catfishes, with 10 species. Only 2 species are called catfish, 3 are called bullheads and the remainder are all **madtoms**. There are 34 families and over 2400 species of catfishes in the world, with 2 families mostly marine and the rest principally freshwater. South America and southern Asia are rich in catfishes.

See **black bullhead**
brindled madtom
brown bullhead
channel catfish
flathead catfish
margined madtom
northern madtom
stonecat
tadpole madtom
yellow bullhead

central mudminnow

Scientific name: *Umbra limi* (Kirtland, 1840)
Family: **Mudminnow**
Other common names: western minnow,
    mudfish, mudpuppy, dogfish, Mississippi
    mudminnow
French name: umbre de vase

Distribution: Found in central North America west of the Appalachian Mountains south to Tennessee and Arkansas. In Canada it is found in southern Manitoba and adjacent areas of western Ontario and south of a line from the southeastern corner of Lake Superior across to about Québec City.

Characters: This is the only species in the family in Canada and is easily recognised by the anal and dorsal fins being close to the tail and by the vertical bar at the tail fin base. There is no lateral line. Dorsal fin rays 13–17, anal rays 7–10, pectoral rays 11–16 and pelvic rays 6–7. Lateral scales 30–37. The head and body are brown, black or olive-green above, the flanks brown with traces of numerous bars

central mudminnow

in some fish and the belly white to yellowish. Fins are brown, sometimes tinged with pink or orange. Spawning males have iridescent green or blue-green anal and pelvic fins. Size attained is 13.2 cm.

Biology: Mudminnows feed on bottom-dwelling animals such as crustaceans, insect larvae, molluscs, rarely small fish but certainly other mudminnows, and other small inhabitants of weedy, detritus-rich ponds and small creeks. Curiously only female mudminnows ate fish in a Manitoba study and older females consumed mostly fishes. During winter this diet may contribute to egg development so that spawning can occur soon after ice break-up, and so young have longer to grow before facing their first winter. Prey is attacked by a swift dart from con-

cealment in vegetation. Mudminnows are common prey for many larger fishes such as **catfishes** and members of the **Pike** and **Sunfish** families. Even birds, muskrats and foxes have been recorded as eating them. Spawning occurs in early spring and 220–2286 eggs are produced which probably stick to vegetation. Females live longer than males and may attain 9 years of age, but this is uncertain as mudminnow scales are difficult to "read" for age. They have been used as bait fish and are excellent aquarium fishes as they do not require an air pump.

central stoneroller

Scientific name: *Campostoma anomalum*
    (Rafinesque, 1820)
Family: **Carp**
Other common names: Mississippi
    stoneroller, stone lugger, racehorse chub,
    greased chub, blue sucker, steel-backed
    chub, rotgut minnow, doughbelly,
    mammy, tallow-mouth minnow
French name: roule-caillou

Distribution: Found from New York west through the southern Great Lakes to Wisconsin and south to Georgia and Mexico. In Canada found in the Thames River of the Lake St. Clair drainage, the Niagara River and probably in a Lake Ontario drainage, in southwestern Ontario.

Characters: This species is unique in Canada by having the intestine wrapped around the swimbladder. The upper and lower jaws have a cartilaginous, chisel edge and the snout projects slightly. Pharyngeal teeth 4–4 or 1,4–4,1, slightly hooked at the tip. Dorsal fin branched rays 7, anal branched rays 6, pectoral rays 15–19 and pelvic rays 8. Lateral line scales 43–64. Gill rakers 21–35. The back and flanks are brown, brassy, dark olive or greyish and the belly is white. There may be a pale golden stripe along the upper flank. Some scales on the flank are darkened apparently where they have been lost and regenerated. There is a dark bar in the anal and dorsal fins. In breeding males the dorsal, anal, pectoral and pelvic fin bases are orange below the black central bar and a paler orange or yellow at the edge of the fin. The caudal fin has a basal orange bar. Upper lips are bright white. Iris red-brown. Breeding males also have large tubercles on the head and one on each scale, smaller tubercles on the gill membranes and side of the head, on the first 6 pectoral rays and on the first 5–6 dorsal rays, and broad, large pectoral fins. Tubercles are lost after spawning, as early as 26 May in New York. Peritoneum jet black. Reaches 28.7 cm.

central stoneroller

Biology: The stoneroller is found in clear rapid streams, in both pool and riffle sections. It can be found in *Potamogeton* weed clumps in riffles. It is rare in lakes and large rivers. During winter it may retreat under stones where several fish can be found together. It is tolerant of some poor water quality but requires silt-free gravel for spawning.

The lower jaw is used to scrape algae and associated organisms off rocks. Diatoms are the major food item. The feeding process causes small stones to move, hence the common name, unless it derives from nest building.

It may root for eggs in nests of other species. Scale eating has been reported. The stoneroller is eaten by **smallmouth bass** and aquatic birds. It may compete with **rainbow trout** as nest building destroys **trout** redds.

Life span is 6 years with females maturing mostly at age 2–3 and males at age 4–5. Males grow much larger than females. Spawning occurs from April to July in stream headwaters with nest building starting at 10.8°C or warmer. Males start to develop tubercles in September and October prior to a spring spawning and lose them after spawning. Tubercle scars are obvious in fish caught in summer. Males excavate pits by burrowing with the head so smaller particles are washed downstream and by carrying larger pebbles to the edge of the pit in the mouth.

Large males may drive away smaller males or 2–5 males may excavate a pit together. Dominant males usually move from pit to pit, spending only a few minutes at each pit. Fights between males of equal size consist of "body checks", shoulder to ribs. Females are usually in schools in deeper water. Females may form a queue downstream of a nest area, awaiting their turn at a nest pit. A female will enter the nest pit whereupon nearby males will attempt to press up against her. This stimulates egg deposition. The process lasts only a few seconds and the activity, along with subsequent pit excavation, covers the eggs. Pits are usually under protecting banks but can be in open water. **Creek, river** and **hornyhead chub** nests may be used. In contrast **creek chubs** and **common shiners** may take over stoneroller nests as the stoneroller is easily displaced. Fertilised eggs are up to 2.4 mm in diameter after water hardening, amber in colour, adhesive and number up to 4800 per female.

This species is an excellent bait for **bass, walleyes** and **catfish** and is sold as such in Ottawa although it does not occur around the National Capital, the source being in south-central Ontario in a Lake Ontario drainage. Stonerollers are eaten in the U.S.A, even in preference to **trout**! The central stoneroller was given the status of "rare" in 1985 by the Committee on the Status of Endangered Wildlife in Canada.

chain cat shark

Scientific name: *Scyliorhinus retifer*
(Garman, 1881)
Family: **Cat Shark**
Other common names: chain dogfish
French name: roussette maille

Distribution: Found on southwestern Georges Bank but not yet definitely recorded from the Canadian part. South to Nicaragua.

Characters: This cat shark is distinguished from its Atlantic coast relatives by having crests over the eyes and by the chain

chain cat shark

or net body pattern. Denticles are small and flat so the skin feels relatively smooth for a shark. There are no enlarged denticles along the upper margin of the caudal. The body has strong black lines in a chain-like pattern which is part of 7–8 obscure dusky saddles. The chain pattern may also extend over the flank. The body colour is reddish-brown above and yellowish below. The eye is bright green. Attains 48 cm and probably more.

Biology: This is a common cat shark south of Canada found on the bottom at 58–550 m and temperatures around 10°C on the continental slope and upper slope. It may favour rocky bottoms where trawls cannot operate. Food is unknown but stomach content analyses show small pebbles to be present in about half the sample. The pebbles may act as ballast. Males may mature at 40 cm and females at 38 cm although some studies indicate this does not occur until a length of 50 cm or more. This is an oviparous shark with 8–12 ova up to 1.6 cm in diameter in a single, left ovary. Young hatch at about 10 cm. The egg case is up to 6.3 cm by 2.7 cm, is amber in colour and each corner has a tendril up to 7.6 cm long.

chain pearlfish

Scientific name: *Echiodon dawsoni*
   Williams and Shipp, 1982
Family: **Pearlfish**
Other common names: none
French name: aurin chaîne

Distribution: Found off Florida and in the eastern Gulf of Mexico with larvae straying north to Atlantic Canada.

Characters: Adults of this species are distinguished by the tapering body shape and the very long dorsal and anal fins, and by having 17–21 pectoral rays and 6 nasal lamellae pairs. Nasal lamellae are flaps of tissue in the nostril and are also used to identify larvae. The larval vexillum, an elongate predorsal filament, is also characteristic. It consists of 2 cartilaginous threads which emerge from the bulbous tip of a fleshy sheath. There are about 119–129 dorsal fin rays and about 120–124 anal fin rays. The adult body is pale and translucent with a white sheen in live fish and the stomach is a

light tan. The name chain pearlfish is derived from chain-like brown pigmentation on the vertebrae. Larvae lack the chain pigmentation. Adults reach 9.2 cm.

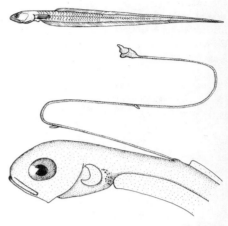

chain pearlfish

Biology: Known only as larval specimens from the Scotian Shelf, first collected in 1977 at the northern limit of the species range. Adults are found at 23–180 m and may be nocturnal. This species and its relatives do not appear to associate with sea cucumbers like other pearlfishes. Larvae feed on small crustaceans such as copepods.

chain pickerel

Scientific name: *Esox niger* Le Sueur, 1818
Family: **Pike**
Other common names: eastern, mud, grass, lake, reticulated or federation pickerel; green, black-chain, river, grass or duck-billed pike; jack, snake, picquerelle
French name: brochet maillé

Distribution: Found in the Eastern Townships of Québec, southern and western New Brunswick and introduced into Nova Scotia and south to Florida and the Gulf Coast and in the southern Mississippi River basin in the eastern U.S.A. Introduced elsewhere in the U.S.A.

Characters: This species is distinguished by having 7–8 or rarely 9 submandibular pores on both lower jaws (usually 4 on each side), scales on the cheeks and opercula,

14–17 branchiostegal rays, and colour pattern. Principal dorsal fin rays 14–15, principal anal rays 11–13, pectoral rays 12–15 and pelvic rays 9–10. Lateral line scales 110–138. Overall colour bright green with the back dark green, olive-green or yellowish-brown, flanks brassy, yellow-green or yellow, with dark lines making a chain or reticulate pattern and a cream or yellowish-white belly. Scales may have gold edges. There are black bars radiating anteriorly and almost vertically downward from the eye. Fins have darkly pigmented rays and clear membranes. The front margin of the anal fin may be orange and the pectoral and pelvic fins may be orange. The eye is yellow. Young fish, less than 25 cm long, have a gold, middorsal stripe and lack the chain marks, being barred and mottled. Hybrids with **northern pike** are known from Québec. Reaches 99.1 cm and 5.6 kg. The world, all-tackle angling record from Homerville, Georgia in 1961 weighed 4.25 kg. The Canadian angling record was caught by Sean D'Entremont in July 1989 from Doctors Lake, Nova Scotia and weighed 2.44 kg.

chain pickerel

Biology: Chain pickerel are found in slow streams, ponds and lakes which have abundant aquatic vegetation. There is some movement into deeper water during the day but they are tolerant of high temperatures up to 37°C. They can tolerate brackish water up to 22‰ but usually 5‰ or less and highly acid water (pH 3.8). Food when adult is crayfish and a wide variety of fishes including their own kind. A 49.5 cm pickerel was found to have eaten a 31.8 cm pickerel. Frogs, snakes and mice are also taken. Chain pickerel feed during both the day and night. Individuals lie in wait for passing prey. Young feed on zooplankton. Females grow larger and faster than males and live longer, to a maximum of 10 years. Maturity is attained at 3–4 years in the north or as early as 1 year in the southern U.S.A. Spawning occurs in Canada in April-May at 6–11°C after the pickerel migrate into flooded, vegetated areas. A female and 1–2 males swim over the vegetation, flex their bodies so their genital openings are close together and eggs and sperm are shed and spread by rapid caudal fin beats. This process is repeated over 1–2 days. The eggs are yellow, up to 2 mm in diameter and adhesive on plants. Up to 30,000 eggs may be shed although most reports are of less than 10,000. The young attach to vegetation with an adhesive gland on the snout until the yolk sac is absorbed after about a week. The chain pickerel is of only minor sport and food interest in Canada but in some U.S. states it is an important sport fish and the white flesh is reputed to be tasty eating. Large numbers are caught through the ice using **minnows** as bait.

- Most accessible June through August.
- Nova Scotia and New Brunswick.
- Light to medium action spinning outfits used with eight- to 10–pound test line.
- Wide variety of 1/4- to 3/8-ounce silver or gold spoons, minnow-imitating plugs and small spinners. The best bait is live **minnows**.

channel catfish

Scientific name: *Ictalurus punctatus* (Rafinesque, 1818)
Family: **Bullhead Catfish**
Other common names: spotted catfish, Great Lake catfish, lake catfish, northern catfish, blue channel cat, lady cat, white cat, fiddler, willow cat, blue fulton, chucklehead
French name: barbue de rivière

Distribution: Found in extreme southern Québec, southern Ontario, Lake of the Woods, southeastern Manitoba and in the Qu'Appelle River and Cumberland Lake in eastern Saskatchewan. South to the Gulf of Mexico in the U.S.A. Widely introduced outside its natural distribution.

Characters: This species is identified by the posterior tip of the adipose fin being free of the back, a characteristic deeply forked caudal fin, mouth corner barbels more than 3 times as long as nostril barbels, and a bony ridge between the back of the head and the dorsal fin. Dorsal fin soft rays 6–7, total anal rays

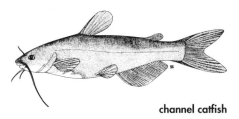

channel catfish

23–32, pelvic rays 8 and pectoral rays 8–9. The dorsal fin spine lacks barbs while the pectoral spine has 16–20 strong barbs posteriorly. Gill rakers 13–18. Males develop a swollen head above and behind the eyes in the spawning season, the bluish back colour is brighter and the belly is whitish-blue. The back and upper flank are steel-blue, blue-grey, slate-brown or grey, fading to a whitish belly. Fins are similar to the adjacent body. Barbels are blackish. Young fish, smaller than 35.6 cm, have olive to blackish dots on the flank and are greenish. A record of this species from Cumberland Lake, Saskatchewan dates back to 1797, a second was caught in that lake in 1820 and the third specimen for Saskatchewan from the Qu'Appelle River in 1983. Reaches 120.2 cm. The world, all-tackle angling record weighed 26.3 kg and was caught in 1964 in Santee-Cooper Reservoir, South Carolina. The Canadian angling record weighed 20.20 kg. and was caught in Red River, Manitoba, in August 1993 by Darryl Landygo.

Biology: Channel cats are found in lakes and the larger rivers favouring deeper, cooler and clearer water than other **bullheads**. However they can survive temperatures up to 35°C. Some enter brackish water. They usually spend the day in deep holes or under rocks and logs. In the St. Lawrence River some channel catfish do not move while others travel as much as 160 km.

Feeding occurs both by day and by night and some items are taken at the water surface. Food includes crustaceans, insects, molluscs, algae and other plants, seeds, fish such as **yellow perch** and **minnows**, and even birds, grapes, chicken necks, canned corn, beef bones and other scavenged items.

Life span is about 40 years although few fish attain this. Populations in the southern U.S.A., where growth is rapid in a warm climate, only reach 7 years and mature at 18 months. In Lake Erie half the females are mature at 25–28 cm and half the males at 28–31 cm. Growth after 8 years of age is slow in Québec waters and maturity is attained there at 8 years at the northern range limit. Catfish can be aged by the growth rings on spines which also reflect water temperatures since catfish do not feed and grow below certain temperatures. This knowledge gained from extant catfish has been used to determine the climate millions of years ago from deposits of fossil catfish spines.

Spawning occurs in late spring to summer at 21–30°C. Some channel catfish move into running water at spawning. The male builds and cleans a nest, using fin and body movements, in holes under rocks, logs or in banks. Females bite other females or males when ready to spawn and both sexes drive other fish away. The female moves over the nest site, wiggling and banging the pectoral and pelvic alternately on the bottom. The male and female position themselves head to tail, wrapping their tails over each other's head, both fish quiver and release eggs and sperm. Eggs are yellow, up to 4.0 mm in diameter and up to 52,000 per female. Males defend, aerate and manipulate the eggs. Manipulation is carried out with the body and fins and may serve to aid in hatching.

Channel catfish have white, flaky flesh which has attracted a commercial fishery in Canada, and it is the principle catfish on farms in the U.S.A., in an attempt to meet demand. It is said to be one of the best tasting freshwater fishes in North America. The Canadian catch reached 564,322 kg in 1964. This catfish is an important sport species. Their large size, fighting abilities and tastiness make them attractive to anglers.

- Most accessible May through July.
- The Red River and Lake Winnipeg in Manitoba and the watershed of the Great Lakes.
- Medium to heavy bait-casting and spinning outfits used with 14- to 20-pound line.

• Whole or cut pieces of forage fish such as **smelt**, **alewife (= gaspereau)**, **goldeye**, animal livers and worms.

channel darter

Scientific name: *Percina copelandi*
(Jordan, 1877)
Family: **Perch**
Other common names: Copeland's darter
French name: dard gris

Distribution: Found in the upper St. Lawrence River basin east and west of Montréal and at Ottawa, and along the shores of lakes Erie and Huron. It is only found west of the Appalachians in the U.S.A., south to the Gulf of Mexico.

Characters: This darter is recognised by the small mouth not extending beyond the anterior eye margin, a smooth edge to the preopercle bone on the side of the head, a large anal fin at least as large as the soft dor-

channel darter

sal fin, belly midline either naked or with enlarged scales, 2 anal fin spines and a deep groove between the snout and lip (premaxillaries protractile). Dorsal fin spines 9–13 (usually 10–11), dorsal soft rays 10–14 (usually 11–12), anal fin rays 7–10 (usually 8–9). Lateral scale rows 43–61. Males have 6–11 enlarged, modified, star-shaped scales in a row on the belly where females are unscaled or scaled only posteriorly. Overall colour is brown to olive, semi-translucent, with about 5–9 faint saddles. The flank has 8–18 brown to black oblong and partly confluent blotches linked by a faint, thin brown to black stripe. Fins are mostly clear. There is usually a spot at the caudal fin base and 2 bars radiating down and forward from the eye. Breeding males have black basal and marginal bands with white at the tip on the spiny dorsal fin, a black head, throat and pelvic fins, a greenish cast to the upper flank and a bluish one to

the lower flank. The basal part of the anal fin is blackish. Tubercles are present. Females have an elongate tubular papilla in the genital area. Reaches 6.1 cm standard length.

Biology: An uncommon Canadian darter found over sand, gravel and rock mixes in stream pools and on lake shores. Insects and crustaceans are the major foods, and large amounts of algae and detritus are also swallowed. Males grow larger than females. Spawning occurs in running water in July in the northern U.S.A. at temperatures over 20°C. Males have a territory based on a central rock. Females join the male over gravel or small rocks behind the central rock. The female partly buries herself in the gravel, the male presses down on her from above with his pelvic fins on each side and his tail area paralleling hers, and adhesive eggs are released and fertilised into the gravel. Several females may spawn with 1 male, depositing 4–10 eggs. Each female may have over 720 eggs up to 1.4 mm in diameter. The eggs are not guarded by the parents. This darter was given the status "threatened" in 1993 by the Committee on the Status of Endangered Wildlife in Canada.

channel flounder

Scientific name: *Syacium micrurum*
Ranzani, 1840
Family: **Lefteye Flounder**
Other common names: none
French name: fausse limande pâté

Distribution: Found from Nova Scotia to Brazil and off tropical West Africa.

Characters: This species is distinguished from other Canadian Atlantic adult **lefteye flounders** by having both pelvic fin bases short and the eyed side base on the belly midline, the lateral line is not strongly arched over

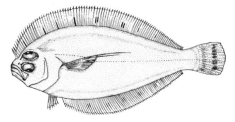

channel flounder

the eyed side pectoral fin, no caudal fin spots, and jaws extending to at least the middle of the eye. Dorsal fin rays 83–92, anal rays 64–74, pectoral rays on the eyed side 10–12, and lateral line scales 54–68. Lower arm gill rakers 7–9. Eyes are close together in both males and females. Males have the upper 2 pectoral fin rays elongated. Larvae have 5–8 elongate, dorsal fin rays known as tentacles. Eyed side brownish with or without spots, with rings containing dark spots, and blotches. There is usually a dark blotch under the tip of the pectoral fin and on the lateral line level with the end of the dorsal fin. Blind side white. Fins are flecked and spotted. Reaches 30 cm.

Biology: Known only from stray larvae caught off the Scotian Shelf. Adults are known only as far north as Florida at depths down to 412 m on mud, sand and gravel bottoms.

chars

Chars (also spelt charrs) are members of the genus *Salvelinus* in the **Salmon Family**. There are about 20 species found in fresh and salt waters of the northern part of the Northern Hemisphere. There are 6 members of the genus in Canada although only one, the **Arctic char** is commonly called by that name, the others being referred to as **trouts**. The **aurora trout** is a subspecies related to the **brook trout**. It has been suggested that the adoption of the spelling "char" over the older "charr" was owing to the rivalry of two ichthyologists at the British Museum in the late nineteenth century with Albert Günther using charr and Francis Day insisting on char. The origin of char is possibly Celtic and more recently Gaelic (*ceara*) meaning red or blood-coloured or possibly from the Old English for turner, a fish that swims to and fro.

Chars are characterised by a short vomer bone in the roof of the mouth with teeth well-developed on its head but not the shaft, scales are minute (190 or more in the lateral line), the flanks have pale grey or red spots on a darker background, and the pectoral, pelvic and anal fins usually have a white leading edge bordered behind by contrasting black.

Chars are important food and sport fishes and are often beautifully coloured. They show a great amount of variation between lakes and many of these forms have received scientific names. Their taxonomy and systematics have yet to be fully worked out. Variation is partly genetic and partly environmental in species found in landlocked, riverine and anadromous populations with wide geographical distributions and histories since the last ice age.

See　**Arctic char**
　　aurora trout
　　bull trout
　　brook trout
　　Dolly Varden
　　lake trout

checker eelpout

Scientific name: *Lycodes vahli*
　　Reinhardt, 1831
Family: **Eelpout**
Other common names: Vahl's eelpout,
　　lycode de Vahl
French name: lycode à carreaux

Distribution: Found in the North Atlantic Ocean; in the west from Davis Strait, off Labrador, in the Gulf of St. Lawrence and south to the northern Scotian Shelf.

Characters: This species is separated from its Canadian Atlantic relatives by having small pelvic fins, a mouth under the snout, no large pores around the mouth, crests on the chin, a single lateral line running down towards the anal fin origin or paralleling the

checker eelpout

anal fin base, a long tail (preanal length 38–41% of total length), and bands on the body. Dorsal fin rays 104–113 and anal rays 96–102 (counts include half the continuous caudal fin rays). Pectoral fin rays 17–20. Scales are absent from the head to dorsal fin origin and from the pectoral fin base. Vertebrae 112–119 in the western Atlantic Ocean. Overall colour is brownish-grey with 7–12 dark bands on the dorsal fin and flank, most apparent in young fish. There are 1–3 black spots on the anterior dorsal fin of adults. Peritoneum black. Reaches 52 cm.

Biology: Reported in Canadian waters at 201–650 m and 2.1–4.5°C. Food includes worms, crustaceans and molluscs. **Greenland sharks** have been reported as predators of this eelpout. Eggs attain 4.5 mm in diameter and number up to 93, but little else is known of biology.

checkered wolf eel

Scientific name: *Lycenchelys kolthoffi* Jensen, 1902
Family: **Eelpout**
Other common names: none
French name: lycode quadrillée

Distribution: Found in Hudson Strait, northern coasts of Greenland, and northern Eurasia.

Characters: This species is distinguished from its Canadian Arctic-Atlantic relatives

checkered wolf eel

by having short pelvic fins, a mouth under the snout, large pores around the mouth, no crests on the chin, no bony plates along the dorsal and anal fin bases, and colour pattern. The body is very elongate and compressed. Branchiostegal rays 6. Vertebrae 116–119. The body is covered with scales except for the belly and the back in front of the dorsal fin. The lateral line has midflank and ventral branches. Dorsal fin rays about 124 and anal rays about 110 (each including half the caudal fin rays). Pectoral fin rays 14–15. Overall colour is yellowish, spotted and blotched dark brown on the flank and dorsal fin. Peritoneum black. Reaches 19 cm.

Biology: Reported from sand and mud bottoms with stones at 202–903 m and temperatures of –0.5 to –0.9°C. Food is small clams.

chestnut lamprey

Scientific name: *Ichthyomyzon castaneus* Girard, 1858
Family: **Lamprey**

Other common names: western, northern, silver, and brown lamprey, hitchhiker, seven-eyed cat, bloodsucker
French name: lamproie brun

Distribution: Found in central North America from southeastern Saskatchewan, west-central Manitoba and eastern Lake Huron tributaries of Ontario south to the Gulf of Mexico centred on the Mississippi-Missouri basin.

Characters: There are 49–56 trunk myomeres. Teeth are sharp, strong and curved. The band of teeth below the mouth is a broad, curved bar with 6–11 tooth cusps. There are 4 pairs of inner lateral teeth, usually bicuspid and sometimes tricuspid. This lamprey is distinguished from Canadian relatives by having a single, notched dorsal fin and with 1 or more lateral disc teeth with 2 cusps. Adults are dark grey to olive, or yellow-brown, sometimes mottled, occasionally a chestnut colour which gives them their name. They become blue-black when spawning. Ammocoetes are overall lighter in colour. Attains 38 cm.

chestnut lamprey

disc view

Biology: Found mostly in medium-sized streams. It is not as economically significant as the **sea lamprey** and **silver lamprey** because of its habitat, size, abundance and distribution in Canada. Elsewhere it is known to attack **brook trout** and can stay attached for over 18 days, killing the host. Trout destruction has been reported as reaching 23.5 kg/ha or about one-third of the trout available to anglers. Peak spawning is in mid-June at 16–22°C and takes place at night in small to large groups (up to 50). A female attaches to a stone and begins rapid quivering motions. A male attaches to the head of the female and wraps its tail around her body. Up to 5 lampreys can attach, each to the head of the one before it. A large female had 42,000 eggs. Eggs are elliptical, 0.64 mm by 0.56 mm. Ammocoetes prefer vegetated areas with current unlike other species. Ammocoete life span is unknown, but is presumed to be 5–7 years. They are a favoured food of **burbot** as well as other fishes. Transformed adults do not feed over their first, and one subsequent, winter and feed most heavily from April to October. They spawn and die the following summer. Adults are eaten by **trouts**. This lamprey was accorded a status of "vulnerable" in 1991 by the Committee on the Status of Endangered Wildlife in Canada.

chevron scutepout

Scientific name: *Lycodonus mirabilis*
  Goode and Bean, 1883
Family: **Eelpout**
Other common names: none
French name: lycaspine à chevrons

Distribution: Reported from eastern Hudson Strait and Davis Strait, the Grand Bank and south to North Carolina.
  Characters: This species is distinguished from its Canadian Arctic-Atlantic relatives by having pelvic fins, large pores around the mouth, and a row of small bony plates along the dorsal and anal fin bases. The body is rounded and there are 5 branchiostegal rays.

chevron scutepout

Scales are absent from the nape and fins. Dorsal fin rays 99–107, anal rays 93–102, and pectoral rays 15–18. Head and fins black, belly bluish-grey, and the rest of the body light. Reaches 28.2 cm.
  Biology: Depth range is 620–2020 m in and near Canadian waters, elsewhere to 2394 m.

chilipepper

Scientific name: *Sebastes goodei*
  (Eigenmann and Eigenmann, 1890)
Family: **Scorpionfish**
Other common names: johnny cod

French name: sébaste de Goode
  Distribution: Found from the Gulf of Alaska to Vancouver Island and Baja California.
  Characters: This species is characterised by the lack of head spines and the longest

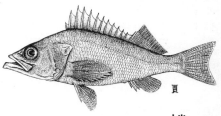

chilipepper

anal ray equal to or less than the eye size. The space between the eyes on top of the head is convex. The chin projects. The upper jaw reaches back to about the middle of the eye. Dorsal fin spines 13, soft rays 13–14, usually 14. Anal fin soft rays 8–9, usually 8, second anal spine not much thicker than third and shorter. Pectoral fin rays 16–18, usually 17, with 7–9 unbranched. Gill rakers 34–39. Vertebrae 26. Lateral line pores 48–57, scale rows below lateral line 60–77. Nasal and parietal spines weakly present in young only. Body pinkish-red, fins pink with soft dorsal and caudal fins dusky. Belly white. Lateral line white. Young are olive on back. Peritoneum silvery-white but black-dotted in young. Reaches 56 cm.
  Biology: Rare in British Columbia. Usually found on sand and mud bottoms and around rocks at 61–330 m. Young fish are in shallower water. Food is krill, squids and fish such as **hake, lanternfish** and **anchovies.** Life span exceeds 16 years. Precocious females in California may mature at 2 years of age although half the population is mature at 4 years. Females may have up to 538,000 eggs. Commercially important in California.

Chimaera Family

Scientific name: Chimaeridae
French name: chimères

Chimaeras, shortnose chimaeras or **ratfishes**, are found in the Atlantic and Pacific oceans. There are about 20 species with 2 in

Canadian waters, 1 on the Pacific coast and 1 on the Atlantic coast.

These fishes are characterised by the blunt snout, diphycercal tail (internally and externally symmetrical), 2 dorsal fins, the first having a venomous spine and being erectile, the second being much longer, lower and not erectile, an inferior mouth, and a tadpole-shaped or spindle-shaped egg capsule with a long, posterior filament. Unlike most other fishes, chimaeras breath water through the nostrils, not the mouth. Unlike the related **sharks**, there is a fleshy gill cover over 4 gill openings, no spiracles, usually naked skin and males have a clasping organ on the head and clasping organs in front of the pelvic fins as well as pelvic bifid or trifid claspers. The lateral line is an open groove, or a closed groove with pores at intervals.

Chimaeras are relatives of the **Longnose Chimaera Family**, sometimes classified as one family, and are part of the **Chimaera Order** which is characterised by a few, large tooth plates used for grinding food, 2 pairs of plates in the upper jaw and 1 pair in the lower. Chimaeras are so named because of their bizarre appearance in allusion to the mythical Greek monster which had a lion's head, a goat's body and a serpent's tail.

These fishes have been used as a fish meal and for oil when caught incidental to other fishes. They can be caught from intertidal areas down to several hundred metres. They swim poorly using the pectoral fins and feed on various invertebrates and fishes. The head clasper is used to hold the female's pectoral fin during mating. Only 2 egg capsules are laid, 1 from each ovary. The embryos take 9–12 months to develop. The head pores are homologous with the ampullae of Lorenzini in **sharks** and can detect electrical fields.

See **deepwater chimaera**
spotted ratfish

Chimaera Order

Chimaeras, **ratfishes**, ghost sharks and elephant fishes are members of the Order Chimaeriformes comprising 3 living families and about 35 species usually in deep, cold temperate to tropical marine waters. The 3 families are combined as 1 family by some scientists. There are representatives of 2 families in Canada with 5 species.

The characters of this order include 2 dorsal fins, the first being short, erectile and with an erectile, venomous spine at the front and the second being long and lower than the first, cartilage skeleton, naked skin in most adults (young have dermal denticles), pelvic and head claspers in males used to grasp females during copulation, an inferior mouth, internal fertilisation and egg case production, grinding tooth plates which may protrude from the mouth like rat teeth (hence ratfishes), tooth replacement is slow as opposed to the rapid process in **sharks**, the palatoquadrate bone is fused to the cranium (holostyly or fusion of the upper jaw mechanism with the skull as in **bony fishes**), no spiracle, 4 gills overlain by a gill cover so there is 1 gill opening on each side of the head as in **bony fishes**, separate anal and urogenital openings, no stomach or ribs, no vertebrae, and the branchial basket below the neurocranium. Fossils date back to Devonian times, over 275 million years ago.

The order is related to the **sharks** and the **Ray Order** which together form a subclass of the **cartilaginous fishes** with chimaeras forming the only other subclass. Chimaeras have diverged markedly from **sharks** particularly in respect to the gill cover, upper jaw and separate gut and urinogenital openings, characters similar to **bony fishes**. Other characters are found in **cartilaginous fishes** and this mixture lead to their name of "chimaera", a monster or cross-breed.

These fishes have little or no economic importance but are intriguing to scientists because of their anatomy.

See **Chimaera Family**
Longnose Chimaera Family

China rockfish

Scientific name: *Sebastes nebulosus*
Ayres, 1854
Family: **Scorpionfish**
Other common names: yellow-striped rockfish, pelican
French name: sébaste à bandes jaunes

Distribution: Found from southeast Alaska to southern California including British Columbia.

Characters: This species is distinguished by colour, a marked concave space between the eyes on top of the head, head spines and lateral line canal pores. Dorsal fin spines 13, soft rays 12–14, usually 13. Anal fin soft rays 6–8, usually 7, second spine twice as thick as third and longer. Pectoral fin rays

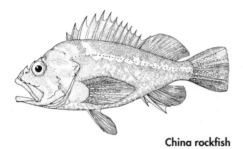

China rockfish

17–19, usually 18. Gill rakers 26–31. Vertebrae 26. Lateral line pore 37–48, scale rows below lateral line 43–48. The supraocular, coronal and nuchal spines are absent, other spines strong and covered by thick skin. The overall colour is black to blue-black including fins, with some yellow, light blue or white mottling. The belly is whitish. There is usually a distinctive, broad, irregular yellow stripe on the third to fourth dorsal fin spine sloping down to the lateral line and along it to the tail base. The peritoneum is pale. Reaches 45.3 cm. The world, all-tackle angling record weighed 1.67 kg and was caught in 1992 in Neah Bay, Washington.

Biology: Found from 3 to 128 m at inshore rocky areas where it can take refuge in crevices. A territory is maintained. This species lives up to 40 years. Food includes brittle stars, squid, octopus, bryozoans, crustaceans and fishes. Females with eyed larvae have been collected in Alaska in July and August. This is one of the best tasting rockfishes and is caught by sport fishermen from boats using squid, shrimp, small live fish or jigs as bait. It is in particular demand by oriental specialty markets, hence its name.

chinook salmon

Scientific name: *Oncorhynchus tshawytscha*
   (Walbaum, 1792)
Family: **Salmon**

Other common names: spring salmon, king salmon, tyee, quinnat, blackmouth, blackjaw, hookbill, winter salmon, chub salmon
French name: saumon quinnat

Distribution: Found from the western Canadian Arctic east to the Mackenzie and Coppermine rivers (rare), the Bering Strait south to California, running up British Columbian rivers and in the upper Yukon River in Canada. Also south to Japan in the western Pacific Ocean. Introduced elsewhere in North America and world-wide but mostly unsuccessful. Some captures in New Brunswick and Nova Scotia are probably strays from U.S. introductions. Widely stocked in the Great Lakes and found also in the St. Lawrence River.

Characters: This species is distinguished by having 130–165 lateral line scales, 13–19 principal anal fin rays, pupil-sized or smaller, oblong black spots on the back, upper flank and all the caudal fin, gums around teeth of lower jaw black and 90–240 pyloric caeca. Principal dorsal fin rays 10–14, pectoral rays 14–17 and pelvic rays 10–11. Males have a kype or hooked lower jaw with enlarged teeth when spawning and the adipose fin is larger. The back and upper flank is iridescent green or blue-green to black with a golden sheen, the lower flank is silvery and the belly silvery-white. The tongue is dark. The adipose fin has a dark margin and a clear central area. Spawning males are pinkish-brown to olive or even a dull yellow with a purple sheen and are much darker than fish in the sea. Young have 6–12 high, wide parr marks which are centred on the lateral line and are wider than

chinook salmon

intervening pale areas. The first anal fin ray is elongated and white. Reaches 160.0 cm and 61.2 kg, the largest Pacific coast **salmon** species. Tyee is the Chinook Indian word for chief or large. The world, all-tackle angling record from the Kenai River, Alaska in 1985 weighed 44.11 kg. The Canadian angling record from the Skeena River, B.C. was caught by Heinz Wichman in July 1959 and weighed 41.77 kg.

Biology: Chinooks live 1–5 years at sea, usually 2–3 years before entering larger rivers to spawn. The longest river migration is 4827 km. Northern populations remain at sea longer than southern ones. Long coastal movements occur northwestwards, reversing to return to the river of birth. Some fish go 1600 km or more out to sea. They may descend to 200 m, possibly 375 m, in the ocean. Only about 260 streams in British Columbia have a chinook run and 14 of these account for half the production of chinook. They prefer freshwater temperatures of 12–14°C.

Young may go to sea immediately or 2–3 months later as smolts, but most spend 1–2 years in fresh water. The former are "ocean-type" chinook and are predominant in coastal populations south of 56°N. The latter are "stream-type" chinook and predominate in inland areas north and south of 56°N and in coastal populations north of 56°N. Stream-type fish are found in areas distant from the sea or those which have low growth opportunities. They have a longer time to grow and be strong enough for a long migration and to be large enough to avoid freshwater predators on a short migration.

Food in fresh water is aquatic and terrestrial insects and crustaceans. Sea-dwelling adults feed predominately on fish including **herrings, sand lances, anchovies, capelins, smelt, eulachons** and many others. Some squids and crustaceans are also taken.

Chinook in fresh water are eaten by **rainbow trout, cutthroat trout, Dolly Varden, coho salmon, rockfishes, northern squawfish, sculpins** and various birds. Adults at sea are taken by marine mammals and, on the spawning run, by bears and birds.

Maximum life span is 9 years and spawners are 3–9 years old. Small three-year-olds are called jacks and are usually males. Mature chinook start on spawning runs throughout the year, usually earlier in the north or in rivers where the run upriver is the longest. Some rivers have more than one run since

these fish are headed for different spawning grounds. These are often spring or winter chinooks. Some runs reach just into fresh water while the Yukon River run is about 2000 km. Spawning times vary with the migration length. The Yukon River spawning time is July–August, in the Fraser River July–November, and October on Vancouver Island.

Spawning sites are large rivers near riffles in water deeper and over gravel larger than for other Pacific salmons. The Fraser and the Yukon are the main Canadian chinook rivers. The female excavates a redd by lashing the tail while lying on her side. Landlocked populations may spawn on gravel shoals as well as streams tributary to their lake of residence. Redds may be 3.7 m long and over 30 cm deep. A dominant pair spawn in the redd while gaping and vibrating. Smaller, "sneaky" males often rush in to fertilise some eggs. The female dislodges gravel at the head of the redd to cover and protect the eggs. The displaced gravel may be twice her body depth. Females may dig other redds and spawn again. Eggs are orange-red, 7.0 mm in diameter and each female may have 13,619. The adults die a few days to 2 weeks after spawning, some males surviving 5 months. Eggs hatch the following spring after overwintering in the gravel. The alevins spend 2–3 weeks in the gravel before emerging.

Chinook are the most important ocean sport fish in British Columbia taken on trolled plugs, spoons, by mooching herring, or on stationary live or dead bait fished deeper than for other Pacific salmons. It does not leap as much as **coho** but is a very strong fighter which makes long sounding runs. As many as 93,000 are taken each year, mostly in the Strait of Georgia. Yukon River chinook are important in the subsistence fishery, taken by fish wheels and gill nets. Commercial operations use trollers, purse seines, gill nets and longlines, taking up to 1.74 million fish (in 1934). Recent catches average about 5500 metric tonnes when fishing is good. The 1988 catch was 5108 tonnes, worth over $37 million. Some are sold fresh or frozen and much is canned. The flesh is red or white, the former receiving a higher price.

Dams, pollution and overfishing all affect detrimentally the stocks of this salmon. Continual stocking operations occur in the Great Lakes where this species provides an exciting sport fish for anglers, the largest salmonid there. However the species is not fully established and replenishment with fingerlings is necessary. Occasionally spawning fish are found in tributaries even in spring in Lake Superior rather than the usual fall spawning. Some stocked chinook in lakes Huron and Superior have been heat-shocked at 32.5°C for 10 minutes about 10 minutes after fertilisation. This results in sterile triploid chinook which are expected to live longer and grow larger since they do not spawn and die at the usual age. Farming operations using pens are being developed on the Pacific coast.

- Most accessible in saltwater during August, in freshwater during June.
- The coastal waters of the Queen Charlotte Islands in British Columbia and the coastal rivers of northern British Columbia.
- Medium to heavy action $10^1/_2$–foot salmon mooching rods and reels for saltwater fishing and medium to heavy action salmon spinning rods and casting rods used with 14- to 20-pound test line.
- For coastal fishing, live **herring** or a trolled cut-plug **herring**, for river fishing 1/4- to 1/2-ounce casting spoons, large spinners and fluorescent coloured wobbling plugs. Best bait for river fishing — treated skeined **salmon** eggs or spawn sacks.

chiselmouth

Scientific name: *Acrocheilus alutaceus*
   Agassiz and Pickering, 1855
Family: **Carp**
Other common names: hardmouth, squaremouth
French name: bouche coupante

Distribution: Found in the Fraser and Columbia river basins of British Columbia, Washington, Oregon, Nevada and Idaho.

Characters: This species is distinguished by having a hard, cutting edge almost straight across the underslung lower jaw (hence the common name). The chisel is not developed in young fish up to 1.5 cm. There is a fleshy

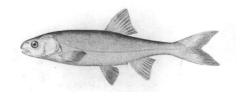

chiselmouth

lip on the upper jaw and a straight, cartilaginous plate. Dorsal fin branched rays 9, branched anal rays 8–9, pectoral rays 15–18 and pelvic rays 9–10. Lateral line scales 85–93. Gill rakers 13–17 and pharyngeal teeth 4–4, 4–5, 5–5 or 5–4 with grinding surfaces. The gut is more than twice the body length. Overall colour dark brown fading ventrally. The flanks are covered with small black spots. The dorsal and caudal fins are grey-brown. The pectoral and pelvic fins may have orange to reddish axils. Young fish have a black spot at the caudal fin base. The peritoneum is jet black. Attains 30 cm.

Biology: Chiselmouths are found in lakes and rivers in Canada. Stomachs contain algae, diatoms and associated invertebrates scraped off rocks in 2.0–2.5 cm long patches by the chisel mouth. Algae are not completely digested and diatoms appear to be the main energy source. The fish darts suddenly onto the substrate to effect the scraping action. Young chiselmouths up to 10 cm long feed on surface insects. The long gut and grinding pharyngeal teeth aid in digestion of food. Sexual maturity is attained at age 3 for males and 3–4 for females. Maximum life span is 6 years. Lake populations spawn in streams in June–July at temperatures above 16°C. Egg numbers average 6200 and are shed over the bottom.

chocolate skate

Scientific name: *Raja bathyphila*
   Holt and Byrne, 1908
Family: **Skate**
Other common names: deepwater ray, abyssal skate, raie bathyale

French name: raie chocolat

Distribution: Found in the North Atlantic Ocean including off the eastern Grand Bank and the Flemish Cap in Canada.

Characters: This species is separated from its Canadian Atlantic relatives by having a rigid snout with its cartilaginous support thick and stiff, cartilaginous supports of the pectoral fin do not reach the snout tip, resembling **Bigelow's skate** but having 31–44 (33 or more in adults) thorns in the midline of the back and tail, and no snout thorns. Dorsal fins joined at the base. The upper surface is prickly with bare patches on the middle of the pectoral fins and along each side of the midline in males. There are a few thorns around the eyes and spiracles, 2–3 thorns on

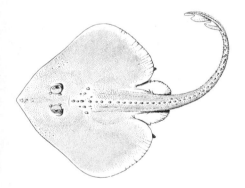

chocolate skate

the nape, 1 on the middle of the shoulder and 3 on each side of the shoulder. There is an additional, parallel row of 10–30 thornlets on each side of the tail midline anteriorly. The underside of the disc is smooth. Egg cases are about 9 cm by 5 cm without the horns included. The upper surface of the disc is dark grey-brown in young but with large white markings on midbody and adults are uniformly white. The tail in young is white, becomes dark in half-grown fish and is greyish in adults. Reaches about 90 cm.

Biology: Canadian depth range is about 770–1920 m, elsewhere 600–2050 m. This species is not common and Canadian records have recently been shown to be mostly **Bigelow's skate**.

chordates

The phylum Chordata is one of the major divisions of the Animal Kingdom, related perhaps to the phylum Echinodermata which includes starfishes, sea urchins and their relatives. The chordates are divided into several subphyla, the Hemichordata or acorn worms, the Urochordata or sea-squirts and salps, the fossil Calcichordata, the Cephalochordata or lancelets, and the **Vertebrata** or **fishes**, amphibians, reptiles, birds and mammals. All **fishes**, therefore are both **vertebrates** and chordates.

Chordates are characterised by having a hollow, dorsal nerve cord, a body cavity which is a true coelom (a body cavity containing internal organs such as those of the digestive system — animals without a coelom are less efficient since body and gut movements cannot be carried on independently), gill slits and a tail behind the anus although some of these characters are only evident in the larvae.

chub mackerel

Scientific name: *Scomber japonicus* Houttuyn, 1782
Family: **Mackerel**
Other common names: hardhead, bulleye, Pacific mackerel, Spanish mackerel, maquereau espanol
French name: maquereau blanc

Distribution: Found world-wide in warmer waters including off British Columbia and Atlantic Canada.

Characters: This species is distinguished from its Canadian relatives on both coasts by having well separated dorsal fins (distance between them greater than snout length), 5–6

chub mackerel

dorsal and anal finlets, no median keel on the caudal peduncle and 8–10 first dorsal fin spines. A swimbladder is present. There is a small pointed flap on the belly between the pelvic fins. Second dorsal fin with 1 spine and 12 rays. Anal fin with 2 spines and 11 rays. Pectoral rays 18–21. Gill rakers 38–46. The body is covered with small, cycloid scales and there is no corselet. The back is a metallic or greenish-blue and the flanks silvery. The upper flank has about 30 wavy, black, diagonal bars which become interrupted below the lateral line in western Atlantic fish but are usually faint or absent on the belly in Pacific fish. There are 3 or more lines radiating from behind the eye. There is a black spot in the axil of the pectoral fin. Reaches 64 cm and 2.9 kg. The world, all-tackle angling record weighed 2.17 kg and was caught in 1986 in Mexico.

Biology: Usually quite abundant off the west coast of Vancouver Island and has entered the Strait of Georgia. Occurs along the coast of Nova Scotia almost every year and even as far north as Anticosti Island. There are northward migrations as temperatures increase in summer along the coasts of North America. This is both a surface and deeper water species and may descend below 360 m. It is found in large schools, often around kelp beds in coastal waters. Food is various other schooling fishes, crustaceans and squid. **Tunas, billfishes, yellowtails**, seals, porpoises and seabirds are predators on chub mackerel. Life span is at least 11 years but some fish mature in their second year. Spawning occurs in March to October, peaking in April to August, in California down to 91.5 m at 15–20°C. Over 1 million, pelagic eggs of 1.3 mm diameter can be produced. Several batches of eggs are released. This mackerel is a good food species used extensively in California. Anglers there may take more fish than the commercial fishermen and it is used as bait for larger, pelagic fishes. It is sold fresh, smoked and canned. The world catch in 1978 was 2,861,264 tonnes. The principal fishery method is purse-seining although a variety of other methods are used.

chubs

The term chub has been applied to a variety of unrelated fishes which have short, thick, rounded bodies and large heads. There is a **Sea Chub Family** with 1 Canadian species (the **Bermuda chub**), the **chub mackerel**, and 7 species of the **Carp Family**, namely the **creek chub, flathead chub, gravel chub, hornyhead chub, lake chub, river chub** and **silver chub**.

In addition, the 4 species of **ciscoes** unique to the Great Lakes, namely the **deepwater** and **shortnose ciscoes** and the **kiyi** and **bloater**, along with the **blackfin cisco** and the **shortjaw cisco** were known as chubs and sold as smoked fish, mostly in the U.S.A. These chubs were caught in deepwater gill nets and were an important fishery in the great lakes until about 1950. Only the **bloater** is still caught regularly and the fishery for the other species has collapsed owing to overfishing and habitat destruction.

Other species of Canadian fishes may be called chub as a local name, e.g. the **mummichog** in the Miramichi River region.

chum salmon

Scientific name: *Oncorhynchus keta*
    (Walbaum, 1792)
Family: **Salmon**
Other common names: dog salmon, keta,
    calico salmon, autumn salmon, qualla
French name: saumon kéta

Distribution: Found from Great Bear and Great Slave lakes down the Mackenzie River to the Arctic and Bering coasts and drainages of Alaska, the Pacific coast and coastal rivers of southeast Alaska and British Columbia south to California. Also in eastern Arctic Siberia and south to the Sea of Japan.

Characters: This species is distinguished by having 124–153 lateral line scales, 13–17 principal anal fin rays, flanks and caudal fin without distinct black spots, short, stout gill rakers 18–26 and pyloric caeca 140–249. Dorsal fin with 10–14 principal rays, pectoral rays 14–16 and pelvic rays 10–11. Breeding males develop hooked jaws and large teeth and a slight hump in front of the dorsal fin. Marine fish are steel-blue on the back and upper flank, silvery on the flank and silvery-white on the belly. The upper flank and back may have fine black speckles. The pectoral, pelvic, anal and caudal fins have dark edges. Spawning males in fresh water are dark olive to black above, greyish-red to brick-red on the flank with greenish to purplish bars or blotches and a dark grey belly. The anal and pelvic fins are often tipped with white. Females are less strongly marked. Young chum are iridescent, mottled green on the back and silvery iridescent green on the flanks and belly. There are 6–14 parr marks which do not descend much below the lateral line and are narrower than the space between them. Fins are clear to white. Hybrids with **pink salmon** are known. "Chum" may be derived from a Chinook Indian word for spots or writing. Reaches 102 cm and 20.4 kg. The world, all-tackle angling record from Behm Canal, Alaska in 1985 weighed 14.51 kg. The Canadian angling record from Rivers Inlet, B.C. was caught by Robert P. Caldow on August 28, 1989 and weighed 12.14 kg.

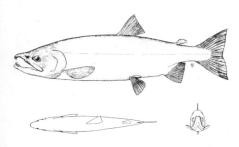

chum salmon

Biology: Chum salmon enter streams on the spawning migration and often travel less than 150 km, stopping at the first barrier as they are not strong jumpers. Some fish even spawn in tidal areas. However some rivers, like the Yukon, have a run which travels about 3200 km and takes from early June to the end of September. Chums appear at the Mackenzie River mouth in August and reach Great Slave Lake by late September or October. A migratory speed of up to 115 km/day has been recorded. Most runs are in the fall but some are in the summer. Very rarely a chum will become trapped in a lake if an outlet stream dries up but normally adult chum are only found in freshwaters on the spawning run. During their sea life they live in offshore waters of the Bering Sea and North Pacific Ocean, moving over a vast

area and from the surface to 60 m before returning to their spawning streams. Spawning varies with locality, July in northern British Columbia, September to July in other areas. Food in the sea includes crustaceans, arrow worms, sea squirts, pelagic snails, squid and fishes. Adults on the spawning run do not feed. Young fish in freshwater eat aquatic insects, such as chironomids, crustaceans and worms. Various insects, fish, **lampreys**, birds and mammals prey on both young and adult chum. Life span is about 7 years, perhaps 9 years, with fish in British Columbia maturing at 1–6 years with age 3 fish dominant. They spend 2–7 years at sea before returning to spawn. Males grow faster and larger than females. Females excavate a redd by lying on their sides and lashing the tail. The redd is a trough up to about half a metre deep and up to 3.2 m long and 2.1 m wide bordered by a ridge of gravel at the downstream end. In some cases no redd is excavated and eggs are shed over and between boulders. Females may excavate more than one redd and males may spawn with more than one female. A female and one dominant male lie in the redd, gape their mouths, vibrate and release eggs and sperm. The dominant male may have several accessory males accompanying him. The female dislodges gravel at the upstream end of the redd to cover the eggs. The orange eggs are up to 5.9 mm in diameter (perhaps 9.5 mm when fertilised) and each female may shed up to 7779. Chum stocks on Vancouver and Queen Charlotte islands have lower fecundities (averages less than 3200 eggs/ female) than mainland stocks (3200–3450 eggs/female). There is also an annual variation in fecundity which is reflected in abundance of adults. The fish die after spawning and may live only a week after first entering fresh water.

The eggs hatch from December to February in British Columbia but only emerge from the gravel in April to May. They migrate to sea during the night and hide in gravel during the day. Some populations which migrate long distances will also travel by day in schools. By late July and early August most have dispersed in the sea.

Chum are not sought extensively by anglers since they spend only 2–3 weeks in fresh waters, but are caught commercially with gill nets and purse seines in sheltered marine waters. The peak catch is made during September or October in British Columbia. As many as 7.7 million fish were caught in Canada in 1928 but catches of less than a million have also occurred. The Canadian catch is usually less than 10% of the world catch. In 1988 the Canadian catch was 29,998 tonnes, worth nearly $72 million. Some are sold fresh but most are canned. It is not as important as some other Pacific salmons, ranking third after **sockeye** and **pink salmon**. The flesh is white. Coastal Indians favour this **salmon** for smoking and it is the most important **salmon** to their economy in northern rivers. It was often used as sledge-dog food, hence the common name "dog" salmon. In Japan it is very important in an ocean ranch industry.

- Most accessible in saltwater during August, in freshwater during June.
- The coastal waters of the Queen Charlotte Islands in British Columbia and the coastal rivers of northern British Columbia.
- Medium to heavy action 10^1/$_2$-foot salmon mooching rods and reels for salt-water fishing and medium to heavy action salmon spinning rods and casting rods used with 14- to 20-pound test line.
- For coastal fishing, live **herring** or a trolled cut-plug **herring**, for river fishing 1/4- to 1/2-ounce casting spoons, large spinners and fluorescent coloured wobbling plugs. Best bait for river fishing — treated skeined **salmon** eggs or spawn sacks.

Cichlid Family

Scientific name: Cichlidae
French name: cichlidés

Cichlids are found in fresh and brackish waters of Central and South America, Africa, Madagascar, the Levant, southern Iran and southern India. There are about 1300 species, probably more, of which 1 has become established by introduction in Canada in the Banff

Cave and Basin Hotsprings, Alberta. Two other species, the convict cichlid (cichlide à bande noire, *Cichlasoma nigrofasciatum* (Günther, 1867)), and the freshwater angelfish (scalaire, *Pterophyllum scalare* (Lichtenstein, 1823)) were also introduced to the hotsprings but have died out. The jaguar guapote (*Cichlasoma managuense* (Günther, 1867)) and the oscar (astronotus, *Astronotus ocellatus* (Agassiz, 1831)) have been recorded from Ontario but the introductions died out.

Cichlids have only a single nostril on each side; practically all other fishes have two nostrils. The lateral line is in 2 parts, an anterior and higher portion ending under the soft dorsal fin and a lower, midflank, posterior part beginning below where the first part ends and continuing to the tail base. Body form varies greatly between species and many are colourful and highly prized as aquarium fishes. There are usually 7–25 spines in the dorsal fin followed by 5–30 soft rays. The anal fin usually has 3 spines, but some species have 4–9 or 12–15 spines, followed by usually 4–15 soft rays. Scales are ctenoid or cycloid and extend onto the head. There is a specialised pharyngeal bone in the throat which breaks up food by pressing it against a hard pad on the skull base. Mouth dentition is highly specialised in relation to diet with scraping (for algae on rocks), pointed (to seize fish), crushing (for hard-shelled molluscs), winkling (for removing snails from their shell) or reduced and embedded (for egg eating).

Cichlids are members of the **Perch Order** classified close to the **Surfperch Family**. "Cichlid" is derived from the Greek word for **wrasses**.

Some cichlids are important food fishes but they have attracted scientific attention for their elaborate breeding behaviour and evolutionary history. Certain cichlids, for example, are mouthbrooders, carrying eggs and fry in their mouths to protect them, while others spawn on the substrate, build nests or nourish young from a skin secretion. African lakes contain rich species flocks of cichlids which show various feeding behaviours. How these species arose and adapted to different ways of life have been important to scientists in understanding the mechanisms of evolution and adaptation. Generally cichlids show a wide range of biology, some being predators, others omnivores while others feed on algae or plants. Some specialise in tearing scales or picking eyes out of other fishes.

See **jewelfish**

ciscoes

Ciscoes, or lake herrings, are members of the **Salmon Family** and are related to the **whitefishes**. There are 9 Canadian species which carry this name but the **kiyi** and the **bloater** are also members of this group (the subgenus *Leucichthys*). Ciscoes are characterised by jaws of equal length and high gill raker counts, more than 32. Ciscoes are difficult to study taxonomically as their characters vary considerably from lake to lake depending on environmental conditions and they may not be a natural group. These variable characters include size, body proportions, scale and gill raker counts and even aspects of their biology, such as growth rate. There is evidence that spawning times have changed in the Great Lakes because of the pressures listed below. This has led to genetic mixing as normally isolated spawning seasons overlapped. Cisco species are no longer as distinct as they used to be. In addition a species may shift its gill raker count, a key identification character, to fill in for a species lost through overfishing or pollution. Ciscoes and other **whitefishes** have been called chameleons because of this plasticity in characters.

Four cisco species are found only in the deeper waters of the Great Lakes. These are the **bloater**, **deepwater cisco**, **kiyi** and **shortnose cisco**. Two other deepwater species, the **blackfin cisco** and the **shortjaw cisco**, are more wide ranging. These 6 ciscoes were known as **chubs** in the Great Lakes commercial fishery, which has declined drastically in recent years because of overfishing, competing species, predatory **sea lampreys,** pollution and habitat destruction. For example, even the **bloater**, regarded as relatively common 10 years ago, now has a proposed status of rare in Canada. The **deepwater cisco** is probably extinct.

Other Canadian ciscoes are the **spring cisco**, found only in southwestern Quebec,

the widely distributed **lake cisco**, the **Arctic cisco** and the **least cisco**, found along the western Arctic coast and in tributary rivers, and the **Bering cisco** which may be found in Yukon coastal waters.

Cisco is derived from ciscoette, a French Canadian word, itself taken from an Ojibwa word meaning that which has oily flesh. The Canadian angling record from Cedar Lake, Manitoba, was caught by Randy Huff on April 11, 1986 and weighed 3.35 kg.

• Most accessible between January and March.

• The northern ranges of Ontario, Manitoba and Saskatchewan.

• Ice fishing tip-ups and jigging rods used with eight- to 12-pound test.

• Small, tear-drop ice fishing jigs and a variety of 1/8- to 1/4-ounce vertical jigging spoons. A popular ice fishing lure rig to use is a flashy spoon to which a leader of line is attached with a small treble hook and plastic bead or pearl. The spoon acts as an attractor while the ciscoe hit the bead or pearl. The best bait, small minnows fished on a hook at different depths between the water's surface and the bottom.

Clingfish Family

Scientific name: Gobiesocidae
French name: crampons

Clingfishes are found world-wide in tropical to temperate waters of all oceans, with a few species in fresh water. They are small fishes, the largest only reaching 36 cm and most being 10 cm or less. There are about 120 species, with 2 on the Pacific coast of Canada.

These small fishes are characterised by a sucking or adhesive disc on the breast formed from the pelvic fins, a flattened head and tapering body, and 3 unique characters — a condyle on the cleithrum bone of the pectoral girdle which fits into a concave process of the supracleithrum, a joint between the epihyal and interopercle, and the heart structure. The disc is covered with papillae and is used for attachment to rocks or algae. It is formed mostly from the pelvic fins but includes a small part of the pectoral girdle and skin flaps. Only the **Snailfish** and **Goby** families also have sucking discs, but in the former the dorsal fin origin is just behind the head and the latter have spines in their dorsal fin. The dorsal and anal fins are opposite each other and positioned in the rear half of the body. Scales, a swimbladder, ribs, a spiny dorsal or anal fin, certain bones such as the circumorbitals after the lachrymal, basisphenoid, orbitosphenoid and basibranchials 1 and 2 are all absent. There are 3–7 branchiostegal rays. The premaxilla bone of the upper jaw has its articular process absent or, if present, fused to the ascending process. There is a genital papilla behind the anus. The hypural bones of the tail skeleton are fused into a single plate. The naked skin is smooth and can be slimy. Some species are capable of colour changes to match the habitat.

This family is a member of the **Perch Order** but once constituted its own order. Clingfishes are thought to be relatives of the **Toadfish Order**.

The sucking disc is used for attachment to rocks in the surge zone of shallow waters although some species live on seaweeds or between the spines of sea urchins. The flattened head and generally stream-lined shape helps them to cling in strong waves and in currents. The larger clingfishes have such a grip that they can be picked up together with a large rock without detaching. A species from Chile even feeds on vertical rock walls in strong surf. They lay large eggs which are guarded by either or both parents.

See **kelp clingfish**
northern clingfish

Clinid Family

Scientific name: Clinidae
French name: clinides

The clinids, kelpfishes, scaled blennies or clipfishes, are found in the Atlantic, Indian and Pacific oceans mostly in temperate waters. There are about 75 species with 2, possibly 3, reported from the Pacific coast of Canada.

They have small embedded, cycloid scales with radii (radiating lines) on all parts of each scale. There is a ligament connecting the dentary symphysis to the ceratohyal. The dorsal fin has more spines than soft rays. It is very long but does not join the caudal fin. Fin rays are usually unbranched. The anal fin has 2 spines. Cirri (feathery outgrowths) are present on the head but not the nape region. There is usually 1 spine and 3 soft rays in the thoracic pelvic fins. Teeth are small and conical and there are no long canines.

They are related to the **Combtooth Blenny Family** which lack scales or have them modified and usually have fewer spines than soft rays in the dorsal fin. Clinids are identified by colour patterns and fin ray and scale counts. A microscope may be needed. This family is a member of the **Perch Order**.

The giant kelpfish (*Heterostichus rostratus* Girard, 1854) is tentatively reported from British Columbia, although its confirmed range is California and Baja California. It is the only kelpfish with a forked tail fin.

Clinids are shallow water species living on the bottom among seaweed and are well camouflaged. Colour matches the habitat and can confuse attempts at identification. They may live in holes and crevices, defending this territory. They are easily captured when discovered and can be kept in aquaria. They are predators on crustaceans and other small marine animals. Most lay eggs, which the male guards, although some are live bearers and the male has an intromittent organ.

See **crevice kelpfish**
striped kelpfish

closespine snipe eel

Scientific name: *Avocettina infans*
(Günther, 1878)
Family: **Snipe Eel**
Other common names: spaced snipe eel, blackline snipe eel, avocet snipe eel
French name: avocette immature

Distribution: Found in all oceans in warmer waters but mostly in the northern hemisphere. Found off the Pacific coast of Canada.

Characters: This species is distinguished from its Canadian relatives, the **carinate** and **slender snipe eels**, by its lack of a caudal filament, only 1 pore on each segment of the lateral line, the presence of elongate sensory ridges on the head behind the eyes, and the anus well to the rear of the pectoral fin level.

The anterior nostrils are tubular in unripe specimens. The upper jaw is much longer than the lower jaw. Dorsal fin rays 279–432,

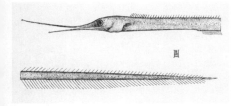

closespine snipe eel

anal fin rays 240–372. Lateral line pores 181–201. Overall colour is brown to black, darker when mature, with the jaws, pectoral fins and belly pale. Attains 80 cm.

Biology: Found off Pacific Canada as shallow as 510–595 m, this species is usually found between 1400 and 2600 m, but it may be as deep as 4575 m. Not a common species. Spawning probably occurs through much of the year.

coastal cutthroat trout

Scientific name: *Oncorhynchus clarki clarki* (Richardson, 1836)
Family: **Salmon**
Other common names: red-throated trout, Clark's trout, sea trout, short-tailed trout, black- spotted trout, harvest trout
French name: truite fardée côtière

Distribution: Found from southeast Alaska south to California including British Columbia as far inland as the Skeena River headwaters. Introduced elsewhere in the U.S.A.

Characters: This species is identified by the low number of principal anal fin rays (8–12), small dark spots without halos on the whole flank, teeth on the head and shaft of the vomer bone in the roof of the mouth and on the back of the tongue, and the two unique red to orange streaks on the underside of the jaw — the "cut throat." This is one of two subspecies of cutthroat trout in Canada (see **west-slope cutthroat trout**) mostly easily separated by distribution. Dorsal fin with 8–11 principal rays, pectoral rays 12–15 and pelvic rays 9–10. Lateral line scales 116–230 and pyloric caeca 24–57. Males develop a slight kype or

hooked lower jaw when in breeding condition. Colour is extremely variable and both subspecies have been introduced into the other's range. Hybrids with **rainbow** and **golden trout** further confuse colour patterns and complicate identifications. The "cut throat" marks may be absent in sea dwelling fish or recent migrants to fresh water. These fish have more silvery flanks, are more bluish on the back, have yellowish lower flanks and fins, and spots are less evident. Generally the back is dark green to greenish-blue, the upper flank olive-green and the rest of the flank and belly is silvery. The gill covers are pinkish. Flank spots below the lateral line are more numerous anteriorly (cf. **west-slope cutthroat**). The outline of spots is irregular, not rounded. Spots are present on the dorsal, adipose and caudal fins and the anal, pectoral and pelvic fin bases. Young have 10 oval, grey-violet parr marks along the lateral line covered with small black dots which extend onto the back and tail. The back may have 5 dark ovals and is olive. The leading edge of the dorsal fin is dark. The dorsal and anal fins may have white patches. The adipose fin has a few black spots. "Cut throat" markings develop on fish over 7.6 cm long. Formerly in the genus *Salmo*. Reaches 99.0 cm in non-migrating fish, usually smaller in sea run fish. The world, all-tackle record for a "cutthroat trout" weighed 18.59 kg and was

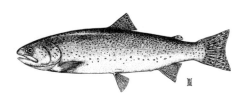

coastal cutthroat trout

caught in Pyramid Lake, Nevada in 1925. The Canadian angling record from Castle River, Alberta, was caught by Ernest Brazzoni in 1988 and weighed 4.34 kg.

Biology: This subspecies is found in fresh and salt waters, migrating between them but not extending into the higher reaches of major rivers like the Columbia in British Columbia. Some populations remain in fresh water. This **trout** prefers smaller streams or those that have long slow reaches before entering the sea. It is also found in small, coastal bog lakes in British Columbia.

Food is aquatic and terrestrial insects, crustaceans, small fishes and **salmon** eggs. Migrating **salmon** are an important food, taken when cutthroats go to sea at the same time, and other fishes eaten include **trout, sculpins, flatfishes, rockfishes** and **sticklebacks**.

Maximum life span is 10 years. Sea run trout are not always larger than stream resident fish because they may not spend long in the sea. Males mature earlier than females, as early as 2 years compared to as late as 6 years. Most fish spawn at 2–4 years.

Spawning occurs in January to May in British Columbia after a migration in late autumn and early winter. There may be late runs in December and January in short streams. Small gravel streams are favoured. The female excavates a redd by lying on her flank and lashing her tail. Redds are about 30 cm across and 10–13 cm deep. Males court females with nudges and by quivering. The female lies in the redd with head and tail bent up, the male joins her, they gape, vibrate and release eggs and sperm. The fertilised eggs fall between the gravel. The female dislodges gravel at the upstream rim of the redd to cover the eggs with up to 20 cm of gravel. The spawning pair may have other males sneaking in to shed sperm. Females may dig more than one redd and both sexes spawn with more than one other fish. Each female may have 2000 or more orange-red, adhesive eggs of 5.1 mm maximum diameter. The red cut throat may be used in aggressive displays. Sea run cutthroat often survive to spawn again, 12% spawning a fourth time in one study.

The fry emerge from the gravel in April and can run to the sea in the spring of their second or third year at about 13–20 cm in British Columbia. They live mostly in estuaries or near shore areas for one or more years, re-entering rivers to spawn in the fall or to feed on migrating **salmon** in the spring. Growth in the sea can be 25 mm per month. There is variation in migration times, sea life span and spawning time between stocks and geographical areas.

This is an important sport fish caught on flies, spoons and live bait and often leaps when hooked. In the Bella Coola system, B.C., runs of **chum** and **pink salmon** in April attract cutthroats which are caught using flies that imitate the salmon fry. Federal and provincial authorities are endeavouring to improve tenfold cutthroat populations in southern British Columbia and Vancouver Island by improving stream conditions where these have deteriorated in populated areas. The flesh is orange-red to pink and best when smoked, fried or baked.

- Most accessible May through September.
- The lower sections of the coastal rivers of British Columbia and the surrounding estuary waters where they enter the Pacific Ocean.
- Ultralight to light action spinning outfits used with four- to eight-pound test line. Fly rods from seven-and-a-half to nine-and-a-half feet long in four- to eight-weight, loaded with weight-forward floating lines and sinking lines.
- 1/8- to 1/4-ounce brightly coloured spoons, a variety of small spinners and jigs, small silver streamers and wet flies.

coastrange sculpin

Scientific name: *Cottus aleuticus* Gilbert, 1896
Family: **Sculpin**
Other common names: none
French name: chabot côtier

Distribution: Found in coastal drainages from the Aleutian Islands to California including British Columbia, notably up the Fraser River to Lillooet. There is an isolated population in a Chukchi Sea drainage of Alaska.

Characters: This and related species in the freshwater genus *Cottus* are distinguished from the **deepwater sculpin** by the gill membrane being attached to the isthmus and the dorsal fins touching. It is separated from its relatives by having 1 pore on the chin tip, a complete lateral line bent downward on the caudal peduncle, the first 2 dorsal fin spines close together, no palatine teeth in the roof of the mouth and a tubular posterior nostril. First dorsal fin spines 8–10, second dorsal rays 16–20, anal rays 12–16 and pectoral rays 13–16. Scales absent except for prickles behind the pectoral fin. Lateral line pores 32–44. Males have a long genital papilla. Overall colour brown to blue-grey with blotches fading to a white belly. There are 2–3 dark saddles under the second dorsal fin. Fins have thin bars. There is often a light bar across the top of the caudal peduncle. The chin is heavily speckled. Spawning males have an orange stripe on the first dorsal fin margin. Reaches 17 cm.

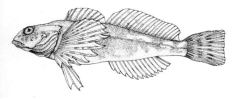

coastrange sculpin

Biology: This species is usually found in fast, gravel-bed streams along the coast but also over sand or mud in lakes and in estuarine and nearshore environments. In lakes it is adapted to a pelagic existence with a daily vertical migration to the surface at night and to the lake bottom in the day. In Cultus Lake, B.C. there is a dwarf population which has a maximum total length of 49 cm, lives 3–4 years, feeds on plankton and minute bottom organisms, spawns throughout summer and is eaten by **Dolly Varden**. Food is generally aquatic insects, molluscs and **salmon** eggs and fry. However these sculpins are food for **Coho salmon, cutthroat trout** and **Dolly Varden**, so it is debatable who gains in this predator-prey relationship. Feeding takes place mostly at night, peaking at or just before dawn. Life span is about 7 years but varies between streams. Spawning occurs February to June (April–May on Vancouver Island) in streams where about 800, orange, adhesive, 1.5 mm diameter eggs are laid on the undersurface of rocks to be guarded by the male. Males may court and spawn with more than 1 female. Up to 7000 eggs at different stages of development may be found under one rock. The young are planktonic in estuaries or lakes and settle to the bottom about 5 weeks after hatching.

cobia

Scientific name: *Rachycentron canadum*
    (Linnaeus, 1766)
Family: **Cobia**
Other common names: sergeant fish, runner, crabeater, mafou, ling, lemonfish, black salmon, cabio
French name: cobilo

Distribution: World-wide in warmer seas and rarely in Atlantic Canada.

Characters: This species has an elongate body with a flattened head. Jaws are large and the lower one projects. Teeth are short and conical and are found on the jaws, tongue and roof of the mouth. The dorsal fin has 6–10 short spines which are free of a membrane and can be depressed and 1–3 spines attached to 26–36 soft rays. The anal fin has 2–3 spines and 20–28 soft rays. The caudal fin is forked in adults with the upper lobe longer, and rounded in young. The pectoral fins are scythe-shaped in adults and have 21–22 rays. Pelvic fins have 1 spine and 5 soft rays. Scales are very small, cycloid and embedded, over 300 in the lateral line. The lateral line is wavy anteriorly. There is no swimbladder. The back is dark brown and the flanks have a dark, midlateral stripe. The dark stripe fades with age. All fins are black except the caudal has white margins. Belly silvery-white to yellowish. Young fish have 2 white or silvery-iridescent stripes separated

cobia

by a broad black to brown stripe along the flank. Reaches 2 m standard length and 68 kg. The world, all-tackle angling record from Western Australia in 1985 weighed 61.5 kg.

Biology: This species has been caught only once in Canada east of Emerald Bank at the surface in 1976. The fish was a juvenile, 42.7 mm in standard length, and was a stray from southern waters. They are common in southern coastal waters especially around floating objects such as buoys and seaweed. Also found in the open ocean. They may be solitary or in small schools. Food is mainly fishes but also crabs, shrimps and squids, easily seized by this fast swimming fish. Cobia live at least 13 years and mature at 2 years for males and 3 years for females. Spawning occurs from April to October in the Gulf of Mexico. Eggs are pelagic. Mature ova are up to 1.31 mm in diameter and fecundity is up to 5.4 million eggs. This species is sold fresh and is variously reported as average to good eating. Anglers catch it with handlines, bottom fishing, jigging, chumming, and by trolling with lures and various live and cut baits. It is a strong fighter and often leaps out of the water.

Cobia Family

Scientific name: Rachycentridae
French name: cobilos

The **cobia** is the only member of its family and is found world-wide in tropical seas. Characteristics and biology are summarised in the species account.

The **cobia** is related to the **Remora, Bluefish** and **Jack** families. It is named, according to one authority, for Canada, but has only recently been found here. This family is a member of the **Perch Order**.

See **cobia**

Cod Family

Scientific name: Gadidae
French name: morues

Cods are mostly northern marine fishes with 1 species in fresh water of North American and Eurasia and a few southern hemisphere species. There are about 30 species and in Canada 3 Arctic coast species, 6 Arctic-Atlantic species, 11 Atlantic species, 3 Pacific species and the fresh water species, a total of 24 species.

Cods have a first dorsal fin behind the head and 1–3 distinct dorsal fins. There are 1–2 anal fins. There are no fin spines. The caudal fin usually extends around the dorsal and ventral tip of the caudal peduncle often framing a pointed end to the body. The vomer bone in the roof of the mouth bears teeth. The swimbladder is not connected to the auditory

capsules and has 2 slender, anterior processes. There is usually a barbel at the tip of the lower jaw. Scales are small and cycloid. There is an obvious lateral line. The first vertebra and neural spine are attached to the skull.

Cods are related to the **Mora, Arrowtail** and **Hake** families and are in the **Cod Order**. These families share such characters as a caudal fin usually separated from the dorsal and anal fins, pelvic fins anterior to the pectoral fins, 4–6 pectoral radial bones and wide gill openings extending above the pectoral fins.

Most cods live on or near the bottom in cold shelf and slope waters in large schools and are of immense commercial importance as food and sport fishes. A few species are found in the deep sea to 1300 m while others live intertidally or enter brackish water. Eggs and larvae are usually pelagic. A long pelagic life and spawning and feeding migrations result in the wide distribution of many species. Egg production can exceed 60 million in some species. Adults feed on other fishes and various invertebrates. Cods are the principal food fish consumed by humans as, although **herrings** have a larger catch, most is processed into fish meal. Overfishing continues to be a problem. The Grand Bank catch of **Atlantic cod** in 1956 had declined to a fifth of that made 50 years before and the Georges Bank **Atlantic cod** biomass has been reduced by 65% since 1977. In 1989 it was estimated by scientists that 45% of the available northern stock of cod was being caught, much more than the 20% which is regarded as allowable for maintaining that stock. The recommended Canadian cod quota was 137,500 tonnes, half of the 293,500 tonne quota for 1988. A rollback to 258,500 tonnes was eventually implemented but even that has severely affected the Maritime economy. A moratorium in the 1990s devastated the economy. Canada was practically founded on the **Atlantic cod** fisheries. The Grand Bank was fished by Europeans long before the voyage of John Cabot in 1497 to these waters. As early as 1620 the cod fleet numbered more than 1000 ships. Some made a summer trip to secure dry cod and a winter trip for pickled or "green" cod.

See **Arctic cod**
     Atlantic cod
     Atlantic tomcod

blue ling
blue whiting
burbot
cusk
European ling
fourbeard rockling
haddock
longfin hake
ogac
Pacific cod
Pacific tomcod
polar cod
pollock
red hake
saffron cod
silver rockling
spotted hake
threebeard rockling
toothed cod
walleye pollock
white hake

Cod Order

The cods or Gadiformes (= Anacanthini) contains 12 families and about 482 species predominately in marine waters world-wide, mostly in colder waters inshore or the deep sea. There are representatives of 5 families with 54 species in Canada on all coasts with 1 species in fresh waters.

These fishes are small to moderately large, have pelvic fins usually well forward below or in front of the pectoral fins, generally no fin spines (**grenadiers** have a spine-like second ray in the first dorsal fin), long dorsal and anal fins which may be in 1–3 separate dorsal or 1–2 separate anal fins, the tail is reduced or confluent with the dorsal and anal fins, chin barbels often present, cycloid scales (but grenadiers have spinules on their scales), swimbladder not connected to the gut, 5–8 branchiostegal rays, the first neural spine close to the skull, the mouth is bordered above by the premaxilla bone, a notch in the premaxilla bone posteriorly, no teeth on the ectopterygoid bone, no orbitosphenoid and basisphenoid bones in the skull, no mesocoracoid bone in the pectoral girdle, and the dorsal and anal fin supports (= pterygiophores) outnumber the caudal vertebrae.

Cods are thought to be closely related to the **Trout-perch Order** because they share such characters as the olfactory bulb of the brain being at the olfactory organ and distant from the brain and the pterosphenoid and parasphenoid bones in the skull are in contact. Cods are intermediate between the **soft-rayed** and the **spiny-rayed fishes** with a mixture of characters belonging to both these groups. **Soft-rayed fishes** lack spines, have cycloid scales and many rays in the pelvic fins. **Spiny-rayed fishes** lack a duct between the gut and the swimbladder, have no orbitosphenoid and mesocoracoid bones, and the upper jaw is bordered by the premaxilla bone only. The **Cusk-eel Order** has been included within the **Cod Order**. The **Cod Order** contains a number of very important food fishes as well as rare, deepsea species. Fossils date back to the Eocene.

See **Arrowtail Family**
Cod Family
Grenadier Family
Hake Family
Mora Family

coho salmon

Scientific name: *Oncorhynchus kisutch* (Walbaum, 1792)
Family: **Salmon**
Other common names: silver salmon, sea trout, blueback, hooknose, silversides, white salmon, medium red salmon, hoopid salmon
French name: saumon coho

Distribution: Found from the Bering Strait to California penetrating inland in much of western British Columbia and parts of the upper Yukon River basin in Yukon. Also in the western Pacific Ocean south to Japan. Introduced to the Great Lakes and to Alberta and Saskatchewan and to waters in the U.S.A. and South America. Coastal Québec, Nova Scotia and New Brunswick records are probably strays from the U.S.A. Some St. Lawrence River records are strays from Lake Ontario.

Characters: This species is distinguished by having 112–148 lateral line scales, 12–17 principal anal fin rays, pupil-sized or smaller black spots on the back, upper flank, dorsal fin base and upper caudal fin lobe only, 18–25 gill rakers, 45–114 pyloric caeca and lower jaw gums pale (although black in some Great Lakes fish). Dorsal fin principal rays 9–13, pectoral rays 12–16 and pelvic rays 9–11. Breeding males have a thickened snout hooked at the tip, an enlarged, hooked lower

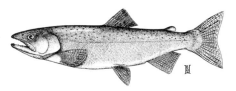

coho salmon

jaw, enlarged teeth, a slight hump and embedded scales. The back is steel-blue to greenish, flanks silvery and belly white. In spawning males the back and head darken or are bright green, the flanks are duller and have a bright red stripe, and the belly is grey to black. Young fish have 8–12 narrow, tall parr marks centred on the lateral line. The intervals between parr marks are wider than the marks. The adipose fin is evenly dusky. The anal fin has elongate, white anterior rays with contrasting black behind. The rest of the anal fin, the pectoral, pelvic and caudal fins are red-orange. Reaches 108.0 cm and 17.7 kg. The world, all-tackle angling record from the Salmon River, New York in 1989 weighed 15.08 kg. The Canadian angling record from Cowichan Bay, B.C. was caught by Mrs. Lee Hallberg in 1947 and weighed 14.07 kg.

Biology: Coho live in the sea and run up rivers and small streams in the summer and fall to spawn in small tributaries. Some fry run to sea immediately after birth but most spend a year in fresh water, 2 years for those in the remote Yukon River. A mild winter allows rapid development of fry and thus an earlier run to the sea. Some fish, known as residuals, remain in fresh water but never spawn. Sea run fish stay inshore for a few months but then enter the open ocean. Some travel as far as 2000 km at 5–7 nautical miles/day but most do not go long distances in a sea life of about 18 months. Adults on the spawning run are usually 3–4 years old although 4–5 year old fish are commoner in

the north and some southern males, known as "jacks" are only 2 years old. Most fish (85%) home to their birth stream, others being strays. Adults stray more frequently in the Great Lakes where the lake replaces the ocean phase of the life cycle. The young fix a memory of their birth stream by odour within 48 hours. Young in rivers are found in pools below riffles or lake shallows at preferred temperatures of 12–14°C.

Food of young is aquatic insects, worms, and even spiders. **Chum, pink** and **sockeye** fry are eaten in large amounts. Smolts entering the sea take various fishes, particularly **salmon** fry and **sand lances**, squids and crustaceans. Adults feed mostly on a wide variety of fishes with some crustaceans and jellyfish. **Herring** and **sand lance** form three-quarters of this diet and feeding frenzies have been reported. **Cutthroat** and **rainbow trout, Dolly Varden,** coho, **northern squawfish, sculpins,** birds and some mammals such as seals and killer whales eat coho. **Lampreys** regularly attack coho.

There is a long and late spawning migration up rivers during the daytime. They usually do not travel further than about 240 km. Spawning takes place in fast, gravel streams from October to March, usually October–November or November–January. Both sexes are aggressive. The female excavates a redd by lying on her side and lashing the tail. There is a dominant pair in the redd who gape, vibrate and shed eggs or sperm. Sneaky males may also rush in and fertilise eggs. The female covers the eggs by dislodging gravel from the upstream edge of the redd. Egg diameters are up to 7.1 mm, number up to 5700 per female and are orange-red. Fecundity varies between stocks and between years. Alaskan stocks are more fecund than B.C. ones, perhaps because of older ages at maturity and slower growth. Stocks in large rivers are more fecund than those in small rivers, perhaps in response to high exploitation rates in the former. The female guards the eggs but both she and the male soon die.

Eggs hatch in spring, the alevins emerging from the gravel after 2–3 weeks in March to July. Migration to sea or a lake occurs in February to June of their first or second year of life, often at night on freshets. These smolts turn silvery and move in small schools.

Coho are important sport and commercial fish in British Columbia. The commercial catch can average over 3 million fish and was worth $10.45 million in 1968. The 1988 catch for Canada weighed 6122 tonnes and was worth over $32 million. They are taken by gill nets, purse seines and trollers from July to September. Trollers use plugs, spoons or feathered jigs and are very effective. The catch is sold fresh, frozen, cured or smoked and is also canned as medium red salmon. Flesh is pink to red but turns white during spawning. Anglers catch this species from June to October in their first or last year of ocean life.

Coho fight strongly and leap dramatically. Similar but smaller gear to commercial trollers is used but also flies and pickled or frozen **herring** as bait. Young fish may be caught in April to June, are called "bluebacks" and weigh only a few kilograms. Later in the year they are about 10 kg and a better catch. Anglers take close to 200,000 fish a year on the Pacific coast.

The wild coho population in the Strait of Georgia is less than half of what it was in the mid-1970s, then about 1 million adults. The population is declining by about 66,000 fish a year and will be extinct in 20 years.

Coho were first introduced to Lake Erie in 1873 and more recently to lakes Huron, Michigan and Superior in 1966 and Ontario in 1968 on the American shore. Recent releases were soon being caught on the Canadian side. Ontario also introduced coho in 1969 to lakes Ontario and Superior and they are also found in Lake Erie. Growth is rapid as the coho feed on **gaspereau** and **smelts** and some stocks are reproducing but most have to be maintained by introduction. The Great Lakes coho now support an important sport fishing industry. In Lake Ontario the peak season is mid-April to mid-May on the southern shore, late summer to early fall throughout the western basin when the coho are deep and downrigger gear is needed to catch them, and near river mouths in the fall as they gather for the spawning run. However PCBs, DDT and other chemical pollutants may exceed acceptable levels in these coho, commercial sales

have been stopped in some areas and anglers are advised not to eat more than one meal per week. Atlantic coast introductions are potentially dangerous for **Atlantic salmon** stocks which they may displace.

- Most accessible June through August on the Pacific coastal waters, August to October in coastal rivers.

- The coastal waters of Vancouver Island and the Queen Charlotte Islands in British Columbia as well as the coastal rivers flowing into the Pacific Ocean in the Terrace, B.C. region.

- Medium to heavy action 10 1/2-foot salmon mooching rods and reels for saltwater fishing used with 14- to 20-pound test line. Medium action spinning and baitcasting outfits between seven to nine feet in length with 14- to 20-pound test line for river fishing.

- For coastal fishing, live **herring** or a trolled cut-plug **herring**. Best bait for river fishing include 1/4- to 3/8-ounce casting spoons and a variety of spinners (blue/silver). Fluorescent-coloured wobbling plugs and an assortment of hair jigs are effective. Best bait for river fishing, treated skeined **salmon** eggs or spawn sacks.

combfishes

The combfishes comprise 2 species on the Pacific coast of North America with 1 recorded from British Columbia. They used to be placed in their own family (Zaniolepididae) but are now placed in the **Greenling Family**.

See **longspine combfish**

Combtooth Blenny Family

Scientific name: Blenniidae
French name: blennies

Combtooth blennies are found in all warmer seas world-wide and enter fresh waters rarely. There are about 345 species, but only 1 occurs in Atlantic Canada.

These small blennies have comb-like or incisor-shaped teeth in an often blunt head. There may be a canine tooth on each jaw half. The mouth is low on the head, small and horizontal or sloping downwards. Scales are absent and the skin is rich in mucous glands. Crests and cirri decorate the head in many species and can be used in identification. Males often have different crests and cirri, colour pattern and anal spine shape (swollen) than females. The dorsal fin is spiny anteriorly but the spines are soft and easily bent. Soft rays are unbranched and are usually more numerous than spines. Pelvic fins are anterior to the pectorals and have 1 short spine, which is embedded and difficult to see, and 2–4 soft rays. There are 1–2 spines in the anal fin.

Combtooth blennies are related to **Clinid Family** members which, in Canada, are found only on the Pacific coast. These families are characterised by an anal fin with 1–2 spines and simple soft rays, pelvic fins with 1 spine and 2–4 simple soft rays inserted ahead of the pectoral fins, two nostrils on each side and often cirri (feathery flaps) on the head. This family is a member of the **Perch Order**.

These fishes are often excellent mimics of other fishes. Some mimic species which are distasteful and escape being eaten on that basis (Batesian mimicry). Others are themselves unpalatable but resemble another, unpalatable fish species and reduce the chances of being taste-tested and perhaps damaged by uneducated predators (Müllerian mimicry). Yet others are aggressive mimics, predators that resemble a harmless species such as a cleaner fish, and so get close to a prey without alarming it.

Blennies are found inshore around rocks and reefs, in shell beds, in mangroves and in seagrass. Some species can leave the water for short periods and sit on rocks, disconcerting the casual observer. They often maintain territories and are found nesting in holes, crevices and empty shells, or even cans. Egg clumps are guarded by one or both adults. The Canadian Museum of Nature once received a call from a surprised gourmand whose raw oyster had a blenny coiled up in its shell.

They are popular aquarium fishes because of their colour patterns, which can change quickly, the ornamentation on the head and their abrupt movements and attentive behaviour.

See **feather blenny**

common carp

Scientific name: *Cyprinus carpio* Linnaeus, 1758
Family: **Carp**
Other common names: German, European, king, mirror or leather carp; German bass, buglemouth bass
French name: carpe

Distribution: Found in Québec, Ontario, Manitoba, Saskatchewan and British Columbia from introductions. Also introduced worldwide in suitable waters. The native distribution is from eastern Europe to western China.

Characters: This species is characterised by having 15–23 branched fin rays, 2 pairs of upper jaw barbels, 21–27 gill rakers and 3

common carp

rows of pharyngeal teeth. The dorsal fin has the last unbranched ray developed as a toothed spine. The anal fin has a similar spine and 4–6 branched rays. Pectoral fin rays 14–19 and pelvic rays 8–9. Lateral line scales 32–41. Scales may be absent (leather carp) or restricted to a few, enlarged scales (mirror carp) but Canadian fish are usually fully scaled. Pharyngeal teeth usually 1,1,3–3,1,1 and molar-like. Breeding males have fine tubercles on the head and pectoral fins. The back is olive-green to grey, the flanks gold or bronze to silvery and the belly yellowish-white. Fins are dusky olive except the anal fin and lower caudal fin lobe may be reddish to orange and have a dark spot at their base. Scales on the upper flank have dark margins and bases. Peritoneum dusky. Reaches 121.9 cm and 37.88 kg. The world, all-tackle angling record from France in 1987 weighed 34.35 kg. The Canadian angling record from Cootes Paradise, Ontario, was caught by Tim Elzinga on June 19, 1994 and weighed 16.29 kg.

Biology: First introduced to Canada in the late nineteenth century, as early as 1880 in Ontario and about 1897 in British Columbia. The carp is primarily a freshwater fish but has been caught in brackish water of the St. Lawrence River, the Fraser and other rivers in British Columbia and even in the sea in the Strait of Georgia. They can tolerate a salinity of 18.6‰ and temperatures up to 35.5°C. Carp are probably capable of colonising Vancouver Island from the mainland on a plume of brackish water from the Fraser River. Carp are found in rivers, lakes, canals and marshes and tolerate turbid and low oxygen conditions. They can often be seen basking at the surface or feeding on algae and their dorsal fins break the water surface. Large fish often move into shallows in the afternoon and evening. Carp also leap from the water but the reason is unknown. They rarely descend below 30 m in lakes and avoid fast water in streams.

Mouthfuls of bottom ooze are taken up, spat out and the food items selected. These include aquatic insects, crustaceans, worms and molluscs, and more rarely, fish. Plant material is ground up by the molar pharyngeal teeth and includes algae, seeds, wild rice, leaves and various aquatic plants. Organic sewage is also eaten. Some surface feeding on algal mats or insects will also occur. A wide variety of other fishes and birds eat smaller carp as do predatory aquatic insects, frogs and toads. Carp eggs are eaten by **minnows, catfishes** and **sunfishes**. Adult carp are too large for most predators except parasitic **lampreys**.

Life span may reach 47 years with males maturing generally at 2–4 years and females at 3–5 years. Most fish live 9–16 years. Growth rates vary markedly, even in adjacent waters. Spawning occurs in groups of 1–3 females and 2–15 males in shallow, weedy waters. Temperatures of 17°C or warmer are necessary and the season lasts several days to several weeks. Spawning may occur any time between May and August in Canada and is easily observed with some fish having their backs out of the water and much audible splashing. Eggs adhere to vegetation and are about 2.0 mm in diameter. A large female can contain 2,208,000 white to yellowish eggs.

An exotic species, carp are a nuisance because they uproot vegetation used by native species for cover, food and spawning. This activity also increases water turbidity to levels which many native species cannot tolerate. Stirred up silt may also smother eggs of native species. Carp also compete with **largemouth bass** and other species for food. Various methods have been employed to eradicate carp from netting to poisons and electric shockers, usually without success except in the smaller, enclosed ponds and lakes.

In the U.S.A. it is sought by anglers but is not fished for extensively in Canada. In England, carp are a premium game fish with angling societies, newsletters, specialised rods and other gear devoted to this species. Some carp are caught in Canada using bow-fishing, spears or spear-guns and scuba gear. In many parts of the world, carp are raised in ponds and are an important food fish. A commercial fishery in Ontario has taken up to 454,000 kg annually valued at $100,000. The total Canadian catch in 1988 was 780 tonnes. The fish are sold alive, fresh or smoked and are often baked. Gefilte fish and caviar are also carp products. In recent years carp have been found to harbour high levels of the toxic chemicals PCBs, and in Wisconsin it is recommended that carp not be eaten more than once a week. Brightly coloured varieties of carp are known as "koi" and are kept as ornamental fish. Colours include red, orange, white, black, blue and yellow in various combinations.

- Most accessible May through July.
- The Great Lakes and its watersheds.
- Medium to heavy action spinning and baitcasting outfits used with 14- to 20-pound test lines.
- Boiled or fresh corn kernels, dough balls made with corn meal, fructose and other flavour additives and worms.

common dolphin

Scientific name: *Coryphaena hippurus* Linnaeus, 1758
Family: **Dolphin**
Other common names: dorade, dorado, mahi mahi
French name: coryphène commune

Distribution: World-wide in warmer waters and from P.E.I. south to Brazil in the western Atlantic Ocean.

Characters: Distinguished from its only relative, the **pompano dolphin**, by having about 245–280 lateral line scales, 56–67, usually 58–66, dorsal fin rays and an oval tooth patch on the tongue. Young less than 20 cm

common dolphin

standard length have dark bars on the body which extend onto the dorsal and anal fins, dark pelvic fins, and white tips to the caudal fin. This pattern provides camouflage among seaweeds. The adult pectoral fin is longer than half the head length and the maximum body depth is less than in the **pompano dolphin** (less than one quarter of the standard length). Anal fin with 25–31 rays, its outer edge concave, pectoral rays 17–21. The male, or bull, has the characteristic steep head while in the female it is more rounded. One of the most beautifully coloured fishes in the ocean, the dolphin is turquoise blue or yellowish-green above and silvery below. The head and body have many small, dark blue to green spots. The pectoral and caudal fins are yellowish. The anal fin often has a pale margin. It changes colour in dramatic waves when removed from the water and becomes mostly a golden yellow, but also tinged with blue and green. The colours fade rapidly on death. Reaches 2.07 m. The world, all-tackle angling record, weighed 39.46 kg and was caught in Costa Rica in 1976.

Biology: This dolphin is a stray in warm months and has been caught in Halifax Harbour in 1901, near Sable Island in 1930, off North Rustico, P.E.I. in 1945, near Georges Bank in 1961, and as young off the southern Scotian Shelf in 1976. An oceanic fish but not uncommon inshore. Western North Atlantic populations may follow a circular migration route from the Caribbean to the U.S. coast and out into the Atlantic Ocean. Young are often found in estuaries or in sar-

gassum weed. This species follows ships and may be found in small groups under floating objects. Food includes fishes of many kinds, including **flyingfish**, which are sometimes caught during a leap of several metres out of the water. When the dolphin attacks, broad dark bars appear on its anterior flanks. Life span is only about 3 years. Unlike most other fishes, females are smaller than males. A very famous game fish often caught by trolling surface baits. It will leap and "tail walk" when hooked. This is the most important sport fish in Florida and North Carolina in terms of numbers and charter boat trips.

common shiner

Scientific name: *Luxilus cornutus*
    (Mitchill, 1817)
Family: **Carp**
Other common names: eastern shiner, redfin
    shiner, silver shiner, silverside, rough-head,
    hornyhead, creek shiner, dace, skipjack
French name: méné à nageoires rouges

Distribution: Found from Nova Scotia and New Brunswick through southwestern Québec and southern Ontario (rare in lower James Bay tributaries) and the Great Lakes but not the northeastern shore of Lake Superior, to southern Manitoba and southeastern Saskatchewan. In the U.S.A. south to Virginia and Colorado.

Characters: This species and its relatives in the genus *Notropis* (typical **shiners**) are separated from other family members by usually having 7 branched dorsal fin rays follow-

common shiner

ing thin unbranched rays, protractile premaxillaries (upper lip separated from the snout by a groove), no barbels, large lateral line scales (fewer than 50), and a simple, s-shaped gut. It is distinguished by having anal fin branched rays 7–9, usually 7–8, exposed part of anterior lateral line scales twice as high as wide, dorsal fin origin over or in front of pelvic fin insertion level, predorsal scale rows 16–30, usually 18–24 (counted from below dorsal fin origin to head, 3–6 scale rows up from the lateral line), and the chin is not pigmented. Dorsal fin branched rays 7, pectoral rays 15–17 and pelvic rays 8–9. Lateral line scales 34–44. Pharyngeal teeth hooked at the tip, usually 2,4–4,2 with such variants as 2,4–4,0 or 1,4–4,1. Males have nuptial tubercles on the snout, in a single row on each lower jaw, sparsely on the nape back to the dorsal fin including the first ray and on the anterior pectoral fin rays. The back is olive-green to olive or bluish-olive with a purple to grey-blue middorsal stripe, flanks are silvery with bronze tinges and some darkened scales, and the belly is silvery-white. There are 3–5 grey-blue, parallel wavy lines on the upper flank but these do not meet in a V behind the dorsal fin as in the closely related **striped shiner**. Upper flank scales are not outlined with pigment as in **striped shiners**. Fins are clear. Young are more silvery. Breeding males have pink to red on the distal third of all fins, the anterior flanks and head are pink and there is a golden stripe on the upper flank. The head is darkened to a lead blue. Peritoneum black to brown. Formerly in the genus *Notropis*. Reaches 20.8 cm.

Biology: Common shiners are found abundantly in streams, rivers and lake margins. Food is taken from the surface and the bottom and includes aquatic insects, algae, other plants, desmids, and small fishes. As much as 71% of the food may be plant material. These fish have been characterised as roving opportunists, taking whatever food is available. They are food for various other fishes and birds.

Life span in Québec is about 7 years, perhaps up to 9 years elsewhere, with maturity attained at 2–3 years. Males grow faster than females and in a Québec study were 1.8 cm longer at age 5 and weighed more than twice as much.

Spawning takes place by day over stream riffles from May to July when water temperatures exceed 16°C. A nest may be excavated in gravel beds of streams or the nests of other species may be used. Males clean a nest area by using their heads to move stones. Each male defends his nest site against other males using his head tubercles to butt opponents. Fin raising may scare away an opponent or pairs of males may parallel swim for up to 2 m with the caudal peduncle and tail slightly raised, followed by butting. The winner returns to the nest site. Males "tilt" to attract a female onto the nest site, inclining the body to one side then the other. The female takes up a position on the side of the male which makes the acutest angle with the bottom. Males may aggregate in masses of 100 fish, all fighting, butting, biting and chasing. Spawning occurs on the fourth day after the mass forms. Injuries often result and become infected with fungus. A dominant male can spawn 8 times in 5 minutes with 36 courting tilts. He may occupy an outlying area from the mass association, using the area for only a day or two at a time. Once the female moves onto the nest site, the male curves around her with his pectoral fin under her breast and his caudal peduncle over her back, and squeezes so eggs and sperm are shed. The female darts forward abruptly after the spawning clasp and often breaks the water surface. This process is repeated many times as less than 50 eggs are shed during each spawning. Hybrids are common because other species' nests are used, notably with the **creek chub, river chub, hornyhead chub, fallfish, central stoneroller** and the **rosyface shiner**. Eggs are about 1.5 mm in diameter and orange when laid, and adhere to the gravel. Each female can have up to 3940 eggs.

This species is often used as a bait fish for **northern pike** and **walleye**. It will rise to a dry fly and is said to be an acceptable food item.

common wolf eel

Scientific name: *Lycenchelys paxillus* (Goode and Bean, 1879)
Family: **Eelpout**
Other common names: none
French name: lycode commune

Distribution: Found from off Nova Scotia south to Virginia.

Characters: This species is separated from its Canadian relatives by having short pelvic fins, a mouth under the snout, large pores around the mouth, no crests on the chin, no bony plates along the dorsal and anal fin bases, and by colour. Dorsal fin rays about 116, anal rays about 104. Scales are present on the body and dorsal and anal fins. Overall colour is a uniform light brown. Reaches 21.0 cm.

common wolf eel

Biology: This species was first described from a specimen caught between LaHave and Sable Island banks. Depth range is 46–1097 m on mud and sand.

cone-chin

Scientific name: *Nesiarchus nasutus* Johnson, 1862
Family: **Snake Mackerel**
Other common names: black gemfish, escolier long nez
French name: menton-pointu

Distribution: Found world-wide in tropical to subtropical waters with some straying into cold-temperate areas such as Atlantic Canada.

Characters: This species is distinguished from other Canadian snake mackerels by having the lower jaw tip projecting markedly, no caudal peduncle keel, 1 spine and 5 branched rays in the pelvic fins, a single, straight lateral line, and 19–21 first dorsal fin spines. The body form is elongate. The soft dorsal fin has 19–24 rays followed by 2–3 finlets. The anal fin has 2 spines, 16–21 soft rays, and is followed by 2–3 finlets. Gill rakers degenerate. Overall colour is dark purplish-brown or chocolate-brown to black with purple tinges.

cone-chin

The eye is light brown. The inside of the mouth is dark brown and the anus margin black. Fin membranes are black. Small preserved specimens (25 cm) have silvery flanks

and belly, a light mouth, a black spot between the first 2 dorsal fin spines, and finlets are not developed. Attains 130 cm standard length.

Biology: First reported from Canada on the LaHave Bank under a different scientific name, now placed in this species. It may descend from the surface to depths of 1300 m near the bottom. This species is usually bentho- or meso-pelagic at 200 m or more. Larvae and young are epi- to meso-pelagic in tropical waters only. Food is fish, squid and crustaceans. Reproduction is year round in warm waters. It is eaten by **longnose lancetfish**.

conger eel

Scientific name: *Conger oceanicus* (Mitchill, 1818)
Family: **Conger**
Other common names: American conger eel, sea eel, congre d'Amérique
French name: congre à museau aigu

Distribution: Found in the eastern Atlantic Ocean and from the Caribbean Sea north to LaHave and Georges banks and the Bay of Fundy in Atlantic Canada.

Characters: This species is distinguished from other Canadian congers by having segmented dorsal and anal fin rays, and jaw teeth

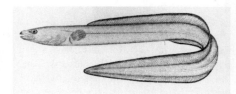

conger eel

form a cutting edge. Adults have the dorsal fin origin over the rear half or slightly behind the pectoral fin. The upper jaw projects beyond the lower jaw. There is one supratemporal pore. The gill slit is large, diagonal and its upper opening begins below the upper third of the pectoral fin base. The eyes are oval. Adults are dark brown or blue-grey to grey or black, with a white chin and a dirty white belly. There is a pale area behind the eye. The dorsal, anal and caudal fins are pale but darkly edged. Pectoral fins are blue-grey, edged with blue-white, or pale blue. Larvae have 140–151 myomeres, a crescent-shaped pigment patch under a golden eye and a row of dots along the flank and along the ventral surface. Larvae attain a maximum length of 160 mm. Adults reach 2.3 m and 40 kg.

Biology: This is the only conger eel found as adults in Canadian waters. Larvae are not encountered frequently either offshore or inshore although a leptocephalus believed to be this species was taken in Passamaquoddy Bay in 1956. On the American coast, this eel is often caught by anglers at docks and piers and is found around coral reefs down to at least 55 m. Conger eels may be found as deep as 577 m. Spawning occurs offshore in summer and up to 6 million eggs are released. Adults die after spawning. Food is small fishes, crustaceans and molluscs. Not commercially important in Canada, conger eels are an excellent food fish.

Conger Family

Scientific name: Congridae
French name: congres

The conger eels are marine fishes of all warmer oceans. There are about 150 species world-wide of which 4 occur on Canada's Atlantic coast. Three of the Canadian species only occur as larvae, strays from southern waters. Several other conger larvae have been collected off the Atlantic coast of Canada but their identity has not been determined accurately.

Congers have a scaleless body and pectoral fins are usually present. There are 8–22 branchiostegal rays. Teeth are strong but there are no long canines. There is a pored lateral line. The posterior nostril is not on the upper lip but well above it near the anterior edge of the eye. The dorsal, anal and caudal fins are well-developed and continuous. Congers have a subdued body colour without the spots found in some **eel** families. Congers are difficult to identify and the number and arrangement of pores in the sensory head canals must be determined along with tooth patterns and gill opening position.

The **Pike Conger Family** is classified with the congers by some authors. This family is a member of the **Eel Order**.

Some conger eels are burrowers, or nocturnal, but many are free-swimming predators that take food near the sea bed during the day. They are often found near seagrass and reefs. Food is fishes, crustaceans and molluscs.

Spawning is believed to take place at depths of about 2500 m in the open ocean for some species. Feeding ceases and the gut degenerates.

The larger species are eaten in Europe and the Far East, but they are not economically important in Canada.

See **bandtooth conger**
conger eel
purplemouthed conger
threadtail conger

copper redhorse

Scientific name: *Moxostoma hubbsi*
Legendre, 1952
Family: **Sucker**
Other common names: none
French name: suceur cuivré

Distribution: Found in the St. Lawrence, Ottawa, Richelieu and Yamaska river systems around Montréal, Québec.

Characters: This species is distinguished by a short dorsal fin, a swimbladder with 3 chambers, lateral line scales 44–48, scales around

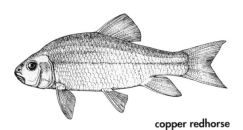

copper redhorse

the caudal peduncle usually 16 (rarely as low as 12–13), scales over the back just in front of the dorsal from lateral line to lateral line 15–16 (excluding lateral line scales), and pharyngeal teeth large, molar-shaped and numbering 4–6 on the lower half of the tooth row. The body is deep, maximum body depth entering body length to end of scales less than 3.5 times in most fish. The snout is short, its length being less than the postorbital length. The snout overhangs the small mouth slightly. The lower lip is deeply cleft, the halves meeting at about 105°. Plicae are weak and long without cross striations. Gill rakers 18–19. Total pharyngeal teeth 18–21. Dorsal fin rays 12–14, anal rays 7, pectoral rays 15–18 and pelvic rays 8–10. The gut has 4 long coils. Males have nuptial tubercles on the head, body and fins. The anal fin has the largest tubercles. Overall colour is copper, which may vary to golden or olive. Scale bases are heavily pigmented. The belly is paler or whitish. Fins are generally similar to the adjacent body or dusky, but the anal fin may have a trace of red and the pelvic fin a trace of orange. Caudal fin red. Peritoneum black. Reaches 69.8 cm total length and 5.67 kg.

Originally described from Lac des Deux-Montagnes, near Montréal. The rivalry between two scientists involved in the description of a new, purely Canadian fish species makes an interesting study in human psychology. Local fishermen were aware of the species. Two scientists set out to collect material independently, the younger having once been an assistant of the older. The younger scientist found a specimen first and published the species description. The older scientist maintained he should have had the honour to publish on this new species, having trained the younger scientist in the mysteries of redhorse taxonomy and having told him of its existence.

Biology: Found in lakes, and from deeper rivers below about 4.0 m and down to 7.0 m usually. Food is mostly (90%) clams and snails crushed by the heavy, molar throat teeth, with some insect larvae. Life span is estimated at 21 years and growth rate is high compared to other redhorses. Maturity is attained at 10 years. Spawning occurs in mid to late June and early July at about 18°C in moderate current at 1.5–2.0 m over a stony bottom. The mean number of eggs per female is 32,747 and the probable maximum is estimated as 111,858, more than other redhorses. This species occurs in an industrialised area which is also susceptible to acid rain. Archaeological investigations show that it used to be more common. The Committee on the Status of Endangered Wildlife in Canada assigned the status of "threatened" to this species in 1987.

copper rockfish

Scientific name: *Sebastes caurinus* Richardson, 1845
Family: **Scorpionfish**
Other common names: yellow-backed rockfish, white rock cod
French name: sébaste cuivré

Distribution: Found from the Gulf of Alaska to Baja California including British Columbia.

Characters: The copper colour of the body with dark fins is characteristic of this species. Dorsal fin spines 13, soft rays 11–14, usually 13. Anal fin soft rays 5–7, usually 6, the sec-

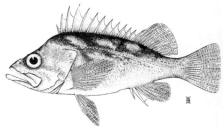

copper rockfish

ond anal spine being twice as thick as the third and about equal in length. Pectoral fin rays 16–18, usually 17. Gill rakers 26–32. Vertebrae 25–26, usually 26. Lateral line pores 37–47, scale rows below the lateral line 39–43. The supraocular, coronal and nuchal spines are absent. The other head spines are thick and prostrate. The overall colour is variable but a copper-brown is usually evident. The upper body is dark to olive-brown or pink to orange-red. There are patches of copper-pink and occasionally dull yellow. Two yellow or copper-orange bands radiate back from the eye. The cheek may have some yellow on it and the chin some orange. There may be a light blotch on midflank. Fins are copper to copper-black or dusky. The lateral line may have a pale stripe and faint bars may be present behind the head. The peritoneum is white. Reaches 57 cm. The world, all-tackle angling record weighed 2.6 kg and was taken by Norman R. Clark on 4 August 1989 at Discovery Island, British Columbia.

Biology: Common in shallow waters in British Columbia in rocky areas and rock-sand bottoms down to 183 m. These rockfish hide among rocks in winter but not in summer. Found also around wharves and jetties and, when young, stranded in tide pools. In the Strait of Georgia they are usually found at less than 20 m. Food is fish and crustaceans. **Shiner perch** are taken as they move into shallow water at night. Young are born in spring and a female of 47 cm produces 640,000. Life span is up to 40 years. Half the male population is mature at 25 cm and half the female population at 24 cm (at about 4 years of age). This species is caught by otter trawls and handlines and is sold as fresh fillets or live to restaurants in Vancouver's Chinatown. It is often seen by SCUBA divers and is a popular sport fish, on light tackle using bait or lures. This rockfish is the one most likely to be caught by anglers. It forms hybrids with the **brown rockfish**

Cornetfish Family

Scientific name: Fistulariidae
French name: fistulaires

Cornetfishes or flutemouths are mostly found in tropical waters in the Atlantic, Indian and Pacific oceans. There are only 4 species, 1 of which enters Atlantic Canada.

They have a characteristic elongate shape with a very long snout with a small mouth at the tip bearing tiny teeth. The dorsal and anal fins each have 13–20 soft rays and are at the end of the body near the tail. The anus is immediately behind the pelvic fins. The caudal fin has a long, trailing central filament formed from the central 2 fin rays. There are no scales and the body is naked or has small prickles and scutes. The lateral line has a strong anterior arch and runs along the whole body length and onto the caudal filament.

Cornetfishes are related to the **Snipefish** and **Pipefish** families in the **Stickleback Order**. The scientific name is derived from the Latin for pipe, alluding to the body shape.

They are usually found in shallow waters and around coral reefs, swimming in small schools, often head downwards. Their camouflage is excellent, enabling them to get close enough to suck up prey fishes with the long snout. They may search through mud and seaweed for food.

See **bluespotted cornetfish**

Cornish blackfish

Scientific name: *Centrolophus medusophagus* (Cocco, 1839)
Family: **Ruff**
Other common names: brown ruff, barrelfish, saw-cheeked fish
French name: pompile brun

Distribution: Found from the Grand Bank and Flemish Cap north to eastern Greenland and south to North Carolina.

Characters: This species is distinguished from other ruffs and medusafishes by having weak dorsal fin spines and about 12 major but weak spines on the preoperculum. The skeleton is poorly ossified, spongy and oil-filled. The dorsal fin originates before the pectoral fin insertion, and has spines grading into soft rays, total count 44–51. Total rays in the anal fin are 25–33. There are 16–21 pectoral fin rays. The lateral line is arched at the front and becomes straight over the anal fin. There are 160–230 scales in the lateral line, the number increasing with growth. The roof of the mouth is toothless. Overall colour is dark brown or pale olive with a paler lateral line. The flanks are often mottled in

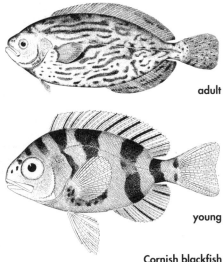

adult

young

Cornish blackfish

young and the back is greenish-brown. In preserved fish the scale pockets are outlined in brown giving a finely mottled appearance.

The peritoneum is black, giving a violet sheen to the belly area. Reaches 58 cm.

Biology: This is a rarely caught species. Six specimens were captured in Canadian waters from 1958–1964. Adults are quite rare and often damaged on capture because of their fragile body. The young fish associate with jellyfish but at about 20 cm they leave the jellyfish and descend to deeper water. They are also associated with flotsam. The external skin layer in young fish may be keratinised as a protection against jellyfish stings. Food includes jellyfish and crustaceans. Tentacles and gonads of jellyfish are twisted off with a relaxed movement. The oil-filled bones may serve to make the fish neutrally buoyant so little energy is needed to float at the desired depth. The oil may also be an energy reserve. This fish is reported to void large clouds of purple matter from the anus, perhaps in response to a threat in hopes of confusing a predator.

cosmopolitan dreamtail

Scientific name: *Oneirodes eschrichti*
    Lütken, 1871
Family: **Dreamer**
Other common names: none
French name: queue-de-rêve cosmopolite

Distribution: Found in all oceans including the Atlantic from Greenland southward.

Characters: This species of deepsea **anglerfish** is part of a group of dreamers including the **westnorat** and **forefour dream-**

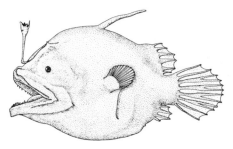

cosmopolitan dreamtail

tails on the Atlantic coast. The females of this group are distinguished by having sphenotic spines, a deeply notched operculum posteri-

orly, a short and broad pectoral fin lobe, the tip of the lower jaw with a spine, the illicium or fishing rod emerging from between the frontal bones on the head, the dorsal edge of these bones being strongly curved, usually 4 anal fin rays and the caudal fin not covered by skin beyond the base. Females of this species are distinguished from Canadian Atlantic relatives by having an esca or bait with well-developed medial appendages and no lateral or anterolateral appendages. Dorsal fin with 5–7 rays and pectoral fin rays 15–19. Overall colour is black with parts of the esca unpigmented. Females reach 29.7 cm total length.

Biology: Three specimens were caught off Newfoundland in 1968. This species is meso- to bathypelagic. Females use the fishing apparatus to attract prey within striking distance. Food includes crustaceans and squids. Females are solitary and males track them down using their well-developed sensory system. Eggs are laid in a jelly veil.

Cow Shark Family

Scientific name: Hexanchidae
French name: grisets

The cow sharks are a small family with only 4 species having a world-wide distribution from cold-temperate to tropical seas. There are 2 Canadian species, 1 on both the Atlantic and Pacific coasts and 1 on the Pacific coast only.

Their family name comes from the bulky body shape. They are easily recognised by the 6–7 gill slits, presence of an anal fin and only one dorsal fin, a stout body and mouth on the underside of the head. A spiracle is present. The teeth of the upper and lower jaws are dissimilar in shape.

Their only related family with one species, not yet found in Canadian waters, is the rare, deepwater, frilled shark. Cow sharks are members of the **Cow Shark Order**.

They are small to very large (1.4 to 6.8 m as adults) and sluggish to active. Most species are deepwater, down to at least 1875 m, but some are seen close inshore and near the surface. Cow sharks are ovoviviparous. They feed on large items such as bony fishes, sharks, rays, crustaceans and carrion including whales.

See **sevengill shark**
        sixgill shark

Cow Shark Order

Cow sharks, comb-tooth sharks, sixgill sharks, sevengill sharks and frilled sharks, of the Order Hexanchiformes, comprise 2 families with only about 6–7 species. In Canada there are 2 species in 1 family on the Atlantic and Pacific coasts. These are medium to large, benthic sharks found world-wide in cold to tropical, shallow to deep waters. The frilled shark, (requin lézard, *Chlamydoselachus anguineus* Garman, 1884) is the only representative of the non-Canadian family. It may eventually be reported from Canada although it is a rare, deepsea shark.

The members of this order are characterised by 6–7 gill slits, 1 spineless dorsal fin and 1 anal fin. Small spiracles are present, there are no nictitating lower eyelids, the intestinal valve is a spiral or ring type and lower jaw teeth are sawtoothed.

The order is thought to be the most primitive of living sharks.

Biology is summarised under the family and species accounts.

See **Cow Shark Family**

crappies

There are 2 species of crappie in Canadian fresh waters, the **black** and the **white crappie**. They are members of the **Sunfish Family**.

creek chub

Scientific name: *Semotilus atromaculatus*
(Mitchill, 1818)
Family: **Carp**
Other common names: horned dace, common chub, brook chub, tommycod, silvery chub, mud chub, blackspot chub
French name: mulet à cornes

Distribution: Found from Nova Scotia westward through southern Québec and Ontario, including the Great Lakes and upper James Bay drainages, to southern Manitoba. Sporadic records in northern Québec. South to Gulf coast drainages and west to Montana in the U.S.A.

Characters: This species is distinguished by having protractile premaxillae (a groove between the upper lip and the snout), a flat barbel in advance of the mouth corner in the groove above the upper lip, lateral line scales 47–66 (usually 52–63) and a black spot at the anterior dorsal fin base. The upper jaw

creek chub

extends back to a level with the front of the eye so the mouth is large. Pharyngeal teeth 2,5–4,2, 2,4–5,2, 2,5–5,2 or 2,4–4,2 with a strongly hooked tip. Dorsal fin branched rays 7–8, usually 7, anal fin branched rays 6–8, pectoral rays 13–20 and pelvic rays 7–9. Breeding males have up to 12 very large tubercles in a line on each side of the head from in front of the lip to over the eye. Smaller tubercles are present on the sides of the head and in a single row on up to 8 pectoral fin rays. Posterior flank scales have tubercles lining their margins and tubercles extend along the upper, anterior caudal fin lobe margin. The back is olive, sometimes with a steel-blue tinge, the flanks silvery and the belly silvery-white to white. Flanks have iridescent purplish or greenish tinges. Scales are outlined with pigment. Fin rays are edged with pigment. The dorsal and caudal fins are dusky. Young are more silvery and have a flank stripe ending in a spot at the tail base. Breeding males may have rosy, orange or yellow tints on the head, body and dorsal fin base. Lower fins are orange and the lateral head surface is blue. Peritoneum silvery with some speckling. Hybrids are formed with **redside dace, common shiner, longnose dace** and **central stoneroller**. Reaches 33.0 cm.

Biology: The creek chub is very common in clear, smaller streams but may also be found rarely along lake shores. Food varies from plankton when young to aquatic and terrestrial insects, crayfish, frogs and small fishes, such as **johnny darter** and **brook stickleback**, and even berries as they grow larger. Some algae and higher plants may also be eaten. In a Québec lake young fed on small adult flies and aquatic beetles during the day while adults were nocturnal and fed on larger prey, crustaceans and insect larvae. More benthic prey are available at night. Creek chub are eaten by a wide variety of fish and birds.

Life span is about 8 years with females maturing at age 2 and males at age 3. Males grew more rapidly than females in a study near Peterborough, Ontario.

Spawning occurs in April–July at about 12°C or higher near stream riffles. In the Mink River, Manitoba and near Peterborough, Ontario, most spawning occurs between the middle and the end of May. Males excavate a pit by violent body movements which dislodge smaller particles and by picking stones up in the mouth and dropping them upstream. This creates a pit which is continually filled in by the current covering and protecting the eggs. The pit is about 30 cm wide but can be more than 5 m long. Several males may collaborate on a single nest. A female approaches a male defending his nest and is tossed into an upright position by the male inserting his head and pectoral fin under her body. The male instantly embraces her in a horizontal curve in about a tenth of a second and about 50 eggs are shed into the gravel and fertilised. Tubercles help the male to grip the female. After this embrace, the female turns belly up as though stunned but soon swims off to spawn again in the same or other nests. A female continues spawning over several days until all eggs are shed. The male covers the eggs with gravel. A male may not lift a female up but instead press her to the bottom or against the pit side when eggs are released. Females have up to 7539 eggs of 1.7 mm diameter.

Some males are "nest-watchers" who may spawn with a female while the dominant male is chasing away another rival. Fights appear to use the head tubercles as weapons although injuries have not been observed. Usually contending males parallel swim for several metres upstream from the nest, with fins erect, mouths open and tails beating slowly but strongly. Tail beats are meant to intimidate. Male **common shiners** often crowd around a creek chub nest involved in their own reproductive behaviour. They may even bump into the creek chub who will use his massive, tuberculate head to drive them away momen-

tarily. **Shiners** and other fishes however can enter nest sites without eliciting a response from the chub unless he is spawning. All intrusions by other male chub result in aggression.

Creek chub are used extensively in Canada as a bait fish and can be caught on a baited hook. They are good eating except for the nuisance of small bones.

crescent gunnel

Scientific name: *Pholis laeta* (Cope, 1873)
Family: **Gunnel**
Other common names: bracketed blenny
French name: sigouine lunée

Distribution: Northern California to the Bering Sea including the British Columbia coast.

Characters: Distinguished from other Pacific coast gunnels with pelvic fins by having 74–81 dorsal fin spines, 32–39 anal fin rays preceded by 2 spines, a median interorbital pore and black bracket-shaped or crescent-shaped markings along the base of the dorsal fin, each enclosing a yellow or orange area. Pectoral fins relatively large with 11–13 rays. Yellowish-green body with mottling on sides. The side of the head has a light area edged with black. The opercle may have a green spot. The anal and caudal fins may be orange. Mature males have an orange or reddish colour on the throat, cheeks, pectoral fins and belly anterior to the anal fin. Attains 25 cm.

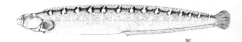

crescent gunnel

Biology: Found in tide pools and down to 73 m associated with seaweed and near exposed rocky headlands. Spawning occurs in January when mature pairs are found under each rock. Only the left ovary is developed and contains up to 1598 eggs. Eggs are initially white but change to a cream colour as they develop. They are laid in a mass and adhere to each other but not the substrate. A single or both parents may be found coiled around the egg mass to protect it. In more northerly waters cold conditions are avoided by moving into deeper water.

crescent loosejaw

Scientific name: *Aristostomias lunifer*
    Regan and Trewavas, 1930
Family: **Barbeled Dragonfish**
Other common names: none
French name: drague lunée

Distribution: Reported from all warmer seas including off the Canadian Atlantic coast.
Characters: This species is distinguished from Canadian relatives by having a pectoral fin, a suborbital light organ, a barbel on the

crescent loosejaw

throat without a distinct bulb at the tip, 2 pairs of nostrils, light organs between the pectoral and pelvic fins evenly spaced (not in groups), and 7–8 pectoral fin rays. Head and body black. The barbel bulb is pale but the stem is black (pale brown to whitish in some preserved fish). Teeth are white. Light organs are white to bluish in preserved fish. There is a crescent of luminous tissue in front of and below the eye, but no solid streak between the eye and the postorbital light organ. Attains about 17 cm.
Biology: Known from a single specimen caught in 1979 at 500 m south of the Grand Bank at the northern range limit. A rare species with only a few specimens caught.

crested ridgehead

Scientific name: *Poromitra crassiceps*
    (Günther, 1878)
Family: **Ridgehead**
Other common names: crested bigscale,
    rhino à petits yeux
French name: heaume à crête

Distribution: Almost cosmopolitan; not found in the Arctic Ocean or the Mediterranean Sea. Found off both the Atlantic and Pacific coasts of Canada.

Characters: Dorsal fin with 1–3 spines and 11–16 soft rays. Anal fin with 1–2 spines and 8–11 soft rays, pectoral fin slender with

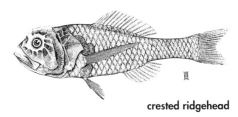

crested ridgehead

13–15 rays, and pelvic fin with 1 spine and 7–8 soft rays. There are about 23–31 scale rows. Distinguished from the related **largeye rhinofish** by having more than 28 gill rakers and a moderate-sized eye (diameter less than one-sixth head length) and from the related **bull rhinofish** by having a weak spine at the lower corner of the preopercle. There is an obvious spine between the nostrils and 2 high, transparent crests on top of the head. The eye is surrounded by radiating ridges. The opercles have radiating ridges also. Gill membranes are free from the isthmus and not joined to each other. Overall colour is black. Attains 15.5 cm standard length.
Biology: Rare in Canadian Atlantic waters and known from only 2 specimens caught on the Flemish Cap in 1968. More common off British Columbia, perhaps because of the proximity of deeper water. This species is found as deep as 3300 m but is not found on the bottom. It rises to near the surface at night. It may live 10 years. Food is small crustaceans.

crested scabbardfish

Scientific name: *Lepidopus altifrons*
    Parin and Collette, 1993
Family: **Cutlassfish**
Other common names: none
French name: poisson sabre crénelé

Distribution: Found from off the Scotian Shelf of Atlantic Canada south to off southern Brazil.
Characters: This species is distinguished from related species by lacking a notch between the spiny and soft parts of the dorsal fin, by a prominent crest on top of the head

commencing over the eye and extending back to the dorsal, and by lower fin rays counts. Dorsal fin elements 90–97. Anal fin

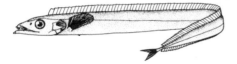

crested scabbardfish

with 2 spines and 52–58 soft rays. Vertebrae 98–107. The body is silvery to brown with a dark lateral line. The gill cavity is black. Reaches 66 cm standard length.

Biology: Juveniles are pelagic but adults are benthopelagic at 200–500 m.

crested sculpin

Scientific name: *Blepsias bilobus*
  Cuvier, 1829
Family: **Sculpin**
Other common names: none
French name: chabot bilobé

Distribution: Found from the Sea of Japan to northern British Columbia.

Characters: This species and its relative, the **silverspotted sculpin**, are separated from other Pacific coast sculpins by the

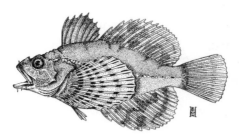

crested sculpin

deep, compressed body and 3 simple, large cirri on each lower jaw. The crested sculpin lacks the deep notch in the spiny dorsal fin found in its relative, has a different colour pattern without light spots and has 15–17 pectoral fin rays. There are prominent cirri and tubular nostrils on the snout. The nasal spine is weak, low and curves backward. There are 4 preopercular spines and the sec-

ond spine is the largest and is broad. The head bears frontal, occipital, supraocular and postocular ridges. First dorsal fin spines 7–9, second dorsal fin rays 20–22. Anal rays 18–20 and pelvic fin with 1 spine and 3 soft rays. Ctenoid scales are in the form of small plates with a small spine in a fleshy papilla. They cover the body, fin bases and side of the head and give the fish a frosty appearance. There are 52–53 lateral line pores. Simple cirri are on each side of the snout and on the upper jaw. The body is olive-green to brown with 4–5 blotches over the back. The belly is paler. The dorsal, caudal and pectoral fins have dusky bars. Reaches 25 cm.

Biology: This is a comparatively rare species of inshore waters of which little is known.

crevalle jack

Scientific name: *Caranx hippos*
  (Linnaeus, 1776)
Family: **Jack**
Other common name: common jack, toro, horse crevalle, cavally
French name: carangue crevallée

Distribution: From Nova Scotia south to Uruguay, and in the eastern Atlantic Ocean and possibly world-wide in warmer waters.

Characters: This species is distinguished from its Canadian Atlantic coast relatives by having a moderately deep body, greater than 28% of fork length, scutes (enlarged scales) in the lateral line posteriorly, and an upper jaw extending back to the rear of the eye or beyond. The front of the head is steep. First

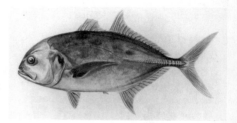

crevalle jack

dorsal fin spines 8, second dorsal fin with 1 spine and 18–22 soft rays. Anal fin with 3 spines and 16–18 soft rays. Gill rakers 15–19 on lower limb of the gill arch. The chest area is mostly scaleless. The adipose eyelid is best developed posteriorly. Metallic green to blue on the back, silvery on the sides. Fins and belly often yellowish. The edge of the gill cover has a vertical, oval black spot. The lower pectoral fin rays have a broad black band. Young fish have 4–6 flank bars. Reaches a reputed 1.5 m. The world, all-tackle angling record weighed 26 kg and was caught in Angola in 1992. "Crevalle" is derived from the Spanish for horse as in horse-mackerel, a related species.

Biology: A rare visitor to Canadian waters first caught from Musquodoboit Harbour, Nova Scotia, in 1933 and subsequently from Prospect in 1970 and Porters Harbour in 1984. Young fish may enter river mouths and are common in shallow inshore waters as schools over reefs. Adults are common along the American coast in large, fast-moving schools and may descend to 350 m offshore. Food is mainly fishes and some invertebrates. Prey fishes have been pursued so vigorously that they leap ashore or into boats. A school of jacks will herd prey fish into a mass before attacking from all sides. Large crevalle jacks are excellent sport fish but poor-eating. They are caught on light tackle by rapid spinning, trolling, surf-casting or fly-fishing. Live fish can be used as bait. They may grunt or croak when caught. Spawning takes place in July in the Caribbean area. This species may show ciguatera poisoning, making the flesh dangerous to eat.

crevice kelpfish

Scientific name: *Gibbonsia montereyensis* Hubbs, 1927
Family: **Clinid**
Other common names: spotted kelpfish
French name: clinide de crevasse

Distribution: From Baja California to British Columbia.

Characters: This species is distinguished from its relative, the **striped kelpfish**, by having fewer than 176 scales (130–175) along the flank above the lateral line, 5–8, usually 6–7, dorsal fin soft rays, and one or more dark spots along the flank. Gill membranes are joined but free of the isthmus.

Dorsal fin spines 34–36 before the few soft rays. Dorsal fin soft rays are more widely spaced at the rear. Anal fin with 2 spines and 23–28 rays. Pectoral fin with 11–13 rays and short, not reaching the anal fin. There are cirri at the dorsal fin spine tips, over each eye and over the nostrils. The cirri over the eye are shaped like a hand with fingers. Red to brown or green or lavender, quite variable. May be uniform or bear spots, bars and stripes. There is usually a large eye spot above the pectoral fin and various other spots distributed on the upper flank. Attains 11 cm.

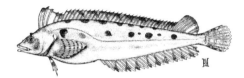

crevice kelpfish

Biology: Associated with algae on exposed, rocky coasts down to 21 m. This species is often immobile and changes colour to match its background so it is difficult to see.

croakers

Croakers are members of the **Drum Family** and there is a single species, the **white croaker**, in Canada on the Pacific coast. Drums and croakers produce sound by contraction of muscles attached to the swimbladder which is used as a resonating chamber.

crossthroat sawpalate

Scientific name: *Serrivomer jespersoni* Bauchot-Boutin, 1953
Family: **Sawpalate**
Other common names: none
French name: serrivomer à gorge croisée

Distribution: Found in the Pacific and Indian oceans and off British Columbia.

Characters: This is the only Pacific Canadian sawpalate and is characterised by the blade of saw-shaped teeth in 2 rows in the roof of the mouth. The dorsal fin has 141–170 rays, the anal fin 127–161, caudal 6 and pectorals 6–7 rays. Vertebrae are about

148–150. Overall colour is dark with the mouth and gill cavities black. Attains 64 cm standard length.

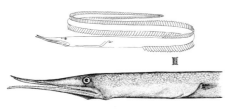

crossthroat sawpalate

Biology: The 2 Canadian specimens were caught off Vancouver Island and Queen Charlotte Sound at depths approximately between 360 and 825 m. One specimen was caught in midwater over depths down to 2290–2380 m.

cubera snapper

Scientific name: *Lutjanus cyanopterus*
  (Cuvier, 1828)
Family: **Snapper**
Other common names: Cuban snapper
French name: vivaneau cubéra

Distribution: Found from Nova Scotia south to Brazil.

Characters: This species is distinguished from the **wenchman**, its only Canadian relative, by having scales on the soft dorsal and

cubera snapper

anal fins and the last dorsal and anal fin ray is shorter than adjacent rays. There are 10 dorsal fin spines and 14 soft rays. Anal fin spines 3, soft rays 7–8, usually 8. Pectoral rays 15–18. Lateral line scales 43–50. The body, head and fins are grey to dark brown with reddish tinges, lighter below. Young

cuberas have irregular shaped, pale bars on the upper flank. Reaches 1.6 m and more than 57 kg. The world, all-tackle angling record weighed 55.11 kg and was caught in 1982 at Cameron, Louisiana.

Biology: A large specimen (112.4 cm total length and 19.1 kg) was caught in a trap net at Tuffin Island, off Ecum Secum, Nova Scotia in 1975. A second specimen was caught in a mackerel trap set in St. Margarets Bay, N.S. in 1988. These records are strays of a species usually found 1400 km or more south of Nova Scotia. This species is only common from southern Florida and southward. It prefers rocky ledges at 18–55 m when adult, but young have been recorded as entering fresh water. Food is mostly fishes, with some crustaceans. Eggs and larvae are pelagic. Anglers catch this species on hooks and bottom longlines and it is spear-fished. The cubera snapper is fished commercially in the tropical western Atlantic Ocean where several thousand tons are caught annually. However it has been reported as causing the tropical fish poisoning known as ciguatera.

cunner

Scientific name: *Tautogolabrus adspersus*
  (Walbaum, 1792)
Family: **Wrasse**
Other common names: sea perch, chogset, bergall, bengal, nipper, blue perch, bluefish, chogy, baitstealer, conner, achigan de mer, tanche, vieille
French name: tanche-tautogue

Distribution: Found from northern Newfoundland and the Gulf of St. Lawrence south to Chesapeake Bay.

Characters: This wrasse is distinguished from its only Canadian relative, the **tautog**, by having 18 dorsal fin spines, a pointed snout, and scales on the lower half of the operculum. Dorsal fin with 9–10 soft rays, anal fin with 3 spines and 9 soft rays. There are about 40 lateral line scales. Overall colour varies with the background and age and possibly diet, often greenish-grey to a dull brown or even reddish or bluish, with various darker blotches. The flanks have iridescent blue-green or red spots. Lips and mouth cavity may be yellowish. The lower jaw is white. The belly is white to bluish. Males develop a spawning colouration which involves the blue-white belly colour becoming more widespread, sometimes the lower flanks become silvery, the head becomes a bright light blue, median fins are blue, and the back is deep blue to purple. Females remain a dull brown, some with 6–7 pale bands. Young fish up to 10 cm have a black spot at the spiny-soft dorsal fin junction and are a bright orange-copper colour. Reaches 43.2 cm and 1.5 kg.

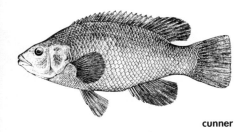

cunner

Biology: Cunners are found around rocks and seaweed clumps and artificial structures such as harbours, wharves, seawalls and pilings. Some specimens have been caught on offshore banks and down to 128 m. They occur in schools but do not enter brackish water. In Newfoundland winters, cunners become torpid under rocks in shallow water when temperatures fall below 5°C and are inactive for 5–6 months of each year. Mass mortalities have been reported when temperatures fall too low. Cunner have a small home range and will return to it if moved.

Food is hard-shelled animals such as molluscs, crustaceans and sea urchins, but any animal or plant food will be consumed including those found in the water column and such unusual items as sea slugs. Mussels take 10–14 hours to pass through the digestive tract and some emerge alive! Cunners feed actively during the day and hide in crevices or lie against rocks at night. In Newfoundland, males feed mostly in the morning and females during both morning and afternoon. Territorial males, non-territorial males and females have different diets reflecting different foraging behaviours. Dominant males take abundant food items

with a low handling time like snails and sea urchins. Females take calorie rich items like clams and fish remains. Non-territorial male diet overlaps that of females and territorial males. Feeding forays from refuges under boulders in the intertidal zone may be as short as 5 seconds or as long as 14 minutes and over 12 m away from the refuge. These fish are mature at 8–11 cm and females grow faster than males. They may live 10 years or more. Spawning occurs in the summer months, June to August, in Canadian waters and floating eggs measure 0.85 mm. Spawning occurs during midflood to high tide and several spawnings per day can take place, mostly in the afternoons. Males strongly defend a territory in which courtship occurs. The borders of this territory are patrolled, particularly in the afternoon and early evening when intrusions by females and young males without territories are common. Courtship involves the male swimming in an arc over a stationary female with fins erect and head turned towards her. The male approaches a responsive female, passes over her several times, places his belly against her back and begins to quiver from head to tail. This is followed by the spawning pair swimming vertically at high speed with eggs and sperm released as both fish flex suddenly into a u-shape with vents close together. Some females spawn with only one male, while others spawn with several males. Group spawning also occurs with more than 150 fish involved and takes place in Newfoundland waters most frequently between 1800–1900 hours.

Cunners are caught and enjoyed by younger anglers using clams as bait, but are often a nuisance as they steal bait meant for other fishes. The bones, and even the flesh, have a bluish tinge which is harmless but discourages some people from trying to eat this fish.

curlfin sole

Scientific name: *Pleuronichthys decurrens*
    Jordan and Gilbert, 1881
Family: **Righteye Flounder**
Other common names: curlfin turbot,
    California turbot

French name: plie à nageoires frisées

Distribution: Found from Alaska to Baja California including British Columbia.

Characters: This species is recognised among Pacific Canadian **flatfishes** by the first 9–12 dorsal fin rays being on the blind side

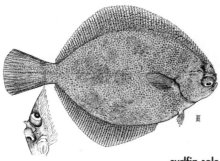

curlfin sole

and the fin origin being at the mouth corner. The ridge between the eyes has large tubercles or spines at each end. Scales are cycloid on both sides of the body, embedded and number 80–96 in the lateral line. An accessory or branch lateral line runs close to the dorsal fin to about midbody level. Dorsal fin rays long, 67–79, anal rays long, 45–53, preceded by a sharp spine. The caudal fin is rounded. The mouth is small and asymmetrical and teeth are mainly on the blind side of the jaws. Total gill rakers 9–13. Eyed side deep olive-green, brown to black or red-brown, with mottling and fine spots. Blind side cream-white but may be completely brown except for head. All fins dark. Reaches 37 cm.

Biology: Abundant in Canada and reported generally at 7.6–350 m on mud bottoms. Elsewhere to 532 m. Food includes worms, molluscs and crustaceans but also brittle stars and nudibranchs. Eggs are pelagic and 1.5 mm in diameter. They are laid in April-August. A commercial species in California, where it is sold as mink food, but not utilised in Canada.

cusk

Scientific name: *Brosme brosme*
(Ascanius, 1772)
Family: **Cod**

Other common names: tusk, torske, scrod
French name: brosme

Distribution: Found from southern Labrador, the outer Gulf of St. Lawrence, the Grand Bank and south to New Jersey. Also found off southern Greenland, Iceland and northwestern Europe.

Characters: This species is uniquely characterised among Canadian **cods** by the single dorsal fin which, with the anal fin, is joined to the caudal fin, separated only by a notch. Dorsal fin rays 85–108, anal rays 62–75. Scales are minute and deeply embedded. The chin barbel is well-developed. Overall colour dark red-brown, green-brown, light brown or brownish-grey fading to cream or dirty white on the belly. The flanks may be mottled with brown. The median fins have a white margin highlighted by a black band immediately below. Young fish may have about 6 yellow bands along the flanks. Reaches 110 cm. Cusk and tusk are Scandinavian words for this fish. The world, all-tackle angling record weighed 14.9 kg and was caught in Norway in 1988.

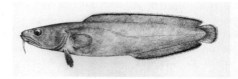

cusk

Biology: The cusk is restricted to rough, rocky bottoms at 18–1000 m, usually at 100–400 m, and 0–12°C. This is a sluggish species found in small schools or alone. Its centre of abundance in Canada is the Scotian Shelf. Food includes crustaceans, molluscs, starfishes and fishes. Hooded seals may eat them. Males are usually larger than females of the same age and life span is about 20 years. Half the population of males is mature at 4.7 years and 43.5 cm and females at 6.5 years and 50.7 cm. Spawning occurs from May to August, peaking in June, in water at the shallow end of its range. Egg numbers are as high as 3,927,000 Eggs are 1.5 mm in diameter and pelagic. The egg surface is finely pitted and the oil globule in the egg is pink or brown. Cusk are taken as a by-catch mainly from the western Scotian Shelf, usually on longlines because of their rocky habitat which is not easily accessible to trawlers. They are a good food fish with firm, white flesh tasting like lobster In 1982, 6290 tonnes worth $2,664,000 were landed. The 1988 catch weighed 2870 tonnes. Cusk are occasionally caught by anglers but live too deep to be regularly sought after.

Cusk-eel Family

Scientific name: Ophidiidae
French name: donzelles

Cusk-eels are found in most temperate to tropical seas world-wide and rarely in fresh waters. There are about 164 species with 4 on the Atlantic coast and 1 on the Pacific coast of Canada.

These fishes have long dorsal and anal fins confluent with the tail fin. Dorsal fin rays are equal in length, or longer, than the anal fin rays opposite. The anus and anal fin origin are usually to the rear of the pectoral fin. Scales are small and cycloid. There may be 1 or more opercular spines. Pelvic fins, comprised of 1–2 slender rays, are rarely absent and are far forward on the throat.

Cusk-eels are related to the **Pearlfish Family** with which they share the continuous dorsal, anal and caudal fins tapering to a point, an anterior nostril distinctly above the upper lip in most species and lack of an intromittent organ in males. However, larvae lack the vexillum of **Pearlfish Family** members. This family is a member of the **Cusk-eel Order**.

Cusk-eels may be found on sandy bottoms, in shallow water, into which they burrow tail first, but others occur at great depths down to more than 8000 m. All larvae are pelagic. Some members of this family have a foam-like substance, rich in cholesterol and phospholipids, in their swimbladders when brought to the surface. The swimbladder of these deepsea fishes is filled with 90% oxygen gas at pressures up to 380 atmospheres. As the fishes decompress on the way to the surface, the expanding oxygen gas turns the swimbladder contents to a foam. Some of the largest species off Chile and South Africa are used as food fishes.

See **Agassiz' cusk-eel**
    blackgut tendrilfin
    fawn cusk-eel
    giant cusk-eel
    mooneye cusk-eel

Cusk-eel Order

The **cusk-eels**, **pearlfishes**, pyramodontines, **livebearing brotulas** or viviparous brotulas, false brotulas and their relatives are members of the Order Ophidiiformes and comprise small to large, principally marine fishes of the Atlantic, Indian and Pacific oceans occupying shallows to the deep sea. There are a few freshwater species and there are many undescribed species. There are 5 families and over 355 species with 3 families and 7 species in Atlantic and Pacific coast waters of Canada.

These fishes are characterised by an elongate tapering body, the anterior position of the pelvic fins on the throat or chin (jugular or mental position), each pelvic fin has 1–2 soft rays and sometimes a spine (pelvic fins are absent in some species), scales small and cycloid or absent, large mouth with the maxilla bone usually reaching back beyond the eye, long dorsal and anal fins usually joined to or continuous with the rounded or tapering caudal fin, paired nostrils, and the dorsal and anal fin ray supports or pterygiophores outnumber the adjacent vertebrae.

The relationships of these fishes are uncertain so their grouping in this order is a matter of convenience. They have been placed in the **Perch Order** and the **Cod Order**, and are probably most closely related to the latter on the basis of caudal skeleton and larval characters.

Most species have no economic importance. Some members of the order are live bearers while others lay eggs. Certain members are inquilines, living within the body cavities of invertebrates.

See **Cusk-eel Family**
    Livebearing Brotula Family
    Pearlfish Family

cuskpout

Scientific name: *Derepodichthys alepidotus* Gilbert, 1895

Family: **Eelpout**
Other common names: none
French name: lycode-donzelle

Distribution: Found in British Columbia, southern California and northwestern Mexico.

Characters: This species is uniquely characterised by the pelvic fins below the eye, each with 3 joined rays on a single, erectile

cuskpout

base and the cleithrum bone of the pectoral girdle extending far forward. Teeth are large, recurved fangs. Dorsal fin rays 110–116, anal rays 94–101, and pectoral rays 10–11. The gill slit is vertical and partly in front of the pectoral fin. Scales and a body lateral line are absent. Bones are fragile and the skin gelatinous. Preserved specimens are light to dark brown. The anal fin margin and the posterior dorsal fin margin are black or brown. The lips and peritoneum are black. Mouth, gill cavity and stomach lining brown. The anus is surrounded by a white ring. Attains 15.1 cm.

Biology: This species was described from a single specimen dredged off the Queen Charlotte Islands at 2904 m in 1890. No more have been caught in Canada and it was only in 1965 that the second and third specimens were caught off Baja California. Only 13 specimens have been caught. The peculiar pelvic fins are used to forage for food in the sediment. Worms are a food item. Females contain up to 25 orange eggs up to 2.4 mm in diameter.

Cutlassfish Family

Scientific name: Trichiuridae
French name: trichiures

Cutlassfishes, scabbardfishes, frostfishes or hairtails, are found in the Arctic, Atlantic, Indian and Pacific oceans. There are 32 species with about 6 species on Canadian coasts.

They have a very long and compressed body, rather like a fragile ribbon. There are fang-like teeth in a large head. The snout is pointed, and the lower jaw projects. The dorsal fin is extremely long and contains anterior spines separated usually by a notch from posterior soft rays but spines and soft rays are difficult to distinguish. The anal fin is low and poorly developed compared to the dorsal fin. It is preceded by a small and a large spine. The caudal fin is small and forked, or absent, in which case the body tapers to a point. The pelvic fin is reduced to a scale-like spine and 0–2 soft rays, or is absent. The gill cover is splintered. There may be as many as 192 vertebrae. There are no scales. There is only one nostril on each side. Gill rakers are spiny.

Cutlassfishes are most closely related to the **Snake Mackerel Family** with which it is sometimes combined, and also to the **Mackerel** and **Swordfish** families. This family is a member of the **Perch Order**. The bigeye frostfish (sabre d'argent à grands yeux, *Benthodesmus elongatus* (Clarke, 1879)) is no longer recorded for Canada. Two subspecies of the bigeye frostfish are now recognised as distinct species (**North Pacific frostfish** and **Simony's frostfish**). A sixth species, *Aphanopus intermedius* Parin, 1983 (intermediate scabbardfish, poisson sabre tachus) may be found on the Atlantic and Pacific coasts of Canada but its systematic status is uncertain. If it is a valid species, then the black scabbardfish is restricted to the northern Atlantic Ocean.

These are mostly deepwater fishes which may be washed ashore or found in the stomachs of marine mammals and large fishes. As a result, specimens are often damaged and difficult to identify. They may descend to 2000 m or rise to 10–20 m. Cutlassfish are fast-swimming voracious predators on smaller fishes and on shrimps and squids. They spawn year round in warmer waters and produce pelagic eggs and larvae. Some species are commercially important in the eastern Atlantic Ocean but not in Canada.

See **black scabbardfish**
      crested scabbardfish
      North Pacific frostfish
      Simony's frostfish
      smalleye frostfish

cutlips minnow

Scientific name: *Exoglossum maxillingua*
(Le Sueur, 1817)
Family: **Carp**
Other common names: eye-picker, little sucker
French name: bec-de-lièvre

Distribution: Found from the St. Lawrence River and its tributaries south to Virginia east of the Appalachian Mountains. In Canada it is found only in southwestern Québec and southeastern Ontario from Lac St. Pierre to eastern Lake Ontario.

Characters: This minnow is uniquely characterised by the lower jaw having 3 lobes, the central lobe being bony and the lateral lobes fleshy. The premaxillaries are not protractile. Dorsal fin branched rays 7, anal branched rays 6, pectoral rays 13–16 and pelvic rays 8–9. Lateral line scales 48–57. Pharyngeal teeth 1,4–4,1. The back is olive-green to blackish, the flanks silvery with an olive or lavender sheen, and the belly whitish. The eye is golden. Only fin rays are pigmented although dorsal, anal and caudal fins may be tinged red. Young fish have a spot at the base of the caudal fin and a stripe along the midflank. The peritoneum is silvery. Reaches 16.0 cm.

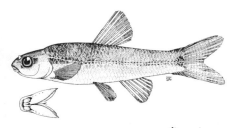

cutlips minnow

Biology: Cutlips prefer warm, clear, gravel streams where they are found under stones or among vegetation in quiet stretches. Food is principally insect larvae, with some molluscs and worms. Crayfish, fish eggs and lamprey larvae may also be taken. Food is scraped from the bottom or poked out of crannies using the shovel-like lower jaw. Sand is sucked in and spat out, presumably retaining the food content. Food drifting in midwater is also eaten.

Males grow larger than females and life span is over 5 years. Spawning takes place from May to July at temperatures over 16°C. A male builds a circular flat-topped nest almost half a metre in diameter and over 15 cm deep by carrying and piling up stones using his mouth. Males may steal stones from other nests if the supply runs short. A female is only allowed to approach a completed nest, the pair lie side by side, curve their bodies and release eggs and sperm. A male may repeat spawning with the same or different females in a 3–6 day spawning period. Eggs are 2 to 4 mm in diameter, and yellow, when they fall into the gravel of the nest. A female may have up to 1177 eggs. Males continue to clean the nest of silt after spawning and to guard the nest where the hatched young remain for about 6 days.

This species is sensitive to habitat changes which add silt or vegetation to the stream. **Common shiners** are known to harass spawning cutlips since **shiners** often spawn in other species nests. The harassment can lead to the cutlips abandoning their spawning.

Cutlips have been used as a bait fish but in the confined space of a bait pail they readily pick out the eyes of other fishes. They also do this in streams but success rate is much lower.

Cutthroat Eel Family

Scientific name: Synaphobranchidae
French name: anguilles égorgées

This family contains about 26 species in the depths of temperate and warmer oceans. Two are found on the Atlantic coast and 1 on the Atlantic and Arctic coasts of Canada. The family includes the mustard or arrowtooth eels and the snubnose parasitic eel.

All family members share a larva with telescopic eyes. Adults have gill openings on the throat region, giving the family its name. In some it is a single slit. Otherwise adults are quite variable. Scales and pectoral fins are present or absent. The snout is blunt or pointed. A lateral line is present but may be very short. The mouth may be large or small. Teeth may be needle-like, incisors or relatively elongate. The dorsal and anal fins are confluent with the caudal fin. Scales are often arranged in a basketwork pattern.

Branchiostegal rays 8–19. The rear nostril is close to the front of the eye. Overall colour is usually dark brown, grey or black.

This family is related to the **Snake Eel** and **Conger** families, among others, by having the frontal bones on top of the head fused. It is a member of the **Eel Order**.

Cutthroats are bottom-living eels found between 100 and 4800 m. Most are predators on fishes. Cutthroat eels have no commercial importance.

See **brown cutthroat eel**
    slatjaw cutthroat eel
    snubnose eel

cutthroat trout

Cutthroat trout are divided into two subspecies in Canada, each with a separate account. There is an inland form known as the **west-slope cutthroat trout** and one on the coast of British Columbia, known as the **coastal cutthroat trout**.

D

dabs

Canada has only a single species of dab, the **longhead dab,** found on the Arctic coast. The **Canadian plaice** and other **flatfishes** are sometimes called dabs. The origin of the word is unknown.

daces

Dace are members of the freshwater **Carp Family**. There are 9 species and 1 subspecies in Canadian fresh waters, not all of them closely related. The name is derived from the Middle English and Old French and refers to the darting motion of these small fishes.

See **Banff longnose dace
blacknose dace
finescale dace
leopard dace
longnose dace
northern redbelly dace
pearl dace
redside dace
speckled dace
Umatilla dace**

daggertooth

Scientific name: *Anotopterus pharao*
    Zugmayer, 1911
Family: **Daggertooth**
Other common names: javelinfish
French name: pharaon

Distribution: World-wide in cooler water outside the tropics, an anti-tropical distribution. On both coasts of Canada and into Arctic waters.

Characters: The large jaws with about 11 strong blade-like teeth give this fish its English name. The French name alludes to the chin projection which is reminiscent of the false beard of Egyptian Pharaohs. The absence of scales and a dorsal fin and the presence of a large adipose fin are characteristic. The anal fin has 13–17 rays, the pectoral fin 12–16 and the pelvic fin 9–11. The bone skeleton of this fish is fragile despite its ferocious appearance and the skin is easily ripped.

Colour is dark-grey to brownish-yellow on the back to yellowish-white or silvery on the belly with silvery sides, and tips of the jaws, branchiostegal membranes, tail fin and tips of pectoral fins black. The jaw, and gill and peritoneal cavities are black. Young are transparent. Attains 146 cm and 1.65 kg.

daggertooth

Biology: The daggertooth can be found at the surface or at great depths. Younger fish are found in temperate waters such as the California coast but the largest specimens come from cold waters in the Antarctic and the northern Atlantic and Pacific oceans. Many specimens have been recovered from the stomachs of other fishes such as **Greenland halibut, Atlantic cod, blue shark, albacore** and even whales. Some have been caught by fishermen trolling for salmon. They are found at 500–2250 m and are bathypelagic. Daggertooths eat fishes, including each other, and the stomach is expandable to allow large prey to be ingested. Pacific **salmons** have been caught for many years with a peculiar, single slash mark, usually attributed to the **salmon shark**. A jaw fragment retrieved from a **sockeye salmon** proved to be from a daggertooth. Daggertooths are therefore a significant predator of salmon, perhaps slicing through the body muscles to disable this prey before feeding. Daggertooths live at least 6 years. They are hermaphrodites.

Daggertooth Family

Scientific name: Anotopteridae
French name: pharaons

The family contains a single bathypelagic species, the **daggertooth,** found in the cooler waters of the Arctic, Antarctic, Atlantic and Pacific oceans including the Canadian east and west coasts. It may reach depths below 2000 m.

The **daggertooth** has no dorsal fin, no scales except some on the lateral line and no light organs. There is a well-developed adipose fin and the pelvic fins are minute. The tip of the lower jaw has a projection. It is a relative of the **Lancetfish** and **Barracudina** families and is a member of the **Flagfin Order**.

See **daggertooth**

dainty mora

Scientific name: *Halargyreus johnsonii*
Günther, 1862
Family: **Mora**
Other common names: slender codling
French name: more délicat

Distribution: Found from sub-arctic waters in the Pacific and Atlantic oceans to sub-antarctic waters. Found off all 3 Canadian coasts.

Characters: This species is distinguished from its Pacific coast relative, the **Pacific flatnose**, by having a rounded snout and by lacking a chin barbel. It is separated from Canadian Arctic-Atlantic species by its lack of a small, dark scaleless area on the belly in front of the anus covering a light organ, and

dainty mora

by its lack of teeth on the vomer bone in the roof of the mouth. The lower jaw projects and has a bony knob at the tip. There are 6–9 first dorsal fin rays and 47–59 second dorsal fin rays. Anal fin rays 41–52 in a deeply-notched fin. Overall colour is a pale bluish- or reddish-brown, darker around the eyes, lips and gill openings. Mouth, gill cavity and peritoneum are black. Reaches 44 cm standard length.

Biology: Canadian specimens have been caught at 585–785 m near the Grand Bank, and elsewhere the species is reported down to at least 1400 m. It is relatively rare in the western North Atlantic with only 3 Canadian specimens reported. The Pacific coast record is of a single fish at Ocean Station Papa (50°N, 145°W), and the Arctic record is of 4 fish taken at 700–720 m in the Davis Strait.

This species swims over the bottom on the continental slope. Food is pelagic crustaceans such as shrimps. Life span may be at least 7 years.

Damselfish Family

Scientific name: Pomacentridae
French name: demoiselles

Damselfishes are found world-wide mainly in shallow, tropical seas. There are about 315 species with only 1 reported from Atlantic Canada.

Damselfishes are almost unique among **bony fishes** in usually having 1 nostril on each side. Only the freshwater **cichlids** and the very distinctive **cutlassfishes** have this character in Canada. The lateral line is incomplete or interrupted and in 2 parts. The mouth is small and its roof lacks teeth. The dorsal fin usually has 8–17 spines and 11–18 soft rays. The anal fin has 2, or rarely 3, spines. The pelvic fin has 1 spine and 5 soft rays. A shelf under the eye is present. Scales are ctenoid and usually extend onto the soft dorsal and anal fins. Branchiostegal rays 5–6.

Damselfishes are **Perch Order** members related to the **Surfperch** and **Cichlid** families. They are difficult to identify and classify partly because colour patterns vary between localities and within a species.

These fishes exhibit a variety of lifestyles, often around coral reefs but also in floating seaweed. One of the familiar ones is shown by the anemonefishes which associate with sea anemones. This relationship is called commensalism, the fish receives protection from predators among the stinging arms of the sea anemone. The anemonefish's skin probably secretes a chemical which inhibits the stinging cells from discharging. Other damselfishes are "cleaners", picking parasites off other fishes. Eggs are usually laid in clumps attached to a hard surface, cleaned and guarded by the male. They produce sounds, likened to chirps, which are used during courtship, in fights, defending territory and as a species recognition. Damselfish have only a local importance as food but are used extensively in the aquarium trade and often in behavioral research.

See **sergeant major**

Dana viperfish

Scientific name: *Chauliodus danae*
    Regan and Trewavas, 1929
Family: **Barbeled Dragonfish**
Other common names: none
French name: chauliode de Dana

Distribution: Found on both sides of the North Atlantic Ocean including off Atlantic Canada and in the South Atlantic.

Characters: This viperfish is distinguished from its Pacific coast relative by the postorbital photophore (light organ behind

Dana viperfish

the eye) being rounded posteriorly. It is separated from its Atlantic coast relative, the **manylight viperfish**, by size and the dorsal fin origin being over the ninth to eleventh photophores in the lateral series. There are 5–6 dorsal fin rays, 10–12 anal rays, 12–14 pectoral rays and 6–7 pelvic rays. A short, stiff chin barbel is present only in very young fish. Colour is an iridescent silver-grey. Reaches about 15 cm standard length.

Biology: A single specimen has been caught in 1979 off the Scotian Shelf at 500 m. Elsewhere it is common and has been caught below 3500 m and can migrate to surface waters at night. Young fish come nearer the surface than adults. Food is fishes and crustaceans, principally the latter. Spawning occurs year round with a peak in spring.

darkbelly skate

Scientific name: *Raja hyperborea*
    Collett, 1879
Family: **Skate**
Other common names: Arctic skate, blackbelly skate, raie arctique
French name: raie boréale

Distribution: Found at Baffin Island in the Canadian Arctic, around Greenland and east to the Barents Sea.

Characters: This species resembles the **thorny skate** which is also found in Arctic waters but has 22–32 thorns in the midline of the disc and tail compared to 12–19 for the **thorny skate**. Colouration also differs with this species having a predominantly dark underside. There are 0–2 thorns between the dorsal fins. The shoulder has 2–4 large thorns. The back is covered with prickles and thornlets but adults have bare areas at the centre of the pectoral fins and along each side of the midline. The lower surface of the disc is smooth. Tooth rows 33–48. Egg cases are 8.1–12.5 cm by 5.4–7.7 cm excluding the horns. They are blackish-brown to golden yellow. There is a lateral flange and the case is covered with silk-like hairs when newly laid. Adult upper surface dark grey to brown, sometimes with light or dark spots. Adults have a dark lower surface which develops gradually with age from a juvenile white. Attains 87 cm.

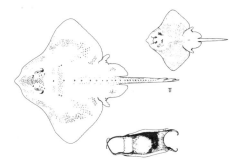

darkbelly skate

Biology: Depth range is about 300–2500 m in cold northern waters at about 0°C. Reputed to be moderately common. Food includes crustaceans, fishes and cephalopods.

darkblotched rockfish

Scientific name: *Sebastes crameri*
    (Jordan, 1897)
Family: **Scorpionfish**
Other common names: blackblotched rockfish, blackmouth rockfish
French name: sébaste tacheté

Distribution: Found from the Bering Sea to southern California including British Columbia.

Characters: The colour pattern and a deep body distinguish this species. There is a moderate knob at the tip of the lower jaw

darkblotched rockfish

directed downwards. Dorsal fin spines 12–14, usually 13, soft rays 12–15, usually 15. Anal fin soft rays 5–7, usually 7, second anal spine twice as thick as third but shorter. Pectoral fin rays 18–20, usually 19. Gill rakers 29–34. Vertebrae 26. Lateral line pores 40–51, scale rows below lateral line 48–62. The coronal spine is absent and the nuchal and parietal spines may coalesce. The overall colour is pinkish with 3–5 dark saddles on the back and dorsal fins (usually 3 below the spiny dorsal fin, 1 below the soft dorsal fin, and 1 on the caudal peduncle). Saddles may fade in large fish. Fins are red to orange. Peritoneum brown with black dots, to black. Young fish have yellow-green tinges on the body. Reaches 58 cm.

Biology: Found on soft bottoms between 29 and 549 m, usually deeper than 76 m. Food is krill, salps and octopi. Rarely **anchovies** are eaten. Half the population is mature at 34 cm for males and 37 cm for females in Canadian waters. Maximum age is estimated to approach 50 years. Young are born in February off British Columbia. Females may have up to about 600,000 eggs in their ovaries.

darter sculpin

Scientific name: *Radulinus boleoides*
Gilbert in Jordan and Evermann, 1898
Family: **Sculpin**
Other common names: none
French name: chabot-dart

Distribution: Found from near Langara Island in the Queen Charlotte Islands to California.

Characters: This species and its relative, the **slim sculpin**, are characterised by the dorsal body profile being straight, no scales below the lateral line on the midflank, the largest of 4 preopercular spines is simple, there is a fold of the branchiostegal membranes over the isthmus, and there are 3 soft pelvic fin rays. This species is distinguished from its relative by the snout length being greater than the eye diameter and nasal spines being long and needle-like. The anal papilla is large and cone-like. First dorsal fin spines 8–11 (long and finger-like in males), second dorsal soft rays 20–22. Anal rays 21–23, pectoral rays 18–20. Lateral line pores 39–40. A row of scales runs above the lateral line from the eyes to under the soft dorsal fin. There are also scales under the pectoral fin, between and behind the eyes, and on the operculum and occiput. There is a small cirrus above each eye posteriorly and sometimes a small cirrus on the occiput. Overall colour is olive-grey to grey with 3–4 brown saddles over the

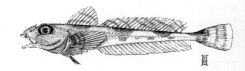

darter sculpin

back. The flank has small, dark blotches. The underside is silvery to white. The dorsal, caudal and upper pectoral fins are barred with brown. Reaches 14 cm.

Biology: Depth range is 15–146 m. This is a rare species with few specimens found in museums. A darter sculpin was seen and caught by scuba divers in Howe Sound at about 21 m, the fifth specimen for British Columbia. Darter sculpins spawn on top of the egg masses of buffalo sculpins, a case of nesting parasitism since the buffalo sculpin eggs are partially smothered. Pigeon guillemots have been recorded as catching this species in California.

darters

Darters are members of the northern hemisphere **Perch Family** which includes those large, familiar sport fishes, the **walleye**, **sauger**, and **yellow perch**. Darters are found only in North America where there are around 148 species, about 20 of which remain to be described scientifically. There are 12 species in Canada.

See **blackside darter**
 channel darter
 eastern sand darter
 fantail darter
 greenside darter
 Iowa darter
 johnny darter
 least darter
 logperch
 rainbow darter
 river darter
 tesselated darter

Darwin's slimehead

Scientific name: *Gephyroberyx darwini* (Johnson, 1866)
Family: **Slimehead**
Other common names: none
French name: hoplite de Darwin

Distribution: Found world-wide in warmer waters including the North Atlantic Ocean and off Nova Scotia.

Characters: This slimehead is distinguished from the only other Canadian member of the family, the **rosy soldierfish**, by having more dorsal fin spines (8, rarely 7, as opposed to 4–7). Dorsal fin soft rays 13–14. Anal fin with 3 spines and 11–12 soft rays. Body scales are small and irregular with lat-

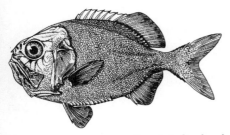

Darwin's slimehead

eral line scales only slightly enlarged and bearing a median spine. Teeth are present on the vomer and palatine bones in the roof of

the mouth (absent in adult **rosy soldierfish**). There is a single row of enlarged teeth posteriorly in the lower jaw. There are 11–13 abdominal scutes in the western Atlantic population. Overall colour can be an intense red, or rosy on the back and sides with silvery overtones on the latter, and fins red. The tongue and gill cavities are black, while the palate is white to red. Reaches 60 cm.

Biology: This species was first reported from Canada in 1993 from southeastern Browns Bank, the northern range limit, at a depth of 110 m. Depth range is 60–1000 m. It seems to prefer hard bottoms with rocks and crevices. Food includes crustaceans such as mysids and **bristlemouths**.

daubed shanny

Scientific name: *Leptoclinus maculatus* (Fries, 1837)
Family: **Shanny**
Other common names: none
French name: lompénie tachetée

Distribution: Found in the North Pacific, Arctic and North Atlantic oceans including all the Canadian coasts.

Characters: This species is 1 of 8 related Canadian shannies which have very elongate bodies, large pectoral fins and pelvic fins

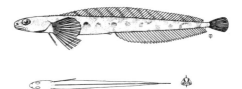

daubed shanny

with 1 spine and 2–4 soft rays. It is distinguished by distribution, 1–2 anal fin spines and 34–38 soft rays, 57–61 dorsal fin spines and the lower 5 rays of the pectoral fin extended and finger-like. Pectoral rays are 14–16. Scales cover the body and sides of the head except the cheeks but the lateral line although complete is not evident. The snout protrudes over the mouth. Overall colour is grey-green to yellowish or reddish-brown, with irregular and rounded darker blotches on the lower flanks and back, about 4–5 bars on the caudal fin, about 10 oblique bars on the dorsal fin, and about 5 bars on the pectoral fins. Reaches 17.8 cm.

Biology: Found on hard, sandy bottoms usually, and on mud or rock down to 240 m but as shallow as 2 m in the subtidal zone. The free lower rays of the pectoral fins are used to support the body on the sea bed and perhaps are used in movement. Food is worms and crustaceans. Spawning is believed to occur in winter with up to 970 eggs being produced.

daubed tonguefish

Scientific name: *Symphurus pterospilotus* Ginsburg, 1951
Family: **Tonguefish**
Other common names: none
French name: sole tachetée

Distribution: Known from Nova Scotia south to Uruguay.

Characters: This **flatfish** is distinguished from its relative, the **largescale tonguefish**, by fin ray and scale counts. Dorsal fin rays

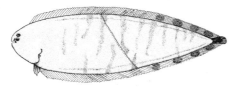

daubed tonguefish

about 93, anal fin rays about 75. Caudal fin rays 11. Scales in lateral series about 88. The overall colour is dusky with faint, incomplete cross bands. The posterior parts of the dorsal and anal fins are dark with 4 black spots. There is an elongate black spot on the caudal fin. Scales are outlined by pigment. Reaches 12.7 cm standard length.

Biology: Known from 3 specimens caught in 1978 and 1982 in 172–263 m near the Scotian Shelf. A poorly known species.

decorated warbonnet

Scientific name: *Chirolophis decoratus* (Jordan and Snyder, 1902)
Family: **Shanny**
Other common names: decorated blenny, decorated prickleback

French name: toupet décoré

Distribution: Found from Washington to the Bering Sea including the coast of British Columbia.

Characters: This species is 1 of 5 related Canadian shannies which have cirri and pelvic fins. It is distinguished from other

decorated warbonnet

warbonnets and the **pearly prickleback** by having 61–63 dorsal fin spines and 44–51 anal fin rays. The lateral line is short, ending about midway along the pectoral fin.

Large cirri are fused on the head just in front of the eyes. There are also 2 large cirri just behind the eye. There is a single cirrus on the middle of the snout. There are many cirri in dense masses between the eyes and dorsal fin and on the upper sides of the head. The first 4 or more dorsal fin spines have prominent cirri. Cirri are also found on the side of the head and under the lower jaw.

Overall colour is pale brown with lighter blotching. Dark bars radiate from the eye, and the dorsal, caudal, anal and pectoral fins are broadly barred. Reaches 42 cm.

Biology: Found at 18–91 m inshore among seaweed. It may hide in rock crevices or sponges, looking out from the opening and often photographed in this "frame." Crustaceans are a major food item.

Deepherring Family

Scientific name: Bathyclupeidae
French name: harengs de profondeur

Deepherrings are found in oceanic waters of the Atlantic, Indian and west Pacific Oceans. There are only about 4 species with 1 reported from Atlantic Canada.

These fishes resemble **herrings** in appearance but are not related. The body is fragile. The lower jaw projects in an oblique mouth. Premaxillae and maxillae bones border the mouth. The body has cycloid, easily detached scales which extend onto the dorsal and anal fins. The dorsal fin is on the rear half of the body and is spineless. The anal fin is much longer than the dorsal fin and has 1 spine. Teeth are in narrow bands on the jaws and roof of the mouth. There are 7 branchiostegal rays and the membranes are separated and free from the isthmus. There is a connection between the swimbladder and the intestine.

Despite their name, deepherrings belong to the **Perch Order** as evidenced by the minute pelvic fins being in advance of the pectorals and having 1 spine and 5 soft rays, the anal fin spine, protrusible jaws, shape and number of branchiostegal rays, and low number of branched caudal fin rays (15). However other characters (cycloid scales, swimbladder-intestine duct, spineless dorsal fin) resemble less advanced fishes and have made this family difficult to classify. Cycloid scales may have lost ctenii secondarily, but the swimbladder-gut duct is a puzzle. They are classified close to the **Goatfish** and **Sea Chub** families.

Deepherrings are rare, deepsea fishes found between 261 and 3000 m.

See **silver deepherring**

deepsea cat shark

Scientific name: *Apristurus profundorum* (Goode and Bean, 1896)
Family: **Cat Shark**
Other common names: deepwater catshark, holbiche papoila
French name: roussette de profundeur

Distribution: Found on the Scotian Shelf and possibly the southern Grand Bank, and off Delaware Bay. Also possibly from Mauritania.

Characters: This cat shark is recognised among its Atlantic relatives by lacking crests over the eyes, dorsal fins are about equal in size, the space between the dorsal fins is longer than the length of the first dorsal fin base, the distance between the pectoral and pelvic fin bases is less than the snout tip to spiracle distance, the inner pectoral margin is equal to about half the pectoral fin base, the caudal fin has a crest of enlarged denticles, dorsal fin tips are not whitish, and flank denticles are nearly overlapping. The body is slender, not tapering strongly to the head.

The snout is longer than the mouth width and labial furrows are very long. The skin has a fuzzy texture. Teeth are tricuspid with

deepsea cat shark

smooth edges. Nostril openings are elongate ovals. Overall colour is grey-brown to dark brown or black.

It is possible that Canadian records are wholly or partly composed of two other deepwater sharks, the **ghost catshark** and the **Iceland cat shark**. However this latter species may be a synonym of the deepsea cat shark. Reaches 62.5 cm but possibly larger.

Biology: This species is poorly known. The deepsea cat shark is found at depths in excess of 256 m down to at least 1600 m. Egg cases, which may have been from this species, have been collected from the Grand Bank. They had curved tendrils arising from bases very close together at one end of the case only. This species is only caught in deep exploratory trawls.

Deepsea Smelt Family

Scientific name: Bathylagidae
French name: garcettes

This family is found in all oceans from the Arctic to Antarctica. There are about 15 species and 9 are found in Canada, 5 off the Pacific coast, 3 off the Atlantic coast and 1 off the Atlantic and Arctic coasts.

Members of this family are also called blacksmelts and smoothtongues. The French name alludes to the body shape which supposedly resembles a blackjack. They are relatives of the **Argentine** and **Pencilsmelt** families in the **Smelt Order**, but are distinguished by having only 2 branchiostegal rays on each side and the small mouth has compressed teeth in single rows, absent from the upper jaw bones (maxilla and premaxilla). The postcleithra and mesocoracoid are absent. The parietal bones do not meet in the midline. Pectoral fins are low down on the side of the body. There is no swimbladder and no light organs. The adipose fin may be present or absent. Eyes are large. Scales are easily lost. The **Pencilsmelts** are sometimes placed in this family. Deepsea smelts were placed in the **Salmon Order**.

Deepsea smelts are oceanic, found in midwater and near the bottom. They can be quite abundant. Some species migrate vertically. Eggs and larvae are pelagic and the larvae can be distinctive with eyes on stalks in some species.

See **goitre blacksmelt**
      Grey's smoothtongue
      northern smoothtongue
      popeye blacksmelt
      slender blacksmelt
      smalleye blacksmelt
      southern smoothtongue
      starry blacksmelt
      stout blacksmelt

deepsea sole

Scientific name: *Embassichthys bathybius*
    (Gilbert, 1890)
Family: **Righteye Flounder**
Other common names: none
French name: plie de profondeur

Distribution: Found from Japan to California including British Columbia.

Characters: This species is characterised among Canadian Pacific **flatfishes** by the upper and lower thirds of the body being greatly compressed compared to the middle third. The body is flabby and slimy. There is a high ridge between the eyes. Pectoral fins

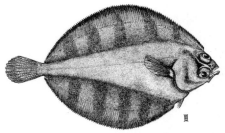

deepsea sole

are shorter than the head. The mouth is small and almost symmetrical. Dorsal fin rays 108–120, anal rays 93–102. The caudal fin is

small and rounded. Lateral line scales in the range 210–250 but the original specimens were described with about 165 scales. Scales are cycloid. The eyed side is brown becoming black towards the dorsal and anal fin tips. The upper and lower thirds have 5 broad bands formed of light bluish spots. Jaw tips, gill rakers and branchiostegal membrane tips are black. Blind side a dusky brown with fins black. Reaches 47 cm.

Biology: Generally found at 320–1433 m and usually deeper than 730 m.

deepwater chimaera

Scientific name: *Hydrolagus affinis*
    (Capello, 1857)
Family: **Chimaera**
Other common names: rabbitfish, ratfish,
    smalleyed rabbitfish, chimère à petits yeux
French name: chimère de profondeurs

Distribution: Found in the North Atlantic Ocean including the southeastern Grand Bank, off the Nova Scotian banks and south to Cape Cod.

Characters: This is the only Canadian Atlantic coast chimaera with a short, rounded snout and with claspers in males bifid (forked)

deepwater chimaera

or trifid (in three parts). The dorsal fin spine is venomous. The eyes are large. The caudal filament is short. The second dorsal fin is continuous without a deep notch. The anal fin is continuous with the caudal fin. The back and upper flanks are dark brown to violet or lead grey with white spots. The lower flanks and belly are white. Fins are paler with dark edges. The snout is greyish. Eyes reflect a shiny blue. The tongue is purple. Attains about 130 cm.

Biology: This bottom living chimaera is found from coastal waters to the continental slope and depths below 2400 m. Deepwater chimaeras have been observed from submersibles and swim mostly with their pectoral fins but also undulate the body. They may be nocturnal judging from the large eyes. Food is invertebrates and fish. Fertilisation is internal. Eggs are laid in a brown, horny capsule. This chimaera is not commercially important in Canada but elsewhere the liver oil has been used in high grade machinery.

deepwater cisco

Scientific name: *Coregonus johannae*
  (Wagner, 1910)
Family: **Salmon**
Other common names: deepwater chub
French name: cisco de profondeur

Distribution: Found in lakes Huron and Michigan.

Characters: This member of the **Salmon Family** was distinguished from its relatives by having large scales (110 or less), no parr marks, teeth absent from the jaws and roof of

deepwater cisco

the mouth, forked tail fin, 2 flaps of skin between the nostrils, the upper and lower jaws were about equal, giving the front of the head a pointed appearance, the premaxilla bone of the upper jaw curved backwards, gill rakers 25–36, usually less than 33, and lateral line scales 74–95. Characters among ciscoes (q.v.) overlap and so the species cannot be easily separated. The lower jaw was equal to the upper jaw and the rear end of the upper jaw usually reached the anterior pupil edge. Dorsal fin rays 9–11, anal rays 10–16, pectoral rays 14–20 and pelvic rays 11–12. Males had 1 nuptial tubercle per flank scale and 1 tubercle on each side of the lateral line pore. Small tubercles were present on the head and pelvic fin rays.

Overall colour was silvery with pink to purple iridescences on the flanks. The back was blue-green and the belly silvery-white. Fins were usually clear or only lightly pig-

mented. Reached 30.0 cm average size. This may have been the same species as the **shortjaw cisco**.

Biology: Deepwater ciscoes were found at 11–183 m, usually below 64 m and perhaps deeper than 200 m. Food was mostly opossum shrimps, with some amphipods, fingernail clams, aquatic insects and fish scales. Maturity was attained between 16.5 and 19.5 cm. Spawning in Lake Huron took place between mid-August and the end of September. Some females spawned perhaps every second year. This was an important component of the Great Lakes "chub" fishery but is now extinct (see **ciscoes**). It was probably swamped genetically as the few remaining deepwater ciscoes hybridised with numerous spawning **bloaters**. Deepwater cisco numbers declined from overfishing and depredations of **sea lampreys** after **lake trout** populations were depleted. The last deepwater cisco from Lake Huron was caught in 1952. The Committee on the Status of Endangered Wildlife in Canada gave this species the status of "extinct" in 1988.

deepwater flounder

Scientific name: *Monolene sessilicauda*
  Goode, 1880
Family: **Lefteye Flounder**
Other common names: none
French name: cardeau de profondeurs

Distibution: Found from Nova Scotia to the Gulf of Mexico.

Characters: This species is distinguished from other Canadian Atlantic adult **lefteye flounders** by having both pelvic fin bases

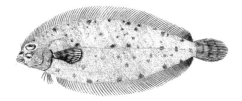

deepwater flounder

short and the eyed side base on the belly midline, lateral line strongly arched over the eyed side pectoral fin, and no blind side pectoral fin. Dorsal fin rays 92–107, anal rays 76–84, eyed side pectoral rays 11–14, and lateral line scales 88–94. Lower arm gill rakers 8–10. Larvae have an elongate dorsal fin ray known as a tentacle. Eyed side brown with blotches arranged as 4 bands across the body. There may be scattered, small blotches over the whole eyed side. There is a large, central blotch on the caudal fin which may be broken into 2 bands. The dorsal and anal fin bases have several large blotches. The lower half of the pectoral fin is barred. Reaches 18 cm.

Biology: Known only from a stray larva caught in 1979 off the Scotian Shelf. Adults are found as far north as New England at 110–457.

deepwater redfish

Scientific name: *Sebastes mentella*
Travin, 1951
Family: **Scorpionfish**
Other common names: ocean perch, redfish, rosefish, beaked redfish, sharp-beaked redfish
French name: sébaste atlantique

Distribution: North Atlantic Ocean including from off Baffin Island south to Nova Scotia. Also in the eastern Atlantic Ocean.

Characters: This species is distinguished from other Atlantic coast scorpionfishes by having 14 or 15 dorsal fin spines and from its

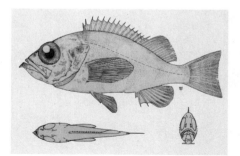

deepwater redfish

closest relatives, the **Acadian** and **golden redfishes**, by a combination of overlapping characters, some of which are internal and require dissection to see. Easily misidentified. This is a less robust redfish with a larger eye than the

golden redfish. Anal fin soft rays 8–10. The lower unbranched pectoral fin rays are usually 8 or less (rarely 9). Total vertebrae 30–32, usually 31. The knob at the tip of the chin is long and sharp. A key internal character is the muscles attaching to the gas bladder. In this species there are 1 or 2 muscle heads with tendons passing between ribs 2 and 3, the muscle is narrow and the posterior tendon is not branched and is attached to the seventh vertebra. Larvae have 5–10 ventral row melanophores. Overall colour is bright red. The region between the pectoral base and the operculum, the cheeks and the pelvic region are silvery. Reaches 55 cm but usually to 40 cm.

Biology: This redfish is found further north, further offshore and in deeper water than related species. It is found over rock or clay and silt bottoms from 200–1100 m. The biology of redfishes has not yet been fully worked out because of the difficulties in separating the species. It rises higher in the water column at night to feed than the other two redfish species. Food is crustaceans and, when larger, fishes. This is a slow-growing and long-lived species which may attain 48 years. Half the population is mature at 18.5 cm for males and 29.5 cm for females. Spawning occurs in March-July and this species is the first of the redfishes to do so in the deeper water it inhabits. An important commercial species making up the bulk of the catch in Newfoundland-Labrador waters. The commercial fishery is a recent development with a maximum catch of 389,000 tonnes in 1959. Catches since then have been less as quotas were imposed to prevent overfishing. In 1979 the catch was worth 15.5 million dollars and weighed 81,587 tonnes. All three redfish species are managed as a single unit and often appear on the market, fresh or frozen, as "ocean perch."

deepwater sculpin

Scientific name: *Myoxocephalus thompsoni*
(Girard, 1851)
Family: **Sculpin**
Other common names: lake sculpin, deepwater blob, Great Lakes fourhorn sculpin, scorpionfish
French name: chabot de profondeur

Distribution: The Canadian populations are in lakes of southwestern Québec, southeastern and northwestern Ontario, the Great Lakes and northward in an arc through Manitoba, Saskatchewan, southern Alberta, Great Bear and Great Slave lakes and on Victoria Island in the Arctic. Also in Lake Michigan.

Characters: This sculpin is distinguished from its freshwater relatives by the separated dorsal fins, gill membranes free of the isth-

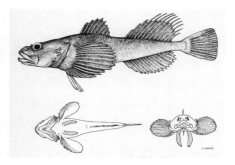

deepwater sculpin

mus and a strong, second preopercular spine pointing backwards. Large head spines absent but if present they are not club-shaped as in the related **fourhorn sculpin**. First dorsal fin spines 7–10, second dorsal rays 11–16, anal rays 11–16 and pectoral rays 15–28. Some prickles are present above the lateral line but scales are absent. Lateral line complete or incomplete but often extends past the end of the second dorsal fin. The back and upper flank are grey-brown and the belly is whitish. There are 4–7 saddles over the back and the back and flanks are spotted or mottled. Fins are thinly barred. Pelvic fins are white. The second dorsal fin is enlarged in adult males and, with the pectoral fin, bears small tubercles. In addition the pelvic fins and upper caudal rays of males are elongated. Reaches 23.5 cm.

Biology: This species is a relative of the **fourhorn sculpin** and was once considered to be the same species or a subspecies of it. The deepwater sculpin is regarded as a glacial relict, once found in marine or brackish Arctic waters and forced to retreat south as the ice sheets advanced. The sculpin was left behind as the ice retreated along with certain crus-

taceans (opossum shrimps and amphipods) which are its food supply. The saline lakes left behind gradually freshened by ice melt and river runoff. There may also be some active movement of marine fish into fresh water in Arctic regions: these would be best described as **fourhorn sculpins**. The deepwater sculpin is more distinct and much older. A 10,000 year old fossil deepwater sculpin had characters as distinct from **fourhorn sculpins** as modern ones. Depth range is 4–366 m and it can be quite common in cold, deep lakes.

Food includes relict crustaceans, copepods, chironomids and **whitefish** eggs. It is eaten by **lake trout** and **burbot** and is an important item in their diets.

Spawning may be year round in the Great Lakes but peaks in late August and early September. In Heney Lake, Québec spawning is thought to occur in June–July at 6–7.2°C. Females have up to 1187 orange eggs of 2.1 mm diameter. Life span is 7 years with females maturing at 3 years and males at 2 years.

It has been extirpated in Lake Ontario, and perhaps Lake Erie, because of pollution or perhaps competition combined with predation by **gaspereau** or **slimy sculpins**. The Committee on the Status of Endangered Wildlife in Canada gave Great Lakes populations of this species a status of "threatened" in 1987.

deepwater skate

Scientific name: *Bathyraja richardsoni*
 (Garrick, 1961)
Family: **Skate**
Other common names: Richardson's skate
French name: raie de profondeurs

Distribution: Found from off southern Labrador to off Georges Bank in Atlantic Canada. Also in the northeastern Atlantic Ocean and at New Zealand, possibly worldwide in deep waters.

Characters: This species is distinguished from its Canadian Atlantic relatives by having a soft and flabby snout with its cartilaginous support thin and flexible, cartilaginous supports of the pectoral fin reaching the snout tip, the upper disc surface lacks distinct spines except for a median row on the tail, and the lower disc surface is prickly and dark coloured. There is no thorn between the dorsal fins. There are 15–20 thorns on the tail midline. Upper teeth rows 21–32 and lower teeth 16–25 in males, and 24–40 and 18–32 respectively in females. Males have 25–31 transverse rows of alar spines with 5–9 spines in a row. Upper disc colour grey, brownish-grey or light brown with an occasional white or black spot. The clasper tips are white and there is some white in the pectoral fin axils and the posterior axils of the pelvic fins. The lower surface is similar to the upper but may be dark grey when the upper disc is light grey. White areas are found around the mouth, nostrils, cloaca, tail base and sometimes gill slits. Reaches 174 cm in length and 37.7 kg.

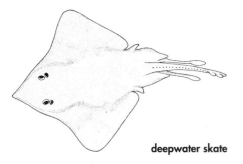

deepwater skate

Biology: Canadian specimens, 18 in number, were caught at 1370–2360 m and 2.8–3.9°C during the 1960s but none have been caught since. Only about 10 other specimens are known. Food is fishes, pelagic shrimps, whelks and alcyonarians.

deepwater slipskin

Scientific name: *Lycodapus endemoscotus*
    Peden and Anderson, 1978
Family: **Eelpout**
Other common names: none
French name: lycode abyssale

Distribution: Found from the Bering Sea to Peru including British Columbia.

Characters: This species is distinguished from its Pacific coast relatives by having the branchiostegal membranes free of the isthmus posteriorly, gill rakers blunt and stout touching the adjacent raker only when depressed, gill opening extending above the upper base of the pectoral fin, vertebrae 86–95, and teeth on the vomer bone of the roof of the mouth usually 16–21. Scales and

deepwater slipskin

pelvic fins are absent. The flesh is gelatinous. Dorsal fin rays 79–91, anal rays 70–81 and pectoral rays 6–9. Preserved specimens have translucent skin with the muscles underneath a light tan, sometimes lightly spotted. Mouth and gill cavities, jaws, peritoneum and stomach are black. Reaches 13.2 cm standard length.

Biology: Reported from British Columbia off northern Vancouver Island. Depth range 933–2225 m.

Diamond Dory Family

Scientific name: Grammicolepididae
French name: poissons-palissades

Diamond dories, or tinselfishes, are found in the Atlantic, Indian and Pacific oceans. There are only 4 species, and 2 are found on the Canadian Atlantic coast.

These fishes have vertically elongate, paper-like scales unlike closely related families. The body is deep and compressed. The mouth is very small and almost vertical. There is a row of bony knobs, each with a spine, along the dorsal and anal fin bases. The caudal fin has 13 branched rays while related families have 11.

Diamond dories are related to the **Boarfish**, **Dory**, **Eyefish** and **Oreo** families in the **Dory Order**.

These fishes are found in deep water from 300 m to over 900 m and are rarely caught.

See **thorny tinselfish**
    tinselfish

diamond stingray

Scientific name: *Dasyatis brevis*
    (Garman, 1880)
Family: **Stingray**
Other common names: none
French name: pastenague à deux queues

Distribution: Found along the Pacific coast of the Americas, from Peru north to California and possibly to British Columbia.

Characters: This species is distinguished from its Pacific coast relative, the **pelagic stingray**, by its diamond-shaped body with a pointed snout. The tail is long and whip-like with a long spine which lies nearer to the tail base than to the tail tip. The upper surface is brown or blackish and the lower surface white. Up to 183 cm long and 122 cm wide. Males are smaller than females.

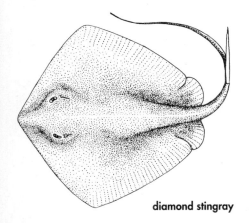

diamond stingray

Biology: Its presence in British Columbia has not been confirmed by specimens. Usually found in sandy areas, around rocks and in kelp beds down to 17 m. This species has been implicated in at least 1 death in the Gulf of California.

diamondcheek lanternfish

Scientific name: *Lampanyctus intricarius*
    Tåning, 1928
Family: **Lanternfish**
Other common names: none
French name: lanterne à joue pailletée

Distribution: Found in the Atlantic, Indian and Pacific oceans including off the Scotian Shelf in Atlantic Canada.

Characters: This species and 7 relatives in the genus *Lampanyctus* are separated from other Atlantic species by lacking photophores close to the dorsal body edge, the PLO photophore is well above the pectoral fin base level while the second PVO pho-

tophore is at or below the upper pectoral base level, there are 4 Prc, the first PO and two PVO photophores are not on a straight

diamondcheek lanternfish

line, both males and females have caudal luminous glands composed of overlapping, scale-like structures without a black pigment border, the fourth PO photophore is highly elevated, there are no luminous, scale-like structures on the belly between the pelvic fin bases or these bases and the anus, there are 4 VO photophores and the SAO series is strongly angled. This species is distinguished from its relatives by having 15–16 gill rakers, long pectoral fins extending beyond the anal fin origin, 1–2 (rarely 3) cheek photophores, luminous tissue at the adipose fin base, 8–9 AOa photophores and 39–40 lateral line organs. Dorsal fin rays 14–16, anal rays 17–20 and pectoral rays 13–15. AO photophores 16–18. The supracaudal luminous gland has 2–3 scale-like segments and the infracaudal 8–10. Reaches 20.0 cm.

Biology: This is a temperate or subpolar-temperate species in both hemispheres. First reported from Canada in 1988. Depth distribution by day is 550–750 m, and by night 40–550 m with a maximum abundance mostly of young at 75 m.

Dogfish Shark Family

Scientific name: Squalidae
French name: chiens de mer

The dogfish sharks have about 10 species found in most seas from inshore waters down to great depths. One species is found on the Atlantic, Arctic, and Pacific coasts.

Dogfish sharks are distinguished from other sharks by their cylindrical bodies, short noses, the absence of an anal fin, by 2, low dorsal fins which have an ungrooved spine at the front margin, small to moderately large denticles, and the first dorsal fin origin in front of the pelvic origins. Fish should be handled with care as the spines contain venom in the tissues of a posterior groove which can cause a painful wound. Teeth on the lower jaw are only slightly larger than those on the upper jaw. An upper precaudal pit is usually present.

Dogfish sharks are members of the **Dogfish Shark Order**.

Some members of this family are found in very large schools which lend themselves to fisheries exploitation. Others are solitary. They are ovoviviparous. Food is a wide variety of fishes, squids, crustaceans and other invertebrates.

See **spiny dogfish**

Dogfish Shark Order

Dogfishes, bramble sharks, sleeper sharks and rough sharks of the Order Squaliformes comprise 4 families with about 74 species found in all oceans. These are moderate to large-sized sharks found mainly on the sea floor from inshore to deep waters. In Canada there are 2 families with 8 species on the Atlantic and Pacific coasts, and entering Arctic waters

This order is characterised by having a cylindrical or compressed body, lacking an anal fin, a spine at the leading edge of the 2 dorsal fins present or absent, a small, ventral mouth with sharp teeth, a deep groove at the mouth corner, no nictitating lower eyelid, 5 gill slits, spiral intestinal valve and small to large spiracles.

These are ovoviviparous fishes. They include the unusual cookie-cutter shark (not in Canada) which chops segments out of larger fishes and whales, the commercially important dogfishes, and the large, somnolent sleeper sharks.

See **Dogfish Shark Family**
    Sleeper Shark Family

dogtooth lampfish

Scientific name: *Ceratoscopelus townsendi*
    (Eigenmann and Eigenmann, 1889)
Family: **Lanternfish**
Other common names: fangtooth lanternfish
French name: lampe à sourcils lumineux

Distribution: Found from Japan to California including British Columbia.

Characters: This lanternfish is distinguished from its Pacific coast relatives by having 4 Prc photophores, the first four PO photophores on the same level but the fifth is elevated, the infracaudal gland is long with

dogtooth lampfish

6–8 scales, and there is a Y-shaped series of luminous scales between the pelvic and anal fins. There is a large luminous organ over each eye but this is easily lost in captured specimens. Dorsal fin rays 13–15, anal rays 13–15, pectoral rays 13–14, and vertebrae 35–38. Total gill rakers 14–16 and AO photophores 10–13. Lateral line scales 36–39. Reaches 18.4 cm. If, as some researchers believe, this species includes populations recognised as the **southseas lampfish** it would then have a cosmopolitan distribution.

Biology: First reported off southern Vancouver Island in 1985 at 40–60 m based on fish caught in 1958. Depth range is from the surface down to 800 m. Food is crustaceans.

Dolly Varden

Scientific name: *Salvelinus malma*
    (Walbaum, 1792)
Family: **Salmon**
Other common names: Dolly Varden char, red-spotted Rocky Mountain trout, Pacific brook trout, bull char, western brook trout, sea-trout, salmon-trout
French name: Dolly Varden

Distribution: Found from Arctic Alaska south to Washington. In Canada in the upper Mackenzie River basin of British Columbia and the far western N.W.T., southwestern Yukon and northern coastal rivers and southwestern parts of British Columbia. Also introduced to Alberta west of Calgary. Probably more widespread but long confused with the **bull trout**. Also in eastern Asia south to Korea.

Characters: This species is characterised by having 105–142 lateral line scales, 9–12 major anal fin rays, pectoral, pelvic and anal fins with white leading edges, followed by a thin black and then a red line in contrast, teeth on the head not the shaft of the vomer bone on the roof of the mouth, caudal fin squarish, body spots small, numerous and cream, yellow, pink or red, gill rakers usually 3–10 on the upper and 8–14 on the lower limb (total 11–26), and pyloric caeca 13–47 in Canada. Dolly Varden are distinguished from **bull trout** by a series of characters described under that species. Major dorsal fin rays 10–12, pectoral rays 14–16 and pelvic rays 8–11.

Colour varies markedly with habitat. Freshwater fish are dark blue, olive-green to brown on the back paling to a white to dusky belly. The back may have some vermiculations ("worm track" markings) in fish from north Vancouver Island and the northern B.C. coast. Dorsal and tail fins are dusky to brown and may bear a few pale spots. Sea run fish are dark blue on the back, flanks are silvery and the belly silver to white. Spawning males are bright orange to red on the belly, lower flank, lower fins and snout, dark green or brown on the back and upper flank, black on the operculum and lower jaw, flank spots are a bright orange-red, and a kype or hooked lower jaw develops. Some populations have red lower sides year round. Young fish (and dwarfs) have 8–12 dark, parr marks, wider than the spaces between them. The lower flank has fine, dark speckles. Dorsal and adipose fins are dusky.

Dolly Varden

This species is named for a female Dickensian character in "Barnaby Rudge" who was colourfully dressed. A pink-spotted calico was called Dolly Varden during Charles Dickens' visit to North America and the **char** was likened to the material. Hybrids

with **brook trout** are reported in Alberta. Reaches about 128.0 cm and 18.3 kg. The world, all-tackle angling record from Mashutuk River, Alaska was caught in 1993 and weighed 8.41 kg.

Biology: This **char** is found in both salt and fresh water of Canada. Data on biology may be based in part on that of the related **bull trout**. The sea run fish stay close to river mouths. Annually, anadromous fish migrate to the sea in late May and early June, spending 2–5 months there. Sea run populations spend 3–4 years in fresh water (and 2–3 years in the sea) and inland populations spend from several months to 3–4 years in streams before going into a lake.

Food includes terrestrial and aquatic insects, snails, worms, crustaceans, leeches, and **salmon** eggs and young as well as other fishes both marine and fresh water, and frogs, moles, mice and small birds. It has long been considered a predator of other, more valuable **salmons** and **trouts** and was even the subject of a bounty in Alaska. However this is controversial and anthropomorphic since in a natural system the fish will be in ecological balance.

Life span is about 20 years but about half this is more common. Maturity is attained at 3–6 years, males often a year before females. Some anadromous populations are quite small and freshwater populations may be stunted.

Spawning occurs from September to November. Anadromous fish migrate into fresh water from May to December, usually July to September, and lake fish enter streams at the same time. Eggs are shed over gravel at water temperatures above about 8°C. The eggs are orange-red, up to 5.6 mm in diameter and can number 8845 per female. Numbers vary with locality and between sea run and freshwater populations. An isolated population in southern Alaska averaged 66 eggs per female while nearby anadromous fish averaged 1888. The female excavates a redd with the tail, either when lying on her side or in some purely freshwater populations when vertical by side-to-side sweeps. Males defend the redd by charges and nips against other males. The redd is up to 61 cm across and 30.5 cm deep. The fish usually pair off but a female may have up to 5 males around her. The eggs and sperm are shed when the female and male(s) are touching, backs are arched, mouths gaped and their bodies vibrating. After spawning the female covers the eggs by dislodging gravel upstream of the redd. Eggs hatch in spring (March to April) and young emerge from the gravel in April to May.

This is a sport fish caught on flies, baits and lures but is not as popular with anglers in Canada as other **Salmon Family** members. Its fighting qualities are less and it seldom leaps. The pink flesh is excellent eating.

- Most accessible May through September.
- The coastal rivers of British Columbia.
- Ultralight to light action spinning gear used with four- to six-pound line. Fly rods ranging from seven-and-a-half to eight-and-a-half feet, four- to seven-weight outfits loaded with weight-for-ward floating or sinking lines.
- A selection of 1/8- to 1/4-ounce spoons, spinners and an assortment of small hair jigs. The best flies are minnow-imitating streamers and salmon egg imitation flies.

Dolphin Family

Scientific name: Coryphaenidae
French name: coryphènes

Dolphins or dolphinfishes are found world-wide in warmer waters. There are only 2 species and both are recorded from Atlantic Canada.

Dolphin fishes resemble the familiar dolphin mammals in the rounded, steep and high forehead. Adult males develop a bony crest on the front of the head. The dorsal fin origin is on the head and it extends back nearly to the tail. The dorsal fin contains 46–67 rays. There are no spines in the dorsal and anal fins. The caudal fin is very deeply forked. The pelvic fin has 1 spine and 5 soft rays and can be folded back into a groove. Scales are minute and cycloid. The complete lateral line curves upward over the pectoral fin. Teeth in the mouth are small and comb-like.

Dolphins are classified close to such **Perch Order** fishes as the **Jack** and **Pomfret** families.

Adult dolphins are open ocean fishes, often encountered near drift lines or following ships. Young associate with floating debris and sargassum weed and may be found inshore. They are important food and game fishes, particularly the **common dolphin**. Anglers catch these fishes by trolling. Dolphins are efficient predators on other fishes and less frequently on squids and crustaceans. They can attain speeds of over 80 km/hour. They may hunt prey in pairs or small packs. Despite their size, life span is short at about 4 years and dolphins grow quickly. Eggs and larvae are pelagic.

See **common dolphin**
   pompano dolphin

doormat parkinglightfish

Scientific name: *Diaphus rafinesquii*
   (Cocco, 1838)
Family: **Lanternfish**
Other common names: none
French name: lampe-veilleuse paillasson

Distribution: Found in the North Atlantic Ocean and Gulf of Mexico including east of the Flemish Cap and off Nova Scotia.

Characters: This species and its relatives, the **bouncer**, **eventooth**, **flashlight**, **square**, **straightcheek**, and **Taaning's headlight-fishes** and the **slanteye parkinglightfish**, are separated from other Atlantic coast lantern-

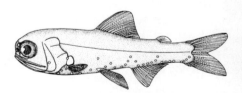

doormat parkinglightfish

fishes by not having photophores near the dorsal body edge, the PLO photophore is well above the upper pectoral fin base level while the second PVO photophore is at or below this level, there are 4 Prc photophores, the PO and two PVO photophores form a straight, ascending line as do the first 3 VO photophores, supracaudal luminous glands are absent, and there is more than 1 pair of luminous head organs. This species is separated from its relatives by having the So photophore present, inner series of teeth on rear part of premaxillary obviously recurved, vomer naked or with only a few, minute teeth, AOa 6 (rarely 5 or 7), first AOa elevated, and gill rakers 22–25. Dorsal fin rays 12–14, anal rays 13–15 and pectoral rays 9–11. AO photophores 9–11. Lateral line organs 35–36. Males have a larger Vn photophore than females. Reaches 9.0 cm.

Biology: This species is more temperate in its distribution than the **straightcheek headlightfish**. Depth distribution is 325–750 m by day with maximum abundance centring at 500 m, and 40–275 m (usually young) and 300–600 m (adults) with a maximum at 100 m. Large fish do not migrate. Maturity is attained at about 5.0–6.5 cm.

Dory Family

Scientific name: Zeidae
French name: zées

Dories are found in the Atlantic, Pacific and Indian oceans. There are 13 species of which 2 occur on the Atlantic coast of Canada.

These fishes have small spines or bucklers at the base of the dorsal and anal fin rays and 8–9 spiny plates along the abdomen. The body is deep and compressed. Some have a distinctive large, round black spot edged with a yellow ring in the middle of the flank. This is known as the mark of St. Peter, supposedly marking the thumb and forefinger of that saint when he took tribute money from its mouth. Its function is unknown. Adults develop very long filaments from the edges of the dorsal fin spine. The mouth is large and oblique with a very protrusible upper jaw. The eyes are large. The facial expression appears lugubrious or gloomy! Scales are small to absent, and not vertically elongate, unlike the **Diamond Dory Family**. There are no spines on the side of the head unlike many superficially similar fishes.

Dories are related to the **Boarfish**, **Diamond Dory**, **Eyefish** and **Oreo** families in the **Dory Order**. "Dory" is derived from the Latin for gilded.

They are found in midwater or on the bottom, from inshore to more than 600 m, often at depths shallower than related fami-

lies and so are more likely to be captured. They can be caught in schools or individually. Dories feed mainly on other fishes, but also take crustaceans. They have been reported to swim on their side as well as vertically. The larger species make good eating.

See **buckler dory**
    red dory

Dory Order

Dories and their relatives comprise the Order Zeiformes with about 39 species found world-wide in shallow to deep marine cold to tropical waters. There are 6 families of which 5 are represented in Canada. These are small fishes reaching a maximum length of about 1 m, generally of little economic importance.

The order is characterised by a compressed and deep body, jaws which can be greatly extended, a pelvic fin with or without a spine and 5–10 soft rays, a distinct, spiny anterior part to the anal fin with 0–4 spines, separate spiny (5–10 spines) and soft-rayed parts to the dorsal fin, soft rays of the dorsal, anal and pectoral fins not branched, caudal fin with 11 or 13 branched rays, a swimbladder, ctenoid or cycloid scales, 7–8 branchiostegal rays, no orbitosphenoid bone in the skull, and the posttemporal bone is fused to the skull. These characters place the Dory Order structurally between the **Alfonsino Order** and the **Perch Order**. Recent studies suggest that these fishes should be placed in the **Puffer Order**. Dories may be ancestral to the **Flatfish Order**. It has been suggested that the **Boarfish Family** be placed in the **Perch Order**. Fossils date to the early Tertiary.

See **Boarfish Family**
    Diamond Dory Family
    Dory Family
    Eyefish Family
    Oreo Family

Dover sole

Scientific name: *Microstomus pacificus* (Lockington, 1879)
Family: **Righteye Flounder**
Other common names: slime sole, slippery flounder, shortfinned sole, rubber sole, Chinese sole
French name: sole à petite bouche

Distribution: Found from the Bering Sea to Baja California including British Columbia.

Characters: This species is characterised by an almost straight lateral line and a short, but unconnected, accessory branch. The gill

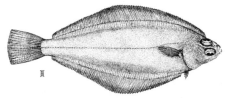

Dover sole

opening extends only a little above the pectoral fin. The body is slimy, slender and flaccid. Mouth small, asymmetrical with teeth on blind side. Dorsal fin rays 88–116, anal fin rays 75–96. Caudal fin rounded. Scales are cycloid and the skin is smooth. Lateral line scales 137–146. Eyed side brown, mottled, with yellow spots in some areas. Blind side light to dark grey with dull red blotches. Fins dusky to black. Reaches 76 cm and 4.7 kg.

Biology: This species is found from the surface down to 1189 m, usually on soft bottoms. There is a winter migration to deep water. Food is burrowing or surface-dwelling invertebrates such as clams, brittle stars, sea pens, worms and anemones. Males mature at 39 cm, females at 45 cm. Females grow faster than males. Maximum age is over 20 years. Each female can produce over 266,000 eggs up to 2.57 mm in diameter. April and May are peak hatching months. Young are pelagic for up to 2 years and reach as long as 10 cm before settling to the bottom. Metamorphosis is delayed to facilitate onshore transport during winter storms. This species was not accepted as a commercial item because of its flaccid, slimy body, but the flesh is excellent and freezes well. Up to about 1360 tonnes are now landed annually in Canada. It is also a good sport fish on light tackle but is not commonly caught.

Dragonet Family

Scientific name: Callionymidae
French name: dragonnets

Dragonets are found world-wide in warmer seas and there are about 130 species. Three

species have been reported from Atlantic Canada.

These fishes have highly protrusible jaws at the end of a depressed body, large upward-directed eyes, often bulging above the head, usually 2 dorsal fins, the first with 1–4 spines and a fleshy membrane connecting the innermost pelvic fin ray to the body in front of the pectoral fin. The preopercle usually has a spine with barbs but the subopercle and operculum are spineless. There are 2 postcleithra. The gill opening is unusual in that it is a small pore near the top of the head. There are no scales but a pored lateral line is present.

The relationships of this family are not fully worked out. Identification can be confused by differences in colour and anatomy between males and females. Atlantic coast dragonets can be distinguished by fin ray and preopercular barb counts. The family is a member of the **Perch Order**.

Most dragonets are found in the tropical Indo-West Pacific Ocean and many have brilliant colours when associated with coral reefs. They swim swiftly and smoothly, scooting over the sandy substrate in shallow waters. They may also be found under rocks or partially buried in sand or gravel. Males are territorial and aggressive, and there is a complex courtship display in the breeding season. The young are pelagic. They are not commercially important except for some use as fish meal.

See **lancer dragonet**
     spotfin dragonet
     spotted dragonet

dragonfishes

Dragonfishes are deepsea fishes of bizarre appearance belonging to the **Barbeled Dragonfish** family, with 30 species. A member of this family, the **large-eye snaggletooth**, is also known as the straightline dragonfish.

Dreamer Family

Scientific name: Oneirodidae
French name: rêveurs

Dreamers are found world-wide in the deeper parts of the oceans. There are about 60 species and 14 of these occur in Canadian waters, 10 off the Atlantic coast, 3 off the Pacific coast and 1 off both the Atlantic and Arctic coasts.

Dreamers are deepsea **anglerfishes** and have a stout body, ranging from oval to globular in shape. The first dorsal fin spine is modified into the fishing apparatus and is directed forwards, sometimes with a joint. The esca or bait at the tip of the illicium contains luminescent bacteria. The second dorsal spine is minute and covered by skin. Females have naked skin, sometimes containing short spines. Dorsal fin rays are 4–8 and anal fin rays 4–7. The jaws are of equal length.

Males are dwarfs less than 2.5 cm long but they probably do not attach permanently to females in most species. Females can reach 30 cm in length. Males lack jaw teeth but have denticles on the snout and lower jaw tips. The male olfactory organs are large to facilitate locating the female by smell. Larvae are found in surface waters but adults are meso- to bathypelagic, down to about 3000 m.

Dreamers are so-named because they are thought to resemble something out of a dream or nightmare. Many species are quite rare and known only from a few specimens. They are members of the **Anglerfish Order**.

Dreamers are related to the **Fanfin**, **Seadevil**, **Whipnose**, **Leftvent**, **Wolftrap**, **Footballfish** and **Werewolf** families which all lack pelvic fins, scales and a pseudobranch, have bones at the front of the head (frontals) which are not united, have the lower pharyngeal bones reduced and toothless, and have 8–9 caudal fin rays. They are identified in part by details of the esca, a structure which requires some expertise to understand and which may be missing or damaged. Males and juveniles are often unknown.

See **bulbous dreamer**
can-opener smoothdream
cosmopolitan dreamtail
dreamteeth
forefour dreamtail
nightmare dreamer
plainchin dreamarm
prickly dreamer
shorthorn dreamer
smooth dreamer
spiny dreamer
toothy dreamer
westnorat dreamtail
whalehead dreamer

dreamteeth

Scientific name: *Microlophichthys microlophus* (Regan, 1925)
Family: **Dreamer**
Other common names: none
French name: dents-de-rêve

Distribution: Found in all oceans including off the Atlantic coast of Canada.

Characters: This species of deepsea **anglerfish** is distinguished as the female from other family members by having sphenotic spines, a curved edge to the frontal bones on the head, a short and broad pectoral lobe, skin extending beyond the base onto the caudal fin, a very short illicium or fishing rod, and an esca or bait without filaments. Dorsal fin rays are 5–7, anal fin rays 4–6, and pectoral fin rays 17–23. Overall colour is black with the esca having unpigmented areas. Females reach 11.8 cm.

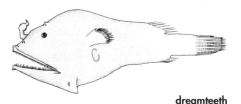

dreamteeth

Biology: Known from 4 Canadian specimens taken in 1968 off Newfoundland, where they are northern records. They may be found below 2000 m. Females use the fishing apparatus to attract prey close enough to be seized.

Driftfish Family

Scientific name: Nomeidae
French name: physaliers

Driftfishes, flotsamfishes or shepherdfishes, are found in tropical and subtropical seas world-wide. There are about 15 species with 3 species reported from Atlantic Canada.

These fishes have 2 dorsal fins, the first with 9–12 spines, which can be retracted into a groove, and the second with 0–3 spines and 14–32 soft rays. The anal fin has 1–3 spines and 14–31 soft rays. Pelvic fins are small in adults but long in the young while the pectoral fins are longer in adults. Pelvic fins fold into a groove. There are no lateral keels on the caudal peduncle. The roof of the mouth has minute teeth. Scales are deciduous (easily detached), cycloid or weakly ctenoid.

This family is related to the **Ruff**, **Sequinfish**, **Squaretail** and **Butterfish** families, all of which share toothed, sac-like outgrowths of the gut. If the gill cover is lifted, the sacs may be seen behind the last gill arch. These families are distinguished by number of dorsal fins, presence/absence of pelvic fins in adults, number and size of dorsal fin spines, presence/absence of keels on the caudal peduncle and whether there are teeth on the roof of the mouth. The **Cape**, **slender** and **fewray fatheads** of the **Ruff Family** are included in this family by some ichthyologists. Driftfishes may be included in the **Butterfish Family**. Driftfishes are members of the **Perch Order**.

These are oceanic fishes which are rare near coasts. Adults are found in deeper water, often in schools, while young live near the surface associated with jellyfish, which provide protection and food. The jellyfish may drop scraps from its meal which are seized by the driftfish. It may paralyse more food fishes than it needs, and release some to the driftfish, although this is speculative. The driftfish is also protected by the stinging cells of the jellyfish from any would-be predator. The jellyfish may also benefit if the presence of driftfish in and around its tentacles attracts other fish species which become a meal. The driftfish are at least partially immune to the stinging cells of the jellyfish.

See **bluefin driftfish**
      man-of-war fish
      silver driftfish

Drum Family

Scientific name: Sciaenidae
French name: tambours

Drums or croakers are found in the Atlantic, Indian and Pacific oceans and some species are permanent residents of fresh water. There are about 270 species with 3 species on Canada's Pacific coast, 2 on the Atlantic coast, and 1 in freshwater Arctic and Atlantic drainages.

These fishes have long dorsal fins with a short section having 6–16 spines separated by a deep notch or gap from 1 spine and 20–35 soft rays. The anal fin has only 1–2 spines and 6–13 soft rays. The tail fin is deeply forked. The mouth is usually on the lower side of a rounded head. Jaw teeth are small but some species have massive throat teeth for crushing molluscs and crustaceans. The lateral line scales run to the tip of the caudal fin. Scales are cycloid or ctenoid and cover the head and body. The chin may have small barbels or conspicuous pores and slits. The head has large canals as part of the lateral line system. The upper edge of the opercle bone is forked, with a bony flap over the gill cover. The swimbladder is complex often with many twig-like or finger-like branches; some have been likened to a carrot, others are hammer or anchor-shaped. The sagittal otolith is very large in many species.

Drums are members of the **Perch Order**. The Atlantic croaker (grondeur atlantique, *Micropogonias undulatus* (Linnaeus, 1766)) has been recorded from Canada but this is an error.

Drums are common shallow water species in warmer areas of the world around estuaries, in bays and on banks. Some are found as deep as 600 m. Freshwater species are common in South America. The swimbladder is used as a "drum" or resonating chamber to produce sound by the action of the drumming muscles. The sounds include quacks, tapping, grunting and snoring as well as drumming and croaking. These noises were understandably a source of confusion to the first sonar operators. Sounds made by Japanese submarines before the Pearl Harbour attack were thought to be drums. The sounds are used in courtship by males. Some species without swimbladders grind their throat teeth to make sounds. The large sagittal otolith or earstone of one of the inner ear canals has been used as jewellery and a good luck charm. Scales are also used to make jewellery. Some drums are used in aquarium displays. They are popular sport fish and are excellent food fish.

See **black drum**
      freshwater drum
      queenfish
      weakfish
      white croaker
      white seabass

duckbill barracudina

Scientific name: *Paralepis atlantica*
  Krøyer, 1891
Family: **Barracudina**
Other common names: Krøyer's barracudina
French name: lussion à bec de canard

Distribution: Found in all oceans including off the coasts of Atlantic and Pacific Canada.

Characters: This species is distinguished from its Canadian relatives by having pectoral fins shorter than the anal fin base, smooth-edged lower jaw teeth, body scales (but easily lost), pelvic fin origin below the dorsal fin origin, 20–26 anal fin rays, and the rear tip of the premaxilla bone of the upper jaw behind the nostril. Dorsal fin rays 9–11, pectoral rays 15–18, pelvic rays 9. Lateral line scales 55–64. Vertebrae 60–73 (63–66 in the North Atlantic, 65–68 in the eastern North Pacific).

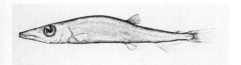

duckbill barracudina

Colour is brownish above with silvery flanks and dark spots. The gill cavity and peritoneum are black. Reaches 50 cm.

Biology: Reported in the Atlantic from off the Flemish Cap where 8 specimens were caught in 1968 and from off the Scotian Shelf where 1 specimen was caught in 1978. Also known off the coast of British Columbia at Deep Big Bank north of Cape Flattery taken in 1985, and at Ocean Station Papa (50°N, 145°W), taken by angling prior to 1979, from single specimens. This species is usually found in deep midwaters but may be cast ashore in temperate to polar areas. Recorded down to 2166 m. Occurs in the Sargasso Sea in the Atlantic Ocean.

duckbill eel

Scientific name: *Nessorhamphus ingolfianus*
  (Schmidt, 1912)
Family: **Neckeel**
Other common names: duckbill oceanic eel,
  spoonbill eel

French name: nesso

Distribution: Found world-wide in temperate to tropical oceans including off Atlantic Canada.

Characters: This species is distinguished from its only Canadian relative, the **neckeel**,

duckbill eel

by having a greatly elongate, flattened, pointed snout with the upper jaw much longer than the lower. Dorsal fin rays 276–300, anal rays 152–175. Lateral line pores about 132, vertebrae 147–159. The dorsal fin origin is just behind the pectoral fin tip. Overall colour is black to dark brown, with bluish tinges. Reaches 67.3 cm.

Biology: Found on the southwest edge of the Grand Bank and along the Scotian Shelf in Canada and first caught in 1962. Capture depths were 155–352 m, in midwater. Elsewhere reported down to 1829 m. Adults are rarely caught but leptocephali and adolescents are commonly taken by research ships. It is thought to spawn in the Sargasso Sea in spring and summer.

dusky rockfish

Scientific name: *Sebastes ciliatus*
  (Tilesius, 1810)
Family: **Scorpionfish**
Other common names: dark dusky rockfish,
  rock cod
French name: sébaste cilié

Distribution: Found from the Bering Sea to northern Vancouver Island.

Characters: This species is distinguished by colour, convex roof of the head between the eyes, black peritoneum, a knob at the tip of the chin, and the posterior edge of the anal fin vertical or slanted anteriorly. There are 3 distinct pores on each side of the lower jaw which the related **black rockfish** lacks. There is a spine on the lower margin of the opercular flap. Dorsal fin spines 13, rarely 14, soft rays 14–17, usually 15. Anal fin soft rays 6–10, usually 8, second anal spine more than twice as thick as third but shorter. Pectoral fin rays 17–19, usually 18, with

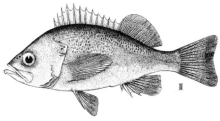

dusky rockfish

9–11 unbranched. Gill rakers 30–37. Vertebrae 28. Lateral line pores 42–53, scale rows below the lateral line 46–63 but the latter varies with locality. Head spines are all weak with only the nasals and parietals evident, sometimes all spines are absent. Branchiostegals are covered with scales.

The overall colour is often blue-black or blue-grey, sometimes grey-brown or greenish-brown above with brown to red-brown or orange spots on the higher sides. Light grey or pink on the belly. The pectoral and pelvic fins and the lower jaw are tinged pink. All fins are dusky to black with blue or purple sheens. Brown streaks radiate back from the eye. Peritoneum black. Reaches 49 cm.

Biology: First recorded in Canadian waters in 1968. Found on and off the bottom, inshore and from 95 to 525 m. Birth takes place in May or later in British Columbia. Life span is up to 30 years. Half the population of males is mature at 25–26 cm and 7–8 years and of females at 25–31 cm and 7–10 years. This species is caught by sport fishermen in British Columbia. When approached by divers they retreat into rocky crevices. Dusky rockfish are taken by commercial trawlers in the Gulf of Alaska. Specimens currently recognised as dusky rockfish may in fact be two species, but this remains to be demonstrated clearly. There is a "dark" shallow water form associated with rocks or kelp and usually found in small schools of less than 100 fish. The "pink" dusky form is found above the bottom in large schools along with **black** and **yellowtail rockfishes**.

dusky sculpin

Scientific name: *Icelinus burchami*
    Evermann and Goldsborough, 1907
Family: **Sculpin**
Other common names: none
French name: icéline obscure

Distribution: Found from southeastern Alaska to California including British Columbia.

Characters: The 5 Pacific coast members of the genus *Icelinus* are characterised by having 25 or more lateral line scales or pores, 2 pelvic fin soft rays, scales in 2 rows close to the dorsal fins and an antler-like preopercular spine. This species is separated from its relatives by the first 2 dorsal fin spines about equal in length to remainder, and 20–26 scale rows not extending beyond the end of the soft dorsal fin. Head pores are large. Pelvic fins are very small. There is a strong nasal spine, 4 preopercular spines with the uppermost having 3 sharp spinules directed dorsally. There is a flat opercular spine. First dorsal fin spines 9–11, second dorsal soft rays 16–18. Anal fin rays 12–14 and pectoral rays 16–19 with lower rays finger-like at their tips. Lateral line scales 35–39.

There is a large, flat, fringed cirrus over the eye. Dorsal fin spines have cirri at their tips. There is a simple cirrus at the middle of the frontal-parietal ridge and a branched cirrus at the rear end of the ridge. Other small cirri include on the suborbital stay, in front of the upper end of the gill opening, base of the opercular flap and end of the upper jaw.

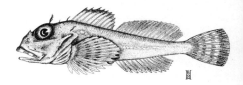

dusky sculpin

Overall colour is yellowish-brown to blackish with light and dark spots and blotches. Fins are dark with white blotches. The cirrus at the end of the upper jaw is white. Colour based on preserved fish only. Reaches 12.7 cm.

Biology: Reported at 61–567 m, mostly near dropoffs and usually caught in prawn traps. Not a well-known species with only about 18 specimens in museum collections.

dusky shark

Scientific name: *Carcharhinus obscurus* (Le Sueur, 1817)
Family: **Requiem Shark**
Other common names: shovelnose, bay shark, requin sombre, réquiem de sable
French name: requin obscur

Distribution: Found off the Atlantic coast of Canada south to South America. Possibly in Europe, and in southern California, southern Africa, Australia and the Far East.

Characters: This shark may be distinguished from other **requiem sharks** in Canada by its pointed or narrowly rounded

dusky shark

pectoral and first dorsal fins, fins not mottled white, no black saddles on the caudal peduncle (distinguishes **ocean whitetip shark**), there are no caudal peduncle keels (distinguishes **tiger shark**), the pectoral fin is not very long and narrow, the body is not a brilliant blue and the first dorsal fin origin is opposite the pectoral fin rear tip (distinguishes the **sandbar, silky** and **blue sharks**), and teeth are serrated (distinguishes the **Atlantic sharpnose shark**). The upper teeth are broad, triangular, heavily serrated and with a slightly oblique cusp. The lower teeth have an erect, serrated cusp rising from a broad root. There is an obvious middorsal ridge and the second dorsal fin is over the anal fin. The denticles overlap in contrast to the **sandbar shark**. The snout is short and rounded. The anterior nasal flaps are very short.

Usually grey above but may be bluish or bronze with a faint white band on the flank. Tips of fins dusky or black-tipped in smaller

fish less than about 1 m. The belly is white or grey-white.

Possibly in excess of 4 m. The all-tackle, rod-caught record weighed 346.54 kg and was caught at Longboat Key, Florida in 1982.

Biology: Rare in Canada, this species is common elsewhere in inshore and offshore warm waters from the surface to 400 m. It may even be found in the surf or sunning itself at the surface. Dusky sharks are strong migrators, heading north in summer when they may reach Canada, and south as winter approaches. Young dusky sharks may form large feeding aggregations. Dusky sharks eat a wide range of fish including **menhaden, sardines, herring, anchovies, eels,** and others as well as crabs, lobsters, shrimp, cuttlefish, octopus, squid, starfish, barnacles and garbage. A 2 m long dusky shark exerts a pressure of 3 tonnes/sq cm (21 tons/sq in) with its teeth. This species is viviparous with a yolk-sac placenta and 3–14 young in a litter. Size at birth is 69–102 cm. Mating seems to occur in alternate years in the spring and gestation may last 16 months. Females drop their young inshore and then leave the nursery. Males mature at about 2.8 m and females between 2.5 and 3.0 m when they are about 6 years old. They live to at least 18 years. Where it is common this species is often caught on longlines, in set bottom nets and on hook and line. It is used fresh, dried and salted, frozen and smoked. The skin has been used for leather, the fins for soup, and the liver oil for vitamins. This shark is dangerous to people because of its size and habitat. Anglers have caught this species with baits set in deep water. It puts up a hard fight.

dusky slickhead

Scientific name: *Alepocephalus agassizi* Goode and Bean, 1883
Family: **Slickhead**
Other common names: Agassiz' smoothhead
French name: alépocéphale obscur

Distribution: Found on both sides of the North Atlantic Ocean including the Davis Strait, off Labrador and off the Scotian Shelf, Nova Scotia.

Characters: This species may be distinguished by the absence of teeth on the maxilla bone of the upper jaw, the dorsal fin origin lying above the anal fin origin, 80–90 lateral line scales and 16–18 anal fin rays. Dorsal fin rays 15–18 and pectoral fin rays 10–12. Gill

dusky slickhead

rakers 23–29. The overall colour is black, which may change to purplish-brown on capture, and it reaches 79 cm standard length.

Biology: The dusky slickhead is found over sandy or clay bottoms at depths of 600–2400 m, in schools. Its food is mainly comb jellies, but also includes crustaceans, starfish and marine worms. Eggs are up to 2.8 mm in diameter and number up to 9150.

dusky snailfish

Scientific name: *Liparis gibbus* Bean, 1881
Family: **Snailfish**
Other common names: polka-dot snailfish
French name: limace marbrée

Distribution: Found across the southern Arctic from the Bering and Chukchi seas to western Greenland and south to the estuary and Gulf of St. Lawrence and the Saguenay River and south to off northern Nova Scotia.

Characters: This snailfish is distinguished from its Arctic-Atlantic relatives by having an adhesive disc, 2 pairs of nostrils, dorsal fin without a notch, dorsal fin rays 38–46, anal fin rays 32–37, pectoral fin rays 35–45 with gill

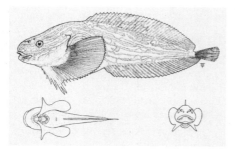

dusky snailfish

opening opposite rays 8–16, peritoneum light and posterior teeth with a large central lobe, anterior teeth with 3 equal lobes. Pyloric caeca

15–42. Males have prickles. The overall colour varies and may be uniform reddish-brown to reddish-pink both with yellowish tints or alternately striped light and dark on the head and body. Fins have black margins. The caudal fin may have 2–3 bands. Peritoneum with a few pigment spots. Reaches 52.4 cm.

Biology: Found on rock, sand and mud bottoms down to 364 m and usually deeper than 100 m. Food is crustaceans including amphipods and crabs. Some food associated with plants is taken above the bottom. Reproduction may occur in spring and summer in the St. Lawrence River estuary but during winter in the Arctic. This snailfish is eaten by **Atlantic cod**.

dwarf wrymouth

Scientific name: *Cryptacanthodes aleutensis* (Gilbert, 1896)
Family: **Wrymouth**
Other common names: red devil
French name: terrassier nain

Distribution: Found from northern California to the Bering Sea including British Columbia.

Characters: This wrymouth is distinguished from its relative the **giant wrymouth** by lacking scales and by colour. The

dwarf wrymouth

elongate body with loose skin, long spiny dorsal fin beginning behind the head and confluent with the caudal and anal fins, eyes high on the head and the almost vertical jaws are characteristic. There are no pelvic fins. The nostril is a tube which extends over the upper jaw. There are 60–69 dorsal fin spines, 3 anal fin spines followed by 45–49 soft rays and the small pectoral fins have about 12 rays. The transparent skin allows the bright pink or red of blood to show. Attains 30 cm.

Biology: Found in bottom mud on the sea bed at 28–350 m. Spawning may extend from spring to summer but little detail is known about life history.

E

Eagle Ray Family

Scientific name: Myliobatidae
(= Myliobatididae)
French name: aigles de mer

Eagle rays, cownose rays, devil rays and mantas are found in the Atlantic, Pacific and Indian oceans. There are about 42 species with 1 found off the Atlantic coast of Canada.

The family has the head higher than the disc, disc width about twice its length, eyes and spiracles laterally, teeth are large and plate-like in 1 or 7–9 or over 100 rows in each jaw, gill openings under the disc may be as long as the eye or much longer, small dorsal fin on the tail base, pectoral fins reduced or absent at the eye level, and the slender tail longer than the disc. They are members of the **Ray Order**.

These rays are very strong swimmers, "flying" through the water with their large "wings." Some have a venomous spine at the tail base and their powerful jaws can crush fingers easily.

See **manta**

eastern sand darter

Scientific name: *Etheostoma pellucidum*
(Agassiz in Putnam, 1863)
Family: **Perch**
Other common names: none
French name: dard de sable

Distribution: Atlantic drainages of Canada in southern Ontario around Lake Erie and southern Lake Huron and the upper St. Lawrence River around Montréal. Also south of the Great Lakes in the Ohio River basin to Kentucky and West Virginia.

Characters: This darter is recognised by the small mouth not extending beyond the anterior eye margin, a smooth edge to the preopercle bone on the side of the head, a large anal fin at least as large as the soft dorsal fin, body very pale when alive, 1 anal fin spine, and scales may only be present on midflank. The first dorsal fin has 7–12 (usually 9–11) weak spines and is widely separated from the 8–12 (usually 10) soft rays of

the second dorsal fin. Anal fin soft rays 7–11. There are 62–84 scales in lateral series. The lateral line is, or is almost, complete.

eastern sand darter

Overall colour is pellucid-white with a yellowish tint on the back and upper flank and silvery-white on the lower flank and belly. Fins are clear but there are dusky markings on the head. The midflank has 8–19 small, dark green to brown horizontal spots or blotches, on the midback there are 11–19 small, dark green spots which separate on each side of the dorsal fins. Scales on the upper flank have a black posterior edge. The iris is golden. Breeding males develop black pelvic fin bases and anal and ventral pelvic fin tubercles, and the overall colour is more yellowish. Formerly in the genus *Ammocrypta*. Reaches 8.4 cm.

Biology: Uncommon in Canadian waters. Found usually in sandy areas of streams, rivers and lake shores where it may be buried with only the eyes showing. This darter plunges head first into sand and completely covers itself. Insects and crustaceans may be captured by a dash from this hiding place but the small mouth and the bottom-dwelling types of food eaten suggest that this species is a "picker" and has no need to ambush prey which have no defence against it. Burying may enable the darter to maintain itself on a suitable habitat without expending energy to keep position against a current flow. Sandy areas are easily silted up in populated and farming areas, so much suitable habitat for this species has been lost in Canada. Spawning occurs in June-July. Translucent, slightly adhesive eggs are up to 1.7 mm in diameter. The males chase a female, resting their pelvic fins and chin on her back. A single male will position himself on top of the female, the pair vibrate, burying their tails and caudal peduncles in the sand, and a single egg is shed and fertilised at a time. A second male may join the spawning pair alongside the female and vibrate with them. The male's ventral pelvic fin tubercles assist in gripping the female below him.

eastern silvery minnow

Scientific name: *Hybognathus regius* Girard, 1856
Family: **Carp**
Other common names: méné bleu
French name: méné d'argent de l'est

Distribution: Found in Lake Ontario drainages, the lower Ottawa and upper St. Lawrence river basins south to Georgia east of the Appalachian Mountains.

Characters: This species resembles the **shiners** (genus *Notropis*) but has an elongate intestine which has coils on the right, and a

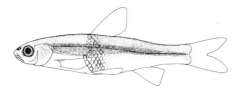

eastern silvery minnow

subterminal mouth. It is distinguished from its relative, the **brassy minnow**, by its falcate dorsal fin, silvery colour and 12 or less radii on adult scales and from the **western silvery minnow** by distribution. Dorsal fin branched rays 7, anal branched rays 7–8, pectoral rays 14–16 and pelvic rays 7–8. Lateral line scales 38–40. Pharyngeal teeth 4–4 with a flat, grinding surface. Males have breeding tubercles on the head, back, flank scales, particularly abundant on anterior scales, and on both sides of all fins, best developed on the upper pectoral and pelvic fins.

The back is olive with the flanks silvery and the belly silvery-white. There is a broad stripe along the midline of the back. The mid-flank stripe has a sharp upper edge and begins half way between the head and the level of the dorsal fin origin. It extends to the base of the tail fin where it is widened. The

preorbital bone of the head has a silvery spot. The lower margin of the caudal fin is white. Dorsal and caudal fin rays and the rear edges of anal rays 2 and 3 are outlined with pigment. Pectoral fin rays 1–7 are also outlined with pigment but the rest of the fin is clear. Pelvic fins clear. Breeding males become yellowish on the flanks and lower fins. Peritoneum black.

Reaches 15.7 cm total length. This species was formerly regarded to be the same species as the **western silvery minnow** and both were combined with the central silvery minnow (not in Canada) under the name *Hybognathus nuchalis*.

Biology: This minnow is common in lakes and streams where there are pools and backwaters. It is a schooling species. Food includes bottom ooze and algae. Life span is 3 years. Males are mature in their second year, females spawn at 1 year of age in New York. Spawning occurs in late April to mid-May in New York at about 13–21°C, starting at 10:00 a.m. and lasting until 4:00 p.m. In Delaware, spawning takes place in April and May at 10–20°C. Females may contain 6600 eggs. The spawning behaviour in New York commences with a concentration of males inshore with females in deeper water. A female ready to spawn moves towards shore and is escorted by 1–10 males. A female may jump out of the water and return to deeper water without spawning. Usually 2 males flank her and the fish quiver strongly in very shallow water (5–15 cm deep). Non-adhesive, demersal eggs of 1.0 mm diameter are shed onto the ooze bottom. Spawning activity stirs up the ooze bottom. The female returns to deeper water and the males remain to wait for another female. This species has been used as a bait fish in Ontario and in Québec for **yellow perch** in winter. About 15,600 kg are caught around Montréal in the fall.

Eel Order

The term eel is often used for any fish with a snake-like body. However there is a group of fish families which are correctly classified as true eels, the Order Anguilliformes. There are 15 families with about 738 species world-wide of which 10 families and over 35 species are reported from Canada. They are mostly of moderate size but some attain 4 m. Most eels live in shallow marine waters although some live in fresh waters or the deep sea.

They are characterised by the absence of pelvic fins, no fin spines, no oviducts, small gill openings, 6–49 branchiostegal rays, a swimbladder with a duct to the intestine, often no pectoral fins, usually an elongate anal fin, usually dorsal and anal fins continuous around the tail, cycloid scales in some, gills displaced posteriorly, and various internal bony characters such as usually no symplectic and the hyomandibular united with the quadrate. Scales are often absent or are minute. The young eel differs markedly from the adult and this larva is known as a leptocephalus. Many leptocephali were originally described as distinct species until it was realised that they were larval eels. Even today, scientists may know distinct eel species as adults and as larvae, but not know which larva develops into which adult.

The leptocephalus is a thin, leaf-like or filamentous, translucent larva which drifts for a few months to several years on ocean currents, preying on plankton with tiny, sharp teeth. Fully-grown leptocephali are about 50–100 mm long although some giants are known at 1800 mm. The leptocephalus transforms into a young eel of typical shape, shrinking to a third of its size in the process, and developing pigment. Eels are related to the **Gulper Eel**, **Tarpon** and **Bonefish** orders which also possess a leptocephalus larva.

Many eels are more active at night than in the day and are predators on other fishes and crustaceans. The eel shape is an adaptation to burrowing or hiding in crevices. Eels can be a very nutritious food and even the leptocephali are eaten in some parts of the world.

See **Conger Family**
Cutthroat Eel Family
Freshwater Eel Family
Moray Family
Neckeel Family
Pike Conger Family
Sawpalate Family
Snake Eel Family
Snipe Eel Family
Spaghetti Eel Family

Eelpout Family

Scientific name: Zoarcidae
French name: lycodes

Eelpouts or viviparous blennies are found from the Arctic to the Antarctic in cold to temperate marine waters with most species in the Northern Hemisphere and almost none in the tropics. A few occur in brackish waters in the Arctic. There are about 225 species with 49 in Canada, 23 on the Pacific coast, 10 on the Arctic coast, 7 on the Arctic-Atlantic coasts and 9 on the Atlantic coast.

These fishes have eel-like bodies with long dorsal and anal fins continuous with the caudal fin. Fins usually lack spines. The pelvic fins are small, with only 2–3 rays, and in front of the pectoral fins on the throat when present. Pectoral fins are large. Scales are minute and cycloid or absent. There is a single pair of tubular nostrils. The swimbladder is absent. Sensory pore patterns on the head are usually species specific. The large mouth is usually under the snout and has thick lips. Teeth are small.

Eelpouts are members of the **Perch Order** and are probably related to the **Ronquil**, **Prickleback** and **Gunnel** families. However relationships are uncertain and eelpouts have been placed in the **Cod Order**. Since the dorsal and anal fins are continuous with the caudal fin, fin ray counts of the former two often include half the caudal fin rays each.

Most eelpouts live in deep water on the bottom but some are intertidal. A few are middle-water dwellers for part of their life and some live only around hydro-thermal vents at several thousand metres depth. They lay few, large demersal eggs and a common European species is a live-bearer. They are of little commercial importance.

See **Adolf's eelpout**
Alaska eelpout
archer eelpout
Arctic eelpout
Atlantic eelpout
Atlantic soft pout
aurora unernak
bigeye unernak
bigfin eelpout
black eelpout

blackbelly eelpout
blackmouth slipskin
checker eelpout
checkered wolf eel
chevron eelpout
common wolf eel
cuskpout
deepwater slipskin
eyebrow eelpout
fish doctor
glacial eelpout
greater eelpout
Labrador wolf eel
Laval eelpout
longear eelpout
longsnout eelpout
looseskin eelpout
naked-nape eelpout
Newfoundland eelpout
ocean pout
Pacific soft pout
pale eelpout
pallid slipskin
polar eelpout
saddled eelpout
scaled-nape eelpout
shortfin eelpout
shortjaw eelpout
shulupaoluk
slipskin
snakehead eelpout
snubnose eelpout
soft eelpout
stout slipskin
stubraker slipskin
threespot eelpout
twoline eelpout
wattled eelpout
wolf eelpout

Electric Ray Family

Scientific name: Torpedinidae
French name: torpilles

Electric rays are found in temperate to tropical waters of the Atlantic, Indian and Pacific oceans. There are about 15 species, with one each on the Atlantic and Pacific coasts of Canada. They are members of the **Ray Order**.

The disc, comprised of the body and pectoral fins, is round and thick. The skin is smooth, without denticles, soft and loose. Eyes are small, and some species are blind (not in Canada). There is a caudal fin and the dorsal fin may be absent or present, and number 1 or 2. The tail is short and thick. Teeth are small, some are rounded, others pointed. Jaws are very slender and there are no labial cartilages. Nasal, gill and mouth openings are all ventral. The rostrum is absent or reduced. The electric organs lie at the base of the pectoral fins on each side of the head. They may account for a quarter of the body mass. They are kidney-shaped muscle tissues and can often be seen through the skin as a honeycomb-shape. The honeycomb is the upper layer of a series of columns, each column made up of plates with a positive charge on top and a negative one below.

Electric rays are found over, or partially buried in, mud or sand in shallow waters, although some species may be found deeper than 1000 m. They are not very active and move by using the tail, not the pectoral fins. Young are born alive. Food is crustaceans, molluscs, worms and fishes. Fish and other food items are stunned by the electric organ. The electricity may also be used to orient the ray or detect the same and other species by disturbances in electrical fields. Most species are not dangerous to humans, but some can produce up to a reputed 300 volts and 2000 watts, which will render a person unconscious. Several shocks can be delivered rapidly but these soon weaken and it may take days to recharge fully. They are not of economic importance but in the past liver oil was burned to give light and used as a folk remedy for cramps. The Greeks and Romans held that the electric shock had medicinal benefits.

See **Atlantic torpedo**
    Pacific electric ray

emerald shiner

Scientific name: *Notropis atherinoides*
    Rafinesque, 1818
Family: **Carp**
Other common names: lake shiner,
    lake silverside, buckeye shiner,
    Milwaukee shiner, Lake Michigan shiner,
    grands yeux, vitreux, épingle
French name: méné émeraude

Distribution: Found from southwestern Québec, through much of Ontario and Manitoba, throughout Saskatchewan, most of Alberta except the southwestern part, in the northwestern part of British Columbia and adjacent parts of the N.W.T. around Great Slave Lake and the upper Mackenzie River. In the U.S.A. south to the Gulf Coast west of the Appalachian Mountains.

Characters: This species and its relatives in the genus *Notropis* (typical **shiners**) are separated from other family members by

emerald shiner

usually having 7 branched dorsal fin rays following thin unbranched rays, protractile premaxillaries (upper lip separated from the snout by a groove), no barbels, large lateral line scales (fewer than 50), and a simple, s-shaped gut. It is separated from its relatives by having 8–12 branched anal fin rays, anterior flank scales rounded, dorsal fin origin behind the level of the pelvic fin insertion, slender body (body depth usually less than head length), snout length less than eye diameter, pectoral fin rays usually 15–17 and flank pigment ends above the lateral line. Dorsal fin branched rays 6–7, pectoral rays 13–17 and pelvic rays 8–9. Lateral line scales 35–43. Pharyngeal teeth are hooked, 2,4–4,2 with occasional loss of teeth in both major and minor rows. Breeding males have tubercles on the upper pectoral fin rays 2–10 and minute tubercles on the head and sometimes the body.

The back is blue-green to greenish-yellow and iridescent, flanks silvery and the belly is silvery-white. There is an emerald green or metallic silver midflank stripe and narrow middorsal stripe on the back. Upper flank scales have dusky edges. Fins are clear except for white areas on the anal and caudal fins.

The overall silvery colour is lost in preserved fish and midflank stripe is most apparent, best developed posteriorly. Peritoneum silvery and speckled brown. Reaches 12.4 cm.

Biology: Emerald shiners are found in large rivers or lakes where they school in open, surface waters. They overwinter in deeper water after moving inshore in the fall.

Food is plankton, some insect larvae and surface insects, fish eggs and fry, worms and algae. There may be a migration with the plankton as it rises to the surface in the evening and descends in the morning. These shiners are an important food source for a wide range of predators including **lake trout, smallmouth bass, rainbow trout, northern pike** and various surface-feeding birds.

Life span is about 4 years. Spawning occurs in June to August in Canada, probably at temperatures over 20°C. In Wisconsin the spawning season may run from May to August, peaking in June-July. Lake Erie spawners gather offshore in schools over gravel shoals numbering in the millions at about 2–6 m. Eggs sink to the bottom and are not adhesive. A male appears to pursue a female for a few seconds until he overtakes her, presses against her perhaps with interlocked pectoral fins, the pair arch upward and roll, releasing eggs and sperm. Females may spawn more than once in a season. Eggs are up to 0.7–0.9 mm in diameter and mature yellow eggs average 3410 for all age classes in Lake Simcoe, Ontario to as high as 8733 eggs for an age 3 fish. Some females survive to spawn in their fifth summer.

This is the most important bait fish because of the immense schools which can be caught commercially. It is even pickled and sold preserved in jars as bait. In Québec, despite its abundance, it is relatively little used, except in fall for the winter fishing season, because of its fragility in captivity and on the hook.

English sole

Scientific name: *Pleuronectes vetulus* (Girard, 1854)

Family: **Righteye Flounder**

Other common names: lemon sole, pointed-nose sole, common sole, California sole

French name: sole anglaise

Distribution: Found from Alaska to Baja California including British Columbia.

Characters: This species is distinguished from Canadian Pacific relatives by the scales on both sides of the body being cycloid and

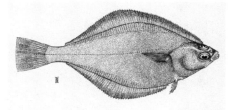

English sole

smooth anteriorly and ctenoid and rough posteriorly. The lateral line is only slightly arched and has 89–105 scales. The accessory lateral line extends back to a level over the pectoral fin. The mouth is small, asymmetrical and teeth are strongest on the blind side. The head is pointed, and the upper eye is visible from the blind side. Dorsal fin rays 71–93, anal fin preceded by a spine and with 52–70 rays. Caudal fin truncate. The eyed side is brown and the blind side white to yellow. The head on the blind side is reddish-brown. Fin tips are dark. Attains 57 cm.

Biology: Common in Canada at less than 128 m, even in the intertidal zone, on soft bottoms. Older fish move to deeper water. There is also a migration into deep water in winter. Maximum reported depth is 550 m. Some English sole undergo migrations as long as 1100 km. Food is clams and their siphons, molluscs, worms, crustaceans, brittle stars and **sand lances**. English sole feed opportunistically and so take a wide variety of food items. Half the females in a population are mature at 29.5 cm and half the males at 26.0 cm. Spawning in British Columbia is from January to March. Large females produce 1.9 million eggs with a diameter of 0.93 mm. Young are pelagic for 6–10 weeks. Anglers regularly catch this fish from piers and boats on light tackle. This species is commercially important in British Columbia with catches exceeding 1100 metric tonnes.

Some populations have an "iodine" or "lemon" flavour, which is accepted by consumers. Some dense populations of English sole develop a myxosporidian infection which turns the flesh "milky" and soft. In this condition it can no longer be marketed although it is not poisonous. This species hybridises with the **starry flounder**.

Enos stickleback

Scientific name: *Gasterosteus* sp.
Family: **Stickleback**
Other common names: Enos Lake stickleback
French name: épinoche d'Enos

Distribution: Found only in Enos Lake, eastern Vancouver Island, British Columbia.

Characters: This lake contains a limnetic form which is reproductively isolated from a benthic form. The 2 forms act as good species. It is not clear which form is the **threespine stickleback** since both forms fall within the current limits of the **threespine stickleback**. They may both be species distinct from the **threespine stickleback**. The divergence between the 2 species occurred less than 12,500 years ago since the lowland area was under the sea until then. Other lakes on Vancouver Island have species pairs, some of which are also reproductively isolated but others are less distinct and probably

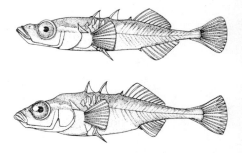

Enos stickleback

have some gene flow. Most lakes, however, contain a single form usually regarded as the **threespine stickleback**. The limnetic form is slimmer, has a narrower mouth and more (22–28 compared to 16–21) and longer gill rakers. There are also biochemical differences. The limnetic form has a dark back and silvery flanks, the benthic form has disruptive colouration. Limnetic breeding males have red throats and blue backs (as in **three-spine sticklebacks**) but benthic males are black. Enos Lake is a valuable resource for studying speciation in fishes. This is only 1 of several unusual stickleback populations in British Columbia not all of which have been described (see as some other examples the **giant stickleback** and **Texada stickleback**). Reaches 5.9 cm.

Biology: One of the sticklebacks is a limnetic form, i.e. pelagic plankton feeder, found near the surface in summer and in deeper water in winter. This limnetic form has protruding eyes, and is presumably better adapted to locating plankton. The other form is a benthic species feeding in the littoral zone in summer and dispersing over the lake bottom in winter. Limnetic females are obligate plankton feeders and males are facultative plankton feeders (females feed on plankton only, males switch to bottom foods during breeding season). The benthic form has no feeding variation. Females are smaller (3.5 cm standard length on average) than males (4.5 cm) in the limnetic form but the benthic form shows no sexual size differences. Males of both forms build nests in the littoral zone during May and June. Females of the limnetic form only enter the littoral zone to spawn. Both sexes select mates of their own form. Male colour and body shape helps in this selection. There are also differences in early courtship behaviour which maintain separation between the 2 forms. Male limnetics nest in the open while benthics nest in dense cover. The Committee on the Status of Endangered Wildlife in Canada gave this (or these) species the status of "threatened" in 1988. Introductions of **brown bullheads** and **pumpkinseed** have eliminated sticklebacks from other small lakes in 2 years. The **bullhead** preys on stickleback nests at night and **pumpkinseed** males may interact territorially with stickleback males. Any regulations to prevent this happening to Enos Lake will probably be ineffective because of the activities of children catching and releasing these fishes as pets unwittingly between drainage basins.

escolar

Scientific name: *Lepidocybium flavobrunneum*
   (Smith, 1849)
Family: **Snake Mackerel**
Other common names: escolier noir
French name: escolar

Distribution: Found world-wide in tropical waters and in Atlantic Canada.

Characters: The tuna-like body is characteristic. The dorsal spines fit into a groove on the back. Dorsal fin soft rays number 15–24, followed by 4–6 finlets. There are 2 anal spines and 12–19 soft rays, followed by 4–6

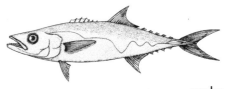

escolar

finlets. This is the only Canadian snake mackerel with keels on the caudal peduncle, 7–12 (usually 8–9) dorsal fin spines and a sinuous lateral line. Dark to purplish-brown above becoming almost black with age, with a mosaic pattern, lighter below. The eye is greenish-gold. Juveniles are lighter in colour than adults which become almost black. Attains almost 2 m and about 45 kg. "Escolar" is the Spanish for scholar in reference to spectacle-like rings around the eyes.

Biology: Found off the Scotian Shelf and Georges Bank where it is caught on baited hooks by longliners after **swordfish**. This pelagic species is found down to 300 m or more. Food is squid, crustaceans and oceanic fishes such as small **tuna**. Fish food items may be longer than the escolar itself. Escolars are cannibals and are also eaten by **swordfish** and **yellowfin tuna**. Females grow faster than males and females of 33 cm length are mature. Spawning south of the Cape Verde Islands begins at the end of July. The flesh is very oily and has a purgative effect when eaten, but is said to be tasty.

eulachon

Scientific name: *Thaleichthys pacificus*
   (Richardson, 1836)

Family: **Smelt**
Other common names: ooligan, candlefish,
    oilfish, salvation fish, fathom fish,
    Columbia River smelt
French name: eulakane

Distribution: Found from the Bering Sea
to California including British Columbia.

Characters: This species is distinguished
from other smelts by having only 4–6 gill
rakers on the upper part of the first arch and
by having obvious, concentric striae on the
operculum and suboperculum bones on the
side of the head. Dorsal fin rays 10–13, anal
rays 17–23 and pectoral rays 10–12. Total
gill rakers 17–23. Lateral line scales 70–86.
Pyloric caeca 8–12. The mouth extends
beyond the middle of the eye. Spawning
males have elongate pelvic fins reaching the
anus, a midlateral ridge formed by swollen
muscles, and tubercles on the head, scales

eulachon

and pelvic, pectoral and anal rays. Back
bluish to bluish-brown, brown or bluish-
black, with flanks and belly silver-white. The
back has fine black pigment dots. The pectoral and caudal fins may be dusky or speckled. The peritoneum is light with dark pigment spots. Eulachon is the Chinook Indian
name for this fish. Reaches 30.5 cm.

Biology: This smelt is commonly found in
coastal waters down to 300 m, perhaps deeper,
and enters rivers up to 160 km from the sea
but usually much less.

Food is crustaceans, particularly euphausiids and copepods, and cumaceans. Feeding
ceases on the spawning run. Eulachon are an
important food for **spiny dogfish, white
sturgeon, salmons, Pacific cod, Pacific halibut**, whales, seals and seabirds. Life span
may exceed 7 years and maturity is attained
at 3 years.

Males are larger than females on the
spawning migration through the Fraser River

estuary in April. The spawning run is mostly
up the larger rivers from March to May. Males
precede females. Eggs number up to 60,600
and are up to 1.0 mm in diameter. When
deposited an outer membrane ruptures, turns
inside out but remains connected to the egg by
a stalk and sticks to sand on the river bed. The
larvae are taken out to sea by the river current.
Many eulachon die after spawning and litter
river banks but some survive to spawn again.

So oily is this fish that when dried and fit-
ted with a wick thrust in the mouth it can be
used as a candle. The oil is, unusually, solid at
lower temperatures and has the consistency of
soft butter and is pungent and golden.
Eulachon caught in March to April are allowed
to "ripen" in large stink boxes and then rendered. It has long been used by native peoples
as a food and medicine. The trails used to
reach the traditional fisheries and to carry the
rendered oil back for trade were known as
"grease trails." This fishery was a major social
event involving large scale migrations, intricate ceremonies and specialised fishing methods. The grease is used as a condiment, in
bread and stews and formerly as a preservative
for dried berries. In recent years, the fat content of eulachons has led to recommendations
that these fish be used as monitors of pollutants. High lipid content absorbs low levels of
organic compounds. The native catch probably
exceeds the commercial fishery.

There are commercial fisheries on spawning runs such as that of the Fraser River which
has rendered as much as 203 tonnes in the
early 1950s. Drift gill nets are used. The fish
are sold for human consumption and for fur-
farm animals, mostly the latter. They are delicious when fried but native peoples maintain
that eating a lot makes one sleepy. They have
been sold as a vitamin supplement in place of
cod liver oil. Salted and smoked eulachon
have also been marketed. The total Canadian
catch in 1988 was 40 tonnes.

European flounder

Scientific name: *Platichthys flesus*
    (Linnaeus, 1758)
Family: **Righteye Flounder**
Other common names: North Atlantic flounder
French name: flet d'Europe

Distribution: Reported from Lake Erie, Lake Huron and Lake Superior as an exotic species. Normally found from the White Sea to the Black Sea on European coasts.

Characters: This is the only species of **flatfish** in the Great Lakes. The almost straight lateral line has bony tubercles at its

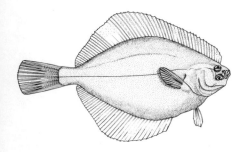

European flounder

anterior end. There are modified, tubercular scales along the dorsal and anal fin bases also. Lateral line scales about 80. Scales are cycloid. The mouth is small, asymmetrical and teeth are best developed on the blind side. Dorsal fin rays 52–67, anal rays 35–46. Caudal fin truncate. The eyed side is brown, grey or olive and may be darkly mottled. Faint red or orange-yellow spots are present. Reaches 51 cm standard length.

Biology: This European species was introduced to the Great Lakes on at least 6 separate occasions in the ballast water of ships. Specimens contained Canadian foods and were evidently feeding in the Great Lakes. In Europe it is found on soft bottoms at shallow depths, entering rivers and lakes but reproducing in the sea. Food is small fishes and invertebrates. Males are mature at 11 cm, females at 17 cm. Up to 2 million eggs are produced in a February-June spawning period after an offshore migration to 27–54 m depths. Eggs are 1.02 mm in diameter and float, but sink as development progresses. They take on adult form at 1.5–3.0 cm and live on the bottom. In Europe about one third of the fish are left-eyed. The early Lake Erie specimens consisted of 1 dextral and 1 sinistral fish. This flounder is an important sport and commercial fish in Europe. This species

may continue to be caught in Canada as more fish are brought in, but it is unlikely to establish breeding populations in fresh water.

European ling

Scientific name: *Molva molva*
(Linnaeus, 1758)
Family: **Cod**
Other common names: grande lingue
French name: julienne

Distribution: Found in Atlantic Canada on the Grand and St. Pierre banks off Newfoundland. Mainly found from Greenland to Iceland and Europe.

Characters: This species and its relative, the **blue ling**, are distinguished from other **cods** by having 2 dorsal and 1 anal fin, no elongate dorsal fin ray, 6–7 pelvic fin rays, a well-developed barbel and over 54 anal rays. It is separated from its relative by marbled flanks, a white margin to the median fins outlined by black below especially to the rear of these fins, a dark spot at the rear edge of the first dorsal fin, 57–70 second dorsal fin rays and 55–67 anal rays. Vertebrae 62–67. First dorsal fin rays 13–16. The upper jaw projects. The back is dark bronze or bronze-green to dark slate. The belly is yellowish-grey. There is a dark spot at the rear of the second dorsal fin. Reaches 2 m and 40 kg. The world, all-tackle angling record weighed 37.2 kg and was caught in 1993 in Norway.

European ling

Biology: Reported in Canadian waters on the southwest Grand Bank from a specimen caught in 1953 at 88–101 m. Also recorded on St. Pierre Bank off southern Newfoundland at 201 m in 1972. Young fish in Europe are found inshore over rocks at 15–20 m and adults at 300–400 m. Life span is up to 15 years for females which live longer than males at about 10 years. Food is mainly fishes, such as **herrings, cods** and **flatfishes**, as well as crustaceans and starfishes. Males are mature at 80 cm and females at 90–100 cm Spawning occurs in March to July at 50–300 m. Egg numbers are extremely high, an estimated 28,361,000 in one female, with a diameter of 1.1 mm, and as high as 60 million. In Europe it is caught by trawlers and is commercially important. Some anglers also catch this species and large ling may be taken in shallow water occasionally.

eventooth headlightfish

Scientific name: *Diaphus perspicillatus*
(Ogilby, 1898)
Family: **Lanternfish**
Other common names: none
French name: lampe-de-tête unidentée

Distribution: Found in the Atlantic, Indian and Pacific oceans including off Nova Scotia.

Characteristics: This species and its relatives, the **bouncer**, **flashlight**, **square**, **straightcheek**, and **Taaning's headlight-**

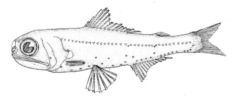

eventooth headlightfish

fishes and the **doormat** and **slanteye parkinglightfishes**, are separated from other Atlantic coast lanternfishes by not having photophores near the dorsal body edge, the PLO photophore is well above the upper pectoral fin base level while the second PVO photophore is at or below this level, there are 4 Prc photophores, the PO and two PVO photophores form a straight, ascending line as do the first 3 VO photophores, supracaudal luminous glands are absent, and there is more than 1 pair of luminous head organs. This species is separated from its relatives by having the So photophore absent, vomer with a small, round to oval patch of teeth on each side, Dn photophore well-developed in a deep cup, directed forward and equal to or

larger than the nasal rosette, the Vn photophore not extending under the eye as far as midpupil level, head longer than deep, photophores not small, Dn not markedly above upper eye level, and total gill rakers 26–29. Dorsal fin rays 15–17, anal rays 14–16 and pectoral rays 10–12. AO photophores 10–12. Lateral line organs 36–38. Adult males have a larger Ant photophore than females. The "headlights" first develop at 1.2–1.3 cm body length when the Dn is apparent but it is only in the size range 2.6–3.2 cm that the Dn and Vn grow rapidly and acquire an adult shape. Reaches 7.1 cm.

Biology: This is a tropical species which enters the Gulf Stream and is sometimes carried to Canada. Depth distribution by day is 375–750 m with most fish caught at 400–500 m and by night is from the surface to 125 m with a maximum abundance at 75 m. Sexual maturity is attained at 5.0–5.5 cm. The main spawning area is probably south of the Sargasso Sea.

eyebrow eelpout

Scientific name: *Lycodes perspicillus*
Krøyer, 1845
Family: **Eelpout**
Other common names: none
French name: lycode sourcillier

Distribution: Found from Greenland southward in the eastern Atlantic Ocean.

Characters: This species is distinguished by the yellowish eyespot over each eye. Body colour is yellowish with 9–11 brownish bands. Each band has a margin darker than the centre. Bands extend onto the dorsal fin and, posteriorly, onto the anal fin. Attains at least 8.3 cm.

eyebrow eelpout

Biology: A single specimen has been reported for Canada in 1985. It was caught in Carson Canyon at the southeast Grand Bank at 283 m. Depth range elsewhere is reported as 108–157 m.

eyed flounder

Scientific name: *Bothus ocellatus*
   (Agassiz, 1831)
Family: **Lefteye Flounder**
Other common names: none
French name: plie oculée

   Distribution: From Nova Scotia south to Brazil.
   Characters: This species is uniquely characterised among adult Canadian Atlantic **lefteye flounders** by the long pelvic fin base

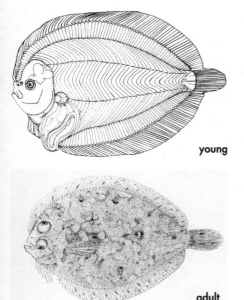

young

adult

eyed flounder

of the eyed side being on the midline of the belly and the blind side base being short. Dorsal fin rays 76–91, anal rays 58–69, eyed side pectoral rays 8–10 and lateral line scales 70–78. Upper arm gill rakers 7–10. Males have eyes further apart and longer upper pectoral rays than females. Larvae have an elongate anterior dorsal fin ray known as a tentacle. The eyed side in adults is pale brown to grey with spots, rings and mottles. There are 2 spots on the caudal fin, one above the other, and a dark blotch on the lateral line on the rear half of the body. Males have blue

lines interspersed with yellow dashes in front of the eyes. Reaches 20 cm.
   Biology: This species is known only from stray larval specimens caught off the Scotian Shelf, and on Georges Bank and Browns Bank. Adults only occur as far north as Long Island, New York, and are found at 3.6–108 m over or burrowing in sand and mud.

Eyefish Family

Scientific name: Macrurocyttidae
French name: mégalopes

   This family is found off southern Africa, in the tropical western Pacific Ocean and the Caribbean and North Atlantic Ocean, including Atlantic Canada. There are about 4 species with 1 found in Canadian waters.
   The eyefishes have a large eye in a large head. The pelvic fin has a long, serrated and strong spine and 5–6 soft rays. The dorsal fin has 6–7 spines and 25–29 soft rays. There is one lateral line. The upper jaw is very protrusible. The jaws have minute teeth.
   This family is related to the **Boarfish**, **Dory**, **Diamond Dory** and **Oreo** families and is a member of the **Dory Order**. Formerly called Zeniontidae.
   Eyefishes are found in waters 300–600 m deep in midwater or near the bottom.
   See **red eyefish**

eyelight lanternfish

Scientific name: *Benthosema suborbitale*
   (Gilbert, 1913)
Family: **Lanternfish**
Other common names: none
French name: lanterne feu-avant

   Distribution: Found in the Atlantic, Indian and Pacific oceans and off the Scotian Shelf and Banquereau Bank in Atlantic Canada.
   Characters: This Atlantic species is distinguished by the PLO photophore being more

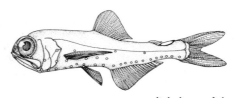

eyelight lanternfish

than its diameter above the upper base of the pectoral fin, no photophores near the dorsal body edge, the second PVO photophore is at or below the upper base of the pectoral fin, the PVO series is almost horizontal, 2 Prc photophores with the second much higher than the first, the second VO photophore is elevated, and small, simple premaxillary and dentary teeth. It is separated from its relative, the **glacier lanternfish**, by having a suborbital photophore and the second Prc photophore at the lateral line. Dorsal fin rays 11–14, anal rays 16–19 and pectoral rays 12–15. Total gill rakers 13–15. AO photophores 10–12. About 34 lateral line organs. Vertebrae 33–35. Males have a single supracaudal and females 2 infracaudal luminous glands which are developed in fish 1.9 cm long. The female glands coalesce into one with growth. Reaches 3.9 cm.

Biology: First reported from Nova Scotia in 1988. Elsewhere reported from near the surface to 250 m at night with most being caught at 10–50 m and in the day at 375–750 m. Sexual maturity is reached at about 2.8 cm. Spawning may occur year round near Bermuda with a peak in spring.

F

fallfish

Scientific name: *Semotilus corporalis*
(Mitchill, 1817)
Family: **Carp**
Other common names: American chub,
silver chub, mohawk, white chub, rough-
nosed chub, windfish, corporal, chivin,
whiting, shining dace
French name: ouitouche

Distribution: Found from New Brunswick
to southern James Bay drainages of Québec
and Ontario south to Lake Erie through eastern Ontario and east of the Appalachian
Mountains to Virginia.

Characters: This species is distinguished
by having protractile premaxillae (a groove
between the upper lip and the snout), a flat

fallfish

barbel in advance of the mouth corner in the
groove above the upper lip, lateral line scales
43–50, no black spot at the dorsal fin base
and each scale base is dark. The barbel may
be absent on 1 or both sides in smaller fish.
Pharyngeal teeth 2,5–4,2, 2,4–5,2 or 2,4–4,2.
Dorsal fin branched rays 7, anal branched
rays 6–8, usually 7, pectoral rays 15–19 and
pelvic fin rays 7–9. Males have small nuptial
tubercles on the snout, over the eye, in a
patch on the postero-ventral edge of the opercle and on the branchiostegal rays, fine tubercles on the opercular flap and on up to 9 pectoral fin rays.

The back is olive-brown to blackish,
flanks are silvery, occasionally with purple to
blue tinges, and the belly is white. There is a
dark bar along the shoulder girdle at the edge
of the gill opening. Scales above the lateral
line are outlined with pigment. Young fish

have a wide flank stripe running from behind
the eye to the tail, ending in a spot at the tail
base. Breeding males have a darkened back
and pink opercles and pectoral fins.
Peritoneum silvery with darker speckles.

Reaches 51 cm. The world, all-tackle
angling record weighed 0.5 kg and was
caught at Orangeville, Pennsylvania in 1986.

Biology: Fallfish live in clear streams and
rivers with gravel bottoms and in lakes. Food
includes aquatic insects, terrestrial insects
taken at the water surface, crustaceans and
fishes. Kingfishers and mergansers are
known to eat them.

Life span is estimated to be 10 years.
Males grow faster than females after age 4.
Males mostly mature at age 3 and females at
age 4. Spawning takes place in May in eastern Québec at 16.6°C. Males begin nest
building at 12°C, carrying stones by mouth.
Nests can be 92 cm high and 183 cm across
and are elongate in flowing water or domed
in quiet water. A nest can weigh up to 81.8
kg. Nests can be in midstream or at stream
edges protected by overhanging vegetation.
Common shiners may use the nest and
hybrids result. Eggs are adhesive after shedding and 2.7 mm in diameter, and are covered with gravel by the male after deposition. A female may have up to 12,321 eggs.

This species is unusual among its relatives because communal spawning occurs.
Several fish of both sexes are found over
nests. Males establish a hierarchy among
themselves by parallel swimming, lateral
displays, head butting and tail biting. Other
fish species are tolerated. A dominant male
starts the communal spawning by swimming
to the nest with a stone in his mouth and
dropping it, or by "rushing" onto the nest
from downstream. Other fallfish are stimulated to rush onto the nest and spawn. There
is no clasping of the female as eggs and
sperm are shed into the gravel. Other male
fallfish often break up the dominant male
spawning couple. Communal spawning
enables many males to fertilise eggs without
having to construct nests.

Fallfish can be caught by fly fishing and give good sport but are a nuisance to anglers trying for **trout**. They are good eating.

fanfin

Scientific name: *Caulophryne jordani*
  Goode and Bean, 1896
Family: **Fanfin**
Other common names: none
French name: nageoire-éventail

Distribution: Found world-wide and reported from Atlantic Canada.

Characters: The very elongate rays in the dorsal and anal fins and large pectoral fins characterise females of this **anglerfish**. The

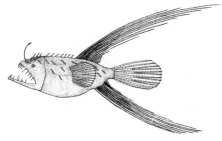

fanfin

dorsal fin has 16–19 rays and the anal fin 14–18. This is a high anal ray count compared to related **anglerfishes**. There are 16–18 pectoral rays. The short illicium has less than 15 filaments and filaments cover the body. The mouth is large and has sharp teeth. Males are minute and parasitic on females. Colour overall is black to brown. Attains 10.9 cm.

Biology: Known only from a single Canadian specimen taken off Newfoundland in 1968 at the northern limit for this species in the Atlantic Ocean. There are only 11 female specimens collected world-wide. Found from waters down to 1510 m, but upper limit unknown.

Fanfin Family

Scientific name: Caulophrynidae
French name: nageoires-éventails

These **anglerfishes** are found in the deep sea of the Atlantic, Indian and Pacific oceans. There are 4 species with 1 reported from Atlantic Canada.

The female fanfin develops the fishing rod and lure, while males are dwarfs, being only about 2 cm long, slender and parasitic on the females. Larvae and free-living males are unique among related **anglerfishes** in having well-developed pelvic fins. There is no bulb or photophore on the illicium. The very elongate dorsal and anal fin rays are characteristic of adult females.

Fanfins are related to other families in the **Anglerfish Order** such as the **Seadevils** and **Whipnoses**. Parasitic males cannot be identified to species. These are meso- and bathypelagic fishes living alone at depths of 500–3000 m. Males search for females using highly-developed sense organs. The adult female feeds on fish, cephalopods and crustaceans. Eggs are released in a gelatinous mass known as a veil.

See **fanfin**

fangtooth

Scientific name: *Anoplogaster cornuta*
  (Valenciennes in Cuvier and
  Valenciennes, 1833)
Family: **Ogrefish**
Other common names: ogrefish, common
  sabretooth
French name: ogre

Distribution: World-wide in warmer waters and entering Atlantic Canada including off the Flemish Cap, south of the Grand Bank and near Sable Island.

Characters: Dorsal fin with 16–20 rays, anal fin with 7–10 rays, pectoral fin with 13–17 rays and pelvic fin with 1 spine and 6 soft rays. The large lower jaw fangs fit into sockets in the palate. The head has obvious

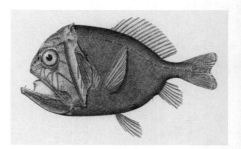

fangtooth

mucous cavities covered by skin. Gill rakers 14–23, long and slender in young, shorter and tooth-like in adults. Young fish have a long head and preopercular spines, which gradually reduce in size with growth and are absent in adults. Dark brown to black overall with a blue iris. Young are silvery with transparent fins. Attains about 16 cm.

Biology: Found between 46 and 4898 m and not uncommon, even in Canadian waters. Adults are deeper than young. Food is small fish and crustaceans and sometimes squid, eaten whole and infrequently. **Tunas** and **marlins** eat fangtooths. They swim by sculling with the pectoral fins, only using the caudal fin when disturbed. Aquaria observations indicate that fangtooths locate food simply by bumping into it and sensing it chemically. A prompt reaction with the fangs secures the prey. The pectoral fins are used to fan water over the gills while digesting large prey which block the mouth.

fantail darter

Scientific name: *Etheostoma flabellare*
  Rafinesque, 1819
Family: **Perch**
Other common names: striped fantail darter,
  barred fantail darter
French name: dard barré

Distribution: Found from southern Québec and eastern New York across the southern Great Lakes to Iowa and Kansas and south to Louisiana and Mississippi. In Canada it is recorded from the upper St. Lawrence River drainage in southernmost Québec, along the lower Ottawa River and tributaries of Lakes Ontario, Erie and southern Lake Huron.

Characters: This species is distinguished from other **darters** in Canada by having the anal fin smaller than the soft dorsal fin, the snout and upper lip joined (i.e. premaxillaries not protractile), belly is scaled, dorsal fin spines short, about eye diameter or less, 5–10, usually 7–8, soft rays 10–15, lateral scales 38–60 with 11–59 pored. Anal fin with 2 spines and 6–10 soft rays. Pectoral rays 10–14. The nape, cheek, opercle and breast lack scales.

Overall colour is olive-brown with 5–15 dark flank bars or sometimes thin stripes, or both on a yellow-brown background. There are about 8–10 dark brown to black saddles. Belly cream, yellowish, yellow-orange or

fantail darter

dusky. The second dorsal fin has 6 narrow stripes and the caudal fin has 4–7 wavy, dark bars. Bars are present before and behind the eye but the one below the eye is weak to absent. Spawning males develop white to yellow-orange, fleshy knobs at the tips of the dorsal fin spines. The base of the fin becomes thickened, perhaps to produce an anti-bacterial and anti-fungal mucus. Cheeks are olive-green and the rest of the head black or dusky. The breast is dusky. The spiny dorsal fin develops basal and marginal orange stripes and the flanks are yellowish. Attains 8.6 cm.

Biology: The preferred habitat is streams with slow to moderate or even fast current. Riffles and raceways are use by this species. Deep areas are used for a winter retreat and gravel and boulder bottoms for spawning. Also found in lakes.

Food is aquatic insects, such as net-spinning caddisflies, blackflies and stoneflies, and crustaceans taken from between and under rocks in the morning and evening. The fantail spends most of its time on the bottom in crevices waiting for prey. Food items can be almost as long as the fish.

Males live longer than females and are larger. Males usually reach 4 years and females 3 years of age, but these fish are mature at 1 year of age. Maximum age is 5 years.

Males set up a territory in spring (April to June) under a rock, cleaning the rock surface with the fleshy knobs of the dorsal fin spines. The male becomes very dark when chasing away intruders. Males threatened by other fishes "freeze" for 2–3 minutes and then resume normal activity. Females enter male territories, poking their heads under rocks and darting from rock to rock.

Courtship involves leading a female to the rock cavity with circling, figure-of-eight swimming, nudging and prodding, and entry and exit from the cavity until the female turns upside down. The swimming patterns are repeated with the male right side up and head to tail with the female. The female eventually quivers and lays 1–3 eggs which stick to the rock, the male flips over to quiver and fertilise the eggs and then flips back again. Up to 45 eggs are laid and fertilised in this manner with the female inverted for up to 2 hours. The cavity under the rock is narrow enough so that the female's dorsal fin contacts the bottom and offers some support. The male may mate with several females and the female with up to 5 males in each spawning season. He guards the eggs and brushes them with his dorsal fin knobs. It is probable that the male is smearing mucus on the eggs to prevent bacterial and fungal attack. The number of eggs in a nest can vary from 8 to 562. The eggs are up to 2.7 mm in diameter.

This darter makes an excellent aquarium fish.

fathead minnow

Scientific name: *Pimephales promelas* Rafinesque, 1820

Family: **Carp**

Other common names: northern fathead minnow, blackhead minnow, Tuffy minnow

French name: tête-de-boule

Distribution: Found from western New Brunswick through southwestern Québec, Ontario, southern and central Manitoba and Saskatchewan, Alberta and southern tributaries of Great Slave Lake, N.W.T. South in central regions of North America to Mexico.

Characters: This species is identified by having premaxillaries protractile (lip separated from the snout by a groove), no barbel, the first, unbranched dorsal fin ray is short and separated by a membrane from the next, longer ray, scales in front of the dorsal fin are much smaller and more crowded than flank scales, the back is flattened, the lateral line is incomplete to nearly complete, the mouth is at the tip of the body and a caudal fin base spot is faint to absent. Dorsal fin branched rays 7, rarely 8, anal branched rays 6, sometimes 7, pectoral rays 14–18 and pelvic rays 8–9. Pharyngeal teeth 4–4, slightly hooked at the tip with elongate cutting surfaces. The gut is elongate with several loops. Scales in lateral series 39–56, lateral line pores usually ending before the

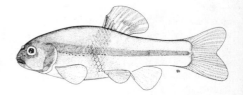

fathead minnow

dorsal fin origin. Large tubercles in males are found on the snout in 3 rows with 4–15 in the lower row, and with up to 11 tubercles on the lower jaws. There are also smaller tubercles on top of the head and pectoral rays. Tubercles first develop in early April near Ottawa and males begin to lose them in late July. By early September only scars remain. Males also develop a blue-black to grey, spongy, wrinkled pad on the back between the head and dorsal fin. Fin membranes swell.

The back and upper flank are dark olive-green to brown, silvery to golden flanks and a whitish belly. There is a midflank stripe. Breeding males darken, particularly the head and dorsal fin, and the stripe is not apparent. The body can be completely black with a white band at the head-body region and under the dorsal fin. This occurs only during aggression or sexual activity. The lateral banding enhances the robust appearance of fish which must maintain a territory over several weeks without much opportunity to feed. Weight loss is replaced by water to help maintain the image of a fat and vigorous male. Very frightened fishes blanch. Peritoneum black. The rosy-red minnow with orange-red body and fins is an aquarium variety. Reaches 10.2 cm.

Biology: Fathead minnows are found in ponds, small lakes and slow-flowing brooks. They tolerate turbidity, high temperatures, pH variations, salinity and low oxygen.

Food is bottom sediment for its organic content including plant material, aquatic insects and zooplankton. It is an important food for many other fishes and aquatic birds. Fatheads sharing a lake with pike show sheltering, dashing and freezing behaviours more often than fatheads from lakes without pike. They also show stronger fright responses to water which pike have lived in — a chemical response.

Males grow faster and larger than females, typical of nest defending species. Life span is about 3 years with maturity attained as early as 1 year, rarely in the year of birth. Spawning runs from April to August, once water temperatures reach 14°C and light-dark hours are 16–8. Males choose a spawning site under a log, rock, plant stems or even a lily pad or any solid artificial structure in shallow water. Cavity spawning in mud-bottomed habitats prevents the eggs from being smothered as well as offering the relatively few eggs spawned from a small fish protection from predators. The male will clean out the cavity, spending up to 10 hours on the task, using his tubercles to scrape, pulling debris with his mouth and sweeping with his tail fin. The spongy pad on the back may serve to test spawning sites and eggs chemically. The pad secretes a mucus which is smeared on the spawning site perhaps to improve it for egg survival since mucus protects against disease and parasites. Diseased eggs are eaten by the male. The mucus may also serve to indicate ownership of a nest site.

Spawning male fatheads lose their ability to produce alarm or fright chemicals on skin injury, otherwise the continual pad rubbing would disturb spawning activities by releasing alarm substance and scaring away females. Females may enter the spawning site casually, be chased there by a male or enticed by a face to face encounter and leading to the nest. He lifts and presses the female on her side between himself and the roof of the spawning site. Egg deposition is thought to use the same unusual mechanism as in the **bluntnose minnow** (q.v.).

Males court females by swimming rapidly up to them and then freezing at 3–5 cm away, and by leading females with a zig-zag or straight-line motion from the female to the nest site. Males will also display to females by erecting their fins for 2–3 seconds and by jump-swims in which a male swims upwards to a female then rolls on his side and swims back down. Butting and lateral quivering also occur, perhaps attempts to assess spawning condition of the female.

Males defend the eggs against other fishes including female fatheads using the snout tubercles to butt and tail swipes to intimidate by sending a pressure wave sensed by the lateral line system. Chasing and biting are common and 2 males may carousel (or circle head-to-tail) trying to contact each other. Leeches and turtles are also driven away. Some eggs are lost while the male is distracted chasing away predators. Repeat spawning may be necessary to replace lost eggs. Males also aerate and clean the eggs with fin movements. A nest will contain eggs in various stages of development as the male will spawn with several females. Females will deposit eggs in several nests. Orange, mature eggs are up to 1.6 mm in diameter with 12,000 or more per nest. A female will release up to 10,164 eggs in a season but from 9 to 1136 at a time. Spawning intervals are 2 to 16 days.

In the U.S.A. fatheads are raised as bait fish and as forage fish for introduction into **bass** fishing lakes. They are also used extensively as a laboratory animal for tests of toxic compounds. They have even been used to evaluate the biological effects of materials from the moon.

fawn cusk-eel

Scientific name: *Lepophidium profundorum*
  (Gill, 1863)
Family: **Cusk-eel**
Other common names: none
French name: donzelle fauve

Distribution: From Nova Scotia south to Florida and the Gulf of Mexico. Also in the Mediterranean Sea.

Characters: This species has a scaly head and body scales are arranged in regular rows. It lacks the unique characters found in its Atlantic coast relatives, such as an enlarged anterior nostril, basket-weave scale arrangement, and elongate lower pectoral fin rays. The tip of the snout has a forward pointing spine under the skin. Dorsal fin rays about

fawn cusk-eel

134–137, anal rays about 114–118 and pectoral rays about 22–24. Gill rakers 8–9. Background colour is brownish with 14–23 large, round white or pale brown spots along the upper flank. There is an irregular series of smaller spots above the large ones anteriorly. The dorsal and anal fins have narrow dusky or black margins. Young fish lack the spots. Pectoral fins yellowish. The gill chamber, gill bars and oesophagus are blackish and the peritoneum is silvery. Reaches over 27 cm total length.

Biology: Found from Sable Island to Georges Bank and first reported in 1967. Usually found at 55–365 m. This species is eaten by **white hake**.

feather blenny

Scientific name: *Hypsoblennius hentz*
(Le Sueur, 1825)
Family: **Combtooth Blenny**
Other common names: spotted seaweed blenny
French name: blennie plume

Distribution: Found from Nova Scotia south to the Gulf of Mexico.

Characters: This species is characterised by having 13–16, usually 14, soft, segmented dorsal fin rays, 3 soft, segmented pelvic fin rays, 11–13, usually 12, stiff and robust dorsal

feather blenny

fin spines and an upper lip without a free dorsal margin. The lower lip is narrow. Anal fin with 2 spines and 14–17, usually 16, soft rays. Pectoral fin rays with 13–15, usually 14, rays. The cirrus above the eye has numerous side branches. The body is yellowish-brown above with many dark brown spots and 5 vague dark bars may be present running obliquely across the flank. There is a large oval, dark area behind the eye. The underside of the head has 2–3 dark, v-shaped bands. The pelvic fins are dusky to dark. The anal fin is barred in females and young but in males is dark, except for a pale edge. Males have a blue spot on the anterior part of the dorsal fin. The belly is whitish. Reaches 10.4 cm.

Biology: Known from only 2 specimens collected in 1973 from Shelbourne Harbour, Nova Scotia, the northern limit of the range for this species. It is found on rocky shores and oyster beds, and sometimes in seagrass beds. In winter it moves to deeper water at 24–30 m. If picked up by hand it will clasp firmly onto the skin using the comb-like teeth. It has a large gape among western Atlantic blennies, used in taking crustaceans and worms for food. Algae and hydroids are also found in stomach contents. Eggs are laid in empty oyster shells near the low-tide mark from May to August. There may be up to 3750 eggs, the result of several spawnings, and they are guarded by the male.

ferocious lizardfish

Scientific name: *Bathysaurus ferox*
Günther, 1878
Family: **Lizardfish**
Other common names: deep-sea lizardfish
French name: poisson-lézard féroce

Distribution: Found in the Atlantic and Pacific oceans including the Atlantic coast of Canada.

Characters: This lizardfish lacks an adipose fin when adult (present in post-larvae) and has been placed in a separate family. It has a unique larva, once described as a distinct species since it is so dissimilar in its appearance: the fins are greatly enlarged and the mouth and head lack the typical lizardfish shape. In adults, the dorsal fin is twice as long as the anal fin. Pectoral fins have one or two elongate, specialised rays. Dorsal fin rays 15–19, anal rays 11–15 and pectoral rays 13–16, with rays 6 or 7 elongate and upturned in life. Lateral line scales 65–78. The teeth are recurved and barbed. The colour is grey to grey-black or brown and the fish is darker below than on the back. Scale pockets are black-lined. The fins are darker than the body and the pectoral and pelvic fins are almost black. Attains about 61 cm.

ferocious lizardfish

Biology: Only recently reported from Canada as a post-larva off Nova Scotia collected in 1980. The ferocious lizardfish lives on the bottom as an adult at depths of 862–3460 m in the abyss and lower continental slope and rise at 1.1–5.3°C. It rests on the bottom with the head raised by the pelvic fins and has been observed from submersibles to swim rapidly if disturbed. The elongate pectoral rays may be sensory. Food is fish and crustaceans. It is a synchronous hermaphrodite, male and female at the same time. Spawning season is probably in November-January.

fewray fathead

Scientific name: *Cubiceps pauciradiatus*
    Günther, 1872
Family: **Ruff**
Other common names: bigeye cigarfish
French name: pompile paucirayonné

Distribution: Found in temperate to tropical waters world-wide including the Scotian Shelf and Georges Bank of Atlantic Canada.

Characters: This species is distinguished from the related **Cape** and **slender fatheads** by having fewer dorsal and anal fin soft rays. Teeth on the vomer bone in the roof of the mouth are knobby. There is a bony keel on the breast. Vertebrae number 31 and there are 2 anal fin spines. Dorsal fin spines 10–12, followed by 1–2 spines and 15–18 soft rays.

Anal fin with 14–17 soft rays. Pectoral fin rays 17–20. Lateral line scales 49–57. Upper procurrent (= inclined forward) caudal rays

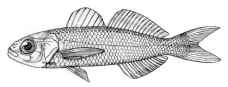

fewray fathead

8–10. Preserved fish are brown on the back, yellowish-tan on the flanks and belly, and the fins are clear. Black to cinnamon brown in life. Reaches about 20 cm, possibly 25 cm.

Biology: First collected in Canada in 1979 as young strays from the south. Found at 100–300 m depth. Fecundity of a female is recorded as 35,800 eggs.

filamented rattail

Scientific name: *Coryphaenoides filifer*
    (Gilbert, 1895)
Family: **Grenadier**
Other common names: filamented grenadier
French name: grenadier filamenté

Distribution: Found from the Bering Sea to California including British Columbia and at Ocean Station Papa (50°N, 145°W).

Characters: This species is distinguished from its Pacific Canadian coast relatives by having the anus immediately in front of the

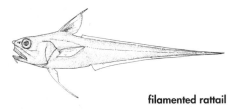

filamented rattail

anal fin, no black, scaleless area on the abdomen, 6 branchiostegal rays, pelvic fin rays 9–10, usually 9, teeth in the upper jaw not in 1–2 distinct rows, a large eye (more than one-fifth head length), scales over much of the head except under the snout, first dorsal fin soft rays 11–14, usually 12–13, the eye rim black only antero-ventrally, a long outer pelvic fin ray (greater than 70% of head length), enlarged scales only at the tip and lateral angles of the snout, and no thorn-like branch to the ventral edge of the subor-bital shelf. Pectoral fin rays 18–23. Scales have small, oblique spines arranged in 3–7 rows. Overall colour is dark brown with black fins, nostrils, underside of the snout, lips and gill membranes. Peritoneum brown-ish-black. Reaches 86 cm.

Biology: This rattail was described from 3 fish caught at 2904 m off Moresby Island in the Queen Charlottes. Also recorded from off Triangle Island and Cape Cook of northern Vancouver Island at 2189 m. The Ocean Station Papa fish are tentatively identified juveniles. Juveniles are pelagic and these were caught at less than 450 m. Eggs are up to 2.2 mm in diameter and number up to 51,110.

Filefish Family

Scientific name: Monacanthidae
French name: limes

Filefishes are tropical to warm-temperate fishes of the major oceans. There are about 95 species, with a majority in Australia, of which 4 are found on the Atlantic coast of Canada.

These fishes have 2 dorsal spines although the second can be absent and is usually much smaller than the first. The first dorsal spine is barbed and file-like, and can be locked into an erect position using the second spine when present. The spines can also be collapsed into a groove on the back. The second dorsal and anal fins are long and broad and used for swimming by undulating waves. Teeth are developed for nibbling and the upper jaw has two rows of protruding incisor-shaped teeth. There are no pelvic fins as such, although a spine or tubercle may be present. The eyes can rotate independently of each other. True scales are absent and small tubercles make the body feel like sandpaper. The gill openings are small slits in front of the pectoral or above the fin base.

This family is closely related to the **Leatherjacket Family** in the **Puffer Order** and is often included within it rather than being a separate family. Its common name is derived from the dorsal file-like spine, and possibly the sandpapery skin.

Some filefishes can produce sounds. They can also distend the belly, probably to increase their apparent size and deter preda-tors. Both the enlarged belly and the dorsal spine are used to wedge tightly into crevices. The flesh of some species is extremely poi-sonous. Filefishes are found from shallow weed beds down to depths over 150 m. The young are camouflaged and drift in floating seaweed. Adults feed on sponges, hydroids, algae, sea whips and other soft bodied inver-tebrates. Filefishes are some of the few fishes which feed directly on coral reefs.

See **fringed filefish**
orange filefish
planehead filefish
scrawled filefish

finescale dace

Scientific name: *Phoxinus neogaeus*
Cope in Günther, 1868
Family: **Carp**
Other common names: bronze minnow,
New World minnow, rainbow chub,
leatherback
French name: ventre citron

Distribution: Found from Maine, New Brunswick and southwestern Québec throughout the Great Lakes and adjacent U.S. states and all of Ontario, in southern Manitoba, in most of Alberta, the southwest-ern corner of Saskatchewan, northeastern British Columbia and down the Mackenzie River valley. Also in Wyoming, Colorado, the Dakotas and Nebraska.

Characters: This species has protractile premaxillaries (a groove between the upper lip and the snout), no barbels, an incomplete

finescale dace

lateral line with scales in lateral series 63–92, mouth extending to below the ante-rior eye margin, a black peritoneum, a short, s-shaped gut, and no upper flank stripe. Dorsal fin branched rays 6–8, usually 7, anal branched rays 6–8, usually 7, pectoral rays 12–16 and pelvic rays 7–8. Pharyngeal teeth hooked, 2,5–4,2, 2,5–5,2, 2,5–4,1 or 1,5–4,1. The lateral line usually ends above the pelvic fin origin and has 9–34 pores. Scales are small and have radii on all fields. Spawning males have 4–5 scale rows on the breast edged with tubercles in comb-like rows and 4–5 rows of tubercles on scales above the anal fin base and on the lower caudal peduncle. The first 4–5 pectoral rays are thickened and darkened and membranes are swollen in breeding males. The first ray has a distinct notch about one-quarter of the fin length from the base.

The back and upper flank are brown to black, below is an olive-green to gold stripe and then a dark midflank stripe which extends onto the head and lips but not the chin, and ends in a spot at the caudal fin base. A thin dark line extends obliquely from the dark back to the flank stripe. The body has numerous, small, black speckles. Breeding males are bright chrome yellow to red below the dark midflank stripe. The lower flank is silvery-white to cream. Fin rays are outlined by dark pigment, most intensely during the breeding season.

This species hybridises readily with the **northern redbelly dace** (q.v.). Reaches 10.7 cm.

Biology: This schooling dace favours bogs, ponds, lakes and slow streams. Food is aquatic insects, crustaceans, molluscs and plankton. Terrestrial insects taken at the water surface, such as ants, as well as spiders can be eaten. Life span is 6 years with both sexes mature at 2 years. Spawning occurs in April–July at 11°C water temperatures or higher. Both males and females initiate chases, with males nipping at the anal and caudal region of a female. The females initiate chases by swimming in a zig-zag fashion. A male swims alongside a female and places his enlarged pectoral fin under the anterior part of the female's body, so that he can direct her swimming to some degree. The male tries to press the female against a rock or perhaps in holes under logs or branches, curling his tail

over her tail so that his tubercles above the anal fin are close to her vent. The pair vibrate for several seconds and sperm and about 20–40 eggs are shed. A female can have up to 3060 eggs of 1.5 mm diameter when water hardened. Finescale dace have been used as bait fish in Québec and Ontario.

fish doctor

Scientific name: *Gymnelus viridis* (Fabricius, 1780)
Family: **Eelpout**
Other common names: green ocean pout, coogjannernak, koupjhaun-ohuk, kugsaunak, unernak
French name: unernak caméléon

Distribution: Circumpolar including Arctic Canada, and south to the St. Lawrence River and off Nova Scotia.

Characters: This species is distinguished from its Canadian Arctic-Atlantic relatives by lacking pelvic fins, having a terminal mouth,

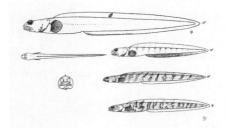

fish doctor

gill opening extending to middle of pectoral fin base, firm skin, no scales, body colour variable but when faintly barred running below lateral line, vertebrae 92–105 and pectoral rays usually 11–13, and dorsal fin origin over the pectoral fin. There are 0–2 pterygiophores (internal fin ray supports) without rays at the front of the dorsal fin. Dorsal fin rays 81–101, anal rays 66–84 and pectoral rays 10–14. Colour may be uniform brown or green, or banded and mottled. Bands and mottles may be bluish, yellowish or white on contrasting backgrounds of yellowish, orange, greenish-brown or red. The anal fin is blue-black to black in males and yellow to light brown in females. There may be several blue-black eye spots on the dorsal fin. Peritoneum blue-black. Reaches 30 cm. The reason for the name "fish doctor" is unknown. It may be that this fish "cleans" parasites from other fishes.

Biology: This species is reported from sand and mud bottoms and is often among brown kelp. It may be caught intertidally, and is common under sea ice in Resolute Bay, N.W.T. Temperature range is –1.9 to 4°C and depth range is 2–256 m. Southern populations are found at warmer temperatures. Food is crustaceans, worms and clams. Polychaete worms can make up 99.4% of the total diet weight. Spawning occurs in late summer to autumn. Pairs of fish doctors share a burrow. Females are mature at 11–12 cm standard length and contain up to 106 eggs of 4.6 mm diameter. This species is prey for **cod, wolffish** and various seabirds and seals. This is one of the most northern fishes known, reaching 82°29'N.

fishes

The word fish is used in the singular for an individual organism and in the plural for many individuals of the same species. Fishes refers to more than one species.

Fishes is a general term for 5 Classes of **vertebrate** animals showing great diversity in form. Some are thought to be more closely related to mammals than to other fishes! The 5 Classes are the Myxini (**hagfishes**), Cephalaspidomorphi (**lampreys**), Chondrichthyes (**sharks**, **skates**, **rays**, **chimaeras** etc.), Sarcopterygii (lobe-finned fishes — not in Canada), and Actinopterygii (**ray-finned fishes**). Other vertebrate classes are the Amphibia, Reptilia, Aves and Mammalia, which may be included within Sarcopterygii in some classifications.

Fishes are cold-blooded, aquatic **vertebrates**, possessing gills throughout their life and limbs, if present, as fins. Some amphibians have gills when young, but these are lost as adults, or if, unusually, gills are retained then legs are present, not fins.

The number of living fish species exceeds that of the tetrapods (the "four-footed" amphibians, reptiles, birds and mammals). New species of fish are still being discovered in numbers exceeding new tetrapods. A com-

puterised listing of world fishes, as yet incomplete, exceeds 24,000 nominal species (D.E. McAllister, pers. comm. 1991).

Canada has 199 of 482 fish families in the world (41%) and 1150 species (about 4.7%).

flabby whalefish

Scientific name: *Gyrinomimus* sp.
Family: **Flabby Whalefish**
Other common names: none
French name: poisson-baleine flasque

Distribution: Caught at Canadian weathership known as Ocean Station Papa at 50°N, 145°W off British Columbia.

Characters: This is probably an undescribed species. The genus *Gyrinomimus* is characterised by having well-developed

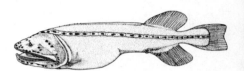

flabby whalefish

eyes, gill rakers reduced to bony plates, the lower jaw reaching back to the opercular opening, only 3 gills and less than 20 rays in the dorsal and anal fins, among other characters. Attains at least 13.9 cm standard length.

Biology: Unknown.

Flabby Whalefish Family

Scientific name: Cetomimidae
French name: poissons-baleines flasques

The flabby whalefishes are found throughout the warmer oceans of the world down to 3200 m. There are about 35 species with an undescribed, new species reported from off the British Columbia coast.

There are no pelvic fins, unlike other whalefishes. There are no scales, except in the lateral line canal, and the body and skin are flabby. Eyes are small or rudimentary. A white organ called cavernous tissue is often present around the anus, dorsal and anal fin bases and end of the upper jaw. It may be luminescent but this has yet to be proved and one scientist suggested that it is a growth medium for bacteria which serve as food for young whalefish.

An alternative explanation for this organ is that in females it may produce pheromones to attract males. The lateral line is formed into a continuous tube with a series of chambers and acts in place of a swimbladder as a hydrostatic organ. The anal fin has lappets or flaps of tissue which hang over the anal fin base. Their function is unknown.

These whalefishes are related to the **Whalefish** and **Redmouth Whalefish** families and are members of the **Pricklefish Order**. All are characterised by a whale-shaped but very small body, very large mouth and a distensible stomach. The dorsal and anal fins are opposite each other near the rear of the body. There is no swimbladder. The typical orange-brown colour of these fishes is probably derived from their crustacean food, and serves as camouflage. Male whalefish are much smaller than females, about one-tenth the length when adult.

Most flabby whalefishes are known from only a few specimens caught on scientific fishing expeditions. They can eat fish as large as themselves because of their distensible stomach and absence of ribs, scales and pelvic fins. In addition the pectoral girdle has only 1 attachment to the skull, also allowing expansion as large food is swallowed.

See **flabby whalefish**

Flagfin Order

The flagfins or Aulopiformes comprise 13 families and about 219 species in marine waters from subarctic to tropical and subarctic waters. In Canada there are representatives of 10 families for a total of 26 species.

This order is uniquely characterised by the second pharyngobranchial bone of the gill arch being elongated posterolaterally thus leaving a gap between the second epibranchial and the third pharyngobranchial which is bridged by an uncinate process of the second epibranchial. This may add strength to the upper pharyngeal jaw apparatus. There is considerable variation in body form and size but generally these fishes lack fin spines, nave 8–12 rays in a pelvic fin lying under or in front of the dorsal fin position, an adipose fin is usually present, the dorsal fin is well in advance of the anal fin, no swimbladder, large

mouth with well-developed teeth, and a maxilla bone not bordering the upper jaw.

This order has been included within the **Lanternfish Order**.

The order includes both benthic and pelagic deepsea species, mostly predatory. Many are hermaphrodites. They are not of great commercial importance.

See **Barracudina Family**
   Daggertooth Family
   Greeneye Family
   Halterfish Family
   Lancetfish Family
   Lizardfish Family
   Pearleye Family
   Sabertooth Fish Family
   Tripodfish Family
   Waryfish Family

flamefish

Scientific name: *Apogon maculatus*
   (Poey, 1860)
Family: **Cardinalfish**
Other common names: none
French name: apogon flamboyant

Distribution: Found from Nova Scotia south to Brazil.

Characters: This species is distinguished from its adult relative, the **twospot cardinalfish**, by having a broad, black saddle on the caudal peduncle extending below the lateral line and by having 17–20 scales around the caudal peduncle. Gill rakers on the lower limb of the arch 13–16, usually 14. The

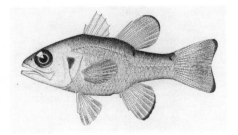

flamefish

overall colour is red or a deep orange-red (hence flamefish). Two parallel white lines pass through the top and bottom of the eye back to the operculum. There is a dark band between the lines. A round, black spot lies below the soft dorsal fin. The second dorsal, anal and caudal fins are often tipped with black. The saddle on the caudal peduncle may fade with age. Reaches 10.5 cm.

Biology: Canadian records are of 3 larval specimens caught off Sable Island and Emerald Bank in 1980. They are strays from warmer waters to the south where this species is common around coral reefs and harbours, and down to 128 m. They have been seen hiding in crevices during the day. Spawning occurs in June and July and larval specimens have been caught off Nova Scotia in August to September. Flamefish are oral brooders, keeping the eggs in the mouth and even as far back as the oesophagus. This species is commonly used in the aquarium trade.

flashlight headlightfish

Scientific name: *Diaphus dumerili*
    (Bleeker, 1856)
Family: **Lanternfish**
Other common names: none
French name: lampe-de-tête lampion

Distribution: Found in the Pacific and Atlantic oceans including off the Scotian Shelf in Atlantic Canada.

Characters: This species and its relatives, the **bouncer**, **eventooth**, **square**, **straight-cheek**, and **Taaning's headlightfishes** and

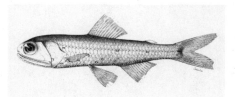

flashlight headlightfish

the **doormat** and **slanteye parkinglight-fishes**, are separated from other Atlantic coast lanternfishes by not having photophores near the dorsal body edge, the PLO photophore is well above the upper pectoral fin base level while the second PVO photophore is at or below this level, there are 4 Prc photophores, the PO and two PVO photophores form a

straight, ascending line as do the first 3 VO photophores, supracaudal luminous glands are absent, and there is more than 1 pair of luminous head organs. This species is separated from its relatives by having the So photophore absent, inner series of rear premaxillary teeth variable in size with only some recurved, vomer with a small, oval to round patch of teeth on each side, and the Dn photophore is small and directed laterally (larger in males than females). The Dn "headlight" is a minute spot at body lengths of 1.2–1.5 cm and grows with the fish. The Vn "headlight" is present from metamorphosis of the larvae at 0.8–0.9 cm. Dorsal fin rays 14–15, anal rays 14–16 and pectoral rays 10–13. Total gill rakers 19–27. AO photophores 10–14. Counts vary with locality. Lateral line organs 36–38. Reaches 8.7 cm.

Biology: This is a common tropical species carried into Canadian waters by the Gulf Stream from spawning areas in the Caribbean Sea where it is very abundant. Depth distribution by day is 225–750 m, most abundantly at 450–500 m, and by night from the surface to 125 m, most abundantly at 50 m. Sexual maturity is attained at 5.2 cm in the Caribbean Sea and life span is 18–24 months.

flatbarbel rearfin

Scientific name: *Melanostomias valdiviae*
    Brauer, 1902
Family: **Barbeled Dragonfish**
Other common names: none
French name: nageoires-reculées
    à barbillon aplati

Distribution: Found in the Atlantic, Indian and Pacific oceans and from Nova Scotia southward into the South Atlantic Ocean.

Characters: This species is distinguished from its Canadian Atlantic relatives by having 4–5 equal length pectoral fin rays with tips unbranched and without luminous material, dorsal and anal fin bases about equal in length, pelvic fins low on the flank, no luminous organs before (preorbital) or below (suborbital) the eye, 24–28 photophores between the pectoral and pelvic fin insertions, and by the barbel tip being flattened and about 2–3 times as long as wide. In addition, there are at least 2 prominent bulbs on one side of the central axis of the barbel tip and 1 or more on the other side. Dorsal fin rays 12–16, usually 13–15, anal rays 17–19, pelvic rays 7. The barbel is shorter or longer than the head. Overall colour is black. No white spots as in the related **bluenose rearfin**. The barbel stem is black and the tip pale. Reaches 24.1 cm, this specimen being the Canadian one.

flatbarbel rearfin

Biology: A single specimen has been caught southwest of Sable Island in 1982 at about 500 m. Elsewhere reported from 40–1600 m.

Flatfish Order

Flatfishes are a group of related species belonging in the Order Pleuronectiformes (= Heterosomata). There are 47 Canadian species found along the 3 coasts and 1 other species has been introduced into the Great Lakes (the **European flounder**). World-wide there are 11 families of flatfishes with about 570 species.

These fishes are unique in that as larvae each eye is on opposite sides of the head as in other fishes, but one eye moves to the other side during development. As adults, both eyes are on the same side of the head and the fish comes to lie on its eyeless side. Depending on which eye migrates, flatfish can be right-eyed or left-eyed. In some species this can vary individually with part of the population right-eyed and the rest left-eyed. Teeth are strongest on the blind side, since these fish are mostly bottom feeders, and the pectoral fin is strongest on the eyed side, where it can move more freely.

Adults live on the sea bed, often with their flattened bodies buried in sand with only the eyes exposed. The fins are used to dig into the sea bed and the sand or mud falls back onto the fish. An ability to change colour rapidly helps conceal the flatfish which endeavours to match its surroundings. Flatfish placed on chess boards have made valiant attempts to

match the checkered pattern.

Partially buried flatfish can breath by taking in water through the mouth, passing it over both gills but ejecting it only on the upper, eyed side of the body. A special channel connects the two sets of gills allowing water which would normally exit on the blind side to be transferred to the eyed side.

Many flatfishes are commercially important including **dabs, flounders, halibuts, plaices, soles** and **turbots**. These names may be applied to unrelated flatfishes found in different families. Some of the larger species exceed 3 m in length while others are only 5 cm long. Flatfish fossils date back to the late Tertiary. Their ancestry lies with the **Perch Order** or possibly a pre-perciform group. There have been suggestions that they have a multiple origin, implying a large measure of convergence of diverse ancestors into the typical flatfish body form.

See **Lefteye Flounder Family**
Righteye Flounder Family
Tonguefish Family

flathead catfish

Scientific name: *Pylodictis olivaris* (Rafinesque, 1818)
Family: **Bullhead Catfish**
Other common names: mud cat, yellow cat, shovelnose cat, shovelhead cat, Johnny cat, goujon, Appaluchion, Hoosier, granny cat, Opelousas cat, Morgan cat, flatbelly, Mississippi cat, bashaw, Russian cat, pieded cat
French name: barbue à tête plate

Distribution: Found principally in the Mississippi, Missouri and Ohio basins south to Mexico and in some southern Great Lakes tributaries. Also in Lake Erie in Canadian waters. Introduced to the Pacific coast drainages of the U.S.A.

Characters: This catfish is identified by having a band of teeth on the premaxillary bones of the upper jaw u-shaped, a free posterior tip to the adipose fin, often fewer than 16 anal fin rays and the upper tip of the caudal fin white, especially in young. The head is flattened between the eyes and the lower jaw projects. Dorsal rays usually 6, anal rays 13–20, pelvic rays 9–11. The pectoral fin spine has teeth both anteriorly and posteriorly. Colour varies with size and habitat. Usually back and upper sides are brown to yellow

flathead catfish

with darker mottling. Lower flanks and belly yellow to cream. Barbels are lighter to darker than the body, fins are similar to the nearby body except for a dark caudal fin. The white tip to the caudal disappears with age. Young fish have more contrasting colours. Reaches a reputed 1.7 m and 56.7 kg. The world, all-tackle angling record caught at Lake Lewisville, Texas in 1982 weighed 41.39 kg.

Biology: First caught off Point Pelee in Lake Erie in 1978 and since then only in 1989 in Lake St. Clair off the mouth of the Thames River. In the U.S.A. flatheads prefer deep pools in large rivers and reservoirs, often being found among submerged logs. They prefer high temperatures, over 30°C, and so are unlikely to become numerous in Canada. Adults are solitary. Young fish prefer riffle areas in streams.

Larger flatheads feed on fish including various **minnows, suckers, sunfish, darters**, other **catfish** and even **northern pike**, seized by a sudden lunge. Crayfish are also eaten. Some fish, when frightened, have been reported to dash into the open mouth of a flathead which gobbles them up.

Age attained is 24 years, and probably more. Most mature at age 4 or 5 years. Spawning occurs in June–July at 22–24°C. Nests are dug out of banks or in river beds by both male and female using their tails and mouths. Courtship involves gentle rubbing of the female's back and sides by the male using his belly. The male caudal peduncle and fin encircle the head of the female and the male quivers strongly. The female deposits 30–50 eggs at a time, which the male fertilises while the pair lie side by side. The male fluffs, ventilates and guards the eggs, even going as far

as killing the female in hatchery or laboratory situations. Eggs are up to 3.7 mm in diameter and an egg mass may contain an estimated 100,000 eggs. The young flatheads maintain a tight school, guarded by the male, until the yolk sac is absorbed.

This species is eagerly sought after by American anglers as its flesh is very tasty (it is called "candy bar" in Wisconsin). They are also a limited part of the commercial catfish harvest in the Mississippi River. As much as 103.6 kg/ha has been raised in ponds. Flatheads are efficient predators and have been used to control numbers of other, unwanted fish species.

flathead chub

Scientific name: *Platygobio gracilis*
 (Richardson, 1836)
Family: **Carp**
Other common names: Saskatchewan dace
French name: méné à tête plate

Distribution: Found from the Mackenzie River delta upstream to Great Slave Lake, northeastern British Columbia, Alberta, central and southern Saskatchewan and Manitoba and south to New Mexico.

Characters: This species has protractile premaxillaries (a groove between the upper lip and snout), a barbel at each mouth corner, and a large gape reaching back to the anterior eye margin or further. The body is elongate, pectoral fins are long and pointed, often reaching the pelvic fins, and the snout over-

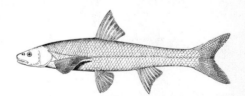

flathead chub

hangs the mouth and is long and pointed, all adaptations to life in fast water. Lateral line scales 42–59. Dorsal fin branched rays 7, rarely 6, anal fin branched rays 7, rarely 6 or 8, pectoral rays 14–20 and pelvic rays 7–9. Pharyngeal teeth 2,4–4,2 or 2,4–4,3. Breeding males have small tubercles on the head, snout, nape, anterior body and rarely on the caudal peduncle, pectoral fin rays 2–8 and anterior dorsal, anal and pelvic fin rays. The back is brown to dusky, flanks silvery and the belly white. The lower lobe of the caudal fin is darker than the upper. Other fins are mostly clear. Young fish have a midflank stripe ending in a spot at the caudal fin base. Peritoneum silvery. Reaches 36.7 cm total length.

Biology: Flathead chubs are found in the faster waters of muddy rivers, but also backwaters, and are rare in lakes and ponds. Food includes such aquatic insects as free-swimming water boatmen and various bottom dwelling larvae, terrestrial insects such as ants, beetles and flies, and fishes. There is a record of a small mammal being eaten. Both sight and smell are used for finding food. Life span in Iowa is at least 4 years and most fish mature at age 2 and a length over 10.5 cm standard length. In the Peace River, B.C. life span is at least 10 years with maturity attained at 4 years and 18.2 cm fork length. Spawning takes place from June to August in Canada, sometimes in smaller streams, but possibly in pools. An average number of eggs was 4974 in Iowa. Egg diameters up to 1.4 mm have been reported. This chub is occasionally caught on baited hooks or artificial flies and has been used as food in British Columbia by native people.

flathead sole

Scientific name: *Hippoglossoides elassodon*
    Jordan and Gilbert, 1880
Family: **Righteye Flounder**
Other common names: cigarette paper
French name: plie à tête plate

Distribution: Found from Japan to California including British Columbia.

Characters: This species is separated from its Pacific Canadian relatives by having a large, symmetrical mouth extending back to the pupil of the eye with upper jaw teeth in 1 series, a truncate caudal fin with a pointed centre, i.e. wedge-shaped, a spine at the anal fin origin, and a very thin body. There are small pores below the lower eye. Dorsal fin rays 72–94, anal rays 55–72. Gill rakers on the lower arch 15–24. Scales in an almost straight lateral line 86–94. Eyed side

scales are ctenoid, blind side scales cycloid except on the caudal peduncle and in a band across the lateral line. Eyed side grey to olive-brown, with dusky brown blotches in some extending onto the dorsal and anal fins. Blind side white with a silvery sheen extending above the lateral line. Reaches 56 cm.

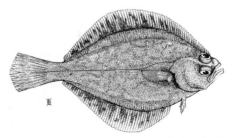

flathead sole

Biology: The flathead sole is usually found at 275–366 m in British Columbia but ranges from the surface to 1050 m. Young are found in the shallows. Food is clams, worms, crustaceans and small fish. They may mature at 1 year but usually in southern British Columbia males mature at 2 years and females at 3 years. Life span is about 12 years. Spawning is from March to April. A large female lays up to 600,000 eggs with a diameter of 3.75 mm. This is a good food fish.

flexfin dragonfish

Scientific name: *Chirostomias pliopterus*
    Regan and Trewavas, 1930
Family: **Barbeled Dragonfish**
Other common names: none
French name: dragon à nageoires ployées

Distribution: Found in the North Atlantic Ocean including from off the Scotian Shelf and southward.

Characters: This barbeled dragonfish is the only Canadian Atlantic species with an adipose fin. The anal and dorsal fin bases are about the same length, pelvic fins are low on the flank, no luminous organs (the preorbital and suborbital) before and below the eye, lower jaw not projecting or curved upwards strongly, 6 pectoral fin rays of about equal length with branched tips and luminous material on some rays, 25–28 photophores between the pectoral and pelvic fin insertions, and the bulb at the end of the barbel is a complex structure with 2–3 lobes and many fila-

flexfin dragonfish

ments. The barbel is about three-quarters of the head length. Dorsal fin rays 18–20, anal rays 22–26 and pelvic rays 7. Overall colour a velvety-black to dark brown, with green, blue or bronze iridescences. The pectoral fins are black except for yellow luminous tissue. The barbel is black or dark brown except the tip and filaments are yellowish. Reaches 20.1 cm standard length or more.

Biology: Several specimens have been caught at 100–500 m off the Scotian Shelf over deeper water.

flounders

Flounders are **flatfishes** belonging to the **Lefteye** and **Righteye Flounder** families. There are 21 species in Canada with flounder in their name and many are not closely related. Flounder is a general term for flatfishes and is apparently of Scandinavian origin.

Some flounders have an anti-freeze gene which facilitates their survival in cold waters. Canadian scientists have synthesised a gene based on that of flounders for splicing into canola or rape-seed plants. It is hoped that the plants will be able to use the gene to produce frost-resistant proteins to protect them from cold weather.

fluffy sculpin

Scientific name: *Oligocottus snyderi*
    Greeley, 1898
Family: **Sculpin**
Other common names: cirriated sculpin
French name: chabot pelucheux

Distribution: Found from Alaska to Baja California including British Columbia.

Characters: This sculpin, and its relatives the **saddleback** and **tidepool sculpins**, are distinguished from other Pacific coast species by having 3 pelvic fin rays, the branchiostegal membranes form a fold over the isthmus, the upper preopercular spine is not antler-like, scales are absent, the anal fin origin is below the end of the spiny dorsal fin and the anus is close to the anal fin. This species lacks body spines, the upper preopercular spine has 2–3 points, there is a nasal spine base cirrus, and body cirri are in groups of 3–4 including at the dorsal fin base. First dorsal fin spines 7–9, second dorsal rays 17–20, anal rays 12–15 and pectoral rays 12–15 with lower 6 finger-like. The first anal ray in males is thickened and there is almost no membrane between rays 2 and 3 or 3 and 4. Lateral line pores 36–39 with 1–2 on the tail. Cirri are found along the anterior three-quarters of the lateral line, along the dorsal fin bases from about the centre of the first to the centre of the second, on the upper midflank anteriorly, on the top of the head, at the dorsal fin spine tips, on the nasal and preopercular spines and lining the edges of the preopercle and opercle. Overall colour varies from green to reddish-brown, pink or lavender. The underside of the head is spotted white. The back has 4–6 saddles. The flank has dark circles and mottles. Fins are barred except the clear pelvics. The belly may be bluish. Attains 8.9 cm.

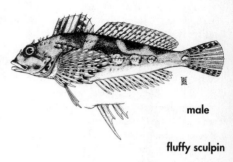

male

fluffy sculpin

Biology: Common in intertidal and subtidal zones on rocky, exposed coasts. It is found in lower pools than the **tidepool sculpin** and has less tolerance of wide temperature regimes. However, it can respire in the air for several hours. It is more secretive and favours surf-grass and coralline algae in pools. Food is crustaceans and worms. Life span is only about 1.5 years in California with a few males perhaps attaining 2 years. Life span in Canada may be longer. The male uses the prehensile, anterior section of the anal fin to clasp the female during spawning in spring or perhaps fall in northern populations.

flying gurnard

Scientific name: *Dactylopterus volitans*
    (Linnaeus, 1758)
Family: **Flying Gurnard**
Other common names: poule de mer
French name: dactyloptère

Distribution: From Argentina to Nova Scotia and also in the eastern Atlantic Ocean and Mediterranean Sea.

Characters: The fan-like pectoral fins almost reaching the tail are distinctive. The

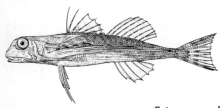

flying gurnard

first dorsal fin has 2 free spines followed by 4 spines joined together by a membrane. The second dorsal fin has 1 spine and 8 soft rays. The anal fin has 6 rays. There are 60–62 scales in lateral series. Overall colour varies with habitat but is usually yellowish-brown to orange-brown, often with blue spots on the back and pink tinges to the lower flank. The pectoral fin has bright blue to lavender spots with black edges and blue lines. Attains 50 cm standard length. The world, all-tackle angling record weighed 1.81 kg and was caught in 1986 at Panama City, Florida.

Biology: This species is a stray in Canada during warmer months with about 4 fish reported from 1973–1977. Usually found on mud and sand bottoms down to 80 m. Food is crustaceans, clams and small fishes. The pectoral fins are spread when the fish is alarmed, giving a sudden flash of colour and increase in size, which may well deter predators.

Flying Gurnard Family

Scientific name: Dactylopteridae
French name: dactyloptères

Flying gurnards are found mainly in the tropical Atlantic, Indian and Pacific oceans. There are only 7 species with 1 reported from Atlantic Canada.

The family is characterised by the extremely long pectoral fins, which almost reach the tail, and which have the inner rays separate and not joined by a membrane. They were believed to be able to fly with this fin even in Greek and Roman times, but this is now considered unlikely. The head is a blunt, bony box, covered by spines and keels. There are 2 spines ahead of the spiny dorsal fin. Pelvic fins are thoracic (under the pectoral fins) and have 1 spine and 4 soft rays. Scales are scute-like on the body and there is no lateral line. The caudal fin skeleton has 5 hypural bones, no free second ural centrum and 17 principal caudal rays.

Young flying gurnards have small pectoral fins and were once identified as distinct species. Flying gurnards may be related to the **Pipefish Family** and its relatives but are classified in the **Mail-cheeked Order**. "Gurnard" is derived from the Latin to grunt.

The pelvic fins are moved alternately to walk the fish across the sea bed. A bone behind the eye produces sound by stridulation. The large pectoral fins are used in gliding underwater and for signalling in reproductive and territorial behaviour and for confusing predators. Flying gurnards do not fly and they are not even true gurnards.

A dried specimen was washed ashore near Country Harbour, Nova Scotia in September 1939 and its rare appearance in Canada was thought to have been the result of it flying onto a steamer deck in southern waters and washing off near Nova Scotia!

See **flying gurnard**

Flyingfish Family

Scientific name: Exocoetidae
French name: exocets

Flyingfishes are found world-wide in warmer waters. There are 52 or more species with 4 reported on the Atlantic coast of Canada.

These fishes do not fly by flapping the enlarged pectoral fins but do erupt from the water surface to glide using the outstretched pectoral fins. Some species have enlarged pelvic fins also and species are called two-winged (monoplane) or four-winged (biplane) flyingfish. The caudal fin has a deep fork and the lower lobe is largest, as a propulsive aid. Jaws are equal in length. The fins lack spines. The abdominal pelvic fins have 6 soft rays. The lateral line runs along the lower edge of the body. Scales are large, cycloid and deciduous. The nostril is shaped like a pit and has a tentacle sticking out of it. Young flyingfish may have a longer lower jaw, a pair of long, flaplike, fleshy barbels and a different colour pattern from adults. Some were originally described as distinct species of fish until scientists realised they were juveniles.

Flyingfishes are related to the **Halfbeak Family** in the **Needlefish Order**. They share large scales (38–60 in the lateral line), a small mouth with small or absent teeth, and usually 8–16 dorsal and anal fin rays without finlets with the **Halfbeaks**. Flyingfishes and halfbeaks are placed in the same family by some scientists.

These are open ocean fishes which are found inshore rarely except when young. Food is crustaceans and plankton. They are attracted to lights at night. Eggs have sticky filaments and become attached to plants. Young are pelagic. Adults are common enough to be used as food in some parts of the world and sometimes as bait for such fishes as **marlins, billfishes** and **tunas**.

The gliding flight of these fishes usually skims the waves for quite long distances but some fly high enough to land on passing ships. Flights occur when the fish builds up speed just below the surface, then angles upward to break out of the water, spreading the pectoral and pelvic fins to begin gliding if the wind conditions are right. They may break out of a wave surface which helps launch them into the air. Often there is insufficient momentum and the lower lobe of the caudal fin remains in the water to help by rapid sculling at 50 beats per second. Free flights may last 13 seconds or more, and touch-and-go flights 42 seconds or more. Speeds reach

55 km/hour and cover up to 200 m. A height of 5 m or more may be reached depending on the wind conditions but usually 1 m or so is the average height. The monoplane flyingfish are more erratic flyers than the biplane ones.

See **Atlantic flyingfish**
blackwing flyingfish
fourwing flyingfish
spotfin flyingfish

Footballfish Family

Scientific name: Himantolophidae
French name: poissons-football

Footballfishes are found world-wide usually in the deep ocean of temperate to tropical waters (larvae, males and juveniles) while some species extend into subarctic and subantarctic waters (large expatriate females). There are 18 species with 2 recorded from the Atlantic coast of Canada.

These are deepsea anglerfishes characterised by the females being globular (hence the name footballfish), by having bony plates, each with a median spine, embedded in the skin, and by having the snout and chin with a dense covering of papillae. The illicium or fishing rod is short and stout and the esca or bait is large, bulbous and has numerous filaments. The body muscles are soft and the bones spongy. The parietal bones are absent, unique among Canadian anglerfishes. Adult males are not parasites on the females as in some anglerfishes, but are dwarfed, reaching 39 mm standard length, compared to 465 mm standard length of females. Males are thought to locate females by the species-specific pheromones that females emit. The males have well-developed nostrils and their jaws are small.

Footballfishes are related to the **Fanfin**, **Seadevil**, **Whipnose**, **Leftvent**, **Dreamer**, **Wolftrap** and **Werewolf** families, which all lack pelvic fins, scales and a pseudobranch, have bones at the front of the head (frontals) which are not united, have the lower pharyngeal bones reduced and toothless, and have 8–9 caudal fin rays. They are members of the **Anglerfish Order**.

Adult footballfishes are found down to 1800 m or more, but also as shallow as 50 m and they are occasionally washed ashore.

Larvae are found mainly in the upper 50 m of the ocean. Food is attracted by light emitted by the esca and by movements of the filaments. The prey is sucked into the mouth when it is close enough. The snout and chin papillae may serve to provide a poor surface for the attachment of suction discs when a struggling squid is caught.

Footballfish may eject a luminous cloud of mucus from the esca to confuse predators attempting to eat them.

See **lightlamp footballfish**
    Maul's footballfish

forefour dreamtail

Scientific name: *Oneirodes schmidti*
    (Regan and Trewavas, 1932)
Family: **Dreamer**
Other common names: none
French name: queue-de-rêve quatravant

Distribution: Probably found in all oceans including off the Atlantic coast of Canada.

Characters: This species of deepsea **anglerfish** is part of a group of dreamers including the **cosmopolitan** and the **westnorat dreamtails**. The females of this group are distinguished by having sphenotic spines, a deeply notched operculum posteriorly, a short and broad pectoral fin lobe, the tip of the lower jaw with a spine, the illicium or

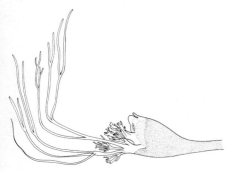

esca of forefour dreamtail

fishing rod emerging from between the frontal bones on the head, the dorsal edge of these bones being strongly curved, usually 4 anal fin rays and the caudal fin not covered by skin beyond the base. Females of this species are distinguished from their Atlantic

relatives by having an esca or bait with 2 pairs of anterolateral appendages. There are 60 upper jaw and 76 lower jaw teeth. The vomer bone in the roof of the mouth has 6 teeth. Females are black with parts of the esca unpigmented. Females reach 4.5 cm.

Biology: One specimen was caught off Newfoundland in 1968. Known from very few specimens world-wide. Females attract prey using the fishing apparatus.

forgotten argentine

Scientific name: *Nansenia oblita*
    (Facciolà, 1887)
Family: **Pencilsmelt**
Other common names: none
French name: argentine oubliée

Distribution: Found off Atlantic Canada and in the eastern North Atlantic Ocean and Mediterranean Sea.

Characters: This species is separated from the **bluethroat** and **large-eyed argentine** by having 4 branchiostegal rays. There are

forgotten argentine

28–30 gill rakers. Dorsal fin rays 10–11 and anal fin rays 9–10. The overall colour is silvery with some pigment on the caudal fin base. Reaches 18 cm.

Biology: Three larval specimens identified as this species were taken south of the Grand Bank in 1979 at 300–500 m.

forkbarbelthroat

Scientific name: *Linophryne lucifer*
    Collett, 1886
Family: **Leftvent**
Other common names: forkbarbel netdevil
French name: gorge à barbe fourchue

Distribution: Found in the Atlantic and Indian oceans including off Newfoundland.

Characters: Females of this species of deepsea **anglerfish** are distinguished from Canadian relatives by having a barbel not divided at the base but its tip divided into a pair of compressed branches with a pair of short branches before these. The esca has 1–8 short filaments at the tip. Males have

forkbarbelthroat

sharp sphenotic spines. Females are brown to black overall with lighter areas on the esca. Females reach 23.0 cm with parasitic males reaching 2.9 cm.

Biology: Known from 3 specimens off Newfoundland and near the Flemish Cap with only 12 female specimens reported world-wide up to 1982. The 3 Canadian fish are a significant part of our knowledge of this species. Females attract prey using the fishing apparatus.

fourbarbelthroat

Scientific name: *Linophryne algibarbata*
    Waterman, 1939
Family: **Leftvent**
Other common names: fourbarbel netdevil
French name: gorge à quatre barbes

fourbarbelthroat

Distribution: Found in the northwest Atlantic Ocean including off Newfoundland.

Characters: Females of this species of deepsea **anglerfish** are distinguished by having a barbel branched at the base into four main arms. These arms bear additional filaments each with a photophore at the tip. The esca or bait is a globular bulb without appendages or filaments. Males have sharp sphenotic spines. Overall colour of females brown to brown-black, some without pigment on the caudal fin. The esca is partly unpigmented. Females reach 23.1 cm total length with attached males at 4.1 cm total length.

Biology: Known from several specimens in Canadian waters off Newfoundland. Females use the fishing apparatus to entice prey within reach of the mouth.

fourbeard rockling

Scientific name: *Enchelyopus cimbrius*
    (Linnaeus, 1766)
Family: **Cod**
Other common names: none
French name: motelle à quatre barbillons

Distribution: Found from the Strait of Belle Isle throughout Atlantic Canada and south to the Gulf of Mexico. Also in southwestern Greenland, Iceland, northwestern Europe and Mauritania.

Characters: This species is separated from its Atlantic coast relatives by having 2 dorsal and 1 anal fins, an elongate first ray in the

fourbeard rockling

first dorsal fin, the remaining first dorsal rays very short and in a groove, and 3 barbels on the snout. The upper jaw has 6–8 large teeth anteriorly. First dorsal fin with 1 long ray and about 50 short, hair-like rays, second dorsal fin with 37–55 rays. Anal rays 36–49 and pectoral rays 15–19. Gill rakers 5–13. The back is sandy-brown, yellow-olive or light yellow-brown fading to a white belly with brown spots. The second dorsal fin and flanks may have a series of large spots. The first dorsal fin ray is black. The posterior second dorsal and anal fin bases and the lower lobe of the caudal fin have a black blotch. The pectoral fins are blackish. The mouth is dark purple or bluish. Reaches 41 cm.

Biology: This rockling is found on mud, sand or gravel bottoms occasionally at extreme low tides but usually at 50–550 m. It burrows head first in the bottom during the day in Newfoundland but may rest on the bottom at night, propped up by its pectoral fins and with the barbels pointing forwards. There may be some movement out of shallower water when winter approaches. Food is crustaceans, worms and molluscs, occasionally fish fry. Food is taken by vigorously disturbing the bottom mud and gulping in mud or small organisms displaced by the digging. It is eaten by **Atlantic cod** and **white hake**. Most fish in a Newfoundland study at Bonavista Bay were 2–3 years old. Life span is 9 years. Spawning extends from May to October, peaking at a water temperature of 9–10°C. Eggs are released preferentially at high tides. Eggs are pelagic, transparent, 1.0 mm in diameter and number up to about 45,000. Fry settle to the bottom at a length of about 4.5 cm.

fourhorn poacher

Scientific name: *Hypsagonus quadricornis* (Cuvier, 1829)
Family: **Poacher**
Other common names: none
French name: agone à quatre cornes

Distribution: From the Sea of Okhotsk and the Bering Sea to British Columbia and Washington.

Characters: This species is distinguished from the related **kelp poacher** by having 12–14 pectoral fin rays with the lower 6–10 rays obviously finger-like, a smooth or slightly prickly leading edge to the first dorsal fin base and the dorso-lateral row of plates with tubercles not spines. There are no prickles on the belly and the spine on the bony rim of the eye does not have a prickly tip. The first dorsal spine is rough on its anterior margin. Gill membranes are not joined to the isthmus. First dorsal fin spines are 9–11, second dorsal fin

soft rays 5–7. Anal fin rays 9–11. The lower lobe of the caudal is larger than the upper lobe. The eye protrudes above the top margin of the head. The head bears large spines and there is a single large cirrus on the snout. There is a single cirrus at the rear of the upper jaw. Overall colour is brown to reddish-brown with yellow, carmine and brown blotching. Paler below but spotted on the belly and breast. The snout cirrus is barred. Broad dark bars are present on the flanks and thinner bars on the pectoral and anal fins. The caudal fin has a dark rear edge. Reaches 10.5 cm.

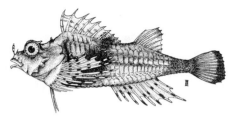

fourhorn poacher

Biology: Found on stone and pebble bottoms at 49–223 m and temperatures as low as −1.2°C. Its appearance is often hidden by a growth of hydroids, a colonial attached invertebrate which has a featherlike or plumose form and may be mistaken for a fungal infection.

fourhorn sculpin

Scientific name: *Myoxocephalus quadricornis* (Linnaeus, 1758)
Family: **Sculpin**
Other common names: four-spined sculpin, four-horned sea scorpion, kanayuk
French name: chaboisseau à quatre cornes

Distribution: Found across the Canadian Arctic north to Ellesmere Island and south into James Bay and to Hebron Fjord, Labrador. Also in Greenland and northern Eurasia.

Characters: This species and its Arctic-Atlantic relatives are distinguished from other sculpins by the upper preopercular spine being a simple straight point, the vomer bone in the roof of the mouth bears teeth but palatine teeth are absent, there are no oblique folds on the lower flank, and the lateral line lacks plates. It is separated from its relatives by having 4 preopercular spines (2 pointing forward and 2 backward), and 4 blunt, rough edged spines on top of the head,

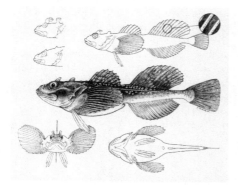

fourhorn sculpin

2 between the eyes and 2 further back. First dorsal fin spines 6–10, second dorsal rays 13–17. Anal fin rays 13–17, and pectoral rays 14–18. There is a row of rough scales from below the first dorsal fin origin to the caudal fin and a second row below the second dorsal fin and sometimes below the first dorsal fin. The colour is dark brown to grey on the back, the flanks are brassy to golden brown and the belly is white. There are 4–7 saddles. The pectoral fins have up to 3 bands. Males develop a rosy colour under the head, on the lower pectoral fin and on the anal and pelvic fins. The second dorsal fin and pelvic fins are larger in mature males and males have tubercles on the second dorsal and pectoral fins. Reaches 36.5 cm.

Biology: This sculpin is found in shallow, coastal areas usually near or in estuaries and seldom below 20 m. However it avoids the spring freshet of the Mackenzie River and moves offshore. Overwintering occurs in bays and inlets and possibly offshore. It may enter rivers for some distance, up to 200 km in the Mackenzie River. It is found at temperatures less than 0°C and up to 9°C. There are isolated populations in Arctic lakes which are not distinct enough to be named as a separated species (see **deepwater sculpin**).

Food consists of crustaceans, molluscs and small fishes. It is a major predator on eggs of other fishes and on its own eggs.

Life span is 14 years. Females grow faster, live longer and are larger than males. Spawning occurs from late fall to winter and as late as spring and it may occur under ice. Timing varies with temperature, salinity and locality. The eggs are up to 2.9 mm in diameter, number up to 6150 and can be green, brown-green or brown. A nest is excavated in mud or algae and adhesive clumps of eggs are laid. The male guards the eggs. Larvae are pelagic and abundant in May to June in shallow, pelagic areas.

This sculpin is said to have been used as food along the shores of Hudson Bay. Populations of the fourhorn sculpin in fresh waters and euryhaline lakes of the Arctic Archipelago are vulnerable and that of Garrow Lake, Cornwallis Island is in danger of extirpation or already lost because of lead-zinc mining waste.

fourline snakeblenny

Scientific name: *Eumesogrammus praecisus* (Krøyer, 1837)
Family: **Shanny**
Other common names: snakeblenny, Atlantic fourline
French name: quatre-lignes atlantique

Distribution: Found from the Sea of Okhotsk and Bering Sea into the Beaufort Sea, Coronation Gulf, Hudson Bay, Baffin Island and south to the Gulf of St. Lawrence, i.e. the Arctic and Atlantic coasts of Canada.

Characters: The relatively deep, compressed body and 4 lateral lines (1 above and 2 below complete midflank lateral line) distin-

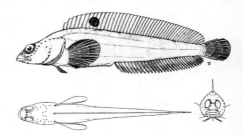

fourline snakeblenny

guish this species form other Arctic-Atlantic shannies and from the related **Arctic** and **radiated shannies**. The dorsal fin has 47–49 spines, the anal fin 1–2 spines and 33–35 soft rays with the last 3 rays spine-like. The large pectoral fins have 16–19 rays. Overall body colour brown to grey, lighter below, with vague broad bars on the flanks. There are 3 dusky bars across the cheek. A large black spot with white margins is on the anterior part of the dorsal fin between spines 8–11, sometimes with a similar smaller spot in front of it. The anal, caudal and pectoral fins are dark with a white margin. Attains 22 cm.

Biology: A poorly known species found over mud and rock at depths of 18–33 m in Labrador for example, but they have been taken from the tidal zone down to 400 m. Water temperatures may be as low as −1.34°C. Food is probably crustaceans and other small bottom organisms. Spawning may occur in late summer in the Arctic.

fourspine stickleback

Scientific name: *Apeltes quadracus*
  (Mitchill, 1815)
Family: **Stickleback**
Other common names: pinfish, mud-perch,
  mud-pouch, bloody stickleback
French name: épinoche à quatre épines

Distribution: Found from the Gulf of St. Lawrence including the Strait of Belle Isle and southern and western Newfoundland south to Virginia. Also introduced to Thunder Bay, Lake Superior, probably in a ship's bilge.

Characters: This species is distinguished by usually having 4–5 (range 1–7) dorsal fin spines angled alternately left and right, and no obvious flank plates. The first and second dorsal fin spines and the pelvic spines are

fourspine stickleback

much longer than the eye diameter. Soft dorsal rays 9–13 and anal fin with 1 spine and 7–10 soft rays. Pelvic fins with 1 spine and 2

soft rays and pectoral fin with 11–12 rays. The back is olive-green to brown, flanks are darkly mottled and the belly is silvery-white. The eye is brown. Spawning males are black with bright, crimson red pelvic fins. Female pelvic fins are orange. Reaches 6.6 cm.

Biology: This is a coastal marine and estuarial brackish water species with some populations rarely in fresh water. It is usually found in vegetated areas with little wave or tidal action.

Food is plankton, aquatic insects, crustaceans, clams, snails, fish eggs, worms, and plant material. Spine number and length varies with the presence of predators, vegetation and other environmental factors, and other **stickleback** species.

Life span is just over 2 years and maturity is attained at 1 year. Many adults die after spawning the year after birth. Spawning occurs from May to August in vegetated, intertidal areas. Some nests are exposed to the air at low tides. The male builds a basket- or cup-shaped nest from selected plant fragments on or between plant stems. Fragments are held together by glue-like kidney secretions. This takes 2–4 hours and the nest is 1–2 cm in diameter.

Males court a female by swimming rapidly in circles around her or in front of her. The courtship involves halting and erecting the red pelvic fins, prodding the side of the female and spiralling around her. A female ready to spawn adopts a head-up attitude and swims towards the male and under his erect pelvic fins which serve as a fixation point. The male leads her to the nest, nudges the nest perhaps to indicate its position and she pushes into it through the upper rim. Once positioned in the nest in a head up position, the female is gently seized by the male on her caudal fin or peduncle and the male quivers for about 1 second. She then deposits eggs in adhesive clusters of about 15–50 at 3–4 day intervals. The eggs are amber and up to 2.2 mm in diameter. The male picks up egg masses which are not deposited accurately and places them in the nest. The male fertilises the eggs by creeping through the nest and roofs over the nest. The female is chased away.

Freshwater populations on the Québec north shore have a very low fecundity with only 10–19 maturing eggs in fish in the second year of life and in the rare females in their third year 39–54 eggs. At a brackish Isle Verte, Québec locality fecundity was 16–60 eggs. A hole in the side of the nest enables the male to insert his snout and suck water over the eggs to aerate them at intervals of 10–30 seconds. This is known as opercular pumping and a male spends half his time in aerating. As many as 4 nests are constructed in a vertical array (apartments) and are defended against predators. Nests may also be scattered throughout the male's territory.

This is the only **stickleback** species to defend more than 1 nest at a time. Intruders are met with a head-down display at 20–30° with the horizontal and the red pelvic fins conspicuously extended. The male will attack the intruder by ramming, nipping and chasing. Multi-layer nesting and air exposure are thought to be a method of confusing egg predators.

fourspot flounder

Scientific name: *Paralichthys oblongus*
　　(Mitchill, 1815)
Family: **Lefteye Flounder**
Other common names: none
French name: cardeau à quatre ocelles

Distribution: Found from Nova Scotia to Florida.

Characters: This species is identified among its Canadian Atlantic relatives by the pelvic fin bases being short and not on the

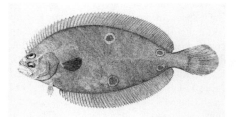

fourspot flounder

midline of the belly, 4 large ocelli (or eye spots), 9–13 gill rakers and large eyes. Dorsal fin rays 71–86, anal rays 58–76, eyed

side pectoral rays 10–12, and lateral line scales about 95. Lower arm gill rakers 7–10. Eyes are very large and almost touch. The 4 ocelli or eyespots comprise 2 on either side of the midflank and 2 near the caudal peduncle. Attains 40.6 cm.

Biology: Occasionally caught in the Bay of Fundy and on the Scotian Shelf in summer. Northern populations are in shallower water (down to 27 m off Massachusetts) than southern ones (deeper than 274 m in Florida) although in Nova Scotia they are known down to 311 m. Shrimps and fish, such as **silver hake**, are important food items. Various other crustaceans like crabs are also taken along with molluscs and squids. Spawning occurs from late spring to fall and perhaps as late as December. Eggs float and are up to 1.1 mm in diameter.

fourtoplamps

Scientific name: *Notolychnus valdiviae*
　　(Brauer, 1904)
Family: **Lanternfish**
Other common names: none
French name: quatre-lampes-hautes

Distribution: Found in all warmer seas world-wide including off Atlantic Canada.

Characters: This species is separated from its Atlantic Canadian relatives by having soft, flexible rays at the caudal fin bases

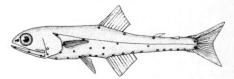

fourtoplamps

without luminous tissue, the AO photophores in 2 rows, a distinct Pol photophore and 3 photophores above the lateral line close to the back. These photophores can be rubbed off during capture and the species may then be identified by the protuberance on top of the head and by fin and gill raker counts. A luminous gland on top of the caudal peduncle is larger in males than females. Dorsal fin rays 10–12, usually 11, anal rays 12–14, usually 13, pectoral rays 11–13, and pelvic rays uniquely 6. Gill rakers 10–11. Reaches only 2.5 cm, a small species.

Biology: Rare in Canadian waters but common to abundant in temperate waters to the south. First reported from the LaHave Bank in 1969. Found off Bermuda at 400–700 m by day and 50–350 m at night. Young fish migrate but adults can be migratory or not, or only partially migratory. There is a spawning peak in spring or early summer and fish are mature at 19–24 mm. Females grow larger than males.

fourwing flyingfish

Scientific name: *Hirundichthys affinis* (Günther, 1866)
Family: **Flyingfish**
Other common names: exocet hirondelle
French name: exocet à frange blanche

Distribution: Found from Nova Scotia to Brazil and elsewhere in the tropical Atlantic Ocean.

Characters: This species is distinguished by the dorsal and anal fin ray counts being about equal within 1–2 rays, and by pectoral

fourwing flyingfish

fin colour pattern. Dorsal fin rays 11–12, usually 11, anal fin rays 11–13, usually 11–12. The second pectoral fin ray is branched and rays number 16–18. The young lack barbels. The back and upper flanks are dark, iridescent blue or green, and the lower flanks and belly silvery white. The dorsal fin is clear, except in young where there is a dark area near the edge. The pectoral fin is dusky and has a transparent area near midfin. Reaches 30 cm.

Biology: Only 2 specimens recorded, 1 off Sambro, Nova Scotia, in 1974 at the northern range limit and 1 off Sable Island Bank in 1976. Ripe females have been caught in midwinter in tropical areas and

have eggs 1.5–1.6 mm in diameter with 8–14 long filaments. This flyingfish is caught by handlines or gill nets in Barbados and is sold fresh.

freshwater drum

Scientific name: *Aplodinotus grunniens* Rafinesque, 1819
Family: **Drum**
Other common names: sheepshead, silver bass, grunter, Red River bass, thunderpumper, white perch, goo, gray perch, lake drum, river drum, jewel-head, bubbler, grinder, crocus, gaspergou
French name: malachigan

Distribution: Found from Hudson Bay south to Guatemala, but not in Atlantic coast drainages south of the St. Lawrence River basin. This is the greatest range in latitude of any North American freshwater fish. In Canada from the upper St. Lawrence River basin, Ottawa River, at Abitibi in the James Bay drainage, in the Great Lakes except for Lake Superior, in Manitoba to Hudson Bay and in southwestern Saskatchewan.

Characters: This is the only freshwater species of this family in Canada. The massive second anal fin spine and lateral line running to the end of the tail are diagnostic. The first dorsal fin has 8–10 spines, the second dorsal fin with 1 spine and 24–33 soft rays. The anal fin has 2 spines and 7–8 branched rays. The lateral line to the tail base has 48–53 scales.

The back is dark green to olive-brown, bronze or silvery-bluish. Flanks are silvery

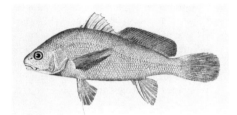

freshwater drum

and the belly white. Fins are dusky except for white to cream or orange-tinged pelvics and clear pectorals.

"Gaspergou" or casburgot from "casser" (to break) and "burgeau" (a kind of shellfish) is a Cajun word. Reaches 1.2 m and 27.7 kg. The world, all-tackle angling record weighed 24.72 kg and was caught in 1972 at Nickajack Lake, Tennessee. The Canadian angling record from the French River, Ontario was caught by Arron Mohr in 1991 and weighed 9.35 kg.

Biology: The favoured habitat of this species is large and shallow waters including both lakes and rivers. Both clear and turbid water is occupied. Freshwater drums retire to deeper waters in winter and in summer are found at less than 10 m in Lake Erie for example.

Food is fish, crayfish and molluscs. River populations are said to favour clams and snails, which are crushed by the throat teeth, but molluscs are not as significant a part of the diet as might be expected from the specialised throat teeth. However, the exotic zebra mussels are eaten by drums which may help control this pest. The young eat crustaceans and aquatic insects.

Females attain larger sizes than males and grow faster after the first 5 years. Males can be mature at 2 years and all are mature at 6. Females mature 1 year later than males. Most drums in Lake Erie are 3–8 years old but they live at least 17 years. Spawning occurs in July and September in southern Canada but comparatively little is known about it. It may take place over sand or mud in shallows or in open water far from shore. Courtship is accompanied by the drumming sounds of the males. Up to 686,000 eggs of 1.7 mm diameter are found in each female. Eggs float to the surface, an unusual feature in freshwater Canadian fishes.

An angler catch of 129,327 drums was made in Ontario waters of Lake Erie from June to August 1978. It is also a commercially important species and is marketed as "white perch." Over half a million kg have been caught annually from Lake Erie in Canadian waters.

- Most accessible May through September.
- The Great Lakes and the St. Lawrence River watershed.

- Medium action spinning and baitcasting outfits used with eight- to 14–pound test lines.
- A variety of 1/4– to 3/8–ounce spinners, wobbling spoons, deep-diving crankbaits, minnow-type baits and jigs and worms, **minnows** and crayfish fished on the bottom.

Freshwater Eel Family

Scientific name: Anguillidae
French name: anguilles d'eau douce

Freshwater eels are found world-wide in temperate to tropical waters except for the south Atlantic Ocean and the whole eastern Pacific Ocean. There are 16 species with 1 or 2 occurring in Atlantic Canada.

The term eel-like is based on the body shape of freshwater eels and includes the muscular slipperiness associated with this fish and its mucus-producing skin. Both dorsal and anal fins are long and join the tail fin. The dorsal fin begins well behind the pectoral fin level. There are no pelvic fins and the pectorals, when present, are on midflank. Scales are absent or when present small, embedded and cycloid. There is a lateral line. Jaws are strong and toothed. The gill openings are small and just in front of the pectoral fins. The anterior nostril is tubular.

The **Freshwater Eel Family** is related to other members of the **Eel Order**.

The life cycle of eels was unknown until Johannes Schmidt published his 1922 study based on years of collecting. Where the adults went on their seaward migration and where the elvers ascending rivers came from were a mystery. These eels are catadromous, living in fresh water but migrating to the sea to spawn and die. In the North Atlantic Ocean spawning occurs in the Sargasso Sea. The young eels or leptocephali (= thin head larvae) are distinctive being transparent and leaf-like. A newspaper can be read through the body of a leptocephalus. In this form they drift to the shores of America and Europe, transform into elvers with the more familiar eel-shape and move into rivers and lakes to feed and grow.

Some scientists believe that the European

eel is not a distinct species but merely **American eels** which develop in cooler areas of the Sargasso Sea and are carried by different ocean currents to the shores of Europe. Differences between the American and European eels overlap and include such characters as vertebral number which is known to vary with development temperature. Larval European eels (*Anguilla anguilla* (Linnaeus, 1758)) have been reported southeast of Halifax, Nova Scotia below 175 m and south of the Grand Bank. If European eels are a distinct species their presence is rare in Canadian waters. Recent studies using mitochondrial DNA showed no genetic divergence among samples of **American eels** along 4000 km of North American coastline reflecting a single spawning population. However European eels had a distinct mt DNA genotype and the conclusion to be drawn is that American and European eels have separate spawning sites such that larval dispersal ends up on different continents. The mt DNA differences are marked but do not prove species distinction as this level of distinction is known to occur among fishes which are a single species (though some authorities would argue that these "single" species are themselves complexes of two or more species). However Icelandic eels seem to be hybrids between the two putative species. All other evidence (vertebral and other counts, body proportions, biology, electrophoresis) suggests that the American and European eels are the same species but have different spawning sites. Only the **American eel** is treated here.

The biology of eels is based almost entirely on the freshwater phase of their life. Adults in fresh water develop large eyes, the gut degenerates and coloration changes in preparation for the migration to the Sargasso Sea. Adults were only caught in the deep ocean, at nearly 2000 m near the Bahamas, in 1977. The Sargasso spawning ground is deduced from collections of larvae across the Atlantic Ocean — the smallest and youngest larvae are found around the Sargasso Sea. The spawning grounds are at about 400 m, at a 17°C temperature and in saltier water than usual sea conditions according to some authors but since spawning adults have never been caught this remains dubious.

The theory advanced by D.W. Tucker in 1959 maintained that European eels lack the energy resources in their migratory, spawning phase to reach the Sargasso Sea 7000 km from Europe. They are presumed to be following an instinct to head out to sea, dating from an earlier geological age when the Atlantic Ocean was narrower before the separation caused by Continental Drift. All European eels die at sea and Europe is restocked by larvae drifting there spawned from American parents. The American populations are closer to the Sargasso and can make the journey easily. Differences between American and European eels are merely the consequence of different environmental regimes in different parts of the Sargasso. This theory has not found general acceptance but, if true, means that all European eels can be harvested for food without depleting stocks. Eels are valued as food, particularly in Europe and Japan, but are not used as extensively in North America.

See **American eel**

fringed filefish

Scientific name: *Monacanthus ciliatus*
  (Mitchill, 1818)
Family: **Filefish**
Other common names: bourse émeri
French name: lime frangée

Distribution: North and South Atlantic oceans, including Atlantic Canada.

Characters: Dorsal fin rays 29–37, anal fin rays 28–36. The gill slit is nearly vertical. The presence of an obvious spine at the pelvic fin position and 2–4 pairs of enlarged spines on each side of the caudal peduncle distinguish this filefish from other Canadian species. The dorsal spine is strong and well-barbed. The belly is distended and a dewlap is developed. The snout profile is concave. Males have 2–3 recurved scutes on the caudal peduncle. Tan, brown, olive-grey or greenish with broad black stripes along the body. General body colour changes to match the surroundings. The caudal fin has 2 black bars, the second at the edge of the fin. The dewlap is black at the base and golden yellow at the margin in males. The dorsal and anal fins are pinkish. Attains 20 cm.

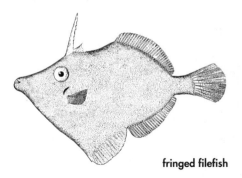

fringed filefish

Biology: Strays from southern and warmer waters are caught in late summer in Canada, as far north as off Argentia, Newfoundland. Common in seagrass beds and often rests head downwards. Food when young is planktonic crustaceans, switching to seagrass and associated crustaceans and worms with growth. About half the diet is seagrass.

fringed flounder

Scientific name: *Etropus crossotus*
    Jordan and Gilbert, 1882
Family: **Lefteye Flounder**
Other common names: none
French name: cardeau frangé

Distribution: Found from Nova Scotia south to Brazil.

Characters: This species is distinguished from other Canadian Atlantic adult **lefteye**

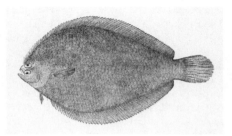

fringed flounder

flounders by having both pelvic fin bases short and the eyed side base on the belly midline, the lateral line is not strongly arched over the eyed side pectoral fin, no caudal fin spots, jaws extending back to the anterior edge of the lower eye and body scales without small secondary scales. Dorsal fin rays 73–87, anal rays 55–68, eyed side pectoral rays 8–10, and lateral line scales 38–48. Lower arm gill rakers 6–9, usually 7–8. Scales are ctenoid on the eyed side and cycloid on the blind side. There are no scales on the snout. Larvae have 2 elongate, dorsal fin rays known as tentacles. Eyed side dark brown to olive-brown. Usually only dorsal, anal, pectoral and pelvic fins with dark spots and blotches but may be blotched or with a dark spot on the caudal peduncle. The caudal fin may have a black margin in large fish. Reaches 16.9 cm.

Biology: Known only from a stray larval specimen caught on Georges Bank in 1982. Adults occur only as far north as Chesapeake Bay at depths of 6–64 m but usually in shallow water and often in brackish water. Found on mud, sand and shell-silt bottoms feeding on worms and crustaceans, including some items found off the sea floor like arrow worms. Females mature at about 8.9 cm, males at about 9.1 cm. Females produce about 155,000 eggs in March-June along the U.S. east coast. This species is used for cat food and fish meal in the U.S.A.

fringed sculpin

Scientific name: *Icelinus fimbriatus*
    Gilbert, 1890
Family: **Sculpin**
Other common names: none
French name: icéline à grandes yeux

Distribution: Found from northern British Columbia to California.

Characters: The 5 Pacific coast members of the genus *Icelinus* are characterised by having 25 or more lateral line scales or pores, 2 pelvic fin soft rays, scales in 2 rows close to the dorsal fins and an antler-like preopercular spine. This species is separated from its relatives by the upper scale row extending onto the caudal peduncle and 2 pores on the chin. The pelvic fin is short, extending up to one third of the distance to the anal fin. The nasal spines have long, fringed cirri at their base. There are 2 low spines and 2–3 bony ridges behind the eye on top of the head. First dorsal fin spines

10–11, second dorsal soft rays 15–17. Anal rays 12–13 and pectoral rays 16–18. Lateral line scales 36–37. There are 1–8 cirri at the end of the upper jaw, with larger specimens having the most. There are 1–3 cirri between

fringed sculpin

the pectoral fin base and lateral line. The eye-ball has 0–5 cirri. The body is a pale olive-brown to grey with yellowish-green spots and reticulations. The back has 3–5 saddles. The belly is silvery-white. The dorsal, caudal and pectoral fins have brown bars on a yellowish-green background. Reaches 19 cm.

Biology: This is a rare sculpin found in the depth range 30–265 m on soft bottoms.

Frogfish Family

Scientific name: Antennariidae
French name: antennaires

Frogfishes, anglerfishes or toadfishes are found world-wide in warmer waters. There are about 43 species with 2 reported from Atlantic Canada.

These are small, globe-shaped members of the **Anglerfish Order** with stalked pectoral fins used for grasping objects. The gill opening is a small pore below the pectoral fin. The mouth is large and oblique with numerous small teeth in bands. The fishing apparatus arises on the snout and is derived from the first dorsal spine. The second and third spines are also separate but are usually obscured by skin. The skin is covered with prickles, denticles, flaps or warts, or it may be naked. Flaps serve to camouflage the fish as does colour. This provides both protection against predators and conceals the frogfish from food items it attempts to lure with its fishing apparatus. A pseudobranch is present.

Some frogfish can swallow air into the stomach to increase their size and deter predators. They live mostly on the seabed but some clamber among floating *Sargassum* weed using the pectoral fins. They are very fast movers when striking a prey item. By expanding the mouth cavity they create a suction effect which swallows prey in less than 0.004 of a second. The females lay eggs in a large, gelatinous, floating mass. They are sought after by the aquarium trade.

See **ocellated frogfish**
   sargassumfish

fur-bearing trout

The cold waters of Canada harbour that unusual fish, the fur-bearing trout or furfish — or so the taxidermists would have us believe. It is characterised by a layer of usu-ally white fur enveloping the body with head and fins protruding. This tribute to the taxi-dermist's art can still occasionally be found and some are sold to travellers from warmer climes. The three-eyed **haddock** of the Maritimes is a distant relative.

G

Gar Family

Scientific name: Lepisosteidae
French name: lépisostés

Gars are found in fresh waters of North and Central America and Cuba, sometimes entering brackish water and rarely the sea. There are 7 species with 2 in Canada.

Gars have elongate jaws ("gar" is Old English for spear) filled with needle-like teeth. The ganoid scales are heavy, peg and groove hinged, non-overlapping, rhombic and plate-like, forming an effective armour. The tail is abbreviate heterocercal, externally appearing symmetrical but heterocercal internally. An upper tail lobe disappears with growth. There are 3 branchiostegal rays. The swimbladder has a rich blood supply enabling the fish to breathe air through a connection to the gut. A school of gars will break the water surface to breathe air at the same time and reduce the chances of attack by predators. Vertebrae are peculiar in having an opisthocoelous shape — anterior end convex, posterior end concave, a kind of ball and socket joint — which is almost unique in fishes and more usually associated with amphibians and reptiles. Dorsal and anal fins are near the tail. They lack spines but have fulcra (angled scales) on their anterior edge. The alligator gar of the southern U.S.A. and central America is the largest species at 3 m and over 158 kg.

These fishes are members of the **Gar Order** and are grouped along with the **bowfin** as a primitive group of fishes. Cretaceous and Eocene fossil gars are known from North America, Europe, India and West Africa. Fossil gars have been reported from Ellesmere Island in the Canadian Arctic Archipelago, well north of their modern distribution. An Upper Cretaceous coprolite (fossil faecal matter) from Alberta contained remains of gar scales and vertebrae. The gar was probably eaten by a crocodile, an indication of the different faunas that gar species have lived with in Canada.

Gars favour shallow, weedy areas of lakes and rivers. They are ambush predators,

lying still or quietly stalking prey until it can be seized by a sudden rush. Their food is almost entirely fishes. They make excellent subjects for home aquaria when young and for public aquaria when large. Gars are not sought after by anglers since they are hard to hook in their elongate, bony jaws, but a few enthusiasts specialise in their capture. They are not a commercial fishery item. Gar scales and skins are occasionally made into jewellery, picture frames, purses and boxes. The scales can be highly polished.

See **longnose gar**
    spotted gar

Gar Order

This order, the Semionotiformes (formerly Lepisosteiformes), contains only a single family, the **Gar Family**. There are 7 living species, with 2 being found in Canada. Some characters are considered under the family account, including the archaic ganoid scales which have a chemical composition different from the usual fish scales. Others include a rudimentary spiral valve, absence of the gular and interopercle bones, 2 or more supratemporal bones, no supramaxilla or myodome, a paired vomer and other skeletal characters. Gars are usually classified with the **bowfin**, but this is not a natural, related group. Both represent a particular stage or level of evolution, the lower bony fishes, or Holostei, between more "primitive" and more "advanced" fishes. Gars are more advanced than **sturgeons** but more primitive than the **bowfin** and higher bony fishes. Their long history has led them to be regarded as "living fossils."

See **Gar Family**

garnet lanternfish

Scientific name: *Stenobrachius nannochir* (Gilbert, 1890)
Family: **Lanternfish**
Other common names: none
French name: lanterne grenat

Distribution: Found across the North Pacific Ocean from the Okhotsk Sea to off

British Columbia and south to California. Also at Ocean Station Papa (50°N, 145°W).

Characters: This species is related to the northern lanternfish and they are distinguished from other Pacific lanternfishes by having 3–5 Prc in an evenly spaced curve, caudal luminous glands divided into platelets

garnet lanternfish

or scales often appearing joined, the fourth PO photophore is greatly elevated, the first 3 of 3–5 VO photophores are not in an ascending, straight line, there are no luminous, small scales at the dorsal and anal fin ray bases, 1 Pol photophore, luminous caudal glands in both sexes, and the SAO series is straight or only slightly angled. The two related species are separated by the garnet lanternfish having 2–4 scales in the supracaudal gland, 5–6 in the infracaudal, a darker body colour, black fins and red photophores. Dorsal fin rays 13–14, anal rays 14–16, pectoral rays 8–10, total vertebrae 36–39. Total gill rakers 17–20, including rudiments 21–25, and AO photophores 13–15. Lateral line scales 37–38. Attains 11 cm.

Biology: This species has been captured at about 500–2900 m off British Columbia and was first reported in Canada in 1975. It occurs generally in deeper water than its relative.

gaspereau

Scientific name: *Alosa pseudoharengus*
   (Wilson, 1811)
Family: **Herring**
Other common names: alewife, mulhaden,
   sawbelly, spreau, kyack, grey herring,
   glut herring, branch herring, spring herring,
   golden shad, river herring
French name: gaspareau

Distribution: Found from the Gulf of St. Lawrence and northeastern Newfoundland to South Carolina in the sea and tributary rivers. Also in the Great Lakes and tribu-

taries having entered the higher lakes via canal systems.

Characters: This herring is distinguished from its Canadian Atlantic coast relatives by the dorsal fin origin not being far forward of the pelvic fins, no enlarged scales before the dorsal fin on the back, back grey-green, branched pelvic rays 8, the belly has a sharp, saw-tooth edge, there are no teeth on the roof of the mouth, lower limb gill rakers 38–46, lower jaw projecting and not fitting into the upper jaw notch, silvery, pearl or pinkish-grey peritoneum, eye diameter longer than snout length, and no diamond-shaped scale pattern. The pigment on the exposed scale base ends in a straight line in contrast to the arch in the **blueback herring**; hence no diamond-shape but a scallop-like pattern. Dorsal fin rays 12–19, anal rays 15–21 and pectoral rays 12–16. Scales along flank 42–54. Belly scales before the pelvic fin 17–21, behind 12–17.

The back is grey-green and the sides and belly are iridescent silver. The flank may have copper tinges in sea run specimens or violet tinges in young. Lines run along the flank above the midline in some adults. There is a black spot behind the head on the upper flank. Fins are pale yellow or green. Attains 40 cm.

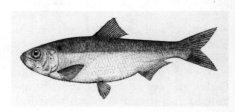

gaspereau

Biology: The gaspereau is a marine species which enters fresh water to spawn. It has been caught 120 km offshore. Some freshwater populations are landlocked and no longer return to the sea. The spread of gaspereau through the Great Lakes via canals has been rapid. The first appearance in Lake Erie was in 1931, in Lake Huron 1933, and it is now abundant in both these lakes. The first report for Lake Michigan was 5 May 1949 and within 20 years it was a commercial fishery item and the dominant fish species is the lake. In the sea it is found deeper, on average, than the **blueback herring** at 56–110 m. The movement of this species in the sea is generally northward and inshore in spring and southward and offshore in the fall, governed by zooplankton concentrations and bottom temperatures greater than 5°C.

Food is the larger zooplankton such as euphausiids, items of which may be selected individually, by a dart and suck, as well as filtered indiscriminately while swimming along with the mouth open. Gaspereau may choose either method depending on available food size. They may also gulp concentrations of plankton. There is a daily vertical migration following the zooplankton to surface waters at night. In fresh water zooplankton is eaten too but some bottom amphipods are also taken and the diet may include aquatic insects in late summer when zooplankton numbers fall off. Larval fishes are part of the zooplankton and in fresh waters gaspereau may be an important predator on commercial and sport fishes. Introduced **coho salmon** are an important predator on gaspereau in the Great Lakes and have reduced mass die-offs.

Gaspereau mature at ages 3–5 with males maturing earlier than females, sometimes as young as 1–2 years. Females are longer and heavier than males of the same age. Life span exceeds 10 years.

Spawning occurs in fresh water in spring and early summer (April–July) at water temperatures as low as 8.9°C. The pre-spawning migration in the St. John River, N.B. starts 3 months before spawning. Slow rivers are favoured but spawning does occur in lakes, ponds and streams. In lakes there is a spawning migration from deep water onto beaches in April–July, the timing being dependent on temperature. Spawning occurs in Lake Ontario at 13–16°C. Two or more fish swim in tight circles with flanks touching, rising to the surface. After circling once or twice at the surface, the fish dive and presumably release eggs and sperm. Spawning takes place in the evening and at night. Older fish spawn first and may be spawning for the fifth time. Eggs are 1.3 mm in diameter and each female may produce 450,000 eggs. Young return to the sea

in late summer and fall. The downstream migration is triggered by increasing rainfall, rapid decrease in water temperature (below 12°C) and the moon phase (dark nights).

Gaspereau are commercially important and are caught on the spawning run using weirs, gill nets, dip-nets and traps. The 1980 catch, which included **blueback herring**, was 9738 tonnes valued at $2,482,000. The 1988 catch of gaspereau alone was 5560 tonnes. They are sold fresh, frozen, smoked, salted or pickled. Some is used as pet food, fish meal or bait in angling and for lobster and snow crab. The flesh is good but bony. Landlocked specimens are thinner and smaller and so are not used much as food for people.

In the Great Lakes mass die-offs of gaspereau strew beaches with immense numbers of decaying fish, rendering the area unsuitable for human use and a health hazard. They can clog water intake pipes. Recovery of populations is rapid, almost sevenfold in 3 years. Die-offs are caused by sudden temperature changes from cold, deep to warm, shallow waters.

gelatinous snailfish

Scientific name: *Liparis fabricii*
   Krøyer, 1847
Family: **Snailfish**
Other common names: gelatinous seasnail
French name: limace gélatineuse

Distribution: Found around the shores of the Arctic Ocean including Canadian waters. Also off Labrador, on the Grand Bank and in the Gulf of St. Lawrence.

Characters: This snailfish is distinguished from its Arctic-Atlantic relatives by having an adhesive disc, 2 pairs of nostrils, dorsal fin without a notch, dorsal fin rays 41–50, anal fin rays 36–42 (usually 37–40), pectoral rays 32–39, peritoneum dark and posterior teeth usually simple with only anterior teeth obviously trilobed. Lower pectoral fin lobe rays are finger-like. The gill slit extends down to pectoral rays 5–11 usually. Pyloric caeca 19–34. Males develop skin prickles. Colour varies, becoming darker shades of brown with age. The dorsal, anal and pectoral fins are dark brown to black. Mouth and gill cavities, and the stomach, are dark.

Peritoneum with spots in young which become so dense in adults that the peritoneum is black. Attains 18.2 cm.

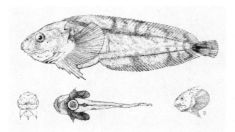

gelatinous snailfish

Biology: This snailfish is found usually on mud, mud and sand or shell and detritus bottoms, and sometimes pelagically, at 40–1800 m and, in Arctic Canada, at temperatures of –1.5 to 0.6°C. The main distribution is at 100–300 m. It may be caught under pack ice over depths of 2 km. Food is crustaceans and worms. Spawning in Arctic waters may be in September–October with egg diameter reaching 2.7 mm and egg numbers 735. This snailfish is eaten by **Atlantic cod**, seals and seabirds.

gem snaggletooth

Scientific name: *Astronesthes gemmifer*
  Goode and Bean, 1896
Family: **Barbeled Dragonfish**
Other common names: none
French name: dragon-saumon précieux

Distribution: In all major oceans. Reported from south of Newfoundland in the stomach of a halibut, presumably an **Atlantic halibut**. This specimen was the holotype or the individual from which this species was first described scientifically.

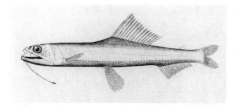

gem snaggletooth

Characters: The gem snaggletooth differs from its Canadian relatives by teeth on the maxilla bone of the upper jaw being comblike, close together and slanted rearward, a ventral adipose fin, 62–70 light organs in the ventral row, not having the lower row of light organs forming a u-shaped bend at the pectoral fin level, 18–19 anal fin rays, and a barbel with a swelling at the tip and black on one side. There are fang-like teeth in the jaws. The head and body are black. Maximum size is about 17 cm.

Biology: Feeds on fishes and crustaceans and undergoes vertical migrations. Larger fish are found in deeper waters, perhaps to 2400 m, with younger fish even coming to the surface.

ghost cat shark

Scientific name: *Apristurus manis*
  (Springer, 1979)
Family: **Cat Shark**
Other common names: none
French name: holbiche fantôme

Distribution: Found on Georges Bank. Also known west of Ireland and possibly off Mauritania.

Characters: This cat shark is distinguished from its Atlantic coast relatives by lacking crests over the eyes, dorsal fins are

ghost cat shark

similar in size, the space between the dorsal fins is longer than the length of the first dorsal fin base, the distance between the pectoral and pelvic fin bases is less than the snout tip to spiracle distance, the caudal fin has a crest of 3 or more enlarged denticles, dorsal fin tips are whitish, and flank denticles are sparse and non-overlapping. The body is stout and tapers strongly to the head. Nostril openings are rounded. Eyes are very small. Denticles are prickly but not fuzzy. Overall colour is grey to blackish with light margins to the dorsal and pectoral fins, at least in young. Attains 85.2 cm.

Biology. This is a poorly known, solitary cat shark found on continental slopes at 658–1740 m. There has been some confusion in identity with the **deepsea cat shark** (q.v.).

ghost shiner

Scientific name: *Notropis buchanani*
Meek, 1896
Family: **Carp**
Other common names: none
French name: méné fantôme

Distribution: Found in Lake St. Clair and Lake huron drainages of southwestern Ontario and in the Mississippi River and western Gulf of Mexico drainages of the U.S.A.

Characters: This species and its relatives in the genus *Notropis* (typical **shiners**) are separated from other family members by usu-

ghost shiner

ally having 7 branched dorsal fin rays following thin unbranched rays, protractile premaxillaries (upper lip separated from the snout by a groove), no barbels, large lateral line scales (fewer than 50), and a simple, s-shaped gut. This species usually has 7 branched anal fin rays (range 6–8), no lateral stripe, is mostly unpigmented (hence common name), and has no infraorbital canal under or behind the eye. Pharyngeal teeth 4–4. Gill rakers short, about 6. Dorsal fin branched rays 7, pectoral rays 12–14 and pelvic rays 8–9. Lateral line scales 30–35. Males have large tubercles on the top of the head and snout and finer ones over the rest of the head, anterior body and on pectoral fin rays. Overall colour is a pale yellowish-white to pale olive and the only darker pigment is some lining the top 3–4 scale rows on the back, a patch of melanophores on the rear of the head and melanophores along the lateral line, often one above and one below

each pore. Fins are transparent. Peritoneum silvery. Reaches 6.4 cm.

Biology: This minnow was first reported from Canada in 1981. It was probably released from an angler's bait bucket. The ghost shiner favours large quiet rivers and streams where it occupies eddies, creek mouths, and areas near vegetation where the current is slow. Rather like **trout**, this species will rest out of the current behind a rock and then dart out to seize drifting food items. Life span is about 2 years and some months. Spawning is from May to August.

ghostly grenadier

Scientific name: *Coryphaenoides leptolepis*
Günther, 1877
Family: **Grenadier**
Other common names: none
French name: grenadier à écailles minces

Distribution: Found in deep waters of both the Pacific and Atlantic oceans including British Columbia waters and off Nova Scotia.

Characters: This grenadier is distinguished from its Pacific Canadian coast relatives by having the anus just in front of the anal fin, 6 branchiostegal rays, no scaleless, black "window" for a light organ on the belly, 9–11 pelvic fin rays, teeth in a broad band in the upper jaw, small eye (less than one-fifth head length), and no scales on the areas under the eye, on the preopercle and on the lower jaws. These characters and the following separate this grenadier from its Atlantic Canada relatives. Second dorsal fin rays shorter than anal rays, scaleless areas on each side of the upper snout surface, and origin of second dorsal fin

ghostly grenadier

behind the anus. The snout is blunt and protrudes little beyond the mouth. First dorsal fin with 2 spines and 8–10 soft rays, usually 9. Second dorsal spine with upward pointing spines on its anterior margin. The second dorsal fin has about 114 rays and the anal fin about 113. Pectoral fin rays 18–22. Scales are thin, with weak spines in 2–5 rows, and are easily detached. There are about 145 along the lateral line. Overall colour is dirty-whitish or pale with pink tinges in fish which have lost their scales. They may be dark brown when scaled. The peritoneum, lower jaw, barbel, lips, mouth and gill cavities and underside of the head are black. Fins are dusky to pale. Exceeds 62 cm in total length.

Biology: Specimens have been caught off Triangle Island in British Columbia in 1964 and off Georges Bank near the Canadian 200-mile limit. This species has been observed at 2400–2507 m from submersibles in the western Atlantic Ocean. It has a depth range of 610–4000 m.

giant cusk-eel

Scientific name: *Spectrunculus grandis* (Günther, 1877)
Family: **Cusk-eel**
Other common names: none
French name: donzelle géante

Distribution: Found in the North and South Atlantic oceans and in the Pacific Ocean, including off the coast of British Columbia and off the Atlantic coast just south of Canadian waters.

Characters: This species is distinguished from its Atlantic coast relatives by its large anterior nostril and fin ray counts. Dorsal fin rays 121–148, anal rays 90–113. Pectoral fin rays 23–33. Developed gill rakers 5–10. There is a strong opercular spine. The anterior nostril has a fleshy rim which is raised above the snout. The lateral line is short. The head and body are covered by scales with about 216 along the flank. Males are a dusky cream,

giant cusk-eel

females light to deep brown. The tail may have irregular greyish-pink blotches. The edges of the dorsal and anal fins are brown.

The caudal fin, edge of the opercular membrane and the posterior half of the pectoral fin are brown. Reaches 138 cm and 16.5 kg.

Biology: First reported from west of southern Vancouver Island at 2520 m in 1981, but also off Tasu Sound, Queen Charlotte Islands at 2835 m and Moresby Island also at 2835 m. Reported from 3188 m south of Georges Bank in the Atlantic Ocean. Elsewhere reported from 800 m to 6273 m close to the sea floor.

giant stickleback

Scientific name: *Gasterosteus* sp.
Family: **Stickleback**
Other common names: none
French name: épinoche géante

Distribution: Found only in Mayer Lake, Graham Island, Queen Charlotte Islands, British Columbia.

Characters: This species is related to the **threespine stickleback** but is distinguished by being more than twice as large on average (8.4

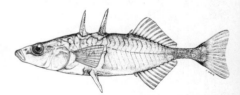

giant stickleback

cm compared to 3.1 cm) as threespines in the same lake, with a more streamlined body, an overall black colour (compared to yellowish with irregular dark flank bars) and in 6 countable and measurable characters. The giant stickleback has 17–27 gill rakers, mean 21.2 (compared to 13–21, mean 16.6 for threespines), 4–8, mean 6.8, lateral plates on the body (3–7, mean 4.7), and long pelvic spines mean 5.3 times in standard length (mean 6.4). The appearance of this fish has resulted from natural selection by such predators as **cutthroat trout** and common loons. This is only 1 of several, unusual stickleback populations in British Columbia, not all of which have been described (see as some other examples the **Enos stickleback** and the **Texada stickleback**). There are about 10 other Queen

Charlotte Island watersheds with "giant" sticklebacks, some black, others grey-black or grey which have yet to be described in the literature. They are of great interest to scientists studying the mechanisms of speciation and evolution. Overall colour is black except for the gill cover and anteroventral region which are bright silver. In the breeding season, males lose the silver colour and become drab, with a light grey or sooty black throat. Some males develop a red throat similar to **threespine stickleback** males. Reaches 11.6 cm.

Biology: This is a limnetic species found in open lake waters and not entering streams. Males apparently prefer shallow, littoral waters. Food is zooplankton for females in the limnetic zone. Predators of adults include **cutthroat trout** and of eggs and juveniles the **prickly sculpin**. Spawning takes place in the third summer of life, starting in May and lasts about 3 months. Females produce an average of 257 eggs per clutch with an unfertilised diameter of 1.9 mm. Males are known to complete about 5 nesting cycles of 18 days before dying. Each cycle includes 1 day to build a nest and court a female, 9 days egg incubation and 8 days of protecting the fry. Nests are built by males where the bottom is sand or gravel, gently sloping and there is shelter afforded by rocks or weeds. The mean clutch size per nest is 773 with the largest being 2001. The Committee on the Status of Endangered Wildlife in Canada gave this species the status of "rare" in 1980. Overfishing of **cutthroat trout** and disturbance of loons by tourists would remove the selective pressures maintaining this species. The spread of beaver is also a threat since beavers cause water-level fluctuations which are detrimental to shallow water nesting or increases water depths allowing access of **cutthroat trout** to the nesting sites.

giant wrymouth

Scientific name: *Cryptacanthodes giganteus*
  (Kittlitz, 1858)
Family: **Wrymouth**
Other common names: none
French name: terrassier géant

Distribution: Found from California to the Bering Sea including British Columbia.

Characters: This wrymouth is distinguished from its relative, the **dwarf wrymouth**, by having exposed scales on the pos-

giant wrymouth

terior part of the body (buried in the skin anteriorly) and by colour. The elongate body, long spiny dorsal fin beginning behind the head and confluent with the caudal and anal fins, eyes high on the head and the almost vertical jaws, are characteristic. There are no pelvic fins. There are 72–77 dorsal fin spines, 2 anal fin spines followed by 43–49 soft rays and about 11 pectoral fin rays. Overall colour is pale brown with touches of yellow or violet. The flanks may be blotched. Some horizontal stripes or spotting may develop. The top of the head and the lower jaw tip may be white. Attains 117 cm or more.

Biology: Found on soft bottoms at 6–128 m. It may spend part of its life buried, but its biology is poorly known.

gizzard shad

Scientific name: *Dorosoma cepedianum*
  (Le Sueur, 1818)
Family: **Herring**
Other common names: hickory shad, lake shad, jack shad, skipjack, mud shad, sawbelly, hairy back, stink shad
French name: alose à gésier

Distribution: Found from the Great Lakes basin of southern Ontario and the St. Lawrence River near Québec City south to Gulf of Mexico drainages.

Characters: This species is distinguished by the last dorsal fin ray being elongated, the mouth is subterminal and anal rays are 25–36. The upper jaw has a deep, central notch. There are muscular sacs behind the upper gills used for food storage. Dorsal fin rays 10–13, pectoral rays 14–17 and pelvic rays 7–10. Scales 52–70 along the flank. Belly scales number 17–20 before the pelvic fin, 10–14 behind. Gill rakers are long, slender and about 90–400, increasing with growth. The stomach has a thick wall, hence "gizzard" shad.

gizzard shad

The back and upper flank are silver-blue, the flanks are silvery and the belly is cream-white. Flanks have a golden, brassy, bluish or greenish tinge. Upper flanks may have 6–8 dark stripes. Smaller fish have a strong, dark, purplish spot on the upper flank just behind the head, fading early in the second year of life.

Reaches 52.1 cm. The world, all-tackle angling record weighed 1.81 kg and was caught in 1993 in Lake Michigan, Indiana.

Biology: Its presence in the Great Lakes is attributed to movement through canals although it may be in Lake Erie naturally. It was first recorded from Lake Superior in 1961. This shad is found in lakes, slower rivers and swamps and may enter brackish water. When startled they will skip over the water surface. Older fish are found in deeper water down to 33 m, especially in winter. Life span is about 10 years. Most fish are mature at 2 years but a few mature at age 1.

Food is initially zooplankton but changes at an early size (about 3 cm) to microscopic algae which are filtered out of the water by the numerous gill rakers and carried by a mucus stream to the muscular sacs where they are concentrated and passed to the gizzard and elongate gut which aid in digestion of this plant food. Few Canadian fishes feed on plant food. There may be selection for certain blue-green algae. Sand is said to be eaten to help in breaking up plant food. Gizzard shad are eaten by many other sport and commercial fishes, particularly when young.

Spawning occurs principally at night in spring or early summer, the timing depend-

ing on water temperature. A school of males and females swim and roll around near the surface ejecting eggs and sperm. Spawning may occur after ascending small streams as well as in lakes over shallow bars. The eggs sink and attach to plants or the bottom. Eggs are up to 1.1 mm in diameter and over half a million are produced.

This shad is of little commercial importance in Canada since the flesh is soft and bony. It is a nuisance to fishermen in that it entangles nets meant for other species. In reservoirs it can become the dominant species and a considerable nuisance through mass die-offs. Gizzard shad have been used as pig and cattle food and as fertiliser.

glacial eelpout

Scientific name: *Lycodes frigidus*
   Collett, 1878
Family: **Eelpout**
Other common names: cold water eelpout
French name: lycode glaciale

Distribution: Found in the Laptev, East Siberian and Chukchi seas and between Greenland and northwestern Europe. In Canada northwest of Ellesmere Island.

Characters: This species is separated from its Canadian Arctic-Atlantic relatives by having small pelvic fins, a mouth under the snout, no large pores around the mouth, crests on the chin, scales on the body and dorsal and anal fins, lateral line single, running below midline along the flank, tail long (preanal length 43–47% of total length), peritoneum dark brown, pectoral fin rays 19–21 and 42–48 scales across the body at anal fin origin level. Dorsal fin rays 99–104, anal rays 85–90 (both

glacial eelpout

including half the caudal fin rays) and vertebrae 103–107. Overall colour is uniform grey or brown. The abdomen and branchiostegal membranes are blue-black. Dorsal and anal fin margins are blue-black. Attains 69 cm.

Biology: The Canadian record is from drifting ice station CESAR about 350 km south of the North Pole (at 85°48'26.8"N, 110°43'39.3"W). Depth range is 475–3000 m at temperatures below 0°C on mud bottoms. Food is crustaceans, molluscs, fishes, brittle stars and squids. Eggs number about 500 and are 7 mm in diameter. Spawning probably occurs in autumn or winter.

glacier lanternfish

Scientific name: *Benthosema glaciale*
   (Reinhardt, 1837)
Family: **Lanternfish**
Other common names: mikiapic kapisilik
French name: lanterne glaciaire

Distribution: North Atlantic Ocean and Mediterranean Sea including eastern Arctic Canada at southern Baffin Bay and southward off Atlantic Canada to off Cape Hatteras.
Characters: This Atlantic species is distinguished by the PLO photophore being more than its diameter above the upper base

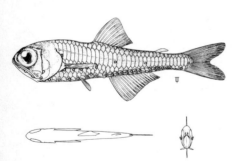

glacier lanternfish

of the pectoral fin, no photophores near the dorsal body edge, the second PVO photophore is below the upper base of the pectoral fin, the PVO series is almost horizontal, 2 Prc photophores with the second much higher than the first, the second VO photophore is elevated, and small, simple premaxillary and dentary teeth. It is separated from its relative, the **eyelight lanternfish**, by not having a suborbital photophore and by the second Prc photophore being below the lateral line. Dorsal fin rays 12–15, anal rays 17–19 and pectoral rays 10–13. Total gill

rakers 15–20, visible in the open mouth. AO photophores 11–14 and vertebrae 35–37. Lateral line organs 36–37. The supracaudal luminous gland is best developed in males and the infracaudal in females. The glands begin to develop at a length of 2.5 cm. Reaches 10.3 cm, but probably 6.8 cm is the maximum in Canada.
Biology: This is probably the most abundant North Atlantic lanternfish. It is found from near surface waters at night down to 1250 m during the day. Temperature range is 0–21°C but this species is most abundant at 4–16°C. Off Nova Scotia it migrates from depths of 250–800 m during the day into the upper 50 m at night, feeding usually between 2000 hours and 0400 hours. In Davis Strait about 46% of the population feeds at night in the upper 65 m having migrated from depths of 300–900 m. Here water temperatures are around 0°C even in summer. Older fish are found deeper than young fish at night. The prey items are selected by the lanternfish and are oil-rich. Food is principally copepods and euphausiid crustaceans. The glacier lanternfish is eaten by many other fishes and by ivory gulls in the southwest Davis Strait. The photophores emit repetitive flashes for a few seconds at 10–15 second intervals. This species is mature at age 2 and lives about 4–5 years. Spawning probably occurs in spring to summer months.

glowingfish

Scientific name: *Neoscopelus macrolepidotus*
   Johnson, 1863
Family: **Blackchin**
Other common names: none
French name: lanterne à grandes écailles

Distribution: In all oceans and as a single specimen from off the Queen Charlotte Islands, B.C.
Characters: The dorsal fin lies in advance of the midbody and the anal fin lies behind it. The tongue of the glowingfish has light organs. The roof of the mouth is dark and the floor light. The tongue is dark overall. The pectoral fins are large and reach back to the anus. There are light organs on the lower body in two rows in addition to a midbelly row. The upper of these 2 rows does not reach the anal

fin origin. The side of the head and the flanks are dark red, the belly silvery-white with blue tinges and the fins pink. Reaches 25 cm.

glowingfish

Biology: The glowingfish lives on the bottom at depths of 300–900 m and does not appear to migrate vertically. The illuminated tongue presumably serves to attract prey right to the mouth.

Goatfish Family

Scientific name: Mullidae
French name: surmulets

Goatfishes, surmullets or red mullets are found in the Atlantic, Indian and Pacific oceans, usually in subtropical to tropical waters. There are about 55 species but only 1 has been reported from Atlantic Canada.

Goatfishes are easily recognised by the pair of long barbels under the chin. The barbels can be folded back into a chin groove. Each barbel can be moved independently. The first dorsal fin has 6–9 spines and is separate from the soft dorsal fin which has 1 spine and 7–9 soft rays. The pelvic fins have 1 spine and 5 soft rays. The caudal fin is forked. Scales are large and weakly ctenoid. They are colourful fish but colour changes to match the habitat and with the time of day.

Goatfishes are classified with the **Drum Family** in the **Perch Order**.

Goatfishes are found inshore, usually in shallow water and can be solitary or in schools. The barbels are used to probe for food, such as worms, molluscs and crustaceans, in mud or sand. The barbels use both touch and taste to locate food items. Some goatfishes use the barbels to excavate the food item or to probe into crevices to dislodge food animals. Other species back away and blow sand off the food item to expose it,

or burrow into the sand with the snout. Young goatfishes are pelagic and are easily attracted to lights at night.

These are often important food fishes. In ancient Rome they were particularly esteemed and Lucullus, the famous gourmand, kept them in saltwater ponds. These goatfish were worth their weight in silver and were shown alive to banquet guests before being cooked, the changing and brilliant colours of the fish as they died supposedly stimulating the appetite.

See **red goatfish**

Goby Family

Scientific name: Gobiidae
French name: gobies

Gobies are found world-wide in warmer seas and the family is the largest marine fish family with an estimated 2000 species. Some enter fresh water. Only 3 species are found in Canada on the Pacific coast although unidentified larval gobies have been caught along the Atlantic coast and an introduced species, the **tubenose goby**, is known from the American side of the St. Clair River which flows between Ontario and Michigan. Another introduced species, the **round goby** is found naturally in the Black and Caspian seas and their tributary rivers. It was first reported from the St. Clair River in 1992.

The family has the pelvic fins modified to form an adhesive disc or cup by fusion of the two fins. There is usually a short spiny dorsal fin (2–8 spines) separated from a soft dorsal fin. Scales may be cycloid or ctenoid. No obvious lateral line. The head is usually blunt. Most are quite small (5–10 cm) and they are often very abundant.

Identification depends on fin ray counts, colour, and where species are numerous, on head pore and papillae patterns. Gobies are members of the **Perch Order**. "Goby" is derived from Latin and Greek words for a **minnow**, the gudgeon, found in Europe which resembles some gobies.

The world's smallest vertebrates are gobies from the Indian Ocean, mature at 8 mm. Other gobies are the familiar tropical mudskippers which can move quickly over land. Gobies tend to rest on the bottom and move in sudden, characteristic dashes. The male goby guards a nest. Food is crustaceans, worms, molluscs and small fishes.

Many gobies are important in the aquarium trade since they are beautifully coloured, small and tough. A few are used as food.

See **arrow goby**
bay goby
blackeye goby
round goby
tubenose goby

goitre blacksmelt

Scientific name: *Bathylagus euryops*
Goode and Bean, 1895
Family: **Deepsea Smelt**
Other common names: none
French name: garcette-goître

Distribution: Found in the North Atlantic Ocean from Labrador and the Davis Strait southward to Bermuda. May be found in other oceans.

Characters: The goitre blacksmelt is distinguished from its Atlantic Canadian relatives by having a gill opening not extending half way up the side of the body and by hav-

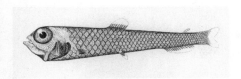

goitre blacksmelt

ing about 40 lateral line scales. Dorsal fin rays 9–11, anal rays 16–19, pectoral rays 7–12 and pelvic rays 7–9. Gill rakers 17–18 on the lower arch. The scale pockets are outlined in black and sometimes lined with purplish tissue. The overall body colour is light brown to light purple. The opercle is blue-black and the snout dusky. Reaches about 20 cm. The common name refers to the heavily-developed lower part of the head, said to resemble a goitre.

Biology: Juveniles and adults are found between 500 and 1800 m, while post-larvae are found at 20–500 m. Food is small, planktonic crustaceans. Pelagic eggs and larvae are produced.

golden redfish

Scientific name: *Sebastes norvegicus*
(Ascanius, 1772)
Family: **Scorpionfish**
Other common names: redfish, ocean perch, rosefish
French name: sébaste orangé

Distribution: Found on both sides of the North Atlantic Ocean including on the northern and Grand banks of Newfoundland, the Flemish Cap and the Gulf of St. Lawrence.

Characters: This species is distinguished from other Atlantic coast scorpionfishes by having 13–17, usually 15, dorsal fin spines

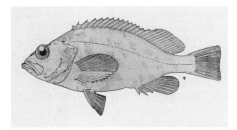

golden redfish

and from its closest relatives, the **Acadian** and **deepwater redfishes**, by a combination of overlapping characters, some of which are internal and require dissection to see. Easily misidentified. This is the most robust of the 3 redfishes with the smallest eye. Anal fin soft rays 7–10, usually 8. The lower unbranched pectoral fin rays are 9 or more (rarely 8). Total vertebrae 30–32, usually 31. The knob at the tip of the chin is blunt and weak. A key internal character is the muscles attaching to the gas bladder. In this species there are 3 or 4 muscle heads with tendons passing between ribs 2 and 3 or both ribs 2 and 3, and 3 and 4, the muscle is wide and the posterior tendon usually has 6 branches. Larvae have 9–24 ventral row melanophores. Overall colour is an orange or golden yellow. Attains 1 m but usually 35–55 cm and 6.4 kg. The world, all-tackle angling record weighed 2.65 kg and was caught in 1982 at Holsteinsborg, Greenland.

Biology: Of the three redfish species, this is the least common and is rare south of

Cabot Strait. It is found over rock or clay and silt bottoms from less than 300 m to over 750 m but intermediate between the depths of the other two redfish species. The biology of redfishes has not yet been fully worked out because of the difficulties in separating the species. Food is crustaceans and, when larger, fishes, and the redfish rises in the water column at night to feed on pelagic prey. This is a slow-growing and long-lived species which may attain 48 years. Half the female population is mature at 40.5 cm. Spawning occurs in April–May off the south coast of Newfoundland. This species probably forms only a minor part of the commercial catch. The commercial fishery is a recent development with a maximum catch of 389,000 tonnes in 1959. Catches since then have been less as quotas were imposed to prevent overfishing. In 1979 the catch was worth 15.5 million dollars and weighed 81,587 tonnes. All three redfish species are managed as a single unit and often appear on the market, fresh or frozen, as "ocean perch."

golden redhorse

Scientific name: *Moxostoma erythrurum*
  (Rafinesque, 1818)
Family: **Sucker**
Other common names: golden mullet, golden
  sucker, smallheaded mullet, white sucker
French name: suceur doré

Distribution: Found from New York to North Dakota through the southern Great Lakes and south to Georgia and Texas. In Canada it is found in drainages of lakes Erie, St. Clair, southern Huron and the Niagara River basin in Ontario, and the Red River of Manitoba.

Characters: This species is distinguished by a short dorsal fin, a swimbladder with 3 chambers, lateral line scales 37–45, scales around the caudal peduncle usually 12, occasionally 13 (rarely as high as 15–16), lower lip thick, posterior edge forming an obtuse angle and lips nearly as wide as snout, pharyngeal teeth not molar-like but blade-like, pelvic fin origin opposite dorsal fin midpoint, eye large (diameter about two-thirds or more of lip width), nostrils behind maxillary tip, and snout slightly overhanging mouth. The dorsal fin is emar-

ginate. The front of the head is flattened and squarish. Gill rakers 25–32. Dorsal fin rays 10–15, anal rays 7, pectoral rays 15–19 and pelvic rays 7–10. The gut has 2–3 coils. Males have large nuptial tubercles on the snout, anterior cheek, anal fin and lower caudal fin lobe. Pectoral and pelvic fins, upper head and body scales bear minute tubercles.

Overall colour is bronze, olive or grey paling to a silvery or whitish belly. The upper flank is golden or brassy. Adults have a golden-green base to flank scales. The young have upper flank scales dark at the margin and pale in the centre in contrast to evenly coloured scales in **black redhorse**. The smallest young have 3 dusky saddles and a pale orange caudal fin. The dorsal and caudal fins are grey in adults. The anal, pelvic and pectoral fins are usually pale orange to reddish with the leading edge white. Peritoneum silvery.

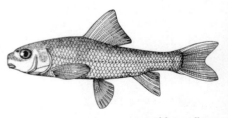

golden redhorse

Reaches 66.0 cm and 2 kg. The world, all-tackle angling record weighed 1.22 kg and was caught at Franklin, Pennsylvania in 1992.

Biology: Golden redhorses are often found in deep pools of streams and rivers with slow current and mud bottoms. They are also found in faster waters with gravel bottoms and rarely in lakes. Golden redhorses appear to be more tolerant of turbid conditions, fluctuating oxygen levels, intermittent flow and temperatures than other **redhorses**.

Food is aquatic insects, worms, molluscs and algae taken from the bottom deposits.

Life span is 11 years and maturity is attained at 3 years in males and 4 years in females. Spawning occurs in the spring (May in Wisconsin) at 15°C and higher water temperatures. These fish spawn during the day and at night. Males arrive first on riffle areas and defend a territory. The large snout tubercles are used to butt other males. No nest is built and females shed up to 35,000 eggs with a diameter up to 2.5 mm which are then abandoned. There is some reproductive behaviour involving runs through the water, rolling and jumping. Each female is flanked by 2 males during spawning.

It does not appear to be in jeopardy in Canada according to the Committee on the Status of Endangered Wildlife in Canada in 1989. In the U.S.A. some golden redhorse are taken by bait fishing or spearing. They are said to be excellent eating, better than many more familiar sport fishes.

golden shiner

Scientific name: *Notemigonus crysoleucas*
  (Mitchill, 1814)
Family: **Carp**
Other common names: eastern golden shiner, roach, bream, American roach, American bream, butterfish, sunfish, windfish, goldfish, dace, chub, bitterhead, gudgeon, young shad, méné plat, petite laquaiche
French name: chatte de l'est

Distribution: Found from P.E.I. (introduced) and Nova Scotia westward through southern Québec, the James Bay drainage at Lake Abitibi and the Great Lakes to southern and central Manitoba and southeastern Saskatchewan, and south to Florida, the Gulf states and Mexico. Widely introduced in the U.S.A. outside this range.

Characters: This species is identified by the strongly decurved lateral line with 39–57

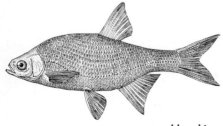

golden shiner

scales, a naked, fleshy ventral keel between the pelvic fins and the anus on the belly mid-

line and 7–18 (usually 11–13 in Canada) branched rays in the anal fin. Pharyngeal teeth 5–5 with a grinding surface and hooked tips. Dorsal fin branched rays 6–8, pectoral rays 15–18 and pelvic rays 8–9. Males have nuptial tubercles on the scales with up to 15 tubercles lining each scale margin with an occasional 1–2 tubercles on the central part of the scale. The largest tubercles are on midflank below the dorsal fin. Much smaller tubercles are scattered over the top and sides of the head, tip of the upper lip, branchiostegal rays, central caudal fin rays and weakly on other fins. There is a patch of larger tubercles on the chin.

Overall colour golden with the back olive-green to dark brown. The belly is silvery-yellow. Fins yellowish. Young fish are more silvery and can be darkly pigmented around each scale. There is also a dark lateral stripe in young. Breeding males develop orange-red pelvic fins and a black edge to the anal fin. The nape swells to a hump. Peritoneum dusky to silvery with dark melanophores.

Golden shiners hybridise with **rudd**, an exotic species from Europe which is easily confused with this species. Reaches 30.5 cm.

Biology: Golden shiners are found in large schools in clear, weedy areas, particularly in lakes but also in embayments of large rivers favouring temperatures in Canada in the low 20s°C but tolerating up to 34°C. The highest lethal temperature is 40°C, unusually high for a North American minnow.

Food is principally crustaceans and flying insects taken in mid to surface waters. Other aquatic insects, molluscs, water mites, small fishes, phytoplankton and filamentous algae are also utilised. Usually only 2–3 items dominate in the diet and the dominant items vary with locality and season. Cladocerans and filamentous algae are recorded as particularly important in several studies. Shiners use 2 methods to forage on zooplankton. Large items like Cladocera (water fleas) are usually located and seized individually. Small, high density items are taken by pump filter-feeding. The shiner can switch between the 2 feeding modes as conditions dictate. This minnow may eat **bass** fry in ponds. Many sport fishes find this abundant shiner an important food source including **large-mouth bass, crappies** and **muskellunge**. A wide variety of birds also eat this minnow. In Ontario, population densities of this shiner are strongly influenced by predator densities. Food abundance does not appear to influence numbers of shiners.

Maturity is usually attained at ages of 1–2 years and life span may be 10 years. Females grow faster, larger and live longer than males. Growth varies with latitude but also variations within a similar climate zone are great. Spawning takes place from May to August in New York when water temperatures exceed 20°C. Adhesive eggs are scattered over filamentous algae or other plants when 1–2 males chase and nudge a female. Yellow eggs are about 1.2 mm in diameter and a female can have up to 200,000. **Largemouth bass** nests have been used by golden shiners as a spawning site. The male bass does not interfere and his presence serves to protect the eggs from predators.

This minnow is the leading bait fish in North America and is even pond cultured in the U.S.A. for bait sales or for food in fish hatcheries. Around Montréal, 15,600 kg are caught each fall for bait. Some authors report it to be excellent eating.

golden trout

Scientific name: *Oncorhynchus aguabonito* (Jordan, 1892)
Family: **Salmon**
Other common names: Kern River trout, California golden trout
French name: truite dorée

Distribution: Found in Arctic drainages of southern Alberta as an introduction. Also reported for British Columbia. This species originated in the Kern River drainage of California but has been introduced widely.

Characters: This species is distinguished from its relatives, the **cutthroat** and **rainbow trouts**, by having 150–212 lateral line scales, scales above lateral line 34–45, no teeth on the shaft of the vomer bone in the roof of the mouth, and by colour. These 3 species often hybridise and can be very difficult to distinguish. Pyloric caeca 21–41. Pelvic rays 8–10. Gill rakers 17–21.

The back is a deep olive-green. The pale flank has few, large, round, dark spots without halos above the lateral line. There is a red streak along the flank. The flanks are overall yellowish-green or golden. The belly and cheeks are bright red to reddish orange. Adults usually have about 10 parr marks, an unusual feature. The dorsal fin has a white to orange tip and there is a white margin on the anal and pelvic fins with a black bar below. The dorsal and adipose fins are golden and heavily spotted. The anal, pectoral and pelvic fins are overall orange to reddish without spots. The tail and dorsal fins have large black spots. Formerly in the genus *Salmo*, this species may be classified as a subspecies of **rainbow trout**.

golden trout

The world angling record from Cooks Lake, Wyoming in 1948 and reached 71.1 cm total length and 4.99 kg.in weight. The Canadian record from Castle River, Alberta, is 1.93 kg. and was caught by Campbell Barnaby in 1965.

Biology: This species has a native distribution in California in cool streams over 3000 m and was introduced to high-altitude lakes in Alberta. It is reproducing in Lower South Fork and Rainy Ridge lakes. Food is insect larvae and some planktonic crustaceans. Life span is 7 years and most fish mature at 3–4 years. Spawning in Alberta is recorded for July. Eggs are shed in stream gravels at 7–10°C. Up to 2280 eggs are produced. This species has a great attraction for sport fishermen because of its colour, rarity and difficulty of access in mountain areas. Anglers catch it using small lures, flies and various live baits. The flesh does not keep well but is delicious.

• Most accessible July and August.

- The Rocky Mountain lakes in British Columbia and Alberta.

- Ultralight to light action spinning outfits used with four- to six-pound line. Fly rods between seven-and-a-half to eight-and-a-half feet in length, four- to seven-weight outfits loaded with weight-forward floating or sinking lines.

- An assortment of 1/8–to 1/4–ounce spoons, small spinners and small hair jigs. The best flies are a wide variety of streamers, wet flies and nymphs.

goldeye

Scientific name: *Hiodon alosoides*
(Rafinesque, 1819)
Family: **Mooneye**
Other common names: toothed herring, northern mooneye, Winnipeg goldeye, western goldeye, yellow herring, shad mooneye
French name: laquaiche aux yeux d'or

Distribution: Found from the Mackenzie River basin southward including northeast British Columbia, eastward draining rivers of Alberta, much of Saskatchewan and Manitoba except the northeastern parts, and in Ontario close to the southeastern Manitoba border. There is an isolated population in northeastern Ontario and northwestern Québec in rivers draining to southern James Bay. It occurs in the U.S.A. south to Mississippi from the main Canadian distribution.

goldeye

Characters: This species is separated from its only relative, the **mooneye**, by having a fleshy keel from the isthmus to the anal fin, the dorsal fin origin is over or behind the anal fin origin and the mouth extends back beyond the middle of the eye. Major dorsal fin rays 9–10, major anal rays 29–35 and 11–12 pectoral rays. Lateral line scales 56–65. The anal fin base has 1–3 rows of small scales. There are 15–19 short, knob-like gill rakers.

The back is dark blue or blue-green, flanks silvery and the belly milky-white. The anterior flank is tinged gold and near the tail blue to pink. Fins are usually clear but may be yellowish to pink. There is a black line following the anterior edge of the pectoral fin. The peritoneum is silvery. The iris of the eye is yellow to golden in adults (hence the name), but silvery in young, and has a golden eyeshine in the dark like a cat. Males have the anterior end of the anal fin expanded so the margin behind is notched.

Reaches over 50.0 cm. The world, all-tackle angling record weighed 1.72 kg and was caught at Pierre, South Dakota in 1987. The Canadian angling record from Battle River Dam, Alberta was caught by R. Weber in 1993 and weighed 1.88 kg.

Biology: Goldeye inhabit turbid waters of lakes, ponds, marshes and quiet, large rivers. They overwinter in the depths of lakes.

Food includes surface and submerged insects, particularly water boatmen, crustacean zooplankton, molluscs, small fishes, frogs, mice and shrews. Surface insects include beetles which fall on the water during dispersal flights. Feeding is thought to occur mostly at night, aided by the large eyes which only have light-sensitive rods in the retina. **Northern pike, yellow walleye, sauger, inconnu,** cormorants and other birds, and mammals eat goldeye.

Goldeye defend an individual space around themselves by charging, chasing, nipping and lateral displays to keep other goldeye at a distance. Their density in the Peace-Athabasca Delta has been estimated at 1 fish per 50 sq m.

Life span is 17 years. Maturity varies with latitude, being as early as 1 year in the south but 6–9 years for males and 7–10 years for females in Alberta. There is a spawning migration to shallow water from overwintering grounds. In rivers there is an upstream migration in spring to spawn, a feeding migration further upriver and a downstream migration in fall. Goldeye migrate to the Peace-Athabasca Delta for spawning beginning in March and adults return to the Peace River in August, young as late as December. The round trip is 700–800 km. One fish travelled 2000 km in 15 days. Spawning takes place in May–July after ice breakup at 10.0–12.8°C, probably at night but the turbid water makes observations difficult. Eggs are steel blue in the female, number up to 25,238 and are about 4 mm in diameter. They become translucent when laid and are semibuoyant, an unusual feature in North American freshwater fishes. The eggs float until they hatch.

Goldeye are marketed as a gourmet item and demand exceeds supply. Most are sold around Winnipeg (hence Winnipeg goldeye) and achieved fame as a delicacy when served on transcontinental trains. Annual catches once reached 454,000 kg in the 1920s when there was a fishery on Lake Winnipeg. Modern catches are much less and are taken mostly from the Saskatchewan River with some from Sandy Lake, Ontario and from Alberta and Québec. Smoked goldeye is red, orange or gold, once formed by the willow wood used in smoking but now obtained with aniline dyes.

Goldeye are a sport fish taken on light tackle baited with insects or small fish, by using small lures and can be caught by wet and dry fly fishing. Goldeye in the North Saskatchewan River, Alberta had high mercury levels, from chlor-alkali plants in Saskatoon, encountered on their migrations, as well as local, natural sources.

goldfish

Scientific name: *Carassius auratus*
(Linnaeus, 1758)
Family: **Carp**
Other common names: golden carp
French name: cyprin doré

Distribution: Originally found in China, now widely introduced in Canada by design or accident. Reported from British Columbia, Alberta, Saskatchewan, Manitoba, Ontario, Québec and New Brunswick. They have been found in North America for over 100 years.

Characters: This species is identified by having 14–20 dorsal fin branched rays, a ser-

rated spine at the dorsal and anal fin origins and no barbels. Anal fin branched rays 5–6, usually 5, pectoral rays 14–17 and pelvic rays 8–10. Lateral line scales 25–34. Gill rakers 37–50. Pharyngeal teeth 4–4, with one tooth conical and the others with expanded crowns. Breeding males have small nuptial tubercles on the operculum, back and pectoral fin rays. The gut is elongate with several loops.

The golden or orange colour of artificially bred aquarium goldfish is distinctive. However populations in the wild, if they breed successfully, gradually revert to a wild-type of colour as golden fish are readily eaten by birds and other fishes. Wild-type colour is an overall olive-green fading to a white belly. Young goldfish are green, brown or bronze to almost black. Peritoneum dusky to black. Reaches 45.7 cm and 1.6 kg; larger fish being hybrids with the **common carp**.

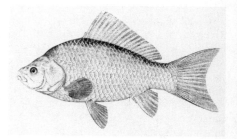

goldfish

Biology: Goldfish appear to favour ponds or pools in streams with aquatic vegetation but are often introduced into small bodies of water as ornamental fish or out of curiosity to see if they will survive. They are tolerant of turbidity, polluted waters and very high temperatures (upper lethal limit 41.4°C).

Food includes aquatic insects, crustaceans, molluscs, worms, detritus and plants. Goldfish have a palatal organ on the roof of the mouth used to taste and touch food.

Life span, at least in captivity, is 30 years or more but about 7 years is more normal in the wild. Sexual maturity is attained at 1–3 years. Spawning occurs in warmer summer months at temperatures above 16°C and eggs are shed over plants or willow roots, often on sunny mornings. Each female is accompanied by 2 or more males and chases are reported. Eggs are adhesive and up to 1.6 mm in diameter. A female will spawn 3–10 batches of eggs at 8–10 day intervals, with up to 4000 eggs being laid in each batch. Total fecundity is 380,000 eggs. Population numbers in confined areas are limited by a chemical released by the goldfish which represses more spawning.

Goldfish are familiar aquarium pets with many exotic varieties having been developed. These include Comets, Veiltails, Fringetails, Telescopes, Lionheads, Orandas, Shubunkins and others, often with bizarre shapes. They are also extensively used as an experimental fish, perhaps more than any other fish species. Studies include physiological and biochemical work and toxic chemical bioassays. They have been used in many U.S. States as bait fish and form an important aquaculture industry. Carp-goldfish hybrids have been used to demonstrate pollution in the Welland River near Niagara Falls. Fish from industrial areas had a higher frequency of cancers than those from a rural area. This hybrid is, therefore, a "sentinel" species or an advance warning system of deteriorating environmental conditions.

Goosefish Family

Scientific name: Lophiidae
French name: baudroies

Goosefishes or monkfishes are found in the Arctic, Atlantic, Indian and Pacific oceans. There are 25 species with 1 in Atlantic Canada.

They are members of the **Anglerfish Order** which have pelvic fins, a pseudobranch, no scales and the frontal bones of the head united. A characteristic feature is an enormous, wide and flattened head with strong, depressible, curved teeth in the mouth, and large spines, knobs and ridges on top. The lower jaw projects. The pectoral fins are on stalks and are arm-like. A fringe of skin flaps runs along the lower jaw, along the lower head side and onto the body and aids in camouflage. The skin is loose and scaleless. The fishing apparatus has a fleshy flap at the tip to attract prey close to the mouth. A second and third dorsal spine on the head are also elongate but are not lures.

Goosefishes live in shallow to moderately deep waters often in temperate parts of the world. Prey is engulfed by the huge mouth when it is in striking distance. As well as fishes and crabs, they have been recorded as eating small sharks and seabirds taken at the surface (hence the name goosefish, although capturing a goose strains the imagination). The females lay large pelagic egg masses or veils more than 60 cm wide and 12 m long. Larvae have very long pelvic fins which shrink as the fish grows. These remarkably ugly fishes are nevertheless commercially important.

See **monkfish**

grapnel compleat-angler

Scientific name: *Lasiognathus beebei*
    Regan and Trewavas, 1932
Family: **Wolftrap**
Other common names: none
French name: parfait-pêcheur à grappin

Distribution: North Atlantic Ocean including off Newfoundland.

Characters: The greatly elongate upper jaw separates this species from all other deepsea **anglerfishes**. There are 3 hooks on the bulb of the esca or bait. The head is narrow with a long fishing apparatus. The skin is naked. Dorsal and anal fin rays are 5. Overall colour is black with parts of the esca unpigmented. Females reach 11.5 cm total length.

grapnel compleat-angler

Biology: This is a little known species with 2 specimens caught off Newfoundland in 1968, 1 off Bermuda and 1 off Madeira. It has been suggested that the escal hooks help impale squid tentacles and certainly the luminescent esca is used to entice prey in reach of the mouth.

grass carp

Scientific name: *Ctenopharyngodon idella*
    (Valenciennes in Cuvier and
    Valenciennes, 1844)

Family: **Carp**
Other common names: white amur
French name: carpe de roseau

Distribution: Found in Lake Erie in Canada from U.S. introductions and being introduced to ponds in Manitoba and Alberta. Its normal range is in eastern Asia from the

grass carp

Amur River of the former U.S.S.R. south to the West River of China and Thailand.

Characters: This species is identified by the eyes being low on the side of the head, the anal fin is far back on the body close to the caudal fin, and pharyngeal teeth have large, parallel grooves on the grinding surface. Dorsal fin branched rays 6–8, anal rays 7–9 and pectoral rays 15–20. Pharyngeal teeth 2,5–4,2, or 2,4–5,2, 2,4–4,2, 1,4–5,2 and other combinations. Lateral line scales 34–47. Nuptial tubercles are evident on male pectoral fins. The overall colour is silvery-green to light golden with a white belly and olive-brown or greyish back. Upper scales are outlined with dark pigment to give a cross-hatching effect. Pelvic fins are whitish while other fins are dark. Peritoneum brownish black. Reaches 121.9 cm and 45.5 kg.

Biology: The natural habitat of this species is large rivers but it can be raised in ponds. It tolerates brackish waters. It has been widely introduced (to at least 40 U.S. states) to control excess aquatic vegetation as it is one of the few fish that eat large plants, taking more than its body weight daily. It may also take some animal material. Pond-cultured grass carp will eat the waste from crops and lawn cuttings. Grass carp tolerate a large temperature range of 0–35°C.

Maturity is attained at 6–10 years in the Amur River and as early as 10 months in Malaysia. Life span is up to 21 years. Spawning in China occurs in spring and summer in the temperature range 19–31°C. Each

female lays up to 1,276,000 floating eggs which require a minimum water velocity of 0.23 m/second or more to support them and hatch. This is found in large rivers where the eggs hatch as they drift downstream. At 20°C and a not unusual velocity of 1.2 m/second hatching requires 180 km of river. Eggs are up to 2.5 mm in diameter before fertilisation.

Aquatic weeds in irrigation ditches of Alberta can block up to 80% of water flow. Poisoning, dredging and cutting have generally proved ineffective. Grass carp are being tested as weed controllers. To prevent disease introductions and breeding of an exotic species, the fish are sterilised, quarantined for a year and given extensive health tests. Sterility is induced by means of a pressure shock to fertilised eggs. Triploid fishes result, which are unable to reproduce.

These fish are usually good eating but may become tainted with an algal flavour. Stocking of grass carp is prohibited in some U.S. states because of the potential for wild fowl and fish habitat destruction should breeding populations become established.

grass pickerel

Scientific name: *Esox americanus vermiculatus*
    Le Sueur in Cuvier and Valenciennes, 1846
Family: **Pike**
Other common names: western grass, mud,
    slough, little or central redfin pickerel;
    grass or mud pike
French name: brochet vermiculé

Distribution: Found from Montréal to Belleville in the St. Lawrence River and eastern Lake Ontario and their tributaries, in the upper Niagara River, Lake Erie, Lake St. Clair and southern Lake Huron, and in the Severn River and Muskoka Lakes area draining to southern Georgian Bay. In the U.S.A. south to Texas and Louisiana, west of the Appalachian Mountains, probably intergrading with **redfin pickerel** from Mississippi to Florida.

Characters: This species is identified by the 7–8 pores on the lower jaws (4 on each jaw, rarely 3 or 5), cheeks and opercula covered with scales, snout concave above, cardioid or notched scales between the pelvic fins less than 5, and pectoral, pelvic and anal fins dusky or yellow-green. There are fewer (5 or less) notched or heart-shaped scales in the diagonal row between the dorsal and anal fins. Dorsal fin with 14–17 principal rays, anal fin with 13–15 principal rays, pectoral rays 14–15 and pelvic rays 9–10. Lateral line scales 92–118. Back and upper flank dark olive-green to yellowish-brown with a reddish-brown middorsal stripe, flank with 15–23 olive, brown or black wavy bars and a pale midlateral stripe, and belly yellow to whitish. Black bars radiate from the eye. The lateral jaw edges are pale. The eye is yellow. The anterior margin of fins is black with the remainder of the fin dusky or amber. Reaches 38.1 cm.

grass pickerel

Biology: Grass pickerel are found in sluggish streams and in ponds with a lot of aquatic plants and neutral to basic silty water, rarely in vegetated lakes. It tolerates high temperatures up to 29°C, an adaptation to shallow, still waters which rapidly heat up. Food is invertebrates when young, switching gradually to fish and crayfish with some larger aquatic insects. Most feeding occurs in the late afternoon or early evening. Life span is 8 years with maturity attained at 1–2 years, 15.7 cm for females and 14.1 cm for males. Females live longer, grow faster and are larger than males. Spawning takes place in March to May, usually April in Ontario, at 4–12°C and probably for a few adults in the fall. Eggs are broadcast on vegetation to which they adhere. Up to 756 mature, amber to yellow eggs are shed, up to 2.4 mm in diameter. There are 3 sizes of eggs in this pickerel's ovaries, totalling 4584. This is not a sport fish in Canada but can be caught on baited hooks, spinners, spoons and plugs.

gravel chub

Scientific name: *Erimystax x-punctatus*
(Hubbs and Crowe, 1956)

Family: **Carp**
Other common names: spotted chub
French name: gravelier

Distribution: Found from Pennsylvania to Ohio and south to Arkansas and Oklahoma. In the Thames River basin of southern Ontario.

Characters: This species is distinguished from other minnows by having protractile premaxillae (upper lip separated from snout by a groove), a barbel at each mouth corner, 37–47 lateral line scales, snout overhanging mouth, and dark, x- (or y- or w-) shaped marks on the flank formed by pigment outlining scales. Pharyngeal teeth 4–4, slender and hooked at the tip. Gill rakers about 9. The gut is longer than the body and has several loops. Dorsal fin branched rays 7, anal branched rays 6–7, pectoral rays 13–19 and pelvic rays 7–9. Males have small nuptial tubercles on the head, branchiostegal rays, on all scales but particularly anterior scales (up to 25 tubercles per scale), in comb-like rows on the isthmus scales, in a single row on pectoral fin rays 2–11, on the anal fin distally, on all pelvic rays except the first ray, and on the dorsal fin and to a lesser extent the caudal fin. There is a nuptial pad on the lower cheek through which several tubercles protrude. Tubercles are also present, unusually, on the lips.

gravel chub

The back is olive to olive-green or grey and the flanks silvery. There may be a dusky midflank stripe. The belly is white, cream or silvery-white. Fins are clear. There is usually a black spot at the caudal fin base. There is a continuous middorsal stripe on the back. Peritoneum dark brown to black. Formerly in the genus *Hybopsis*. Reaches 10.2 cm.

Biology: The gravel chub appropriately prefers gravel-bottomed or rocky, moderate to large streams without silt and with swift water. It can also be found in larger slower rivers where bottom silt is absent. It lives in small cavities beneath rocks which are soon filled in by any silt. It has only been collected in Canada in 1928 and in 1958. Siltation has probably extirpated it.

Food is aquatic insects, snails, and encrusting plants on rocks. It probes under rocks, in crevices and mollusc shells with the long snout and well-developed taste buds on the barbels.

Life span is about 3 years. Spawning occurs in spring in swift riffles over gravel at 16°C or warmer. The nuptial pad is used to maintain contact with females during spawning. A female lies motionless on the bottom, often in a natural depression. A male moves above or alongside her without touching, the female responds with slow body undulations and the male touches cheeks. Rapid body vibrations follow and eggs and sperm are shed. Eggs have a diameter up to 2.0 mm and number over 500 in one female.

The gravel chub is now (1987) "extirpated" in Canada according to the Committee on the Status of Endangered Wildlife in Canada.

graveldiver

Scientific name: *Scytalina cerdale*
    Jordan and Gilbert, 1880
Family: **Graveldiver**
Other common names: burrowing blenny
French name: blennie fouisseuse

Distribution: Found from southern California to northwestern Alaska including the coast of British Columbia.

Characters: This species and the family are characterised by an elongate, compressed and eel-like body, with loose skin, the very

graveldiver

small eyes near the top of the head, the large opercles reaching the top of the head, the absence of scales and pelvic fins, and the continuous dorsal, anal and caudal fins,

without spines, on the rear half of the body. The body is deepest posteriorly. The gill membranes are united and free of the isthmus. Teeth on the jaws are small and conical with 2 canines at the front of the upper and lower jaws. Both the upper and lower jaws have prominent pores with 4 pairs on the lower jaw. There are 41–51 dorsal fin rays and 36–41 anal fin rays. Pale pink, violet, brown-purple, reddish-brown or yellow with darker mottles. Attains 15.2 cm.

Biology: Found in shallow water, including tide pools and beaches, to about 7.6 m where it burrows in loose gravel, sand or broken shells. This fish is rarely seen because of its habit of burrowing, although clam diggers may encounter it. However, up to 3.5 fish/sq m. may be found. Wave action in winter limits its distribution. The Latin *cerdale* means "wary one." They may live 8–9 years, maturing at 3 years of age. Reproduction probably occurs sub-tidally.

Graveldiver Family

Scientific name: Scytalinidae
French name: blennies fouisseuses

The **graveldiver** is the sole member of this family which is found on the Pacific coast of North America.

The family and species are described under the species account.

The **graveldiver** is related to the **Gunnel** and **Shanny** families and is a member of the **Perch Order**.

See **graveldiver**

gray starsnout

Scientific name: *Bathyagonus alascanus*
    (Gilbert, 1896)
Family: **Poacher**
Other common names: none
French name: astérothèque gris

Distribution: Found from the Bering Sea through British Columbia to northern California.

Characters: This poacher is one of 4 related species called starsnouts (**bigeye, blackfin, gray** and **spinycheek starsnouts**) for an arrangement of 5 or more small spines at the tip of the snout on a moveable plate which form, supposedly, a star. Three spines point vertically and 2 laterally. The gray starsnout is distinguished by having a small pit on the back of the head, plates in a single row or single pair in front of the pelvic fins, no spines on the bones under the eye centre and the anal fin origin lying below the space between the 2 dorsal fins. There is a row of strong spines on the eyeball. The first dorsal fin has 5–8 spines, the second 5–7 soft rays. The anal fin has 6–8 rays and the pectoral fin about 15 rays with the lower 5–6 obviously finger-like. There are 35–39 plates in the dorsal row. Cirri are found as 1 large and 1 small one at the rear of the upper jaw with 1 or more cirri on each lower jaw. Gill membranes are joined to the isthmus. Brown to a greenish grey above to a light brown on the belly. The back and flanks have 5–6 brown saddles. The pectoral, dorsal and caudal fins are barred. Reaches 13 cm.

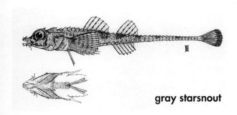

gray starsnout

Biology: A common species in British Columbia. Habitat is in rocky areas at 18–252 m.

gray triggerfish

Scientific name: *Balistes capriscus* Gmelin, 1789
Family: **Leatherjacket**
Other common names: baliste gris
French name: baliste capri

Distribution: Found from Newfoundland south to Argentina and in the eastern Atlantic Ocean and Mediterranean Sea.

Characters: This species is distinct from the **ocean triggerfish** by having enlarged flexible scales above the pectoral fin base and from the **queen triggerfish** by colour and fin ray counts. Dorsal fin rays 26–29, usually 27–28, anal fin rays 23–26, usually 24–25, and pectoral fin rays 13–15, usually 14. Outer

caudal fin rays only slightly elongated. The lateral line is complete. Body colour is variable, brown to grey or greenish. Dorsal, anal

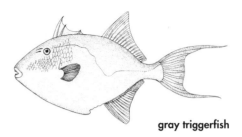

gray triggerfish

and caudal fins with occasional blue spots or lines, marbled. There is usually a ring of blue spots around the eye interrupted by olive-green streaks. There are 4 dark patches at the second dorsal fin base. Four irregular vertical bars are usually most distinct on young fish. Young have many, small rounded spots and dark patches on the body. The pectoral fins are greenish. Teeth are orange. Reaches 49.2 cm. The world, all-tackle angling record weighed 6.15 kg and was caught in 1989 at Murrells Inlet, South Carolina.

Biology: An occasional stray into Canadian waters from the south as far as Newfoundland. Adults may be open water species and the young are found in floating *Sargassum* weed. Also found over rocky bottoms at 10–100 m. They are usually solitary. Food is molluscs and crustaceans. Eggs are laid in a cavity excavated by the female and are guarded by the male. This triggerfish is said to be excellent eating.

graylings

Graylings are members of the **Salmon Family**. There are 4 species found across the Northern Hemisphere with 1 species, the **Arctic grayling**, in Canada. Graylings are a silvery-grey. The **Atlantic salmon** is sometimes referred to as a grayling in Nova Scotia and the **mountain whitefish** may also be called grayling.

great sculpin

Scientific name: *Myoxocephalus polyacanthocephalus* (Pallas, 1814)
Family: **Sculpin**

Other common names: none
French name: grand chaboisseau

Distribution: Found from Japan to Washington including British Columbia.

Characters: This sculpin is separated from its Canadian Pacific relatives by the separated dorsal fins, gill membranes attached to the

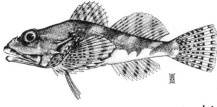

great sculpin

isthmus but with a free fold posteriorly, the upper preopercular spine is very long (longer than eye), sharp and strong and projects outward and upward, and body and head scales are scattered in fleshy papillae. There are spinate scales above and below the lateral line. Lateral line pores about 35–45 with pores in parallel above and below. There is a small cirrus above and behind each eye and papillae at dorsal fin spine tips. First dorsal fin spines 9–10, usually 9, second dorsal rays 10–16, anal rays 8–13 and pectoral rays 16–19 with lower rays finger-like at their tips. The back is a dark olive to blackish with 4 dark saddles and interspaces progressively lighter posteriorly. The flanks are mottled. The belly is pale. Fins are thinly barred or spotted in rows. The spiny dorsal fin is mottled dark anteriorly while posteriorly membranes are paler. Pectoral fins may be dark basally and light at the tip with some clearer areas in between, or barred. Barred pectorals are found most strongly in males. Males also have papillae on the inner pectoral fin surface of rays ventral to the uppermost 2–4 rays and above the lowermost 6–8 rays. Pelvic fin rays may also have papillae. Attains 76 cm and perhaps larger.

Biology: Common in Canadian waters along the coast in shallow to deep water (0–775 m). Bottom sediments are usually hard but this fish has been caught over sand where eelgrass and sea lettuce are abundant. Food includes fishes, but biology is not well

known. This species is often caught by anglers from piers, jetties and wharves when in pursuit of other species.

great white shark

Scientific name: *Carcharodon carcharias* (Linnaeus, 1758)
Family: **Mackerel Shark**
Other common names: white shark, white pointer, blue pointer, white death, maneater shark, mangeur d'homme
French name: grand requin blanc

Distribution: In Atlantic Canada as far north as Newfoundland and the Gulf of St. Lawrence. First reported from British Columbia in 1961 from the east coast of the Queen Charlotte Islands. Rare on our Pacific coast. Generally found in tropical and warm temperature oceans of the world but has reached Alaskan waters. Most Canadian records are from Nova Scotia.

Characters: Distinguished from other **mackerel sharks** by having distinctive, large serrated teeth, the upper teeth being almost triangular in shape and up to 8 cm long. Specimens under 150 cm in total body length have slender teeth, sometimes with smooth edges and basal cusplets. The body is heavy and cylindrical. Both the second dorsal and

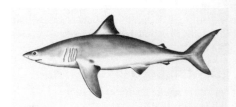

great white shark

anal fins are small and can pivot. The snout is conical and pointed (hence white pointer). The 5 gill slits are about half the body depth in height. The scales are minute with 3 weak ridges and almost flat so the skin is not very rough to touch.

Despite its name, the great white shark is not white, except in very large specimens which are a dull grey-white. The back is lead-grey, grey-brown, slate blue or black and fades to a dirty-white on the belly. The pectoral fins have black tips and there may be a black spot on the body near their base. Large adults lack this spot. The dorsal and tail fins are dark along their rear margins while the pelvics are darkest along their front margins.

Said to reach 11.3 m but this record is now known to be an error. It was based on a specimen from White Head Island, near Grand Manan, New Brunswick, taken in a herring weir in mid-June, 1930, and cannot now be verified. It was not seen or measured by an ichthyologist and a tooth from this specimen was only comparable to that of a shark 5.0–5.3 m in length. Nevertheless it crushed the side of a large dinghy "like an eggshell." The world record rod-caught great white shark was caught on 21 April 1959, weighed 1208.38 kg, measured 513.08 cm and came from South Australia. A 1556 kg and 5.27 m long specimen was caught by Captain Frank Mundus and Donald Braddick off Montauk, Long Island on 6 August 1986, the largest fish ever caught on rod and line. Maximum size reports in the literature are sometimes exaggerated and 6.0 m is probably the largest size attained. A great white 5.26 m fork length in a straight line, was caught in gill nets or a cod net off northwestern P.E.I. and landed at Alberton on 4 August 1983. This is one of the longest accurately measured great white sharks. One taken in a herring weir at Campobello Island, New Brunswick in 1932, was said to measure 7.92 m but this was probably an exaggeration. A specimen about 5.2 m long was found beached at Long Inlet, Graham Island, B.C. on 16 December 1987.

Biology: It is found in coastal and offshore waters from the surface down to 1280 m. It has entered saltwater creeks in the U.S.A. and is often found close inshore near the surf line. In the western North Atlantic great white sharks are found in a ratio of 1 to 2,046 other sharks based on longline and rod and reel data. Found in Canadian waters during warmer weather in April to November, most frequently in August. They appear to be more frequent in warm-water years and favour temperatures between 12 and 25°C.

Great whites are mature between 3.3 and 4.3 m and live at least 20 years. Pregnant females have seldom been caught so little is known about reproduction in this species. Pups number up to 9 and are about 100–110 cm.

Their diet consists of harbour seals, sea lions, harbour porpoises, other **sharks, sturgeons, tunas,** a variety of other fishes, shell fish, sea turtles and sea gulls. Whale carcasses are an important food off the northeastern U.S. coast. Sea otters are often killed on the Pacific coast of the U.S. but it is not known if the shark eats them. At Grand Manan, N.B., a large great white was dispatched by several bullets, towed to shore and on being cut open was found to contain two large harbour seals, one intact and the other "cut in two as though with an axe." Various unusual items have been found in their stomachs including a whole sheep, a cuckoo clock, a bulldog, and many bottles and cans.

They also attack people at bathing beaches, given the chance, although there have been no records of fatalities in Canada. There are usually fewer than 5 attacks on humans along the U.S. Pacific coast each year. A great white shark 4.5 m in length can bite a man in two and one 6 m long can swallow a man whole. Small boats have been attacked in Canadian waters with 1 fatality by drowning. There have been no direct fatal attacks by this species in Canada. A great white shark attacked the gear of a salmon fisherman off the west coast of Vancouver Island near Ucluelet but Pacific coast incidents are very rare. These sharks have been known to take a larger boat by the propeller and shake it.

The flesh is edible though seldom eaten and is said to be one of the best tasting in sharks with a reddish colour like that of salmon. It should be filleted and well soaked to remove the urea. However muscle and liver tissue from great white sharks taken in the Bay of Fundy-Gulf of Maine area have higher levels of PCBs and chlorinated hydrocarbon pesticides than other fish. Top predators like great white sharks concentrate harmful chemicals and their flesh should be eaten sparingly. It has been eaten fresh, dried and salted, or smoked. This shark has also been used for fish meal, leather and shark-fin soup. The liver oil can be used for its vitamin content. Large jaws command a high price in the thousands of dollars. Great whites are not common enough to support a commercial fishery and are usually caught incidental to other fisheries. They may be caught by bait fishing while chumming or by trolling. They have been known to jump out of the water and can make sudden dashes. It is the world's largest game fish and adults fight so strongly that few are captured. In the northeast U.S. it is an important sport fish. Baits include **tuna** and other oily fishes.

greatbarbelthroat

Scientific name: *Linophryne coronata* Parr, 1927
Family: **Leftvent**
Other common names: blacktail netdevil
French name: gorge à grande barbe

Distribution: Found in the Atlantic and Pacific oceans including off Newfoundland.

Characters: Females of this species of deepsea **anglerfish** are distinguished by having a barbel not branched at the base and with its end divided into 4 short branches, each with photophores often on stalks. The esca or bait has 2 pairs of short, distal appendages. Males have strong sphenotic spines. Overall colour of females is black. The esca has light patches. The lower half of each fang in the jaws is black. The caudal fin

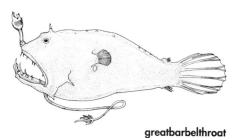

greatbarbelthroat

has a central clear spot. Males are brownish to black. Females reach 22.5 cm, with parasitic males 2.6 cm.

Biology: There are 3 specimens from off Newfoundland but since there were only 12 female specimens of this species known worldwide up to 1982, they are quite significant in

our understanding of this species. Females attract prey using the fishing apparatus.

greater amberjack

Scientific name: *Seriola dumerili* (Risso, 1810)
Family: **Jack**
Other common names: greater yellowtail, sériole couronnée,
French name: grande sériole

Distribution: From Nova Scotia to Brazil and in all warmer oceans.

Characters: This species is distinguished from its Canadian Atlantic coast relatives by the moderately deep but not highly com-

greater amberjack

pressed body, a lateral line without enlarged scales (scutes), a fleshy lateral caudal peduncle keel, a short upper jaw extending only to the middle of the eye and 7 first dorsal fin spines. Anterior spines may be embedded in the flesh in large fish and difficult to see. The second dorsal fin has 1 spine and 29–35 soft rays. The anal fin has 3 spines and 18–22 soft rays. Gill rakers number 18–24 when fish are 2–20 cm fork length and 11–19 when over 20 cm fork length. Adults are blue-grey to olive on the back with sides and belly silvery to white. There may be brownish or pink tinges on the lower surfaces and a yellow to amber stripe along the flank. There is a dark olive-brown stripe from the snout through the eye to the first dorsal fin origin. Fins are mostly dusky. Young fish have 5 bars. Reaches 188 cm and 80.6 kg. The world, all-tackle angling record weighed 70.59 kg and was caught at Bermuda in 1981.

Biology: First recorded from Canada in 1973 from off Prospect, Nova Scotia with a second specimen caught in a mackerel trap in St. Margarets Bay in 1984. These are northern range records. It is common in the western Atlantic Ocean south of our waters. This species is usually found at 18–72 m but can go as deep as 360 m. It may be found in surface or near bottom schools or be found as individuals. Adult greater amberjacks are often found near reefs, deep holes offshore and drop-offs. Young are associated with debris or floating seaweed in offshore waters. Food is mostly fishes and some invertebrates. Maximum age is about 15 years. Spawning takes place in August and November in the Caribbean. This is an important game and commercial fish to the south but the flesh has been contaminated with ciguatera poisoning.

greater eelpout

Scientific name: *Lycodes esmarki*
    Collett, 1875
Family: **Eelpout**
Other common names: Esmark's eelpout,
    lycode d'Esmark
French name: grande lycode

Distribution: Found in the North Atlantic Ocean, in the west from Greenland and the Labrador shelf south perhaps as far as Virginia.

Characters: This species is separated from its Canadian Arctic-Atlantic relatives by having small pelvic fins, a mouth under

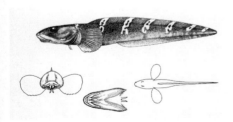

greater eelpout

the snout, no large pores around the mouth, crests on the chin, a double lateral line with one complete and midlateral and the other on the lower flank, long tail (preanal length 38–44% total length), pectoral fin rays 21–24, and colour. There are no pyloric caeca, a unique absence in Canadian *Lycodes* species. Dorsal fin rays 113–118 and anal rays 97–102 (each including half of the continuous caudal fin rays). Vertebrae 115–118.

The belly, dorsal and anal fins and pectoral fin base are scaled. Overall colour is variable with age and locality but is often brown dorsally becoming yellowish ventrally. The upper flank and dorsal fin have 5–9 white to yellowish bands which may be inverted Y-shapes in young. The nape may be crossed by a light band. Bands may have a dark centre. Peritoneum black. Attains 75 cm.

Biology: This species is usually caught at 151–550 m on mud bottoms at a temperature range of –0.4 to 5°C. It may be caught as shallow as 51 m or as deep as 750 m. Typically this eelpout sits on a soft bottom in a coiled position. Food includes starfishes, sea urchins and brittle stars. Eggs number about 1200 in large females and have a diameter of 6 mm.

greater redhorse

Scientific name: *Moxostoma valenciennesi*
    Jordan, 1885
Family: **Sucker**
Other common names: common redhorse
French name: suceur jaune

Distribution: Found in southern Ontario and southwestern Québec in the St. Lawrence River, Richelieu River and Ottawa River, lakes Ontario, Erie, St. Clair and Huron and their tributaries. In the U.S.A. in the southern Great Lakes, St. Lawrence River and upper Mississippi River basins.

Characters: This species is distinguished by a short dorsal fin, a swimbladder with 3 chambers, lateral line scales 41–45, scales around the caudal peduncle usually 15–16,

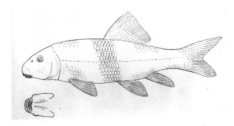

greater redhorse

scales over the back just in front of the dorsal from lateral line to lateral line usually 12–13 (excluding lateral line scales), and pharyngeal teeth small, comb-like and 12–30 on lower half of the tooth row. The maximum body depth enters body length to the end of the scales 4 times or more. The dorsal fin usually has a convex margin. The snout is longer than the postorbital length. The mouth is not overhung by the snout. The upper lip is wide with coarse plicae. The lower lip is deeply cleft and wide, plicae are coarse, deep and lack cross striations. Gill rakers 25–31. Dorsal fin rays 11–15, anal rays 7, pectoral rays 15–19 and pelvic rays 8–10. The gut has 5–8 coils. Males have nuptial tubercles on the anal and caudal fins and also on the pectoral and pelvic fin rays. The head and body scales are also minutely tuberculate.

Overall colour is dark olive-green, or greyish, with bronze or golden tints, fading ventrally to a milky-white belly. The dorsal, anal and caudal fins are dark red. The caudal may be mostly grey. Median fins may be red only at their margins. Scales have a dark crescent of pigment on the base. The anterior tip of the dorsal fin is white to pink and the anterior rays of the pelvic and pectoral fins white, yellowish or reddish-orange. The pectoral fin is olive and the pelvic fin is pale red.

Reaches 66.0 cm total length and 5.4 kg or more. The world, all-tackle angling record weighed 4.16 kg and was caught in the Salmon River, New York in 1985.

Biology: This redhorse favours clear, clean, hard-bottomed streams and lake margins but also occurs over softer bottoms in muddy areas. It may be sensitive to turbidity, siltation and pollution. Food is principally crustaceans and aquatic insects, with some molluscs and worms. Eggs of this redhorse are eaten by **American eels, fallfish** and **yellow perch**. Life span is 15 years with sexual maturity attained at 9 years. Spawning occurs over a 2 week period in late June and early July at 16–19°C in the upper St. Lawrence River. There are up to 51,434 eggs per female. The spawning habitat is less than 2 m deep and has a gravel, sand or rubble bed and moderate to swift current. Males move slowly on the spawning ground, often gently nudging and pushing each other. The female selects a spawning site and is flanked by 2 males. Other males attempt to join in.

The female is nuzzled by males in the genital area. Eggs and sperm are shed as the fish quiver and tremor for 2–8 seconds, the males pressing against the female.

greater silver hatchetfish

Scientific name: *Argyropelecus gigas* Norman, 1930
Family: **Silver Hatchetfish**
Other common names: none
French name: grande hache d'argent

Distribution: Found in all oceans except the North Pacific. Reported off the Atlantic coast of Canada.

Characters: This species is distinguished by having a hatchet-shaped body, 12 abdominal light organs, telescopic eyes directed upwards and a large blade anterior to the dorsal fin. In addition the lower light organs are

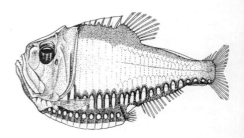

greater silver hatchetfish

in a nearly continuous row and the body profile below the dorsal blade spines 3 and 4 is raised. Pigmented with small spots along the midflank on a light brown background, partially outlining muscle blocks, in preserved specimens. Light organs silvery and edged with black. Overall colour is silvery. A large species exceeding 12 cm standard length.

Biology: One specimen was caught off the Scotian Shelf in 1952 at 622–640 m. Found chiefly between 400 and 600 m without any evidence of vertical migration.

greateye

Scientific name: *Epigonus denticulatus* Dieuzeide, 1950
Family: **Greateye**
Other common names: pencil cardinal
French name: grands-yeux

Distribution: Found world-wide in warmer seas and in Atlantic Canada.

Characters: This fish resembles **Cardinalfish Family** members but has more scales and scales extending onto the soft dorsal and anal

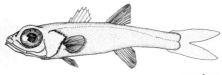

greateye

fins. There are 3–7 membranous projections at the top of the operculum. Lateral line scales 46–51. Scales detach easily. First dorsal fin spines 7, second dorsal fin with 1 spine and 9–10, usually 10, soft rays. Anal fin with 2 spines and 8–9, usually 9, soft rays. Pectoral rays 18–20. Gill rakers on the lower limb of the arch 20–25, total rakers 28–34. Pyloric caeca are 10–14. Overall body colour is reddish-brown with a light yellow head. Fins are light. The iris is black. Scale pockets have brown-black pigment spots. Reaches 20 cm.

Biology: Found at depths of 180–830 m, but most common at 300–600 m. Young are pelagic at 130–425 m. This species does not appear to be a mouthbrooder like **cardinalfish**. It is a commercial species in the Mediterranean Sea.

Greateye Family

Scientific name: Epigonidae
French name: grands yeux

Greateyes or deepwater cardinalfishes are found world-wide in warmer marine waters. There are about 15 species, with 1 reported from Atlantic Canada.

These are small, large-eyed fishes with usually 2 dorsal fins. The first dorsal fin has 7–8 spines and the second dorsal fin 1 spine and 7–10 soft rays. Both fins are covered with scales. There are 1–3 anal fin spines and 7–9 soft rays. There are usually 25 vertebrae and more than 6 infraorbital bones. Scales are ctenoid and the complete lateral line extends onto the caudal fin.

Greateyes are closely related to the **Cardinalfish Family** and are included within it by some authors. The family is a

member of the **Perch Order**. Greateyes have scales on the soft dorsal and anal fins, at least on the base, and there are always more than 30 pored scales in the lateral line.

These fishes are found in deeper water than most **cardinalfishes**. Some species are commercially important.

See **greateye**

green moray

Scientific name: *Gymnothorax funebris*
Ranzani, 1839
Family: **Moray**
Other common names: none
French name: murène verte

Distribution: Found in the Atlantic Ocean south to Brazil and rarely in Atlantic Canada.

Characters: Colour and size will separate the adults of this species from the **pygmy moray**, its relative in Atlantic Canada. The anal fin begins just behind the anus and the dorsal fin origin lies near the gill opening. The posterior nostrils are simple openings without tubes, the anterior nostrils are tubular and near the snout tip. Teeth lack serrations on the anterior and posterior margins. Dorsal fin rays 340–361, anal rays 217–237. Adults are dark green or greenish-grey to brown. Young fish are blackish without a white lower jaw as in many small morays. Reaches 2.5 m, the largest Atlantic coast moray.

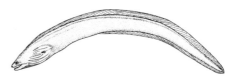

green moray

Biology: One specimen was speared in Halifax Harbour in 1952 and a second observed under water near Bathurst, New Brunswick in 1972. The captured specimen was 169 cm long and weighed 15 kg. This is a species usually found in tropical waters and is common from Florida to Brazil in the western Atlantic Ocean, around harbours, coral reefs, rocks and mangroves. It has been used as a food fish in the Bahamas and is marketed fresh and salted. Large green morays have caused ciguatera poisoning and its bite is dangerous. It is reported to be aggressive to divers without being provoked.

green sturgeon

Scientific name: *Acipenser medirostris* Ayres, 1854
Family: **Sturgeon**
Other common names: none
French name: esturgeon vert

Distribution: Found around the North Pacific Ocean from Taiwan to Baja California including British Columbia.

Characters: This species is distinguished from its Pacific coast relative, the **white sturgeon**, by having 22–36 lateral scutes of shields along the midflank, a greenish colour

green sturgeon

and the barbels are nearer to the mouth than the tip of the snout. The snout is concave with the tip turned up. The dorsal fin has 33–42 rays and the anal fin 22–30. The dorsal row of scutes numbers 7–11 to the dorsal fin with 1–2 behind the dorsal fin, and the lower row has 6–10 scutes with 1 plate between the anal and caudal fins. Gill rakers 18–20. Colour is an olive-green or dark green with olive stripes on the whitish-green belly and lower flank. Scutes are paler than the adjacent body. Fins are dusky to grey or pale green. The internal organs of the abdomen are pale. Reaches 213 cm and 159 kg.

Biology: Green sturgeons are found on soft bottoms down to 122 m and are more common in the ocean than **white sturgeon**. They are often found in brackish water of river mouths. Food includes fishes such as **sand lances**, crustaceans and molluscs. Young fish eat mostly crustaceans. Spawning occurs in the spring after a late summer to fall migration into fresh water. They have no commercial importance in Canada. The Committee on the Status of Endangered Wildlife in Canada approved a status of "rare" for this species in 1987.

green sunfish

Scientific name: *Lepomis cyanellus* Rafinesque, 1819
Family: **Sunfish**
Other common names: green perch, black perch, logfish, blue-spotted sunfish, little redeye, blue bass, sand bass, creek sunfish, rubbertail, bream, sunperch, goggle-eye, branch perch, rock bass, pond perch, shade perch, ricefield slick, blue and green sunfish, buffalo sunfish
French name: crapet vert

Distribution: Found in southwestern Ontario in Lake St. Clair and Lake Erie tributaries and in northwestern Ontario in Quetico Provincial Park in the Hudson Bay drainage. In the U.S.A. from New York and North Dakota, south to Florida and northeastern Mexico, west of the Appalachian Mountains. Introduced outside this natural range in North America and Germany.

Characters: This species is characterised by having 9–11 dorsal fin spines, 3 anal fin spines, 40–53 lateral line scales, a black opercular or "ear" flap with a red, pink or yellow margin, about as long as deep and with an entire bony edge (not crenate or wavy), and 8–10 rows of scales on a diagonal between the lateral line and dorsal fin origin. Dorsal fin soft rays 10–12, anal soft rays 8–10 and pectoral rays 12–15.

Back and upper flank brown to olive overlain with emerald or bluish green, fading to yellow-green on the flank with iridescent

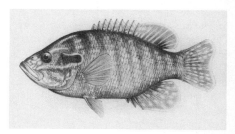

green sunfish

green or blue flecks, and white to yellow-orange or pale olive on the belly. The upper flank has 7–12 dark bars. Scales have a paler centre than margin giving an impression of thin horizontal stripes. The head may be spotted emerald green or iridescent blue and may have wavy emerald lines radiating backwards. The rear base of the dorsal and anal fins has a dark blotch. Pectoral fins are clear. Breeding males are more intensely coloured with the dorsal, anal and caudal fins, and sometimes pelvic fins, dusky to olive overall but membranes are darker than rays and the fin margin is white, yellow or orange. Peritoneum silvery-white.

Reaches 30.5 cm. The world, all-tackle angling record weighed 0.96 kg and was caught in Stockton Lake, Missouri in 1971.

Biology: Green sunfish are found in lake shallows, ponds and small streams with abundant vegetation. They are quite tolerant of turbid and silty conditions and can survive temperatures up to 36°C. In highly turbid conditions green sunfish "cough" to unclog their gills. Food is aquatic insects, crustaceans, molluscs and small fishes.

Life span is about 10 years. Crowded populations show stunting. Maturity is attained as early as 1 year in the south and probably 3 years in Canada. Spawning occurs from May to August in the north, peaking at 15–28°C.

Males excavate shallow nests in areas sheltered by rocks, logs or vegetation and a colony of males can be found together. The male swims vertically above the nests and lashes his tail to clear sand and gravel from the nest. Larger pebbles are picked up and removed with the mouth. Nests are 15–38 cm in diameter. Nests are defended against other males by head on or opercle-mouth encounters and males may grasp each other. Spawning occurs over 1–2 days when a male and female enter the nest site. The male adopts a vertical position, the female inclined on her side so her genital area is in contact with that of the male. Both sexes vibrate and eggs and sperm are shed. Each female carries up to 10,000 eggs. Males and females will spawn with more than one individual. The male guards and fans the eggs and guards the young for about a week until they leave the nest. Eggs are yellow, up to 1.4 mm in diameter, and attach to gravel or vegetation. Males make grunting noises as part of their courtship ritual, rushing repeatedly toward a female and backing toward the nest.

An important game fish in some parts of the U.S.A. caught with worms, flies and small spinners, but too uncommon to be sought after in Canada. The flesh is white, flaky and good tasting.

Greeneye Family

Scientific name: Chlorophthalmidae
French name: yeux-verts

Greeneyes are found in all warmer oceans. There are about 20 species with 2 reported from the Atlantic coast of Canada.

This family possesses a single, elongate supramaxilla bone in the upper jaw and 8 branchiostegal rays. The tip of the upper jaw does not extend beyond the orbit. Eyes are large. There is a single dorsal fin and usually a small adipose fin. A pseudobranch and pyloric caeca are present. Members are hermaphrodites. The species vary considerably in appearance. The greeneyes have large eyes with a keyhole-shaped pupil, a pseudobranch, pyloric caeca, moderate-sized mouth and short fins.

This family is related to the **Pearleye** and **Waryfish** families of the **Flagfin Order**. Members of this family are benthic fishes usually in deep water down to 6000 m although some are found as shallow as 100 m. Most are quite rare although some species can be abundant.

Greeneyes are named for the metallic green light reflected by the tapetum lucidum, a layer in the eye. They have green or yellow eye lenses which filter the camouflaging light emitted by luminous crustaceans, making this prey more visible. Greeneyes (*Chlorophthalmus* species) have an organ around the anus which produces a dim light from bacterial action. It may well serve to maintain contact between individuals and perhaps in mating. The *Chlorophthalmus* eye has specialised, twin cones which detect upper and forward light emitted by the perianal organ.

These fishes are not commercially important in Canada but are captured and used as food in the Mediterranean Sea and eastern Atlantic Ocean.

See **longnose greeneye**
    shortnose greeneye

Greenland halibut

Scientific name: *Reinhardtius hippoglossoides*
(Walbaum, 1792)
Family: **Righteye Flounders**
Other common names: Greenland turbot,
   turbot, Newfoundland turbot, black halibut,
   blue halibut, lesser halibut, mock halibut,
   bastard halibut, flétan noir, nat-ah-nuh,
   natarnak
French name: flétan du Groenland

Distribution: Found from Japan to the
Chukchi Sea and south to Baja California in
the Pacific Ocean including British Columbia,
and from 77°N off Greenland, to southern
Baffin Island, northern Hudson Bay, Davis
Strait and Labrador southward throughout
maritime Canada to the Gulf of Maine.

Characters: This species is distinguished
from related **flatfishes** by having a nearly
symmetrical, large mouth extending beyond

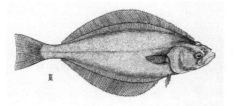

Greenland halibut

the lower eye, an upper eye at the top of the
head far removed from the lower eye and
visible on the blind side, a slightly forked to
truncate caudal fin, no spine in front of the
anal fin, simple teeth in a single row in each
jaw, and a straight lateral line. The preopercular bone on the side of the head has a right
angled lower corner with a series of pores.
Dorsal fin rays 83–108, anal rays 62–84.
Pectoral rays 11–15. Gill rakers 10–12 on the
lower arch. Lateral line scales about
109–119. Scales are cycloid on both sides.

The eyed side is black to dark brown or
rust-coloured, blind side white becoming
grey to dark grey or blue-greenish in adults.

Pacific coast stocks may be a distinct subspecies based on biochemical genetic analyses. See the discussion under **halibuts** about
the naming of this species. Reaches 119 cm.

Biology: Reported from La Pérouse Bank
in British Columbia as a single stray specimen
from the north caught at 550 m. Biology is
based on the Atlantic stocks. Only strays are
in southern Canadian waters like the Bay of
Fundy, entering in cold periods. This is a
species favouring temperatures at or below
7°C, either in shallow northern waters or deep
southern ones. Off Labrador and northern
Newfoundland this species is deeper than 457
m but the range is 90–2000 m. The preferred
depth on the Scotian Shelf is 165–273 m.
Larger and older fish predominate in deeper
waters and are more numerous in northern
areas. In the northern Gulf of St. Lawrence
they are found at 150–450 m, most abundantly at 300–350 m where the temperature
range is 4.5–6.0°C. Greenland halibut have
been tagged in White Bay, Newfoundland and
recovered at Baffin Island.

This fish is a major predator on other fishes
and it leaves the bottom to do so. Species
eaten include **Atlantic** and **polar cod, capelin,
roundnose grenadier, witch flounder, barracudinas, redfishes, sand lances** and even
their own young. Various crustaceans, squids
and bottom invertebrates are also eaten. In
their turn they are eaten by **Greenland shark,
cod, salmon**, whales and seals.

Older fish are found in deeper, northern
waters. The Baffin Bank may be a nursery
area. Females grow faster and live longer than
males and all fish over 90 cm are female.
Growth rate varies with area. The bulk of the
male population in the Gulf of St. Lawrence is
40–85 cm and 6–9 years of age and females
are 43–64 cm and 6–10 years. Maximum life
span is about 19 years but larger fish are difficult to age.

Spawning takes place in winter and early
spring in Davis Strait at 650–1000 m and
temperatures of 0–4°C and probably in the
Laurentian Channel. Fish move north to
spawn in Davis Strait but do not return south.
Each female produces up to 300,000 eggs
with a diameter of 4.5 mm. The young rise to
30–250 m and live pelagically, drifting south
to populate the shelf and slope of Labrador
and Newfoundland. Some stocks show little
mixing as subadults and adults, for example
those in the Gulf of St. Lawrence, Saguenay

Fjord and off Labrador. The stocks can be separated by using their parasite fauna as biological "tags."

Greenland halibut are caught in gill nets and trawls and sold as fresh-frozen fillets. They are also smoked and salted for local use. The 3 fisheries are Baffin Island-West Greenland with a total allowable catch (TAC) in 1986 of 25,000 tonnes, Labrador-East Newfoundland (TAC 100,000 tonnes) and Gulf of St. Lawrence (TAC 5000 tonnes). The annual catch in the 1980s had an average value of about $45 million but could reach $140 million if the total allowable catch was taken. The 1988 Canadian catch was 16,070 tonnes.

Greenland manefish

Scientific name: *Caristius groenlandicus* Jensen, 1941
Family: **Manefish**
Other common names: none
French name: cariste de Groenland

Distribution: Found from the Davis Strait south to the waters off Nova Scotia. Also in the eastern and South Atlantic Ocean. It has been reported from off British Columbia but the relationships of these manefishes are unclear and this may be the **manefish**.

Characters: This species is distinguished by its high, long dorsal fin originating on the head, by the scale sheaths for the dorsal, anal and pelvic fins and the high, steep slope to the front of the head. Dorsal fin rays 32–36, anal rays 18–22, pectoral rays 16–19. The

posterior nostril is a slit and the anterior nostril circular. The jaws have 1 row of canine teeth along the sides and 2–5 rows at the front. Overall colour a pinkish-brown with fins black. The eye is golden. The peritoneum is black and since the body wall is thin this is visible externally. Reaches at least 30 cm, largest Canadian specimen 25.4 cm.

Biology: Captured down to 1660 m in Davis Strait and as shallow as 146 m in Atlantic Canada. About 9 specimens have been recorded from Atlantic Canada. A rare species of which little is known. Food includes squid and probably fishes and crustaceans.

Greenland shark

Scientific name: *Somniosus microcephalus* (Bloch and Schneider, 1801)
Family: **Sleeper Shark**
Other common names: sleeper shark, ground shark, gurry shark, grey shark, large sleeper, requin dormeur, eqalukjuaq, iqalukuak, iqalujjuaq, eqaludjuaq
French name: laimargue atlantique

Distribution: Throughout Atlantic Canada and as far south as Cape Cod and north to Ellesmere Island in the Arctic. Found also at 76°30'N in Greenland, the south Atlantic and the Antarctic.

Characters: The Greenland shark is distinguished from other sharks by the absence of an anal fin, the body not being flattened, and

Greenland shark

the absence of spines at the front margin of the dorsal fins. The space between the dorsal fins is at least as long as the prebranchial length while in the Pacific sleeper shark it is about two-thirds this length. The gill slits are small, low on the body and in front of the pectoral fin. The snout is short, thick and rounded and the eye is circular and very small. The upper teeth are pointed while the lower teeth are broad, smooth and oblique thus forming a cutting edge.

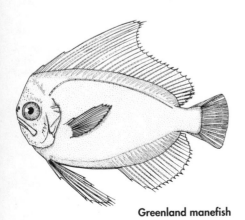

Greenland manefish

Grey or blue-grey to coffee brown or black with some vague dark bands on the back and flanks. Albinos have been reported in Greenland.

Possibly up to 8 m and 1012.5 kg. This is the largest Arctic fish. The largest, all-tackle rod-caught fish was 775 kg and was taken at Trondheimsfjord, Norway in 1987.

Biology: It is commonly found in coastal waters including river mouths at the surface in winter and retreats to deeper and cooler water in summer. It may descend to depths of at least 1200 m. This shark is characterised as sluggish although it may be able to move quickly on occasion since its foods include large and active prey.

These sharks eat fish such as **herring, Atlantic salmon, Arctic char, capelin, flatfishes** and various other species. At Pond Inlet one of these sharks was found to have eaten another shark which had eaten a third. They may also eat seals, common porpoise, sea birds, squid, snails, pelecypods, crabs, jellyfish, and seaweed, and will scavenge for scraps near fishery operations. Also known to gouge out flesh from dead whales. They were called gurry sharks from the waste or *gurry* resulting from the processing of whales at whaling stations. One 4.85 m specimen contained the jaws of a 2.33 m blue shark in its stomach. One entire reindeer has been found in a Greenland shark.

The Greenland shark gives birth to live young. One female 5 m long had 37 cm young in one uterus. Growth may be very slow. A specimen caught off West Greenland in 1936 measured 2.77 m and was only 2.86 m long when recaptured 16 years later.

Greenland sharks often have a parasitic copepod, *Ommatokoita elongata*, usually attached to the eyes, one to each eye, and over 6 cm long. Of 1505 sharks examined in east Greenland waters, only 17 were not infested. These parasites are very obvious and possibly luminescent. It has been suggested that they act as lures to attract prey species closer to their hosts but this remains unproven. Arctic char from Greenland shark stomachs have been recovered with only the tail missing, suggesting they are taken head on, perhaps attracted by the white copepod which stands out against the dark background colour of the shark.

Extensive commercial operations have not been tried by Canadians but it has been valued in Greenland and Europe for its hide, liver oil and as human and dog food. Large fishing vessels in Canadian waters, like freezer factory-trawlers, dump any Greenland sharks they catch. A years catch has reached 50,000 fish in the 1950s in West Greenland. Up to 400 are caught each year by Pangnirtung fishermen along the east coast of Baffin Island while fishing for turbot.

There has been some promotion of this shark in a Montreal fish store as an Arctic seafood, and continuing efforts to market the skin. The flesh is poisonous when fresh unless washed, dried or boiled. The poison is derived from pelecypods which are common in Arctic waters. Ravens and fulmars scavenging shark carcasses have become too ill to fly and stumble around as though intoxicated. The flesh is used as dog food in Greenland but, unless treated to remove the poison, dogs become "shark drunk" — drowsy and giddy — and may die. However dogs at Pond Inlet, Baffin Island ate fresh shark meat without any such symptoms.

Over 477 litres of oil has been taken from one individual. The skin can be used as a leather in book binding, for shoes, and for heavy upholstery. These sharks damage seals, eat bait meant for other fishes and destroy nets during the fall fishery. It is said to give little fight when hooked. It is caught with hook and line, on longlines or by gaffs as well as in cod traps. In winter it may be lured to the surface by a light.

In Labrador "several portions of the vitals are preserved by the people with the greatest of care, under the supposition that the wearing or carrying of them or the simple having them in the house will prove sure protection against not only the rheumatism, but several diseases peculiar to the male sex" (Stearns, 1884).

Greenling Family

Scientific name: Hexagrammidae
French name: sourcils

This family is found only in the North Pacific Ocean and the adjacent Arctic Ocean, where there are 11 species, 8 in Canada.

There is usually more than one lateral line, a cirrus or feathery flap of skin over the eye and elsewhere on the head and a long dorsal fin with about equal numbers of spines and soft rays separated by a notch. Scales may be cycloid but are usually ctenoid and are comb-like in the combfishes. The posterior nostril is absent or reduced to a small pore. Pelvic fins are thoracic, ie. positioned below the pectoral fins, and have 1 spine and 5 soft rays. Teeth are usually small and gill membranes are joined and free of the isthmus. There are 6 branchiostegal rays. The swimbladder is absent.

The French name of this family refers to the cirri or "eyebrows" above the eye. Greenlings are related to the **Sculpin** family but lack spines on the head. The combfishes are sometimes placed in a separate family, the Zaniolepididae. Greenlings are members of the **Mail-cheeked Order**.

Family members are inshore fishes. They are said to be good eating but only the **lingcod** is commercially important.

See **Atka mackerel**
    kelp greenling
    lingcod
    longspine combfish
    masked greenling
    painted greenling
    rock greenling
    whitespotted greenling

greenside darter

Scientific name: *Etheostoma blennioides*
    Rafinesque, 1819
Family: **Perch**
Other common names: none
French name: dard vert

Distribution: Found in the Lake St. Clair, southern Lake Huron and rarely Lake Erie drainages of southwestern Ontario in Canada. Elsewhere in the lower Great Lakes basin, the Potomac and Mississippi basins as far south as Arkansas and northern Alabama.

Characters: This darter is recognised by the small mouth not extending beyond the anterior eye margin, a smooth edge to the preopercle bone on the side of the head, an anal fin smaller than the soft dorsal fin, lip and snout not separated by a groove (pre-maxillaries not protractile), 2 anal fin spines, belly fully scaled, dorsal fin spines 11–16, usually 12–14, dorsal soft rays 11–16, and lateral line scales 51–86. Anal fin soft rays 6–10, usually 7–9. Pectoral rays 13–16. This darter is unique in that the skin over the pre-orbital bone at the side of the snout is fused to the skin over the maxilla bone of the upper jaw.

The back is olive-green to olive-brown, flanks pale green and the belly white. The upper body has brown to orange-red spots. Anal, caudal and pelvic fins pale green. The dorsal fins are green and often have an orange-red stripe at their bases. The back has 5–8, usually 7, brown saddles obscured in older fish by the background. The flanks at and below the lateral line have 5–10 olive-brown, u-,v- or w-shaped marks. Two bars extend down and anteriorly from the eye. Breeding males are bright green, bars on the back and flanks are dark green and the spiny dorsal fin has a brick-red stripe at the base. There are tubercles on the belly posteriorly and the lower caudal peduncle scales. The pelvic spine becomes covered in spongy tissue and is bent. Females are yellow-green. Females have smaller fins than males. The genital papillae of both sexes form a short tube. Reaches 14.0 cm standard length, the largest member of its genus.

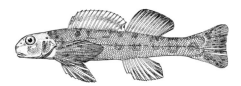

greenside darter

Biology: Found in rivers and streams over rocks and gravel where current is medium to fast. Food is mainly insect larvae, with some crustaceans. A few fish reach 4 or more years of age. Most live only 3 years. Males grow faster and are larger than females. Maturity can be attained at 1 year in both sexes after rapid growth; females may attain over two-thirds of their growth in 1 year. Spawning occurs in April to June in the northern U.S. when water temperatures exceed 10°C. Eggs are often deposited in filamentous algae. Males select a territory but the females choose the specific spawning site. The female sits on an algae-covered rock at a distinct angle and the male lies on top of the female, both vibrate and 3–15 eggs are laid. Up to 1832 adhesive eggs of about 1.85 mm diameter are produced by each female, in 10–12 spawnings over 4–5 weeks. Several females spawn with one male. Males threatened by other fishes "freeze" for 2–3 minutes before resuming normal activity. The Committee on the Status of Endangered Wildlife in Canada gave this species "vulnerable' status in 1990.

greenstriped rockfish

Scientific name: *Sebastes elongatus*
  Ayres, 1859
Family: **Scorpionfish**
Other common names: strawberry rockfish,
  striped rockfish, poinsetta
French name: sébaste à bandes vertes

Distribution: From the Gulf of Alaska to Baja California including British Columbia.
Characters: This species is recognised by its slender body and the horizontal green stripes. Dorsal fin spines 13, soft rays 12–14, usually 13. Anal fin soft rays 5–7, usually 6, second anal spine twice as thick as third and longer. The posterior edge of the anal fin is almost vertical. Pectoral fin rays 16–18, usually 17. Gill rakers 29–33. Vertebrae 26. Lateral line pores 37–47, scale rows below lateral line 42–55. The supraocular, coronal and nuchal head spines are absent, remaining

greenstriped rockfish

spines strong. The upper body is pink with 2 green stripes on each side of the lateral line but often broken by flank blotches. The caudal fin also has green stripes on its membranes. The

head and fins are greenish. Peritoneum grey with black dots. Reaches 38 cm.
Biology: Common on rocky and soft bottoms at 61–402 m. The highest concentrations in the Strait of Georgia were observed below 80 m on fine sediment interspersed with rocky areas. Young are born in June or later in British Columbia. Half the population is mature at 23 cm in Canadian waters. It is occasionally caught on hook and line but is said not to be a good tasting fish. Commercial bottom trawlers catch large numbers of this rockfish, but since many are small they are processed into fish meal or animal feed.

Grenadier Family

Scientific name: Macrouridae
French name: grenadiers

Grenadiers, **rattails** or whiptails are found world-wide in deeper waters including the Arctic and Antarctic oceans. There are about 285 species of which 7 are found on the Pacific coast, 5 on the Atlantic coast, 1 on the Pacific and Arctic coasts and 5 on the Atlantic and Arctic coasts.
These fishes are characterised by the second dorsal and anal fins being continuous with the elongate, tapering and pointed tail (hence "rattail" or "whiptail"). The caudal fin is absent in most species although a broken tail tip may regenerate and give the appearance of a caudal fin. There is usually a barbel on the chin and the snout protrudes over the mouth sometimes markedly as a shovel-like structure. The snout may be armed with spiny scutes. The short first dorsal fin may have a spine-like second ray. There are 7–14 rays in this fin and 80 or more in the second dorsal fin, but true spines are not present in the fins. The pelvic fins are thoracic, lying more or less below the pectoral fin base and have 5–18 rays with the outermost often elongated. The pelvic fins may be absent. Scales are small and cycloid but have small spines sometimes arranged in rows to form a ridge. Scales are present on the head as well as the body. Small teeth are present on the jaws. There may be a light organ under the skin of the abdomen opening in front of the anus. The organ contains luminous bacteria.

Grenadiers are **Cod Order** members related to the **Hake** and **Cod** families.

Grenadiers swim over the bottom at water depths between about 200 and 2000 m. They are the most common fish on the continental slope. Their snout is used to plough up bottom sediments and reveal food which is taken in by the underslung mouth. Males of some species can make noises using drumming muscles on the swimbladder. Grenadiers often have a fat-rich foamy deposit in the swimbladder, like that in the **Cusk-eel Family**. This deposit is associated with maintenance of a high oxygen pressure in these deepsea fishes. Deepsea fishes have been shown to have a decreased metabolic activity compared to shallow water fishes. This may be the combined effects of low food availability, high pressures and low temperatures. Larger grenadiers were fished commercially using deepwater trawls, traps and setlines. However catches have declined and are now incidental to other fisheries.

See **American straptail grenadier**
 bearded rattail
 carapine grenadier
 filamented rattail
 ghostly grenadier
 Günther's grenadier
 lamp grenadier
 longnose grenadier
 marlin-spike
 pectoral rattail
 popeye
 rock grenadier
 roughhead grenadier
 roughnose grenadier
 roughscale grenadier
 russet grenadier
 shortbeard grenadier
 smooth grenadier

Grey's smoothtongue

Scientific name: *Bathylagus greyae*
 Cohen, 1958
Family: **Deepsea Smelt**
Other common names: none
French name: garcette de Grey

Distribution: Known from Bermuda and off Atlantic Canada.

Characters: This species is distinguished from its Atlantic Canadian relatives by hav-

ing,a gill opening extending at least half way up the side of the body and by having 13 anal fin rays. There are about 45–50 lateral line scales. Dorsal fin rays 11–13, and pectoral rays 12–13. Body colour in preservative is brown dorsally, paler ventrally. The opercle and snout are dusky. Scale pockets have traces of purple pigment. Reaches 7.9 cm standard length.

Grey's smoothtongue

Biology: A single, possibly immature, specimen was caught off Browns Bank in 1982. A poorly known species.

Ground Shark Order

Ground sharks, **cat sharks**, finback catsharks, false catsharks, barbelled hound sharks, smoothhounds, **houndsharks**, weasel sharks, **requiem sharks** and **hammerhead sharks**, of the Order Carcharhiniformes comprise 8 families with about 193 species found world-wide in warm-temperate to tropical waters. A few enter fresh waters. In Canada there are 3 families and 17 species on the Atlantic and Pacific coasts.

The order is characterised by having an anal fin, 5 gill slits, 2 dorsal fins without spines, the long mouth extends back behind the front of the eyes which have lower nictitating eyelids, and there is a spiral or scroll intestinal valve. Spiracles are large, small or absent. There is no deep furrow between the nostril and the mouth. **Hammerhead sharks** are sometimes placed in a separate family.

These are small to very large **sharks**, the most speciose order of living **sharks**. They are found inshore, in the open ocean and on the bottom in deep water. Ground sharks are oviparous with the eggs laid in small cases with tendrils, or live-bearing with or without a placental attachment. There is a single, functional ovary. The majority of **sharks** dangerous to humans are classified within this order.

A number of species are commercially important for flesh, shark fin soup, vitamin content of liver oil and for skin as leather. Jaws are often cleaned and sold as curios. Some species are recognised sport fishes.

See **Cat Shark Family**
Hound Shark Family
Requiem Shark Family

grubby

Scientific name: *Myoxocephalus aenaeus*
(Mitchill, 1814)
Family: **Sculpin**
Other common names: little sculpin
French name: chaboisseau bronzé

Distribution: Found from the Strait of Belle Isle south throughout Atlantic Canada to New Jersey.

Characters: This species and its Arctic-Atlantic relatives are distinguished from other sculpins by the upper preopercular

grubby

spine being a simple straight point, the vomer bone in the roof of the mouth bears teeth but palatine teeth are absent, there are no oblique folds on the lower flank, and the lateral line lacks plates. It is separated from its relatives by having 3 preopercular spines (1 pointing forward to downward, 2 pointing backward), the uppermost preopercular spine is less than twice as long as the one below, and the spiny dorsal fin origin is in front of the rear edge of the operculum. First dorsal fin spines 8–11, second dorsal rays 13–15. Anal fin rays 10–12 and pectoral rays 14–17. There are a few scales along each side of the lateral line. Overall colour is grey, sometimes greenish-grey to brown with darker mottles on the flanks and pale grey to white below. There is a dark, wide saddle under the front of the spiny dorsal fin and 2 smaller saddles under the second dorsal fin. The fins have thin bars. Males have contrasting black

and cream areas on the body and fins, especially the pelvic fins, during the spawning season. Attains 19.4 cm.

Biology: Grubbies are found abundantly on mud, sand, gravel or rock bottoms from tide pools down to about 130 m in coastal waters at a wide range of temperatures and salinities. They may enter estuaries and are found among eelgrass. Food includes crustaceans, molluscs, sea squirts, sea urchins and a variety of small fishes such as **gaspereau, cunners, eels, sand lances, mummichogs, silversides, sticklebacks** and **tomcods**. Spawning takes place in winter to spring, and possibly summer. At Cape Cod some females spawn during their first year of life. Eggs are up to 2.0 mm in diameter and can be clear or coloured red, green or yellow. The eggs are laid in clumps which stick to seaweed or rocks. The blood of this sculpin has an antifreeze protein which increases in November to a peak level in January. This protein depresses the freezing point and allows the fish to tolerate low environmental temperatures, a necessity for a shallow water, winter spawning species. This common species often takes bait meant for sport fishes and can be a nuisance to all but the youngest anglers.

grunt sculpin

Scientific name: *Rhamphocottus richardsoni*
Günther, 1874
Family: **Sculpin**
Other common names: grunt-fish, pugfish,
Richardson's sculpin, northern sea horse
French name: chabot grogneur

Distribution: Found from Japan and the Bering Sea to California including British Columbia.

Characters: This species has an unusual body form for a member of the sculpin family with the head length about half the standard length and a unique colour pattern. The gill opening is small. Nasal, postocular, nuchal, cleithral and supracleithral at the upper gill slit edge, clavicular and preopercular spines present. All are sharp except the nuchal which is blunt. Scales are in the form of small plates covered with many-branched spines and covered in skin. They are found on the head, body and fin bases and rays except the caudal fin, on the first dorsal spine and in 4–5 rows on the upper eyeball. The body feels velvety to touch. The lateral line has about 25 pores. Large fish have a flap-like cirrus on the upper lip. First dorsal

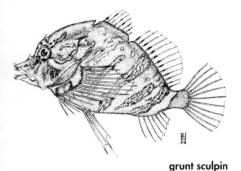

grunt sculpin

fin spines 7–9, which can fold back into a groove, second dorsal fin with 12–14 soft rays. Anal fin rays 6–8, pectoral rays 14–16 with the lower 8–9 finger-like, and pelvic fin with 1 spine and 3–4 soft rays. Vertebrae few, 26–28. Overall colour is a creamy yellow to creamy brown with dark brown markings extending downward and forward across the flanks. The belly may be lemon yellow to pale red. The head has dark streaks radiating from on the eyes. The caudal peduncle is bright red posteriorly. The dorsal, anal, caudal and pectoral rays are coral red with crimson margins. The finger-like pectoral rays and pelvic rays are orange. The first dorsal fin has black spots on the rays and there is a row of spots near the base of the soft dorsal fin rays. Reaches 8.5 cm.

Biology: Common in coastal waters of British Columbia where it is caught in tide pools and on sand and shell-sand beaches but also reported down to 200 m elsewhere. This fish may be seen swimming head up, crawling over rocks using the finger-like pectoral rays, or moving in a series of short jumps. Swimming is mainly accomplished by use of the pectoral fins. Its eyes move independently and, coupled with the jerky motion, give this fish a comical appearance. Grunt sculpins can often be found in empty giant barnacle casings or in a discarded can under piers. Young (1.4–1.8 cm) are caught in brackish water of

the Fraser River estuary in April-June. Food is crustaceans and worms when adult and crustaceans and fish larvae when young. Eggs are produced in winter, number up to 150 and are yellow to orange. The female chases a male until she corners him in a crevice, keeping him prisoner there until her eggs are laid and fertilised. The female guards the eggs. Life span may be about 5 years. Grunt sculpins are named for the grunting sound they make when picked up.

gulf snailfish

Scientific name: *Liparis coheni* Able, 1976
Family: **Snailfish**
Other common names: Cohen's snailfish
French name: limace de Cohen

Distribution: Found from the St. Lawrence River estuary and Gulf of St. Lawrence south to the Bay of Fundy and Gulf of Maine.

Characters: This snailfish is distinguished from its Atlantic coast relatives in Canada by having an adhesive disc, 2 pairs of nostrils, dorsal fin without an anterior notch, posterior teeth with 3 equal lobes, light peritoneum, dorsal fin rays 36–41, anal rays 30–35, pectoral rays 32–40 and pyloric caeca 14–29. Lower pectoral fin lobe rays are finger-like. The gill opening extends downward opposite pectoral rays 0–7. Teeth are in bands. Males have skin prickles. Overall colour is light brown with dark brown posteriorly on the dorsal and anal fins. Caudal fin with 4–5 bars. Some specimens are striped. The peritoneum has a few brown spots. Reaches 11.8 cm.

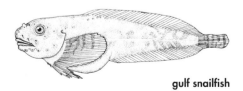

gulf snailfish

Biology: This snailfish has been caught at a depth range of 4–210 m. Larvae enter estuaries. It is mature at 2 years. Spawning may occur over an extended period from winter to spring judging by capture of females with eggs nearly 1 mm in diameter.

Gulf Stream flounder

Scientific name: *Citharichthys arctifrons*
Goode, 1880
Family: **Lefteye Flounder**
Other common names: none
French name: plie du Gulf Stream

Distribution: Found from Nova Scotia to Yucatan.

Characters: This species is distinguished from its Canadian Atlantic relatives by having short pelvic fin bases with that of the eyed side being on the midline of the belly, and a bony protuberance on the snout. Dorsal fin rays 75–86, anal rays 58–67, eyed side pectoral rays 9–11, and lateral line scales 37–43. Lower arm gill rakers 6–8. Larvae up to 12 mm long have 3 elongate, dorsal fin rays known as tentacles. Eyed side brown without spots, blind side whitish brown. Reaches 18 cm.

Gulf Stream flounder

Biology: Usually found at 46–366 m but occasionally as shallow as 22 m over its American range. Reported as common on the Scotian Shelf, and on Georges Bank at 73 m in Canada. Food is various bottom invertebrates such as worms and crustaceans. Spawning may occur throughout much of the year. Eggs are translucent and up to 0.8 mm in diameter. Eye migration occurs at 13–15 mm standard length. This is a good food fish but is too small to be a commercially viable species. Incidental catches are converted to fish meal.

Gulper Eel Order

This order, the Saccopharyngiformes, comprises 4 families, two of which, the **Gulpers** and **Swallowers**, have Canadian representatives. There are 26 species in the order and they are rare, deepsea fishes.

The anatomy of the **Gulpers** and **Swallowers** is regarded as perhaps the most highly modified of all vertebrates. The jaws and the hyomandibular and quadrate bones are elongated to form an immense gaping mouth capable of swallowing fish larger than themselves. The pharynx and stomach are elastic and can be distended to accommodate the prey. The eyes are tiny and near the tip of the snout. Many structures are lost including scales, ribs, pelvic fins, swimbladder, pyloric caeca, branchiostegal rays, opercular bones, and the symplectic bone. Some also lack an upper jaw, pectoral fins and internal support to the dorsal and anal fins. The jaws and their suspension are elongate and project backwards. The lateral line on the body has papillae instead of pores. Median fin rays are not branched or segmented. Gill openings are small and ventral and the caudal fin is absent or rudimentary. They range in size from small (10 cm or less) to large (over 2 m) and are eel-shaped.

Gulper eels have a leptocephalus larva, with v- rather than w-shaped myomeres, and are related to, and sometimes classified with, the **Eel Order**. They may spawn only once, dying afterwards.

See **Gulper Family**
Swallower Family

Gulper Family

Scientific name: Eurypharyngidae
French name: grandgousiers

Found in the Atlantic, Indian and Pacific oceans and on the Atlantic coast of Canada. Only 1 species in the family.

This family is highly unusual, lacking various skeletal elements such as opercular bones, ribs and branchiostegal rays, and also the scales, pelvic fins, pyloric caeca and a swimbladder. The caudal fin is absent or rudimentary. The eyes are tiny and placed far anterior. The most obvious feature is the enormous mouth and distensible pharynx which can take in very large fish. Gill openings are small and closer to the anus than the snout tip. This is the only **teleost** fish with 5 gill arches and 6 visceral clefts.

The **pelican gulper** is a relative of the **Swallower Family** and they both have a leptocephalus larva which relates them to the **eels** with which they are sometimes classified. It is a member of the **Gulper Eel Order**. The French name is taken from a character of the 16th century author, Rabelais. Grandgousier was the father of the giant Gargantua who had a prodigious appetite.

This species is found in the deep sea and is bathypelagic.

See **pelican gulper**

Gunnel Family

Scientific name: Pholidae
French name: sigouines

Gunnels are found principally in the North Pacific Ocean with a few species in the North Atlantic Ocean. There are about 14 species with 6 on the coast of British Columbia and 2 on the Atlantic coast. One species is found in the Arctic and Atlantic oceans and in the North Pacific Ocean but not as far south as British Columbia.

These fishes have eel-like, elongate, compressed bodies with 73–100 spines in the long dorsal fin and no soft rays. The anal fin has 2 spines and 32–53 soft rays and is about half as long as the dorsal fin. The dorsal and anal fins are joined to the caudal fin. The pectoral and pelvic fins are small or absent. Even when present, the pelvic fin is only 1 spine and 1 soft ray. Scales are minute and embedded with an incomplete or absent lateral line. There are no ribs. Gill membranes are attached to each other but free from the isthmus. Teeth are small and conical.

Gunnels are related to the **Prickleback Family** which however has a longer anal fin and 1 or more complete lateral lines. The family is a member of the **Perch Order**.

These fishes are common inshore and can often be found under rocks at low tide or amongst seaweed. They are easily caught by hand, if a little slippery to hold. Their movement is eel-like. They are often eaten by various sea bird species and are intermediate hosts for parasites which reach their adult form in the sea birds. Eggs are laid in masses on the bottom and larvae are pelagic.

See **banded gunnel**
crescent gunnel
longfin gunnel
penpoint gunnel
red gunnel
rock gunnel
rockweed gunnel
saddleback gunnel

Günther's grenadier

Scientific name: *Coryphaenoides guentheri*
(Vaillant, 1888)
Family: **Grenadier**
Other common names: none
French name: grenadier de Günther

Distribution: Found in the North Atlantic Ocean including in Davis Strait off northern Labrador.

Characters: It is distinguished from other Canadian Atlantic coast grenadiers by having

Günther's grenadier

second dorsal fin rays shorter than anal fin rays, 6 branchiostegal rays, 7–8, rarely 9, pelvic fin rays, pectoral fin rays 19–21, serrated anterior edge to the first 1–2 rays of the first dorsal fin, origin of the second dorsal fin behind the anus level, no scaleless areas on each side of the upper snout surface, and anal fin origin behind end of first dorsal fin. The underside of the snout is scaleless. The first dorsal fin has 11–12 rays. Scales have about 10 rows of large, broad spines. Overall colour when preserved is brown. The mouth and gill cavities are dark brown. Reaches at least 48 cm.

Biology: Davis Strait specimens were caught at 1400–1960 m. Elsewhere it is found at 1200–2600 m. Food is small, bottom-dwelling invertebrates.

H

haddock

Scientific name: *Melanogrammus aeglefinus*
(Linnaeus, 1758)
Family: **Cod**
Other common names: gibber, chat, pinger,
jumbo, scrod, ping pong, snapper haddock,
églefin, poisson de St. Pierre
French name: aiglefin

Distribution: Found in Europe and the
western Atlantic Ocean from the Strait of
Belle Isle across to Gaspé and southward
encompassing the Grand Bank to North
Carolina.

Characters: This species is separated
from other Canadian Arctic-Atlantic cods by
having 3 dorsal and 2 anal fins, the first dor-

haddock

sal having a pointed tip, a projecting snout,
the upper jaw does not reach the eye, a large
black blotch on the flank above the pectoral
fin and a black lateral line. The chin barbel is
very small. First dorsal fin rays 14–18, second dorsal rays 20–26 and third dorsal rays
19–24. First anal fin rays 21–28, second anal
rays 20–25. The back is a dark to purplish-
grey, the lower flank silver-grey and the
belly is white. There may be iridescent pink
tinges on the lower flank. Dorsal, pelvic and
caudal fins are dark grey or dusky. The anal
fins are silvery-grey with black, basal spots.
Attains 112 cm and 16.8 kg. The world, all-
tackle angling record weighed 4.5 kg and
was caught in 1988 in Perkins Cove, Maine.

Biology: Haddock are found over sand,
clay or gravel bottoms at 10–450 m and
1–13°C. In summer they are found on shallow, warm banks and inshore areas and in

winter in deeper, cooler water and on banks.
For example in the Sable Island-Emerald
Bank region haddock are found at 70–125 m
and 4–6°C in winter and migrate inshore off
Cape Breton or onto shallower banks at
35–70 m and 6–8°C in summer. Haddock in
the Gulf of St. Lawrence migrate south to the
Scotian Shelf for winter. There are a number
of stocks separated by deep waters in Atlantic
Canada. Young haddock are commensals with
jellyfish in the open sea which offers shelter
and probably protection from predators.

Adult haddock feed on crustaceans, molluscs, starfishes, worms and fishes found on
the sea bed. There are seasonal and locality
specific foods where certain items predominate. Occasionally they feed on sponges
which taint the flesh. Haddock are food for
other **Cod Family** members as well as other
fishes and seals.

Both males and females become mature at
2–7 years. This varies with the stock — all
age 3 and older haddock on Georges Bank
are mature. Females grow faster than males
after age 3. On Georges Bank half the population is mature at 37 cm for males and 40 cm
for females. Age at maturity has decreased in
recent years because of overfishing. Northern
stocks grow more slowly than those in the
south. Maximum age is 15 years.

Spawning occurs from January to July on
banks in Canada, progressively later in more
northerly areas. On Georges Bank peak
spawning occurs in late March or early April
mostly at 4–7°C. Eggs are up to 1.7 mm in
diameter, number over an estimated 2 million
and are pelagic. At about 5.0 cm young aban-
don surface waters for a bottom existence.

Haddock are of significant commercial
importance and are caught using otter trawls
by Canadian and foreign ships. Some inshore
traps, gill nets, handlines and longlines are
also used. They are sold fresh, frozen, salted,
canned, or smoked as "finnan haddie."
Catches in the northwest Atlantic Ocean
have been as high as 249,000 tonnes but
overfishing and poor recruitment reduced
this to 47,000 tonnes in 1970. There has

been some recovery since 1970 and a 50,000 tonne Canadian catch in the early 1980s was valued at about $25 million. The southern Grand Bank stock for example grew from a small fishery and declined to a negligible catch in the period 1946–1975 with several peaks in this period. The Georges Bank stock of age 2 and older haddock numbered an estimated 530 million fish (427,000 tons) in 1965 but declined to 8 million fish (22,000 tons) in 1972. The total Canadian catch in 1988 was 30,800 tonnes.

Occasionally three-eyed haddock are shown to gullible tourists or scientists by fishermen. These fish are made by careful surgery, implanting the third eye from one fish above the gill opening on the side of head in a dead fish or even a living fish. In the latter case there is some healing over several months which makes the fake even more realistic.

Haeckel's chimaera

Scientific name: *Harriotta haeckeli*
    Karrer, 1972
Family: **Longnose Chimaera**
Other common names: none
French name: chimère d'Haeckel

Distribution: Found in Davis Strait on the Greenland side and off the U.S. coast, probably occurs within Canadian waters too.

Characters: This chimaera is distinguished from other Atlantic Canadian species by the long snout, the arched head

Haeckel's chimaera

profile, mouth below the eyes, tooth plates broad, blunt edged, knobbed and ridged, and a smooth, short and curved dorsal fin spine. The tail filament is very short, and the body is longer than the tail. The space between the dorsal fins is greater than the length of the first dorsal fin base. The suborbital head canal is s-shaped. The pectoral fin does not reach back to the pelvic fin origin. The snout is turned up at the tip. Overall colour is brownish. Reaches 65 cm at least.

Biology: Found at 1813–2603 m, but biology is unknown.

Hagfish Family

Scientific name: Myxinidae
French name: myxines

Hagfishes are temperate to sub-tropical marine fishes found world-wide, usually on and in mud bottoms. In tropical waters they are limited to deep, cool areas.

There are 6 genera with about 43 species, of which 1 is found on the Atlantic coast and 2 on the Pacific coast of Canada. They are often classed as relatives of the **Lamprey Family** and, like them, are characterised by an eel-shaped body and the absence of jaws (see **jawless fishes**). They are members of the **Hagfish Order**. There are no paired fins, no true fin rays, the skeleton is cartilage, there is one semicircular ear canal, and the gill openings are pores rather than slits. "Hagfish" is derived from the Old English for witch.

Hagfishes lack a true dorsal and anal fin and the fin on the posterior part of the body is a finfold, or fold of skin. The mouth is surrounded by 3–4 pairs of barbels and horny teeth are restricted to two rows on the tongue and a single one on the palate. Eyes lack a lens and eye muscles, and are variably developed depending on habitat. Deepwater species have a weakly-developed retina and the eye is not visible through the skin. In shallow water species, the retina is well-developed, there is a vitreous body and the overlying skin is unpigmented, presumably to allow the entry of light. There are also light sensitive patches near the cloaca.

These fishes have both blood vessels and open spaces, or sinuses. This presents problems in movement of blood around the body, as blood pressure drops in the sinuses. There are separate hearts to pump blood into the gills, from the gills into the liver and so on, wherever a sinus occurs. Hagfishes have the lowest blood pressure of any vertebrate and heart metabolic rates are low so the heart is very resistant to low oxygen levels. Up to 80% of heart energy can be generated anaerobically. These features have attracted scientists who hope to gain a better understanding of how hearts work.

Water passes over the gills after entering through a special opening at the front of the body, known as the nasohypophysial opening. There are 1–16 pairs of gill openings behind the head. Hagfishes produce a large amount of slime containing strengthening threads from a row of mucous pores low on the flank. The slime may serve in defense and in suffocating food fishes. Hagfishes obtain their food by scavenging, and eat the insides of dead or dying fishes, supplemented by invertebrates. The teeth are used to rasp a hole and to tear up flesh. Hagfish may enter through the mouth or anus, and eat all the internal organs, leaving a "bag of skin and bones." As many as 123 hagfish have been found at one **Atlantic cod** corpse. When a strong grip is needed to enter a tough-skinned corpse, or detach a piece of flesh, the hagfish can throw its eel-shaped body into a knot,

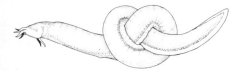

Hagfish Family

sliding it along the body to the head, to increase its purchase. Knots are also used to clean the body of excess slime by sliding through the loop. The force exerted by the knot is sufficient to escape a human grip. The clogged nasohypophysial opening is cleared by a "sneeze." Hagfishes also throw the body into a figure eight shape, a flexibility made possible by the cartilage skeleton.

Eggs are large (2.5 cm), elongate, and number up to 30, each in its own horny shell. Hooked fibres attach the eggs to each other and the sea bottom. They do not metamorphose like lampreys, and young are like the adults. Each hagfish has a single gonad composed of both ovary and testes, but only one becomes functional in the adult.

Hagfishes are often a nuisance to commercial fishermen, damaging or destroying fish in nets and leaving the nets covered in slime, hence their other name, "slime eels." Reputedly, other fish will not come near slimed nets.

A fine leather is made from their skin, and often used in wallets. These were once thought to de-magnetise bank cards! — but magnetic clasps are to blame. The value of "eelskin" products is now about $100 million annually and may become an important Canadian fishery as stocks in Asian waters have been depleted. Hagfishing licences have been issued by Nova Scotia and New Brunswick.

Hagfishes have a remarkable resistance to disease. Wounds remain clean and uninfected for weeks and, peculiarly, do not heal. Biomedical studies have been made on their immune systems which may reveal valuable pointers relevant to human physiology.

See **Atlantic hagfish**
    black hagfish
    Pacific hagfish

Hagfish Order

This is 1 of 2 orders of living **jawless fishes**, the Myxiniformes. The other is the **Lamprey Order**. There is only 1 family in the order and it has Atlantic and Pacific coast representatives in Canada.

The order is characterised by lacking bone, the body skeleton being a fibrous, cartilaginous material, no eye muscles, 1–16 external gill openings, no scales, no paired fins, a single semicircular canal in the internal ear, a single, simple olfactory capsule with only a few folds of sensitive tissue, olfactory nerves with separated bundles, an unsegmented notochord and the adenohypophysis has undifferentiated cellular elements not arranged in separate areas unlike all other vertebrates.

Biology and other peculiarities of this order are summarised in the family account.

See **Hagfish Family**

hagfishes

Hagfishes belong to the Class Myxini even though the class contains only a single order and family and very few species (about 43). This emphasises the great structural differences between hagfishes and the many thousands of **cartilaginous** and **bony fishes**. Hagfishes are one of the 4 classes in Canada which comprise those organisms known generally as **fishes**. The other 3 classes are the **ray-finned fishes**, **cartilaginous fishes** and **lampreys**. Anatomical and life history detail are summarised in the order and family accounts.

Hagfishes are thought to be descendants of early **jawless fishes** which flourished in Ordovician to Late Devonian times about 450 million years ago. These early relatives were heavily armoured with bony plates and quite different in appearance from their living, eel-like descendants. The exact relationships of hagfishes to these early fishes is uncertain since many of the shared characters are primitive ones and not indicative of relationships. Other hagfish characters are more recent specialisations or losses such as that of bone and paired fins which are of no use in assessing ancestral relationships. Hagfishes are thought to be descendants of the early pteraspids and are placed by some authors in the Class Pteraspidomorphi. Others include them with **lampreys** in the Class Cephalaspidomorphi.

Hagfishes are probably the most primitive **jawless fishes** and **lampreys** are more closely related to **jawed fishes** than to hagfishes. The similarities between hagfishes and **lampreys** are primitive characters and do not indicate a close relationship.

See **Hagfish Order**

Hake Family

Scientific name: Merlucciidae
French name: merlus

The hakes are found in the Atlantic and eastern Pacific oceans and around New Zealand. There are about 13 species with 4 reported for Canada from the Atlantic (3) and Pacific (1) coasts.

Their general body form resembles the **Cod Family**. There are 2 dorsal fins (1 species has a single dorsal fin) and 1 anal fin. The first dorsal fin is much shorter than the second dorsal fin. The second dorsal and anal fins have a notch which in some species almost divides these fins into two. The first large dorsal fin ray is spiny. There are 7–9 pelvic fin rays. The tail fin may be absent, cod-like or confluent with the dorsal and anal fins. The mouth is large and has obvious

teeth. There is no chin barbel and no pyloric caeca. The vomer bone in the roof of the mouth has teeth. Scales are cycloid. There are 7 branchiostegal rays. The frontal bones of the head are separate (joined in the **Cod Family**). The first vertebra and neural spine are fused to the skull. There is a v-shaped ridge on top of the head. The swimbladder is not attached to the skull.

This family is closely related to the **Cod Family** in the **Cod Order** and is sometimes classified within the **Cod Family**. The term hake is also used for 4 members of the **Cod Family**, namely the **longfin, red, spotted** and **white hakes**. The Merlucciidae are therefore sometimes referred to as the "true" hakes. "Hake" is derived from an Old English word for hook.

Hakes are relatively deepwater (50–1000 m) predators of **herrings** and **mackerels**. In warmer tropical waters they are found deeper than in cooler waters. They form large schools which migrate in- and offshore with the seasons. Eggs are pelagic and reproduction by family members encompasses the whole year. Some species are commercially important in colder waters like Canada but the flesh is soft and does not keep well.

See **offshore hake**
    Pacific hake
    silver hake
    winged hake

Halfbeak Family

Scientific name: Hemiramphidae
French name: balourous

Halfbeaks are found world-wide in warmer oceans and some live in fresh water in the Indo-Australian region. There are about 85 species with 2 on the Atlantic coast of Canada.

These fishes are characterised by an elongate lower jaw and short, triangular upper jaw. Some species show characters intermediate between halfbeaks and **flying fishes**. However the pectoral and pelvic fins are short. The lower lobe of the caudal fin is slightly to much longer then the upper lobe. The fins lack spines and the dorsal and anal fins are far back on the body, opposite each other. There are 6 soft rays in the abdominal pelvic fins. Scales are large, cycloid and deciduous. The lateral line runs from the throat along the lower edge of the body and has 1–2 branches to the pectoral fin origin. The nostril is a pit with a tentacle sticking out.

Halfbeaks are related to the **Flyingfish Family**, with which they share large scales (38–60 usually in the lateral line), a small mouth with small or absent teeth, and usually 8–16 dorsal and anal fin rays without finlets. Flyingfishes and halfbeaks are placed in the same family by some scientists. They are members of the **Needlefish Order**.

Marine halfbeaks are found at the surface in coastal waters and often leap out of the water or skip and skitter along the surface. One species even glides like a **flyingfish**. Halfbeaks feed on floating algae or on crustaceans and fishes. Their eggs attach to plants by means of sticky filaments. Some halfbeaks have internal fertilisation and bear live young. They are used commercially for their excellent flesh in warm areas and are also popular bait fish for **billfishes** and **tunas**.

See **ballyhoo**
    silverstripe halfbeak

halfmoon

Scientific name: *Medialuna californiensis*
    (Steindachner, 1875)
Family: **Sea Chub**
Other common names: none
French name: demi-lune

Distribution: Found from Vancouver Island south to the Gulf of California.

Characters: This species is the only member of its family on the Pacific coast and is identified by its colour, teeth, fin ray counts

halfmoon

and internal anatomy. There are 9–11 dorsal fin spines and 22–27 soft rays. The anal fin

has 3 spines and 17–21 soft rays. There are 50–53 lateral line pores. The back is dark blue, flanks light blue and whitish on the belly. Fins are dark. The postero-dorsal corner of the gill cover is dusky. Young fish are blue dorsally and silvery below. When frightened, halfmoons develop a dark grey stripe along the middle flank with a narrow white stripe above, probably to reduce visibility to predators from above or below. Reaches 48.3 cm and over 2 kg.

Biology: First caught in Canadian waters west of Vancouver Island in 1979 during an exploratory squid fishing survey. This fish is usually found in small schools around rocks and in kelp inshore and to depths of 40 m. Food is seaweed, bryozoans, sponges and small invertebrates. In California females spawn from May to September. Young are pelagic under debris and floating seaweed, often many kilometres from shore. Life span may exceed 8 years and most fish are mature by 2 years of age and 20 cm length. Young halfmoons have been observed in a "floating leaf" posture, lying on their side near the surface with head and tail downward. The unrelated **tripletail** also exhibits this behaviour. This species is known to "clean" parasites off other fishes in California. Halfmoons may be caught on hook and line or spearfished, with about 67,000 taken this way annually in California. It is a good fighter. There is also a commercial fishery and the flesh is fine and flavourful.

halibuts

Halibuts are **flatfishes**. There are 3 Canadian species with this name in the **Righteye Flounder Family**. Despite its name, the **Greenland halibut** is found on all three coasts. These large fish and their European relatives have long been popular food fishes. The name is derived from holy flounder in Low German since they were commonly eaten on holy days.

In 1968, the *Pacific* halibut industry requested that "halibut" not be used to describe the *Greenland* halibut, whose Atlantic populations were a significant source of competition for the commercial "halibut" market, being a cheaper species.

However the name "Greenland halibut" has long been in use and appears in various books, reports and scientific papers. It was allowed to keep its name in scientific works, but Greenland halibut exported to the U.S.A. from Canada must now be marketed as "Greenland turbot."

See **Atlantic halibut**
Greenland halibut
Pacific halibut

Halosaur Family

Scientific name: Halosauridae
French name: halosaurs

Halosaurs are found world-wide usually in deep water, sometimes to 5200 m. There are 3 genera with 15 species but only 2 occur off Atlantic Canada.

These fishes have an elongate, probing snout, an underslung mouth, teeth in bands on the premaxillae and maxillae bones in the upper jaw, separated branchiostegal membranes with 9–23 rays, the dorsal fin short, spineless, with 9–13 rays and anterior to the anus, large, cycloid, deciduous scales with less than 30 rows longitudinally and a lateral line positioned below the midline of the flank and having a large canal. There is no caudal fin.

They are related to the **Tapirfish Family** and are in the **Bonefish Order**. They have an elongate, leptocephalus larva like **eels**. The eyes of the larva are tubular and directed dorsally.

The main habitat is the continental slope, rise and abyssal plain at 400 m or deeper where these fishes swim just above the bottom. Food is various invertebrates such as crustaceans and worms from the sea floor and occasionally squid. Populations are predominately females. Males have enlarged and dark-coloured nostrils.

See **bald halosaur**
longfin halosaur

halterfish

Scientific name: *Omosudis lowei*
Günther, 1887
Family: **Halterfish**
Other common names: none
French name: poisson à licou

Distribution: Found in warmer parts of the world's oceans including the Atlantic coast of Canada.

Characters: The lower jaw is uniquely deep, strong and truncate and bears an enlarged fang on each side. The head is markedly compressed. There are 9–12 dorsal fin rays, 14–16 anal fin rays, 11–13 pectoral fin rays and 8 pelvic fin rays. Colour is brown to black on the back with silvery, iridescent sides through which a black body cavity lining can be seen in some fish, while others are reported as having a silvery peritoneum. The gut is covered by deep black tissue. There are small, dark spots over the whole body. The tip of the snout and the anterior jaw edges are black. The caudal peduncle has a black horizontal band like a keel but not raised. Dorsal and anal fins vary from dusky to black. Halterfish reach about 25 cm in length.

halterfish

Biology: Known from the northwest Flemish Cap and south of Browns Bank in Canada, each time from a single specimen. The halterfish is a predator on fishes and squids including specimens larger than itself. It has been caught at depths of 100–1300 m where it must be a fast swimmer as it is hard to catch in nets. However, as with other small deepsea fishes, scientists have captured halterfish by proxy in the stomachs of other fish. These larger and faster fish include **yellowfin tuna**, **longnose lancetfish** and **albacore**.

Halterfish Family

Scientific name: Omosudidae
French name: poissons à licou

This family contains only one species found in the warmer parts of all oceans including the Atlantic coast of Canada.

Scales are absent and the body lacks pores. A lateral line is present in the young but is lost in adults. There are no light organs and no swimbladder. Head bones are very thin and soft and the skin is delicate and easily torn as in many deepsea fishes. The silvery, iridescent flanks may reflect light from other deepsea organisms and help the **halterfish** see its prey. In addition, the iridescence may break up into flashes of light and help to confuse predators. The **halterfish** is a close relative of the **Lancetfish Family**. It is a member of the **Flagfin Order**.

The fangs and jaw structure indicate that **halterfish** feed on fishes and similar large prey and a distensible stomach is needed to accommodate this food. Young **halterfish** are found nearer the surface than adults and show a vertical migration. The adults are synchronous hermaphrodites, carrying a dorsal testis and ventral ovarian tissue.

See **halterfish**

hammerhead sharks

The hammerhead sharks are easily recognised because of their unusual head shape which gives these fishes their name. They are members of the **Requiem Shark Family** but are sometimes classified as a distinct family (Sphyrnidae). There is only 1 Canadian species.

See **smooth hammerhead**

harlequin rockfish

Scientific name: *Sebastes variegatus* Quast, 1971

Family: **Scorpionfish**

Other common names: none

French name: sébaste arlequin

Distribution: Found from the Aleutian Islands to Queen Charlotte Sound and off Flores Island, Vancouver Island, British Columbia.

Characters: This species is recognised in part by its colour pattern, particularly the clear lateral line not bordered by red, and by head spines and fin ray counts. The knob at the tip of the chin is weak. Dorsal fin spines 13–14, usually 13, dorsal soft rays 13–15. Anal fin soft rays 6–7, usually 7, second spine thicker and longer than the third. Pectoral fin rays 17–19, usually 18. Gill rakers 36–41. Vertebrae 27. Lateral line pores 42–52, scale rows below lateral line 46–58.

Supraocular, coronal and nuchal spines absent, nuchals occasionally present. Overall colour is a pinkish-red with large dark patches on the back and flanks. Broad dark bands radiate back from the eye high on the head. The lateral line is pale on its posterior two-thirds. The spiny dorsal fin is black at the outer edge and the membranes of the anal and caudal fins are black. The margin of the caudal fin is pink or red. The peritoneum is dark brown to black. Reaches 37 cm.

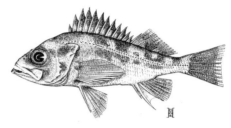

harlequin rockfish

Biology: Found on the bottom at 70–549 m. A poorly-known species. Half the population is mature at 24 cm for males and 23 cm for females in Canadian waters. Young are born in June in British Columbia. A large catch, over 46 tonnes, was made on the Bowie Seamount of the Queen Charlotte Islands in 1993.

hatchetfishes

Hatchetfishes are members of the **Silver Hatchetfish Family** which has 8 species bearing that name. The name describes the body shape which is compressed, has a sharp lower edge and a thin tail to form the handle of the hatchet.

See **greater silver hatchetfish**
highvelo hatchetfish
longspine silver hatchetfish
lowcrest hatchetfish
short silver hatchetfish
silvery hatchetfish
slender hatchetfish
transparent hatchetfish

headlightfishes

Headlightfishes are members of the marine **Lanternfish Family**. In Canada 7 species have this name, 6 off the Atlantic coast and 1 off the Pacific. They are close relatives of the 2 Canadian parkinglightfishes, the **doormat** and **slanteye**, all being in the same genus, *Diaphus*. There are about 60 species world-wide in this genus. They are named for the 1 or more pairs of light organs on the head.

See **bouncer headlightfish**
California headlightfish
eventooth headlightfish
flashlight headlightfish
square headlightfish
straightcheek headlightfish
Taaning's headlightfish

Herring Family

Scientific name: Clupeidae
French name: harengs

Herrings, **shads**, **sardines**, pilchards and **menhadens** are found world-wide in warmer marine waters with some species anadromous or permanent freshwater residents. There are about 180 species with 9 found in Canada, 1 on the Pacific coast (with a second species, the **American shad**, introduced to the Pacific coast and its rivers from the Atlantic coast), 3 on the Atlantic coast, 3 on the Atlantic coast and in its rivers, 1 in Atlantic rivers and 1 on the Pacific and Arctic coasts.

These fishes have modified scales on the belly forming abdominal scutes with a saw-like edge. The lateral line is usually absent or on only a few scales. Silvery cycloid scales are easily detached and are found only on the body. Teeth are small or absent but gill rakers are long and numerous for sieving plankton. Fins lack spines. There is no adipose fin. The pectoral and pelvic fins have a large axillary scale. The caudal fin is deeply forked. The eye is partly covered by an adipose eyelid. The flesh is particularly oily and is highly nutritional.

Herrings are related to the **Anchovy** family and are members of the **Herring Order**. "Herring" is derived from an Old English word for the **Atlantic herring**.

Members of this family often form immense schools in surface waters of the ocean where they feed on plankton. Schooling is an anti-predator device making it difficult for a predator to pick out an indi-

vidual from a tight mass of fish. There is also a "sentry effect" where awareness is increased by the presence of many fish. The school is maintained by a balance between visual attraction and lateral line stimulus repulsion.

Herring can feed on the smaller plankton, less than 300–400 mm, at night by filter-feeding but during the day can also use particulate feeding. In the latter they select larger plankton using the area temporalis, a specialised ventro-posterior region of the retina which improves vision as herring approach food items from slightly below.

Herring are easily caught and are extremely valuable to commercial fisheries. They are the most important fishes economically, both as food for man and also for many other commercial fish species. Wars have been fought over fisheries for herrings and governments and states have been terminated. Records of herring fisheries date from 709 A.D. in England and archaeological sites in Europe show evidence that herring were eaten 5000 years ago. An estimated 10 billion **Atlantic herring** are caught each year and in one year members of the herring family made up 37.3% of all fish caught in the world. Some are used for fish meal, as fertiliser and as an oil source.

See **American shad**
Atlantic herring
Atlantic menhaden
blueback herring
gaspereau
gizzard shad
Pacific herring
Pacific sardine
round herring

Herring Order

The Order Clupeiformes, containing the **herrings, round herrings, shads, sardines, menhadens, anchovies**, denticle herrings and wolf herrings, comprises 5 families and over 350 species found in fresh and salt waters world-wide. There are 2 families in Canada with 12 species.

These fishes are all uniquely characterised by a recessus lateralis, a chamber of the neurocranium where the infraorbital and preopercular sensory head canals join. Three other unique characters are the nature of the connection between the swimbladder and the ear, the presence of 2 foramina — 1 in the temporal region and 1 in the auditory region of the skull, and the caudal fin skeleton. The swimbladder forks anteriorly to form 2 large vesicles or sacs each of which lies within a bony swelling (ossified bulla) or expansion of the prootic and pterotic bones. The caudal fin skeleton has a urostyle (a major bone) composed of uroneural one and the last vertebral centrum, and hypural one is separated by a gap from the urostyle. In addition there are no parasphenoid teeth, no leptocephalus larva, abdominal scutes are present, gut connected to the swimbladder via a duct, pelvic fins are abdominal and pectoral fins low on the body, no dorsal adipose fin or fin spines, scales are cycloid, no lateral line on the body, no large foramen or opening on the anterior ceratohyal bone and the parietal bones are separated by the supraoccipital on the roof of the skull. Fossils date back to the Early Cretaceous. Round herrings are sometimes placed in a separate family, Dussumieriidae.

These fishes are essentially plankton feeders with long gill rakers. Many are very important food fishes occurring in large, pelagic schools, making this the most economically important order.

See **Anchovy Family**
   Herring Family

high cockscomb

Scientific name: *Anoplarchus purpurescens*
   Gill, 1861
Family: **Shanny**
Other common names: crested blenny,
   cockscomb prickleback
French name: crête-de-coq pourpre

Distribution: From southern California to Alaska including British Columbia.

Characters: This species is related to the **slender cockscomb**, which also lacks pelvic fins and has a median crest on top of the head. It usually has fewer anal rays than its relative and is also distinguished by the width between the posterior gill membrane attachments to the isthmus being 1.7–4.1% of standard length. Both these characters overlap in

the 2 species, making their identification difficult. There are 54–60 dorsal fin spines and 36–42 anal fin rays. Anal fin ray numbers are higher in the north of the species range. Scales are confined to the posterior part of the body. The lateral line canal is faint. Colour varies and the body may be blackish, purple, brown or grey. There is often mottling and reticulate patterns, particularly in females. There is a grey bar at the caudal fin base. The cheek usually has 2 dark streaks. Breeding males develop orange to deep red fins, and the anterior dorsal fin spot becomes outlined in gold, while females develop patterned pectoral, anal and caudal fins. Attains 20 cm.

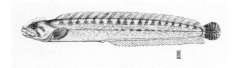

high cockscomb

Biology: Usually found under rocks intertidally, but also down to 30 m. They are also found under algae when the tide is out and can survive several hours to slightly more than one day without being covered by water. In Oregon their rock microhabitat has a temperature range of 4–24°C annually and this shanny is known to produce anti-freeze compounds in its body during winter.

Food includes green algae but is mainly worms, molluscs and crustaceans. Garter snakes search for and eat high cockscombs at low tide.

They are mature at 2–3 years of age. Females are larger and grow faster than males. A territory is defended by males in the spawning season and these fish usually do not move more than 15 m from their capture site. Males display laterally with fins and crest erect or in spasms when the body jerks 1–3 times. During spawning, the male positions himself upside down under the female who is pressed against a rock. Spawning occurs in late winter (January to March) with up to 2700 white eggs of 1.57 mm diameter being deposited in an hour-glass shaped egg mass under rocks or shells. The female guards and fans the eggs by wrapping herself around them and undulating the rear part of the body. Guarding lasts for about one month. The egg mass may be moved. Larvae are planktonic.

highfin dragonfish

Scientific name: *Bathophilus flemingi*
  Aron and McCrery, 1958
Family: **Barbeled Dragonfish**
Other common names: none
French name: dragon à haute nageoire

Distribution: Found from British Columbia to Baja California and at Ocean Station Papa (50°N, 145°W).

Characters: This species is distinguished from its Canadian Pacific coast relatives, the **longfin dragonfish** and the **pitgum lanternfish**, by the presence of delicate pectoral fins, a very long barbel, pelvic fins on mid-flank, and the first tooth on the lower jaw not piercing the premaxillary bone of the upper jaw. Teeth are large and spaced out in the mouth. Dorsal fin rays 15–16, anal rays 16–17. Pectoral fin rays 4–7, pelvic rays 15–19. There is a postorbital light organ. An upper row of belly photophores is in 2 sections, one from the pectoral fin base to above the pelvic fin insertion (15–17 photophores) and one continuing at a lower level to a point between the dorsal and anal fin origins (12–14 photophores). A lower row of belly photophores numbers 16–32 and is continued above the anal fin in a short row of 4–6 photophores. Overall colour is black to dark brown. Reaches 16.5 cm.

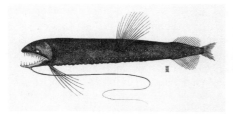

highfin dragonfish

Biology: Ocean Station Papa fish were taken at night in less than 60 m of water. Also found off the Queen Charlotte Islands. Elsewhere reported in the range 225–1370 m. Life span is thought to be 8 years. Spawning occurs in spring or early summer.

highfourthpo lampfish

Scientific name: *Lampadena luminosa*
  (Garman, 1899)
Family: **Lanternfish**
Other common names: none
French name: lampe à haut-po-quatre

Distribution: Found in temperate to subtropical waters of the Atlantic, Indian and Pacific oceans, including off Atlantic Canada.

Characters: This species is distinguished from its Canadian Atlantic coast relatives by the large luminous glands, outlined with heavy, black pigment, on the upper and lower caudal peduncle, and the pelvic fin origin under the front of the dorsal fin; and from its close relative, the **toothnose lampfish**, by having photophore PO4 over photophore PO3, hence the common name. Dorsal fin rays 14–15, usually 15, anal rays 13–15, usually 14, and pectoral rays 15–17,

highfourthpo lampfish

usually 16. Photophores: PO 5, VO 4–5, usually 5, AO 5–6, rarely 7, + 2, total 7–9. Attains about 20 cm, large for a lanternfish.

Biology: Known in Canadian waters off the Scotian Shelf from only 2 specimens caught in 1984 at 204–207 m. These are probably strays from the south and are northern range limits for the species in the northwest Atlantic Ocean. In the Atlantic Ocean found mostly at 425–850 m during the day and 40–225 m at night with a maximum catch around 75 m. Reported as deep as 1300 m.

highlight hatchetfish

Scientific name: *Sternoptyx pseudobscura*
  Baird, 1971
Family: **Silver Hatchetfish**
Other common names: none
French name: hache d'argent à haute épine

Distribution: World-wide in tropical to temperate oceans. First reported from

Canada in 1975 off southern British Columbia and in 1991 on the Flemish Cap off Newfoundland.

Characters: The body is shaped like a hatchet, there are 10 abdominal light organs, but only 3 at the anal fin, the eyes are normal

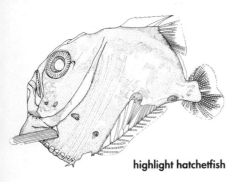

highlight hatchetfish

and the first anal fin support is enlarged supporting a transparent membrane above the anal fin rays. This species differs from its relative, the **transparent hatchetfish**, by having a high supra-anal light organ and spines on the gill raker tooth plates. The back is dark with an overall silvery colouration to the body and light organs outlined in black. Exceeds 5.5 cm standard length.

Biology: Usually found between 800–1500 m and does not migrate vertically. The Flemish Cap specimen was caught at 568–591 m. Food is small crustaceans.

highseas lightfish

Scientific name: *Vinciguerria poweriae*
(Cocco, 1838)
Family: **Lightfish**
Other common names: none
French name: poisson étoilé de Power

Distribution: Found world-wide in warmer seas and entering Atlantic Canada.

Characters: This species is distinguished from its Canadian Atlantic relatives by having the end of the dorsal fin opposite or

highseas lightfish

behind the anal fin origin, a photophore or light organ below the rear eye margin, 12–15 photophores over the anal fin and back to the tail, no photophore at the tip of the chin, and 14–16 gill rakers. The anal and dorsal fin bases are about equal in length. The anal fin has 12–14 rays. The eyes are normal. There is a dark streak at the tip of the lower jaw and over the upper jaw margin. The back is dark and the flanks silvery. Reaches about 43 cm.

Biology: Found off the Scotian Shelf and northeast Georges Bank in Canada. First reported in 1988 and these records represent a northern range extension for the species in the northwest Atlantic Ocean. Found mainly at 300–600 m by day and 50–350 m by night. Food is small crustaceans. Spawning occurs in spring and summer.

highsnout ridgehead

Scientific name: *Melamphaes lugubris*
Gilbert, 1890
Family: **Ridgehead**
Other common names: none
French name: heaume triste

Distribution: From Baja California to the Bering Sea and off the Queen Charlotte Islands.

Characters: The head is large and heavily sculptured and bears numerous pore rows. There are 2 vertical ridges on the side of the

highsnout ridgehead

head behind the eye. The operculum is unique in having 8 scales behind the second ridge (usually missing, however). The top of the head and in front of the first ridge are covered by longitudinal striations. The flank has 32–36 scale rows. There is no lateral line. Dorsal fin spines 1–3, usually 3, soft rays 14–16. Anal fin with 1 spine and 7–9 , usually 8, soft rays. Pectoral fin not slender and 15–17 rays, usually 16, reaching past anus. Pelvic fin with 1 spine and 7 soft rays. Gill membranes free from isthmus and not joined to each other. The preopercle has 2 weak spines at its lower corner. Dark brown to black with a black throat and branchiostegal rays. Attains 8.9 cm.

Biology: Little is known. In the subarctic young fish are found nearer the surface (50–75 m) than adults (200–250 m) and in southern regions both young and adults remain below 200 m, down to 1500 m.

highvelo hugo

Scientific name: *Hygophum hygomi*
  (Lütken, 1892)
Family: **Lanternfish**
Other common names: none
French name: hugo haut-velo

Distribution: Found in the Atlantic, Indian and Pacific oceans, and off the Scotian Shelf in Canada.

Characters: This species and its relatives, the **longnose** and **upmouth hugos**, are distinguished from other Atlantic coast lantern-

highvelo hugo

fishes by having no photophores close to the dorsal body edge, the PLO photophore is well above the pectoral fin level, the second PVO photophore is below the upper end of the pectoral fin base, there are 2 Prc photophores, the PVO photophores are inclined, not horizontal, while the VO photophores are horizontal and there are 2 Pol photophores. This species is separated from its relatives by the second Prc photophore being at or close to the lateral line and the VLO photophore being at the lateral line. Dorsal fin rays 13–15, anal rays 20–23 and pectoral rays 14–17. Total gill rakers 18–23. AO photophores 12–14. Lateral line organs 38–39. Males have a single, luminous supracaudal

gland appearing at 3.2–4.0 cm. Females have 1–3 small, elongate, luminous infracaudal patches appearing at 4.3–5.0 cm. Reaches at least 6.8 cm.

Biology: Depth occurrence in the Atlantic Ocean generally is 400–850 m by day with some fish as deep as 1550 m. By night fish are found from the surface down to 1050 m with concentrations at various levels above 235 m and at 500–600 m. The latter are juveniles. Growth of males is slower than that of females and females grow larger. Only a few fish live more than 1 year. Spawning occurs in late autumn to winter off Bermuda.

hippo combchin

Scientific name: *Holtbyrnia rostrata*
  (Günther, 1878)
Family: **Tubeshoulder**
Other common names: none
French name: menton-peigne tocson

Distribution: Found in the Atlantic Ocean including off the coast of Atlantic Canada.

Characters: This species is recognised by the family character of a tube projecting from the flank above the pectoral fin, by having an evident lateral line with enlarged scales and by having scales on the head overlapping normally (scales may be lost in captured specimens). In addition pelvic fin rays are 9 and enlarged teeth or tusks are present on the premaxillary bone of the upper jaw. It is unique among related species in its lack of photophores or light organs. Colour is probably dark. There is no white tissue behind the eye. Records of this species are often uncertain because of difficulties in identification. Attains 14.6 cm.

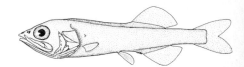

hippo combchin

Biology: Six specimens were caught in 1968 at the northwest Flemish Cap and identified as this species. Little is known but like its relatives this species lives in the deep ocean.

horned lampfish

Scientific name: *Ceratoscopelus maderensis*
(Lowe, 1839)
Family: **Lanternfish**
Other common names: horned lanternfish
French name: lampe cornée

Distribution: Found in the North Atlantic Ocean and Mediterranean Sea including off the Scotian Shelf in Atlantic Canada.

Characters: This species and its relative, the **southseas lampfish**, are separated from other Atlantic species by lacking pho-

horned lampfish

tophores close to the dorsal body edge, the PLO photophore is well above the pectoral fin base level while the second PVO photophore is at or below the upper pectoral base level, there are 4 Prc, the first PO and two PVO photophores are not on a straight line, both males and females have caudal luminous glands composed of overlapping, scale-like structures without a black pigment border, and the fourth PO photophore is not elevated. It is distinguished from its relative by having 17–22 gill rakers and no scale-like, luminous structures in a series between the pelvic fins and anus. Dorsal fin rays 13–15, anal rays 13–15 and pectoral rays 13–14. AO photophores 11–14. Lateral line organs 38–39. Reaches 8.1 cm.

Biology: This is a temperate and partially subtropical species. Its distribution overlaps that of the **southseas lampfish**. Depth distribution by day is 100–1000 m and by night from the surface to 400 m and 600–1000 m. Adults are found at 330–600 m during the day south of New England. A particular sound-scattering layer in the ocean off Canada and the northeastern U.S.A. was investigated using the Deep Submergence Research Vehicle *Alvin*. Visual identification showed the layer to be made of horned lamp-

fish. Horned lampfish are food for **cod, silver hake** and **pollock** in Canadian waters. Sexual maturity is reached at 6.2 cm. Spawning occurs in spring to summer.

horned whiff

Scientific name: *Citharichthys cornutus*
(Günther, 1880)
Family: **Lefteye Flounder**
Other common names: none
French name: limande cornée

Distribution: Found from Nova Scotia south to Brazil.

Characters: This species is distinguished from its Canadian Atlantic adult relatives by having short pelvic fin bases with that of the eyed side being on the midline of the belly, no bony snout protuberance, a partially scaled snout, and 40–45 lateral line scales. Dorsal fin rays 74–83, anal rays 59–66 and eyed side pectoral rays 10–11. Lower arm gill rakers 11–15. Males have strong head spines and the upper pectoral fin rays are greatly elongated. Larvae have 3 elongate, dorsal fin rays known as tentacles. The eyed side is brown. The pectoral fin axil has a dark blotch and the fin is barred. Dorsal and anal fins may be spotted. The caudal fin often has 2 spots, one above the other. Reaches 10 cm.

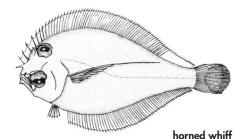

horned whiff

Biology: Known only from a stray larval specimen from the south caught on Georges Bank in 1982. Adults are usually found below 140 m down to 400 m only as far north as Georgia.

hornyhead chub

Scientific name: *Nocomis biguttatus*
(Kirtland, 1840)
Family: **Carp**

Other common names: river chub, jerker, horned chub, Indian chub, redtail chub
French name: tête à taches rouges

Distribution: Found from New York to Colorado and south to Arkansas. Reported from Canada only in drainages of lakes Ontario, St. Clair and Erie, southern and northwestern Lake Huron drainages and in southeastern Manitoba.

Characters: This species is recognised by having protractile premaxillae (upper lip separated by a groove from the snout), a barbel

hornyhead chub

at each mouth corner, 38–48 lateral line scales, pectoral fins do not reach to the pelvic fins, the snout projects only a little over the mouth, there is a stripe along the middle of the back and along the flank, and the spot at the caudal fin base is round and black. Pharyngeal teeth 1,4–4,1, 4–4 or 4–3, with hooked tips. Gill rakers short and about 9. Dorsal fin branched rays 6–7, usually 7, branched anal rays 5–6, usually 6, pectoral rays 14–17 and pelvic rays 8. Males have up to 130 large, pointed tubercles on top of the head, as well as on the pectoral fin rays.

The back is olive-brown, flanks are silvery or iridescent green and the belly yellowish to white. Caudal fin yellow. Upper flank scales are outlined with pigment and have a dark bar at their base. Dorsal and anal fins are orange to reddish in breeding males, there is a red spot behind the eye and a strong, black lateral flank stripe develops. The head and upper body have pink and blue tinges. Females have a lateral stripe at spawning but this fades after she leaves the nest area. Young fish have a red caudal fin. Peritoneum brown to dusky with black melanophores. Reaches 25.0 cm total length.

Biology: This chub prefers slow, clear, gravel or sand bottomed streams. It is found in pools and riffles and may hide under rocks.

Food is vascular plants, filamentous algae, aquatic insects, worms, crayfish, snails and fish. Feeding is mainly by sight. Young fish also eat a lot of algae including diatoms, and aquatic insects and snails. Plant material is probably not absorbed because the gut is too short but associated animal life is utilised.

Life span is 4 years. Males grow faster and reach a larger size than females since they build and defend a nest. Females are mature at age 2 in New York, or age 3 in Ontario. Spawning starts at water temperatures over 16°C, usually in May to July, when males begin to build the nest of pebbles and stones in shallow water, often below a riffle. The male moves pebbles by rolling them along using the head and mouth or by carrying them in the mouth. There was 1 nest/100 sq m in a Wisconsin creek. A nest may be up to 1 m wide and 1 m long and 15 cm deep, although usually smaller. A spawning trough is excavated on the top of the nest. Nests provide protection, a clean substrate and oxygenated water for the eggs. Females are led or driven over the nest during construction, eggs are shed and fertilised in a few seconds and the eggs fall into the pebble trough. Eggs are adhesive. The male subsequently adds more pebbles to protect the eggs and excavates a new trough downstream of the first. The male presses the female's genital area into the trough by placing his caudal peduncle over hers. Both vibrate, the female gapes and eggs and sperm are shed. A male may spawn with more than 1 female both at the same time and consecutively. Each female contains up to 995 eggs of 2.0 mm diameter but these are shed at intervals and a single nest can have eggs from up to 10 females. The eggs are adhesive.

Male and female hornyhead chubs make raids on nests to steal and eat eggs. Some males are believed to mimic female behaviour in order to have a chance at fertilising eggs. Accessory males, small non-spawning individuals, are found around nests adding and removing stones. They may be practising reproductive behaviour as nest sites and gravel are probably limited and larger males nest earlier than smaller, reproducing males.

Males of several other species of fish use the chub nest as a spawning site, 1 male of each species to each nest. **Common shiners**, for example, defend the nest against smaller species while the chub drives away larger fishes, such as **northern hog suckers**. The large, sharp tubercles are used to butt intruders on the head. Other species using the nest include **blackside dace, rosyface shiner, bluntnose minnow, rainbow** and **johnny darters**.

Hornyhead chubs have been used as bait for **northern pike, walleye, bass** and **catfish** in the U.S.A. and in Canada. Bait fish releases have increased its range in southern Ontario. Anglers can catch this chub on baited hooks and dry flies. They are said to be quite tasty. The Committee on the Status of Endangered Wildlife in Canada has classified this species as not in jeopardy in 1988.

horsehair eel

Scientific name: *Gordiichthys irretitus*
    Jordan and Davis, 1891
Family: **Snake Eel**
Other common names: none
French name: serpenton poil-de-cheval

Distribution: Found from the Scotian Shelf of Canada south to the Gulf of Mexico and Suriname.

Characters: This species is distinguished as a larva by having 192–214 total myomeres (muscle blocks), 110–127 nephric myomeres, 11 or less low, gut loops, dorsal fin originating

horsehair eel

anterior to myomere 23, little or no body wall pigment below the gut except under the liver lobes and the last 2 major, vertical blood vessels are widely separated. Preanal myomeres 112–128 and predorsal myomeres 13–21. Adults have a hard, blunt tail tip, no pectoral fin, crescentic gill openings low on the body, dorsal fin originating on the head, and 186–189 lateral line pores. Colour is pallid overall. Reaches 84 mm as a larva and 79.0 cm total length as an adult.

Biology: This species was first recorded from Canada in 1989 as a leptocephalus larva. Adults are rarely caught and are found at 90–200 m over sand and mud.

Hound Shark Family

Scientific name: Triakidae
French name: émissoles

The hound sharks, smooth hounds and topes are small to moderate-sized fishes with 39 species in all warm and temperate coastal seas with a few deepwater species. Only two species are reported from Canada, one on each coast.

They are distinguished from other shark families by the presence of an anal fin, 5 gill slits, 2 dorsal fins, no fin spines, horizontally elongate eyes, nictitating eyelids, a spiral intestinal valve, normal head, first dorsal fin base in front of pelvic bases, moderately long labial furrows, precaudal pits absent and no wavy margin to the upper tail fin. Teeth are small to large with strong basal ledges and grooves. They may be blade-like, molariform or cusped. Spiracles are small.

Hound sharks are members of the **Ground Shark Order** and are relatives of the **Cat Shark** and **Requiem Shark** families.

Their chief habitat is sand, rock and mud inshore areas. They often form large schools but may occur as individuals. Some species are very active and probably swim continuously while others can rest on the bottom. They are more active during the night than the day. Food is bottom and midwater crustaceans, fishes and cephalopods. These sharks are ovoviviparous or viviparous, and with or without a yolk-sac placenta. Some members of this family are numerous in both tropical and temperate inshore waters and are important to small commercial and artisanal fisheries. They are used as food, for fish meal and oil, and for shark fin soup.

See **smooth dogfish**
    soupfin shark

hugos

Hugos are members of the **Lanternfish Family** with 3 species off the Atlantic coast of Canada.

See **highvelo hugo**
    longnose hugo
    upmouth hugo

I

Iceland cat shark

Scientific name: *Apristurus laurussoni*
(Saemundsson, 1922)
Family: **Cat Shark**
Other common names: none
French name: roussette d'Islande

Distribution: Found in the North Atlantic Ocean including off Atlantic Canada.

Characters: This species is distinguished from its Atlantic coast relatives by lacking a crest over the eye, by the first and second

Iceland cat chark

dorsal fins being about equal in size, by the space between the dorsal fins being greater than the length of the first dorsal fin base, and by the caudal fin lacking a crest of denticles. There are 8–9 rows of pores along the undersurface of the snout. Teeth number 70 to 90 in the upper and 54 to 64 in the lower jaw. Flank denticles are flat, overlapping and are not fuzzy to touch. Colour is an overall dark brown to black or dark grey, with a reddish belly. This species may be the same as the **deepsea cat shark**. Attains 68 cm.

Biology: This cat shark is found on or near the bottom of the upper continental slopes from 550 to 1462 m. It is thought to be oviparous.

inconnu

Scientific name: *Stenodus leucichthys*
(Güldenstadt, 1772)
Family: **Salmon**
Other common names: sheefish, connie, conny, shovelnose whitefish, Eskimo tarpon, si-airryuk, sierak, tierak, tiktalerk
French name: inconnu

Distribution: Found across northern Eurasia, in the Caspian Sea basin and in Bering and Beaufort sea basins of North America. In Canada this includes the Mackenzie and Yukon river systems of the Yukon, N.W.T. and northern British Columbia and in rivers east to Cape Bathurst, N.W.T. on the Beaufort Sea.

Characters: This member of the **Salmon Family** is distinguished from its relatives by having large scales (115 or less), no parr marks, teeth absent from the jaws and roof of the mouth, forked tail fin, 2 flaps of skin between the nostrils, the lower jaw projects in a pike-like head, the premaxilla bone of the upper jaw curves forward, gill rakers 19–24, and lateral line scales 90–115. Small teeth are present on the anterior lower jaw, premaxilla and head of maxilla bones, tongue and roof of the mouth. Dorsal fin rays 11–19, anal rays 15–18, pectoral rays 16–17 and pelvic rays 11. Pyloric caeca 150–202.

The back is brown to pale green, flanks silvery and the belly silvery-white. The dorsal and caudal fins have black tips.

Attains 1.5 m and over 28.5 kg, the largest **whitefish** (up to 40 kg in Eurasia). The world, all-tackle angling record weighed 24.04 kg and was caught in 1986 in the Pah River, Alaska. The French name for this fish "unknown" was applied by early voyagers since it is unknown in southern Canada.

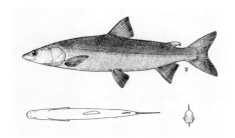

inconnu

Biology: Inconnu live in coastal areas and run up rivers to spawn or live in lakes such as Great Bear and Great Slave and run up streams entering the lakes to spawn.

Food of adults is fishes such as **Pacific herring, cod, pond smelt, whitefishes, chinook salmon, northern pike, sticklebacks, Carp Family** species, **sculpins, flounders** and **Arctic lampreys** and ammocoetes. Young inconnu eat aquatic insects and planktonic crustaceans. Inconnu are cannibals and are eaten by **northern pike** and **burbot**.

Life span is about 11 years in Great Slave Lake but fish up to 22 years are reported from elsewhere in the Mackenzie River basin. Maturity is attained at 6–10 years. The spawning migration takes place over summer and spawning occurs in the late summer and fall at temperatures of 1.5–4.6°C. Spawning occurs at intervals of 2–4 years for individuals. Up to 420,000 eggs are produced by each female. Young inconnu remain in streams and rivers for 2 or more years before descending to a lake or the sea where they grow rapidly on fish food. Inconnu overwinter in deep embayments of the Mackenzie River estuary. They can be caught easily on the return run from spawning in the fall by gill nets. At this time, the fish are concentrated, returning en masse from the spawning grounds which were reached over several months.

Inconnu were locally split and dried, or smoked because of the oily flesh. The Great Slave Lake commercial catch is frozen and sold to the U.S. for smoking. As much as 156,176 kg has been taken annually in Great Slave Lake. They have also been used as dog food. In Alaska there are some sport fisheries using mostly artificial baits. Small inconnu leap and large inconnu run deep and strong.

• Most accessible June and July.
• Isolated regions of the Yukon and the northwest region of the Northwest Territories.
• Medium action spinning or baitcasting outfits used with 10– to 20–pound line, fly rods in the eight-and-a-half to nine-and-a-half-foot length, eight-weight and nine-weight outfits loaded with weight-forward sinking lines and shooting heads.
• Wide range of 1/4– to 3/8–ounce flashy spoons and spinners. Best flies are large, saltwater streamers used for snook and **tarpon**.

Innes' tubeshoulder

Scientific name: *Holtbyrnia innesi*
(Fowler, 1934)

Family: **Tubeshoulder**
Other common names: none
French name: circé d'Innès

Distribution: Found in the Atlantic and Pacific oceans. Reported from Ocean Station Papa (50°N, 145°W) in the North Pacific Ocean.

Characters: This species is recognised by the family character of a tube projecting from the flank above the pectoral fin, by having an evident lateral line with enlarged scales and by having scales on the head overlapping normally. In addition pelvic fin rays are 9 and enlarged teeth or tusks are present on the premaxillary bone of the upper jaw. It is distinguished from its relatives by having a light organ at least 1.5 organ diameters behind the lower jaw tip,

Innes' tubeshoulder

short gill filaments united at the base and 22–23 gill rakers. Scales number 94–104 in lateral series. Overall colour is dark. There are patches of white tissue behind the eye. Reaches 21.3 cm.

Biology: Nothing is known of its biology.

Iowa darter

Scientific name: *Etheostoma exile*
(Girard, 1859)
Family: **Perch**
Other common names: yellowbelly, red-sided darter, weed darter, dard d'herbe
French name: dard à ventre jaune

Distribution: Found from eastern and southern Québec westward through the Great Lakes basin and tributaries of Hudson Bay to Alberta and across the northern U.S.A. paralleling this distribution. Also reported from northern Alberta.

Characters: This species is distinguished from other **darters** in Canada by having the anal fin smaller than the soft dorsal fin, the snout and upper lip joined (i.e. premaxillaries not protractile), belly scaled, cheeks scaled, dorsal fin spines longer than eye diameter, 7–12 (usually 8–9), soft rays 9–13 (usually 10–11), lateral scales 45–69 (usually

Iowa darter

48–60) with 18–35 pored. Anal fin with 1–2 spines and 6–9 soft rays. Pectoral rays 12–14. The opercles are scaled. Overall colour is olive-brown to dark brown fading to cream or yellowish on the belly. There are bars radiating from the eye. The back has 7–12 vague saddles and the midflank 9–14 short bars or squarish blotches. The caudal fin is barred and there is a basal spot, flanked by a spot above and sometimes one below. Breeding males have a first dorsal fin with a blue basal band or a series of blue spots each surrounded by a clear halo, a transparent band, an orange-red band and a deep blue or blue-green marginal band. The bars on the flank are dark blue or blue-green and the spaces between them yellow, orange or brick red. The belly is yellow, orange or red. The pectoral and anal fins are orange-yellow or yellow-red. Males have larger first dorsal and anal fins than females. Reaches 7.5 cm.

Biology: The habitat of this darter is weedy areas of lakes or rivers with clear water. At night it hides in crevices, holes and under logs and branches. Food is aquatic insects and crustaceans, snails and fish eggs. Iowa darters may live 4 years and females are larger than males. Spawning occurs in May-June in Canada preferentially on roots, usually those under banks, or on sand. Males have territories and females spawn with several males. The male lies over the female with his tail depressed and paralleling hers and his pelvic fins over her dorsal fin. Eggs are laid in groups of 3–7 and are 1.1 mm in diameter. Eggs attach to roots and weeds. The male continues to guard his territory but does not care for the eggs directly. Large females may lay up to 2048 eggs. Iowa darters have an alarm substance in their skin. Damage to the skin as in a predator's attack releases the alarm substance which other darters can detect, initiating predator avoidance behaviour.

J

Jack Family

Scientific name: Carangidae
French name: carangues

Jacks, **scads**, trevallies, **pilotfish** and pompanos are found in all warmer oceans. There are about 140 species with 11 on the Atlantic coast, 2 on the Pacific coast and 1 on both coasts.

These fishes vary considerably in body form from torpedo-shaped to extremely thin and compressed. Most lack bright colours and patterns, and are silvery, orange or yellowish. Scales are usually small and cycloid but a few species have ctenoid scales. Lateral line scales may be developed into distinctive, enlarged spiny scutes. The lateral line is usually arched anteriorly. Some areas of the body may be scaleless. There is a first dorsal fin with 3–9 spines, a second dorsal fin with 1 spine and 15–44 soft rays and, in some species, a series of up to 9 finlets (also behind the soft anal fin). The anal fin has 3 spines and 15–31 soft rays. The first 2 anal fin spines are separate from the rest of the fin, but may be overgrown by flesh and difficult to detect in large adults. Nevertheless these spines are a particular characteristic of jacks. The pectoral fin has 1 spine and about 14–24 soft rays and the pelvic fin 1 spine and 5 soft rays. The caudal peduncle is slender and the caudal fin deeply forked. Jaw teeth may be small or large and are in bands. There may be an adipose eyelid.

Jacks are relatives of the **Cobia, Remora** and **Dolphin** families in the **Perch Order**.

Jacks are primarily marine fishes but a few do enter brackish water. They are often offshore spawners and produce pelagic eggs in summer months. The banded young hide under jellyfish and debris and in seaweed clumps. Young fish also differ in shape, the body being deeper than in adults, and in having elongate fin spines developed in some species while others have shorter fins than adults. As adults they form schools inshore. The pilotfish retains its bands and follows larger fishes. Jacks feed on various invertebrates and fishes and are fast swimmers. They are important game and food fishes but not in Canada. Some are reported to cause food poisoning because of the ciguatera toxin.

See **Atlantic moonfish**
     banded rudderfish
     bigeye scad
     blue runner
     crevalle jack
     greater amberjack
     jack mackerel
     lookdown
     mackerel scad
     pilotfish
     redtail scad
     rough scad
     round scad
     yellowtail

jack mackerel

Scientific name: *Trachurus symmetricus*
    (Ayres, 1855)
Family: **Jack**
Other common names: mackereljack, horse
    mackerel, saurel, rough scad
French name: carangue symétrique

Distribution: Found from southeast Alaska to the Galapagos Islands including the British Columbia coast and at Ocean Station Papa (50°N, 145°W).

Characters: This jack is distinguished from its Canadian Pacific coast relatives by having scutes (enlarged scales) along the lateral line. Lateral line scales 87–111. There is an additional lateral line along the base of the spiny

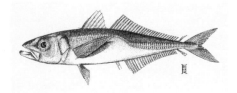

jack mackerel

dorsal fin, ending between the level of the fourth and fifth spines. First dorsal fin with 8 spines, second dorsal fin with 0–1 spine and

28–38 soft rays. There may be an anteriorly directed spine in front of the first dorsal fin in young fish. Anal fin with 1–2 spines and 22–33 soft rays. Both the dorsal and anal fins break up into a finlet posteriorly. Pectoral fin rays 22–24. Colour is metallic blue or olive-green on the back with silvery sides and belly. There is a dark spot on the postero-dorsal corner of the gill cover. The tailfin is yellowish or reddish. Reaches 81 cm.

Biology: This jack is quite common off southern Vancouver Island in early fall and is a schooling species. It has been caught as deep as 403 m in British Columbia. It may be found around reefs and kelp beds and in the open ocean. Food is larger plankton and smaller fishes. Jack mackerels have been observed to select a prey item and chase it down. A jack mackerel can cover 139 cm/second or almost 28 times their total length each second. Their vision is exceptional and they can feed by the light of the moon. They are eaten by sealions, porpoises, **swordfish** and other large fishes and various seabirds. Half the population of females mature at 28 cm and all are mature at 31 cm and 3 years of age. They can live over 30 years. Unusually in a long-lived fish, maturity can be reached at 1 year of age. Pelagic eggs are spawned in February–May off Baja California and number over 50,000 even in females only 21.5 cm long. Larger fish may have about half a million eggs of about 1 mm diameter. Spawning jacks off Washington have been caught almost 1000 km out to sea. These fish can be caught from piers and boats on hook and line using live anchovy bait and by trolling. They are a popular sport fish with as many as 200,000 caught yearly in California. There is a commercial canning operation for this species in California where they are caught with purse seines. The name horse mackerel was changed by U.S. authorities to jack mackerel in 1948 and this is believed to have given the fish more consumer appeal.

Japanese lanternfish

Scientific name: *Notoscopelus japonicus* (Tanaka, 1908)
Family: **Lanternfish**
Other common names: none

French name: lanterne japonaise

Distribution: Found at Ocean Station Papa (50°N, 145°W) and possibly off southern British Columbia waters. Elsewhere in the western North Pacific Ocean.

Characters: This is the only species on the Pacific coast characterised by stiff, spine-like rays at the upper and lower caudal fin bases, no large glands on the upper and lower caudal peduncle outlined by heavy black pigment, and a dorsal fin base longer than the anal fin base. It is related to the Atlantic species **Bolin's lanternfish, northern sail-lamp, patchwork lanternfish** and **spinetail lanternfish**. This species has ctenoid scales. Dorsal fin rays 20–22, anal rays 18–20, pectoral rays 10–12 and total vertebrae 40–42. Lateral line scales 41–43. Total gill rakers 23–28. Total AO photophores 14–16, Prc photophores 2+2. Reaches 14 cm.

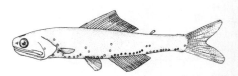

Japanese lanternfish

Biology: There is some confusion in the Canadian literature on the identity of *Notoscopelus* in waters off British Columbia so biology is poorly known. In Japan this lanternfish is an important item in the diet of fur seals.

Jasper longnose sucker

Scientific name: *Catostomus catostomus lacustris* (Bajkov, 1927)
Family: **Sucker**
Other common names: none
French name: meunier de Jasper

Distribution: Found in Pyramid Lake, Jasper Park, Alberta.

Characters: This subspecies is distinguished from the typical form, the **longnose sucker**, by having smaller lateral line scales (96–110) on average and fewer gill rakers (20–23, mean 21.6). Dorsal fin branched rays 7–8, anal branched rays 6–8, pectoral rays 14–17 and pelvic rays 7–10. The upper lip is thick with 3–4 rows of papillae. The flanks are dark grey with a metallic sheen, obscured by dark olive spots. The belly is white. Dorsal

Jasper longnose sucker

and caudal fins grey. Anal fin brownish and pectoral fin brownish to grey-brown. It may be a relict which survived the Wisconsin glaciation in a montane-foothill refugium. Originally described from Annette, Beauvert and Patricia lakes as well as Pyramid Lake, specimens from the former two lakes are not different from **longnose sucker** and Patricia Lake fish have not been re-examined. The situation is complicated by the knowledge that **longnose suckers** from elsewhere may have been dumped in Pyramid Lake while being used illegally as live bait by anglers (see also **Banff longnose dace**). Usually less than 15.0 cm standard length, but up to 41.2 cm.

Biology: This sucker hides under stones during the day, emerging in the evening to enter shallow waters. Food of young is mostly zooplankton while older fish larger than 5.0 cm take mostly crustaceans, and some aquatic insects and molluscs. Spawning occurs in June in streams entering Pyramid Lake, or in lake shallows, at 8–14°C. All fish are mature by age 6 although some mature at 4 years. Life span is 14 years. A removal programme from 1940 to 1945 took 33,097 suckers out of Pyramid Lake in an effort to improve **rainbow trout** fishing. This may have affected the sucker population since **mountain whitefish** predominated in the 1980s while the suckers comprised 75% of fish caught prior to 1946.

javelin spookfish

Scientific name: *Bathylychnops exilis* Cohen, 1958
Family: **Spookfish**
Other common names: none
French name: revenant javeline

Distribution: Found in the temperate northeast Pacific Ocean including Canadian waters and rarely in the Atlantic Ocean.

Characters: This species is distinguished from other spookfishes by an elongate, rounded body, numerous vertebrae (78–84), teeth on the roof of the mouth in a single row and eyes with pearly accessory corneal bodies. There may be as many as 4 lenses in each eye, a unique character. While the eyes protrude they are not markedly tubular. The larger, primary eyes are directed dorsally and auxiliary eyes ventrally. There are about 13–16 dorsal and 10–14 anal fin rays. Pectoral rays 10–13 and pelvic rays 7–8. Lateral line scales have dorsal and ventral flaps pointing anteriorly. Body colour is light orange-yellow and the flesh is nearly transparent. A light brown stripe runs from the

javelin spookfish

head to the adipose fin high on the flank. The snout is dark. The eyes are iridescent silvery-green. Reaches 48.7 cm standard length.

Biology: There is little information on biology. Eggs and larvae are pelagic and adults are found in the middle depths of the deep ocean. The additional eye lenses serve to detect movement from below. The binocular eyes are restricted to dorsal vision and predators or prey from below would not be seen without the additional lenses. Food is crustaceans, probably jellyfish relatives and possibly microscopic organisms.

jawed fishes

Fishes with jaws far outnumber the few **jawless fishes** by about 300 to 1. The jaws are actually derived from gill arches, which have undergone major modifications. Paired fins (pectorals and pelvics) are usually present, there are 3 semicircular canals in the ear, the gill openings are usually slits, nerve fibres are myelinised, and vertebral centra are present. Most jawed fishes have scales. The jawed fishes are part of the Gnathostomata which has 2 fossil (placoderms and spiny sharks) and 2 living classes (see below) The Amphibia (amphibians), Reptilia (reptiles), Aves (birds) and Mammalia (mammals) are also Gnathostomata.

Jawed fishes first appeared in the Early Silurian, over 450 million years ago. The relationships of the various groups of jawed fishes is uncertain. The two major groups are the **cartilaginous fishes**, or Chondrichthyes, which includes **sharks** and **rays** and the **Chimaera Family**, and the **bony fishes**. Since there are only about 850 species of **cartilaginous fishes**, most fishes (ca. 23,650) are **bony fishes**.

jawless fishes

The jawless fishes (also called Superclass Agnatha) comprise the living **Hagfish** and **Lamprey** families (which are also orders and classes), and the heavily-armoured, extinct ostracoderms. As well as lacking jaws, there are no pectoral or pelvic fins, no scales, no bone and therefore no vertebral centra but only a notochord, only 1–2 vertical semicircular canals in the ear, and pores, rather than slits, as gill openings.

Jawless fishes may have first emerged in the Late Cambrian, over 500 million years ago, and were most diverse in the Silurian and Lower Devonian. There are about 84 living species world-wide in marine and fresh waters, compared with about 24,500 species of **jawed fishes**.

The **jawed fishes**, and about 23,600 species of amphibians, reptiles, birds and mammals, make up the bulk of the living jawed **vertebrate** animals (or Gnathostomata).

The precise relationships of the two jawless fish families with each other and the various fossil forms remains contentious. Hagfishes are probably the most primitive and lampreys more closely related to Gnathostomata.

jewel lanternfish

Scientific name: *Lampanyctus crocodilus* (Risso, 1810)
Family: **Lanternfish**
Other common names: none
French name: lanterne-joyau

Distribution: Found in the North Atlantic Ocean and Mediterranean Sea. In Canada from Ungava Bay southward off the Atlantic coast.

Characters: This species and 7 relatives in the genus *Lampanyctus* are separated from other Atlantic species by lacking photophores close to the dorsal body edge, the PLO photophore is well above the pectoral fin base level while the second PVO photophore is at or below the upper pectoral base level, there are 4 Prc, the first PO and two PVO photophores are not on a straight line, both males and females have caudal luminous glands composed of overlapping, scale-like structures without a black pigment border, the fourth PO photophore is highly elevated, there are no luminous, scale-like structures on the belly between the pelvic fin bases or these bases and the anus, there are 4 VO photophores and the SAO series is strongly angled. This species is distinguished from its relatives by having 15–18 gill rakers, long pectoral fins extending back beyond the pelvic fin bases but not reaching the anal fin origin, 2–3 cheek photophores, luminous tissue at the adipose fin base, 38–39 lateral line organs and 5–7 AOa photophores. Dorsal fin rays 13–15, anal rays 16–18 and pectoral rays 13–16. AO photophores 13–16. The supracaudal luminous gland consists of 3–4 poorly-defined segments while the infracaudal gland is about 3 times as long and has 8–10 scale-like segments. Reaches 30 cm, a very large lanternfish.

jewel lanternfish

Biology: Distribution is temperate and partially subtropical and it is the commonest lanternfish in the temperate Atlantic Ocean. Some specimens enter subarctic waters. Depth distribution by day is usually 275–1000 m with a maximum abundance at 600–800 m. At night from near the surface to

1000 m with maximum abundance varying with locality. Near Bermuda the night maxima were at 100–250 m and at 400–1000 m. Only juveniles migrate. Spawning occurs in the fall in the Atlantic Ocean.

jewelfish

Scientific name: *Hemichromis bimaculatus* Gill, 1862
Family: **Cichlid**
Other common names: jewel cichlid, red cichlid, African jewelfish
French name: cichlide à deux taches

Distribution: Restricted to the Cave and Basin Hotsprings, Banff National Park, Alberta. Specimens were aquarium stock, probably from Liberia, Africa. Elsewhere in North America only known from introductions to Florida.

Characters: Readily identified by its single nostril opening on each side of the head and the colour pattern. Dorsal fin spines

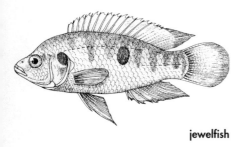

jewelfish

13–15, soft rays 9–13. Anal fin spines 3 and soft rays 7–9. Pectoral fin rays 14–15. Lateral scale rows 24–29. Overall colour is red with 6–7 sky-blue rows of flank speckles in the breeding season. The dorsal fin has a double row of blue spots on a red background. The pelvic and anal fins have blue spots and a black anterior edge. The caudal fin has a dark red edge. Outside the breeding season flanks are greenish-yellow with the back dark olive to grey-brown with greenish tinges. Fins are yellowish-brown to greenish. A flank stripe is apparent and 5–6 bands may be developed. There is a blue-black spot on the gill cover and on the upper midflank. There are aquarium varieties of this species in which colour patterns vary although the

red with blue speckles is a common theme. Reaches 20 cm.

Biology: The habitat consists of several hotsprings which feed into a shallow pond or marsh which in turn empties into the Bow River. The population of jewelfish in the hotsprings area is thought to be the offspring from a single breeding pair, indicative of how easily exotics can become established. The pond has widely varying temperatures depending on season and distance from the various hotspring inflows, but jewelfish have been caught at over 21°C when the Bow River was at 5.5°C. Jewelfish are relatively rare in this habitat, mortality being high when water levels are low. Food is any small organisms and they are recorded as eating snails, amphipods, insects, fish, diatoms and algae in the hot springs. The adult pairs are territorial and aggressive and show parental care in the spawning season. Sexual maturity is attained at about 7 cm. Jewelfish dig up the habitat during the spawning season to form pits in which up to 500 eggs are deposited. Fry may be moved to several new pits as they grow. Fry are identified by the parents on visual and chemical cues.

johnny darter

Scientific name: *Etheostoma nigrum* Rafinesque, 1820
Family: **Perch**
Other common names: central johnny darter
French name: raseux-de-terre

Distribution: Found in southern Québec, Ontario, Manitoba and eastern Saskatchewan. Occurs southward to Mississippi and Alabama.

Characters: This **darter** is recognised by the small mouth not extending beyond the anterior eye margin, a smooth edge to the preopercle bone on the side of the head, an anal fin smaller than the soft dorsal fin, belly scales present or absent but no enlarged scales in midline, premaxillaries protractile, i.e. a deep groove separates the upper lip from the snout, 1 thin anal spine, 1–11, usually 9 or less, pores in the preoperculo-mandibular canal (the head sensory canal running from the lower jaw onto the preopercle bone), and 9–15, usually 12 or less, dorsal fin soft rays. Dorsal fin spines 6–10, anal soft rays 6–10. Pectoral fin rays 10–14. Lateral line scales 35–59. The breast, cheek

johnny darter

and nape are usually scaleless. Overall colour is pale brown or sandy with yellowish or greenish tints depending on habitat. The back has about 4–7 dark brown saddles. The flanks have 7–12 distinctive x-shaped pigment marks which may also resemble m- or w-shapes. The caudal fin usually has 2–4 complete bars. Breeding males are black and flank markings are not always visible or appear as bars. The dorsal, anal and pelvic fin spine tips may be swollen white knobs. Reaches 7.7 cm.

Biology: The johnny darter occurs in lakes, large rivers and streams although preferring the latter. It is found in relatively fast water or in still water and is most frequent over sand, gravel or boulder bottoms. In competition with other darters, it dominates weed beds. It may also be found in lakes down to 64 m. Food is various aquatic insects and crustaceans taken from the bottom. This common darter is eaten by many other fishes. Females live about a year longer than males, to age 4, but males are larger. Spawning occurs from April to June in Canada, the peak depending on environmental conditions (temperature range 10–25°C). Males clean the undersurface of rocks with their fins and maintain a territory, defending it against other males by a display with erect fins. Male fights involve head butting and fin nipping. Males also defend the nest site against crayfish which favour territories under rocks and eat fish eggs. Crayfish with a carapace length up to 3.2 cm were chased away by johnny darter nips to the abdomen. Females are courted by the male's invitation under the rock and his movements there upside down. The pair move over the rock surface together inverted and an adhesive egg is deposited and fertilised every few seconds. Should the female turn upright, the male prods her into inverting and continuing the egg laying. The female may deposit 30–200 eggs at each site and visit 5–6 sites. A single site may have up to 1150 eggs, collected from a series of females. Males guard the eggs and fan them with their pectoral fins to keep them clean and aerated. The eggs are also rubbed with the swollen dorsal fin spines. Eggs which develop a fungal infection are eaten. Eggs are up to 1.5 mm in diameter. This species is an excellent aquarium denizen and has been used in behavioural studies.

K

kelp clingfish

Scientific name: *Rimicola muscarum*
(Meek and Pierson, 1895)
Family: **Clingfish**
Other common names: slender clingfish
French name: crampon de varech

Distribution: Found from Baja California to the Queen Charlotte Islands.

Characters: The sucking disc on the breast and the spineless, posteriorly positioned dorsal and anal fins are characteristic

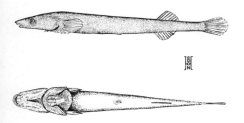

kelp clingfish

of clingfishes. This species is distinguished from its relative, the **northern clingfish**, by having 6–8 dorsal rays and a small, narrow head. Anal fin rays number 6–8. Pectoral fin rays number 14–17. There are 4 pelvic rays on each side which join to form a wrinkled anterior edge to the disc. Overall colour is variable with habitat, from a vivid green to a pale olive-green or brown. There may be a reddish or orange flank stripe. Females may have brown-red spots. Attains 7 cm.

Biology: Found adhering to kelp or eelgrass with its disc. Food is small copepods, associated with kelp blades, which are seized when they move into range. Moving detritus may also be attacked but is spat out. Life span is thought to be 1 year with adults dying after an April spawning at Vancouver Island. Egg masses are found on kelp in May and early June.

kelp greenling

Scientific name: *Hexagrammos decagrammus*
(Pallas, 1810)
Family: **Greenling**

Other common names: greenling sea trout, chirus, bodieron, boregat, bluefish, tommy cod, rock trout, speckled sea trout
French name: sourcil de varech

Distribution: From southern California to Alaska including British Columbia.

Characters: Dorsal fin with 20–23 spines and 22–26 soft rays. Anal fin with 0–1 spine and 21–26 soft rays. Ctenoid scales cover the body and top of the head. The lateral lines are found along the base of the dorsal fin from the head to the middle of the soft rays, from the head to the tail fin, from the top of the gill opening to the tail fin, from the gill opening below the pectoral fin above the pelvic fin to a level opposite the end of the anal fin, and from the isthmus branching behind the pelvic fin to pass on each side of the anal fin to the tail. This species is distinguished from other Canadian greenlings by having 5 lateral lines, a cirrus above each eye and another between the eye and the dorsal fin origin in a small pit, and a short, strong spine at the anal fin origin. Colour is variable. A brown, slate-grey or olive background has large blue spots ringed with small reddish-brown spots in the male, while the female has numerous fine reddish-brown to golden spots or many, large, dark-brown blotches. The inside of the mouth is yellowish. A large eye-spot is found at the end of the soft dorsal fin. Attains 61 cm and 2.1 kg. The world, all-tackle angling record weighed 1.24 kg and was caught in 1988 at Chugach Passage, Alaska. The Canadian angling record

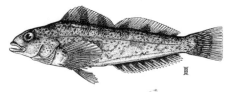

kelp greenling

from Port Renfrew, B.C. in 1992 was caught by Judy Lam and weighed 1.56 kg.

Biology: Common along rocky shores, in kelp beds and on sandy bottoms down to 46

m. Moves offshore in winter in northern areas. Females tend to live in shallower water than males and probably have their year-round distinctive colour to blend in with the algae there. Males in deeper water are not as exposed to surface predators and do not require concealing colouration. Food is crustaceans, worms, sea cucumbers and small fishes. They may live up to 12 years and spawn as early as 3 years of age. Spawning is in October to November when pale blue or mauve eggs are laid in masses on empty barnacle shells, coral colonies and other epifauna, rarely on rocks. Each male may guard up to 10 masses of neighbouring spawn, the masses being golf to tennis ball size. Each mass may have up to 9660 eggs of 2.5 mm diameter. This species is sought by sport and spear fishermen and is good eating. It follows divers around and will accept hand-held food.

kelp perch

Scientific name: *Brachyistius frenatus*
  Gill, 1862
Family: **Surfperch**
Other common names: kelp sea-perch,
  brown sea-perch
French name: perche de varech

Distribution: From northern British Columbia to Baja California.

Characters: This surfperch is distinguished from other Canadian species by having 37–44 lateral line scales and a frenum.

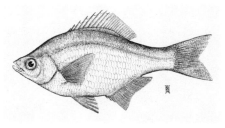

kelp perch

Dorsal fin spines 7–10, soft rays 13–16. Anal fin spines 3–4, soft rays 20–25. Pectoral fin rays 16–18. Caudal fin forked. Head concave over eye. Males have an enlarged, anterior anal fin, the gonopodium. Overall colour above olive to copper-brown or golden,

resembling kelp, sometimes with blue spots or streaks, or white blotches. Flank with a pale central stripe. Belly paler or silvery and often tinged red. Flanks may be rosy. Pectoral fin base finely spotted blue. Fins pale to a faint rosy colour. Anal fin anterior edge dark. Reaches 22 cm.

Biology: Found among kelp down to about 30 m although usually higher in the kelp canopy. Food is small crustaceans living on kelp and parasites which are cleaned off other fishes. The clients of the kelp perch keep still and erect their fins so that this surfperch can freely pick off parasites. Young are born in the spring. Large and small male kelp perch preferentially court large females but may also court small ones too. Courtships were brief, less than half a minute. Males are aggressive in competition for females.

kelp poacher

Scientific name: *Agonomalus mozinoi*
  Wilimovsky and Wilson, 1978
Family: **Poacher**
Other common names: none
French name: agone de varech

Distribution: Found from central California to the west coast of Vancouver Island.

Characters: This recently discovered species is distinguished from other related poachers, such as the **fourhorn poacher**, by having 11–12, usually 12, pectoral fin rays with the lower 1–2 rays thickened and finger-like, a prickly leading edge to the dorsal fin base and 4 rows of plates including a spiny dorso-lateral row. The belly has prickles and the spine on the bony rim of the eye

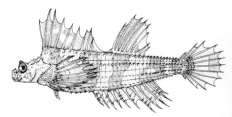

kelp poacher

is prickly at the tip. The first dorsal spine is straight on its anterior margin. Gill membranes are not joined to the isthmus. The first dorsal fin has 8–9 spines, the second dorsal fin 6–8 soft rays. Anal fin rays are 11–12. The caudal fin is crenulate. There is a long flap of skin on the snout. The dorsal fins, snout flap, pectoral fins, caudal fin and various parts of the head, body and other fins have a remarkable and unique scarlet-red colour interrupted with brown and white blotches. Attains 8.9 cm.

Biology: Found in shallow rocky areas and down to 11 m. This species can climb rock faces aided by its pectoral fins. It is camouflaged by pieces of seaweed and sponge on its body. In California it is mainly nocturnal. A female has produced clusters of 6 to 25 red eggs in an aquarium, deposited in crevices such as barnacle orifices and tube worm coils. Each egg is about 1 mm in diameter and adheres to its neighbours but not the substrate.

kelp snailfish

Scientific name: *Liparis tunicatus*
    Reinhardt, 1837
Family: **Snailfish**
Other common names: Greenland snailfish,
    nipishah, nee-fitz-shak, nipi-sak
French name: limace des laminaires

Distribution: Found across the whole Canadian Arctic from the Chukchi Sea and Alaska to western Greenland, and from northern Ellesmere Island south to the Labrador coast.

Characters: This snailfish is distinguished from its Arctic-Atlantic relatives by having an adhesive disc, 2 pairs of nostrils, dorsal fin without a notch, posterior teeth with 3 equal

lobes, light peritoneum, dorsal fin rays 37–44 (usually 41–43), anal rays 31–38 (usually 34–36), pectoral rays 32–39 and pyloric caeca 10–49. The gill opening extends downward opposite pectoral rays 0–7. Males have prickles on the tip of the head from the nostrils back to the anterior dorsal fin. Overall colour varies with habitat, usually grey-brown or reddish-brown to black. Some may be striped or speckled and mottled on the flank. There may be orange-reddish dorsal and anal fins with 6–8 bars. The caudal fin has 1–3 bars. Peritoneum pale with numerous small dots dorsally. Reaches 16.1 cm.

Biology: Usually found in shallow, shore waters attached to kelp fronds, even under sea ice. Rarely collected below 50 m. Temperatures vary between –1.5 and 2.1°C. Food is principally amphipods and copepods, with some other crustaceans. Spawning probably occurs in winter and spring. This species is eaten by seals in the Canadian Arctic.

key worm eel

Scientific name: *Ahlia egmontis*
    (Jordan, 1884)
Family: **Snake Eel**
Other common names: none
French name: serpenton d'Egmont

Distribution: From Brazil north to the Scotian Shelf in Canada.

Characters: Larvae have 147–165 myomeres (muscle blocks) with pigment spots along the dorsal body margin, a single spot at

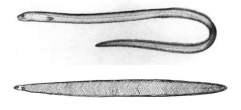

key worm eel

each anal ray base, dorsal fin origin posterior to myomere 60, and dashes on most myosepta. There are 4–6 gut swellings and 4–7 subcutaneous spots below the midline on the tail. In adults, the dorsal fin lies above or slightly behind the origin of the anal fin. The

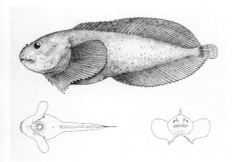

kelp snailfish

snout is rounded when viewed from above. The caudal and pectoral fins are well developed. Jaw teeth are in a single row and vomer teeth in the roof of the mouth are absent. The body is a uniform brown, sometimes finely and darkly spotted. Larvae are 79–84 mm long in Canada. Adults attain 43.3 cm.

Biology: Known only as stray larvae (or leptocephali) in Canadian waters and first reported in 1988. Adults are found in beds of seagrass and on reefs, from depths of 6 cm to 37 m. Spawning occurs in offshore waters and adults migrate. The eye increases in size, the body becomes silvery and the pectoral fins become longer. Adults can be attracted to lights at night.

Killifish Family

Scientific name: Fundulidae
French name: fondules

Killifishes or topminnows are found in fresh, brackish and coastal marine waters of North and Central America where there are about 48 species. There are 3 species in Canada, 1 on the Atlantic coast and in Atlantic drainages, 1 in Arctic and Atlantic drainages including brackish waters of the Atlantic coast, and 1 in fresh waters of the Atlantic drainage.

These small fishes are distinguished by a series of osteological characters such as the autopalatine bone projecting anterior to the lateral ethmoid and the anteriorly directed ventral arms of the maxillary bones of the upper jaw often have strong hooks. Scales are cycloid and extend onto the top of the head. The snout is pointed and elongate compared to related families. The head is flattened on top and the mouth upturned and protrusible. Lateral lines are absent on the body but can be well-developed on the head. The caudal fin is truncate and fins lack spines. Pelvic fins are abdominal. The swimbladder lacks a duct to the gut.

Killifishes are members of the **Killifish Order**. "Killifish" is derived from a Dutch word for a creek or channel in reference to their habitat.

Killifishes lay eggs but lack the modified anal fin or gonopodium of the similar-appearing **Livebearer Family**. Food is usually sur-

face items taken by the oblique mouth. The flattened head may be an adaptation to poor oxygen conditions enabling killifish to live as close to the air-water interface as possible in oxygen-rich conditions. Some are colourful and their tolerance of warm temperatures and wide salinities make them attractive aquarium fishes. Others have been used extensively as experimental animals.

See **banded killifish**
blackstripe topminnow
mummichog

Killifish Order

The **killifishes** or topminnows, rivulines, splitfins, four-eyed fishes, pupfishes or tooth carps and **livebearers** or Cyprinodontiformes comprise 9 families and about 800 species. These are small fishes of shallow brackish and fresh waters. There are 2 families with 5 species in Canada, 3 of which are native to eastern Canada and 2 of which are introduced to hotsprings at Banff, Alberta.

The order is characterised by a lateral line restricted to the head (on the body only as pitted scales), the nostrils are paired, the swimbladder is not connected to the gut, branchiostegal rays 3–7, the upper jaw is toothed and protrusible and is bordered only by the premaxilla bone, the vomer bone in the roof of the mouth is usually present, the supracleithrum bone in the skull-pectoral girdle attachment is present, the pectoral fin is set low on the flank, the metapterygoid bone is usually absent, the ectopterygoid bone is absent, the caudal fin skeleton is symmetrical internally, the caudal fin is not lobed, and parietal bones in the skull roof are present or absent.

This order is related to the **Silverside** and **Needlefish** orders by the possession of a large, demersal egg with many oil droplets and adhesive filaments, spermatogonia in the testes are confined to the terminus of tubules, infraorbital bones 3–5 under the eye and the fourth pharyngobranchial bone of the gill arch are absent, the heart develops in larvae in front of rather than under the head, and a specialised jaw mechanism where the rostral cartilage is not connected to the premaxilla bone in the upper jaw and where there are crossed palatomaxillary ligaments and a ligament from the maxillary to the cranium. These 3 orders are related to the higher fishes grouped with the **Perch Order**. These fishes are oviparous or viviparous. One species, a rivuline, (not in Canada) is unique among all fishes in being a hermaphrodite with internal fertilisation. The livebearers include all-female species which mate with males of another species merely to stimulate egg development, the sperm contributing no genetic material. Some rivulines are "annual" fishes. Adults spawn in the rainy season, and die, the eggs survive the dry season buried in mud and hatch in the next rainy season. Some species have the smallest reported fish eggs, perhaps only 0.1 mm in diameter. The four-eyed fishes have each eye divided into 2 parts, one for vision above the water surface and one for vision below. Many species are popular, colourful and easy to keep aquarium fishes.

See **Killifish Family**
Livebearer Family

king mackerel

Scientific name: *Scomberomorus cavalla* (Cuvier, 1829)
Family: **Mackerel**
Other common names: thazard barré
French name: tassard royal

Distribution: Found in the western Atlantic Ocean from Nova Scotia south to Brazil.

Characters: This species is distinguished from its Atlantic coast relatives by having the dorsal fins close together (separated by a

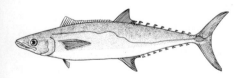

king mackerel

distance less than snout length), 12–18 (usually 15–18) first dorsal fins spines, 7–16 gill rakers, flanks not spotted and the first dorsal fin is not black anteriorly. The lateral line has a strong and abrupt downward curve under the second dorsal fin. Second dorsal fin with 15–18 rays and 7–10 finlets. Anal

fin with 16–20 (usually 18–19) rays and 7–10 finlets. Pectoral rays 21–23. There is no corselet. The back is dark to grey and the flanks silvery. Young fish may have small, bronze, yellowish or dark grey spots in 5–6 rows along the flank. Reaches 173 cm fork length and 45 kg. The world, all-tackle angling record weighed 40.82 kg and had a fork length of 170 cm. It was taken off Key West, Florida in 1976.

Biology: Reported from only 3 specimens in St. Margarets Bay, N.S. from 1974–1977. This is a coastal species. There is a northward movement in spring along the Atlantic coast from Florida for some fish although others are caught in Florida year round. Food is fishes, particularly **herrings**, crustaceans and squid. In Florida females mature at 4 years and 83.7 cm and males at 3 years and 73 cm. Life span is at least 14 years for females but only 9 years for males. Spawning in Florida occurs in late summer and in the western Gulf of Mexico from May to September at 35–183 m. Fecundity reaches 2,280,000 eggs. This is an important sport and commercial species along the U.S. coast year round with seasonal peaks. A peak catch was 4764 tonnes in 1974 taken with hook and line and gill nets. Anglers take this species from boats using trolled lures or small bait fish. Young can be caught from shore. Most of the catch is sold fresh as steaks although some has been canned.

king-of-the-salmon

Scientific name: *Trachipterus altivelus* Kner, 1859
Family: **Ribbonfish**
Other common names: none
French name: roi-des-saumons

Distribution: Found from Alaska to Chile including British Columbia.

Characters: The unique shape of the caudal fin, sticking upwards from the body and comprising the upper caudal lobe only, is distinctive. The body is ribbon-like, width about one-tenth of the depth. The pelvic fin is long in young fish but regresses to almost nothing in adults. The long dorsal fin has 160–188 rays. The lateral line is comprised of 262–306 small, separate tubes. The belly and tail midline are spiny. Body silvery with crimson fins. Black above the eye. Young have 3–5 blotches anteriorly on the flank. Attains 1.83 m but weighs only about 4 kg.

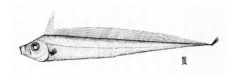

king-of-the-salmon

Biology: The common name is based on an Indian legend that these fish lead salmon runs into rivers. May be caught by anglers trolling for salmon but they are usually bathypelagic. They have been caught from the surface down to 650 m. They may live up to 7 years. Food is small invertebrates and fishes. Spawning occurs year round but peaks in spring. Egg densities off the American coast reach 25 per 10 sq m.

kitefin shark

Scientific name: *Dalatias licha*
    (Bonnaterre, 1788)
Family: **Sleeper Shark**
Other common names: darkie charlie,
    black shark, black jack
French name: squale liche

Distribution: World-wide in colder waters with a single record from Atlantic Canada.

Characters: This species is distinguished by its chocolate brown colour with some blackish spots, lack of an anal fin, no fin

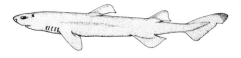

kitefin shark

spines, the second dorsal fin slightly larger than the first, the first dorsal fin origin clearly behind the pectoral fin tips, and the upper teeth slender and conical, lower teeth blade-like, triangular and serrated. The snout is short and blunt and lips are thick, fringed and papillose. Chocolate brown, greyish,

black or violet with black spots. The caudal fin is black-tipped, other fins with pale edges. The skin is probably luminescent. Reaches 182 cm.

Biology: Recorded as a single specimen taken on the northern edge of Georges Bank on the 19 August 1937. Common in deep waters of temperate and tropical continental and island slopes and shelves at 37–1800 m or more. It is occasionally washed ashore. It is a bottom shark but has an oily liver and may be found in midwaters. It is apparently solitary. Kitefins are ovoviviparous producing litters of 10–16 young born at about 30 cm. Food is mostly deepwater fishes such as **deepwater smelt, barracudinas, viperfishes, scaly dragonfishes, greeneyes, lanternfishes, bristlemouths, sharks** and various others but also squid, octopi, crustaceans, brittle stars, worms and jellyfish. It may ambush fast moving prey like bonito or perhaps scavenge dead ones. It cuts large pieces of flesh out of its prey. In the eastern Atlantic it is caught by bottom trawls and used for fish meal and leather. Off Japan it is a food fish and the liver oil is prized. This shark used to be caught specifically for the use of the skin as a polishing or abrasive agent by jewellers and cabinet makers.

kiyi

Scientific name: *Coregonus kiyi* (Koelz, 1921)
Family: **Salmon**
Other common names: chub, waterbelly,
    mooneye
French name: cisco kiyi

Distribution: Found in lakes Ontario, Huron, Michigan and Superior.

Characters: This member of the **Salmon Family** is distinguished from its relatives by having large scales (110 or less), no parr marks, teeth absent from the jaws and roof of the mouth, forked tail fin, 2 flaps of skin between the nostrils, the upper and lower jaws are about equal, giving the front of the head a pointed appearance, the premaxilla bone of the upper jaw curves backwards, gill rakers 34–48, usually 36–41, and lateral line scales 71–91. Characters among **ciscoes** (q.v.) overlap and so the species cannot be easily separated. The lower jaw usually projects a little, is thin and has a knob at its tip. Gill rakers are about equal in length to gill filaments, paired fins are very long (the pelvics usually reach to or past the anus), the eye is large and about equal in length to the snout, and the body is deepest anteriorly. Dorsal fin rays 9–11, anal rays 9–16, pectoral rays 15–18 and pelvic rays 11–12. Overall colour is silvery with pink, purple or blue iridescent areas. The back is dark and the belly white. Dorsal and caudal fins have dark margins, other fins clear. The middle rays of the caudal fin are black. The pectoral fins are black on the dorsal margin. The tip of the lower jaw is dark. This species has been suggested to be the same species as the **lake cisco** or the same as the **bloater**. Reaches 35.1 cm total length.

kiyi

Biology: Kiyi are usually found below about 100 m although depth range is 37 m to 180 m or more. Opossum shrimps and amphipods are the main food items with some insects and molluscs. Females are larger than males and usually live longer, to 10 years rather than 8 years. Growth is slow. Maturity is attained at 2–3 years. Spawning takes place from late September to January, probably at about 91–168 m and 1.7–3.4°C. This species formed part of a commercial fishery in Lake Ontario (see ciscoes) but is now probably extirpated there and from Lake Huron. It is still abundant in Lake Superior. **Rainbow smelt** and **gaspereau** were competitors of this **cisco** in Lake Ontario and heavy fisheries contributed to its loss. The Committee on the Status of Endangered Wildlife in Canada gave this species the status of "rare" in 1987.

knifenose chimera

Scientific name: *Rhinochimaera atlantica* Holt and Byrne, 1909

Family: **Longnose Chimaera**
Other common names: straightnose rabbitfish, chimère à nez mou
French name: chimère-couteau

Distribution: Found in the North Atlantic and North Pacific oceans and off Atlantic Canada. Found south to Virginia in the western Atlantic Ocean.

Characters: This chimaera is recognised by its long snout, almost straight head profile, mouth in front of the eye, tooth plates

knifenose chimera

narrow, sharp-edged and smooth, and a smooth dorsal spine in adults. The snout is straight at the tip. The pectoral fin is long and narrow. There are no tubercles on the snout. The caudal fin is thickened in males and has 25–30 enlarged, knob-like denticles. The head clasper is small. Overall colour is chocolate brown but may be whitish. Fins are darker and brown in preserved fish. Gill opening dark. Reaches about 140 cm.

Biology: Found off Labrador, northern Newfoundland, southwestern Nova Scotia and Georges Bank at 529–1100 m, elsewhere to 1500 m. Fertilisation is internal. Egg cases are large, 15 cm, and tadpole-shaped. The cases have a narrowed area anteriorly, a long posterior tube and wide lateral membranes with cross ribs.

kokanee

The kokanee is a landlocked form of the **sockeye salmon** (q.v.). It has been referred to as a separate species from the **sockeye** until it was realised they were the same. Even a proposed subspecies status is not now generally accepted. Kokanee stocks are probably of independent origin, there are different stocks within lakes, there are intermediate forms called "residuals" in lakes which are sockeye that do not migrate and kokanee may even migrate with **sockeye**. Separating the two forms serves no purpose.

L

Labrador wolf eel

Scientific name: *Lycenchelys labradorensis*
  Geistdoerfer, Hureau and Rannou, 1970
Family: **Eelpout**
Other common names: none
French name: lycode du Labrador

Distribution: Found in the Labrador Sea.

Characters: This species is separated from its Canadian relatives by having short pelvic fins, a mouth under the snout, large pores around the mouth, no crests on the chin, no bony plates along the dorsal and

Labrador wolf eel

anal fin bases, and by colour. The mouth is small and does not extend back to the eye. There is a single lateral line. Dorsal fin rays 120, anal rays 115 (each including half the continuous caudal fin rays). Pectoral rays 17. The body is pale, almost colourless or with bluish tinges. Head, dorsal and anal fins bluish. The pectoral and pelvic fins are brown. Dorsal and anal fin margins brown. Peritoneum black. Reaches 21.9 cm. This may be the same species as *Lycenchelys albus* (Vaillant, 1888) found in the eastern Atlantic Ocean off France and Spain.

Biology: Reported on mud bottoms at 3365–3975 m.

lake chub

Scientific name: *Couesius plumbeus*
  (Agassiz, 1850)
Family: **Carp**
Other common names: northern chub, creek chub, chub minnow, Moose Lake minnow, bottlefish
French name: méné de lac

Distribution: Found across Canada and north in the Mackenzie River, absent only from Newfoundland, P.E.I., Cape Breton, Anticosti Island, the Arctic Islands and the adjacent mainland and from the coast and

islands of British Columbia. In the U.S.A. in northern states along the Canadian border and south to Colorado.

Characters: This species is characterised by the presence of a barbel at the end of the upper jaw, lateral line scales 53–79, mouth not extending back to the eye, no axillary scale or fleshy stays at the pelvic fins and rounded pectoral fins. Occasional specimens may have a pelvic axillary process. Dorsal fin branched rays 7, branched anal rays 6–8, usually 7, pectoral rays 13–19 and pelvic rays 7–9. Pharyngeal teeth hooked, 2,4–4,2 with a wide range of variants including complete loss of minor row teeth. Breeding males have small tubercles on the top and sides of the head extending back to the dorsal fin, on flank scales down to the lateral line with up to 6 on each scale margin, on breast scales and on the upper pectoral and pelvic fin rays. Males have longer pectoral fins than females and the anterior rays are thickened.

The overall colour is silvery with a leaden tinge (hence "plumbeus"). The back is olive, dark green, brown, grey or blackish, the flanks silvery and the belly silvery-white. Some scales on the flank are darkened and upper flank scales have dark margins. A mid-flank, lead-coloured stripe is evident in young but fades in adults although some retain it. The stripe extends onto the snout and upper lip in young. Breeding males have variable amounts of red or red-orange at the pectoral and pelvic fin bases, in a stripe just above the pectoral, pelvic and anal fins,

lake chub

mouth corners, upper lip, snout and behind and just inside the gill slit at the lateral line origin. Pacific populations are said to lack these. Peritoneum silvery and speckled. Hybrids with **longnose dace** are reported from Alberta. Reaches 22.7 cm total length.

Biology: Lake chub, despite their name, occur in the cool waters of streams and rivers as well as lakes. In British Columbia they are found in the Liard Hot Springs where they may be distinct from other populations. Lake populations retreat to deeper water in summer as shallows heat up.

Food includes aquatic and terrestrial insects, some planktonic crustaceans, snails, algae, and small fishes. Most food is detected by sight. Various predatory fishes and birds consume lake chub. The common loon has been observed flying with a lake chub in its bill.

Life span is about 7 years with maturity attained at 3–4 years. Females grow faster and live longer than males. Spawning occurs from April to August at 10°C or higher, the time depending on latitude. In the Montreal River, Saskatchewan most spawning takes place during the afternoon, although some continues to midnight. There is usually a migration into streams but spawning may occur along rocky shores or on lake shoals. The bottom varies from silt to rocks. Eggs are yellow, non-adhesive, average 1.6 mm in diameter and up to 11,440 are found in each female. No nest is built and there is no parental care of eggs and young. Courtship involves a male pursuing a female and nudging her vent region often forcing her to break the water surface. The male flank stripe is dark and distinct and the mouth opens and closes rapidly. Several males may swim side by side near the female, competing for position. Once a female nears a rock or swims under it, the male presses against her, vibrates and eggs are shed and fertilised. Several spawning acts occur in each minute, lasting about 1 second, and only a few eggs are shed each time.

This species is used as live bait in Canada.

lake chubsucker

Scientific name: *Erimyzon sucetta*
　　(Lacepède, 1803)
Family: **Sucker**
Other common names: western lake
　　chubsucker, pin sucker, sweet sucker

French name: sucet de lac

Distribution: Found only in western Lake Erie and adjacent ponds and in Lake St. Clair in Canada. In the U.S.A. south to Texas and Florida.

Characters: This sucker is identified by the short dorsal fin, absence of a lateral line, oblique and subterminal mouth without a strongly overhanging snout, and a midflank, black stripe. Pharyngeal teeth are short and club-shaped. The lower lip has a 90–100° angle, only a short cleft, and coarse papillae in long ridges. Gill rakers 31–35. Dorsal fin rays 10–13, anal rays 7, pectoral rays 15–16 and pelvic rays 8–9. Scales in lateral series 33–42. Males have 3–4, large nuptial tubercles on the snout and the anal fin rays have rows of small tubercles. The back and head are olive-green to brown, the flanks are golden brown to silvery and the belly yellow to greenish-yellow. Scales are outlined in black. Large fish may lack a flank stripe and have 6–8 bars. Dorsal, anal and caudal fins are olive-green, pectoral and pelvic fins are dusky or whitish. Young may have a reddish tail and the anterior dorsal fin edge is black. Attains 43.2 cm.

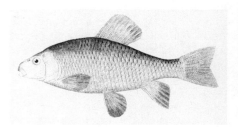

lake chubsucker

Biology: This sucker is found in ponds in Canada and in vegetated lakes and slow-moving streams elsewhere. Food is crustaceans and aquatic insects. Life span is up to 8 years. Maturity is attained at 1–2 years. Spawning takes place in March to July in streams. The male clears a gravel area as a nest or eggs are simply scattered. Each female produces up to 20,000 non-adhesive, 2 mm diameter eggs.

lake cisco

Scientific name: *Coregonus artedi*
　　Le Sueur, 1818

Family: **Salmon**
Other common names: cisco, lake herring,
 tullibee, freshwater herring, blueback,
 sand herring, shallowwater cisco,
 grayback tullibee, Bear Lake herring,
 blueback tullibee, herring salmon,
 arnaqsleq, kapisilik, kaviselik
French name: cisco de lac

Distribution: Found from eastern Québec,
including Ungava Bay and southern Hudson
Bay west to northern Alberta and much of
the N.W.T., north to Great Slave Lake and
the lower Mackenzie River. Also in U.S.
states adjacent to the Great Lakes.

Characters: This member of the **Salmon
Family** is distinguished from its relatives by
having large scales (110 or less), no parr

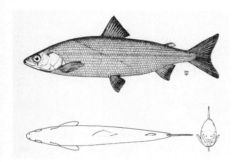

lake cisco

marks, teeth absent from the jaws and roof of
the mouth, forked tail fin, 2 flaps of skin
between the nostrils, the upper and lower jaws
are about equal, giving the front of the head a
pointed appearance, the premaxilla bone of
the upper jaw curves backwards, gill rakers
38–64, usually 46–50, and lateral line scales
63–94. Characters among **ciscoes** (q.v.) overlap and so the species cannot be easily separated. The lower jaw is usually about the same
length as the upper jaw which extends back to
the anterior eye margin, there is a knob at the
lower jaw tip, the body is deepest at the middle and is elongate and rounded in cross section. Dorsal fin rays 9–15, anal rays 10–15,
pectoral rays 14–18 and pelvic rays 8–12.
Males have one nuptial tubercle in the centre
or near the edge of each scale.

Overall colour is silvery with pink to purple iridescence. The back may be grey, light

brown, bluish, greenish or almost black and
the belly is white. The dorsal and caudal fins
may be darkly pigmented on the distal half or
on the margin. Pelvic and anal fins are milky.
The pelvic fins have dark tips. Fins are generally clear with limited pigmentation.

This species shows considerable variation
over its wide range and some variants have
been given scientific names, 24 subspecies
being described in 1931. In some lakes there
are two forms, a small and a large one with
different biology and anatomy. The confusion
of genetic identity through man-induced
changes and extinction of some forms (see
ciscoes) and lack of study makes a resolution
of these names difficult. Lake cisco have been
referred to as a *Coregonus artedi* "complex"
which indicates that there is not a single,
clearly defined species but a complex of
forms. Hybrids with **lake whitefish** (q.v.) are
reported for Canada.

Reaches 57.2 cm total length and 3.63 kg.

Biology: This widespread freshwater, lake
species is also found in coastal salt water of
Hudson Bay where they feed in summer. It is
also known from large rivers. Lake cisco are
pelagic in lake midwaters, at 18–53 m in Lake
Superior for example, with movements into
deeper, cooler water in summer and into shallower waters in fall. There are reports of daily
vertical migrations with cisco coming to the
surface at night under winter ice to feed on
crustaceans. It is rarely found at temperatures
above 18°C.

Food is mainly plankton and large crustaceans such as opossum shrimps and
amphipods but can include aquatic insects and
molluscs in shallow waters or terrestrial
insects taken at the surface. Eggs of their own
and other species are eaten, as well as fry and
minnows. A variety of other fishes eat lake
cisco including **lake trout, northern pike,
yellow perch, walleye** and **burbot**. Strongly
swimming prey is taken by a dart and suck
action. Gulping is also used where the fish
open and close the mouth 2–3 times per second, taking more than 1 prey at a gulp. Even
buried prey can be taken.

Life span is 31 years of age and maturity
is attained at 1–6 years depending on locality,
later in the north. Spawning takes place from

September to December, earliest in the north, when large schools form, usually at 6°C or less. The spawning ground is often gravel shallows at 1–3 m but can occur pelagically at 9–42 m over deep water. Males arrive on the spawning grounds first, 2–5 days before females. As many as 12 males will follow a single female but at spawning time the female is usually accompanied by 2 males. She descends to 15–20 cm above the bottom, leading the males whose heads are level with her anus. Eggs are shed, mostly at night, fall to the bottom and are abandoned. The eggs are slightly adhesive and become attached to the bottom. Ripe females produce up to 29,000, 2.1 mm diameter eggs. These eggs hatch the following spring at ice break-up.

This **cisco** was once very abundant and of great commercial importance with as much as 21.8 million kg being taken from Lake Erie in 1918. Local fisheries still catch this species for food, for fur farms and for dogs in the north. It is sold fresh, frozen or smoked and is very good eating. The total Canadian catch in 1988 was 1400 tonnes. Anglers may catch it on live bait including **minnows**, artificial lures and flies, and by ice fishing and spearing. Cisco populations are declining. In addition to overfishing and other factors outlined under **ciscoes**, this species is sensitive to enrichment of lakes since it thrives in infertile waters. Enriched or eutrophic waters have depleted oxygen levels in summer in the deep, cool waters favoured by cisco. The cisco is forced into surface waters where temperatures are too high and summerkills are common.

lake lamprey

Scientific name: *Lampetra macrostoma*
  Beamish, 1982
Family: **Lamprey**
Other common names: none
French name: lamproie à grand disque

Distribution: Found only in lakes Cowichan and Mesachie on Vancouver Island, British Columbia.

Characters: The limited distribution of this species is a key identification character. There are 3–4 cusps on the band above the mouth, 4 teeth on each side of the mouth with a cusp formula of 2–3–3–2, 5–6 cusps on the band

below the mouth, and the disc and eye are large compared to the **Pacific lamprey**. There are 59–70 myomeres. Velar tentacles number 11–15. Overall almost black as adults. Velar tentacles are weakly pigmented. Ammocoetes resemble the **Pacific lamprey**. Attains 25.6 cm as adults, 27.3 cm when immature.

lake lamprey

disc view

Biology: This is the only freshwater parasitic lamprey in British Columbia. It was classed as "rare" in 1986 by the Committee on the Status of Endangered Wildlife in Canada. Spawning is assumed to occur from May to August over shallow gravel bars in the lakes. Ammocoetes are found in silt of the lakes or lower reaches of inlet streams where they live for about 6 years. Ammocoetes metamorphose into adults from July to October. Adults probably live 2 years. Known to parasitise **coho salmon**, **cutthroat trout** and **Dolly Varden**. Eighty per cent of fish examined in Lake Cowichan have been recorded as having lamprey scars and 50% of **Salmon Family** members in Mesachie Lake. Fifteen per cent of **Salmon Family** members had wounds penetrating the body cavity and this probably was fatal.

lake sturgeon

Scientific name: *Acipenser fulvescens*
  Rafinesque, 1817
Family: **Sturgeon**
Other common names: freshwater, common, Great Lakes, red, ruddy, black, rock, stone, dogface, shellback or bony sturgeon; smoothback, rubber nose, esturgeon de lac, camus; or for young — escargot maillé, charbonnier
French name: esturgeon jaune

Distribution: Found from western Québec including James Bay, all of Ontario and most of Manitoba and westward in the North

Saskatchewan River to Alberta. South to Alabama, northern Mississippi and Arkansas west of the Appalachian Mountains.

Characters: This species is characterised by having 1 large plate between the caudal fin and the anal fin in addition to the fulcrum, 25–40 gill rakers, 29–43 lateral scutes or plates and 25–30 anal fin rays. Dorsal fin rays 35–40, dorsal plates 8–17, ventral plates 6–12.

Back and upper flank dark brown, olive-green or grey and belly white to yellow-white. Flanks may be reddish. Fins are dark brown or grey. Body cavity organs are black but the peritoneum is silvery and only slightly pigmented. Specimens smaller than 30 cm have 2 black blotches on the upper snout, a black blotch between the dorsal and lateral plates above the pectoral fin base and another similarly positioned below the dorsal fin, and smaller spots on much of the rest of the head and body. Lower parts of the body are greenish.

Reaches 274.5 cm and 140.62 kg, the largest freshwater fish in North America. The world, all-tackle angling record is recognised as a 41.84 kg fish caught in the Kettle River, Minnesota in 1986 although much larger fish have been caught on rod and line. The Canadian angling record from Georgian Bay, Ontario in 1992 was caught by Edward Paszkowski and weighed 76.10 kg.

lake sturgeon

Biology: Lake sturgeon are found in shallow areas of lakes and large rivers at about 5–9 m although they may descend to 43 m. Populations in the St. Lawrence River and the Hudson Bay drainage may enter brackish water. Food is slurped from bottom sediments and includes a wide variety of animal and plant material found in and on the bottom. Sediment is also taken in and ejected from the gill slits or the mouth. The food is detected by the barbels which lightly touch the bottom as the sturgeon swims slowly along. The tubular mouth is protruded as soon as food is detected. Recorded food items are crayfish, other crustaceans, clams, snails, aquatic insects, fish eggs, algae and rarely fish. It is not considered to be a serious predator on the eggs of other fishes.

Sturgeon may leap out of the water, a habit attributed to efforts to rid themselves of parasitic **lampreys**. 61 **silver lampreys** have been recorded on a single lake sturgeon, 1.3 m long and 16 kg in weight, caught in the St. Lawrence River, although these were not considered to be enough to kill the sturgeon.

Accurate age determination is difficult in long-lived species like sturgeons. Maximum female age is estimated to be 96 years and for males 55 years. There is a report of one fish aged at 154 years from Lake of the Woods. Growth is slower in the north than the south and fish are older. Maturity has been estimated at 8–20 years for males and 14–33 for females, varying with locality. St. Lawrence River female sturgeon reach sexual maturity at an estimated 27 years and 1.33 m and the mean interval between spawnings is 9.4–9.7 years, higher than reports for other populations.

Spawning occurs in April to June at 12–18°C in flowing water or rocky lake margins with wave action. Lake populations may migrate up rivers for 400 km to reach spawning grounds although the distance travelled is usually less and fish are generally sedentary outside spawning. Males arrive first on the spawning grounds. The large female is in spawning condition for a short time and is flanked by 1–2 males. The spawning process may involve splashing, vibrations and leaps clear of the water. Eggs and sperm are shed at intervals over a few days and the eggs adhere to rocks. The spawning act lasts only 5 seconds. The eggs are black, up to 3.5 mm in diameter and in very large fish could exceed 3 million. Spawning occurs at estimated intervals of 1–7 years in males and 4–10 years in females, with longer intervals in the north.

This species has been used for food fresh or smoked, the eggs as caviar, the swimbladder as isinglass (a form of gelatin) and skin as leather. Dams, pollution and overfishing have reduced populations in Canada. 88,287 kg were caught in 1961 in Canadian waters but the Lake Erie catch alone in the late nineteenth century exceeded 2,268,000 kg. In the

Québec portion of the St. Lawrence River commercial yields are very high, up to 3.4 kg/ha with 138.8 tonnes being taken in 1986. These stocks have been over-exploited. They are caught with gill nets, longlines with up to 600 hooks, and seines.

It is not a major sport fish in Canada but large specimens are occasionally hooked or snagged to the great surprise of the angler. Some anglers do pursue this giant fish using **minnows**, meat or worms as bait or spinning gear and handlines. Sturgeon fight strongly and may leap. There are catches of one sturgeon for every 4 hours fishing effort near Medicine Hat, Alberta. There are winter spear fisheries in the U.S.A.

One unexpected detrimental factor to sturgeon survival is discarded rubber bands used by Canada Post to bind mail. These are washed through storm sewers into the St. Lawrence River where they become threaded onto the pointed snouts of sturgeon grubbing in the mud for food. Out of 800 fish studied near Québec, 64 had elastic bands. The bands become embedded in the sturgeon's head, interfere with feeding and leave the fish open to infection. Sturgeon with bands weigh one-third less than normal.

lake trout

Scientific name: *Salvelinus namaycush*
    (Walbaum, 1792)
Family: **Salmon**
Other common names: lake char; Great Lakes, forktail, mackinaw, salmon, fat lake, grey or mountain trout; laker, landlocked salmon, siscowet, taque, togue, truite grise, namaycush, isok, ihok, nauktoq, näluarryuk, isuuq, isuuraaryok, isuuqiq, siuktuuk, sigguayaq, ilortoq, ivitaruk, iqluq and others
French name: touladi

Distribution: Found from Labrador and Nova Scotia west to British Columbia and Alaska (but absent from most of the Hudson Bay lowlands, southern Saskatchewan, southeastern Alberta and southwestern B.C.), north to Banks, Victoria and Baffin islands (but rare on the last) and south to Idaho and Pennsylvania. Also introduced in the U.S.A., Europe, South America and New Zealand.

Characters: This species is distinguished by having 116–138 lateral line scales, 8–10 principal anal fin rays, teeth on the anterior end only of the vomer bone in the roof of the mouth, pectoral, pelvic and anal fins with a white leading edge but no black contrasting bar behind, head, flank, dorsal, adipose and caudal fin spots white to cream but never red, and the caudal fin has a deep fork. Dorsal fin principal rays 8–10, pectoral rays 12–17 and pelvic rays 8–11. Pyloric caeca 81–210. Males and females have tiny nuptial tubercles around the anus.

Overall colour is light to dark green, dark olive, brown, grey or black with some fish very silvery masking spots. The back may have pale grey worm-tracks or vermiculations. The belly is dirty white to yellowish. Pectoral, pelvic and anal fins orange. Breeding males develop a black, flank stripe and more reddish brown body and reddish lower fins. The jaw tips and roof of the mouth become whitish. Young have 5–12 parr marks with the spaces between equal or greater in width. Fins are clear except dark bars develop on the dorsal fin of larger parr.

Reaches 126 cm and 46.3 kg from Lake Athabasca, Saskatchewan in 1961. The world, all-tackle angling record was caught in Great Bear Lake on July 19, 1991 by Rodney Harback and weighed 30.16 kg. This fish is also recognized as the Canadian record.

A deepwater (80+ m), fatter form in Lake Superior known as "siscowet" is considered by some scientists to be a distinct species or subspecies but since intermediates exist it is

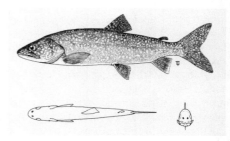

lake trout

not distinguished taxonomically here. Another form is the "humper" which lives over mounts at about 50 m depth. There are genetic and morphological differences between forms but reproductive isolation is incomplete. A lake trout and **brook trout** artificial hybrid is known as **splake**.

Biology: Lake trout are found, naturally enough, in lakes where they are solitary but may also be found in some northern rivers and rarely in brackish water. Southern populations are found only in deep lakes where they can retreat to cooler depths in summer since they prefer waters about 10°C or less. They have been reported down to 467 m in Great Bear Lake. Northern populations may be found in shallow waters.

Food includes plankton, sponges, aquatic insects, terrestrial insects when abundant, fishes including their own species and occasionally small mammals such as mice and shrews, and confused yellow warblers which fell onto the water surface in fog. The diet emphasis varies with habitat and plankton feeders grow more slowly than those which eat mostly fish. In smaller lakes fish may not be readily available in the cooler depths and such plankton as opossum shrimps are the mainstay. Opossum shrimps are 82–95% of the food volume of young (up to age 2) trout in Lake Superior but trout over 40 cm long have a diet which is 94% fish. **Ciscoes** are the most important fish in lake trout diet but **sculpins** are particularly important to younger trout. A wide variety of other fishes are taken as opportunity permits.

Sea lampreys have caused a major decline in trout of the upper Great Lakes, having gained access via canals. DDT was another major factor in decline of this species, causing embryo death. Lake trout also accumulate PCBs and other toxic chemicals and in 1976 Wisconsin banned human consumption of this fish from Lake Michigan. Overfishing has also caused a decline and natural populations of lake trout are extinct in lakes Ontario, Erie and Michigan and only 2 small, remnant stocks survive in Lake Huron. Lake trout are now a small part of the Great Lakes sport fishery, having been replaced by introduced **rainbow trout** and Pacific salmons. Stocking of lake trout and lamprey control by chemicals have enabled Lake Superior trout to recover to some degree.

Life span may exceed 53 years with maturity attained at 4–7 years in the south and 8–22 years in northern areas like Great Bear and Great Slave lakes. Growth varies over the wide range of this species, generally being slower in the north.

Spawning occurs from August to December, principally in October, and earlier in the north than the south. Temperatures are about 8–11°C and spawning occurs between 1900 and 2200 hours in the dark. Spawning is triggered, at least in part, by sudden temperature drops, cloud cover and onshore winds. Spawning lasts about 2–20 days at any one site. Up to 18,051, 6.0 mm diameter eggs are shed over boulders, rubble, or clam shell beds, falling into crevices in moderately deep (to 60 m) to very shallow (a few centimetres) water. There is no redd construction unlike other **salmons** and **trout**. The spawning ground is cleaned with body or tail brushes or by rubbing with the snout. Most fish spawn in lakes but rarely river spawning is reported. The female spawns with 1–2 males or a group of males and females spawn together. The male nudges or nips the female, presses against her flank with the vents close together, the male erects his dorsal fin and they gape and quiver. Some populations home to spawning sites and disperse over 160 km, to return again in subsequent years. Spawning intervals for females vary, every third year in Great Bear Lake and every second year in Great Slave Lake. Eggs hatch in February to June depending on latitude.

Lake trout are an important sport fish taken with flies or lures in cool seasons or by deep trolling in summer. Whole or cut fish can be used as bait when bottom fishing. Northern trout remain in cool, near-surface waters even in summer and deep trolling is not required. They can then be caught by spinning or on bucktails and streamers. Trout are also caught through the ice. The Northwest Territories have several expensive, trophy, sport fisheries requiring float plane transport to reach. They must be carefully managed to avoid over-exploitation by rod-and-line fishing. Catch-and-release is favoured with catch limits and fishery zones. Stockings in some Ontario lakes in efforts to improve catches over the natural return have been shown to be of no help. Limitations on take and shortened fishing seasons are probably the best way to maintain a sport fishery. There is a major planting programme in the Great Lakes with about 9 million yearlings being released annually. The flesh is white, pink or orange-red and is very tasty. Commercial catches in some lakes are taken with gill nets and are particularly important in the Northwest Territories. Lake trout and **lake whitefish** make up 95% of the total catch there. The total Canadian catch in 1988 was 1050 tonnes.

- Most accessible June through September.
- Great Bear and Great Slave Lake in the Northwest Territories, northern Manitoba and northern Saskatchewan.
- Medium action spinning and baitcasting outfits used with 12- to 20-pound test line.
- A wide variety of trolling and casting spoons between 1/4 and one ounce, large wobbling plugs and yellow/white jigs between 1/4 and 1/2 ounce. The best bait is live or dead bait fish and larger forage fish.

lake whitefish

Scientific name: *Coregonus clupeaformis*
(Mitchill, 1818)
Family: **Salmon**
Other common names: common whitefish, Sault whitefish, eastern whitefish, Great Lakes whitefish, inland whitefish, gizzard fish, lake herring, Labrador whitefish, sead, humpback, buffalo back, whitebait, pi-kok-tok, jikuktok, anahik, kapihilik, pikuktuuq, kakiviatktok, kavisilik, anâdlerk, kakiviartût, keki-yuak-tuk, anadleq, qelaluqaq
French name: grand corégone

Distribution: Found from New Brunswick and some Nova Scotia lakes, and Labrador west to British Columbia and throughout the Yukon and N.W.T. including Victoria Island. Also introduced into Newfoundland and parts of British Columbia and Alberta. Also in Alaska and U.S. drainages of the Great Lakes and St. Lawrence River basin.

Characters: This member of the **Salmon Family** is distinguished from its relatives by having large scales (110 or less), no parr marks, teeth absent from the jaws and roof of the mouth, forked tail fin, 2 flaps of skin between the nostrils, the mouth is under the snout, premaxilla bone of the upper jaw curves backward making the snout rounded, the adjacent maxilla bone is twice or more longer than wide, lower fins clear but sometimes with dark spots, gill rakers 19–37, and lateral line scales 70–97. Dorsal fin rays 10–13, anal rays 10–14, pectoral rays 14–17 and pelvic rays 10–12. Nuptial tubercles are found on 3 or more scale rows above the lateral line and 6 rows below, and sparsely on the head. Each scale has 1 central tubercle with smaller tubercles on each or either side on some scales. Large fish develop a hump on the back, particularly in northwestern Canada. Lake whitefish produce more mucus than **ciscoes** and feel slipperier.

Overall colour is silvery with a light to dark brown, greenish or black back and a silvery-white belly. Scales are outlined with pigment in northwestern Canada. Flanks may have a bluish-tinge. Fins vary from clear in the Great Lakes to black-tipped in the north.

This species has been referred to as the *Coregonus clupeaformis* "complex" because of its wide range in variation, particularly in northwestern North America, which may encompass more than one species. Some lakes, for example in Algonquin Park, Ontario, contain both dwarf and normal forms which differ in biology but not in anatomy,

lake whitefish

apart from size. In Lake Como, Ontario dwarfs are 170–179 mm and normals 280–289 mm fork length. In the Yukon several lakes have 2 forms of whitefish, a benthic form with low gill raker counts feeding on the bottom and a pelagic form with higher gill raker counts feeding on zooplankton throughout the water column. High raker fish have shorter life spans and mature earlier: they are the more unique member of the 2 forms. Samples from 5 Ontario lakes showed differences in gill raker numbers, pyloric caeca numbers, in size of the tail, dorsal fin and eye, and in biochemistry, evidence of genetic separation since they spawn at the same place and time. Evidence from mitochondrial DNA studies shows that different genetic structures correlate with the Pleistocene glaciations.

Hybrids between lake whitefish and **lake cisco** exist in the Great Lakes and elsewhere and are known as "mule whitefish." They are bright green in colour and intermediate in anatomical characters. Reaches 91 cm total length and 19.05 kg.

The world angling record from Meaford, Ontario caught in May of 1984 by Dennis M. Laycock weighed 6.52 kg. The Canadian angling record from Clear Lake, Ontario was caught by Chris T. D. Webster in May 1983 and weighed 6.97 kg.

Biology: Lake whitefish are found, appropriately enough, in lakes but are also in large rivers. They enter brackish waters of Hudson Bay and the N.W.T., and rarely in New Brunswick, feeding there in summer months. Their depth range depends on temperature. In southern Canada they retreat to cooler, deeper waters in summer, down to at least 128 m but in northern Canada summer temperatures are probably cool enough in surface waters.

Food is various bottom invertebrates, small fishes and fish eggs although some may feed pelagically on plankton or take terrestrial insects fallen on the water surface. Fishes eaten include **johnny darters, spottail minnows, ninespine sticklebacks, gaspereau** and **deepwater sculpins**. Variation in gill raker number and length in any population indicates the main feeding mode. Lake whitefish are eaten by **lake trout, northern pike, yellow walleye, burbot, yellow perch** and others. They eat their own eggs.

Females live longer and mature later than males. Life span is at least 30, perhaps over 50, years. Maturity is attained as late as 8 years in Great Slave and Great Bear lakes but southern populations mature earlier, as early as age 2 for males and 3 for females. Age at first maturity declines with exploitation as growth rate increases. In Lake Winnipeg, age-groups 5, 6 and 7 accounted for 81% of the catch from 1944 to 1948 but by 1969 88% of the catch was age-groups 3 and 4.

Spawning takes place over 2–6 weeks from September to January, earlier in the north than the south, when water temperatures fall below 8°C. Some spawning may occur under ice. Northern populations may only spawn at 2–3 year intervals. The fish enter shallow waters, less than 8 m deep, and release eggs over hard, sandy, silty or weedy bottoms. Some fish spawn in deep water however. The spawning process often takes place at night with much splashing and jumping out of the water. Pairs of fish or 1 female and 2 males rise to the surface and shed eggs and sperm. Yellowish eggs are about 2.6 mm in diameter when shed and may exceed 415,000 per female or 27,460 eggs/kg body weight. The eggs hatch in the following spring, usually April or May, and receive no care from the parents. Post-spawning adults move to overwintering sites, such as the delta in the Mackenzie River. Stocks of this **whitefish** in different lakes vary considerably in diet, growth rate, movement patterns, fecundity, and egg and larval size.

This is a very important commercial species in Canadian fresh waters although numbers are declining through overfishing, pollution and the depredations of **sea lampreys**. An annual catch in the Great Lakes has been as high as about 8 million kg, caught with gill nets and trap nets. In western Canada gill nets are set through holes in the ice with a "jigger" which bounces the end of the net from an entry hole to another hole a net's length away. Along with **lake trout**, this species is the principal recreational and commercial fish in northern Canada. The total Canadian catch in 1988 was 9600 tonnes worth about $12 million. Whitefish are marketed dressed, fresh or frozen and in such categories as "jumbo," "large" and "medium." They may also be canned and the eggs made into "golden" caviar. They are considered to be better eating than **lake trout**.

- Most accessible in open water lakes or river fishing during the months of November and December; for ice fishing, December and March.
- Southern to mid-central Ontario, Quebec and the northern ranges of Manitoba and Saskatchewan.
- Open water fishing includes ultralight to light action spinning gear used with six- to 12–pound lines. Ice fishing gear includes tip-ups and jigging rods loaded with 10– to 14–pound line.
- For open water fishing, an assortment of 1/8– to 1/4–ounce flashy spoons, small spinners as well as hair and plastic body jigs. For ice fishing, 1/8– to 1/4–ounce vertical jigging spoons. The best bait, small live and salted minnows fished on the bottom.

lamp grenadier

Scientific name: *Nezumia stelgidolepis* (Gilbert, 1890)
Family: **Grenadier**
Other common names: California grenadier, California rattail
French name: grenadier-lampe

Distribution: Found from off Vancouver Island south to southern Peru.

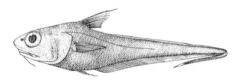

lamp grenadier

Characters: This grenadier is distinguished from its Pacific Canadian coast relatives by having 7 branchiostegal rays, the anus well in advance of the anal fin origin, and a small, black scaleless "window" to the light organ between the pelvic fin bases. There is a larger "window" anterior to the anus. The second dorsal spine in the first dorsal fin is strongly serrated along its anterior edge. Scales along the shelf below the eye are well-developed and firmly attached and have 3–5 ridge-like rows of spines. First dorsal fin with 2 spines and 8–11 soft rays, followed by

138–153 rays. Pectoral fin rays 20–26. Pelvic rays 9–11, usually 10. Scales are covered with slender to conical spines arranged in an irregular quincuncial pattern. These spines give the fish a velvety and shiny appearance. Teeth are in broad bands in both jaws. Overall colour is dark brown and bluish on the belly. The lips, gill membranes, lower snout surface, underside of the head, fins and the area beneath the eye are black. The mouth cavity is pale to dusky except for blackish to grey oral valves. Only the outer edges of the gill cavity are black. The peritoneum is pale. Exceeds 44.5 cm in total length. *Nezumia* is from the Japanese word for rat, *nezumi* and *stelgidolepis* means "scraper scale" in reference to the spiny body scales.

Biology: British Columbian specimens were taken at 470 m. Mostly caught between 291 and 640 m, but sometimes as shallow as 91 m. Little is known of their biology although they are quite common and are caught in bottom trawls and traps. They may live about 4 years.

lampfishes

Lampfishes are members of the **Lanternfish Family**. There are 3 Canadian species (**dogtooth**, **horned** and **southseas lampfishes**) belonging to the genus *Ceratoscopelus*, 3 Canadian species (**highfourthpo**, **sunbeam** and **toothnose lampfishes**) belonging to the genus *Lampadena*, and 2 Canadian species (**lesser** and **smoothbrow lampfishes**) belonging to the genus *Taaningichthys*. The term lampfish has also been applied to other **Lanternfish Family** members, now generally called lanternfishes.

Lamprey Family

Scientific name: Petromyzontidae
French name: lamproies

Lampreys are found in cooler waters of the northern and southern hemispheres. There are 41 species with 11 recorded from Canadian fresh waters and along all three coasts.

Lampreys are **jawless fishes**, lacking bone in the skeleton and having 7 pairs of pore-like gill openings. The eel-like body has no pectoral or pelvic fins. There are 1 or 2 dorsal fins and a caudal fin. An anal fin-like fold develops in spawning females. Eyes are large. The mouth is a suctorial disc armed with rows of horny teeth. There are also teeth on the tongue. The median nostril, or nasohypophysial opening, is not connected to the mouth in contrast to members of the **Hagfish Family**. There is a light-sensitive pineal organ or "third eye" behind the nostril. The skin is covered in mucus which is poisonous to fishes and humans. Lampreys are edible if the mucus is cleaned off.

They are often classified with the **Hagfish Family** which also lacks jaws but are not closely related. They are members of the **Lamprey Order**. Their origins lie at least 300 million years in the past. Their tooth arrangement is used in classification and identification along with the number of myomeres (muscle blocks along the body). Both tooth counts and the number of cusps are used, in particular those on the supraoral lamina (bar above the "mouth," the oesophageal opening), the infraoral lamina (bar below the "mouth") and the row of teeth on both sides of the "mouth." There are various series of smaller teeth and of course teeth on the tongue. Larval lampreys lack teeth and are particularly difficult to identify and their determination often requires specialist knowledge. Characters for the larvae include counts of myomeres and pigmentation patterns.

Lampreys have an unusual life cycle. Adults die after spawning and the eggs develop into a larva, known as an ammocoete, which lacks teeth, has an oral hood, eyes covered by skin, a light-sensitive area near the tail, and is a filter-feeder while buried in mud and silt. Fleshy tentacles in the oral hood are used to extract minute organisms from the water, such as algae (desmids and diatoms) and protozoans. After several years (up to 19 but usually 7 or less), the ammocoete transforms into an adult with enlarged eyes, teeth, a different colour and pronounced dorsal fins. The body shrinks during this metamorphosis and adults are only larger than ammocoetes if they feed. The adult may be a parasite on other fishes and marine mammals, or non-feeding. Individuals of a species may or may not be parasitic and different species may be parasitic or non-parasitic. The non-parasitic

species are believed to have evolved from a parasitic species so there tends to be closely related parasitic/non-parasitic species pairs. There are 7 parasitic species in Canada and 4 non-parasitic species.

Parasitic adults feed mostly on other fishes, attaching to their bodies by suction and using their toothed tongue to rasp through the skin and scales to take blood and tissue fragments. Prey is detected by sight but some lampreys attach to hosts during the night. Perhaps this reduces their own predation risks and enables them to approach their quiescent hosts more easily. Lampreys tend to select larger fish as these survive longer and ensure a good food supply. The flow of blood is aided by an anti-coagulant in lamprey saliva called lamphedrin, which also serves to break down muscle tissue. Large, anadromous lampreys, such as the **sea lamprey** and the **Pacific lamprey**, are usually attached ventrally near the pectoral fins while small, freshwater species, such as the **chestnut lamprey** and the **silver lamprey**, are usually attached dorsally. The **river lamprey**, which feeds on muscle tissue, also favours dorsal attachment. Dorsal attachment reduces abrasion of the lamprey in shallow water. Ventral attachment results in greater food intake for the lamprey. Lamprey attacks leave a characteristic round scar and can be a major problem for commercial fisheries by damaging food species and leaving them too unsightly to market. The attack may weaken or even kill the host. Weakened fishes are more prone to diseases and the wound provides an easy path of entry for them. The fish (and marine mammal) species parasitised are varied and reflect availability in the habitat. Even fishes with heavy scales like **Gar Family** members are attacked. A single 16 kg **lake sturgeon** has been recorded with 61 **silver lampreys** parasitising it, although it was estimated that this would not kill the host by draining its blood.

Niagara Falls was a barrier to the **sea lamprey** until the Welland Canal was built in 1829. The **sea lamprey** gained access to the upper Great Lakes and devastated the fish stocks. The **lake trout** catch declined in Lake Michigan from 2948 tonnes in 1944 to

181 kg in 1953. Immense sums have been spent on poisoning streams with "lampricides" and using electrical and mechanical barriers in attempts to control the numbers of lampreys during the concentrated and accessible ammocoete stage of their life cycle.

Marine lampreys enter fresh water to spawn and freshwater species may move into or up streams. The scientific name of the family means "stone sucker" and the adult mouth is used to hold or suck onto stones as well as on prey. This suction enables the lamprey to maintain position in fast-flowing streams when spawning and even to climb over rapids and small waterfalls. Usually spawning occurs in shallow water with a moderate current, a bottom of gravel and nearby sand and silt for the ammocoetes to live in. Either or both sexes build a nest by moving gravel around with their sucking mouths and by thrashing their bodies. A shallow depression is formed, about 0.5–1 m long. Spawning often occurs in groups and several males may attach to a female with the sucking disc. The process takes several days as only a few white to yellow eggs are laid at a time. The eggs are adhesive.

Adult lampreys are usually caught when attached to a host or when spawning. Electro-shocking will force ammocoetes out of their u-shaped burrows to the surface and immobilise adults. They sometimes attach to boats and occasionally to swimmers when their skin is cool but are easily removed, perhaps because nobody has left a lamprey on their skin long enough to see if the tongue starts rasping flesh!

Lampreys have been used for food by various native peoples in Canada and are popular in Japan. They have been considered a delicacy and can be smoked, set in aspic or cooked in a variety of ways. Henry I of England is said to have died of a "surfeit of lampreys."

See **Alaskan lamprey**
American brook lamprey
Arctic lamprey
chestnut lamprey
lake lamprey
northern brook lamprey
Pacific lamprey
river lamprey
sea lamprey
silver lamprey
western brook lamprey

Lamprey Order

Lampreys belong to the Order Petromyzontiformes which has 1 family in fresh and salt waters of temperate areas of the world. There are about 41 species of which 11 occur in Canada.

The order is characterised by having an elongate body, round, suctorial mouth which contains horny teeth, lacking bone and having a cartilaginous skull, having a long dorsal fin or fins, 7 lateral pairs of gill openings, a single nasal opening on top of the head between the eyes, not connected to the pharynx, eyes usually lateral, no paired fins and no scales, vertebrae lack centra, and an isocercal tail (internally and externally symmetrical) in adults and a hypocercal tail (lower lobe longer and supported by tail skeleton — asymmetrical internally and externally) in the larvae or ammocoetes.

Their relationships are discussed under **lampreys** and other anatomical features, along with biology, in the family account.

See **Lamprey Family**

lampreys

Lampreys belong to the Class Cephalaspidomorphi which contains a single order and family and very few species (about 41). That so few species constitute a class on the same level as **ray-finned fishes** with many thousands of species, indicates how unique is their anatomy. Some of this anatomy is summarised in the order account. Lampreys comprise 1 of the 5 classes known generally as **fishes**. The 3 classes in Canada are the **ray-finned fishes**, the **cartilaginous fishes** and the **hagfishes**. Lampreys have 2 semicircular canals in the inner ear, true bone cells are present in some fossil members, there is a single nostril in the midline of the head (nasohypophysial) with a pineal eye behind it and pectoral fins are present in some, fossil members.

The similarity between **hagfishes** and lampreys is thought to be superficial and owed to possession of primitive characters which cannot be used to confirm a close relationship. These two groups of organisms, with few living members, are placed in different classes and have had a long and separate history. Lampreys are thought to be more closely related to the **jawed fishes** since they share possession of more than 1 semicircular canal, highly differentiated kidney collecting tubules, no accessory heart, spiral intestine or fold in the intestine, absence of a persistent pronephros in the kidney anatomy, a large exocrine pancreas, a photosensory pineal organ, certain vertebral, eye and muscular structures, the histology of the adenohypophysis, and composition of insulin and haemoglobin, none of which are found in the **hagfishes**.

Lamprey ancestors date back to the Ordovician, about 450 million years ago. These ancestors had bodies covered in plates and were superficially unlike modern lampreys. However they did have such features as a terminal mouth supported by a cartilage ring and a cartilaginous gill skeleton similar to that found in modern lampreys and their larvae. The first recognisable lamprey fossils are from the Carboniferous rocks of Illinois 325–280 million years ago although an earlier Silurian fossil may be a relative.

See **Lamprey Order**

lancer dragonet

Scientific name: *Paradiplogrammus bairdi*
    (Jordan, 1887)
Family: **Dragonet**
Other common names: coral dragonet
French name: dragonnet de Baird

Distribution: From the Caribbean Sea north to off Sable Island and the Scotian Shelf in Atlantic Canada.

Characters: This species can be distinguished from its relatives, the **spotfin dragonet** and the **spotted dragonet**, by the second dorsal fin having 9 rays and the anal fin 8 rays, and by the preopercular spine having a forward-directed barb as well as 3–9, usually 3, barbs on the upper surface. The first dorsal fin has 4 spines. Pectoral fin rays number 19–20. The male has a higher dorsal fin and larger anal fin than the female. Overall colour is mottled red with some brown, black and white. There are 4 prominent dorsal blotches. Some fish are iridescent pink. Males have a bright yellow to orange

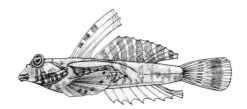

lancer dragonet

patch on the first dorsal fin and blue spots around the lower part of the eyes. There are dark blue bars with orange margins on the preopercle. Attains 11.4 cm.

Biology: Canadian records are of stray larvae caught in 1979–1980. Adults are found at coral reefs, rubble and rocks, often buried in sand down to 91 m.

lances

Lances (or launces) are members of the **Sand Lance Family** with 2 species along the coasts of Canada, the **northern sand lance** and the **stout sand lance**. Their name is taken from the elongate, thin body with a pointed head.

Lancetfish Family

Scientific name: Alepisauridae
French name: cavalos

Lancetfishes are found in all oceans including Arctic seas. There are only 2 species in the family and both are reported from Canada.

Lancetfishes or handsawfishes have a strong mouth armed with hollow, fang-like teeth. The skeleton is weak, the skin translucent and the body flaccid but they are voracious predators. There is no swimbladder, scales or light organs and the body is covered with pores. Their most characteristic feature is the remarkable high dorsal fin which can fold back into a deep groove. The function of this fin is uncertain; it may be used to round up shoals of small fish as food.

Lancetfishes are members of the **Flagfin Order**.

These fish are hermaphrodites, perhaps an adaptation to a solitary life. Despite this and an oceanic life, they have been used as food. A gorged lancetfish may become bloated and forced to the surface. Parasitic worms can have the same bloating effect. They make daily vertical migrations. Lancetfish have been very useful to scientists since they catch many small fishes from the open ocean without damaging them, despite their fangs. Many new species of fish, squid and octopus were first described from lancetfish stomachs! Lancetfish can be found as deep as 3656 m. They are occasionally caught by trolling lures and their ferocious appetite has been recognised by the name "wolves of the sea."

See **longnose lancetfish**
　　shortnose lancetfish

Lanternfish Family

Scientific name: Myctophidae
French name: poissons-lanternes

Lanternfishes are found in all seas from the Arctic through the tropics to the Antarctic with 235 species world-wide. There are 62 species in Canadian waters, 44 on the Atlantic coast, 4 on the Atlantic and Arctic coasts and 14 on the Pacific coast. Diverse, oceanic and deepwater families like lanternfishes probably have a number of other species which remain to be discovered in Canadian waters.

Lanternfishes are small (mostly less than 10 cm), have large eyes and a blunt snout, possess between 50 and 80 light organs (hence "lanternfish"), have an adipose fin, a dorsal fin on the middle of the back, fins usually lacking strong spines except for a rudimentary spine at the anterior base of the dorsal, anal, pectoral and pelvic fins, and have abdominal pelvic fins. They have dark brown, black or bluish-black backs and silvery scales along the flanks. Scales are easily detached and are usually lost when fish are brought up from deep water. Instead of lateral line scale counts, the horseshoe-like organs left on the flank by detached scales are counted. Scales are usually cycloid and only 4 species have ctenoid scales.

Lanternfishes are members of the **Lanternfish Order**.

Photophores produce a bluish light by a reaction in which the chemical luciferin is oxidised by the enzyme luciferase in the presence of oxygen. Each photophore has its own blood and nerve supply and consists of a scale embedded in the skin and modified into a shallow cup to support the tissues. The tissues include a reflector layer backed by dark pigment and, within the cup, the luminous tissue. The scale cup has a modified scale over it, forming a lens. The photophores, in their species specific patterns, are believed to be important to the lanternfishes in recognising members of their own species. They may also block out the lanternfish's silhouette to predators from below by emitting a continuous, low intensity light which matches that coming from the surface of the sea. Some authors maintain that photophores can be switched on or off so that an illuminated fish can suddenly "vanish" in the dark ocean depths and so that a rhythmical pattern can be emitted to help in species recognition. Certainly the intensity of light emitted can be varied.

A second, common type of light organ in lanternfishes is the supracaudal and infracaudal luminous glands found on the upper and lower caudal peduncle at the base of the tail. These glands have been called "stern chasers" and are believed to function to deflect predators. The blue flash of these organs has been likened to a spark of electricity. The flash attracts the predator to the tail of the fish but by the time the predator strikes in that region the light is out and the lanternfish has departed into the dark ocean with a flick of its tail. The flash of light may also serve to blind the predator. A predator attacking a school of lanternfishes would be even more confused.

Lanternfishes are relatives of the **Blackchin Family** in the **Lanternfish Order**. They are identified by the number and position of light organs, fin ray counts and fin positions. The complex pattern of light organs and photophores on the body of lanternfishes has led scientists to make a standard set of abbreviations as a convenient summary.

These fishes are very common offshore at depths of about 300–1200 m, although many reach the surface at night in a vertical migration of several hundred metres to feed on zooplankton. They can be attracted to lights and are then easy to catch. Young lanternfish are found higher in the water column than adults and larvae of most species are in the upper 125 m. Larval lanternfish differ from adults in pigmentation and light organ arrangement. Larvae may be stylophthalmoid, in which the eyes are on long stalks. Lanternfishes feed on such plankton as copepods, ostracods, krill, arrow worms, and fish eggs and larvae.

Lanternfishes are not caught by anglers and only a few are commercially important. Their potential importance is high because of their numbers and their possible use in fish oil and meal production. They are, however, a numerous and important food for many other species of fish such as **cod**, **swordfish**, **tuna** and **salmon** as well as seals and whales, and have been studied by biologists for this reason.

See **Arctic telescope**
bigeye flashlightfish
bigfin lanternfish
blue lanternfish
Bolin's lanternfish
bouncer headlightfish
broadfin lanternfish
brokenline lanternfish
California headlightfish
Caribbean divinglamp
diamondcheek lanternfish
dogtooth lampfish
doormat parkinglightfish
eventooth headlightfish
eyelight lanternfish
flashlight headlightfish
fourtoplamps
garnet lanternfish
glacier lanternfish
highfourthpo lampfish
highvelo hugo
horned lampfish
Japanese lanternfish
jewel lanternfish
lesser beaconlamp
lesser lampfish
linestop lanternfish
longfin lanternfish
longnose hugo

lunar lanternfish
Mediterranean divinglamp
metallic lanternfish
North Atlantic cornerlantern
northern lanternfish
northern saillamp
patchwork lanternfish
penlight fish
pinpoint lanternfish
rakery lanternfish
roughscale lanternfish
seven-aoa platelamp
shortcheek tail-light
shortplate willothewisp
shortwing lanternfish
sickle-ear slimlantern
sidelight lanternfish
slanteye parkinglightfish
smoothbrow lampfish
smoothcheek lanternfish
southseas lampfish
spinecheek lanternfish
spinetail lanternfish
spotted lanternfish
square headlightfish
straightcheek headlightfish
sun flashlightfish
sunbeam lampfish
tail-light lanternfish
Taaning's headlightfish
toothnose lampfish
toplights lanternfish
upmouth hugo

Lanternfish Order

Lanternfishes and **blackchins** or Myctophiformes are found world-wide in marine waters. There are 2 families with about 241 species. Canadian waters contain 63 species, all but 1 from the **Lanternfish Family**.

These fishes are characterised by a compressed body, usually a large, terminal mouth, cycloid scales, no fin spines, the maxilla bone does not border the mouth and is toothless, the premaxilla borders the mouth, abdominal pelvic fins, usually 7–11 branchiostegal rays, an adipose fin containing cartilage, usually 8 pelvic rays, usually photophores and light organs arranged in distinctive patterns on the head and body, no mesocoracoid bone in the pectoral girdle, and the second preural neural spine in the tail skeleton is reduced to a low crest with the first epural over this crest. The third pharyngo-branchial bone has the largest tooth plate in the upper pharyngeal jaw. The fourth tooth plate is only half the size and is connected to the third by a hinged joint. The muscles attached to these bones are modified appropriately, the beginnings of a process where more advanced fishes have the third pharyngobranchial emphasised as the main toothed element in the upper pharyngeal jaw. Lanternfishes are intermediate between more primitive lower fishes and the advanced fishes.

Members of the **Flagfin Order** are closely related to this order and are sometimes placed within it. The lanternfishes are similar in many respects to the **Salmon Order** and have been included with them. All these fishes are regarded as the group from which most higher fishes evolved but their relationships still remain to be worked out in detail.

Members of this order are deepsea pelagic and benthopelagic fishes mostly of small size, adapted for exploiting the vast open ocean by daily vertical migrations in search of food. Their large numbers make them an important link in the ocean food chain.

  See **Blackchin Family**
       Lanternfish Family

large-eye snaggletooth

Scientific name: *Borostomias antarcticus*
  (Lönnberg, 1905)
Family: **Barbeled Dragonfish**
Other common names: straightline dragonfish
French name: dragon-saumon à grands yeux

Distribution: Found in all major oceans including the Southern Ocean and along the Atlantic and Arctic coasts of Canada. As far south as 65°S and as far north as 66°N.

Characters: Teeth on the maxilla bone of the upper jaw are clearly separated and do not slant rearward in contrast to those in related Atlantic coast species. In addition there is no adipose fin ventrally. There are fang-like teeth in the jaws also. There is a double light organ behind the eye. Lateral photophores 40–46, ventral row 64–68. Dorsal fin rays 9–13, anal rays 12–17 and pectoral rays 7–9. The head

and body are black but the skin often becomes detached after being hauled up from great depths. The single, chin barbel has a bulb with

large-eye snaggletooth

1–2 filaments and is pale distally. Reaches more than 35 cm standard length.

Biology: Found in the Newfoundland Basin of Atlantic Canada at depths between 489 and 1018 m and north and east of Cape Chidley in Labrador at 900–980 m. Elsewhere found at 350–2500 m. Food is crustaceans and mesopelagic fishes.

large-eyed argentine

Scientific name: *Nansenia groenlandica*
  (Reinhardt, 1839)
Family: **Pencilsmelt**
Other common names: Greenland argentine
French name: serpe de Groenland

Distribution: Found in Arctic and subarctic waters of the North Atlantic Ocean including the Atlantic coast of Canada.

Characters: The large-eyed argentine is distinguished from the **bluethroat argentine** by having 37–45 gill rakers (instead of 25–31) and by having the dorsal fin origin in front of the midpoint of the body. It is distinguished from the **forgotten argentine** by having a low number of branchiostegal rays (3) which also separates it from similar fishes in other families. Dorsal fin rays are 9–10 and anal rays 8–10. Material preserved in alcohol is brown to light brown. Young fish have a barred tail. In life probably a silvery fish. Attains about 24.5 cm.

large-eyed argentine

Biology: Found chiefly in the deep open ocean from 300–1000 m. Probably feeds on zooplankton. One Canadian record was from the stomach of a **black swallower** caught south of Browns Bank, and this is the largest known specimen of this argentine species. Also known from east of the Flemish Cap. Spawns in spring and early summer.

largemouth bass

Scientific name: *Micropterus salmoides*
  (Lacepède, 1802)
Family: **Sunfish**
Other common names: northern largemouth, black, green, bigmouth, jumper, mossback, Oswego, cow, lake, straw, river and mud bass; line side, green trout
French name: achigan à grande bouche

Distribution: Found from southwestern Québec, southern Ontario and through all the Great Lakes to southeastern Manitoba. Also introduced to southern British Columbia, Alberta and Saskatchewan. In the U.S.A. south to the Gulf states and widely introduced. Introduced to Europe, Africa, South America and Southeast Asia.

Characters: This species is distinguished by having 9–11 dorsal fin spines, 58–77 (usually less than 70 in Canada) lateral line scales, the upper jaw extends back beyond the eye and the pelvic fins are not joined by a membrane. There are no scales on the bases of the soft dorsal and anal fins. Second dorsal fin soft rays 11–14, anal fin with 3 spines and 10–12 soft rays and pectoral rays 13–17.

The back is bright green to olive or dark green, the flanks dark to light green or sometimes golden green, and the belly is yellowish to white. The flank has a black midlateral stripe sometimes extending to the snout, particularly prominent in young but breaking up irregularly into blotches or even absent in adults. The upper and lower flank are irregularly spotted with dark brown, sometimes forming short stripes. The eye is golden brown. The inside of the mouth is white. Dark bars radiate from the eye and snout backwards. Pectoral fins are mostly clear or lightly pigmented. Other fins are green to olive or dusky. Young are similar to adults but have a broad black margin to the caudal fin and more mottled upper flank. Rare, golden forms of

this bass occur in nature, similar to a **goldfish** in colour. Peritoneum silvery.

Reaches 97.0 cm. The world, all-tackle angling record from Montgomery Lake, Georgia in 1932 weighed 10.09 kg. The Canadian angling record from Preston Lake, Ontario was caught by Mario Crysanthou in 1976 and weighed 4.75 kg.

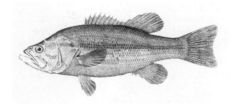

largemouth bass

Biology: Largemouths are found in still, shallow areas of lakes and some large river bays, usually at depths less than 6 m. Small schools of 5–10 fish are common. Unlike its relative, the **smallmouth bass**, it favours heavy, aquatic vegetation and submerged logs, and it can survive higher temperatures, up to 38°C although it then rests in shade. Young bass divide into two sub-populations in summer, one inshore and the other offshore, and this may persist through life with some mixing in spring. In the nutrient-poor, Precambrian Shield lakes of Ontario, the size of bass populations is limited by the extent of warm, weedy shallows. This bass is found on the bottom in winter and may then be caught by ice fishermen unlike the inactive **smallmouth bass**. Experimental studies show largemouth bass to be quiescent and non-feeding at 3°C but able to react well to a stimulus.

Food is a wide variety of fishes, crayfish, molluscs, frogs and large insects, with smaller insects and plankton when small. Some are recorded as having eaten leeches, salamanders, snakes, turtles and mice. Largemouths are sight feeders, taking prey at the surface around dusk and dawn and in midwater or on the bottom during the day. They rest on the bottom at night. This species is cannibalistic. Bass catch individual **minnows** quite easily but were confused by schools of 8 or more fish, unless one or two members are distinctive in some way. Food items may be pursued or simply sucked in while lying in wait.

Life span is 16 years with maturity attained at 3–5 years for females and 3–4 years for males in Canada (8 months in Cuba). Growth varies with locality, generally slower in the north where fish live longer. Some populations become stunted through overcrowding.

Spawning occurs from May to August once water temperatures reach 17°C or warmer. The male sweeps out a circular nest, a little before this temperature is attained, on gravel, sand or even mud among reeds, stumps, or water lilies. The nest bed often has roots of the vegetation exposed or other hard materials for the eggs to adhere to. The nest is up to 1 m across and 30 cm deep, about twice the bass's body length. Males are very aggressive and defend territory up to 7 m from the nest. Courtship involves parallel swimming, nudges, nips and bites. The male assumes an upright position in the nest with the female at a 45° angle so their genital areas are in contact. Eggs are scattered over the nest and even outside it. Each female can have up to 145,000, yellow and adhesive eggs with a maximum diameter of 2.0 mm. Females may spawn with several males, depositing portions of her egg complement in each nest. The male guards and fans the eggs which hatch in 3–7 days. The male also guards the pale green, free-swimming fry for as long as a month. The large swarm of young spread out as time goes by, keeping the male busy to defend them all, until they disperse. **Golden shiners** may spawn in bass nests.

This bass was once commercially important in Canada but is now reserved for anglers. It is a major sport fish in eastern Canada taken with minnows, frogs, worms, both live and plastic, surface plugs and other lures. Bass strike strongly and fight well. Swimming ability decreases as temperature falls so anglers may find bass put up less of a fight early and late in the year. Their successful capture is made more difficult by their habitat of dense vegetation and logs. They are reputed to be very intelligent, able to distinguish a lure from the real thing after one encounter. Some "fished out" lakes are said to be really full of fish familiar with all the usual lures. The flesh is flaky, white and excellent eating. Size limits are imposed in many waters to preserve the stocks. Studies on return of hooked juveniles show that most survive, with significant mortality only in fish hooked deep in the oesophagus.

In the U.S.A. this fish is stocked in ponds and reservoirs for sport and for food and is probably that country's most important freshwater game fish. Introductions to Saskatchewan before 1950 failed to reproduce but more recent attempts are apparently more successful. Warm temperatures needed for spawning and low winter oxygen levels are often limiting factors to the spread of this fish in Canada. British Columbia populations came across the border from introductions in neighbouring U.S. states.

- Most accessible July through to October.
- Southern Ontario and southern Quebec.
- Medium to heavy action spinning and baitcasting outfits used with eight- to 30–pound test lines.
- A wide variety of spinnerbaits, plastic worms, crankbaits, plastic jigs, living rubber jigs, surface spoons, surface plastic frog imitations and surface plugs. The best live bait includes frogs, **minnows**, crayfish, leeches and worms.

largescale sucker

Scientific name: *Catostomus macrocheilus* Girard, 1856
Family: **Sucker**
Other common names: none
French name: meunier à grandes écailles

Distribution: Found in the Peace River basin of northwestern Alberta and British Columbia, the Fraser, Columbia and coastal river systems of British Columbia. Also in Washington, Oregon, Montana, Idaho, Utah and Nevada.

Characters: This sucker is distinguished by the short dorsal fin, 62–83 lateral line scales, 2 swimbladder chambers, lower lip completely cleft with rarely 1–2 rows between the cleft and the mouth — usually none, no notch where the upper and lower lips meet, upper lip papillae obvious and can be seen from in front, lower lip almost as long as wide, scales from lateral line to dor-

largescale sucker

sal fin origin 11–15, and dorsal fin rays usually 13–15 (range 12–17). Lip papillae are large and oval. The pelvic fins have a fleshy connection to the body. The cartilaginous edges of the jaws are not visible in the open mouth. The mouth is not markedly overhung by the snout. Gill rakers 25–37. Anal fin rays 7, pectoral rays 16–18 and pelvic rays 9–12. Males have strong tubercles on the anal fin and lower caudal fin lobe. The back is black, olive or blue-grey fading to a white or yellow-white belly. There is a dark stripe along the flank below the lateral line. The leading edge of the dorsal, pectoral and pelvic fins is white with contrasting dark behind, or dark. Young fish, up to about 15 cm, may have 3–4 flank blotches. Breeding males have an iridescent olive-green to yellowish stripe above the lateral line and a yellowish stripe between the dark stripe and the white belly. Females are similar but the colour is not as heightened or as contrasting between stripes. Peritoneum dusky silvery to dusky black. Largescale and **white suckers** form hybrids. Reaches 61.0 cm and 3.2 kg.

Biology: Largescale suckers are found in lakes and large rivers from shallows to 27 m, in weedy areas. Food includes crustaceans, aquatic insects, molluscs, eggs of **salmon**, and algae. It is not thought to be a serious predator on **salmon** eggs. Largescale suckers are eaten by **northern squawfish**, various birds and even bears. Life span is up to an estimated 15 years. Sexual maturity is attained at 5 years for males and 6 years for females. Spawning occurs in April to June in British Columbia at

about 8–9°C on sand bottomed streams or lake outlets or on gravel and sand lake shoals. Timing is about 1 week later than that of **white suckers**. Eggs are 2.5 mm in diameter before fertilisation and a female may shed over 20,000 yellow, adhesive eggs. Larvae develop in the gravel or on the sand surface for several weeks before becoming pelagic. At this time the mouth is at the head tip facilitating capture of pelagic plankton. The mouth migrates ventrally and the sucker settles to a bottom dwelling existence. This sucker is edible and it has been suggested that it may be sold "incognito" in fish-'n-chips.

largescale tapirfish

Scientific name: *Notacanthus chemnitzi*
    Bloch, 1787
Family: **Tapirfish**
Other common names: spiny eel, snubnosed
    spiny eel, swordtail eel
French name: tapir à grandes écailles

Distribution: World-wide in cooler waters. Found from the Labrador coast south to the Gulf of Mexico in the western North Atlantic Ocean.

Characters: Dorsal fin with 5–12 spines, usually 10–11. Anal fin with 13–21 spines and 110 or more soft rays. Pelvic fin with a fulcral spine, 2–4 fin spines and 6–11 soft rays. Pectoral fin with 10–17 rays. Grey to blue-grey becoming dark brown overall with age. Peritoneum and pharynx black giving a bluish tinge externally when seen through skin. Attains 122 cm.

largescale tapirfish

Biology: Found just above the bottom usually from 128 to 1000 m, down as far as 3285 m. In Arctic waters found at the shallower depths. Not occurring in schools. Females are larger than males. Food is principally large pink sea anemones thought to be eaten by browsing head down. A commercially important species off Japan.

largescale tonguefish

Scientific name: *Symphurus minor*
  Ginsburg, 1951
Family: **Tonguefish**
Other common names: none
French name: sole à grandes écailles

Distribution: Found from Nova Scotia south to Florida and the northeastern Gulf of Mexico.

Characters: This **flatfish** is distinguished from its relative, the **daubed tonguefish**, by fin ray and scale counts. Dorsal fin rays 69–76, anal fin rays 54–63. Caudal fin rays 10–11. Scales in lateral series 55–66. Overall

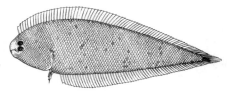

largescale tonguefish

colour is dusky or brown, fins lighter. The body is mottled with some scales darker than others. There may be vague cross bands posteriorly. Reaches 9 cm.

Biology: Larvae occur off Nova Scotia and on the Scotian Shelf as strays from the south. One of the adult specimens used to describe this species is from "off Halifax, Nova Scotia" at a depth of 170 m, but some authors doubt this is a correct record. Adults may be found on the Scotian Shelf but if this is so they are most probably recruited from drifting larvae and do not breed there. The spawning season for this species in the south is late spring to early summer. Food is crustaceans and worms.

largeye

Scientific name: *Pachystomias microdon*
  (Günther, 1878)
Family: **Barbeled Dragonfish**
Other common names: none
French name: drague grands-yeux

Distribution: Found mostly in the tropical North Atlantic to Atlantic Canada but also reported from the Indian and Pacific oceans.

Characters: Distinguished by a large, crescent-shaped light organ under the eye which is part of a cushion of luminous tissue

largeye

on the roof of the mouth. Light organs are often violet, red or rose and some are green-yellow. There is a membranous floor to the mouth. The body colour is dark brown to black. It exceeds 22 cm in length.

Biology: In Canada reported from southeast of Nova Scotia. Food is presumed to be fish and crustaceans. This loosejaw may descend to 4465 m. The red light organs are rare among sea fishes.

largeye lepidion

Scientific name: *Lepidion eques*
  (Günther, 1887)
Family: **Mora**
Other common names: North Atlantic codling
French name: lépidion à grands yeux

Distribution: Found in the North Atlantic Ocean. From Davis Strait and Greenland to the southeast Grand Bank in Canada.

Characters: This species is separated from its Atlantic coast relatives by its lack of a flattened snout and of a small, dark scaleless

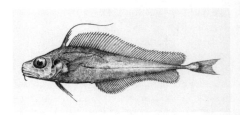

largeye lepidion

patch over a light organ in front of the anus, by having some teeth on the head of the vomer bone in the roof of the mouth, and 7–8 pelvic fin rays with the second and third rays longest. First dorsal fin rays 5, second dorsal fin rays 52–60. Anal fin with a short first ray followed by 49–54 rays. A chin barbel is present and the anal fin is partly indented. Overall colour is pale. Reaches 44 cm.

Biology: Found from 127–1880 m in the Atlantic Ocean but in Canada at 385–775 m. Individuals or schools may be caught. Food is shrimps and worms, apparently pelagic species, although this species is assumed to be a bottom feeder. Spawns near Iceland in April at lengths of 28–29 cm and temperatures of 5.2–6.5°C. Females begin to mature at 22–23 cm. Males are larger than females. Fecundity exceeds 100,000 eggs.

largeye rhinofish

Scientific name: *Poromitra megalops*
    (Lütken, 1877)
Family: **Ridgehead**
Other common names: none
French name: rhino à grands yeux

Distribution: World-wide in tropical and warm-temperate waters including off the Atlantic coast of Canada, the northwest Flemish Cap and in the Newfoundland Basin.

Characters: Distinguished from the related **crested ridgehead** and **bull rhinofish** by having fewer than 28 gill rakers and a large eye (diameter more than one-fifth

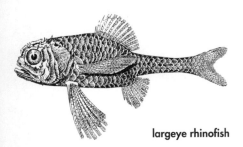

largeye rhinofish

head length). Scales in 25–29 rows. Dorsal fin with 2–3 spines and 10–12 soft rays. Anal fin with 1 spine and 8–10 soft rays. Pectoral fin rays 13–15 and pelvic fin with 1 spine and 7 soft rays. There is a serrated crest on top of the head and a spine between the nostrils. Overall colour is probably dark. Gill and mouth cavities are dark. Scale pockets

are outlined in brown in preserved fish. Attains 6.2 cm standard length.

Biology: First caught in Canadian waters in 1968 but only known from 3 specimens. Adults are usually caught below 400 m where they are bathypelagic.

Laval eelpout

Scientific name: *Lycodes lavalaei*
    Vladykov and Tremblay, 1936
Family: **Eelpout**
Other common names: Newfoundland
    eelpout, lycode du Labrador
French name: lycode de Laval

Distribution: Found from Hudson Bay to off central Labrador south to the Gulf of St. Lawrence and Saguenay Fjord, the Grand Bank and the Scotian Shelf. Also from the Jan Mayen Islands.

Characters: This species is separated from its Canadian Atlantic relatives by having small pelvic fins, a mouth under the

Laval eelpout

snout, no large pores around the mouth, crests on the chin, lateral line single and on midflank, tail short (preanal distance in the range 45–55%, usually about 50%, of total length), body markings and fin ray counts. Dorsal fin rays 97–104 and anal rays 77–82 (each including half the continuous caudal fin rays). Pectoral fin rays 18–20 and vertebrae 100–102. Scales on the body and dorsal and anal fins except the margin. No scales on the back, abdomen or pectoral fin base. The body is brownish-grey or grey with black blotches or a black network on the upper flank. Young fish have 8–9 light flank bars and a light band on the nape. There may be pink tinges on the pectoral and anal fins. Peritoneum is light. Reaches 55.2 cm.

Biology: Depth range is 24–535 m on mud and sand bottoms. Temperatures off Labrador were −1.2 to 2.5°C. Food includes various bottom organisms and small fishes such as **eelpout** species. Spawning is thought to occur in summer or early autumn.

least cisco

Scientific name: *Coregonus sardinella*
 Valenciennes in Cuvier and Valenciennes,
 1848
Family: **Salmon**
Other common names: lake herring, big-eye,
 Mackenzie herring, kraaktak, kapahilik
French name: cisco sardinelle

Distribution: Found around Alaska and in
northern British Columbia and the Yukon
and in Arctic Canadian rivers and coastal
waters east to Bathurst Inlet and north to
Banks, Victoria and Prince of Wales islands.
Also across northern Eurasia.

Characters: This species is distinguished
from other **salmons** by having 78–98 lateral
line scales, a strongly forked tail, no parr
marks, 2 skin flaps between the nostrils,
mouth terminal but lower jaw protruding,
and 41–53 gill rakers. Characters among **cis-**

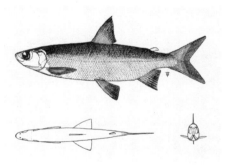

least cisco

coes (q.v.) overlap and so the species cannot
be easily separated. The lower jaw projects
further back than the upper jaw when the
mouth is closed. Migrating populations have
48–53 gill rakers and non-migrating populations 41–47 rakers. Dorsal fin rays 12–14,
anal rays 11–13, pectoral rays 14–17 and
pelvic rays 8–12.

Overall colour is silvery with a brown to
olive-green back. Pelvic fins have black tips
in non-migrating fish while migrating fish
have dark spots on the head, back, dorsal and
adipose fins, and sometimes on the pectoral
fins. All fins have dark tips.

Reaches 41.9 cm for the migratory form
and 22.9 cm for the non-migratory form in

one study but lake-dwelling fish can reach
42.8 cm fork length and are longer at a given
age than coastal fish. A "jumbo" spotted form
reaches 45.2 cm fork length. Differences
between populations have led to this species
being called the *Coregonus sardinella* complex, indicating that there may be more than
one species among the populations currently
recognised as the least cisco. Differences
include size, spotting patterns, gill raker
counts and migratory habits. Some lakes may
contain two forms of this "complex." The
"jumbo" spotted form in lakes of the upper
Yukon River drainage are large, spotted, have
higher gill raker counts (48–52) and are probably non-migratory. There is also a large,
spotted, anadromous form in the lower Yukon
River but most "typical" least cisco, abundant
in lakes and larger rivers of northwestern
Canada and Alaska, are small, unspotted, and
have 41–47 rakers.

Biology: There are small, freshwater, non-
migrating populations and larger, marine,
migrating ones. The latter tolerate a wide
range of salinities and temperatures.

Food is aquatic insects, terrestrial insects
stranded at the water surface, worms, molluscs, crustaceans and fish. These ciscoes are
eaten by **lake trout, inconnu, northern pike**
and **burbot**. Least cisco can probably
exclude **lake whitefish** with high raker
counts owing to competition for food. In
Trout Lake, Yukon dwarfs feed on surface
insects and zooplankton while normal fish
feed on bottom invertebrates.

In one study, life span was 11 years in
migratory fish which were older and grew
faster than non-migratory ones which attained
9 years. In Trout Lake, Yukon dwarfs mature
at 3–6 years and normal fish at 6–9 years. In
the Mackenzie River minimum age at maturity is 4 years. Maximum life span may be 26
years. Females are larger than males.

The migratory form ascends rivers in
spring and summer to spawn in fall and then
descends to the coast. The upriver migration
in the Mackenzie begins in the delta in late
August through September. Spawning takes
place in the upriver areas, such as the Peel
River, in late September to early October.
Eggs are laid over gravel or sand bottoms at

1.0–1.5°C in rivers or on lake shores in the non-migrating form. A female can have up to 23,600 eggs. Repeat spawning is known to occur at intervals perhaps greater than a year. Eggs hatch in spring after overwintering under the ice and the young of the migratory form move downstream. Young least cisco are found in the Mackenzie delta and in coastal habitats.

This is an important commercial species in Siberia but is only an incidental catch or a native fishery in Canada.

least darter

Scientific name: *Etheostoma microperca*
Jordan and Gilbert in Jordan, 1888
Family: **Perch**
Other common names: northern least darter
French name: petit dard

Distribution: Found centred on the southern Great Lakes from southern Ontario to northwest Minnesota and southward to southern Ohio. There are isolated populations from central Missouri to southeast Oklahoma. In Canada only in southwestern Ontario from Lake Ontario across to southern Georgian Bay and southward.

Characters: This species is distinguished from other **darters** in Canada by having the anal fin smaller than the soft dorsal fin, the snout and upper lip joined (i.e. premaxillaries not protractile), anterior belly scaleless, dorsal fin spines 5–8, usually 6–7, soft rays 7–11, usually 8–10, and lateral scales 30–39.

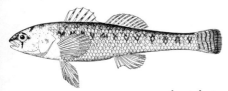

least darter

The anal fin has 1–2 spines and 4–7, usually 5–6, soft rays. Pectoral rays 9–12. The lateral line is absent and only 0–3 scales are pored. The cheeks and breast lack scales. The opercles are partly scaled.

Overall colour is olive-green to brown with darker spots extending onto the belly and dorsal and caudal fins. There are 3–11 weak, dark green saddles in some fish. The midflank has 7–15 small, black to green blotches on a straw-coloured background. Belly cream to yellowish-white. The anal, pectoral and pelvic fins are dusky. There is a short stripe on the nape in front of the dorsal fin and black bars below and before the eye. Breeding males have an ochre suffusion in addition to the green body, a red-orange spot between each dorsal fin spine surrounded by metallic green flecks and black or grey bars at the edge and base of this fin. The second dorsal fin has 4–5 grey bands. The iris is red. The belly, pectoral fin base and opercle are a metallic green. Anal and pelvic fins are a rusty or reddish orange. The caudal fin has 6–7 grey bars. The male pelvic fins become enlarged in order to clasp the female. The third ray is elongated, the spine has an extra fold and the pelvics form a cup-shape. The second dorsal and caudal fins and the top of the head become milky-white. Breeding tubercles are found on the anal and pelvic fins and rarely and uniquely on the dorsal fins. Females develop a yellowish or amber colour to the anal, pectoral and pelvic fins.

Attains a maximum of 4.6 cm. This fish is the smallest fish and smallest vertebrate in Canada with mature adults being 2.2 cm long.

Biology: The least darter is found in weedy areas over mud and sand bottoms in lakes and slow streams. It is reputed to burrow into the bottom to avoid dry periods.

Food is small crustaceans, insects and other invertebrates taken from around plants rather than from the bottom as the **johnny darter** does.

Least darters are mature at 1 year of age. Females live longer than males but life span is only 18–20 months and most fish die after their first spawning. A few fish reach 2 years of age.

Spawning occurs in May-June in Canada with a male migration into weedy areas and establishment of territories. These territories are three-dimensional and include the vertical height of the weeds. Other darters have two-dimensional territories. Females enter the weeds later and may be courted by several males until one is successful. The female orients herself vertically along a plant stem, and the male clasps the female just in front of the dorsal fin with his enlarged pelvic fins. Both fish quiver, 1–3 eggs are laid and fertilised and the fish move to a new position. The female may repeat the spawning process with the same or a new male. Females may contain up to 1102 eggs and about 30 are laid each day. Eggs are up to 1.1 mm in diameter.

leatherfin lumpsucker

Scientific name: *Eumicrotremus derjugini* Popov, 1926
Family: **Lumpfish**
Other common names: none
French name: petite poule de mer arctique

Distribution: Found in the Arctic Ocean, including across the Canadian Arctic, and adjacent waters north of 58°N including the Labrador coast, and in the northern Sea of Okhotsk.

Characters: This species is separated from its Arctic-Atlantic relatives by having the gill opening above the pectoral fin, many large,

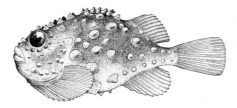

leatherfin lumpsucker

pointed tubercles each with many spines on the head and body, supplemental pores above the lateral line, rounded anterior body, first dorsal fin rays covered with skin and not visible and pectoral fin base without tubercles. Dorsal fin spines 6–7, soft rays 11–13, anal rays 10–13, and pectoral rays 25–27. Chin and throat naked or with a few tubercles under the lower jaw in very large fish. Lateral line pores developed. No barbel-like chin flaps. Tubercles low, conical and covered with prickles. Tubercles distant from each other by at least diameter of bases. Olive on the flanks, darker on the back. Reaches 10 cm standard length.

Biology: Found on mud, gravel or stone at 50–274 m, with young in shallow water, at temperatures in the range –2 to 1.6°C. Food

is amphipods, oikopleura, copepods, caprellids and barnacle nauplii. This lumpfish is eaten by thick-billed murres in Hudson Strait. Spawning is in late summer to fall. Eggs attain 4.3 mm.

Leatherjacket Family

Scientific name: Balistidae
French name: balistes

Leatherjackets or triggerfishes are found world-wide in warmer waters with about 40 species, 3 of which enter Atlantic Canada.

Leatherjackets have a compressed body and head covered with non-overlapping or slightly overlapping plate-like, rough scales (hence "leatherjacket"). Pelvic fins are reduced to a spine or tubercle. There are 3 dorsal fin spines although the third can be very small. The first spine can be locked erect with the second spine forming the locking mechanism (hence "triggerfish"). Soft fin rays are branched. There are 4 outer and 3 inner teeth in each upper jaw adapted to form a powerful beak for crushing. The protruding eyes can be moved independently.

Leatherjackets are close relatives of the **Filefish Family** which is often included within the Leatherjacket Family. They are members of the **Puffer Order**.

These fishes are usually found on coral reefs, in eelgrass beds or in open waters in the tropics. The trigger mechanism of the dorsal spines forms an effective way of instantly increasing the size of the fish, reducing the number of predators large enough to swallow it and discomforting those which try. The erect dorsal spine is also used to "lock" the fish into a crevice so it cannot be dislodged. The belly can be expanded to help in wedging the fish firmly. Triggerfishes swim slowly by sculling with the dorsal and anal fins but can move quickly when disturbed by using the caudal fin.

Leatherjackets eat, among other things, long-spined sea urchins which are turned over and attacked with the strong teeth. Their main diet is crustaceans and molluscs which are revealed by puffs of water on sandy bottoms or pulled out of crevices. The eggs of triggerfishes settle to the bottom and are guarded by the male, who may even bite painfully any divers who approach too close. Young are pelagic. Triggerfish are good to eat but some may contain flesh toxins. **Queen triggerfish** are baked and regarded as a delicacy in the Bahamas. Some species produce grunting, purring or clicking sounds. These are made by the teeth or pharyngeal teeth, or by the tympanum, an area of enlarged scales behind the gill openings, which can be vibrated. The swimbladder amplifies the sound.

See **gray triggerfish**
   ocean triggerfish
   queen triggerfish

Lefteye Flounder Family

Scientific name: Bothidae
French name: turbots

Lefteye flounders are found in the Atlantic, Indian and Pacific oceans. There are about 115 species with 17 reported from Canada, 15 on the Atlantic coast and 2 on the Pacific coast.

These fishes have the typical **flatfish** body plan. Eyes are on the left side of the head (= sinistral) although some individuals are reversed. The pelagic egg has a single oil globule in the yolk. Fins do not have spines. The dorsal fin origin is above or anterior to the eye. The pelvic fin on the eyed side is on the midline of the belly and often longer than the one on the blind side. Branchiostegal membranes are connected. The preopercle bone on the side of the head has a free mar-

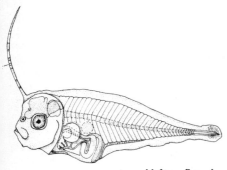

Larval lefteye flounder

gin. The anus is on the blind side. Males often have longer pectoral fins, longer anterior dorsal fin rays, spines on the snout and

eyes set further apart. The lateral line does not have a dorsal branch but may be forked above the upper eye. Scales may be both ctenoid and cycloid.

Lefteye flounders are members of the **Flatfish Order** and are related to the **Righteye Flounder Family**.

These are commercially important fishes also sought by anglers although some are relatively small and of little interest. They are common in shallow, coastal waters, but some species descend to several hundred metres. They often bury themselves in bottom sediment with only the eyes and nostrils protruding. However they are active hunters of prey and swim well. Most species are capable of intricate colour changes to match the background.

See **angelfin whiff**
   channel flounder
   deepwater flounder
   eyed flounder
   fourspot flounder
   fringed flounder
   Gulf Stream flounder
   horned whiff
   Pacific sanddab
   sash flounder
   slim flounder
   smallmouth flounder
   speckled sanddab
   spiny flounder
   spotfin flounder
   summer flounder
   windowpane

Leftvent Family

Scientific name: Linophrynidae
French name: pores-gauches

Leftvents or netdevil anglerfishes are found in the Pacific, Indian and Atlantic oceans where there are 47 species. Atlantic Canada has 5 species.

These deepsea members of the **Anglerfish Order** are characterised by having the anus on the left side not in the midline as is usual in fishes, by having usually 3 dorsal and anal fin soft rays, and by having 4–5 branchiostegal rays. There are strong sphenotic spines on top of the head. Barbelthroats (genus *Linophryne*) have a remarkably developed barbel hanging down from the hyoid region of the throat. The barbel may bear photophores. The light is produced by a chemical process in photocytes (light-producing cells) which are controlled by oxygen in the blood. The bait, or esca, of the fishing apparatus contains luminous bacteria and in one species emits a bright turquoise light.

Leftvents are related to the **Fanfin**, **Seadevil**, **Whipnose**, **Dreamer**, **Wolftrap**, **Footballfish** and **Werewolf** families, which all lack pelvic fins, scales and a pseudobranch, have bones at the front of the head (frontals) which are not united, have the lower pharyngeal bones reduced and toothless, and have 8–9 caudal fin rays. They are identified by the presence/absence of the hyoid barbel and by its shape and form.

Males are parasites on the females and their eyes and olfactory organs, among other organ systems, degenerate once they are attached. Males have tubular eyes and the skin is naked. Unattached males are smaller than parasitic ones.

Leftvents are found from 200–4000 m.

See **forkbarbelthroat**
  fourbarbelthroat
  greatbarbelthroat
  Schmidt's leftvent
  twohorn barbelthroat

leister sculpin

Scientific name: *Enophrys lucasi*
  (Jordan and Gilbert, 1898)
Family: **Sculpin**
Other common names: none
French name: chabot de leister

Distribution: Found from the southern end of Queen Charlotte Strait in British Columbia to the Bering Sea and Bering Strait.

Characters: This sculpin is distinguished from the related **buffalo sculpin** by having 1–5 barbs on the large upper preopercular spine. In addition, the lower edge of the bone under the eye is a large flange which covers part of the upper lip. Nasal spine sharp and preorbital spine forked with rounded points. There is a knife-edged nuchal ridge which rises to a point and has a steep posterior edge. First dorsal fin spines 7–8, second dorsal soft rays 12–14, anal rays 9–11, pectoral rays 15–19 and pelvic fin with 1 spine and 2–3 soft rays. Lateral line with 34–37 plates with 1–2 keels and tubercles. The head

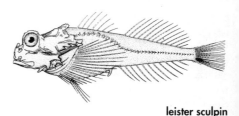

leister sculpin

bones are covered in small tubercles. There are 2–3 irregular rows of cirri on the body under the lateral line behind the pelvic fins and many cirri on the edge of the upper jaw, mouth corner and preopercle. Males have 2–3 light bands on the body and the flank cirri are surrounded by a white blotch. Females are lighter in colour than males. Fins in both sexes are barred and spotted pale yellow. The belly in both sexes is pale yellow. Reaches 25 cm.

Biology: Leister sculpins are found in rocky areas where they hide in bryozoan and hydroid colonies, down to 18 m.

leopard dace

Scientific name: *Rhinichthys falcatus*
  (Eigenmann and Eigenmann, 1893)
Family: **Carp**
Other common names: silvery grey minnow
French name: naseux léopard

Distribution: Found in the Fraser and Columbia river basins of British Columbia and adjacent U.S. states.

Characters: This species is uniquely characterised by well-developed fleshy stays connecting the pelvic fin ray bases to the adjoining body. The body is slender and delicate.

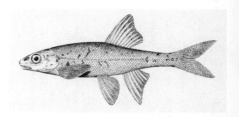

leopard dace

The dorsal fin has a concave margin. There is a large, flattened, protruding barbel at each mouth corner. Dorsal fin branched rays 8, anal branched rays 6, pectoral rays 13–15 and pelvic rays 8. Lateral line pores 49–66 and scales around the caudal peduncle 20–33. Scales on the body are conspicuous in living fish. Pharyngeal teeth 2,4–4,2. Males develop nuptial tubercles on the top of the head, back, flank scales and pectoral and pelvic fin rays. Scale tubercles are near the margin and line up in rows along the body. The back is dark, the flanks creamy and the belly silvery-white. The flanks have many large spots and blotches. Spawning males have orange-red lips and pelvic fin bases. This colour may be present year round. The peritoneum is silvery-white with a few speckles. Reaches 12.0 cm.

Biology: Leopard dace prefer slow moving currents in rivers near shorelines and are also found in lakes. They prefer habitats with temperatures between 15 and 18°C in August. Food is aquatic and surface, terrestrial insects. Worms washed into rivers at high water are also eaten. Females are larger than males and life span is over 4 years. Spawning occurs in July. The Committee on the Status of Endangered Wildlife in Canada accepted a report on this species in 1990 but no status designation was required.

lesser beaconlamp

Scientific name: *Lampanyctus alatus*
    Goode and Bean, 1896
Family: **Lanternfish**
Other common names: none
French name: petite lampe-bouée

Distribution: Found in the Atlantic, Indian and Pacific oceans and off the Scotian Shelf in Atlantic Canada.

Characters: This species and 7 relatives in the genus *Lampanyctus* are separated from other Atlantic species by lacking photophores close to the dorsal body edge, the PLO photophore is well above the pectoral fin base level while the second PVO photophore is at or below the upper pectoral base level, there are 4 Prc, the first PO and two PVO photophores are not on a straight line, both males and females have caudal luminous glands composed of overlapping,

scale-like structures without a black pigment border, the fourth PO photophore is highly elevated, there are no luminous, scale-like

lesser beaconlamp

structures on the belly between the pelvic fin bases or these bases and the anus, there are 4 VO photophores and the SAO series is strongly angled. This species is distinguished from its relatives by having 13–15 gill rakers, long pectoral fins extending to first Pol photophore, VLO photophore near lateral line, 1 cheek photophore, luminous tissue at adipose fin base, and lateral line organs 35–36. Dorsal fin rays 11–13, anal rays 16–18 and pectoral rays 11–13. AO photophores 11–14. The supracaudal luminous gland has 2–4 weak segments and the infracaudal has 4–5 scale-like segments. The head, body and fins are covered by secondary photophores. Reaches 6.1 cm.

Biology: This species is probably tropical in its distribution. First reported from Canadian waters in 1969. Depth distribution in the Atlantic is 275–1000 m by day and 40–300 m at night. Maximum abundance by night is at 50–100 m. Sexual maturity is attained at about 4.0 cm.

lesser lampfish

Scientific name: *Taaningichthys minimus*
    (Tåning, 1928)
Family: **Lanternfish**
Other common names: none
French name: petit poisson-lampe

Distribution: Found in the Atlantic, Indian and Pacific oceans and off Atlantic Canada.

Characters: This species is distinguished from its Canadian Atlantic coast relatives by the large luminous glands, outlined with heavy black pigment, on the upper and lower caudal peduncle, and the pelvic fin origin in front of the dorsal fin origin, and from its close relative, the **smoothbrow lampfish**, by photophore counts of VO 8–10, AO 4–7 + 4–6, total 9–13, and the Pol photophore lying

lesser lampfish

under or in front of the adipose fin base. There are hook-like teeth near the tip of the lower jaws. Dorsal fin rays 11–13, usually 12, anal rays 11–14, usually 13, and pectoral rays 15–17, usually 16. The upper caudal peduncle gland is twice as big on males as on females, and the lower gland is larger than the upper in both sexes. There is a crescent of whitish tissue on the posterior half of the iris. Attains about 6.5 cm.

Biology: A relatively uncommon species known from 3 Canadian specimens caught in 1979 from south of the Grand Bank and a fourth specimen from the stomach of a **swordfish** caught off the Scotian Shelf and reported in 1968. Near Bermuda it has been caught at 600–850 m by day and 200–600 m by night. The night records are as shallow as 51 m in some areas. Sexually mature females are 4 cm and longer. A spawning peak in late winter-early spring is reported for Hawaii and in fall for Bermuda.

Lightfish Family

Scientific name: Photichthyidae
French name: poissons étoilés

Lightfishes are small, delicate, bioluminescent, deepsea fishes of the tropical and temperate Atlantic, Pacific and Indian oceans. There are about 18 to 25 species in the world of which 7 occur in Canada.

They are relatives of the **Bristlemouth** and **Silver Hatchetfish** families in the **Widemouth Order** and, like them, carry photophores or light organs on their heads and bodies. The photophores have a lumen and a duct. In Canadian species there are photophores on the isthmus, 2 rows of photophores on the belly, and one over the anal fin

back to the tail. The body carries easily detached (or deciduous) scales and usually an adipose fin. There is a large mouth with fine teeth and gill rakers are well-developed. There is no lower jaw barbel. Eyes vary in size from moderate to large and may be tubular and telescopic. Lightfishes are usually black on the back with silvery sides. Most specimens are damaged on capture, losing skin and scales.

They are identified by the position and shape of the fins, by counts of fin rays and by the number and arrangement of photophores. They are common but are seldom seen except by ichthyologists using special midwater trawls. Some important material studied by ichthyologists comes from the stomachs of other fishes — this gives an idea of how little is known about the smaller fishes which inhabit open midwaters of the oceans.

Lightfishes are mesopelagic or bathypelagic, living at depths of 200–800 m during the day, rising higher in the water at night and returning to the depths for the day. The younger fish, known as post-larvae, live nearer the surface and undergo a metamorphosis which involves shrinkage of the body and development of photophores to become adult when they sink to lower level.

See **highseas lightfish**
    oceanic lightfish
    ovate lightfish
    sailor lightfish
    slender lightfish
    slim lightfish
    star-eye lightfish

lightlamp footballfish

Scientific name: *Himantolophus groenlandicus* Reinhardt, 1837
Family: **Footballfish**
Other common names: Atlantic footballfish, football atlantique
French name: football fine-lampe

Distribution: Found in the Atlantic Ocean from West Greenland to South Africa, including the Grand Bank, south of Sable Island and Georges Bank of Atlantic Canada. It may also occur in the western Indian Ocean.

Characters: This anglerfish is distinguished from its relative, **Maul's footballfish**, by the short filaments on the tip of the esca or bait of the fishing apparatus. The illicium and esca are heavily tuberculate. Dorsal fin rays 4–6, anal fin rays 4 and pectoral fin rays 14–18. The skin has large plates, each with a central spine. Adults are ashen to black or black-brown and young are a deep brown colour overall. Fins are greyish-brown with blackish tips. Females reach 46.5 cm, and males are less than 4 cm.

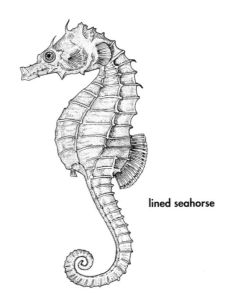

lined seahorse

lightlamp footballfish

Biology: Known from Canadian waters as shallow as 137–146 m. Reported down to 1830 m. This is the commonest footballfish accounting for more than half the known specimens for the family. Food includes fishes, cephalopods and coelenterates, which are attracted by the luminescent esca or bait of the fishing apparatus.

lined seahorse

Scientific name: *Hippocampus erectus*
  Perry, 1810
Family: **Pipefish**
Other common names: none
French name: hippocampe rayé

Distribution: Found from Argentina to Nova Scotia.

Characters: Unmistakeable by its erect position when alive and prehensile tail. There are 16–21 dorsal fin rays. Pectoral rays are 14–19 and anal rays 3–4. There are 10–12 trunk rings and 32–39 tail rings. Colour is variable, light brown, olive-brown, brick-red, orange, yellow or grey to nearly black. There are usually large pale blotches and dark lines on the back. May be dotted white or golden. Attains 17.7 cm.

Biology: The only Canadian seahorse is found as a stray in the summer. Specimens found in seaweed often have bony outgrowths and fleshy tabs, presumably as camouflage. Seahorses cling to vegetation with the tail and in aquaria to each other, sometimes requiring untangling. They swim with the aid of the dorsal fin which may beat up to 35 times per second. They are commonest in deeper water where there is abundant vegetation. They have been caught at 73 m. The female uses an ovipositor to deposit brick-red eggs in the male's pouch. The male may receive eggs from more than one female. The developing embryos absorb calcium and probably oxygen from the surrounding fluid in the brood pouch. About 250–700 young, about 6 mm long are squeezed out of the male's brood pouch in summer. The young grow to 75 mm in 4 months and may breed at this early age. Food is the smaller crustaceans sucked into the tube snout. Seahorses are sold for aquaria and dried as curios.

linen skate

Scientific name: *Raja lintea* Fries, 1838
Family: **Skate**
Other common names: white skate, sailray, raie voile
French name: raie linon

Distribution: Found in the North Atlantic Ocean including off the Flemish Cap in the west. Also on the west Greenland coast.

Characters: This species is separated from its Canadian Atlantic relatives by having a rigid snout with its cartilaginous support thick and stiff, cartilaginous supports of the pectoral fin do not reach the snout tip, dorsal

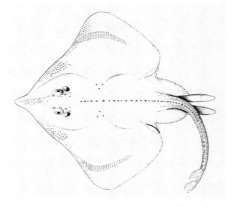

linen skate

fins separate or joined at the base, large thorns on the back, snout angle usually less than 90°, more than 10 spines along the tail midline posterior to pelvic fin axils, 40–51 thorns along the body and tail midline, and upper jaw teeth in 47–50 rows. The median row of tail spines contains the largest thorns. There are 2–4 spines in front of the eyes, 1 at the inner eye edge, 4 spines behind the eyes and 3 spines on the shoulder. The lower disc is smooth. The outer edge of the pectoral fins are prickly. Egg cases are 10.7 cm by 7.7 cm excluding the horns. Horns terminate in fine points. The case has longitudinal striations and cross-hatching. The upper disc is brown-grey. The underside is white in some. In others, the rear borders of the pectoral and pelvic fins are darkened grey. The vent is surrounded by grey and the tail has a median grey band. Reaches 119 cm. The world, all-tackle angling record weighed 9.06 kg and was caught in 1987 in Norway.

Biology: Known from 2 specimens taken on the northern slope of the Flemish Cap in 1958–1961 at depths of 635–750 m. Elsewhere reported at 150–650 m. Food includes crustaceans, worms and fishes such as **lancetfish**.

linestop lanternfish

Scientific name: *Gonichthys cocco* (Cocco, 1829)
Family: **Lanternfish**
Other common names: none
French name: lanterne boute-ligne

Distribution: Found in the Atlantic Ocean and Mediterranean Sea. In Canada along the Atlantic coast from near the Grand Bank and the Scotian Shelf.

Characters: This species is separated from its Atlantic coast relatives by lacking photophores near the dorsal body edge, the PLO photophore is at or slightly above the level of the upper pectoral fin base, the mouth is subterminal and gill rakers are present. Dorsal fin rays 10–13, anal rays 20–23 and pectoral rays 13–16. Total gill rakers 9–13. AO photophores 16–20. Lateral line organs 26–30. Adult males have 5–8, rounded, luminous supracaudal organs which develop at about 2.4 cm. Adult females have an infracaudal series of 3–6 oval patches which first appear at 3.1 cm. Reaches 6.0 cm.

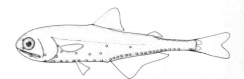

linestop lanternfish

Biology: An early record of this species was made in 1913 off Newfoundland and it is common near the Grand Bank. This is the most abundant surface-visiting lanternfish in the main part of its distribution. It is known from the surface down to 1500 m with a maximum catch at 425–650 m during the day and from the surface to 175 m at night. This lanternfish is sexually mature at 3.8 cm and few fish live more than 1 year. A spawning peak occurs in winter or early spring.

lingcod

Scientific name: *Ophiodon elongatus* Girard, 1854

Family: **Greenling**
Other common names: cultus cod, buffalo
  cod, blue cod, green cod, leopard cod,
  cuttus cod
French name: morue-lingue

Distribution: From Baja California to
Alaska including British Columbia.
Characters: The dorsal fin has 24–28
spines and 19–24 soft rays. The anal fin has 3
spines and 21–25 soft rays. Scales are cycloid

lingcod

and there are 150–180 pored scales. This
species is unique among Canadian greenlings
for its canine teeth and separated gill membranes. It is also distinguished by having 1
lateral line canal and the mouth extending
beyond the anterior eye margin. There are
also 4–5 preopercular spines and a large,
branched cirrus over each eye. The flesh may
be green in younger fish.
Colour varies with the environment but
consists of dark mottling and dark, light or
golden spotting over brown, grey, green or
blue shades. The belly is grey-white.
Attains 1.52 m and 47.6 kg, possibly
larger. The world, all-tackle angling record
weighed 31.29 kg and was caught on the 16
June 1992 at Langara Island, British Columbia
by Murray M. Romer.
Biology: Found from the surface down to
427 m or deeper but mostly inshore near
rocks. Young are found in bays. Males are
commoner than females in shallow water.
Food is a variety of other fishes, crustaceans and octopus. They are also cannibals.
Males establish territories during early winter
in rocky areas where there is a strong current
from tides or ocean swells. Displaced fish
home at a speed of up to 1.2 km/day.
Spawning occurs from December to
March at night and pink or whitish eggs, up
to 3.5 mm across with hardened shells, are
deposited under rocks or in crevices. These

egg masses may weigh 13.6 kg and be 76 cm
across. The eggs are initially pink to yellowish-white but turn completely white within a
week and grey as the embryo develops. Large
females spawn first. The male guards and
fans the eggs. Growth varies from 0.8 kg for
males to 1.2 kg for females per year. Males
are mature at 46–51 cm and age 2, females at
61–76 cm and age 3–5 and they may live as
much as 20 years. Large females produce
over half a million eggs.
Lingcod are caught in British Columbia
off the west coast of Vancouver Island by
trawlers and in the Strait of Georgia by hand-
liners and also in Queen Charlotte Sound.
The 1985 catch was 5688 tonnes, the highest
recorded, and was worth almost $3 million.
They are also a sport fish caught on large
jigs, spoons or live bait and by spear fishermen. Fishermen report "triples", where a
hooked, small lingcod is grabbed by a larger
one which is in turn seized by an even larger
one. Lingcod are good eating despite the
green flesh (the green colour disappears on
cooking). Indian fisheries for lingcod may
date back 5000 years. Recent catches and
average size have declined and tighter fishery
regulations have been imposed.

• Most accessible July and August.

• The coastal waters on the west coast of
Vancouver Island, the Queen Charlotte
Islands and the waters off the northern
coast of British Columbia.

• Heavy action saltwater rods and reels.
The most common outfits are Penn 20–
to 50–pound saltwater rod and reel
combinations used with the same line
weights.

• One- to six-ounce vertical jigs fished
near the bottom. The best bait is octopus, **herring** and **anchovy** fished near
the bottom.

lings

Lings are members of the **Cod Family**
and there are 2 species on the Atlantic coast,
the **blue ling** and the **European ling**. The
freshwater **burbot** is another Cod Family
member, commonly called ling. The **white
hake**, also a Cod Family member, is some-

times called ling. The French word lingue has been used for the unrelated **Greenling Family** but this was changed to sourcil to avoid confusion. Ling derives from the Middle English and probably refers to the elongate body form.

little skate

Scientific name: *Raja erinacea*
(Mitchill, 1825)
Family: **Skate**
Other common names: tobacco box,
hedgehog skate
French name: raie hérisson

Distribution: Found from southeastern Newfoundland along the Scotian Shelf, in the Bay of Fundy and on Georges Bank. Reported south to North Carolina.

Characters: This species is separated from its Canadian Atlantic relatives by having a rigid snout with its cartilaginous support thick

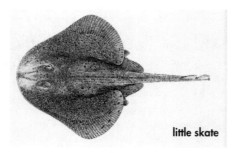

little skate

and stiff, cartilaginous supports of the pectoral fin do not reach the snout tip, dorsal fins joined at the base, snout blunt and angle greater than 90°, well-developed spines along body and tail midline but adults lack spines on the tail midline, and upper jaw teeth 30–64, increasing with age and usually less than 54 at 35–50 cm. Very similar to the **winter skate** but differs in having pelvic spines near the cloaca in females (nearer the edge of the pelvic fins in **winter skate** females). Male little skates do not have pelvic spines but male **winter skates** do. There are 2–4 rows of large spines on each side of the disc and tail midline, a heavy concentration of 30–60 nape and shoulder spines, 3–8 spines behind the eye, 8–15 in front of the eye, 9–12 along the inner

margin of each eye and several between the eyes. The lower disc is smooth except for the snout. Males develop claspers at 36 cm and are fully developed when over 50 cm. Egg cases are 5.5–6.3 cm by 3.5–4.5 cm. The horns are 6.3–7.6 cm and 4.1–5.5 cm. Upper disc grey to dark brown, often with dark spots. Lower disc white to grey. Attains 60 cm.

Biology: Once thought to occur in the Gulf of St. Lawrence, specimens there are now thought to be a similar species, the **winter skate**. The little skate is found over sand and gravel usually in shallow water but reported down to 329 m on Georges Bank. It has been found over a wide range of temperature, 1.2–21°C, but in Passamaquoddy Bay it moves inshore for the winter and offshore in summer suggesting a preference for cooler temperatures. On the Scotian Shelf preferred depth is 37–90 m and preferred temperature range is 5–10°C. Food is principally crustaceans such as crabs, shrimps and amphipods, followed by worms, molluscs and fishes, taken throughout the day and night from the sea bed surface. **Sharks, winter skates** and grey seals eat little skates. This skate lives at least 8 years and about one-third of the population is mature at about 4 years or 42–44 cm. Mating and egg production occur year-round with peaks in June–July and late October–early January. Hatching takes 6–9 months. The egg case is often partly buried in sand. Young skates are about 10 cm at birth and reach 21.5 cm at 1 year of age. This species is frequently caught in trawls and weirs incidental to commercial fisheries. Some is converted to fish meal but it is not a major fishery item in Canada.

little tunny

Scientific name: *Euthynnus alletteratus*
(Rafinesque, 1810)
Family: **Mackerel**
Other common names: little tuna
French name: thonine commune

Distribution: Found in the Atlantic Ocean, the Mediterranean and Black seas and around Australia. Reported from Atlantic Canada.

Characters: This species is separated from its Atlantic coast relatives by the dorsal fins being close together (separated by a distance less than snout length), first dorsal fin spines usually about 15 (range 10–15), 37–45 gill rakers, 4–5 black spots below the pectoral fin and straight to wavy blue-green stripes between the dorsal fins and the lateral line. The second dorsal fin has 12–13 rays and is followed by 8 finlets. The anal fin has 11–15 rays followed by 7 finlets. Scales are restricted to the lateral line and corselet. The back is dark blue to steel blue and the lower flanks and belly silvery to white. Reaches 1.22 m. The world angling record weighed 15.95 kg and was taken in Algeria in 1988.

little tunny

Biology: Caught only once in Canada from southeast of Tignish Run, P.E.I. in 1983. This is a coastal species found in large schools in fast waters near shoals and off-shore islands and it is common south of Canada. Food is small fishes such as **herrings** as well as squid and crustaceans. **Sharks, yellowfin tuna** and **billfishes** are predators of this species. Life span is over 7 years. Maturity is attained at 35 cm off Florida. Spawning occurs in spring to summer (March to November off Florida) with up to 1.75 million eggs being shed in several batches. Anglers report this species to be a good fighter. It is used as bait for sailfishes. Little tunnies are caught with other **tunas** and **bonitos**. The world catch has reached 10,731 tonnes in 1981.

Livebearer Family

Scientific name: Poeciliidae
French name: poecilies

Livebearers are found in fresh and brackish waters from the eastern United States south through the Caribbean to northeastern Argentina and in Africa. There are about 293 species. They do not occur naturally in Canada, but 2 species are found in the Cave and Basin Hotsprings, Alberta, as introductions from aquarium stock coming from the United States. The guppy (queue de voile, *Poecilia reticulata* Peters, 1859) and the green swordtail (queue d'épée, *Xiphophorus helleri* Heckel, 1848), both livebearers, were also introduced to this hotspring but no longer survive there.

Livebearers in the Americas have the first 3 anal fin rays unbranched and the male has rays 3–5 elongated and highly modified into a gonopodium which is used for transferring sperm packets into the female. It is moveable to the side or forward to allow copulation to occur. The sperm packets release sperm when placed in the female and some can be stored for future use. Details of gonopodium anatomy are important in identifying and classifying species. Pectoral fins are high on the flank, pelvic fins are anterior and there are pleural ribs on the first several haemal arches. The supraorbital pores have neuromasts embedded in fleshy grooves. Young are born alive, a condition known as ovoviviparity where the eggs develop and hatch in the mother.

Livebearers are related to the **Killifish Family** and are members of the **Killifish Order**.

Livebearers are found in habitats from mountain streams to brackish coastal marshes and river mouths. Food is mostly encrusting algae and the associated, small invertebrates. Males tend to be smaller than females and more brightly coloured. These colours are best seen during the courtship display.

Some species are important in the aquarium business, such as the guppy and swordtail, while the mosquitofish has been used world-wide as a predator on aquatic mosquito larvae, the adult fly being a carrier of malaria. They have also been used extensively in genetics research, research on tumours and in immunology. Some livebearers are all-female species and egg development is stimulated by spermatozoa from another species, without any genetic contribution. Young are identical to the mother. This unusual form of reproduction is called gynogenesis. Others have superfetation where eggs are at different developmental stages within the mother and are born over a period of several days rather than all at once.

See **mosquitofish**
    sailfin molly

Livebearing Brotula Family

Scientific name: Bythitidae
French name: donzelles vivipares

Livebearing or viviparous brotulas are found in the Atlantic, Indian and Pacific oceans. There are about 90 species, some yet undescribed, with 1 found on the coast of British Columbia.

There are no spines in the fins. Pelvic fins are thoracic when present (on the breast ahead of the pectoral fin level). Scales are usually present and cycloid, or may be absent. A swimbladder and pyloric caeca are present. There is usually a strong spine on the operculum. Males have a penis and these fishes bear live young rather than shedding eggs. Skin is loose and is thick over the dorsal and anal fins.

These fishes are relatives of the **Cusk-eel Family** in the **Cusk-eel Order**.

Livebearing brotulas are found mostly in coastal waters near shore or at moderate depths but some are deepsea fishes while others are found in fresh water. They are secretive, hiding in crevices and caves or in burrows.

See **red brotula**

Lizardfish Family

Scientific name: Synodontidae
French name: poissons-lézards

Lizardfishes are found in all oceans and on both the Atlantic and Pacific coasts of Canada. There are about 55 species of which 4 are reported from Canada.

These fishes, as their name suggests, resemble lizards in the appearance of the head, which has a large mouth with many, small, canine-like teeth along both jaws and in the possession of shiny scales. The small to medium-sized body is cylindrical and usually has an adipose fin. A larval lizardfish is very distinct in form from the adult being transparent, scaleless, elongate and having large black spots under the skin on the belly.

They are relatives of the **Barracudina**, **Daggertooth**, **Sabertooth Fish**, **Halterfish** and **Lancetfish** families in the **Flagfin Order**.

They mostly occur in shallow waters but some have been captured at 4800 m. They sit quietly on the bottom with the head end raised by the pelvic fins waiting for a small fish to swim by. This prey is quickly seized by a sudden darting motion, reminiscent of land lizards and usually swallowed whole. Some lizardfish will bury themselves in sand with only the eyes showing.

See **ferocious lizardfish**
    red lizardfish
    smallscale lizardfish
    snakefish

lobefin snailfish

Scientific name: *Liparis greeni*
    (Jordan and Starks, 1895)
Family: **Snailfish**
Other common names: Green's liparid
French name: limace à nageoire lobée

Distribution: Found from the Bering Sea to Washington including British Columbia.

Characters: This species is characterised by having over 300 pyloric caeca and an obvious anterior lobe to the dorsal fin. Teeth are in bands. The eye is small. The gill opening is mostly above the pectoral fin and does not descend below the fourth pectoral ray. There is a nearly round adhesive disc. The nostril is double. Dorsal fin rays 37–40, anal rays 31–32. The pectoral fin has 33–37 rays with the lower 6 thickened, partly free of their membrane and elongated into a small lobe. The back is light brown, golden-brown or blue-black, the belly with cream to light brown blotches. Its colour matches the habitat. Reaches 31 cm. This species was named for Ashdown Green, a Canadian naturalist.

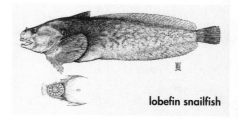

lobefin snailfish

Biology: Very little is known about this species. In Canada it has been collected in tide pools and waters less than 3 m deep over mud, sand, gravel and rocks with associated kelp and other seaweeds.

logperch

Scientific name: *Percina caprodes*
(Rafinesque, 1818)
Family: **Perch**
Other common names: zebra fish, jackfish, Manitou darter, rockfish, hogmolly, hogfish
French name: fouille-roche

Distribution: Found from east-central Alberta, central Saskatchewan, Manitoba, Ontario and southeastern Québec south to the Gulf of Mexico. Also reported from the north shore of the Gulf of St. Lawrence opposite Anticosti Island as an isolated population.

Characters: This **darter** is separated from its Canadian relatives by having an obviously protruding snout, a large anal fin at

logperch

least as large as the soft dorsal fin, belly midline either naked (females) or with 20–37 enlarged scales (males), 2 anal fin spines, no groove between the snout and lip (premaxillaries not protractile), 67–103 lateral line scales and 14–25 flank bars. First dorsal fin spines 12–17, usually 14–16, second dorsal rays 13–18, usually 15–16, soft anal fin rays 8–13, usually 10–11. Pectoral fin rays 12–16, usually 14–15. The cheeks and opercles are scaled and the breast is naked.

Overall colour is yellow-green to grey-green. The back has 8–10 saddles. The flank bars may terminate in a ventral tear-drop. Alternate bars reach to, and pass below, the lateral line. The dorsal fins are striped orange and black and the caudal fin has 3–4 bars. The caudal fin has a large black basal spot. The ventral scales develop tubercles in spawning males which are darker than females but have no bright colours except sometimes for orange around the caudal

spot. This **darter** is very variable in characters over its wide range. Reaches 17.8 cm.

Biology: This species has the widest distribution of any **darter** and is found in streams, rivers and lakes over a variety of bottoms. It may even be found buried in sand with only the eyes showing. Reported down to 40 m in Lake Erie.

Food includes aquatic insects and crustaceans revealed when stones and debris are overturned by the snout. Logperch also eat fish eggs and non-spawning males are fond of eggs of their more successful siblings.

Maximum age is about 4 years. Spawning occurs in June when males move into sandy shallows of lakes in schools of up to several hundred fish or into streams with shallow rapids. Females swim through this school, and if one stops on the sand, a male will settle on her back, clasping with his pelvic fins and depressing his caudal fin alongside hers. Both fish quiver and eggs are fertilised in a cloud of sand which coats the eggs. The eggs are not guarded and males do not defend a territory. In streams males have a moving territory around a female as she swims onto the spawning bed. Both lake and stream spawning behaviours of logperch are very primitive among **darters**. About 10–20 colourless eggs are released each time and the female may spawn with several males. Eggs are 1.3 mm in diameter and number up to 3085 in large females. Young logperch are poorly developed in contrast to other darters and must drift from flowing to still waters where suitable small plankton is available as prey. Other darters can start feeding immediately on small insects.

Logperch thrive in an aquarium and are used as bait fish in Canada.

longear eelpout

Scientific name: *Lycodes seminudus*
Reinhardt, 1837
Family: **Eelpout**
Other common names: none
French name: lycode à oreilles

Distribution: Found in the Canadian Beaufort Sea and off Ellesmere Island. Also in the northern North Atlantic, Barents Sea and Kara Sea.

Characters: This species is separated from its Canadian Arctic-Atlantic relatives by having small pelvic fins, a mouth under the snout,

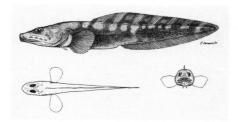

longear eelpout

no large pores around the mouth, crests on the chin, lateral line single and on midflank, tail short (preanal distance in the range 48–52% of total length), scales are present only on the flank posterior to the pectoral fin tip, usually a dusky peritoneum, and a gill opening reaching below the pectoral fin base. Dorsal fin rays 91–97, anal rays 73–78 (each including half the continuous caudal fin rays). Pectoral fin rays 19–22. Vertebrae 96–98. Overall colour a light grey-brown with belly darker than rest of body. There are usually 4–8 light bars on the flank and dorsal fin. Scales are lighter than the background. Pectoral fin dark with light edge. Reaches 51.7 cm.

Biology: This species has been caught at 335–610 m and temperatures of -0.6 to 0.3°C in Canada on mud and clay bottoms. Elsewhere reported at 130–1400 m. Food is worms, crustaceans and fishes. Reproduction is in June with about 300 demersal eggs up to 8.2 mm diameter being laid.

longear sunfish

Scientific name: *Lepomis megalotis*
　　(Rafinesque, 1820)
Family: **Sunfish**
Other common names: northern longear,
　　Great Lakes longear, big-eared sunfish,
　　red-bellied bream, blue and orange sunfish,
　　cherry bream, bloody sunfish, red perch,
　　blackears, creek sunfish, redeyed sunfish,
　　brilliant sunfish, tobaccobox
French name: crapet à longues oreilles

Distribution: Found from the upper St. Lawrence River basin in Québec and Ontario, the Ottawa River basin in Québec, tributaries of lakes St. Clair, Huron and Georgian Bay, and west of Lake Superior in Ontario. Recently reported from southeast Manitoba. In the U.S.A. south to northeast Mexico west of the Appalachian Mountains, east to western Florida. Also introduced outside native range.

Characters: This species is distinguished by having 10–11 dorsal fin spines, 3 anal fin spines, 33–46 lateral line scales, with 4–6 in a row between the lateral line and dorsal fin origin, and the black opercular or "ear" flap has a pale red, yellow or white margin and is elongate. The bony margin of the flap is crenate. Soft dorsal fin rays 10–12 and soft anal rays 9–12. Pectoral fin rays 10–15.

The back and upper flank are olive, blue-green to reddish-brown, flanks have 8–10 bars variably developed but most evident in young, and have yellow, orange or blue-green spots on an olive or rusty background. Cheeks are orange, the sides of the head have horizontal wavy blue-green streaks on an orange background, and the breast and belly are red, orange or yellow. Most fins are brown to orange, dark at their bases. Pectoral fins are clear to dusky. Breeding males have an overall reddish head and body with blue to blue-green streaks on the head and spots on the body dorsally. Pelvic fins are black in breeding males and dorsal and anal fin membranes have reddish-brown speckles and the iris is red to orange.

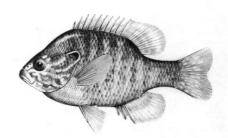

longear sunfish

Reaches 23.6 cm. The world, all-tackle angling record weighed 0.79 kg and was caught in Elephant Butte Lake, New Mexico in 1985.

Biology: Longears are found in shallow, pooled waters of rivers, and in ponds and lakes where there is vegetation They survive temperatures up to 37.8°C but are intolerant of silt.

Food includes terrestrial and aquatic insects, crustaceans and other invertebrates such as snails as well as small fishes and fish eggs. "Coughing" serves to eject excess gravel from the mouth after eating eggs.

Life span is about 10 years with maturity attained at 1–4 years, males probably a year earlier than females. Northern populations, such as those in Canada, are smaller in body size than southern populations. Growth in rivers is slower than in lakes.

Spawning occurs from late May to August in northern waters at water temperatures over 22°C. The male excavates a shallow, rounded nest in gravel, sand or mud in faster water with less vegetation than **pumpkinseeds**. Nests are excavated with lateral tail sweeps. Nests are up to 46 cm across and found in colonies of 5–13 in the shallows. Nest colonies are a result perhaps of the limited availability of preferred habit but experimental evidence in the laboratory suggests the social attraction between members of the same species is more important. The nesting cycle lasts about 2 weeks and eggs hatch in 1 week. The male defends the nest, eggs and the young, principally against other longears. Nest intruders are mostly female longears intent on eating eggs or males trying to fertilise eggs. Male longears show contact injuries such as split dorsal fins and torn "ear flaps."

Courtship involves pairs swimming in circles until the male comes to rest over the nest with the female inclined at about 45° so their genital regions are in contact, the pair vibrates and 7–20 eggs are shed and fertilised. The male grunts during courtship and may spawn more than once. The amber to yellow eggs sink and adhere to the bottom. Eggs are 1.0 mm in diameter and number up to 22,119 per female although the total spawned may only be up to 4213. Several females may spawn in one nest. The male fans the eggs first in a normal position using his paired fins but then stands on his tail. The first fanning method is thought to mix eggs and sperm while the sec-

ond pushes the fertilised eggs deep into the gravel for protection from predators.

Hybrids with **pumpkinseeds**, which have an overlapping but generally earlier spawning season, are found in Ontario. Ripe but small female **pumpkinseeds** approach male longears late in their season when male **pumpkinseeds** are no longer defending nests and when favoured small male **pumpkinseeds** are unavailable. This may be the source of hybrids. Hybrids may result from sperm drifting from one species' nest to the others.

The flesh is white, flaky and good eating. Anglers catch this species on live baits, flies and spinners. The Committee on the Status of Endangered Wildlife in Canada believes this species is not in jeopardy in Canada.

longfin armorhead

Scientific name: *Pseudopentaceros pectoralis* Hardy, 1983
Family: **Armorhead**
Other common names: none
French name: tête-casquée à longues nageoires

Distribution: Found at Ocean Station Papa (50°N, 145°W), a Canadian weathership, and within Canadian territorial limits off the coast of British Columbia. Also found from Hawaii to the Aleutian Islands and along the Pacific coast to California.

Characters: The head bones are not covered in skin but exposed and striated with radiating lines. The body is deeper than in related species. Dorsal fin spines 14, soft rays 8–9. The spiny dorsal fin is better developed than the soft-rayed part and can be folded down into a groove. Anal fin spines 3–4, soft rays 6–8. The pectoral fin has 16–19 rays and is exceptionally long. There are 65–77 scales

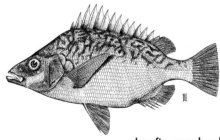

longfin armorhead

in the lateral line. Scales on the midline from throat to pelvic fin base 22–29. Back and fins dark, flanks silvery with slight mottling. Young have irregular dark blotches on the flanks. Reaches 42.5 cm.

Biology: An offshore species of colder waters from the surface to at least 201 m. It may feed at night on moving food.

longfin dragonfish

Scientific name: *Tactostoma macropus*
    Bolin, 1939
Family: **Barbeled Dragonfish**
Other common names: arrowfish, arrow
    dragonfish
French name: dragon à longues nageoires

Distribution: Found from Japan and Alaska to California including off all the British Columbia coast and at Ocean Station Papa (50°N, 145°W).

Characters: This species is distinguished from its Canadian Pacific coast relatives, the **highfin dragonfish** and the **pitgum lantern-**

longfin dragonfish

fish, by its lack of pectoral fins, very short barbel and the pelvic fins being low on the body. The body is particularly elongate. The lower jaw projects and curves upwards. Fang-like and minute teeth are found in the mouth. Teeth are also present on the tongue. Dorsal fin rays 14–17, anal rays 19–22, pelvic rays 8–10. The belly photophore rows number about 66 above and about 57 below, joining near the tail with about 12–17 photophores. There is a large suborbital photophore, luminous patches around the eye and on the operculum and small photophores between each pair of branchiostegal rays. Overall colour is jet black with some grey on the rear part of the lower jaw. The outer skin is often lost in captured specimens and the colour is then a lead-grey. Reaches 34.3 cm.

Biology: Found from 500 to 1000 m at Ocean Station Papa. Captures elsewhere have been made from 31–1830 m.

longfin gunnel

Scientific name: *Pholis clemensi*
    Rosenblatt, 1964
Family: **Gunnel**
Other common names: none
French name: sigouine à longue nageoire

Distribution: From northern California to Alaska including the coast of British Columbia.

Characters: Distinguished from other Pacific coast gunnels with pelvic fins by having 87–92 dorsal fin spines and 48–53

longfin gunnel

anal fin rays preceded by 2 spines. The relatively large pectoral fins have 11–14 rays. Colour is magenta to silver overall, but can be very pale. There are about 13–15 lighter areas along the base of the dorsal fin forming saddles, each enclosing some dark spots. The flanks have patches of lighter colour and are mottled with faint spots which may form a series of chain-like markings. A silver bar with dark borders runs back from the eye. Attains 14.0 cm. This species is named for Dr. W.A. Clemens, a Canadian zoologist.

Biology: Found in water 7–64 m deep associated with rocks and algae but also over sand bottoms. They may be seen by divers on rock surfaces but soon hide in crevices if disturbed. An adult has been found wrapped around a circular clutch of white eggs in a chimney sponge. It may be a cleaner fish, picking parasites off other fishes.

longfin hake

Scientific name: *Urophycis chesteri*
    (Goode and Bean, 1878)
Family: **Cod**
Other common names: none
French name: merluche à longues nageoires

Distribution: Found from the mid-Labrador Shelf south to the Straits of Florida.

Characters: This species and its relatives, the **red, spotted** and **white hakes,** are distinguished from other Arctic-Atlantic **cods** by having 2 dorsal and 1 anal fin, no snout barbels, pelvic fins with only 2, long, filamen-

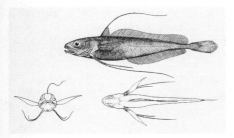

longfin hake

tous rays, and no canine teeth on the lower jaw and vomer bone in the roof of the mouth. Longfin hake are distinguished from their relatives by the first pelvic fin filament reaching almost as far as the end of the anal fin. First dorsal fin rays 8–11, the third 5 times as long as any other ray, second dorsal rays 50–63. Anal fin rays 43–56 and pectoral rays 14–17. Lateral scales 90–91. The barbel is long and the anal fin margin is slightly concave. There are 4–5 upper gill rakers. The back and upper flank olive-brown to olive fading to a silvery-white on the belly. Fins similar to adjacent body colour but margins are dusky to black. Caudal fin dark. Reaches 42 cm.

Biology: This species is restricted to deep water at 160–1290 m, most commonly at 300–450 m and 3.5–6.5°C in Canadian waters and deeper in the warmer U.S.A. Overall temperature range is 1.6–12.0°C. It is mainly caught along the edge of the continental shelf or in deep fjords such as one near the southern coast of Newfoundland. It is sedentary on the bottom or swims several centimetres above the bottom. Larger, older fish tend to be found in deeper water than young fish. Food is mostly crustaceans but large longfin hake may take **lanternfishes, bristlemouths** and **silver hatchetfishes.** They are eaten by **white hake** and probably **Atlantic cod**. Females are larger than males and maturity is attained at 22.4 cm for males and 29.2 cm for females in the U.S.A. Spawning is reported for Canadian waters in October and may peak in winter. Off Virginia spawning occurs from late September to April. Eggs are

pelagic, number up to 1,305,700 and have a diameter of 0.8 mm. Young remain pelagic through winter and spring and descend to the bottom at 13.6 cm after some time in midwater. The flesh is soft and this species has limited commercial importance. It is a by-catch of bottom trawling for other species and is usually processed as fish meal and for oil.

longfin halosaur

Scientific name: *Halosauropsis macrochir*
(Günther, 1878)
Family: **Halosaur**
Other common names: none
French name: halosaure à longues nageoires

Distribution: Found off the Atlantic coast of Canada and in the Atlantic, Pacific and Indian oceans outside the tropics.

Characters: This species is distinguished from its relative, the **bald halosaur**, by having a broad, black stripe along the lateral line and unpigmented pyloric caeca. Dorsal fin rays 10–13, anal rays about 158–194, pectoral fin with 10–14 rays and pelvic with 8–10. The pectoral fin is long, reaching the dorsal fin. There are 25–32 scales anterior to the anus. The opercle bears scales. There is a row of organs on top of the head which may be taste buds. Pyloric caeca number 7–13 in a double row and are creamy white. The body is a grey to bluish-black with the top of the head, branchiostegal membranes and gill isthmus black. The mouth is blue-grey. The peritoneum is brown. Reaches about 90 cm, the largest **halosaur.**

longfin halosaur

Biology: A single specimen was recorded for Canada from Carson Canyon at the southeast Grand Bank in 1985 at 2215 m. Elsewhere depth range is 1100–3200 m at 2–4°C. This fish is not uncommon and in the western Atlantic has been observed from the submersible ALVIN to number 2.37 fish per thousand square metres. This species rests on the bottom or swims just above it. The long pectoral fins are held high and directed forward and may have a sensory function. The tail is curled up and undulations of the tail region keep the fish in a head-down position for feeding. It can swim backwards. Food is crustaceans, molluscs, worms and starfishes. Bottom sediment is also found in stomach contents, presumably taken in with food items. Females outnumber males by 2 to 1.

longfin lanternfish

Scientific name: *Diogenichthys atlanticus* (Tåning, 1928)
Family: **Lanternfish**
Other common names: none
French name: lanterne à longues nageoires

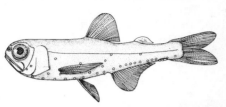

longfin lanternfish

Distribution: Found in the Pacific, Indian and Atlantic oceans and off the Scotian Shelf and Grand Bank in Canada.

Characters: This species is separated from its Atlantic coast relatives by having no photophores near the dorsal body edge, the PLO photophore is obviously above the upper pectoral fin base, the second PVO photophore is below the upper pectoral fin base and the PVO series is horizontal, 2 Prc photophores are present with the second slightly higher than the first, premaxillary teeth are lanceolate, flattened and often bear a denticle on each side at the widest point, and the anterior, outer dentary teeth are flattened while the posterior ones are hooked forward. Males have a large supracaudal luminous gland first appearing at 1.5 cm and females have 2–4 patches in an infracaudal gland which appears at 1.6 cm. The Dn photophore of males is larger than that of females. Dorsal fin rays 10–12, anal rays 14–18 and pectoral rays 10–14. Total gill rakers 12–15. AO photophores 8–11. Vertebrae 31–34. Reaches 2.9 cm.

Biology: First reported for Canada in 1988. Off Bermuda it is caught at 25–1250 m by day, mostly at 600–650 m, and at 18–1050 m at night, mostly at 50–100 m and 850–900 m. Sexual maturity is attained at about 2.2 cm. Spawning occurs year round but peaks in spring and fall near Bermuda. Life span is only about 1 year.

longfin mako

Scientific name: *Isurus paucus* Guitart Manday, 1966
Family: **Mackerel Shark**
Other common names: taupe longue aile
French name: petit requin-taupe

Distribution: Reported from the Tail of the Grand Bank in Atlantic Canada and along the outer coast of Nova Scotia to Georges Bank. Probably world-wide in tropical to temperate seas.

Characters: This species is very similar to the **shortfin mako** but has a longer pectoral fin (equal to pectoral fin base to snout tip distance) and the belly is dark blue to blackish with only a small part white. The snout is more blunt than in the **shortfin mako** and the cusps of anterior teeth in both jaws are

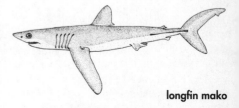

longfin mako

straight, not curved. The caudal peduncle has strong keels. The eye is large. The back and upper flank are dark blue to blue-black. The belly is dark. The undersides of the snout and mouth are dusky or blue-black. Reaches 4.17 m.

Biology: This species is usually found below the thermocline and so is not as visible as other sharks. It will approach the surface at night. This species is said to be slower and less active than the **shortfin mako**. Food is fish and squid. This species is adult at 2.45 m. Young are about 92–97 cm before birth. There is uterine cannibalism and litters number 2. This is a poorly known

---

species only recently distinguished from the **shortfin mako**. It is fished for off Cuba for animal feed and fish meal.

longfin pearleye

Scientific name: *Benthalbella linguidens*
  (Mead and Böhlke, 1953)
Family: **Pearleye**
Other common names: none
French name: oeil-perlé à longues nageoires

Distribution: From northern Japan to Oregon including off British Columbia at Ocean Station Papa (50°N, 145°W).

Characters: This pearleye is separated from its Pacific relative, the **northern pearleye**, by higher fin rays counts. In addition

longfin pearleye

the adipose fin is over the anal fin. Dorsal fin rays 7–10, usually 9, anal rays 28–30 and pectoral rays 24–27. Lateral line scales about 66. Short, sharp spines precede the caudal fin on the upper and lower caudal peduncle. Overall colour is a dull brown with scale pockets outlined slightly with pigment. Fins heavily pigmented. Adipose fin a creamy yellow at the base in preserved fish. Peritoneum black. Attains 30.2 cm.

Biology: First reported for Canada in 1981. A poorly known species apparently found in the upper levels of the ocean, some within a few metres of the surface.

longfin sawpalate

Scientific name: *Serrivomer parabeani*
  Bertin, 1940
Family: **Sawpalate**
Other common names: thread eel
French name: serrivomer à nageoire longue

Distribution: Found in Atlantic, Indian and possibly the Pacific oceans and from waters off Labrador and in Davis Strait.

Characters: This species may not be distinct from the **stout sawpalate**. It was characterised by the first branchiostegal ray not

possessing a process projecting beyond the hyoid arch. **Stout sawpalates** sometimes have the process on one side of the head, but

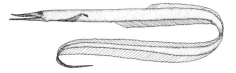

longfin sawpalate

not the other, suggesting this character is individually variable. Other characters do not differ between the 2 species.

Biology: Found from 150–3000 m, and even as deep as 4500 m. In Canada reported at 800–1120 m.

longfin sculpin

Scientific name: *Jordania zonope*
  Starks, 1895
Family: **Sculpin**
Other common names: bandeye sculpin
French name: chabot à longues nageoires

Distribution: Found from southern Alaska and British Columbia south to California.

Characters: This sculpin is separated from its Canadian Pacific relatives by the high first dorsal fin spine count of 17–18. There is a long, recurved nasal spine and 2 preopercular spines with the lower one strongest and directed upward. The second dorsal fin has 15–18 soft rays and the anal fin 22–24 rays with the last 4 elongated and finger-like. Pectoral fin rays 13–15 with lower 6 finger-like and pelvic fin with 1 spine and 4–5 soft

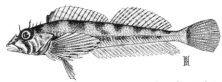

longfin sculpin

rays. Ctenoid scales cover the body above the lateral line with some fused together while below the lateral line scales are fused into serrated ridges sloping obliquely back and down. Lateral line with 48–51 rows. There are 2 small cirri on either side of each nasal spine, large, jet-black cirri over the front and rear of the eye and 3 long cirri behind the eye on top of the head. Overall colour is olive-green to orange-tan with red markings. The back has 6–8 saddles and the flank a series of dark spots. The side of the head and eye have light, yellow, wavy bands. The dorsal and pectoral fins have dark bands with membranes dark and rays lighter. The dorsal fin may be reddish. The caudal fin is bright orange and the pelvic fins are dusky. The base of the pectoral fin has a strong yellow blotch in some fish. The eye rim is red. Breeding adults darken in colour. Reaches 15 cm.

Biology: Longfin sculpins often cling to rock faces at depths of 2–38 m and are common in British Columbia. This species is also reported to hang upside down in caverns. Some may be captured among seaweeds where the red bands blend with red algae to conceal this sculpin. They maintain territories of up to 0.5 sq m and are aggressive. Food is gammarid crustaceans, shrimps and worms and this sculpin is eaten by **smoothhead sculpins**. Preferred prey is copepods but these are not abundant in fall and a new feeding method is employed. The longfin sculpin tends to take bites out of prey items such as sedentary worms, barnacles and hydroid colonies but also mobile crustaceans. Prey is searched for visually, "walked" towards using the pelvic and pectoral fins and then bitten after a sudden burst of speed once within striking distance. Spawning occurs in October and 20–30 eggs are laid in each of several clusters. Eggs are guarded by the female.

longfin smelt

Scientific name: *Spirinchus thaleichthys*
    (Ayres, 1860)
Family: **Smelt**
Other common names: Sacramento smelt,
    Pacific smelt, Puget Sound smelt
French name: éperlan d'hiver

Distribution: Found from the Gulf of Alaska to California including British Columbia.

Characters: This species and its relative, the **night smelt**, are distinguished from other smelts by having 8–14 upper arch and 24–32 lower arch gill rakers, medium conical to large

canine teeth on the tongue, 4–8 pyloric caeca, and minute pointed teeth across the vomer bone on the roof of the mouth. This species is difficult to distinguish from its relative. It has a longer pectoral fin (84% or more of distance to pelvic insertion), 54–63 scales along flank with 14–21 pores, a blunt snout, and the length of the longest anal fin ray enters 1.4–2.2 times in head length. Mouth large, extending to rear or beyond of eye. Dorsal fin rays 8–10, perhaps as few as 6, anal rays 15–22 and pectoral rays 10–12. Total gill rakers 36–47. Breeding males develop enlarged first rays to the pectoral and pelvic fins and the dorsal and anal fins are enlarged. The lateral line protrudes because the underlying muscles swell, a shelf develops at the anal base and tubercles appear on the scales and paired fins. The back is olive-brown and the flank and belly are silvery-white. Breeding males are darker with scales outlined by pigment and the back a rich dark green. Peritoneum silvery with some dark speckling. Attains 20.0 cm.

longfin smelt

Biology: This smelt is found inshore down to 137 m in the sea and is occasionally caught in shrimp trawlers. There is a landlocked population in Harrison Lake, B.C. which is smaller than marine populations. The only other freshwater population is in Lake Washington, Washington. Female fish at 3 years in Harrison Lake may carry up to 2425 eggs. Males precede females on the spawning run. Longfin smelt are mature at 2 years and live 3 years. Spawning occurs from October to December in the lower reaches of streams. Each female may produce up to 23,634 adhesive eggs of 1.2 mm diameter. Food is crustaceans in both marine and freshwater populations. This species is said to be good eating but is not common enough in Canada to be used commercially.

longfin snailfish

Scientific name: *Careproctus longipinnis*
Burke, 1912
Family: **Snailfish**
Other common names: none
French name: limace à longues nageoires

Distribution: Found from Labrador to Nova Scotia. Also in the northeastern Atlantic Ocean.

Characters: This snailfish is separated from its Atlantic coast relatives in Canada by having a small adhesive disc, 1 pair of nos-

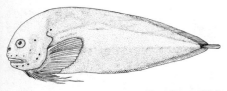

longfin snailfish

trils, lower pectoral fin lobe rays longer than head, and a deep body, equal to or greater than head length. Dorsal fin rays 51–55, anal rays 44–49 and pectoral rays 30–31. The gill slit is above the pectoral fin. Overall colour is reddish or white. Reaches 27 cm. This may be the same species as the **sea tadpole**.

Biology: Found on sand or mud bottoms at 500–800 m feeding on amphipods and other crustaceans.

longhead dab

Scientific name: *Pleuronectes proboscideus*
(Gilbert, 1896)
Family: **Righteye Flounder**
Other common names: none
French name: limande carline

Distribution: Found from the Sea of Okhotsk and Bering Sea to Bathurst Inlet, N.W.T.

Characters: This Arctic species is characterised by a small, almost symmetrical mouth, a lateral line with a steep bend over the pectoral fin and a long, pointed head. Dorsal fin rays 62–74, anal rays 46–53 and pectoral rays 9–13. Lateral line scales 73–95. Gill rakers 9–11 on the lower arch. The margin of the head above the eye is strongly concave and there is a rough crest behind the

eye. Eyed side a light, greyish or olive-brown with speckles. Blind side bright yellow. Attains 41 cm.

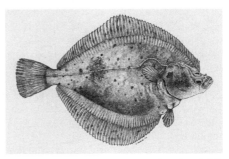

longhead dab

Biology: Found at 10–125 m. Not commercially important and little is known of its biology.

longhorn sculpin

Scientific name: *Myoxocephalus octodecemspinosus* (Mitchill, 1814)
Family: **Sculpin**
Other common names: long-spined sculpin, toadfish, bullhead, hacklehead, common sculpin, gray sculpin
French name: chaboisseau à dix-huit épines

Distribution: Found from the Strait of Belle Isle south to Virginia including Banquereau and Sable Island banks.

Characters: This species and its Arctic-Atlantic relatives are distinguished from other sculpins by the upper preopercular spine being a simple straight point, the vomer bone in the roof of the mouth bears

longhorn sculpin

teeth but palatine teeth are absent, there are no oblique folds on the lower flank, and the lateral line lacks strong plates. It is separated from its relatives by having 3 preopercular spines (1 pointing forward to downward, 2 pointing backward) and the uppermost spine is about 4 times longer than the one below. First dorsal fin spines 7–10, second dorsal rays 15–17. Anal rays 12–15 and pectoral rays 16–19. The lateral line has weak plates. Overall colour is dark olive-grey, greenish-brown or greenish-yellow fading to a white belly. The flanks are blotched and may have 3–4 irregular bars. The first dorsal fin is dusky, the second dorsal fin has 3–4 bars and there are bars on the caudal, anal and pectoral fins. The anal fin is a pale yellowish colour. Reaches 45.7 cm.

Biology: Longhorn sculpins are shallow water residents in spring and summer and retreat to deeper water in winter, down to 127 m. The winter migration avoids very low temperatures and this species lacks a blood anti-freeze found in some other **sculpins** such as the **grubby**. It is found at a wide range of temperatures. Food is crustaceans, molluscs, squids, sea squirts, and small fishes such as **herrings, scups, mackerels, puffers, smelts, menhadens, sand lances, mummichogs, cods** and **silversides**. It also scavenges in harbour areas. This sculpin may be seen sat on the sea bottom with its mouth gaping. Sexual maturity is attained in the third year of life and life span is 9 years. Spawning takes place in winter from December to January. Eggs are adhesive and are laid in masses on sponges and in depressions on hard surfaces. The eggs are up to 2.3 mm in diameter, number as many as 8000 and can be green, orange, brown or red. This sculpin has been used for fish meal, oil and in pet food in Canada.

longjaw cisco

Scientific name: *Coregonus alpenae*
(Koelz, 1924)
Family: **Salmon**
Other common names: longjaw chub
French name: cisco à grande bouche

Distribution: Found in lakes Huron, Michigan and rarely in Erie.

Characters: This **cisco** is distinguished from other **salmons** by having 68–96 lateral line scales, a strongly forked tail, no parr marks, 2 skin flaps between the nostrils,

mouth terminal and lower jaw usually projecting, and 30–46 gill rakers. Characters among **ciscoes** (q.v.) overlap and so the species cannot be easily separated. Dorsal fin rays 9–13, anal rays 9–14, pectoral rays 12–18 and pelvic rays 10–13. Males developed nuptial breeding tubercles. Overall colour was silvery with iridescent pink or purple on the upper flank. The back was green to bluish and the belly was white. Fins and jaws were weakly pigmented. Reached 54.6 cm and 1.86 kg. This species may be the same as the **shortjaw cisco**.

longjaw cisco

Biology: This species in now considered to be extinct in Canada, a status approved by the Committee on the Status of Endangered Wildlife in Canada in 1988. It was last reported from Lake Michigan in 1968 and Georgian Bay in 1975. Overfishing and the depredations of the introduced **sea lamprey** led to its demise. Hybridisation may also have effectively removed populations with characters of longjaw ciscoes. The ecology of the Great Lakes changed by removal of predators such as **lake trout** and **burbot** by the **sea lamprey**, pollution, and fishing out of some stocks. Some **ciscoes** became more widespread and genetically swamped once isolated species. The recorded depth range was 5.5–183 m. Food included crustaceans such as the opossum shrimp and some bottom organisms such as aquatic insects and small clams. This cisco was eaten by **lake trout** and **burbot**. Sexual maturity was attained at 3–4 years and life span was 9 years or more. Spawning occurred in October to November in fairly shallow water at 18–46 m. Development occurred over winter and the eggs hatched in spring. A large female could lay an estimated 20,000 eggs. This species was commercially important under the name chub and was sold smoked. It was caught with gill nets at about 30–100 m. As the population decreased so was the legal net mesh size so that younger fish were caught and the population was depleted further.

longnose chimaera

Scientific name: *Harriotta raleighana*
Goode and Bean, 1895
Family: **Longnose Chimaera**
Other common names: bentnose rabbitfish,
chimère à nez rigide
French name: chimère-spatule

Distribution: Found in the Atlantic and Pacific oceans including off southwestern Nova Scotia and south to Chesapeake Bay.

Characters: This chimaera is distinguished from other Atlantic Canadian species by the long snout, the arched head profile, mouth below the eyes, tooth plates broad, blunt edged, knobbed and ridged, and a serrate, straight dorsal fin spine. The snout is curved up at the tip. The caudal fin ends in a long filament, sometimes lost. Pectoral fin short but reaching the origin of the pelvic fins, and broad. Adults have tubercles on the snout. Males lack denticles on the caudal fin. The head clasper is small. Overall colour is chocolate brown with fins lighter but edged in dark brown. Pelvic fins are blackish. The iris is a pale green. Females have pale areas. Attains 1.2 m.

longnose chimaera

Biology: Found at depths of 360 to 2603 m. In Canada, not uncommon on the continental slope off Nova Scotia including Georges Bank. A poorly-known species. Females reach larger sizes than males. Food is invertebrates and fishes. Fertilisation is internal. Females have been reported with copulation scars. The spindle-shaped egg capsule is brown to almost black, has amber, ribbed flanges on each side and is 16.5 cm

long. Young hatch in summer. Catches of this species in Canada are incidental to other fisheries but have been used as fish meal.

Longnose Chimaera Family

Scientific name: Rhinochimaeridae
French name: chimères à long nez

Longnose chimaeras or rabbitfishes are found in the Atlantic and Pacific oceans and the southern Arctic. There are 6 species with 2 reported from Canada's Atlantic coast and 1 from immediately neighbouring Arctic and Atlantic waters.

These fishes are distinguished by a long and pointed snout, a diphycercal tail (internally and externally symmetrical), 2 dorsal fins, the first having an erectile, venomous spine, the second being longer, lower and not erectile, an inferior mouth, and eggs deposited in a horny, spindle-shaped capsule. Water is breathed in mainly through the large nostrils in front of the mouth. Unlike the related **sharks**, there is a fleshy gill cover over 4 gill openings, no spiracle, usually naked skin and males have a clasping organ on the head and clasping organs in front of the pelvic fins, as well as simple rod-like pelvic claspers.

Longnose chimaeras are relatives of the **Chimaera Family** (and have been classified with them as one family) and are in the **Chimaera Order**. They are characterised by a few large tooth plates used for grinding food, 2 pairs in the upper jaw and 1 pair below.

These fishes have been used for fish meal and oil when caught incidental to other fishes. They swim poorly and feed on various invertebrates and fishes. Longnose chimaeras are usually found in deeper waters down to over 2600 m. The head clasper is used to hold the female's pectoral fin during mating. Only 2 egg capsules are laid, 1 from each ovary. The long snout is covered with chemical and electrical sensory organs and may be used to detect prey or mates.

See **Haeckel's chimaera**
knifenose chimaera
longnose chimaera

longnose dace

Scientific name: *Rhinichthys cataractae*
(Valenciennes in Cuvier and Valenciennes, 1842)

Family: **Carp**
Other common names: Great Lakes longnose
dace, stream shooter
French name: naseux de rapides

Distribution: Found from Labrador and
the upper St. Lawrence River basin north to
Hudson Bay, west through the Great Lakes,
to British Columbia and north in the
Mackenzie River basin. Absent from northern Manitoba, Saskatchewan and northwestern Alberta and to the north. In the south it
reaches Virginia east of the Appalachians,
Iowa to the west and in a long western arm
extends into Mexico.

Characters: This species is distinguished
by the premaxillaries not being protractile (no
groove between the upper lip and snout), a

longnose dace

barbel at each mouth corner and an elongate
snout projecting beyond the ventral mouth.
Dorsal fin branched rays 7, anal fin branched
rays 6, pectoral rays 12–17 and pelvic rays
7–9. Lateral line scales 55–76. Pharyngeal
teeth hooked, 2,4–4,2, 1,4–4,1 or 1,4–4,0.
Breeding males have nuptial tubercles on the
top of the head, posterior scale edges, and on
the pectoral, pelvic, anal and dorsal fins.

The back is olive-green to brown, grey or
black fading to a cream or whitish belly. The
lower flank and belly may be golden. Some
scales may be darkly pigmented and there
may be a dark stripe in front of the eye. The
lateral line is wholly or partially dark, or not
dissimilar from the background, varying with
locality. The origin of the dorsal fin and the
upper origin of the caudal fin are white to
cream. Fin rays are outlined by dark pigment.
Young fish have a dark stripe on the head and
body. Breeding males have orange-red mouth
corners, cheeks, pectoral fin axils and on the
pelvic fins and anterior anal fin base. Dorsal
and caudal fin membranes dull to dark red.
The back and upper flank are dark olive.

Peritoneum silvery with brown spots.

Hybrids are formed with **lake chub** and
redside shiners in Canada. Reaches 17.8 cm.
The species was described from fish collected at Niagara Falls, hence "*cataractae.*"

The longnose dace may comprise the type
subspecies east of the Rockies and another,
unnamed subspecies is in British Columbia
(see also **Nooky dace** and **Banff longnose
dace**). There are colour and behavioural differences between eastern and western longnose dace. The western form lacks the crimson red to orangish patches found in eastern
males and spawns at night.

Biology: Longnose dace are found in fast,
clear streams with gravel, rock, and boulder
beds. It can live in very fast water by taking
advantage of holes and crevices between
rocks. The swimbladder does not grow with
the fish so large specimens have relatively
small swimbladders, are less buoyant and are
able to hug the bottom. Fish which develop in
still water have larger swimbladders than
those in fast water. This affects the buoyancy
range that can be adjusted in response to
varying current speeds. Lake dwelling fish
adjust their swimbladder volume in response
to wave action.

Food is principally aquatic insects such as
blackflies, caddisflies, midges and mayflies
taken at night, an unusual feeding time for a
minnow. Some worms, terrestrial insects,
crustaceans, molluscs and fish eggs are also
eaten. Algae and diatoms may predominate in
some populations during the summer.
Smallmouth bass and **brook trout** are predators of this **dace**. During the day this **dace**
remains under stones, hiding from predators.

Life span is 5 years with sexual maturity
attained at 2 years, rarely at 1 year. Spawning
occurs from April to August at temperatures
over 11°C over riffles, and sometimes over
river chub nests. Males defend a territory up
to 20 cm across and butt or bite intruders.
When a female enters a male's territory he
vibrates rapidly for 0.5–2.0 seconds at
0.75–1.0 second intervals and pushes his
snout against rocks with his body sloping at
45–90°. The female responds by adopting the
same angle. The two fish come together and
push against the bottom, quiver for 1–2 sec-

onds and release eggs and sperm. Eggs are adhesive, transparent, 1.7 mm in diameter and number up to 9953 per female. Young are pelagic and live near shore in slow or still waters for about 4 months before settling to the bottom.

Used as a bait fish in the U.S.A. for **bass** and **catfish** but not in Canada to any marked extent.

longnose gar

Scientific name: *Lepisosteus osseus*
(Linnaeus, 1758)
Family: **Gar**
Other common names: garpike, northern
    longnose gar, billy gar, billfish,
    needlenose, northern mailed fish,
    pin-nose gar, bonypike, scissorbill
French name: lépisosté osseux

Distribution: Found in the Mississippi River, Great Lakes and southern Atlantic coastal basins, absent from the eastern American mountains. In Canada from the St. Lawrence River basin, the Great Lakes, but rare in Lake Superior, across southern Ontario.

Characters: This species is distinguished from its relative, the **spotted gar**, by the long, narrow snout 14–18 times longer than minimum width, 57–66 lateral line scales and spots only on the body from the pelvic fins to the caudal peduncle and on the dorsal, anal and caudal fins. Gill rakers 14–31. Dorsal fin rays 6–9, anal rays 7–10, pectoral rays 10–13 and 6 pelvic rays. Young fish have dorsal and ventral filaments on the caudal fin. The swimming young fish appears to be moved by a propeller as these filaments vibrate rapidly.

longnose gar

Adults are grey or olive-brown to dark green fading to pale green or silver on the flanks and white on the belly. Colour is variable with habitat. Flank scales often outlined in black. The dorsal, anal and caudal fins are pale brown to yellow and spotted. Pectoral and pelvic fins are dusky without spots. Young have a narrow reddish-brown or black stripe on the back, and one on the midflank which has a wavy upper edge. Above the flank band they are brown to black, below brown with white or cream areas.

Reaches over 2 m. The world, all-tackle angling record weighed 22.82 kg and came from the Trinity River, Texas in 1954, but this may have been a distinct undescribed species. The Canadian angling record in 1993 from the Ottawa River, Ontario was caught by Ed Lalonde and weighed 6.31 kg.

Biology: This freshwater species occasionally enters brackish water and has been caught in the St. Lawrence River estuary at Ste-Anne-de-la-Pocatière in 1926 and 1945 at a salinity range of 13–20‰ at the surface and 25‰ at the bottom (sea water = 35‰). It is usually found in quiet, weedy shallows of lakes and larger rivers and, because of its air-breathing ability, enters hot stagnant waters to feed where other predators could not survive. Gars can be seen in summer hovering motionless at the surface although they dive rapidly out of sight if disturbed.

Food is all fishes of suitable size, frogs, crayfish and even small aquatic mammals. Prey is seized by a sideways slash of the snout after a dart or drift from cover. The prey, impaled on the teeth, is manoeuvred so that is can be swallowed head first.

Maximum age is 17 years for males and more than 30 years for females. Females grow faster and the sex ratio of males to females changes from about 262 to 100 in early life to only 8 males per 100 females after age 10.

Spawning occurs in spring and summer at 20°C or warmer in weedy shallows. The female is approached by up to 15 males which she leads in an elliptical path. The males nudge the female's belly area with their snouts while oriented head down. Males and female quiver and eggs and sperm are released. The eggs are scattered and attach to vegetation. The eggs are dark green, perhaps as camouflage, and measure 3.2 mm in diameter. The number of eggs may be as high as 77,156.

Eggs are poisonous and can kill smaller mammals. In Ontario gar eggs have been found in the nests of **smallmouth bass** and such nests had a higher success rate than nests with only bass eggs. Whether gar are deliberately spawning over bass nests is uncertain, they may merely be in the same area. However they do gain an advantage because the bass defends the nest against predators. Curiously, gar eggs are eaten by other fish despite being poisonous to mammals. The bass may benefit by having larger gar eggs and larvae in the nest to distract predators from the smaller bass eggs and larvae. Also more eggs and larvae of whatever species lessens the chance of individual loss to a single predatory attempt. Conversely, the male bass has more eggs to guard and the larger gar eggs are more attractive to predators, but on balance both fish species benefit.

The young gar have an adhesive pad on the snout tip which attaches them to weeds. After about 9 weeks the yolk-sac is absorbed, the gar no longer hangs vertically from vegetation and is free-swimming. They grow very rapidly, as much as 3.9 mm a day, much faster than most other Canadian freshwater fishes.

Gar are considered a pest because they eat other fishes and are often killed by fishermen.

longnose greeneye

Scientific name: *Parasudis truculenta*
(Goode and Bean, 1896)
Family: **Greeneye**
Other common names: none
French name: oeil-vert à long nez

Distribution: Found from Atlantic Canada south to Brazil.

Characters: This species is distinguished from its Canadian relatives by having large eyes, no greatly elongate fin rays and the anus separated from the pelvic fin bases by 8–10 scales. The snout is very long. Dorsal fin rays 10, anal rays 9, pectoral rays 14–16 and pelvic rays 9. Lateral line scales number 78–85. Overall colour is a light brown or yellowish tan with the dorsal fin tip blackish. The eye is an iridescent green in life. There are 3 saddles across the back in young fish. Attains 25 cm.

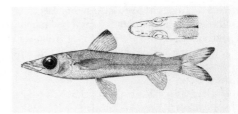

longnose greeneye

Biology: Reported from the southeast LaHave Bank and Sable Island Bank at depths of 154–440 m. Fairly common offshore from the U.S.A. over mud bottoms. It feeds in midwater, principally on **lanternfishes** and **bristlemouths**. The long thin stomach can be expanded to fill the whole abdominal cavity and fish up to one-third the size of this greeneye may be swallowed. Spawning probably occurs in spring in northern waters and this species is a hermaphrodite.

longnose grenadier

Scientific name: *Caelorinchus caelorhincus*
(Risso, 1810)
Family: **Grenadier**
Other common names: saddled grenadier, blackspot grenadier, hollowsnout grenadier, grenadier raton
French name: grenadier à long nez

Distribution: Found from the Grand Bank south to Brazil. Also in the eastern Atlantic Ocean.

Characters: This species is represented in Canada by the subspecies *C. caelorhincus carminatus* (Goode, 1880). It is distinguished

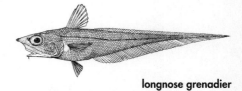

longnose grenadier

from other Canadian Atlantic coast grenadiers by having second dorsal fin rays shorter than anal fin rays, 6 branchiostegal rays, 7 pelvic fin rays and the first ray of the first dorsal fin not serrated. The first dorsal fin has 10–11 rays and the pectoral fin 17–20 rays. The scales have small oblique spines arranged in diverging rows. There is a large, black, scaleless area on the abdomen, the "window" for the light organ. Colour is brown to black with some purple tinges. The back bears 3 saddle marks, under the origins of the first dorsal and second dorsal fins with the third equally spaced behind the second. The gill and mouth cavities are black or dark grey. The first dorsal fin is usually dusky to blackish. Other fins are dusky except the pelvic which has black inner rays and the outer, elongate ray whitish. Reaches 43.0 cm.

Biology: First reported from Atlantic Canada in 1971. This species may occur in shallow waters, often less than 366 m, but is found in the range 89–849 m. Food is crustaceans, worms and snails. Life span is at least 16 years and females mature at about 26 cm. The spawning period is probably prolonged and in Europe may be most evident in September to November. It is common in by-catches in some areas and is used for fish meal and oil.

longnose hugo

Scientific name: *Hygophum benoiti*
(Cocco, 1838)
Family: **Lanternfish**
Other common names: none
French name: hugo à long nez

Distribution: Found in the North Atlantic Ocean, Mediterranean Sea and Gulf of Mexico. Off the Scotian Shelf in Atlantic Canada.

Characters: This species and its relatives, the **highvelo** and **upmouth hugos**, are distinguished from other Atlantic coast lanternfishes by having no photophores close to the dorsal body edge, the PLO photophore is well above the pectoral fin level, the second PVO photophore is below the upper end of the pectoral fin base, there are 2 Prc photophores, the PVO photophores are inclined, not horizontal, while the VO photophores are horizontal, and there are 2 Pol photophores. This species is separated from its relatives by the second Prc photophore being midway between the lateral line and the lower body edge. Dorsal fin rays 12–14, anal rays 19–21

and pectoral rays 13–15. Total gill rakers 17–20. AO photophores 11–13. Lateral line organs 36–37. Males have a supracaudal luminous gland outlined in black. Females have an infracaudal luminous gland with 2–4 elements which may be indistinct, and occasionally a weak supracaudal gland. Glands develop in males at 1.7–2.0 cm and in females at 2.4–2.5 cm. Reaches 5.5 cm.

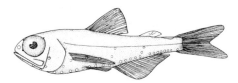

longnose hugo

Biology: First reported from Canada in 1919. Reported at 100–1050 m by day and by night from the surface to 1000 m, but depth abundance varies with locality and season. Migration rates average about 145–165 m/hour and the fish take about 3.0–3.5 hours to rise and to descend. Sexual maturity is reached at about 4.0–5.0 cm. Spawning peaks in March-May at Bermuda when most fish are 1 year old. Life span is a little more than 1 year.

longnose lancetfish

Scientific name: *Alepisaurus ferox*
Lowe, 1833
Family: **Lancetfish**
Other common names: Atlantic lancet fish, handsawfish, longsnout lancetfish
French name: cavalo féroce

Distribution: All major oceans including both Canadian coasts.

Characters: The high dorsal fin and slender body characterise a lancetfish. This species differs from the **shortnose lancetfish** by having the dorsal fin high in front with usually several free rays, and by having a long snout (a third to half of head length). The dorsal fin has 32–48 rays, the anal fin 13–18 and the pectoral fin 12–15. The back is dark and the sides pale and iridescent. A keel on the rear part of the flank is black and fins are brown to black. There are no spots on the dorsal fin. Attains 215 cm in length but only 6.8 kg in weight and so, although it is one of the largest deepsea predators, its thin body weighs comparatively little.

longnose lancetfish

Biology: This lancetfish is a fast swimmer and can be found from the surface including inshore down to 1280 m in Canadian waters, probably deeper elsewhere. It eats many kinds of fishes, as well as pelagic molluscs and worms, squids, tunicates and crustaceans. It is reported to be an hermaphrodite with both testicular and ovarian tissue developed at the same time. Lancetfish are eaten by **sharks**, **opahs**, **albacores** and **yellowfin tunas**. It is said to be good eating with sweet flesh.

longnose skate

Scientific name: *Raja rhina*
   (Jordan and Gilbert, 1880)
Family: **Skate**
Other common names: pocheteau noir
French name: pocheteau long-nez

   Distribution: Found from Alaska to Baja California including British Columbia.
   Characters: This species is distinguished from Canadian Pacific relatives by having a rigid snout with its cartilaginous support

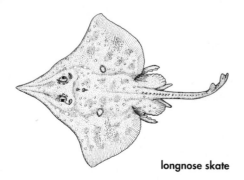

longnose skate

thick and stiff, cartilaginous supports of the pectoral fin do not reach the snout tip, no enlarged snout tip thornlets or scapular (= shoulder) spines, pelvic fins deeply notched, and no lateral tail thornlets. The snout is long and pointed. There are 1–2 middorsal spines behind the eyes and about 20 spines along the middle of the tail. The eyes have spines around their inner edge. The lower surface is smooth except for prickles on the snout and anterior disc margin in adults. Egg cases are 8–13 cm long by 5.7–7.6 cm wide. They contain only 1 embryo. The case surface is weakly striated. The horns are slender and short. The anterior margin is concave and the posterior edge is almost straight or convex. There are many attachment fibres along the edges. The upper disc surface is brown with a small, dark ring on each pectoral fin. A light spot may be present behind each ring. The lower surface is bluish, grey, black or light brown, with brown spots or flecks anteriorly. Attains 1.4 m.
   Biology: This is a common species in Canadian trawl catches. Depth range is 25–675 m. Life span is at least 13 years with maturity attained at 6–9 years. The pectoral fins may be sold fresh as skate wings.

longnose sucker

Scientific name: *Catostomus catostomus*
   (Forster, 1773)
Family: **Sucker**
Other common names: sturgeon, northern,
   finescale, red, black or red-sided sucker;
   milugiak, nannilik, miluiak, miluqiaq
French name: meunier rouge

   Distribution: Found from Labrador and New Brunswick to British Columbia, Alaska and into eastern Siberia. Absent from Nova Scotia and the Atlantic, Pacific and Arctic islands of Canada. In the U.S.A. in states close to the Canadian border and south to Idaho and to West Virginia.
   Characters: This species is identified by having 9–11 principal dorsal fin rays, 91–120 scales in a complete lateral line, no membranous stays between the pelvic fins and the body, and the lower lip is completely cleft in the midline. Anal fin principal rays 7, pectoral rays 16–18 and pelvic rays 9–11.

Gill rakers 23–30. Breeding males have nuptial tubercles on the head, anal fin and lower caudal fin lobe.

The back is dark olive, brown, grey or black fading to a cream or white belly. The scales are outlined with dark pigment on the back and upper flank. Both sexes have a head and midflank pink to red stripe bordered below by black and abruptly set off from the light belly when breeding, and males have a black back, females a gold to copper-brown back. The underside of the head is yellow to orange in both sexes and the belly pinkish. Fins are similar to the adjacent body. Peritoneum dusky black. Young may have 3 black blotches on the flank, sometimes forming saddles over the back.

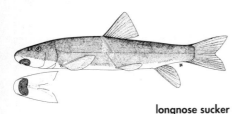

longnose sucker

Hybrids with **white suckers** are reported from Alberta. Reaches 64.2 cm and 3.31 kg for a specimen from Great Slave Lake. The world, all-tackle angling record weighed 2.86 kg and was caught in the St. Joseph River, Michigan in 1986.

Biology: This sucker is common in clear northern waters but is restricted to cool areas in the south such as deep lakes, as deep as 183 m in Lake Superior. In the Arctic it may enter brackish water.

Food is crustaceans, aquatic insects, clams, worms, and plant material. Algae may comprise up to 95.5% of gut contents in medium-sized suckers of the Matamek River, Québec and about 2% of the annual periphyton production in the river is consumed. Once regarded as an egg predator of sport fish, this is now discounted. It is commonly eaten by other fishes, birds, bears and other mammals.

Life span is about 24 years. Females live longer and grow larger than males. Maturity is attained at 2–10 years. There is a wide range in growth and in maturity patterns,

reflecting the broad distribution of this species and the various habitats. Growth tends to be slower and life span longer in the north. However growth in Great Slave Lake is faster than in smaller, southern lakes. Some populations are dwarfed.

Spawning takes place in streams or lake shallows once water temperatures exceed 5°C. This is usually April–July in Canada and the spawning run peaks several days before that of **white suckers**. The spawning process may only extend over 5 days. Males remain on the spawning grounds longer than females. Most fish migrate in the evening but spawning on gravel bottoms occurs during the day. The males occupy faster water near the stream middle, females slower water at the edge. A female approaches the males and is flanked by 2–4 of them. Eggs and sperm are shed as males clasp the female with their pelvic fins or vibrate against her with the anal fin. Each thrashing and splashing spawning act lasts only 3–5 seconds but is repeated up to 40 times an hour. The eggs are white and adhere to the gravel. Each female may have up to 60,000, 3.0 mm diameter eggs in her ovaries. Fry emerge from the gravel after 1–2 weeks and when 1.0–1.2 cm total length start to migrate downstream during nights.

This species has been used for food for humans and dogs. The flesh is good eating, being white and flaky. It is excellent smoked. Great Lakes catches are sold as "mullet" with other **suckers**.

longnose tapirfish

Scientific name: *Polyacanthonotus challengeri*
  (Vaillant, 1888)
Family: **Tapirfish**
Other common names: spiny eel
French name: tapir à nez long

Distribution: Found world-wide in temperate waters and off British Columbia.

Characters: Distinguished from the related **shortspine tapirfish** by the mouth ending at or posterior to the anterior edge of the eye and the dorsal fin origin (first spine) being over or posterior to the pectoral fin. Also the gill raker counts differ. Dorsal fin spines 32–46. Pelvic fin with a fulcral spine and 8–10 rays.

Pectoral fin with a fulcral spine and 9–15 rays. Gill rakers 11–21. Light grey to off-white or tan. Anal fin soft rays and tail dark

longnose tapirfish

brown. The opercle margin and posterior part of the mouth black. Opercle, underside of head and mouth anteriorly are bluish. Lateral line dark. Attains 54.5 cm. The species is named for H.M.S. Challenger, a ship which was used for oceanographic studies.

Biology: Found near the bottom at 1302–3753 m in cooler water. Food is bottom invertebrates such as amphipods, worms and mysids.

longsnout eelpout

Scientific name: *Bothrocara remigerum*
    Gilbert, 1915
Family: **Eelpout**
Other common names: none
French name: lycode à long nez

Distribution: Found from British Columbia to California.

Characters: This species is separated from its Canadian Pacific relatives by lacking pelvic fins, having a large gill opening, minute scales present, eyes oval, 1 indistinct lateral line, gill rakers long and pointed, and eye diameter shorter than snout length. Nape scales are present. The flesh is firm. The upper jaw projects and has an upturned tip. Pectoral fins reach back to the anal fin. Dorsal fin rays 107–117, anal rays 93–94, and pectoral rays 13–16. Dorsal and anal fins

longsnout eelpout

are covered in gelatinous tissue anteriorly. There are large head pores. Overall colour is brownish. The anterior dorsal and anal fin

margins are black, posteriorly the whole of these fins is black. Mouth and gill cavities dark, peritoneum black. Reaches 56 cm. This species may be the same as the **soft eelpout**.

Biology: Depth range is 1500–1920 m, and in Canada is found at the deep end of this range in Queen Charlotte Sound.

longsnout manypitshoulder

Scientific name: *Normichthys operosus*
    Parr, 1951
Family: **Tubeshoulder**
Other common names: multipore searsiid
French name: épaule-criblée long nez

Distribution: An Atlantic Ocean species reported off Canada.

Characters: This species is recognised by the family character of a tube projecting from the flank above the pectoral fin, by distribution, the lack of enlarged scales in the lateral line and an upper jaw extending to just behind the pupil. In addition, there are very large pores behind the shoulder girdle.

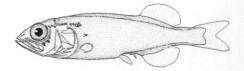

longsnout manypitshoulder

There are 7–8, usually 8, pelvic fin rays. The frontal bones on top of the head are widest behind the eye. Photophores are usually absent. Uniformly dark in colour. Reaches 16.4 cm in length.

Biology: Twenty specimens were caught off the Flemish Cap in 1968 and 3 east of the Grand Bank in 1981. Found at 780 m and down to below 1000 m, but little else is known.

longsnout prickleback

Scientific name: *Lumpenella longirostris*
    (Evermann and Goldsborough, 1907)
Family: **Shanny**
Other common names: long-snouted blenny
French name: stichée à long nez

Distribution: Found from British Columbia to southeastern Alaska.

Characters: This species is 1 of 8 related Canadian shannies which have very elongate bodies, large pectoral fins and pelvic fins with 1 spine and 2–4 soft rays. It is distinguished by distribution, 2–5 anal fin spines, the snout longer than the eye and protruding over the mouth and by the absence of white flank bars. There are 61–71 dorsal fin spines, and 36–42 soft anal rays. Dorsal spines are free from the membrane at their tips and are stronger than in related species. Scales cover the body and head and the lateral line is short and indistinct. Bluish-brown or olive above changing to silvery or sooty-blue below. The upper flank may have darker blotches but

longsnout prickleback

these are faint. The dorsal and anal fins are dark at their margins. The caudal fin is mostly black. Reaches 31 cm.

Biology: Found at 91–141 m offshore, with young pelagic, but little else is known.

longspine combfish

Scientific name: *Zaniolepis latipinnis*
　Girard, 1857
Family: **Greenling**
Other common names: longspine greenling
French name: sourcil à longues épines

Distribution: From Baja California to Vancouver Island in British Columbia.

Characters: The second dorsal fin spine is very elongate, about twice the head length, and the first 3 rays are all long and free of a membrane. Dorsal fin spines 20–21 followed by a deep notch and 1 spine and 11–12 soft rays. The anal fin has 3 spines and 15–17 branched rays. The first 2 pelvic fin rays are thickened and reach past the anal fin origin. A small cirrus is sometimes found above the eye. Gill membranes are joined anteriorly but are free of the isthmus. There are a pair of spines on the nasals and 3–4 spines on the lower part of the preoperculum. There is one lateral line. Scales extend onto the head

except for the snout. Scales are comb-like and ctenoid. Overall colour is green to yellow-brown with the flanks spotted. Fins are

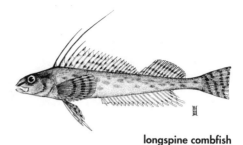

longspine combfish

reddish with various spots and bars. A black bar runs from the eye to the tip of the snout. Attains 30.5 cm.

Biology: This is a bottom species found at depths of 27–201 m. Food is crustaceans, molluscs and worms. The combfish is a cannibal. Life span exceeds 7 years with sexual maturity attained at 11.0–11.5 cm. Growth is slow at the low temperatures where it lives. Eggs are up to 2.1 mm in diameter and number up to 6530. There may be a spawning movement into shallower water. The spawning season is in winter. In California, 3 egg clutches may be produced in a reproductive season. They have a peculiar behaviour when first caught, bending the body to take the tail in the mouth.

longspine silver hatchetfish

Scientific name: *Argyropelecus aculeatus*
　Valenciennes in Cuvier and Valenciennes,
　1849
Family: **Silver Hatchetfish**
Other common names: Atlantic silver
　hatchetfish, silver hatchetfish
French name: hache d'argent à grandes épines

Distribution: In all major oceans and off the Atlantic coast of Canada from the Grand Bank southwards.

Characters: This species is distinguished by having a hatchet-shaped body, 12 abdominal light organs, telescopic eyes directed upwards and a large blade anterior to the dorsal fin. In addition the lower light organs are not in a continuous row, there are 2 spines of unequal size on the posterior tip of the abdomen, 9 dorsal fin rays, and enlarged teeth in the lower jaw. Pigmentation is diffuse but overall colour is silvery, underlain with black. Light organs

longspine silver hatchetfish

are silvery-white to yellow and edged with black. Reaches 10.4 cm total length.

Biology: Found mostly at 200–550 m during the day rising to 80–200 m at night. Some Canadian specimens taken off the Flemish Cap were caught at 2000 m, and this species has been caught at less than 50 m. Feeds on small crustaceans such as crab larvae, ostracods and copepods, and on fish larvae at dusk. Spawning occurs at 2 years of age in summer or fall. Some adults live to spawn again but most die.

longspine snipefish

Scientific name: *Macrorhamphosus scolopax* (Linnaeus, 1758)
Family: **Snipefish**
Other common names: trumpet fish
French name: bécasse de mer

Distribution: Atlantic, Indian and Pacific oceans including southern Nova Scotia.

Characters: The body shape is distinctive with the long, thin snout and very large second

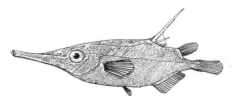

longspine snipefish

dorsal fin spine (sometimes more than a third of standard length). Dorsal fin spines 3–8, soft rays 10–14. The anal fin has 19–20 soft rays. The small mouth at the end of the snout is toothless. The young are silvery with a blue-black back but adults become pink or red, blue-grey, or intermediate in colour. Female genital papillae are black. Up to 20 cm long.

Biology: Occasionally caught in Canadian waters where it is at the northern limit of its range. Young are pelagic in the open ocean while adults are found near the bottom at 25–150 m, sometimes down to 600 m. In aquaria, they have been observed swimming slowly, head-down. Food is pelagic or bottom invertebrates. Life span is at least 5 years. Reproduction occurs over winter. Males raise their dorsal spines when they meet, parallel swim and push against each other. In some cases the erect spine is thrust at the other male. A male courts a female by parallel swimming and locking his caudal peduncle under hers. They rise in the water column for about 1 minute, the female dragging the male, and spawn. At the surface they separate. This fish is commercially important in Morocco.

longspine thornyhead

Scientific name: *Sebastolobus altivelis* Gilbert, 1896
Family: **Scorpionfish**
Other common names: longspine channel rockfish, idiotfish
French name: sébastolobe à longues épines

Distribution: Found from the Aleutian Islands to Baja California including British Columbia.

Characters: This fish and the related **shortspine thornyhead** are distinguished from other Pacific coast scorpionfishes by their higher dorsal fin spine and vertebral counts (28) and by having a sharp, spiny ridge under the eye. This species usually has 15 dorsal fin spines (range 15–16) with the third, or rarely the fourth, spine longest and more than a third of the head length. Branchiostegals usually with scales. Soft dorsal fin rays 8–10, anal fin with the second spine twice as thick as third and slightly longer, and 4–6 soft rays. Pectoral fin with 22–24 rays, the lowest 6–7 forming a distinct lobe. Gill rakers 21–26. Scale rows below the lateral line 32–38, lateral line pores 28–32. All head spines except coronal are present and sharp. Body colour red. There is black on the spiny dorsal fin. Gill cavity lining dark grey to black. Peritoneum white with black dots. Juveniles are mostly black, including the peritoneum. Reaches 38 cm.

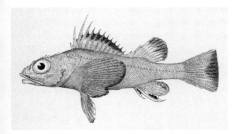

longspine thornyhead

Biology: First recorded off Vancouver Island, Marble Island and the Queen Charlotte Islands in 1968. A common species on soft bottoms offshore in deeper water than its relative at 200 m to 1750 m or more. They may be found resting on the bottom in depressions or in a shallow furrow around large white sponges. Young fish are found in midwater. An egg laying species in which eggs are enclosed in a gelatinous veil. Spawning probably occurs in March to May. Males and females are mature at 27–28 cm. Caught in trawls and traps and on setlines.

longtail whipnose

Scientific name: *Gigantactis longicirra*
Waterman, 1939
Family: **Whipnose**
Other common names: none
French name: tact géant à queue filamenteuse

Distribution: Found in temperate to tropical waters of the Atlantic and Pacific oceans including Canada's Atlantic coast.
Characters: Females of this deepsea **anglerfish** have lower jaw teeth and 8–10 dorsal fin rays which distinguish it from all other whipnoses. The esca or bait has 3 or less distal filaments. Males have 3 upper and 4 lower denticular teeth, 11 olfactory lamellae and a naked unpigmented skin. Overall

female colour is dark with parts of the esca unpigmented. Females reach 22.1 cm standard length and males reach 1.4 cm.

longtail whipnose

Biology: A single Canadian specimen has been caught in the Gulf of St. Lawrence. Adult females have been caught between 1000 and 2300 m.

longtooth anglemouth

Scientific name: *Gonostoma elongatum*
Günther, 1878
Family: **Bristlemouth**
Other common names: gonostome nu
French name: gonostome à grandes dents

Distribution: Found in temperate to tropical waters world-wide including off Atlantic Canada from the Grand Bank southward.
Characters: This anglemouth is distinguished from its Atlantic coast relative, the **spark anglemouth**, by having 18–21 gill rakers, obvious photophores or light organs, and no glandular mass at the rear of the upper jaw. It is separated from other Atlantic bristlemouths by lacking isthmus photophores, 14 or less branchiostegal rays, and the anus nearer to the anal fin base than the pelvic fin bases. Photophores: SO 1, ORB 1, OP 3, BR 8–9, IV 5 + 10, VAV 4–6, OA 13–15, AC 21–23, IC 41–43. Dorsal fin rays

longtooth anglemouth

12–15, anal rays 28–33. Overall colour is black with faint silvery, bluish and greenish iridescence on the flanks and speckled rays. Females reach 27.5 cm and males 17.8 cm.

Biology: Canadian specimens have been caught from 152–1025 m. Young and adults are usually found at 500–1200 m, stratified by size. Off Bermuda reported down to 1500 m. There is a daily vertical migration to 50–400 m at night, although some fish remain at great depths. Food is crustaceans and young fish. Males are mature at 11 cm and females at about 20 cm and spawning occurs in spring to summer.

lookdown

Scientific name: *Selene vomer*
    (Linnaeus, 1758)
Family: **Jack**
Other common names: horsehead, moonfish,
    musso panache
French name: sélène

Distribution: Possibly from Nova Scotia, and south to Uruguay. Also in the eastern Atlantic Ocean.

Characters: This species is distinguished from its Canadian Atlantic coast relatives by the very compressed, deep body with an almost vertical head margin, and by the anterior soft dorsal and anal fin rays being elongate. Undoubtedly the most supercilious fish! The first dorsal fin has 7–8 spines, the second 1 spine and 20–23 soft rays. The anal fin has 3 spines and 17–20 soft rays. Young fish have dorsal fin spines and pelvic fin rays elongated into "streamers." The overall colour is an iridescent silver with some golden tinges. The back is bluish-green. The caudal fin is yellowish and the pelvics dusky brown. Reaches 41 cm. The world, all-tackle angling record weighed 1.67 kg and was caught in 1987 at Galveston, Texas.

Biology: Nineteenth century records are uncertain and may be mis-identified **Atlantic moonfish**. There are no recent records but lookdowns have been caught in the Gulf of Maine as strays from the south. This is a shallow water species found over sand and mud bottoms. Food is fish, worms and crustaceans. Spawning is in April in the Caribbean. It may be caught by anglers but is usually captured in seines and trawls. Despite its thin body, it is good eating.

loosejaws

Loosejaws are deepsea fishes found in all oceans. There are 13 species of which 9 occur in Canada, 6 on the Atlantic coast, 2 on the Pacific coast and 1 on both coasts. They have been placed in their own family (Malacosteidae) but are now classified as **Barbeled Dragonfish Family** members. Their most characteristic features are the elongate jaws, which are longer than the head, the absence of a floor to the mouth, and the very flexible neck vertebrae. These adaptations coupled with the large, barbed teeth enable the aptly named loosejaws to thrust out their lower jaw and impale prey. The dorsal and anal fins are placed far back on the body. There is no adipose fin and scales are absent. Light organs are found on the head and body and are largest on the head. Some head light organs produce a red light while others produce the more usual green light. These fishes are usually black overall.

See **bigmouth loosejaw**
    crescent loosejaw
    largeye
    Pleiades loosejaw
    shining loosejaw
    shortnose loosejaw
    stoplight loosejaw
    tenrayed loosejaw
    Tittmann's loosejaw

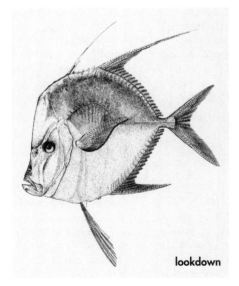

lookdown

looseskin eelpout

Scientific name: *Taranetzella lyoderma*
Andriashev, 1952
Family: **Eelpout**
Other common names: none
French name: lycode flasque

Distribution: Found from Kamchatka to Oregon including off southern British Columbia.

Characters: This species is distinguished from its Pacific coast relatives by having scales mostly on the posterior section of the tail, by having pelvic fins, no lateral line, gelatinous flesh, a gill slit extending down to the pectoral base, slender body, terminal mouth and enlarged pores anteriorly on the head. Jaw teeth are large canines. Dorsal fin rays 86–91, anal rays 72–79 and pectoral rays 15. Body pinkish-grey in preservative. The skin is loose and transparent. Peritoneum black. The gill and mouth cavities are light. Reaches 14.5 cm.

looseskin eelpout

Biology: Reported at 986–3000 m. Biology is unknown.

louvar

Scientific name: *Luvarus imperialis*
Rafinesque, 1810
Family: **Louvar**
Other common names: none
French name: louvereau

Distribution: World-wide in tropical to temperate seas including off Vancouver Island, just outside the Canadian fishery zone.

Characters: Oval, compressed body with a slender, keeled caudal peduncle. The head is blunt and the mouth minute. The eye is low on the head. There is a deep groove above the eye. The caudal fin is lunate. The dorsal fin has 13 spines and the anal fin 14 spines. The anus lies near the pectoral fin base and is covered by a flap, the remnant of the pelvic fins. Scales are minute and irregularly arranged and shaped giving the fish a "frosted" appearance.

There are only 19–24 vertebrae with the last two being fused. The skeleton is weakly developed but the swimbladder is large. Young are

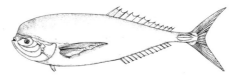

louvar

markedly different from adults, having teeth and a larger eye, dorsal and anal fins, and with large flank spots and black dorsal and anal fins. The scales in young are starfish-shaped and raised on a pedicel. Larvae have 2 long dorsal and 1 long pelvic fin spines. Adult body pink in life (silvery-grey when dead) on the flanks with some dark spots. Back metallic blue. Dorsal and anal fin rays are pink or red with the membranes black. A row of 5–7 pink spots runs along the dorsal fin base. The pectoral fins are red or yellowish. The pelvic fins are whitish. The caudal fin is dark blue with reddish tinges. Attains 1.88 m and 140 kg.

Biology: Found in the open ocean, often near the surface. Food is jellyfish and other planktonic gelatinous invertebrates such as salps and comb jellies. These are digested by a long gut and elongate absorptive projections in the stomach, just as in the leathery turtle which shares the same diet. One of the most fecund fishes producing an estimated 47.5 million eggs in late spring and summer. Although rarely caught, they are excellent eating.

Louvar Family

Scientific name: Luvaridae
French name: louvereaux

The louvar is the only member of this world-wide tropical to temperate family. It is reported from off the coast of British Columbia.

Characters and biology are summarised under the species account.

Louvars are related to the surgeon fishes and their allies in the **Perch Order**. It is one of a number of unrelated oceanic fishes which cause great interest when caught or washed ashore because of their unusual appearance and rarity.

See **louvar**

lowcrest hatchetfish

Scientific name: *Argyropelecus sladeni*
Regan, 1908
Family: **Silver Hatchetfish**
Other common names: none
French name: hache d'argent mince

Distribution: Found in all major oceans. Reported from southern British Columbia.

Characters: This species is distinguished by having a hatchet-shaped body, 12 abdominal light organs, telescopic eyes directed upwards and a large but low blade anterior to the dorsal fin. In addition the lower light organs are not in a nearly continuous row, there are 2 spines of equal size on the posterior tip of the abdomen and no enlarged teeth in the lower jaw. Dorsal fin rays 9–10, anal rays 12–13 and pectoral rays 10–11. Gill rakers 17–21. Large pigment spots are found along the midline. Overall colour is silver with black-edged silvery light organs. Attains 6 cm standard length.

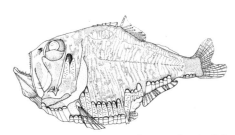

lowcrest hatchetfish

Biology: Mostly at 350–600 m by day rising to 100–350 m at night.

lowfin snailfish

Scientific name: *Paraliparis calidus*
Cohen, 1968
Family: **Snailfish**
Other common names: none
French name: limace ardente

Distribution: Found from the Gulf of St. Lawrence south to the Gulf of Mexico.

Characters: This snailfish is separated from other Canadian Atlantic species by the lack of an adhesive disc and pelvic fins, by having 1 pair of nostrils, teeth in bands, a horizontal mouth and 6 caudal fin rays. Dorsal

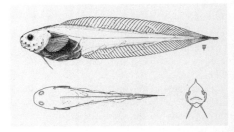

lowfin snailfish

fin rays 58–63, anal rays 54–58 and pectoral rays 15–18 in an upper lobe (total 20–22). The pectoral fin is below the level of the eye centre. Head, fins and belly black. Body paler, a dusky white, with small pigment spots. The mouth is not darkly pigmented. Peritoneum dark. Reaches 14.2 cm standard length.

Biology: This species has been caught at 150–400 m in the Gulf of St. Lawrence and on the U.S. coast down to 1207 m. Food is probably comb jellies, cnidaria, possibly salps, and crustaceans. Spawning is thought to occur almost year round. Eggs are up to 3.2 mm in diameter.

lumpfish

Scientific name: *Cyclopterus lumpus*
Linnaeus, 1758
Family: **Lumpfish**
Other common names: sea cock, sea hen, henfish, lumpsucker, sea owl, paddle-cock, red lump, blue lump, grosse poule de mer, poule de l'eau, nipisa, lepisuk
French name: lompe

Distribution: Found from southern Baffin Island and Hudson Bay to Chesapeake Bay and Bermuda in the western Atlantic Ocean. Also in Europe.

Characters: This species is distinguished from its Arctic-Atlantic relatives by having the gill opening extending below the upper edge of the pectoral fin, tubercles in 3 rows on the flank and the first dorsal fin covered by a humped crest of skin in adults. Dorsal fin with 6–8 spines, 9–11 soft rays. Anal fin with 9–11 rays and pectoral fin with 19–21 rays.

Overall colour is grey, grey-blue to yellow-green or brown. Belly yellowish to white. Spawning males have a grey-black body and reddish belly, sides and fins. Young may be brown, dark purple-red, brown spotted or red.

Attains 61 cm and 9.5 kg.

lumpfish

Biology: Found from tidal pools and floating seaweed down to 470 m and common in Canadian waters. Young lumpfish (less than 5.5 cm) live primarily in the top few centimetres of the ocean during summer in the Bay of Fundy. Adults are also pelagic in Canadian waters at depths of 0–80 m over water as deep as 380 m and many kilometres from shore. Lumpfish are mostly seen as adults when breeding in shallow water or as young when living in tidal pools before dispersing.

Food is crustaceans, comb jellies jellyfish, arrow worms, worms and small fishes such as **herring** and **sand lance**.

Growth is rapid, to 5.3 cm, in the first year. Males are about 4, and females 5, years old when spawning. Males are much smaller than females. They live to 14 years of age.

Spawning occurs inshore after a migration in spring to summer at about 8°C. A territory is established in shallow water by the male which arrives first on the spawning ground. Females mate indiscriminately with males but there is a courtship involving quivering, nest cleaning and fin brushing. Up to 300,000 sticky eggs, 2.2–3.1 mm in diameter, are laid in crevices or among seaweed. Each female may lay several egg masses at intervals of 8–10 days which hatch in 14–70 days depending on temperature.

The male guards, fans and puffs water over the eggs and is very aggressive. Fanning shortly after eggs are laid disperses waste ammonia which results from egg adhesion.

Oxygen is not in short supply in turbulent shore waters. Spent females retire to deeper water. Eggs may take up to 70 days to hatch in cold northern waters. Puffing water at the egg mass increases in frequency near hatching and may help larvae break free. Egg masses are individually variable in colour, from black to brown, red, pink, orange, yellow, green or purple. The young are pelagic, but on hatching have long been said to attach themselves to the male or to seaweed and so be carried into deeper water. This "peripatetic nursery" is not now believed.

Seals are predators on lumpfish and will sometimes peel their skin off before eating them. They are also eaten by sperm whales and **Greenland sharks**. **Cunners** are effective egg predators since they swarm over the guardian male.

An inshore fishery off Newfoundland processed about 200 tonnes for caviar in 1972 but catches are often in the 2–4 tonnes range for Canada. The flesh of the male is considered a great delicacy in Newfoundland. Lumpfish have been evaluated as an aquaculture species in Canada. Lumpfish are the only known intermediate host for a parasite which attaches to the gills of the commercially important **Atlantic cod**. Lumpfish can be present in sufficient numbers to be a nuisance to weir operators.

Lumpfish Family

Scientific name: Cyclopteridae
French name: poules de mer

Lumpfishes or **lumpsuckers** are found in cold to temperate marine waters of the Northern Hemisphere. There are 28 species with 8 in Canada, 2 on the Pacific coast, 2 on the Arctic coast, 1 on the Atlantic coast and 3 on the Arctic-Atlantic coast.

The body is usually globular in shape and is often covered with tubercles of various sizes on a wrinkled skin. The pelvic fins are modified into an adhesive, sucking disc. The lateral line is absent. There are 2 short dorsal fins although the spiny first dorsal may be embedded in thick skin or absent. The anal fin is short. The gill slit is small and usually above the pectoral fin base. The skeleton is semi-cartilaginous. There are 2 pairs of nostrils.

Lumpfishes are closely related to the **Snailfish Family** which is sometimes classified in the Lumpfish Family. Young lumpfish are often hard to identify as they differ in appearance from adults, lacking some of the key characters. They are members of the **Mail-cheeked Order**.

The disc is used to cling to rocks and seaweeds. A force of 13.3 kg is necessary to overcome the suction of a 39 cm **lumpfish**. Adults are found as deep as 900 m but are usually at 100–400 m. Females lay eggs in spongy masses which adhere to rocks and seaweeds and males of some species guard the eggs.

Fossil **lumpfish** have been reported from Green Creek, Ottawa, relics of the post-Pleistocene marine invasion of eastern Canada.

The **lumpfish** is used as a source of "caviar" and the flesh of male **lumpfish** is tasty when smoked.

See **Atlantic spiny lumpsucker**
  Arctic lumpsucker
  leatherfin lumpsucker
  lumpfish
  Newfoundland spiny lumpsucker
  Pacific spiny lumpsucker
  smooth lumpfish
  smooth lumpsucker

lumpsuckers

Lumpsuckers are members of the **Lumpfish Family** and the word has been used as a common name for most of the 8 Canadian species, including the **lumpfish** itself. The name is taken from the heavy, bulky body and the adhesive apparatus on the belly.

lunar lanternfish

Scientific name: *Myctophum selenops* Tåning, 1928
Family: **Lanternfish**

Other common names: none
French name: lanterne lunaire

Distribution: Found in the Atlantic, Indian and Pacific oceans and from off Nova Scotia.

Characters: This species and its Atlantic coast relatives, the **metallic, roughscale** and **spotted lanternfishes**, are distinguished by

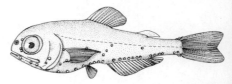

lunar lanternfish

lacking photophores near the dorsal body edge, the PLO photophore is above the upper pectoral fin base while the second PVO photophore is below this base, there are 2 Prc and 1 Pol photophores, the PVO photophores are not horizontal but inclined while the VO series is level, the SAO series is straight or almost so, and the first SAO is behind the third VO. This species is separated from its relatives by having 7 or less AOp photophores with 0–1 over the anal fin base, 21–25 gill rakers, AO photophores 9–12 and pectoral fin rays 15–18. Dorsal fin rays 12–14 and anal rays 17–19. Lateral line organs 36–38. Scales are ctenoid. Both males and females have overlapping scale-like structures (5–7 in males, 2–4 in females) forming a supracaudal luminous gland. The gland appears at 3.0 cm in males and 3.4–3.6 cm in females. Reaches 7.5 cm.

Biology: Known only from 3 specimens taken off the Scotian Shelf and reported in 1988. Depth range in the Atlantic Ocean generally is 225–450 m by day and 40–225 m at night. It does not approach the surface. Its biology in the western Atlantic is poorly known. Spawning at Bermuda probably occurs in spring and summer.

M

Mackerel Family

Scientific name: Scombridae
French name: maquereaux

The **mackerels**, **tunas**, **tunnies**, **bonitos** and **Spanish mackerels** are found world-wide in the open waters of warmer seas with some species in coastal waters. There are 49 species with 13 reported from Canada, 8 from the Atlantic coast, 1 on the Pacific coast and 4 on both coasts.

These fishes are characterised by a stream-lined body, pectoral fins high on the flank and often sickle-shaped, 5–12 finlets behind the dorsal and anal fins, 2 dorsal fins which can fold down into grooves, pelvic fins below the pectorals with 1 spine and 5 soft rays, and gill membranes free from the isthmus. Teeth vary from weak to strong. Some species have an adipose eyelid. Scales are small and cycloid, or absent. The caudal peduncle is slender with 2 keels.

Mackerels are members of the **Perch Order**. "Mackerel" may be derived from the Middle French word for pimp and is used today in Québec for a lecher.

Members of this family are important sport and commercial fishes. Their importance is such that specially designed ships travel long distances to capture them and even a hook-and-line method can be profitable. Purse seines, drift nets, gill nets and trap nets are also used. As much as 6.1 million tonnes are caught annually world-wide. The flesh of these fishes is dark and oily and does not keep well. Histamine develops in the flesh of fish left out in the sun, imparting a characteristic peppery taste which should be taken as a warning of inedibility. Many species are eaten immediately on capture or canned.

Various tunas have been found to have high levels of mercury in their flesh, a result, it was believed, of man-made pollution. Tuna catches have been confiscated for health reasons. However mercury content analyses of **skipjack tuna** from museum specimens dated 1878 and other species show some levels higher than modern (1970–1971) samples, and

on average about equal, although there is some confusing contamination of specimens by mercury from the lead glass preserving jars.

The large tunas have a high metabolic rate and a countercurrent heat exchanger which keeps their body temperature warmer than the surrounding sea. The stream-lined body makes them some of the fastest fishes in the ocean, capable of bursts of speed up to 90 km/hour. The dorsal, pectoral and pelvic fins can be retracted into grooves to increase the stream-lining. In addition the head is pointed, the caudal peduncle narrow with 1–3 stabilising keels, the caudal fin is broad and deeply forked for propulsion, known technically as a high aspect ratio, the skin is smooth and elastic with small, cycloid scales or no scales except for a corselet of larger scales near the pectoral fins, and there is usually no swimbladder.

These fishes have long migrations connected with feeding and reproduction. Some species form large schools. Food of larger species is fishes and squids while the smallest take plankton. Eggs and larvae are planktonic. Canadian species are often visitors from the warmer waters to the south.

See **albacore**
Atlantic bonito
Atlantic mackerel
Atlantic Spanish mackerel
bigeye tuna
bluefin tuna
bullet tuna
chub mackerel
king mackerel
little tunny
Pacific bonito
skipjack tuna
yellowfin tuna

mackerel scad

Scientific name: *Decapterus macarellus*
(Cuvier in Cuvier and Valenciennes, 1833)
Family: **Jack**
Other common names: comète maquereau
French name: décaptère faux-maquereau

Distribution: From Nova Scotia south to Brazil and world-wide in warmer waters.

Characters: This species is distinguished from its Canadian Atlantic coast relatives by not having a deep, compressed body but an elongate one with maximum depth 20–25% of fork length, by having 110–147 scales and posteriorly enlarged scutes in the lateral line, a short pectoral fin not extending to the last

mackerel scad

dorsal fin spine, and 27–32 soft anal fin rays. There are 8 first dorsal fin spines and 1 spine preceding the soft dorsal fin. Soft dorsal fin rays 31–37 and soft pectoral rays 21–23. There is 1 dorsal and 1 anal finlet. The lateral line is only slightly arched anteriorly. Scutes become gradually larger posteriorly but are not as well developed as in **round scad**. The back is metallic blue to blue-black with silvery-white flanks and belly. There is a small, black spot at the edge of the gill cover. The membrane just inside the upper jaw (the oral valve) has an obvious white blotch. The caudal fin is yellow-green. The dorsal fin may be tipped with black. Reaches about 35 cm fork length.

Biology: An occasional visitor to Nova Scotia and New Brunswick waters, this scad was first reported in 1907 from Chedabucto Bay, Nova Scotia, the northern range limit. Only about 5 specimens have been reported since then. This fish is primarily a pelagic and offshore species which occurs in large schools around islands at depths of 40–200 m. Food is planktonic invertebrates. This species is used mostly as bait but is also eaten locally in the Caribbean.

Mackerel Shark Family

Scientific name: Lamnidae
French name: lamnies

The mackerel shark family comprises 5 species found in almost all seas from shallow waters down to about 1280 m. They are all large, fast species of open waters. In Canada,

all 5 species have been reported, 2 on the Atlantic coast, 1 on the Pacific coast and 2 on both coasts.

They are readily distinguished from the **sleeper, dogfish** and **angel sharks** by having an anal fin. There are 5 gill slits which separates them from the **cow sharks. Cat sharks, hound sharks, requiem sharks** and **hammerhead sharks** all have nictitating eyelids and a spiral or scroll intestinal valve while mackerel sharks lack the eyelid and have a ring intestinal valve. Their name derives from the narrow, streamlined shape of the body with a pointed nose, a thin caudal peduncle and an almost symmetrical tail, in which characters they resemble the fast-swimming **Mackerel Family**. This tail shape and very strong lateral keels on the caudal peduncle distinguish them from **sand tiger** and **thresher sharks** while the teeth numbering less than 40 in each jaw separates them from the **basking shark** and the **whale shark**. Teeth are large and blade-like. There are precaudal pits on the upper and lower caudal peduncle in contrast to the **sand tiger**.

Mackerel sharks are members of the **Mackerel Shark Order**.

The eggs of these sharks develop within the body and the young are born alive. Developing foetuses feed on fertilised eggs and possibly on their siblings before birth, a uterine cannibalism. Food is a variety of fishes, **sharks, rays**, squids, crustaceans, and marine reptiles, birds and mammals. Carrion is an important item for some species. A complex circulatory system using counter-current heat exchangers reduces loss of heat from the gills and body surface. They are warm-blooded and this maintenance of a body temperature 7–10 C° above their surroundings probably enables them to enter the colder waters of Canada. These sharks are important to fisheries because of their tasty flesh and are usually caught on pelagic long-lines among other methods. There is also a market for their jaws and teeth as well as fins, hides and oil. These large, fast sharks are some of the most dangerous predators in the sea and are known to attack humans.

See **great white shark**
　　longfin mako

porbeagle
salmon shark
shortfin mako

Mackerel Shark Order

Mackerel sharks, **sand tigers**, goblin sharks, crocodile sharks, megamouth sharks, **thresher sharks** and **basking sharks** of the Order Lamniformes comprise 7 families with 16 species in cold-temperate to tropical waters world-wide. They are mostly large sharks found from inshore to deep waters. In Canada there are 4 families and 8 species on the Atlantic and Pacific coasts.

The order is characterised by having an anal fin, 5 gill slits, 2 dorsal fins without spines, the mouth extends back beyond eye level, there are no nictitating eyelids and the intestinal valve is of ring type. Spiracles are present or absent. There is no groove between the nostril and the mouth. Teeth at the front of the mouth are the largest and are separated by a gap or by smaller teeth from the side teeth.

These sharks show considerable variety in body form and include threshers with greatly elongate tail fins, the large-eyed crocodile sharks, the goblin sharks with a prolonged, dagger-like snout and the recently discovered megamouth which has a large, terminal mouth. These are live-bearing sharks some of which have uterine cannibalism.

See **Basking Shark Family**
Mackerel Shark Family
Sand Tiger Family
Thresher Shark Family

madtoms

Madtoms are small members of the **Bullhead Catfish Family** and are found only in North America. There are about 25 species of madtoms with 5 species in Canada including the closely related **stonecat**. These 5 species all have venomous tissues associated with the pectoral spine. Pain from a spine penetrating the skin lasts about 30 minutes or less and is usually compared to that of a bee sting. The injured part may swell and a sting on the finger can result in sharp pain as far as the elbow. Stings are not fatal to humans. Madtoms are named for their hyperactive swimming behaviour and perhaps the effect of their stings.

See **brindled madtom**
margined madtom
northern madtom
stonecat
tadpole madtom

Mail-cheeked Order

The Order Scorpaeniformes is made up of 25 families and about 1270 species found in marine and fresh waters world-wide. In Canada there are 10 families and 194 species.

The order is characterised by the suborbital stay, a prolongation of the third suborbital bone which runs across the cheek to brace against the preoperculum (hence "mail-cheeked"). There is some dispute as to whether this stay defines the order so the order is a provisional arrangement of families. The stay may have evolved independently more than once. A second character is 2, plate-like hypurals attached to the last half centrum in the tail skeleton. Other characters found in some members include a spiny head, sometimes with bony plates, bony plates on the body, rounded pectoral and caudal fins and the lower pectoral fin rays are often finger-like. Red is a common colour for these fishes. Fossils are reported from the early Tertiary.

The **scorpionfishes** and **sculpins** comprise more than half the species in the order and are well represented in Canada. Some species in the order are extremely venomous, the most deadly fishes known. Scorpionfishes have internal fertilisation while other families shed eggs. Certain species are economically important although many species are small.

See **Flying Gurnard Family**
Greenling Family
Lumpfish Family
Poacher Family
Sablefish Family
Scorpionfish Family
Sculpin Family
Searobin Family
Snailfish Family
Soft Sculpin Family

makos

Makos are members of the **Mackerel Shark Family** with 2 species in Canada on the Atlantic coast, the **longfin** and **shortfin makos**. Mako is derived from a Maori word.

man-of-war fish

Scientific name: *Nomeus gronovii*
(Gmelin, 1788)
Family: **Driftfish**
Other common names: bluebottle fish
French name: physalier

Distribution: Found in the Pacific, Indian and Atlantic oceans. In the western Atlantic from the Grand Bank south to Brazil.

Characters: This species is identified by the colour pattern, insertion of the pelvic fins usually ahead of the pectoral fins and, in par-

man-of-war fish

ticular, the fan-like pelvic fins with the inner edge attached to the belly. Dorsal fin spines 9–12, folding into a groove, soft rays 24–28. Anal fin spines 1–2, soft rays 24–29. The back is dark blue with triangular extensions of this colour on the flanks. The lower flank is blotched and spotted blue. The anal, caudal and second dorsal fins are also blotched blue. The first dorsal fin and the pelvic fins are black. The background colour is silvery or white. Larger fish are a more uniform dark colour. Reaches 25 cm standard length.

Biology: There is only one Canadian record of this species, caught in 1952 in deep water east of the Grand Bank. The man-of-war fish is a subtropical species and strays into northern waters are rare. It is usually found with the Portuguese man-of-war, *Physalia* (hence the French common name), a large jellyfish with tentacles 10 m long,

and with other jellyfishes. The colour pattern of the fish resembles the tentacles of the jellyfish when these are retracted into a clump. Large fish may live in deep water without associating with jellyfish. The man-of-war fish is said to be immune to the jellyfish toxin, relative to other species which associate with poisonous jellyfishes. The fish usually avoids being stung by its swimming abilities. It eats jellyfish and jellyfish have been reported to eat it. The fish will also take arrow worms and other pelagic invertebrates.

manacled sculpin

Scientific name: *Synchirus gilli* Bean, 1890
Family: **Sculpin**
Other common names: none
French name: chabot emmenoté

Distribution: Found from the western Gulf of Alaska to California including British Columbia.

Characters: This sculpin is recognised by the pectoral fins being joined ventrally (hence "manacled"). There is a strong anal papilla which lies in a groove between the anus and the anal fin. There is a sharp nasal spine and a sharp preopercular spine with 2 widely-separated points. First dorsal fin with 8–10 spines, second dorsal with 19–21 soft rays. Anal rays 18–21, pectoral rays 21–24 and pelvic with 1 spine and 3 soft rays. The pelvic rays in males are turned forward and can be used, with the opened lower jaw, to clasp the female. A dark pad on the lower jaw of males helps in clasping the female.

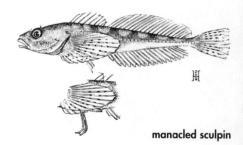

manacled sculpin

Ctenoid scales are found at the dorsal fin base in a row and number 38–42 in the lateral line. There is a small postocular cirrus, a cirrus at each dorsal spine tip and about 7 cirri along the lateral line. Overall colour is green to yellow-brown or red-brown with 7 light saddles over the back. There is a silvery lateral stripe in males. Fin rays have dark pigment while membranes are clear. This species was originally discovered and described from Barkley Sound, B.C. Reaches 8 cm.

Biology: Manacled sculpins use their pectoral and pelvic fins to cling to rocks or algae in shallow water of bays and tidepools. This sculpin is sensitive to high temperatures. Food is small crustaceans such as isopods and gammarids. Maturity is attained at 5.1 cm and spawning occurs in May or possibly throughout winter and spring since ovaries contain eggs in several stages of development. Eggs are pink, adhesive and are attached to kelp holdfasts in egg masses of 15–30 eggs. Mating pairs can be lifted out of the water attached to each other.

manefish

Scientific name: *Caristius macropus*
    (Bellotti, 1903)
Family: **Manefish**
Other common names: veilfin
French name: cariste

Distribution: Found in the North Pacific Ocean including off British Columbia. Also in other oceans but the relationships of these fishes are poorly known. Possibly the Atlantic coast species, the **Greenland manefish**, is the same species as on the Pacific coast.

manefish

Characters: This species is recognised by its high, long dorsal fin originating on the head, the scaly sheaths for the dorsal, anal and pelvic fins and the high, steep slope to the front of the head. Dorsal fin rays 32, anal rays 22 and pectoral rays 14–19. The body is a dark purplish-brown to pinkish-brown, or possibly silvery in life when scales have not been rubbed off on capture. The head is not as dark as the body. Fin membranes are black. Reaches 33 cm.

Biology: Rare in Canada but occasionally caught in midwater and even bottom trawls. Caught at 305–610 m along the coast of North America. Food is crustaceans and fish and the manefish is itself eaten by such fishes as **lancetfishes** and **albacore**.

Manefish Family

Scientific name: Caristiidae
French name: caristes

Manefishes are found world-wide in the open ocean. There are only about 4–6 species in the family and there is a different species on the Atlantic and Pacific coasts of Canada.

They have a deep body, a long dorsal fin which originates on the head and folds into a fleshy sheath, 7 branchiostegal rays, 15 branched caudal fin rays and a pelvic fin with 1 spine and 5 elongate soft rays. There are no anal fin spines. The anal fin has a groove but this extends forward to the base of the pelvic fins and thus can accommodate the latter also. Scales are cycloid. The skeleton is weak and captured fishes are often damaged.

The relationships of this poorly-known family are not clear; some authors place them with the more primitive spiny-rayed fishes, others with the more advanced spiny-rayed fishes. They may be relatives of the **Dory Family** or the **Pomfret Family** and are in the **Perch Order**. The identity of the species reported from Canadian waters is also in doubt; there may be two species or only one.

These are rare fishes of the open ocean where they are bathypelagic down to 500 m, or near the surface. Some species are known from only a few specimens.

See **Greenland manefish**
     manefish

manta

Scientific name: *Manta birostris*
(Walbaum, 1792)
Family: **Eagle Ray**
Other common names: Atlantic manta,
giant devil ray, manta atlantique
French name: mante

Distribution: Found world-wide in warmer waters and from Georges Bank to Brazil in the western Atlantic Ocean.

Characters: The 2 large, cephalic fins or head flaps are unique among Canadian fishes. The dorsal fin is at the tail base.

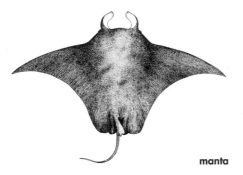

manta

There are 130–200 tooth rows in the lower jaw only and the mouth is terminal. The body and pectoral fins are covered with small denticles both above and below. Dark brown, greenish-brown or even reddish to blue-black or black above and white below. There may be white shoulder patches above and occasionally other light areas. The lower surface may be blotched. Manta comes from the Spanish word for blanket in reference to the huge enveloping size. Reaches 6.7 m, with a disc width of 9.1 m, and 1820 kg.

Biology: Occasional specimens have been spotted or harpooned on Georges Bank. They may be found inshore but mantas are open-ocean pelagic fishes using their gill rakers to strain small fish and crustaceans out of the water. The gills have special filter plates to remove food items from the inflowing water without clogging the gills' ability to extract oxygen. They flap their huge pectorals to swim, and appear to fly through the water. They may be seen resting at the surface with pectoral fin tips curled out of the

water. They are often seen swimming in pairs. Young are born alive, 1 or 2 at a time. They feed on uterine "milk" during development. Despite their size, mantas are harmless and only become dangerous if hooked, when their size and weight can destroy a small boat. Mantas leap, somersault or cartwheel from the water surface behind fishing boats, landing with a loud cannon-like report, and this activity is potentially dangerous to humans. **Remoras** are often attached to the pectoral fins or inside the mouth of mantas. Leaps are thought to be an attempt to remove parasites, stun small fishes or even to be play. Occasionally caught and sold as food with the liver giving oil and the skin being used as an abrasive. Manta flesh is said to be tasty but there is no commercial fishery.

manylight viperfish

Scientific name: *Chauliodus sloani*
Bloch and Schneider, 1801
Family: **Barbeled Dragonfish**
Other common names: Sloane's viperfish
French name: chauliode très-lumineux

Distribution: World-wide in tropical to temperate seas including the Atlantic coast of Canada.

Characters: This viperfish is distinguished from its Pacific coast relative by the postorbital photophore (light organ behind the eye) being rounded posteriorly. It is separated from its Atlantic coast relative, the **Dana viperfish**, by size and the dorsal fin origin being over the fourth to eighth photophore in the lateral series. Photophores emit a bluish light in life. Dorsal fin rays 5–7, anal rays 10–13, pectoral rays 11–14 and pelvic rays 6–8. A slender, flexible chin barbel is present

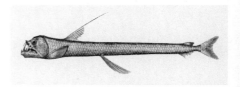

manylight viperfish

in fish up to about 100 mm standard length. Colour is an iridescent silver-blue, greenish, black or dark brown above. Fins are lighter than the body, the membranes mostly transparent. Reaches 30.5 cm.

Biology: Not uncommon on and off banks in Canada at depths of 55–475 m. In the North Atlantic it has been caught at less than 500 m down to 1800 m during the day, ascending to the upper 800 m at night, as shallow as 50 m. Food is small fishes, particularly **lanternfishes**, and crustaceans with some algae. It hovers head up and fins extended waiting for prey. **Atlantic cod** eat this viperfish. The photophores have been studied in the laboratory and found to flash or emit continuous luminescence when stimulated electrically. They serve to obliterate the shadows cast by daylight from above and the fish's body. It spawns year round with a peak in late winter to early spring.

manyray smoothhead

Scientific name: *Alepocephalus bairdi*
Goode and Bean, 1879
Family: **Slickhead**
Other common names: Baird's smooth-head
French name: alépocéphale multirai

Distribution: On both sides of the North Atlantic Ocean including from off Greenland and Labrador to the Grand Banks and off the Scotian Shelf.

Characters: This species may be distinguished by the absence of teeth on the maxilla bone of the upper jaw, the dorsal fin origin lying above the anal fin origin, 62–70 lateral

manyray smoothhead

line scales and 21–25 anal fin rays. Dorsal fin rays 18–23 and pectoral fin rays 10–13. Gill rakers 26–27, pyloric caeca 14–18. The overall colour is a purplish-brown with the gill and mouth cavities very dark. Young fish are darker than adults. Reaches 100 cm.

Biology: Not common in Atlantic Canada. Found over sandy and ooze bottoms at about 590–1700 m in schools. Food is comb jellies,

sea squirts, fish, such as deepsea **anglerfishes**, and crustaceans. Eggs are reported to be as large as 4.6 mm in diameter and spawning may occur in winter. Up to 160,000 whitish to light orange eggs are produced. Fish are mature only at 55 cm or more for males and 70 cm or more for females.

marbled snailfish

Scientific name: *Liparis dennyi*
Jordan and Starks, 1895
Family: **Snailfish**
Other common names: Denny's liparid
French name: limace à petits yeux

Distribution: Found from Alaska to Washington including British Columbia.

Characters: This species is distinguished from its Pacific coast relatives by having an adhesive disc with its rear edge behind the

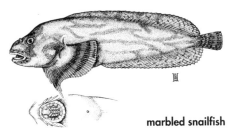

marbled snailfish

level of the gill slit, 2 pairs of nostrils, gill slit partly in front of the pectoral fin down to between rays 10–18, dorsal fin rays 37–40, anal rays 30–34 and pectoral rays 36–39. The dorsal and anal fins extend onto the first third of the caudal fin. The lower 4 or more pectoral rays are thickened and lower rays are elongated to form a lobe. Teeth are trilobed and in bands. The eye is small. Pyloric caeca 19–31. Overall colour is olive, dark brown or black with dark mottling on the flanks in the form of wavy lines. White spots may also be present. The pectoral fin may be barred black and white. Fin margins are black. Caudal barred. Peritoneum silvery with dots. Reaches 30.5 cm.

Biology: Common in Canada in the depth range 8–225 m over rubble, rock and shell with associated algae. May be caught in shrimp trawls. Spawning occurs in January in Canada. Eggs are pink.

margined madtom

Scientific name: *Noturus insignis*
(Richardson, 1836)
Family: **Bullhead Catfish**
Other common names: none
French name: chat-fou livré

Distribution: Found in Atlantic coastal streams from New York south to Georgia, upper Ohio, Tennessee and Kanawha tributaries, southern tributaries of Lake Ontario. In Canada reported from Gatineau Park, Québec, and in Ontario from the Fall River, Lanark County and Lake Joseph, Muskoka District.

Characters: This species is identified by the posterior tip of the adipose fin not being free but attached to the back, pectoral spine

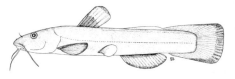

margined madtom

nearly straight to moderately curved, without anterior teeth, posterior teeth present, not recurved, colour pattern dark without blotches or saddles on the body, premaxillary band of teeth without lateral processes extending backwards, pectoral radials usually fused, pectoral rays usually 9, pelvic rays usually 9, lower jaw included, 11 preoperculomandibular pores, and vertical fins with a black margin. Dorsal fin soft rays are 5–7, usually 6, anal rays number 15–21. Pectoral ray range is 7–10, pelvic ray range 8–10. Overall colour is olive, slate-grey or yellowish fading to cream on the belly. Chin barbels are light and other barbels dark. A narrow dark band crosses the belly in front of the pelvic fins. The dark band just below the edge of the dorsal, anal and caudal fins give this species its name. The extreme edge of these fins is clear. The pelvic fins are clear and the pectorals have a marginal band. Reaches 15.8 cm total length.

Biology: Canadian records are probably the result of bait fish releases by anglers from the U.S. However the species is now known from 3 separate localities in Canada and may

just be uncommon, having arrived here through interconnecting postglacial lakes 8–10,000 years ago. It was designated as "threatened" in 1989 by the Committee on the Status of Endangered Wildlife in Canada. It prefers clear streams with riffles of gravel and stones and disappears when these silt up. It is also recorded from a rubble shoal in Lake Joseph. This madtom is secretive and nocturnal. Food is insects, crustaceans and fish, usually taken at night. Females are mature at 2 years, males a little earlier. Maximum age is 4–5 years. Most growth occurs in the summer after spawning. Adhesive eggs are deposited in a mass in a nesting cavity and are placed such that a current of water brings oxygen to them. The male cares for the eggs. Spawning occurs in June-July and females have up to 223 orange eggs with a diameter of 4.0 mm. The sting is painful.

margined snake eel

Scientific name: *Ophichthus cruentifer*
(Goode and Bean, 1896)
Family: **Snake Eel**
Other common names: serpent de mer
French name: serpenton livré

Distribution: Known from Florida to the Scotian Shelf of Atlantic Canada.

Characters: Adults have a hard, pointed tail tip with the dorsal and anal fins ending in front of the tail tip. The mouth extends

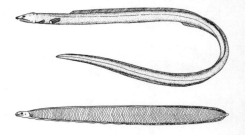

margined snake eel

beyond the posterior eye margin and bears strong teeth. The head is sharply pointed. Light brown, darkening with age. Many have a mesh-like pattern of black and white. The inside of the mouth is white. Young may be pale and speckled. Larvae have 114–162 myomeres with flank pigment, spots along the dorsal body margin, and a looped gut with 8–9 pigment spots dorsally and ventrally and clusters of pigment ventrally behind the anus. A postlarval Canadian specimen was 12 cm long. Attains 41.6 cm when adult.

Biology: Known from stray larvae (or leptocephali) in Canada. Adults are found offshore down to 2000 m, but as shallow as 36 m. A burrowing species reputed to be a parasite which chews into the body cavity of large fishes and feeds on their muscles. The finding of snake eels in the body cavities of other fishes may be a result of them being eaten and then burrowing out of the gut using their sharp pointed tail. Capable of a nasty bite when adult. Often caught by anglers.

Markle's ray

Scientific name: *Breviraja marklei*
    McEachren and Miyaki, 1987
Family: **Skate**
Other common names: none
French name: raie de Markle

Distribution: Known only from off Nova Scotia.

Characters: This species is distinguished from its Canadian Atlantic relatives by having a soft and flabby snout with its cartilaginous support thin and flexible, cartilaginous supports of the pectoral fin reaching the snout tip, and the upper disc surface has distinct spines on the nape, shoulder, eye margins and body and tail midline. There are 1–5 thorn rows on the tail. The adult upper

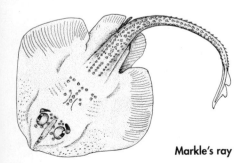

Markle's ray

surface is brownish-grey with lighter areas on the snout and on the disc margin. Dorsal fins are darker. The lower surface is creamy-white but is brownish-grey along the disc margin, snout base, around the nostrils and gill slits, pelvic fins and tail base. Smaller fish are tan or grey with numerous brownish-grey eye spots over the upper surface of the disc and tail and around the lower disc margin. The tail has a basal brownish-grey band. Reaches 45.1 cm.

Biology: Capture depths are 443–988 m but biology is unknown.

marlin-spike

Scientific name: *Nezumia bairdi*
    (Goode and Bean, 1877)
Family: **Grenadier**
Other common names: common grenadier, common rattail
French name: grenadier du Grand Banc

Distribution: Found in the North Atlantic Ocean, principally in the west from the Gulf of St. Lawrence and the southwestern Grand Bank south to the Caribbean Sea. Possibly in the Davis Strait also.

Characters: This species is distinguished from its Canadian Atlantic coast relatives by having second dorsal fin rays shorter than

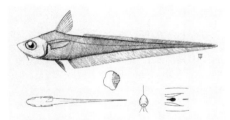

marlin-spike

anal rays, 7 branchiostegal rays, a small mouth which is strongly inferior, 6–7, usually 7, pelvic fin rays with the first ray being obviously elongated. The first dorsal fin has 11–13 rays, the second ray serrated anteriorly and usually filamentous at the tip. The second dorsal fin has about 137, the anal fin about 120 and the pectoral fin 17–20 rays. The small scales are covered in spinules or small spines. There is a "window" of the light organ on the belly between the pelvic fin bases. Overall colour is bluish-grey or brown-grey. The flanks may be silvery above and bluish to blackish ventrally. The orbit is an iridescent silver-grey or dark blue and the head may have pink or violet tinges. The first dorsal fin is pink with blackish spines. Mouth and gill cavities are black. Reaches 40 cm.

Biology: The marlin-spike lives on mud bottoms from 90–2285 m although most are caught at depths of about 200–800 m. Shallower records are probably discards from fishing vessels. Larger fish occur deeper than smaller ones. On the Scotian Shelf they are found at a temperature range of 4–13°C. Food is bottom-living crustaceans. **Swordfish** have been recorded as eating this grenadier. Spawning probably occurs in summer and autumn, judging by capture of ripe males, when mature fish are at their deepest levels. Eggs and larvae have not been described. Eggs probably rise and develop on their way to just below the thermocline, a food-rich area for the young to grow in. Young are pelagic until their second winter when they settle to the bottom. It is probably a long-lived and slow-growing species like other grenadiers. Life span is believed to be 11 years. The small size of this species makes it unattractive as a commercial item.

marlins

Marlins are famous sport fishes. There are 2 species in Canada, the **blue** and the **white marlin**, members of the **Swordfish Family**. Marlin is a shortened version of marlinespike, an elongate, pointed instrument used for separating strands of rope, in allusion to the elongate, pointed upper jaw of these fishes.

masked greenling

Scientific name: *Hexagrammos octogrammus*
(Pallas, 1814)
Family: **Greenling**
Other common names: none
French name: sourcil masqué

Distribution: Northern British Columbia in the Queen Charlotte Strait to the Okhotsk Sea.

Characters: Dorsal fin with 17–20 spines and 22–25 soft rays. Anal fin with 22–26 rays. Scales are ctenoid on the body and top of the head. The lateral lines are found along the base of the dorsal fin, from the head to the tail on the upper flank, from the top of gill opening to the tail, and from the throat to beyond the pelvic fins dividing to pass on

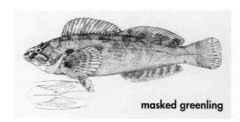

masked greenling

each side of the anal fin to the tail. Distinguished from other Canadian greenlings by having 4 lateral lines on the flanks, a small mouth and a large branched, black cirrus over the eye. There are 5 lateral lines but the fourth is very short and does not extend onto the flank. Green to brown with darker saddles and spots on the back and flanks. Fins may have bars or be quite dark, with the dorsal and anal fins dark edged. Attains 28 cm.

Biology: Rare in British Columbia where found in shallow rocky areas. It is active mainly in the early hours of the day. There appears to be little information on its biology but this fish is unusual in having "goggles." These are two, orange-red, crescent-shaped bodies in the upper and lower parts of the eye cornea. These migrate towards each other under strong light to form a natural filter.

matcheek warbonnet

Scientific name: *Chirolophis tarsodes*
(Jordan and Snyder, 1902)
Family: **Shanny**
Other common names: none
French name: bonnet à joues touffues

Distribution: Found from the Bering Sea south to the Queen Charlotte Islands.

Characters: This species is 1 of 5 related Canadian shannies which have cirri on the head and have pelvic fins. Like other Pacific coast **warbonnets** it has masses of cirri on top of the head and on the first dorsal fin spines, but it also has dense, matted cirri on the cheeks and side of the head. The gill membranes are joined but free of the isthmus. The 2 rows of teeth in the jaws form a cutting edge. The lateral line is short, ending above the gill opening. Dorsal fin rays 58–60, anal rays 43–45. Pectoral rays are 14–15. Overall colour is yellowish-brown in preservative. The dorsal fin has a series of blotches and about 12 bars and spots along the flank below it. There is a median stripe along the anal fin or a series of broad bars, and bands on the caudal fin. Pelvic fins may be black. Reaches 19 cm.

matcheek warbonnet

Biology: Found in shallow rocky areas below low tide. A poorly known species.

Maul's footballfish

Scientific name: *Himantolophus mauli*
    Bertelsen and Krefft, 1988
Family: **Footballfish**
Other common names: none
French name: football de Maul

Distribution: Found in the North Atlantic Ocean including the Gulf of St. Lawrence and off southern Nova Scotia.

Characters: This anglerfish is distinguished from its relative, the **lightlamp footballfish**, by the very long filaments on the tip of the esca or bait of the fishing apparatus. Dorsal fin rays 5, anal fin rays 4 and

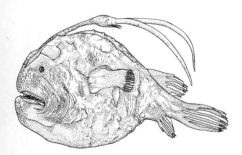

Maul's footballfish

pectoral fin rays 15–17. Colour is dark brown to black on both body and fins when adult. Females reach 15.5 cm.

Biology: Known from 3 Canadian specimens taken at 411–765 m and only 7 specimens of the species have been collected. Nothing is known of biology, but it undoubtedly captures other fishes using its esca to attract them close enough to be gulped down.

Maul's waryfish

Scientific name: *Scopelosaurus mauli*
    Bertelsen, Krefft and Marshall, 1976
Family: **Waryfish**
Other common names: none
French name: guetteur de Maul

Distribution: Mostly in the Western North Atlantic Ocean from the Caribbean Sea north to southeast of Nova Scotia and the Grand Bank. Also recorded from the Indian and Pacific oceans but much rarer.

Characters: Maul's waryfish has fewer (12–13) pyloric caeca than other Canadian waryfish (16–30). These structures are fin-

Maul's waryfish

ger-like attachments to the digestive tract. Adults of this species have not yet been captured. Large juveniles are brown in preservative with black gill covers and spots at the caudal fin base. Size to 99.5 mm SL.

Biology: Very little is known, see **Waryfish Family** account.

Mediterranean divinglamp

Scientific name: *Lobianchia dofleini*
    (Zugmayer, 1911)
Family: **Lanternfish**
Other common names: none
French name: lampe-de-plongée de la Méditerranée

Distribution: Found in all temperate and warmer seas including off Atlantic Canada.

Characters: This species is distinguished from other Canadian Atlantic species by having soft flexible rays at the caudal fin bases, the AO photophores in 2 series, a distinct Pol photophore, anal fin base about equal in length to the dorsal fin base, and by having luminous glands on top of and under the caudal peduncle. In contrast to its relative, the **Caribbean divinglamp**, this species has the Pol photophore closer to the lateral line than the anal fin. Dorsal fin rays 15–17, usually 16, anal rays 13–15, usually 14, and pectoral rays 10–13, usually 12. Photophores: AO 4–6, usually 5, + 4–6, usually 5, total 9–12, usually 10. Males have a gland on top of the caudal peduncle with 7–8 scale-like structures with small triangular ones along the margin. Females have a luminous gland under the caudal peduncle with 2–4 overlapping scale-like structures flanked by 1–2 pairs of smaller triangular ones. Reaches about 5 cm, a small lanternfish.

Mediterranean divinglamp

Biology: Common in Canadian waters from east of the Flemish Cap and along the edge of the Scotian Shelf. Near Bermuda it is caught at 350–750 m during the day and at 20–250 m at night, but depths also vary with the seasons, and with the size of the fish. This species spawns principally from January–June, peaking in winter, off Bermuda at about 3.1 cm. Life span is only 1 year.

medusafish

Scientific name: *Icichthys lockingtoni*
    Jordan and Gilbert, 1880
Family: **Ruff**
Other common names: brown rudderfish
French name: stromatée-méduse

Distribution: Found from Japan through British Columbia to Baja California.

Characters: The only Canadian Pacific coast medusafish, this species is identified by its limp, compressed body, with the top of the head spongy. The bony skeleton is poorly ossified. The dorsal fin has 3 weak spines grading into 34–42 soft rays. The anal fin has 3 weak spines and 20–29 soft rays. The small pectoral fin has 18–21 rays. There are 100–130 lateral line scales. Young lack scales and have a deeper body. The roof of the mouth is toothless. Bluish-grey to brown with dusky to black fins. Scale pockets are darker than the general background colour. Young are pinkish or bluish and almost transparent. Reaches 46 cm.

medusafish

Biology: Not uncommon near the surface, but may be normally deeper, to at least 91 m, in oceanic waters. The young live under and in the bell and gut cavity of jellyfishes or inside the tunic of salps. They feed on the trailing tentacles of this host by a rolling and twisting motion which tears off chunks of flesh. A captive specimen has been observed to swim and feed upside down and at various angles, apparently a normal behaviour well-adapted to living with jellyfish.

menhadens

Menhaden are members of the **Herring Family** with a single species in Canada, the **Atlantic menhaden**. There are 3 other menhaden species on the east coast of the U.S.A. Menhaden is derived from an Algonquian word meaning "fertilises." These fishes can be so numerous they were used to fertilise fields.

metallic lanternfish

Scientific name: *Myctophum affine*
    (Lütken, 1892)
Family: **Lanternfish**
Other common names: none
French name: lanterne rude du nord

Distribution: Found in the Atlantic Ocean including Atlantic Canada.

Characters: This species and its Atlantic coast relatives, the **lunar, roughscale** and **spotted lanternfishes**, are distinguished by lacking photophores near the dorsal body edge, the PLO photophore is above the upper pectoral fin base while the second PVO photophore is below this base, there are 2 Prc and 1 Pol photophores, the PVO photophores are not horizontal but inclined while the VO series is level, the SAO series is straight or almost so, and the first SAO is behind the third VO. This species is separated from its relatives by having 7 or less Aop photophores with 0–1 over the anal fin base, 18–22 gill rakers, AO photophores 12–15 and pectoral fin rays 13–14. Scales are ctenoid and there are 41–42 lateral line organs. Dorsal fin rays 12–13 and anal rays 18–20. Adult males have 7–8 overlapping, scale-like structures in the supracaudal luminous gland. The gland develops at 2.5 cm.

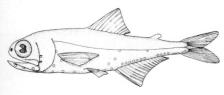

metallic lanternfish

Adult females have 3–4 oval or lanceolate patches in the infracaudal gland, developing at 2.8–3.0 cm. Reaches 7.9 cm.

Biology: This is regarded mainly as a tropical species but Canadian records from the Flemish Cap and southward are not uncommon. Canadian records are probably expatriates. Depth distribution in the Atlantic Ocean by day is 300–650 m and by night 0–275 m, mostly at the surface.

mimic shiner

Scientific name: *Notropis volucellus*
  (Cope, 1865)
Family: **Carp**
Other common names: channel mimic shiner
French name: méné pâle

Distribution: Found from southwestern Québec through southern Ontario and the Great Lakes to northwestern Ontario and southern Manitoba. South to Mexico and Alabama.

Characters: This species and its relatives in the genus *Notropis* (typical **shiners**) are separated from other family members by usually having 7 branched dorsal fin rays following thin unbranched rays, protractile premaxillaries (upper lip separated from the snout by a groove), no barbels, large lateral line scales (fewer than 50), and a simple, s-shaped gut. This species is separated from its relatives by having 7 (rarely 8) anal fin branched rays, a dusky lateral band on the flank, black pigment around the anus and anal fin base, no clearly defined middorsal stripe and pigment extends below the lateral line. Dorsal fin branched rays 6–7, pectoral rays 12–16 and pelvic rays 8–10. Lateral line scales 32–39. Pharyngeal teeth 4–4, slightly to strongly hooked. Breeding males have minute tubercles on top of the head, snout and to a lesser extent on the preopercle and lower head, and on the pectoral rays. Back with dark outlined scales on a straw-yellow to yellowish-olive background. Flanks are silvery with the dark lateral stripe poorly developed anterior to the dorsal fin level but sometimes ending at the caudal base in a triangular spot. Lateral line scales have a spot above and below each pore. The belly is white. Peritoneum silvery with some darker speckles, or dusky. Reaches 7.7 cm.

mimic shiner

Biology: Mimic shiners prefer still water and school at mid- to surface levels. They may also be found in fast current of streams and rivers. During the night, mimic shiners remain on the lake bottom scattered on bare areas. They aggregate into schools of up to 20,000 fish during the day. Food is crustaceans, aquatic and terrestrial insects, and algae and detritus browsed from the bottom. Most feeding occurs at dawn and dusk. Predators include **smallmouth** and **largemouth bass**, other fishes and various birds. Life span is rarely 3 years and maturity is attained at 1 year. Spawning occurs from May to August in Wisconsin and orange eggs are thought to be broadcast over vegetation at night, up to 960 per female. Egg diameter is 1.0 mm.

minnows

The term minnow has been used in three ways. In Europe it refers to a particular species of fish, closely related to the **finescale dace** of North America. It is often used to refer to any member of the freshwater **Carp Family**, many of which are small fishes. And finally, it is applied to any group of small fishes.

Mola Family

Scientific name: Molidae
French name: môles

Molas, headfishes or sunfishes, are usually found in subtropical to tropical waters of the Atlantic, Indian and Pacific oceans. There are only 3 species and 1 is reported from both the Atlantic and Pacific coasts of Canada.

The shape of molas is unique. The scientific name means millstone and refers to this shape. The body appears to have been chopped off behind the dorsal and anal fins and is rounded. The rudder-like structure at the rear is called a clavus and has 5–13 lobes. There is no tail but the dorsal and anal fins are long and provide the means of locomotion. The dorsal and anal fins are spineless. A pseudocaudal or gephyrocercal fin may be present in place of the caudal fin. It is formed from a few rays of the dorsal and anal fins which have moved into the tail position. The jaws have 2 fused teeth. There is no lateral line and no swimbladder. Nostrils are minute.

Molas are relatives of the **Porcupine** and **Puffer** families which all share an absence of true jaw teeth but have a cutting edge which may be split into 2, 3 or 4 "teeth." The pelvic fins are absent. Molas are members of the **Puffer Order**.

These fishes are often sighted floating at the surface when their large size and peculiar shape attracts attention.

See **ocean sunfish**

monkfish

Scientific name: *Lophius americanus*
Valenciennes in Cuvier and Valenciennes, 1837
Family: **Goosefish**
Other common names:goosefish, American angler, allmouth, fishing frog, greedigut,

molligut, mud-fish, bellyfish, rape, sea devil, abbot, molykite, diable de mer, poisson-pêcheur, lotte
French name: baudroie d'Amérique

Distribution: Found from the Gulf of St. Lawrence and Newfoundland south to northern Florida.

Characters: The large, flattened head with a wide mouth full of recurved teeth, the flaps along the lower head and flank margin, and the fishing apparatus identify this **anglerfish**. The first dorsal fin has 3 spines on the head, the first being the illicium. There is a series of 3 shorter spines connected by a membrane and a second dorsal fin of 9–12 rays. The anal fin has 8–10 rays and the pectoral fin 19–28 rays. Dark brown to tan above with various blotches becoming lighter to white on the belly. Membrane of spines black. Pectoral fins have a dark tip and the pelvic fins are reddish. Eyes are green. Reaches 1.2 m and 31.5 kg. The world, all-tackle angling record weighed 16.8 kg and was caught in 1988 at Perkins Cove, Maine.

monkfish

Biology: Monkfish may be found from the tideline down to 668 m over gravel, sand or clay bottoms. On the Scotian Shelf they are found at 27–366 m. Cooler temperatures are preferred, between 3–6°C in winter and 5–9°C in summer, although they tolerate 0–21°C. They migrate to deeper waters in winter. Food includes many species of fishes and invertebrates along with the occasional unwary seabird sitting on the surface. There is an old report of 7 wild ducks being found in a monkfish stomach. They may partially bury themselves in the bottom as concealment from prey. They live at least 12 years, females longer than males, and grow quickly when young, reaching 11.4 cm by 1 year of age. Maturity is attained at 3+ years (37 cm total length) in males, and 4+ years (48.5 cm) in females. Spawning occurs in June-September in Canada and eggs are laid in a pink, violet-grey or purple-brown veil or mucous sheet. Each egg is 1.6–1.8 mm in diameter and there are up to 3 million. The **swordfish** has been reported to eat monkfish. The monkfish is not sought after in Canada but may be taken incidentally in trawls and on longlines and used as fish meal. The Canadian catch in 1985 was 1845 tonnes but none were reported for 1987–88. It is said to be good eating. In the U.S.A., monkfish are landed "tails-only." Specimens have been used by scientists as an experimental animal in physiological and biochemical research.

mooneye

Scientific name: *Hiodon tergisus*
    Le Sueur, 1818
Family: **Mooneye**
Other common names: toothed herring,
    river whitefish, freshwater herring, cisco,
    white shad
French name: laquaiche argentée

Distribution: Found from the James Bay lowlands of northeastern Ontario and adjacent Québec, south through the Ottawa River basin to the upper St. Lawrence and Lake Champlain, and lakes Ontario and Erie. Also in Lake of the Woods, southern Manitoba and Saskatchewan and the North and South Saskatchewan, Battle and Red Deer rivers of Alberta. In central U.S.A. south to the Gulf coast.

Characters: This species is distinguished from its only relative, the **goldeye**, by having a fleshy ventral keel only from the pelvic to

mooneye

the anal fins, a dorsal fin origin in front of the anal fin origin and the mouth extending at most to midpupil level. Dorsal fin rays

10–14, anal rays 26–31 and pectoral rays 13–15. Scales in lateral line 52–60. The anal fin base has 2–3 rows of small scales and, in males, the anterior anal fin is greatly enlarged leaving the margin behind strongly concave. Colour is olive to brown on the back with a steel-blue sheen, flanks are silvery and the belly white. Fins are dusky, and a black stripe margins the leading edge of the pectoral fin. The eyes are golden above and silvery below but not as bright golden as in **goldeye**. Reaches 47 cm and 1.1 kg.

Biology: Mooneye are found in both running and still shallow waters and appear to be sensitive to turbidity. They are usually taken at less than 11 m depth. There is a migration up rivers to spawn in the spring. Food includes insects, crustaceans such as crayfish and plankton, molluscs and small fishes. Feeding often occurs at the surface in the evening and during the night when insects fallen on the water surface are taken aided by the light-sensitive eyes. Males mature as early as 3 years while females are mature at 4–5 years. Life span is 11 years. Spawning takes place in April–June and each female may produce up to 20,000 blue-grey eggs of 2.1 mm diameter. This species is of limited commercial importance, mostly on the U.S. side of Lake Erie. Various **herrings** and **whitefishes** have been listed erroneously as mooneye in catch statistics. It is caught by anglers who specialise in catching this unusual sport species using flies, worms, grasshoppers, minnows or lures on light tackle. It is best eaten spiced or smoked as it is dry and tasteless when fresh.

mooneye cusk-eel

Scientific name: *Ophidion selenops*
    Robins and Böhlke, 1959
Family: **Cusk-eel**
Other common names: none
French name: donzelle à grands yeux

Distribution: Found from Nova Scotia south to Florida and the Gulf of Mexico.

Characters: This species lacks head scales and body scales are elongate and oriented alternately to form a basket-weave pattern, a distinctive character. The snout tip has a forward pointing spine under the skin. The eye is large. Dorsal fin rays 132–140, anal rays

123–129 and pectoral rays 15–16. The body is silvery and may have a dusky stripe along the flank. The iris, gill cavity and peritoneum are silvery. There is an anchor-shaped mark on the nape. Reaches 10 cm.

mooneye cusk-eel

Biology: Known as larvae first reported in 1980 from off the Scotian Shelf as northern range records. Usually found at 20–320 m.

Mooneye Family

Scientific name: Hiodontidae
French name: laquaiches

The mooneyes are found only in North American fresh waters in central Atlantic, Arctic and Gulf of Mexico drainages. There are only 2 species, both found in Canada.

These moderate-sized fishes are similar in appearance to **herrings** but have teeth on the tongue, roof of the mouth and jaws, and a dorsal fin far back over the elongate anal fin. There are 7 pelvic fin rays, a pelvic axillary process, 7–10 branchiostegal rays, a subopercular bone is present on the side of the head and scales in the lateral line number 52–62. There is a ventral keel to the body but no scutes as in **herrings**. Scales are cycloid. The swimbladder is connected to the skull. The eyes are large and far forward on the head near the rounded snout. There are adipose eyelids. There is a single pyloric caecum.

This family is a member of the **Bony-tongue Order**. It has no close, living relatives in Canada. Tropical relatives include the knifefishes, elephantfishes and freshwater butterflyfishes often found in aquarium stores. Fossil relatives are found in the Palaeocene of Alberta of 65–53 million years ago.

Their biology is summarised in the species accounts. A unique feature is that eggs are ovulated directly into the body cavity and not carried externally via oviducts as in most **bony fishes**. One species, the **goldeye**, is commercially important in Canada.
See **goldeye**
     mooneye

Mora Family

Scientific name: Moridae (= Eretmophoridae)
French name: mores

Moras, deepsea, flatnose or morid cods are found in deep water of all seas including polar ones, rarely in brackish water. There are about 98 species, 3 reported from the Atlantic coast, 2 from the Arctic and Atlantic coasts, 1 from the Pacific and 1 from all three coasts of Canada.

These fishes have 1 or 2, more rarely 3, dorsal fins, 1–2 anal fins, a narrow caudal peduncle, no fin spines, cycloid scales, a chin barbel may be present, and pelvic fins are in front of the pectoral fins. The distinctive features are internal and include a vomer bone in the roof of the mouth either toothless or with minute teeth and the swimbladder has 2 extensions which connect with the auditory capsules. Some have light organs.

Moras are related to the **Arrowtail, Cod** and **Hake** families, all of which are **Cod Order** members.

Many moras, being deepsea fishes, are known from only a few specimens and little is known of their biology. Others are quite abundant and several species are commercially important in Australia and New Zealand.
See **blue antimora**
     brown peeper
     dainty mora
     largeye lepidion
     Pacific flatnose
     smallscale mora
     smoothchin mora

Moray Family

Scientific name: Muraenidae
     (= Heteromyridae)
French name: murènes

Morays are found world-wide in warmer marine waters, occasionally entering fresh water. There are about 200 species and 2 are rare strays in Atlantic Canada. Other species than these 2 are known to occur in Atlantic Canada as larval strays (see for example **moray species**) but they have not been identified to species.

A characteristic feature of morays is the lack of pectoral fins, unlike most **eels**. The dorsal, anal and caudal fins are continuous. The body is strongly muscled and the jaws bear well-developed, often canine, teeth. There is no lateral line on the body or scales. The gill opening is almost round, and there are several branchial pores above the gills on the side of the head. The posterior nostril is usually at the upper part of the front of the eye and the anterior nostril is tubular. Other characters used to define the family include extremely reduced gill arches, few, non-overlapping branchiostegal rays, temporal pore canal absent and various other osteological characters.

Morays are relatives of the **Snipe**, **Spaghetti** and **Freshwater Eel** families of the **Eel Order**, all of which have frontal bones on top of the head divided by a suture. "Moray" is derived from the Portuguese and Latin for these fishes.

These fishes are usually found associated with rocks and coral reefs and also harbours. A few are found down to 500 m. Some attain over 3 m in length. Food is fishes or any dead animal. Morays are chiefly nocturnal. They may cause ciguatera poisoning if eaten. In this type of poisoning, a toxin in algae is concentrated up the food chain. Plant-eating fish are eaten by carnivores like the morays which pass on the poison to humans. Some cases are fatal. There are also toxins in the skin of some morays. However it is not true that their bite is venomous, although dirty wounds can become infected, nor is it true that once bitten by a moray it is impossible for the moray to let go. Nevertheless a large moray can inflict a nasty wound, even crushing bone in their powerful jaws. Divers in warmer waters should be circumspect about thrusting their hands into holes and crevices where morays are apt to hide. Morays may have poor vision and regard a hand with fingers as a tasty octopus meal.

The scientific family name is taken from that of a wealthy Roman of the 2nd century B.C., Licinius Muraena. He kept morays in captivity as a symbol of wealth. At one time another Roman, Gaius Herius, had 6000 of them in a special pond! These fish were even lent to Julius Caesar for display at a banquet. Caesar had wanted to buy them but Gaius refused to surrender this status symbol. Morays were decorated with jewels and even, it is said, fed rebellious slaves.

See **green moray**
moray species
pygmy moray

moray species

Scientific name: *Gymnothorax* sp.
Family: **Moray**
Other common names: none
French name: murène

Distribution: Found south of the Grand Banks, Newfoundland.

Characters: This species is known only from 32 premetamorphic larvae which cannot be identified with any known adult. It is characterised by the dorsal fin beginning about 35 myomeres (muscle blocks) in front of the anus, pigment on top of the head, no pigment on the oesophagus or on the back midline before the dorsal fin and myomere counts. Total myomeres 136–140, preanal myomeres 73–75 and predorsal myomeres 40. Reaches 48 mm standard length.

Biology: Biology is unknown. First reported from Canada in 1989.

mosquitofish

Scientific name: *Gambusia affinis* (Baird and Girard, 1853)
Family: **Livebearer**
Other common names: western mosquitofish, silver gambusia, spotted gambusia, Texas gambusia
French name: gambusie

Distribution: Naturally occurring from New Jersey to Mexico and inland. Introduced to the Cave and Basin Hotsprings at Banff.

Characters: Males are easily recognised by the anal fin rays 3–5 being specially modified into an elongate gonopodium for intromittent fertilisation. Males direct their gonopodium anteriorly when mating, in contrast to some other species of mosquitofishes. This prevents excessive production of infertile hybrids between different species. Males have the end of the anal fin base well ahead of the beginning of the dorsal fin. Females lack a gonopodium and the end of the anal fin is under the beginning of the dorsal fin. The related **sailfin molly** has more dorsal fin rays. Dorsal fin with 5–8 rays, anal fin with 8–10

mosquitofish

rays and pectoral fin with 12–14 rays. Lateral scale rows number 26–33. Males are translucent grey with a blue sheen on the sides. The back is olive-brown to yellowish-brown and the belly silvery or yellowish. A dark bar passes through the eye. The flanks may be spotted. Pigment margins the scales to form a diamond pattern on the body. Dorsal and caudal fins are spotted but others are clear. Females have a large triangular blotch on the lower flank behind the pectoral fin. The black peritoneum can be seen through the body wall. The species in the hotsprings may be *Gambusia holbrooki* Girard, 1859, the eastern mosquitofish, which has recently been separated from *G. affinis*, the western mosquitofish. Males attain 4 cm, females 7.0 cm.

Biology: This species is more abundant and widespread than the **sailfin molly** in the hotsprings and neighbouring marshes. It occurred there in a temperature range of 18–27°C when the nearby Bow River was 5.5°C. This species can survive low temperatures and has been observed under ice at Banff. It has also been seen in the marsh at 30°C. Mosquitofish are normally inhabitants of clear and weedy streams and ditches, weedy margins of large rivers and lakes, marshes and brackish coastal lagoons.

Food is taken from, at, or near the surface and off plants and includes crustaceans, worms, snails and algae.

Sexual maturity can be reached in only 3 months. The small male approaches the female from the side or behind and with a rapid motion inserts his gonopodium tip into the female. The dark female flank blotch serves to identify receptive females and as a target for male thrusting. Sperm are transferred in a spermatophore. During mating the gonopodium is angled forward at 140–150°. Up to 226 young are born after 3–8 weeks gestation. A female may produce 3–4 broods each season. One fertilisation may fertilise several broods in succession. Numbers of each sex in a population vary between localities, mostly females predominate over males. Males are more sensitive to temperature extremes, starving and overcrowding.

This species has been introduced to waters world-wide in an effort to control malaria by destruction of the aquatic larvae and pupae of the mosquito carrying the disease. Unfortunately it also consumes eggs and fry of valuable, native fish species. Also used as a research species and sometimes seen in aquaria.

mosshead sculpin

Scientific name: *Clinocottus globiceps* (Girard, 1857)
Family: **Sculpin**
Other common names: globe-headed sculpin, round-headed sculpin
French name: chabot à tête moussue

Distribution: Found from Alaska to California including British Columbia.

Characters: This species and its relatives, the **calico** and **sharpnose sculpins**, are separated from other Pacific coast sculpins by hav-

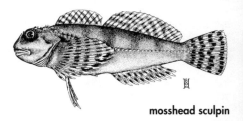

mosshead sculpin

ing 3 pelvic fin rays, branchiostegal membranes joined and forming a fold over the isthmus, largest preopercular spine not antler-like, no scales, and the anal fin origin is below the second dorsal fin. This species is separated from its relatives by lacking a pelvic fin membrane attached to the belly, no cirri on the end of the upper jaw, there is no fleshy tubercle in the upper lip groove and there is a small patch of cirri between the pectoral fin base and lateral line. The head is blunt. First dorsal fin spines 8–10, second dorsal fin soft rays 13–17, anal rays 10–12 with tips finger-like, and pectoral rays 13–15 with the lower 6–8 finger-like. Lateral line canal with 34–40 pores. The anterior third of the lateral line canal has branched cirri and there are branched cirri in many rows on top of the head such that the area between the eyes is covered. Larger specimens may have cirri on the end of the upper jaw. Males have a strong anal papilla which ends in a horn. Colour is olive or reddish brown on the back with 5–6 dark saddles. The belly is brown to yellowish. Fins have olive, brown or black bars. Attains 19 cm.

Biology: Common in tide pools and subtidally, it can also be found in areas exposed to strong surf. Some fish may even be seen "sitting" on rocks out of the water but they quickly jump back into tide pools when approached. They can respire in the air for several hours. Mossheads have a home pool to which they return if displaced. Life span is 6 years. Larger fish tend to live in lower tidal pools. Densities of this species were 1.9–2.5 fish per sq m at Helby Island, B.C.

mosshead warbonnet

Scientific name: *Chirolophis nugator*
(Jordan and Williams, 1895)
Family: **Shanny**
Other common names: ornamented blenny,
mosshead prickleback
French name: toupet élégant

Distribution: From southern California to Alaska including the British Columbian coast.

Characters: This species is 1 of 5 related Canadian shannies which have cirri on the

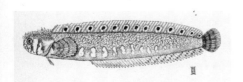

mosshead warbonnet

head and possess pelvic fins. It is distinguished from the **warbonnets** and the **pearly prickleback** by having 53–55 dorsal

fin spines and 37–42 anal fin soft rays following 1 anal spine, teeth arranged in a cutting edge and about 12–13 ocelli (or eye spots) along the dorsal fin. The lateral line is short and does not pass the end of the pectoral fin. Cirri form a dense but even mat from the anterior eye margin back to the dorsal fin. Colour varies with males overall a more reddish or orange brown than females, and with pale spots and brown streaks. The pelvic fins and the anterior part of the anal fin are white. Other fins are faintly barred. The ocelli are replaced by bars in females. There is a dark bar below the eye and bars on the cheeks. Reaches 15 cm or more.

Biology: Found under rocks in the intertidal zone and down to 80 m. It may hide in tubeworm holes with only the head protruding. Around jetties it uses discarded bottles, cans and pipes as a home. The cirri may act as camouflage in this habitat. They may live about 5 years. Food includes sea slugs and doubtless other small marine organisms. Spawning occurs in winter, about January, and eggs are large with a diameter of about 2 mm.

mottled sculpin

Scientific name: *Cottus bairdi* (Girard, 1850)
Family: **Sculpin**
Other common names: Miller's thumb,
Columbia sculpin, muffle-jaw, spoonhead,
blob, gudgeon, freshwater sculpin, muddler,
springfish, lake sculpin
French name: chabot tacheté

Distribution: Found in the Columbia and Milk River drainages of southern British Columbia and Alberta, and in adjacent U.S. states. This distribution is separated from an eastern one stretching from northeastern Labrador, Ungava, western Québec, Ontario and the Great Lakes, to southern Manitoba. In the U.S. it is found south to Georgia and Alabama.

Characters: This sculpin, and related species in the freshwater genus *Cottus*, are distinguished from the **deepwater sculpin** by the gill membrane being attached to the isthmus and the dorsal fins touching. It is separated from its relatives by having 2 pores on the tip of the chin, an incomplete lateral line, prickles only behind the pectoral fins, palatine teeth in the roof of the mouth, last 2 dorsal and anal rays close together, the fourth pelvic fin ray about three-quarters as long as the longest ray,

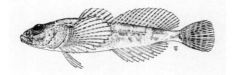

mottled sculpin

3 preopercular spines, usually 14–16 (range 12–17) pectoral rays and head length in standard length 2.9–3.2. Caudal peduncle length is less than postorbital length. First dorsal fin spines 6–9, second dorsal rays 15–19 and anal rays 10–16. There are 15–36 lateral line pores. Males have a thin, elongate genital papilla.

Overall colour light to dark brown or olive with back and sides darkly mottled. The belly is white. There are 2–3 saddles at the second dorsal fin and 2 fainter saddles at the first dorsal fin. There is a dark bar at the base of the caudal fin. Fins are thinly barred brown or dusky. The first dorsal fin has an anterior and a posterior spot. The chin has some speckling. The breeding male develops a dark stripe on the first dorsal fin with a broad orange stripe above it to the edge of the fin. His overall colouration is darker than the female, being blue-black. The western Canadian "mottled" sculpins may represent a species distinct from the eastern Canadian mottled sculpin. Reaches 17.7 cm.

Biology: This sculpin favours cool streams and lakes over sand or gravel bottoms. They will burrow in the bottom if approached. Depth range is from the shallows down to about 16 m.

Food is mainly aquatic insects with some crustaceans, worms, rarely small fishes, and fish eggs. However they are not a major predator on eggs of **trout** and other sport species. Mottled sculpins feed in the open at night and hide among rocks during the day. Food includes both swimming prey and prey buried in the substrate. The latter can be located by detecting prey movement using the mandible or large lower jaw bone. The sculpin places its lower jaw on the bottom to detect prey vibrations, "hops" towards the stimulus and bites into the sand. The mandible has very large neuromasts which aid in reception of the signal. This ability to detect vibrations may also be used to locate potential predators and in communication among members of a species. They are eaten by **brook trout** and water snakes.

Maturity is reached at age 2–3 years and life span is 6 years. Spawning takes place in spring, mainly in May in Canada at 5–16°C. Males defend a nest under a rock, and entice females there by a courtship display which involves head shaking and nodding, expanding the gill cover and undulating the body. Knocking sounds are produced by head nods and slaps to the substrate, and drum rolls are produced by a rapid series of knocks followed by a head slap. Spawning takes place at night so sound is very important as a signal in nest defense and possible female choice of males. The male will also bite the female or take her head into his mouth and shake her.

Females select larger males to mate with as these have a higher breeding success and favour those with nests under larger rocks. They spend about a week searching for a large male as too long a delay in selection leads to high egg mass failures because of late egg laying. However too large a male will eat the female. Eggs are deposited on the roof of the nest, the female is driven away and the male guards and fans the eggs. Up to 12 females may breed with 1 male but females breed only once per season. Large males succeed in hatching more eggs than small males. Each female may produce up to 635 eggs of up to 3.0 mm diameter and a nest can contain up to 2874 eggs.

mountain sucker

Scientific name: *Catostomus platyrhynchus*
 (Cope, 1874)
Family: **Sucker**
Other common names: northern mountain
 sucker, plains mountain sucker,
 Jordan's sucker
French name: meunier des montagnes

Distribution: Found from southwestern Saskatchewan, southern Alberta and southern British Columbia south to California.

Characters: This species is distinguished by having a short dorsal fin, 60–108 (often 78 or more in Canada) lateral line scales, 2 swimbladder chambers, the lower lip does not have a complete cleft and there are usu-

mountain sucker

ally 3–5 papillae between the cleft and the mouth, the cartilaginous jaw edges can be seen inside the mouth, and there is a notch where the upper and lower lips meet. The upper lip has papillae only close to the mouth so papillae are not visible from the front of the head. Dorsal fin rays 8–13, anal rays 7, pectoral rays 15 and pelvic rays 9–10. The gut is very long with 6–10 coils. Males have large nuptial tubercles on the anal fin, lower caudal fin lobe, caudal peduncle and upper pectoral and pelvic fins. The back and upper flanks are green, grey or dusky brown with black speckling and spotting, lower flanks and belly yellowish to white. The midflank stripe is dark green to black, and breeding males have an orange to red stripe above it. Fins are clear to pink. Young have 3 dark, upper back and flank bars. Peritoneum dusky to black. Reaches 23.1 cm.

Biology: This sucker is not common in some Canadian waters and it may prove to be "vulnerable," although it is reported as common in southern Alberta. The Committee on the Status of Endangered Wildlife in Canada decided in 1991 not to give it a status. It is found in deep pools of streams and rivers and is rare in lakes. Its usual habitat is high, swift mountain streams up to about 2560 m. Young fish may be found in moderate current. Food is scraped off rocks with the cartilaginous jaws and includes algae such as diatoms, insect larvae and other invertebrates. Some fish turn upside down to scrape algae off the underside of boulders. Most fish become mature between 3 and 5 years of age although some males may mature as early as

1 year in Montana. Life span is at least 9 years. Spawning takes place in riffles during June-July at 10.5–18.8°C. The yellow eggs are up to 2.2 mm in diameter and each female has up to 3710 in her ovaries. The eggs are adhesive and there is no parental care. This species is reared as a bait fish in the U.S.A. and is used as food on fur farms.

mountain whitefish

Scientific name: *Prosopium williamsoni*
   (Girard, 1856)
Family: **Salmon**
Other common names: Rocky Mountain
   whitefish, Williamson's whitefish, grayling
French name: ménomini de montagnes

Distribution: Found from most of main-land British Columbia and southern Alberta south to Nevada.

Characters: This species and its relatives, the **round** and **pygmy whitefishes**, are distinguished from other **Salmon Family** members by having a single flap of skin between the nostrils, large scales (108 or less in the lateral

mountain whitefish

line) and a forked caudal fin. It is separated from its relatives by having usually 19–26 gill rakers, 74–92 lateral line scales, scales around the caudal peduncle 20–24, and 50–146 pyloric caeca. Teeth are found only on the tongue and gill rakers of adults and addition-ally on the premaxilla bone of the upper jaw in young. Dorsal fin rays 11–15, anal rays 10–13, pectoral rays 14–18 and pelvic rays 10–12. Nuptial tubercles develop on 3–4 scale rows above and below the lateral line, most obviously in males but also in females.

The back is brown to olive or grey-blue, the flanks silvery and the belly is white. Scales are outlined in black, particularly on the back. The dorsal fin is dusky and the pec-toral and pelvic fins are tinged orange or amber. Young fish have 7–11 large, dark spots along the lateral line and 1 or more rows or spots in a row above this. Spawning males develop a dark stipe on the midflank.

Reaches 58.5 cm. The world, all-tackle angling record weighed 2.43 kg and was caught by John R. Bell on 15 June 1988 in the Rioh River, Saskatchewan. The Canadian record, a 2.57 kg fish was caught in Gap Lake, Alberta in June 1991 by Peter Zebroff.

Biology: This **whitefish** inhabits the shallows of colder lakes (20 m or less) and the colder larger streams and rivers. There are spring feeding movements into small Alberta streams which are clearer than other water bodies and make visual feeding easier. Other, complex movements associated with feeding and spawning occur through summer and fall.

Food is aquatic insect larvae, crustaceans, molluscs, eggs of its own and other fish species and rarely fishes. It may take surface insects and probably zooplankton where conditions for the usual bottom feeding are poor. **Lake trout** and probably **burbot** are predators.

Life span is exceptionally 29 years but maturity is reached at 3–4 years, some fish maturing as early as 1–2 years. Spawning occurs at night from October to February, although this long spawning season represents spawning times for 2 or more different populations within a single lake, e.g. Kootenay Lake. In the Sheep River, Alberta spawning occurs from late September to mid-October in shallow, fast midstream. Eggs are up to 3.7 mm after fertilisation with up to 24,143 eggs per female. Hatching takes place in spring at about the time of ice break-up after a winter spent in the gravel. Spawning usually occurs in streams but can occur on gravel shoals in lakes. Young fish travel in schools.

It is an excellent food fish, fresh and smoked, and is a sport fish in western Canada caught on flies and lures or using such bait as maggots, corn, **salmon** eggs or insect larvae such as stoneflies.

- Most accessible May through July.
- The lakes, rivers and tributary streams in Northern Alberta and central to northern British Columbia.
- Ultralight to light action spinning outfits used with four- to six-pound test line. Fly rods from seven-and-a-half to

eight-and-a-half feet in length rated for four- to seven-weight and loaded with weight-forward and level floating or sinking fly lines.

- Small, 1/16 to 1/8 ounce spoons, spinners and jigs, wet flies and nymphs, small worms, larval stages of insects and invertebrates found in the same aquatic environment.

moustache sculpin

Scientific name: *Triglops murrayi* Günther, 1888
Family: **Sculpin**
Other common names: mailed sculpin
French name: faux-trigle armé

Distribution: Found from Baffin Island, Davis Strait and Hudson Bay south to the Gulf of Maine. Also in Greenland and northern Europe.

Characters: This species is distinguished from its eastern Arctic and Atlantic relatives by having the upper preopercular spine a sim-

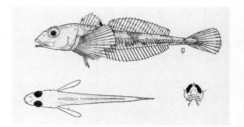

moustache sculpin

ple point, the vomer is toothed, the lateral line plates have backward pointing spines, the lower flank has oblique skin folds with serrated edges, 16–19 pectoral fin rays, colour pattern and a rounded snout. The eye diameter is less than the postorbital distance. First dorsal fin spines 9–12, second dorsal rays 18–26 and anal rays 18–27. The lower 6–7 pectoral rays are finger-like. The middle and inner pelvic rays are equal in length or the middle ray is shorter. Lateral line plates 45–49. There are small, spiny scales below the dorsal fin. The overall colour is olive or pinkish with yellowish, orange or white lower flanks and belly. The back has 3–4 large saddles or blotches, small spots or blotches, or both. The head is often spotted. The black iris of the eye is rimmed with a fine gold line. The first dorsal fin has a black spot at the margin between spines 1 and 2. The dorsal and pectoral fins have thin bars. The caudal fin has 2–3 bars. In males the dorsal fin spot is well-developed, there is a separate spot in the posterior part of the same fin, and white patches develop on the breast and flanks. There is a black bar above the upper jaw (the "moustache"). Peritoneum lightly spotted and silvery. Reaches 20 cm.

Biology: This sculpin is found on sandy bottoms at 7–320 m at 1–12°C. Food is various crustaceans and worms, some taken above the bottom. It is eaten by **Atlantic cod** and thick-billed murres in Canada. Females grow larger than males. Spawning occurs in summer and fall, perhaps into winter. In the Gulf of Maine in October, ripe females have amber eggs numbering up to 2739. There may be several spawnings in a season. Eggs may be up to 2.2 mm in diameter.

Mudminnow Family

Scientific name: Umbridae
French name: umbres de vase

Mudminnows are freshwater fishes of the Northern Hemisphere found in Alaska, central and eastern North America, and in Europe and Siberia. There are only 5 species with 1 reported from Canada.

They are characterised by the dorsal and anal fins being far back on the body near the tail as in the **Pike Family**, no adipose fin, a toothless maxilla bone in the upper jaw, no pyloric caeca (finger-like gut branches), infraorbital canal pores 3 or less, branchiostegal rays 5–8, rounded tail fin, absence of a duck-billed snout and no groove between the upper lip and the snout.

The closest relatives of this small, innocuous fish are members of the large, predatory **Pike Family**. Another family member, the Alaska blackfish (dallia, *Dallia pectoralis* Bean, 1880) was introduced to Ontario but died out. Mudminnows are members of the **Pike Order**. Fossils date back to the Oligocene.

Mudminnows, as their name indicates, are found in muddy or swampy areas. They can survive low oxygen conditions by breathing air. They can survive drying by burying themselves in the soft ooze and detritus. It is doubtful that they can survive complete desiccation of the habitat. There is evidence that some species can survive being frozen in ice and certainly the Canadian species remain active in winter under an ice cover, using oxygen directly from gas bubbles under the ice.

See **central mudminnow**

Mullet Family

Scientific name: Mugilidae
French name: muges

Mullets or grey mullets are found worldwide in temperate to tropical coastal areas readily entering estuaries and even resident in fresh waters. There are up to 80 species with 2 reported from Atlantic Canada.

Mullets have an unusual feature of the pelvic girdle for a **spiny-rayed fish** detailed below. The first dorsal fin has 4 strong spines and is well-separated from the second soft rayed dorsal fin with its 1 spine and 7–8 soft rays. The anal fin has 2–3 spines and about 7–10 soft rays. The pelvic fins have 1 spine and 5 soft rays. The eye has adipose or fatty eyelids forming a vertical, slit-like opening. The lateral line is absent or difficult to discern. Scales are cycloid and extend onto the top and sides of the head. Teeth are small or absent in a small, triangular mouth which has the corners turned down. Gill rakers are long. The stomach wall is strongly muscled and the gut is very long.

Mullets are members of the **Mullet Order**. They are unusual in that they lack a connection between the pelvic girdle and the cleithrum bone of the pectoral girdle. They are probably most closely related to the **Barracuda Family**. "Mullet" is derived from the Latin for these fishes.

Mullets are schooling fish which feed on microscopic algae and the minute animals associated with the algae. They grub, gulp or suck (hence "Mugil") bottom deposits, spitting out some of the debris and extracting nutrient from the remainder. The long gill rakers filter the food, the strong gizzard-like stomach crushes it and the long intestine (about 7 times body length) aids in digestion. Their bottom feeding leaves long patches of disturbed sediment readily visible from a distance. Young mullet are pelagic. These fishes are very important economically as food eaten fresh, smoked or canned, as bait, and as cultured fish in ponds.

See **striped mullet**
     white mullet

Mullet Order

The mullets or grey mullets (Mugiliformes) comprise a single family of 80 species with 2 Canadian species. They are found world-wide in tropical to temperate seas and in some fresh waters.

There has been considerable dispute about the placement of the single family; it is often included in the **Perch Order**. The characters are those of the family.

See **Mullet Family**

mummichog

Scientific name: *Fundulus heteroclitus*
    (Linnaeus, 1776)
Family: **Killifish**
Other common names: common killifish,
    saltwater minnow, chub, barbel, mummy,
    gudgeon, mud dabbler, saltmarsh killifish
French name: choquemort

Distribution: Found from southwestern Newfoundland and the Gulf of St. Lawrence south to Texas.

Characters: This mummichog is separated from the **banded killifish** by having 8–12 gill rakers. Dorsal fin rays 10–13, anal rays 9–12 and pectoral rays 16–20. Lateral

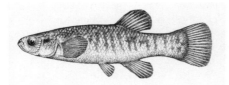

mummichog

scale rows 31–39. No lateral line. There are 4 pores on the lower jaw. Males have larger dorsal and anal fins than females.

Males are a dark green, olive-green or steel blue on the back and upper flank, the flank has white and yellow spots and faint

silvery and dark blue bars, and the belly is white to orange-yellow. There may be an eye-spot on the rear of the dorsal fin and a yellow spot on the back at the front of the dorsal fin. The leading edge of the pelvic and anal fins is yellow. In spawning males the belly is a bright yellow and scales develop finger-like contact organs. Females are a lighter olive-green and have about 13–15 faint flank bars. Colours change markedly in response to background.

Canadian populations belong to the sub-species *F. h. macrolepidotus* (Walbaum, 1792). Hybrids with **banded killifish** are known from Digby Neck and Porters Lake, N.S. and Lake of Shining Waters, P.E.I. Attains 15.2 cm.

Biology: Mummichogs are extremely common in shallow marshy areas, estuaries and creeks along the coast extending into brackish water areas. Landlocked freshwater populations are reported from Nova Scotia. They can survive high temperatures, up to 35°C (and to 42°C for 2 minutes) and are very tolerant of low oxygen so that they may be found in stagnant ponds. Should the pond dry out, they can survive some time in the mud. During winter they may bury themselves in mud or in holes in tidal streams. Schools are regularly spaced with an average distance to the nearest neighbour less than 1 fish length.

Food includes crustaceans, worms, diatoms, molluscs, larval insects such as mosquitos, spiders, mites, fish eggs, including its own, and small fishes. Predators include a wide variety of fishes, bullfrogs, birds and some small mammals such as mink and otter. In Nova Scotia some populations of mummichog move into marshes with the high tide to feed.

Life span is 4 years. Females are mature at 3.8 cm and males at 3.2 cm, at about 2 years of age although some may spawn at 1 year. Spawning occurs from February to October along its whole range when temperatures are favourable, tides are high and the moon is new or full. In Nova Scotia spawning begins at the end of May and ends in the middle of June. Multiple spawnings, up to 8, are known in Florida. The male chases the female and clasps her with his dorsal, anal and pelvic fins, pressing her against a rock and probably using the contact organs at this time. The clasp is brief, 1–2 seconds, both fish quiver and eggs and sperm are extruded. Eggs are laid in groups on plants, algal mats, sand, mud or shell bottoms in tidal areas. There is a limited salinity range in which eggs and sperm can survive despite the adult's wide environmental tolerances.

In the southern U.S.A. eggs are deposited in empty ribbed mussel shells and lack the filaments found in northern populations. The eggs find protection from predators and shell distribution is in areas with sufficient oxygen. The 2 types of eggs and spawning behaviour correspond to the 2 subspecies of mummichog.

The fertilised eggs are pale yellow, up to 2.5 mm in diameter, adhesive and number up to 740. The eggs are deposited in clutches of 10 to 300. The eggs can be stranded at low tide but survive to hatch. Eggs laid high on plants have reduced exposure to predators, and have a reduced risk of being dispersed or covered by silt in strong tides.

The wide tolerance to oxygen and temperature levels make mummichog an easily carried bait fish. Some have even been flown to central Canada from Halifax by commercial bait dealers. Mummichogs have long been used as a convenient source of fish eggs and sperm used to study embryology and the effects of chemicals. They have also been used to study the functions of various glands, such as the thyroid, adrenal and pineal glands, leading to an understanding of growth, reproduction, calcium metabolism and osmoregulation. Their easy maintenance in laboratories has made them important in studies on cancer, steroids, stress, survival at sub-zero temperatures, circadian rhythms, and in bioassays. They have even been sent into space to analyse the effects of weightlessness on development and movement behaviour. Since mummichogs do not migrate they are a good test animal for the presence of pollutants in coastal environments. All-female hybrids with **banded killifish** are reported from Nova Scotia. They reproduce clonally and so are important for experiments requiring fish with a constant genetic background.

muskellunge

Scientific name: *Esox masquinongy* Mitchill, 1824
Family: **Pike**
Other common names: musky, lunge, jack, chatauqua; tiger, spotted, barred, great, leopard, Great Lakes, Ohio or Wisconsin muskellunge; maskinonge
French name: maskinongé

Distribution: Found from southwestern Québec and southern Ontario west to western Lake Superior but only south of this lake to western Ontario and introduced to southern Manitoba. In the U.S.A. south to northern Georgia.

Characters: This species is distinguished by having a total of 12–20 pores on the lower jaws (usually 6–10 on each jaw), cheeks and

muskellunge

opercula are not fully scaled (upper halves only) and colour pattern. Dorsal fin with 15–19 principal rays, anal fin with 14–16 principal rays, pectoral rays 14–19 and pelvic rays 11–12. Lateral line scales 130–176.

The bank and upper flank are golden green to brown, or yellowish, flanks similar or grey or silvery and the belly is whitish with small brown or grey spots and blotches. The head has spots on the sides or bars radiating from the eyes. Flanks have dark brown to black spots, bars, blotches or worm tracks (vermiculations) on a lighter background. The dark markings vary considerably between and within populations. Very large fish are more silvery and such markings are obscured. Fins are green to redbrown and the dorsal, anal and caudal fins in particular are blotched with dusky spots. Young have a gold or gold-green stripe down the middle of the back, upper flanks and back are bluegreen to tan fading to white below and the flanks have irregular, dark blotches or oblique bars. Hybrids with **northern pike** are strongly barred and called tiger muskellunge.

Reaches over 1.83 m and possibly 45.0 kg but most are much smaller. The world, all-tackle angling record from Blackstone Harbour, Ontario was caught on 16 October 1988 by Kenneth J. O'Brien and weighed 29.48 kg. This fish is also recognized as the Canadian record. Muskellunge and maskinongé have been variously attributed to Latin or Québecois for long mask (masca longa, masque allongé) and various Indian words.

Biology: Muskellunge are found in the warm shallows of lakes and rivers where there is abundant vegetation such as pondweed. Large fish often occur in deeper water along rocky shores, down to 12 m. They are more common in slower streams and rivers than **northern pike**. They are tolerant of high temperatures up to 32°C and low oxygen. However they prefer temperatures below 26°C.

Food is mainly fishes seized by a rapid dart from motionless concealment in vegetation or near fallen logs and stumps. A musky may watch a prey item for many minutes before striking. The prey is impaled crossways on the large canine teeth, taken back to concealment and rotated in the mouth so it can be swallowed head first. This prevents injury if the prey has spiny fins. As well as fish, frogs, crayfish, snakes, muskrats, mice, shrews, chipmunks and various waterfowl are taken. Young and adults are cannibals; a 71.1 cm fish was found to have a 40.6 cm musky in its stomach. They are reported to make occasional lunges at bathers who claim to have been bitten.

Life span has been estimated at over 30 years but even trophy fish are mostly less than 23 years old. Growth is rapid in the first few years but the rate varies with locality being slower in northern Ontario than the south. Both sexes mature at 3–5 years although males are smaller. Females live longer than males.

Spawning occurs in April to May after ice melt and later than **northern pike**. Water temperature is usually over 9°C in shallow, vegetated or debris-rich flooded areas. The fish home to specific spawning grounds and to areas on these grounds. Some fish have been caught at the same place for 7 years in Stony Lake, Ontario. Such fish may well have summer home ranges distinct from other spawning groups and are reproductively isolated. This could be very important in managing muskellunge stocks.

The large female swims over the vegetation with one, sometimes two, males, both sexes rolling to bring their genital areas close together when eggs and sperm are shed as the fish vibrate. Their tails lash to spread the eggs which fall into the vegetation. The spawning season usually lasts a week with many such spawning acts. A female may have 265,000 amber eggs up to 3.5 mm in diameter.

Commercial landings of muskellunge in Ontario and Québec reached an estimated 447,578 fish in 1888–1897 but commercial fisheries were closed in 1936 to protect the developing sport fishery. This large sport fish is avidly sought by residents and visitors to Canada and it is a mainstay of the angling industry. Large muskellunge are more common in Canadian than U.S. waters. An estimated 100 person-hours of angling is required to capture a musky large enough to keep. However 74 keen musky anglers in Lake St. Clair caught 1273 fish in 1017 days of fishing. There are a number of fishing clubs in Canada and the U.S. devoted to catching muskellunge. They are caught by trolling or by using a large, live fish as bait. They are very strong fighters and will leap out of the water. There are strict fishing regulations in regard to size, season and bag limits in order to maintain stocks of this species. However about 30% of all angled muskellunge die because of stress, including many apparently fit fish released by anglers. The flesh is white and flaky and musky can be baked, poached or fried but most larger fish are mounted as trophies.

- Most accessible June and November.
- Southern Ontario including the Lake Huron shorelines, Georgian Bay and the St. Lawrence River as well as southern Quebec including the Ottawa River and the St. Lawrence River.
- Heavy-action baitcasting outfits used with 20– to 30–pound test lines.
- Best trolling lures include the largest wobbling plugs. The best casting lures include a wide variety of jerkbaits and large, flashy in-line spinners. The best bait includes large live forage fish such as **chubs** and **suckers** rigged live and fished near the bottom or under a float.

N

naked-nape eelpout

Scientific name: *Pachycara gymninium*
    Anderson and Peden, 1988
Family: **Eelpout**
Other common names: none
French name: lycode à nuque nue

Distribution: Found from the Queen Charlotte Islands south to Mexico.

Characters: This species is separated from its Pacific coast relatives by having pelvic fins, a large gill opening usually extending to about the lower edge of the pectoral base, terminal mouth and blunt snout, robust body, scales present on body, tail and on vertical fins to about half their height and usually absent from pectoral base, midlateral branch of lateral line originating in pectoral fin axil and running to the tail, usually 6 suborbital pores, firm flesh, and no scales on the nape. There is a lower lateral line from the head to the tail tip. Dorsal fin rays 96–103, anal rays 77–84 and pectoral rays 14–18. Vertebrae number 102–109. Overall colour dark brown, head and pectoral fin almost

naked-nape eelpout

black. Mouth and gill cavities dark brown to black. Peritoneum and vertical fin margins black. Reaches 42.2 cm standard length.

Biology: This species was first described from a specimen caught in a trap west of Tasu Sound, Queen Charlotte Islands at 2744 m. Depth range is 1829–3219 m over mud bottoms. Food is crustaceans and worms. A mature female had 80 eggs up to 7.2 mm in diameter.

narrowside alfonsin

Scientific name: *Beryx splendens*
    Lowe, 1834
Family: **Alfonsino**
Other common names: Alfonsin a Casta, Alfonsin de Costa Estreita, slender beryx, slender alphonsino
French name: béryx allongé

Distribution: World-wide. Found off the Atlantic coast of Canada.

Characters: Distinguished from the **wideside alfonsin** by having fewer pyloric caeca (23–36), more scales along the flank (74–82),

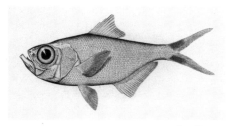

narrowside alfonsin

fewer dorsal fin soft rays (13–15), and a less deep body. The upper head and body and fins are bright red. The iris of the eye is pink and its upper margin is dark blue. The gill cavity is bright red. The flanks are pink and the belly is silvery-white. Size up to about 63 cm.

Biology: Known from a single specimen taken at 585 m in 1955 off the southern tip of Nova Scotia. A deepwater fish found commonly at 183–732 m and also below and above these depths, often in rocky areas. It eats fish and crustaceans and migrates near to the surface in the evening to feed. This alfonsino begins to mature in it second year of life and most are mature by 5–6 years. Life span is at least 14 years. A narrowside alfonsin has been found in the stomach of a **longnose lancetfish**.

neckeel

Scientific name: *Derichthys serpentinus*
    Gill, 1884
Family: **Neckeel**
Other common names: narrownecked oceanic eel, narrowneck eel
French name: anguille à col

Distribution: Found world-wide in temperate to tropical oceans including off Atlantic Canada.

Characters: This species is distinguished from its only Canadian relative, the **duckbill eel**, by having a short, blunt snout with the

neckeel

upper jaw slightly longer than the lower. Dorsal fin rays 226–262, anal rays 155–180. Lateral line pores 80–90, vertebrae 126–134. The dorsal fin origin is well behind the pectoral fin. The "neck" is constricted in front of the pectoral fins. Olive to grey or black with a bluish sheen on the neck. Fins mostly clear. Lateral line pores are lighter than surrounding tissue. Reaches 40 cm.

Biology: First reported in 1973 from midwater at 183 m over a depth of 338 m off Georges Bank. Other specimens were taken off the Flemish Cap in 1968. Elsewhere found down to 2000 m. Spawning is thought to occur south of Bermuda, judging by the distribution of larvae. Large eggs numbered about 4100 in one female. It is believed this eel breeds more than once since both large and minute eggs are found in one individual.

Neckeel Family

Scientific name: Derichthyidae
French name: anguilles à col

Neckeels, longneck eels or oceanic eels are found in the deep waters of the Atlantic, Indian and Pacific oceans. There are only 3 species with 2 reported from Atlantic Canada.

Neckeels are named for a narrowing of the head in front of the pectoral fins in one species, giving the appearance of a neck. Two other species have a flattened, duck-like snout. The dorsal fin origin lies well behind the head and the anal fin origin is after the body's midpoint. There are large pores around the eyes and on the lower jaw. The head may have parallel striations, part of a sensory system. The dorsal, anal and caudal fins are continuous. Jaws are long. The anterior nostrils are short, anteriorly directed

tubes. Teeth are small and in broad bands on the jaws and roof of the mouth. Gill openings are separate, nearly horizontal and are under the throat. The lateral line is clearly marked and has 80–132 pores. Scales are absent.

Neckeels are related to other **Eel Order** families such as the **Sawpalate** and **Pike Conger** families. The **neckeel** and the 2 **duckbill eels** were once classified in separate families.

These eels are found in the midwaters of the open ocean, usually below 500 m. Food is mainly crustaceans. Reproduction occurs at warmer times of the year and there is a leptocephalus larva.

See **duckbill eel**
     neckeel

Needlefish Order

Needlefishes, **flying fishes**, **halfbeaks**, **sauries**, medakas or ricefishes and their relatives belong to the Order Beloniformes. These are small to medium-sized fishes. There are 5 families with about 191 species found in marine, fresh and brackish waters world-wide in temperate to tropical latitudes. In Canada there are 3 families with 8 species, all but 1 on the Atlantic coast and that 1 on the Pacific coast.

They are characterised by an elongate body, a beak develops at some stage in most species, the upper jaw is not protrusible, the lateral line being absent or low on the body, nostril openings paired or single, 4–15 branchiostegal rays, dorsal and anal fins are placed rearward on the body, pelvic fins are abdominal with 6 soft rays, the interarcual cartilage is small or absent, in the gill arch there is a large, ventral flange on the fifth ceratobranchial bone, the second and third epibranchials are small, the second pharyngobranchial is re-oriented vertically, the interhyal is lost, and the lower caudal fin lobe has more rays than the upper lobe.

This order is related to the **Killifish** and **Silverside** orders by the possession of a large, demersal egg with many oil droplets and adhesive filaments, spermatogonia in the testes are confined to the terminus of tubules, infraorbital bones 3–5 under the eye and the fourth pharyngobranchial bone of the gill arch are absent, the heart develops in larvae in front of rather than under the head, and a specialised jaw mechanism where the rostral cartilage is not connected to the premaxilla bone in the upper jaw and where there are crossed palatomaxillary ligaments and a ligament from the maxillary to the cranium. These 3 orders are related to the higher fishes grouped with the **Perch Order**.

Medakas are often used in studies of development while other, larger species are used for food in tropical regions. Gliding flight or high jumps are characteristic of most members of the order. Most species have some commercial importance in tropical waters.

See **Flyingfish Family**
Halfbeak Family
Saury Family

Newfoundland eelpout

Scientific name: *Lycodes terraenovae*
Collett, 1896
Family: **Eelpout**
Other common names: none
French name: lycode de Terre-Neuve

Distribution: Found from the Davis Strait to the Grand Bank.

Characters: This species is separated from its Canadian Arctic-Atlantic relatives by having small pelvic fins, a mouth under

Newfoundland eelpout

the snout, no large pores around the mouth, crests on the chin, a single lateral line running down towards the anal fin origin or paralleling the anal fin base, a long tail (preanal length about 35–43% of total length), and uniform brown colour. Dorsal fin rays about 109, anal rays about 97, and pectoral rays about 23. Reaches 35.6 cm.

Biology: Reported down to 870 m on the Canadian side of Davis Strait but little is known of its biology.

Newfoundland spiny lumpsucker

Scientific name: *Eumicrotremus terraenovae*
Myers and Böhlke, 1950
Family: **Lumpfish**
Other common names: none
French name: petite poule de Terre-Neuve

Distribution: Found on the Newfoundland Grand Bank.

Characters: This species is separated from its Arctic-Atlantic relatives by having the gill opening above the pectoral fin, many

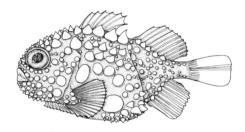

Newfoundland spiny lumpsucker

large, pointed tubercles each with many spines on the head, body and tail, supplemental pores above the lateral line, rounded anterior body, first dorsal fin rays free of skin, pectoral fin base with tubercles, 6 tubercle rows between the eyes and tubercles on the posterior part of the body irregularly arranged. Dorsal fin spines 7, soft rays 12, anal rays 11 and pectoral rays 25. Mid-occipital row of tubercles well-developed. Chin densely tuberculate. Colour not known. Reaches 4.1 cm.

Biology: Known only from a single specimen caught in 1885 at 71 m. This species is regarded by some authors as the same as the pimpled lumpsucker, *Eumicrotremus andriashevi* Perminov, 1936 of the northwest Pacific Ocean, and closely resembles the **Atlantic spiny lumpsucker**. No new specimens have been caught in over 100 years which suggest that it is probably an aberrant **Atlantic spiny lumpsucker**. The pimpled lumpsucker is benthic at 20–75 m on stony or pebbly bottoms or occasionally sand at −1.7 to 3.2°C.

night smelt

Scientific name: *Spirinchus starksi*
  (Fisk, 1913)
Family: **Smelt**
Other common names: none
French name: éperlan nocturne

Distribution: Found from southeastern Alaska to California including British Columbia.

Characters: This species and its relative, the **longfin smelt**, are distinguished from other smelts by having 8–14 upper arch and

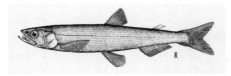

night smelt

24–32 lower arch gill rakers, medium conical to large canine teeth on the tongue, 4–8 pyloric caeca, and minute pointed teeth across the vomer bone on the roof of the mouth. This species is difficult to distinguish from its relative. It has a shorter pectoral fin (84% or less of distance to pelvic insertion), 60–66 scales along flank with 16–24 pored, pointed snout, and the length of the longest anal ray enters 2.2–3.1 times in head length. The mouth is large, extending to the rear of the eye. Dorsal fin rays 8–11, anal rays 15–21 and pectoral rays 10–11. Total gill rakers 32–45. Males have longer pectoral fins than females and tubercles on the head, scales and lower fins. Overall colour green to brown with flanks silvery. Peritoneum silver with a few pigment spots. Reaches 23.0 cm.

Biology: This species is found from the surface to 128 m. Food is crustaceans. Many predators feed on these smelt including a wide variety of fishes, birds and seals. Life span is at least 3 years. Spawning is said to occur at night in the surf of sandy beaches during May in northern areas, January to September in California. Males gather in dense schools in shallow water and females dash in, lay eggs and return to deeper water. Males outnumber females 8 to 1 at the spawning peak and at the end of spawning

by 100 to 1. Eggs adhere to sand grains and become partially buried in the sand. These fishes are occasionally caught on hook and line but are usually taken in California by jump nets. Two fishermen jump over incoming surf to place a net stretched between poles and catch the fish as the wave recedes. This type of net was invented by North Coast Indians. Commercial quantities are also taken. They are excellent eating when pan-fried.

nightmare dreamer

Scientific name: *Oneirodes epithales*
  Orr, 1991
Family: **Dreamer**
Other common names: none
French name: rêveur cauchemar

Distribution: Found in the western North Atlantic south of Newfoundland.

Characters: This dreamer is distinguished from all its relatives in the same genus by its escal appendage pattern. The pattern comprises a single, short, unpigmented medial appendage with 16 short filaments, an elongate anterior appendage which is branched at the tip, and no lateral and antero-lateral appendages. The medial appendage is about 40% of escal bulb length and the illicium length is 15.6% SL. The posterior appendage is short, unpigmented and bears 3 short fila-

esca of
nightmare dreamer

ments. Upper jaw teeth number 44 and vomerine teeth 6. Dorsal fin rays 5, anal rays 4 and pectoral rays 15. The anterior appendage has pigment internally for about one-half its length, with a paired eye-spot at the tip of the pigment. There is also a paired eye-spot in the dorsal pigment patch of the escal bulb. Females attain 12.8 cm.

Biology: First described in 1991 from a single specimen caught in 1986 at 41°05'39"N, 56°25'33"W, approximately 800 km south of Newfoundland. This specimen was caught in an open trawl between the surface and 1829 m.

ninespine stickleback

Scientific name:*Pungitius occidentalis*
   (Cuvier in Cuvier and Valenciennes, 1829)
Family: **Stickleback**
Other common names: tenspine stickleback,
   pinfish, tiny burnstickle, many-spined
   stickleback, kakilahaq, kakiva, kakilasak,
   kakidlautidlik, kakilusuk, kakilishek
French name: épinoche à neuf épines

Distribution: Found from all eastern Canada to northern and eastern Alberta, northeastern British Columbia, the Mackenzie valley and all the N.W.T., Baffin, Banks and Victoria islands. In the U.S.A. south to New Jersey on the Atlantic coast, in Great Lakes drainages and around coastal Alaska but not far south on the Pacific coast.

Characters: This species is characterised by 6–12 (usually 8–11) dorsal fin spines alternately leaning to the left and right, no obvious, large bony plates on the flank and colour. Bony plates are present but are small and often 0–8 in fresh water, along the whole flank and onto the caudal peduncle in the sea. The caudal peduncle is long and slender. Dorsal fin soft rays 8–13, anal fin with 1 spine and 6–11 soft rays, pectoral rays 10–11 and pelvic fin with 1 spine and 1 soft ray. The pelvic skeleton is absent in many fish from Wood Buffalo National Park, Alberta and many populations across Canada contain a few fish which have a reduced or absent pelvic skeleton.

Overall colour is dark to light green, yellow-green, olive, brown or grey with dark bars, mottles and blotches on the flank and a silvery to yellowish-white belly. Fins are clear. Breeding males are overall jet black and have white to light blue pelvic fins. Fish

from Lake Huron have a black ventral patch rather than being black overall.

Formerly named *Pungitius pungitius* (Linnaeus, 1758), this name is restricted to a European species and *P. occidentalis* is correct based on fish from Newfoundland. Reaches 9.0 cm.

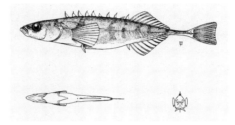

ninespine stickleback

Biology: Ninespines are found in both fresh and salt waters but usually enter fresh waters to spawn. Marine populations are commonest in estuarine conditions or marshes. Hudson Bay populations are believed to winter in the sea. Some ninespine populations may be catadromous. In lakes it is found down to a maximum of 110 m and it is believed to overwinter in deep water, but it is commonest in shallow bays. It is also common in slow streams and ponds.

Food comprises aquatic insects, crustaceans, molluscs, worms and eggs and larvae of their own and other fish species. Females feed mostly in the early morning at Isle Verte, Québec. Male diet is more diverse than other **sticklebacks** because they spend more time away from their nests. This stickleback is commonly eaten by sport fishes.

Life span may be over 3 years and maturity is attained at 1 year for 90% of males but only 40% of females in Lake Superior. All are mature at age 3. In the Matamek River, Québec life span is 1 year and some months but in Matamek Lake over 2 years. In a tidal creek at Isle Verte, Québec, most fish appear to live about 1 year although some may survive to reach 2 years and some months.

Spawning takes place in May to July. The male builds a nest off the bottom in dense vegetation, gluing plant fragments together with extruded kidney secretions. In areas without vegetation the nest is built on the bottom and even on turbulent, rocky lake shores. The male defends his nest territory by charges, nipping, biting and chasing. Other encounters involve a slow approach with pelvic spines erect and the head angled slightly down followed by a retreat or the two combatants circling rapidly biting each other's tail. Mouth fighting may also take place in the most energetic fights. Males may drag other males, **sculpins** or small **suckers** away by the dorsal or tail fins. The nest is a tunnel open at both ends and about 3–4 cm long. Nests are reported to be open at one end only in Lake Superior, the fish entering and turning around to deposit eggs or sperm.

The male courts a female with a complex dance. He angles his body head down, an aggressive position, erecting his spines, twisting his body into a slight s-bend, and zig-zagging towards her. The female assumes a submissive, head up position and follows the male to the nest. The male indicates the nest entrance with his snout, the female pushes past to enter the nest and the male vibrates near her tail to stimulate egg deposition.

Each female lays 20–80 eggs and is chased away by the male. He may mate with up to 7 females. Eggs are up to 1.5 mm in diameter and fecundity can reach 136 eggs at Isle Verte, Québec, a tidal creek, compared to only 71 eggs in the freshwater Matamek River system, Québec. Nests at Isle Verte had a mean number of 331 eggs or fry. The male swims through his nest without stopping, but fertilises the eggs. The eggs are fanned and so aerated by the male. A male may build a second nest while still guarding the first one. The young move away from the nest when about 2 weeks old but up till then he catches them in his mouth and spits them back into the nest. Marine ninespines may remain in tidal rivers of Québec until freeze-up in November while **threespine** and **blackspotted sticklebacks** leave in July.

Nooky dace

Scientific name: *Rhinichthys* sp.
Family: **Carp**
Other common names: Nooky longnose dace, Nooksack dace

French name: naseux Nooky

Distribution: Found in the Nooksack River system of southwestern British Columbia. Also in Puget Sound drainages and Pacific coast drainages of the Olympic Peninsula.

Characters: This species (or subspecies) is distinguished from neighbouring **longnose dace** populations by fewer lateral line scales (50–61), fewer scales around the caudal peduncle (21–28), a narrower caudal peduncle, and by biochemical differences. The systematics of **longnose dace** (*Rhinichthys cataractae*) populations has not been fully worked out and several species and/or subspecies may exist in western Canada.

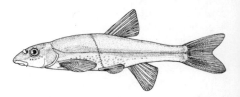

Nooky dace

Biology: This **dace** is found in the moderate current of riffles. Food is aquatic insects. Spawning occurs in April. Agriculture and gravel pit operations may threaten the survival of this species.

North Atlantic cornerlantern

Scientific name: *Symbolophorus veranyi*
  (Moreau, 1888)
Family: **Lanternfish**
Other common names: largescale lanternfish
French name: lanterne-de-coin nord-atlantique

Distribution: Found in the North Atlantic Ocean and Mediterranean Sea. In Atlantic Canada from the Scotian Shelf and its edge and on Georges Bank.

Characters: This species is separated from its Atlantic coast relatives by lacking photophores near the dorsal body edge, the PLO photophore is above the pectoral fin base level, the second PVO photophore is at or below the upper pectoral fin base level and PVO photophores are not horizontal but inclined, there are 2 Prc photophores, VO photophores are level, 1 Pol photophore, and the SAO photophores are strongly angled

with the first in front of the third VO photophore. Dorsal fin rays 12–14, anal rays
21–23 and pectoral rays 12–14. Total gill

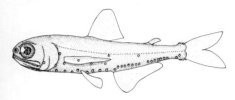

North Atlantic cornerlantern

rakers 18–21. Lateral line organs 41–42. AO
photophores 14–17. Adult males have a
supracaudal luminous gland made up of 1–3
small, coalescing patches which appears in
fish 5.2 cm long. Adult females have 2–4
patches infracaudally which appear at 5.8
cm. Reaches at least 13.0 cm.

Biology: This lanternfish favours temperate waters and is not uncommon off the
Canadian coast. Found at 100 m and at
550–800 m during the day and most commonly at the surface at night but also more
rarely down to 800 m. Eaten by **swordfish** in
Canadian waters.

North Pacific frostfish

Scientific name: *Benthodesmus pacificus*
  Parin and Becker, 1970
Family: **Cutlassfish**
Other common names: none
French name: poisson sabre nord-pacifique

Distribution: Found from southern Japan
to California including off British Columbia.

Characters: This species is distinguished
from related species by having a notch
between the spiny and soft parts of the dorsal

North Pacific frostfish

fin, the spiny part of this fin is about half as
long as the soft part, no crest on top of the
head commencing over the eye and extend-

ing back to the dorsal fin, and by the total
dorsal fin rays being 142–148 and total vertebrae being 149–153 (these last two characters overlap with **Simony's frostfish** but that
species occurs only on the Atlantic coast of
Canada: note also that the total dorsal ray
count conflicts with the dorsal fin spine
count from the same source given below;
minimum count can only be 143). Dorsal fin
spines 44–46 and soft rays 99–104. Anal fin
with 2 spines and 90–94 soft rays. The body
is silvery and the jaws, opercle, and mouth
and gill cavities black. Reaches 112 cm standard length.

Biology: The adults of this species are
benthopelagic below 304 m, sometimes
migrating to the surface, while young are
mesopelagic from 100 to 500 m and as deep
as 1000 m.

northern anchovy

Scientific name: *Engraulis mordax*
  Girard, 1854
Family: **Anchovy**
Other common names: Californian
  anchoveta, California anchovy, plain
  anchovy, Pacific anchovy
French name: anchois du Pacifique

Distribution: Found from the Queen
Charlotte Islands south to Baja California.

Characters: This is the only Canadian
Pacific anchovy and is easily recognised by

northern anchovy

its extremely long upper jaw, the gill covers
extending backwards, the round body in
cross section and a short snout. Scales are
large, cycloid, easily detached and number
41–50. There is no lateral line canal. Dorsal
fin rays 14–19, anal rays 19–26 and pectoral
rays 13–20. Lower gill rakers 37–45, long
and slender. Blue-green on the back and silvery on the flanks and belly. There is a faint
silver stripe along the side. Reaches 24.8 cm.

Biology: Adults are pelagic in dense schools. Found from the surface down to 310 m or deeper from inshore waters to 480 km offshore as eggs and larvae. Adults prefer water temperatures between 13 and 18°C for breeding. Food is various planktonic crustaceans, such as euphausiids, copepods and decapod larvae, which are caught by filter-feeding and "pecking" individual prey. Anchovies are an important food for many other fish species. Spawning occurs in July and August in Canada and fish are 10 cm long at 1 year of age. They may live 7 years. Growth in the first year is faster in B.C. than in California. Eggs are elliptical in shape and about 1.55 mm long. The eggs float perpendicularly at first and then horizontally. Up to 30,000 are produced, many more in California. Hatching occurs in 2–4 days and maturity is attained as early as 1 year old. In California these anchovies spawn about 20 times per year. A 4 year old female produced nearly 5 times as many eggs per unit of body weight than a 1 year old since she spawned an average of 23.5 times compared to 5.3 times over a longer spawning season. Anchovies are used as "chum" to attract game fish in California and as bait for **salmon** in northern waters. Purse seiners capture large quantities of this anchovy in California. Some is sold fresh or canned but most are processed as fish meal and for their oil content. Northern anchovies are not found in consistently large numbers to be a permanent, commercial product in British Columbia. They were abundant in the late 1940s in the Strait of Georgia and some were canned.

northern brook lamprey

Scientific name: *Ichthyomyzon fossor*
  Reighard and Cummins, 1916
Family: **Lamprey**
Other common names: Michigan brook
  lamprey, blood sucker
French name: lamproie du nord

Distribution: Found in the Hudson Bay drainage of Manitoba, the Great Lakes basin of Ontario and the upper St. Lawrence River basin in Québec, south to Kentucky and Missouri.

Characters: Trunk myomeres number 50–58. The sucking disc is narrower than the body. This species is distinguished from other Canadian lampreys by having a single dorsal fin, teeth along the side of the mouth with 1 cusp, 2 knob-like and blunt cusps on the bar above the mouth, 6–11 knob-like and blunt cusps on the bar below the mouth. Adults are grey to brown above, silvery or

northern brook lamprey

disc view

white on the belly. The area under the gill pores may be orange. Fins are grey to yellow or brown. The eye is bluish. Attains 25.4 cm.

Biology: This is a non-parasitic species found in warmer streams and smaller rivers than the **American brook lamprey** or along the margins of larger rivers. Spawning occurs in May to June at 13–22°C without a migration. The nest is constructed among large stones to create a cavity. Unusual vertical body movements, and transport of gravel using the sucking disc, excavate a 10 cm long nest. Up to about 2,000 eggs of 1.0–1.2 mm diameter are produced. Ammocoetes live 5–7 years and may "rest" for a year without feeding before transformation to the adult in August to September. Ammocoetes have been sold as bait in Quebec. This species was accorded the status of "vulnerable" in 1991 by the Committee on the Status of Endangered Wildlife in Canada.

northern clingfish

Scientific name: *Gobiesox maeandricus*
  (Girard, 1858)
Family: **Clingfish**
Other common names: common clingfish,
  flathead clingfish
French name: crampon bariolé

Distribution: Found from Baja California

to southeastern Alaska including the coast of British Columbia.

Characters: The sucking disc on the breast and the spineless, posteriorly positioned dorsal and anal fins are characteristic of clingfishes. This species is distinguished from its relative, the **kelp clingfish**, by having 12–16 dorsal fin rays and a large, broad, flattened head. The anal fin has 11–15 rays. The pectoral fin has 21–23 short rays and there is a fleshy flap between the gill opening and the fin base. There are 4 pelvic fin rays and the fins are joined by a papillose membrane which is part of the disc rim. Overall colour is grey to light greenish-brown to pink or red with lighter mottling or white spotting often in a reticulate pattern. Dark thin bars radiate from the eyes. The side of the head has a faint reticulate pattern. There are white bars between the eyes. The dorsal, anal and caudal fins have white spots at their tips. Attains 17 cm.

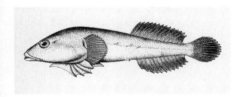

northern clingfish

Biology: Found in the intertidal zone among algae, including areas of strong current where the adhesive disc enables it to cling to rocks and kelp. It may go as deep as 7.9 m or be high among seaweed intertidally. In Baja California found on drifting kelp. Attachment by the disc is mostly passive but muscular activity is used to increase adhesive power in emergencies. However the fish tires rapidly and can be popped off a rock with moderate force exerted by a finger under the head. Adhesion also helps as an anchor while forcing prey off the rock. Food is small crustaceans and molluscs. Mollusc shells are wrapped in mucus to protect the gut from perforation. This clingfish is a cannibal. The yellow eggs are adhesive and are deposited on the underside of rocks in the spring. The male guards the eggs and several females may contribute eggs to the same site.

northern hog sucker

Scientific name: *Hypentelium nigricans* (Le Sueur, 1817)
Family: **Sucker**
Other common names: hognose sucker, mud sucker, black sucker, riffle sucker, bighead sucker, stoneroller, hogmolly, hammerhead, boxhead, hog mullet, stonetoter, stonelugger
French name: meunier à tête carrée

Distribution: Found from New York to Minnesota and south to Louisiana. In Canada reported from tributaries of lakes Huron, St. Clair, Erie and western Ontario.

Characters: This species is distinguished by its short dorsal fin, 44–54 lateral line scales, a broad head which is depressed between the eyes on the top, the eyes are high on the side of the head, and the snout is elongate and curved down (hence hog). The lips are large, fleshy, papillose and almost circular in outline. Gill rakers about 21. Dorsal fin rays 10–13, anal rays 7–8, pectoral rays 15–17 and pelvic rays 9. The gut has 5 anterior coils. Males have large nuptial tubercles on the anal fin, lower caudal fin and caudal peduncle, and smaller tubercles on the dorsal, pectoral and pelvic fins, some scales, and the head. Males have longer anal fins than females. The back and upper flanks are dark olive to red-brown fading to yellowish-brown or greenish-yellow on the lower flank and white on the belly. Flanks are blotched and spotted. Young and some adults have 3–6 dark saddles sloping down and forward on the back and upper flank. Fins are dusky to yellowish or olive. The anal, pectoral and pelvic

northern hog sucker

fins and lower caudal fin lobe have a white leading edge. Peritoneum dusky with some blackish areas. Reaches 61.0 cm and 2.3 kg.

Biology: This sucker inhabits swift streams and is found in riffles and pools with gravel and stone bottoms. It is rare in lakes and is intolerant of turbidity. Large pectoral fins low on the body, a tapering body and reduced swimbladder are adaptations for life in fast water, similar to that seen in **daces** (*Rhinichthys* species). Food is aquatic insects, crustaceans and algae obtained either by scraping rocks in riffles or turning them over using the long snout to root out food with the rubbery lips. This process dislodges some food items which drift downstream to be seized by expectant **minnows** and turtles. **Smallmouth bass** eat hog suckers and **blacknose dace** and **creek chub** eat their eggs. Females mature at 3–4 years and life span is about 11 years. Males grow faster than females up to 4 years, after which females grow faster. Males mature at 2 years. The largest fish are female. Spawning occurs in April-May beginning at about 11°C in riffles. The males are on the riffle and females leave pool areas to settle on the gravel. Two to 11 males close in on each female, sometimes covering her flanks and back so only the head and tail are visible. They all vibrate, releasing eggs and milt. Males may stand on their heads with their lashing tails out of the water, creating a dramatic splashing. The splashing helps hide the eggs in the gravel. Mating lasts only 2 seconds and the process is repeated at intervals of 4–7 minutes. Eggs are non-adhesive and settle in the gravel which has been cleaned somewhat by the vigorous male splashing. Hog suckers have been used as bait in the U.S.A., and can even be caught on worms or wet flies but it is too restricted in distribution to be used in Canada. They may be caught by hand during the spawning period. A record from eastern Lake Ontario was probably a bait fish release.

northern lanternfish

Scientific name: *Stenobrachius leucopsarus*
(Eigenmann and Eigenmann, 1890)
Family: **Lanternfish**
Other common names: smallfin lanternfish
French name: lanterne du nord

Distribution: Found from Kamchatka and the Bering Sea to off British Columbia and south to Baja California. Also at Ocean Station Papa (50°N, 145°W).

Characters: This species is related to the **garnet lanternfish** and they are distinguished from other Pacific lanternfishes by having 3–5 Prc in an evenly spaced curve, caudal luminous glands divided into platelets or scales often appearing joined, the fourth PO photophore is greatly elevated, the first 3 of 3–5 VO photophores are not in an ascending, straight line, there are no luminous, small scales at the dorsal and anal fin ray bases, 1 Pol photophore, luminous caudal glands in both sexes, and the SAO series is straight or only slightly angled. The two related species are separated by the northern lanternfish having 5–8 scales in the supracaudal gland, 7–9 in the infracaudal, a silvery body colour, light grey fins and bluegreen or yellow-green photophores. Dorsal fin rays 12–15, anal rays 14–16, pectoral rays 8–11, and total vertebrae 35–38. Total AO photophores 12–14. Total gill rakers 17–20, including rudiments 20–22. Exceeds 9.5 cm.

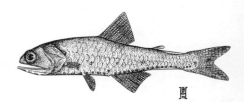

northern lanternfish

Biology: A common species off British Columbia with a wide depth range from the surface down to 2900 m. There is a daily migration from near surface waters to depths of 300 m or more during daylight. Not all fish migrate each night and about half the population assumes a vertical position, apparently conserving energy and trying to be inconspicuous to predators. The largest fish are always deepest on average. Food is small fishes and crustaceans. **Yellowtail rockfish** and **salmon** are known to eat this lanternfish. Maximum age is about 8 years, with maturity attained at 4 years. Spawning occurs in December to March.

northern madtom

Scientific name: *Noturus stigmosus*
Taylor, 1969
Family: **Bullhead Catfish**
Other common names: none
French name: chat-fou du nord

Distribution: Found in the upper eastern tributaries of the Mississippi River and in western Lake Erie drainages of the U.S.A. In extreme southwestern Ontario.

Characters: This species is identified by the posterior tip of the adipose fin not being free but attached to the back, pectoral spine usually

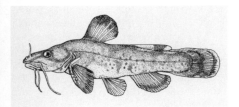

northern madtom

curved, scimitar-like with small anterior and large posterior teeth, posterior teeth recurved towards spine base, colour pattern of dark blotches or saddles on the back, caudal fin rays usually 49–53 (range 47–56), typically two internasal pores, black blotch on adipose fin not usually extending to margin, dorsal fin white-edged, dark midcaudal band present, and eye diameter enters 1.7–2.4 times in snout length. Dorsal fin with 5–7, usually 6, soft rays, anal rays 13–16, pectoral rays 7–9 and pelvic rays 8–10, usually 9. Preoperculo-mandibular pores 11. The body has large yellow to pink or tan areas on a black to olive background. The belly is white. Two pale yellow spots are behind the eyes, a yellow saddle is on the back of the head, followed by a dark saddle, and there are dark saddles below the dorsal fin and between the dorsal fin and the adipose fin. There is a dark crescent on the midcaudal fin with lighter areas on each side and both a basal and a sub-marginal dark crescent. Breeding males have bulging cheeks and a blue-black to black head. Attains 17.8 cm.

Biology: Usually found in large streams and small rivers over sand and mud bottoms but avoiding very silty conditions. Egg masses of 61–141 eggs are found under stones or in discarded cans. Spawning takes place at night and eggs and young are guarded by the male. Only 1 specimen from Canada taken in Lake St. Clair, Ontario near the Detroit River. Biology is poorly known. The Committee on the Status of Endangered Wildlife in Canada considered in 1993 that there was insufficient scientific information for status designation on this species.

northern pearleye

Scientific name: *Benthalbella dentata*
(Chapman, 1939)
Family: **Pearleye**
Other common names: none
French name: oeil-perlé du nord

Distribution: Found in the western Pacific Ocean and from Alaska to Baja California including British Columbia.

Characters: This pearleye is separated from its Pacific coast relative, the **longfin pearleye**, by lower fin ray counts. In addition the adipose fin is behind the anal fin level. Dorsal fin rays 6–8, usually 7. Anal fin rays 17–21, pectoral rays 21–25. Lateral line scales 54–58, larger than other flank scales. Overall colour is brown, lighter below. Scale pockets are outlined with dense pigment. Gill membranes are purple. The eye is in a black cylinder. Peritoneum black. Reaches about 24 cm.

northern pearleye

Biology: Found between 100 and 1000 m particularly off the Queen Charlotte Islands. Adults are usually deeper than 500 m.

northern pike

Scientific name: *Esox lucius* Linnaeus, 1758
Family: **Pike**
Other common names: great northern pike,
    pickerel, snake, wolf, gator, slinker,
    Great Lakes pike, Canada pike, shovelnose

pike, channel pickerel, short pickerel, marsh pickerel, hammer handle, grass pike, or jack (young pike), sjulik, ihok, siun, hiulik, siolik, kikiyuk, idlûlukak
French name: grand brochet

Distribution: Found from Labrador and Québec (but not the Maritimes and Gaspé) west to Alberta, northern and northeastern British Columbia, Yukon, mainland N.W.T. and Alaska. In the U.S.A. south to Missouri east of the Appalachian Mountains. Also across northern Eurasia.

Characters: This species is distinguished by having 9–11 pores on the lower jaws (usually 5 on each jaw), the cheeks are fully scaled but the opercula usually on the top half only, and colour. Dorsal fin principal rays 15–19, principal anal rays 12–16, pectoral rays 13–17 and pelvic rays 10–11. Lateral line scales 105–148.

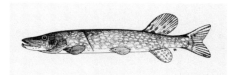

northern pike

The overall colour is dark with light spots, the reverse of that in **muskellunge**. The back and upper flank are dark green, olive-green or brownish, fading to a whitish belly. The flank has 7–9 rows of greenish, yellow to whitish blotches along it. Scales have a golden tip. The head sides have wavy, golden or yellow blotches and lines and the eyes are bright yellow to golden. The dorsal, anal and caudal fins are green, yellow, orange or pale red, blotched and barred irregularly with black. The pectoral and pelvic fins are dusky to orange. Young have 8–15, wavy, white or yellow bars which become the bean-shaped blotches in adults as they gradually break up. There is a gold to green stripe along the middle of the back in some fish but others are completely dark green. There is a stripe below the eye in young less than 4 cm long. Adults have a vertical bar below the eye. A variety, known as silver pike, has an overall silvery colour without flank spots.

Reaches 133.3 cm total length and perhaps 34.0 kg. The world, all-tackle angling record weighed 25 kg and was caught in Germany in 1986. The Canadian angling record from Delaney Lake, Ontario, was caught by Harry Bell in 1946 and weighed 19.13 kg.

Biology: Pike are solitary and are found in lakes and rivers where the water is still or flowing slowly. Vegetation is heavy and the water warm but they usually retire to deeper, cooler water at the height of summer. However pike are active in winter as anglers can testify. Summer distribution is usually within 300 m of shore and less than 4 m deep. On windy days, pike retreat offshore in surface waters. Pike tolerate brackish water. Food is initially zooplankton and aquatic insects but fish begin to predominate at 5.0 cm after about 1 month's growth. Over 90% of the diet of adults is fish, but frogs, crayfish, mice, muskrats and ducklings are taken. The delta areas of the Saskatchewan and Athabasca rivers lose an estimated 1.5 million waterfowl to pike each year, about one-tenth of the annual production. In Lac Ste. Anne, Alberta, pike feed on **yellow perch, spottail shiners, burbot** and **white suckers** in order of importance. Both sexes fast during spawning but females have rations 1.5–2.3 times as much as males in summer and winter. The daily ration was high from May to August with a June peak and very low in winter. Food is seized after a rapid dart from concealment. Cylindrical fish like **yellow perch** are preferred over more deep-bodied species like **bluegills** as being easier to swallow. Adults are attacked by **lampreys** and on the spawning grounds by bears and large, predatory birds. Young are eaten by various other fishes, birds and even large aquatic insects.

Life span is up to 26 years but is less than half this in fast-growing southern populations in Canada compared to Arctic fish. Some aquarium fish have lived 75 years. Maturity, like growth, varies with latitude and habitat. Males mature at 1–6 years and females at 2–6 years. Females grow larger, faster and live longer than males. Growth is best at 19–21°C and is very efficient.

Spawning runs occur in the late evening and early night, several days before spawning occurs. Spawning takes place during the day, often in mid-afternoon, in shallow bays or flooded fields just after ice melt in late March to May. Water temperatures on the spawning run are as low as 1.1°C. Spawning itself takes place at temperatures several degrees warmer than this, up to 17.2°C. The spawning period is about 10 days at any one site.

Each female is accompanied by 1–2 males as she swims over vegetation in the shallow water. Both sexes roll to bring their genital regions close together, vibrate and release 5–60 eggs and the sperm. Tail sweeps scatter the eggs. This 3–10 second process is repeated many times each day. Eggs are amber, 3.2 mm in diameter, adhesive and each female can produce up to 595,000. Eggs hatch 12–14 days later and the fry attach to vegetation by an adhesive head gland until the yolk sac is absorbed 6–10 days later.

Pike form a significant part of the fresh-water commercial catch in Canada, about 4100 tonnes in 1988 worth almost $3.3 million. They rank after **lake whitefish, lake trout** and **yellow walleye** in Saskatchewan. In Alberta pike were used for mink food and are exported to French consumers. They are sold fresh and make excellent eating, having white, flaky flesh, perhaps not as good as **walleye** or **Salmon Family** members. A muddy taste in summer is attributed to the skin mucus and can be avoided by removing the skin before cooking.

Pike are good sport fish taken by trolling spoons, plugs, fishes and worms near or off weed beds. They may also be taken with **minnows** suspended below a float. Wire leaders are used because of the pike's sharp teeth. They are also an important element of the winter ice fishery taken with live or salted fish as bait or by jigging. Size limits are imposed on anglers but research shows this must be done with care. A large limit might seem to protect young fish so more survive to reproduce, but often more large females are taken and egg production decreases. A careful balance must be struck.

One of the more fascinating aspects of pike lore is the stories which have accumulated over the centuries. The Emperor's Pike, 579.5 cm long and 250 kg, was purportedly caught in a lake near Württemburg in 1497 and found to have a copper ring around its gill region relating in Greek its release by the Emperor Frederick II on 5 October 1230. The skeleton of this monster was kept in Mannheim Cathedral but was shown to have extra vertebrae taken from several pike. The story itself is untenable even without the physical disproof. The pike would have had trouble growing with a copper ring around its gill region and a pike 579.5 cm long should have weighed more like 1.5 tons. A general belief in giant pike made stories of people being pulled into ponds, hands being severed, infants in the pike stomach, and so on more acceptable. While these European tales can be discounted by the practical North American, one pike myth current in Canada is that they lose their appetite and their large canine teeth in midsummer when one would expect them to be actively feeding and biting on anglers' lures and baits. Scientists regard this as an angler's excuse. Pike do lose teeth but replace them regularly and always have an efficient set. Pike don't bite well in August because prey is abundant and they are well fed, and they tend to retreat to cooler waters at this time.

- Most accessible May through September.
- The Northwest Territories, northern Alberta, northern Saskatchewan, northern Manitoba, northern Ontario and northern Quebec.
- Medium to heavy action spinning and bait casting outfits used with 12– to 20–pound test line.
- A wide variety of 1/4– to one-ounce casting and trolling spoons, large spinners, spinnerbaits and an assortment of crankbaits and wobbling lures. The best bait includes large live or dead forage fish such as **chubs**, rigged live and fished near the bottom or under a float.

northern pipefish
Scientific name: *Syngnathus fuscus*
  Storer, 1839
Family: **Pipefish**
Other common names: common pipefish
French name: syngnathe brun

Distribution: Found from Texas and Florida to the Gulf of St. Lawrence.

Characters: This species is distinguished from its straight-bodied relatives by having 18–21, usually 19, trunk rings and its dorsal

northern pipefish

fin ray count. A caudal fin is present. The snout is moderately long (length enters head length 1.7–2.3 times). Dorsal fin rays 33–49. Pectoral fin rays 12–15, usually 13–14. Tail rings 33–42. The anal fin is absent in males, and is minute with only 3 rays in females. Body dark and mottled or with 12–13 brown bands. Usually green to brown or red. Flanks covered in white dots. Caudal fin brown and dorsal and pectoral fins pale. The dorsal fin may have diagonal bands. Colour changes to match surroundings. Attains 30.5 cm.

Biology: Found in seaweeds and eelgrass beds in salt marshes, harbours, estuaries and along the coast. The commonest Atlantic Canada pipefish. Capable of rolling their eyeballs separately. Food is principally the smaller crustaceans, fish eggs and fry but also includes worms. Prey is taken by a dart and suck method. Females deposit eggs into the male brood pouch a few at a time through a slit. A male may have up to 570 eggs in 1–3 layers arranged in 2–8 cross rows. Eggs are 0.75–1.0 mm in diameter. Breeding occurs in summer and incubation takes about 10 days. Young emerge from the brood pouch at 8–9 mm. They mature at about 1 year, or perhaps as late as 2 years. Some populations migrate to deeper water for the winter, become torpid and may even be partially buried in the sea bed. They may be eaten by **Atlantic cod**.

northern puffer

Scientific name: *Sphoeroides maculatus*
    (Bloch and Schneider, 1801)
Family: **Puffer**

Other common names: sea squab, swellfish, swelltoad, bellowsfish, sugar toad, globefish, balloonfish, compère bigarré
French name: sphéroïde du nord

Distribution: Found from southern Newfoundland south to Florida.

Characters: This species has a four-toothed beak in the mouth and is distinguished from related species by fin ray counts and prickles on the belly. Dorsal fin rays are 7–8, anal fin rays 6–7, and pectoral fin rays 15–17, usually 16. There is one lateral line. The back is a dark olive-green, brown, grey or dusky, the flanks greenish-yellow or orange and the belly is white to yellow. The body, and cheeks in particular, are peppered with small black spots. There are 6–8 flank bars. Attains 36 cm.

northern puffer

Biology: A rare stray in Canada but reported from as far north as Newfoundland. Found from inshore down to 183 m in Canadian waters. They eat crustaceans and molluscs using their powerful beak and also take other invertebrates and fish. They also bite readily at a baited hook and can be a nuisance to anglers where common. Spawning occurs in spring and summer in the U.S.A. Eggs number up to about 449,200, are small (0.9 mm) and sink when laid, sticking to each other and the substrate. The left ovary is larger than the right ovary. Life span is about 5 years but sexual maturity is reached at 1 year of age. Sometimes sold as food under the name "sea squab" in the U.S.A. It is not toxic like some of its relatives.

northern redbelly dace

Scientific name: *Phoxinus eos* (Cope, 1862)
Family: **Carp**
Other common names: red-bellied dace

French name: ventre rouge du nord

Distribution: Found from P.E.I. and Nova Scotia west through New Brunswick, southwestern Québec, probably all of Ontario but only southern Manitoba, and southwestern Saskatchewan, much of Alberta except eastern parts, the eastern Peace River basin of British Columbia and in the N.W.T. only south of Great Slavia Lake. In the U.S.A. south to Pennsylvania and Colorado.

Characters: This species has protractile premaxillaries (a groove between the upper lip and the snout), no barbels, an incomplete lateral line and minute scales in lateral series 66–95, mouth not extending past the anterior eye margin, a black peritoneum, 2 extra major loops in the long gut, and a stripe or series of spots between a dark upper flank stripe and the back. Dorsal fin branched rays 6–8, anal branched rays 6–8, pectoral rays 13–16 and pelvic rays 8–9. Scales have radii on all fields. The lateral line usually does not pass the level of the pelvic fin origin. Pharyngeal teeth 5–5 with variants 5–3 and 5–4. Males have tubercles lining breast scales to form 4–6 comblike rows. Minute tubercles are found on the head, above the anal fin, lower half of the caudal peduncle and pectoral fin rays.

The back is olive, dark brown or even black, lower flank silvery to cream below a broad, dark, midflank stripe. The upper flank stripe breaks up into spots behind the dorsal fin. Between the two flank stripes the body is silvery-yellow and there is a thin oblique line trending posteriorly, below the dorsal fin. There is a stripe on the middle of the back. Breeding males have a brilliant red lower flank and belly below the midflank stripe. The lower flank is yellow before and after

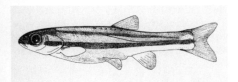

northern redbelly dace

the peak spawning period. Females are yellowish-green below the midflank stripe in the spawning season. Fins are yellowish.

Hybridises freely with the related **fine-scale dace**, with the hybrids interbreeding, making some populations a mixture of intermediate forms, none clearly one **dace** or the other. In an Albertan lake, the hybrids proved to be all-female. They may be produced continually by the parental species or be a distinct, self-perpetuating lineage. Such hybrids are also known from Québec, and in the U.S.A. where research has shown them to be a unisexual, clonal hybrid species perpetuated by gynogenesis, i.e. the females produce eggs identical genetically to themselves but require sperm from a related species (often one of the parental species) to stimulate development. The male makes no genetic contribution. This explanation of the all-female species is borne out by some populations now having only one of the parental species present so hybrids can no longer be produced. Reaches 7.7 cm.

Biology: This species inhabits the brown waters of bogs, ponds and small streams over silt or detritus bottoms. Food is diatoms, filamentous algae, zooplankton and aquatic insects. Various fish eating birds and **brook trout** eat this **minnow**. Life span is 8 years for females and 6 years for males. Maturity may be attained as early as 1 year of age. In southern Canada spawning occurs in June and in August in northern Alberta. Some populations in central Ontario have an extended spawning season, from mid-June to mid-August. These fish were fractional spawners, releasing eggs in batches over a long period. Temperatures are usually above 13°C. A female, with 1–8 males in attendance, darts in and out of filamentous algae, depositing non-adhesive eggs in a struggling mass. About 5–30 eggs are shed at each dart into the algae. A female can contain up to 6450 eggs of 1.24 mm diameter. This **dace** is used as a bait fish in eastern Canada.

northern rockfish

Scientific name: *Sebastes polyspinis*
    (Taranetz and Moiseev, 1933)
Family: **Scorpionfish**
Other common names: none
French name: sébaste à quatorze épines

Distribution: Found from Kamchatka in the former U.S.S.R. to the Queen Charlotte Islands.

Characters: This species is recognised by its dorsal fin spine count of 14. Soft dorsal fin rays 13–16, usually 15. Anal fin soft rays 7–9,

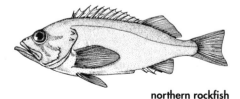

northern rockfish

usually 8, anal spines 3–4, with the second spine thicker and shorter than the third. Pectoral fin rays 17–19, usually 18, with 8–11 unbranched. Gill rakers 34–39. Vertebrae 28. Pores in the lateral line 40–53, scale rows below the lateral line 46–53. The branchiostegals are covered by scales. Head spines are weak to absent, the supraocular, tympanic, coronal and nuchal spines always absent. Overall colour is reddish or olive-brown with dark grey mottles and orange flecks. The lower part of the head is orange-red. The mouth and gill cavities are white with olive speckles. The belly is white. Three olive bands radiate back from the eye. The dorsal fin is reddish-olive on the membranes with a blackish edge. The pectoral fin is olive dorsally and reddish-orange or paler below. The pelvic and anal fins are reddish-orange, with red margins. Caudal fin rays reddish with olive membranes. The peritoneum is black, or silvery with black dots. Reaches 38 cm.

Biology: Found on soft bottoms from 73 to 358 m. This species is much less abundant than **Pacific ocean perch**. The maximum age for this species is 15 years. Females 21.9 cm and larger and older than 7 years are mature.

northern ronquil

Scientific name: *Ronquilus jordani*
   (Gilbert, 1889)
Family: **Ronquil**
Other common names: none
French name: ronquille du nord

Distribution: From California to the Bering Sea including British Columbia.

Characters: This species is distinguished from its relatives the **blue-eyed searcher** and the **bluefin searcher** by having the first 20–30 dorsal fin rays unbranched (the rest branched), cycloid or weakly ctenoid scales smooth to touch, tiny scales on the cheek, no large black patch on the front of the dorsal fin, and an upper jaw reaching the middle of the eye. Dorsal fin rays 41–48, anal fin rays 31–34 and pectoral fin rays about 17. Pores are evident on the head, but are not well-developed. Males are orange above and olive-green below, with the top of the head black. The flanks have vague dark bars. The dorsal and caudal fins are black with a yellow margin. The pectoral fin is yellow dorsally, black ventrally. Pelvic fins are black. The anal fin is iridescent blue with a black margin and golden spots near the body. The area below the eye and the cheek have golden to orange streaks. Females are olive-green above and lighter below. The back behind the head is reddish. The dorsal and caudal fins have orange margins while the anal fin has a brown margin to a light blue fin. Pelvic fins have some white on them. There are fine yellow lines below and paralleling the lateral line in both sexes. Some smaller fish may be a light, flesh-pink except for the black eyes. Attains 17.1 cm.

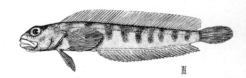

northern ronquil

Biology: Found on the bottom at 3 to 275 m depending on latitude with shallows being preferred in the north. Often associated with sandy bottoms near rocks, using the rocks as a refuge. Spawning occurs in February to March and eggs are pink or amber. Eggs are deposited on rocks. Young are pelagic close to shore.

northern saillamp

Scientific name: *Notoscopelus kroeyeri*
   (Malm, 1861)
Family: **Lanternfish**

American eel

Arctic char

Arctic grayling

Arctic lamprey

rowtooth flounder

Atka mackerel

antic bonito

Atlantic cod

Atlantic wolffish

Aurora trout

Banded gunnel

Big skate

Black crappie

Blackeye goby

Blacknose shiner

Bluegill

Bluntnose minnow

Bottlelight

Bowfin

Broad whitefish

Brook silverside

Brook trout

Brown rockfish

Brown trout

Buffalo sculpin

Burbot

Canary rockfish

Central mudminnow

Chain pickerel

Channel catfish

Channel darter

China rockfish

Chinook salmon

Chum salmon

Coastal cutthroat trout

Common shiner

Copper rockfish

Creek chub

Daubed tonguefish

Decorated warbonnet

Dolly Varden

Dover sole

English sole

Fallfish

Fish doctor

Freshwater drum

Gaspereau

Gizzard shad

Golden shiner

Graveldiver

Gray triggerfish

Grunt sculpin

Kelp greenling male

Kelp greenling female

Lake trout

Lake whitefish

Largemouth bass

Logperch

Longfin gunnel

Longfin sculpin

Longnose dace

Longnose gar

Longspine snipefish

Lumpfish

Monkfish

Mooneye

Northern hog sucker

Northern pearleye

Northern pike

Northern ronquil

Northern spearnose poacher

Ocean pout

Opah

Pacific cod

Pacific sleeper shark

Pacific spiny lumpsucker

Pacific viperfish

Padded sculpin

Pile perch

Pink salmon

uget Sound rockfish

Pumpkinseed

uillback

Quillback rockfish

uillfish

Rainbow smelt

inbow trout

Red Irish lord

Red hake, white hake

Rock bass

Rock sole

Rockweed gunnel

Rosylip sculpin

Rough pomfret

Round whitefish

Saddleback gunnel

ffron cod

Sailfin sculpin

rgassumfish

Sea raven

iner perch

Shorthorn sculpin

rtnose sturgeon

Showy snailfish

Silverspotted sculpin

Slim lightfish

Slimy sculpin

Smallmouth bass

Spinynose sculpin

Spotted ratfish

Starry flounder

Stout eelblenny

Stout sand lance

Striped seaperch

Sturgeon poacher

Swordfish

Tadpole madtom

Thornback sculpin

Threespine stickleback

Tube-snout

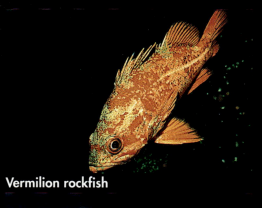

Vermilion rockfish

White bass

White hake

Whitespotted greenling

Yellow perch

Yellow walleye

Yelloweye rockfish

Yellowtail rockfish

Other common names: Krøyer's lanternfish
French name: lampe-voilière du nord

Distribution: Found only in the North Atlantic Ocean in temperate to subpolar waters as far north as the Arctic Circle.

Characters: This is 1 of 4 Atlantic coast species characterised by stiff, spine-like rays at the upper and lower caudal fin bases, no

northern saillamp

large glands on the upper and lower caudal peduncle outlined by heavy black pigment, and a dorsal fin base longer than the anal fin base. It is distinguished from its relatives (**Bolin's lanternfish, patchwork lanternfish** and **spinetail lanternfish**) by having 26–30 gill rakers visible in the open mouth, 21–22 dorsal fin rays, a large luminous gland on top of the caudal peduncle in males but no luminous tissue on the cheek or above the eye. Anal fin rays are 18–20, usually 19, and pectoral rays 12–13. Photophores: AO 8–10, usually 9, + 6–8, usually 7, total 15–18, usually 16. In adult males the gland occupies most of the upper caudal peduncle and is divided into 8–9 segments. Attains 16.5 cm or more.

Biology: Reported off Labrador, in the Gulf of St. Lawrence, off the Scotian Shelf and south of the Flemish Cap. Found at 325 m to more than 1000 m by day and from the surface to 125 m at night. Euphausiid crustaceans are the most important food item. In Canadian waters it is food for **swordfish, silver hake** and **Atlantic cod**. Spawning occurs mainly in February-March in Canadian waters of the Flemish Cap when fish are about 3 years old. Maximum age is 6 years.

northern sand lance

Scientific name: *Ammodytes dubius*
    Reinhardt, 1837
Family: **Sand Lance**

Other common names: Greenland sand lance,
    Arctic sand lance, offshore sand lance
French name: lançon du nord

Distribution: Found from Baffin Island and Hudson Bay along the Labrador coast and south to Virginia. Also in the western Canadian Arctic in the Beaufort Sea.

Characters: This species is distinguished from its only Canadian relative, the **stout sand lance**, by having usually 56–69 dorsal fin rays, 27–36 anal rays and 68–78 vertebrae. Overlaps occur in these counts and some fish may be difficult to assign to species. However Canadian offshore populations of sand lances with slender bodies and high vertebral counts (mean 73.8) are the northern sand lance. The number of oblique, lateral plicae or skin folds is 124–147. The sides are silvery with an iridescent green or blue lustre and the belly white. The back is bronze, blue-green or olive. Reaches 37.2 cm.

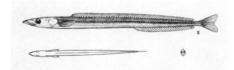

northern sand lance

Biology: This is an offshore, bottom-living species usually found at 15–108 m and 1–11°C (on the Scotian Shelf) over sand or fine gravel, into which they burrow. It has recently been reported to spawn in coastal waters of southern Newfoundland and may hibernate over winter in shallow waters in the north. Food is mainly copepod crustaceans which undergo a migration towards the surface at night and the sand lance probably follows the copepods to feed. Copepods are strained by filter feeding from the water using long gill rakers, but larger food items like worms are picked selectively. Sand lances are food for **Atlantic cod, haddock, pollock, silver hake, white hake, redfishes,** and **yellowtail flounder** among other species of fish as well as whales and sea birds. They are the most important food for **Canadian plaice**. Spawning begins in Canadian waters in late November and peaks in December-January but extends to May-June in Fortune Bay, Newfoundland. Eggs are up to 1.23 mm in diameter, but numbers spawned are unknown. Young are planktonic. Males and females grow at about the same rate but growth rates differ at different localities. Maximum age is at least 10 years and maturity is reached at 1–2 years. During the 1970s, the numbers of sand lance on the Grand Bank increased owing to a decline in the numbers of **Atlantic cod** because of overfishing.

northern sculpin

Scientific name: *Icelinus borealis*
　　Gilbert, 1896
Family: **Sculpin**
Other common names: comb sculpin
French name: icéline boréale

Distribution: Found from the Bering Sea to Washington including British Columbia.

Characters: The 5 Pacific coast members of the genus *Icelinus* are characterised by having 25 or more lateral line scales or

northern sculpin

pores, 2 pelvic fin soft rays, scales in 2 rows close to the dorsal fins and an antler-like preopercular spine. This species is separated from its relatives by the first 2 dorsal fin spines about equal in length to remainder, upper scale row extends onto caudal peduncle, no bump between the stout nasal spines, and a single chin pore. The uppermost of the 3 preopercular spines has 3–6 points directed upward. First dorsal fin spines 9–11, second dorsal soft rays 14–17. Anal rays 11–14 and pectoral rays 14–17. Lateral line scales 37–40. There is a simple, large cirrus at the base of the nasal spine, a large and branched cirrus over the rear of the eye, 1 cirrus at the end of the upper jaw, several on top of the head behind the one at the eye, filamentous cirri along the lateral line and cirri at the lower preopercular spines. The back and

upper flank is dark olive-grey or brown with 4 dark saddles. The belly is lighter. Fins have brown bars except for the anal fin. The head has thin brown bars. The spiny dorsal fin has 2 black spots on the margin, darkest in males. Reaches 10.2 cm.

Biology: Depth range is 5–247 m on soft, shell or rock bottoms, possibly deeper. It is common in British Columbia waters. A principal food item is shrimps and it may be caught in prawn traps.

northern searobin

Scientific name: *Prionotus carolinus*
　　(Linnaeus, 1771)
Family: **Searobin**
Other common names: green-eye, common gurnard, common searobin, cuckoo fish, pigfish, flying toad, grunter, web-fingered searobin, grondin carolin
French name: prionote du nord

Distribution: Found from Nova Scotia to Florida.

Characters: This species is distinguished from its Canadian relatives by having scales rather than plates, 3 short, stout, lower, finger-like pectoral rays, no forked snout, by colour pattern, and by a short pectoral fin reaching back level with rays 5–6 of the second dorsal fin. First dorsal fin with 10, rarely 9, spines and second dorsal fin with 12–14 soft rays. Anal fin soft rays usually 11–12. The pectoral fin tip is rounded or square. The caudal fin is concave posteriorly. There are some chest scales. The body is mottled greyish or reddish on the back and upper flank, and is dirty white or yellowish below. There

northern searobin

are about 5 dark saddles across the back. The first dorsal fin has a black eye-spot between spines 4 and 5. The caudal fins and the branchiostegal rays are black, grey or brown. The anal fin is brown. The finger-like pectoral rays are orange and the rest of the fin is crossed by 2 broad, dusky bars on a yellow to orange background. The pelvic fins are white. Reaches 43 cm.

Biology: Expatriates or strays from the south are found occasionally in the Bay of Fundy and offshore on the Scotian Shelf at 145 m. Generally found inshore and down to 170 m. They retire to deeper water in winter, re-appearing in the shallows in May–June on the U.S. coast. If disturbed they will bury themselves in sand with only the eyes and top of the head exposed. Food is crustaceans, squids, molluscs, worms and small fish. They are known to be prey for sharks. Sexual maturity is reached at 2–3 years, sometimes as early as 1 year, and this searobin lives at least 11 years. Spawning occurs from June to September, peaking in July–August. Eggs are buoyant, yellowish and about 1.5 mm in diameter. This searobin has the reputation of being one of the noisiest fish along the Atlantic coast of N. America. It is particularly loud in the spawning season when staccato calls replace the usual grunts. It is edible but is more of a nuisance to anglers where common, taking bait meant for other fishes. Although a bottom fish, they have been hooked near the surface by anglers trolling for **mackerel**. Commercial catches in the south are taken by trawlers and used for food and fish meal, for bait, pet food and fertiliser.

northern sennet

Scientific name: *Sphyraena borealis*
  DeKay, 1842
Family: **Barracuda**
Other common names: none
French name: barracuda du nord

Distribution: Found from Nova Scotia south to Uruguay.

Characters: The characteristic shape distinguishes this species. The mouth is large and has fangs. The dorsal fins are small and widely spaced. The lower jaw projects and has a fleshy tip. The pelvic fin origin lies under the origin of the first dorsal fin. There are 118–135 lateral line scales. The overall colour is silvery on the sides, olive-brown on

the back. The second dorsal, caudal, anal and pelvic fins are yellowish. Young fish have dark, elongate to squarish blotches along the back and lateral line. Reaches 46 cm.

northern sennet

Biology: Known only from one Canadian specimen caught in Halifax Harbour in 1928, the northern limit for this species in the western Atlantic Ocean.

northern smoothtongue

Scientific name: *Bathylagus schmidti*
  (Rass, 1955)
Family: **Deepsea Smelt**
Other common names: none
French name: leuroglosse luisant

Distribution: Found from southern British Columbia including the Strait of Georgia to the Bering and Okhotsk seas.

Characters: This species has been confused with the **southern smoothtongue** but has many more vertebrae and differences in larval pigment patterns. There are probably more scales in this species, although this character has yet to be investigated thoroughly (scales are easily lost). Colour is silvery with a dusky back and fins. Reaches sizes greater than 20 cm standard length.

northern smoothtongue

Biology: This species is very abundant in coastal waters being the third most common eggs and larvae in southeastern Alaska and the Strait of Georgia. Adults have been caught from the surface down to 732 m, and observers in submersibles in the Strait of

Georgia have seen the fish hanging motionless and head down! Food is small crustaceans, marine worms and fish eggs. This smoothtongue is eaten by **Pacific herring**, **eulachon**, **stout sand lance** and **chinook salmon**. Females may live more than 5 years, but males die at a smaller and younger age. The spawning season starts in the Strait of Georgia in late January and peaks in March–April with two or more egg batches laid in the season. Eggs are most abundant between 200 and 260 m with older larvae found between 40–90 m.

northern spearnose poacher

Scientific name: *Agonopsis vulsa*
(Jordan and Gilbert, 1880)
Family: **Poacher**
Other common names: windowtail poacher
French name: agone foncé

Distribution: Found from southeastern Alaska to southern California including British Columbia.

Characters: This species is distinguished from other Canadian Pacific poachers by having a pointed snout with 2 forward-point-

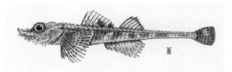

northern spearnose poacher

ing spines at its tip, and by caudal and pelvic fin colour patterns. Cirri are found on the snout, upper jaw end (3) and sides, under the lower jaw, near the operculum edge and on the branchiostegal rays. The first dorsal fin has 7–10 spines, the second dorsal fin has 7–9 rays. The anal fin has 10–12 rays. The pectoral fin has 13–15 rays with about 6–8 of the lower rays obviously thickened and finger-like. The gill membranes attach to the throat or isthmus. Overall colour is brown fading to white below. The caudal fin has a clear, light, central area. The pelvic fins are dark brown with white tips. The back and flanks have 6 or more dark saddles which extend onto the adjacent fins. Reaches 20 cm.

Biology: A bottom-living species at depths from 18–163 m over sand near rock outcrops, and also reported from the surface. Young are attracted to lights on piers and jetties. Adults use the pectoral fins to move but are generally motionless except when grubbing for worms and clams in the substrate.

northern squawfish

Scientific name: *Ptychocheilus oregonensis*
(Richardson, 1836)
Family: **Carp**
Other common names: Columbia squawfish, Columbia River dace
French name: sauvagesse du nord

Distribution: Found in British Columbia from the Nass, Fraser and Columbia river systems to central and southern coastal river systems, and from the Peace River basin entering northwestern Alberta. Also in adjacent U.S. states.

Characters: This species is characterised by the long snout, large mouth reaching back under the eye, no barbels and 64–80 lateral line scales. Dorsal fin branched rays 8 (range 7–9), anal fin branched rays 7 (range 7–9), pectoral rays 15–18 and pelvic rays 9. Pharyngeal teeth with slightly hooked tips, usually 2,5–4,2. Males have small tubercles on the head, back, pectoral, pelvic and caudal fins. The back is dark green, grey-green or green-brown, fading through silvery or pale yellow flanks to white on the belly. Young fish have a faint midflank stripe posteriorly, ending in a spot at the caudal fin base, best seen in preserved fish. Breeding males have yellow to orange pectoral, pelvic

northern squawfish

and anal fins and a white line below the lateral line. Peritoneum speckled. Reaches 63.0 cm fork length and 13.0 kg.

Biology: Northern squawfish are found offshore in lakes down to 36 m as adults while young fish enter shallows in summer. They may be found in slower rivers. Food when adult is various fishes and crayfish. This **minnow** replaces **northern pike** as a top predator in western Canada where the pike is absent. Terrestrial insects, aquatic insects, molluscs and some plankton are eaten when young. Squawfish also eat their own eggs and the occasional toad. Peak feeding activity is at dusk and during the night. It is a predator on **salmon** and also eats similar food. Some attempts have been made to reduce squawfish numbers. Life span may be as much as 20 years with maturity attained at about 6 years and 30.5 cm in one study. Females grow slightly faster and live longer than males. Spawning occurs from late May to July in gravel shallows at temperatures over 12°C. There may be some courtship behaviour with the male nudging the female's anal area. Each female is surrounded by several to many males, she arches her back, adhesive eggs are shed and fall to the bottom. Egg diameter is about 1.0 mm and they are greenish or pale orange and each female can produce up to 27,500. Hybrids with **peamouths** and **redside shiners** are known in Canadian waters and also **chiselmouths**. Squawfish can be angled for using flies and it is edible though not particularly tasty. A related species in the Colorado River reaches 180 cm and 45 kg.

northern wolffish

Scientific name: *Anarhichas denticulatus*
  Krøyer, 1845
Family: **Wolffish**
Other common names: bull-headed catfish,
  broad-headed catfish, Arctic wolffish,
  jelly-cat
French name: loup à tête large

Distribution: Found in the North Atlantic Ocean and adjacent Arctic seas. In Canada reported from Prince Patrick Island and possibly Victoria Island, N.W.T., and from off Baffin Island and the Flemish Cap, Newfoundland, the Gulf of St. Lawrence and south to Sable Island Bank and to Cape Cod.

Characters: This species is distinguished from its Arctic-Atlantic relatives in Canada by colour and by the teeth on the vomer bone in the mouth roof extending less far back than the palatine bones. Dorsal fin spines 76–81,

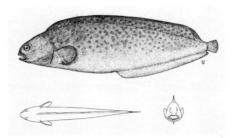

northern wolffish

anal rays 45–47, pectoral rays 20–22, vertebrae 78–82. Caudal fin rays 18–22, usually 20. The body is yellowish-grey, grey-brown, dark brown or blue-back and may be darkly spotted. Spots may not be clearly defined and may form a weak bar. However some fish do have sharp, distinct spots and superficially resemble **spotted wolffish**. Reaches 143.8 cm and 19.5 kg. The world, all-tackle angling record weighed 17 kg and was caught in 1982 at Holsteinsborg, Greenland.

Biology: This wolffish has been found from the surface down to 600 m, but prefers deeper waters with temperatures below 5°C. Elsewhere to 970 m. It does not school. Young have an extended pelagic period and adults probably migrate considerable distances to counteract drift away from adult spawning grounds. Food includes both bottom and free-swimming invertebrates, from crabs, brittle stars, starfish, sea urchins and molluscs to comb jellies, jellyfish and small fishes. Apparently eaten by ringed seals in the Arctic and by **cod** and **golden redfish** in the Atlantic and elsewhere by **Greenland sharks**. This species lives at least 12 years. Spawning probably occurs in Canadian Atlantic waters in late autumn and early winter. Up to 29,290 eggs are laid on the bottom and are 8 mm in diameter. The flesh develops a "jelly" condition or watery flesh, making this species unsuitable for sale. The skin is also unsuitable as leather.

numerous helmetfish

Scientific name: *Melamphaes microps*
  (Günther, 1878)
Family: **Ridgehead**
Other common names: none
French name: heaume nombreux

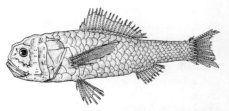

numerous helmetfish

Distribution: Found north and south of the tropical Atlantic Ocean, in the Indian Ocean and parts of the Pacific Ocean. Off the Canadian Atlantic coast near the Flemish Cap and in the Newfoundland Basin.

Characters: This species is distinguished from its relatives, the **highsnout ridgehead** and **shortspine helmetfish**, by having usually 8, rather than 7, branched rays in the pelvic fin. Scale rows number 32–35 from nape to caudal fin base. Dorsal fin spines 3, soft rays 16–18. Anal fin spine 1, soft rays 7–8. Pectoral rays 14–16. Teeth in 2–5 rows in jaws. The eye is surrounded by radiating ridges. The few captured specimens have faded in preservative and colouration is not recorded. Attains 9.9 cm.

Biology: Biology is little known. This species has been caught down to over 2500 m.

O

oarjaw wingmax

Scientific name: *Bellocia michaelsarsia*
(Koefoed, 1927)
Family: **Slickhead**
Other common names: Michael Sars
  smooth-head
French name: maxailé aviron

Distribution: Found in the North Atlantic
Ocean including off the Atlantic coast of
Canada.

Characters: This species is distinguished
by having teeth on the maxilla bone of the
upper jaw, the dorsal fin origin in front of the
anal fin origin, the lower jaw without a
prominent knob, 9–11 anal fin rays and the

oarjaw wingmax

forehead and snout straight over the eyes.
Pectoral fin rays number 15–17. It is brown
in colour. Attains at least 37 cm.

Biology: This species has been trawled at
2600–4000 m. Other aspects of its biology
are unknown.

ocean perches

Ocean perches are members of the
Scorpionfish Family and include the **Pacific
ocean perch** and the **golden redfish** which
used to be known as the ocean perch.
However "ocean perch" is most commonly
encountered as the market name for 3 redfish
species, the **Acadian**, **deepwater** and **golden
redfish** which are very similar in appearance
and are not distinguished commercially. An
alternative commercial name is **redfishes**.

ocean pout

Scientific name: *Macrozoarces americanus*
(Schneider, 1801)
Family: **Eelpout**
Other common names: muttonfish, mother-
  of-eels, eelpout, congo eel, laughing jack
French name: loquette d'Amérique

Distribution: Found from southern
Labrador, the Gulf of St. Lawrence and
through Atlantic Canada as far south as off
North Carolina.

Characters: This species is distinguished
from its Canadian Atlantic relatives by having pelvic fins and scales and the rear part of

ocean pout

the dorsal fin having short spines abruptly
lower than the rest of the fin. Dorsal fin soft
rays 95–100 followed by 18 short spines,
anal rays 105–124 and pectoral rays 18–21.
Vertebrae 131–144.

Overall colour variable but usually a yellowish to red-brown background with grey or
olive-green mottles. Lips are a dull yellow.
Dorsal fin with a yellow margin. Pectoral fins
often reddish or orange as are rear dorsal and
anal fin margins. Belly white to yellowish.

Reaches 107 cm and 5.4 kg.

Biology: Ocean pouts are found from the
intertidal zone down to 364 m, usually on a
hard bottom but also over sand and mud.
Temperature range is 0–17°C. They overwinter in deeper water and come inshore in the
spring.

Food is scooped in mouthfuls from the
bottom during daylight or seized when drifting past and includes worms, crustaceans such
as crabs, shrimp, barnacles and amphipods,
various clams and snails, sea squirts and sea
urchins as well as the occasional **herring** and
smelt. In Newfoundland 62% of the diet is
green sea urchins. **Cunners** will follow ocean
pout to feed on organisms exposed by the disturbance of sediments and overturned rocks.
Ocean pout are eaten by various other fishes
and by harbour seals.

Life span is up to 18 years and growth is
slow. Copulation occurs vent to vent with the
male on his side and the female at a 45° angle
to the bottom. Pectoral fins interlock and tails
are coiled. Quivering and arching of the back

occurs in the male. Fertilisation is internal. A large, sticky egg mass is deposited in crevices or under boulders in August in Newfoundland waters. Eggs are large, 6 mm in diameter, and number up to 4200. The female guards the eggs which take 2–3 months to hatch. The eggs hatch as juveniles, rather than larvae, and are very similar to adults in appearance. Most ocean pout leave shallow water before the onset of winter.

Incidental catches are processed as fish meal in Canada but the flesh is white and flaky and makes good eating. Some scientists have used the ocean pout in physiological studies of the heart and muscles. It has also been evaluated as an aquaculture species in Canada.

ocean sunfish

Scientific name: *Mola mola*
(Linnaeus, 1758)
Family: **Mola**
Other common names: headfish, moonfish, trunkfish, millstone
French name: môle commun

Distribution: Found in temperate to tropical waters world-wide and from the Gulf of St. Lawrence and Newfoundland southward in the Atlantic and from Alaska and British Columbia southward in the Pacific Ocean.

Characters: The peculiar shape of this fish is distinctive. There is no caudal or pelvic fins. The dorsal and anal fins are large, fixed in a vertical position and placed posteriorly. The jaws have cutting edges divided into two "teeth." The mouth is small. The dorsal fin has 15–20 soft rays and the anal fin 14–19 soft rays. Scales are tubercles set in a tough, leathery skin which has a thick layer of cartilage beneath it. There is a pore-like gill opening in front of the upward-directed pectoral fin. Young fish are covered in large spines and have a normal caudal fin. Colour is dark grey or blue above to silvery grey-brown on the flanks and dusky or dirty-white below. Flanks may be spotted. It is said to luminesce at night. Reputed to exceed 4 m and 2000 kg but at these sizes hard to measure and weigh accurately.

Biology: A summer stray to Canadian waters but not rare, it occasionally becomes stranded in weirs. It may be seen floating or swimming lazily at the surface by flapping its dorsal and anal fins. Such fish may be

ocean sunfish

sick, but they can swim strongly. They may be warming the body to speed up digestion. It is even reported to jump clear of the water, perhaps in an attempt to dislodge the numerous skin parasites. It has been hit by ships. The bottom limit for this fish is uncertain but it descends to at least 570 m. Food is principally jellyfish, comb jellies and salps, but also crustaceans, algae, molluscs, squids, fishes and brittle stars. This is the most fecund fish with a single female of 1.37 m producing up to 300 million eggs, and one of the most disparate in larval and adult size, an increase by 60 million times. The skin is tough, being made of collagen fibres. In the nineteenth century, children wrapped sunfish skin in twine to make bouncy balls.

ocean triggerfish

Scientific name: *Canthidermis sufflamen*
(Mitchill, 1815)
Family: **Leatherjacket**
Other common names: sobaco

French name: baliste océanique

Distribution: Found from Nova Scotia south to the Caribbean Sea and South America.

Characters: This species is distinguished from other Canadian leatherjackets by its lack of enlarged, flexible scales above the pectoral fin base. There are 25–28, usually 26–27, dorsal fin rays, 23–25, usually 24, anal fin rays and 15–16 pectoral fin rays. The dorsal and anal fins are very high. Caudal fin lobes are only slightly elongated. Overall colour is brown to grey, lighter ventrally. The base of the pectoral fin is blackish. Young fish have dark grey to brown spots on the body, second dorsal, anal and caudal fins. The first dorsal fin membrane is dark. Reaches 60 cm. The world, all-tackle angling record weighed 4.42 kg and was caught in 1989 at Key West, Florida.

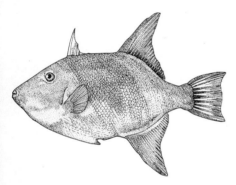

ocean triggerfish

Biology: Known only from immature strays in Canadian waters collected in 1978–1979.

ocean whitefish

Scientific name: *Caulolatilus princeps*
(Jenyns, 1842)
Family: **Tilefish**
Other common names: none
French name: tile océanique

Distribution: Found from Peru north to British Columbia.

Characters: This species is recognised by the continuous dorsal fin with 7–10, usually 9, spines and 23–27, usually 25–26, soft rays, the lack of teeth in the roof of the mouth and the finely serrate margin to the preopercle bone on the side of the head. The anal fin has 1–2 spines and 20–26, usually

ocean whitefish

24–25, soft rays. Lateral line scales number about 99–115 or 116–134 according to different authors. The jaws have an outer row of canines with bands behind. The body is yellowish to brown above and whitish below. Fins are yellow or yellow-green and the dorsal and anal fins have a central blue stripe. The pectoral fin is bluish centrally and is streaked with yellow. Pores on the flank are white. Attains 102 cm and 5.4 kg.

Biology: Found offshore between Barkley Sound and Clayoquot Sound, Vancouver Island, in British Columbia, but this species is uncommon north of California. It inhabits rocky reefs and banks at depths of 10–150 m. In the U.S.A. they are most abundant around offshore islands. Food is crustaceans, fishes, worms, squids and octopi. This fish lives longer than 13 years. Spawning occurs in winter in California and young are planktonic. Ocean whitefish are caught by sport fishermen in California. The commercial fishery is small and has not been helped by some catches having a bitter taste, likened to raw olives, and occasioned perhaps by some item in the diet of the whitefish.

ocean whitetip shark

Scientific name: *Carcharhinus longimanus*
(Poey, 1861)
Family: **Requiem Shark**
Other common names: oceanic whitetip shark, requin océanique, requin à longues nageoires, réquiem océanique
French name: rameur

Distribution: Common in warm oceanic waters around the world including off Atlantic Canada.

Characters: This requiem shark is distinguished from its Canadian relatives by its serrated teeth with a single cusp, long and broad

ocean whitetip shark

paddle-shaped pectoral fins, broad and rounded dorsal fin, and white fin tips in adults (black in juveniles but these have black saddles on the caudal peduncle). The snout is very short and blunt and the body stocky. The head is very broad. The tip of the anal fin reaches nearly to the precaudal pit. There is usually a middorsal ridge.

Olive-grey to brown or slaty-blue above with a dirty white or yellow belly. The dorsal fins, pectoral fins, pelvic fins and tail fin lobes are white tipped but this may be absent. There is a faint white band on the flank. Young fish have black tips to the dorsal, pectoral and pelvic fins but also have black saddles on the caudal peduncle, upper margin of the caudal fin and in front of the second dorsal fin. The undersurface of the pelvic fins, lower lobe of the caudal fin and apices of the anal and second dorsal fins are often spotted black.

Up to 3.95 m. The world, all-tackle angling record from Hawaii caught in 1992 weighed 66.45 kg.

Biology: Very rare off the Atlantic coast of Canada; caught once south of Newfoundland in the Gulf Stream on 12 June 1950, once in October 1961 on Georges Bank and one was caught on 25 July 1953 just off Georges Bank. Found at the surface down to at least 152 m but is usually offshore in the open sea. This is an open ocean, pelagic species usually found in waters warmer than about 20°C and therefore rare in Canada. It is one of the three most common oceanic sharks in warmer waters. The sexes are segregated in some areas. It is slow-moving but capable of sharp bursts of activity and is an aggressive shark in pursuit of prey.

Food is mostly fish and squid. Fish items in its diet include **barracuda, tuna, marlin, dolphins** (the fish), **jacks** and **threadfins**. Also consumed are dolphins, sea birds, turtles, snails, crustaceans, carrion and garbage. Although they eat **dolphins** (the fish) a whitetip has been seen swimming with 8–10 of them. They have been observed casually cruising around with mouths open in schools of actively-feeding small **tuna**. Since these sharks were found to have tuna in their stomachs it seems they merely waited for the frenzied tuna to blunder into their open mouths. They are also reported to feed at the surface, lifting their heads out of the water to grasp the prey.

Ocean whitetips are viviparous with a yolk-sac placenta. Litters number 1 to 15 with a mean of about 6 and young are 60–75 cm at birth. Gestation is about one year with mating and birth in early summer in the western North Atlantic. Males mature at 1.75–1.98 m and females at 1.8–2.0 m.

This shark is eaten fresh, smoked and dried, and salted. It is also used for fish meal, shark fin soup, for hides and for the vitamin content of its liver oil. It is caught on pelagic longlines, handlines and in pelagic and bottom trawls. Ocean whitetips cause a lot of damage to the **tuna** and **swordfish** longline fisheries as they persist in following boats and devouring hooked catches. This shark can be caught on hook and line but is highly suspicious of baits and gives a poor fight when hooked. This species is dangerous to man for its persistent curiosity and unlike the great white shark it cannot be frightened off. Whitetips were seen by frogmen around the wreck of the "Andrea Doria" which sank near the Nantucket lightship in 1956.

oceanic lightfish

Scientific name: *Vinciguerria nimbaria*
(Jordan and Williams in Jordan and Stark, 1895)
Family name: **Lightfish**
Other common names: none
French name: poisson étoilé océanique

Distribution: Found in all the major oceans in warmer waters including Atlantic Canada.

Characters: This species is distinguished

from its Canadian Atlantic relatives by having the end of the dorsal fin opposite or behind the anal fin origin, a photophore or light organ below the rear eye margin, 13–14 photophores over the anal fin and back to the tail, and a photophore at the chin tip. The anal and dorsal fin bases are equal in length. There are 13–16 anal fin rays. The eyes are normal and the upper jaw margin is pigmented. The back is dark and the flanks silvery. Reaches 48 mm in standard length.

oceanic lightfish

Biology: First caught in Atlantic Canada at Browns Bank in 1978 and since recorded several times on the Scotian Shelf. Juveniles and adults are found at 200–400 m by day and in the upper 100 m at night. This species may be thrown up on shore by storms because it enters the surface ocean layers. Food includes small crustaceans principally copepods, and feeding takes place mostly in the afternoon and early evening with a peak between 7–8 p.m. in the tropical Atlantic Ocean.

oceanic puffer

Scientific name: *Lagocephalus lagocephalus*
(Linnaeus, 1758)
Family: **Puffer**
Other common names: toby
French name: orbe étoilé

Distribution: Found world-wide in subtropical to tropical waters. In the eastern Atlantic Ocean there are only 2 records, one from Bermuda and one from Newfoundland.

Characters: This species has a four-toothed beak in the mouth and is distinguished from related species by fin ray counts. Dorsal fin rays are 13–15, anal fin rays 11–14 and pectoral fin rays 13–16. Spines are restricted to the belly. Belly spines have 4 prongs at the base. The lower caudal fin lobe is longer than the upper one. There are 2 separate lateral lines. Adults are dark green, dark blue, pur-

plish-black or brown-grey fading through silvery to purplish sides to white below. Flanks are spotted anteriorly but these fade in larger

oceanic puffer

fish. Fish less than 18 cm long have 9 or fewer bars on the back between the eye and the dorsal fin. Reaches at least 61 cm. The world, all-tackle angling record weighed 2.99 kg and was caught in England in 1985.

Biology: Only 1 specimen has been collected in Canada from Placentia Bay in 1961. This species, as its names suggests, is usually found in the open ocean near the surface but may be cast up on beaches.

ocellated frogfish

Scientific name: *Antennarius ocellatus*
(Bloch and Schneider, 1801)
Family: **Frogfish**
Other common names: none
French name: antennaire ocellé

Distribution: Found from Atlantic Canada south to Venezuela and in the eastern Atlantic Ocean.

Characters: This **anglerfish** is distinguished from the related **sargassumfish** by its lack of cirri on the snout in front of the short

ocellated frogfish

fishing apparatus. The esca or bait is a fleshy bulb with many filaments. There are usually 13 soft dorsal fin rays, 8 anal fin rays and

11–13, usually 12, rays in the pectoral fin. The skin has a frosted appearance because the head, body and fins are covered with fine tubercles having an narrow base, flaring dorsally and sometimes with fine points at each tip. There are 3 large black eyespots or ocelli, one on the rear of the dorsal fin, one in the middle of the caudal fin and one on the midflank. The rest of the body is spotted or mottled with dark brown on a tan, pink or yellow background. Reaches 38 cm.

Biology: Three larval specimens have been collected on the Scotian Shelf in 1977 and 1979. These are strays from the south.

offshore hake

Scientific name: *Merluccius albidus*
  (Mitchill, 1818)
Family: **Hake**
Other common names: merlu argenté du large
French name: merlu blanc

Distribution: Found from the Scotian Shelf of Atlantic Canada south to Brazil.

Characters: This species is distinguished from its relative, the **silver hake**, by having more lateral line scales (130–148) and fewer

offshore hake

gill rakers (8–12, usually 9–11). First dorsal fin rays 10–13, second dorsal rays 35–41. Anal fin with 35–42 rays and pectoral with 12–17 rays. Jaws are large with several rows of recurved teeth. Overall colour an iridescent silver when alive fading to dark grey to blue on the back, silvery flanks and silvery-white belly. The inside of the mouth and tongue are dark blue. The cheek is pigmented in contrast to **silver hake**. Peritoneum dark brown to black. Attains 70 cm.

Biology: This hake is usually found in water deeper than 183 m down to 1170 m at temperatures of 5–10°C. Young, males and young females are found at less than 550 m while large females are found deeper. Food

includes fishes, particularly **hakes** and **lanternfishes**, squid and crustaceans, particularly those which can be caught near the sea bed. Feeding occurs throughout the day except near dawn. There is some cannibalism. Growth is rapid when young and females grow much larger than males. Life span exceeds 5 years but offshore hake are difficult to age accurately. Spawning occurs from April to October in the Gulf of Mexico and April to July in New England at 330–550 m on or near the bottom. Eggs are 1.2 mm in diameter, greenish-white and number about 500,000. This species is not commercially important in Canada but it is caught in the Gulf of Mexico by U.S. and Cuban fishermen and sold fresh, frozen or smoked.

ogac

Scientific name: *Gadus ogac*
  Richardson, 1836
Family: **Cod**
Other common names: Greenland cod,
  rock cod, pilot, fjord cod, morue de roche,
  morue ogac
French name: ogac

Distribution: Found from Alaska throughout the southern Canadian Arctic to Hudson Bay, Labrador, Newfoundland and the Gulf of St. Lawrence south to include Cape Breton Island, N.S.

Characters: This species and its relative, the **Atlantic cod**, are separated from other Canadian Arctic-Atlantic cods by having 3 dorsal and 2 anal fins, the first dorsal fin being rounded, a projecting snout, the upper jaw extends back beyond the front of the eye, a slender well-developed chin barbel,

ogac

about twice the pupil diameter, no large, black blotch on the flank, a light lateral line and a large eye entering 4.0–5.5 times in head length. The ogac is distinguished from its relative by the unspotted body and jet black peritoneum. First dorsal fin rays 13–17, second dorsal rays 14–20 and third dorsal rays 15–20. First anal fin rays 18–23, second anal rays 15–20. Males bear many, long, club-shaped breeding tubercles on body scales. Overall colour brown to black with lighter, yellowish blotches and marbling on the flanks and a grey to white belly. Ovaries are blue-black. Attains 71.1 cm and 7 kg. Ogac is an Inuktitut word for this fish.

Biology: This cod is an inshore species although in warmer southern waters it may be found offshore down to 400 m. It also enters estuaries and the brackish Bras d'Or Lake, N.S. where it is found in deep, cold holes. In Hudson Bay ogac are bottom-living, non-schooling and non-migrating and are not found under ice like **Arctic cod**. Life span there is 12 years. Food is principally fishes such as **capelin, polar cod, Greenland halibut** and also crustaceans, molluscs, starfishes and worms when fish are not available. Ogac are cannibals but have few other predators. Maximum life span is about 21 years but not all populations live so long — James Bay fish only reach 9 years. Maturity is attained at 2–4 years. Spawning occurs in February, March and April (April to June in James Bay) with about 1–2 million, large eggs being produced. Some spawning may occur in brackish water. Spawning is repeated in each year after maturity is attained. Unlike its relative, the **Atlantic cod**, this species has little commercial importance although 6 tonnes were caught in 1985 in Canada. The flesh is tougher than that of **Atlantic cod**.

Ogrefish Family

Scientific name: Anoplogastridae
French name: ogres

This family, also called fangtooths, is found bathypelagically in most oceans between 46°N and 46°S. There are only 2 species and 1 is found in Atlantic Canada.

The head has an ogre-like appearance. The short, deep body is covered with small, thin, cycloid scales, with many spines. Each scale is on a short pedicel embedded in the skin. The lateral line is an open groove occa-

sionally covered with scales at intervals. There are no spines in the fins except the caudal base. The pelvic fin has 7 soft rays. The jaws have characteristic and numerous fangs which are depressible in young but fixed in adults. The neural spines are strongly slanted. There are 8–9 branchiostegal rays. There is no subocular shelf.

Ogrefish are relatives of the **Spinyfin** and **Slimehead** families. They are members of the **Alfonsino Order**.

Young are different from adults in having a big eye, long head spines, smaller teeth and slender gill rakers and were once described as a distinct species.

This fish is remarkable for its ability to survive in aquaria for up to 23 days. Most meso- and bathypelagic fish die within minutes or hours of capture so that most of our knowledge of them is based on dead specimens.

See **fangtooth**

oilfish

Scientific name: *Ruvettus pretiosus*
    Cocco, 1829
Family: **Snake Mackerel**
Other common names: castor oil fish,
    scourfish, plaintail
French name: rouvet

Distribution: Found world-wide in warmer oceans and off Newfoundland and Nova Scotia.

Characters: The body form somewhat resembles a **tuna**. The spiny dorsal fin with 13–15 spines folds down into a groove. The

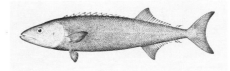

oilfish

soft dorsal fin has 15–19 rays, followed by 2 finlets. The anal fin has 1–2 spines, 14–18 soft rays, and is followed by 1–2 finlets. The belly is keeled between the pelvic fins and the anus. This is the only Canadian snake mackerel with its scales interspersed with spiny tubercles. There is no caudal peduncle keel and there is 1 spine and 5 soft rays in the pelvic fin. The overall colour is violet or purplish-brown to dark-brown with pectoral and pelvic fin tips black. The eye is greenish. Juveniles have white margins on the soft dorsal and anal fins. Attains a reputed 3 m and 50 kg.

Biology: Canadian records are strays from warmer waters. This species is usually found between 182 and 732 m. It may rest head upward, supported by the oil in the flesh at neutral buoyancy. Food is fish, cephalopods and other invertebrates. It is caught accidentally while longlining for **tuna**. Anglers may catch it using powered reels to fish in deep water. The oily flesh has a purgative effect when eaten, hence the common names, although grilling will remove the oil. The flesh spoils rapidly and food poisoning has resulted on occasion.

opah

Scientific name: *Lampris guttatus*
    (Brünnich, 1788)
Family: **Opah**
Other common names: spotted opah,
    moonfish, Jerusalem haddock, kingfish,
    poisson lune, opa
French name: opah

Distribution: World-wide in cool-temperate to tropical seas. On both the Atlantic and Pacific coasts of Canada.

Characters: The body shape and upwardly directed pectoral fin along with colour are dis-

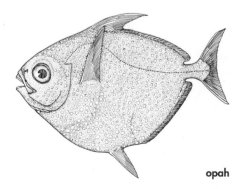

opah

tinctive. There are no teeth. Scales are cycloid and minute. The dorsal fin is greatly elongated anteriorly, its length almost matched by

the sickle-shaped pelvic fins. Dorsal fin with 48–56 rays, anal fin with 33–42 rays, pectoral fin with 20–25 rays, and pelvic fin with 12–17 rays. Back dark violet, steel blue or green. Flanks iridescent silver-blue with white or silver spots. Belly rose. Fins and mouth deep scarlet. Golden around eyes. Up to 1.85 m long and reputedly 273 kg. The world, all-tackle angling record weighed 55.33 kg and was caught in Mexico in 1993.

Biology: This is an oceanic species found from shallow to perhaps quite deep water. It is not common and excites a lot of attention when caught because of its size and colouring. Strays into Atlantic Canada in warm summer months, reaching the Grand Banks. On the Pacific coast reported from off southern Vancouver Island. Food is unusual in that it is often squids and octopuses along with fishes and crustaceans. They have been caught by anglers after **salmon** and **albacore**, and on **tuna** longlines. The flesh is red and quite tasty, if dry, and is especially good when smoked.

Opah Family

Scientific name: Lamprididae (= Lampridae)
French name: opahs

This family is found world-wide in temperate and tropical waters. There are 2 species and 1 is found on both the Atlantic and Pacific coasts of Canada.

The oval and compressed shape of the body is distinctive with the high anterior arch to the lateral line and the deep scarlet fins and mouth. The pectoral fin points upward rather than rearward. The pectoral fins are used for fast swimming by a rapid up and down motion, and the opah appears to "fly" through the water to catch its food. More characters and biology are given under the species description.

Opahs are relatives of the **Ribbonfish Family** in the **Opah Order**. Opah is apparently an African word for these fish.

See **opah**

Opah Order

Opahs, oarfishes, crestfishes, **ribbonfishes**, tube-eyes, hairyfish, tapetails, largenoses and their relatives or Lampridiformes (= Lampriformes or Allotriognathi) comprise

7 families with about 19 species found in most oceans, often in the deep sea. There are 2 families with 2 species on the Pacific and Atlantic coasts of Canada.

These fishes have a wide variety of body and fin shapes, often compressed yet very elongate fishes, lack true fin spines, have 0–17 pelvic rays in a thoracic to jugular fin, the pelvic girdle is attached to a large, specialised hypocoracoid bone in the pectoral girdle, the premaxilla bone borders the upper jaw, the swimbladder is not connected to the gut when present, scales are small and cycloid or absent, teeth are weak to absent, and the orbitosphenoid skull bone is present in some species. The order is usually defined by the protrusion mechanism of the upper jaw. The maxilla bone slides in and out with the premaxilla instead of being attached by a ligament to the ethmoid and palatine bones.

Opahs are related to the **Alfonsino** and **Dory** orders. Some families (not found in Canada) have been included within the **Alfonsino Order**. Fossils date to the Tertiary period. Much remains to be learned about fishes in this order since museum specimens are rare for many species and the fish themselves are fragile.

One member of the order, the oarfish (*Regalecus glesne*) not reported from Canada, attains over 8 m in length, is ribbon-like, and has a bright red dorsal fin with elongate rays. It is probably the basis for many sea-serpent legends.

See **Opah Family**
    Ribbonfish Family

Opeongo whitefish

Scientific name: *Coregonus* sp.
Family: **Salmon**
Other common names: none
French name: corégone de l'Opéongo

Distribution: Known only from Opeongo Lake, Algonquin Provincial Park, Ontario.

Characters: This is a dwarf form related to the **lake whitefish**. It differs in lateral line scale counts (average 77.3 in the Opeongo whitefish and 83.3 in **lake whitefish**), in gill raker counts (average 25.4 compared to 27.7) and also in vertebral counts. However immature **lake whitefish** had counts of lateral line

scales which were not different from Opeongo whitefish and a third group of fish had an even lower lateral line scale count, around 72. The Opeongo whitefish has a

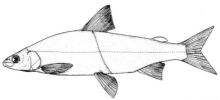

Opeongo whitefish

lower raker count compared to **lake whitefish** in contrast to the **Squanga whitefish** of the Yukon. The taxonomy of the Opeongo whitefish is uncertain; it may be a distinct species or merely a spawning stock. Attains an average length of 12.0 cm total length, half that of **lake whitefish** in the same lake.

Biology: Opeongo whitefish are caught below 15 m in July–August at 7–11°C while **lake whitefish** are between 8 and 15 m at 11–18°C. At other times of the year, distribution is similar. Life span is 5 years compared to 14 in **lake whitefish** and growth is slower. Spawning takes place at a peak in the first 2 weeks of November at 4–7°C. Eggs hatch in the first 2 weeks of May. Competing introduced **lake cisco** and acid rain have led to the Opeongo whitefish being endangered.

orange filefish

Scientific name: *Alutera schoepfi*
    (Walbaum, 1792)
Family: **Filefish**
Other common names: alutère orangé, turbot, hogfish, sunfish, unicornfish
French name: bourse orange

Distribution: Found from Brazil to Nova Scotia.

Characters: The dorsal fin has 32–39 rays, the anal fin 35–41 rays. The gill slit is very oblique. The absence of an obvious spine at the pelvic fin position and the low fin ray counts distinguish this species among Canadian filefish. The dorsal spine is very slender, weakly barbed and often bent. The dorsal snout profile is slightly concave to straight. The skin is rough. Adults are usually brown or olive-grey with fine orange to yellowish spots but may be bright yellow overall. Attains 61 cm.

orange filefish

Biology: Rare in Canadian waters with two specimens caught in Nova Scotia one in 1938 and one in 1955. This is the northern limit for this species. Young are common in floating algae and adults are often seen floating head down looking for food while being propelled slowly by the dorsal and anal fin. Food includes algae and sea grasses. Spawning occurs in April, July, August, November and December in the Caribbean. The large pelvic bone of adults has been used as a letter opener.

orangespotted sunfish

Scientific name: *Lepomis humilis*
    (Girard, 1858)
Family: **Sunfish**
Other common names: orangespot, redspotted
    sunfish, dwarf sunfish, pygmy sunfish
French name: crapet menu

Distribution: Found in Cedar Creek and Pelee Island in the Lake Erie basin and the Canard River, a Detroit River tributary, in southwestern Ontario. In the U.S.A. from south of the Great Lakes Canadian distribution west to the Dakotas and south to Gulf drainages.

Characters: This species is distinguished by having 3 anal fin spines and 7–10 soft rays, usually 10 (range 10–12) dorsal fin spines, Second dorsal fin soft rays 9–11, 32–41 lateral line scales, compressed body, no teeth on the tongue, ectopterygoid or entopterygoid, long pointed pectoral fins (about 3 times in standard length and reaching anterior edge of eye when folded forward) and opercular bone extending only to middle of "earflap", which has a light orange to red margin surrounding a black spot. The single, most characteristic fea-

ture is the large, sensory cavities on the head - those above the upper lip are slit-like and larger than the nostril diameter. There are also 2 pits between the eyes and large pores along the preopercle. Males have an olive-green back, lighter flanks and a yellow to white belly. Flanks with 4–7 dark olive broad bars, especially in young. The head and body have orange spots. Fins have a red-orange margin. Females are brown without orange spots, and soft dorsal and caudal fins have brown spots. Breeding males have heightened orange colours, an orange-red eye, belly and median fins orange, flanks and sides of head iridescent sapphire blue with orange to red streaks and spots, and the anterior pelvic fin and the whole anal fin have a black margin. Hybrids with **pumpkinseeds** are reported from Canada. Reaches 16.0 cm total length.

orangespotted sunfish

Biology: This species is found in rivers, streams, ponds and lakes and is tolerant of silt, low oxygen levels and some pollution. It was first reported from Canada in 1981. Food is aquatic insects, crustaceans such as crayfish, mites, with some algae and small fishes and terrestrial insects. Life span is 7 years and maturity is attained primarily at 2–3 years of age. Spawning in Wisconsin is from late May to August when water temperatures reach about 18°C. It takes place in shallow water where the male constructs a bowl-shaped nest by tail flicks and trembling of fins. The nest is 15–18 cm wide and 3–4 cm deep. Males produce courtship sounds which are species specific. The male and female manoeuvre around each other, even splashing, eventually coming to lie together with bellies touching. Eggs and sperm are then shed. Males remain on the nest until eggs hatch. The eggs are amber, 0.5 mm in diameter and number up to 4,700. They are adhesive and stick to pebbles and sand grains in the nest where the male aerates them by fin quivering. The male defends the eggs but may lose some as he drives away one predator. The bright colour of this sunfish has led to its use as an aquarium fish.

Oreo Family

Scientific name: Oreosomatidae
French name: oréos

Oreos are found in the Atlantic, Indian, Pacific and Antarctic oceans. There are about 9 species, with 1 species definitely known from the Pacific coast of Canada, and possibly a second species from the weathership Ocean Station Papa at 50°N, 145°W (juveniles are hard to identify).

This family has a deep, compressed body, an upturned, moderate-sized protractile mouth, an anteriorly arched lateral line, small cycloid or ctenoid scales, and conical scutes and protuberances on the body when young. Jaw teeth are small and in 1–2 rows. The eye is very large. The strong fin spines bear longitudinal grooves. Often young fish with their scutes and leathery skin are mistaken for species different from the scaled

oreosoma

adults. This juvenile appearance is known as the oreosoma. Oreos are related to the **Boarfish**, **Diamond Dory**, **Dory** and **Eyefish** families in the **Dory Order**.

Adults are usually found below 150 m and are rarely caught. These oreos are not a brand of cookie.

See **oxeye oreo**

ovate lightfish

Scientific name: *Ichthyococcus ovatus* (Cocco, 1838)
Family: **Lightfish**
Other common names: none
French name: poisson étoilé oval

Distribution: Widely distributed in all oceans usually in subtropical waters but also including off Atlantic Canada.

Characters: This species is distinguished from the related **slim lightfish** and other Canadian lightfishes by distribution, absence

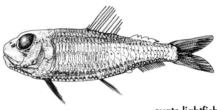

ovate lightfish

of the SO photophore, gill rakers number 19–25, the anal fin origin being well behind the end of the dorsal fin, and by the large, tubular and telescopic eye turned obliquely upwards. Dorsal fin rays 10–13, anal fin rays 12–17, lateral line scales 33–38. A ventral adipose fin is present. Photophores: ORB 2, OP 3, BR 11–12, OA 23–27, IV 23–26, VAV 8–11, AC 12–14. Overall colour is a brownish-yellow with silvery flanks. Scale pocket edges and fin bases are black. The peritoneum is silvery but the black gut is visible through the body wall. Reaches 54.5 mm.

Biology: First reported as a single specimen for Canada from the Flemish Cap off Newfoundland in 1990. Adults are found mostly at 200–500 m and do not migrate vertically. Post-larvae are found in the upper 150 m before metamorphosis and at 400–750 m after metamorphosis. Reproduction is probably year round with a late spring to early summer peak.

oxeye oreo

Scientific name: *Allocyttus folletti* Myers, 1960
Family: **Oreo**
Other common names: none

French name: oréo occulé

Distribution: Found from California to Japan including off the British Columbia coast, at or near the weathership Ocean Station Papa (50°N, 145°W), in the Hecate Strait, and off Englefield Bay, Queen Charlotte Islands.

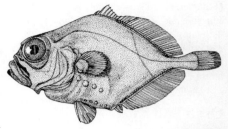

oxeye oreo

Characters: The deep compressed body and large eye are distinctive when combined with granular belly scales and granular scales between the eye and dorsal fin. Flank scales are cycloid. There are 5–7 dorsal fin spines and 30–33 soft rays. The anal fin has 3 spines and 31–32 soft rays. The dorsal and anal fin bases have rows of spiny scales. Young have flexible spines over each eye. Young differ from the adults in having a leathery skin because of minute tubercles, a row of enlarged plate-like scales near the pelvic fin and very large tubercles on the lower flank. Adults are dusky but young have obvious, oval dark spots on the upper flank. Attains 38.3 cm standard length.

Biology: A poorly known species quite rare in scientific collections. Adults are near the ocean bottom at 366–732 m while the young are found in the open ocean in surface waters.

P

Pacific angel shark

Scientific name: *Squatina californica*
   Ayres, 1859
Family: **Angel Shark**
Other common names: none
French name: ange de mer du Pacifique

   Distribution: Not reported from Canada but found in southeastern Alaska and California and so expected to occur in British Columbia. Also in the southern hemisphere.

   Characters: The absence of an anal fin and the flattened body immediately separate this species from all other Canadian sharks. The five gill slits extend onto the under side of the

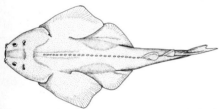

Pacific angel shark

head, eyelids are movable, and eyes are on top of the head with large spiracles behind them. There are two small dorsal fins near the tail. The lower lobe of the caudal fin is larger than the upper lobe. The Pacific angel shark is separated from all its relatives by the anterior nasal barbels being simple in shape with a spatulate tip, the dermal folds on the side of the head are without lobes, the distance from the eye to the spiracle is less than 1.5 times eye diameter, and the posterior tips of the pectoral fins are not rounded but subangular. Teeth are pointed with a broad base. There are small spines on the back and tail in the midline and moderate-sized spines on the snout and above the eyes. Overall colour is grey-brown to reddish-brown, dark brown or blackish, speckled with darker dots. The belly is white. Attains 155 cm and 27 kg but average size is about 100 cm and 10 kg.

   Biology: Found from shallows down to 183 m, this species is partially buried in sand

or mud near rocks in shallow waters with its eyes and back exposed. The body colour blends well with the background. It is sluggish and not very active. It is most active at night when it swims about but returns to the same spot to rest during the day. Angel sharks are ambush predators shooting out their jaws to grab active fish and squid prey. These sharks are ovoviviparous with a litter size of 1–13, average 7, and a birth size of 21–26 cm. Most specimens have only the left ovary functional. Gestation lasts about 10 months and birth occurs in March–June in California. Mating takes place soon after birth. Males begin to mature at 75–80 cm and females at 86 cm. Fresh or frozen, this species has recently become a high-priced food item in California where it is caught with gill nets. A catch of 277,400 kg was taken in 1984. It may be caught on hook and line or speared by skindivers. Its powerful jaws make it a potential danger to anglers and fishermen.

Pacific barracuda

Scientific name: *Sphyraena argentea*
   Girard, 1854
Family: **Barracuda**
Other common names: California barracuda
French name: barracuda argenté

   Distribution: Found from Alaska to Baja California including British Columbia.

   Characters: The characteristic shape distinguishes this species. The mouth is large and has fangs. The dorsal fins are small and widely spaced. The first dorsal fin has 5 spines, the second dorsal fin 1 spine and 8–10

Pacific barracuda

soft rays. The anal fin has 1 spine and 8–10 soft rays. There are about 16 pectoral fin rays. The lateral line has about 166 scales. The back is brownish or bluish becoming silvery below. The upper flank may have oblique bars. The lateral line is dark. The caudal fin is yellowish. Reaches 1.22 m and 8.2 kg.

Biology: An inshore species which goes down to about 18 m. It may occur in small schools. It is most common in California and Mexico and northern occurrences are sporadic. This species migrates south during the winter. A major food item is **sardines** but diet includes other pelagic fishes. Seals, sea lions and porpoises and large fishes feed on barracuda. Life span is over 12 years and fish begin maturing in the second year of life. Spawning occurs from April to September and eggs are pelagic. Females spawn several times each year. Large females produce up to 484,000 eggs each spawning. Each egg is 1.2–1.6 mm in diameter. It is an important sport and commercial fish in California and Mexico, and is caught on hook and line and in gill nets. A total catch peaked in 1920 at 3724 tonnes. It is not known to be dangerous in Canada.

Pacific bonito

Scientific name: *Sarda chiliensis lineolata*
(Girard, 1858)
Family: **Mackerel**
Other common names: California bonito,
eastern Pacific bonito, skipjack, belted
bonito, shortfinned tunny
French name: bonite du Pacifique

Distribution: Found in the eastern Pacific Ocean from Baja California to British Columbia and Alaska.

Characters: This species is distinguished from its Pacific coast relatives by the dorsal fins being close together (separated by a distance less than snout length) and first dorsal

Pacific bonito

fin spines 17–20. Second dorsal fin with 1 spine and 13–17 soft rays followed by 7–9 finlets. Anal fin with 2 spines and 10–15 soft

rays followed by 6–8 finlets. Pectoral rays 22–27. Gill rakers 20–27. Cycloid scales cover the body and there is a corselet around the pectoral area, first dorsal fin base and throat as well as other enlarged scales around the pelvic fin bases. There is a double-pointed skin flap on the belly between the pelvic fins. The back is metallic blue to greenish-blue and the flanks silvery. The flank has 8–10 oblique, black stripes, occasionally absent. Reaches 102 cm and 11.3 kg. The world angling record weighed 10.07 kg, measured 91.4 cm fork length and was caught off Malibu, California in 1978. The type subspecies is found off Chile and Peru.

Biology: This pelagic species can be found inshore off the west coast of Vancouver Island and in the Strait of Georgia or Queen Charlotte Sound. They are often in large schools in warmer waters. Younger fish live closer to shore than older fish. Food includes **sardines, anchovies**, other pelagic fishes and squid. Sexual maturity is attained at 2 years. Spawning in California occurs in January to May. Fecundity is about half a million eggs spawned in batches. This bonito is an important sport fish in California and is used in canning when caught by purse seiners. It is a "white meat" species. The world catch was 21,308 tonnes in 1977.

Pacific cod

Scientific name: *Gadus macrocephalus*
Tilesius, 1810
Family: **Cod**
Other common names: gray cod, true cod,
Alaska cod, whisker cod
French name: morue du Pacifique

Distribution: Found from Korea to California including British Columbia. Also in the Chukchi Sea.

Characters: This species is distinguished from other Pacific **cods** by having 3 dorsal and 2 anal fins, a moderate chin barbel about equal to eye diameter, the lower jaw included in the upper jaw and the first anal fin origin under the second dorsal fin. First dorsal fin rays 10–13, second dorsal rays 13–18 and third dorsal rays 14–17. First anal rays 16–19, second anal rays 15–18. Pectoral rays 18–22. Tubercles in males are few and very small. The back and upper flank are brown to grey. The back and flanks have many brown spots and pale areas. Fins are

Pacific cod

dusky. The margin of the median fins is white. Reaches 114 cm. The world, all-tackle angling record weighed 13.6 kg and was caught in 1984 at Andrew Bay, Alaska.

Biology: This species occurs from the shallows down to 875 m on mud or reef bottoms, usually at less than 300 m. Cod migrate to remain in favourable, cool water, 6.4 to 7.2°C in Queen Charlotte Sound and 6.7 to 7.9°C off southwest Vancouver Island for example. Canadian stocks have a spawning migration into coastal bays of 15–50 m during December-February after the bays cool from 12–13°C. In March–April post-spawning cod migrate offshore to depths below 100 m where temperatures are cooler (1–7°C) for feeding. The cod has several, distinct populations in British Columbia. Food includes crustaceans such as crabs, worms, molluscs, **Pacific herring, sand lances, walleye pollock, flatfishes** and others. Life span is 12 years but few fish are caught past age 5–6 in the commercial fishery. Fish are mature at about 45–55 cm fork length and 2–3 years. Spawning takes place in winter to spring, peaking in January-March at 5–9°C. Up to 6.4 million, 1.0–1.6 mm, demersal eggs are produced. This cod is an important commercial species caught by trawlers in British Columbia. The catch in 1988 was 11,014 tonnes, and it is marketed fresh or frozen, often as fish sticks.

Pacific electric ray

Scientific name: *Torpedo californica*
    Ayres, 1855
Family: **Electric Ray**
Other common names: none

French name: torpille du Pacifique

Distribution: Found in the North Pacific Ocean from Dixon Entrance, northern British Columbia to Baja California.

Characters: This is the only electric ray on the Pacific coast of Canada and it is recognised by the rounded, thick, smooth and spineless disc, short thick tail with 2 dorsal fins, the anterior one larger, and a large tail fin. Teeth are small with a small cusp and there are 4–5 rows in each jaw. The top is dark or brown-grey or bluish and is covered with small, black spots. The underside is white to slate-grey. Reaches 137 cm and 41 kg.

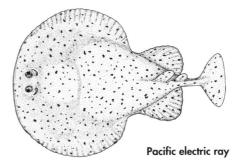

Pacific electric ray

Biology: This electric ray is usually found in shallow water but may descend to 421 m. It is common buried in or swimming over sand bottoms, but may also be found around rocks and kelp. It swims using the tail, not the pectoral fins as with most rays. Food includes **herring, anchovies, coho salmon, halibut** and other fishes. Feeding has been observed in California at night where the electric ray lunges at prey in mid-water from about 5 cm away, enveloping it with the pectoral fins, and doing barrel rolls or forward somersaults which further envelop the prey. Undulations of the disc margin force the prey to the mouth where it is swallowed head first. From lunge to swallow, only 10 seconds may elapse. The initial envelopment immobilises the prey with electrical discharges. During the day, electric rays remain partially buried in sand and ambush passing prey. There are no records in Canada of humans being injured by the electric shock of this species but they have been aggressive to divers in California. This species has been studied extensively by physiologists interested in the electrical and chemical transmission of nerve impulses.

Pacific flatnose

Scientific name: *Antimora microlepis*
   Bean 1890
Family: **Mora**
Other common names: longfin cod,
   finescale antimora, finescale codling
French name: antimore à petites écailles

Distribution: Found from Japan through the North Pacific Ocean to British Columbia and south to Central America.

Characters: This species is distinguished from its Pacific coast relative, the **dainty mora**, by having a flattened snout forming a broad, pointed plate with a ridge on its side, and a chin barbel. Gill filaments on the first

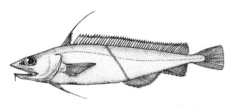

Pacific flatnose

gill arch number 90–103. The first dorsal fin has 4–5 rays, the second 50–55. The anal fin has 37–42 rays and is deeply notched. There are about 115 scale rows along the flank. Pale blue-grey or olive-green to deep violet or blue-black overall. The fin margins, lower gill cover and branchiostegals are dark. The skin is often rubbed off during capture by trawlers. Reaches 75 cm, probably larger.

Biology: Found in Canadian waters from 457 to 1900 m and elsewhere down to 2896 m or as shallow as 175 m.

Pacific hagfish

Scientific name: *Eptatretus stouti*
   (Lockington, 1878)
Family: **Hagfish**
Other common names: none
French name: myxine brune

Distribution: Found from Baja California to southeastern Alaska including British

Columbia. Northern range limit may be Nootka Bay, Vancouver Island, B.C.

Characters: The Pacific hagfish is distinguished from other Canadian species by having 10–14 gill pores, 4 pairs of barbels, an

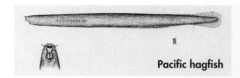

Pacific hagfish

indistinct eye spot and 10–16 (usually 12–14) slime pores before the branchial region. Total slime pores 71–88. The ventral finfold is large. Colour is dark brown, brownish-red, tan or grey, but never black, and brown when preserved in alcohol. Light patches giving a piebald pattern are common. Some fish are albinos. The ventral finfold has a pale margin. The eye is lighter in colour but not as large as in the **black hagfish**. Attains 63.5 cm.

Biology: Found as shallow as 16 m and down to 732 m on mud bottoms. A common species in Canada. Known to feed on **Pacific cod**, **spiny dogfish**, **Salmon Family** members and **flatfishes** among others. Maturity is attained at 35 cm or longer. Eggs are spindle-shaped, 33 mm long and 10 mm wide, with tufts of hooked spines at each end. Mature eggs number 11–48. The sex ratio in this species is about equal in some populations in contrast to some other hagfish species in which females predominate. However collections at Bamfield, B.C. had a female/male ratio at different times of 1.5 to 2.9. This species has been observed to tie itself in knots to remove excess slime from the body.

Pacific hake

Scientific name: *Merluccius productus*
   (Ayres, 1855)
Family: **Hake**
Other common names: Pacific whiting,
   California hake
French name: merlu du Pacifique

Distribution: Found from the Bering Sea to Baja California including British Columbia.

Characters: This is the only Canadian Pacific hake species and has deeply incised second dorsal and anal fins. The mouth is large with strong teeth on both jaws and on the vomer bone in the roof of the mouth. The lower jaw projects. First dorsal fin with 10–13 rays, second dorsal with 37–44 rays. Anal fin rays 37–44 and pectoral rays 14–16. There are 147–166 lateral line scales. The back is dark or silvery-grey and has black speckles. The flanks are silvery. Pectoral fins are brown. The mouth and gill cavities are black. Attains 91 cm.

Pacific hake

Biology: Pacific hake are very common in Canadian waters from the surface to 980 m or more. Hake have been called "one of the most abundant species of fish in the northeastern Pacific Ocean." Usually shallower than 230 m. During the day they are often found in compact schools near the sea floor but rise and disperse somewhat at night in pursuit of euphausiid crustaceans. There are seasonal inshore and offshore movements. A north-south movement involves a coastal stock which spawns in Baja California in winter and feeds in Queen Charlotte Sound in summer. Males arrive off Canada later than females and leave earlier. Females are from 60–82% of the stock and so any fishery must be carefully managed. The coastal stock is the main hake stock but there is also a spawning stock in the Strait of Georgia. This latter stock is smaller but lacks a myxosporean parasite found in the other stock which rapidly degrades the flesh. Most hake in Canada are 4 years or older and many migrate south for the winter.

Food is principally euphausiid crustaceans, and **sand lances** and **Pacific herring** along with other fishes and crustaceans. Older hake eat more fishes. Most feeding occurs at night. Pacific hake are eaten by **spiny dogfish, walleye pollock, Pacific cod**, various other fishes and by seals, sea lions and small whales.

Half the male population is mature at 33 cm and half the female population at 37 cm in the Strait of Georgia. Most fish are mature by age 4. Females grow larger than males and live 2–3 years longer. Growth of both sexes is rapid in the first 3 years. Life span is 20 years.

Spawning occurs in January-February in California to Baja California and March to May in the Strait of Georgia. Up to about 500,000 eggs of 1.2 mm diameter are produced at depths of 130–500 m. Eggs are assumed to ascend in the water to a shallower level of neutral buoyancy.

This hake was not used extensively as a commercial species because of the soft and tasteless flesh. However the catch off Canada in 1969 was 65,000 tonnes. It is processed into animal food as fish meal. Hake are frozen by former Soviet ships for human consumption. Hake may be a considerable nuisance in that they clog gill nets and trawls meant for more important species. Pacific whiting is a commercial or marketing name. Anglers may catch hake while trolling for **salmon**.

Pacific halibut

Scientific name: *Hippoglossus stenolepis* Schmidt, 1904
Family: **Righteye Flounders**
Other common names: halibut, common halibut, whitesided paltus
French name: flétan du Pacifique

Distribution: Found from Japan to California including British Columbia.

Characters: This species is distinguished from its Canadian Pacific relatives by the symmetrical mouth extending back to the middle of the lower eye, a slightly forked or indented caudal fin and no spine in front of the anal fin. The upper eye is not visible from the blind side. Dorsal fin rays 89–109, anal rays 64–81. There are 145–190 scales in the lateral line, which is arched over the pectoral fin. Scales are cycloid on both sides of the fish.

Eyed side blackish, dark brown or grey with paler markings. Blind side white. Ambicoloration is not unusual where the blind side is pigmented, either partially or wholly.

Pacific halibut

Reaches 2.67 m and 363 kg and is the largest Pacific coast **flatfish**. The world, all-tackle angling record weighed 166.92 kg and was caught at Gustavus, Alaska in 1991. The Canadian angling record from Langara Island, B.C., was caught by Glen Oliver on June 21, 1992 and weighed 78.09 kg. This halibut is related to the **Atlantic halibut** and was thought to be only a subspecies of it. However recent studies of enzyme proteins indicate that the Pacific and Atlantic populations became reproductively isolated in the Pliocene 1.7–4.5 million years ago and they are now regarded as distinct species.

Biology: Common in British Columbia from shallow, coastal waters down to about 1100 m, most commonly at 55–422 m on soft bottoms. Surface currents carry young fish to inshore bottoms at age 6–7 months. As they grow they move into deeper water and become part of a commercial offshore fishery at 5–7 years of age. Spawning migrations of 1600 km have been recorded.

Food is various fishes, crabs and other crustaceans, clams and squids.

Females mature at 8–16 years, average 12 years, males much earlier at about 7–8 years. Females grow much faster and larger than males. They live at least 15 years. Spawning is from November to March at 275–412 m. Each female can produce over 4 million eggs of 3.5 mm diameter. Eggs and larvae are pelagic for 5 months mainly between 100–200 m.

This is an important commercial species taken by a deepsea fishery using longlining. Smaller halibut, which are caught commercially, are known as "chickens." Overfishing led to a decline in stocks but in 1923 an International Fisheries Commission began regulating the fishery. Stocks have recovered in part because of this action, and also because of improving ocean conditions for halibut. Prince Rupert is known as the "Halibut Capital of the World", since about half a billion kg have been landed there from 1908 to 1975. The Canadian catch in 1988 weighed 5847 tonnes and landings were worth almost $29 million. Pacific halibut are an excellent food although some stocks have mercury contamination.

It may be caught by surprised anglers, but should be handled with care as the large, thrashing tail can inflict a severe injury. Smaller halibut are often taken on plug-cut herring drift-fished (or mooched) or trolled for **salmon**.

- Most accessible July and August.

- The coastal waters of the west coast of Vancouver Island, the Queen Charlotte Islands and the waters off the northern coast of British Columbia.

- Heavy action saltwater rods and reels. Common outfits are Penn 20– to 50–pound saltwater rod and reel combinations used with the same line weights.

- Four- to eight-ounce vertical jigs fished near the bottom. The best baits are octopus, **herring** or **anchovy** fished near the bottom.

Pacific herring

Scientific name: *Clupea pallasi*
 Valenciennes, 1847
Family: **Herring**

Other common names: Easter herring,
California herring, seld, pirkroartitak,
krolleliprark, iituuq, kavisilâq
French name: hareng du Pacifique

Distribution: Found from the White and
Laptev seas to the Beaufort Sea and Bathurst
Inlet in the Arctic and south to Baja
California in the eastern, and Korea in the
western, North Pacific Ocean.

Characters: This herring is distinguished
from its Canadian Pacific coast relatives by
the lack of large scales on the caudal fin, no
flank spots and no striations on the gill
cover. Dorsal fin rays 15–21, anal rays
13–20, pectoral rays 17 and pelvic rays 9.
There are 38–54 scale rows along the side.
There is no median notch in the upper jaw.

The back and upper flank is blue-green to
olive and the flanks and belly are silvery.
Attains 46 cm.

Some scientists place this herring as a
subspecies of the **Atlantic herring** but
recent biochemical genetic studies and life
history data indicate that they are distinct
species. Herring entered the Pacific Ocean
about 3.0–3.5 million years ago in the mid-
Pliocene after the Bering Strait opened. The
gradual cooling of the Arctic Ocean since
then has eliminated the continuous distribution from the Pacific across the Arctic to the
Atlantic Ocean.

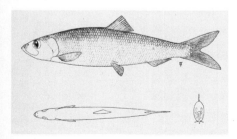

Pacific herring

Biology: Adults migrate to the surface in
the evening and to deeper water at dawn.
They are found in large schools offshore, and
in harbours, bays and estuaries when spawning. British Columbia is the centre of abundance in the eastern Pacific Ocean. Reported
down possibly to 475 m.

Adult herring eat crustaceans and such
fishes as **eulachon, herrings, starry flounder, ronquils, sand lances, hakes** and **rockfishes**. Younger fish eat smaller crustaceans
and fish larvae. Herring are of great importance as food for **chinook** and **coho salmon**
as well as other fishes, seabirds, sea lions
and whales. **Pacific cod** are an important
predator, each cod eating several hundred
herring each year, thereby affecting both the
cod and herring fisheries depending on the
numbers of each present. **Pacific hake** and
sablefish are also important predators and
the 3 species can consume 22–42,000 tonnes
of adult herring accounting for the average
annual mortality of 36%. Herring eggs are
eaten by a wide variety of predators, particularly gulls which flock in the tens of thousands at low tide, and crabs which take up to
18% of the eggs at one site.

Herring mature at 2–4 years of age and
may live 19 years. Spawning is preceded by
an inshore migration to shallow bays in the
autumn when feeding stops after a summer
spent fattening offshore. The winter is spent
fasting and in ripening sexual products using
the energy from stored oil. Strait of Georgia
fish have ovary weights 2.1 times larger than
Beaufort Sea fish.

Spawning occurs in February–July with a
peak in March on the Pacific coast and June–
July in the Beaufort Sea. Temperatures are
3–12.3°C. In Arctic waters of the Mackenzie
River estuary spawning occurs in June–July
under the ice. In open water temperatures are
2.5–3.5°C. As many as 134,000 eggs are
produced with diameters 1.2–1.5 mm when
exposed to sea water. Average fecundity is
usually below 50,000 eggs.

The eggs adhere to seaweed or rocks but
may be arranged in rows on the sea bed as the
females extrude the eggs aided by contact
with the substrate. The spawning area is often
white and opaque with milt from the males
over a distance of 450 km in British
Columbia. This cloud helps protect the eggs
from predatory seagulls. Spawning fish are
sometimes so numerous they must enter bays
in successive waves. Eggs may be so numerous that those laid first are suffocated by those
laid on top of them. In 1962 an estimated 2

trillion eggs were laid. Egg densities can exceed 4 million per square metre. Egg mortality is high. The young herring develop and remain in schools and they leave for deeper water in the autumn at 7–10 cm in length.

Pacific herring are excellent eating fresh or as kippers, bloaters and roll mops, canned and salted but this is a minor use for this fish. There is a lucrative fishery for roe with eggs harvested by purse seines for export exclusively to Japan. The landed value of roe in 1979 was $126.6 million. The carcasses are made into fish meal. The roe fishery must by carefully monitored to ensure survival of stocks by allowing enough fish to spawn in each year. The concentration of spawning herring and the purse seine fleet is such that the fishing season in a particular area can be over in 15 minutes.

In 1976, 78,832 tonnes of herring were caught in the roe fishery in British Columbia. Catches in British Columbia have been as high as 264,007 tonnes in 1963 but stocks are now depleted by overfishing. The 1988 Canadian catch was 31,601 tonnes. It ranks second after the **salmons** in commercial value on the Pacific coast and landings were worth $56 million in 1989. The adult stocks in B.C. average about 350,000 tonnes or 33 billion fish.

Considerable scientific effort is put into assessing herring spawnings in order to predict future stocks. Egg samples are collected by SCUBA divers and the area covered by spawn measured. It has even been shown that recruitment of herring in B.C. is related to long-term (5–6 year) temperature and salinity oscillations associated with long-period waves.

This species is the most important bait fish for anglers in British Columbia, used in trolling or "mooching" for **salmon**. It emits an oily trail when dragged through the water which attracts the **salmon**.

Pacific lamprey

Scientific name: *Lampetra tridentata*
(Gairdner in Richardson, 1836)
Family: **Lamprey**
Other common names: three-toothed lamprey, tridentate lamprey, sea lamprey

French name: lamproie du Pacifique

Distribution: From Baja California to Japan including British Columbia.

Characters: Myomeres number 58–76. The tooth formula is 3 cusps on the bar above the mouth, 4 teeth on each side of the mouth,

Pacific lamprey

disc view

some tricuspid and some bicuspid, and 5–8 cusps on the bar below the mouth. This species is distinguished from other Canadian lampreys by having 2 dorsal fins and 3 cusps on the bar above the mouth. Adults are blue-black to brown or reddish when spawning. Velar tentacles are darkly pigmented at the base. Teeth are orange or yellow. Ammocoetes are a pale brown with the central tail area lightly pigmented and the head moderately pigmented. Attains 76 cm when adult and 12.2–30.3 cm at transformation.

Biology: This species has both marine and landlocked populations. In the sea it has been reported down to 250 m and is common on west coast fishing grounds. It is a parasitic species which migrates into fresh water from April to June and completes the migration by September. These lampreys overwinter hidden under rocks and mature, build nests and spawn from April to July and then die. Nests are usually built in rivers but have been seen in shallow waters of Babine Lake, B.C. The adults shrink by 20% over winter. The migration may cover hundreds of kilometres and they apparently do not feed. The nest is about 53–58 cm in diameter and receives up to 106,000 oval eggs about 1.1–1.2 mm long. Males may spawn with more than one female in different nests. Ammocoetes spend 4–6 years in the stream mud. Adults spend 1–3.5 years as a parasite, entering salt water from December to July after beginning metamorphosis in July. They are eaten by whales and seals. Pacific lamprey scars have been found on 1.8% of a **sockeye salmon** stock at the mouth of the Fraser River and on 76% of **rainbow trout** in a lake. Scars are also found on a variety of whale species with frequencies up to 89%. These lampreys have been eaten smoked, salted or sun-dried and are used as bait for **trout** and **sturgeon**. They were an important food source for natives along the Columbia River and were fished for along with **salmon**.

Pacific ocean perch

Scientific name: *Sebastes alutus*
  (Gilbert, 1890)
Family: **Scorpionfish**
Other common names: longjaw rockfish, pop
French name: sébaste à longue mâchoire

Distribution: Found from Japan to southern California including British Columbia.

Characters: The chin has a strong, protruding knob which is characteristic. Dorsal fin spines 13–14, usually 13, dorsal soft rays 13–17, usually 15. Anal fin soft rays 6–9, usually 8, second spine thicker but shorter than third. Pectoral fin rays 15–19, usually 18. Gill rakers 30–40. Vertebrae 26–28, usually 27. Lateral line pores 44–56, scale rows below lateral line 49–55. Head spines are weak with the coronal and nuchal spines absent and sometimes the tympanic or supraocular spine. The body and fins are a bright carmine red. The belly is whitish with

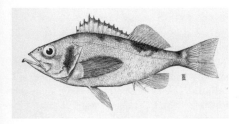

Pacific ocean perch

some silver. There are olive-brown saddles on the back, particularly evident below the soft dorsal fin and across the tail base. These saddles may be absent. The spiny dorsal fin has a dark edge. The lower lip and the mouth

lining are dark. Peritoneum grey with black dots, or black. Reaches 51 cm.

Biology: Abundant offshore between 73 and 640 m but usually near the 180 m contour over gravel and rocky, and sometimes soft, bottoms. They prefer gullies and canyons. The Canadian population off Vancouver moves into deeper water (> 250 m) for winter. Young fish are in shallower water than adults. This slow-growing species is believed to live almost 60 years and is the most important scorpionfish commercially. The total catch in 1968 was nearly a quarter of a million metric tonnes. The catch declined in the 1970s in Queen Charlotte Sound because of Japanese and Soviet exploitation in 1966–1969. The Canadian catch in 1988 was 26,707 tonnes. It is trawled and marketed as fillets. There are various stocks of this species, each with their own growth characteristic. They are mostly caught in the temperature range 4.5–7.7°C. Catch rate may be as high as 11.1 metric tonnes per hour. Young fish are pelagic several hundred kilometres from shore and do not settle to the bottom until 2–3 years of age. Young are born in January to March in Canadian waters. Half the population is mature at 34 cm for males and 35 cm for females in Canadian waters. A 20 year old female, 43.6 cm long, produces 305,000 young. They feed on crustaceans, squids and other fishes. This perch is an important food for **albacore** and **Pacific halibut**.

Pacific pomfret

Scientific name: *Brama japonica*
  Hilgendorf, 1878
Family: **Pomfret**
Other common names: pomfret
French name: castagnole mince

Distribution: Found in the North Pacific Ocean from Japan to Baja California, on the British Columbia coast and at Ocean Station Papa (50°N, 145°W). Also south to Peru.

Characters: This species is distinguished from its Canadian relatives by having the adult dorsal and anal fins covered with scales, a rounded head profile, a strongly compressed head such that the lower jaw bones touch each other at the ventral midline, caudal peduncle scales not abruptly larger than those on the caudal fin base, and fewer dorsal and anal fin rays on average than the **Atlantic pomfret**. Dorsal fin rays 33–36, anal rays 27–30, and pectoral rays 21–23. Scales in the lateral series 65–75. Overall colour is a silvery-black, with the back darkest. The snout is black. The mouth lining is black. Fins are generally black, except the pelvic fin in which the first 2 rays are black and the remainder clear. The innermost pectoral rays are also clear. The caudal fin is pale edged. Reaches 1.22 m.

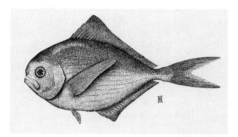

Pacific pomfret

Biology: An open ocean species which is caught occasionally but unpredictably in near-shore waters. Not uncommon in British Columbia and extremely abundant from July to November in the open ocean at Ocean Station Papa. Fish, squid and crustaceans are food items. It may live at least 6 years. It has been caught by gill nets and on hook-and-line and is a good food fish.

Pacific pompano

Scientific name: *Peprilus simillimus*
　(Ayres, 1860)
Family: **Butterfish**
Other common names: Pacific butterfish,
　California pompano
French name: pompano du Pacifique

Distribution: Found from central British Columbia south to the Gulf of California.

Characters: This species is distinguished from the related **butterfish** by distribution, by lacking pores below the anterior half of the dorsal fin and by having simple pointed teeth at the front of the upper jaw. Dorsal fin with 2–4 spines and 41–48 soft rays. Anal fin with 2–3 spines and 35–44 soft rays. No

pelvic fins. The body is an iridescent green or bluish on the back with silvery flanks. Fins are dusky. Reaches 28 cm. "Pompano" is a Spanish word for this fish.

Pacific pompano

Biology: A common species over sand from 9–90 m. It is tolerant of varying salinities. The bones are poorly developed but are oil-filled with the skull alone being 68% lipid. The oil contributes to buoyancy (and this fish lacks a swimbladder when adult) but may also serve as an energy reserve. Jellyfish, small fishes, crustaceans and worms are eaten. Young Pacific pompanos associate with jellyfish or other floating objects. The excellent flesh is best eaten freshly caught. It is marketed in small quantities in California and is caught by anglers from piers.

Pacific sanddab

Scientific name: *Citharichthys sordidus*
　(Girard, 1854)
Family: **Lefteye Flounder**
Other common names: mottled sanddab,
　soft flounder, melgrim
French name: limande sordide

Distribution: Found from the Bering Sea to Baja California including British Columbia.

Characters: This species is separated from its only Pacific coast relative, the **speckled sanddab**, by having a bony ridge over the lower eye and the lower eye diameter is greater than snout length. The space between the eyes is concave. Dorsal fin rays 86–102, anal rays 67–81. Caudal fin rounded. Gill rakers on the lower arch 12–16. Lateral line scales 61–70. Scales ctenoid on the eyed side of the body and cycloid on the blind side. Overall colour on the eyed side brown with darker, irregular mottles. Dorsal, anal and caudal fins marked with black. Males have dull orange or yellow spots. Blind side pale brown to white. Young fish are a light olive-

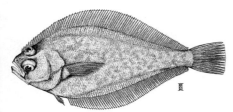

Pacific sanddab

green with brown, black and orange speckles, concentrated on the fins. Reaches 41 cm.

Biology: Common in shallow waters of British Columbia but may descend to 549 m elsewhere. Adults prefer coarse bottoms in shallower water than young, which are found on deeper silty bottoms. Food includes small fish, crustaceans, squid, worms and other bottom and pelagic invertebrates. Half the female population is mature at 19.1 cm in California. Life span exceeds 10 years and females grow larger than males. Spawning occurs in February in waters adjacent to British Columbia and there may be a second spawning in the same season. Eggs are up to 0.84 mm in diameter. This species is used for food in Canada and is particularly popular in California. It is marketed under the name "sole." They may be caught on hook and line and are popular in boat fishing. Righteyed individuals are not uncommon.

Pacific sandfish

Scientific name: *Trichodon trichodon*
  (Tilesius, 1813)
Family: **Sandfish**
Other common names: tobiefish
French name: trichodonte

Distribution: Found from Kamchatka around the North Pacific Ocean as far as San Francisco including the coast of British Columbia.

Characters: The fringed lips are unique. There are also fringed flaps on the throat. There are about 46 pores in the lateral line which is high on the flank. Spiny dorsal fin with 13–15 rays, second dorsal fin with 1 spine and 18–20 soft rays. Anal fin with 1 spine and 28–29 soft rays. Pectoral fin with 21–22 rays and lower edge turned anteriorly. Pelvic fin with 1 spine and 5 soft rays. There is a slender anal papilla and a pair of palps on each side of the anus. The body is dusky or brown on the back and upper flank becoming silvery below. The back has dark, irregular patches. There is a dark stripe along the lateral line. The spiny dorsal fin has dark horizontal streaks. The pectoral and caudal fins have darkened upper edges while the anal and pelvic fins are light. Attains 30.5 cm.

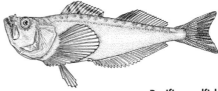

Pacific sandfish

Biology: Found on or in sand and mud down to depths of 55 m. They may be 30 cm below the sand surface. They can be caught by hand. Food is other fishes which they lie in wait for, concealed by the sand with only the eyes and mouth showing. They may live 8–9 years, maturing when 2–3 years old. Spawning may occur in late winter (February) and a gelatinous, amber, egg mass is attached to rocks. There may be about 1000 eggs in each mass with a diameter of 3.5 mm. The eggs incubate for a year which is why they are attached to stable rocks and not spawned in the normal sandy habitat of this fish. Eggs may be found on rocks in surge channels. Pacific sandfish are eaten by **chinook salmon**, harbour seals and sea lions. However young sandfish are found in schools with hundreds of thousands of young **pink salmon**, probably gaining protection from predators in this mass of fish.

Pacific sardine

Scientific name: *Sardinops sagax caeruleus*
  (Girard, 1854)
Family: **Herring**
Other common names: pilchard, California
  pilchard
French name: sardine du Pacifique

Distribution: Found from Kamchatka and Alaska to Baja California including British Columbia. Also in the southern hemisphere below the tropics as a distinct subspecies.

Characters: This species is separated from its Canadian Pacific coast relatives by having spots on the flanks, striations on the

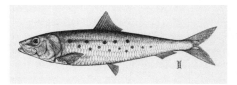

Pacific sardine

gill cover, large scales on the caudal fin, an elongate, rounded body and weak scutes on the belly. Dorsal fin rays 17–20, anal rays 17–20, pectoral rays 17 and pelvic rays 9. Gill rakers on the lower arch 45–110, increasing in number with growth. There are 52–60 scales along the flank. The back and upper flank are dark metallic blue or green. The sides and belly are silvery. Black spots on the sides are in a variety of sizes and arrangements. Attains 41 cm but usually less than 30 cm. This subspecies is sometimes regarded as a distinct species.

Biology: Large schools containing 10 million fish have been reported for this sardine. Food is mainly diatoms with some crustaceans off Vancouver Island. This sardine does not spawn in Canadian waters but is recruited from California stocks which migrate further northward each year as they grow, entering Canadian waters in summer. Some fish apparently overwinter in inlets on the west coast of Vancouver Island rather than migrating southward. This species is mature at 24 cm. Females grow faster than males. Life span is up to 25 years. Night spawning occurs from January to June with an April–May peak at 15–18.3°C. Each female produces several batches of 30–65,000 eggs each with up to 200,000 each season. Eggs are 1.6 mm, float and hatch in about 3 days. Young are found inshore in large schools. Canadian landings of this species have been as high as 80,504 tonnes. The Canadian stocks have not produced a big brood of young since 1939. This

has been variously attributed to changes in ocean currents, overfishing and ecological replacement by the **northern anchovy**. The catch was used for oil and fish meal with some being canned. The Committee on the Status of Endangered Wildlife in Canada approved the status of "rare" in 1987. Sardine remains have been found in sediments of Saanich Inlet, Vancouver Island dating back to 8850–9840 B.P. and archaeological digs along the Pacific coast show that this fish has long been used by native peoples.

Pacific saury

Scientific name: *Cololabis saira*
(Brevoort, 1857)
Family: **Saury**
Other common names: none
French name: balaou japonais

Distribution: Found in the North Pacific Ocean from Japan to Mexico including British Columbia.

Characters: The only saury in Pacific Canada with both jaws somewhat elongated into blunt beaks and with 5–7 finlets behind the posteriorly placed dorsal and anal fins. The lower beak is slightly longer than the upper beak. Teeth are in a single row on the upper beak and develop on the lower beak only in adults. Scales number 128–148 in midline. Gill rakers number 32–43. Dorsal fin rays 14–18 and anal rays 18–21 (counts

Pacific saury

include finlets). Pectoral rays 12–15. The body is green to blue above and silvery on the side and belly. The flanks have blue blotches. Reaches 40 cm.

Biology: Found offshore from the surface down to 229 m and also in brackish water in the Ain River, Queen Charlotte Islands. The northernmost populations, in Alaska for example, are seasonal and this part of the range is a feeding area with reproduction occurring in warmer, southern waters. Food is plankton, particularly crustaceans. Pacific sauries may live for 6 years although recent studies indicate fish 33 cm long are only 14 months old. The eggs are about 2 mm in diameter and have many filaments at the pole and a single, long one at the opposite end. Filaments anchor the egg to seaweed or rocks. About 1800 eggs are released at each spawning and each fish will spawn 6–7 times from December to fall in California. This species is attracted to lights at night and can then be caught easily with a dip net. Pacific sauries are an important food for a variety of fishes, including **albacores** and **marlins**, seabirds and marine mammals. Attempts to escape predators lead to surface skipping which may project them into boats. It is a commercial species in the western pacific Ocean; fortunately the green or blue flesh turns white on cooking! Many large sauries are infested with hairy, parasitic copepods or have scars from copepods and are rendered unattractive for sale.

Pacific sleeper shark

Scientific name: *Somniosus pacificus*
  Bigelow and Schroeder, 1944
Family: **Sleeper Shark**
Other common name: laimargue dormeur
French name: laimargue du Pacifique

Distribution: North Pacific Ocean from Japan across to British Columbia and south to California and Mexico.

Characters: This is the only shark on our Pacific coast which lacks an anal fin, is not flattened, and lacks spines in the dorsal fins. The space between the dorsal fins is about two-thirds the prebranchial length rather than the same length or longer as in the **Greenland shark**. The gill slits are small,

Pacific sleeper shark

low on the body and in front of the pectoral fin. The eye is small. The snout is short, thick and rounded and the eye is circular and

very small. The body is heavy and cylindrical but flaccid when out of the water. The upper teeth are pointed while the lower teeth are broad, triangular, smooth and oblique thus forming a cutting edge. Scales have hooked cusps giving the skin a rough texture. Blackish-brown, slate-grey or slate-green or light-grey with darker streak-like mottling. Said to reach at least 7.6 m based on underwater photographs but the largest captured specimen was 4.4 m.

Biology: Found from tide pools (!) down to at least 2000 m especially in warmer, southern waters. A sluggish, usually deepwater shark like its relative on the Atlantic coast but a voracious feeder. Diet includes **chinook salmon, rockfish, flatfish** such as **rex** and **dover soles** and **halibut**, harbour seals, octopi, squid, crabs, tritons, and carrion. It is not clear if prey items like salmon and seals, which are fast swimmers, are caught alive or picked up dead as carrion. The head and mouth cavity are long and the mouth small which suggests they may be able to feed by suction, pulling in unsuspecting prey by a sudden inrush of water to the mouth cavity. Pregnant females are rarely caught but this species is probably ovoviviparous. Females may have up to 300 eggs. This species has little economic importance apart from taking some **salmon** and **halibut** from longlines. It is occasionally caught on longlines or in trawls.

Pacific soft pout

Scientific name: *Melanostigma pammelas*
  Gilbert, 1895
Family: **Eelpout**
Other common names: midwater eelpout
French name: mollasse noire

Distribution: Found from British Columbia to Mexico.

Characters; This species is distinguished from its Pacific coast relatives by lacking scales, lateral line and pelvic fins, and the gill slit is a small pore above the pectoral fin. Dorsal fin rays 73–88, anterior rays covered by skin, anal rays 64–75 and pectoral rays 6–8. The flesh is gelatinous. The head is small and rounded. Overall colour is variable and may be silvery-blue, grey or dark brown, with the head and belly black. Young are clear. Peritoneum black. Attains 11 cm, reports of 30.4 cm probably in error.

Pacific soft pout

Biology: This is a pelagic species in coastal waters at 96–1984 m. Food is crustaceans, some fishes, salps and worms seized by a lunge. Eggs number about 30 and are 2 mm in diameter.

Pacific spiny lumpsucker

Scientific name: *Eumicrotremus orbis*
  (Günther, 1861)
Family: **Lumpfish**
Other common names: none
French name: petite poule de mer ronde

Distribution: Found from northern Japan to the Chukchi Sea and south to Washington including British Columbia.

Characters: This species is distinguished from its Pacific coast relative, the **smooth lumpsucker**, by having large, horny, conical skin protuberances. These tubercles are larger and more numerous in females. The tubercles, remainder of the skin and dorsal fin spines are covered by small, spiny scales. Gill opening smaller than the eye, well above the pectoral fin. First dorsal fin rays 5–7, second dorsal rays 9–12, anal rays 8–11, and pectoral rays 19–27. Overall

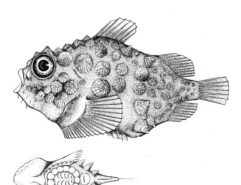

Pacific spiny lumpsucker

colour light to dark green, yellow or brown, and sometimes purplish. Lips are a lavender colour. The bony plates are dull orange to reddish-brown in males and pale green in females. Anal and caudal fins and flanks may be tinged bluish. Attains 12.7 cm.

Biology: Occurs commonly in tide pools and down to 575 m attached to rocks in fast tidal currents. When swimming, it quivers its fins rapidly while the body is held stiff. Found at temperatures as low as –1.7°C. This lumpfish is eaten by **longnose lancetfish**, a midwater predator, suggesting that the lumpfish spends some time off the bottom. Females may mature at 3.3 cm. Eggs are red and number up to 477 with an average diameter of 2.0 mm. They are laid in winter, November to February. This species is often caught in shrimp trawls.

Pacific staghorn sculpin

Scientific name: *Leptocottus armatus*
  Girard, 1854
Family: **Sculpin**
Other common names: staghorn sculpin, cabezon
French name: chabot armé

Distribution: Found from the Bering Sea to Baja California including British Columbia.

Characters: This species is recognised by having 37–42 lateral line pores, gill membranes broadly joined to the isthmus without a

Pacific staghorn sculpin

fold, no scales or cirri, and the uppermost of 3 preopercular spines is very large, sometimes extending above the dorsal head profile, and has 2–5 recurved spinules. This spine can inflict a nasty wound. There is no nasal spine but there is a central bump on the snout. First dorsal fin spines 5–9, second dorsal soft rays 15–21 and pelvic soft rays 4. Anal soft rays 14–20. The back is olive-grey to green with yellow areas or brown. The belly is orange-yellow to white. The dorsal, caudal and pectoral fins have green or dark bars on a creamy-yellow or golden-yellow background. Pectoral fin bars are particularly broad and evident. The spiny dorsal fin has an orange edge and a large, dark spot posteriorly. The anal fin is clear. Mature females have a deep red tinge to the caudal fin and a light red margin to the anal fin. Reaches 48 cm but usually smaller.

Biology: This is a very common Canadian sculpin of shallow waters, eelgrass beds, tidal pools and lower sections of streams along the coast. Maximum depth is 91 m. It may bury itself in sand with only the eyes protruding. When picked up or threatened the gill covers are flared and a low humming sound may be heard. Food is various invertebrates, particularly amphipods, and fishes. Clam siphons are cropped. It is eaten by various shore birds and by sea lions. Even foxes catch them in the surf. Great blue herons swallow staghorns without breaking off the spines which are supposed to be protective and are raised when the fish is disturbed. Life span is over 3 years. Spawning takes place in February. There is an average of 3200 eggs per female. This sculpin is often caught on hook and line by anglers and it can be a nuisance in gill nets.

Pacific tomcod

Scientific name: *Microgadus proximus* (Girard, 1854)
Family: **Cod**
Other common names: tomcod, wachna
French name: poulamon du Pacifique

Distribution: Found from the Bering Sea south to California including British Columbia.

Characters: This species is distinguished from other Pacific **cods** by having 3 dorsal and 2 anal fins, a small chin barbel about equal to pupil diameter, the lower jaw included in the upper jaw and the first anal fin origin under the first dorsal fin. First dorsal fin rays 11–15, second dorsal rays 16–21, third dorsal rays 18–22. First anal rays 20–29 and second anal rays 18–24. Pectoral rays 19. Gill rakers 26–28. The back is olive-green to brown with the belly cream to white. Fin tips are dusky. Reaches 30.5 cm.

Biology: Reported from shallows near beaches down to 275 m, but usually at 27–92 m, on sand and mud bottoms. Young are found in shallower water and may approach the surface. Food includes crustaceans, mol-

Pacific tomcod

luscs and small fishes and it is food for a variety of larger fishes and marine mammals. Life span is about 5 years. Spawning occurs in late winter to spring and eggs are demersal. This cod is not common or large enough to support a commercial fishery but it is tasty and edible. Some is trawled for fish meal and anglers may catch it from piers. It often has copepod parasite in the mouth.

Pacific viperfish

Scientific name: *Chauliodus macouni* Bean, 1890
Family: **Barbeled Dragonfish**
Other common names: fanged viperfish
French name: chauliode féroce

Distribution: Found from Japan to the Gulf of Alaska and south to Baja California including British Columbia.

Characters: This species is distinguished from its Atlantic coast relatives by having the postorbital (behind the eye) light organ triangular or pointed posteriorly. The hexagonal pigment pattern on the flank, both dorsal and ventral adipose fins, two rows of photophores on the lower flank, the immense fangs and the

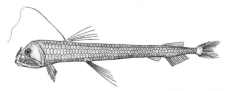

Pacific viperfish

long, filamentous first dorsal fin ray are all characteristic. Dorsal fin rays 6–7, anal fin rays 10–12, pectoral fin rays 10–12 and pelvic rays 7–8 and very elongate. Gill rakers are absent. There is a series of photophores between the bases of the branchiostegal rays, a single photophore below the eye and one in front of the eye. All the photophores emit blue light. In living fish, but not preserved ones, there are spherical patches of pink luminous tissue along the upper and lower edges of the body and on all fins, embedded in the gelatinous sheath which encloses the fish. Overall colour is dark brown to black. This species is named for J. C. Macoun of the Geological Survey of Canada, a precursor to the Canadian Museum of Nature. Reaches 25 cm.

Biology: Found from 76 m down to perhaps 1600 m. Small fish are common at 500 m or deeper, while large fish are not found until at least 600 m. This is a pelagic fish sometimes found on or near the bottom. Pacific viperfish feed on arrow worms, crustaceans, squids and fishes. It lives at least 8 years. There are perfectly preserved fossils of a *Chauliodus* from Miocene rocks of California, some with their last meal visible in the stomach position. This fossil viperfish is very similar to modern forms.

padded sculpin

Scientific name: *Artedius fenestralis*
　Jordan and Gilbert, 1883
Family: **Sculpin**
Other common names: none
French name: chabot rembourré

Distribution: Found from the Gulf of Alaska to California including British Columbia.

Characters: This species and its Pacific coast relatives, the **Puget Sound, scalyhead, and smoothhead sculpins**, are distinguished by having 2–3, mostly 3, pelvic fin soft rays, simple or branched uppermost preopercular spine but not antler-like, (except in the **padded sculpin**) and 3–16 scales in the rows above the lateral line. This species is separated from related species by having scales on the head and scale rows extending onto the caudal peduncle, no cirrus on the upper front eye margin and the uppermost of 3 preopercular spines with 2–3 spinules. The nasal spine is short and blunt. First dorsal fin spines 8–10, second dorsal soft rays 16–18. Anal fin rays

12–14, pectoral rays 14–16 with lower 7 finger-like. Upper flank scale rows number 26–29 with 9–11 scales in the longest row. There are scales behind and below the front of the eyes on the sides of the head. Lateral line scales 35–37. There is a single or double cirrus along the lateral line as far back as the anterior third of the soft dorsal fin. There are cirri on the end of the upper jaw, the anterior nostril, on the upper rear operculum, 3 on the preoperculum edge and several in a row on top of the head behind the eye level, large anteriorly and smaller posteriorly. Colour is pale orange, yellow, light green or even cream on the back and cream to pale brown on the belly. There are 7 green, brown or blackish saddles over the back. Except for the pelvics, all fins have dark bars. Males have a small, weak anterior spot and a large, dark posterior spot on the spiny dorsal fin. Males become dusky to blackish during spawning with 3 dusky, pale blue or golden yellow bands on the spiny dorsal fin. Reaches 14 cm.

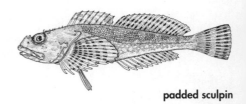

padded sculpin

Biology: Reported down to 56 m from the intertidal zone and abundant in British Columbia. Food is crustaceans, such as shrimps, and small fishes. Spawning takes place in January–March, and eggs are salmon-pink, purplish or grey and are laid under rocks.

paddlefish

Scientific name: *Polyodon spathula*
　(Walbaum, 1792)
Family: **Paddlefish**
Other common names: spoonbill cat, spade-
　fish, duckbill cat, shovelfish, oarfish
French name: spatulaire

Distribution: Now restricted to the Mississippi River basin and adjacent Gulf-coastal rivers, but formerly also in the Great Lakes.

Characters: The paddle-like snout is unique. In adults it may be a third of the fish's length. There are 2 minute barbels on

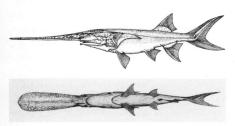

paddlefish

the snout in front of the mouth. The mouth cannot be protruded. The gill cover has a long, posterior projection. Rhomboidal scales are found on the caudal peduncle. There are also dorsal and ventral fulcra on the caudal fin, denticles over the pectoral fin and on the trunk and anchor-shaped plates on the paddle. Teeth are very small. Gill rakers are very long and number over 400.

The back and flanks are grey to blue-black, the belly whitish. Up to 2.24 m and 83.5 kg and perhaps over 90 kg.

Biology: Early Canadian records are from Sarnia and the Spanish River of Lake Huron, Lake Helen on the north shore of Lake Superior, and Lake Erie. Paddlefish are found in backwaters of large rivers and in lakes. Upriver spawning migrations occur when rivers are low and currents weak in contrast to most other fishes. Dams have severely restricted this movement. Other authors note migrations at flood times for spawning. The open mouth of a paddlefish is cavernous and food is plankton strained from near the water surface by the many, fine gill rakers. The paddle may help in detecting food by sensing disturbances in electrical fields, as a planing device to keep the head up when the mouth is open and causing drag, as a probe for use in mud, or a beater to free minute food organisms attached to plants. These last two are considered the least likely functions. Paddlefish are most active at night and rest on the bottom in deep pools during the day.

Spawning occurs on stony or sandy river bottoms in rapidly flowing water or in lake shallows. Timing depends on latitude,

February in the south, May in the north. Over 608,000 greenish-black eggs are laid but spawning is at intervals of 2 years or more. The fertilised eggs have a diameter of up to 4 mm and must become attached to the bottom by their adhesive surface to hatch properly. Young only develop a distinct paddle at 3.5 cm. Sexual maturity is attained at 7 years of age for males at about 102–127 cm, and for females at 7–14 years and 107–140 cm. Life span may exceed 60 years.

Paddlefish often leap out of the water falling back on their side with a tremendous splash. This is probably an effort to detach parasites, such as **lampreys**.

Dams, pollution, overfishing and other factors of an industrial age have severely reduced populations of this interesting fish. It is now extirpated in Canada. Paddlefish have been sold as food and eggs were used as a kind of caviar. There is even a sport fishery in some parts of the U.S. where fish are caught by blind snagging. In 1899 the total reported U.S. commercial harvest was 1,105 tonnes and in 1975, 431 tonnes. In the U.S.A. artificial propagation of paddlefish has been attempted. Fish caught on the spawning migration were taken to hatcheries and injected with pituitary hormone to stimulate egg production. Eggs were hatched in jars and young restocked in rivers.

Paddlefish Family

Scientific name: Polyodontidae
French name: spatules

Paddlefishes are found only in fresh waters of the Yangtze River, China, and the Mississippi River, U.S.A., with a distinct species in each area.

These fish are unmistakeable because of the paddle-like snout. The skeleton is cartilaginous, the intestine has a spiral valve, and the caudal fin is heterocercal, i.e. its skeleton turns upwards into the upper fin lobe. These are characters of more primitive fishes and are also found in **sharks**, for example.

Paddlefishes are related to the **Sturgeon Family** in the **Sturgeon Order** and these 2 families are the only survivors of an ancient group of fishes dating from the Early Cretaceous more than 135 million years ago.

Details of biology are given in the species account.

See **paddlefish**

painted greenling

Scientific name: *Oxylebius pictus* Gill, 1862
Family: **Greenling**
Other common names: convictfish
French name: sourcil à tête pointue

Distribution: From Baja California to southern Alaska including British Columbia.

Characters: The dorsal fin contains 15–17, usually 16, spines and 14–16 soft rays. The anal fin has 3–4 spines and 12–13 soft rays.

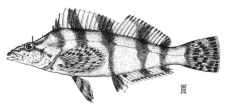

painted greenling

Scales are ctenoid and extend between the eyes. There are about 76 along the flank. Cheek scales are cycloid. There are 2 red cirri on each side of the head, one over the eye and one mid-way between the eye and dorsal fin origin. The snout is pointed. This species is distinguished from other Canadian greenlings by having 1 lateral line, the mouth not reaching back to the anterior eye margin and by the dark bars on the flank and tail. The bars are a dark, rich red-brown, number about 5–7 and extend onto the dorsal and anal fins. There may be clumps of white spots outside the bands. Overall colour is gold, brown or grey or very dark and white-spotted. A bar runs from the eye along the snout and 2 bars radiate posteriorly from the eye. The pectoral, pelvic and caudal fins have rows of dark spots making thin bars. Breeding males may be almost black overall. Breeding females are more brightly coloured with yellow and light orange fins, the pectoral, pelvic and caudal fins have burnt orange and brown bars, and the anterior belly and lower head surface are white and yellow flecked with orange or light brown. Reaches 25 cm.

Biology: This species has been observed in a vertical position along rock faces. It is found from the intertidal zone down to 57 m, and around piles and wharves, at densities as high as 0.3 per square metre. Fish become torpid from December to March. Food is selected crustaceans, worms and molluscs. They may live 8 years. Males maintain territories of about 2 sq m. Spawning takes place almost all year round and orange, walnut-shaped, egg masses are attached to algae or invertebrate encrustations. Females produce 3 clutches each with up to 5000 eggs during each breeding cycle of 10 days mating and 20 days parental care. Eggs are 1.4 mm in diameter. The males defend the eggs, even from passing skin divers, for 2.5–3.5 weeks. However this requires a lot of energy and the male's condition declines. He may compensate by eating some of the eggs. Males are usually 18 cm and 4 years old when they guard eggs. Females mature at age 3. This species is said to be immune to the stinging cells of the giant sea anemone, *Tealia*, which is found in this greenling's habitat. Young painted greenlings may be seen nestling among the tentacles of this sea anemone, and 2 other anemones of the genus *Urticina*. Greenlings fed on crustaceans associated with the latter anemone and took refuge there.

pale eelpout

Scientific name: *Lycodes pallidus*
    Collett, 1878
Family: **Eelpout**
Other common names: none
French name: lycode pâle

Distribution: Circumpolar including the Canadian Arctic, and south to off Prince Edward Island, possibly to Cape Cod.

Characters: This species is separated from its Canadian Arctic-Atlantic relatives by having small pelvic fins, a mouth under the snout, no large pores around the mouth, crests on the chin, a double lateral line with one incomplete midlateral and the other on the lower flank, long tail (preanal length 41–45% of total length), pectoral fin rays 17–21, usually 18–20, and colour. Dorsal fin rays 92–101 and anal rays 79–86 (both including half of the continuous caudal fin rays). Vertebrae 96–104. The belly, nape and anal and dorsal fins lack scales. Overall colour is creamy to light brown. Young have 8–10 dark bars crossing the body and including the dorsal and anal fins. Older fish lose the bars on the dorsal fin. Peritoneum brownish-black. Reaches 26 cm.

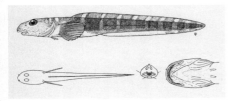

pale eelpout

Biology: Total depth range is 11–1750 m on mud bottoms in a temperature range of -2 to 1.1°C. In the Kara Sea of the former U.S.S.R. spawning probably occurs in October–November and eggs number about 35 and are 6.1 mm in diameter. Food there is worms, molluscs and amphipods.

pale lathfish

Scientific name: *Lestidiops jayakari*
 (Boulenger, 1889)
Family: **Barracudina**
Other common names: none
French name: poisson-latte pâle

Distribution: Found world-wide except perhaps the eastern Pacific Ocean. Canadian records are from off Nova Scotia.
Characters: This barracudina is distinguished from its Canadian relatives by having a pectoral fin shorter than the anal fin base, smooth-edged lower jaw teeth, scales restricted to the lateral line, the pelvic fin before the dorsal fin, an adipose fin between

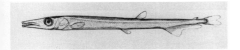

pale lathfish

the pelvic and anal fins, and its Atlantic coast distribution. Dorsal fin rays 9–10, anal rays 28–33, pectoral rays 11–12 and pelvic rays

9. Lateral line scales 63–72. Vertebrae 76–85. Overall colour is light with a dark upper flank stripe. Reaches about 20 cm.
Biology: Larvae and post-larvae have been caught off the Scotian Shelf and Georges Bank at 200–300 m. Young are usually in the upper few hundred metres but adults are known down to more than 2000 m. Spawning in the Atlantic occurs in August to October.

palespotted eel

Scientific name: *Ophichthus puncticeps*
 (Kaup, 1860)
Family: **Snake Eel**
Other common names: none
French name: serpenton ocellé

Distribution: Found from Suriname north to the Scotian Shelf in Canada.
Characters: This species is distinguished as a larva by having 9 low to moderate gut loops, the nephros never ending on the ninth gut loop, 126–142 total myomeres (muscle blocks), 62–68 nephric myomeres, 69–77

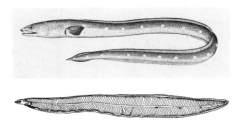

palespotted eel

preanal myomeres and 49–58 predorsal myomeres. Adults have a hard, pointed tail tip and no caudal fin. There is a large mouth with strong, pointed teeth. Vomer teeth in the roof of the mouth are in a single row. The dorsal fin has its origin over the end of the pectoral fin. Body dark grey, brown or yellowish, paling ventrally. Pores on head are darker than the background. Flanks with white, yellowish or buff, eye-sized spots at wide intervals, numbering 18–21. Larvae are up to 89 mm long and adults reach 92.7 cm total length.
Biology: Known from Canada only as stray larvae (or leptocephali) first reported in

1988. Adults are found down to 150 m but are rare in shallow water. Capable of a nasty bite when adult. Often caught by anglers.

pallid sculpin

Scientific name: *Cottunculus thomsoni*
(Günther, 1882)
Family: **Soft Sculpin**
Other common names: none
French name: cotte blême

Distribution: Found on both sides of the North Atlantic Ocean and in the western Atlantic from Davis Strait south to South Carolina.

Characters: This species is separated from its Arctic-Atlantic relative, the **polar sculpin**, by its smooth skin with only a few spines and

pallid sculpin

no bands on the body. Dorsal fin spines 6–8, flexible, dorsal soft rays 14–17. Anal fin rays 13–14, pectoral rays 22–23. Lateral line pores 18. The head is knobbed and ridged. Overall colour is a grey-brown with translucent skin. The body is dark posteriorly. The tips of the pectoral fin membranes are black. Reaches 35.5 cm standard length.

Biology: Reported at depths of 100–1600 m at temperatures of 3.12–4.4°C, somewhat warmer than its relative. Little is known of its biology.

pallid slipskin

Scientific name: *Lycodapus mandibularis*
Gilbert, 1915
Family: **Eelpout**
Other common names: pale eelpout, pallid eelpout
French name: lycode à longues branchiospines

Distribution: Found from Alaska to California including British Columbia.

Characters: This species is distinguished from its Pacific coast relatives by having the branchiostegal membranes free of the isth-

mus posteriorly, gill rakers blunt and stout touching the adjacent raker only when depressed, gill opening extending above the

pallid slipskin

upper base of the pectoral fin, vertebrae 81–97, and teeth on the vomer bone of the roof of the mouth 0–5. The upper rim of the orbit is high and interrupts the concave dorsal head profile. Scales and pelvic fins are absent. The flesh is gelatinous. Dorsal fin rays 76–100, anal rays 65–79 and pectoral rays 6–9. Vertebral counts are lower in British Columbia than in Oregon and California probably because of unusual oceanographic conditions in Canada causing higher temperatures and lower salinities below 200 m. Mature males have an outer row of large jaw teeth. Colour is a translucent cream to silvery white with some speckling. The mouth, gill cavity and stomach linings are dark. Lips are pale or darkened. Peritoneum silvery or dark. Tail and posterior vertical fin margins darkened. Reaches 19.8 cm standard length.

Biology: Usually found at 50–800 m in submarine canyons or deep inlets, rarely at the surface and down to 1370 m. It is a pelagic species with a daily vertical migration, at least in southern populations. Food is planktonic crustaceans and some squid. Life span is 5 years. Spawning may occur year round. Eggs are 1.9 mm in diameter and when mature number up to 125.

patchwork lanternfish

Scientific name: *Notoscopelus resplendens*
(Richardson, 1845)
Family: **Lanternfish**
Other common names: patchwork lampfish
French name: lampe-voilière sao-en-coin

Distribution: Found in all warmer seas including off Atlantic Canada.

Characters: This is 1 of 4 Atlantic coast species characterised by stiff, spine-like rays at the upper and lower caudal fin bases, no large glands on the upper and lower caudal peduncle outlined by heavy black pigment, and a dorsal fin base longer than the anal fin base. It is distinguished from its relatives (**Bolin's lanternfish, northern saillamp** and **spinetail lanternfish**) by having 19–23 gill rakers, AO photophores 12–14 and 39–40 lateral line organs. Dorsal fin rays 21–24, anal rays 17–20, usually 19, and pectoral rays 11–13. Adult males have a large luminous gland occupying most of the upper caudal peduncle and consisting of 8–9 segments. Reaches 9.5 cm.

patchwork lanternfish

Biology: First reported from Canada in 1969 and quite common along the outer limit of the Scotian Shelf. At Bermuda, this lanternfish is found at 650–1150 m by day and 50–300 m by night. Individuals may be found as deep as 2000 m. Larvae are found at 50–100 m and are non-migratory. Spawning begins in late autumn to winter and fish are mature at about 6.6 cm.

peamouth

Scientific name: *Mylocheilus caurinus*
    (Richardson, 1836)
Family: **Carp**
Other common names: peamouth chub,
    northern dace
French name: méné deux-barres

Distribution: Found in British Columbia, Alberta, Washington, Oregon, Idaho and Montana. In Alberta from the Athabasca River, in British Columbia from the Fraser, Columbia, upper Peace river systems, Pacific coast rivers, Vancouver, Nelson and Bowen islands and in the adjacent sea.

Characters: This species is distinguished by the barbel at each mouth corner, the small mouth, protractile premaxillaries (groove

above upper lip), lateral line scales 66–84 and a well-developed pelvic axillary scale. The snout overhangs the mouth. Dorsal fin branched rays 7, anal branched rays 7–8, pectoral rays 14–18 and pelvic rays 7–10. Gill rakers 8–12. Pharyngeal teeth usually 1,5–5,1 but sometimes 2,4–5,2 or 2,5–4,2, with grinding surfaces in adults and hooked tips in young. Nuptial tubercles in males are on the back and sides of the head, on the back and on the dorsal, pectoral and pelvic fins.

The back is dark olive brown and the flank is silvery with a head to tail stripe, and one below it ending above the anal fin base. The belly is silvery-white or yellowish. Breeding males have a green back, females a brown back. Both sexes have red lower lips, red lateral stripes and a red stripe from the mouth across the cheek and opercle. The pectoral fins are darker and longer in males. Peritoneum dusky.

This species hybridises with the **northern squawfish** and the **redside shiner**. Reaches 36.0 cm.

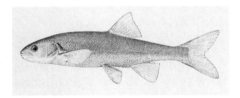

peamouth

Biology: The peamouth favours weedy, shallow areas of lakes and rivers when young, deeper water as adults except at night when they move into shallow water. Unusually in members of the **Carp Family** it tolerates brackish water and this tolerance enabled it to reach Vancouver Island on a plume of low salinity water from the Fraser River estuary. This colonisation of Vancouver Island was by a process that biogeographers call a "sweepstakes" dispersal route where colonisation is highly improbable for most fish but does occur for some. It is a schooling species.

Food is mainly aquatic insects with some terrestrial insects, crustaceans, molluscs and small fishes such as **sculpins**. Some populations feed mainly on snails. Feeding during the day in lakes may be at 20 m depths followed by a rise to surface waters at night to take advantage of emerging insects.

Females are larger than males. Life span is about 13 years. Males mature at age 3 and females at age 4. Spawning occurs from late April to July at 11–22°C. A school of 50–400 fish enters shallow water in a lake or stream mouths, outlets or rarely riffles. A female is pushed by 2 or more males onto the shoreline where their backs stick out of the water. Eggs and sperm are shed as the fish quiver with the tail of one or both males curved sharply over the caudal peduncle of the female. Grey-green, adhesive eggs attach to the bottom rocks. There are up to 18,900 eggs per female.

Peamouths have been used in the past as food in hotels. They have been caught by anglers using **salmon** eggs, flies or grasshoppers as bait.

pearl dace

Scientific name: *Margariscus margarita*
  (Cope in Günther, 1868)
Family: **Carp**
Other common names: nachtrieb dace,
  northern pearl dace, northern minnow,
  northern dace
French name: mulet perlé

Distribution: Found from Nova Scotia and central Labrador west to Alberta, eastern British Columbia and the south of Great Slave Lake, N.W.T. In the U.S.A. south to Virginia, west to Montana with relict populations in South Dakota, Nebraska and Wyoming.

Characters: This species is distinguished by having protractile premaxillae (a groove between the upper lip and the snout), a flat barbel in advance of the mouth corner in the groove above the upper lip, lateral line scales 46–79 (usually 65–75) and no black spot at the dorsal fin base. The barbel may be absent or very small on one or both sides in which case the high scale count in a complete lateral line, short s-shaped gut, silvery peritoneum, small mouth and lack of unique characters found in other **minnows** distinguish this species. The upper jaw does not reach back to a level with the front of the eye. Pharyngeal teeth hooked, 2,5–4,2, 2,4–4,2, or 2,4–4,1. Dorsal fin branched rays 6–7, usually 7, anal

fin branched rays 6–7, usually 7, pectoral fin rays 14–19 and pelvic rays 8–9. Males have large nuptial tubercles on up to 8 pectoral fin rays in a double row, with a few, very small ones on the head, lining scale edges, and densely tuberculate on the first 2 branchiostegal rays. Tubercles are also present on other fins, varying greatly in number and extent. Pectoral fins are longer and wider in males than in females.

The back is dark brown to almost black, greyish or green, the flanks are olive to silvery and the belly silvery-grey to white. Flanks may have dark scales. Young fish have a brown-black stripe ending in a spot at the tail base. Breeding males and some females are orange-red below the midflank. This colour persists from fall to the spawning season. Peritoneum silvery with some darker speckles dorsally.

Possible hybrids with **lake chub** are reported from Wood Buffalo National Park, Alberta. Formerly in the genus *Semotilus*. Reaches 15.8 cm.

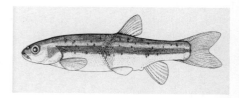

pearl dace

Biology: Pearl dace are found in clear streams, pools and channels of headwaters, bogs, ponds and small lakes.

Food is aquatic and terrestrial insects, crustaceans, young fish, detritus and possibly algae and larger plant debris. Life span is 4 years for females and 3 years for males in Maryland. Females grow faster than males in Québec and both sexes mature at 2 years.

Spawning occurs in late March to June at 17°C or more in clear, shallow water over sand or gravel in weak to moderate current. Spawning in Lake Gamelin, Québec occurred in the first half of May. A male defends a territory about 20 cm wide against other males. Ripe females are allowed into the territory or driven into it by the male.

The male places his pectoral fin under the anterior part of the female's body, lifting it up at an angle of about 30°, and his caudal peduncle over that of the female, pressing her belly down. This may stretch the female's belly and help release the eggs. The pectoral fin tubercles of the male aid in grasping the female. The fish vibrate for about 2 seconds and eggs are shed. Females repeat spawning numerous times with different males. Each female may have up to 4240 eggs of 1.4 mm diameter.

Pearl dace produce an alarm substance from skin cells when injured. Other pearl dace react in 2 phases. The first phase is rapid, unpredictable swimming which serves to remove the fish from danger and the second phase is several hours of inactivity on the bottom which is thought to reduce the chance of detection by a predator after the first, confusing flight phase. Pearl dace are normally schooling midwater fish.

It is used as a bait fish in Canada.

Pearleye Family

Scientific name: Scopelarchidae
French name: yeux-perlés

Pearleyes are found in the Atlantic, Indian, Pacific and Antarctic oceans. There are 17 species with 2 reported from the Pacific coast and 2 from the Atlantic coast of Canada.

Their eyes are large and tube-shaped, pointing upwards or upwards and forwards. Each eye bears an unusual, glistening pearly-white spot, or lens pad, hence the family name. Cycloid scales cover the body and rear part of the head behind the eyes. There are 40–66 lateral line scales. Dorsal fin rays are 5–10 and anal rays 17–39. Pectoral fin rays are 18–28. The pelvic fins have 9 rays. There is no swimbladder. Luminous tissue, derived from muscle blocks, is found in some pearleyes along the belly. The tongue has large teeth which are usually hook-shaped. There are 2 rows of teeth in the lower jaw with the inner row being large, depressible canines. There are no normal gill rakers which have been replaced by teeth on bony plates.

Pearleyes are relatives of the **Greeneye** and **Waryfish** families in the **Flagfin Order**.

These are fishes of the open ocean's mid-water and are usually found between 500 and 1000 m when adult, and at 100–200 m when larvae. Some are found as deep as 3000 m. They are only seen by scientists using mid-water trawls. Pearleyes are fast swimmers but are nevertheless food for **albacore** and **Salmon Family** members as well as many other midwater fishes. Pearleyes are hermaphrodites and eggs and sperm mature simultaneously.

See **blackbelly pearleye**
longfin pearleye
northern pearleye
Zugmayer's pearleye

Pearlfish Family

Scientific name: Carapidae
French name: aurins

Pearlfishes or fierasfers or carapids are found in all warmer seas. There are about 32 species and 1 has been reported from Atlantic Canada.

This family is characterised by very long dorsal and anal fins which join with the caudal fin to appear as a continuous fin tapering to a point at the tail. Anal fin rays are longer than the dorsal fin rays opposite them. The anus and anal fin origin are usually below or even anterior to the pectoral fin base, just behind the head. The dorsal and pelvic fins are absent in most species and the pectoral fins are absent in some. Scales are absent. The gill openings extend far forward under the head. Teeth are present on the jaws and roof of the mouth. There are no opercular spines nor a supramaxilla.

These fishes have a unique, elongate, pelagic larva called the vexillifer. Vexillifers are elongate larvae with a long, usually ornamented, predorsal filament (or vexillum) which dangles over the front of the head. This larva develops into the tenuis larva in which the vexillum has degenerated and the head is relatively small. Tenuis larvae are benthic. The vexillum may function to forewarn the larva of predators or approaching prey by touch or by sensing a disturbance in the water. It may also increase the apparent size of the larva to a predator, distract a predator's attention, or deflect an attack to this expendable body part.

Pearlfishes are related to the **Cusk-eel Family** in the **Cusk-eel Order**.

Some members of this family, like the Canadian species, are free-living. Others however are most unusual in that they hide inside the bodies of other animals. This is known as inquilinism. These other animals include sea cucumbers, starfish, sea urchins, clams and sea squirts. They enter sea cucumbers through the anus, tail or head first. Entry may be by a corkscrew motion. Some enter head first when young and tail first when adult. The fish may remain in the respiratory tree (a branch of the sea cucumber cloaca) or bite through it and enter the body cavity. As many as 15 fish can be found in 1 sea cucumber. As few as 1% to as many as 90% of hosts may have fish in them in a given area. The name pearlfish is derived from the pearl shell host in which the fish occasionally becomes embedded in the shell wall and covered in mother-of-pearl. They may be parasitic, eating the internal organs of the sea cucumber. Some pearlfishes are cannibals.

See **chain pearlfish**

pearlsides

Scientific name: *Maurolicus muelleri*
(Gmelin, 1788)
Family: **Silver Hatchetfish**
Other common names: Müller's pearlsides
French name: marguerite perlée

Distribution: In all oceans including subpolar and temperate waters. Off the Atlantic coast of Canada.

Characters: This species is distinguished from other silver hatchetfishes by having a

pearlsides

more normal-shaped body and only 3 (rather than 6) cartilaginous pelvic radials. These radials are skeletal elements in the girdle, which supports the pelvic fin. In addition there are light organs at the tip of the lower jaw and the upper row of light organs along the lower flank number 9–10 (as opposed to 3–8 in all other hatchetfishes found in Canada). Colour is brilliant silvery on the flanks with a greenish-blue back. Light organs are yellow or green. Reaches about 7.6 cm.

Biology: This is a common hatchetfish which is sometimes found washed up on beaches after a storm. Adults live below 200 m, during the day, down to about 400 m, migrating at night into the upper 100 m. Food is small crustaceans such as copepods and euphausiids. This species is sexually mature at an age of 1 year and lives about 3 years. Spawning occurs in spring to summer in northern waters. The female lays up to 596 eggs which float to the surface. The larvae sink as they develop. Pearlsides are food for innumerable other fishes in the ocean.

pearly prickleback

Scientific name: *Bryozoichthys marjorius*
McPhail, 1970
Family: **Shanny**
Other common names: none
French name: stichée perlée

Distribution: Known only from British Columbia, southeastern Alaska and the Aleutian Islands.

Characters: This species is 1 of 5 related Canadian shannies which have cirri on the head and possess pelvic fins. It is distinguished from its relatives, the **warbonnets**, by having 66–71 dorsal fin spines. The anal fin has 1 spine and 51–59 soft rays and the pectoral fin 14–16 rays. The lateral line canal is short and extends only to a point above the middle of the pelvic fins. Teeth are conical and in bands on the jaws and roof of the mouth. Two cirri over the eye are large and branching. There is also a cirrus on the snout, 3 short cirri between the eyes in a row, about 18 short cirri on top of the head behind the eye, branching cirri at the tip of the first 4 dorsal fins, a short cirrus at the posterior end of the upper and of the lower jaw, and sometimes cirri between the lateral line pores. Colour is an overall light brown with

9–11 dark blotches or saddles over the back and pearly-white areas along the flanks. A band runs from the eye to the mouth corner. Pectoral, pelvic and anal fins are dusky with pale margins. Anal fin with a long central stripe. Caudal fin with 2–5 bars. All cirri are brownish although the large ones over the eye may have pale bands. Reaches 26.5 cm.

pearly prickleback

Biology: A rarely collected species of which little is known. Canadian specimens are from La Pérouse Bank off southern Vancouver Island, Portland Channel and Dixon Entrance off the northern Queen Charlotte Islands, and northwest of Langara Island. Found down to 308 m. Females have eggs in September.

pectoral rattail

Scientific name: *Albatrossia pectoralis*
(Gilbert, 1892)
Family: **Grenadier**
Other common names: giant grenadier
French name: grenadier pectoral

Distribution: Found from Japan to California including off British Columbia and at Ocean Station Papa (50°N, 145°W).

Characters: This species is distinguished from its Pacific Canadian coast relatives by the anus being immediately in front of the anal

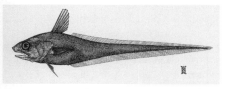

pectoral rattail

fin, no scaleless black area on the abdomen, 6 branchiostegal rays, pelvic rays 6–8, usually 7, and no stout, scute-like scales on the snout tip. First dorsal fin with 2 spines and 7–9 soft rays, second dorsal fin with about 126 rays. Anal fin

rays about 131. Pectoral rays 16–21. The lateral line is obvious with about 264 scales. Scales are small and have 1–5 ridge-like rows of small spines decreasing in development and sharpness with age. Teeth have arrowhead-shaped tips. Overall colour is brown with fins, gill membranes, mouth and gill cavities, lips and lower snout surface blackish. The peritoneum is black. Scale margins and the lateral line are dark. Often caught with scales lost, these fish then appear pale with a pink to violet tinge. Reaches at least 150 cm, the largest member of the family.

Biology: Found from 200–2170 m generally, perhaps in midwaters at Ocean Station Papa. Also recorded off Vancouver Island at 1371–1463 m. Food is fishes, squids, combjellies and crustaceans. Females are larger than males and are found in shallower water. Spawning occurs over an extended period but is most active in fall and winter. Young are probably pelagic. They may live over 17 years. There is a Bering Sea fishery by former Soviet vessels, the eggs and liver being vitamin rich. The flesh is watery but can be processed.

pelagic stingray

Scientific name: *Dasyatis violacea*
(Bonaparte, 1832)
Family: **Stingray**
Other common names: violet stingray
French name: pastenague violette

Distribution: Found world-wide in warmer waters and on both the Atlantic and Pacific coasts of Canada.

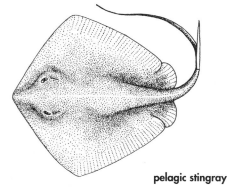

pelagic stingray

Characters: This species is separated from its Pacific coast relative, the **diamond stingray**, by the rounded snout. It lacks the ventral finfold of its Atlantic coast relative, the **roughtail stingray**. The tail is longer than the disc. There is no caudal fin. The upper surface is a dark purplish to black or greenish-blue colour and the lower surface is purplish to grey or greenish-blue. Reaches 164 cm in length and 81 cm wide.

Biology: In Atlantic Canada this species has been caught quite frequently from the Flemish Cap and south to Georges Bank. On the Pacific coast a pelagic stingray was caught west of Nootka Island in 1985. This stingray takes its name from its pelagic existence over the deep ocean or inshore. It has been caught at depths of 37–238 m over much deeper water in the Atlantic Ocean. Food is small pelagic fishes, including **sea horses**, squids, coelenterates and shrimps. Mating occurs in March-June and birth as late as September. Longlines meant for **tuna** and **swordfish** often capture this stingray in Atlantic Canada.

pelican gulper

Scientific name: *Eurypharynx pelecanoides*
　　Vaillant, 1882
Family: **Gulper**
Other common names: umbrellamouth gulper,
　　pelican eel
French name: grandgousier pélican

Distribution: Found in all oceans and from the Davis Strait southwards in Canadian waters.

Characters: The enormous mouth and the tiny eyes near the snout tip are characteristic.

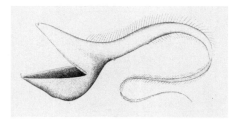

pelican gulper

The body is quite fragile. The gill openings are small and nearer the anus than the snout

tip in contrast to the related **taillight gulper**. Jaw teeth and the pectoral fins are minute. The dorsal fin originates on the head. The male has a large, circular, knob-like nasal rosette. The caudal fin has a luminescent organ at the tip. Black overall with a white groove on each side of the dorsal fin. Caudal organ black dorsally and white ventrally. Rarely exceeds 100 cm.

Biology: Found from 711–2682 m and quite common in Canadian waters but also descends to 7625 m or deeper elsewhere. It may approach the bottom. The leptocephalus phase lasts up to 2 years and these larvae are found at 100–200 m. Food is plankton, squid and fishes that may be attracted to the huge open mouth by dangling the luminescent caudal fin tip in front of it or even by swimming in a circle! It is unlikely that prey is chased, since most is swallowed head first and the pelican gulper is a poor swimmer. This fish probably lunges at its prey with its mouth closed, the mouth is opened very close to the prey and the huge gape is unfolded like a parachute by the pressure of the water. The prey is engulfed in a pool of water and this water is gradually removed through the narrow gill openings, enabling the prey to be swallowed. Eaten by **lancetfish** among others. Males probably use their large nasal organs to detect the pheromones emitted by females.

Pencilsmelt Family

Scientific name: Microstomatidae
French name: microbecs

The pencilsmelts are found in all the major oceans from the subarctic to the subantarctic. There are 13 species of which 3 have been reported from Canada, two on the east and one on the west coast.

They resemble the **Argentine Family** and the Canadian species are characterised by having an adipose fin, the dorsal fin in front of the pelvic fins, pectoral fins on the sides of the body (not low down) and lateral line scales extending onto the tail fin. Anal fin ray counts are generally 7–10 compared to 10–28 in the **Deepsea Smelt Family** and branchiostegal rays are 3–4 compared to 2. The postcleithrum bones in the pectoral fin supporting skeleton are present but the mesocoracoid is absent. Their soft bodies and weak bones mean that captured specimens are often in poor condition for study.

Pencilsmelts are relatives of the **Argentine Family** and are sometimes classified in that family or with the **Deepsea Smelt Family**. They are members of the **Smelt Order** and have been placed in the **Salmon Order**.

These fishes are found both in midwater and near the bottom in the open ocean.

See   **bluethroat argentine**
      forgotten argentine
      large-eyed argentine

penlight fish

Scientific name: *Protomyctophum crockeri* (Bolin, 1939)
Family: **Lanternfish**
Other common names: California flashlightfish
French name: télescope californien

Distribution: Found from Japan to Baja California including off the coast of British Columbia.

Characters: This lanternfish and its relative, the **bigeye flashlightfish**, are distinguished from other Pacific coast species by having 2 Prc photophores and the PLO photophore at about the level of the lowest pectoral fin ray. This species is separated from its relative by the SAO photophore series

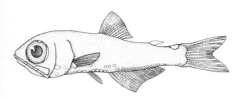

penlight fish

being in a straight line, the first SAO photophore is over or slightly before the fourth VO photophore and the AO series rarely exceeds 12–14 photophores but may reach 16. There are no lateral line pores. Dorsal fin rays 11–13, anal rays 19–24, pectoral rays 13–17 and total vertebrae 36–38. Total gill rakers 18–24. Males develop supracaudal luminous glands at 2.5 cm. Females have infracaudal glands with 2–4, usually 3, small oblong spots. Reaches 4.6 cm.

Biology: Reported off Vancouver Island in 1985 at several localities. It is often caught at night but does not reach the surface.

penpoint gunnel

Scientific name: *Apodichthys flavidus* Girard, 1854
Family: **Gunnel**
Other common names: pen-point blenny, band-shaped blenny
French name: sigouine jaunâtre

Distribution: Southern California to Alaska including British Columbia.

Characters: This species, and the related **rockweed gunnel**, lack pelvic fins. They are distinguished by dorsal fin spine counts and the pen nib-shaped anal spine in this species.

penpoint gunnel

Dorsal fin spines 86–96. Anal fin with 1 large spine and 35–43 soft rays. Pectoral fin large with 14–17 rays. Colour depends on diet and habitat and is very variable. The basic colours are green-yellow and red, with brown or orange when these two are mixed. Dark or light dots along midflank. Narrow, dark bar stretching obliquely downward from eye to operculum. Sometimes a second bar runs obliquely upwards from the upper rear corner of the eye. Sometimes a silver stripe with an orange or black border runs from the mouth through the eye to the end of the head. Attains 46 cm.

Biology: Found in shallow water among algae in tide pools and over rock, sand and mud. Retreats to rocks when plants die back in winter. Colour was thought to be adjusted in response to the colour of the background algae, green fish in shallower water where green algae are most common and red fish in deeper water with predominant red algae. An alternative theory suggested that diet determines fish colour. However it has been shown that planktonic gunnel larvae which metamorphose and settle to the bottom from high in the water column turn green while those lower down in the water column are red-brown. Light and depth are the factors involved in determining colour. High larvae tend to end up in the high intertidal zone with green algae and lower larvae in the low and subtidal zone with brown and red algae. Food is small crustaceans and molluscs. Spawning occurs in winter and white eggs are laid in a mass, protected by the parents. Should the egg mass be dislodged by currents, the parents will wrap around it and ease it back under cover.

Perch Family

Scientific name: Percidae
French name: perches

Perches, darters, pike-perches and their relatives are found in fresh waters across the northern hemisphere. There are about 162 species total with 148 in North America. The Canadian members number 16, including 1 exotic species from Europe. The walleye has 2 subspecies.

Perches have 2 dorsal fins, the first spiny (6–9 spines) and the second soft rayed, which are usually separate or only slightly joined. The anal fin has only 1–2 spines (rather than 3 as in related families). The pelvic fins are under the pectorals (thoracic) and have 1 spine and 5 soft rays. There are 5–8 branchiostegal rays and the branchiostegal membrane is not attached to the isthmus. Scales are ctenoid. Teeth may be long and sharp or small and in bands. The premaxillae are protractile or not, the supramaxilla is absent, the pseudobranch is large or rudimentary, 0–1, rarely 2, predorsal bones, and there is no subocular shelf. The operculum has a sharp spine. There are 2 kinds of perches — large species with compressed bodies and a swimbladder, and derived from them small species with depressed bodies and reduced or absent swimbladders. This condition is believed to have arisen twice within the family. In North America the larger species include the yellow perch, sauger and walleye and the smaller species are the darters. In darters the mouth is small, not extending back past the anterior eye margin, and the lower edges of the preop-

ercle bone on the side of the head are smooth.

Perches are of course members of the Perch Order and are regarded as the "typical" family. They are close relatives of the Sea Bass Family. "Perch" is derived from the Latin and Greek for these fishes.

Perches are found in warm southern waters to subarctic ones, in both flowing and still water. Some larger species are commercially important in Canada while smaller species make attractive aquarium fishes. The small darters rival coral reef fishes for colour when in breeding condition.

Darters are sensitive to environmental change and are useful indicators of the health of aquatic ecosystems. The snail darter, not found in Canada, achieved a measure of fame when it was discovered in 1973 in a limited area of the lower Little Tennessee River, and placed on the U.S. Federal Endangered Species List. Construction of the Tellico Dam was halted to protect this minute fish. The sauger, walleye and yellow perch are very important species in sport fisheries in Canada.

Perches have a variety of reproductive strategies which include broadcasting, stranding, burying, attaching, clumping and clustering. During the breeding season tubercles develop, particularly on the male. These may be on the body, fins or head and are used to maintain contact and enhance grip between males and females during the spawning act. Darters in the genus *Percina* have enlarged and strongly toothed scales between the pelvic fin bases and along the belly midline in males. The male probably uses these scales during spawning to stimulate the female. Female darters often have enlarged genital papillae and in those species which lay eggs in gravel or plants the papilla is an elongate tube. Some darter males have egg-shaped knobs on the dorsal or paired fins and these are used to attract females to a nest site. Females are thought to be more likely to spawn with successful males, which already have eggs or convincing mimics of eggs, in their nests.

Certain darters, such as the Iowa and johnny darter, have large secretory cells in their skin. These release a chemical alarm substance into the water when damaged in a predator's attack. The chemical signals other **darters** to "freeze", hopefully avoiding detection by the predator. Studies in southern Ontario indicate that darters are not often food for other fishes, despite their small size, but they are an important food for common mergansers during the spring migration of this bird.

See **blackside darter**
blue walleye
channel darter
eastern sand darter
fantail darter
greenside darter
Iowa darter
johnny darter
least darter
logperch
rainbow darter
river darter
ruffe
sauger
tesselated darter
yellow perch
yellow walleye

Perch Order

Perches and their relatives comprise the Order Perciformes with about 150 families and over 9290 species world-wide in both salt and fresh waters and from cold to tropical waters. In Canada there are 58 families and 262 species. This order dominates the seas and many freshwaters, particularly in the tropics and marine shore waters. About one-third of all fishes are perciforms. It is the largest **vertebrate** order. The **yellow perch** is often used in schools and universities to represent a **bony fish**.

This order is not a completely homogenous group but can be taken to represent a level of evolution from which many other groups arose. It cannot be characterised by unique characters but rather by contrasting it with lower **teleosts**. In this large, diverse group of fishes there are many exceptions to these generalisations. Members of the order have spines in the dorsal, anal and pelvic fins (absent in lower **teleosts**), 2 dorsal fins but no adipose fin (1 dorsal fin and sometimes an adipose fin),

scales are usually ctenoid (cycloid), pelvic fins are thoracic or jugular in position (abdominal), the pelvic girdle is attached to the pectoral girdle (unattached), the posttemporal bone is usually forked (not forked), the pelvic fin has 1 spine and 5 or less soft rays (no spine and 6 or more soft rays), usually 15 or fewer branched caudal fin rays (16 or more), the pectoral fin base is high on the flank and aligned vertically (low and horizontal), physoclists where the swimbladder is not connected to the gut by a duct (physostomes where it is connected), the orbitosphenoid, mesocoracoid and intermuscular bones are absent (present), branchiostegal rays 7 or less (usually more), the upper jaw border is formed by the premaxilla (premaxilla and maxilla), and no bone cells in adult bone (present). Fossils may date to the Late Cretaceous over 70 million years ago and by the Eocene this order was extremely diverse.

The biology of this order is highly varied and is covered in the family accounts.

See **Armorhead Family**
Barracuda Family
Bigeye Family
Black Swallower Family
Bluefish Family
Butterfish Family
Butterflyfish Family
Cardinalfish Family
Cichlid Family
Clingfish Family
Clinid Family
Cobia Family
Combtooth Blenny Family
Cutlassfish Family
Damselfish Family
Deepherring Family
Dolphin Family
Dragonet Family
Driftfish Family
Drum Family
Eelpout Family
Goatfish Family
Goby Family
Graveldiver Family
Greateye Family
Gunnel Family
Jack Family
Louvar Family
Mackerel Family
Manefish Family

Perch Family
Pomfret Family
Porgy Family
Prowfish Family
Quillfish Family
Ragfish Family
Remora Family
Ronquil Family
Ruff Family
Sand Lance Family
Sandfish Family
Sea Bass Family
Sea Chub Family
Sequinfish Family
Shanny Family
Snake Mackerel Family
Snapper Family
Squaretail Family
Sunfish Family
Surfperch Family
Swordfish Family
Temperate Bass Family
Temperate Ocean Bass Family
Tilefish Family
Tripletail Family
Wolffish Family
Wrasse Family
Wrymouth Family

petrale sole

Scientific name: *Eopsetta jordani*
    (Lockington, 1879)
Family: **Righteye Flounder**
Other common names: brill, round-nosed sole,
    Cape sole, English sole
French name: plie de Californie

Distribution: Found from Alaska to Baja
California including British Columbia.

Characters: This species is separated from
its Pacific Canadian relatives by having a
large, symmetrical mouth extending back to
the rear part of the eye and with 2 rows of
teeth in the upper jaw, a wedge-shaped or
broad v-shaped caudal fin, a spine preceding
the anal fin, and small, firmly attached scales.
Dorsal fin rays 82–103, anal rays 62–80.
Lateral line slightly arched over the pectoral
fin, with 88–100 scales. Olive brown on the
eyed side. Blind side white with faint pink
tinges. Dorsal and anal fins with dusky, faint
blotches. Reaches 70 cm and 3.6 kg.

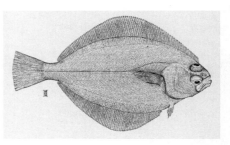

petrale sole

Biology: Common in Canadian waters,
from the surface down to 550 m. In winter
fish are concentrated at 310–460 m and in
summer at 73–128 m. Food includes **sand
lances, herrings** and crustaceans, but a variety of bottom invertebrates is also consumed.
Females grow larger and faster than males,
attaining ages of 25 years compared to 19
years. Half the males in a population are
mature at 38 cm and 7 years, while half the
females mature at 44 cm and 8 years. Large
females produce 1.2 million pelagic eggs of
1.3 mm diameter in late winter and early
spring. This occurs in Esteban Deep at about
366 m off central Vancouver Island and after
spawning fish disperse to return in subsequent years. The summer inshore fishery of
Vancouver Island also receives sole from
spawning deeps off Washington. This is a
very valuable commercial species, second
only to the **Pacific halibut**, because of its
large size, good quality as fresh or frozen fillets and the liver being a rich source of vitamin A. Trawl catches fluctuate widely
because of overfishing and varying oceanographic factors, but reached a peak of 3040
tonnes in 1948

pickerels

Pickerels are, strictly speaking, the smaller
members of the **Pike Family**. Canada has the
chain pickerel and two subspecies, the **grass**
and **redfin pickerels** in rivers draining to the
Atlantic Ocean. Pickerel is a diminutive name
for pike.

Pickerel is also commonly used for the
walleye and also the **sauger**, members of the
Perch Family, since there is a supposed

resemblance in the teeth and head shape of these fishes.

Pike Conger Family

Scientific name: Muraenesocidae
French name: congres-dorés

Pike congers, or knife-teeth eels, are found in tropical and warm temperate seas world-wide. There are about 8 species with one found on the Pacific coast of Canada.

These eels are scaleless but have a well-developed lateral line. The snout is often elongate. They have obvious pectoral fins, no pelvic fins, and thick, muscular bodies. The posterior nostril is a pore in front of the eye. The gill opening is large. The eyes are large and skin covered. The dorsal fin origin lies over the base of the pectoral fin. Teeth are large, especially on the roof of the mouth where there 4–8 fang-like teeth.

Pike congers have been classified with the **Conger Family** and are closely related to them. They can only be distinguished from congers by osteological characters. They are members of the **Eel Order**.

These eels may enter fresh waters and are common in warm, shallow seas.

See **twinpored eel**

Pike Family

Scientific name: Esocidae
French name: brochets

The **pikes**, **pickerels** and **muskellunge** are found in fresh waters of the Northern Hemisphere. They are moderate to large-sized fishes. There are only 5 species and 4 of these occur in Canada. One of the Canadian species has 2 subspecies. The fifth species is found in eastern Siberia. The **northern pike** is found in Europe, Asia and North America.

The family is characterised by a flattened, elongate, duck-billed snout, teeth on the tongue and on the basibranchial bones behind the tongue are small, branchiostegal rays 10–20, nasal bones are present, the swimbladder is connected to the gut by a duct, jaws have large teeth, intermuscular bones are forked or y-shaped, no fin spines, pelvic fins are abdominal, cycloid scales, the infraorbital sensory canal on the head has 8 or more pores,

gill rakers are present as sharp denticles in patches, no mesocoracoid bone in the pectoral girdle, no orbitosphenoid or mesethmoid bones in the skull, no pyloric caeca, a single uroneural bone in the tail skeleton, the lateral line is complete and the forked caudal fin has mostly 17 branched rays. Fossils date back to the Cretaceous, and *Esox* dates to about 62 million years ago in the Palaeocene of Alberta.

Pikes are members of the **Pike Order** and are related to the **Mudminnow Family** by such characters as no adipose fin, dorsal and anal fins far back on the body near the tail, the upper jaw is bordered by a toothless maxilla, and pyloric caeca and the mesocoracoid bone in the pectoral girdle are absent. "Pike" are named for their pointed snout and "pickerel" is a Middle English word for a small pike.

Pikes are predators on other fishes aided by the posterior dorsal and anal fins which facilitate rapid darts forward. They are important sport fishes, much sought after by anglers for their fighting ability, but are not very good eating because of the intermuscular bones.

See **chain pickerel**
grass pickerel
muskellunge
northern pike
redfin pike

Pike Order

Pikes, **pickerels**, **muskellunge** and **mudminnows** belong to the Order Esociformes (= Haplomi, Esocae). There are about 10 species in northern hemisphere fresh waters. They are small to large fishes comprising 2 families with 5 species in Canada.

They are characterised by having the dorsal and anal fins located posteriorly on the body near the tail, no pyloric caeca, no breeding tubercles, no adipose fin and the maxilla is without teeth but is included in the gape. These characters contrast with the members of the **Salmon Order** where these fishes were once classified. Fossils date back to the Palaeocene.

The **Pike Family** members are of great economic importance as sport fishes while the small **mudminnows** have been used as bait.

See **Mudminnow Family**
Pike Family

pile perch

Scientific name: *Rhacochilus vacca*
(Girard, 1855)
Family: **Surfperch**
Other common names: dusky sea-perch, pile
surfperch, splittail perch, forktail perch,
silver perch, porgy
French name: perche de pilotis

Distribution: From southeastern Alaska
through British Columbia to Baja California.

Characters: This surfperch is distinguished from other Canadian species by having a frenum, a low spiny dorsal fin and a

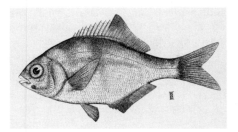

pile perch

high soft rayed dorsal fin, no blue horizontal
stripes and 58–69 lateral line scales. Dorsal
fin spines 9–11, soft rays 21–25. Anal fin
with 3 spines and 27–30 soft rays. Pectoral
fin with 19–22 rays. The caudal fin has a
deep fork. Brown, grey or black above with
silvery flanks and belly. The flanks may be
blotched or have a broad dark bar in the middle. Lower flank scales are dusky and stand
out. There is often a dark spot low on the
head below the eye. Pelvic fins have black
tips. Breeding males are dark while young
are pinkish. Reaches 44.2 cm.

Biology: This is a species of rocky shores
and kelp beds, often found near pilings and
jetties. It may go as deep as 46 m. Food is
molluscs, hard-shelled crabs, brittle stars and
barnacles which are crushed by the throat
teeth and after digestion covered in mucus to
be released in the faeces. It searches for food
in a head-down position and carefully selects
prey items. In California it is known to
"clean" parasites off other fishes. Life span is
at least 10 years. After age 4 females are
larger than males. Most fish are mature at age

3 although some fish of both sexes mature at
2 years. Mating occurs in the fall but fertilisation is delayed 3 months. Gestation is about 6
months. Fecundity is 7–61 embryos. Young
are born in August in Canada. Often caught
by anglers. Commercially important in
California and sold as "perch."

pilotfish

Scientific name: *Naucrates ductor*
(Linnaeus, 1758)
Family: **Jack**
Other common names: shark pilot,
poisson pilote
French name: fanfre

Distribution: Found world-wide in warmer
waters and off both the Atlantic and Pacific
coasts of Canada.

Characters: This species is distinguished
from its Canadian relatives by the 5–8 distinct
vertical bars on the body. The 3–6 dorsal fin
spines are short and not connected by a membrane in adults. They are only readily visible
in young fish. There are no scutes (enlarged
scales) in the lateral line but there is a fleshy
lateral keel on the caudal peduncle. The caudal peduncle is grooved above and below.
Scales are ctenoid. There is 1 spine in the second dorsal fin and 24–29 soft rays. The anal
fin has 3 spines and 15–18 soft rays.

pilotfish

Overall colour is blackish-silver to bluish.
The flank bars are bluish and 2–3 extend onto
the dorsal and anal fins. The caudal fin is
banded and has white tips. Pectoral and
pelvic fins are black tipped or may be dark
overall. The dorsal and anal fin lobes are
white tipped. An excited pilotfish becomes
silvery white, the bars vanish and 3 broad,
blue patches appear on the back. Reaches 70
cm, but usually smaller.

Biology: First reported from off Vancouver Island in 1981, a northern range extension. Not uncommon off Nova Scotia as a summer and fall migrant, and reported once from Placentia Bay, Newfoundland, the northern limit of their range. This species is an unusual member of its family in that it follows sharks, large fishes, whales, turtles, or even rides the bow waves of ships and boats, feeding off scraps. A leatherback turtle caught in Placentia Bay had 9 pilotfish in attendance, having been tagged in French Guiana 128 days before and covering over 5000 km at 39 km/day. Legend has it that they lead sharks to their prey but the reverse is the true state of affairs. They do not receive any protection from the shark in return for their supposed piloting, and indeed are careful to stay well clear of the shark's mouth. In contrast they have been seen to enter the mouth of **rays** which are known not to feed on fishes.

They may serve as "cleaner" fishes, removing parasites from their host. They feed mostly on plankton and small fishes which are foraged independently of their host's feeding. Their association with ships has led to the parallel legend that they guide ships to a safe port. Young pilotfish are found in association with jellyfish and seaweeds.

The characteristic barred colouration is very obvious and serves as a warning device to potential predators much as a bee or wasp colour pattern does. The danger warned of is the presence of the **shark** nearby, perhaps enabling the pilotfish to make extensive feeding forays on its own. The loss of bars is usually associated with an aggressive threat display aimed at driving smaller pilotfish away from the shark host, thus reducing competition for space and food. The colour change only occurs when another shark is present to which smaller, subordinate pilotfish could retreat.

pink sabertooth

Scientific name: *Evermannella balbo*
  (Risso, 1820)
Family: **Sabertooth Fish**
Other common names: balbo sabertooth
French name: dents-de-sabre rose

Distribution: Mostly found in the North and South Atlantic and Mediterranean Sea and probably around the globe in the southern oceans. Found off the Atlantic coast of Canada.

Characters: The tubular eyes slanting upwards and forwards along with a high anal fin ray count (33–37) distinguish this species. There is a glistening green-white spot on the side of the eye which may be a light reflector, but little is known of its function. Colour is a glistening light brown in preserved specimens with 7–13 irregular rows of pigment spots along the sides but colour patterns are highly variable and some are almost completely brown to black. The operculum is heavily spotted with pigment in some fish. Life colours are probably silvery with a faint pink tint. Size is up to 171 mm standard length.

pink sabertooth

Biology: Reported from 2 specimens off the northwest Flemish Cap taken in 1968 and 2 specimens on the Scotian Shelf in 1978. Rare in the northwest Atlantic Ocean. Adults are usually found at depths over 400 m but some have been reported from 100 m. Food is small fishes.

pink salmon

Scientific name: *Oncorhynchus gorbuscha*
  (Walbaum, 1792)
Family: **Salmon**
Other common names: humpback, autumn salmon, dog salmon, haddo, holia
French name: saumon rose

Distribution: Found from the Mackenzie River delta around Alaska and south through British Columbia to California. Also south to Japan in the western Pacific Ocean. Also introduced to Lake Superior and now reaching Lake Ontario and to Europe and Asia. Atlantic Canadian captures are strays from cage rearing operations on the U.S.A. as introductions in Canada have been unsuccessful.

Characters: This species is distinguished by having 147–205 lateral line scales, 12–19 principal anal fin rays, large eye-sized black spots on the back, upper flank, and adipose and caudal fin and 24–35 gill rakers. Dorsal fin principal rays 10–16, pectoral rays 13–19 and pelvic rays 9–11. Pyloric caeca 95–224. Spawning males have a narrow snout with a turned down end, an enlarged and turned up lower jaw, enlarged teeth, embedded scales and a marked hump on the back before the dorsal fin. The adipose fin is always larger in males than in females.

The back is steel blue to blue-green, flanks are silvery and the belly white. Breeding males have a dark back and pale red flanks blotched brown to olive-green. Young lack parr marks and spots.

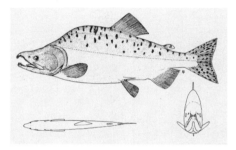

pink salmon

Reaches 76.0 cm and 6.4 kg. The world, all-tackle angling record from St. Mary's River, Ontario weighed 5.94 kg and was caught on 23 September 1992 by Ray Higaki. This fish is also recognized as the Canadian record.

Biology: This Pacific salmon spends about 18 months at sea, entering small coastal streams or lower reaches of large rivers to spawn. Fish tend to return to their birth stream but wandering is not uncommon and accounts for the rapid spread of pink salmon from Lake Superior through the Great Lakes. Young fish may run to sea soon after hatching and many do not feed in fresh water. Adults do not feed on the spawning migration except in the Great Lakes.

Food in the sea is crustaceans, squids, pteropods and a wide variety of fishes. Those young which feed briefly in fresh water take aquatic insects. Other **Salmon Family** mem-

bers, **northern squawfish**, and **sculpins** as well as birds and mammals feed on pink salmon. They are also cannibals. **Lampreys** are frequently parasitic on pink salmon.

Life span is usually 2 years, some living 3 years particularly in the Great Lakes. A 2 year life span means spawning runs consist of even- and odd-numbered year stocks. These stocks may use the same river or one stock is dominant in a particular river. The Fraser River has an odd-year stock for example and even-year stocks are found in northern B.C. and the Queen Charlotte Islands. The Great Lakes stock is an odd-year one. Males run first and are larger. Runs occur from June to September and reach lower tidal areas or a maximum of about 500 km up larger rivers but usually less than 160 km even in large rivers. Spawning occurs from July to October at 10–16°C, later runs at a lower temperature.

Males are aggressive and defend a territory against other males. Females are aggressive towards females and small males but to a lesser extent than adult males. Females are particularly territorial when digging redds. The female excavates a redd about 1 m long and up to 0.5 m deep by lashing her tail while lying on her side. Females may build and spawn in more than one redd and males may spawn with more than one female. A spawning pair, sometimes accompanied by up to 10 or more other males, position themselves in the redd, gape and release eggs and sperm, usually at night. The spawning pair consists of the female and the longest, most hump-backed male with the other males arranged by size behind them. There is much fighting and jockeying for position by the other males and some fish have deep cuts from the enlarged teeth. There may also be an outlier male, small and coloured like a female, which maintains a position to one side of the nest. The other males and the outlier all release sperm when the pair spawn. The female dislodges gravel at the upstream edge of the redd to cover and protect the eggs. This takes 2–3 hours. The eggs are orange-red, 6.0 mm in diameter and number over 2000 per female.

Adults die within a few days or weeks of spawning. Eggs hatch from December to

February and the young or alevins leave the gravel in April to May when the yolk is absorbed. The fry may move to sea in a single night while those far upriver drift passively or swim actively at night and hide in the gravel during the day. Some may move downstream actively in schools during the day. The young fish stay in coastal waters for several months before heading out to the open sea.

Along with **chum salmon**, this species was less regarded in native and commercial fisheries. However it has become more appreciated and catches may exceed 10 million fish annually in Canada. Most is canned. Catches are made with purse seines, gill nets and by trolling as the fish return to the coast. The 1988 Canadian catch was 31,355 tonnes, the largest by weight of the Pacific salmons, and was worth almost $42 million. The flesh is pink (hence its name) and tasty although reputedly not as good as **sockeye, coho** or **chinook**. Anglers take this species by trolling bait in the ocean or large lakes or on the spawning run with flies or artificial lures. It is the third most important Pacific salmon for anglers after **coho** and **chinook**.

This species, like so many other migratory fishes, is very susceptible to environmental changes. In British Columbia 75% of the production occurs in only 8% of the pink salmon spawning streams. A major rock slide in Hells Gate Canyon of the Fraser River eliminated most of the stock but it later recovered after the slide was cleared. The failure of the transplant operation to Newfoundland of 15.35 million eggs between 1959 and 1966 is suggested to be owing to predators, unfavourable river temperatures, unsuitable stocks in respect of homing behaviour and too few eggs. In contrast the 1956 introduction to Lake Superior was successful and has spread throughout the Great Lakes, reaching Lake Ontario by 1979.

- Most accessible June through August.
- For saltwater fishing areas, include the waters of Vancouver Island and the Queen Charlotte Islands, for freshwater fishing the coastal rivers of northern British Columbia.

- Top saltwater outfits include standard 10 1/2–foot salmon rods equipped with a mooching reel used with eight- to 14–pound test line. Lighter spinning and baitcasting outfits can be used with eight- to 14–pound test line. Fresh water fishing outfits include ultralight to light action spinning rods and reels used with six- to 10–pound test line.
- Live **herring** or trolling with a cut-plug **herring**. The best artificial lures for fresh water rivers are an assortment of 1/4– to 3/8–ounce flashy spoons, spinners and jigs.

pink snailfish

Scientific name: *Paraliparis rosaceus*
Gilbert, 1890
Family: **Snailfish**
Other common names: none
French name: limace rosâtre

Distribution: Found from British Columbia to Baja California.

Characters: This snailfish is identified among its Canadian Pacific relatives by the lack of pelvic fins and an adhesive disc, by having 6 branchiostegal rays, no barbels or papillae on the snout and no laterally directed opercular spine, mouth horizontal, and teeth in a single row of blunt canines with bands only at the jaw tips. Dorsal fin rays 57–69, anal rays 53–60. The pectoral fin has 18–22 rays, with an upper lobe of 13–16 rays separated by a deep notch from a lower lobe of

pink snailfish

2–4 rays. Notch rays are gradually reduced to rudiments with increase in fish size. Pyloric caeca 6–9 and pale. Specimens over 10 cm are rosy or pinkish on the body with a brown to black snout. Young fish are dark brown. Fins have a dark margin. The mouth cavity is dusky. Gill cavity and peritoneum black, stomach pale. Reaches 40 cm standard length.

Biology: Canadian specimens were caught in **sablefish** traps set at 2195 m off Tasu Sound in the Queen Charlotte Islands and at 1920 m off Vancouver Island in 1978 and 1979. Elsewhere depth range is 1050–3358 m. Largest eggs are 3.7 mm in diameter and ripe eggs in a female number an estimated 1277.

pinpoint lanternfish

Scientific name: *Lampanyctus regalis* (Gilbert, 1892)
Family: **Lanternfish**
Other common names: small-eyed lanternfish, pinpoint lampfish
French name: lampe royale

Distribution: Found from Japan to Baja California including off British Columbia and at Ocean Station Papa (50°N, 145°W).

Characters: This species is separated from other Pacific coast lanternfishes by having 4 Prc photophores, the fourth PO

pinpoint lanternfish

photophore is elevated above the others, 2 Pol photophores, the SAO series is angled, and there are scale-like, luminous caudal glands. It is distinguished from its relatives, the **broadfin** and **brokenline lanternfishes** by the short, narrow-based pectoral fin, small photophores, and the VLO photophore is well above a line from SAO photophores 1 and 2. The third SAO photophore is over the anal fin origin. Dorsal fin rays 14–17, anal rays 16–19, pectoral rays 11–14 and vertebrae 36–39. Total gill rakers 16–19 and AO photophores 13–15. Lateral line scales 36–39. The inner rays of the pelvic fins are whitish. Reaches about 19 cm.

Biology: Caught below 600 m down to 1100 m at the Canadian weathership. Found at 99–891 m and most common off the northern coast of British Columbia. Elsewhere reported

to rise to 50 m at night and descend to 1630 m in the day. Food is euphausiid crustaceans.

Pipefish Family

Scientific name: Syngnathidae
French name: hippocampes

This family includes both the pipefishes and the **seahorses**. The family is mostly marine, with some brackish and freshwater species, and is found in all cold-temperate to tropical oceans. There are about 200 pipefish species and about 30 seahorse species. The Atlantic coast of Canada has 5 pipefishes and 1 seahorse and there is 1 pipefish on the Pacific coast.

These fishes are characterised by a body enclosed in a series of bony rings. The snout is an elongate tube with a small mouth at the tip. There are no true jaw teeth. The gill opening is small and pore-like, the gills are lobe-shaped. There are 1–3 branchiostegal rays. There is no supracleithrum. There are no pelvic fins. The anal fin is always small with only 2–6 rays. The dorsal, anal and caudal fins are absent in some species. Those without a caudal fin may have the tail prehensile, able to grasp and hold onto objects. Pipefishes and seahorses have only one kidney, on the right side.

Pipefishes and seahorses are related to the **Cornetfish** and **Snipefish** families and are members of the **Stickleback Order**. They are identified partly by the number, form and arrangement of bony rings. The body is divided into a trunk and a tail. The first trunk ring has the pectoral fin base and the last has the anus in it.

Pipefishes have a straight body and often a caudal fin. Seahorses have a vertical posture, the head bent down, no caudal fin and a coiled tail. The **pipehorse** is intermediate in form. Their most remarkable feature is that males care for the eggs. The female attaches eggs to the male belly or places them in a pouch (or marsupium). Here the eggs develop and eventually leave after about 4–6 weeks through a slit or pore so the male "gives birth."

Pipefishes and seahorses are found mostly in shallow coastal areas and in estuaries but also occur down to about 400 m and in the open ocean often associated with floating seaweed. They are slow-moving and easily picked up by hand. Propulsion is by undulating the dorsal and pectoral fins. Since they cannot outswim most predators, they are often very well camouflaged. Their food is small crustaceans sucked into the tube-like snout. Many species have a life span of only about 2 years.

Dried seahorses are commonly sold as curios and some family members have been used as medicines or aphrodisiacs in the East. They are popular aquarium fishes. Certain species are endangered by collecting for curios and aquaria.

See **bay pipefish**
bull pipefish
lined seahorse
northern pipefish
pipehorse
pugnose pipefish
sargassum pipefish

pipehorse

Scientific name: *Acentronura dendritica*
(Barbour, 1905)
Family: **Pipefish**
Other common names: seahorse pipefish
French name: syngnathe dendritique

Distribution: Found from Brazil to Nova Scotia.

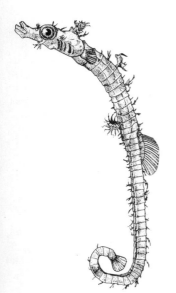

pipehorse

Characters: This species is identified by being intermediate in appearance between a **pipefish** and a **seahorse**. A small caudal fin is present but the tail is curved. The head is nearly straight. The body is covered with fleshy tabs arranged in clusters. Trunk rings number 13–15, usually 14, tail rings 37–41, usually 39. Dorsal fin rays 15–18, pectoral fin rays 12–15 and anal fin rays 2–3. Variable from light to dark, often blotched. Attains 8.1 cm.

Biology: Only found as strays on the Scotian Shelf in Canada; two fish were caught in 1977 in floating brown algae. These are northern records for the species. This is a rare species known from less than 40 specimens and not found inshore on the mainland of North America. Swims with the head up and rests with the tail curled around an object like **seahorses**. The smallest male with a brood pouch was 46.5 cm long.

pitgum lanternfish

Scientific name: *Opostomias mitsuii*
Imai, 1941
Family: **Barbeled Dragonfish**
Other common names: pitgum dragonfish
French name: dragon japonais

Distribution: Found from Japan to California including off the coast of Vancouver Island, British Columbia.

Characters: This species is distinguished from its Canadian Pacific relatives, the **highfin** and **longfin dragonfishes**, by having pectoral fins, a moderately long barbel, pelvic

pitgum lanternfish

fins on the lower flank, and the first tooth on the lower jaw piercing the premaxillary bone of the upper jaw. The eye pupil is circular. Dorsal fin rays 21–24. Anal fin rays 22–24. Pelvic rays 7–8 and pectoral rays 5. The barbel is shorter than or about equal to head length. Reaches 20.8 cm standard length.

Biology: A single specimen was caught off southern Vancouver Island in 1972; a northern range extension for the species. Two more specimens were caught in 1991, 88 km off Vancouver Island in a midwater net fished at the surface.

pitted tubeshoulder

Scientific name: *Maulisia argipalla*
   Matsui and Rosenblatt, 1979
Family: **Tubeshoulder**
Other common names: palegold searsiid
French name: circé troué

Distribution: Found in all oceans including off the Pacific coast of Canada.

Characters: This species is recognised by the family character of a tube projecting from the flank above the pectoral fin, the lack of

pitted tubeshoulder

enlarged scales in the lateral line and a large upper jaw extending past the eye. In addition pores behind the shoulder girdle are small. Pelvic fin rays are 7–8, usually 7. The frontal bones on top of the head are widest over the eye. In anterior view the fish appears to be frowning. There is a round photophore below the pectoral fin. Dark to pale gold in colour over the whole body. There is white tissue behind and under the eye. Scales are outlined with dark brown pigment in preserved fish and the canal system on the head is dark brown on a white background. Reaches about 19 cm.

Biology: Found at 475–1000 m or lower in the mesopelagic zone. Little else is known.

pixie poacher

Scientific name: *Occella impi* Gruchy, 1970
Family: **Poacher**
Other common names: none
French name: lutin

Distribution: Known only from the mouth of the Skonun River, Graham Island, British Columbia.

Characters: This species is related to the **warty poacher** but has 9 anal rays and 18

pectoral fin rays. In addition the nasal spine is sharp and hooked backwards and the anus is nearer the origin of the anal fin than the pelvic

pixie poacher

fin. There are spiny plates on the breast. The lower jaw and the area below the eye have broad pits. The first dorsal fin has 9 spines and the second dorsal fin 6 soft rays. There is a flap at the rear of the upper jaw. Gill membranes are not joined to the isthmus. The preserved specimen is brownish overall. The tips of the dorsal fins are brown. The caudal fin is brownish and the pectoral fin has a broad brown stripe on its upper third. Reaches 2 cm.

Biology: The only known specimen was collected in brackish water on a sand and pebble beach between high and low tide. It may be a juvenile **pricklebreast poacher** but this remains to be proven. The Committee on the Status of Endangered Wildlife in Canada considered in 1991 that there was insufficient scientific information about this species to accord it any status.

plaices

Plaices are **flatfishes** of the **Righteye Flounder Family**. In Canada there is 1 species, the **Canadian plaice**, also known as the American plaice although it is mostly found in Canadian Arctic and Atlantic waters. The word comes from a Greek root meaning flat. The plural plaices is not in common use and the singular serves for the individual and for many plaice.

plainchin dreamarm

Scientific name: *Leptacanthichthys*
   gracilispinis (Regan, 1925)
Family: **Dreamer**
Other common names: none
French name: bras-de-rêve menton-uni

Distribution: Found in the North Atlantic and Pacific oceans including the Atlantic coast of Canada.

Characters: This species of deepsea **anglerfish** is unique among dreamers in having a well-developed mandibular spine which is longer than the quadrate spine (these spines lie at the rear of the lower jaw) and by having a very elongate and narrow pectoral fin lobe. Well-developed sphenotic spines are also present and the operculum is deeply notched posteriorly. Dorsal fin rays 4–6, anal fin rays 5–6, and pectoral fin rays 18–21. Overall colour is dark with the esca unpigmented in patches. Females reach 6.9 cm while the male is only 7.5 mm.

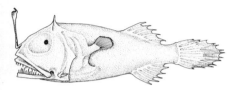

plainchin dreamarm

Biology: Known from only 3 Canadian specimens taken off Newfoundland in 1968. Most specimens are caught below 1000 m. The male in this species is parasitic on the female. Females use the fishing apparatus to attract prey close enough to be gulped down.

plainfin midshipman

Scientific name: *Porichthys notatus*
   Girard, 1854
Family: **Toadfish**
Other common names: midshipman,
   singing fish
French name: pilotin tacheté

Distribution: Found from the Gulf of California to southeast Alaska including the coast of British Columbia.

Characters: The body bears more than 840 photophores (light organs), arranged in rows — 2 dorsal rows, a midlateral row, lower lateral row, anal row, 2 rows joined on the belly, 2 rows on the throat and lower jaw, plus various rows on the head. Those on the underside of the head are in a v-shape. British Columbia midshipmen are not bioluminescent probably because the appropriate luminescent diet items are not found in the north, in particular certain small ostracod crustaceans. The body lacks scales but there are 4 lateral line canals, near the dorsal fin, midlateral, lower flank and near the anal fin. The

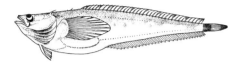

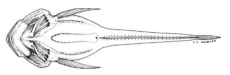

plainfin midshipman

first dorsal fin has 2 spines and the second dorsal fin 33–38 rays. The anal fin has 28–37 rays. The pelvic fin has 1 spine and 2 soft rays. There is a sharp opercular spine which can cause a painful wound. There are numerous head cirri.

The body is dark brown, olive or iridescent purple on the back, silvery on the side and golden-yellow or yellow-white on the belly. The flanks and back have some blotching. There is a white blotch under the eye edged by a ventral black crescent. Attains 38 cm.

Biology: The name of this species derives either from its whistling ability, likened to that of a junior naval officer, or from the rows of light organs looking like buttons on a naval uniform. Sound production can be heard 12 m away and is produced by forcing air in the swimbladder through a small opening between 2 chambers. The resulting hum can be very annoying to houseboat owners as it lasts overnight. The sound has been recorded as high as 20 decibels above the ambient level where 5 dB is considered a nuisance.

During the day this species buries itself in mud and emerges at night to feed on fishes and crustaceans. Some food may be seized while the fish is concealed in the mud. Found commonly from the shore down to 366 m. An important food item for seals and sea lions.

This species is unusual in that males grow larger and live longer than females. Males may reach 4 years of age.

The light organs are used in southern populations in courtship but may also flash when the fish is picked up or disturbed. Yellow or pink eggs are spawned in crevices, under rocks or on hard surfaces in late spring and are guarded by the male. The male will excavate a cavity and eggs are attached to its roof, kept clean and moist until hatching up to 40 days later. Up to 789 eggs may be laid and fish in British Columbia produce greater numbers of larger eggs than more southern populations. Some males are sneak-spawners, fertilising eggs produced by a female member of a spawning pair.

The flesh is edible but is not sold except for pet food and for animals on fur farms. Anglers often catch this unusual fish.

planehead filefish

Scientific name: *Stephanolepis hispidus* (Linnaeus, 1766)
Family: **Filefish**
Other common names: none
French name: lime à grande tête

Distribution: North Atlantic Ocean from Atlantic Canada south to Brazil in the west.

Characters: Dorsal fin rays 27–35, anal fin rays 26–35. The gill slit is nearly vertical. The presence of an obvious spine at the pelvic fin position but no caudal peduncle paired spines distinguish this filefish. The dorsal spine is strong and well-barbed. The snout profile is slightly concave to straight.

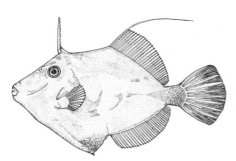

planehead filefish

Males have bristly spines on the caudal peduncle and the first ray in the soft dorsal fin is thread-like. Tan, olive, brown or greenish with or without dark brown blotches, spots and lines. The dorsal and anal fins are dark along their bases. The dorsal spine and the caudal fin are green. The soft dorsal fin and anal fin are pale. Attains 25 cm.

Biology: Stray adults have been caught in Nova Scotia and New Brunswick and larvae are not uncommon off Nova Scotia. Young are often found in floating seaweed. Smaller fish (2.1–4.0 cm) feed mostly on amphipods but older fish feed on seagrass and clams, and other organisms associated with seagrass beds.

Pleiades loosejaw

Scientific name: *Aristostomias polydactylus* Regan and Trewavas, 1930
Family: **Barbeled Dragonfish**
Other common names: none
French name: drague Pléiades

Distribution: Found in all major oceans including off the Canadian Atlantic coast.

Characters: This species is distinguished from Canadian relatives by having a pectoral fin, a suborbital light organ, a barbel on the

Pleiades loosejaw

throat, 2 pairs of nostrils, light organs between the pectoral and pelvic fins in 5–9 groups or clusters, and 14–17 pectoral fin rays. Head and body black. There is a solid streak of luminous tissue between the eye and the postorbital light organ. Attains 22 cm.

Biology: Reported from just outside Canadian waters south of the Grand Bank in 1988, a northern range limit. It occurs in depths from 25 m to 1000 m. Quite a rare species.

Poacher Family

Scientific name: Agonidae
French name: agones

Poachers and alligatorfishes are found mainly in the North Pacific Ocean with a few species in the North Atlantic Ocean and 1 species off southern South America. There are about 50 species with 19 on the Pacific coast and 3 on the Atlantic and eastern Arctic coasts of Canada.

They are easily recognised by their elongate bodies covered in bony plates which are non-overlapping, fused together in rows and often spiny or toothed. The pelvic fins are thoracic (under the pectorals) and have 1 spine and 2 soft rays. There may be 1 or 2 dorsal fins. The anal fin lacks spines and all fins, unusually in fishes, lack branched rays. The pectoral fins are large and fan-like, sometimes with the lower rays elongated. The head may have various spines and the area around the mouth may have various barbels. Males usually have larger pelvic and anal fins than females. The anus is between the pelvic fins. The basihyal is small to absent, the predorsal bone and swimbladder are absent, and there are 0–1 tabular bones. Branchiostegal rays 5–6.

Poachers are relatives of the **Sculpin Family** and members of the **Mail-cheeked Order**.

These are small bottom living fishes at shallow to moderate depths with some down to 1280 m. Barbels are used to help locate food.

See **Arctic alligatorfish**
      Atlantic alligatorfish
      Atlantic poacher
      bigeye starsnout
      blackfin starsnout
      blacktip poacher
      bluespotted poacher
      fourhorn poacher
      gray starsnout
      kelp poacher
      northern spearnose poacher
      pixie poacher
      pricklebreast poacher
      pygmy poacher
      rockhead
      sawback poacher
      smooth alligatorfish
      smootheye poacher
      spinycheek starsnout
      sturgeon poacher
      tubenose poacher
      warty poacher

polar cod

Scientific name: *Arctogadus glacialis* (Peters, 1874)
Family: **Cod**
Other common names: Arctic cod, Arctic Greenland cod, morue arctique
French name: saïda imberbe

Distribution: Found from Ellesmere Island and northern Baffin Island west to the Beaufort Sea. Also off northern Greenland, in the Barents Sea and off northeastern Siberia in the Chukchi Sea.

Characters: This species and its relative, the **toothed cod**, are distinguished from other western Arctic **cods** by having the jaws

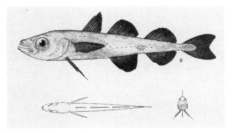

polar cod

about equal or the lower protrudes slightly, an emarginate to forked caudal fin, sensory head canals poreless or with few, very small pores, the lateral line is not continuous before the second dorsal fin, and the palatine bones in the roof of the mouth have strong teeth. This species is separated from its relative by the chin barbel being absent or very tiny, less than pupil diameter. The lateral line is straight behind the level of the middle of the second dorsal fin. First dorsal fin rays 9–16, second dorsal rays 15–24 and third dorsal fin rays 19–25. First anal fin rays 16–24 and second anal rays 15–26. Pectoral rays 18–22. Gill rakers 27–35. The back and upper flank are blackish-brown. The belly is silvery and all fins are black. Young are a light grey with the head and fins chocolate-brown. Reaches 41 cm standard length.

Biology: This cod is usually caught under drifting ice at 0–25 m over great depths but may descend to about 1000 m. It may be caught in ice cracks. It occurs in schools and is pelagic. Food is mainly **Arctic cod**, and amphipod crustaceans which live on the underside of ice. Females may mature at 3–4 years and life span is at least 9 years. There is a fishery in the East Siberian Sea, off east Greenland and north of the Baffin Sea. The catch is used as fish meal and oil.

polar eelpout

Scientific name: *Lycodes polaris*
 (Sabine, 1824)
Family: **Eelpout**
Other common names: Canadian eelpout
French name: lycode polaire

Distribution: Almost circumpolar in the Arctic Ocean and from the Beaufort Sea to Labrador in Canada, and south to the Gulf of St. Lawrence and the Saguenay River.

Characters: This species is separated from its Canadian Arctic-Atlantic relatives by having small pelvic fins, a mouth under the

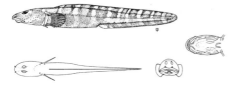

polar eelpout

snout, no large pores around the mouth, crests on the chin, lateral line single and on midflank, tail short (preanal distance in the range 45–56% of total length), scales are usually absent or very few on the posterior midflank, pointed teeth on the vomer bone in the roof of the mouth 2–7, 90–93 vertebrae, and 9–12 dark flank bars. Dorsal fin rays 89–94, anal rays 69–76 (each including half of the continuous caudal fin rays). Pectoral fin rays 15–19. The flanks and dorsal fin have alternate narrow light and broad dark bars. Light bars number 9–12 but in older fish they become interrupted. Reaches 25 cm.

Biology: This eelpout is found on mud bottoms at 5–300 m, sometimes close to the tidal zone. It is one of the most common species in trawls made deeper than 40 m in

the Beaufort Sea. It is usually found at temperatures colder than −1°C. Food is mainly amphipods but includes other crustaceans, clams, worms and brittle stars. **Arctic cod** are also eaten. Clam siphons are nipped off. Mouthfuls of mud are taken in and food items extracted, including crustaceans, worms, brittle stars and even **Arctic cod**. Life span is over 5 years. Spawning may occur in autumn or early winter and females have up to 187 eggs with a diameter approaching 5 mm. This species is known to burrow into mud tail first.

polar sculpin

Scientific name: *Cottunculus microps*
 Collett, 1875
Family: **Soft Sculpin**
Other common names: Arctic sculpin,
 cotte arctique, crapaud de mer,
French name: cotte polaire

Distribution: Found on both sides of the North Atlantic Ocean and in Canada from Smith Sound at the north of Baffin Bay south to the Saguenay River and Browns Bank off Nova Scotia, and to New Jersey.

Characters: This species is separated from its Arctic-Atlantic relative, the **pallid sculpin**, by having a rough, spiny skin and 3–4 bands on the body. Dorsal fin spines are weak and number 6–8, soft rays 13–15. Anal fin rays 10–11 and pectoral rays 17–19. Lateral line pores 13–15. Overall colour is pale but the bands are broad and dusky. The head is blotched and spotted and often has a dark band across the snout. The pectoral fin has small dark spots. Reaches 30 cm but usually 9–14 cm standard length.

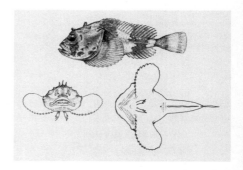

polar sculpin

Biology: Usually caught at 170–895 m in waters at 1.3–4°C, somewhat cooler than its relative. Elsewhere it is reported to eat worms, amphipods, mysids and sea spiders. Spawning in the Barents Sea takes place in June and July and 124–220 eggs are released, each with a diameter of about 4.5 mm. Females grow to larger sizes than males.

pollock

Scientific name: *Pollachius virens* (Linnaeus, 1758)
Family: **Cod**
Other common names: Boston bluefish, harbour pollock, scrod, merlan, merlannoir, lieu noire, coley, colin, blister back, rock salmon, black cod (and coalfish, saithe and green cod in Great Britain)
French name: goberge

Distribution: Found in Europe, Greenland and in Canada from southern Labrador and throughout the Maritimes, south to North Carolina.

Characters: This species is separated from other Canadian Arctic-Atlantic cods by having 3 dorsal and 2 anal fins with short

pollock

interspaces, the first anal fin origin under the second dorsal fin origin, the lower jaw projects, a chin barbel which is small in young and disappears in adults, scales overlapping and both the pectoral and pelvic fins are short, the latter being less than three-quarters the length of the former which extends only to the end of the first dorsal fin. First dorsal fin rays 12–14, second dorsal rays 20–23 and third dorsal rays 19–24. First anal fin rays 24–32, second anal rays 19–24.

The back is brown to green or olive, flanks greenish, olive, grey or yellowish and the belly grey or silvery to white. Green is always a predominant colour. Dorsal and

anal fins are olive-grey or greenish. Pelvic fins have reddish tinges. The mouth is dark. The lateral line is white or grey.

Attains 1.5 m and reputedly 31.5 kg. The world, all-tackle record rod-caught fish was 21.06 kg and was caught at Brielle, New Jersey in 1975.

Biology: Pollock are found in a depth range of 35–364 m and a temperature range of 0–18°C but preferring mid-ranges of both of these. Unlike other **Cod Family** members it is often found above the sea bed. There is a summer inshore and winter offshore migration of pollock up to 20 cm long (hence harbour pollock). Older fish, 2 years or more, are in deeper water near shore or on offshore banks. There are also north-south movements in and out of the Bay of Fundy where schools are made up of fish of similar size. Curiously larger fish, 65–85 cm long, preferred the New Brunswick shore of the Bay while smaller fish, 45–65 cm, were off Nova Scotia.

There is no spawning in the Bay of Fundy and fish there are recruited from the Gulf of Maine and Scotian Shelf. On the Scotian Shelf there is a year-class variability. Fishes born in a given year are more numerous in some years than others. This has important implications for fishery management. Year-class strength may depend on the association of spawning activities with Gulf Stream gyres.

Life span is 25 years. Maturity is attained at 3–7 years and 46–70 cm but both age and length at maturity has fallen in recent years because of overfishing and variation in environmental conditions such as temperature.

Food includes crustaceans and fishes, the latter increasing in the diet with age. Pollock are cannibals.

Spawning occurs from September to March in Canada. Over 4 million, 1.2 mm diameter pelagic eggs are produced.

Pollock are commercial fishes in Canada, caught principally by otter trawls but also longlines, purse seines, handlines and occasionally in traps and weirs. Catches have averaged 41,900 tonnes for 1960–1987 and values of $11.6 million. Most catches are made around southern Nova Scotia. They are also sport fishes caught on lures as "harbour pollock."

Pomfret Family

Scientific name: Bramidae
French name: castagnoles

Pomfrets or breams are found in oceanic waters of the Atlantic, Indian and Pacific oceans. There are 18 species, of which 3 are found off the Atlantic and 2 off the Pacific coasts of Canada.

These fishes have a long, single dorsal fin with a few unbranched anterior spines. There are no anal fin spines. The body is compressed and oval in shape and the head is rounded and blunt. Adults have keels on their scales. The pelvic fins have a scaly sheath and are thoracic or jugular in position. Scales cover the top and sides of the head, except the snout and the exposed maxilla bone of the upper jaw. Scales also extend onto the fins in some species while in others they are restricted to the fin base. The posterior nostril is slit-like.

Pomfrets are related to the **Manefish Family** in the **Perch Order**. The name pomfret comes from a Portuguese word for these fishes.

These fishes are found in temperate to tropical waters in the open ocean near the surface. Some may form schools. They are only rarely caught by **salmon** and **albacore** trollers and on longlines, most are only seen by scientists.

Young pomfrets are pelagic and differ in fin shapes and body form from adults making their species identity uncertain. The caudal fin in young can be rounded (forked in adults), the preopercle bone on the side of the head serrated (smooth in adults), scales bear spines (lost in some adults), and so on.

Pomfrets are important food fishes off Spain and the Canary Islands.

See **Atlantic fanfish**
 Atlantic pomfret
 bigscale pomfret
 Pacific pomfret
 rough pomfret

pompano dolphin

Scientific name: *Coryphaena equisetis*
 Linnaeus, 1758
Family: **Dolphin**

Other common names: none
French name: coryphène dauphin

Distribution: Found world-wide in warmer waters and straying into Atlantic Canada.

Characters: Distinguished from its only relative, the **common dolphin**, by having about 160–200 lateral line scales, 46–60,

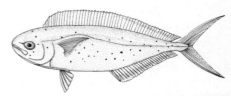

pompano dolphin

usually 52–59, dorsal fin rays and a squarish tooth patch on the tongue. Young do not have bars but a dark body with clear pelvic fins. The dorsal fin may show faint bars in young fish and the caudal fin is unpigmented on its edge. The adult pectoral fin length is half the head length and maximum body depth is greater than in the **common dolphin** (more than one quarter of the standard length). Anal fin with 23–29 rays, its outer edge convex, pectoral rays 18–21. The head is only slightly steeper in males than in females and generally resembles that of a female **common dolphin**. Overall colour is silvery or yellowish. Dorsal, anal and caudal fins yellowish and flank spots pronounced. Reaches 76 cm and 2.3 kg.

Biology: Known only from 3 larval specimens taken in 1981 on the Scotian Shelf at the northern range limit in the western Atlantic Ocean. This species is generally rarer than its relative, perhaps because it has long been confused with it. It is more confined to oceanic waters, but may come inshore. It is attracted by lights at night. Food is small fishes, crustaceans and squids.

pond smelt

Scientific name: *Hypomesus olidus*
 (Pallas, 1814)
Family: **Smelts**
Other common names: smallmouth smelt
French name: éperlan à petite bouche

Distribution: Found from Korea northward to Arctic drainages of Siberia and in coastal southern Alaska and the Peel River, Yukon and in the Mackenzie River, Rae River and Great Bear Lake, N.W.T.

Characters: This species and its relative, the **surf smelt**, are distinguished from other smelts by having 8–14 gill rakers on the upper arch, minute brush-like teeth on the tongue, and an incomplete lateral line with 73 or fewer scales. This species has fewer pyloric caeca (0–3, rarely 4 and usually 2 in Canada) than the **surf smelt** and the length of the adipose fin base is equal to or longer than the eye diameter. Dorsal fin branched rays 7–10, anal branched rays 11–18 and pectoral branched rays 9–13. There are 7–16 scales in a short lateral line and 51–62 scales along the flank. There are 8–12 upper gill rakers, 26–34 total gill rakers. The swimbladder connects to the gut by a duct from behind the swimbladder tip. Males develop tubercles on the head, scales and fin rays. The male pelvic fins almost reach the anus, much longer than in females. Overall body colour brownish to olive-green with dorsal scales outlined. The belly is silver-white. A faint speckled stripe on the caudal peduncle fades anteriorly. There is a silver stripe on the midflank. Snout and operculum speckled. Peritoneum light with a few pigment spots. Attains 20.0 cm.

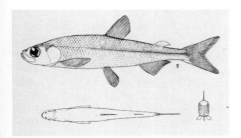

pond smelt

Biology: Found mainly in freshwater lakes and streams, entering brackish water along the Tuktoyaktuk Peninsula. Food is crustaceans, insects and perhaps algae. **Inconnu**, **northern pike** and various **salmons** eat pond smelt. Life span is rarely

longer than 4–5 years but a few fish reach 8–9 years. Growth rates vary markedly with some reaching 7.0 cm at age 2 and others only at 5 years or more. Age at first maturity is 2–3 years in Canada. Adults are pelagic. Spawning in Alaska occurs in June in shallow areas over debris. Eggs are adhesive and attach to roots or other objects in shallow water. There is a spawning run into streams in some populations and in a Canadian lake repeat spawning in subsequent years is known. It is said to be excellent eating. The total Canadian catch in 1988 was 7700 tonnes (13,429 in 1983).

popeye

Scientific name: *Coryphaenoides cinereus*
 (Gilbert, 1893)
Family: **Grenadier**
Other common names: none
French name: grenadier cendré

Distribution: Found from western North Pacific Ocean to Oregon including British Columbia and at Ocean Station Papa (50°N, 145°W).

Characters: This species is distinguished from its Pacific Canadian coast relatives by having the anus immediately in front of the

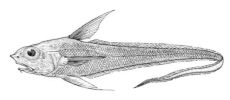

popeye

anal fin, no black, scaleless area on the abdomen, 6 branchiostegal rays, pelvic fin rays 8–10, usually 9, teeth in the upper jaw not in 1–2 distinct rows, a large eye (more than one-fifth head length), scales over much of the head except under the snout, first dorsal fin soft rays 10–14, usually 10–11, the eye rim black only antero-ventrally, a long outer pelvic fin ray (greater than 70% of head length), enlarged scales only at the tip and lateral angles of the snout, and a small, thorn-like branch to the ventral edge of the suborbital shelf. Pectoral fin rays 19–23. Scales bear 3–10 rows of fine spines, the number increasing with size. Overall colour is a dirty-white when scales are lost. Scale pockets are margined with brown. The second dorsal fin and anal fin are dusky to grey. Other fins darken with age, eventually becoming black. The gill and mouth cavities are black. The peritoneum is black. The barbel and gill membranes are blackish. Reaches 56 cm.

Biology: A single specimen was caught off Queen Charlotte Sound at 2760 m in 1965 (see **bearded rattail**), 3 specimens off Triangle Island at northern Vancouver Island in 1964 at 2103–2195 m, and a single juvenile from Ocean Station Papa, tentatively identified as this species. Found from 630 to 2832 m.

popeye blacksmelt

Scientific name: *Bathylagus ochotensis*
    Schmidt, 1938
Family: **Deepsea Smelt**
Other common names: eared blacksmelt
French name: garcette à oreilles

Distribution: Found in the northern Pacific Ocean including from Baja California to British Columbia.

Characters: Distinguished from other Pacific coast species of deepsea smelts by having 12–16 anal fin rays, about 46 scales

popeye blacksmelt

along the lateral line, concentric lines on the operculum and a blunt snout. Dorsal fin rays 9–12 and pectoral rays 6–10. Colour in alcohol is brown with the mouth, tongue and gill cavity black. Size to 12.6 cm standard length.

Biology: Caught at the surface and down to 900 m. Food is presumed to be crustaceans.

porbeagle

Scientific name: *Lamna nasus*
    (Bonnaterre, 1788)

Family: **Mackerel Shark**
Other common names: mackerel shark, blue dog, salmon shark, herring shark, bonito shark, beaumaris shark, blue mako
French name: maraîche

Distribution: North coast of Newfoundland and the Gulf of St. Lawrence south to Nova Scotia and on to New Jersey and probably South Carolina. Also found on the coasts of Europe and in the southern hemisphere.

Characters: Distinguished from the **great white shark** by the smooth teeth which have a cusp on each side near the base unlike those

porbeagle

in the **shortfin mako**. Lateral cusps may be absent from sharks smaller than 1.2 m. The anal and second dorsal fins lie opposite each other and there is a secondary keel below the main keel on the tail fin while the **shortfin mako** has the origin of the second dorsal fin well in front of anal fin origin and no secondary keel. The body is stout and deep. The snout is conical, pointed and longer than in the **salmon shark** (distance from snout tip to eye 2 times or less in distance from eye to first gill opening). The 5 gill slits are moderate in size, about equal to the snout length.

Dark blue-grey to blue-black on the back, changing abruptly to white on the belly without dark spots and blotches as in the **salmon shark**. The posterior base of the first dorsal fin has a distinguishing white patch. The lower pectoral fin surface is dusky to black on its outer half, mottled with white on its inner half.

Up to 3.72 m, but usually smaller. The world record rod-caught porbeagle caught in 1993 in the Pentland Firth, Scotland weighed 230 kg. "Porbeagle" is a Cornish dialect word for this shark.

Biology: Found from the surface down to at least 366 m. An open water species preferring water colder than 18°C but also reported in the Bay of Fundy and Passamaquoddy Bay in shallow water. This is the commonest large shark along the Atlantic coast of Nova Scotia in the summer but is also caught in winter. It is common in southern Newfoundland from July to September. They are often seen breaking the surface with their dorsal and tail fins.

Food consists of various fishes as the common names suggest, including **herring, mackerel, gaspereau, cod, cusk, hakes, redfish** and **flounders** as well as squid. Eggs develop within the female for about 8 months and up to 5 young are born in late summer at 60–75 cm in length. The oldest young, while still unborn within the mother, eat the unfertilised eggs and the younger embryos to become immensely fat. This shark may live 30 years or more and take 5 years to become mature.

Porbeagles have a heat-exchanger mechanism which raises body temperature up to 8.3C° above sea temperature, making them more efficient in colder waters.

Sometimes reported as a sluggish fish when hooked, other authors maintain that it is an excellent sport fish which may leap. The flesh is white and said to taste like **swordfish**, although some find it distasteful. They may be caught by trolling or bait fishing while chumming. Baits include **mackerel, herring**, squid and **bonito** and should be deeply set. Long wire leaders (5 m) should be used because porbeagles tend to roll up the line causing it to break.

A commercial fishery in Canadian waters resulted in over a million kilograms being caught by Norwegian, former U.S.S.R. and other vessels starting in 1961 and over 24,000 tonnes were landed in 1972. High mercury levels were discovered in porbeagle muscle and the fishery has ceased. The liver oil has been used in the U.S.A., the flesh for fish meal and the fins used for shark fin soup. They are often a nuisance because they will remove commercially important species like **cod** from hooks by biting through the line.

Porcupinefish Family

Scientific name: Diodontidae
French name: atingas

Porcupinefishes, burrfishes or spiny puffers are found world-wide in warmer waters. There are 19 species with 2 reported from Atlantic Canada.

These fishes are recognised by the sharp spines or quills covering the body. These modified scales may be fixed and erect, or moveable and only erected when the body is inflated by swallowing air or water. The teeth are fused to form a crushing, parrot-like beak (hence Diodontidae, two-toothed, one in each jaw). Teeth lack the median groove seen in **Puffer Family** members. Porcupinefish are relatives of the **Mola** and **Puffer** families in the **Puffer Order** which all share an absence of true jaw teeth but have a cutting edge which may be split into 2, 3 or 4 "teeth." The pelvic fins are absent.

Young porcupinefish are pelagic but adults are mostly found inshore down to about 90 m. Food is shelled invertebrates which are crushed with the beak. Porcupinefish inflate their bodies when disturbed. This increases their size and, with the spines, deters predators, an asset in such slow swimmers. They are, however, very agile and can manoeuvre their bodies very easily. They are often dried and sold as curios. They have even been used as lamps in the Far East since a candle will shine through the inflated and stretched skin. They are common aquarium exhibits. They soon become tame and will shoot water from the tank surface at their keeper when hungry. Their flesh is often very poisonous and can be fatal if eaten.

See **balloonfish**
striped burrfish

Porgy Family

Scientific name: Sparidae
French name: spares

Porgies or seabreams are found in all warmer seas and rarely entering brackish or fresh waters. There are about 100 species with 2 found in Atlantic Canada.

Porgies can be recognised by their 2 types of jaw teeth, the front ones being incisors or canines and those at the rear molars. There are also molar teeth in the pharyngeal "mill" which crush shellfish. The maxilla bone of the upper jaw is covered by a sheath when the mouth is closed. The preopercle bone on the side of the head has a smooth margin. The forehead is often steep. Many species have the rear nostril slit-like, including all but one of the American species. The mouth is small but the eye is large. The dorsal fin is continuous and has 10–15 spines and 8–17 soft rays. The anal fin has 3 spines and 7–16 soft rays. The pelvic fins have 1 spine and 5 soft rays. Scales are cycloid or weakly ctenoid. There are 6 branchiostegal rays. Young porgies are often very different in colour and patterns than adults.

Porgies are members of the **Perch Order**. "Porgy" is derived from the Latin and Greek for these fishes.

These fishes are most common in shallow waters wherever molluscs occur. This may be coral reefs, eelgrass beds, bays or sandy and rocky beaches. Porgy species may be hermaphrodites with both sexes developing at the same time, protandrous with a sex change with age from male to female or protogynous with a sex change from female to male. Porgies are important food fishes in several parts of the world and some species are sought after by anglers.

See **scup**
sheepshead

Portuguese shark

Scientific name: *Centroscymnus coelolepis*
Bocage and Brito Capello, 1864
Family: **Sleeper Shark**
Other common names: Portuguese dogfish,
pailona commun
French name: pailona

Distribution: From the Grand Bank south to Delaware Bay. Also in Europe, Africa, and the western Pacific and possibly New Zealand.

Characters: The absence of an anal fin, very small dorsal fin spines, dark brown body, very short snout, lanceolate upper teeth

with one cusp and blade-like lower teeth with short oblique cusps, and large, flat denticles distinguish this shark. The dorsal fins are about equal in size. Dark chocolate brown over the whole body and fins. Maximum length 1.14 m.

Biology: This sluggish species is common in deep water on or near to the bottom of continental slopes. Mostly deeper than 370 m down to 3675 m but may rise to 270 m. This is the deepest known shark. Water temperatures are 5–13°C. The Portuguese shark eats bony fishes and squid. Whale flesh has been found in the stomach contents of this shark, but it is uncertain whether this was scavenged or taken from a living whale during its feeding dive. It is ovoviviparous with 13–16 young in a litter, less than 20 cm long at birth. Adults are mostly 90–95 cm. It is caught in bottom trawls, deepwater fixed nets and on line gear such as that used for halibut. It has been dried and salted for human food and processed for fish meal. It was fished commercially off Portugal, hence the common name but it is not important in North American waters. This fish is too deep to be caught by anglers.

pouts

Pouts are members of the **Eelpout Family** and include the **ocean pout**, the **Atlantic soft pout** and the **Pacific soft pout**. The **aurora unernak** may also be known as the aurora pout and the **fish doctor** as the green ocean pout.

Pout is derived from an Old English root meaning "to inflate" in reference perhaps to the muscular, protruding cheeks.

pouty snailfish

Scientific name: *Paraliparis garmani*
Burke, 1912
Family: **Snailfish**
Other common names: pouty seasnail
French name: limace pote

Distribution: Found from the Davis Strait in Canadian waters south to Cape Hatteras and assumed to occur along Canada's Atlantic coast.

Characters: This snailfish is separated from other Canadian Atlantic species by the lack of

Portuguese shark

an adhesive disc and pelvic fins, by having 1 pair of nostrils, teeth in bands, an oblique mouth and 8 caudal fin rays. Dorsal fin rays 54–59, anal rays 49–53 and upper pectoral fin lobe rays 13–14 (total 19–22). There are 6 pyloric caeca. The body is a dusky white with scattered, black, pigment spots. The mouth is not pigmented. Peritoneum black. Reaches 14.2 cm standard length.

pouty snailfish

Biology: This species has been caught in the range 226–915 m. They have been observed from submersibles swimming 1–3 m above the sea floor, angled upward at 15–30° to the horizontal. Swimming is by rhythmic fin movements. Food is pelagic crustaceans but amphipods scavenging dead fish lying on the sea bottom may also be eaten. Females with up to 317 eggs greater than 2 mm in diameter have been caught in January and September off the U.S. coast. Maximum egg size is 3.5 mm.

pricklebacks

Pricklebacks are members of the **Shanny Family** and are named for the long dorsal fin composed almost entirely of spines. There are 9 species of prickleback on the Pacific coast and 1 on the Arctic coast.

See **black prickleback**
blackline prickleback
bluebarred prickleback
longsnout prickleback
pearly prickleback
ribbon prickleback
rock prickleback
snake prickleback
whitebarred prickleback
Y-prickleback

pricklebreast poacher

Scientific name: *Stellerina xyosterna*
(Jordan and Gilbert, 1880)
Family: **Poacher**
Other common names: none

French name: agone à poitrine épineuse

Distribution: Found from southeastern Alaska and the Queen Charlotte Islands south to Baja California.

Characters: The upturned mouth is characteristic and the many small prickles on the breast, rather than plates, are unique. Plates are in 4 rows on each side, bearing prominent spines. First dorsal fin with 6–8 spines, second dorsal fin with 5–7 soft rays. Anal fin rays 7–9. Pectoral fin rays 16–19. The anal fin origin lies below the first dorsal fin. A barbel or cirrus at the rear of the upper jaw is rounded and not flap-like. Gill membranes are not joined to the isthmus. Olive-brown overall, often darkly spotted on the back. Caudal fin black. Pectoral fin with large, black blotch formed by pigmentation on distal membranes but the fin margin is clear. Anal fin spotted and blotched black posteriorly. Reaches 16 cm.

pricklebreast poacher

Biology: Found on a mud or sand bottom at 1.8–91 m.

Pricklefish Order

The pricklefishes, gibberfishes, **ridgeheads** or bigscales, **redmouth whalefishes**, **whalefishes**, **flabby whalefishes**, hairyfishes, tapetails or ribbonbearers, and largenose fishes of the Order Stephanoberyciformes comprise about 86 marine species in 9 families. There are 12 species in 4 families in Canada.

They are characterised by a rounded body, absence of teeth on the roof of the mouth, very thin skull bones, orbitosphenoid usually absent, subocular shelf absent, and the supramaxilla absent or reduced. They were formerly included in the **Alfonsino Order**.

Most of the species are oceanic and deepsea fishes.

See **Flabby Whalefish Family**
Redmouth Whalefish Family
Ridgehead Family
Whalefish Family

prickly dreamer

Scientific name: *Spiniphryne gladisfenae* (Beebe, 1932)

Family: **Dreamer**

Other common names: none

French name: rêveur piquant

Distribution: Found in the North Atlantic Ocean including northeast of Labrador.

Characters: The prickly dreamer is unique within its family by having numerous, obvious, close-set skin spines covering

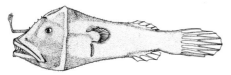

prickly dreamer

the body and fins. Dorsal fin rays 6, anal fin rays 4–5 and pectoral fin rays 15–17. Sphenotic spines are well-developed and the profile of the frontal bones on the head dorsally is convex. Males and larvae are unknown. Overall colour dark-brown to black. The tips of the distal escal appendages are dark red and the posterior three-lobed appendage is a bright red-orange. The distal appendage colour may be due to the presence of blood. Females reach 10.5 cm standard length.

Biology: Only a single specimen has been caught near Canadian waters in 1974 at a depth of 1950–1955 m.

prickly sculpin

Scientific name: *Cottus asper* Richardson, 1836

Family: **Sculpin**

Other common names: prickly bullhead

French name: chabot piquant

Distribution: Found from Alaska to California including British Columbia in coastal drainages. Also in the Peace River drainage in northeastern British Columbia and just entering Alberta.

Characters: This and related species in the freshwater genus *Cottus* are distinguished from the **deepwater sculpin** by the gill membrane being attached to the isthmus and the dorsal fins touching. It is separated from its relatives by having 1 pore on the chin tip, a complete lateral line, the first 2 dorsal fin spines close together, palatine teeth in the roof of the mouth and the posterior nostril is not tubular. First dorsal fin spines 7–11, second dorsal rays 18–23, anal rays 12–19 and pectoral rays 14–18. Prickles may occur over the whole body (particularly in inland populations), or be restricted to the pectoral fin axil (more common in coastal populations). Lateral line pores 28–43. The male genital papilla is long and v-shaped and in the female short and round.

Overall colour dark brown or greyish-brown fading to white or yellowish-white on the belly. The flanks are mottled black and there are 3 dark bands under the second dorsal fin. Fins are thinly barred. The first dorsal fin has an elongate black blotch posteriorly. The chin is lightly speckled. Both males and females have an orange margin to the first dorsal fin in the spawning season but males are darker overall.

The freshwater form has been recognised as *C. a. asper* and the coastal form as *C a. parvus* (Girard, 1854). Reaches 19.2 cm standard length with a questionable report of 30.5 cm total length.

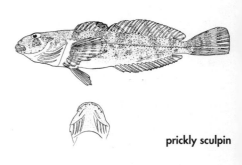

prickly sculpin

Biology: This species is found both in coastal rivers and in inland rivers and lakes. It prefers quieter waters like pools in contrast to the **coastrange sculpins**. It may enter the sea in estuaries and nearshore areas and will set up house in discarded beverage cans.

Food includes aquatic insects, molluscs and, when larger, small fishes. They are known to eat **salmon** and **rainbow trout** eggs. Feeding takes place mostly at night, peaking at or just before dawn. A variety of fishes and birds eat this sculpin including **trout** and **northern squawfish**.

Life span is about 7 years with maturity attained at age 3, but life span varies between streams. Spawning occurs from March to July in Canada, inland and northern populations spawning later than coastal and southern ones. The favoured temperature range is 8–13°C. Coastal populations migrate downstream and may spawn in brackish water returning up stream in the summer and fall. Males choose a nest site under a rock and court a female to lead her to the site. Up to 10,000 (usually less), 1 mm diameter, adhesive, orange eggs are attached to the undersurface of the rock. Since a male may entice up to 10 females under the rock 1 at a time, there can be as many as 30,000 eggs there in various stages of development. The male guards the eggs and fans them using his large pectoral fins. Larvae are pelagic for 4–5 weeks before settling to the bottom.

prickly snailfish

Scientific name: *Paraliparis deani*
Burke, 1912
Family: **Snailfish**
Other common names: prickly liparid
French name: limace épineuse

Distribution: Found from Alaska to California including British Columbia.

Characters: This snailfish is identified among its Canadian Pacific relatives by the lack of pelvic fins and an adhesive disc, by having 6 branchiostegal rays, no barbels or papillae on the snout and no laterally directed opercular spine, a horizontal mouth, teeth in

prickly snailfish

bands, a gill slit extending from above the pectoral fin and down at least 10 rays in front, a dark stomach and a pale, dotted or silvery peritoneum. Dorsal fin rays 56–59, anal rays 44–49, and pectoral rays 18–22 with the lower rays elongate and not joined by a membrane. Prickles are present on the lower pectoral fin surface. Pale brown or whitish overall with pink lips and fins. The belly is silvery with black pigment spots. Peritoneum silvery but darkened by pigment spots. Stomach black. Reaches 10 cm.

Biology: Reported from 64–203 m in British Columbia but may descend over 1000 m elsewhere. Usually caught in bottom trawls. Spawning may take place in February when fish with mature, 2 mm eggs have been caught.

prowfish

Scientific name: *Zaprora silenus*
Jordan, 1896
Family: **Prowfish**
Other common names: none
French name: zaprora

Distribution: Found from California to Japan and along the coast of British Columbia.

Characters: The long dorsal fin has 54–57 spines, the anal fin is poorly developed with 3–4 weak spines and 24–27 soft rays, the

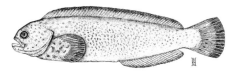

prowfish

pectoral fin has 20–25 rays and there are about 36 pyloric caeca. Prowfish lack pelvic fins. The gill membranes are united. Scales are small but very elongate and cover the body. There is no lateral line. The head has large mucous pores ringed with white or blue. Dark green to brown or grey, fading to tan on the belly. The head and body are spotted irregularly or mottled. The flanks may have yellow spots. The head and pectoral fin bases are yellowish and the inside of the mouth is yellow or orange. Fins are dark edged. Attains 89 cm.

Biology: The prowfish is rarely encountered. Adults are bottom dwellers at 29–457 m while larvae and young are planktonic. They may live at least 12 years and spawn at 4 years. Young fish have been found with the large orange jellyfish *Cyanea* and adults are known to feed on jellyfish. It is of no commercial importance but the red flesh is quite edible.

Prowfish Family

Scientific name: Zaproridae
French name: zaproridés

Prowfish are found in the North Pacific Ocean from California to Japan, including Canadian waters. There is only one species in the family and the account under **prowfish** gives information on biology and characters. Its closest relatives appear to be the **Shanny Family** and the **Wolffish Family** in the **Perch Order**. The **prowfish** was first described from a specimen caught in November 1895 near Nanaimo, B.C.

See **prowfish**

Puffer Family

Scientific name: Tetraodontidae
French name: sphéroïdes

Puffers, toadfishes, toados, helicopterfish, or tobies are warm-water fishes found worldwide in seas and occasionally in fresh water. There are about 121 species with 3 recorded from Atlantic Canada.

Puffers are able to inflate the body by swallowing air or water which expands a sac attached to the stomach. The absence of ribs and pelvic fins facilitates this expansion. The fish then floats on the surface for several minutes or more before it can expel the air. They lack obvious spines and have only small prickles usually restricted to the belly. Jaw "teeth" have a median suture so that there is a pair in each jaw, forming a parrot-like beak (hence *Tetraodon* - four-toothed).

Puffers are relatives of the **Porcupinefish** and **Mola** families in the **Puffer Order** which all share an absence of true jaw teeth but have a cutting edge which may be split into 2, 3 or 4 "teeth."

These are agile fishes but they are unable to swim quickly. They can turn easily and even swim backwards, hence the name helicopterfish. The ability to inflate increases

their size and decreases the number of predators who can accommodate them in their mouths. However the helpless, floating fish is easy prey for seabirds so the advantages of this defence are suspect.

Puffers may contain a poison, tetrodotoxin, which is deadly to humans. It is often concentrated in the gonads, probably as a defense mechanism for the eggs. The preparation of puffers in restaurants in Japan is carried out by specially licensed chefs who carefully excise the dangerous parts. People die every year from eating "fugu" but this no doubt adds a certain spice to the lives of those who continue to indulge in this food. It is reported that in one year 211 cases of fugu poisoning resulted in 118 deaths. In 1984, a single puffer appropriately prepared cost $200 and fugu sales were in the tens of millions of dollars.

The beak-like mouth is adapted for feeding on hard-shelled animals like crabs, molluscs and coral. They may feed in groups. Puffers will shoot a stream of water at a sandy bottom to expose prey hidden there.

See **blunthead puffer**
northern puffer
oceanic puffer

Puffer Order

Puffers or Tetraodontiformes (= Plectognathi) comprise 8 families found worldwide mostly in warmer seas with a few species in fresh waters. These are the spikefishes, triplespines, **leatherjackets**, **triggerfishes**, **filefishes**, **boxfishes**, cowfishes, **trunkfishes**, **puffers**, spiny puffers, **porcupinefishes** and **molas** or **ocean sunfishes**. There are over 339 species in 9 families ranging in size from a few centimetres to over 2 m and 1000 kg. There are 15 species in 6 families in Canada.

Puffers are diverse in external appearance but are defined by a complex of characters of which the key ones are internal. These include a skin more commonly with spines and plates or shields than scales, although some are naked, small gill openings, a nonprotrusible mouth, teeth may be distinct or fused into a parrot-like beak, the parietal, circumorbital and nasal bones are absent, the opercular bones and branchiostegal rays are covered by thick skin or hexagonal plates, there are no sensory canals in the skull bones, lower ribs are usually absent, the hyomandibular and palatine bones are fused to the skull, the posttemporal is present or absent — if present it is fused to the pterotic bone of the skull, the urohyal is present or absent, the maxilla and premaxilla bones of the upper jaw are usually united, no anal fin spines, swimbladder usually present, and the pelvic girdle and fins are present or absent.

The order derives its name from the ability of some members to gulp water (or air) and puff up their size. Water is gulped into a ventral branch of the stomach. Increased size thwarts the smaller predators or tightens the skin and helps erect defensive spines. The fish deflates by expelling the water. Other members of the order enlarge their body slightly by moving the pelvic bone to expand a ventral flap. Puffers make sounds by grinding their teeth or by vibrations of the swimbladder.

Fossils are reported from the Eocene and possibly even the middle Cretaceous. Puffers are derived from the **Perch Order**, although some scientists believe they may be related to the **Dory Order**.

Most puffers are tropical to subtropical in coastal waters and can be colourful. A few are food fishes but some are dangerous to eat because of the poison, tetrodotoxin, in the muscles, skin, blood or internal organs but particularly in the ovaries. About half the tetrodotoxin poisonings are fatal.

See **Boxfish Family**
 Filefish Family
 Leatherjacket Family
 Mola Family
 Porcupinefish Family
 Puffer Family

Puget Sound rockfish

Scientific name: *Sebastes emphaeus*
 (Starks, 1911)
Family: **Scorpionfish**
Other common names: rock cod
French name: sébaste paradeur

Distribution: Found from Alaska to Baja California including British Columbia.

Characters: This species is recognised by size, colour and a combination of anatomical features. Dorsal fin spines 13, soft rays 13–15, usually 14. Anal fin soft rays 6–7, usually 7, second anal spine thicker than third (but not twice as thick) and longer. Pectoral fin rays 16–18, usually 17. Gill rakers 37–41. Vertebrae 27–28, usually 27. Lateral line pores 37–45 and scale rows below lateral line 38–45. Supraocular, coronal and nuchal spines absent. Overall colour reddish-brown to copper-red with dusky to greenish-brown bars and blotches on the flanks. Pink to white on the belly. Greenish bands radiate back from the eye. Spiny dorsal fin dark green with red spine tips. Base of soft dorsal fin black and the edge bright red. Other fins light red. Mouth red. Peritoneum black. Reaches 18.3 cm.

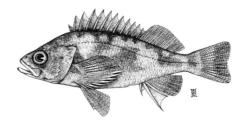

Puget Sound rockfish

Biology: Found on rough bottoms, hiding in crevices in strong currents at 9–366 m. Large concentrations have been found at 10–25 m in Washington State. Not uncommon but rarely caught because of its habitat. These fish become restless if they are not touching a solid object with their pectoral fins, an adaptation to avoiding predators by always having a refuge close "at hand." In winter this fish huddles in crevices and is very inactive. Spawning occurs later than in related species, August-September. A 17.9 cm female produced 57,103 young. Ripe females have a semi-transparent belly and divers can see the eyed larvae inside. Maturity is reached at ages 2–4 years and life span is up to 22 years. They are eaten by **yelloweye**, and various other, **rockfishes**. Prey items are small planktonic crustaceans and salps.

Puget Sound sculpin

Scientific name: *Ruscarius meanyi*
    Jordan and Starks, 1895
Family: **Sculpin**
Other common names: none
French name: chabot à joue écailleuse

Distribution: Found from northern California to southeast Alaska including British Columbia.

Characters: This species and its Pacific coast relatives, the **padded, scalyhead,** and **smoothhead sculpins**, are distinguished by

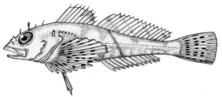

Puget Sound sculpin

having 2–3, mostly 3, pelvic fin soft rays, simple or branched uppermost preopercular spine but not antler-like, (except in the **padded sculpin**) and 3–16 scales in the rows above the lateral line. This species is separated from related species by having scales on the head and scale rows extending onto the caudal peduncle, a slender cirrus on the upper front eye margin, and snout scales. The nasal spine is sharp and recurved. There are 4 preopercular spines with the uppermost large and forked and the remainder becoming smaller ventrally. First dorsal fin spines 9–11, second dorsal soft rays 14–17. Anal rays 10–13 and pectoral rays 14–16. Scales in 3–5 rows on the upper eye surface. Lateral line with 34–38 scales. A cirrus with 3–4 branches is on the upper rear eye margin and there is a cirrus before and behind the upper gill opening. There is a row of cirri along the ridge below the eye and each dorsal fin spine has a cirrus at its tip. Small cirri are found along the lateral line, on the eye and near spines on the side of the head. Overall colour is green to cream with darker saddles on the back and blotches or vermiculations ventrally. The dorsal, caudal and pectoral fins have brown bands or streaks. Breeding males

have a clear area on the first 2 anal fin rays with the rest dusky and dusky dorsal and pelvic fins. Reaches 6.0 cm.

Biology: Reported down to 82 m off the Queen Charlotte Islands, but also as shallow as 1 m elsewhere. It is an uncommonly to rarely caught species, perhaps because of its habit of resting on vertical rock faces.

pugnose minnow

Scientific name: *Opsopoeodus emiliae*
    Hay, 1881
Family: **Carp**
Other common names: small-mouthed minnow
French name: petit-bec

Distribution: Found from western Lake Erie to Wisconsin and Minnesota and south to Texas and Florida. In Canada reported from Lake St. Clair and Lake Erie drainages and Lake St. Clair itself in southwestern Ontario.

Characters: This minnow is distinguished by having 8 branched dorsal fin rays and a very small, almost vertical mouth. A barbel at one or both mouth corners is not unusual in this minnow. There are 7, rarely 6, branched anal rays, 15 pectoral and 8 pelvic rays. Lateral line scales 35–41. Pharyngeal teeth 5–5, rarely 5–4, slender, and serrated on the crown below a hooked tip. Males develop acute nuptial tubercles in dense patches around the mouth above the upper lip and on the lower jaw. Smaller tubercles cover the rest of the head and are in double rows on pectoral rays 5–7. Males have longer pectoral fins than females.

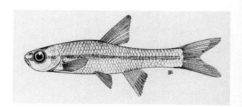

pugnose minnow

The back is light olive to yellowish overlain by silver, the flanks silvery with a midlateral stripe which extends onto the head, through the eye and onto the upper lip but not around the snout. The belly is silvery with a faint emerald sheen. Scales on the upper flank and back are outlined with dark pigment each forming a diamond shape. Some fish have an almost translucent appearance. The dorsal fin has dusky patches between the first 4 major rays and the last 3 rays leaving a clear area between. Breeding males have a dark silver-blue body and bright white tips to the anal and pelvic fins. Small white knobs develop on the first three dorsal fin rays. Peritoneum silvery with numerous melanophores.

Formerly in the genus *Notropis*. Reaches 6.4 cm.

Biology: Pugnoses prefer clear, weedy streams, rivers and lakes with little current creating a pond-like environment. They avoid highly turbid or silted waters where plants cannot grow. Young are found in shallower water than adults. Food is aquatic insects, crustaceans, and some fish eggs and larval fish. The upturned mouth suggests that surface insects may be taken. Life span is 3 years. Spawning in Canada occurs probably in spring and summer; in the southern U.S.A. gravid females can be caught from January to September. Eggs are up to 1.5 mm in diameter when water hardened and number 340 per female. Males defend a territory under a flat rock, cleaning the rock undersurface and swimming in figure eights. The dorsal fin white knobs mimic eggs. The female follows a leading male after an erected fin display to the rock shelter. She tests the rock surface with her mouth while the male nudges and lifts her belly with his snout. The pair eventually come to lie side by side, invert and spawn. Spawning only takes a second but is repeated up to 15 times. The eggs are laid in strings of 2–5 as a single layer with up to 120 eggs each spawning session. Spawning occurs every 6–7 days. This species was assigned the status of "rare" in 1985 by the Committee on the Status of Endangered Wildlife in Canada.

pugnose pipefish

Scientific name: *Bryx dunckeri*
(Metzelaar, 1919)
Family: **Pipefish**
Other common names: none

French name: syngnathe camus

Distribution: Found from Brazil to east of Georges Bank in Atlantic Canada.

Characters: This species is distinguished by lacking an anal fin and by having few dorsal fin rays (21–27). A caudal fin is pre-

pugnose pipefish

sent. Trunk rings 15–18, usually 17, tail rings 30–36, usually 31–33. Pectoral fin rays 9–13, modally 11. The body is mottled pale to reddish brown or dark overall to black, sometimes with white rings around the body. A pale spot behind the eye. Males are darker than females. Attains 9.5 cm.

Biology: Known only from a single stray in Canadian waters collected in 1978. Found in shallow water such as reefs and estuaries usually down to 11 m, but as deep as 72 m, and in the open ocean when young. Males begin to develop a brood pouch at 42 mm and eggs are in 2–8 cross rows in 1–3 layers. Eggs may be as few as 8 or as many as 50. Breeding occurs almost year round.

pugnose shiner

Scientific name: *Notropis anogenus*
Forbes, 1885
Family: **Carp**
Other common names: none
French name: méné camus

Distribution: Found in the Great Lakes, northern Mississippi River and U.S.A. Hudson Bay basins and in Canadian waters at Gananoque, eastern Lake Ontario, several localities along the Lake Erie shore, Lake St. Clair and southern Lake Huron.

Characters: This species and its relatives in the genus *Notropis* (typical **shiners**) are separated from other family members by usually having 7 branched dorsal fin rays following thin unbranched rays, protractile premaxillaries (upper lip separated from the snout by a groove), no barbels, large lateral line scales (fewer than 50), and a simple, s-shaped gut. It is separated from its relatives by having 6–9, usually 7, anal fin branched rays, the dark or grey flank stripe extends

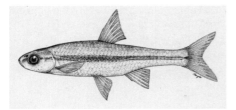

pugnose shiner

onto the head and through the eye to include the lips and chin but not extensively on the snout, and a short, vertical mouth extending only back to the anterior nostril. Pharyngeal teeth 4–4 with slightly to strongly hooked tips above weak serrations. Dorsal fin branched rays 6–8, pectoral rays 11–13 and pelvic rays 7–8. Lateral line scales 34–38. Nuptial tubercles in males are found on top of the head and upper surfaces of the pectoral and pelvic fin rays. The back is pale yellow to olive, the flanks are silvery and the belly whitish. Upper flank scales are darkly outlined with pigment and the space between them and the lateral stripe is unpigmented. Fins are transparent to slightly dusky. There is a dark, pear-shaped spot at the caudal fin base. Breeding males are bright yellow dorsally. Peritoneum, dark brown to black (visible through the body wall in preserved fish). Reaches 6.0 cm total length.

Biology: The pugnose prefers clear, weedy waters usually with sandy beds whether lakes or streams. It is very intolerant of turbid water and weed removal. Canadian populations appear to be very small and localised. Pugnoses occur in schools of 15–35 fish which quickly conceal themselves in bottom vegetation when threatened. Food is very small crustaceans and filamentous algae. Life span is about 3 years. Spawning probably occurs in June in Ontario, May to July in Wisconsin at 21–29°C. There may be up to 1275 eggs in each female with diameters up to 1.3 mm. The Committee on the Status of Endangered Wildlife in Canada classed this species as "rare" in 1985.

pumpkinseed

Scientific name: *Lepomis gibbosus*
   (Linnaeus, 1758)
Family: **Sunfish**
Other common names: yellow sunfish, common sunfish, round sunfish, sunny, punky, sun bass, pond perch, bream, flatfish, kivvy, yellow belly, tobacco box, quiver, roach
French name: crapet-soleil

Distribution: Found in southern New Brunswick, southwestern Québec, southern Ontario but not northern and western Lake Superior drainages, southeastern Manitoba. Also on Vancouver Island, the Columbia River basin of southern British Columbia and the Oldman River drainage of Alberta as introductions. In the U.S.A. south to Georgia in the east and Ohio in the west but widely introduced elsewhere. Also introduced to Europe.

Characters: This species is characterised by having 9–12 dorsal fin spines, 3 anal fin spines, 35–47 lateral line scales, gill rakers are short (length about equal to width) and knob-shaped, or bent, and the short opercular or "ear" flap is black with a white to yellow or orange margin and a red spot at the rear edge. Second dorsal fin soft rays 10–13, anal soft rays 8–12 and pectoral rays 11–14. The pectoral fin reaches the front of the eye when folded forward.

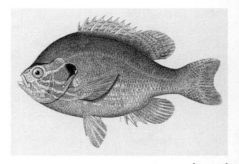

pumpkinseed

The back and upper flank are brown or golden green to olive and the lower flank has wavy blue-green lines. The belly is a very distinctive and colourful orange to red-orange. The flank has 7–10 vague bars most evident in females, and is variously spotted olive, orange, red, blue or emerald. The head has alternating, wavy blue-green and orange-brown stripes on its sides and is also spotted with olive, orange or red. The red "ear" flap spot may be orange or yellow and is white in preserved fish. The dorsal spines have a black leading edge. Fin membranes are spotted brown or are black except for the pectorals which are clear to amber. The second dorsal and caudal fin membranes additionally have orange to olive spots. The pelvic fin has a white leading edge. The posterior margins of the second dorsal, anal and caudal fins are blue-green to yellow. Peritoneum silvery.

Hybrids with **bluegill**, and other **sunfishes**, are common and may even hybridise with the parents and other hybrids making identification very difficult. The name pumpkinseed is said to be derived from the body outline resembling these seeds.

Reaches 40.0 cm. The world, all-tackle angling record from Mexico, New York in 1985 weighed 0.63 kg. The Canadian angling record from the Nottawasaga River, Ontario, was caught by Bruce Stanley on July 14, 1992 and weighed 0.85 kg.

Biology: Pumpkinseeds are extremely common and numerous in weedy bays of lakes, ponds, and slower areas in streams and rivers where the water is clear. They prefer denser vegetation than **bluegills**. They are common around docks. Their distribution is centred further north than other sunfishes and they favour cooler waters.

Food is aquatic and terrestrial insects, crustaceans, worms, snails, salamander larvae and small fishes. Feeding involves a wide variety of foods taken during the day, with peaks at dawn and in the late afternoon, by quick darts from a tail-up, head-down position. During the night they rest on the bottom, in rocky areas or near logs, and become pale with prominent bars. Pumpkinseeds are eaten by all larger predatory fishes including a wide variety of sport fishes.

Life span is 10 years (12 in captivity) with maturity attained at age 1–3. Parental males mature about 1 year later than females. Stunting is not uncommon in crowded conditions and has been recorded for 14 years or

more in Lac Hertel, Québec and transplants show this is environmental and not genetic. Annual mortality on Lac Vert, Québec is 81% between ages 4 and 7. Studies of pumpkinseed growth in lakes suffering from acid rain shows increases because of reduced competition as young pumpkinseed do not survive well, or conversely decreased growth because of effects on food supplies.

Spawning occurs form May to August when water temperatures reach values over 12.5°C and daylength exceeds 12 hours. Female pumpkinseed choose between several males so male courtship is important in increasing the probability of females visiting their nest. Larger males are preferred since they can better defend the brood against predation by snails, for example. The male excavates a nest in shallows near shore using his tail or his mouth for large objects. A nest has a shallow bowl shape about 3.5 times male length, on clay, silt, sand, gravel or rock bottoms in areas with aquatic vegetation. The male and female swim in circles, 11 per minute, nip and bang into each other. The male is vertical but the female inclines so their genital areas are in contact. Eggs and sperm are shed during the circling. Males and females spawn more than once with different partners. Cuckoldry is common where small males rush in to spawn with adults (sneakers) or mimic females (satellites) to achieve the same end.

The eggs are amber, about 1.0 mm in diameter and adhesive to vegetation, hard substrate or even small particles. A large female may have as many as 7000 eggs. A nest may contain up to 14,639 eggs from several females. The male guards and fans the eggs and watches over the young for up to 11 days, capturing strays in his mouth and putting them back in the nest. A reproductive phase, however, may occupy on average 10 days, 2 for nesting, 3 for spawning, 4 for brooding and 1 day for vacating the nest. Territory defense around a nest involves puffing out the gill covers, rushes, bites, chases and mouth-fighting. They will nip fingers placed close to the nest.

Pumpkinseeds are often the first fish caught by the youngest anglers and will take any live or artificial bait. Even bare hooks are attacked. They are tasty with white, flaky flesh but are seldom eaten by anglers. There is a minor commercial catch in Ontario and Québec which is combined with **bluegills** as "sunfishes." The brilliant colours of this fish make it an excellent aquarium denizen. They may be significant competitors with such sport fish as **yellow perch** as studies in Lake Memphremagog, Québec show a marked reduction in perch growth as pumpkinseed abundance increased.

- Most accessible June and September.
- Southern Ontario including the Kawartha Lake system and the Rideau system.
- Ultralight spinning outfits used with four- to six-pound test lines.
- Small 1/16– to 1/8–ounce plastic jigs and small worms fished under a float.

purplemouthed conger

Scientific name: *Pseudophichthys splendens*
    (Lea, 1913)
Family: **Conger**
Other common names: none
French name: congre splendide

Distribution: Found on both sides of the Atlantic Ocean in tropical waters and on the Canadian coast.

Characters: This species is distinguished as an adult from other Canadian Atlantic congers by having segmented dorsal and anal fin rays, jaw teeth in bands and vomer teeth in the roof of the mouth in a broad patch. Adults have 33–39 preanal lateral line pores, 7 prepectoral pores and no supratemporal pore. The dorsal fin origin lies posterior to the tip of the pectoral fin. The gill opening is crescentic and lies below and in front of the pectoral fin. The anterior upper and lower jaws

purplemouthed conger

have a series of both small and very large pores. Adult colour is light brown to grey or ochre. The dorsal and anal fins become

darker posteriorly. The peritoneum, gill cavity, gill openings, mouth cavity and lips are a purple-black. Larvae are distinguished by the dorsal fin beginning before the anus, 131–137 myomeres (muscle blocks) and a complex pigment pattern scattered over the whole body surface. Canadian larvae are 65–107 mm long. Adults attain 50 cm.

Biology: Canadian records are of stray larvae taken at depths of 50–200 m in 1979. Adults are found on muddy bottoms at depths of 37–1647 m.

pygmy moray

Scientific name: *Anarchias similis*
    (Lea, 1913)
Family: **Moray**
Other common names: none
French name: murène pygmée

Distribution: Found from waters off Atlantic Canada as strays and south to Brazil. Also in the eastern Atlantic Ocean.

Characters: Colour and size will separate adults of this species from the **green moray**, its relative in Atlantic Canada. The rear nos-

pygmy moray

tril is above the eye next to a large head pore. The dorsal and anal fins are poorly developed and begin just in front of the caudal fin, well rearward of the anus. Dorsal fin rays 23–34, anal rays 11–22. Overall colour is tan to brown with white markings on the head and chin. Head pores are in white spots. Rare specimens have a dark ladder-like pattern on the body. Larvae also have the dorsal and anal fins restricted to the posterior part of the body, a total myomere (muscle block) count of 105–114, and only 1–3 small melanophores restricted to near the brain base. Adults attain 20.6 cm, the smallest Atlantic coast moray. Larvae reach 60 mm.

Biology: Two larval specimens have been caught just outside Canadian waters south of the Grand Bank at a depth of 200 m or less.

This is a rare species in the western North Atlantic Ocean. Adults are found on shallow coral reefs, deep rocky areas and in eel grass, down to 180 m. Ripe females have been caught from July to November and males in February, September and October. Eggs are 1.0 mm in diameter.

pygmy poacher

Scientific name: *Odontopyxis trispinosa* Lockington, 1880
Family: **Poacher**
Other common names: none
French name: agone pygmée

Distribution: Found from southeastern Alaska to central Baja California including British Columbia.
Characters: This poacher is recognised by having a heart-shaped pit on the top of the head which is divided into two parts by a longitudinal ridge, and by having a single vertical spine at the snout tip. There are 2 backward pointing spines behind this vertical spine. There are no cirri except 1 at the rear of the upper jaw. The first dorsal fin has 3–6 spines and the second dorsal fin 5–8 soft rays. The anal fin has 5–7 rays and the pectoral fin 13–15 rays with the lower 5–7 slightly finger-like. Gill membranes are joined to the isthmus. Colour is grey to olive-green with 6 or more saddles on the back and flanks. The dorsal, pectoral and caudal fins have dusky bars. Reaches 9.5 cm.

pygmy poacher

Biology: Habitat is soft bottoms from 9 to 373 m. Young are pelagic.

pygmy rockfish

Scientific name: *Sebastes wilsoni* (Gilbert, 1915)
Family: **Scorpionfish**
Other common names: Wilson's rockfish, slender rockfish

French name: sébaste pygmée

Distribution: From southeast Alaska to southern California including British Columbia.
Characters: This species is a small rockfish distinguished by a complex of characters including colour, lateral line canal pores, gill

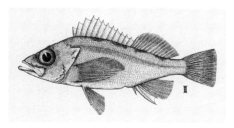

pygmy rockfish

rakers, and head spine arrangement. Dorsal fin spines 13–14, usually 13, soft rays 13–15, usually 14. Anal fin soft rays 5–7, usually 6, second anal spine not quite twice as thick as third and longer than third. Pectoral fin rays 16–18, usually 17. Lateral line pores 37–46, scale rows below lateral line 45–50. Gill rakers 37–43. Vertebrae 27–28, usually 27. Supraocular, coronal and nuchal spines absent, others strong. Overall colour a light brown with red tinges. There are 4–5 dark saddles on the back and adjacent fin. A brown-red stripe runs below the lateral line. The lower flank and belly are silvery and clearly demarked from the upper flank. Peritoneum black. Reaches 21 cm, usually smaller.
Biology: Found offshore from surface waters down to 274 m. Young are born in June in Canadian waters.

pygmy smelt

Scientific name: *Osmerus spectrum* Cope, 1870
Family: **Smelt**
Other common names: none
French name: éperlan nain

Distribution: Found in Heney Lake, Québec, Lake Utopia, N.B. and in lakes of southern Maine. Probably in various other Québec, N.B. and Maine lakes. Introduced to Meach and Ouimet lakes, Québec.

Characters: This smelt is distinguished from the other lake smelt in eastern North America, the **rainbow smelt**, by being less

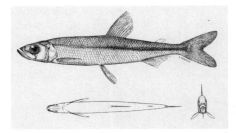

pygmy smelt

then 13.5 cm standard length, usually 34–36 (range 32–36) gill rakers and eye diameter 4.4–6.5% of standard length. Midlateral scales 58–66. Overall coloration silvery. Preserved fish have a dark flank stripe and speckled fins with the anal fin being almost clear. Recent studies maintain that the dwarf and large forms of smelt in lakes should be regarded as stocks rather than species. Attains perhaps 13.5 cm standard length.

Biology: This smelt lives in lakes along with the larger **rainbow smelt**. Food is principally plankton and aquatic insects unlike **rainbow smelt**, which take fish when larger, including pygmy smelt. Young pygmy smelt are found in schools and are attracted to artificial lights at night. During the day they retreat to deeper water. Adults form schools beneath the ice in January. Maturity is reached at age 2 and life span is 5 years. Growth is slower in pygmy smelt than in **rainbow smelt**. Spawning occurs in April and May during and after spring breakup, and later than **rainbow smelt**. Temperatures are 4–8°C and eggs are shed on sand and gravel beaches. Up to 3774 eggs of 0.7 mm diameter are found in preserved females. The Committee on the Status of Endangered Wildlife in Canada is considering a status of "rare" for this species. Numbers of pygmy smelt in Heney Lake appear to have declined.

pygmy snailfish

Scientific name: *Lipariscus nanus*
    Gilbert, 1915

Family: **Snailfish**
Other common names: none
French name: limace naine

Distribution: Found from Alaska to California including British Columbia.

Characters: This snailfish is separated from its Canadian Pacific relatives by lacking pelvic fins and an adhesive disc, by having 5 branchiostegal rays and by the gill slit being above the uppermost pectoral fin ray. Teeth are in narrow bands. Dorsal fin rays 40–52, anal rays 37–49, pectoral rays 13–15 with a notch (2–3 rays) making an upper (9–10 rays) and a lower (2–3 rays) lobe. Lower lobe rays are free of the membrane for up to half their length. Black pyloric caeca number about 6. Prickles are found over the body and pectoral fin. The skin is transparent but has scattered pigment spots, most densely near the tail. The snout, mouth and gill cavities, peritoneum and stomach are black. Reaches 5.4 cm standard length.

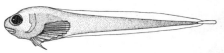

pygmy snailfish

Biology: Generally caught at 100–810 m in British Columbia where it is a midwater species. Not uncommon off Vancouver Island.

pygmy whitefish

Scientific name: *Prosopium coulteri*
    (Eigenmann and Eigenmann, 1892)
Family: **Salmon**
Other common names: Coulter's whitefish, brownback whitefish
French name: ménomini pygmée

Distribution: Found in Lake Superior and in western Canada, Montana, Washington and western Alaska. In the Columbia, Fraser, Liard, Peace and Skeena river systems of British Columbia, the Teslin and Alsek river systems of British Columbia and the Yukon, Elliott Lake in the Yukon, Great Bear Lake in the N.W.T., Lake Athabasca in Saskatchewan, and in Waterton Lakes and Solomon Creek, Alberta.

Characters: This species and its relatives, the **round** and **mountain whitefishes**, are distinguished from other **Salmon Family**

pygmy whitefish

members by having a single flap of skin between the nostrils, large scales (108 or less in the lateral line) and a forked caudal fin. It is separated from its relatives by having 11–21 gill rakers, 50–70 lateral line scales, 18–20 scales around the caudal peduncle and 13–33 pyloric caeca. Teeth are found only on the tongue and are small. Dorsal fin rays 10–14, anal rays 10–14, pectoral rays 13–18 and pelvic rays 9–11. Both sexes have nuptial tubercles, best developed in males on the top of the head, flank and back scales and pectoral and pelvic fins. Males have larger fins than females. The back is brown, flanks silvery and belly white. The back has 12–14 dark spots along its midline. The flank midline has 7–14 dark spots which may be absent in adults. The dorsal, caudal and anal fins are clear and colourless, the anal and pelvic fins are whitish. The caudal fin may have a dark spot at its base. This whitefish may have survived glaciation in up to 6 different refugia so there are complex differences between various forms. Attains 27.1 cm fork length. Some lakes in Alaska have 2 forms of this whitefish, differing in gill raker counts.

Biology: This **whitefish** is found in both lakes and in moderate to swift rivers. In lakes it is usually deeper than about 6 m, and in Lake Superior is found at about 18–89 m, usually below 55 m. Food is crustaceans, aquatic insects and molluscs, and also **salmon** and **whitefish** eggs. **Arctic char, lake trout, Dolly Varden** and fish-eating birds take this whitefish. Life span is at least 9 years and females grow faster and live up to 3 years longer than males. Maturity is attained at 2–3 years of age, sometimes as early as 1 year. Spawning occurs in October to December in Canada, presumably in shallow water. Eggs are shed over gravel and hatch in the spring. Orange eggs are up to 2.6 mm in diameter and average up to 1153 eggs per female.

Q

queen triggerfish

Scientific name: *Balistes vetula*
    Linnaeus, 1758
Family: **Leatherjacket**
Other common names: old wench, old wife,
    baliste vieille
French name: baliste royal

Distribution: Found from Nova Scotia
and Sable Island south to Brazil and in the
eastern Atlantic Ocean.

Characters: This species is distinct from
the **ocean triggerfish** by having enlarged,
flexible scales above the pectoral fin base

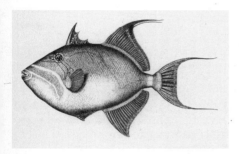

queen triggerfish

and from the **gray triggerfish** by colour and
fin ray counts. Dorsal fin rays 29–32, usually
30, anal fin rays 27–29, usually 27, pectoral
fin rays 13–15, usually 14. Outer caudal fin
rays greatly elongated. The spiny dorsal fin
has 3 spines and folds into a groove. Scales
are outlined with pigment and by grooves
between them. The head has 2 characteristic,
broad blue bands below the eye and several
narrow gold or blue bands radiating in all
directions from the eye. There is a bright
blue ring around the mouth. Several wavy,
dark reticulate lines are found on the dorsal
and anal fins. Body colour is yellowish-
brown to blue-green to deep brown and is
often bluish. The ventral surface is a dull
yellow. There is a broad blue ring around the
caudal peduncle. Young fish have broken
lines running obliquely across the body. The
head bands in young may be indistinct. Blue
head bands are a constant feature but body

colour changes with background and light
intensity. Reaches 60 cm. The world, all-
tackle angling record weighed 5.44 kg and
was caught in 1985 at Ponce Inlet, Florida.

Biology: Rare in Canadian waters as strays
from the south. Only 3 specimens reported
since 1882. A common species on reefs and in
seagrass beds from the surface down to 275 m.
It feeds on various invertebrates such as molluscs and worms and including the long-
spined sea urchin *Diadema*, turning the urchin
over to attack the unprotected underside. One
queen triggerfish was seen to pick up an
urchin by one spine using its teeth and drop it
so it fell with the underside up. The trigger
fish may even "play" with the sea urchin. Life
span is at least 12 years. There is a peak
spawning in February in the Caribbean.
Fecundity is high, over 600,000 eggs. It is
caught in the Caribbean on handlines, in traps
and by bottom trawls. Marketed fresh, it is
said to be an excellent food fish but may be
slightly poisonous.

queenfish

Scientific name: *Seriphus politus*
    Ayres, 1860
Family: **Drum**
Other common names: none
French name: tambour royal

Distribution: Found from Baja California
to British Columbia.

Characters: This drum is separated from
its Canadian Pacific relatives by the high anal
fin ray count and the large gap between the

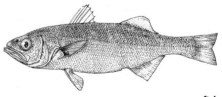

queenfish

spiny and soft dorsal fins. First dorsal fin with
7–9 spines, second dorsal fin with 1 spine and
18–21 soft rays. Anal fin with 2 spines and

21–23 soft rays. Pectoral fin rays 18. Lateral line scales about 60-65. No chin barbels. The back and upper flank are bluish or tan, silvery below. Fins are yellowish. Reaches 30 cm.

Biology: Known only from a single specimen caught near the mouth of Burrard Inlet, off Vancouver, in 1981. Habitat in California is inshore shallow areas (1.2–8.2 m) like bays over a sand bottom. Also found down to 55 m. This species lives in schools and moves into deeper water at night. Food is crustaceans and fishes taken at night. Females mature in their first spring or second summer at about 10 cm standard length. Spawning occurs from February to August in late afternoons and early evenings, with peaks during the waxing moon. Spawning occurs once a week in season and large females begin earlier and end later than smaller ones to produce 12–24 batches of eggs. An average female produces 300,000 eggs but a large female can produce nearly 2.3 million in a 6 month period. In California it is commonly caught by anglers from piers and even fished commercially despite the relatively small size.

quillback

Scientific name: *Carpiodes cyprinus*
(Le Sueur, 1817)
Family: **Sucker**
Other common names: carpsucker, lake quillback, eastern quillback, long-finned sucker, broad mullet, white carp, silvery carp, drum, plains carpsucker
French name: couette

Distribution: Found in the St. Lawrence River around Montréal, Ottawa River up to Ottawa, Richelieu River, Lake Champlain, lakes Erie and Huron and Georgian Bay, Lake of the Woods, central and southern Manitoba and Alberta. In the U.S.A. south to Louisiana and west to the Florida Panhandle, west of the Appalachian Mountains and south to Virginia east of these mountains from Pennsylvania.

Characters: The quillback is recognised by the long dorsal fin with 22–32 major rays which has the anterior rays elongated into a high, sickle-shape. The longest dorsal fin ray is 4–6 times the length of the shortest. The small mouth is overhung by the snout. The caudal fin is deeply forked. The lips have transverse plicae and the lower lip halves meet at an acute angle and have no knob at the tip. Pharyngeal teeth are thin, small and comb-like with pointed tips. The gut is elongate with 6–9 loops. Gill rakers 25–29. Major anal fin rays 6–9, pectoral rays 15–16 and pelvic rays 8–10. Lateral line scales 33–42.

quillback

Males have nuptial tubercles on the side of the head below the top of the eye level, on top of the head, on the underside of the head to the anterior branchiostegals and on the first dorsal fin ray, first 11 pectoral rays and 8 pelvic rays. Anal and caudal fins are tuberculate in some males. There are up to 18 tubercles per scale on the 3–4 rows above and below the lateral line. There may even be tubercles on the cornea, completely surrounding the pupil. Females may have fewer tubercles than males. The back and upper flank are olive to dark or light brown or tan, the flanks are silvery often with a golden yellow tinge, and the belly cream to white. Scales have silver, green or blue reflections. The eye is silvery. The upper fins are dusky, lower fins more transparent, sometimes with basal orange or yellow tinges and a white leading edge. The anterior edge and dorsal margin of the dorsal fin are black. The snout tip and lips are often a milky-white. Reaches 66.0 cm and 5.4 kg. The world, all-tackle angling record from Lake Michigan, Indiana weighed 2.94 kg and was caught in 1993.

Biology: This species is found in clear and turbid waters of rivers and lakes preferring warm temperatures as high as 29–31°C. Food is bottom fauna such as aquatic insects, crustaceans and molluscs and any organic matter in bottom sediments. Life span is 12 years. Maturity is attained at 4 years. An upstream spawning migration in the Ochre River, Manitoba takes place once water temperatures reach 5°C but only when discharges are high. Spawning occurs in streams, flooded areas or bays of lakes in April to July, perhaps later to September. Water temperatures are 7–18°C in Manitoba, 19–28°C in other studies. Eggs are broadcast over sand or mud and number up to 360,000 per female. This sucker is of minor commercial importance in the Mississippi River and Lake Michigan, where it is caught with gill nets, and has white, tasty flesh. Anglers catch them in the U.S.A. by using dough balls, bread, worms and grubs as bait or by snagging.

quillback rockfish

Scientific name: *Sebastes maliger*
(Jordan and Gilbert, 1880)
Family: **Scorpionfish**
Other common names: orange-spotted
rockfish, yellow-backed rockfish,
brown rockfish, speckled rockfish,
gopher rock cod
French name: sébaste à dos épineux

Distribution: Found from the Gulf of Alaska south to central California including British Columbia.

Characters: This species is distinguished from its Canadian relatives by the high spines in the dorsal fin and the membranes between these spines being deeply notched. The colour pattern is also unique. Dorsal fin

quillback rockfish

spines 13, soft rays 12–14, usually 13. Anal fin soft rays 6–7, usually 7, second anal spine twice as thick as third and about equal in

length. Pectoral fin rays 16–18, usually 17. Lateral line pores 34–48, scale rows below lateral line 39–45. Gill rakers 29–33. Vertebrae 26. Nuchal, coronal and usually supraocular head spines absent. The overall colour is brown to almost black with yellow, tan or orange mottling in large patches and spots on the anterior flanks, back, rear of the head and spiny dorsal fin. The breast and lower head have orange-brown spots on a pale orange background. Fins are dark brown to blackish. Peritoneum is silvery-white. Reaches 61 cm. The world, all-tackle angling record weighed 2.58 kg and was caught in 1988 at Warmhouse Beach, Washington.

Biology: Found from inshore rocky areas and inlets and down to 275 m. Submersible observations in the Strait of Georgia show this species favours complex rocky habitats shallower than 60 m. In the Saanich Inlet, B.C., this is the dominant rockfish between 21 m and 100 m with a median density of 5.7 fish per 100 sq m. Northern populations are in shallower waters than southern ones and adults are in deeper water than young. Often found as solitary individuals in caverns or large cloud and chimney sponges and where kelp cover is extensive. Food includes various crustaceans, snails and fish. Young are born in January to April in British Columbia, earlier in the southern Strait of Georgia than the north. Life span is up to 40 years. Maturity is attained at 26 cm for female and 27 cm for males when half the population is mature. Sought after as a sport fish by anglers and spear fishermen and appearing in the commercial catch where it is filleted. Inshore vessels catch mostly this species using handlines and fish are sold live to restaurants in Vancouver's Chinatown. It can be a nuisance to salmon anglers.

quillfish

Scientific name: *Ptilichthys goodei*
Bean, 1881
Family: **Quillfish**
Other common names: none
French name: fouette-queue

Distribution: Found from Oregon to northwestern Alaska and the Okhotsk Sea and along the coast of British Columbia to Oregon.

Characters: The body is extremely long and slender. The pelvic and caudal fins are absent and there are no scales and no lateral

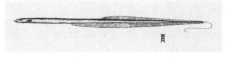

quillfish

line. The dorsal fin has 83–90 separate, hooked, short spines and 137–148 longer soft rays. The anal fin has 180-196 long soft rays. There are 13 pectoral fin rays. The tail tapers to become a filament. The lower jaw projects. Gill membranes are free from the isthmus. Pale greenish, orange or yellow with a dark line along the belly and sometimes 2 maroon stripes on the flank and maroon spots on the back. The throat region is orange. Attains 34 cm.

Biology: The biology of the quillfish is poorly known. They are attracted to lights at night but may normally burrow in mud or sand. Caught at depths up to about 150 m. This species is most often encountered in the stomachs of other fishes, such as **coho salmon.**

Quillfish Family

Scientific name: Ptilichthyidae
French name: fouette-queues

Quillfish are found from Oregon to northwestern Alaska and the Okhotsk Sea. There is only one species in the family and the account under **quillfish** covers biology and characters. It is a member of the **Perch Order.**

See **quillfish**

R

radiated shanny

Scientific name: *Ulvaria subbifurcata*
(Storer, 1839)
Family: **Shanny**
Other common names: none
French name: ulvaire deux-lignes

Distribution: Found from the Strait of Belle Isle south to Massachusetts in the northwest Atlantic Ocean.

Characters: This species has a relatively deep body like its relatives the **fourline snakeblenny** and the **Arctic shanny** but is

radiated shanny

distinguished by having a midflank lateral line from head to tail and a short lateral line above, extending to the tip of the pectoral fin. There are 43–44 dorsal fin spines and 2 spines followed by 30–31 soft rays in the anal fin. The upper corner of the gill cover is elongated as a rearward pointing flap. Overall colour is brownish with a pale brown or yellowish white belly. There is an elongate, oval blotch on the anterior part of the dorsal fin between spines 5–10, followed by 4–5 oblique, dusky bars. A black bar runs obliquely back and down from the eye. The caudal fin is barred with 3–4 rows of dots. Females become a light yellow with brown body marks and a grey-white belly in the week before spawning. During spawning the female becomes white while the male is almost black. After spawning the female is grey but returns to a normal gold colour with brown markings and a pale yellow belly a few days later. Reaches 18 cm.

Biology: This shanny is found on rocky shores among seaweed and down to about 55 m year round. Adults are most active after dark. They have a particular home site to which they can return from at least 270 m

away using sight and smell. Usually they remain in an area less than 3 sq m. Food appears to be a variety of available items from crustaceans, worms, tube-feet of sea urchins and small fishes to **capelin** eggs. Worms are apparently favoured by larger shannies in Newfoundland. Males live about 10 years and females 8 years. It takes 4 years for size to double from 55 to 110 mm total length. Spawning occurs in spring and early summer, May in Newfoundland. First spawning occurs at 3–5 years of age. The male swims under and around the female, nudging her abdomen with his snout so she tilts to one side. Eggs and sperm are released as both fish are tilted to one side. Eggs may be 1.55 mm in diameter when fertilised and are stuck together in a mass. The male guards, nudges and fans the eggs. The mean number of eggs in the ovary was 1512 and in egg masses 2706 in a Newfoundland study. Males may spawn up to 4 times but females only once as these egg figures indicate. Larvae are pelagic. Radiated shannies are eaten by **Atlantic cod** and the **grubby**.

ragfish

Scientific name: *Icosteus aenigmaticus*
Lockington, 1880
Family: **Ragfish**
Other common names: fan-tailed ragfish, spotted ragfish
French name: torchon mou

Distribution: Found from Japan to southern California including British Columbia.

Characters: This species can be recognised by the unusually limp body, like a rag, because the skeleton is mostly cartilage and it is very compressed (*Icosteus* means "yielding bones"). Eyes are small. Adults lack scales and pelvic fins. There are no fin spines. The caudal fin is slightly forked in adults. There is a humped back before the dorsal fin. Teeth are minute. Dorsal fin rays 52–56. Anal fin rays 34–44. Pectoral fin rays 20–21. Young fish in contrast to adults, have a deeper body, a spiny lateral line, abdominal pelvic fins with 5 rays are present although loosely attached, and have a rounded caudal fin. Adults are chocolate brown, young are brown to yellow and are darkly blotched on the head and body with purple. Attains 2.13 m or more.

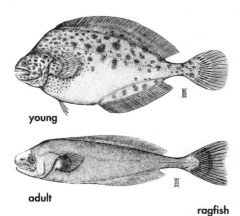

young

adult

ragfish

Biology: Usually found offshore at 18–732 m and captured by trawlers. Food is fish, squid and octopus. Sperm whales are known to eat this species. Spawning may occur in both winter and summer and up to about half a million pelagic eggs are produced. Spawning adults are 7–9 years old.

Ragfish Family

Scientific name: Icosteidae
French name: torchons

The **ragfish** is the only member of this family and is found on the Pacific coast of North America including British Columbia.

The characters and biology of the family are summarised under the species account.

This family is included in the **Perch Order** although some scientists place it in its own order, the Icosteiformes.

The young and adults differ markedly in appearance and were described as separate species.

See **ragfish**

rainbow darter

Scientific name: *Etheostoma caeruleum* Storer, 1845
Family: **Perch**
Other common names: blue darter, banded darter, soldier darter
French name: dard arc-en-ciel

Distribution: From the southern Great Lakes basin from New York to Minnesota, in the Mississippi and Ohio river basins and southward to Mississippi and Alabama. In Canada only in southwestern Ontario in tributaries to lakes Ontario, Erie and southern Huron.

Characters: This species is distinguished from other **darters** in Canada by having the anal fin smaller than the soft dorsal fin, the snout and upper lip joined (i.e. premaxillaries not protractile), belly usually scaled, dorsal fin spines 8–12, usually 10–11, soft rays 10–15, usually 13, lateral scales 36–57 with 12–39 pored. Anal fin with 2 spines and 6–9 soft rays. Pectoral rays 12–14. The opercle is scaled but the cheek and breast are usually naked.

The non-breeding and female colour is a light green with green-brown or black bars and varies with the habitat. The female has a red based and blue-margined spiny dorsal fin. The back has 3–12 saddles and the flank 8–14 bars, the latter most developed on the tail. Three bars radiate from the eye but are diffuse.

Males have brilliant blues and reds on the body, head and fins and orange on the branchiostegal membranes. Some scales have red margins. Bars are a dark blue-green on the flank and the spaces between the bars are red-orange. Tail bars circle the body. The spiny dorsal fin is usually red at the base and blue at the edge margined with greenish-blue. The soft dorsal fin is blue-green at the base and edge with an intervening red-orange bar. The anal fin is blue-green with a central red spot. The pelvic fin is blue-green with anterior ray tips whitish. Tubercles are present on the rear half of the belly and the lower half of the caudal peduncle. Breeding

rainbow darter

males compete successfully with any tropical fish for colour and are perhaps Canada's most colourful fish. Reaches 7.6 cm.

Biology: Rainbow darters are found in clear, sand or gravel bottomed streams, predominately in riffles. Food includes aquatic insects, snails, small crayfish and fish eggs taken particularly from rock surfaces in the morning and evening. Males establish small territories in riffle areas of streams in spring, April to June. They display their bright colours with fins erect and have stylised but non-injurious fights with other adjacent males, sometimes becoming so engrossed in chasing away another male that they lose their mate. Females are courted. When ready to spawn, at peak temperatures of 17–18°C, a female enters the gravel head first, to bury the ventral part of the body, the male lies over her with his tail region bent down to parallel hers, both fish quiver and about 3–7 eggs are extruded and fertilised. The eggs are buried in the gravel and the female continues to spawn in different areas until 800 or more eggs have been laid over a period of several days. Eggs are up to 1.9 mm in diameter. After spawning females remain in quieter pools below the riffles, an area also favoured by young fish. Life span may be up to 4 years but sexual maturity can be attained at 1 year. They can be maintained in well-aerated aquaria and are extremely attractive. Like many darters they are particularly sensitive to pollution and silting of their habitat and therefore make good biological indicators of water quality.

rainbow smelt

Scientific name: *Osmerus mordax*
(Mitchill, 1814)
Family: **Smelt**
Other common names: American smelt,
   Atlantic smelt, Atlantic rainbow smelt,
   Arctic rainbow smelt, freshwater smelt,
   saltwater smelt, frostfish, icefish, leefish,
   lake smelt, spirling, sea smelt, éperlan
   du nord
French name: éperlan arc-en-ciel

Distribution: Found from southern Labrador throughout the Maritimes south to New Jersey in the sea. Also enters rivers and is landlocked in lakes throughout eastern Canada. Introduced and widespread in all the Great Lakes and adjacent inland lakes including Lake Winnipeg (also introduced in the Mississippi River basin). In the Arctic from Cape Bathurst, N.W.T. coastwise around Alaska and south to Vancouver Island but relatively rare in Pacific Canada.

Characters: This species is distinguished by having 8–14 upper arch and 15–24 lower arch gill rakers, medium conical to large canine teeth on the tongue, 4–9 pyloric caeca, and 1–3 large canines on each side of the vomer bone in the roof of the mouth. Dorsal fin rays 8–11, anal rays 11–17 and pectoral rays 9–14. Lateral line scales 56–72 with 13–30 pored. Total gill rakers 26–37. Males have numerous head, body and fin tubercles. The mouth is large and reaches the rear of the eye. Paired and anal fins are larger in males and a lateral ridge may develop.

rainbow smelt

The back is olive-green, steel blue or black and the flank is silvery with purple, blue or pinkish iridescences (hence "rainbow"). Scales on the back are outlined with pigment. There is a silvery stripe along the flank which turns dark in preserved fish. The peritoneum is silvery with dark pigment dots. Landlocked smelt are darker than other populations and may have dusky fins rather than the typical clear fins.

Populations in the Pacific and western Arctic are recognised as *O. m. dentex* Steindachner, 1870 by some authors. Reaches 35.6 cm.

Biology: Rainbow smelt are found schooling in coastal waters entering fresh waters to spawn and having landlocked populations in numerous lakes. Smelt were introduced to Lake Simcoe around 1960. The winter angling harvest rose from 3 fish in 1962 to 234,865 fish in 1973. They are pelagic with a maximum recorded depth of at least 150 m, possibly 425 m in the sea. In the Great Lakes they are commonest at 18–60 m and rarely descend below 75 m. Bay of Fundy fish move offshore in summer to deeper and cooler water. They enter estuarine areas in the early winter to avoid cold waters. In lakes cooler water is preferred, about 7°C. In the St. Lawrence estuary smelt have seasonal, open-water migrations of about 80–160 km.

Food is a wide variety of crustaceans, worms, squid, and small fishes in the sea and opossum shrimps and other invertebrates in fresh waters. Many fishes both in the sea and in lakes depend on smelt as a food source including such economically important species as **Atlantic salmon, Atlantic cod, brook trout, lake trout, yellow walleye** and **yellow perch**, as well as seals.

Females live longer, grow faster and are larger than males. Life span is 5–9 years in most populations but up to 17 years on the Beaufort Sea coast of the Yukon. Beaufort Sea fish live longer and reach larger sizes than Atlantic coastal fish. Maturity is attained at age 3 in Atlantic populations although some fish mature a year earlier. Alaskan and northern Canadian populations mostly mature at ages 4–7, often at 6–7 years and 20–22 cm.

Spawning migrations take place February to June, being later in northern seas and lakes. The run usually starts when water temperatures reach 4°C or higher, just after the ice breaks up and moves out. Spawning itself takes place at 9°C in Lake Erie, at 7–11°C in Lake Simcoe streams but 5–7°C along Lake Simcoe shores when entering rivers for example. Lake populations enter rivers even under ice. The Mackenzie River spawning also takes place under ice. Deepwater spawning takes place in Lake Heney, Québec but fish may spawn offshore on gravel shoals or on shores. Males are first on the spawning grounds in freshwater areas of rivers. Spawning occurs at night.

Eggs are adhesive, 1.0 mm in diameter, and number up to 93,000 per female. The outer membrane of the egg ruptures but remains attached to the egg by a stalk. This outer membrane is the adhesive part and the egg sways in the water at the end of the stalk. They become attached to vegetation or rocks and may be so numerous that some are smothered. As many as 190 eggs/sq cm have been counted. The fry are carried downstream to brackish water or the lake after hatching.

Mass mortalities of adults have been reported in the Great Lakes after spawning, 200 m long, 4.6 m wide and 0.3 m deep. This creates a health hazard, renders beaches unusable and is costly to clean up.

Smelt are important in both sport and commercial fisheries. They can be legally seined or dip-netted at night on the spawning run, caught on hook and line from docks, or through the ice in winter. Commercial catches are taken in the Great Lakes using otter trawls and in the Miramichi River estuary by box nets through the ice. Bag nets, fyke nets, gill nets and seines are also used. In 1979, 2542 tonnes worth $1,065,767 were caught in Atlantic coastal areas of Canada and 10,979 tonnes in the Great Lakes worth $2,035,000. Ontario had a catch of 7289 tonnes in 1966 and smelt occupied first place by weight among all Great Lakes fishes in that year. The total Canadian catch in 1988 was 11,000 tonnes worth about $4.2 million. Smelt are sold fresh, frozen or pre-cooked, are delicious fried and are in high demand by consumers in Japan and the U.S.A. Their cucumber-like odour when fresh is distinctive and probably accounts for the name "smelt."

Fishermen have claimed that smelt are important predators on commercially important species. Although fish are a relatively small part of the smelt diet (as little as 4.3% for males in Lake Simcoe), the numbers of smelt alone lend some weight to this accusation. Whether the numbers of young commercial fishes eaten by smelt are offset by the numbers of smelt eaten by survivors remains to be determined. Rainbow smelt have been widely distributed in southern Ontario as bait fish introductions.

rainbow trout

Scientific name: *Oncorhynchus mykiss*
  (Walbaum, 1792)
Family: **Salmon**
Other common names: steelhead trout,
  Kamloops trout, coast rainbow trout,
  silver trout, half-pounder, redsides,
  Pacific trout
French name: truite arc-en-ciel

Distribution: Found in coastal waters and basins draining to the ocean in British Columbia and extreme southwest Yukon and in the upper Peace and Athabasca river basins. Also from Japan and Alaska to Mexico. Widely introduced outside this natural range in all provinces of Canada and world-wide in suitable waters. Broad areas of introduction are southwestern Québec, southern Ontario, all the Great Lakes and across the southern Prairie provinces but also at various places in the Yukon, N.W.T., the Maritimes and in Newfoundland since 1887.

Characters: This species is distinguished by having 100–161 lateral line scales, 8–12 principal anal fin rays, the vomer bone in the

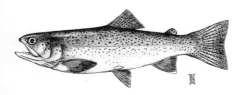

rainbow trout

roof of the mouth has teeth on its head and shaft, no red spots on the body but only small dark ones and radiating rows of black spots on the dorsal and caudal fins, no reddish "cutthroat" marks and no teeth at the tongue base. Dorsal fin principal rays 10–12, pectoral rays 11–17 and pelvic rays 9–10. Pyloric caeca 27–80. Breeding males have an elongated snout, the lower jaw is hooked and the roof of the mouth is white.

Overall colour is very variable and this is reflected in the common names. Stream fish are darker and more colourful (rainbows) than lighter, silvery lake or sea fish (Kamloops or steelhead). Some sea run and lake fish have small orange to red marks below the lower jaw similar to those in **coastal cutthroat trout**. The back and upper flank are steelblue, greenish, silvery-olive or even brown, flanks and belly are silvery, grey, white or yellow-green. The side of the head and the flank are characteristically pink. The flank has a broad pink to red or lilac stripe with small black spots. The adipose fin has a black margin and a few spots. Pectoral, pelvic and anal fins may have a few spots and are dusky without any strong markings. Pectoral and pelvic fins are often orange-red. Spawning fish are very dark and the flank stripe is dark red or

purple. The young have 5–13 dark, oval parr marks centred on the lateral line with the spaces between the marks wider than the marks. There are 5–10 parr marks on the back in front of the dorsal fin. The upper flank has some dark spots. The dorsal fin is tipped white or orange and has a dark leading edge, sometimes broken up into spots. The anal fin has a white or orange tip. Black spots are few to absent on the tail. Some adults in streams do not lose their parr marks.

Golden and palomino trout are genetic variants of rainbow trout reared in hatcheries and released into the Great Lakes. Golden trout (not true **golden trout**) are golden-orange without black spots and palomino trout are golden with a few black spots but much less than normal rainbows.

Fish in the upper Columbia, Fraser, Athabasca and Peace River basins are placed in the redband trout subspecies *O. mykiss gairdneri* (Richardson, 1836) and those from the coast of British Columbia and the lower Fraser River in the coastal trout subspecies *O. mykiss irideus* (Gibbons, 1855). The former subspecies has larger spots, more elliptical parr marks (more rounded in the coastal subspecies), often with additional rows above and below the main parr marks (usually reduced or absent in the coastal subspecies), more yellow and orange tints on the body, a trace of a cut throat mark, and light coloured tips to the dorsal, anal and pelvic fins. The scientific name of the species was formerly *Salmo gairdneri*.

Reaches 122.0 cm and 19.1 kg as sea run or lake fish but smaller in streams. Fish less than 10 kg are trophy-size in most of Canada. A 14.98 kg fish was a Canadian record from Kispiox River, British Columbia. The world, all-tackle angling record from Bell Island, Alaska caught in 1970 weighed 19.1 kg. The Canadian angling inland record from Kootenay Lake, B.C. was caught by George Hill in 1976 weighing 15.94 kg.

Biology: Rainbows are found in rivers or streams where there are pools and riffles. Some live in lakes and are called Kamloops trout while others run to sea and are called steelheads. They can tolerate temperatures up to 24°C, warm for a **trout**, but prefer temperatures below 20°C. Sea run fish spend about 1–4 years usually in inshore waters at middle to surface depths after 1–4 years in fresh water. However one steelhead moved 3840 km from the Aleutian Islands to a Washington river. Some fish (half-pounders) return to streams after a few months at sea. Summer steelhead have spent one winter at sea and return in summer (April-October) to spawn next spring while winter steelhead are larger and return from December to April peaking in January to spawn in March and April. Peaks vary with runoff and weather conditions. Summer and winter steelheads are genetically different stocks. The Great Lakes have introduced steelhead stocks. Lake populations run up streams to spawn while river fish enter headwater streams.

Food includes plankton, crustaceans, aquatic and terrestrial insects, snails, leeches, **salmon** eggs, and fishes (such as **kokanee**, among many others). The fish eaten enhance growth and the species taken depends on what is available. Fish and squid are taken at sea along with some crustaceans. Rainbows are food for various other **Salmon Family** members found in the same habitat as well as various birds and some mammals. **Lampreys** attack this trout, particularly the **sea lamprey** in the Great Lakes, where up to 8.6% of fish bear scars.

Life span varies with habitat, up to 11 years in some lake fish, 8 years in the Great Lakes but only 3–4 years in many streams and small lakes. Growth varies with habitat including such factors as length of sea, stream or lake life, years before spawning, available food supplies, latitude, altitude, temperature regime, competition with other salmonids, and so on. Ageing these fish may be difficult because of the complicated life history pattern of stream and lake residency.

Maturity is also variable with habitat. Some males mature at 9 months in fish introduced to warm southern waters and some females only at 8 years, but generally maturity is reached at 3–5 years in Canada with males maturing a year earlier than females. Repeat spawning can occur for up to 5 years. Spawning takes place from March to August but is usually in spring. Great Lakes fish may spawn from late December to late April.

Water temperature for spawning usually exceeds 10°C but may be 5–13°C. A female excavates a redd by lying on her side and thrashing her tail. Redd excavation occurs during the day and night and dimensions are usually longer and deeper than the female's body. A male courts a female by rubbing his snout and body against her, by vibrating, by swimming over her in the redd and by pressing against her. Several males are found around each female but one male is dominant. The spawning act lasts 5–8 seconds with the pair parallel in the redd pressed together, both fish gape, arch and vibrate. Other males may shed sperm. The female covers the eggs with gravel by dislodging it from the upstream end of the redd. Most spawning takes place in the morning and evening and nests may be abandoned during the day. Females construct several redds and may spawn with several males. Eggs are orange or pink, 5.0 mm in diameter and up to 12,749 in number. Egg numbers are usually a few hundreds to thousands. The eggs hatch in about 8 weeks and fry generally emerge in June to August from spring spawnings. Most migration of steelheads at 1–4 years is in spring and at night.

Rainbow trout are one of the top few sport fishes in North America and of great commercial importance because of the money spent on gear, accommodation, transport, etc. by anglers in pursuit of this fish. Many books and articles have been written on the methods and joy of catching this trout. It may be caught on flies, with lures or with various still-fished or moving baits. It is a strong fighter which bites easily and leaps often, and may "cartwheel" and "tail-walk." Dawn and dusk are the best times to catch rainbows in streams. Trolling a flutter spoon is mainly used on large lakes. Baits and small jigs are used in ice fishing. Steelhead has been called the most prestigious fish of the Pacific rivers, being much larger than stream rainbows. They are caught in winter and early spring as they run up rivers to reach their spawning grounds. Steelhead or **salmon** roe is a popular bait. Various artificial lures are used, often red or orange in imitation of **salmon** eggs. Plastic worms are also used as are various natural baits. Summer steelhead are usually caught on wet flies. Most sea run fish are caught on the spawning migration.

The flesh is excellent eating fresh or smoked and may be red if food is mostly invertebrates or white if food is fishes. The total Canadian catch in 1988 was 3658 tonnes. Farmed fish are sold frozen world-wide, the most important **trout** in this regard, and ironically some of that found in Canada comes from Japan or Europe. Small put-and-take fisheries are common wherever this species is found or has been introduced. Gill net fisheries for steelhead are found in marine U.S. waters on the Pacific coast but generally the wild stocks are not used as a commercial species.

Rainbows have been used extensively as research animals as their requirements are well known and they are readily available from hatcheries. Hatchery fish often have reduced or absent fins and deformed mouths. Cage culture of rainbows is being carried out in Atlantic Canada and the economics of pothole prairie lake aquaculture has been examined. The latter does not appear to be commercially viable.

Introductions of this fish to various waters throughout Canada may have serious consequences for other species. For example, in the Atlantic region steelhead may compete with **Atlantic salmon** since they use similar habitats and foods.

- For inland rainbow trout, May and September; for coastal and Great Lakes rainbow, April to June and October to December.
- For inland rainbows, mid-central to northern British Columbia, for coastal steelhead in rivers, mid-central British Columbia to northern British Columbia including some of the rivers on Vancouver Island, for migratory rainbows in Ontario, the Great Lakes tributary rivers and streams.
- For coastal and British Columbia rainbows is light action to medium action spinning and baitcasting outfits used with six- to 20–pound test lines. Specialized Great Lakes outfits include steelhead noodle rods and float rods and reels used with four- to eight-pound test line.

- For inland rainbows include a variety of 1/8– to 3/8–ounce flashy spoons, spinners and jigs, for coastal steelhead and Great Lakes migratory rainbows include 1/4– to 3/4–ounce flashy spoons, spinners, jigs and a wide assortment of wobbling plugs. Imitation salmon eggs and egg clusters are also popular drifted in fast water. The best bait, treated skeined salmon eggs and spawn sacks.

rakery lanternfish

Scientific name: *Lampanyctus macdonaldi* (Goode and Bean, 1896)
Family: **Lanternfish**
Other common names: none
French name: lanterne-bouée râtelière

Distribution: Found in the Atlantic and Southern oceans and on the Flemish Cap in Atlantic Canada.

Characters: This species and 7 relatives in the genus *Lampanyctus* are separated from other Atlantic species by lacking photo-

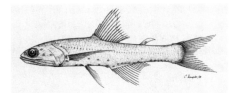

rakery lanternfish

phores close to the dorsal body edge, the PLO photophore is well above the pectoral fin base level while the second PVO photophore is at or below the upper pectoral base level, there are 4 Prc, the first PO and two PVO photophores are not on a straight line, both males and females have caudal luminous glands composed of overlapping, scale-like structures without a black pigment border, the fourth PO photophore is highly elevated, there are no luminous, scale-like structures on the belly between the pelvic fin bases or these bases and the anus, there are 4 VO photophores and the SAO series is strongly angled. This species is distinguished from its relatives by having 21–27 gill rakers. Dorsal fin rays 13–16, anal rays 15–19 and pectoral rays 12–14. AO photophores

13–15 and lateral line organs 36–37. Supra-caudal luminous gland with 3–4, poorly-defined, scale-like structures and infracaudal gland with 7–8 poorly-defined, scale-like structures. Reaches 16.3 cm.

Biology: This species is subpolar-temperate in both hemispheres. Depth distribution is 550 to 1000 m or more by day. At night young are at 60–175 m and adults deeper than 850 m. Food is probably crustaceans.

ratfishes

Ratfishes are members of the **Chimaera Family** with 1 species on the Pacific coast of Canada, the **spotted ratfish**. Ratfishes is an alternative name for this family and has been applied generally to several chimaera species. They are called ratfishes because of the elongate tail.

rattails

Rattails are members of the **Grenadier Family**. There are 3 species in Canada with this name; the **pectoral rattail**, **filamented rattail** and the **bearded rattail**, all on the Pacific coast. They have long, thin, tapering, supposedly rat-like tails. Rattail is also applied to other species in the family as a general name and as another name for the family itself.

Ray Order

Rays, **skates**, thornbacks, **electric rays**, sawfishes, guitarfishes, **stingrays**, freshwater or river stingrays, **eagle rays**, and **manta** or devil rays comprise the Order Rajiformes. These **cartilaginous fishes** are found world-wide primarily in marine waters of the Atlantic, Indian and Pacific oceans but also in polar regions and fresh waters. These are bottom-dwelling fishes found from the shallows to the deep sea. There are 12 families with about 456 species world-wide, with 4 families and 29 species on all 3 coasts of Canada.

Rays are characterised by a flattened body (or disc) with enlarged pectoral fins attached to the side of the head, gill openings are ventral, no anal fin, eyes and spiracles on the upper surface, anterior vertebrae are fused, no nictitating membrane but the cornea of the eye is continuous with the skin of the head,

jaws are protrusible and teeth are pavement-like. Spines on the head, body and tail are important in identifying some species and are described under **Skate Family**.

Rays are sometimes divided into 4 or 5 orders. Along with **sharks** they form one of two subclasses of **cartilaginous fishes** with **chimaeras** forming the other subclass.

Rays are mostly bottom-dwellers generally feeding on molluscs and crustaceans which are crushed by the heavy teeth. They may partially bury themselves in mud or sand. Dorsal spiracles allow water to be taken in for respiration and expelled through the ventral gill slits without the gills becoming clogged by bottom sediment. The wing-like pectoral fins are used in swimming, beating up and down. Most species give birth to live young although **skates** lay eggs covered by a horny capsule. Stingrays carry dangerous venomous spines on their tails and electric rays can shock. The snout may be sensitive to electromagnetic stimuli. Fossils extend back to the Late Jurassic. They are generally of little commercial importance.

See **Eagle Ray Family**
Electric Ray Family
Skate Family
Stingray Family

ray-finned fishes

The ray-finned fishes or Actinopterygii is 1 of 4 classes of **fishes** found in Canada. There are 2 subclasses within the ray-finned fishes, the **sturgeons** with the **paddlefishes** (= Chondrostei) and the **gars** with the **bowfins** and true bony fishes (= Neopterygii). The true **bony fishes** are also known as **teleosts**. Ray-finned fishes share a common ancestor with the coelacanths, lungfishes and tetrapods. Ray-finned fishes are the largest and most diverse group of **vertebrates**, making up more than half the total number of living species and about 97% of the modern fishes. There are 36 orders, 179 families and 1065 species of ray-finned fishes in Canada.

Ray-finned fishes are characterised by dermal, paired, segmented ray-like supports within the fins (lepidotrichia), by these rays being attached to an internal skeleton without that skeleton extending into the fin base, scales are ganoid, cycloid or ctenoid and may be absent, a single dorsal fin (although it may become subdivided), a pectoral propterygium, an anterodorsal peg-like process on the scales, jugal pitlines, mandibular sensory canal enclosed in the dentary bone, usually no spiracle, teeth have acrodin (a tissue forming a cap), interopercle present, branchiostegal rays present, radials (or actinost bones) are attached to the scapulo-coracoid bone region of the pectoral girdle, fusion of internal pelvic cartilages during development, an expanded metapterygium supporting the radials in the pelvic girdle, the gular plate of the throat region is absent, no internal nostrils and nostrils are high up on the head.

rays

Rays are usually listed as members of the **Skate Family**. In Canada there is only 1 species, **Markle's ray**, with this name. In addition the **Electric Ray Family** contains the **Pacific electric ray**, the **Stingray Family** contains the **pelagic** and **roughtail stingrays** and the **Eagle Ray Family** contains the manta. See the account under **Ray Order**.

Ray is from the Latin word "raia" for this kind of fish.

rearfin expatriate

Scientific name: *Scopeloberyx opisthopterus*
(Parr, 1933)
Family: **Ridgehead**
Other common names: none
French name: expatrié rétropinne

Distribution: Found in the western North Atlantic Ocean north to the northwest Flemish Cap off Atlantic Canada. Also known from the tropical Indian Ocean and eastern equatorial Pacific Ocean.

Characters: This species is distinguished from other ridgeheads by having more than

20 scale rows, more than 2 cheek scales and less than 16 spines and rays combined in the dorsal fin. Dorsal fin with 2–3 spines and 11–12 soft rays. Anal fin with 1 spine and 7–8 soft rays. Pectoral fin rays 12–15 and pelvic fin with 1 spine and 7–8 rays. Scale rows 23–25. Overall colour is probably dark. Attains 3.9 cm standard length.

Biology: Rare in Canadian waters with only 7 recorded specimens taken in 1968. Adults are usually found between 850 m and 1050 m off Bermuda where spawning occurs from spring to summer. This species has a 2–year life cycle and dies after spawning.

recto

Scientific name: *Howella brodiei*
Ogilby, 1899
Family: **Temperate Ocean Bass**
Other common names: pelagic basslet
French name: recto

Distribution: Found in the North and South Atlantic Ocean from Iceland and the Flemish Cap and Grand Bank southward. Also in the eastern Atlantic and western Pacific oceans.

Characters: This species is distinguished from its Atlantic coast relatives by having widely separated dorsal fins, pelvic fin

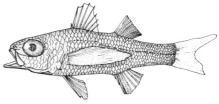

recto

inserted in front of the pectoral fins, and by scale and fin rays counts. First dorsal fin spines 7–8, second dorsal fin with 1 spine and 9–10 soft rays. Anal fin with 3 spines and 7–8 soft rays. Pectoral fin elongated. Lateral line interrupted behind the dorsal origin and below the space between the dorsal fins. Scales in lateral line about 35–39. Overall colour dark brown to black with some silver tints. Reaches 9.0 cm standard length.

Biology: Adults and young are known from 26–1829 m. Young are pelagic and

rearfin expatriate

adults bathypelagic to benthic. Biology in detail is unknown.

red barbier

Scientific name: *Hemanthias vivanus*
(Jordan and Swain, 1884)
Family: **Sea Bass**
Other common names: none
French name: barbier rouge

Distribution: Found from Brazil to North Carolina and off Georges Bank in Atlantic Canada.

Characters: This species is one of the streamer basses, so-called because the dorsal and caudal fins often have 1 or more filamen-

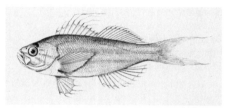

red barbier

tous rays. Colour, scale count and caudal filaments separate this species from the other streamer bass species (**yellowfin bass**). The red barbier has the caudal fin corners extended as long filaments, the longest pelvic fin ray is a filament and there are 1–9 elongate spines in the dorsal fin. Lateral line scales number 45–50. Larvae of this species have deep bodies, large heads, large, ornate spines on the head, serrations on several dorsal and anal fin spines and a serrate crest on top of the head. Adults have a deep red body and head, spotted with yellow and with violet tinges. The dorsal and caudal fins are red and the anal and pelvic fins orange to gold. There are 2 golden stripes on the side of the head, the upper one running from the eye onto the base of the pectoral fin. The anal fin in mature females is mottled blue and olive and in males is bright yellow, and the pelvic fins are pink in females and blood red in males. Reaches 25.0 cm.

Biology: Known only as larval strays in Canadian waters where they are at the northern limit of their range. They were first collected here in 1978. They are the most abundant larvae among the anthiine basses of the

east coast U.S.A. Adults are found at 45–610 m. This species is a protogynous hermaphrodite, changing from female to male during its life cycle, probably at the end of the spawning season.

red brotula

Scientific name: *Brosmophycis marginata*
(Ayres, 1854)
Family: **Livebearing Brotula**
Other common names: red brotulid
French name: donzelle rouge

Distribution: From Baja California to southeastern Alaska including the coast of British Columbia.

Characters: The long dorsal and anal fins are separate from the small caudal fin. Dorsal fin rays 92–110, anal fin rays 70–81. There are about 20 pectoral fin rays. The pelvic fins have only 2 rays, which are slender filaments with the outer ray twice as long as the inner ray. The lateral line is in 2 parts, an anterior arched part over the pectoral fin and ending at midflank above the level of the anus, and a straight posterior part beginning under the end of the arched part and running to the caudal fin. Teeth are moderate in size, conical and in bands on the jaws and roof of the mouth. The gill membranes are joined but are not attached to the isthmus. Overall colour is a warm red, brownish-red or brown, paler below. The pectoral and caudal fins are bright red and the pelvic tips are whitish. The thick mucus secreted by the body is also reddish. Attains 46 cm.

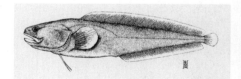

red brotula

Biology: Found in inshore waters at moderate depths, down to 256 m. Not commonly encountered as it is a secretive species, hiding in caves and crevices. This species gives birth to live young, rather than shedding eggs, in spring. Reported to be good eating with sweet flesh.

red dory

Scientific name: *Cyttopsis roseus*
(Lowe, 1843)
Family: **Dory**
Other common names: none
French name: zée rouge

Distribution: Found in the Atlantic, Indian and Pacific oceans including the Atlantic coast of Canada.

Characters: This species is distinguished from the related **buckler dory** by having scales and 9–10 soft rays and no spine in the pelvic fin and 27–30 anal fin soft rays. The anal fin has 1–2 spines, the first short, broad and erect, the second very small. The dorsal fin has 4–8 spines and 26–30 soft rays and the pectoral fin has 13–14 rays. Scales are small and cycloid, 73–84 in the lateral line. The body is deep and compressed. There are two, keeled scutes between the pelvic fin and

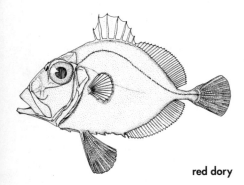

red dory

anus and the bases of the dorsal and anal fins have a row of bony ridges. Deep red to rosy pink to silver with the pelvic rays red or black. Pelvic fin membranes are black distally. Attains 30 cm standard length.

Biology: Only known in Canada from 3 specimens taken in 1974 and 1984 off Nova Scotia. Found in midwater or near the bottom at about 200–690 m. Food is fishes and crustaceans.

red eyefish

Scientific name: *Zenion hololepis*
(Goode and Bean, 1896)
Family: **Eyefish**
Other common names: none

French name: mégalope rouge

Distribution: Known from off the Yucatan Peninsula north to the Scotian Shelf in Atlantic Canada.

Characters: The large eye in a large head and the body colour are characteristic. The dorsal fin has 6–7 spines, the anterior edge of

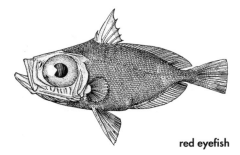

red eyefish

the largest spine having 2 rows of spinules, and 25–28 soft rays. The anal fin has 1 spine and 23–28 soft rays. The pectoral fin has 16 rays. The soft dorsal and anal fins have a row of small scutes along the base forming a groove in which the fins lie. Overall colour is reddish-orange. Attains 10 cm.

Biology: Known only from a single specimen in Canada caught in 1984 at about 485 m. Biology is unknown.

red goatfish

Scientific name: *Mullus auratus*
Jordan and Gilbert, 1882
Family: **Goatfish**
Other common names: surmullet
French name: rouget doré

Distribution: Found from Nova Scotia to Guyana.

Characters: Recognised by the unique pair of barbels under the chin and by colour. First dorsal fin with 7–8 spines, second dorsal fin with 1 spine and 8 soft rays. Lateral line scales 29–37. No spine on the operculum. The body is a bright scarlet or crimson with some blotches. There are 2 yellow to red stripes along the flank. The first dorsal fin has an orange stripe at its base and a red to brownish stripe at its margin. The second dorsal fin is spotted red or yellow and the spots are aligned in stripes. There are 7–8 faint bars on the dark red caudal fin. The pectoral fins are reddish. Reaches 25 cm.

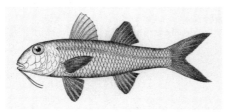

red goatfish

Biology: Known from only a single stray specimen caught in a seine at Eastern Passage, Nova Scotia in 1928. Apparently 1928 was an exceptional, warm-water year and southern species came north to the shores of Nova Scotia. Adults are usually found at 9–91 m over mud. Red goatfish are considered a delicacy in the southern part of their range.

red gunnel

Scientific name: *Pholis schultzi*
Schultz, 1931
Family: **Gunnel**
Other common names: none
French name: sigouine rouge

Distribution: From northern California to southern British Columbia and the Queen Charlotte Islands.

Characters: Distinguished from other Pacific coast gunnels with pelvic fins by having 80–89 dorsal fin spines and 40–44 anal fin rays preceded by 2 spines. The pectoral fins have 10–13 rays. Body usually bright to

red gunnel

dark red, or a light brown to greenish-brown. Flanks plain to spotted, streaked, mottled and blotched. The dorsal and anal fins have light and dark bars. Two dark bars run obliquely downward and back from the eye separated by and preceded by pale areas. Attains 13 cm.

Biology: Found in the intertidal to subtidal zones down to 18 m with various algae, in tidal surge channels, and on the open coast.

red hake

Scientific name: *Urophycis chuss*
(Walbaum, 1792)
Family: **Cod**
Other common names: squirrel hake, ling, merluche écureuil
French name: merluche rouge

Distribution: Found from southern Newfoundland and the Scotian Shelf, but not the Gulf of St. Lawrence, south to North Carolina.

Characters: This species and its relatives, the **longfin, spotted** and **white hakes**, are separated from other Canadian Arctic-Atlantic cods by having 2 dorsal fins, 1 anal fin, no snout barbels, pelvic fins with only 2 long, filamentous rays, and no canine teeth on the lower jaw and vomer bone in the roof of the mouth. The red hake is distinguished from its relatives by the pelvic fin filaments not reaching the

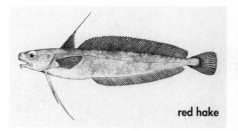

red hake

end of the anal fin, the third ray in the first dorsal fin is an elongate filament, 3 gill rakers on the upper arm of the gill arch and 95–117 lateral line scales (7–10 scales between the first dorsal fin and lateral line). First dorsal fin rays 9–11, second dorsal fin with 53–64 rays. Anal fin rays 45–57 and pectoral rays 14–17. The chin barbel is very small.

Overall colour is reddish-brown to olive-brown or even black fading to yellowish below and white on the belly. The body is often mottled. The lateral line is pale. Dorsal and anal fins not dark-edged. Pelvic fins white, pale pink or yellow. A dusky blotch may be present on the opercle.

Attains 130 cm and 3.2 kg although these figures may be confusion with **white hake** specimens. The world, all-tackle angling record from Brielle, New Jersey in 1993 weighed 3.06 kg.

Biology: This hake is found on sand, mud and silt bottoms at 37–915 m at a temperature range of 3–12°C. Different studies report differing depth preferences probably in response to temperature. There is an inshore migration in spring and an offshore migration in fall in some areas such as Passamaquoddy Bay, but not on the Scotian Shelf where temperatures of 7–10°C are found in the Scotian Gulf where hake aggregate.

Young red hake are pelagic but in the size range 2.3–14.0 cm they live in or under the shell of a dead or living scallop. Hake living in the mantle cavity of live scallops, without harming them, is a phenomenon known as inquilinism, but this only occurs in 3–17% of hake. The hake dart inside the mantle cavity of the scallop through the excurrent siphon. The hake inhabit increasingly larger shells as they grow. The young hake only emerge at night and are protected against predators by the scallop shell.

Their growth strategy is "get mature quick" in contrast with **white hake**. Growth is rapid and life span is short. Red hake mature at about 30 cm and 2 years of age and live about 5 years. Their maximum size may be only about 50 cm.

Young fish forage at night using touch and taste sensitive chin barbel, pelvic fins and dorsal fin filament. Crustaceans are the major food but some fish are eaten.

Spawning occurs from July to September at 10–12°C. Eggs are 1.0 mm in diameter.

There is a commercial fishery for "hake" but species are not distinguished and the term includes **longfin, red, silver** and **white hake**. Foreign trawlers have fished specifically for red hake prior to 1980. The estimated yield for the northwest Atlantic Ocean in 32,000 tonnes. Red hake flesh is white and tasty and is sold as fresh fillets, salted or canned. The liver is processed for oil.

red Irish lord

Scientific name: *Hemilepidotus hemilepidotus*
    (Tilesius, 1811)
Family: **Sculpin**
Other common names: spotted Irish lord,
    red sculpin
French name: chabot trilobé rouge

Distribution: Found from the Bering Sea to California including British Columbia.

Characters: This species and its relative, the **brown Irish lord**, are distinguished from other Pacific coast sculpins by having 4 pelvic fin soft rays and scales in 2 bands, one below the dorsal fin and one around the lateral line. It is separated from its relative by having 4–5 dorsal scale rows and the branchiostegal membranes are united to each other with a fold over the isthmus. The nasal spine is strong and sharp but is covered with skin. There are 4 preopercular spines, the upper 2 being long, sharp and pointing backward and the lower 2 being smaller, blunter and directed down and back. There is a cleithral spine above the pectoral fin base. First dorsal fin spines 10–13, second dorsal soft rays 17–20. The spiny dorsal fin has a notch between spines 3 and 4 and is joined to the second dorsal fin. Anal rays 13–16 with free tips, pectoral rays 15–17 with lower about 9 rays finger-like at their tips. The upper scale band surrounds but does not contact the dorsal fins. The lower band has 1 row above the lateral line and up to 9 rows below it. Lateral line pores 59–71. Pyloric caeca 6–7. The nasal spine has a cirrus with up to 12 branches. There is a large cirrus over the rear eye margin with up to 18 branches, another branched cirrus on the occiput and one on the upper operculum. There are also groups of cirri on the lachrymal bone (4), along the anterior lateral line, on the lower jaw, on the lower edge of the preoperculum, and a broad cirrus at the rear end of the upper jaw.

red Irish lord

Overall colour is red with brown, purple, white and black mottles and spots. The back has 4 dark saddles. The chin is freckled brown. The caudal fin is thinly barred with light colour. In large males the pelvic fins and the pectoral base are darkly spotted and the pectoral axil has contrasting light bars and spots. Females have white pelvic fins.

Reaches 51 cm. The world, all-tackle angling record weighed 1.11 kg and was caught at Depoe Bay, Oregon in 1992.

Biology: Common from tide pools to 275 m. In Barkley Sound kelp beds there are 0.38 red Irish lords per sq m. Their range of movement is small and they may well have a base of activity to which they always return. They are very well camouflaged among algae. Food is crabs, barnacles, gammarids, caprellids, mussels and fishes. Life span is at least 6 years. Spawning takes place in March in southern British Columbia but in Puget Sound, Washington occurs from October to January depending on area and year. Up to 126,000 eggs may be produced by a female, about 30% of their body weight. Pink, yellow, purple or blue egg masses are laid in shallow water on invertebrate growths such as barnacles and mussels. They are very conspicuous but are guarded by the male and female. Should the parents be killed, another red Irish lord may guard the eggs, merely by using the site. Egg masses are 10–20 cm in diameter and 2–4 cm thick. Each egg is up to 1.7 mm in diameter. This sculpin can be caught easily on a baited hook and is reputed to be good eating.

red lizardfish

Scientific name: *Synodus synodus*
    (Linnaeus, 1758)
Family: **Lizardfish**
Other common names: rockspear
French name: poisson-lézard rouge

Distribution: Found on both sides of the Atlantic Ocean but most common on the western shore.

Characters: Distinguished by four dark-red bars on the back and upper sides. Both dorsal and tail fins have red bands and there

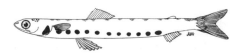

red lizardfish

is a dark spot near the tip of the snout. It has only 8–10 anal fin rays (its relative, the **snakefish**, has 14–16 and a different colour pattern). Dorsal fin rays 12–14, pectoral rays 11–13 and pelvic rays 8. Lateral line scales 54–59. Reaches 33 cm.

Biology: First caught in Canada in 1977 off Nova Scotia as a post-larva. The post-larvae reach Canada in the warm waters of the Gulf Stream. Found as adults in rocky and reef shelf waters down to 90 m, usually on sand. Red lizardfish are said to be good to eat. They feed on fish and crustaceans. Their eggs are unusual in having hexagonal facets on the surface.

redbanded rockfish

Scientific name: *Sebastes babcocki*
    (Thompson, 1915)
Family: **Scorpionfish**
Other common names: bandit, barber pole
French name: sébaste à bandes rouges

Distribution: From the Aleutian Islands to California including British Columbia.

Characters: This species is most easily distinguished by the bars on the body. Dorsal

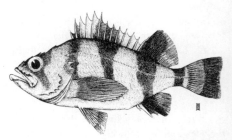

redbanded rockfish

fin spines 13, soft rays 13–15, usually 14. Anal fin soft rays 6–8, usually 7, the second anal spine twice as thick as the third and longer. Pectoral fin rays 17–20, usually 19. Gill rakers 29–33. Vertebrae 26. Lateral line pores 41–51. There are scales on the branchiostegal rays. The supraocular, coronal, and occasionally nuchal head spines are absent. Pink to white background with 4 broad, dark red bars on the flank. The first bar begins at the front of the spiny dorsal fin and slopes down and back to the pectoral fin base crossing the rear of the operculum, while the second bar is vertical. The second 2 bars extend onto the adjacent parts of the spiny and soft dorsal fins. The third bar extends onto the anal fin. The last bar is on the caudal peduncle. The caudal fin is broadly edged in black. A dark band radiates down and back from the eye. The peritoneum is silvery-white to black, or blotched. Reaches 64 cm.

Biology: Found on soft bottoms from 91 to 549 m. Also reported from Hodgkins guyot off the coast of British Columbia. Young are born in April in British Columbia. Half the males in a population are mature at 38 cm while females reach this level at 42 cm. This species is usually caught on hook and line.

redbreast sunfish

Scientific name: *Lepomis auritus*
 (Linnaeus, 1758)
Family: **Sunfish**
Other common names: yellowbelly sunfish, red perch, longear bream, tobacco box, red brim, sunperch, red-bellied bream, red-headed bream, robin, leather ear, blackeared pondfish
French name: crapet rouge

Distribution: Found in New Brunswick and south to Florida and Alabama. Introduced elsewhere in the U.S.A., and overseas, for example to Italy.

Characters: This species is identified by having 3 anal fin spines, 9–11 dorsal fin

redbreast sunfish

spines, 39–54 lateral line scales, no tongue teeth, the ear flap or opercular flap is all black or blue-black, longer than deep and

has a crenate *bony* edge (well forward of the fleshy end to the flap), the preopercle bone is not serrate on its lower edge, and there is no black spot at the rear base of the second dorsal fin. Dorsal soft rays 10–12, anal soft rays 8–10 and pectoral rays 13–15. Overall colour is olive to golden brown. The back is dark olive to dusky. The flanks have reddish spots and blue streaks. The breast is bright yellow to orange-red. Fins are dusky and may be darkly mottled or tinged with red. The front margin and tip of the pectoral fins are dark. Breeding males are red to deep orange on the breast, females yellowish to pale orange. Males have a red or bronze iris and lips are pale blue. Males have a longer and broader ear-flap than females. Reaches 28.0 cm. The world, all-tackle angling record from the Suwanee River, Florida in 1984 weighed 0.79 kg.

Biology: This species is found in the quieter areas of rocky streams, on rocky lake shores and in vegetated areas with sand and mud bottoms. It winters in groups in deeper holes known as hibernia at temperatures below 5°C. During the summer they are most active in warmer weather and dart under rocks when disturbed. Food is preferably the larger aquatic insects but also includes molluscs, crustaceans and small fishes. Life span is 8 years with maturity attained at 1 year. The hibernium breaks up in spring when water temperatures reach 10°C. Spawning occurs from June to August in New York, and peaks in April to June in Florida. The male builds and defends a nest in shallow, shore waters on sand or fine gravel in the shelter of a log or stump. A nest can be about 1 m across and is in the open in still waters or downstream of a rock in running water. Redbreast sunfish may use **largemouth bass** nests. Unlike most **sunfishes** the male does not produce sounds during courtship. Eggs are amber to yellow and adhesive. Large females average 8250 eggs. The male aerates and removes silt from the eggs with fanning movements of his fins and guards the newly-hatched young for a short time. This **sunfish** is a prized as a game fish in the U.S.A.

redeye gaper

Scientific name: *Chaunax stigmaeus*
　Fowler, 1946
Family: **Sea Toad**
Other common names: none
French name: bayeur rouge

　Distribution: Found along the Atlantic coast of North America from Nova Scotia to Florida.
　Characters: The balloon-shaped body with its flabby, thin but rough skin is characteristic of this **anglerfish**. The fishing appa-

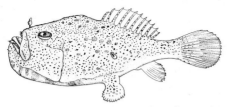

redeye gaper

ratus is short and may be retracted. The gill opening is in the posterior half of the body, below the dorsal fin on the flank. There are 11 dorsal fin rays, 5 anal fin rays and 14 pectoral fin rays. Overall colour is red to orange-red to pink, often with yellow or greenish markings. The anal fin is red. The esca is black and the iris rose. Reaches 25.5 cm total length. This may be the same species as *Chaunax nuttingi* Garman, 1896.
　Biology: Two specimens have been caught off Nova Scotia in 1980 and 1982 and these represent northern range limits.

redfin pickerel

Scientific name: *Esox americanus americanus*
　Gmelin, 1788
Family: **Pike**
Other common names: banded, trout, grass,
　bulldog or mud pickerel; red-finned pike
French name: brochet d'Amérique

　Distribution: Found in Lac St. Pierre of the St. Lawrence River and tributary rivers and the Richelieu River of Québec and south to Georgia and Florida east of the Appalachian Mountains.
　Characters: This species is identified by the 7–8 pores on the lower jaws (4 on each

jaw, rarely 3 or 5), cheeks and opercula covered with scales, snout convex above, cardioid (or notched) scales between pelvic fins 7–16, and pectoral, pelvic and anal fins amber, orange or red. There are more notched or heart-shaped scales on the flank than in the related grass pickerel, 13–22 in the diagonal row of scales between the dorsal and anal fins. Dorsal fin with 15–18 principal rays, principal anal rays 13–17, pectoral rays 14–15 and pelvic rays 8–9. Lateral line scales 102–116. The back and upper flank are light to dark brown to olive-green with a pale stripe from the head to the dorsal fin origin. The flank has 20–36 olive or dark brown, wavy bars and a pale midlateral stripe. The belly is amber to whitish. The eye is yellow to yellow-green. Black bars radiate anteriorly, posteriorly and ventrally from the eye. The lateral edges of the jaws, lower jaw tip and isthmus are dark. The dorsal fin is dark and the caudal fin is amber, orange or red. Attains 33.0 cm. The world, all-tackle angling record from Redhook, New York was caught in 1988 and weighed 0.87 kg.

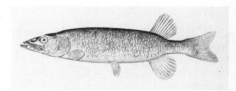

redfin pickerel

　Biology: Redfin pickerel are found in slow, weedy, dark, acid streams and less commonly in ponds, lakes and rivers. Young redfin feed on invertebrates but adults take a wide variety of fishes. Adults feed at dawn and dusk and young in mid-afternoon and after sunset. Life span is 7 years. Females grow faster, are larger and live longer than males. Redfins grow faster than the related **grass pickerel**. Spawning takes place in April when water temperatures reach 10°C. Up to 542 mature eggs are shed by each female, adhering to vegetation or the bottom. Eggs are golden and 1.9 mm in diameter. The female also carries numerous smaller eggs, up to 4364 total. Once sold in Québec in small amounts, it is no longer common enough to be commercially viable. It is caught by anglers in the U.S.A. using spinning gear.

redfin shiner

Scientific name: *Lythrurus umbratilis* (Girard, 1856)
Family: **Carp**
Other common names: compressed redfin
French name: méné d'ombre

Distribution: Found in southern Ontario in Lake Erie, Lake Huron and Lake St. Clair tributaries and rarely in Lake Ontario tributaries, and south from New York and Minnesota to Louisiana and Texas.

Characters: This species is distinguished by having protractile premaxillae (upper lip separated by a groove from snout), no bar-

redfin shiner

bels, lateral line scales 37–56, anal fin branched rays 9–11, dorsal fin origin behind pelvic fin insertion level, anterior midflank scales rounded, body deep (depth about equal to or longer than head length), and a black patch at the anterior dorsal fin base. Pharyngeal teeth slender and hooked at the tip, 2,4–4,2. Dorsal fin branched rays usually 7, rarely 6, pectoral rays 11–13 and pelvic rays 7–9. Males have nuptial tubercles on the snout, cheeks, head to the dorsal fin origin, including the first small dorsal rays, and in 2 rows on each lower jaw. Also present on most scales, pectoral fin rays and leading edge of anal and pelvic fins. The back is brownish-blue or bluish with silvery overtones. There is a dusky spot at the anterior dorsal fin base. Flanks are silvery and the belly white. Flanks have scales outlined with dark pigment but the upper flank and back scales are not outlined and are less obvious. There may be 4–11 diffuse flank bands. Spawning males are bluish-green on the

back, steel-blue on the sides and intense blue or powder blue on the top of the head, and the anal, caudal, pectoral and pelvic fins are bright red and black. Peritoneum silvery with melanophore speckles. Formerly in the genus *Notropis*. Reaches 9.0 cm.

Biology: This shiner prefers weedy pools in streams and rivers over sand, gravel and rock. It tolerates some turbidity and silt and may be expanding its range in Ontario as a result of increasing siltation. Food is aquatic and terrestrial insects, with some plant material. Life span in Mississippi is only about 2 years, rarely to 3 years elsewhere, and many adults die after spawning at 1 year of age. Maturity is attained at 2.8 cm in females. Spawning takes place in June, July and August over sand or gravel-bottomed, slow streams at temperatures of 20°C or warmer. It may use **longear sunfish** nests as spawning sites in Canada. The **sunfish** nest provides a clear, silt-free site for eggs to develop and the male **sunfish** unwittingly defends the eggs from other fishes. Up to a hundred **shiners** may gather at one **sunfish** nest, attracted by the scents released during **sunfish** spawning and by the presence of the male **sunfish**. Male shiners defend a territory over the nest, butting and chasing away other males. Females and males swim alongside each other, over the nest, undulating wildly as eggs and sperm are shed. Most spawning occurred between 1000 and 1430 hours in one study. Females contain up to 887 mature ova but in Mississippi at least have other, smaller ova which indicates more than one clutch may be shed each season. Eggs are up to 0.9 mm in diameter. The eggs are not guarded. This shiner is used as bait in the United States.

redfishes

Redfishes are members of the **Scorpionfish Family**. There are 3 species on the Atlantic coast of Canada, the **Acadian redfish**, **deepwater redfish** and the **golden redfish**. These 3 species are difficult to distinguish and are marketed under the commercial name "redfish" or **"ocean perch."** These fishes are bright red, orange or yellow-red.

redhorses

Redhorses are large members of the freshwater **Sucker Family** and are all in the genus *Moxostoma*. There are about 10 species of redhorses in North America and 7 in Canada. Redhorses have 3 swimbladder chambers instead of the usual 2 in suckers. They are often difficult to capture and their identification presents problems. They are named for their large size and reddish fins.

See **black redhorse**
 copper redhorse
 golden redhorse
 greater redhorse
 river redhorse
 shorthead redhorse
 silver redhorse

redmouth whalefish

Scientific name: *Rondeletia loricata*
 Abe and Hotta, 1963
Family: **Redmouth Whalefish**
Other common names: none
French name: poisson-baleine diable

Distribution: Found in warmer oceans world-wide and off the Scotian Shelf in Canada.

Characters: Dorsal and anal fin rays 13–16, pectoral fin rays 9–11, pelvic fin rays 5–6. Vertical rows in lateral line 14–19. Dark

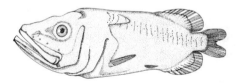

redmouth whalefish

orange-brown in colour overall, with fin tips light. The mouth is reddish-orange. The orange-brown tissue may be luminescent. Attains 11.0 cm total length.

Biology: Known from a single Canadian specimen caught in 1984 taken at 1185 m. This species probably migrates vertically to at least 350 m. It may live 8 years. Food is amphipods and other crustaceans.

Redmouth Whalefish Family

Scientific name: Rondeletiidae
French name: poissons-baleines diables

These small mesopelagic and bathypelagic fishes are found in all the warmest major oceans. There are only two species with 1 reported from Atlantic Canada.

The head is large and the eye small. There are no scales and the skin is smooth. The lateral line is composed of 14–26 vertical rows of pores, rather than the usual horizontal row. The fins lack spines. The pelvic fins are subabdominal and have 5–6 rays. There are 3 epurals and 6 hypural bones in the tail skeleton.

These whalefishes are related to the **Flabby Whalefish** and **Whalefish** families in the **Pricklefish Order**. All are characterised by a whale-shaped body, very large mouth and a distensible stomach. The dorsal and anal fins are opposite each other near the rear of the body. There is no swimbladder. The typical orange-brown colour of these fishes is probably derived from their crustacean food, and serves as camouflage.

This family is named for the French ichthyologist William Rondelet (1507–1566), although he never knew of their existence.

Redmouth whalefishes are rare and only encountered below 1000 m in scientific fishing expeditions. Their biology is poorly known. They can eat fish as large as themselves because of their distensible stomach.

See **redmouth whalefish**

redside dace

Scientific name: *Clinostomus elongatus*
 (Kirtland, 1838)
Family: **Carp**
Other common names: red-sided shiner
French name: méné long

Distribution: Found from New York to Minnesota and south to Kentucky in the Mississippi River basin. In Canada restricted to streams tributary to western Lake Ontario, Lake Erie, southern Lake Huron and Lake Simcoe.

Characters: This species is distinguished by having protractile premaxillae (upper lip separated from snout by a groove) and a large, upturned mouth, scales in a complete lateral line 59–75, pelvic fin origin in front of dorsal fin origin, dorsal fin branched rays 7, rarely 6, and anal branched rays 8, rarely 7 or 9. Pharyngeal teeth usually 2,5–4,2 or

redside dace

2,5–5,2 with slightly hooked tips. Pectoral rays 14–16, pelvic rays 8. Nuptial tubercles in males are large on top of the head, on the body and upper and lower pectoral and pelvic fins. There is 1 tubercle per scale except on the caudal peduncle where there are 3–4 per scale and on the breast where up to 7 comb-like rows of tubercles edge the scales, with up to 4 tubercles per scale. Pectoral fins are longer in males than females. The back is dark olive to blue-green with a thin, golden-green stripe along the whole upper flank and a broader red or scarlet to pink or orange stripe below it terminating at or beyond the dorsal fin level. Males tend to have a brilliant red stripe, females a pinkish to orange one and young a white stripe. Iridescent blue, green and purple tints are found over the whole body. The belly is whitish. The eye is silvery with a dark stripe through the centre. Peritoneum silvery, speckled with dark melanophores. Reaches 11.4 cm.

Biology: Redside dace schools favour clear streams with gravel and stone bottoms, and with overhanging vegetation which supports an insect fauna. They prefer pools and quiet riffles. They are sensitive to turbidity and stream "improvement" where bushes are removed. Food is mainly insects and about 77% are terrestrial insects and spiders, many caught by leaps of several centimetres from the water surface. Life span is 4 years and maturity is attained at age 3. Females are generally larger than males of the same age. Spawning occurs in May at 16–19°C over gravel. Males may defend a territory but usu-

ally school downstream of **creek chub** nests. When a female moves over the nest, 2 or more males join her and eggs are shed in the nest even with the **creek chub** male present. Spawning may be repeated 4–6 times within 1 minute, but more commonly at intervals of several minutes. Eggs are 2.4 mm in diameter after being shed, non-adhesive and number up to 1971. The Committee on the Status of Endangered Wildlife in Canada gave this fish the status of "rare" in 1987. However it has been dispersed outside its natural range in southern Ontario as a bait fish.

redside shiner

Scientific name: *Richardsonius balteatus*
  (Richardson, 1836)
Family: **Carp**
Other common names: none
French name: méné rose

Distribution: Found in the Peace River drainage of northern Alberta and British Columbia, in the Fraser and Columbia river drainages and in northern coastal drainages of B.C., south to Washington, Oregon, Idaho, Montana, Nevada, Wyoming and Utah.

Characters: This species is distinguished by the long anal fin (9–23, often 15, branched rays), a rearward placed dorsal fin with branched rays 7–11, usually 9, 52–67 scales in the lateral line, 2,5–5,2, 2,5–4,2 or 2,4–4,2

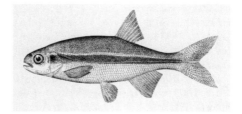

redside shiner

pharyngeal teeth, and a small keel on the belly near the anal fin. Gill rakers 6–9. Pectoral fin rays 13–16 and pelvic rays 8–9. Nuptial tubercles in males are on the head, pectoral, pelvic, dorsal and anal fins (except first dorsal and anal fin ray) and on the central caudal fin rays. Scales have up to 10 tubercles lining their edge particularly on the anterior belly, lower caudal peduncle and midflank. Back scales have scattered tubercles. Males have longer pectoral fins than females.

The back and upper flanks are black, dark brown, olive or bluish, the flanks are silvery and the belly is silvery to white. There is a midlateral stripe, fading near the head, but evident through the eye. Fins are dusky to amber or clear. The eye is golden. Breeding males are golden on the head and fins, yellow above the lateral stripe and orange to crimson red below it from the head to the anal fin. The lower body surface and fins are yellow. The female is golden above and below the lateral stripe. Peritoneum silvery and lightly speckled with melanophores.

Hybrids with the **peamouth chub, longnose dace** and **northern squawfish** are known from British Columbia. Reaches 18.0 cm.

Biology: The redside shiner is a common schooling fish abundant in lakes, ponds, rapid streams, and slow rivers. Smaller fish are found closer to the shore and surface waters than adults. Adults are associated with vegetation in shallow water down to about 4 m during the day but they spread out in surface waters at night. There is a retreat to deeper water in winter. They can survive temperatures as high as 37.5°C for short periods in Harrison Lake, B.C. near the hot springs. Food is various planktonic and bottom crustaceans when young and aquatic and terrestrial insects when adult. Molluscs, fish eggs and small fishes including **trout** are also eaten. Redside shiners are cannibals. They are very numerous and an important food for **cutthroat trout, rainbow trout, Dolly Varden, northern squawfish**, various aquatic birds and mink.

Life span is 7 years with sexual maturity attained at 3 years. Most large fish are female. Spawning takes place from May to August when males arrive on the spawning ground first at temperatures over 10°C. Spawning may occur in stream riffles or in lakes, throughout the day and night. Males, and to a lesser extent females, may spawn more than once in a season. A female and 1–2 accompanying males splash strongly in shallow water, releasing eggs and sperm. Pale yellow eggs are up to 2.2 mm in diameter and number up to 3602. The eggs adhere to vegetation and are shed 10–20 at a time.

Large populations of this **shiner** are serious competitors with young **trout** for food and indeed may eat them, even though **trout** when larger eat the **shiner**. In British Columbia some lakes have been poisoned in an attempt to eradicate the **shiner** and improve **trout** survival. The **shiner** has also been introduced as a forage fish with the same purpose. This tampering with complex, natural ecosystems usually proves costly and ineffective.

redstripe rockfish

Scientific name: *Sebastes proriger*
    (Jordan and Gilbert, 1880)
Family: **Scorpionfish**
Other common names: rock cod
French name: sébaste à raie rouge

Distribution: Found from the Bering Sea to California including British Columbia.

Characters: This species is distinguished by colour, head spines and the toothed knob on the chin. Dorsal fin spines 13, soft rays

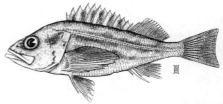

redstripe rockfish

13–15, usually 15. Anal fin soft rays 6–7, usually 7, second anal spine twice as thick as third and equal in length. Pectoral fin rays 16–18, usually 17. Lateral line pores 48–55, scale rows below lateral line 50–60. Gill rakers 36–43. Vertebrae 27. Head spines are weak and the supraocular, coronal and nuchal spines are absent. The overall colour is a light or pale red. The belly is whitish. The lateral line is grey, outlined by red. The back is mottled with olive and there are yellowish tinges to the flanks. The top of the lower jaw is dusky. Olive stripes radiate from the eye. Fins are red with some light green on the dorsal and caudal fins and some yellow on the anal and pelvic fins. Peritoneum black or dark brown. Reaches 51 cm, perhaps larger.

Biology: This rockfish is found from 12 to 366 m but occurs in shallower water in the north. It may hover over the sea bed or perch on a rock. Spawning takes place in July in British Columbia. Half the male population is mature at 28 cm and half the females at 29 cm. Maximum age is estimated to exceed 40 years. It is caught by commercial trawlers and sold fresh or frozen.

redtail scad

Scientific name: *Decapterus tabl*
    Berry, 1968
Family: **Jack**
Other common names: none
French name: comète queue rouge

Distribution: Found from Nova Scotia south to Venezuela, and world-wide in warmer waters.

Characters: This species is distinguished from its Canadian Atlantic coast relatives by not having a deep, compressed body, but an elongate one with maximum depth 20–25% of fork length, by having 103–119 scales and posteriorly enlarged scutes in the lateral line, a long pectoral fin reaching the end of the spiny dorsal fin, and 24–27 anal fin soft rays. There are 8 spines in the first dorsal fin and 1 spine preceding the soft dorsal fin. Soft dorsal fin rays 29–34 and pectoral rays 20–22. There is 1 dorsal and 1 anal finlet. The lateral line is more arched than in the **mackerel scad**. The bright red colour of the caudal fin is also distinctive. Back a metallic blue or greenish, head dorsally dark, flanks a dusky silvery with a silvery or white belly. Dorsal fin rays are dark and membranes clear. The anterior 10 or so second dorsal fin rays and the finlet are red tinged. Pelvic fins

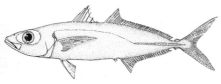

redtail scad

tinged red. Anal fin colourless. Pectoral fin dusky dorsally. The scientific name stands for "*T*ropical *A*tlantic *B*iological *L*aboratory"

of the U.S. Bureau of Fisheries in Florida. Reaches about 41 cm total length.

Biology: First caught on the southwest Sable Island Bank in 1983, a northern range record and the only Canadian specimen. This species lives deeper than its relatives, the **mackerel** and **round scads**, and is usually trawled at 200–360 m. Dolphins are known to eat this scad.

redtail surfperch

Scientific name: *Amphistichus rhodoterus*
    (Agassiz, 1854)
Family: **Surfperch**
Other common names: porgy, redtail seaperch
French name: ditrème rosé

Distribution: From Vancouver Island south to central California.

Characters: This surfperch is distinguished from other Canadian species by having a row of small scales along the posterior

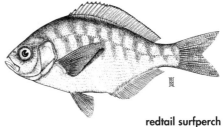

redtail surfperch

half of the anal fin base, no frenum and 60–67 lateral line scales with 4–6 on the tail. Dorsal fin spines 8–10, soft rays 25–29. Anal fin with 3 spines and 26–32 soft rays. Pectoral fin rays 27–28. Caudal fin with a broad fork. Back is pale olive. Silvery to brassy overall with 8–11 reddish to brownish bars on the flanks. These bars are interrupted by the lateral line and re-start in a staggered pattern. All fins except the pectorals are pink or reddish, most noticeably the caudal fin. The dorsal fin has a pink margin but basally may be light blue. Reaches 41 cm or more.

Biology: Sand beaches swept by surf are the habitat of this species but it is also found in quiet bays. Caught down to 7.3 m. Very common. Food is mainly crustaceans but also includes fish, molluscs and worms. Males mature at ages 2–3 and females 3–4.

Maximum age is 9 years. Mating occurs in December-January and young are born July-September. Each female may have 1–39 embryos with larger fish having the most. This is an important sport fish in the U.S.A.

Remora Family

Scientific name: Echeneidae (= Echeneididae)
French name: rémoras

Remoras, diskfishes, or sharksuckers, are found in the warmer waters of the Atlantic, Indian and Pacific oceans. There are 8 species with 2 reported from Atlantic Canada, 1 from Pacific Canada, and 1 probably from both coasts.

These fishes are immediately recognisable by the sucking disc on top of the head. The disc is a highly modified spiny dorsal fin in which the spines have split to form 10–28 moveable plates (laminae or lamellae) lying across the head. The lower jaw projects. Small but sharp teeth are found on the jaws, roof of the mouth and often on the tongue. Scales are small and cycloid. There is no swimbladder. There are 8–11 branchiostegal rays.

Species are distinguished by the number of laminae in the disc and by fin ray counts. Remoras may be placed in their own order or included in the **Perch Order** as here. They appear to be related to the **Cobia** and **Dolphin** families within the **Perch Order**, sharing such characters as the absence of predorsal bones and absence of a beryciform foramen in the anterior ceratohyal, several anal pterygiophores anterior to the first haemal spine, tubular bony structures around the prenasal canals, and very elongate larvae which complete development of dorsal fin rays only when 2–3 times flexion size.

Remoras attach to sharks, other fishes, sea turtles, marine mammals and even ships, using the disc. They may even be found inside the gill cavities of **mantas** and **ocean sunfish**. Remoras also swim freely in surface waters. Certain remoras prefer particular host species. The disc is used to create a partial vacuum by moving the laminae upwards. It requires a considerable force to detach a remora. They feed on discarded fragments from the meals of their larger hosts and also serve to clean their hosts of crustacean skin parasites.

However this service is offset by the abrasive effects of disc attachment which, in some host species, can remove scales and damage skin resulting in death for the host. They will also take small fishes and invertebrates.

Remoras have been used to catch sea turtles. A hole is drilled through the remora's tail and a line attached. Several remoras are released near a sea turtle and one or more will attach to it, enabling it to be gently pulled to the boat. The Latin word "remora" means delay or hindrance. Legends credit remoras with the ability to slow sailing ships, and, as a potion, to stop aging in women, hinder the course of love and delay legal proceedings!

See **black remora**
sharksucker
spearfish remora
whalesucker

Requiem Shark Family

Scientific name: Carcharhinidae
French name: mangeurs d'hommes

This family has about 58 species in the warmer parts of the world's oceans and occasionally fresh water. There are 8 species in Canada, 7 on the Atlantic coast and 1 on both the Atlantic and Pacific coasts.

They are distinguished from other Canadian sharks by a complex of characters including having an anal fin, 5 gill slits, 2 dorsal fins, no fin spines, nictitating eyelids, and a scroll intestinal valve. The head is usually normal, the first dorsal fin base is in front of the pelvic bases, there is a wavy dorsal tail fin margin, well-developed, knife-like teeth with cutting edges, usually no spiracles, and precaudal pits.

Requiem sharks are members of the **Ground Shark Order** related to the **Cat Shark**, and **Hound Shark** families. The family includes the **hammerhead sharks** which used to be placed in their own family, Sphyrnidae.

This is one of the largest and most economically important shark families. Most members are voracious predators as their common names suggest and they are frequently dangerous to man. Some of these species enter rivers and remain there for long periods causing human fatalities but none of these bull or river sharks are found in Canada.

The function of the hammer-head in hammerhead sharks is uncertain but several theories have been advanced. The flattened "hammer" may increase manoeuvrability, enabling rapid banking and quick rises in pursuit of fast-moving squid prey. It may act as a planing surface to provide lift. It may also serve to allow greater development of lateral line canals and ampullae of Lorenzini and thus better pressure and electromagnetic abilities. The wide spacing of the eyes may confer better binocular vision and the nasal capsules can be larger and more widely-spaced giving a more acute and better directional sense of smell. Hammerheads are free-swimming and can be seen in schools numbering in the hundreds off Florida.

These sharks are usually viviparous or ovoviviparous. Food includes a variety of fishes, sharks, rays, squids, crustaceans, marine reptiles, birds and mammals, and carrion and garbage.

See **Atlantic sharpnose shark**
  blue shark
  dusky shark
  ocean whitetip shark
  sandbar shark
  silky shark
  smooth hammerhead
  tiger shark

rex sole

Scientific name: *Errex zachirus*
  (Lockington, 1879)
Family: **Righteye Flounder**
Other common names: longfin sole, witch
French name: sole américaine

Distribution: Found from the Bering Sea to Baja California including British Columbia.

Characters: This species is recognised by a pectoral fin on the eyed side being longer than the head. The body is thin and slimy. Scales are cycloid and the almost straight lateral line has 132–138 scales. The mouth is small and asymmetrical with teeth mainly on the lower side. The head is rounded anteriorly. Dorsal fin rays 87–110, anal rays 78–93, preceded by a spine. Caudal fin a pointed v-shape. Eyed side light brown, white to dusky on the blind side. Fins are dusky with dark edges. The pectoral fin is

blackish. Young are almost translucent but fish 17–25 cm long have blotches on th eyed side. Reaches 61 cm.

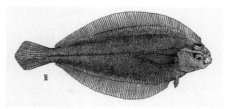

rex sole

Biology: Usually found below 366 m but common in Canada. Depth range is 0–850 m. Food is crustaceans when fish are 15 cm or less in length and worms when larger. The life span of this species is 24 years and growth is slow. Females grow larger and live longer than males. Males are mature at 3 years, females at 4 years. Spawning in Hecate Strait is in March–April. Up to 238,000 eggs are produced. Larvae are pelagic until 7.4 cm long. This species is caught in Canada but is thin and difficult to fillet on a commercial scale. It has been used as animal food.

ribbed sculpin

Scientific name: *Triglops pingeli*
  Reinhardt, 1838
Family: **Sculpin**
Other common names: none
French name: faux-trigle bardé

Distribution: Found from Japan and the Chukchi and Bering seas to Washington including British Columbia and in the North Atlantic Ocean including Atlantic Canada, and across the Arctic as far north as Ellesmere Island.

Characters: This species and its relative, the **roughspine sculpin**, are distinguished from other Canadian Pacific sculpins by the oblique folds of skin below the lateral line running postero-ventrally, tiny scales on the fold edges, fine prickles over the upper eyeball, the slender body tapering to the tail and scales covering the flank above the lateral line, the top of the head and on the dorsal, pectoral and caudal fin rays. The ribbed sculpin is separated from its relative by the row of rough, raised scales along the upper flank and the 3 or more rows of prickles on the eyeball. Pectoral fin ray count and colour p[attern distinguish it from Arctic-Atlantic relatives. Body folds are

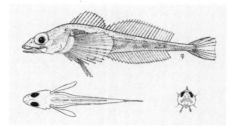

ribbed sculpin

about equal in number to lateral line scutes, and there are folds of skin across the breast. First dorsal fin spines 9–13, second dorsal rays 22–28, anal rays 20–28 and pectoral rays 16–19 with lower 7–8 weakly finger-like. Lateral line plates 47–50, each with a backward pointing spine. There is a sharp nasal spine and 4 blunt preopercular spines. The male anal papilla is long and curved forward. The back is olive-brown to red-brown with 4–5 dark saddles which may be weakly developed. Belly white. The tail fin has small blotches. There is a black bar and silvery area in front of the pectoral fin. Pectoral fins have 4–6 weak, curved bars. Males have a silver line below the lateral line with a narrow black stripe below. In females the stripe is broken into dark blotches. Reaches 20 cm.

Biology: Not uncommon on the bottom over mud and rocks in colder waters at 4–100 m but as deep as 930 m. It may be found at temperatures below 0°C. Food is crustaceans and arrow worms and more rarely some worms and fishes. It actively forages in the water column when young, and to some extent when adult. Life span is at least 5 years. Thick-billed murres eat this sculpin in Hudson Bay. Each female has up to 400, 3 mm diameter eggs which may be spawned in fall or early winter. Eggs are a milky-red and demersal.

ribbon barracudina

Scientific name: *Notolepis rissoi*
  (Bonaparte, 1841)
Family: **Barracudina**

Other common names: none
French name: lussion blanc

Distribution: Found in the Pacific, Indian and South Atlantic oceans including off British Columbia.

Characters: This species is distinguished from its Canadian relatives by the pectoral fins being shorter than the anal fin base, smooth-edged lower jaw teeth, body scales (but easily lost), pelvic fin origin behind the dorsal fin origin, many anal fin rays, and a Pacific distribution. This subspecies has larger teeth then its Arctic-Atlantic relative and, on average, fewer vertebrae and anal fin rays. Dorsal fin rays 8–11, anal rays 28–34, pectoral rays 9–13 and pelvics about 12–13. There is a blunt keel along the belly. Lateral line scales number 59–67. Total vertebrae 76–82. Overall colour is silvery. There is a black spot at the anal and pelvic fin origins and a dark dorsal band or speckling is present in preserved fish. The jaw tip is dark. Reaches 30 cm.

ribbon barracudina

Biology: Found in inshore waters such as the Strait of Juan de Fuca and Puget Sound but also offshore at 155–825 m. Elsewhere reported down to 2200 m. Food is fish and shrimps. Spawning occurs in January to September, peaking in May. Adults are found much further north than post-larvae.

ribbon bristlemouth

Scientific name: *Diplophos taenia*
  Günther, 1873
Family: **Bristlemouth**
Other common names: none
French name: cyclothone ruban

Distribution: Found world-wide in warmer oceans and off the Scotian Shelf in Atlantic Canada, southward.

Characters: This species is distinguished from all other Atlantic coast bristlemouths by its high anal fin ray count (54–69), by having photophores on the isthmus and the dorsal fin origin well in front of the anal fin origin. Dorsal fin rays 9–12. Photophores: SO 1, ORB 1, OP 3, BR 10–13, IV 40–51,

ribbon bristlemouth

VAV 14–17, AC 42–51, OA 66–77, IC 99–113. The back is brown-black and the flanks silvery. Fins are colourless. The inside of the mouth and gill covers are dusky and the jaws are transparent posteriorly and ventrally. Reaches 27.6 cm standard length.

Biology: Known from only a single specimen caught at 210 m northeast of Georges Bank in 1984 and first reported in 1988. Found usually at 300–800 m by day, migrating vertically to approach the surface at night. Larvae are found in surface waters.

ribbon prickleback

Scientific name: *Phytichthys chirus*
(Jordan and Gilbert, 1880)
Family: **Shanny**
Other common names: belted blenny
French name: lompénie ruban

Distribution: From southern California to the Bering Sea including British Columbia.

Characters: This species is related to the **black** and **rock pricklebacks** and like them lacks pelvic fins and a head crest, has 4 lateral line canals and has the anal fin joined to the caudal fin. It is distinguished by having

ribbon prickleback

2–3 anal fin spines. There are 59–78 dorsal fin rays and 40–50 soft anal fin rays. The pectoral fins are very small and have about 15 rays. Scales extend over the whole body. The upper 3 lateral lines run from head to tail, the lowest one ending near the anal fin origin. Vertical branches of these canals can be seen. Olive-green to olive-brown overall

becoming yellow to green on the belly. The flanks may be darkly or white spotted. There are 4 dark lines radiating down and back from the eye defined by light streaks. Attains 21.1 cm total length.

Biology: Found in the intertidal zone under rocks and down to 12 m. Often entwined around the holdfasts of kelp. Food is crustaceans and algae. Used as bait for larger fishes such as **flounders, scorpionfishes** and **greenlings**.

ribbon sawtailfish

Scientific name: *Idiacanthus fasciola*
Peters, 1876
Family: **Barbeled Dragonfish**
Other common names: black dragonfish
French name: idiacanthe ruban

Distribution: Found in all tropical and temperate oceans including the Atlantic off the Grand Bank and Scotian Shelf.

Characters: The family account should be referred to for the many unusual features of this fish. Males and females differ markedly

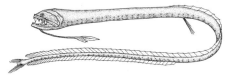

ribbon sawtailfish

in appearance and neither is like the larvae! The very elongate body with elongate dorsal and anal fins nearly reaching the tail and the lack of pectoral fins are characteristic. Males lack pelvic fins, teeth, chin barbel, a functional digestive tract and are much smaller than females. Larvae have eyes at the end of long stalks (see **sawtailfishes**). Females are black and males brown. The female tail fin is yellow with luminous tissue. Males reach 5–7 cm but females can exceed 30 cm and perhaps attain 40 cm.

Biology: Occasionally specimens are caught in Canadian waters. The male does not grow after metamorphosis from the larval form. Spawning probably occurs at some considerable depth as this is where the smallest larvae are caught. Adult females migrate daily from 2000 m to the surface but males apparently live at 1000–2000 m continually. Food for females is fishes. Larvae eat diatoms and minute crustaceans. Males diet.

ribbon snailfish

Scientific name: *Liparis cyclopus*
    Günther, 1861
Family: **Snailfish**
Other common names: Günther's liparid
French name: limace-ruban

Distribution: Found from the Bering Sea to Oregon including British Columbia.

Characters: This species is distinguished from its Pacific coast relatives by having an adhesive disc with its rear edge behind the

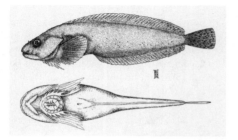

ribbon snailfish

level of the gill slit, 2 pairs of nostrils, gill slit partly in front of the pectoral fin down to between rays 5–10, dorsal fin rays 35–37, anal rays 29–31 and pectoral rays 29–32. The caudal fin is mostly free of the dorsal and anal fin. The pectoral fin has a lower lobe with rays separated from the membrane. Teeth are in bands and are trilobed. Pyloric caeca 39. The body is olive-brown with fine black spots. Larger dark spots are found on the middle and lower flank and there may be 4 pale flank stripes. There are oblique bars on the dorsal and anal fins and vertical bars on the caudal fin. The peritoneum is pale with black dots. Reaches 11.4 cm.

Biology: Not uncommon in British Columbia down to 183 m from nearshore waters. Although it is reported as not common in tide pools, in Canadian waters it is found there associated with algae and kelp over soft sand, muck, mud and rocks. First described from Esquimault Harbour, Vancouver Island.

Ribbonfish Family

Scientific name: Trachipteridae
French name: trachyptères

Ribbonfishes or scythe fishes are found in all oceans and comprise about 9 species with 1 on the Pacific coast of Canada.

They are characterised by the very thin body, which is ribbon-like and fragile, and the unique caudal fin which is long and at right angles to the body. There is no anal fin. The dorsal fin is very long and originates near the level of the eye. There are no ribs and the swimbladder is reduced or absent. Each dorsal fin ray has a lateral spine at the base. The mouth is very protrusible. Adults have tubercles and pores in the skin which are thought to reduce drag when swimming. Scales are absent, or present and deciduous or modified ctenoid scales. Body and fin shapes change markedly as these fishes grow. There are no ribs and the swimbladder is absent or rudimentary.

This family is a relative of the **Opah Family** in the **Opah Order**.

These fishes move by undulating the dorsal fin and keep their head up at a 45° angle rather than horizontally. They are not uncommon and may be caught in nets or seen when washed ashore.

See **king-of-the-salmon**

ridged eel

Scientific name: *Neoconger mucronatus*
    Girard, 1858
Family: **Spaghetti Eel**
Other common names: none
French name: anguille enfaitée

Distribution: Tropical areas of the western Atlantic and eastern Pacific oceans. Found in Atlantic Canada.

Characters: Adults have a dorsal fin origin slightly in front of the anus position. Pectoral fins are small and the eye minute. Dorsal fin rays 151–153 and anal rays about 133. Total lateral line pores 21–41. The head is pale and sharply pointed. Overall colour is grey to brown with some dark reticulations or honeycomb pattern. Larvae have 96–110 myomeres (muscle blocks), 39–56 preanal myomeres, a small melanophore ventrally at segment 20–

28, a large ventral melanophore about mid-body where the gut forms a large loop and a deep melanophore in the mid-part of the caudal region. The larval Canadian specimen was 37 mm long. Adults attain 30 cm.

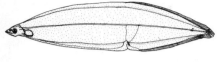

ridged eel

Biology: Known from Canada only as a stray larva (or leptocephalus) and first reported in 1988. Adults have been found on mud bottoms and silty offshore banks at 3–183 m. Spawning apparently occurs off the northeast coast of Brazil in September-November and February-March. Larval life is at least 4 months.

Ridgehead Family

Scientific name: Melamphaeidae
French name: poissons-heaumes

The ridgeheads, bigscales or bluebacks are small, bathypelagic fishes of all oceans and seas except the Arctic and Mediterranean. There are about 33 species with 9 occurring in Canada, 7 on the Atlantic coast and 3 on the Pacific coast. One species is found on both coasts.

Family members have characteristic blunt heads which are sculptured and ridged. The bones and scales are paper-thin, particularly in the deeper water species. Scales are large, cycloid and easily detached. There is no true lateral line and only 1–2 pored scales. The dorsal fin has 1–3 weak spines before 10–18 soft rays. The pelvic fins lie under the pectoral fins (thoracic or subthoracic position) and have 1 spine and 6–8 soft rays. The anal fin has 1 spine and 7–12 soft rays. Spines are developed where the caudal fin meets the body dorsally and ventrally and number 3–4. There are 19–36 gill rakers, often with many spines, and 7–8 branchiostegal rays. Teeth are minute and are found in bands or in single rows.

Ridgeheads are members of the **Prickle-fish Order**.

Ridgeheads are commonest below 1000 m when adult and are rarely found above 100 m except as young and larvae. They may descend below 4000 m. Little is known about their biology but they are eaten by marine mammals and the larger fishes. They are not commercially important as they are only caught on scientific fishing expeditions using special deepsea nets. These fishes are fragile and preserved specimens are often damaged.

See **bull rhinofish**
crested ridgehead
highsnout ridgehead
largeye rhinofish
numerous helmetfish
rearfin expatriate
shortspine helmetfish
squarenose helmetfish
twospine bigscale

Righteye Flounder Family

Scientific name: Pleuronectidae
French name: plies

Righteye flounders are found in the Arctic, Atlantic and Pacific oceans with some occasionally entering brackish water and a few species resident in fresh water. There are about 99 species with 29 from Canadian waters. The Canadian species include 17 on the Pacific coast, 5 on the Atlantic coast, 3 on the Arctic coast, 1 on the Arctic-Atlantic coasts, 1 on the Arctic, Atlantic and Pacific coasts, 1 on the Arctic coast and on the Pacific coast also entering fresh water, and 1 exotic species in the Great Lakes.

These fishes have the typical **flatfish** body plan. Eyes are almost always on the right side of the body (= dextral) although some individuals may be reversed. In some species this reversal is quite common and found in a majority of individuals in a population. There is no oil globule in the egg yolk. There are no fin spines. The dorsal fin origin is above or anterior to the eye. The preopercle bone on the side of the head has a free margin. Pelvic fins are symmetrically placed on each side of the body. The lateral line may have a dorsal branch paralleling the dorsal fin. Scales are often ctenoid on the eyed side and cycloid on the blind side but can be cycloid or ctenoid on both sides.

Righteye flounders are members of the **Flatfish Order** and are related to the **Lefteye Flounder Family**.

This family includes many commercially important fishes, often attaining a very large size. Although typically bottom fish, they migrate long distances and leave the sea bed to hunt food. They often conceal themselves with a thin layer of sand and mud on the bottom with only the eyes and nostrils protruding.

See **Arctic flounder**
    arrowtooth flounder
    Asiatic arrowtooth flounder
    Atlantic halibut
    Bering flounder
    butter sole
    C-O sole
    Canadian plaice
    curlfin sole
    deepsea sole
    Dover sole
    English sole
    European flounder
    flathead sole
    Greenland halibut
    longhead dab
    Pacific halibut
    petrale sole
    rex sole
    rock sole
    roughscale sole
    sand sole
    slender sole
    smooth flounder
    starry flounder
    winter flounder
    witch flounder
    yellowfin sole
    yellowtail flounder

ringtail snailfish

Scientific name: *Liparis rutteri* (Gilbert and Snyder in Jordan and Evermann, 1898)
Family: **Snailfish**
Other common names: ring-tailed liparid
French name: limace annelée

Distribution: Found from the Bering Sea to California including British Columbia.
Characters: This species is distinguished from its Pacific coast relatives by having an adhesive disc with its rear edge behind the level of the gill slit, 2 pairs of nostrils, gill slit above the pectoral fin, dorsal fin not lobed, and a white bar across the caudal fin base. Dorsal fin with a wavy margin and 30–32 rays, anal rays 23–27 and pectoral rays 30–33. Lower pectoral rays are thick-

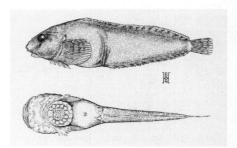

ringtail snailfish

ened and partially separated from the membrane. Teeth are trilobed. Pyloric caeca 23–31. Overall colour black to bluish or brown. The flanks have rows of elongate, black spots or wavy streaks. The caudal fin is speckled. Reaches over 16 cm.
Biology: Not uncommon in Canadian waters. Found from tidal pools down to 73 m over clay, muck, rocks and shell bottoms among algae.

river chub

Scientific name: *Nocomis micropogon*
    (Cope, 1865)
Family: **Carp**
Other common names: crested chub, eastern
    river chub
French name: méné bâton

Distribution: Found from New York to Indiana and south to North Carolina and Alabama. In Canada reported from tributaries of lakes Ontario, Erie, St. Clair and southern Lake Huron and in the Madawaska River of the Ottawa River basin (the latter possibly a bait fish introduction).
Characters: This species is recognised by having protractile premaxillae (upper lip separated by a groove from the snout), a barbel at each mouth corner, 37–43 lateral line scales, pectoral fins do not reach to the pelvic fins, the snout projects only a little over the mouth, there is no stripe along the middle of the back and the flank stripe is vague, and the spot at the caudal fin base is indistinct. Pharyngeal teeth 4–4 or 3–4.

Dorsal fin branched rays 6–7, usually 7, anal fin branched rays 6–7, usually 6, pectoral rays 15–19 and pelvic rays 8. Males have large nuptial tubercles on the snout, usually less than 65 in all. There are fine tubercles on some upper pectoral fin rays. During the breeding season males develop a large swelling between and behind the eyes on top of the head.

The back is olive-brown to greenish-olive with a dusky, yellow stripe, the flanks silvery to iridescent green and the belly white to yellow. Scales on the upper flank are outlined with dark pigment and have a basal spot. Young fish have an obvious midflank, dark stripe ending in a spot but in fish larger than about 6.0 cm the stripe fades. The tail in young fish is grey to orangish. In adults the dorsal and caudal fin rays are outlined in black and anal, pectoral and pelvic fins are white to yellowish. Breeding males may develop pink to red tinges on the head, flanks and belly and olive to yellow dorsal and caudal fins. The pectoral and anal fins are bright yellow and the leading edge of these fins and the pelvics is white. Peritoneum brown to black with dark spots. Reaches 32 cm.

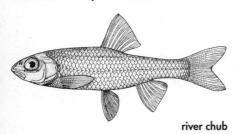

river chub

Biology: River chubs, as the name suggests, favour larger bodies of running water, which are usually clear and have gravel, rubble or rock beds. Food is aquatic insects, crustaceans, snails and possibly fish.

Males grow larger than females and life span is about 5 years. Maturity is attained at 3 years. Male river chubs excavate a depression in stream beds in spring at 15–20°C, filling it with pebbles and stones. Nests may be about a metre wide, 1.2 m long and about 15 cm high. As with the **hornyhead chub**, the current tends to elongate the nest. As many as 7000 pebbles weighing 107 kg form a single

nest which takes 20–30 hours to construct. The male constructs a narrow trough on top of his nest about as wide as his body and up to two-thirds his body length. He lies partly in this trough and vibrates his body to attract the female. The male presses against the female and may clasp her between his flank and upper pectoral fin. A female may have up to 725 eggs which are deposited among the pebbles and covered with more pebbles by the male. **Common** and **rosyface shiners, longnose dace** and **central stonerollers** use river chub nests for their spawning, even when the male chub is guarding his nest. Hybrids are common because of this association. This chub has been used as a bait fish and its distribution in southern Ontario has been widened through releases of such fish. The river chub was listed as not in jeopardy in 1988 by the Committee on the Status of Endangered Wildlife in Canada.

river darter

Scientific name: *Percina shumardi*
  (Girard, 1859)
Family: **Perch**
Other common names: big-headed darter
French name: dard de rivière

Distribution: Found in Hudson Bay drainages in central and southern Manitoba and adjacent parts of northwestern Ontario and in the Lake St. Clair drainage in southwestern Ontario. In the U.S.A. found south of the Great Lakes to Louisiana and Texas.

Characters: This **darter** is distinguished from its Canadian relatives by having a large anal fin at least as large as the soft dorsal fin, belly midline scaleless in females and some

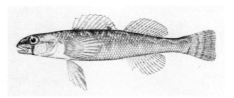

river darter

males and with 1–18 enlarged scales in most males, 2 anal fin spines, a shallow groove present or not between the snout and lip, snout not protruding, lateral line scales 46–62, and 9–12, usually 10, dorsal fin spines. Soft dorsal fin rays 11–16, usually 13–14, anal fin rays 10–13, usually 11. Pectoral fin rays 13–15. Cheek and opercles with scales, breast usually without scales. Overall colour is dark olive-green to brown with 5–12 faint saddles over the back and 8–15 flank blotches. There may be a basal caudal spot. The belly is white to yellow. The eye has radiating bars. The spiny dorsal fin is striped and the soft dorsal fin weakly striped. The first dorsal fin has a small black spot anteriorly and a large black spot posteriorly. The caudal fin has 3–4 wavy bars. Other fins are mostly clear. Breeding males have an elongate anal fin and tubercles on the anal and pelvic rays, ventral caudal fin rays, belly scales and head canals. There are no brightened colours. Reaches 8.9 cm.

Biology: Apparently uncommon in Canada, its biology is poorly known. It is found in large rivers and streams with moderate to fast currents over boulder, rubble, gravel and bedrock bottoms, and also in lakes, often where waves wash over beaches. It is more tolerant of turbidity than most **darters**. Food includes aquatic insects, crustaceans, fish eggs and probably snails. Life span is perhaps as long as 4 years. Spawning may occur in early summer in Canada.

river lamprey

Scientific name: *Lampetra ayresi*
    (Günther, 1870)
Family: **Lamprey**
Other common names: none
French name: lamproie à queue noire

Distribution: Found from California to southern Alaska including British Columbia.

Characters: Myomeres number 60–71. The tooth bar below the mouth has 5–10 cusps, often bicuspid at each end of the bar. This species is distinguished from other Canadian lampreys by having 2 dorsal fins, the tooth bar above the mouth with 2 cusps, teeth along each side of the mouth 3 with at least the middle tooth tricuspid, sharp teeth on the tongue and teeth above the dorsal tooth bar (supraoral lamina) large and sharp. Adults are dark brown to grey or blue-black,

silvery on the lower flanks and silver to white on the belly. Fins are yellowish. Both adults and ammocoetes have a dark spot on the tail, hence the French name. In ammocoetes most of the head is unpigmented, as is most of the tail. Attains 31.1 cm.

adult

ammocoete

river lamprey

disc view

Biology: This is a parasitic species found in both salt and fresh water. Adults live 2 years but their feeding period in the Strait of Georgia is only about 10 weeks. Spawning occurs from April to June after a return to fresh water between September and late winter. They transform to adults in late July but, unusually for a lamprey species, they only migrate to the sea in the following year from late April to early July. This is probably a response to the maximum discharge of the Fraser River where this species has been most studied. Their food is young **Pacific herring** and **Salmon Family** members. In 1975 an estimated 667,000 lampreys in the Strait of Georgia killed between 60 and 600 million juvenile fish!

river redhorse

Scientific name: *Moxostoma carinatum*
    (Cope, 1870)
Family: **Sucker**
Other common names: river mullet, greater redhorse, redfin redhorse, pavement-toothed redhorse, big-jawed sucker, big-toothed redhorse
French name: suceur ballot

Distribution: Found in the St. Lawrence River and nearby waters around Montréal, the Mississippi River near Ottawa, the Ausable River of lake Huron and the Grand River of Lake Erie in Canada. South to Florida and west to Ohio and Arkansas but sporadically distributed.

Characters: This species is distinguished by a short dorsal fin, a swimbladder with 3 chambers, lateral line scales 41–47, scales around the caudal peduncle usually 12–13, (rarely 15–16), lower lip at least 3 times wider than upper lip and almost straight along rear edge and without transverse lines or papillae across long, narrow plicae, pelvic fin origin anterior to midpoint of dorsal fin base, pharyngeal teeth molar-shaped and numbering 6–9 on lower half of tooth row. The mouth is slightly overhung by the snout. Gill rakers 26–30. Dorsal fin rays 12–15, anal rays 7–9, pectoral rays 15–19 and pelvic rays 8–10. Gut with 5–6 coils. Males have nuptial tubercles on the back of the head, snout, cheek and throat. Minute tubercles line scale margins on the upper flank, on dorsal, anal and caudal fin rays and on the anterior pectoral and pelvic fin rays. The back and upper flank are brown or bronze to olive- or lime-green, paling to a white to yellow belly. The flank may be silvery. There is often a golden sheen over the flank and belly. Dorsal, anal and caudal fins are pale red, leading edges of the pelvic fins are pale red, and of the pectoral and pelvic fins are white. Pectoral fins olive. There may be a thin vertical line at the caudal fin base. Upper flank scales have a dark pigment spot at their base. Breeding males have a head and midflank dark stripe ending above the anal

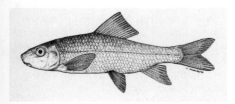

river redhorse

fin. The anal fin is longer in males than females. Females have thickened skin on the lower caudal peduncle. Peritoneum silvery.

Reaches 76.0 cm and 6.4 kg. The world, all-tackle angling record from Limestone Creek, Alabama weighed 2.52 kg and was caught in 1985.

Biology: River redhorses, as the name suggests, are found in moderate to large, fast rivers in deeper water over a silt-free bottom. In Québec they are reported from water less than 2 m deep. They are soon eliminated by pollution.

Food is aquatic insects such as mayflies, and particularly molluscs, crushed by the molar teeth, as well as other bottom invertebrates. Food is detected by sight.

Life span is at least 20 years with maturity at 10 years. Spawning may occur in large rivers or in the upper parts of large tributary streams after a migration. Canadian reproduction probably occurs at the end of May and into June at water temperatures over 18°C. Males arrive on gravel shoals before females and excavate nests using tail sweeps, head pushes and carrying with the mouth. Nests may be up to 2.4 m across and 30 cm deep. A male maintains a stationary position over the nest facing upstream until a female approaches when he darts back and forth across the nest. A second male joins the first synchronising his movements with the first until the female takes up a position between the 2 males. All 3 fish vibrate strongly, eggs are shed and fertilised, and buried in the gravel. Eggs are up to 4.0 mm in diameter and each female can have up to 31,049 eggs.

This species has formed a minor part of a commercial catch near Montréal in the past. It may be caught by sport fishermen in Ontario. Bone remains have been found in Indian middens. The Committee on the Status of Endangered Wildlife in Canada gave this species a status of "rare" in 1983.

river shiner

Scientific name: *Notropis blennius*
(Girard, 1856)
Family: **Carp**
Other common names: poor minnow,
straw-coloured minnow
French name: méné de rivière

Distribution: Found from southern Alberta, Saskatchewan and Manitoba south to Texas and Alabama.

Characters: This species and its relatives in the genus *Notropis* (typical **shiners**) are separated from other family members by usually

river shiner

having 7 branched dorsal fin rays following thin unbranched rays, protractile premaxillaries (upper lip separated from the snout by a groove), no barbels, large lateral line scales (fewer than 50), and a simple, s-shaped gut. It is identified by having 6 branched anal rays (sometimes 7), a mouth under the snout, the midflank stripe is indistinct, and there is no black spot at the caudal fin base. Lateral line scales 32–41. Dorsal fin branched rays 6–7, usually 7, pectoral rays 13–15 and pelvic rays 8. Pharyngeal teeth 2,4–4,2 with such variations as 2,4–4,1, 1,4–4,1, 3,4–4,1. Breeding males have small tubercles on the snout, top of the head, pectoral fin rays 2–7 and the anterior edges of the dorsal and anal fins. The back is straw, olive or light brown in colour, flanks are silvery and the belly white to cream. There is a silvery midflank stripe in living fish. The middle of the back has a stripe which passes on each side of the dorsal fin. Fins are clear. Peritoneum silvery. Reaches 13.2 cm.

Biology: River shiners are a schooling species favouring the main current of large rivers. They stay in deeper water when it is clear, venturing into shallows at night or under turbid conditions. Food is various aquatic insects, such as mayflies, caddisflies, water boatmen, various crustaceans, algae and other plant material. Life span is 4 years with males maturing at 1 year and females at 2 years. Spawning occurs in summer from June to August over sand and gravel. A female may contain over 3000 eggs of 1.0 mm diameter.

rock bass

Scientific name: *Ambloplites rupestris*
    (Rafinesque, 1817)
Family: **Sunfish**

Other common names: redeye, goggle eye, garguncle
French name: crapet de roche

Distribution: Found from southwestern Québec across southern Ontario including upper reaches of James Bay tributaries to Lake of the Woods, southern Manitoba and the Qu'Appelle River of eastern Saskatchewan. In the U.S.A. west of the Appalachian Mountains south to the Gulf Coast. Introduced both east and west of this central American range. Also introduced in England.

Characters: This species is identified by having 6 (range 5–7) anal fin spines and 10–13 dorsal fin spines. Soft dorsal fin rays 10–13, soft anal rays 9–11 and pectoral rays 12–15. Lateral line scales 35–51. The opercular or "ear flap" is short and not brightly coloured but black with a paler margin.

Overall colour above brown with a golden sheen to olive or green with dark saddles and bronze blotches. The belly is silvery to dusky white. Scales below the lateral line have a dark brown spot which line up to form 8–11 or more horizontal rows. The eye is red to orange and can be seen easily from above.

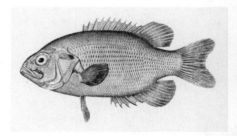

rock bass

The dorsal and anal fin spines are darker than the fin membranes. Anal spine tips are white. The pectoral fin is dusky, pale yellow to olive, and other fins are mottled black to brown with white spots or ovals posteriorly on vertical fins. Rapid colour changes from predominantly black to silvery with black blotches are not unusual. Peritoneum colourless.

Attains 43.0 cm and 1.7 kg. The world, all-tackle angling record weighed 1.36 kg and was caught in the York River, Ontario on 1 August 1974 by Peter Gulgin. This fish is also recognized as the Canadian record.

Biology: Rock bass are found in groups near rocks and docks in shallow, weedy lake margins and streams. In an Ontario lake, bass were observed to school during the day at 1–7 m in rocky areas. At night they were mostly inactive and settled on rocks or logs. Tagging programmes in southern Lake Ontario show that rock bass may disperse 241 km from a release point, although mean distance was only 15.5 km over 238 days. In Lake Erie there is a 35–40 km migration to a spawning site. Stream populations are more sedentary.

Food is a variety of aquatic insects, some surface insects, crustaceans such as crayfish and small fishes such as **yellow perch, Carp Family** members and their own species. Feeding takes place in the evening (1700–2100 hours) and the morning (0930–1200 hours). Life span is up to 18 years in aquaria but most live less than 13 years in nature. Life span in streams is only 5–6 years, much less than in lakes. Growth may be influenced by size of the water body inhabited. Under crowded conditions, stunted populations develop. Acid rain may cause faster growth in some lakes because less young survive to compete for food.

Maturity in an Ontario river was attained at 3–4 years, in lakes at 4–9 years. Spawning occurs in May to June after a movement into shallow water at 16–21°C in Wisconsin. Spawning starts at about 21°C. A river dwelling population in Ontario (Thames River) began spawning earlier at lower temperatures and lasted longer than in lake populations because of flooding which repeatedly stopped breeding. The season lasted from early May to late July while in Lake Opinicon, Ontario the season is late May to mid-June.

Older and larger males spawn earliest and thus have more chances to re-nest. Large males build larger nests and a nest was usually completed the day its construction was started. Nests in flowing water were elliptical, about 39–43 cm long. Lake Opinicon fish had peak reproduction at 21–33°C. The male excavates a circular nest up to about 27 cm across in gravel or swampy areas, adjacent to those of many other males, using his pectoral fins in particular as well as the anal fin. Most **sunfishes** use the tail to sweep debris from the nest site. Some stones are pushed to the nest rim with the open mouth in stream populations. Rooted plants are pulled outside the nest and dropped. Nests are about 1.9 times as large as the male.

There is considerable competition for females. Larger males are preferred by females. Spawning males become black. A male successful in attracting a female will remain next to her while she comes to lie on her side so her genital opening is pressed against that of the male. Both fish vibrate and rock back and forth in a head to tail position. A few (3–5) eggs are shed at intervals for an hour or longer. In Lake Opinicon, Ontario about 500 eggs are laid. A nest may contain eggs from more than 1 female and females will deposit eggs in several nests. Up to 11,000 adhesive, orange to golden eggs up to 2.1 mm in diameter are produced. The male defends the eggs until they hatch and fans them with his pectoral fins. He also protects the larvae for 9–10 days until they leave. Males and females can then spawn again and in Lake Opinicon, 24% of males do so. Defense posture includes erect fins and an open mouth.

It gives a good fight on light tackle and has tasty, white flesh. Rock bass form a minor part of the commercial catch in Ontario but is combined with **crappies** in statistics.

- Most accessible June through September.
- The shores of the Great Lakes and the St. Lawrence watershed.
- Ultralight spinning outfits used with four- to six-pound test line,a variety of 1/16–to 1/8–ounce spoons, spinners and jigs and small one to four-inch minnow-imitating plugs as well as worms or small live **minnows** fished on the bottom or under a float.

rock greenling

Scientific name: *Hexagrammos lagocephalus* (Pallas, 1810)
Family: **Greenling**
Other common names: fringed greenling, red rock trout
French name: sourcil de roche

Distribution: From southern California to the Bering Sea including British Columbia.

Characters: Dorsal fin with 20–23 spines and 20–25 soft rays. Anal fin with 21–24 soft rays. Scales are ctenoid on the body and top of

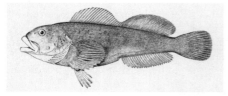

rock greenling

head, cycloid on the side of the head. Lateral lines are from the head below the dorsal fin to the middle of the soft rays, from the head to the tail, from the top of the gill opening to the base of the tail, from the gill opening below the pectoral fin and above the pelvic fins to a level above the rear half of the anal fin, and from the isthmus branching in two behind the pelvic fins along each side of the anal fin to the tail. This species is distinguished from other Canadian greenlings by having 5 lateral line canals, a large cirrus above each eye, and the first lateral line canal reaching beyond the middle of the soft rayed dorsal fin. Colour is variable. The background is green to brown with dark mottling which in males is red. Two red lines radiate back and down from the eye. The inside of the mouth is bluish. Fins are barred or blotched. Young fish have bright red eyes. Attains 61 cm and 1.3 kg. The world, all-tackle angling record weighed 0.83 kg and was caught at Adak, Alaska in 1988.

Biology: Common in shallow rocky areas on exposed coasts in summer at temperatures up to 13°C. In winter in the northwest Pacific it migrates to depths of 50–60 m and 300–400 m. Mature fish are found as deep as 510 m. Temperatures at these depths are –1.4 to 3.7°C. Spawning occurs in coastal areas with strong currents in June to September. Eggs are laid on algae. A sport fish often caught by shore fishermen. It is fished by bottom trawls off the former U.S.S.R.

rock grenadier

Scientific name: *Coryphaenoides rupestris* Gunnerus, 1765

Family: **Grenadier**
Other common names: roundnose grenadier, black grenadier
French name: grenadier de roche

Distribution: Found in the North Atlantic Ocean, in the west from Baffin Island and Davis Strait south to North Carolina and the Bahamas.

Characters: It is distinguished from other Canadian Atlantic coast grenadiers by having second dorsal fin rays shorter than anal fin rays, 6 branchiostegal rays, 7–8, usually 8, pelvic fin rays, pectoral rays 16–19, serrated anterior edge to the first 1–2 rays of the first dorsal fin, origin of the second dorsal fin behind the anus level, no scaleless areas on each side of the upper snout surface, and anal fin origin below the end of first dorsal fin. The first dorsal fin has 10–13 rays and the second dorsal 103–183. The anal fin has 104–193 rays. Scales have small, retrorse spines. The overall body colour is brown with fins grey, brownish-violet, or black. The flanks are a dull silvery-grey. The mouth and gill cavities and the underside of the head are dark brown. Reaches 100 cm.

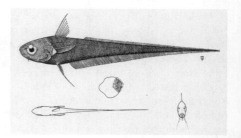

rock grenadier

Biology: This grenadier is found at depths of 350–2500 m and perhaps deeper. Temperature range where many specimens are caught is narrow: 3.5–4.5°C. It was not uncommon off Labrador and northern Newfoundland until overfished. It is known to migrate vertically to feed and most feeding is done in autumn and winter. Food is principally bottom dwelling but pelagic crustaceans with some squids and fish although diet appears to vary with area: Grand Bank rock grenadiers feed mainly on **lanternfish** for example and thalassobathyal populations feed mainly on fishes and large crustaceans. Curiously, the types of parasites found in this grenadier indicate that it must also feed on bottom living organisms which carry these parasites. Spawning occurs at various times of the year, perhaps with spring and autumn peaks. Up to 35,500 eggs may be produced which float and are 2.3–2.4 mm in diameter. Females grow faster and larger than males and both sexes are late maturers. They live at least 30 years. Aging methods using scales and otoliths give contradictory results. Canadian populations may migrate to spawning grounds south of Iceland and eggs and young drift to Canadian shores on the Irminger Current. The former U.S.S.R. had a commercial fishery for this grenadier in the Davis Strait and off Labrador and Newfoundland at 500–1000 m with catches as high as 83,000 tonnes, but the fishery is now incidental to that for **Greenland halibut**. The catch was mostly of 9–14 year old fish of 60–70 cm length. There was a Canadian catch of 9 tonnes in 1986 but usually none is reported. This grenadier produces fillets like those of **Atlantic cod** with a good fillet to total body weight ratio. The flesh is of high quality and rich in vitamins A, B12 and B2.

rock gunnel

Scientific name: *Pholis gunnellus*
   (Linnaeus, 1758)
Family: **Gunnel**
Other common names: butterfish, tansy, tissy,
   rock eel
French name: sigouine de roche

   Distribution: North Atlantic Ocean; in the west from Greenland and Labrador south to Delaware Bay.
   Characters: Dorsal fin with 73–86 spines (usually less than the related **banded gunnel**). Anal fin with 2 spines and 37–48 soft rays.

rock gunnel

Pelvics present. Pectorals with 10–13 rays. Colour varies with the background from yellowish to olive to brown or brown-red. There is a dark bar running obliquely from the eye to the dorsal fin and below the eye to behind the mouth. There is no pale band behind this bar as in the **banded gunnel**. There are 9–15 round, black spots with pale yellow edges along the dorsal fin base. The anal and caudal fins are usually yellow and there are 14–20 dark bars on the anal fin. The eyes may bear reflective white spots. Attains 30 cm.
   Biology: Found intertidally in rock pools hiding among weeds, in crevices and underneath rocks, and also down to 183 m on offshore banks. They may live 5 years. Food is worms, crustaceans, molluscs and fish eggs, with opportunity allowing other items like insect larvae to be taken by visual discovery. Rock gunnels are eaten by various sea birds and by inshore fishes like the **Atlantic cod** and **pollock**. Spawning occurs in winter after an offshore migration. Eggs are 1.7–2.2 mm in diameter and stick together in small balls on rocks, shell debris or in crevices and are guarded by the male and female. The parents roll the eggs together into a ball and curl around them. Larvae hatch after 2 months and are pelagic until they reach about 3 cm. Larval growth is about 2 mm a week in southern Canada. Larval survival is related to the timing of appearance of their food organisms which is itself determined by local oceanography and abundance of phytoplankton.

rock prickleback

Scientific name: *Xiphistes mucosus*
   (Girard, 1858)
Family: **Shanny**
Other common names: rock blenny, rock eel,
   black eel
French name: lompénie de roche

   Distribution: Found from southern California to southeastern Alaska including British Columbia.
   Characters: This species is related to the **ribbon** and **black pricklebacks** and like them lacks pelvic fins and a head crest, has 4 lateral line canals, and has the anal fin joined to the caudal fin. It is distinguished by having no anal fin spines, the dorsal fin origin near the head, and by colour. Dorsal fin spines are 71–78. There is 1 anal fin spine and 46–50 soft rays. The pectoral fins are reduced to

tiny flaps. Scales are found over the whole body. The lateral lines have numerous vertical branches. Colour is variable, from green-

rock prickleback

ish-black to greenish-grey or brown. Young fish have alternate dusky and white bars on the rear of the body. There are 2–3 dusky bars radiating back and down from the eye but these are edged in black (white in the **black prickleback**). Reaches 58.6 cm.

Biology: Found intertidally and down to 18 m or so on rocky coasts where there are masses of algae. They are found under algae when the tide is out and can survive from several hours to a day without being covered by water. Food is predominately red and green algae, which are protein and carbohydrate rich, and benthic diatoms. Some crustaceans and other small invertebrates are also eaten but these may be taken in accidentally with the algae. Fish less than a year old are carnivores but soon become completely herbivorous. They mature at 5 years of age and females probably grow larger and live longer than males, up to 11 years. Females lay eggs in masses approaching 10,000 eggs under rocks, which the male guards by wrapping his body around them. The male may guard 3 egg masses at once from different females. Spawning occurs in winter. Often caught on fish-baited hook and line and also used as bait for larger fish. It can be eaten.

rock sole

Scientific name: *Pleuronectes bilineatus* (Ayres, 1855)
Family: **Righteye Flounder**
Other common names: rock flounder, roughback sole, broadfin sole, white-bellied sole, two-lined dab
French name: sole du Pacifique

Distribution: Found from Korea to California and in British Columbia.

Characters: This species is characterised among Canadian Pacific fishes by the lateral line having both a strong arch over the pectoral fin and a short accessory branch. Scales on the eyed side are ctenoid and some are tuberculate. Blind side scales are cycloid. Scales extend onto the dorsal, anal and caudal fins. Lateral line scales 70–97. Mouth small, asymmetrical and with teeth best developed on the blind side. Dorsal fin with 65–82 rays, anal fin preceded by a sharp spine and with 50–65 rays. Caudal fin a broad v-shape. Gill rakers 6–12 on the first arch. Eyed side dark brown, olive to grey with dark or light, red or yellow mottles. Fins darkly mottled. Blind side white with yellow posteriorly. Reaches 61 cm.

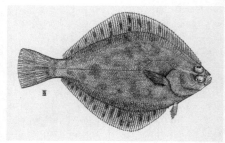

rock sole

Biology: A common Canadian species at 37–55 m but also from the surface to 575 m. Usually on sand or sand/pebble bottoms. The rock sole moves into shallow water in summer. Food is worms, clams, crustaceans, brittle stars, **sand lances** and **herrings**. The siphons of molluscs are an important food. Females live longer (22 as opposed to 15 years) and grow larger than males. Maturity is attained at about 4 years. Spawning occurs in February–April in Puget Sound. Large females lay up to 1.3 million yellow-orange eggs with a diameter of 0.92 mm. The eggs sink. This is an important commercial species with up to 3220 tonnes being caught annually in Canada. It is also popular with anglers.

rockfishes

Rockfishes are members of the **Scorpionfish Family** and are sometimes also called rockcods, as many inhabit rocky areas. The majority of Pacific coast species in this family are named rockfish (31 out of 36 species).

The unrelated **striped bass** may be referred to as rockfish.

rockhead

Scientific name: *Bothragonus swani*
(Steindachner, 1876)
Family: **Poacher**
Other common names: deep-pitted
sea-poacher, pithead poacher
French name: tête-de-roche

Distribution: Found from southeast Alaska through British Columbia to central California.

Characters: The rockhead is unique among poachers for its rounded, smooth plates on the body and the wide, bulging head with a deep pit on top. The pit contains club-shaped processes originating on the rear wall of the pit. There are no spines on the head. Cirri are minute. The first dorsal fin has 2–5 spines and the second dorsal fin 4–5 soft rays. The anal fin also has 4–5 rays. The large pectoral fin has 10–12 rays. Gill membranes are joined to the isthmus. Colour varies with the background. The body may be brown, orange or scarlet with dark brown or bluish bars. The fins are spotted white and the pectoral fin may have a white band at the base. Reaches 8.9 cm.

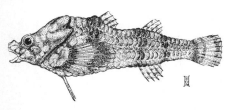

rockhead

Biology: The habitat of this species is from the intertidal zone down to 18 m. Often found in crevices and under weed-covered boulders but well camouflaged. They may live about 3 years. Food is small crustaceans. It is reputed to make a humming sound. There seems to be no confirmed explanation for the unusual pit on top of the head but one suggestion is that it mimics the openings of sponges and sea squirts, disguising the presence of this fish. Colouration of rockheads is similar to common tide pool sponges.

rocklings

Rocklings are found on the Arctic and Atlantic coasts of Canada. Two species, the **silver rockling** and the **threebeard rockling** are closely related and the third, the **fourbeard rockling**, is placed in a different subfamily of the **Cod Family**.

rockweed gunnel

Scientific name: *Apodichthys fucorum*
Jordan and Gilbert, 1880
Family: **Gunnel**
Other common names: rockweed blenny,
fucus blenny
French name: sigouine de varech

Distribution: From Baja California to central British Columbia.

Characters: This species, and the related **penpoint gunnel**, lack pelvic fins. They are distinguished by dorsal fin spine counts and

rockweed gunnel

the pen nib shaped spine in the **penpoint gunnel**. Dorsal fin spines 82–87. Anal fin with 1 spine and 28–38 soft rays. Pectoral fins very small with 11–12 rays. Bright green to red or brown depending on algal background. Occasionally with small spots along midflank. A narrow dark bar from the eye runs obliquely forwards and downwards. Attains 22.9 cm.

Biology: Found in rockweed (*Fucus*) in tidal pools and down to 9.1 m. It will remain under rockweed even out of water. Food is small crustaceans and molluscs. The green colour is apparently taken from the invertebrate food. Mink are known to eat this gunnel.

Ronquil Family

Scientific name: Bathymasteridae
French name: ronquilles

The ronquils or searchers are found in the North Pacific Ocean, where there are about 8 species with 3 reported from Canada's Pacific coast.

These fishes have a high and straight lateral line, just below the dorsal fin. The single, continuous dorsal and anal fins are long and most rays are soft, unbranched and branched. The pelvic fins are thoracic (below the pectoral fin base) and have 1 spine and 5 branched rays. The pectoral fin base is vertical. Both the caudal and pectoral fins are rounded. The palate is toothed.

Ronquils are members of the **Perch Order**. "Ronquil" is a diminutive of the Spanish and Greek words for snore or grunt.

They are bottom dwellers of rocky areas inshore but are not usually seen except by scientists and some divers.

See   **blue-eyed searcher**
       bluefin searcher
       northern ronquil

rosethorn rockfish

Scientific name: *Sebastes helvomaculatus*
    Ayres, 1859
Family: **Scorpionfish**
Other common names: deep-water scratchtail
French name: sébaste rosacé

Distribution: From Alaska to Baja California including British Columbia.

Characters: This scorpionfish is distinguished from its Canadian Pacific relatives by a unique colour pattern and the space

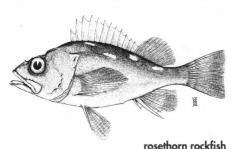

rosethorn rockfish

between the eyes on top of the head being strongly concave. Dorsal fin spies 12–14, usually 13, dorsal soft rays 12–14, usually 13. Anal fin soft rays 6–7, usually 6, with second anal spine thicker and longer than the third. Pectoral fin rays 15–18, usually 16, with 6–8 unbranched. Gill rakers 28–33. Vertebrae 26. Lateral line pores 34–45, scale rows below the lateral line 42–48. Coronal

and, usually, nuchal spines absent. The back and upper flanks are pink or orange-yellow mottled with olive or greenish-yellow. There are 4–5 characteristic white to pink or orange blotches on the upper flank which stand out in contrast to the darker background. The belly is white. The mouth cavity is whitish with some pink traces. The gill cavity is dusky and is black dorsally on the inside of the gill cover. Fins are pink with some yellow-green. There is a dusky patch on the operculum. The peritoneum is black, or grey with black dots. Reaches 41 cm.

Biology: Found on soft bottoms at 92–550 m. Young are born in June in British Columbia. Half the population is mature at 22 cm for males and 20 cm for females in Canadian waters.

rosy soldierfish

Scientific name: *Hoplostethus mediterraneus*
    Cuvier, 1829
Family: **Slimehead**
Other common names: Mediterranean
    slimehead, rough fish, black-mouthed
    alfonsin, poisson-montre
French name: hoplostète argenté

Distribution: Found in the Atlantic Ocean and Mediterranean Sea and off Atlantic Canada.

Characters: The elongate spine at the angle of the preopercle bone on the side of the head, the large mucous head cavities, and the 8–12 scutes on the belly are distinctive. There is a spine above the top of the gill opening. Dorsal fin spines 4–7 (which distin-

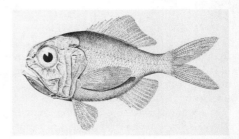

rosy soldierfish

guishes it from **Darwin's slimehead** with 8 spines, the only other family member in Canada), soft rays 12–14. Anal fin with 3 spines and 9–10 soft rays. Pectoral fin rays 14–16. Lateral line scales 25–30. Overall colour is rosy or pale pink on the back, head and upper flank. The lower flanks and belly are silvery or blackish. The iris is iridescent green. The cheeks and head cavity bottoms are silvery. The peritoneum, mouth and gill cavities are black. Fins are bright red with fin rays darker. Reaches 30 cm.

Biology: Known only from a single specimen taken off Browns Bank at 439 m in 1968. Usually found at 250–914 m. Food is bottom-swimming crustaceans, fishes and cephalopods. Often very abundant and frequently caught in trawls or on hooks set at several hundred metres off Europe and Africa. Off Europe spawning occurs in autumn.

rosyface shiner

Scientific name: *Notropis rubellus*
   (Agassiz, 1850)
Family: **Carp**
Other common names: skipjack
French name: tête rose

Distribution: Found from southwestern Québec west to southeastern Lake Superior but absent from the rest of Lake Superior, throughout the southern Great Lakes and southern Ontario, and in the Red River of Manitoba. In the U.S.A. south to Virginia and northern Alabama.

Characters: This species and its relatives in the genus *Notropis* (typical **shiners**) are separated from other family members by usually having 7 branched dorsal fin rays following thin unbranched rays, protractile premaxillaries (upper lip separated from the snout by a groove), no barbels, large lateral line scales (fewer than 50), and a simple, s-shaped gut. It is separated from its relatives by body depth being less than head length, dorsal fin origin is posterior to the pelvic fin insertion, pectoral fin rays usually 11–14, snout length is greater than eye diameter in adults, and flank pigment ends at or below the lateral line. Dorsal fin branched rays 6–7, anal branched rays 8–10, pectoral rays 11–14 and pelvic rays 8. Lateral line scales 36–45. Pharyngeal teeth 2,4–4,2, with a wide range of variants. Breeding tubercles in males found on the head, in a row of about 12 on the lower jaw,

scales predorsally and above lateral line, the latter edged with 1–5 tubercles, and upper pectoral fin surface. The back is olive to yellowish or bluish, often with a thin dusky stripe, flanks silvery with a thin, iridescent green or emerald or orange stripe above the lateral line, and belly is silvery-white. Scales are outlined with pigment. Fins are transparent. Breeding males are orange-red on the head, intense blue on the back, a light red on the belly and pink on the dorsal, anal, pectoral and caudal fin bases. There is a scarlet bar at the gill opening. Peritoneum silvery with dark speckles. Reaches 8.9 cm.

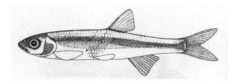

rosyface shiner

Biology: This shiner is found in clear streams and rivers over gravel and sand in fast water. It does not tolerate turbidity or silt. Food comprises aquatic and terrestrial insects, diatoms and algae. Life span is 3 years with maturity attained at 1 year. Spawning females contain up to 1482 eggs which are 1.2 mm in diameter. Fertilised eggs are said to turn bright yellow. Orange or pink-orange eggs are shed over gravel depressions near riffles when groups of 8–25 fish quiver and thrash for 5–6 seconds, breaking the water surface. The eggs are adhesive and fall in between the gravel. Spawning in Ontario is from mid-May to late June at 20–27°C. Spawning may occur over **hornyhead chub** and **lamprey** nests or with **common shiners**. Males engage in head butting and parallel swimming but do not defend a defined territory. This species has been used as a bait fish in the U.S.A. and is a brilliant aquarium fish although difficult to keep.

rosylip sculpin

Scientific name: *Ascelichthys rhodorus*
   Jordan and Gilbert, 1880
Family: **Sculpin**
Other common names: none

French name: chabot à lèvres roses

Distribution: Found from southeast Alaska to California including British Columbia.

Characters: This sculpin is distinguished by its lack of pelvic fins and scales. The anal papilla is small and conical. The belly

rosylip sculpin

between the anus and the anal fin is constricted. There is a stout, skin-covered, preopercular spine with an upward hook. First dorsal fin spines 7–10, second dorsal soft rays 17–20. Anal fin rays 13–16, and pectoral rays 16–18 with the lower 7 finger-like. The lateral line has 34–38 pores. There is a large, branched cirrus at the rear margin of the eye and 5–9 filamentous cirri above the pectoral fin base. Overall colour is black or olive-brown to grey fading to yellowish-grey on the belly. The lateral line canal is pale. The top of the eye and top of the head have fine, light blue vermiculations in some fish. Fin margins are pale except the dorsal fin margin which is bright red. The lips may be a rosy-red and the area behind the pectoral fins may be red. Reaches 15 cm.

Biology: This species is common in tide pools and can be caught under rocks when the tide is out. It can respire in the air for several hours. It is also found on rock reefs, among boulders and rock crevices down to 15 m and in kelp beds. Life span may exceed 3 years. Food is gammarid and caprellid crustaceans.

rough hookear

Scientific name: *Artediellus scaber* Knipowitsch, 1907
Family: **Sculpin**
Other common names: hamecon
French name: hameçon rude

Distribution: Found in the western Arctic of Canada from Somerset Island westwards to the Beaufort Sea. Also west to the Barents Sea across northern Eurasia.

Characters: This sculpin and its Arctic-Atlantic relatives, the **Atlantic** and **snowflake hookears**, are distinguished by having the upper preopercular spine pointed and strongly hooked upwards, the margin of the first dorsal fin is often dark and both dorsal fins in males are spotted or barred. This species has cirri and conical tubercles on the nape and anterior back and lacks nasal spines. First dorsal fin spines 7–9, second dorsal rays 12–14 and anal rays 10–13. Pectoral rays 18–23. Lateral line pores 21–31. The head is greyish-brown and the flanks lighter with large, irregular spots which appear as bands in some fish. The male spiny dorsal fin has a black spot at the rear. All fins have orange bands. Pectoral fin tips white. Reaches 8.4 cm.

rough hookear

Biology: This sculpin is found on mud-sand bottoms often in brackish (10–15‰) waters at 0–100 m and temperatures around 0°C and up to 5°C. It may burrow into bottom sediments. Food is various bottom invertebrates such as crustaceans and worms. Females about 3–4 years old are mature. Life span is about 7 years. Spawning probably occurs in August–September with about 100 eggs of 2.7 mm diameter being produced.

rough pomfret

Scientific name: *Taractes asper* Lowe, 1843
Family: **Pomfret**
Other common names: none
French name: castagnole rugueuse

Distribution: Found from Japan to Alaska in the North Pacific Ocean including off the Queen Charlotte and Vancouver islands but world-wide in temperate to tropical waters.

Characters: This species is distinguished from its Canadian relatives by having the adult dorsal and anal fins covered with scales, the head profile between the eyes being flat or slightly convex and the large scales. Dorsal fin rays 31–35, anal rays 22–26, and pectoral rays 18–20. The lateral

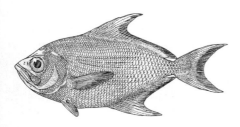

rough pomfret

line is indistinct or absent and there are 43–47 scales in lateral series. Posterior large scales bear sharp, longitudinal ridges and, in young fish, spines. There is no caudal peduncle keel. Overall colour is dark brown with a copper or golden sheen on the flank. There is a white crescent on the caudal fin in some fish. The tongue is dusky in contrast to the mouth lining. The dorsal and anal fins bear alternate pale and dark bands. The pectoral fins are pale and the pelvic fins dark. Reaches 50 cm and probably larger.

Biology: A pelagic, offshore species with little known of its biology. First reported from Canada in 1981.

rough sagre

Scientific name: *Etmopterus princeps* Collett, 1904
Family: **Sleeper Shark**
Other common name: great lanternshark
French name: sagre rude

Distribution: From the Scotian Shelf of Nova Scotia south to New Jersey. Also in Europe and south to Mauritania.

Characters: This species is distinguished by the absence of an anal fin, obvious spines in the dorsal fins, teeth in the upper jaw with

5 cusps the central cusp being largest, and body with hooked, spiny scales. Young fish may have only 3 cusps in the upper jaw.

rough sagre

Lower jaw teeth have a single, very oblique cusp with a notch on its outer margin and form a cutting edge. Brownish-black or black above and darker below with no obvious markings, except the posterior, lower corner of the second dorsal fin can be whitish and the anterior surface of the gill slits are whitish. There is no spot between the eyes. The skin has minute photophores (light-emitting organs). Maximum length about 75 cm.

Biology: This species is found on continental slopes on or near the bottom where it is not uncommon. It is found at depths from 567 m to 2213 m. Males mature at about 55 cm. Diet and other details of biology are not known but it is probably ovoviviparous and feeds on fish. There is no fishery and this shark lives too deep to be of interest to anglers.

rough scad

Scientific name: *Trachurus lathami* Nichols, 1920
Family: **Jack**
Other common names: chinchard frappeur
French name: saurel maxécus

Distribution: Found from Nova Scotia to Argentina.

Characters: This species is distinguished from its Canadian Atlantic coast relatives by not having a deep, compressed body but an elongate one with maximum depth 20–25% of fork length, by having 65–77 enlarged scales or scutes in the lateral line all of the same size and a long pectoral fin extending beyond the soft dorsal fin origin. There are no fleshy tabs on the inside rear edge of the gill cavity. There are no finlets behind the dorsal and anal fins. The first dorsal fin has 8 spines, which can be folded into a groove, the second 1 spine and 25–34 soft rays. The anal fin has 3 spines and 23–30 soft rays. Overall colour is silvery, darker on the back, often bluish or blue-green, and with a black spot on the edge of the gill cover sometimes present. Reaches 40 cm.

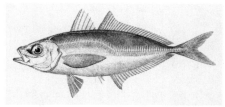

rough scad

Biology: Found first on Georges and Browns banks in 1968, along the Scotian Shelf in 1979 and in a mackerel trap in St. Margarets Bay, Nova Scotia, in 1981. The latter is a northern range record. Little appears to be known of its biology but young are numerous in the Gulf Stream off the Florida Keys. It is a schooling species found near the bottom at 50–90 m but also in near surface waters. Food is small invertebrates. Spawning probably occurs offshore from about April to June in the Caribbean area.

rough trunkfish

Scientific name: *Lactophrys trigonus*
(Linnaeus, 1758)
Family: **Boxfish**
Other common names: buffalo trunkfish
French name: coffre tuberculé

Distribution: Found from Brazil to Massachusetts and possibly into Atlantic Canada.

rough trunkfish

Characters: The rough trunkfish has a curved spine projecting from the lower rear corner of the carapace in contrast to its relative the **smooth trunkfish** which has no horns. The plates are finely tuberculate. Olive above to brown below. The plates are edged in black. A black blotch between the eye and pectoral fin and another blotch in midflank. Upper body plates have rosettes of pale green, bluish or white spots. The largest adults are blue-grey or pale green, and the carapace is covered in white spots, lines and scrawls. The dorsal fin base is dark. Attains 53 cm.

Biology: Reported from off the Nova Scotia Banks in 1953 but no other confirmatory captures made. Usually found in seagrass beds feeding on invertebrates and algae. When removed from the water it makes a loud grunting noise. This a favourite food fish in the Caribbean but has been implicated in ciguatera poisoning.

roughback sculpin

Scientific name: *Chitonotus pugetensis*
(Steindachner, 1876)
Family: **Sculpin**
Other common names: none
French name: chabot à dos rugueux

Distribution: Found from northern British Columbia to Baja California.

Characters: This sculpin is distinguished from its Pacific coast relatives by a very deep notch between rays 3 and 4 of the first dorsal fin, the long first dorsal spine, and the rough, large ctenoid scales covering the body above the lateral line and the upper head. There is a large anal papilla with a curved tip. There are nasal, supraorbital and parietal spines, the latter double. There are 4 preopercular spines, the uppermost the largest and antler-shaped with 3 upper spines. First dorsal fin spines 8–11, second dorsal soft rays 14–18. Anal fin rays 14–17, pectoral rays 16–18 and pelvic fin with 1 spine and 2–3 soft rays. Lateral line scales enlarged, 36–39. Cirri are large and flat on the snout, eyeball and upper rear eye margin. There may be cirri at the end of the upper jaw and on the opercular flap. The back and upper flank are grey-green to brown with 4 dark brown saddles. Lower flank and belly grey to whitish.

The spiny dorsal fin margin is dark. The anal fin has a dark band with the fin margin light. The dorsal and caudal fins have brown

roughback sculpin

bands. Males become dark during the breeding season, there is a red blotch below the lateral line at the soft dorsal fin level and a red, orange or white patch over each eye. Reaches 23 cm.

Biology: Reported down to 142 m but usually common in shallower water. It may bury itself in sand leaving only the back and eyes visible and is active at night. Food is crustaceans such as shrimps. Eggs are pink or light green and about 1.0 mm in diameter. Total number of eggs per female averages 1043 per clutch in California where 3 clutches are produced in an extended spawning season, peaking in spring.

rougheye rockfish

Scientific name: *Sebastes aleutianus*
  (Jordan and Evermann, 1898)
Family: **Scorpionfish**
Other common names: blackthroated rockfish,
  blacktip rockfish, buoy keg
French name: sébaste à oeil épineux

Distribution: Found from the Aleutian Islands south to California including British Columbia.

Characters: This scorpionfish is uniquely characterised on the Pacific coast of Canada by having 2–10 spines lining the lower rim of the eye socket. Dorsal fin spines 13–14, usually 13, dorsal soft rays 12–15, usually 14. Anal fin soft rays 6–8, usually 7, second spine twice as thick as third and about equal in young or somewhat shorter in adults. Pectoral fin rays 17–19, usually 18. Gill rakers 34–39. Vertebrae 27. Lateral line pore count 29–34, scale rows below lateral line

47–55. All head spines are present although the coronal spines may be absent. The body is orange-red, red or red-black, becoming pink below. There are 3 dark cross bands on top of the head. Flanks may have faint bars, blotches, or spots. Fins reddish, tipped with black. Dusky blotch on operculum. Mouth and gill cavity white to pink with black blotches. Peritoneum silvery-grey with black dots. Reaches 96 cm.

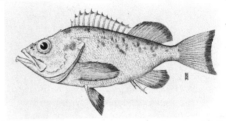

rougheye rockfish

Biology: Common in offshore waters but rare inshore. Reported by Russian trawlers from Dickins, Union and Hodgkins guyots off the coast of British Columbia. Found on the bottom from 92–732 m. Young are born in April in British Columbia. Half the population is mature at 43 cm for males and 45 cm for females in Canadian waters. Maximum age is estimated to be over 100 years. Caught on deep longlines in Japan.

roughhead grenadier

Scientific name: *Macrourus berglax*
  Lacepède, 1802
Family: **Grenadier**
Other common names: smooth-spined rattail,
  onion-eye, ingminniset
French name: grenadier berglax

Distribution: Found in the North Atlantic Ocean, in the west from Baffin Island and Davis Strait south to Georges Bank and New York.

Characters: It is distinguished from other Canadian Atlantic coast grenadiers by having second dorsal fin rays shorter than anal fin rays, 6 branchiostegal rays, 8 pelvic rays, serrated anterior edge to the first 1–2 rays of the first dorsal fin, and origin of the second dorsal fin in front of the anus level. The first dorsal fin has 11–13 rays, the second dorsal fin about 124. The anal fin has about 148 rays. Pectoral fin rays number 17–20. Scales have a median keel of 6–12 small spines

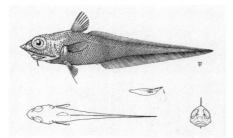

roughhead grenadier

forming obvious ridges along the body. Head scales are non-overlapping. Overall colour is an ash-grey becoming darker on the rear edge of posterior scales and on the chest. The first dorsal and pectoral fins are dusky and the anal fin has a dark, marginal band. Reaches over 100 cm.

Biology: Found principally at about 200–600 m on the bottom of the continental slope but may be found as deep as 2740 m. Most numerous at –2.0–3.5°C. An Inuit name for this species "ingminniset" means "it bellows when dying", and refers to the sounds produced by the drumming muscles on the swimbladder. Spawning occurs in winter and early spring with up to 71,000 eggs being produced. Egg diameter is as large as 4.02 mm. Females grow faster than males and live at least 25 years. Age determination from scales and otoliths is difficult because the growth rings are not clearly defined. Food includes worms, molluscs, amphipods and brittle stars. Larger grenadiers eat fish such as **capelin**, shrimp and bivalve molluscs. This grenadier is eaten by **Atlantic cod**. There is no fishery for this species in particular, but it is caught in other fisheries and used for its liver which is canned and turned into a medicinal oil. The white, flaky flesh is good eating but the hard, thick scales render its preparation difficult on a commercial scale.

roughnose grenadier

Scientific name: *Trachyrhynchus murrayi* Günther, 1887

Family: **Grenadier**
Other common names: Murray's longsnout grenadier
French name: grenadier-scie

Distribution: Found in the North Atlantic Ocean including Atlantic Canada in the west.

Characters: This grenadier is distinguished from its Canadian Atlantic coast relatives by having the fin rays of the second dorsal fin as long or longer than the anal fin rays, and the gill slit lacks a fold of skin over the upper and lower parts. This species also has a true, but small, caudal fin, unique among the Canadian grenadiers. There are 5–11 enlarged scales in front of the anus. The first dorsal fin has 10–11, usually 11, rays. Pectoral fin rays 21, pelvic rays 7. Overall colour is grey-brown. Reaches 45 cm and probably larger.

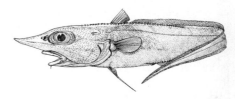

roughnose grenadier

Biology: First reported from a single specimen caught off Hamilton Inlet, Labrador in 1954, this species is now known to occur in the Davis Strait and the Labrador Sea. This species is recorded elsewhere at 530–1630 m. Females are believed to mature at about 30 cm and spawning in Europe takes place in March or April. Little is known of its biology.

roughscale grenadier

Scientific name: *Coryphaenoides acrolepis* (Bean, 1883)
Family: **Grenadier**
Other common names: Pacific grenadier
French name: grenadier à écailles rudes

Distribution: Found from Japan to California including British Columbia and at Ocean Station Papa (50°N, 145°W).

Characters: This species is distinguished from its Pacific Canadian coast relatives by having the anus immediately in front of the anal fin, no black, scaleless area on the abdomen, 6 branchiostegal rays, pelvic fin rays 8–9, usually 8, teeth in the upper jaw not in 1–2 distinct rows, a large eye (more than one-fifth head length), scales over much of the head except under the snout, first dorsal fin soft rays 8–11, the entire eye rim black, outer pelvic ray short (50–70% of head

roughscale grenadier

length), and enlarged, tubercle-like scales on the entire edge of the snout. Pectoral fin rays are 19–22. The second dorsal fin has about 109 or more rays. The anal fin has about 94 or more rays. Spine rows on the scales vary from 3–5. Spines are small but strong. Scales along the flank number about 195. Overall colour is grey-brown to chocolate-brown. Fins darken with age and are black in large adults. The gill cavity and peritoneum are black. Reaches at least 87 cm.

Biology: Specimens have been caught off Vancouver Island at 1998–2189 m, in the Juan de Fuca Strait and off northern British Columbia at 1830–2745 m. Ocean Station Papa records are mostly of pelagic juveniles. This species is found usually from 600–2500 m in the North Pacific Ocean but may be as shallow as 155 m. Some fish have been caught over depths of 8100 m but were probably swimming pelagically above this bottom. Stomach contents bear this out, since they contain bathypelagic food items. Eggs are up to 2.1 mm in diameter and number up to 118,612. It is a by-catch of the longline fisheries and has been sold as fresh fillets in the U.S.A.

roughscale lanternfish

Scientific name: *Myctophum asperum* Richardson, 1845
Family: **Lanternfish**
Other common names: none
French name: lanterne rugueuse

Distribution: Found in the Atlantic, Indian and Pacific oceans including off Nova Scotia.

Characters: This species and its Atlantic coast relatives, the **lunar, metallic** and **spotted lanternfishes**, are distinguished by lacking photophores near the dorsal body edge, the PLO photophore is above the upper pectoral fin base while the second PVO photophore is below this base, there are 2 Prc and 2 Pol photophores, the PVO photophores are not horizontal but inclined while the VO series is level, the SAO series is straight or almost so, and the first SAO is behind the third VO. This species is separated from its relatives by having 7 or less AOp photophores with 0–1 over the anal fin base, 14–16 gill rakers and the SAO photophores in a curved line. Dorsal fin rays 12–14, anal rays 17–20 and pectoral rays 12–16. AO photophores 12–14. Lateral line organs 38–39. Adult males have 5–7 overlapping, scale-like structures forming a supracaudal luminous gland. This gland begins to develop at 3.2 cm. Adult females have 1–3 heart-shaped patches forming the infracaudal luminous gland. This gland begins to develop at 4.8–5.2 cm. Reaches over 8.5 cm.

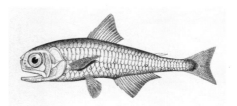

roughscale lanternfish

Biology: First reported east of Georges Bank in 1988 based on only 2 specimens. Depth range in the Atlantic Ocean is 425–750 m by day and from the surface to 125 m by night, mostly at the surface. Little is known of its biology.

roughscale sole

Scientific name: *Clidoderma asperrimum* (Temminck and Schlegel, 1846)
Family: **Righteye Flounder**
Other common names: none
French name: plie rugueuse

Distribution: Found from Korea and Japan to southern British Columbia and Oregon.

Characters: This species is separated from its Pacific Canadian relatives by the absence of scales on the blind side and by the rough tubercles covering the eyed side. The tubercles bear hair-like spines. Large tubercles are arranged in 6 longitudinal rows There are smaller tubercles around the eyes, on the snout and in radiating rows on the dorsal and ventral body edges and on the inner parts of the dorsal and anal fin rays. The lateral line has a low arch over the pectoral fin and a short branch over the eye. The mouth is small and asymmetrical, being longer on the blind side. Teeth are better developed on the blind side of the jaws. Dorsal fin rays long, 75–94, anal rays long, 61–75. Caudal fin rounded. The eyed side is brown and the blind side grey. Reaches 55 cm.

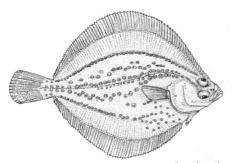

roughscale sole

Biology: The Canadian records are of 2 specimens from Esteban Deep at 339–348 m off western Vancouver Island and 1 specimen in the Dixon Entrance off the northern Queen Charlotte Islands at 439–549 m. This species is found on mud bottoms.

roughscale wirewing

Scientific name: *Bathypterois quadrifilis*
    Günther, 1878
Family: **Tripodfish**
Other common names: none
French name: cran-tactile losange

Distribution: Found in both the North and South Atlantic oceans including off the coast of Canada.

Characters: This species is separated from its Canadian relatives by having minute eyes, the upper 2 pectoral fin rays greatly

elongated, the lowest pectoral ray long and thick, and scales behind the lower pectoral fin have strong spines. Dorsal fin rays

roughscale wirewing

12–15, anal rays 8–10, pectoral rays 10–13 and pelvic rays 9. Lateral line scales 57–63. Overall colour in preservative is black or dark brown with the edges of scale pockets and lateral line pores white. The adipose fin is clear. Attains 18 cm standard length.

Biology: A single Canadian specimen was caught off the Scotian Shelf on the bottom at 1010–1020 m in 1984. This is a northern range extension for the species. It is found from 402 m to 1408 m.

roughspine sculpin

Scientific name: *Triglops macellus*
    (Bean, 1883)
Family: **Sculpin**
Other common names: none
French name: faux-trigle épineux

Distribution: Found from the Bering Sea to Washington including British Columbia.

Characters: This species and its relative, the **ribbed sculpin**, are distinguished from other Canadian Pacific sculpins by the oblique folds of skin below the lateral line running postero-ventrally, tiny scales on the fold edges, fine prickles over the upper eyeball, the slender body tapering to the tail and scales covering the flank above the lateral

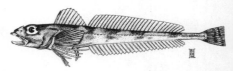

roughspine sculpin

line, the top of the head and on the dorsal, pectoral and caudal fin rays. The roughspine sculpin is separated from its relative by lacking large upper flank scales and by the single row of prickles on the eyeball. Body folds number 1–2 per lateral line scute. First dorsal fin spines 10–11, second dorsal rays 27–31, anal rays 27–31, and pectoral rays 15–17 with the lower 5–7 markedly fingerlike. Lateral line plates 50–53. There is a sharp nasal spine and 3–4 small, sharp preopercular spines. Males have a large papilla which curves forward. The back is olivegreen or light brown fading to a cream or white belly. The back has 5 dark saddles. The throat is silvery. The dorsal, pectoral and caudal fins have faint brown bars. There is a black spot at the tip of the first dorsal fin between the first 2 spines. Males have a dark spot on the side of the snout. Reaches 25 cm.

Biology: This species has been recorded from 18–275 m, but is not common.

roughtail skate

Scientific name: *Bathyraja trachura*
(Gilbert, 1892)
Family: **Skate**
Other common names: black skate
French name: raie à queue rude

Distribution: Found from the Bering Sea to British Columbia and Baja California.

Characters: This species is separated from its Canadian Pacific relatives by having a soft and flabby snout with its cartilaginous support

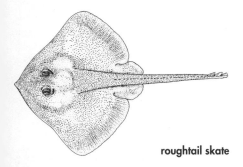

roughtail skate

thin and flexible, cartilaginous supports of the pectoral fins almost reaching the snout tip, no scapular thorns (large shoulder spines), underside almost free of prickles, and no nuchal thorns. There are 21–30 median tail thorns and fine prickles cover the dorsal disc and tail. There are 26–33 pointed teeth rows in the

upper jaw of males and 30–35 flattened teeth in a quincunx in females. The alar thorns of the male are stout, hook-like and in 20–24 longitudinal and 4–8 transverse rows. The egg capsule is smooth with long, slender horns and is about 12 cm by 8 cm. Both sides of disc and tail are a uniform plum brown, black or slate-grey. The tip of the anterior pelvic lobes, cloaca margin, gill slits and mouth are whitish. Reaches 89 cm long and 56 cm wide.

Biology: The depth range for this species is 490–1993 m. The British Columbia specimens are from off southern Vancouver Island at 731–743 m and off the southern Queen Charlotte Islands at 1134–1262 m.

roughtail stingray

Scientific name: *Dasyatis centroura*
(Mitchill, 1815)
Family: **Stingray**
Other common names: stingaree, clam cracker
French name: pastenague à queue épineuse

Distribution: Found from New Brunswick south to Florida and possibly to South America. Also in the eastern Atlantic Ocean and the Mediterranean Sea.

Characters: This species is distinguished from its Atlantic coast relative, the **pelagic stingray**, by the possession of a long, low ventral finfold and the pointed snout. The disc has many spines with a concentration in the shoulder region. The tail has many rows of small spines. The upper surface is olive-brown and the lower surface is off-white. Reaches 4.2 m

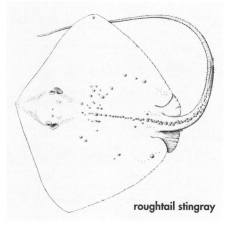

roughtail stingray

in length and 2.1 m wide. The world, all-tackle angling record weighed 133.35 kg and was caught in the Gambia in 1988.

Biology: Known only from a single Canadian specimen from the Northumberland Strait in 1953. It is a summer stray in northern waters. It is found from the shallows down to about 200 m. Food is crabs, clams, snails, squids and worms. Young are produced after a 4 month gestation in autumn and early winter. There are usually 2–4 young with a disc width of 34–36 cm at birth.

round goby

Scientific name: *Neogobius melanostomus*
(Pallas, 1814)
Family: **Goby**
Other common names: Caspian round goby
French name: gobie arrondie

Distribution: Found from the Aegean to the Black and Caspian seas and introduced to the St. Clair River, southwestern Ontario, lakes Superior and Erie and the Welland Canal.

Characters: This goby is separated from the only other goby in the Great Lakes, the **tubenose goby**, by not having a very elongate anterior nostril which hangs over the lip. First dorsal fin spines 5–7, usually 6, second dorsal fin with 1 spine and 11–17 soft rays, anal fin with 1 spine and 9–14 soft rays, and pectoral fin with 16–20 branched rays. Gill rakers 9–12. Vertebrae 31–34. Caudal peduncle depth is two-thirds its length. The tongue is truncate or slightly notched. Females are smaller than the male. Mature males have larger dorsal and anal fins. Overall colour is yellowish-grey or brownish-grey with large,

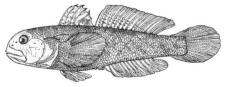

round goby

dark brown flank blotches. The first dorsal fin has a black blotch posteriorly. When spawning, males are black with the dorsal, caudal and anal fins white-edged or yellow, although the first dorsal margin can be black

and there may be practically no margin to the anal fin. The black spot on the first dorsal fin can still be seen against the light. There are no free tips to fin rays. Reaches 25 cm.

Biology: The origin of this species is probably from ballast water discharged from ships coming from Europe. This species is found in inshore waters at depths to about 20 m, sometimes to 60 m, on gravel, shell or sand bottoms. It also enters rivers. Larvae live near the bottom. Maturity is attained in the second year by females and in the third year by males in the native habitat. Life span can exceed 4 years. Males die after spawning. Molluscs predominate with significant amounts of crustaceans in the north Caspian Sea but this can vary annually with crustaceans becoming predominant. They feed most heavily in the post-spawning period in July and August. Other important foods are bivalves, polychaetes, chironomids, fish eggs and small fishes. They eat zebra mussels but then pass chemicals up the food chain to valuable **bass**, **walleye**, and **trout**. Spawning takes place at the end of April to August in near shore areas of the north Caspian Sea. There may be repeat spawning, up to 6 times every 18–20 days, as indicated by captive specimens. Peak spawning occurs at 15°C. Young fish have been found on the U.S. side of the St. Clair River indicating that spawning occurs in fresh water in the Great Lakes. Eggs are attached to rocks and guarded by the male. Fecundity reaches 6,177 eggs. Eggs are ovoid with a sharp apex and measure 3.9 by 2.2 mm. Pike-perch (relatives of **sauger** and **walleye**) are predators in the native habitat. It is an important food species in the Black Sea marketed fresh and canned.

round herring

Scientific name: *Etrumeus teres*
(DeKay, 1842)
Family: **Herring**
Other common names: Atlantic round herring, red-eye round herring, shadine rond
French name: shadine

Distribution: Found off East Africa, in the Red Sea, Japan, southern Australia, east and west coasts of the Americas and Hawaii. Found occasionally in the Bay of Fundy and around southern Nova Scotia.

Characters: This species is unique in its possession of a w-shaped pelvic scute, a modified scale in the pelvic region of the belly. There are no other belly scutes. Branchiostegal rays are 11–15. Dorsal fin rays 16–22. Anal fin rays 10–13. The pelvic fins lie behind the dorsal fin base and have 7 branched rays. Pectoral fin branched rays 13–16. Both the pectoral and pelvic fins have an elongate axillary scale at their bases. Scales in lateral series 48–58 but usually lost on capture. Back olive-green in life to brown in preserved fish, sides silvery and the junction of these two meeting as a clear midlateral line. The snout tip is dark. Fins are clear. Reaches 25 cm standard length.

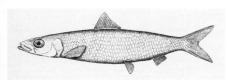

round herring

Biology: Round herrings reach Canada in warmer years. Occasional specimens are caught and sometimes large schools are trapped in weirs. It occurs inshore in the north but offshore in the south along the American coast. Food is zooplankton. Spawning in the southern U.S.A. takes place in winter, offshore in water several metres deep. This species is commercially important in various parts of the world and is caught with purse seines.

round scad

Scientific name: *Decapterus punctatus*
(Cuvier, 1829)
Family: **Jack**
Other common names: none
French name: comète quiaquia

Distribution: From Nova Scotia south to Brazil and in the eastern Atlantic Ocean.

Characters: This species is distinguished from its Canadian Atlantic coast relatives by not having a deep, compressed body, but an elongate one with maximum depth 20–25% of fork length, by having 77–108 scales and posteriorly enlarged scutes in the lateral line, and 3–14 dark spots on the anterior and the

curved parts of the lateral line. There are 8 spines in the first dorsal fin and 1 spine precedes the soft dorsal fin. Soft dorsal fin rays

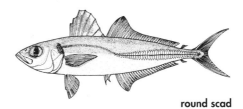

round scad

29–35, soft anal rays 25–31, and pectoral soft rays 18–20. There is 1 dorsal and 1 anal finlet. The lateral line is more strongly arched and caudal peduncle scutes are more vertically enlarged than in the **mackerel scad**. The back is greenish to grey-green, the flanks silvery and the belly is dusky to whitish. There are 1–14 small, black spots along the anterior lateral line. There is a black spot at the edge of the gill cover and a narrow, yellowish stripe along the flank. The membrane just inside the upper jaw (the oral valve) is transparent or dusky. Reaches 30 cm.

Biology: First caught in 1983 off Sable Island during experimental fishing operations. These specimens are northern range records. Small juvenile round scad appear to prefer oceanic waters and are found over 400 km offshore. They are pelagic while adults prefer inshore bottom waters, down to about 183 m. This is a schooling species. Food is small, planktonic invertebrates, mostly copepods but also snail larvae, pteropods and crustaceans. Spawning occurs offshore year round with a peak in spring. This species is used mostly for bait as it is small for sport fishing but it is sold fresh as food.

round skate

Scientific name: *Raja fyllae* Lütken, 1887
Family: **Skate**
Other common names: round ray
French name: raie ronde

Distribution: Found in the North Atlantic Ocean and from Davis Strait and Labrador south to Georges Bank in the west.

Characters: This species is separated from its Canadian Atlantic relatives by having a rigid snout with its cartilaginous support thick and stiff, cartilaginous supports of the pectoral fin do not reach the snout tip, dorsal fins joined at base, snout angle 115° or

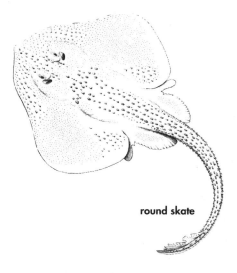

round skate

greater, body and tail with large spines not in a prominent midline but in 2–4 rows, upper jaw teeth in 30–38 rows, and tail longer than the body. Thorns may be absent just posterior to the shoulder area on the mid-back. Large thorns are present on the shoulder, numbering 5–9 around the eyes and in 2–3 rows on the snout. The anterior pectoral fin margin develops thorns with age. Females develop large thorns on the inner posterior part of the pectoral fins. Egg capsules are 3.6–4.4 cm by 2.6 cm excluding the horns. Upper disc ash grey to chocolate brown, with dark blotches in young and tail often barred. Underside white or grey with spots or sooty areas posteriorly on the pectoral and pelvic fins and the tail. Reaches 55 cm.

Biology: This skate is found at 170–2050 m in colder waters (1–7°C). Food is crustaceans.

round whitefish

Scientific name: *Prosopium cylindraceum* (Pallas, 1784)
Family: **Salmon**
Other common names: pilot fish, frost fish, Menominee whitefish, cross whitefish, lake minnow, osungnak, okeugnak, kapisilik

French name: ménomini rond

Distribution: Found in Alaska, Yukon, N.W.T. and far northern British Columbia and the prairie provinces, and in the Great Lakes except Lake Erie, in southern Ontario, in isolated localities in northwestern Ontario tributaries of Hudson Bay, much of Québec and Labrador except northwestern Québec and the Québec-Labrador North Shore and Gaspé, and in northern New Brunswick and the New England states. Also in Siberia.

Characters: This species and its relatives, the **mountain** and **pygmy whitefishes**, are distinguished from other **Salmon Family** members by having a single flap of skin between the nostrils, large scales (108 or less in the lateral line) and a forked caudal fin. It is separated from its relatives by having 13–21 gill rakers, 74–108 lateral line scales, 22–27 scales around the caudal peduncle and 50–130 pyloric caeca. Dorsal fin rays 11–15, anal rays 9–13, pectoral rays 14–17 and pelvic rays 9–11. Nuptial tubercles are found on 5 scale rows above and below the lateral line. There is 1 tubercle on the centre of each scale. The nape also has a few, smaller tubercles. Male tubercles are better developed than in females.

The back is brown or bronze to dark green or blue-grey, the flanks are silvery and the belly silvery-white. The head may be darkly spotted. Scales are outlined with dark pigment, particularly on the back. The dorsal and caudal fins are dusky. The adipose fin is spotted brown. The pectoral fins are orange in spawning fish, less bright, brown or yellowish, out-

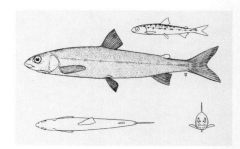

round whitefish

side the spawning season. Fainter orange tinges are also present on the pelvic bases and on the anal fin in the spawning season. Young fish up to 18 cm have 2–3 rows of 7–13 spots along the flank, the lowest at the lateral line.

Attains 56.1 cm. The world, all-tackle angling record weighed 2.72 kg and was caught in the Putahow River, Manitoba on 14 June 1984 by Allan J. Ristori.

Biology: This **whitefish** is found in the Great Lakes most abundantly in shallow waters above about 37 m although rare specimens descend to about 219 m. It is also found in rivers and streams and enters brackish water in Hudson Bay and along the Arctic coast.

Food is aquatic insects and molluscs with some crustaceans and fishes such as **sculpins** and **sticklebacks**. It has been reported to eat **lake trout** and **chum salmon** eggs and possibly its own eggs but it is not a major predator on commercial species. **Lake trout** are predators on round whitefish and a variety of fishes feed on round whitefish eggs and fry.

Life span exceeds 14 years. Growth varies with locality, Great Slave Lake fish growing faster than Koksoak River, Ungava fish. Maturity in Great Bear Lake is attained at 5–7 years, elsewhere as early as 2–4 years.

Spawning takes place in the fall, November–December in the Great Lakes and earlier (October) in the north. Males arrive on gravel shallows in lakes down to 14 m, at river mouths or up streams before the females. Round whitefish also broadcast eggs over silt and weeds but eggs are most abundant on gravel. Pair spawning occurs and the eggs are left untended to hatch in spring about 20 weeks later. Orange eggs are up to 3.5 mm in diameter before fertilisation with up to 20,000 eggs per female. Females may not spawn every year.

There have been Canadian commercial fisheries in lakes Huron and Superior where catches up to 31,780 kg annually have been made in the 1960s. It is occasionally caught by anglers in New Brunswick and is a good food fish.

rudd

Scientific name: *Scardinius erythrophthalmus*
    (Linnaeus, 1758)
Family: **Carp**
Other common names: none
French name: gardon rouge

Distribution: Found in the St. Lawrence River basin of Canada from New York State introductions. The natural distribution is in Europe from England to the Aral Sea basin. Also introduced elsewhere in the U.S.A.

Characters: This species is distinguished by a keel in front of the anus covered by scales and the pharyngeal tooth count and morphology (c.f. **golden shiner** where scales do not cover the fleshy keel and pharyngeal teeth number 5–5). Pharyngeal teeth usually 3,5–5,3 or rarely 2,5–5,2, slightly hooked and strongly serrated. Scales have numerous fine circuli and few large radii on all fields, unlike most Canadian **minnows**. Lateral line

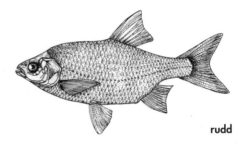

rudd

scales 36–45. The dorsal fin origin is clearly posterior to the pelvic fin origin. Dorsal fin branched rays 7–10, mostly 8–9, anal fin branched rays 9–12, mostly 10–11, pectoral rays 14–16 and pelvic rays 8–9. Gill rakers 10–13. Males develop breeding tubercles on the head and body. Overall colour is golden to silvery on the flanks with a darker back, blue-black to greenish-brown, and white belly. Upper flank scales have dark bases. Dorsal and caudal fins are orange to red, the pelvic and anal fins are red and the pectoral is yellow. The iris is golden or orange with a red spot at the top. Peritoneum silvery. Hybrids with **golden shiner** are known, further confusing identification of this exotic. Reaches 45.0 cm and 2.06 kg. The world all-tackle angling record weighed 1.58 kg and was caught in Sweden in 1988.

Biology: Rudd are usually inhabitants of still waters in midwater or near the surface. Food is principally terrestrial and surface living aquatic insects, crustaceans, snails, fish eggs and some plant material and fishes. Life span is at least 11 years. Females mature in the third year of life. Spawning in Europe occurs in April-July at water temperatures above 18°C. Females broadcast up to 232,000, 1.4 mm diameter eggs on vegetation. The young remain attached to vegetation until the yolk-sac is absorbed. This is a sport fish in Europe and has been fished commercially but is not particularly tasty. The bait fish industry cultures rudd in the Great Lakes region and releases will no doubt spread this exotic further.

Ruff Family

Scientific name: Centrolophidae
French name: pompiles

Ruffs or medusafishes are found in temperate to tropical waters of all oceans except the tropical Pacific and Indian oceans. There are about 27 species, 7 reported from Canada.

These fishes have a special outgrowth of the gut (see below), pelvic fins present in adults, a single, long dorsal fin with 0–9 spines followed by soft rays. There are usually 3 anal fin spines before 15–39 soft rays. Pelvic fins fold into a groove. Scales are cycloid in most species and do not extend onto the head. There are usually no teeth on the roof of the mouth. There are usually no keels on the caudal peduncle. The dorsal and anal fins are never falcate. There are 7 branchiostegal rays.

This family is related to the **Driftfish, Sequinfish, Squaretail** and **Butterfish** families, all of which share toothed, sac-like outgrowths of the gut. If the gill cover is lifted, the sacs may be seen behind the last gill arch. These families are distinguished by number of dorsal fins, presence/absence of pelvic fins in adults, number and size of dorsal fin spines, presence/absence of keels on the caudal peduncle and whether there are teeth on the roof of the mouth. The placement of species in these families is still in dispute among ichthyologists. The **Cape, slender** and **fewray fatheads** are sometimes placed in the **Driftfish Family**. This family is a member of the **Perch Order**.

Their name, medusafishes, is derived from the habit of young fish which live near or inside the bell (or medusa) of jellyfish. They are at least partially immune to jellyfish stings and feed on jellyfishes, in particular on their tentacles and gonads. They may use the jellyfish as protection against predators.

See **barrelfish**
black ruff
Cape fathead
Cornish blackfish
fewray fathead
medusafish
slender fathead

ruffe

Scientific name: *Gymnocephalus cernuus* (Linnaeus, 1758)
Family: **Perch**
Other common names: pope, ruff
French name: grémille

Distribution: Found naturally from England and France east to Siberia. Introduced to the Great Lakes at the western end of Lake Superior, including Thunder Bay, Ontario.

Characters: The ruffe is distinguished by the large sensory cavities under the skin on the top and sides of the head and by having a

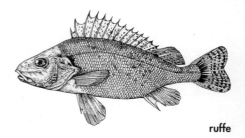

ruffe

long spinous part to the dorsal fin united with a short soft-rayed part. Dorsal fin spines 11–16, soft rays 10–15. Anal fin with 2 spines and 4–6 soft rays. Lateral line with 35–40 scales. Gill rakers 8–13. Back grey-green to green-brown with vague brownish speckles. Gill cover with greenish or bluish tints. Dorsal and caudal fins blotched and speckled, other fins clear. The pectoral fins may be rosy. Belly and flanks yellowish. Attains 50 cm.

Biology: The ruffe is a recent addition to the Great Lakes fauna, brought in the bilges of ships from Europe. Its normal habitat is slow-flowing lowland waters, which are often turbid. Food is small bottom organisms and zooplankton which are seized from ambush, aided by a highly-developed and sensitive lateral line system. In Eurasia, ruffe become mature at the end of their second year, and live at least 7 years. Spawning occurs in spring to summer depending on latitude and temperature, and up to 200,000 eggs are laid, with a diameter of 1.1 mm, on a hard bottom of sand, clay or gravel. Ruffe have an extended spawning period, longer than in **yellow perch**, for example, and this ensures that some eggs meet favourable conditions if there is environmental variation. Unfortunately this ability enhances its survival in places where it is exotic, such as the Great Lakes. This species has no commercial or sport importance and in Europe is known to prey on **whitefish** eggs, reducing the populations of valuable species. It may eventually have serious effects on Great Lakes fisheries and is impossible to eradicate. The U.S.A. has a "Ruffe Control Committee" examining various chemicals as piscicides. In an effort to reduce exotic introductions to the Great Lakes, ships are now required to exchange their ballast water over the continental shelf where depths exceed 2000 m and where potential freshwater invaders and coastal species would not survive. Open-water species could enter with the new ballast water, but are fewer in numbers, intolerant to fresh water and poorly adapted to enclosed and coastal ecosystems. However, this does not solve the problem of secondary ballast water transfers in ports like Montréal, Québec and Halifax, where exotic or native species can be taken on board and transferred into the Great Lakes. The **threespine** and **fourspine stickle-backs** are believed to have reached parts of the Great Lakes in this way.

russet grenadier

Scientific name: *Nematonurus armatus*
(Hector, 1875)
Family: **Grenadier**
Other common names: abyssal grenadier, smoothscale rattail, grenadier de profondeur
French name: grenadier roux

Distribution: Found almost world-wide in deeper waters including off British Columbia and off Nova Scotia. Arctic coast records for Canada are unconfirmed.

Characters: This grenadier is distinguished from its Pacific Canadian coast relatives by having the anus immediately in front of the anal fin, no black, scaleless area on the abdomen, 6 branchiostegal rays, 9–12 pelvic fin rays, and teeth in upper jaws in 1–2 widely separated rows, the outer row teeth being

russet grenadier

much the larger. These characters and the following separate this species from Canadian Atlantic coast grenadiers. Second dorsal fin rays shorter than anal rays, scaleless areas on each side of the upper snout surface, and no strong median keel on trunk and tail scales. The first dorsal fin has 2 spines and 8–10 soft rays and the second dorsal about 67 rays. The anal fin has about 77 rays. Pectoral fin rays 18–22. Scales bear thin, sharp spines in 3–10 or more rows. Overall colour is dark brown, or reddish-brown to blackish. Fins are dusky to pale in young fish but black in adults. The lower head surface, barbel, lips, area under the eye, lower snout surface, mouth and gill cavities, and the peritoneum are all black. Small pores on the dorsal head and body are rimmed in black in contrast to the brown background colour. Reaches 102 cm in total length.

Biology: Reported from off Georges Bank in Canadian Atlantic waters in 1974 from fish collected in 1883 at 2394 m and also off Cape Sable, Nova Scotia. Reported from off British Columbia in 2920 m, off Triangle Island at 2103–2195 m, off Moresby Island in 2904 m and off Graham Island in about 1830–1920 m. Found at depths between 282 and 4700 m, but mostly in the 2500–3500 m, range. It may be the dominant fish species in areas below 2400 m in the western Atlantic Ocean. This species is unusual in that food items include a significant number of pelagic species. It has been observed swimming with eel-like movements from a submersible in the western Atlantic Ocean at 2808 m. It never rested on the bottom but swam above it.

S

Sabertooth Fish Family

Scientific name: Evermannellidae
French name: poissons dents-de-sabre

Sabertooths are small, midwater or mesopelagic fishes of tropical and subtropical waters of all oceans. There are 7 species and one is reported from the Atlantic coast of Canada.

Sabertooths are related to the **Barracudina, Daggertooth, Halterfish** and **Lancetfish** families and are members of the **Flagfin Order**.

Scales are absent and three bands of muscle can be seen particularly on the tail in contrast to the more normal two bands. The eyes are tubular in most species. There are fanglike teeth in the roof of the mouth and large lower jaw teeth. There is no swimbladder. These are delicate species like many deepsea fishes, with paper-thin bones and fragile skin.

Larvae are found in shallower water than adults. There is no apparent vertical migration and adults can reach 1000 m. They are swift swimmers, able to escape most nets. They can swallow large food items such as midwater fishes and squids. Sabertooths are hermaphrodites.

See **pink sabertooth**

sablefish

Scientific name: *Anoplopoma fimbria*
(Pallas, 1814)
Family: **Sablefish**
Other common names: blackcod, Alaska blackcod, coalfish, blue cod, candlefish, skilfish
French name: morue charbonnière

Distribution: Found from Baja California to Japan including the coast of British Columbia.

Characters: This species is distinguished from its relative the **skilfish** by having a slender body, 17–30 first dorsal fin spines and 13–23 anal fin rays. The second dorsal fin has 1 spine and 13–21 soft rays. The soft anal fin is preceded by 3 spines, often embedded and hard to locate as is that in the soft dorsal fin. Scales are weakly ctenoid, small and cover the body and head. Teeth are small and in patches on the jaws and roof of the mouth. There are 62–65 gill rakers.

Colour is an overall grey, grey-black or greenish grey, lighter on the belly, and blotched on the back. The spiny dorsal fin has a black edge and the lining of the gill cover is dark. The outer edge of the pectoral fin is dark black. Young fish are blue or greenish-grey in colour, but they darken with age. Rare specimens may be golden-yellow overall with a black eye. The word sable is derived from a Slavic word for black. Attains 1.07 m and reputedly over 57 kg.

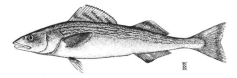

sablefish

Biology: Young sablefish are in shallow water or pelagic in the open ocean, but adults are found on mud between 366 and 915 m, and move into deep water in winter even below 1829 m.

Food is fishes, worms, octopi and crustaceans. Juvenile sablefish are important predators of juvenile **Pacific herring** but strong year classes of sablefish depend on abundant calanoid copepods as food.

Sablefish populations show occasional large year-classes. These are produced when sea surface temperatures are high and oceanographic conditions result in more food or in transport to areas with abundant food supplies. Sablefish are known to travel 4300 km in up to 7 years of life but other authors estimate life span at 70 years. They grow at about 0.5 kg per year. Half the population is mature at 58 cm for females (age 5.2 years on average) and 52 cm for males (age 4.8 years) although this varies locally. Spawning occurs in January to April with a peak in February along the whole B.C. coast. Pelagic eggs may be found several hundred kilometres offshore at depths up to 404 m. Over a million eggs may be produced with a diameter up to 1.2 mm.

A commercial fishery using trawls, traps and longlines, brought in 5229 tonnes in 1988 worth $15.7 million for Canada with landings in other countries in the many thousands of metric tons. The flesh is very oily and sablefish are very tasty when smoked because of this. It has been sold as "smoked Alaska black cod." The skull is 60% lipid and this oil is thought to aid in buoyancy as well as being an energy reserve. Young sablefish are a nuisance to salmon anglers but provide good sport around piers, jetties and wharves. Significant numbers of sablefish caught off the U.S. coast in the 1970s had mercury concentrations above 0.5 p.p.m., the level established by the Food and Drug Administration as the maximum allowable in fish. It has been overfished in southern British Columbia.

Sablefish Family

Scientific name: Anoplopomatidae
French name: morues noires

This family contains only 2 species found in the North Pacific Ocean and both are reported from British Columbia.

These species have 2 dorsal fins, 1 lateral line canal and lack cirri, spines and ridges on the head. The gill membranes are attached to the isthmus. Pelvic fins are thoracic (under the pectoral fins) and have 1 spine and 5 soft rays. Nostrils are well-developed.

The 2 species are distinguished by fin ray counts. The relationships of this family are uncertain but they are usually placed with the **Greenling** and **Scorpionfish** families in the **Mail-cheeked Order**.

These are deepwater fishes which occur near the surface only as young. The **sablefish** is commercially important.

See **sablefish**
    skilfish

saddleback gunnel

Scientific name: *Pholis ornata* (Girard, 1854)
Family: **Gunnel**
Other common names: saddled blenny
French name: sigouine mantelée

Distribution: Northern California to Vancouver Island in British Columbia. Also reported from Japan and the Bering Sea.

Characters: Distinguished from other Pacific coast gunnels with pelvic fins by having 74–80 dorsal fin spines, 32–38 anal

saddleback gunnel

rays preceded by 2 spines, no median interorbital pore and 12–14 black v or u-shaped markings along the base of the dorsal fin enclosing green or brown areas darker then body colour. Pectoral fins are relatively large with 11–13 rays. Olive-green to brown on the back, yellow to orange or red on the belly. A dark bar is in two bands across the head from eye to eye. A dark bar runs down from the eye. A series of dark bars originates at midflank and fades towards the belly. Pectoral, anal and caudal fins often orange. Anal fin can be light green and barred white. Attains 30.5 cm.

Biology: Found on mud or rock bottoms near stream outlets in eelgrass and seaweed, usually at 18–37 m, but down to 50 m. Mud flats and eelgrass beds are favoured by some populations and these have a greater tolerance of thermal stress than other shore species. The under-rock microhabitat has an annual temperature range of 4–24°C in Oregon. They live about 7 years and mature at about 2 years of age. Food is small crustaceans, principally amphipods on rocky bottoms, and molluscs, principally exposed siphon tips of clams, on mud bottoms. Both the male and the female guard an egg mass.

saddleback sculpin

Scientific name: *Oligocottus rimensis* (Greeley, 1899)
Family: **Sculpin**
Other common names: prickly sculpin
French name: chabot mantelé

Distribution: Found from Alaska to Baja California including British Columbia.

Characters: This sculpin, and its relatives the **fluffy** and **tidepool sculpins**, are distinguished from other Pacific coast species by having 3 pelvic fin rays, the branchiostegal membranes form a fold over the isthmus, the upper preopercular spine is not antler-like, scales are absent, the anal fin origin is below the end of the spiny dorsal fin and the anus is close to the anal fin. This species is distinguished by the slender spines covering the body and a single point to the upper preopercular spine (rarely 2 points). First dorsal fin spines 8–10, second dorsal rays 16–19, anal rays 13–15 and pectoral rays 13–15. The first 2 anal rays are lengthened in males. Lateral line pores 35–41. Cirri are found on the anterior half of the lateral line, 4 are present on top of the head from the eye to the dorsal fin, and a small one is at the end of the upper jaw and on the nasal spine. Overall colour is olive-green to reddish-brown. The lower flanks are pale yellow or tan to green. The back has 5 saddles with pale blue edges. The flank has dark markings. Fins are barred red with rays otherwise green. Pelvics clear. Attains 6.4 cm.

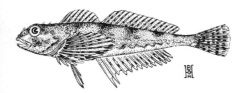

saddleback sculpin

Biology: This sculpin is not as common as its relatives but is found in lower, rocky tide pools and in kelp and eelgrass. Food is crustaceans and worms.

saddled eelpout

Scientific name: *Lycodes mucosus*
    Richardson, 1855
Family: **Eelpout**
Other common names: lightcheek eelpout
French name: lycode à selles

Distribution: Found across the Canadian Arctic from the Beaufort Sea to Baffin Island. Also in the Chukchi Sea.
Characters: This species is separated from its Canadian Arctic-Atlantic relatives by having small pelvic fins, a mouth under the snout, no large pores around the mouth, crests on the chin, lateral line single and on

midflank, tail short (preanal distance in the range 49–55% of total length), scales are absent or present, pointed teeth on the vomer

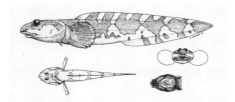

saddled eelpout

bone in the roof of the mouth 2–7, 90–92 vertebrae, 5–8 dark saddles on the back, and a pale peritoneum. Dorsal fin rays 88–93, anal rays 69–73 (each including half the caudal fin rays), and pectoral rays 17–18. Cheeks are light with the upper side of the head very dark and clearly delineated from the cheeks. The first flank light band has distinct dark borders and is arched forward onto the head. Dark bands are clearly delineated on the flank and have light central spots on the dorsal fin. There is an unpigmented area above the anal fin. Reaches 49 cm.
Biology: This eelpout is known to live in burrows in the mud under sea ice in Resolute Bay, N.W.T. but little is known of its biology.

saffron cod

Scientific name: *Eleginus gracilis*
    (Tilesius, 1810)
Family: **Cod**
Other common names: Far Eastern navaga,
    morue boréale, ogavik, ogak, siuryuktuuq
French name: navaga jaune

Distribution: Found in the western Arctic from Cambridge Bay west to the Beaufort Sea, Bering Sea and south to Sitka, Alaska in the east and to North Korea in the west.
Characters: This species is distinguished from other western Arctic **cods** by having the upper jaw projecting, a truncate caudal fin, sensory head canals poreless or with few, very small pores, and the lateral line is not continuous before the second dorsal fin. The chin barbel is as long as the pupil diameter. The lateral line is straight behind the level of the middle of the second dorsal fin. First dorsal

fin rays 11–16, second dorsal rays 15–24 and third dorsal rays 17–24. First anal fin rays 20–27 and second anal rays 18–23. Gill rakers

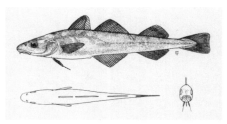

saffron cod

14–25. The back is dark olive, flanks silvery tinged with violet fading to yellowish lower down and the belly is silvery-white. The body may be spotted. The dorsal and caudal fins have a white margin. Reaches 63 cm.

Biology: This species is found at the surface and down to 75 m in coastal areas and it enters river mouths. It may descend to 200 m. There is an inshore migration for spawning in winter and a retreat to deeper water in summer for feeding. Food includes crustaceans, worms and fish fry. Spotted and ringed seals eat this fish in the Bering and Chukchi seas. Life span is at least 11 years. Sexual maturity is attained at 2–3 years and 21–35 cm fork length. Spawning takes place under coastal sea ice in December–February at −1.8 to 0°C where there is a tidal influence over a sand or pebble bottom at 2–10 m. Fecundity is up to 210,000 demersal, nonadhesive eggs with a diameter up to 1.7 mm. Larvae hatch in spring and, for the first 2–3 months, young saffron cod can be found associated with jellyfishes. This species has a commercial potential which has yet to be fully realised in North America. It is fished commercially in Asia.

sailfin molly

Scientific name: *Poecilia latipinna*
 (Le Sueur, 1821)
Family: **Livebearer**
Other common names: none
French name: molliénésie à voilure

Distribution: Found only in Cave and Basin Hotsprings, Banff National Park,

Alberta. Naturally occurring from North Carolina south to Yucatan.

Characters: The most characteristic feature is the enlarged, sail-like dorsal fin which develops in adult males. The related **mosquitofish** has fewer dorsal fin rays. Dorsal fin with 12–18 (male) or 10–12 (female) rays, anal fin with 7–9 rays. Lateral scale rows 23–30. Male mollies have enlarged anal rays forming a gonopodium for intromittent fertilisation. The form introduced to the hot springs was the jet black one produced by artificial breeding for the aquarium trade. Chequered and marbled black strains as well as a very rare golden one have also been reported from Banff. The chequered form predominates at present and probably represents the wild-type colouration. Natural colouration is as follows. The back is olivebrown or dark green and the upper flank is blue. The flank scales have a pearly cast over a brownish to blue background and there are up to 9 flank stripes made up of fine red, blue or green dots. On the rear part of the flank there are 6–7 dark bands. The dorsal fin is dotted black on blue with an orangered to yellowish margin. Females lack these bright colours. The name molly is a short form of *Mollienisia*, the scientific name of a related genus named for Count F.N. Mollien. Males attain 10 cm, females 15.0 cm.

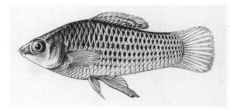

sailfin molly

Biology: This species is less abundant and widespread in the hotsprings than the **mosquitofish**. It occurred there in a temperature range of 18–27°C when the nearby Bow River was 5.5°C. The molly prefers warmer temperatures than the **mosquitofish**. This species is found naturally in coastal waters, ditches and canals from brackish to full sea water. Food is algae with small crustaceans and aquatic insects. Adult females grow 2–3 times faster than males, although some males grow as fast as females. Reproduction in Florida peaks in May–June and August– September. Up to 60 young are born, usually after about 8–10 weeks gestation. In laboratory experiments, the interval between brood production ranges between 21 and 68 days, the shorter intervals occurring at higher temperatures, so there is a potential for rapid population increase. Adult females are more numerous than males in any population although the sex ratio at birth is 1:1. Males are sexually hyperactive and can inseminate a large number of females in a short period of time — a condition which has been called suicidal reproduction. Females respond to male courtship displays only as virgins or just after parturition. Males can recognise that females are not virgins by "gonopore nibbling", sensing by chemical means.

sailfin sculpin

Scientific name: *Nautichthys oculofasciatus*
    (Girard, 1857)
Family: **Sculpin**
Other common names: sailor-fish
French name: chabot à grande voile

Distribution: Found from Japan to California including British Columbia.

Characters: This sculpin and its relative, the **smallsail sculpin**, are distinguished from Pacific coast relatives by the steep rise of the back from the occiput to the dorsal fin origin, an oblique, black bar running from the eye downward on the side of the head, and the spiny dorsal fin has membranes to the end of the spines and is higher than the soft dorsal fin. This species is separated from its relative by having 27–30 second dorsal fin soft rays and a spiny dorsal fin more than twice as high as long. The nasal spine is sharp and strong. The upper rear eye margin has 3–4 blunt spines. There are blunt, flattened spines on a fronto-parietal ridge and a large posttemporal spine. The preopercle has 3 blunt, skin-covered spines with the upper one the largest. First dorsal fin with 8–9 spines, the first 4–5 greatly elongated. Anal fin rays 16–21, pectoral rays 13–14 with lower 5 rays finger-like at tip, and pelvic fin with 1 spine and 3 soft rays. The caudal fin is rounded and bent upwards. Scales are

small spines embedded in papillae and cover the whole body and head except paired fin bases, the anal fin base and the midline of

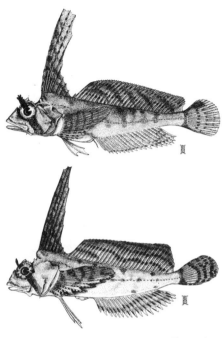

sailfin sculpin

the top of the head. Scales are also on the soft dorsal, caudal, pectoral and pelvic fins. The skin has a velvety touch. Lateral line pores 41–46. There is a large flat cirrus on the eyeball which is also part of the oblique bar through the eye. There are smaller cirri on the eye, upper jaw, head spines, under the eye and along the preoperculum edge. The back and upper flank is brown to grey with vague dark bars or blotches. The belly is pale brown to cream. The spiny dorsal fin is dark. There may be red flecks on the eye and soft dorsal fin. Fins have bars. Reaches 20.3 cm.

Biology: This sculpin is often caught in shrimp trawls at depths to 110 m in southern, coastal waters of Canada. Also recorded from tide pools. Rocky bottoms and algae beds are favoured. It is nocturnal. Divers have observed it hanging upside down in caverns and swimming by slowly flapping the dorsal and anal fins while the body is held stiffly. Food is crustaceans. In aquaria the "sail" is lowered in front of the head and waved over the food before it is seized. Orange eggs are laid in late winter or spring intertidally among mussels. The egg mass adheres to the substrate.

sailor lightfish

Scientific name: *Polymetme corythaeola*
  (Alcock, 1898)
Family: **Lightfish**
Other common names: none
French name: cyclothone matelot

Distribution: Found in all warmer seas and entering Atlantic Canada.

Characters: This species is distinguished from its Canadian Atlantic relatives by having the end of the dorsal fin opposite or

sailor lightfish

behind the anal fin origin and by lacking a photophore or light organ below the rear eye margin. Photophores over the anal fin and back to the tail number 24–25, with 17–18 being over the anal fin. The anal fin is much longer than the dorsal fin, with 30–34 rays. The back is dark and the flanks silvery. The outer caudal fin rays are black. There is transparent tissue on the abdomen between the pelvic fin and the anus. Reaches about 26 cm.

Biology: A single specimen was trawled at 350 m off the Scotian Shelf in 1983. It was a northern range extension for the species and more have been caught. Adults are usually found at 300–500 m swimming over the bottom but may descend to 760 m.

Salish sucker

Scientific name: *Catostomus* sp.
Family: **Sucker**
Other common names: Campbell sucker,
  meunier de Campbell
French name: meunier des Salish

Distribution: Found in the Salmon and Little Campbell rivers in the Fraser River

lowlands, British Columbia. Also in neighbouring Washington.

Characters: This species is distinguished from the **longnose sucker** by having larger scales, a deeper head, lesser lip width, and a shorter snout. Lateral line scales have means in the 84–86 range compared to 103–107 for neighbouring **longnose sucker** populations. In other respects, such as colouration, it resembles the **longnose sucker**. Attains 20.0 cm, usually smaller in Canada.

This distinct species probably evolved in an ice-free area south of Puget Sound which acted as a glacial refugium during the Pleistocene. After the glaciation, about 12,000 B.P., this species spread northward through proglacial lakes and drainage connections into the lower Fraser Valley and what is now Puget Sound but was then above sea level. At this time the Fraser Canyon was blocked with ice and the Fraser flowed into the Columbia until about 11,000 B.P., preventing Columbian fishes from entering the area. The sea flooded into the lower Fraser Valley and Puget Sound in about 11,500 B.P. isolating the Salish sucker in several, now unconnected streams and lakes of B.C. and Washington.

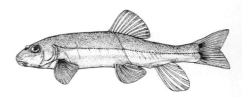

Salish sucker

Biology: This sucker is found in cool streams (and also in lakes in Washington). Food is aquatic insects, particularly chironomids. Males first mature in their third year at about 12.0 cm, females in their fourth year at about 14.5 cm. Life span is at least 6 years. Spawning occurs in March to April at 7–8°C in riffles over fine gravel. The Salish sucker is probably extirpated from the Little Campbell River and is restricted to headwaters of the Salmon River. Habitat change because of urbanisation is the main threat to this sucker in Canada. This species was given the status of "endangered" in 1986 by the Committee on the Status of Endangered Wildlife in Canada.

Salmon Family

Scientific name: Salmonidae
French name: saumons

The salmons, **trouts, chars, graylings, whitefishes, ciscoes** and their relatives are found in the cool and cold, fresh and salt waters of the Northern Hemisphere. There are about 70 species with 37 reported from Canada, and 2 subspecies which have separate accounts here. The huchen (huchon, *Hucho hucho* (Linnaeus, 1758)) was introduced to Québec from Europe but did not establish reproducing populations, nor did the Asian cherry salmon (*Oncorhynchus masou* (Brevoort, 1856)) or the European houting (lavaret, *Coregonus lavaretus* (Linnaeus, 1758)) introduced to Ontario and Québec respectively. British Columbia may have a distinct *Coregonus* sp., the Dragon Lake whitefish, and a distinct *Prosopium* sp., the giant pygmy whitefish, species not yet formally described.

Salmons are medium to large sized fishes up to about 1.5 m. These fishes are characterised by having an adipose fin, 11–210 pyloric caeca, a mesocoracoid bone in the pectoral girdle, the swimbladder is connected to the gut by a duct, the gill membranes are free of the isthmus and extend far forward, the last 3 vertebrae are turned up in the tail skeleton, the eye muscles pass through a deep posterior myodome and attach to trunk muscles and there are 7–20 branchiostegal rays. Scales are cycloid, confined to the body and can be minute. Pelvic, and sometimes pectoral, axillary scales are present. Pelvic fins are abdominal in position. There are no fin spines and the dorsal fin is at midbody. The lateral line is obvious. Breeding tubercles develop in the spawning season in some species. Many have strong teeth on both jaws, the tongue and the roof of the mouth. These fishes are tetraploid.

Salmons are members of the **Salmon Order**. The word "salmon" is from the Latin for **Atlantic salmon**. The limits and relationships of species within the family have long been in contention. Some are discussed under the heading **ciscoes**. A number of species exist which have not been named while others have a name but contain more than a single species. The latter are often referred to as a species "complex" since it is difficult to describe the complex observed variation in simple terms of several, named species. Even the correct scientific name to apply to a species can be in dispute or not open to easy resolution. The familiar **rainbow trout**, long known by the scientific name of *Salmo gairdneri*, is now generally recognised as *Oncorhynchus mykiss*, a relative of the Pacific salmons rather than salmon and trouts of Europe. A less familiar example is the whitefish name *Coregonus prognathus* based on fish from Lake Ontario described by H.M. Smith in 1894. Only a few specimens were ever collected and by 1929 it was considered to be extinct. The name was used again in a 1973 doctoral thesis to include a number of **cisco** species such as the **shortjaw, shortnose** and **deepwater ciscoes** but in 1981 T.N. Todd re-examined all the original material deposited in museums. Some specimens, including the holotype on which this species is founded, were in too poor a condition to be identified. The rest comprised 3 **lake ciscoes**, 12 **bloaters**, 2 **kiyis**, 6 **shortnose ciscoes** and 7 **shortjaw ciscoes**. The name has no taxonomic validity because of this confusion and the deterioration of museum material and should not be used in **cisco** taxonomy.

Young salmons are difficult to identify as their appearance changes with growth and adults can show colour and other character variations related to locality and season.

The salmon family is extremely important for the sport and commercial fisheries it supports. The commercial salmon landings in British Columbia for 1988 weighed 88,000 tonnes worth $312 million. When combined with the fish processing industry the salmon were worth probably over $1 billion and in addition there is an important sport fishery and farming operations. Many thousands of books and scientific papers have been written about these fishes. Members of the family have been widely introduced elsewhere in the world in cool waters, including the Southern Hemisphere. Certain salmonids are entirely resident in fresh water but many are anadromous, spending their life at sea but running up rivers to spawn and die. Migrations can be over thousands of kilometres and adults return to their stream of birth, a remarkable example of accurate navigation and ability to cross obstacles like falls by jumping. The young develop for several years in fresh water. Young salmons, **trouts** and **chars** are known as fry or alevins, when a few centimetres long they have dark blotches (parr marks) along the flank and are called parr, as they run to the sea they become silvery and are called smolt, an adult male returning early from the sea to fresh water is a grilse, and in the **Atlantic salmon**, which can return to spawn several times, the spent fish returning to the sea are called kelt.

See **Acadian whitefish**
Arctic char
Arctic cisco
Arctic grayling
Atlantic salmon
aurora trout
Bering cisco
blackfin cisco
bloater
broad whitefish
brook trout
brown trout
bull trout
chinook salmon
chum salmon
coastal cutthroat trout
coho salmon
deepwater cisco
Dolly Varden
golden trout
inconnu
kiyi
lake trout
lake cisco
lake whitefish
least cisco
mountain whitefish
Opeongo whitefish
pink salmon
pygmy whitefish
rainbow trout
round whitefish
shortjaw cisco

shortnose cisco
sockeye salmon
spring cisco
Squanga whitefish
west-slope cutthroat

Salmon Order

The Order Salmoniformes contains 1 family and about 66 species in marine and fresh waters of the northern hemisphere.

The characters of this order are essentially those of the family. It once included the families **Pike** and **Mudminnow** (now in the **Pike Order**) and the **Argentine, Deepsea Smelt, Pencil Smelt, Slickhead, Spookfish, Smelt** and **Tubeshoulder** families (now in the **Smelt Order**).

See **Salmon Family**

salmon shark

Scientific name: *Lamna ditropis*
    Hubbs and Follett, 1974
Family: **Mackerel Shark**
Other common names: mackerel shark,
    requin-taupe saumon
French name: taupe du Pacifique

Distribution: North Pacific Ocean from Japan across to British Columbia and south to California and Mexico.

Characters: Distinguished from the **great white shark** by the smooth teeth which have a cusp on each side near the base unlike those in the **makos**. The anal and second dorsal fins lie opposite each other and there is a secondary keel below the main keel on the tail fin while the **shortfin mako** has the origin of the second dorsal fin well in front of the anal fin origin and no secondary keel.

salmon shark

The body is stout and deep. The snout is conical and shorter than in the **porbeagle** (distance from snout tip to eye 2.5 times or more in distance from eye to first gill opening). The gill slits are long. Scales are small and the skin almost smooth to the touch. Dark blue-grey, grey-black or mottled grey above with an abrupt change to white ventrally. Adults have dark grey or black blotches on the ventral surface. The first dorsal fin is dark without the white patch found in the porbeagle. There is a black spot at the pectoral fin base. Maximum length 3.05 m.

Biology: Found from the surface down to at least 152 m. A common species offshore and near beaches on Canada's Pacific coast. They occur singly and in schools, swimming quickly, and following **salmon** schools. They are voracious predators on **salmon, lumpfishes, sculpins, pollock, tomcod** and other fishes as well as squid. These sharks maintain a body temperature 7–11C° above sea temperature. Salmon sharks are ovoviviparous with up to 4 young in a litter. There is uterine cannibalism with the oldest young eating their siblings. Young fish have asymmetrical tails and are 65–70 cm long. Males are mature between 1.8 and 2.4 m. A salmon shark may be dangerous to man like its fearsome relative the **great white shark**, because of its size and voracity, but this is unproven. This species has attracted sports fishermen in the Strait of Georgia and will take both surface and bottom baits such as **salmon** and salmon spoons. It can fight enough to pull a small boat around. Japanese coastal longliners catch salmon sharks in the North Pacific and the flesh is sold in Japan. Salmon shark flesh is red. Oil, skin and fins are also used. It is a nuisance to commercial fisheries because it entangles salmon nets by twisting and rolling when it runs into them. The shark usually has to be killed to free the net. **Chinook** and **coho salmon** are torn away from commercial trolling gear by this shark.

Sand Lance Family

Scientific name: Ammodytidae
French name: lançons

Sand lances or launces or sand eels are found in the Atlantic, Indian, Pacific and Arctic oceans. There are about 18 species with 2 in Canada, 1 on all three coasts and 1 on the Atlantic and Arctic coasts.

These fishes are characterised by their elongate shape, 1 long dorsal fin with 40–69 soft rays, which can fold back into a groove, pelvic fins absent in Canadian species, a lateral line running just below the dorsal fin, minute, cycloid scales which seem to form diagonal plates, no teeth, a fleshy ridge low along each side, and a protruding lower jaw. The caudal fin is forked. There is no swimbladder.

Sand lances belong to the **Perch Order** and are not closely related to other families. The taxonomy of some sand lances is poorly worked out and various species names are used. *Ammodytes hexapterus* is often called *A. americanus*.

These fishes often bury themselves in sandy shallows, with only the head protruding. They dive in head first, aided by the pointed lower jaw. Burrowing provides protection from predators. Normal swimming is with an eel-like motion. The sharp lower jaw may perforate the gut of a predator like the **Atlantic cod** and the sand lance then becomes encysted in the body wall. Sand lances occur in very large schools (up to 1800 million fish) and these are of immense importance as food for other fishes, particularly commercial species, and whales and seabirds. Lances can be used as bait by anglers but are not fished commercially for table food but for fish meal and oil. Over 660,000 tonnes were caught in the western Atlantic in 1982.

See **northern sand lance**
      stout sand lance

sand shiner

Scientific name: *Notropis ludibundus*
    (Girard, 1856)
Family: **Carp**
Other common names: shore minnow,
    straw-coloured minnow
French name: méné paille

Distribution: Found from southwestern Québec, southern Ontario but not north of Lake Superior, southern Manitoba and southeastern Saskatchewan. In the U.S.A. south to Gulf drainages and to Mexico west of the Appalachian Mountains.

Characters: This species and its relatives in the genus *Notropis* (typical **shiners**) are separated from other family members by usually having 7 branched dorsal fin rays following thin unbranched rays, protractile premax-

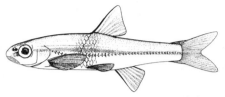

sand shiner

illaries (upper lip separated from the snout by a groove), no barbels, large lateral line scales (fewer than 50), and a simple, s-shaped gut. It is identified by having usually 6 branched anal rays (range 5–7), a weakly developed midflank stripe best developed posteriorly not passing through the eye onto the snout, no black pigment concentrated about the anus or anal fin base, no pigment below the lateral line, and a thin stripe along the middle of the back before and behind the dorsal fin but not encircling it. The pupil has a wedge or "nipple" on its anterior margin. Dorsal fin branched rays 7, pectoral rays 12–18, and pelvic rays 7–8. Lateral line scales 31–39. Pharyngeal teeth 4–4, hooked at the tip. Breeding males have minute tubercles on the head and pectoral rays 1–9 and on pelvic rays.

The back is light yellowish to olive-yellow, often almost transparent, flanks silvery with green and lavender tinges, and belly silvery-white. Back and upper flank scales are outlined in black. There is a narrow, yellow stripe above the silvery flanks. Lateral line pores outlined with pigment, a spot above and a spot below each pore. Fins are colourless although anal fin membranes may be milky-white. Peritoneum silvery with some darker speckles. Reaches 8.1 cm.

This species was formerly named *Notropis stramineus*. Although *N. ludibundus* has priority it has not been used. The International Commission on Zooological Nomenclature may rule to conserve the commonly used *N. stramineus*.

Biology: As the name suggests, this shiner prefers sandy areas of lakes and large rivers. It may descend to 34 m. There are daily movements of this schooling fish from deep water in the day to shallows at night. Food includes aquatic insects, zooplankton, bottom crustaceans, diatoms and terrestrial insects taken at the surface. Life span is at least 3 years with maturity at 1 year. Spawning occurs from April to August depending on latitude and water temperature regime. Temperatures have been reported to be as high as 37°C. July appears to be the spawning peak in Michigan and Wisconsin. A female can contain up to 2660 eggs of 1.0 mm diameter. Eggs are shed over gravel or sand, perhaps under submerged vegetation.

sand sole

Scientific name: *Psettichthys melanostictus* Girard, 1854
Family: **Righteye Flounder**
Other common names: fringe sole, sand flounder, spotted flounder
French name: plie à points noirs

Distribution: Found from the Bering Sea to California including British Columbia.

Characters: This species is characterised among Canadian Pacific **flatfishes** by having the first 8 or more dorsal fin rays elongated and free of the membrane. The caudal fin is rounded, the anal fin is preceded by a forward-directed spine, and the large, symmetrical mouth ends below the middle of the eye. Dorsal fin rays 72–90, anal rays 53–66. Lateral line with 98–112 scales and a dorsal branch. Scales on the eyed side are ctenoid, on the blind side cycloid except ventrally where some ctenoid scales are found. The eyed side is grey to light green to brown and covered

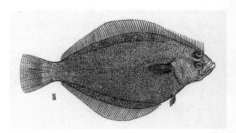

sand sole

with small black spots and speckles. Some fish have dull yellow dorsal and anal fin ray tips. The blind side is white. Reaches 63 cm.

Biology: This is a common shallow water species on sandy bottoms usually not deeper than 183 m, but recorded down to 325 m. Food is **speckled sanddabs, herring, anchovies** and crustaceans, worms and molluscs. Females grow larger and faster than males and live at least 7 years. Spawning occurs from January to July depending on location and latitude. Eggs are pelagic and 1.0 mm in diameter. It is often caught by anglers and forms a minor part of the commercial trawl catch. It is sold fresh or frozen as fillets of "sole."

sand tiger

Scientific name: *Carcharias taurus* Rafinesque, 1810
Family: **Sand Tiger Shark**
Other common names: dogfish shark, ground shark, shovelnose shark, nurse shark, spotted ragged-tooth shark, requin sable tacheté
French name: requin-taureau

Distribution: From the Bay of Fundy to the Caribbean Sea. Also in the Mediterranean Sea, Red Sea, southern hemisphere and Far East.

Characters: This species is recognised by having an anal fin, normal head, tail fin shorter than head and body, small gill slits, first dorsal

sand tiger

fin not far back and only a little larger than the second dorsal fin, and large teeth, sharp, curved and pointed with narrow cusps and 2 or more lateral cusplets on each side. The anal fin is similar in size to the dorsal fins.

Overall colour is light brown or greenish-grey with some reddish, brownish or yellow-brown spots on the body, particularly near the tail. The belly is grey-white. The rear margins of fins may be black-edged.

Reaches up to 3.18 m and over 145 kg. The all-tackle, rod-caught record from Hilton Head Island, South Carolina weighed 145.37 kg and was caught in 1989.

Biology: This is a common, sluggish shark of temperate and tropical waters and can be found at the surf line and in shallow bays down to 191 m or more. It is rare in Canadian waters, entering in warm years. A specimen was caught in a weir near St. Andrews, Passamaquoddy Bay in 1913. In the evening of the 4 August 1975, two unsuccessful fishermen in a 12–foot dory on the Bay of Fundy tossed their mackerel bait overboard to see what it would attract. About 20 minutes later, a 3 m shark, identified as a sand tiger, appeared, "knocked against the side of the boat and slapped the boat a number of times with its tail." A third specimen was caught in the Minas Basin, Bay of Fundy, on 10 August 1986, and was a 79 cm long male. This species is more active at night and is a strong but slow swimmer often near the bottom but also in midwater and at the surface. One unusual habit is swallowing air at the surface and holding it in the stomach so that the shark can hover motionless in midwater like a bony fish. Sand tigers may be encountered individually or in large schools. They migrate northward in summer and southward in winter on the Atlantic coast. Small to large schools develop for feeding, courtship, mating and birth.

Sand tigers are voracious feeders on other fishes such as **herrings, bluefishes, bonitos, gaspereau, mackerel, flatfishes** and many others as well as small **sharks, rays,** squids, crabs and lobsters. A school of sand tigers will surround and crowd together a school of prey fishes to make their food more easily available.

This species shows uterine cannibalism and there are normally only 2 surviving young in a litter, one in each uterus. Each pup in its uterus is fed by the continuing production of thousands of eggs by the female after siblings have been devoured. Foetuses at 17 cm have sharp teeth and are feeding, at 26 cm they can swim in the uterus, and they are born very large at 95–110 cm in length. They already have experience at hunting and attacking prey and so are well equipped to survive. Gestation occupies 8–9 months. Males and females are mature at 220 cm and are about 8 years old.

This shark has been eaten fresh, frozen, smoked and dried salted and is highly esteemed in Japan. It is also used for fish meal, liver oil, and sharkfin soup. Line gear, bottom gill nets and pelagic and bottom trawls have caught this species and it is fished for wherever it is found although its importance varies with the region.

It may attack people, especially spear fishermen, but it is relatively unaggressive and rare in Canadian waters. Sand tigers can be kept easily in aquaria for up to 10 years where it proves popular because of its fearsome appearance. It can be caught with live bait in shallow water at night and is a popular sport fish in warmer waters along the U.S. coast. It also takes surf cast baits meant for other fishes. Sand tigers do not put up as good a fight as **makos**.

Sand Tiger Family

Scientific name: Odontaspididae
(= Carchariidae)
French name: requins-taureau

This family contains only 4 species found world-wide in cool-temperate to tropical waters, and 1 of these occurs on the Atlantic coast of Canada.

It is distinguished by having an anal fin, a long and conical snout, no nictitating eyelids, five gill slits anterior to the pectoral fins, 2 dorsal fins, a ring intestinal valve, an asymmetrical tail and no keels on the caudal peduncle. There is a precaudal pit on the upper caudal peduncle only. Teeth are large with a slim, central cusp and small, lateral cusplets.

Sand tigers belong to the **Mackerel Shark Order**.

These are all large sharks found from tropical to cool-temperate waters both inshore and deep water in almost all seas. Sand tigers are ovoviviparous and have uterine cannibalism. They are voracious predators on other fishes, squids and crustaceans and are potentially dangerous to man. Some species are important in offshore and inshore fisheries.

See **sand tiger**

sandbar shark

Scientific name: *Carcharhinus plumbeus*
(Nardo in Oken, 1827)
Family: **Requiem Shark**

Other common names: brown shark, réquiem plombe
French name: requin gris

Distribution: Found from Atlantic Canada south to Brazil. Also in Europe, the southern hemisphere, Indian Ocean, Australia, Far East and eastern Pacific Ocean.

Characters: This shark may be distinguished from other Canadian requiem sharks by its short, rounded snout, its pointed or narrowly rounded pectoral and first dorsal fins, fins not mottled white, no black saddles on the caudal peduncle (distinguishes **ocean whitetip shark**), no caudal peduncle keels (distinguishes **tiger shark**), the pectoral fin is not very long and narrow and the body is not brilliant blue (distinguishes **blue shark**), teeth are serrated (distinguishes **Atlantic sharpnose shark**), and the first dorsal fin origin over the middle of the pectoral fin (distinguishes **dusky** and **silky sharks**). Teeth are triangular, erect to slightly oblique and have broad cusps in the upper jaw. Lower jaw teeth have narrow, erect cusps. There is a poorly developed interdorsal ridge. The first dorsal fin is very tall and triangular. There are no definite teeth on the free edges of the scales which are widely-spaced and do not overlap.

Grey-brown or bluish-grey above fading to white on the belly. The tips and posterior edges of the fins are dusky. There is a faint white bar on the flank. Scales may be bright blue in some fish.

Up to 3 m. The world all-tackle angling record weighed 117.93 kg and was caught in the Gambia in 1989.

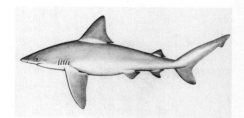

sandbar shark

Biology: Two specimens were caught off southern Nova Scotia on 6 August 1976 by a commercial longliner but the material was not kept. It is also recorded from the tip of

Georges Bank. Rare in Canada but a common shark in temperate and tropical waters both inshore and offshore, down to 280 m. It will enter harbours, very shallow muddy bays, and river mouths but is not common on sandy beaches or in the surf. Migration to the north occurs in summer with a southerly retreat for winter. One shark travelled 2724 km from New York to Mexico and longer travels have been reported. Adults are usually segregated by sex, males moving south earlier and deeper than females. Large schools may form on these migrations.

Food is small fishes such as **sardines, menhaden, shad, anchovies, barracuda, mullet, bonito, mackerel** and many others, and squid, cuttlefish, octopus, molluscs, shrimps and crabs.

Sandbar sharks are viviparous with a yolk-sac placenta. Young number 1 to 14 in a litter, with larger females having more young. Size at birth is 56–75 cm. Gestation lasts about 9 months but young are born only in alternate years. Pups are dropped in shallow bays from May to September. Females and other adults do not stay in the nursery area and this probably reduces cannibalism. Males follow and bite females on the back until they swim upside down allowing mating. Males mature at 131–178 cm and females at 144–183 cm. This shark may live over 30 years and take 12 to 13 years to reach maturity. Growth is 5.2–7.3 cm per year.

This species is abundant south of Canada and is caught on longlines, hook and line, and in bottom nets. It is used fresh, frozen, smoked and dried and salted. The skin has been used as leather, the fins for soup, and the liver oil is rich in vitamins. It is a sport fish which may be caught on cut bait set on the bottom at night in deeper water. Young sandbar sharks can be caught in estuaries and give a good fight on light tackle. This shark is ranked second in large shark catches by anglers in the U.S.

It is one of the few sharks reported in which cancer has been found. An understanding of why sharks so rarely have cancer compared to other vertebrates may be of immense medical benefit to humans.

It is not known to be dangerous to man because it does not frequent beaches and feeds on small prey. However it is potentially dangerous on size alone and cannot easily be distinguished from other, similar, carcharhinid sharks in attack situations.

Sandfish Family

Scientific name: Trichodontidae
French name: trichodontes

Sandfishes are found in the North Pacific Ocean. There are only 2 species, 1 of which is found in British Columbia.

The mouth of sandfishes is moderately large and almost vertical and has the lips conspicuously fringed to form a straining device. There are no scales. The preopercle has 5 sharp spines. There are two dorsal fins.

The family is related to weeverfishes and stargazers (not found in Canada) and the **Black Swallower Family** of the Atlantic coast. It is a member of the **Perch Order**.

The name is derived from the habit of living on or partly buried in sand or mud. The second species is an important food fish in Japan and its biology is better known.

See **Pacific sandfish**

sandpaper skate

Scientific name: *Bathyraja interrupta*
   (Gill and Townsend, 1897)
Family: **Skate**
Other common names: Bering skate,
   black skate
French name: raie rugueuse

Distribution: Found from the Bering Sea to California including British Columbia.

Characters: This species is separated from its Canadian Pacific relatives by having a soft and flabby snout with its cartilaginous support thin and flexible, cartilaginous supports of the pectoral fins almost reaching the snout tip, and 1–2 scapular (= shoulder) thorns present on each side. The median row of thorns from the nape to the first dorsal fin may be interrupted on the body. There are 17–30 median tail thorns. Fine prickles cover the whole upper disc and tail. The lower disc and tail lack prickles except for the tip of snout. Males have stout, hook-like alar thorns in 19–22 longitudinal and 4–5 transverse rows. There are 20–29 parallel rows of pointed teeth in the male upper jaw and 23–30 flattened teeth in a quincunx arrangement in the female. The upper side is dark

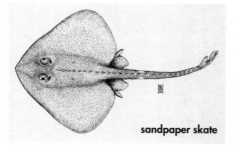

sandpaper skate

brown in adults and light brown in young and the lower surface is white except for a dark tail. The upper surface may be mottled white in adults and have dark specks in young. The cloaca, pectoral margins and pelvic tips are dark. Egg cases are dark brown with a yellowish-brown lateral keel. There are fine attachment fibres along the keels. Length is 4.9–5.9 cm. The surface has numerous, longitudinal rows of prickles. The rectangular case has a rounded to straight anterior margin and a nearly straight to convex posterior margin. The anterior horn tips curve inward and the posterior horns are the longest. Males reach about 70 cm and females 86 cm.

Biology: Canadian specimens have been caught in shallow water and elsewhere at 25–1380 m.

sardines

There is a single Canadian species of this name, the **Pacific sardine** of the **Herring Family**. However young **Atlantic** and **Pacific herring** are canned and sold as "sardines." Confusingly, the **Pacific sardine** is often called and canned as "pilchards" in Canada. Canned sardines from Europe are a different species from the above, and as adults are sold as pilchards. Fisheries for sardines or pilchards have declined world-wide, partly because of climatic changes but also because of overfishing. Sardine is derived from the Latin and Greek words for the island of Sardinia, where fish of this kind were abundant.

sargassum pipefish

Scientific name: *Syngnathus pelagicus*
    Linnaeus, 1758
Family: **Pipefish**
Other common names: none
French name: syngnathe sargassier

Distribution: Found from the Caribbean Sea to off Nova Scotia in the western Atlantic.

Characters: This species is distinguished from its straight-bodied relatives by its trunk ring and dorsal fin ray counts, its long snout and offshore distribution. A caudal fin is present. The snout is long (length enters head length less than 1.9 times). There is a low ridge on top of the head and snout. Dorsal fin rays 25–34. Trunk rings 15–18, usually 17, tail rings 30–35. Variable in colour but often dark green-brown. There is a distinct lateral snout stripe. Each trunk ring has a pale band or spot. There are 15–20 pale rings around the tail. There is a dark stripe on the middle of the dorsal fin and 7–9 cross bars. The caudal fin is brown. Attains 20 cm.

sargassum pipefish

Biology: A pelagic species found in *Sargassum* weed, as the name indicates. Only strays are likely to enter Canadian waters, washed inshore by storms. The male may carry as many as 225 eggs in his brood pouch in 1–2 layers and 2–6 cross rows. Eggs are 0.8–0.9 mm in diameter in the pouch. This pipefish is eaten by the **sargassumfish**.

sargassumfish

Scientific name: *Histrio histrio*
    (Linnaeus, 1758)
Family: **Frogfish**
Other common names: none
French name: sargassier

Distribution: Found in the Atlantic, Pacific and Indian oceans including from near the Grand Bank south to Brazil in the western Atlantic Ocean.

Characters: This **anglerfish** is distinguished from its relative, the **ocellated frogfish**, by having 2 fleshy cirri on the snout in front of the short fishing apparatus. The skin lacks scales but the body is covered with fleshy tabs which help camouflage it. The

sargassumfish

esca or bait is a fleshy bulb with filaments. Colour varies with the habitat with a brown marbled pattern on a yellow to olive background mimicking *Sargassum* weed usually evident. May be almost black or mostly yellow. Even the inside of the mouth mimics the seaweed. Attains 19.5 cm.

Biology: Occasional specimens are found in Canadian waters, having drifted here from the south. This species normally is found in floating *Sargassum* weed through which it clambers aided by its arm-like pectoral fins which are used to clasp the weed. It may propel itself forward by forcing water out of the gill openings. It feeds on other organisms living in the *Sargassum* such as the sargassum shrimp, and has a high growth and assimilation efficiency in this relatively poor environment. It is also a cannibal. An aquarium specimen attempted to devour several fish of a similar size but choked to death. Egg "rafts" are produced which are transparent, have scrolled ends and are about 9 cm long without being spread out. The spawning season extends from January to at least October and may be year round. Females have produced up to 8 egg rafts at intervals of 3–12 days. They become so swollen and buoyant with eggs that they take up a head down position. Males may help to pull the egg raft out of the female. Sargassumfish are sold in the aquarium trade.

sash flounder

Scientific name: *Trichopsetta orbisulcus* Anderson and Gutherz, 1967

Family: **Lefteye Flounder**
Other common names: none
French name: plie à nageoire frangée

Distribution: Found off Nova Scotia, Nicaragua and Venezuela.

Characters: This species is distinguished from other Canadian Atlantic adult **lefteye flounders** by having both pelvic fin bases short and the eyed side base on the belly midline, lateral line strongly arched over the eyed side pectoral fin, blind side pectoral fin present, no spines on the ridge between the eyes and no eye tentacles. Scales are ctenoid on the eyed side and cycloid on the blind side. Gill rakers short and stout, 7–8 on the lower limb. Dorsal fin rays 91–92, anal rays 70–73 and lateral line scales 78–80. Larvae have numerous fine spines on the head and a short second dorsal fin ray. Overall body colour is brown or straw-coloured with a variable number of spots or blotches on the body and fins. There is usually a large blotch at the junction of the curved and straight parts of the lateral line and on the lateral line just anterior to the caudal peduncle. Head furrows are blackish. The male has a large black spot on the dorsal fin between rays 3 and 7. The blind side is light dusky. Reaches 11.7 cm.

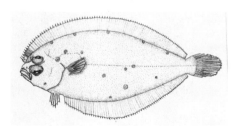

sash flounder

Biology: Larval specimens collected in 1980 at 133 m and in 1981 at 275 m on the Scotian Shelf are the only records of this species in Canada. Two other specimens, 1 from off Nicaragua at 156 m and 1 from off Venezuela at 119 m are the only other known records of this species.

sauger

Scientific name: *Stizostedion canadense* (Smith in Cuvier, 1834)
Family: **Perch**

Other common names: sand, blue, or grey
    pickerel, pike or pike-perch; river pike,
    spotfin pike, pickering, jack salmon,
    horsefish, spotted trout, rattlesnake pike
French name: doré noir

Distribution: Found from southern
Canada southward west of the Appalachians
to Arkansas and Tennessee but introduced
into some eastern and southern areas. In
Canada from the North Saskatchewan River
in Alberta and east to James Bay drainages,
essentially in the southern half of Alberta,
Saskatchewan and Manitoba, to southwestern Quebec and waters southward.

Characters: This species has a large mouth
with the upper jaw extending back to the rear
edge of the pupil, the preopercle bone on the

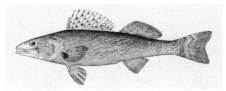

sauger

side of the head is serrated at its outer angle,
there are 11–14 soft rays in the anal fin after 2
spines, 2 canine teeth are present at the lower
jaw tip, the spiny dorsal fin is clear with small
spots and there are 3–4 brown saddles on the
back. First dorsal fin spines 10–15, second
dorsal fin with 1–2 spines and 16–22 soft rays.
Pectoral fin rays 12–14. There are 3–9, usually
5, pyloric caeca attached to, but shorter than,
the stomach. Gill rakers 6–8 on the lower limb
and 3–5 on the upper limb, moderately long
and denticulate. Scales are ctenoid and 79–100
in the lateral line.

Overall colour yellowish-brown, golden
olive, or even grey, saddles are a darker
brown. Flanks may have several large, dark
brown spots. Belly a milky-white. The first
dorsal fin has a dark margin and the membranes are spotted black in 2–3 rows, each
spot being a half-moon shape. The second dorsal fin has 2 rows of spots forming narrow
bands. The caudal fin is also barred and its
lower margin may be white. The anal and
pelvic fins are clearer but have dark specks.
The pectoral fin has a black, basal spot.

Reaches 76.2 cm. The world, all-tackle
angling record weighed 3.96 kg and was
caught in 1971 in Lake Sakakawea, North
Dakota. The Canadian angling record from the
Saskatchewan River, Saskatchewan, was
caught by Alex Foster in 1990 and weighed
3.52 kg. The largest sauger may be hybrids
with **walleye** known as saugeyes.

Biology: Saugers prefer more turbid water
than **walleyes** whether in large, shallow lakes
or large rivers with slow current. Sauger are
abundant in new reservoirs which tend to be
turbid but their numbers decrease as the reservoir stabilises. They were also of increasing
abundance in Lake Erie from higher turbidity
and fertility levels caused by land erosion in
the late nineteenth century. By 1960 they were
almost extinct because spawning sites were
destroyed and the stocks overfished. Recently
their re-establishment in Lake Erie has been
attempted with some measure of success.
Turbid conditions may protect young fish from
predators by reducing visibility, prevent eggs
from sticking together and being deprived of
adequate oxygen supplies and may concentrate plankton to lighted surface waters where
the young sauger can feed easily. Sauger are
usually found in the upper part of the water
column but may descend to 20 m. They may
enter brackish water in the St. Lawrence River.
The tapetum lucidum, a layer in the eye which
causes a silvery eyeshine, serves to stimulate
the visual cells by reflection. In low light conditions of turbid waters, vision is enhanced
and since the sauger's tapetum is better developed than that of a **walleye's**, it is at an advantage in turbid water. Sauger are more active in
shallow water when it is windy, and presumably waves are increasing turbidity.

Food of small sauger is plankton, fish fry
and insect larvae, with larger sauger taking
crayfish, insects and a variety of other fishes.
Sauger are known to favour demersal fish
prey throughout the day in some habitats.
Growth varies with the habitat, richer waters
showing more rapid growth than poor waters
such as those on the Precambrian Shield. Old,
slow-growing populations in the north reach
13 years while young, fast-growing populations in the south are up to 6 years old. Sauger
in rivers draining to James Bay have a slower

growth rate, shorter maximum length but a longer life span than sauger in southern Québec. Males are mature at 2 years and females at 3–4 years of age.

Spawning occurs at the end of May and beginning of June on gravel shoals down to 3.7 m of rivers or lakes at about 4–11°C. Males arrive first on the spawning ground while females are the first to leave. Spawning takes place at night with each female accompanied by one to several males. The eggs are shed, fertilised and fall into interstices of the gravel. A large female may produce up to about 210,000, non-adhesive eggs of 1.5 mm diameter. Sauger and **walleye** have been bred artificially and are known as "saugeye." Sauger are important commercially. They are caught with gill nets, pound nets and trap nets and in Manitoba as much as 2.5 million kg may be caught annually. The catch in Lake Erie has declined from 2.7 million kg to almost nothing. Saugers are strong fighters and although not as popular a sport fish as **walleye,** they are good eating with a firm white flesh sold usually as fillets.

- Most accessible June through November.
- Southern Quebec and the St. Lawrence River.
- Light to medium action spinning gear used with eight- to 12–pound test line.
- Minnow-type plugs from three to five inches in length trolled or cast, a variety of 1/4– to 3/8–ounce crankbaits and a wide assortment of hair and plastic body jigs. The best baits are worms or live **minnows** fished near bottom. A jig and **minnow** combination is a favourite.

Saury Family

Scientific name: Scomberesocidae
French name: balaous

Sauries are found world-wide in temperate to tropical waters. There are only 4 species of which 2 occur in Canada, 1 on the Atlantic and 1 on the Pacific coast.

These fishes have long or short beaks as adults and short jaws as young. Both jaws may be elongated into slender beaks or the beaks, particularly the lower jaw, may be short. Scales are small, cycloid, 70–148 along the flank. The spineless dorsal and anal fins are opposite each other at the rear of the body and each has 4–7 finlets between it and the caudal fin. Dorsal fin rays are 14–18, anal rays 16–21. Pelvic fins have 6 soft rays. The lateral line is low on the side.

Sauries are related to the **Flyingfish** and **Halfbeak** families sharing certain characters of the internal skeleton and the low lateral line. Sauries are members of the **Needlefish Order**. The name saury is derived from a Greek word for a seafish.

These are fishes of surface waters often found in large schools. The lateral line position, low on the body, is an adaptation to surface life, enabling the fish to sense the watery world below. When pursued by predators, sauries skitter over the water surface, sometimes in large numbers forming a "cascade" of fish. The 2 Canadian species are large and differ in various structural aspects from the other 2 dwarf species (6.8–12.4 cm). The dwarf species have a single ovary (2 in Canadian species), no swimbladder (present), 70–91 scales (107–148), pectoral rays 8–11 (12–15) and a long caudal peduncle (short). The dwarf species are thought to be offshoots from the larger species. Sauries are important food fishes and are usually canned. Sauries are important in the diet of such fishes as **tunas** and **billfishes**.

See **Atlantic saury**
      Pacific saury

sawback poacher

Scientific name: *Sarritor frenatus*
      (Gilbert, 1896)
Family: **Poacher**
Other common names: none
French name: agone à dos denté

Distribution: From Japan and the Bering Sea to southeast Alaska and northern British Columbia.

Characters: This poacher is identified by having a spiny snout which projects over the mouth and by having a number of long bar-

sawback poacher

bels at the rear of the mouth. There are often 2 cirri under the snout tip. There are 4 cirri or barbels at the rear of the upper jaw and a branching cirrus midway along each lower jaw. The head bears strong spines behind the eye and on the side. First dorsal fin spines 6–8, second dorsal fin soft rays 6–8. Anal fin rays 6–7. Pectoral fin rays 15–17, lower rays slightly finger-like. Gill membranes are not joined to the isthmus. Overall colour is brown to reddish-brown, with some blotches dorsally on the head and back. The caudal fin is dusky while other fins are lightly blotched to dusky. Dorsal, caudal and pectoral fins have alternating black and white bars on their fin rays forming irregular bars across the fins. The barbels are white. Reaches 27 cm.

Biology: Found on soft bottoms at 18–155 m. Little appears to be known of its biology.

Sawpalate Family

Scientific name: Serrivomeridae
French name: serrivomers

Sawpalates, sawtooth, deepsea or thread eels, are found in the temperate to tropical Atlantic, Indian and Pacific oceans. There are about 10 species, with 2 reported from Canada's Atlantic coast, 1 from the Pacific coast and 1 from the Arctic coast.

Sawpalates are characterised by 2 or more rows of blade-like teeth in the roof of the mouth which gives them their name. Jaws are elongate, reach beyond the eyes and have minute teeth. The lower jaw projects. The dorsal fin begins well behind the head, behind the anal fin origin. The dorsal, caudal and anal fins are continuous. Pectoral fins are rudimentary or absent. Pelvic fins are absent. Gill openings are laterally placed, almost vertical and confluent on the throat. There are no scales and lateral line pores are minute. The tail is thread-like. Vertebrae are numerous, thin and cylindrical. These are fragile fishes, easily damaged, and are usually caught in good condition only by scientific research vessels using special gear.

Sawpalates are members of the **Eel Order** related to the **Neckeel** and other eel families.

These fishes are bathypelagic, swimming in the ocean depths down to 6000 m, but they may migrate to surface waters. Larvae and juveniles are near the surface and hatching is known to occur in the Sargasso Sea for Atlantic species. Larvae are transparent leptocephali, typical of eels. This family has no commercial importance.

See **crossthroat sawpalate**
longfin sawpalate
short-tooth sawpalate
stout sawpalate

sawtailfishes

Sawtailfishes are found in all oceans with about 3 species, 1 of which is found off the Atlantic coast of Canada. They have been classified in their own family (Idiacanthidae) but

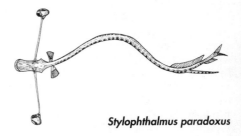

Stylophthalmus paradoxus

are now placed in the **Barbeled Dragonfish Family**. The sawtailfishes (also called blackdragons or stalkeyes) are characterised by being very elongate, deepsea fishes with long dorsal and anal fins nearly reaching the tail fin and with each dorsal and anal fin ray having a short spine on each side. There is no adipose fin, no scales and in adults no pectoral fins. Curiously, the males lack pelvic fins. Females have fang-like teeth while the males lack teeth on the jaws. Light organs are found in 2 rows on the lower part of the body. Females are several (up to 7) times larger than males and have a chin barbel. The digestive system degenerates in males and does not absorb food. Larvae were described as a distinct species, *Stylophthalmus paradoxus* the paradoxical stalkeye, because they were so different from adults with the peculiar eye stalks.

See **ribbon sawtailfish**

scads

Scads are members of the marine **Jack Family**. There are 5 Canadian species with this name, all found on the Atlantic coast. Scads have an elongate body shape in contrast to some other members of their family. The origin of the word scad is unknown.

See **bigeye scad**
mackerel scad
redtail scad
rough scad
round scad

scaled dragonfishes

Scaled or scaly dragonfishes was the common name used for the family Stomiidae when it was restricted to those deepsea fishes with hexagonal scales, elongate body with dorsal fin above anal fin at rear of body, no adipose fin and an elongate chin barbel. They are now included with the **loosejaws, sawtailfishes, scaleless dragonfishes, snaggletooths** and **viperfishes** in the **Barbeled Dragonfish Family**.

See **boa dragonfish**
shortbarbel dragonfish

scaled-nape eelpout

Scientific name: *Pachycara lepinium*
Anderson and Peden, 1988
Family: **Eelpout**
Other common names: none
French name: lycode à nuque écaillée

Distribution: Found from the Queen Charlotte Islands south to Mexico.

Characters: This species is separated from its Pacific coast relatives by having pelvic fins, a large gill opening extending to the

scaled-nape eelpout

lower edge of the pectoral base, terminal mouth and blunt snout, robust body, scales present, midlateral branch of the lateral line originating posterior to pectoral fin margin and running to the tail tip, usually 6 suborbital pores, firm flesh, and scales on the nape. A lower lateral line runs from the head to the tail tip. Dorsal fin rays 99–113, anal rays 85–98 and pectoral rays 15–18. Vertebrae number 105–120. Overall colour dark brown with the head and pectoral fin almost black.

Mouth and gill cavities dark brown or black. Reaches 59.7 cm standard length.

Biology: This species was first described from a specimen caught in a trap west of Tasu Island, Queen Charlotte Islands at 2744 m. Depth range is 1728–2970 m over mud bottoms. Food is worms, clams and crustaceans. Eggs are 4.3 mm in diameter.

scaleless dragonfishes

The scaleless dragonfishes or scaleless black dragonfishes are found in the deep sea of the Atlantic, Indian and Pacific oceans. There are about 200 species with 11 in Canadian waters, 8 on the Atlantic coast and 3 on the Pacific coast. They once comprised a family of their own (Melanostomiidae) but are now included within the **Barbeled Dragonfish Family**. These fishes are characterised by the dorsal fin being over the anal at the rear of the body, no scales or hexagonal areas, no dorsal adipose fin in most species, pectoral fins absent in some species, and most species have a chin barbel. The tip of the barbel is variously swollen and branched and is helpful in identification. Large photophores occur in 2 rows on each side of the belly, and there are numerous small photophores over the head and body as well as various luminous patches. There is a postorbital luminous organ behind the eye but usually no preorbital (before) or suborbital (below) ones. Overall body colour is black. Well developed gill rakers are absent. The mouth is very large and is well-armed with teeth, often fang-like ones.

See **bearded dragonfish**
bluenose rearfin
bronze-green flagfin
flatbarbel rearfin
flexfin dragonfish
highfin dragonfish
longfin dragonfish
pitgum lanternfish
sooty dragonfish
triangle-light dragon
tripletwig smoothgill

scallop snailfish

Scientific name: *Liparis inquilinus*
Able, 1973
Family: **Snailfish**
Other common names: inquiline snailfish

French name: limace des pétoncles

Distribution: Found from the Bay of Chaleur and Magdalen Islands in the Gulf of St. Lawrence south to the Bay of Fundy and to North Carolina.

Characters: This snailfish is distinguished from its Atlantic coast relatives in Canada by

scallop snailfish

having an adhesive disc, 2 pairs of nostrils, a dorsal fin with an anterior notch, dorsal fin rays 33–38, anal rays 28–31, pectoral rays 30–35 and pyloric caeca 14–21. The lower pectoral fin lobe has fleshy, finger-like rays. Teeth are in bands and are weakly trilobed. Colour is variable from light to reddish-brown or black with uniform colour, or mottled, striped or spotted. The caudal fin is usually barred. The eye is brown, black or silvery. Peritoneum pale with a few brown spots. Reaches 7.2 cm.

Biology: This species is not uncommon in Canadian waters at depths of 3–119 m. It has the peculiar habit of hiding for protection during the day in sea scallops, *Placopecten magellanicus*, attached upside down by the adhesive disc to the upper scallop valve. Up to 32 fish may be found in 1 scallop. The scallop is not harmed and recognises the snailfishes, but closes up when touched by other fishes. The phenomenon of living within another animal is called inquilinism. Feeding occurs at night when the snailfish leaves the scallop to forage for crustaceans using taste buds on the lower pectoral fin lobe. This fish may spawn at 1 year of age peaking in February to April, and die afterwards. Eggs are laid in clusters of 20–80. Eggs are up to 1.3 mm and a large female contained 1135 eggs. Male scallop snailfish have prickles on the skin. These may serve in recognition of males by the female when she bumps into them while swimming about excitedly in spawning condition.

scaly hedgehogfish

Scientific name: *Ectreposebastes imus* Garman, 1899

Family: **Scorpionfish**
Other common names: none
French name: sébaste hérisson

Distribution: Found world-wide in warmer seas and off Nova Scotia.

Characters: This species is distinguished from other Atlantic coast scorpionfishes by having 12 dorsal fin spines and a lateral line in a channel covered by thin spines. Colour is also distinctive. The dorsal fin has 9–10, usually 10, soft rays. There are 5–7, usually 6, soft rays in the anal fin after 3 spines (but only 2 in young) and 18–20, usually 19, rays in the pectoral fin. The body and bones are soft and flabby. The first preopercular spine is longest and the second may be almost as long in young fish. Supraocular and postocular spines absent, except in young. Adults have a maroon and black body. Young are black but paler where scales have come off. The mouth cavity is black with bright orange and red patches. Throat teeth are red or orange. Peritoneum dusky with dark spots but pale posteriorly. Reaches 17.1 cm.

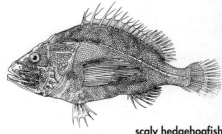

scaly hedgehogfish

Biology: First caught in Canada in 1971 at 475 m on the Scotian Shelf. Only 3 other specimens have been caught along the Atlantic coast of North America. This species has been found as shallow as about 150 m, and as deep as 1000 m in midwater or on the bottom. They appear to feed off the bottom judging by the crustacean species found in their stomach contents.

scaly waryfish

Scientific name: *Scopelosaurus harryi* (Mead in Mead and Taylor, 1953)
Family: **Waryfish**
Other common names: scaly paperbone

French name: lanterne-lézard écaillée

Distribution: North Pacific Ocean including off the British Columbia coast.

Characters: The scaly waryfish is distinguished from other Canadian waryfishes by having 16–21 pyloric caeca (finger-like

scaly waryfish

extensions of the digestive tract), short pectoral fins and a black patch on the pectoral fins. Overall colour is dark including fins. The mouth cavity is black. Reaches 26.6 cm.

Biology: Found at depths of 500–800 m. This is a rare species first described from Japan with the second and third specimens from west of the Queen Charlotte Islands. Little is known of its biology, but see **Waryfish Family**.

scalyhead sculpin

Scientific name: *Artedius harringtoni*
   (Starks, 1896)
Family: **Sculpin**
Other common names: plumose sculpin,
   white-spotted sculpin
French name: chabot à tête écailleuse

Distribution: Found from the Gulf of Alaska south to California including British Columbia.

Characters: This species and its Pacific coast relatives, the **padded, smoothhead** and **Puget Sound sculpins**, are distinguished by having 2–3, mostly 3, pelvic fin soft rays, simple or branched uppermost preopercular spine but not antler-like, (except in the **padded sculpin**) and 3–16 scales in the rows above the lateral line. This species is separated from related species by having scales on the head and scale rows extending onto the caudal peduncle, a cirrus on the upper front eye margin, and no snout scales. Some jaw teeth are enlarged. Males have an enlarged genital papilla. The nasal spine is strong but covered by skin. There are 2 preopercular spines, the upper being strong, flattened or

branched and covered by skin. First dorsal fin spines 8–10, second dorsal fin soft rays 15–18. Anal rays 10–14 and pectoral rays 13–15 with lower rays finger-like. There are 38–51 rows of scales on the upper flank with 8–16, usually 8–10, scales in each row. Lateral line scales 35–39. There is a scale at each dorsal fin soft ray base, scales are arranged irregularly on the operculum and top of the head and there are scales at the rear axillae of the pectoral fin base. The lateral line has long filamentous cirri level with below the middle of the spiny dorsal to the middle of the soft dorsal fin. The top of the head has several long, filamentous cirri and there is a cirrus at the end of the upper jaw. There is a cirrus over the eye in males and a large, branched cirrus over the anterior and over the posterior eye margin with another cirrus behind the latter. Cirri are larger in males.

The back is brown-olive fading to a dusky cream on the belly. There are 5–7 dark saddles over the back. The lower flank has light spots. There is a white spot at the caudal fin base and a red one at the tip of the first 2 dorsal fin spines. The dorsal, caudal and pectoral fins have brown spots on the rays forming bands. Males have bright orange-yellow branchiostegal membranes, red bars radiating from the eyes and a light violet mouth cavity with purple-red or red-brown spots. Anal and pelvic fins are dusky

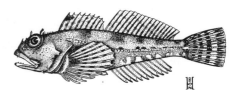

scalyhead sculpin

brown with yellowish-white spots resembling eggs. Females have white to pink or red anal and pelvic fins. Reaches 10 cm.

Biology: This is a very common species of rocky areas with barnacle clusters, loose cobble and around artificial structures down to 22 m with some found in the intertidal zone. The spaces between cobbles or barnacles are exploited as a microhabitat. It is also common in kelp beds although in Barkley Sound kelp 484 females were captured but only 1 male. Density was up to 4 fish per sq m, the most abundant of 22 kelp species. Food is principally caprellid and gammarid crustaceans but also includes other crustaceans, worms and fish. This sculpin hides in crevices, coiling the body and striking out to ambush prey. Prey may also be stalked over clusters of barnacles. Sedentary worms, barnacles and hydroids are nipped at. **Copper rockfish** eat this sculpin.

Males are strongly territorial and have a threat display. They are much larger than females. When a female approaches a male guarding a rock shelter, he rolls his head in a circle and flares the orange branchiostegal membranes. Females respond by horizontal head snapping in rapid succession and sometimes quivering. Males may mate with several females (or the same female at intervals) and guard several egg masses at different developmental stages. Eggs are fertilised while still in the ovary and a female's eggs are fertilised before she arrives at a nest site to lay them. A male would guard these eggs because they were his or, if not his, because he has a chance to fertilise the next clutch from this female. The egg spots on the anal fin may attract a female to an apparently successful male who appears to have eggs in his nest space Females carry mature eggs at 5.4 cm or larger. This species is very unusual in that there is internal fertilisation and male parental care. Only 1 other fish is known to do this, a **cardinalfish** not found in Canada.

Schmidt's leftvent

Scientific name: *Edriolychnus schmidti* Regan, 1925
Family: **Leftvent**
Other common names: none
French name: pore-gauche de Schmidt

Distribution: Found in all oceans including off the Atlantic coast of Canada.

Characters: The females of this species of deepsea **anglerfish** are distinguished from their Canadian relatives the **forkbarbelthroat, fourbarbelthroat, twohornbarbelthroat** and the **greatbarbelthroat** by lacking a barbel, by having numerous small teeth in

the jaws, the fishing apparatus is a rounded bump on the snout with a small, posterior branched appendage, and the skin is unpigmented. Mature males are colourless and have well-developed jaw teeth. Denticles are small and do not meet when the jaw is closed. Females attain 8 cm and attached males about 2.0 cm.

Schmidt's leftvent

Biology: Rare in Canada and only recorded in 1988. Females have been caught with 3 parasitic males attached. The fishing apparatus lures prey close enough to be seized.

Scorpionfish Family

Scientific name: Scorpaenidae
French name: scorpènes

The **scorpionfishes, redfishes, rockfishes,** stonefishes and sailbackfishes or wasp fishes are found world-wide in temperate to tropical seas and rarely in fresh water. There are about 388 species, mostly in the Indo-Pacific Ocean but the genus *Sebastes* has about 100 species in the North Pacific Ocean alone. There are 36 Pacific coast species, 4 Atlantic coast species and 2 Atlantic and Arctic coast species in Canada.

This family and related ones are characterised by a suborbital stay, an elongation of the third bone under the eye which extends across the cheek to the preoperculum. They are known as "mail-cheeked fishes." The head has ridges, spines, tabs, cirri, skin flaps and tentacles on the top and sides. There are usually 2 (1–2) opercular and usually 5 (3–5) preopercular spines. The eye is moderate to large in size. The mouth is large in a broad head. Colour is often reddish or brown. The dorsal fin is continuous with 7–18 spines often separated by a notch from 4–18 soft rays. The anal fin has 1–4, usually 3, spines and 3–14, usually 5, soft rays. The pectoral fin is large with 11–25 rays. There is 1 spine and 2–5, usually 5, branched rays in the pelvic fin. The caudal fin is rounded or emarginate. Scales are usually ctenoid and scale counts are of pored scales in the lateral line and the number of diagonal rows across the flank counted below the lateral line. The latter count is higher than the first.

Scorpionfishes are related to the **Searobin Family** and, more distantly, such large Canadian families as the **Greenlings**, **Sculpins**, **Poachers** and **Snailfishes** among others. They are members of the **Mail-cheeked Order**. The great number of species (34 in the genus *Sebastes* alone) in the North Pacific Ocean, coupled with a similarity occasioned by their relationship, make these fishes difficult to separate and identify. Some experience is needed. Counts and colour are important distinguishing characters as are the number and position of spines on the head. The important head spines number 8 and start near the nostril and run over the eye onto the nape of the head. They are named the nasal, preocular, supraocular, postocular, tympanic, coronal, parietal and nuchal spines. A colour character is that of the peritoneum or body cavity lining which requires dissection to determine. Characters unique to individuals are not always present, and a complex of characters must be used for identification. A scientific key to species is the easiest route to a sound identification.

These fishes are found from the shallows down to over 2000 m. The dorsal, anal and pelvic spines may have a venom gland and some non-Canadian species are deadly, causing agonizing death in a few minutes to anyone unlucky enough to receive a puncture wound. Many Canadian **rockfishes** have venom glands or tissues on their fin spines, particularly the **brown** and **quillback rockfishes**. Pain, swelling and fever can result from **rockfish** stings but they are not dangerous as long as the wound is cleaned of bacterial infection.

Most scorpionfishes are fertilised internally. Some give birth to live young while others lay eggs in a gelatinous balloon up to 20 cm in diameter. *Sebastes* species are live-bearers. A small submarine used to explore rocky areas and boulder fields along the coast of southeastern Alaska down to 240 m found these areas harboured a wide variety of *Sebastes* species where they are safe from trawlers. Many species are commercially important. The three Atlantic coast redfishes (**Acadian, deepwater** and **golden**) rank fourth in importance in Canada among commercial fishes by weight, 73,500 tonnes in 1988.

See **Acadian redfish**
aurora rockfish
black rockfish
blackbelly rosefish
blue rockfish
bocaccio
brown rockfish
canary rockfish
chilipepper
China rockfish
copper rockfish
darkblotched rockfish
deepwater redfish
dusky rockfish
golden redfish
greenstriped rockfish
harlequin rockfish
longspine thornyhead
northern rockfish
Pacific ocean perch
Puget Sound rockfish
pygmy rockfish
quillback rockfish
redbanded rockfish
redstripe rockfish
rosethorn rockfish
rougheye rockfish
scaly hedgehogfish
sharpchin rockfish
shortbelly rockfish
shortraker rockfish
shortspine thornyhead
silvergray rockfish
smoothhead scorpionfish
splitnose rockfish
stripetail rockfish
tiger rockfish
vermilion rockfish
widow rockfish
yelloweye rockfish
yellowmouth rockfish
yellowtail rockfish

Scotian snailfish

Scientific name: *Careproctus ranulus*
(Goode and Bean, 1879)
Family: **Snailfish**
Other common names: none
French name: limace acadienne

Distribution: Found in the St. Lawrence River estuary, east of Newfoundland and off Halifax, Nova Scotia, south to Virginia.

Characters: This snailfish is separated from its Atlantic coast relatives in Canada by having a small, shallow cupped, adhesive disc, 1 pair of nostrils, slender body, and 8–13 pale pyloric caeca. Dorsal fin rays 46–58, anal rays 42–51, and pectoral rays 24–32. Teeth are simple or have weak lateral lobes, and are in bands. Overall colour is white. Peritoneum is silvery, stomach pale. Reaches 8.1 cm. This species was described from a specimen caught off Halifax, Nova Scotia.

Scotian snailfish

Biology: Uncommon in Canadian waters with only about 3 specimens known. Depth range is 95–253 m. Females are mature at a small size, 5.4 cm total length. Eggs number 10–20 and are greater than 3 mm in diameter.

scrawled filefish

Scientific name: *Alutera scripta*
(Osbeck, 1765)
Family: **Filefish**
Other common names: scribbled leatherjacket
French name: alutère écrit

Distribution: World-wide in tropical and temperate waters, reaching Atlantic Canada.

Characters: The dorsal fin has 43–49 rays, and the anal fin 46–52, which distinguish this species from other Canadian filefishes. Pectoral fin rays 13–15. The gill slit is very oblique. There is no obvious spine at the pelvic fin position. The dorsal spine is slender and weakly barbed and often broken when the fish is handled. The dorsal snout profile is obviously concave. The body is olive-brown to grey with many blue or green spots and lines and scattered black spots. The lines may be scrawled, hence the name. The caudal fin is mostly black. Attains about 1 m. The world, all-tackle angling record weighed 0.86 kg and was caught in Hawaii in 1989.

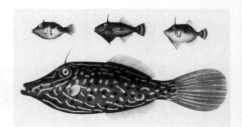

scrawled filefish

Biology: Caught only once in Canadian waters, south of Sable Island Bank in 1941. Food includes hydrozoans, gorgonians, sea anemones, algae and seagrass. Young live in seagrass beds and line up with the grass and sway with it in any current to remain camouflaged. Adults are often seen drifting at odd angles, usually nose down looking for food. Spawning in the Caribbean is recorded for December and May.

Sculpin Family

Scientific name: Cottidae
French name: chabots

Sculpins and bullheads are found principally in marine and fresh waters of the northern hemisphere, with 4 species from Australia and New Zealand. There are about 300 species with 63 in Canada. Most Canadian species are marine and found on the Pacific coast (37), a few entering brackish to fresh water there (5) or confined there to fresh water (2). There are 13 marine Arctic-Atlantic species. Only 2 species are restricted to fresh waters outside the Pacific drainages. One species is found on all 3 coasts and a few others are found in fresh to brackish waters on several coasts. An undescribed species is reputed to exist in Cultus Lake, B.C.

Sculpins have a naked body or have scales, plates, prickles or spines. The head is large and is blunt. It often has spines or knobs particularly 1–4 preopercle spines and the body tapers posteriorly. There is a large, dorsally placed eye. The mouth is large but teeth are generally small. There is 1 lateral line. The dorsal fin usually has separate, short spinous and longer soft portions. Pelvic fins (rarely none) have 1 spine (often embedded and hard to detect) and 2–5 soft rays. There are no anal fin spines. The pectoral fin is large and fan-shaped. The caudal is usually rounded or truncate. The hyomandibular bone has a unique lateral process. Adults lack a swimbladder. The males of some species have a penis-like urogenital papilla to deliver sperm internally to females. Eggs are few, large and demersal and may be guarded by the male. Coloration is usually mottled and drab.

This family is related to the **Soft Sculpin** and **Poacher** families in the **Mail-cheeked Order**. Important characters in identifying sculpins are fin ray counts, the number and arrangement of scales, the shape of the preopercular spines, position of head cirri and body form.

Most sculpins are small, shallow water, bottom-living species abundant in tide pools although some are found down to 2000 m. Food is bottom invertebrates such as molluscs, crustaceans, worms, insects and small fishes.

They are not commercially important except for the **cabezon** although some are used as bait, for dog and cat food or provide young anglers with sport.

See **Arctic sculpin**
Arctic staghorn sculpin
armorhead sculpin
Atlantic hookear
bigeye sculpin
bigmouth sculpin
brown Irish lord
buffalo sculpin
cabezon
calico sculpin
coastrange sculpin
crested sculpin
darter sculpin
deepwater sculpin
dusky sculpin
fluffy sculpin
fourhorn sculpin
fringed sculpin

great sculpin
grubby
grunt sculpin
leister sculpin
longfin sculpin
longhorn sculpin
manacled sculpin
mosshead sculpin
mottled sculpin
moustache sculpin
northern sculpin
Pacific staghorn sculpin
padded sculpin
prickly sculpin
Puget Sound sculpin
red Irish lord
ribbed sculpin
rosylip sculpin
rough hookear
roughback sculpin
roughspine sculpin
saddleback sculpin
sailfin sculpin
scalyhead sculpin
sea raven
sharpnose sculpin
shorthead sculpin
shorthorn sculpin
silverspotted sculpin
slim sculpin
slimy sculpin
smallsail sculpin
smoothhead sculpin
snowflake hookear
spatulate sculpin
spinynose sculpin
spoonhead sculpin
spotfin sculpin
stellate sculpin
thornback sculpin
thorny sculpin
threadfin sculpin
tidepool sculpin
torrent sculpin
twohorn sculpin

scup

Scientific name: *Stenotomus chrysops*
(Linnaeus, 1766)
Family: **Porgy**
Other common names: porgy, northern porgy, sea bream, ironsides, maiden, fair maid

French name: spare doré

Distribution: Found from New Brunswick and Nova Scotia south to Florida.

Characters: The scup is distinguished from its Canadian relative, the **sheepshead**, by having narrow conical teeth at the front of the jaws, a lunate caudal fin with pointed tips and colour pattern. Dorsal fin spines 12–13,

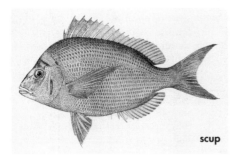

scup

soft rays 11–12. Anal fin with 3 spines and 10–12 soft rays. Pectoral fin rays 15–17. The soft dorsal and anal fins have a scaly sheath at the base. There are 46–55 lateral line scales. Overall colour is a dull silver with blue flecks and faint flank bars. The bar at midflank is the most distinct. There are 12–15 faint flank stripes, and a stripe along the dorsal fin base is blue. The dorsal, anal and caudal fins are dusky with blue flecks. Scup is taken from an Narragansett Indian word, "mishcup", meaning big and close together in reference to the scales. Reaches 46 cm. The world, all-tackle angling record weighed 2.06 kg and was caught in 1992 in Nantucket Sound, Massachusetts.

Biology: Scup are not uncommon visitors to Canadian waters with records dating back to 1866 and numbers high enough in some summers to be fished for deliberately by anglers. Reaches as far north as Passamaquoddy Bay and Sable Island Bank. In the U.S.A., scup schools winter offshore but move into shallow, inshore waters in the warm months to spawn. Food includes crustaceans, worms, molluscs, squid, sea urchins, fish and other bottom organisms. Scup are heterosexual and spawning occurs in spring and summer, peaking in June. Eggs are 0.9 mm in diameter and pelagic. Males and females are mature at 2 years, may live up to 15 years, but populations are dominated by 2–3 year old fish 20–25 cm fork length. Scup are commercially and recreationally important in the U.S.A. Anglers caught 14 million scup north of Cape Hatteras in 1965 from the shore and party boats.

Sea Bass Family

Scientific name: Serranidae
French name: serrans

Sea basses, which includes rockcods, streamer basses and groupers, are found in temperate to tropical seas world-wide with a few species in fresh water. There are about 450 species but only 4 have been reported from Atlantic Canada as strays from the warmer waters to the south.

These fishes are distinguished by a characteristic robust body with a large mouth and by having an opercle with a major spine flanked above and below by a smaller spine. **Temperate Bass** usually have the main spine and the one above it. There are 3 anal fin spines and 6–10 soft rays. The dorsal fin is often notched between a spiny part with 7–13 spines and a posterior part with 10–21 soft rays. The pelvic fin has 1 spine and 5 soft rays. Scales are usually ctenoid, occasionally cycloid. Scales often extend onto the soft dorsal, anal and caudal fins. There is no pelvic axillary scale. There is a complete lateral line, not extending onto the tail fin. The caudal fin is rarely forked as in **Temperate Bass** but is rounded, truncate or lunate. There are usually small canine teeth in the jaws. The maxilla bone of the upper jaw is exposed and does not fit behind the lachrymal bone on mouth closure.

Sea basses are related to the **Temperate Bass Family** in the **Perch Order**.

These fishes are hermaphrodites, capable of developing into either males or females although they are not usually both sexes at the same time. Fertilisation occurs in large groups so eggs and sperm from different individuals mix and ensure genetic diversity. Often they are born as females and some develop into males later. They are large (3 m and over 400 kg) to small (3 cm) fishes. Most sea bass are solitary carnivores found on or just above the sea bed. Some live in caves or crevices. They tend to lie in wait for prey and seize it with a sudden rush. Their habitat is often rough bottoms near rocks and reefs so they also favour shipwrecks and harbours. Large groupers can be tamed and fed fish by hand when diving.

These are important food fishes also sought by anglers and the smaller species are popular in the aquarium trade. Some tropical species may cause a form of food poisoning known as ciguatera.

See **black sea bass**
  red barbier
  snowy grouper
  yellowfin bass

Sea Chub Family

Scientific name: Kyphosidae
French name: kyphoses

Sea chubs, nibblers, rudderfishes, drummers and **halfmoons** are found world-wide in warmer waters. There are about 42 species with 1 on the Atlantic and 1 on the Pacific coast of Canada.

Sea chubs have a small mouth in a blunt head. The body is oval-shaped. The dorsal fin is usually continuous with 9–16 spines and 11–28 soft rays. Teeth are usually incisor-like for cutting and have the shape of a hockey stick with the base horizontal. They are in 1 main row with small, pointed teeth bordering the main row. The spiny dorsal fin may be folded back into a groove. The anal fin has 3 spines. Scales extend onto the fins except the spiny dorsal fin, and onto the head. Scales are small, cycloid or ctenoid. The swimbladder is unusual in that it is divided posteriorly and extends into the tail region.

Sea chubs are members of the **Perch Order** classified close to the **Deeperherring** and **Butterflyfish** families. The rudderfishes, nibblers and halfmoons are sometimes classified as distinct families.

Some sea chubs feed primarily on algae using the incisor-shaped teeth to nibble this food. Their nibbling habit extends to other fishes and they are difficult to keep in aquaria. They are usually found near shore around reefs, rocky areas and harbours as adults with young fish pelagic in association with floating seaweed. Some species (rud-

derfishes) follow ships for long distances, apparently to feed on scraps thrown overboard. These fishes are both food and game fishes but are not often highly esteemed.

See **Bermuda chub**
  halfmoon

sea lamprey

Scientific name: *Petromyzon marinus* Linnaeus, 1758
Family: **Lamprey**
Other common names: lake lamprey, lamprey eel, lamper eel, stone sucker
French name: grande lamproie marine

Distribution: Both sides of the North Atlantic Ocean. In the west from Labrador to the Gulf of Mexico. Although found throughout Atlantic Canada, spawning migrations into streams on P.E.I. have not been recorded. Throughout the Great Lakes.

Characters: This species is the largest lamprey and perhaps the most effective parasite. The sucking disc is large with hard, large and sharp teeth. The bar below the mouth has 6–10 large cusps. There are 4 pairs of bicuspid inner lateral teeth. There are 63–80 trunk myomeres. Spawning males develop a rope-like ridge from the head to the first dorsal fin. This species is distinguished from other lampreys by having 2 dorsal fins and the teeth over the mouth not in a bar but a single tooth with 2 pointed cusps.

sea lamprey

disc view

Adults are blotched dark-brown to black. Landlocked populations are grey-blue (as are newly transformed adults) but become golden-brown when spawning. Ammocoetes are pale grey to brown. Both adults and ammocoetes are lighter below. Teeth and disc are yellow. Attains 1.2 m. Landlocked fish are smaller.

Biology: The sea lamprey is anadromous, entering rivers to spawn but living in the sea. There are, however, landlocked native populations which live and spawn in Lake Ontario and Lake Champlain and introduced populations in other Great Lakes and Big Rideau Lake, Ontario. In the sea, where they spend about 2 years, they are found from inter-tidal areas to the deep ocean at 4099 m.

Spawning occurs in spring and early summer with a migration into running fresh water during night-times. Migrations up to 320 km occur. Migrations take place at 10–18.5°C and spawning at 17–19°C. Adults do not feed prior to and during migration. The gut becomes reduced, sight fails until the fish are blind and the skin begins to fall off. They may be attracted to suitable spawning streams by sensing chemicals given off by larvae resident there from previous spawnings. Barriers almost 2 m high can be crept over using the sucking disc.

Males build the nest, later helped by the female. The nest is up to a metre long and females deposit up to 305,000 small, about 1 mm diameter, eggs. The female attaches to a stone at the upstream end of the nest and the male glides over her to attach to the top of her head. The male curls his body around the female so the genital organs are close together. Contractions expel eggs and sperm. Spawning acts take 2–5 seconds and are repeated every 4–5 minutes. The nest may be fanned by whipping motions of the body to cause sand to drift over and protect the eggs from predators.

The ammocoete stage is reported to last 18 years or more although this seems dubious, and 4–8 years is more likely. They live in u-shaped burrows. Growth is rapid and they more than double in length in 6 months. In the St. John River system, N.B. many lampreys do not feed during the 9–10 months after the beginning of metamorphosis in mid-July. Metamorphosis involves changes for suctorial feeding, resulting in a more active life style as a parasite. During this process length remains much the same but weights decline. Food of adults includes whales and seals as well as large pelagic fishes. Only **swordfish** and **striped bass** are reported to eat these lampreys in the sea.

This species is a major pest in the Great Lakes to which it gained access after the construction of the Welland Canal in 1829. It was first detected in Lake Erie in 1921 and by 1946 had reached Lake Superior. It feeds on several commercially important fishes such as **lake trout** and **whitefishes**. The 3000 ton lake trout catch in Lake Michigan in 1944 fell to 16 kg by 1955. Over 6000 chemicals were tested to find a means of poisoning the ammocoetes which are the most accessible stage of the life cycle. Only 2 chemicals proved practical as lampricides and vast sums have been spent in Canada and the U.S.A. poisoning streams. Even barrier dams to prevent spawning runs have been built and sterile males released to prevent fertilisation of eggs. The lampricide has reduced the spawning phase by 80–90% and rehabilitated a sport and commercial fishery worth billions of dollars. Each lamprey can kill about 20 kg of fish during a 12–20 month feeding period, earning its popular title "vampire of the Great Lakes." Unfortunately other lamprey species in the Great Lakes have been affected by poisoning, particularly the **silver lamprey**, which has disappeared from about half the streams treated. It may prove possible to lure adult lampreys into traps or streams unsuitable for spawning by using the chemical petromygonol sulphate and allocholic acid. These bile acids are released from the gall bladder of ammocoetes and adults may home on spawning streams by detecting these chemicals. As natural components of the environment, these bile chemicals are not detrimental.

sea raven

Scientific name: *Hemitripterus americanus* (Gmelin, 1789)
Family: **Sculpin**
Other common names: toad sculpin, whip sculpin, red sculpin, sea sculpin, gurnet, puff-belly, scratch belly, sea hen
French name: hémitriptère atlantique

Distribution: Found from southern Labrador south to Chesapeake Bay.

Characters: This species is uniquely characterised among its Atlantic coast relatives by having the head, chin and first dorsal spine tips with fleshy tabs and the skin being rough. The tabs on each lower jaw number 4–8. First dorsal fin spines 16–17, second dorsal fin with 1 spine and 12 soft rays, and

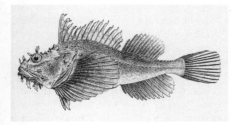

sea raven

anal rays 13–14. The skin has prickles which are enlarged on the upper flank and near the lateral line. Overall colour is usually reddish-brown with darker brown marbling. Fish may be a rich vermilion, grey or brown. The belly is yellow. The fins have light spots, blotches or bars and the pectoral and anal fins often have yellow rays. Reaches 64 cm and 3.2 kg.

Biology: This species favours hard or rock bottoms in shallow to moderately deep water, rarely to 192 m. On the Scotian Shelf they favour 37–108 m depths and 6–9°C temperatures. However they have been caught at the surface and at a temperature range of less than 0°C to 15.6°C. Food is voraciously consumed and includes crustaceans, molluscs, sea urchins and such fishes as **Atlantic herring, sand lances, sculpins** and **silver hake**. Spawning occurs from late autumn to early winter. Eggs are yellow to bright orange, up to 4 mm in diameter and number up to 40,000 per female. The eggs are adhesive and deposited in clusters of 141–478. They may be attached to sponges or even hidden inside them. This sculpin has the unusual ability of inflating its belly with water, presumably as an anti-predator mechanism, but in the process it floats helplessly at the surface. It also contains an anti-freeze in its blood which lowers the freezing point. This may be evidence of an Arctic ancestry since it apparently avoids freezing conditions in Atlantic Canada. This sculpin has been used as bait in lobster traps and in physiological studies of heart performance and chemistry.

sea tadpole

Scientific name: *Careproctus reinhardti* (Krøyer, 1862)
Family: **Snailfish**
Other common names: none
French name: petite limace de mer

Distribution: Found from northern Baffin Island and Hudson Bay to the Gulf of St. Lawrence and St. Lawrence River estuary. Elsewhere in Arctic waters of the northern hemisphere.

Characters: This snailfish is separated from its Arctic-Atlantic relatives in Canada by having a small, deep-cupped adhesive disc, 1 pair of nostrils, slender body, and 16–30 pyloric caeca. Dorsal fin rays 50–58, anal rays 41–58 and pectoral rays 25–34. Overall colour is reddish or whitish. Peritoneum pale. Reaches 21.5 cm.

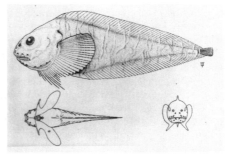

sea tadpole

Biology: This species occurs at 48–384 m in the Gulf, elsewhere down to 1284 m on mud bottoms. Females are mature at sizes larger than 12 cm. Spawning probably occurs in spring and summer in the Gulf. Eggs are about 4 mm in diameter and number 40–50 in each female.

Sea Toad Family

Scientific name: Chaunacidae
French name: crapauds de mer

Sea toads, gapers or coffinfishes are found in the Atlantic, Indian and Pacific oceans where there are 12 species, with 1 occurring on the Canadian Atlantic coast.

These **anglerfishes** have a balloon-shaped body with flabby, thin but rough skin. The body can be inflated by pumping water into sacs under the skin. There is a gill opening in the posterior half of the body below the dorsal fin. The fishing apparatus fits into a depression on the snout. The lateral line and head canals are obvious and open but are protected by enlarged spiny scales. The body is pink to red-orange.

Sea toads are relatives of the **Batfish Family** in the **Anglerfish Order**.

They are usually found in water 90 m to 2000 m deep. Eggs are laid in a large, gelatinous floating mass.

See **redeye gaper**

Seadevil Family

Scientific name: Ceratiidae
French name: poissons-pêcheurs

Seadevils are found world-wide in the deep ocean and there are only 4 species, and 3 are reported from Atlantic Canada.

Females are recognised by having 2–3 rays in front of the soft dorsal fin modified into fleshy knobs or caruncles. Dorsal and anal fin rays are usually 4, range 3–5. The esca or bait is simple with only 1–2 filaments. The skin is spiny. There are no sphenotic spines. The parietal bones are large. Males are parasitic on females when mature. They have a pair of denticular teeth on the snout tip and 2 pairs on the lower jaw tip. The mouth is vertical to strongly oblique. Their eyes are well-developed and they depend on sight rather than smell to locate females.

Seadevils are related to such members of the **Anglerfish Order** as the **Fanfin**, **Whipnose**, **Leftvent**, **Dreamer**, **Wolftrap**, **Footballfish** and **Werewolf** families, which all lack pelvic fins, scales and a pseudobranch, have bones at the front of the head (frontals) which are not united, have the lower pharyngeal bones reduced and toothless, and have 8–9 caudal fin rays. Species are distinguished by the number of caruncles and esca morphology.

Larvae are found in surface waters but adults are in the deep sea either meso- or bathypelagic. The illicium can be withdrawn into a sheath of tissue on the back such that its rear end protrudes from a pore in front of the caruncles. This movement is probably used to draw the esca, and the enticed prey, closer to the mouth.

See **stargazing seadevil**
twoclub angler
warted seadevil

seahorses

Seahorses are familiar fishes often displayed in aquaria or sold dried as souvenirs. Their erect body posture, prehensile tail, a pouch in which males brood the young, and long snout are very distinctive.

There are about 30 species world-wide in shallow, warmer waters, but only 1 is found on the Atlantic coast of Canada. They are classified in the **Pipefish Family**, sharing with the pipefishes an elongated body enclosed by a series of bony rings.

See **lined seahorse**

seaperches

Seaperches are members of the Pacific coast **Surfperch Family** with 2 Canadian species, the **striped seaperch** and the **white seaperch**.

Searobin Family

Scientific name: Triglidae
French name: trigles

Searobins and armored searobins (or gurnards) are found world-wide in temperate to tropical seas. There are about 100 species with 3 on the Atlantic coast of Canada.

These fishes have 2 dorsal fins, obviously separate, the lower 2–3 pectoral rays are enlarged, finger-like feelers and the head is encased in bony armour. There are two groups of searobins: the unarmored ones with ctenoid scales or plates, a row of spines along each side of the dorsal fin bases, usually spines at the snout tip, 3 feelers and a shallower habitat, usually to 180 m; and the armored searobins which have a body enclosed by 4 rows of spiny plates, 2 flattened snout projections, 2 feelers, barbels on the lower jaw and often a deeper habitat, to 1200 m.

Searobins are related to the **Scorpionfish Family** in the **Mail-cheeked Order**. Armored searobins are placed in a family separate from the unarmored searobins by some scientists. The name gurnard is from the Latin, to grunt, because of the sounds they make.

These fishes are bottom dwellers, using the finger-like lower pectoral rays to feel for food. This process looks as if the fish is "walking" along the sea bed. The rays can be used to turn stones and probe shells for food. They may also swim by using the large, upper part of the pectorals which flap like wings and enable searobins to glide through the water. Some species have been seen to leave the water surface propelled by the tail muscles. They can produce a chirping, bird-like sound using the swimbladder and associated muscles when taken out of the water. Sound production also occurs in the water and has been likened to grunts, growls and staccato calls. Young searobins are pelagic but soon settle to the bottom. Food is mostly crustaceans and molluscs. Some species are commercially important.

See **armored searobin**
 northern searobin
 striped searobin

seasnails

Seasnail refers to some members of the marine **Snailfish Family** such as the **black seasnail** and formerly the **Atlantic snailfish** and **dusky snailfish**. Since seasnail is used for a type of mollusc, the name should be avoided for fishes to reduce confusion.

Sequinfish Family

Scientific name: Ariommatidae
French name: poisson pailletés

Sequinfishes or ariommatids are tropical and subtropical fishes found world-wide with about 6 species. Only 1 species is reported from Atlantic Canada.

The caudal peduncle has 2 low, fleshy keels on each side. There are 2 dorsal fins, the first with 10–12 spines and the second with 13–18 soft rays. The pelvic fins fold into a groove. The anal fin has 3 spines and 12–16 soft rays. The roof of the mouth is toothless.

This family is related to the **Ruff**, **Driftfish**, **Squaretail** and **Butterfish** families, all of which share toothed, sac-like outgrowths of the gut. If the gill cover is lifted, the sacs may be seen behind the last gill arch. These families are distinguished by number of dorsal fins, presence/absence of pelvic fins in adults,

number and size of dorsal fin spines, presence/absence of keels on the caudal peduncle and whether there are teeth on the roof of the mouth. The common name is derived from the circular and easily detached scales. This family is a member of the **Perch Order**.

These are deepwater fishes living near the bottom. They are poorly known because they are seldom caught. Young fish are known to live under jellyfish. They have been used as food and are caught at night using lift-nets and attracting lights.

See **silver-rag**

sergeant major

Scientific name: *Abudefduf saxatilis*
 (Linnaeus, 1756)
Family: **Damselfish**
Other common names: coralfish, five-banded
 damselfish, chauffet soleil
French name: sergent-major

Distribution: Found from Nova Scotia south to Uruguay in the western Atlantic Ocean. World-wide in warmer seas although Atlantic populations may be a species distinct from others.

Characters: The single nostril on each side of the head and the 5 bars are distinctive. Dorsal fin with 13 spines and 12–13 soft rays. The anal fin has 2 spines and 10–13 soft rays. Pectoral fin with 18–19 rays. Lateral line scales 21. Shallow water specimens are bright yellow above with 5 dark brown to black bars (hence "sergeant

sergeant major

major"). The belly and lower flank are silvery-grey to greenish-grey. Fins are dusky. There is a dark spot at the upper pectoral fin base. In deeper water specimens are a deep blue or dark grey and bars are hardly evident. Reaches 23 cm.

Biology: A single, stray Canadian specimen, 2.9 cm long, was caught off the Scotian Shelf in 1966. In southern areas, such as the West Indies, this is a very abundant species found around coral reefs, rocky and sandy areas, and artificial structures. It can tolerate very high temperatures, up to 37°C, which few other fishes can, and so may be found in many shallow habitats under tropical heat. It retreats into cavities in reefs when threatened. Young may be found in sargassum weed. Food is anemones, algae, crustaceans, sea squirts and fish. This is an aggressive species when adult, but young are sociable. Males clean a hard surface to which eggs are attached individually by a thread and then guarded until hatching. The egg mass is deep red or purple. In the Caribbean it is taken by shore seines, handlines or cast-nets and is marketed fresh.

seven-aoa platelamp

Scientific name: *Lampanyctus festivus*
　　Tåning, 1928
Family: **Lanternfish**
Other common names: none
French name: lampe-platine à sept-aoa

Distribution: Found in the Atlantic, Indian and Pacific oceans including off the Scotian Shelf in Atlantic Canada.

Characters: This species and 7 relatives in the genus *Lampanyctus* are separated from other Atlantic species by lacking photophores

seven-aoa platelamp

close to the dorsal body edge, the PLO photophore is well above the pectoral fin base level while the second PVO photophore is at or below the upper pectoral base level, there are 4 Prc, the first PO and two PVO photophores are not on a straight line, both males and females have caudal luminous glands

composed of overlapping, scale-like structures without a black pigment border, the fourth PO photophore is highly elevated, there are no luminous, scale-like structures on the belly between the pelvic fin bases or these bases and the anus, there are 4 VO photophores and the SAO series is strongly angled. This species is distinguished from its relatives by having 13–14 large gill rakers, long pectoral fins extending beyond the pelvic fin bases and no cheek photophores. Dorsal fin rays 13–16, anal rays 17–22 and pectoral rays 13–17. AO photophores 14–16. Lateral line organs 39–40. The supracaudal luminous gland has 2–3 scale-like segments and the infracaudal 7–9 segments. Reaches 13.8 cm.

Biology: This species is mostly subtropical. First reported from Canada in 1969. Depth distribution in the Atlantic is 475–1000 m by day with a maximum abundance at 700 m, and 40–325 m by night with a maximum abundance at 75–150 m. Sexual maturity is attained at about 8.4 cm. Life span is at least 2 years. Spawning occurs year round with a peak in winter.

sevengill shark

Scientific name: *Notorhynchus cepedianus*
　　(Péron, 1807)
Family: **Cow Shark**
Other common names: broadnose sevengill
　　shark, spotted cow shark
French name: requin à sept branchies

Distribution: From northern British Columbia to southern California and Mexico on the Pacific coast. Also in the western Pacific and the Southern Hemisphere.

Characters: The only Canadian shark with 7 gill slits. In addition the head is broad and rounded, eyes are small, the body spotted, and the lower jaw teeth are comb or saw-like unlike the smaller, pointed, upper

sevengill shark

jaw teeth. The caudal peduncle is short with the upper length about equal to the dorsal fin base length. Body with many small black spots over blue-grey or brown-grey to reddish brown. The belly is paler. Dorsal fin and upper caudal fin lobe without black tips. Rare specimens are piebald, having a white background with large, dark spots. May reach 4 m but most definite records smaller, e.g. 2.9 m and more than 182 kg.

Biology: Common is shallow waters close to shore even at the surf line, moving with the tides, and down to at least 46 m. This species is active, a strong swimmer, and a noted predator particularly on other sharks like **spiny dogfish**, on **rays**, on **bony fishes** including **salmon**, **herring**, and on carrion including human flesh. It will also take harbour seals. This shark is ovoviviparous with large litters of up to 86 young measuring 45–53 cm, which females drop in shallow bays. Males mature between 150 and 180 cm and females between 192 and 208 cm. This shark is aggressive when provoked and potentially dangerous to man. This species has a high quality flesh considered to be one of the best tasting in sharks. It is fished commercially in some parts of the world, like California, with rods or longlines. Oil and leather are other products. It is often kept in aquaria and one in a California aquarium attacked a diver and bit out a section of flesh from his forearm. The section of flesh was later found floating in the aquarium and surgically re-attached to the diver. Small fish are easy to catch in the shallow waters of nursery bays during the late summer and fall. When pulled out of the water, they will thrash about and attempt to bite anything they can reach. Large specimens often have to be subdued with firearms when boated.

shads

Shads are members of the **Herring Family** with 2 Canadian species, the **American shad** and the **gizzard shad**. The former is found on the Atlantic coast and in rivers draining there but has also been introduced to the Pacific coast and its rivers. The **gizzard shad** is found in freshwater Atlantic drainages. Shad is derived from the Old English for members of the **Herring Family**.

Shanny Family

Scientific name: Stichaeidae
French name: stichées

The shannies or **pricklebacks** are mostly found in the North Pacific Ocean with a few species in the North Atlantic Ocean and the Arctic Ocean. There are about 65 species with 14 reported solely from the Pacific coast, 2 solely from the Atlantic coast, 4 from both the Atlantic and Arctic coasts, 1 from the Arctic coast only, and 2 from the Pacific, Arctic and Atlantic coasts, for a total of 23 species in Canada.

The name prickleback is derived from the long dorsal fin covering most of the back, which is composed wholly of spines in most species. The anal fin is also long with 1–5 spines. The anal fin is longer than the distance from the snout to the anal fin origin. Both the dorsal and anal fins may be joined to the caudal fin, but are usually separate. Pelvic fins are small, thoracic (just in front of the pectoral fin base) and have 1 spine and 2–4 soft rays. Pelvic fins may be absent. There is a long compressed and small body and a small mouth. The lateral line is often indistinct. Scales are very small, cycloid and may be absent. Ribs are present.

This family is related to the **Gunnel Family** which it resembles superficially, but gunnels have a shorter anal fin, the distance from snout to anal fin origin being greater than anal fin length. The family is a member of the **Perch Order**.

Shannies are common in tide pools and shallow waters where there is algae. The Japanese make fish cakes out of some shannies.

See **Arctic shanny**
Atlantic warbonnet
black prickleback
blackline prickleback
bluebarred prickleback
daubed shanny
decorated warbonnet
fourline snakeblenny
high cockscomb
longsnout prickleback
matcheek warbonnet
mosshead warbonnet
pearly prickleback

radiated shanny
ribbon prickleback
rock prickleback
slender cockscomb
slender eelblenny
snake prickleback
snakeblenny
stout eelblenny
whitebarred prickleback
Y-prickleback

sharks

Sharks comprise part of the Class Chondrichthyes or **cartilaginous fishes** along with **chimaeras** and **rays**. Scientifically they are known as Selachimorpha (or Pleurotremata). Sharks and **rays** are one subclass of the **cartilaginous fishes** and **chimaeras** form the only other subclass. There are 8 living orders of sharks with about 350 species and 6 of these have Canadian representatives for a total of 12 families and 37 species.

Sharks are readily identified by their general appearance, including a torpedo-shaped body and ventral mouth. Their characters include 5–7 lateral gill openings partly over or in front of the pectoral fins (1 external opening in **chimaeras**), the anterior margin of the pectoral fin is not attached to the side of the head (as in **rays**), pectoral girdle halves fused ventrally and not joined dorsally, the anal fin is present or absent, 1–2 dorsal fins, usually heterocercal tails (upper lobe longer than the lower and the internal skeleton being turned up), skin with a sandpapery feel owing to the placoid scales (a plate-like bony socket embedded in the skin with a small but sharp tooth bearing cusp(s) protruding out of the skin) which are precursors of **vertebrate** teeth and different from scales of **bony fishes**, nictitating eyelids may be present, teeth in several rows in the mouth with a lost tooth being replaced by a forward migration of the rear row tooth, internal fertilisation by means of male claspers (modified from part of the pelvic fins), a few, large eggs develop internally or externally in horny capsules and long gestation up to 2 years. When eggs are deposited in the sea in a case the shark is called oviparous. Ovoviviparity occurs when the shark retains the eggs which are nourished by yolk from a yolk sac.

Some ovoviviparous sharks show uterine cannibalism where the young feed on eggs or smaller young within the mother after their yolk is absorbed. A single embryo may then survive in each uterus. In viviparity the embryo depends on yolk but once this is used up it becomes attached to the uterus wall by a yolk-sac placenta and is fed through the mother's blood stream. Young sharks, known as pups, are quite large and well-developed when born, well able to survive a hostile world. Fossils date back to the Lower Devonian and they flourished in the Carboniferous. The word "shark" is supposedly derived from the German dialect word for rascal.

Sharks are principally marine although some enter or live in fresh water. They are found from the shallows of tide pools (even very large sharks) down to great depths in the open ocean. They vary greatly in size (15 cm to over 18 m) and many are harmless to man. However all large sharks should be considered potentially dangerous to man. Sharks have formidable teeth in some species which are used to drastic effect on prey and humans. There have been no direct attacks on humans by sharks in Canada although dories have been sunk. Sharks are the most economically important **cartilaginous fishes** used as food, including shark fin soup, a vitamin source from the liver, for leather from the skin, teeth and jaws as curios, and as sport fishes. There was a catch of 101 tonnes of large sharks in Canada in 1988 (in addition to **spiny dogfish** and **porbeagle**).

See **Angel Shark Order**
Carpet Shark Order
Cow Shark Order
Dogfish Shark Order
Ground Shark Order
Mackerel Shark Order

sharksucker

Scientific name: *Echeneis naucrates* Linnaeus, 1758
Family: **Remora**
Other common names: pilot sucker, white-tailed sucker, suckerfish
French name: naucrate

Distribution: World-wide in warm waters and from Uruguay to Nova Scotia in the western Atlantic Ocean.

Characters: This remora is distinguished from its Canadian relatives by having 20–28 disc laminae, pointed pectoral fins, a slender

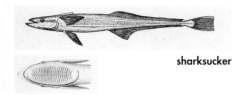

sharksucker

body and a striped colour pattern. There are 31–42, usually 39, dorsal fin rays, and 30–41, usually 36, anal fin rays. There are 21–24 pectoral fin rays. The lower jaw has an obvious fleshy tab. Overall colour is grey to brown or black. There is a distinctive black stripe along the flank edged by white. Fins are black with white margins. Attains 96.5 cm.

Biology: This remora is often found attached to large **sharks**, but is also found on turtles and large **bony fishes**. It has also been reported as attaching to swimmers, and is often caught by fishermen since it swims free of hosts. It is a rare stray found in Nova Scotian waters. Sharksuckers have been caught from the surface to 141 m. When attached to a **shark**, this **remora** uses ram ventilation but when free-swimming or stationary active gill ventilation is used to ensure sufficient oxygen flow over the gills. It may remain attached to **sharks** which enter fresh waters. Food includes crustaceans, squids and even clams. During spawning a male will nudge the female's abdomen and a group of 4–6 males drive the female to the surface where eggs and sperm are released. Pelagic eggs are 2.6 mm in diameter and about 500 are released each day during the spawning season based on aquarium observations. In the Caribbean Sea spawning probably occurs in summer at water temperatures above 25°C while in the Indian Ocean spawning occurs from January to April. The young sharksucker begins attaching to sharks when it is 5.5 cm long.

sharpchin barracudina

Scientific name: *Paralepis coregonides borealis* Reinhardt, 1837
Family: **Barracudina**
Other common names: scaled lancet fish

French name: lussion à menton

Distribution: Found from Arctic waters into the Atlantic Ocean including along the Canadian coast.

Characters: This species is distinguished from its Canadian relatives by having pectoral fins shorter than the anal fin base, smooth-edged lower jaw teeth, body scales (but easily lost), pelvic fin origin below the dorsal fin origin, 22–24 anal fin rays, and the rear tip of the premaxilla bone of the upper jaw under the nostril. Dorsal fin rays 9–11, pectoral rays 14–15 and pelvic rays 9. Lateral line scales 57–61. Vertebrae 67–74. Overall colour is iridescent silver overlain by black to brown, becoming lighter ventrally. Peritoneum black. Reaches over 50 cm. Another subspecies is found in the Mediterranean Sea.

sharpchin barracudina

Biology: Reported from the Davis Strait and Labrador Sea, Flemish Cap, Newfoundland Shelf, Grand Bank and off Georges Bank. Apparently quite common and an important food for **Atlantic salmon**, as well as **cod, tuna, lancetfish** and seals. Barracudina in **cod** and **Atlantic salmon** stomachs point head forward suggesting they were captured tail first by pursuit. Food is shrimps and fishes. Young fish are found from the surface to 200 m, older fish are deeper and seldom caught. Some specimens have been found stranded on beaches, apparently adults which have drifted too far north and frozen to death. Reproduction occurs from March to September in temperate waters. Larvae hatch at 70–140 m.

sharpchin rockfish

Scientific name: *Sebastes zacentrus*
    (Gilbert, 1890)
Family: **Scorpionfish**
Other common names: big-eyed rockfish
French name: sébaste à menton pointu

Distribution: Found from Alaska to California including British Columbia.

Characters: This species is distinguished by a complex of characters including head spines, anal fin spines, a strong knob on the chin and 2 triangular, blunt spines on the lower edge of the bone under the eye. There may be a shelf under the nostrils. Dorsal fin

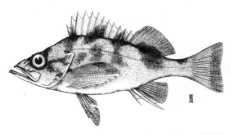

sharpchin rockfish

spines 13, soft rays 13–15, usually 14. Anal fin soft rays 6–8, usually 7, second anal spine twice as thick as third and longer. Pectoral fin rays 16–19, usually 17, with 8–9 unbranched. Lateral line pores 39–47, scale rows below lateral line 43–59. Gill rakers 31–37. Vertebrae 27. Supraocular, coronal and nuchal spines usually absent, other spines strong and sharp. Overall colour is pinkish with or without 5–6 saddles on the back. Flanks are yellowish-red and the belly white. Two dusky bars radiate back from the eye. Peritoneum black. Reaches 33 cm.

Biology: This species lives on soft bottoms at 91–402 m. Also reported by Russian trawlers on Hodgkins guyot off the coast of British Columbia. Half the male population is mature at 24 cm and females at 25 cm in Canada. Maximum age approaches an estimated 50 years. Young are born in July.

sharpnose sculpin

Scientific name: *Clinocottus acuticeps*
   (Gilbert, 1896)
Family: **Sculpin**
Other common names: none
French name: chabot à nez pointu

Distribution: Found from the Bering Sea to California including British Columbia.

Characters: This species and its relatives, the **calico** and **mosshead sculpins**, are separated from other Pacific coast sculpins by having 3 pelvic fin rays, branchiostegal membranes joined and forming a fold over the isthmus, largest preopercular spine not antler-

like, no scales, and the anal fin origin is below the second dorsal fin. This species is separated from its relatives by the inner pelvic ray being attached to the belly by a membrane and by having 1–2 cirri on the end of the upper jaw. First dorsal fin spines 7–9, second dorsal fin rays 13–17, anal rays 9–13 and pectoral rays 13–15. Lateral line pores 33–36. The snout is pointed. Male sharpnose sculpins have a long genital papilla, reaching the anal fin, and with a triple branch at the tip. Females have flanges around the vent. Cirri are found as follows: 1 on the inside of each nasal spine, 1 on the upper eye, 1 pair above and behind the eye, 2–3 pairs between the eye and occiput, 1 or more at the end of the upper jaws, 2 on the preopercle edge, 2 at the upper gill cover edge, along the anterior two-thirds of the lateral line and at each dorsal fin spine tip. Overall colour is olive-green, bright green or light brown. The cheek is silver to white. The back has 6 saddles. Three bars radiate from the eye. The belly is white to cream. The first dorsal fin is dark between the first and third spines. Fins are barred except for the clear pelvics. Reaches 6.4 cm.

sharpnose sculpin

Biology: Common in high rocky intertidal pools and subtidal areas, on sand and also entering areas near fresh water and sometimes streams. Spawning occurs from January to April near Vancouver. Egg masses number 18–98 eggs. Eggs are brown, amber or olive-green. They are laid in a single, circular layer on rocks exposed to the air about half of each day. The eggs are protected from desiccation by a layer of rockweed over them.

sharptail eel

Scientific name: *Myrichthys breviceps*
   (Richardson, 1845)
Family: **Snake Eel**
Other common names: none

French name: serpent de mer à queue pointue

Distribution: From Brazil to the Laurentian Channel of Atlantic Canada. Most common from Brazil to the Florida Keys.

Characters: This species is distinguished by having a tail ending in a hard point, the dorsal fin origin is on top of the head, the

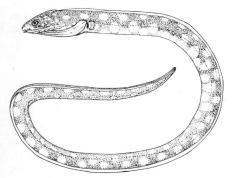

sharptail eel

pectoral fin is small and broad-based, and the colour pattern. The mouth is small with molar teeth in several rows. The body and head are dark brown or olive with a violet tinge in some specimens. The dorsal fin is dusky. The body, head and dorsal fin are covered with large, pale yellow or pale green spots in 2–4 rows on the body. There are 30–35 pairs of spots along each side of the dorsal fin. Adults attain 102 cm.

Biology: This species is known from a specimen, 56 cm long, which was found attached to the stomach of a **swordfish** caught 259 km off Cape Breton. Since **swordfish** are very good swimmers and the snake eel was embedded in the stomach lining, this eel was most probably eaten outside Canadian waters — some ichthyologists claim it as a Canadian fish despite this! Adults are common in clear water near the bottom, particularly in seagrass beds, but also in harbours. Found down to 9 m but usually at 3 m or less. This is a burrowing species but is often seen during the day.

sheepshead

Scientific name: *Archosargus probatocephalus* (Walbaum, 1792)
Family: **Porgy**

Other common names: sheepshead porgy, rondeau mouton
French name: spare tête-de-mouton

Distribution: Found from Nova Scotia south to the Gulf of Mexico and Brazil.

Characters: The sheepshead is distinguished from its Canadian relative, the **scup**, by the broad incisor teeth at the front of the jaws, a shallowly forked caudal fin with rounded tips and colour pattern. The dorsal fin has 10–12 spines and 11–13 soft rays. The anal fin has 3 spines and 9–11 soft rays. There are about 44–49 scales in the lateral line. The back is olive-brown with a black bar across the nape. The flanks are silvery to yellowish with 4–7, slightly oblique and strong bands. Reaches 91 cm. The world, all-tackle angling record weighed 9.63 kg and was caught in 1982 in New Orleans, Louisiana.

sheepshead

Biology: A single specimen has been collected by SCUBA diving in Shelburne Harbour, Nova Scotia in 1973. This species may also stray to the Bay of Fundy. Sheepshead are common in shallow waters, in estuaries and around artificial structures. Food is principally molluscs, but also bryozoans, echinoderms, sea squirts, crustaceans, worms, and barnacles. The volume of barnacles eaten may be so great as to contribute significantly to the sediment content on the sea floor as the broken barnacle plates pass through and out of the sheepshead gut. In Florida this may be 4.9 kg/sq m annually. Spawning in the U.S.A. occurs in February–April. This is an important sport and commercial species in the U.S.A. where 117 tons were marketed fresh in 1975 and 975 tons in 1974.

shiner perch

Scientific name: *Cymatogaster aggregata*
   Gibbons, 1854
Family: **Surfperch**
Other common names: yellow shiner,
   shiner seaperch, seven-eleven perch
French name: perche-méné

   Distribution: From southeastern Alaska
through British Columbia to Baja California.
   Characters: This surfperch is distinguished from other Canadian species by having 36–43 lateral line scales and no frenum.

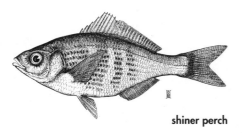

shiner perch

Dorsal fin spines 8–11, soft rays 18–23. Anal fin spines 3, soft rays 22–26. Pectoral fin rays 19–21. Head concave over the eye. The caudal fin is forked. Silvery overall but breeding males are blackish. The back is dark to greenish. Scales bear black spots forming flank stripes. Three yellow bars cross these stripes and give the appearance of the numbers 711, hence one of the common names. There is a dark spot over the lip. Reaches 20 cm.
   Biology: This is a very common schooling marine species which may enter fresh water. In the sea it may be in shallow water of eelgrass and kelp beds and around harbour structures on soft bottoms, or down to 146 m. Food is small crustaceans, barnacles, mussels and algae. Mating occurs inshore in large schools in April–July, fertilisation occurs in November–December and about 8–36 young are born tail first mostly in the following June–July. Young are 5.6–7.8 cm long. Males may defend territories against other males of similar size in competition for large females. Courtship occupies about a third of the male's daily activity, a considerable expenditure of energy. Males may even guard females who are near-term or after birth since multiple spawnings are possible and proximity confers an advantage on the male. Males are mature shortly after birth and breed at about 1 year. Females are larger and do not breed until their second year. Multiple inseminations are common but the benefit of this is unclear. Fecundity is independent of mates since sperm not used to fertilise eggs degenerate and cannot be used for fertilising later broods. However the long period of sperm storage is unusual and multiple insemination may insure successful transfer of viable sperm. Maximum age is probably 4 years. Frequently caught by anglers.

shiners

   Shiners are members of the **Carp Family** named for their silvery sides. Most are members of the genus *Notropis*, with the exception of the **golden shiner** and the **redside shiner** in Canada. *Notropis* is the dominant genus in the family in North America with about 110 species. Shiner is also applied to other silvery fishes, such as the **butterfish**, **Atlantic silverside** and **black crappie** among others.

See **bigmouth shiner**
   blackchin shiner
   blacknose shiner
   bridle shiner
   common shiner
   emerald shiner
   ghost shiner
   golden shiner
   mimic shiner
   pugnose shiner
   redfin shiner
   redside shiner
   river shiner
   rosyface shiner
   sand shiner
   silver shiner
   spotfin shiner
   spottail shiner
   striped shiner
   weed shiner

shining loosejaw

Scientific name: *Aristostomias scintillans*
   (Gilbert, 1915)
Family: **Barbeled Dragonfish**

Other common names: shiny loosejaw
French name: drague scintillante

Distribution: Found in all warm oceans and off southern British Columbia.

Characters: This species is distinguished from Canadian relatives by having a pectoral fin, a suborbital light organ, a barbel on the throat with a distinct bulb lacking filaments, 2 pairs of nostrils, light organs between the pectoral and pelvic fins evenly spaced (not in groups), and 4 pectoral fin rays. The body and head are black. The light organ below the eye is red while the other one behind the eye is blue or green. Emissions of the organ below the eye are near the human visual threshold. Size is up to about 23 cm.

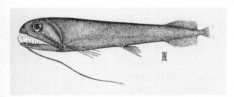

shining loosejaw

Biology: Rarely found close to the surface (29 m in B.C.), most specimens being caught deeper than 300 m. Lives at least 8 years. Food is crustaceans and spawning occurs in the spring.

shining tubeshoulder

Scientific name: *Sagamichthys abei*
    Parr, 1953
Family: **Tubeshoulder**
Other common names: none
French name: circé luisant

Distribution: Found in the Pacific Ocean from Japan to California and in the eastern South Pacific, including off the coast of British Columbia.

Characters: The tube projecting from the flank above the pectoral fin is characteristic of the family. Scales on the head overlap, but not in the usual fashion of those in front over those behind, but the reverse, where each scale overlaps the one in front. There is an evident lateral line with enlarged scales. There are large, white, elongate light organs on the belly. There are 9–10, usually 9, pelvic

fin rays. Enlarged teeth absent or weak on the premaxillary bone of the upper jaw. Adults are dark in colour although young are a light

shining tubeshoulder

blue-grey and lack pigment in the tail region. Reaches 33 cm in length. This species is named for Tokiharu Abe, a Japanese ichthyologist, and Sagami Bay, Japan.

Biology: Descends to depths over 900 m but young will migrate upward to the 200 m level or even as shallow as 37 m, much shallower than any other tubeshoulder. Food is small crustaceans. This is the most abundant tubeshoulder.

short bigeye

Scientific name: *Pristigenys alta* (Gill, 1862)
Family: **Bigeye**
Other common names: none
French name: priacanthe-crapet

Distribution: Found from Nova Scotia south to the northern coast of South America.

Characters: This species is separated from its relatives, the **bulleye** and **bigeye**, by having pelvic fins shorter than the head, the tenth dorsal fin spine not more than twice as long as second spine, and by scale and fin ray counts. Dorsal fin spines 10, soft rays 10–12, usually 11. Anal fin soft rays 9–11, usually 10. Pored lateral line scales 31–40. The body

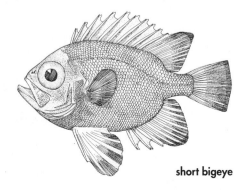

short bigeye

is red or rose and is often blotched. All fins, except the pectoral, are black-tipped. The iris is gold, red or silvery. Reaches 30 cm.

Biology: Canadian specimens are known from Corsair Canyon off southwest Nova Scotia, caught in 1966, and from Sambro Creek and Prospect, N.S. in 1990. This is the northern range limit for the species. Adults are usually found on rock bottoms at 100–200 m. Young, up to 6 cm long, are found in sargassum weed in the Gulf Stream and are often captured for aquaria. Spawning occurs from late June to mid-September along the American coast.

short silver hatchetfish

Scientific name: *Argyropelecus hemigymnus* Cocco, 1829
Family: **Silver Hatchetfish**
Other common names: none
French name: hache d'argent courte

Distribution: Found in all oceans from the tropics to temperate waters. Reported off the Atlantic coast of Canada.

Characters: This species is distinguished by having a hatchet-shaped body, 12 abdominal light organs, telescopic eyes directed upwards and a large blade anterior to the dorsal fin. In addition the lower light organs are not in a nearly continuous row, there is only one spine on the posterior tip of the abdomen and there are 8 dorsal fin rays. Pigment may be distinct or diffuse and change with time of day. The abdomen is dark in preserved fish while the flanks are not pigmented except

short silver hatchetfish

where silvery light organs are outlined in black. Overall colour is silvery with a dark brown band on the anterior back. Reaches

only 40 mm standard length, a dwarf species with males smaller at 28 mm.

Biology: Reported from off the Flemish Cap in Canadian waters. Found mostly at 200–800 m as adults during the day, rising to 100–650 m at night, but has been reported from 3000 m in the Atlantic Ocean east of Canada. Larvae do not migrate but adults do. Depth depends on development stage (larvae tend to be shallower), season and latitude. Feeds at dusk on minute crustaceans and larval fishes. This species is sexually mature at the age of 1 year and adults mostly die after spawning. Mates are located by smell, pheromones being released to aid location. Spawns early to mid-summer in the north, throughout the year south of 40°N. Eggs are up to 1.0 mm diameter.

short-tooth sawpalate

Scientific name: *Serrivomer lanceolatoides* (Schmidt, 1916)
Family: **Sawpalate**
Other common names: black saw-toothed eel
French name: serrivomer à dents courtes

Distribution: Found in the North Atlantic Ocean, including off Nova Scotia and Bermuda in the west.

Characters: This species is separated from its Atlantic/Arctic Canadian relatives by having 175–199 dorsal fin rays, 165–192

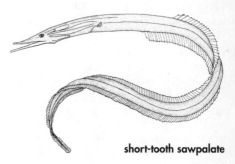

short-tooth sawpalate

anal rays, 7 caudal rays, and 8 branchiostegal rays with only the sixth ray having an anterior process jutting beyond the hyoid arch with which they articulate. The characteristic blade- or saw-like teeth on the roof of the mouth number 30–50 (in adults) in 2 parallel and alternating rows. The anterior part of the body is oval in cross section. Overall colour is blackish-brown. The skin epidermis is easily detached and is iridescent bronze. Reaches 65 cm.

Biology: Known only from a larval specimen 26.8 cm total length caught in 1978 at 80 m off the Scotian Shelf. Adults elsewhere are found at 150–1000 m. Food is crustaceans. Known to breed in the Sargasso Sea in spring and summer. Males lose all but a few, isolated saw teeth as they mature.

shortbarbel dragonfish

Scientific name: *Stomias brevibarbatus*
Ege, 1918
Family: **Barbeled Dragonfish**
Other common names: none
French name: dragon vert

Distribution: North Atlantic Ocean including southwest of Sable Island in Canada.

Characters: Distinguished from the **boa dragonfish** by having 5 rows of hexagonal areas above the light organ rows. The barbel

shortbarbel dragonfish

is less than half head length and has 4 filaments on the bulb at its tip. There are 17–20 dorsal fin rays, 19–22 anal rays and 7–9 pectoral rays. There are 72–76 light organs in the ventral series. Colour is an iridescent dark green. The hexagonal areas form a distinct pattern. Reaches 20 cm in total length, the Canadian record being the largest recorded specimen.

Biology: A single specimen has been caught in Canadian waters in 1982. Less common than other dragonfishes. Found at about 500–1500 m in the day and 100–200 m at night.

shortbeard grenadier

Scientific name: *Chalinura brevibarbis*
Goode and Bean, 1896
Family: **Grenadier**
Other common names: none
French name: grenadier à barbe courte

Distribution: Found in the North Atlantic Ocean including off Georges Bank in Canadian waters.

Characters: It is distinguished from other Canadian Atlantic coast grenadiers by having second dorsal fin rays shorter than anal fin

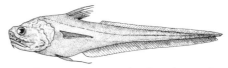

shortbeard grenadier

rays, 6 branchiostegal rays, 8–9 pelvic fin rays, serrated anterior edge to the first 1–2 rays of the first dorsal fin, origin of the second dorsal fin behind the anus level, scaleless areas on each side of the upper snout surface and a long pectoral fin reaching back to overlap the anal fin. The first dorsal fin has 9–10 rays, the pectoral fin 18–20 rays. Scales have small spines arranged in slightly diverging rows. Overall colour a pale brown with lips, peritoneum, mouth and gill cavities black. Reaches at least 35 cm.

Biology: Specimens have been caught at 1645–2294 m off Georges Bank. Elsewhere reported as benthopelagic at 1500–3200 m. Food is small crustaceans.

shortbelly rockfish

Scientific name: *Sebastes jordani*
(Gilbert, 1896)
Family: **Scorpionfish**
Other common names: slim rockfish, slender rockfish, steamer rockfish
French name: sébaste à ventre court

Distribution: Found from Queen Charlotte Sound off northern British Columbia south to Baja California.

Characters: This species is unique in Canadian Pacific scorpionfishes by having the anus anterior to the anal fin by 1.1–1.5 orbit widths, midway between the anal and pelvic fin origins. Dorsal fin spines 13–14, usually 13, dorsal soft rays 13–16, usually 14. Anal fin soft rays 8–11, usually 9, second spine shorter than third and not much thicker. Pectoral fin rays 19–22, usually 20, with 12–15 unbranched. Caudal fin forked.

Gill rakers 40–49. Vertebrae 26. Lateral line pores 52–64, about 65 scale rows below the lateral line. Head spines are weak. The

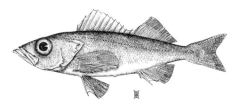

shortbelly rockfish

nasals and parietals always present; preocular, postocular and tympanics may be weakly present; others absent. Olive-pink on the back, light pink on the flanks with fins matching neighbouring body colour. Belly white. Peritoneum silver-grey with black dots, or black. Reaches 32 cm.

Biology: May be found in large schools offshore and in midwater at 91–283 m. Young occur in shallower water than adults. Food is mainly krill. This species is commonly eaten by other fishes, seabirds and marine mammals. They mature at 15–17 cm and 2–3 years of age and live at least 11 years. Females grow larger than males. A 30.5 cm female can produce 50,000 young. Young are born in April in British Columbia. Trawls often catch this species but most individuals are relatively small and unprofitable to market.

shortcheek tail-light

Scientific name: *Lepidophanes guentheri*
  (Goode and Bean, 1896)
Family: **Lanternfish**
Other common names: none
French name: feu-arrière à joue courte

Distribution: Found in the Atlantic Ocean and off southern Nova Scotia.

Characters: This species is distinguished from its Atlantic coast relatives by lacking photophores close to the dorsal body edge, the PLO photophore is above the upper pectoral fin base level, the second PVO is not above the pectoral fin level, there are 4 Prc photophores, the first PO and two PVO photophores are not in a straight line, the caudal luminous glands are a series of overlapping

scale-like structures without a black pigment border numbering 5–7 infracaudally, the fourth PO photophore is highly elevated, there are 5 VO photophores, the SAO series is weakly angulated and there is no crescent of white tissue on the rear half of the iris. The pectoral fin is long, reaching beyond the anal fin origin. Dorsal fin rays 13–15, anal rays 13–16 and pectoral rays 11–14. Total gill rakers 13–15. AO photophores 11–14. Lateral line organs 36–37. There is no difference between the sexes in luminous tissue distribution. Reaches about 7.8 cm.

shortcheek tail-light

Biology: An abundant species in tropical waters but only recorded once from east of Georges Bank where 2 specimens were caught in 1980. Reported elsewhere from 425–950 m by day and 40–175 m at night. Sexual maturity is attained at 4.7 cm.

shortfin eelpout

Scientific name: *Lycodes brevipes*
  Bean, 1890
Family: **Eelpout**
Other common names: none
French name: lycode à courtes nageoires

Distribution: Found from the Okhotsk Sea to California including British Columbia.

Characters: This species is distinguished from its Pacific coast relatives by having prominent ridges on the ventral surface of the

shortfin eelpout

lower jaw known as "mental crests", the pectoral fin has a rounded outline, the eye is smaller than snout length, mouth and gill cavities and peritoneum are not black and pelvic fins are very small (length enters 2.5 times into eye diameter). Pelvic fins are present and there are no mucous pores on the jaws. The flesh is firm. The lateral line is indistinct. There are teeth on the vomer and palatine bones on the roof of the mouth. Dorsal fin rays 85–102, anal rays 74–89, and pectoral rays 19–21, with the lower 7 rays finger-like. There are 99–103 vertebrae. The upper flanks and back are light brown, the belly paler. The flank and dorsal fin have 9–13 white bars, with only the first one in front of the dorsal fin. The dorsal and anal fins have narrow black margins. Pelvic fins are pale. The peritoneum region is white to pink. The mouth and gill cavities are greyish. Reaches 32.8 cm.

Biology: This species has been recorded from the stomach of a **lingcod** in Canada and is found in the Strait of Georgia and Queen Charlotte Sound. Depth range is 25–973 m on mud bottoms.

shortfin mako

Scientific name: *Isurus oxyrinchus*
Rafinesque, 1810
Family: **Mackerel Shark**
Other common names: bonito shark,
 mako shark, blue pointer, mackerel shark,
 sharp-nosed mackerel shark, taupe bleu
French name: mako à nageoires courtes

Distribution: Found on Browns Bank off Nova Scotia and the Tail of the Grand Banks (two specimens in 1962) south to the Gulf of Mexico. There are two records for British Columbia off Vancouver Island. Found south of the Aleutian Islands and rarely from Washington. Also throughout the warmer oceans of the world.

Characters: Distinguished from other **mackerel sharks** by smooth-edged teeth with a triangular cusp and no lateral cusps at the base and short pectoral fins (shorter than the head). Large shortfins have their upper teeth more flattened and triangular in shape. The cusps of the anterior teeth in both jaws are curved labially. The origin of the first dorsal fin is over or behind the rear tips of the pectoral fins and the origin of the second dorsal fin is in front of the anal fin origin. There are no secondary keels on the tail fin. The snout is conical and sharply pointed.

The belly is snow white in contrast to the **longfin mako**. Deep blue-grey or steel blue above and on sides with a snow-white belly and white undersurface to the snout and area around the mouth. Death fades the blue colour to dark grey. There is a black spot at the pectoral fin base.

May attain 4 m and 625 kg but most are 2.1–2.4 m. The world record rod-caught mako weighed 505.76 kg and was caught at Mauritius in 1988. The first British Columbia record was about 3 m long. The scientist who observed the specimen took photographs and retrieved the jaw. Unfortunately the film negative fell overboard during transfer to a patrol vessel and the jaws were stolen from his laboratory. A small specimen was caught in 1992 360 km due west of Cape St. James, B.C.

shortfin mako

Biology: Common in warmer waters offshore but relatively rare where water temperature falls below 16°C (such as Atlantic and Pacific Canada). Shortfin makos have a body temperature 7–10C° higher than the surrounding water. Found in shallow and surface waters down to at least 400 m. The mako catch on the Grand Banks is only about 7% of the longline catch of large sharks. However it is the second most abundant large pelagic shark caught by longlining after blue sharks. A shortfin mako has travelled about 2130 km in 37 days at an average speed of 57.6 km/day. This species is very active, perhaps the fastest swimming shark supposedly at nearly 100 km/h, although this is almost certainly an exaggeration. It is famous for leaping high (several metres) out of the water.

It can show extreme bursts of speed when pursuing prey items like **mackerel, tuna** and **bonito**. It also feeds on **bluefish, anchovies, herring, cod** and cod-relatives, **sauries, swordfish, blue sharks, hammerheads,** squids and sea turtle heads. The stomach's capacity is 10% of body weight and about 2 kg of fish are eaten daily. However a 331 kg mako had a whole, 54 kg **swordfish** in its stomach.

They are ovoviviparous and show uterine cannibalism with 2–16 pups (usually lower numbers), measuring 68–75 cm, in a litter. Gestation is about 1 year. Males are mature at about 2 m and 2 years of age and females at 2.6 m or larger and 6 years of age. Growth is about twice as fast as in **porbeagles** and much faster than **requiem sharks**. Growth rate is about 28 cm per year. Females live as long as 11.5 years and reach 328 cm, but a recent study found the oldest male, at 225 cm, was only 4.5 years old.

An important species for longline fisheries where it is common but low fecundity offsets its rapid growth so limiting the size of the fishery. The flesh is of high quality and is used fresh, frozen, smoked and dried, and salted. It is sold as "swordfish." The oil, fins and skin are also processed for vitamins, soup and leather respectively. The jaws and teeth are sold as ornaments.

It is an important game fish because of its size, speed when hooked and leaping ability. It is known to attack and smash boats, mostly when hooked, and is even reported to leap into boats causing the angler to leap out! Having said this, shortfin makos can be caught with trolled baits and lures, and by live and dead baits. Great care must be exercised when gaffing or boating this species. Reported to attack swimmers, this species must be treated with extreme caution since its size, teeth, and speed are such that there is little chance of fending off an attack.

shorthead redhorse

Scientific name: *Moxostoma macrolepidotum*
(Le Sueur, 1817)
Family: **Sucker**
Other common names: northern redhorse, common redhorse, redfin, red sucker, common mullet, short-headed mullet, bigscale sucker, brook mullet, river sucker, eastern redhorse
French name: suceur rouge

Distribution: Found from southwestern Québec and its James Bay shore, throughout Ontario, southern and central Manitoba and Saskatchewan, and southeastern Alberta. In the U.S.A. south to South Carolina, Alabama and Texas and west to Montana.

Characters: This species is distinguished by a short dorsal fin, a swimbladder with 3 chambers, lateral line scales 38–47, scales around the caudal peduncle 12–13 (rarely 15–16), lower lip thick, posterior edge nearly straight and lips not nearly as wide as snout, pharyngeal teeth not molar-like but blade-like, pelvic fin origin opposite dorsal fin mid-point, eye large (diameter about two-thirds or more of lip width), nostrils behind maxillary tip, and a small mouth overhung by snout. The dorsal fin is emarginate. The front of the head is rounded and subconical. Gill rakers 22–30. Dorsal fin rays 10–15, anal rays 6–8, pectoral rays 14–19 and pelvic rays 8–10. The gut has 6 rounded coils. Males have large nuptial tubercles on the anal and caudal fins with minute tubercles scattered over much of the rest of the body and fins.

The overall colour is brown to olive fading to a whitish or yellowish belly. Scales on the upper flank have black pigment at their base forming a crescent. Variously tinged with reflective golden, bronze, yellow or green. Fins are all reddish to some degree. Pectoral and pelvic fins may be more orange or yellowish, the dorsal fin may have only a red tip with a black margin and dusky to orange over most of the fin and the caudal fin may only be margined with red. Breeding males and females have blood-red caudal fins and lower fins are a brilliant orange-red. Peritoneum silvery.

Attains 75.0 cm and 4.5 kg. The world, all-tackle angling record weighed 2.16 kg and was caught at Island Park, Indiana in 1984.

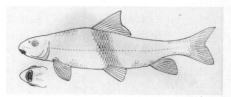

shorthead redhorse

The Canadian angling record from North River, Ontario in 1988 was caught by Bruce Johnstone and weighed 3.99 kg.

Biology: This redhorse may rarely enter brackish waters but is usually found in lakes and the clearer rivers with moderate current, over sand, gravel or rock. It is not tolerant of pollution and siltation but can withstand water temperatures up to 37.2°C and so is found in sluggish, shallow and unshaded rivers.

Food is principally aquatic insects, with worms and molluscs slurped and strained from bottom sediments.

Life span in Canada is 14 years, longer than southern populations. Maturity is attained at 2–5 years depending on locality. Near Montréal life span is reported to be 11 years with maturity attained at age 6. ·

Spawning takes place from May to July, mostly May in Canada, after a migration into riffle areas of streams at about 11°C around Montréal. Males arrive first and defend a territory although no nest is built. Depressions seen in bottom sediments may be incidental to spawning movements and not a nest. Each female is flanked by 2 males who press their caudal regions against her. Spawning takes only 2–3 seconds and is accompanied by vibrations. Eggs are shed and abandoned at night, in the early morning, or during the day. Each female may carry up to 44,000 eggs of 2.1 mm diameter.

This is the most abundant **redhorse** species in Canadian waters and was important in commercial **redhorse** catches, although these catches were minor compared to other fishes. The flesh is good eating but, as with all **redhorses**, there are numerous bones which make them difficult to prepare. The flesh should be scored or turned into ground meat for patties. Anglers catch this species on spawning migrations on hooks baited with worms, grasshoppers, grubs and meat, and on artificial wet flies and plugs.

shorthead sculpin

Scientific name: *Cottus confusus*
  Bailey and Bond, 1963
Family: **Sculpin**
Other common names: none
French name: chabot à tête courte

Distribution: Found in the Puget Sound, Columbia and Snake river basins of the U.S.A. and Canada. In Canada in the Columbia, Flathead, Kettle and Slocan rivers of southeastern British Columbia and in the St. Mary and Milk rivers of Alberta.

Characters: This sculpin, and related species in the freshwater genus *Cottus*, are distinguished from the **deepwater sculpin** by

shorthead sculpin

the gill membrane being attached to the isthmus and the dorsal fins touching. It is separated from its relatives by having 2 pores on the tip of the chin, an incomplete lateral line, prickles only behind the pectoral fins, palatine teeth in the roof of the mouth, last 2 dorsal and anal rays close together, the fourth pelvic fin ray about three-quarters as long as the longest ray, 2–3, usually 2, preopercular spines, usually 13–14 (range 11–15) pectoral rays and head length in standard length 3.2–3.9. There is 1 median occipital pore and papillae on top of the head are well developed. First dorsal fin spines 7–10, second dorsal rays 15–19 (erroneously 11–15 in some works) and anal rays 10–15, usually 12–13. Lateral line pores 18–37.

Overall colour light brownish-yellow with darker mottles. There are 5–6 black saddles. The flanks are lighter and may have 3 dark bars under the second dorsal fin. The chin has light speckling. The spiny dorsal fin is dark at the front and between the posterior rays and may have a central stripe.

The Alberta and Flathead River, B.C. fish show differences from the shorthead sculpins of the Columbia and Kettle rivers. They may be a distinct species. Reaches 12.2 cm standard length.

Biology: This species lives in high cold streams in riffle areas and in the large Columbia River. It is most abundant in stony areas at 13–17°C. Food is aquatic insects and fish eggs including its own. Maturity is reached at 2–3 years, earlier for males than females and life span is 6 years. Spawning is reported in mid-May in Alberta and eggs are laid on the underside of rocks. A female may have up to 690 eggs. This species was recognised as "threatened" in 1983 by the Committee on the Status of Endangered Wildlife in Canada.

shorthorn dreamer

Scientific name: *Dolopichthys allector*
    Garman, 1899
Family: **Dreamer**
Other common names: none
French name: rêveur à petites cornes

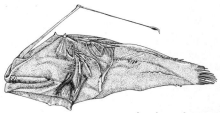

shorthorn dreamer

Distribution: Known from the Pacific and Atlantic oceans including off Newfoundland.

Characters: This deepsea **anglerfish** and its relative, the **toothy dreamer**, are distinguished as females by having the dorsal edge of the frontal bone on the head nearly straight, sphenotic spines present and a deeply notched operculum posteriorly. The pectoral fin lobe is short and broad. The lower jaw has a well-developed spine at its tip. The illicium or fishing rod originates in front of the sphenotic spines. Males have 8–10 denticles on the lower jaw and 10–11 olfactory lamellae. The shorthorn dreamer has no teeth on the vomer bone in the roof of the mouth when larger than 18.5 mm, and lower jaw teeth are fewer than 129 in fish larger than 60 mm. Dorsal fin rays 6–7, anal fin rays 5–6 and pectoral fin rays 19–21. Overall colour is dark brown to black with parts of the esca or bait unpigmented. Females reach 15.4 cm.

Biology: Only a single specimen has been caught in Canadian waters northwest of the Flemish Cap in 1968. This specimen is one of only 2 records for the entire North Atlantic Ocean. As in other **anglerfishes**, the fishing apparatus is used to entice prey close enough to be gulped down.

shorthorn sculpin

Scientific name: *Myoxocephalus scorpius*
    (Linnaeus, 1758)
Family: **Sculpin**
Other common names: Greenland sculpin, daddy sculpin, black sculpin, bull-rout, crapaud de mer à courtes épines, qanirkuutuk
French name: chaboisseau à épines courtes

Distribution: Found from Alaska through the Canadian Arctic north to Ellesmere Island and south to New York on the Atlantic coast. Also in northern Europe and along the Siberian coast.

Characters: This species and its Arctic-Atlantic relatives are distinguished from other sculpins by the upper preopercular spine being a simple straight point, the vomer bone in the roof of the mouth bears teeth but palatine teeth are absent, there are no oblique folds on the lower flank, and the lateral line lacks plates. It is separated from its relatives by having 3 pre-opercular spines (1 pointing forward to downward, 2 pointing backward), the uppermost preopercular spine is less than twice as long as the one below, the spiny dorsal fin origin is not obviously in front of the rear operculum edge, pectoral rays are usually 17–18 (range 14–19) and there are spines over the eyes. First dorsal fin spines 7–12, second dorsal rays 12–20. Anal fin rays 9–16. There is a row of plates above, and a row below, the lateral line. Overall colour dark green to greenish-brown to almost black with dark mottling. The belly is white to yellowish or light orange in females

shorthorn sculpin

and reddish-orange or cherry red in males. Fins are brown, green or yellow and have paler spots or bars. Males have large pale yellowish spots on the lower flank.

Sometimes recognised as distinct sub-species in Greenland and eastern North

America, *M. s. groenlandicus* (Cuvier, 1829). Reaches 90 cm.

Biology: Shorthorn sculpins are found in coastal waters and on banks offshore down to 145 m, or to 250 m in Europe. They are usually caught on mud, sand, pebble or weed bottoms and are common around harbours and wharves. They have been caught in a wide range of temperatures and salinities.

Food includes crustaceans, sea urchins, molluscs, worms and such fish as **herring, eelpouts, sculpins, snailfishes** and small **cod**. Food choice is often governed by availability and by environmental conditions. In Cumberland Sound, Baffin Island shorthorn sculpins were found to be feeding on planktonic amphipods while in nearby Pangnirtung Fjord they were eating snails and clams. Drifting ice in the Sound probably reduced visibility making it difficult for the sculpins to locate food on the sea bed but the illuminated and brightly coloured plankton were easily detected.

Females are larger and older than males at maturity. Half the male population matures at about 30 cm and 5 years while half the females mature at 34–35 cm and 6 years. Life span is 15 years.

Spawning takes place in November and December at Newfoundland when temperatures are about 2.7–3.2°C. Depth range is 6–11 m and adhesive eggs are laid in v-shaped crevices. The eggs are up to 2.5 mm in diameter, pale pink to purplish pink or a reddish-yellow in colour and number up to 60,976 in each female. Males guard the eggs until hatching. The fry are pelagic but may also be found near the sea bed. In Alaska, the fourhorn sculpin spawns during summer.

This species is caught easily by young anglers but is a bait stealer and nuisance to anglers after more desirable species. It will grunt when taken out of the water. It has been utilised for human food on a local basis in Labrador and was once important as a bait for use in lobster traps.

shortjaw cisco

Scientific name: *Coregonus zenithicus*
  (Jordan and Evermann, 1909)
Family: **Salmon**
Other common names: shortjaw chub, long-jaw, light-back tullibee, Lake Superior longjaw, pale-back tullibee, bluefin
French name: cisco à mâchoires égales

Distribution: Found in lakes Huron, Michigan, Superior and Nipigon, in lakes of Algonquin Park, Ontario, in Lake Winnipeg, Manitoba, lakes Reindeer and Athabasca in Saskatchewan, Barrow Lake and possibly Gregoire lake, Alberta and Great Slave Lake, N.W.T.

shortjaw cisco

Characters: This member of the **Salmon Family** is distinguished from its relatives by having large scales (110 or less), no parr marks, teeth absent from the jaws and roof of the mouth, forked tail fin, 2 flaps of skin between the nostrils, the upper and lower jaws are about equal, giving the front of the head a pointed appearance, the premaxilla bone of the upper jaw curves backwards, gill rakers 32–46, usually 38–42, and lateral line scales 58–90. Characters among **ciscoes** (q.v.) overlap and so the species cannot be easily separated. The lower jaw may protrude in fish outside the Great Lakes but is usually a little ventral and shorter than the upper jaw. The snout is long (usually 3.3–3.6 times in head length), the premaxillaries are at 60–70° to the horizontal, paired fins are moderately long and gill rakers are about equal in length to the gill filaments. The maxillary bone of the upper jaw is long, the upper jaw often reaching mid-pupil, hence the confusing English common name, "longjaw." Dorsal fin rays 9–11, anal rays 10–13, pectoral rays 15–18 and pelvic rays 11–12.

Overall colour is silvery with a purple iridescence. The back is dark blue-green to pale green and the belly white. The dorsal fin margin and outer halves of the pectoral and caudal fins may be black but other fins are generally clear or only lightly pigmented. The pelvic and anal fins may darken with age. Dwarf shortjaw ciscoes are found in Algonquin Park maturing at under 10.0 cm. The identification of **ciscoes** presents problems and it is not clear if all populations recorded as shortjaws are that species. Reaches 47.0 cm fork length.

Biology: Shortjaw ciscoes are recorded from the Great Lakes at 18–183 m varying with the season, shallowest in summer, slightly deeper in winter and deepest in spring.

Food is opossum shrimps and amphipods with some planktonic crustaceans, fingernail clams and aquatic insects. **Lake trout** and **burbot** are predators.

Females live longer and reach larger sizes than males. Life span is about 11 years. Fish larger than 24.3 cm are mature, at 2–5 years.

Spawning time is from August to May, the peak varying with the lake. There are spring and fall spawners in Lake Superior. In Lake Superior spawning occurred in late November–early December at 37–73 m over clay. The yellow eggs average 2.14 mm in diameter.

This **cisco** was an important part of the Great Lakes "chub" fishery and the Manitoba "tullibee" fishery. It was an excellent food fish when fresh or smoked. It is probably extirpated from lakes Michigan (last seen in 1975) and Huron (last seen 1982) but is not uncommon, though declining, in Lake Superior. It has been estimated that as much as 90% of the fish catch in Lake Superior was this species in the 1920s but is now less than 5% of the catch. It has suffered from several man-made factors outlined under **ciscoes**. The Committee on the Status of Endangered Wildlife in Canada gave this species the status of "threatened" in 1987.

shortjaw eelpout

Scientific name: *Lycenchelys jordani*
　(Evermann and Goldsborough, 1907)
Family: **Eelpout**
Other common names: none
French name: lycode de Jordan

Distribution: Found from Alaska to Oregon including British Columbia.

Characters: This species is distinguished from its Pacific coast relatives by having scales, a gill slit extending in front of the pectoral fin, pelvic fins present, a low body

depth at the anal fin origin (2.3–8.3% of standard length), anterior suborbital pores parallel with the upper jaw, large pores

shortjaw eelpout

around the mouth and small teeth on the vomer bone in the roof of the mouth. Dorsal fin rays about 116, anal rays about 93 and pectoral rays 16–18. Scales extend onto the bases of the vertical and pectoral fins. There is no distinguishable lateral line canal. Overall colour is brownish-olive with lighter scales giving a finely spotted appearance. The head, pectoral fins and margins of vertical fins are darker. Reaches 33.6 cm.

Biology: Depth range is 1650–2200 m with a specimen from off Queen Charlotte Sound taken at nearly 2200 m. This species is known to eat brittle stars.

shortnose cisco

Scientific name: *Coregonus reighardi*
　(Koelz, 1924)
Family: **Salmon**
Other common names: Reighard's chub or
　cisco, shortnose chub, greaser
French name: cisco à museau court

Distribution: Found in lakes Ontario, Huron and Michigan.

Characters: This member of the **Salmon Family** is distinguished from its relatives by having large scales (110 or less), no parr marks, teeth absent from the jaws and roof of

shortnose cisco

the mouth, forked tail fin, 2 flaps of skin between the nostrils, the upper and lower jaws are about equal, giving the front of the head a pointed appearance, the premaxilla bone of the upper jaw curves backwards, gill rakers 30–43, usually 34–38, and lateral line scales 64–96. Characters among **cisces** (q.v.) overlap and so the species cannot be easily separated. The end of the upper jaw often reaches mid-pupil. The lower jaw is slightly ventral or shorter than the upper jaw, the snout is short (usually 3.4–4.0 times in head length), premaxillaries are up to 90° with the horizontal, gill rakers are shorter than gill filaments and paired fins are very short. Dorsal fin rays 8–11, anal rays 9–13, pectoral rays 15–17 and pelvic rays 10–12. The snout is short (hence the common name). Overall colour is silvery with a pink iridescence. There is a unique yellow-green back. Dorsal and caudal fins are darkened but other fins are clear. The premaxillaries, cutting edge of the maxillaries and lower jaw are dark. Reaches 37.1 cm total length. This species may be the same as the **shortjaw cisco** according to one author, distinct according to others. Reports of this species from lakes Superior and Nipigon are apparently misidentified **shortjaw cisces**.

Biology: This **cisco** was reported from a depth range of 23–91 m in Lake Ontario. Maximum range is 9–165 m. Food is mostly opossum shrimps, amphipods with some copepods, aquatic insects and fingernail clams. Life span is about 8 years for females which live about 2 years longer than males. Maturity is attained at 2–4 years. Spawning occurred in western Lake Ontario in April and May, and perhaps into June, at about 75 m over sand, silt or clay. Fall spawners have been noted in Lake Michigan. Water temperatures are 3.8–4.7°C. Eggs are yellow and 2.0 mm in diameter. The Lake Ontario and Lake Michigan populations are extirpated, since 1964 and 1972 respectively (see **cisces**). Georgian Bay populations are probably the only remaining resource of this species. This was an important commercial species of **cisco** in Canadian waters of Lake Ontario and formed part of the U.S. "chub" fishery before stocks were overfished. A fat fish, it was excellent eating when smoked. The Committee on the Status of Endangered Wildlife in Canada gave this species the status of "threatened" in 1987.

shortnose greeneye

Scientific name: *Chlorophthalmus agassizi* Bonaparte, 1840
Family: **Greeneye**
Other common names: none
French name: oeil-vert camus

Distribution: Found from Nova Scotia south to Surinam and in the eastern Atlantic Ocean and Mediterranean Sea.

Characters: This species is distinguished from its Canadian relatives by having large eyes, no greatly elongated fin rays, and the anus separated from the pelvic fin bases by 2–3 scales. The mouth is large, reaching back below the front of the eye, and superior. Dorsal fin rays 10–12, anal rays 7–9, pectoral rays 15–17 and pelvic rays 8–9. Lateral

shortnose greeneye

line scales number 50–55. The body is blotched dark brown on the sides and has about 5 dark brown saddles across the back. The eye is green. Attains 20 cm, but usually caught at about 12 cm.

Biology: Found off southwestern Nova Scotia and southwest of Sable Island Bank at 128–267 m. It is apparently a resident on the Scotian Shelf although rarely caught. Elsewhere reported down to 1000 m and as shallow as 50 m. It is a schooling species with pelagic larvae. Food is bottom invertebrates such as crustaceans and molluscs. In the Mediterranean Sea it is caught by bottom trawlers and sold fresh and in the eastern Atlantic catches by former Soviet and by Polish trawlers are made into fish meal.

shortnose lancetfish

Scientific name: *Alepisaurus brevirostris* Gibbs, 1960
Family: **Lancetfish**
Other common names: shortsnout lancetfish
French name: cavalo ocellé

Distribution: In all major oceans but not the North Pacific. Found on the Atlantic coast of Canada.

Characters: The high dorsal fin and slender body characterise a lancetfish. This species differs from the **longnose lancetfish** by having

shortnose lancetfish

a dorsal fin low in front without free rays, and by having a short snout (less than a third of head length). There are 40–48 dorsal fin rays, 13–17 anal rays and 12–14 pectoral rays. The back is iridescent brown-black and the sides paler. A keel on the rear part of the flank is black. The dorsal fin is black with a row of white spots. Reaches 96 cm.

Biology: Only a single specimen, 92 cm total length, has been caught in Canadian waters at the northwest Flemish Cap in 1968. Biology is probably similar to that of the **longnose lancetfish** but this species is only recently described and little is known. It is a hermaphrodite and feeds mostly on fishes at 100–300 m.

shortnose loosejaw

Scientific name: *Malacosteus danae*
    Regan and Trewavas, 1930
Family: **Barbeled Dragonfish**
Other common names: none
French name: drague à nez court

Distribution: Found in the North Pacific Ocean including off British Columbia.

Characters: Very similar to the **stoplight loosejaw** from which it may not be distinct. The light organ behind the eye is less than 25% the eye size and this character is said to distinguish the two species.

shortnose loosejaw

Biology: Caught at less than 650 m at Ocean Station Papa (50°N, 145°W) off the coast of British Columbia.

shortnose sturgeon

Scientific name: *Acipenser brevirostrum*
    Le Sueur, 1818
Family: **Sturgeon**
Other common names: pinkster, little sturgeon, roundnoser, bottlenose, mammose, soft shell sturgeon
French name: esturgeon à museau court

Distribution: Found from the Saint John River, New Brunswick south to the St. Johns River, Florida.

Characters: This species is distinguished from other eastern Canadian sturgeons by having 1 large plate between the anal fin and

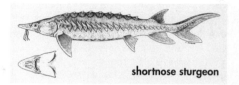

shortnose sturgeon

the caudal fulcrum, 18–24 anal fin rays and the anal fin insertion is opposite the dorsal fin insertion. The short, rounded snout is characteristic. Dorsal fin rays 38–42, dorsal plates 7–13, lateral plates 21–35 and ventral plates 6–11. Gill rakers 22–32.

The back is olive, dark brown or black fading to light brown or yellowish on the lower flank and white on the belly. Pectoral and pelvic fin margins white. Plates are paler than adjacent skin. Young fish have black blotches. The body cavity organs are blackish and the peritoneum is only slightly pigmented.

Reaches 143 cm total length and 23.6 kg. The world, all-tackle record weighed 5.04 kg and was caught on 31 July 1988 by Lawrence Guimond in the Kennebecasis River, N.B.

Biology: Shortnose sturgeons are found in large rivers where there is tidal influence and in the adjacent sea. It is known only from the Saint John River basin in Canada where there are an estimated 18,000 adults. The sturgeon overwinters in the estuary of the Saint John and feeds in the upper estuary. It often enters water less than 1–2 m deep.

Food is bottom invertebrates such as molluscs, worms, insect larvae, crustaceans, small **flounders** and plant material. Occasionally blind but healthy sturgeon are caught indicating that vision is of little importance in finding food.

Life span is 67 years (a female; the oldest male was 32) with 50% of the population of males maturing at age 12 and females at age 17 in Canada. In the St. John River, N.B. males mature at 10–11 and females at 13 years.

Males spawn every 2 years and females at 1–5 years, probably 3 years on average. In Massachusetts a 4–12 year interval between first and second spawning is reported. Spawning occurs from April to June at 9–15°C after a migration to the parental stream of birth as far as 200 km. Spawning occurs over sand, gravel or boulders in fast water. Eggs are dark brown and up to 208,000 are produced by each female. Eggs attach to the substrate. Young remain in the river until they are 45 cm long when they join the seasonal feeding/overwintering migration. Tagged sturgeons have been recaptured together up to 3 years later suggesting that pair-bonding may occur.

This species was given the status of "rare" in 1980 by the Committee on the Status of Endangered Wildlife in Canada. The flesh is edible and eggs can be made into caviar but this species is too uncommon to support a fishery although some were caught and sold incidentally with **Atlantic sturgeon.**

shortplate will-o'-the-wisp

Scientific name: *Lampanyctus pusillus*
    (Johnson, 1890)
Family: **Lanternfish**
Other common names: none
French name: feu-follet à platine courte

Distribution: Circumglobal in the southern hemisphere and in the North Atlantic Ocean and Mediterranean Sea. Found off the Scotian Shelf in Atlantic Canada.

Characters: This species and 7 relatives in the genus *Lampanyctus* are separated from other Atlantic species by lacking photophores close to the dorsal body edge, the PLO photophore is well above the pectoral fin base level while the second PVO photophore is at or below the upper pectoral base level, there

are 4 Prc, the first PO and two PVO photophores are not on a straight line, both males and females have caudal luminous glands composed of overlapping, scale-like structures without a black pigment border, the fourth PO photophore is highly elevated, there are no luminous, scale-like structures on the belly between the pelvic fin bases or these bases and the anus, there are 4 VO photophores and the SAO series is strongly angled. This species is distinguished from its relatives by having 11–13 gill rakers, pectoral fins extending back beyond pelvic fin bases, 1 cheek photophore, no luminous tissue at the adipose fin base and 33–34 lateral line organs. The infracaudal luminous gland covers only half the underside of the caudal peduncle length. There are 3–4 scale-like segments on the infracaudal gland. The supracaudal gland is only half as long as the infracaudal. The Prc and AOp photophores are continuous. Dorsal fin rays 11–13, anal rays 13–16 and pectoral rays 13–15. AO photophores 9–12. The head, body and fins are covered with secondary photophores. Reaches only 4.3 cm.

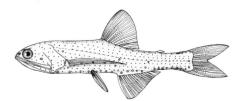

shortplate will-o'-the-wisp

Biology: This species is classed as a temperate to subtropical species. First reported from Canada in 1969. Depth distribution by day in the Atlantic is 33–1000 m and by night 25–1000 m. Day maximum abundance is at 600–700 m and night at 50–200 m. Only a few fish survive into a second year of life. Sexual maturity is attained at 3.6 cm. Spawning occurs year round but mostly in winter and spring.

shortraker rockfish

Scientific name: *Sebastes borealis*
    Barsukov, 1970
Family: **Scorpionfish**
Other common names: buoy keg

French name: sébaste boréal

Distribution: Found from Japan to northern California including British Columbia.

Characters: This species of scorpionfish is distinguished by colour, head spines and lateral line pore count. The lower jaw has char-

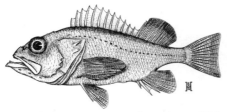

shortraker rockfish

acteristic, very large pores. Dorsal fin spines 12–14, usually 13, dorsal soft rays 12–15, usually 13. Anal fin soft rays 6–8, usually 7, the second spine thickest but shorter than the third. Pectoral fin rays 17–20, usually 19 with 1–9 unbranched. Gill rakers 27–32. Vertebrae 27–28, usually 27. Lateral line pores 27–32, scale rows below lateral line 36–49. Postocular and tympanic head spines absent, other spines moderate to weak. There are 1–3 spines on the lower edge of the gill cover and sometimes one spine on the lower orbit rim. Pink or orange-pink to blood red overall, with vague red to orange bars. The belly is usually greyish. Fins are reddish with the pectoral and pelvic fins sometimes edged with black or dark grey. The mouth and gill cavities are red with white or grey patches and with black spots. Peritoneum silvery-grey with black dots. Reaches 96 cm.

Biology: Found on soft bottoms around 200–560 m. Caught in gill nets and on longlines in Japan. Half the population is mature at 45 cm in Canadian waters. Young are born in April in British Columbia.

shortspine boarfish

Scientific name: *Antigonia combatia*
Berry and Rathjen, 1959
Family: **Boarfish**
Other common names: none
French name: sanglier à courtes épines

Distribution: Found from Brazil to Atlantic Canada.

Characters: The body is deep and compressed. The dorsal fin has 9, rarely 10, spines and 26–30 soft rays. The anal fin has 3 spines and 23–28 soft rays. The pectoral fin has 11–13, usually 12, branched rays. The pelvic fin has 1 spine and 5 soft rays. There are about 49–57 scale rows. Scales are found extending onto the membranes of the pectoral and caudal fins, along all spines, on the soft rays of the pelvic fin and on the lower jaws, cheeks, throat, opercular bones and snout. The scales are ctenoid and have spines on the scale centre giving the fish a velvety texture. Red to pink dorsally, silvery ventrally. Attains 12.5 cm.

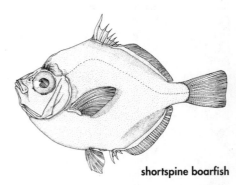

shortspine boarfish

Biology: Found at 120–600 m but rare in Canadian waters and first reported in 1988.

shortspine helmetfish

Scientific name: *Melamphaes suborbitalis*
(Gill, 1883)
Family: **Ridgehead**
Other common names: none
French name: heaume à épine courte

Distribution: Found in the North Atlantic Ocean and also between Australia and New Zealand. Canadian specimens are from the Nova Scotian slope.

shortspine helmetfish

Characters: This species is distinguished from its relatives the **highsnout ridgehead** and the **numerous helmetfish** by having shoulder spines pointing forwards. There are 32–35 scale rows from nape to caudal fin base. Dorsal fin spines 3, soft rays 15–16. Anal fin spine 1, soft rays 7–8. Pelvic fin with 1 spine and 7 branched rays. Pectoral fin rays 15–16. The eye is surrounded by radiating ridges. The body bears 6 wide but faint, dark stripes. Gill and mouth cavities are dark. Scale pockets are outlined in brown in preserved fish. Up to about 10 cm standard length.

Biology: This species was first reported from Canada in 1988. Little is known of its biology as it occurs below 500 m when adult. Young are found at 150–200 m.

shortspine tapirfish

Scientific name: *Polyacanthonotus rissoanus* (de Filippi and Vérany, 1859)
Family: **Tapirfish**
Other common names: spiny eel, smallmouth spiny eel
French name: tapir à petites épines

Distribution: Atlantic and Pacific oceans, from the Davis Strait and Labrador southward in Canada.

Characters: Distinguished from the related **longnose tapirfish** by the mouth ending anterior to the eye and the dorsal fin

shortspine tapirfish

origin (first spine) being obviously anterior to the pectoral fin insertion. Also the gill raker counts differ. Dorsal fin spines 26–36. Pelvic fin with a fulcral spine and 7–11 rays. Pectoral fin with a fulcral spine and 10–16 rays. Gill rakers 23–28. Light grey to off-white or tan. Anal fin soft rays dark brown. The opercle margin and posterior part of the mouth black. Opercle, underside of head and mouth anteriorly are bluish. Attains 39.4 cm.

Biology: Found near the bottom at 540–2875 m, in cooler waters. Food is small bottom crustaceans, particularly amphipods and mysids, and also worms and coelenterates.

shortspine tenplate

Scientific name: *Polyipnus asteroides* Schultz, 1938
Family: **Silver Hatchetfish**
Other common names: none
French name: dix-bards à épines courtes

Distribution: Western Atlantic Ocean from off the Scotian Shelf in Canada to South America.

Characters: The body shape approaches that of a hatchet, there are 10 abdominal light organs, eyes are normal, and there is no

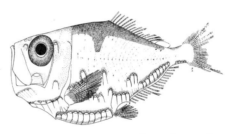

shortspine tenplate

large transparent membrane above the anal fin rays. In addition there are 6 or more anal light organs and 20–24 gill rakers. Colour is bright silvery with a dark back and some spotting and striations on the flank. A tapering bar extends down to the midline of the flank from the dorsal fin origin. Reaches 8.1 cm standard length.

Biology: A midwater fish about which little is known. The Canadian specimen was caught in 256 m and elsewhere this species may descend to 1097 m.

shortspine thornyhead

Scientific name: *Sebastolobus alascanus* Bean, 1890
Family: **Scorpionfish**
Other common names: spinycheek rockfish, shortspine channel rockfish, idiotfish, channel rockcod, hooligan, gurnard
French name: sébastolobe à courtes épines

Distribution: Found from the Bering Sea to Baja California including British Columbia.

Characters: This fish and the related **longspine thornyhead** are distinguished from other Pacific coast scorpionfishes by

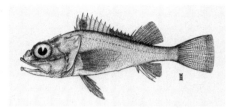

shortspine thornyhead

their higher dorsal fin spine (16, range 15–17) and vertebral counts (28) and by having a sharp, spiny ridge under the eye. The fourth or fifth dorsal fin spine is longest and almost a quarter of head length. The branchiostegals are scaleless. Soft dorsal rays 8–10, anal fin with the second spine twice as thick as third but about equal in length, and 4–5 soft rays. Pectoral fin with 20–23 rays, the lowest 6–7 forming a distinct section of the fin. Gill rakers 18–24. Vertebrae 29–31. Scale rows below lateral line 35–46, lateral line pores 29–33. All head spines except the coronal present and sharp. Colour a translucent red or pink with 1–2 black blotches on the spiny dorsal fin and dusky areas on the body. A dusky blotch on the operculum. Gill cavity lining light with sometimes a dusky blotch on the inside of the opercle. Peritoneum white with black dots, darker in young. Reaches 75 cm.

Biology: Common in British Columbia at 50–800 m on soft bottoms but has been reported as shallow as 26 m and below 1524 m elsewhere. Spawning probably occurs in March to May. Transparent, gelatinous egg masses float at the surface. Each mass has 2 lobes, 15–61 cm long, containing eggs 1.2–1.4 mm in diameter in a single layer. A commercially important species caught in trawls and traps and on setlines.

shorttail skate

Scientific name: *Raja jenseni*
Bigelow and Schroeder, 1950
Family: **Skate**
Other common names: Jensen's skate
French name: raie à queue courte

Distribution: Found from the southwest Grand Bank and Nova Scotia south to New England.

Characters: This species is separated from its Canadian Atlantic relatives by having a rigid snout with its cartilaginous support thick and stiff, cartilaginous supports of the pectoral fin do not reach the snout tip, dorsal fins separate at the base, large thorns on the back, snout angle usually less than 90°, more than 10 spines along the tail midline posterior to the pelvic fin axils, 24–31 thorns along the body and tail midline and teeth in 56–66 rows. The tail is short. There is 1 large thorn on the inner side of each spiracle, 2–3 thorns on the inner side of each eye, and a patch of spines on the snout in young fish, lost in older ones. The underside is smooth. The upper disc in preserved fish is grey-brown with dark margins to the pectoral fins. The underside is white, yellowish or grey. The mouth has white patches in front and behind. Reaches 85 cm.

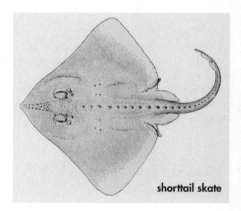

shorttail skate

Biology: Canadian records are in a depth range of 365–840 m but in New England this skate is caught at 1907–2295 m. The shallower end of the Canadian depth range is probably in error. This is an uncommon species in Canadian waters. Food includes crustaceans and fishes such as the **redfishes**.

shortwing lanternfish

Scientific name: *Lampanyctus ater*
Tåning, 1928
Family: **Lanternfish**
Other common names: none

French name: lanterne à pectorale courte

Distribution: Found in the Atlantic, Indian and Southern oceans and off the Scotian Shelf in Atlantic Canada.

Characters: This species and 7 relatives in the genus *Lampanyctus* are separated from other Atlantic species by lacking photophores

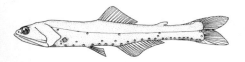

shortwing lanternfish

close to the dorsal body edge, the PLO photophore is well above the pectoral fin base level while the second PVO photophore is at or below the upper pectoral base level, there are 4 Prc, the first PO and two PVO photophores are not on a straight line, both males and females have caudal luminous glands composed of overlapping, scale-like structures without a black pigment border, the fourth PO photophore is highly elevated, there are no luminous, scale-like structures on the belly between the pelvic fin bases or these bases and the anus, there are 4 VO photophores and the SAO series is strongly angled. This species is distinguished from its relatives by having 15–18 gill rakers and short pectoral fins not extending beyond the pelvic fin bases. Dorsal fin rays 13–16, anal rays 16–20 and pectoral rays 11–12. AO photophores 12–16 and lateral line organs 35–39. The supracaudal luminous gland is about half as long as the infracaudal gland. The infracaudal has 5–7 poorly-defined, scale-like structures with 1–2 of them separated anteriorly from the remainder. Reaches about 14.0 cm.

Biology: This species is subtropical in distribution. Depth distribution by day is 550–1550 m with larger fish deeper. By night these fish were taken at 60–1250 m with maximum abundance at 100–150 m and 800–900 m in different localities. Fish smaller than 5.0 cm are migratory but fish of all sizes may not migrate. Sexual maturity is attained at about 9.0 cm and spawning occurs in early summer off Bermuda. Males develop faster but females grow to a larger size. Life span is at least 2 years.

showy bristlemouth

Scientific name: *Cyclothone signata*
    Garman, 1899
Family: **Bristlemouth**
Other common names: none
French name: cyclothone prétentieuse

Distribution: Found in the eastern and central Pacific Ocean and off British Columbia.

Characters: This bristlemouth is distinguished from its Pacific coast relatives by lacking SO photophores, by a basically white body with some black pigment, no scales and no precaudal luminescent glands. Gill rakers 14–15. Photophores: ORB 1, OP 2, BR 9–11, IV 12–14, OA 7, VAV usually 4, sometimes 3, AC 13–14. Dorsal fin rays 12–14, anal rays 17–20. The black eyes and the dark-edged photophores stand out against the white or translucent body colour. The belly appears black in preserved fish (or bluish in life) because the peritoneum lining is visible through the skin. There are vertical bars of dark pigment under the body muscles and between the photophores on the branchiostegals. The dorsal surface of the head lacks pigment spots. Reaches 3.8 cm.

showy bristlemouth

Biology: Reported a number of times west of Vancouver Island, off the Brooks Peninsula in 1983, an El Niño year, and at Ocean Station Papa (50°N, 145°W). Food is copepods and ostracods and there is evidence that this species feeds intermittently, with rest periods for digestion. They may migrate vertically, but not in a daily pattern, to feed and then descend to rest and digest. Food items are selected rather than taken as opportunity presents.

showy snailfish

Scientific name: *Liparis pulchellus*
    Ayres, 1855
Family: **Snailfish**
Other common names: shorttail snailfish,
    continuous-finned liparid

French name: limace prétentieuse

Distribution: Found from the Bering Sea to California including British Columbia.

Characters: This species is distinguished from its Pacific coast relatives by having an adhesive disc with its rear edge behind the

showy snailfish

level of the gill slit, 2 pairs of nostrils, gill slit partly in front of the pectoral fin down to rays 1–7, dorsal fin rays 47–53, anal rays 39–42 and pectoral rays 36–37. The lower pectoral rays are thickened and finger-like. The dorsal and anal fins are joined to the caudal fin. Teeth are trilobed and in bands. Pyloric caeca 32. Overall colour is light to dark brown, becoming paler below. Wavy purplish flank stripes outlined with white may be present, or spots. Fins have a dark margin except for the pectorals which have a light margin. Young fish have oblique dark bars. Peritoneum silvery with dark spots. Reaches 25.4 cm.

Biology: Common in Canadian waters from the shore down to 183 m over mud bottoms. They are often caught in shrimp trawlers but are discarded. Individuals are said to take refuge in bottles, cans and other sea floor junk. Food includes crustaceans, worms, **flatfishes** and **snailfishes**. Larger females contain about 9200 eggs and spawn in winter and spring in California. This species lives at least 5 years.

shrimp eel

Scientific name: *Ophichthus gomesi*
(Castelnau, 1855)
Family: **Snake Eel**
Other common names: none
French name: serpenton chevrette

Distribution: Found from Brazil north to the Scotian Shelf in Canada.

Characters: Larvae have 138–152 total myomeres (muscle blocks) with 4–5 spots below the tail midline, a single spot at each anal ray base, gut with 8 weak swellings and pigment limited to first 2 swellings. Preanal myomeres 67–76, nephric myomeres 56–64 and predorsal myomeres 60–73. Adults have a hard, pointed tail tip and no caudal fin. There is a large mouth with strong, pointed teeth. The vomer teeth in the roof of the mouth are in 2–3 rows. The dorsal fin has its origin at the level of the pectoral fin tip. The tail is about two-thirds of the total length. The upper body is dark or light brown to dark grey, sometimes with bluish or reddish tints, or yellowish. The dorsal and anal fins are dusky or translucent and edged in black and the belly is pale. Head pores are rimmed with black pigment. Largest reported Canadian specimen is 10.3 cm long, smallest 73 mm. Adults attain 91.4 cm.

shrimp eel

Biology: Known from Canada as stray larvae (or leptocephali) but quite common compared to other snake eel records. Reputed to be a parasite which chews its way into the body cavity of large fishes and feeds on their muscles. Found in shallow areas over sand, mud, rock or shell. Capable of a nasty bite when adult. Often caught by anglers or by trawlers, sometimes as deep as 457 m.

shulupaoluk

Scientific name: *Lycodes jugoricus*
Knipowitsch, 1906
Family: **Eelpout**
Other common names: none
French name: lycode plume

Distribution: Found in the Canadian Beaufort Sea at the Boothia Peninsula, and in the Chukchi, Laptev, Kara and White seas.

Characters: This species is separated from its Canadian Arctic-Atlantic relatives by having small pelvic fins, a mouth under the snout, no large pores around the mouth, crests on the chin, lateral line single and on midflank, tail short (preanal distance in the range 46–49% of total length), scales are absent, rounded or flat-topped teeth on the vomer bone in the

---

roof of the mouth 8–14, and 99–102 vertebrae. Dorsal fin rays 96–111, anal rays 78–88 (both including half the caudal fin rays).

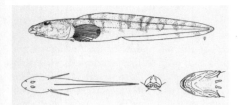

shulupaoluk

Pectoral fin rays 17–18. The top of the head is dark, flanks yellowish and belly white. There are 8–9 dark, v-shaped, widely spaced bars on the flank and dorsal fin. Peritoneum light. Reaches 44.7 cm.

Biology: Usually found inshore in brackish water over mud at depths of 9–15 m, and sometimes down to 90 m. Temperatures are usually below 0°C. Food is crustaceans, clams and worms. Reproduction probably occurs in autumn with about 1280 demersal eggs of about 4.5 mm being produced.

sickle-ear slimlantern

Scientific name: *Centrobranchus nigroocellatus* (Günther, 1873)
Family: **Lanternfish**
Other common names: none
French name: lanterne-fine oreille-faucille

Distribution: Found in the western Indian, the South Pacific and the Atlantic oceans. In Atlantic Canada off the Tail of the Grand Bank and off Nova Scotia.

Characters: This species is separated from its Atlantic coast relatives by lacking photophores close to the dorsal body edge, the PLO photophore is at or above the upper pectoral fin base, the mouth is subterminal and the snout protrudes, and there are no gill rak-

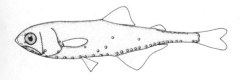

sickle-ear slimlantern

ers. There are clumps of spines on the gill arch. The tail is slender. Dorsal fin rays 9–11, anal rays 16–19 and pectoral rays 13–17. AO photophores 12–17. Vertebrae 35–37. Adult males have 4–7 rounded supracaudal luminous organs which first appear at 1.9 cm. Adult females have 3–6 oval, non-overlapping infracaudal luminous organs which begin developing at 2.3 cm. Reaches about 5.0 cm.

Biology: Near Bermuda and elsewhere, this species is caught at the surface to 200 m at night and 375–800 m by day. Sexual maturity is attained at about 3.4 cm and spawning peaks in late winter to early spring at Bermuda.

sidelight lanternfish

Scientific name: *Bolinichthys supralateralis* (Parr, 1928)
Family: **Lanternfish**
Other common names: none
French name: lampe à feux latéraux

Distribution: Found in the Atlantic, Indian and Pacific oceans, including off the Atlantic coast of Canada.

Characters: This species and its relatives, the **spinecheek** and **smoothcheek lanternfishes**, are distinguished from other Atlantic coast species by lacking photophores close to

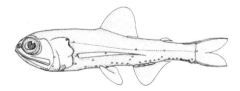

sidelight lanternfish

the dorsal body edge, the PLO photophore is well above the pectoral fin level, the second PVO photophore is not above the pectoral fin level, there are 3 Prc photophores, caudal luminous glands are a series of overlapping, scale-like structures without a black pigment border, the fourth PO photophore is highly elevated, there are 5 VO photophores, and a crescent of whitish tissue on the rear half of the iris. This species is separated from its relatives by having the VLO photophore well below the lateral line and patches of luminous tissue along the anal fin base. The iris tissue is not luminous. Dorsal fin rays 12–15, anal rays 12–15 and pectoral rays 12–15. Total gill rakers 15–22. Vertebrae 33–34. AO photophores 8–11. Supracaudal luminous gland with 2–3 scale-like structures and infracaudal gland with 3–6 scale-like structures. Reaches at least 11.7 cm.

Biology: Reported from Canada in 1988. Caught in the Atlantic at 375–750 m by day and 40–650 m at night, most abundantly at 100 m. Large specimens are usually taken below 500 m and may not migrate vertically. Life span is at least 2 years and sexual maturity is reached at 9 cm. Spawning occurs in late spring to early summer.

silky shark

Scientific name: *Carcharhinus falciformis*
(Bibron in Müller and Henle, 1841)
Family: **Requiem Shark**
Other common names: net-eater shark, grey reef shark
French name: requin soyeux

Distribution: Found world-wide in tropical to temperate seas. Recorded from Browns Bank, off the southern Scotian Shelf and south and southeast of the northeast peak of Georges Bank in Atlantic Canada.

Characters: This species is distinguished from other requiem sharks by lacking spiracles (distinguishes **tiger shark**), the first dorsal fin origin is posterior to the end of the pectoral fin free rear tip (the inner corner of

silky shark

this fin) (distinguishes **dusky** and **sandbar sharks**), there is an interdorsal ridge, the first dorsal fin has a narrow to broadly rounded tip, there are no caudal peduncle keels (distinguishes **tiger shark**), the body is not brilliant blue and the pectoral fins are not very long and narrow (distinguishes **blue shark**),

fins are not mottled white and there are no black saddles on the caudal peduncle (distinguishes **ocean whitetip shark**) and teeth are serrated (distinguishes **Atlantic sharpnose shark**). The second dorsal fin is less than half the height of the first with its inner margin and rear tip more than twice as long as its height and the middle of the first dorsal fin base is closer to the pectoral fin insertion than to the pelvic fin origin. Teeth in the upper jaw have oblique cusps with a deep notch on each side, are serrated and have basal cusplets or well-developed serrations. Lower jaw teeth are erect, narrow and smooth edged except sometimes for serrations near the tip. The snout is fairly long and rounded The eyes are moderately large. The denticles are small and flat, with 3–5 low ridges, making the skin silky to the touch.

Overall colour dark grey to grey-brown, grey-blue or blackish. The flanks may have a greenish tinge. The belly is white. Fin tips dusky but not black except sometimes for the first dorsal fin. The pectoral fins are darker than the adjacent body and dusky below. Reaches about 3.5 m.

Biology: This shark is a summer visitor to waters off Nova Scotia. It is difficult to identify without careful study and may be more common than records indicate. Elsewhere it occurs commonly in warm, open, oceanic waters and in inshore waters as shallow as 18 m. Maximum depth attained is at least 500 m. Young are found offshore in nursery areas while adults are found further offshore.

Food is mostly fishes, especially pelagic ones, but squid, pelagic crabs and paper nautiluses are also taken.

Young number 2–14 in each litter and are 70–90 cm at birth. Little is known about reproduction. Males mature at 187–240 cm and females at 213–260 cm. Life span is over 13 years.

This shark is used in the Gulf of Mexico and Caribbean Sea where it is caught by bottom nets and pelagic longliners. The flesh is eaten, fins are made into soup, skin into leather and the liver is used for its oil and vitamin A content. In the eastern Pacific Ocean it is considered a nuisance by tuna purse seiners as it damages nets and attacks the tuna rendering them unsuitable for market. Divers report a threat display by this species consisting of an arched back, raised head and lowered caudal fin. This species is potentially dangerous to humans.

silver anchovy

Scientific name: *Engraulis eurystole*
    (Swain and Meek, 1885)
Family: **Anchovy**
Other common names: anchois gris
French name: anchois argenté

Distribution: Found from the Scotian Shelf of Atlantic Canada to Florida and the Gulf of Mexico, and to northern Brazil.

Characters: This anchovy is distinguished from its Canadian relative, the **striped anchovy**, by having a short maxilla bone in

silver anchovy

the upper jaw, ending in a rounded or square tip and by fewer anal fin rays. Scales about 40–45 along the flank. There is no lateral line canal. Dorsal fin rays 13–16, anal rays 15–18, rarely 19, and pectoral rays 15–16. Lower gill rakers 27–33. The back is blue-green. The silvery flank stripe has a dark upper border. Reaches 15.5 cm.

Biology: First reported, as post-larvae, for Canada in 1980 as northern range extensions. None of the specimens were adult, indicating that either adults were able to avoid the nets used or that the larvae and young in Canadian waters are strays from the south. In the U.S.A. this species is more common offshore and probably only enters shallow waters at night. It is found down to 65 m. Spawning occurs in summer and the eggs are ellipsoidal in shape. It is caught in the Caribbean with seines, trawls and with liftnets used at night with lights.

silver chub

Scientific name: *Macrhybopsis storeriana*
    (Kirtland, 1847)
Family: **Carp**

Other common names: Storer's chub
French name: méné à grandes écailles

Distribution: Found centred on the Mississippi River basin in the U.S.A. The northern limits are lakes Erie and St. Clair and the St. Clair River in Ontario and the Red and Assiniboine river systems of Manitoba.

Characters: This species is distinguished from other **minnows** by having protractile premaxillae (upper lip separated by a groove from the snout), a barbel at each mouth corner, lateral line scales 35–48, the mouth under a projecting snout, and an unspotted flank. Pharyngeal teeth 1,4–4,1. Gill rakers short, about 10. Dorsal fin branched rays 6–7, anal fin branched rays 6–7, usually 7, pectoral rays 16–18, and pelvic rays 8–9, usually 8. Males have nuptial tubercles on rays 2–8 of the pectoral fin, fine tubercles on top of the head and larger ones on the side of the head. The back is grey-green, or greenish-olive, flanks silvery and the belly white to silvery-white. There is a faint, dusky lateral stripe, most evident posteriorly. The lower 3–4 caudal fin rays are characteristically white. The iris is yellowish-white. Peritoneum silvery. Formerly in the genus *Hybopsis*. Reaches 23.1 cm.

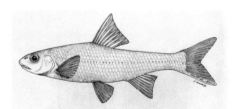

silver chub

Biology: The silver chub is found in lakes down to about 20 m and in pools in running water over sand or gravel bottoms, but also mud and clay. It enters lake shallows at night. Its survival in Lake Erie was in doubt because of the disappearance of mayflies on which it fed. However silver chub switched to other insect larvae, crustaceans and molluscs such as small clams. This chub is eaten by **burbot, yellow walleye, sauger, flathead catfish**, and other fishes. Life span is 4 years and fish over 2 years of age are sexually mature. Spawning occurs in May to July at temperatures above 19°C. Water temperatures above 21°C must last for 3 months or more to ensure growth and reproduction of this chub. This limits the northern distribution of this species. Lake populations may be found inshore but spawning is thought to occur in open water. Ripe eggs are 1.5 mm in diameter, light orange in colour and number up to 12,311. The Committee on the Status of Endangered Wildlife in Canada assigned the status of "rare" to this species in 1985. Silver chub are considered to be excellent bait for **walleye** and **bass**, however they should not be used in this way in Canada because their numbers are low.

silver deepherring

Scientific name: *Bathyclupea argentea*
    Goode and Bean, 1895
Family: **Deepherring**
Other common names: none
French name: hareng de profondeur argenté

Distribution: Found off the Atlantic coast of North America.

Characters: The only member of its family in Canada. It is characterised by having large, cycloid, easily detached scales numbering about 35 in a straight lateral line. A spineless dorsal fin in the rear half of the

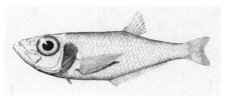

silver deepherring

body has 9 rays. The anal fin has 1–2 spines and about 29 rays. The pelvic fins are in advance of the pectoral fins, between them and the rear eye margin, and have 1 spine and 5 soft rays. Colour is yellowish-silvery. Reaches 33 cm.

Biology: First reported from the Atlantic coast of Canada in 1988 without further details. A rarely caught species with little known of its biology. It has been caught at 668 m off the U.S. coast.

silver driftfish

Scientific name: *Psenes maculatus*
    Lütken, 1880
Family: **Driftfish**
Other common names: none
French name: psène maculé

Distribution: Found in the Pacific, Indian and Atlantic oceans and from south of the LaHave Bank in Canada to northern South America in the western Atlantic Ocean.

Characters: This species is distinguished from the related **bluefin driftfish** by fewer dorsal and anal fin rays and by colour pattern.

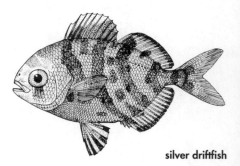

silver driftfish

First dorsal fin spines 9–11, second dorsal fin with 1 spine and 22–24 soft rays. Anal fin with 3 spines and 19–23 soft rays. The muscles are firm. Colour is silvery overall with a translucent aspect. Dark blue curved bands are found on the flanks. The second dorsal and anal fins have dark broad bands on their margins. The first dorsal fin is black. The pelvic fin is black in young fish and becomes pale at the centre in adults. Attains 15 cm.

Biology: Known in Atlantic Canada from only a single specimen caught in 1968 at a depth of 100 m. This species is found associated with jellyfish and, when young, under floating *Sargassum* weed. Adults probably frequent deeper waters.

silver hake

Scientific name: *Merluccius bilinearis*
    (Mitchill, 1814)
Family: **Hake**
Other common names: whiting,
    New England hake, frostfish
French name: merlu argenté

Distribution: Found from southern Newfoundland (and possibly the Strait of Belle Isle) and the southern Gulf of St. Lawrence to South Carolina.

Characters: This hake is distinguished from its Atlantic coast relative, the **offshore hake**, by having fewer lateral line scales (103–130) and more gill rakers (15–22). There are rows of sharp, backward curved teeth in the jaws. The lower jaw projects. The first dorsal fin has 10–14 rays, the second 37–42. The anal fin has 38–42 rays and the pectoral fin 13–17. There are differences in body proportions between hake populations along the Atlantic coast.

Overall colour is iridescent silver, sometimes with golden tints, when fresh but this fades to brown or dark grey on the back, silvery on the flanks with 5–13 faint dark or dusky rose bars or blotches, and silvery-white on the belly. The lateral line is outlined with a thin black line above and below. The dorsal fins are edged with black or green and the anal fin with white or green. The pectoral fin and its axil are black. The inner mouth is dusky blue. The cheek is not pigmented in contrast to **offshore hake**. The peritoneum is dusky and reddish. Attains 76.2 cm and 2.3 kg.

silver hake

Biology: This is a common Canadian species found from low tide strandings down to 915 m but mostly at 54–270 m. It prefers temperatures of 4.6–12.5°C, warmer than most other **Cod** and **Hake Family** members. Lowered water temperatures in winter on offshore fishing grounds have caused the hake to disappear. There is an inshore, northward, summer migration with warming of coastal waters and an offshore, southern migration in fall as inshore waters cool. On the Scotian Shelf smaller fish (< 25 cm) are found closer to shore than adults.

Food is a large variety of other fishes, voraciously pursued and consumed. Squid and euphausiid crustaceans are also taken. Groups of hake have been known to pursue and strand **herring** on the shore. Most feeding occurs between dusk and midnight on Georges Bank and food there is predominantly crustaceans. Silver hake are cannibals and a major cause regulating their own population size. Hake are food for various large pelagic predators such as **swordfish** as well as groundfish like **Atlantic cod** and **spiny dogfish**.

Growth is rapid with maturity attained as early as 2 years and almost all hake are mature at 3 years. Life span is 12 years. Females grow much larger than males.

Spawning occurs from March to September, peaking in July–August on the Scotian Shelf and is strongly influenced by temperature. Eggs are pelagic and 1.0 mm in diameter. Over a million eggs are produced.

This hake is fished commercially off the Scotian Shelf by former Soviet and by Cuban ships using bottom trawls. As much as an estimated 299,530 tonnes was caught in 1973 but only 41,006 tonnes was caught in 1981. Small meshed nets were used and resulted in a by-catch of young fish of other commercial species. A minimum mesh size was instituted in 1977. The Canadian catch in 1988 was 12 tonnes. Fresh or frozen whole fish or fillets are sold to some extent in Canada but most are frozen in blocks for foreign markets because the flesh spoils rapidly. It is a poor sport fish because, although it bites readily, it fights poorly.

Silver Hatchetfish Family

Scientific name: Sternoptychidae
French name: haches d'argent

This family of small, deepsea fishes is found in all oceans including off the Atlantic and Pacific coasts of Canada. There are about 41 species with about 12 found in Canada.

The Silver Hatchetfish Family is divided into two subfamilies, one with an elongate body, 19–38 anal fin rays and light organs on the isthmus, and the other with a hatchet-shaped body, very compressed, an unusual blade in front of the dorsal fin formed from fin spine bases which have fused, 11–19 anal fin rays and a keel-like abdomen. The first subfamily includes the **bottlelight, pearlsides** and **Atlantic constellation fish** and the second includes the **longspine, greater** and **short silver hatchetfishes**, the **silvery, slender, transparent, highlight** and **lowcrest hatchetfishes** and the **shortspine tenplate**.

Scales are easily detached in silver hatchetfishes and there is a well-developed swimbladder. Light organs are large and occur in distinctive patterns. There are 6–10 branchiostegal rays, 3 on the epihyal. A pseudobranch is present. The closest relatives of this family are in the **Bristlemouth Family**. The family is a member of the **Widemouth Order**.

Silver hatchetfishes are numerous and are found usually in oceanic waters down to possibly 3658 m, although generally shallower with younger fish higher in the water column. Some migrate vertically, others not at all. Most are mesopelagic, but some are bathypelagic or even benthic. The distinctive light organ arrangements may enable hatchetfish to recognise their own species and to merge their image with light from the ocean surface so a predator from below cannot separate them from the general diffused light from above. Hatchetfishes are an important food item for many larger fish species.

See **Atlantic constellation fish**
    bottlelight
    greater silver hatchetfish
    highlight hatchetfish
    longspine silver hatchetfish
    lowcrest hatchetfish
    pearlsides
    short silver hatchetfish
    shortspine tenplate
    silvery hatchetfish
    slender hatchetfish
    transparent hatchetfish

silver lamprey

Scientific name: *Ichthyomyzon unicuspis*
    Hubbs and Trautman, 1937
Family: **Lamprey**
Other common names: northern lamprey, brook lamprey
French name: lamproie argentée

Distribution: Found from Manitoba, through southern Ontario around the Great Lakes to western Québec and as far south rarely to Mississippi.

Characters: Trunk myomeres number 47–55. The sucking disc is wider than the body. This species is distinguished from other Canadian lampreys by having a single dorsal fin, all teeth along the sides of the mouth with 1 cusp, a sharp bicuspid tooth on the bar above the mouth and 5–11 sharp, triangular cusps on the bar below the mouth. Adults are brown, blue-grey or bluish with a blue-grey or silver belly. Ammocoetes are paler. Attains 38.1 cm.

silver lamprey

disc view

Biology: This is a parasitic species found in the larger rivers and lakes. The **northern brook lamprey** is its non-parasitic relative. Spawning occurs in May–June and up to 65,000 eggs of 1 mm diameter may be produced. Ammocoetes live 4–7 years before beginning transformation in late fall. Adults live 12–20 months and may migrate to a lake to feed. Females grow faster than males and attain a larger size. It is not as large as the **sea lamprey** and is not as economically important. The ammocoetes are used as bait for sport fish.

silver-rag

Scientific name: *Ariomma bondi*
    Fowler, 1930
Family: **Sequinfish**
Other common names: silver-rag driftfish, ariomme grise
French name: semble-coulirou

Distribution: Found in the Gulf of St. Lawrence and Georges and St. Margarets bays, Nova Scotia, south to the Caribbean Sea and Uruguay. Also in the eastern Atlantic Ocean off Africa.

Characters: This species is distinguished by having 2 dorsal fins, a slender caudal peduncle with lateral keels, adipose tissue

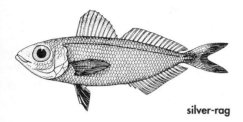

silver-rag

around the eye, no teeth on the roof of the mouth and a stiff, forked caudal fin. The first dorsal fin has 11–12 spines, the second dorsal fin 14–17 rays. The anal fin has 2–3 spines and 12–16 soft rays. Lateral line scales number about 30–45. There are only 2 scale rows between the lateral line and the dorsal fin. Scales extend onto the top of the head as far as the front of the pupil. The body is dark bluish to brown above and silvery on the flanks and belly. The young have 3–6 flank bands. Reaches 30 cm.

Biology: Believed to live and feed on the sea bed at 60–200 m, especially on sand and mud bottoms. Food is crustaceans. The fatty tissue around the eyes and nostrils helps to protect them as food is scooped from the sea floor. Small specimens are pelagic. Adults are often very common. It is caught with bottom trawls and sold fresh or frozen in the Caribbean area.

silver redhorse

Scientific name: *Moxostoma anisurum*
     (Rafinesque, 1820)
Family: **Sucker**
Other common names: silver mullet,
     whitenose redhorse, white nosed sucker
French name: suceur blanc

Distribution: Found in central North America from southern Canada south to northern Alabama and Georgia. In Canada it is found from the upper St. Lawrence River basin in southwestern Québec, west through the Great Lakes and southern Ontario to southern Manitoba, Saskatchewan and over the Alberta border in the North and South Saskatchewan rivers.

Characters: This species is distinguished by a short dorsal fin, a swimbladder with 3 chambers, lateral line scales 38–48, scales around the caudal peduncle usually 12, occasionally 13 (rarely as high as 15–16), greatest body depth enters body length to end of scales 3.5 times of less, the lower lip is thin and the plicae are long and narrow with cross lines. The mouth is overhung by the snout. The dorsal fin edge is convex to straight in shape. The upper lip is narrow and has plicae only on the inside. The lower lip is deeply cleft and the halves meet at 90° or more. Gill rakers 25–28. Pharyngeal teeth are elongate and thick but not molar-shaped. The gut has 5 coils. Dorsal fin rays 13–18, anal rays 7, pectoral rays 16–20 and pelvic rays 8–10. Males have large nuptial tubercles on the anal and caudal fins, and minute tubercles on paired fins, dorsal fin, head and on some scales.

The back is olive-green to bronze or brown with silvery or yellowish-gold flanks and a silvery to white belly. The flank may have bronze tinges particularly in spawning fish. The snout is often white. Scales are outlined with dark pigment but bases are not strongly pigmented. Paired fins are dusky to pale red or orange. Caudal and dorsal fins are slaty to dusky. Young have 2–3 flank blotches. Peritoneum silvery with a few black spots.

Reaches 71.1 cm. The world, all-tackle angling record from Plum Creek, Wisconsin was caught in 1985 and weighed 5.18 kg.

silver redhorse

Biology: This redhorse is usually found in slow, deep pools of streams and large rivers but also occurs in lakes. It is sensitive to siltation and pollution. Food is aquatic insects and occasionally molluscs and crustaceans. Life span is 21 years with maturity attained at 5–8 years. Females grow faster and live longer than males. An upstream spawning run may begin in Lake Erie as soon as the ice goes out. Spawning occurs in May–June at 13°C or more in moderate to fast, turbid, shallow streams with gravel bottoms at less than 2 m depth. Males arrive on the spawning grounds before females and are thought to defend a territory. Eggs number up to 36,340.

silver rockling

Scientific name: *Gaidropsarus argentatus*
  (Reinhardt, 1838)
Family: **Cod**
Other common names: Arctic rockling
French name: mustèle argentée

Distribution: Found from Baffin Island south to the Grand Bank. Also in Greenland, Iceland and northern Europe.

Characters: This species and its relative, the **threebeard rockling**, are distinguished from other **cods** by having 2 dorsal and 1 anal fins, the first ray in the first dorsal fin is elongate and the remaining rays are very short, and 2 snout barbels. This species is separated from its relative by having short, star-shaped gill rakers with teeth at the tip. Second dorsal fin rays 52–65, anal rays 43–51 and pectoral rays 22–24. Lateral line pores enlarged and about 27. Gill rakers 8–11 on the lower arch and 1–2 on the upper arch. The elongate dorsal ray is 5.9–8.5% of total body length. Overall colour is red-brown, brick red to red, or blackish-grey with blue tinges on the head and a pink belly. The barbel tips and median fin tips are red. Young fish are silvery. Reaches 45 cm.

silver rockling

Biology: First caught in Canada off Hawkes Harbour, Labrador in 1956 and rare in Canada with only 4 specimens reported. Usually found at 400–500 m, and down to 2260 m, at 0.5–3.1°C. May be found as shallow as 150 m. Food is crustaceans, occasionally fishes. Spawning probably occurs in spring as pelagic young have been caught in June–August near the Arctic Circle.

silver shiner

Scientific name: *Notropis photogenis*
  (Cope, 1865)
Family: **Carp**
Other common names: none
French name: méné-miroir

Distribution: Found in the Grand and Thames rivers and Bronte Creek in southern Ontario in the drainages of lakes Erie, St. Clair and Ontario. In the U.S.A. from Indiana to New York and south to Georgia.

Characters: This species and its relatives in the genus *Notropis* (typical **shiners**) are separated from other family members by

silver shiner

usually having 7 branched dorsal fin rays following thin unbranched rays, protractile premaxillaries (upper lip separated from the snout by a groove), no barbels, large lateral line scales (fewer than 50), and a simple, s-shaped gut. This species is separated from its relatives by having 8–12 branched anal fin rays, rounded anterior flank scales, body depth less than head length and a crescent-shaped black patch medial to each nostril. The dorsal fin origin lies over the pelvic fin insertion. Lateral line scales 36–41. Pectoral rays 15–17 and pelvic rays 8–9. Pharyngeal teeth 2,4–4,2 or 1,4–4,2. Males develop nuptial tubercles on the head, anterior scales and upper pectoral fin surface. The flanks are silvery with bluish reflections and there is a midflank stripe broadest to the rear. There may be an iridescent gold or blue dorsolateral stripe. The lateral line has spots above and below each pore. The back is green, yellow or slaty-olive, overlain with silvery or steel blue. The belly is white to silvery. The middorsal stripe is narrow and sharply defined and may be iridescent gold or bluish. Fins are generally clear although lower ones may be whitish and the dorsal and caudal fins have dark margins. Reaches 14.2 cm.

Biology: This species was first reported from Canada in 1973. It is found in large, clear streams with swift currents and hard bottoms, favouring deeper pool habitats. Food includes aquatic insects, crustaceans, flatworms, water mites, surface insects, and algae. They may jump to take flying insects. **Smallmouth bass** are known to be predators. Life span is over 3 years with maturity attained in the second year. Spawning occurs in May and June in Ontario over about a 2 week period at about 17–23°C. Maturing eggs are yellow, orange or pink-orange and up to 1.1 mm in diameter. The Committee on the Status of Endangered Wildlife in Canada gave this species the status of "rare" in 1983. It has been used as a bait fish in Canada.

silver surfperch

Scientific name: *Hyperprosopon ellipticum*
(Gibbons, 1854)
Family: **Surfperch**
Other common names: porgy
French name: ditrème argenté

Distribution: From Vancouver Island south to Baja California.

Characters: This surfperch is distinguished from other Canadian species by having pelvic fins not black-tipped, no row of

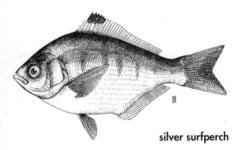

silver surfperch

small scales along the posterior half of the anal fin base, no frenum and 59–67 lateral line scales. Dorsal fin spines 8–10, soft rays 25–29. Anal fin with 3 spines and 29–35 soft rays. Pectoral fin with 26–28 soft rays. Caudal fin with a moderate fork. The back is dark-green to a silver-grey with silvery flanks and belly. The flank has several faint dusky to golden pink bars. The caudal fin is usually pinkish. Dorsal and caudal fins often

have dark margins, on the dorsal fin sometimes concentrated into an anterior spot. The anal fin has a black to orange spot anteriorly. Reaches 27 cm.

Biology: Found on exposed sandy beaches, around rocks and piers and sometimes in the mouths of estuaries. Caught down to 110 m. Mating occurs in late September and young are born from late June to early August, about 9 months later. Up to 30 young are born at a length of 2 cm. Some fish become mature in 1 year and all are mature by age 3. Males attain an age of 7 years and females 5 years in Oregon. Often caught by anglers along the shore.

silvergray rockfish

Scientific name: *Sebastes brevispinis*
(Bean, 1884)
Family: **Scorpionfish**
Other common names: shortspine rockfish, rock salmon
French name: sébaste argenté

Distribution: From the Bering Sea to southern California including British Columbia.

Characters: This species has a large mouth with the upper jaw extending back beyond the eye. There is a strong chin projection. Dorsal fin spines 13, soft rays 13–17, usually 14. Hart (1973) lists 15–17 dorsal fin rays. Anal fin soft rays 7–8, usually 7, second anal spine thicker but usually shorter than the third. Pectoral fin rays 16–18, usually 18, with 9–11 rays unbranched. Gill rakers 33–36. Vertebrae 26. Lateral line pores 44–53, scale rows below

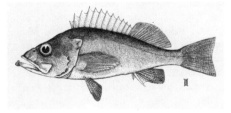

silvergray rockfish

lateral line 58–70. The nasal, preocular and parietal head spines are weak and the others are usually absent. Dark grey to olive or green on the back with silvery or silver-grey flanks and a white belly. Lips are blackened. The lower fins and some of the belly are red-tinged. The peritoneum is white with black dots. Attains 71 cm.

Biology: A common commercial species comprising about 30% of the catch excluding the abundant **Pacific ocean perch**. They are called rock salmon because of the red tinges and body shape. Found from 30–366 m, usually near the bottom around reefs and over soft bottoms. Food includes such fishes as **sand lances** and **herrings**. The young are born in June or later in British Columbia. Half the population is mature at 43 cm for males and 45 cm for females in Canadian waters. Maximum age is estimated to be 80 years.

Silverside Family

Scientific name: Atherinidae
French name: capucettes

Silversides, sand smelts or whitebait are found mostly in temperate to tropical seas with some species in fresh waters. There are about 165 species with 1 on the Pacific coast of Canada, 1 on the Atlantic coast also entering brackish water and 1 in fresh waters of river basins draining to the Atlantic Ocean.

These small, elongate, silvery fishes have a short, spiny first dorsal fin widely separated from the second dorsal fin. The second dorsal often has a spine in front of the soft rays. Pelvic fins are usually abdominal and have 1 spine and 5 soft rays. Pectoral fins are high on the flank. The anal fin has 1–3 spines preceding the soft rays. Cycloid scales are usually large, extend onto the head and there is no lateral line although there may be a row of pits, 1 to each scale. Many species have a broad, silvery, iridescent lateral stripe which turns black in preserved fish. The oblique, terminal mouth is small as are the teeth. The swimbladder is not connected to the gut.

Silversides are members of the **Silverside Order**, and most of their related families are found in southeast Asia and Australia. They are difficult to identify where many species occur together.

These fishes are found in large schools but are not commercially important in a direct sense. However they are major bait and forage fish for commercial species. They are usually found in shallow, inshore waters. Eggs of many species have filamentous outgrowths for attachment to seaweed, sand or rocks. Food is principally plankton. Some species from tropical waters are sold as aquarium fishes.

See **Atlantic silverside**
brook silverside
topsmelt

Silverside Order

Silversides and rainbowfishes or Atheriniformes are found in temperate to tropical marine and fresh waters. All are small, often silvery fishes. There are 8 families and about 285 species. In Canada there is 1 family with 3 species, 1 each on the Pacific and Atlantic coasts and in fresh waters.

The order is characterised by the presence of usually 2 dorsal fins, the first with flexible spines the second far back opposite the elongate anal fin, the anal fin usually has a spine at its origin, the pectoral fin is usually high on the flank, pelvic fins are abdominal (thoracic in some) and usually have 6 soft rays, a small mouth, the lateral line is weakly developed or absent, scales are cycloid, branchiostegal rays 5–7, parietal bones in the skull roof present, paired nostril openings, the preanal length of flexion larvae is short, about one-third of body length, and a single row of melanophores on the dorsal surface of the larva.

The order is related to the **Killifish** and **Needlefish** orders (q.v.) which have been included within the Silverside Order.

Some members of the order from southeast Asia have a peculiar, bony and muscular copulatory organ in males known as a priapium. This organ is located under the throat. The California grunion is the best known member of the order. It spawns on sandy beaches in the many thousands 1–2 days after a new or full moon during spring flood tides. Eggs hatch at the next high tide, 2 weeks later. Most silversides live in shallow, surface waters, often feeding at the air-water interface.

See **Silverside Family**

silverspotted sculpin

Scientific name: *Blepsias cirrhosus*
(Pallas, 1814)
Family: **Sculpin**
Other common names: silver spot, little
dragon sculpin
French name: chabot à taches argentées

Distribution: Found from Japan to
California including British Columbia.

Characters: This species and its relative,
the **crested sculpin**, are separated from
Pacific coast sculpins by the deep, com-

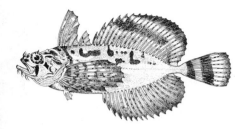

silverspotted sculpin

pressed body and 3 simple, large cirri on
each lower jaw. The silverspotted sculpin is
distinguished from its relative by a notch
between the third and sixth spines of the first
dorsal fin, by colour pattern and by having
11–14 pectoral fin rays. The nasal spine is
blunt and recurved. There are 4 preopercular
spines, the second is the largest but all are
blunt and covered by skin. There are frontal,
occipital and parietal ridges. First dorsal fin
spines 6–10, second dorsal soft rays 20–25.
Anal fin rays 18–22, and pelvic fin with 1
spine and 3 soft rays. Ctenoid scales comprise small plates with a small spine embedded in a fleshy papilla. Scales cover the body
but are absent in patches along the rear lateral line, the caudal peduncle, below the lateral line, under the pectoral fin and are
patchily present on the lower head. Lateral
line pores 43–57. A pair of long cirri are present on the snout and are folded down, and
there is an erect, median snout cirrus. Small
cirri are present on the nasal spines, above
the eyes and on the throat. The back is olive-
brown to green and the belly is white to yellowish. There are vague dark saddles over

the back. The flank has copper-red areas.
The flank anteriorly below the lateral line
has white or silvery patches. Black bars radiate from the eye. Fins are brown to black
with clear areas. Small fish have a dark bar
on the pectoral fin. The inside of the mouth
is blue. Reaches 20 cm standard length.

Biology: This sculpin is moderately common and occurs from the intertidal zone and
weedy bays down to 37 m and off the coast.
It may be nocturnal. It is eaten by the **calico
sculpin**. Spawning occurs in February and
light brown or blue eggs are attached to
rocks. Males mate with females which then
have spermatozoa in the ovary but mating is
followed by external fertilisation, an unusual
behaviour.

silverstripe halfbeak

Scientific name: *Hyporhamphus unifasciatus*
(Ranzani, 1842)
Family: **Halfbeak**
Other common names: common halfbeak,
skipjack
French name: demi-bec africain

Distribution: Found from New Brunswick
south to Argentina. Also in the eastern Pacific
Ocean.

Characters: Distinguished from its only
Canadian relative, the **ballyhoo**, by having
15–18 anal fin rays, the pelvic fin is short
and does not extend back level with the dorsal fin origin, and by colour. Dorsal fin rays
14–16. There is a bony ridge in front of the
eye. Lower caudal fin lobe short. Dorsal and
anal fins are scaly near their bases. The back
and body are green with silvery tinges. A silvery stripe runs along the upper flank. The
dorsal and anal fins have dusky tips anteriorly. The back has 3 dark lines along the
middle. Scales are dark at their edges. The

silverstripe halfbeak

lower jaw tip and upper lobe of the caudal
fin are yellowish-red. The peritoneum is
black. Reaches about 30 cm.

Biology: Known from a single Canadian specimen caught in a herring weir at Chamcook, Passamaquoddy Bay, New Brunswick in 1949. This is a rare stray and a northern record. This species is found in surface waters of bays and estuaries and is not common around coral reefs in southern waters. Food is crustaceans, molluscs and plants. Halfbeaks are used as bait for large game fishes such as **common dolphin** and **billfishes**.

silvery hatchetfish

Scientific name: *Argyropelecus lychnus*
    Garman, 1899
Family: **Silver Hatchetfish**
Other common names: none
French name: hache d'argent à quatre gaffes

Distribution: Found in all major oceans according to some authors (but see below). This species was recorded from the Pacific coast but those records are now believed to be the **lowcrest hatchetfish**. Even the accuracy of Atlantic coast records has been questioned! Hatchetfishes can be hard to identify. Recorded off Nova Scotia.

Characters: This species is distinguished by having a hatchet-shaped body, 12 abdominal light organs, telescopic eyes directed

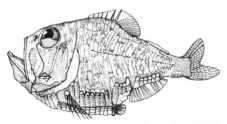

silvery hatchetfish

upward and a large and high blade anterior to the dorsal fin. In addition the lower light organs are not in a nearly continuous row, there are two spines of equal size at the posterior tip of the abdomen, no enlarged teeth in the lower jaw, and 9 dorsal fin rays. The back is dark, the flanks lighter with small spots and the light organs are silvery with black edges. Overall colour is silvery. Attains over 6 cm standard length.

Biology: One specimen was caught near the LaHave Bank at 238 m in 1967, the only Atlantic Ocean record. Usually concentrated at 300–400 m without an obvious vertical migration.

Simony's frostfish

Scientific name: *Benthodesmus simonyi*
    (Steindachner, 1891)
Family: **Cutlassfish**
Other common names: none
French name: poisson sabre ganse

Distribution: Found in the North Atlantic Ocean including off Newfoundland.

Characters: This species is distinguished from related species by having a notch between the spiny and soft parts of the dorsal

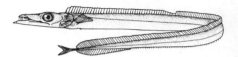

Simony's frostfish

fin, the spiny part of this fin is about half as long as the soft part, no crest on top of the head commencing over the eye and extending back to the dorsal fin, and by the total dorsal fin rays being 148–155 and total vertebrae being 153–158 (these last two characters overlap with the **North Pacific frostfish** but that species occurs only on the Pacific coast of Canada). Dorsal fin spines 44–46 and soft rays 104–109. Anal fin with 2 spines and 93–102 soft rays. The body is silvery and the jaws, opercle, and mouth and gill cavities black. Reaches 130 cm standard length.

Biology: The adults of this species are benthopelagic from 200 to 900 m while young are mesopelagic.

sixgill shark

Scientific name: *Hexanchus griseus*
    (Bonnaterre, 1788)
Family: **Cow Shark**
Other common names: bluntnose sixgill shark, shovelnose shark, mud shark, requin grisé
French name: requin griset

Distribution: From the Aleutian Islands south to California and Mexico including

British Columbia. In the western Atlantic Ocean from Nova Scotia south to the Caribbean Sea and Costa Rica. Also in Europe and the Southern Hemisphere.

Characters: The six pairs of gill openings are unique in Canadian sharks. In addition the snout is short, blunt and broad, the mouth

sixgill shark

large, the eyes are small and the caudal peduncle is short and stout with its upper length about equal to the dorsal fin base length. The lower jaw has 6 rows of comblike or saw-like teeth with short cusps while the upper jaw teeth are smaller and not comb or saw-like. Scales have 3 ridges with the centre ridge largest. Overall colour is dark brown or grey to almost black above becoming paler below. There is often a lighter streak along the flank. They eye is greenish. Attains at least 4.82 m and 590 kg, with reports of 8 m specimens. The all-tackle, world record came from the Azores Islands in 1990 and weighed 485 kg.

Biology: Reported from Nova Scotia as single specimens caught in gill nets off Sambro at 155 m on 19 August 1989, and in the Emerald Basin at 183 m on 22 October 1989. Much commoner in British Columbia. This species is sluggish but can swim strongly. It is found from the surface down to at least 1875 m. It eats a variety of fish including other **sharks, rays, dolphin** fish, **swordfish, marlin, Pacific lamprey, Pacific hagfish, herring** and **cod**, as well as crabs, shrimp, squid, seals and carrion. This shark is sensitive to light and rests on the bottom during the day but may approach the surface at night to feed. Shallow water captures are in colder waters. It is ovoviviparous with large litters of up to 108 pups measuring 60–73.5 cm at birth. Females mature at about 4.5–4.82 m. Most specimens are caught at

night on the bottom but it is not commercially important because of the depths it prefers. However it is locally common and is caught on longlines, in gill nets, purse seines, traps and in bottom and pelagic trawls. It can be eaten but the flesh is said to be a purgative. Some catches have been used for fish meal and oil. This species may snap when caught and should be handled with care. The Vancouver Aquarium had 3 specimens on display for a short time in the summer of 1975. The smallest sharks ate the larger one. These were the largest sharks (3 m) displayed live in Canada. This species has been seen on guided dive trips at 25–70 m off Hornby Island in the Strait of Georgia and at the mouth of Alberni Inlet in Barkley Sound around Vancouver Island.

Skate Family

Scientific name: Rajidae
French name: raies

Skates and **rays** are found world-wide in the ocean from shallows to great depths. Tropical species are often in deeper water than cold and temperate species. There are over 200 species. In Canada there are 13 Atlantic coast species, 7 Pacific coast species, 1 Arctic coast species and 3 Arctic-Atlantic coast species.

Skates are recognised by the disc, comprising body and pectoral fins, a reduced or absent caudal fin, no anal fin, a long, slender tail, 0–3, usually 2, small dorsal fins found near the end of the tail, prickles, spines or thorns on the skin particularly along the centre of the back, and 1 to several eggs laid in a black or dark green horny capsule or egg case which has 4 elongate corners, or horns, used for attachment to bottom weeds and rocks. The capsule is known as a "mermaid's purse." The anterior edge of the neurocranium or skull is extended as a rostral bar. This cartilaginous structure may be slender and soft (softnosed skates — *Bathyraja* species) or thick and stiff (hardnosed skates — *Raja* species). Teeth are small and rounded, or pointed in several rows arranged in a parallel or quincunx pattern. Both sexes may have pointed teeth, or both sexes have rounded teeth but males develop sharp, conical teeth just prior to maturing. In the latter case the quincunx pattern typical of immatures and females changes to more widely spaced teeth in cross rows. The male uses his jaws to hold the female during copulation. Males have a modification of the pelvic fins, known as claspers, which aid in delivering sperm to the females. Female skates are often larger than male skates but males have more and larger spines on the tip of the pectoral fin known as alar spines. Alar spines probably help in grasping the female during mating. The 5 gill openings and the mouth are ventral, on the underside of the disc. The eyes and spiracles are on the upper surface. The spiracle enables clean water to be passed over the gills for respiration. Water entering through the ventral mouth might carry clogging sediment in bottom-dwelling skates. Some skate species have electric organs made of modified axial muscles. These organs have a weak discharge, unlike that of **electric rays**, and they are not used to stun prey. The organs are discharged in contact with other skates suggesting they are used in intra-specific communication.

These fishes are relatives of the **Electric Ray** and **Stingray** families and are members of the **Ray Order**. Skate and ray are both used for members of the Rajidae. Skate is often used for larger and commercial species. The term skate is derived from a Scandinavian word for these fishes. The distribution of various spines are used in identification. The skin thorns are large, strong spines which are often in a row along the middle of the back and tail. Smaller spines, which are larger than the prickles or scales, are called thornlets. Malar spines are those close to the edge of the disc opposite the eyes. Nuchal thorns are on the nape and scapular thorns are on the shoulder behind the eyes on each side of the midline.

Skates use the pectoral fins to swim with a flapping or undulating motion. Some species have elongate pelvic fin rays with which they "walk" over the sea floor. These are mostly bottom-living fishes although some are pelagic. They often flap their pectoral fins to partially bury themselves in sediment, hiding from predators and prey. Food is an assortment of seabed organisms such as crabs, lobsters, shrimp and other, smaller crustaceans as well as worms, clams and small fishes. The embryo in the egg capsule may take up to 14 months to develop. Skates are excellent eating but of low commercial value. The "wings" are cut up and sold as "scallops" but most of the catch is made into fish meal or pet food. In 1981, 4500 tonnes of skates were caught in the northwest Atlantic. The Canadian catch in 1988 was 822 tonnes. However many skates are discarded in favour of commercial species.

See **abyssal skate**
barndoor skate
big skate
Bigelow's skate
broad skate
chocolate skate
darkbelly skate
deepwater skate
linen skate
little skate
longnose skate
Markle's ray
roughtail skate
round skate
sandpaper skate
shorttail skate
skate species
skate species
smooth skate
soft skate
spinytail skate
starry skate
thorny skate
winter skate

skate species

Scientific name: *Bathyraja* sp.
Family: **Skate**
Other common names: none
French name: raie

Distribution: From Franklin Bay, Beaufort Sea in the Canadian Arctic.

Characters: This species is believed to be new but has not yet been scientifically described as it is known only from 5 egg cases, one containing a young skate. Much remains to be learned about Arctic fishes and several new species may eventually be found in the far north.

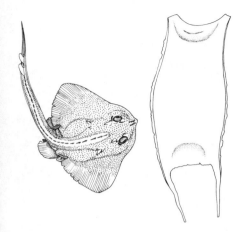

skate species

Biology: The egg cases were collected in 1977 at 335 m.

skate species

Scientific name: *Raja* sp.
Family: **Skate**
Other common names: none
French name: raie

Distribution: Found near the Flemish Cap of Atlantic Canada and the Denmark Strait between Greenland and Iceland.

Characters: This species is not yet scientifically described. It resembles the **darkbelly skate** but has more tooth rows (50–68), is light in colour — sometimes even white above and below, and reaches a larger size at 115 cm. It occurs in deep, cold water, a very Canadian environment which is poorly sampled and may yet yield more species new to science.

skilfish

Scientific name: *Erilepis zonifer*
   (Lockington, 1880)
Family: **Sablefish**
Other common names: fat-priest fish,
   marine monk, priestfish, giant seabass
French name: morue bariolée

Distribution: Found from California to Japan including British Columbia.

Characters: This species is distinguished from its relative the **sablefish** by having a stout body, 11–14 first dorsal fin spines and

11–14 anal fin rays. The first dorsal fin can be retracted into a groove. There are 1–2 spines and 13–17 soft rays in the second dorsal fin. The anal fin has 2–3 spines. Both soft dorsal and anal fin spines may be hard to locate. Scales are ctenoid, small and cover the body, head and lower parts of the soft fins. Lateral line scales 120–124. Teeth are sharp, conical, in 2 lower jaw rows and in a band in the upper jaw. Adults are overall black with dirty-white scale margins. Young are grey-blue to green and heavily blotched white, with bars on the fins, large spots on the spiny dorsal fin and a pale belly. Attains 178 cm and 91 kg, and larger. The English common name is derived from a Haida Indian word for fish.

skilfish

Biology: Young are found at the surface but adults are deep water fish, down to 439 m on rocky bottoms offshore. Young fish are curious as they poke their heads out of the water around ships. Not as important commercially as the **sablefish**, but it is taken by trawling and longlining. The flesh is oily.

skipjack tuna

Scientific name: *Katsuwonus pelamis*
   (Linnaeus, 1758)
Family: **Mackerel**
Other common names: oceanic bonito,
   striped bonito, listao
French name: thonine à ventre rayé

Distribution: Found world-wide in warmer seas entering waters off British Columbia and Nova Scotia.

Characters: This species is distinguished from its relatives on both coasts by the dorsal fins being close together (separated by a distance less than snout length), 14–16 first dorsal fin spines, and 51–63 gill rakers. Second dorsal fin rays 13–16 followed by 7–9 finlets. Anal fin with 2 spines and 12–16 soft rays followed by 7–8 finlets. Pectoral rays 24–28. A corselet of modified cycloid scales encompasses the first dorsal fin base,

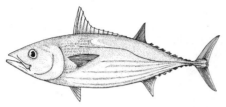

slipjack tuna

pectoral area and throat. The rest of the body has no scales. No swimbladder. There is a flap of skin between the pelvic fins with 2 points. The back is dark blue to purplish-blue with silvery flanks and dirty or shining white belly. First dorsal fin pale, other fins dusky except the pelvics which are white along the margin. The lower flank has 2–6 dark blue or brown stripes, occasionally broken into blotches or absent. There may be light bars on the flank. Reaches 1.08 m and 34.5 kg. The angling record weighed 19 kg and was caught in 1985 at Mauritius.

Biology: British Columbia records are for Barkley Sound and the entrance to the Strait of Juan de Fuca and Nova Scotia records for east of Georges Bank and off Devils Island. This is a surface schooling and migratory species favouring waters of 15–30°C, usually 20–28°C, down to 260 m. Its distribution is limited by a combination of oxygen levels (5 p.p.m.) and temperature (18°C) below which these fish are generally absent. This species is often associated with floating debris, other **tunas**, whales and even sharks. Food is a variety of fishes and invertebrates. Cannibalism is common and major predators are **billfishes** and other **tunas**. Minimum size at maturity is 39.1 cm for males and 34 cm for females. Life span is estimated to be 8–12 years. Spawning occurs in batches year round in the tropics. Up to 2 million eggs of 1.1 mm diameter may be released. This tuna is commercially important and is frozen for canning after capture by purse seines, pole and line gear, or line fisheries. It is also taken with beach seines, gill nets and in traps. Up to 40% of "tuna" catches are this

species. The world catch in 1978 was 796,034 tonnes. It is too rare in Canada to be a commercial species. It is a favourite of anglers where common.

slanteye parkinglightfish

Scientific name: *Diaphus termophilus* Tåning, 1928
Family: **Lanternfish**
Other common names: none
French name: lampe-veilleuse oeil-penché

Distribution: Found in the Atlantic and Pacific oceans and off the Scotian Shelf of Atlantic Canada.

Characters: This species and its relatives, the **bouncer**, **eventooth**, **flashlight**, **square**, **straightcheek**, and **Taaning's headlight-fishes** and the **doormat parkinglightfish**, are separated from other Atlantic coast lanternfishes by not having photophores near the dorsal body edge, the PLO photophore is well above the upper pectoral fin base level while the second PVO photophore is at or below this level, there are 4 Prc photophores,

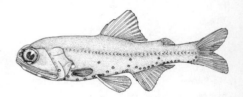

slanteye parkinglightfish

the PO and two PVO photophores form a straight, ascending line as do the first 3 VO photophores, supracaudal luminous glands are absent, and there is more than 1 pair of luminous head organs. This species is separated from its relatives by having the So photophore absent, vomer with a small round to oval patch of teeth on each side, Dn photophore well-developed in a deep cup, directed forward and about half the size of the nasal rosette, first SAO photophore on a level with the fifth VO photophore and pelvic fins extending beyond anal fin origin. Dorsal fin rays 13–15, anal rays 15–16 and pectoral rays 11–13. Total gill rakers 23–26. AO photophores 9–12. Lateral line organs 35–36. Adult males have a Vn photophore about 3 times larger than that of females. "Headlights" or photophores Dn and Vn are apparent at 1.2 cm body length. Reaches about 8.0 cm.

Biology: This species is tropical to subtropical and reaches Canada via the Gulf Stream. A single specimen has been caught south of La Have Bank in 1968. Depth distribution is 325–850 m by day, most abundantly at 400–500 m, and 40–225 m at night, most abundantly at 100 m. Sexual maturity is reached at 6.3 cm.

slatjaw cutthroat eel

Scientific name: *Synaphobranchus kaupi* Johnson, 1862
Family: **Cutthroat Eel**
Other common names: Kaup's deepsea eel, Gray's cutthroat eel, longnose eel, northern cutthroat eel
French name: anguille égorgée bécue

Distribution: Found world-wide including from the Davis Strait and Labrador to South Carolina in the western Atlantic Ocean.

Characters: This eel is distinguished from other family members in Canada by the pointed head, large mouth reaching back beyond the eye and the dorsal fin origin far behind the level of the anus. Pectoral fins present. Scales are minute, rod-shaped and embedded. There are about 30 preanal pores and 8 prepectoral pores in a distinct lateral line. Gill slits are very small, on the throat, joining anteriorly to form a "v." Small, sharp, recurved teeth occur in bands in the jaws and as a single or double row on the roof of the mouth. The anterior nostril is large and tube-shaped. The posterior nostril is a raised pore near the eye. Overall colour

slatjaw cutthroat eel

is black or dark purple-grey to brown. The anterior edges of the dorsal and anal fins are lighter than the posterior edges. The mouth cavity is blue-black. Reaches 81.3 cm.

Biology: Found at 131–4800 m, with the shallowest record off Cape Sable, N.S.. This eel is a dominant element of the deepsea bottom fauna and comprises about 40% of the fish by weight and number at 500–1500 m in the eastern North Atlantic. It has been observed from a submersible swimming along or above the bottom and hovering head up or down. It can swim backwards or forwards. Food is crustaceans, fishes and large cephalopods. Also known to eat octopus eggs. Spawning may peak in spring and summer and orange eggs are about 1 mm in diameter. The leptocephalus larva stage may last 18–22 months and during this stage the eyes are telescopic.

Sleeper Shark Family

Scientific name: Dalatiidae
French name: laimargues

These sharks comprise about 49 species found from the Arctic to the Antarctic Ocean in coastal and oceanic waters. In Canada there are 7 species on the Pacific and Atlantic coasts and entering the eastern Arctic.

Most members lack spines in their dorsal fins and have small luminous organs on the belly. They were once included in the **Dogfish Shark Family** and are members of the **Dogfish Shark Order**.

They range in size from the some of the smallest sharks, the pygmy sharks less than 20 cm when adult, to some of the largest, the sleeper sharks which can exceed 6 m in length.

See **black dogfish**
Greenland shark
kitefin shark
Pacific sleeper shark
Portuguese shark
rough sagre
spined pygmy shark

slender barracudina

Scientific name: *Lestidiops ringens* (Jordan and Gilbert, 1881)
Family: **Barracudina**
Other common names: none
French name: lussion long

Distribution: Found from British Columbia

to Baja California. Also at Ocean Station Papa (50°N, 145°W).

Characters: This barracudina is distinguished from its Canadian relatives by having a pectoral fin shorter than the anal fin base, smooth-edged lower jaw teeth, scales

slender barracudina

restricted to the lateral line, the pelvic fin before the dorsal fin, an adipose fin between the pelvic and anal fins, and its Pacific coast distribution. Dorsal fin rays 9–12, anal rays 26–33, pectorals 11–12 and pelvics 8–9. There are ridges between the pelvic fins and the anus. The back is a greenish-brown and the flanks and belly an iridescent silver. Reaches 21.8 cm.

Biology: Reported from 29–50 m off Vancouver Island, Queen Charlotte Sound, and off Bamfield. Ocean Station Papa fish were taken at less than 60 m. Elsewhere down to 3920 m.

slender blacksmelt

Scientific name: *Bathylagus pacificus*
    Gilbert, 1890
Family: **Deepsea Smelt**
Other common names: Pacific blacksmelt
French name: garcette élancée

Distribution: Found from the Bering Sea to Baja California, including British Columbia.

Characters: Distinguished from other Pacific coast species of deepsea smelts by

slender blacksmelt

having 15–22 anal fin rays, 7–11 pectoral fin rays and 37–42 scale rows along the flank. Dorsal fin rays 8–13, pelvic rays 7–10 and

gill rakers 28–32. Colour is brown to black, with a bluish-black head. Attains 25 cm.

Biology: Found at depths below 300 m to over 1000 m and does not apparently migrate. Spawning occurs in spring. Food is small crustaceans. Many larger species of fish feed on slender blacksmelts.

slender bristlemouth

Scientific name: *Cyclothone pseudopallida*
    Mukhacheva, 1964
Family: **Bristlemouth**
Other common names: phantom bristlemouth
French name: cyclothone mince

Distribution: Found in the Pacific Ocean including off British Columbia and in the Atlantic Ocean off Nova Scotia. Also in the Indian Ocean.

Characters: This species is separated from its Pacific and Atlantic coast relatives by lacking SO photophores, by having a

slender bristlemouth

basically light brown body with scales, a transparent area in front of the anal fin, 8–9 OA photophores, 18–20 gill rakers, and the first 2 VAV photophores close together. Photophores: ORB 1, OP 2, BR 9–11, IV 3 + 10, VAV 4–5, AC 14–15, IC 31–34. Dorsal fin rays 12–14, anal fin rays 17–20. Body on upper flanks light brown, grey or greyish-brown, clearly demarcated from unpigmented lower flank. There are 40–50 small pigment spots on top of the head. Females reach 5.8 cm but males reach only 4.3 cm.

Biology: Found at about 400 m west of Vancouver Island, off Cape Flattery and at Ocean Station Papa (50°N, 145°W) in less than 450 m. Off the Atlantic coast, slender bristlemouths have been caught on the southwest Scotian Shelf at 500 m in 1979 and off Sable Island Bank in 1980. These are northwestern Atlantic Ocean range extensions first reported in 1988. Usually found at 300–900 m depending on the season, latitude and age and reported as deep as 3000 m. There is no daily vertical migration. Up to 1500 yellowish eggs are shed.

slender cockscomb

Scientific name: *Anoplarchus insignis*
   Gilbert and Burke, 1912
Family: **Shanny**
Other common names: none
French name: crête-de-coq mince

Distribution: From northern California to the Aleutian Islands including the coast of British Columbia.

Characters: This species is related to the **high cockscomb**, which also lacks pelvic fins and has a median crest on top of the head. It usually has more anal rays than its relative and is also distinguished by the width between the posterior gill membrane attachments to the isthmus being 0–1.9% of the standard length. Both these characters overlap in the 2 species, making their identification difficult. There are 57–64 dorsal fin spines, 40–46 anal fin rays, and 9–10 pectoral fin rays. Fin spine and ray counts vary with latitude. Scales are only on the posterior part of the body. There is an indistinct lateral line on the midflank and also one between it and the dorsal fin. Dark brown to black, occasionally bright red, sometimes mottled.

slender cockscomb

There are usually dark and light bars on the cheek and saddles over the back. Reaches about 12 cm.

Biology: Found intertidally and down to 30 m, often among rocks.

slender eelblenny

Scientific name: *Lumpenus fabricii*
   (Valenciennes in Cuvier and
   Valenciennes, 1836)
Family: **Shanny**

Other common names: lompénie élancée
French name: lompénie de Fabricius

Distribution: Circumpolar in Arctic waters, across Arctic Canada and as far south as Nova Scotia in the western Atlantic Ocean.

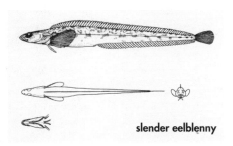

slender eelblenny

Characters: This species is 1 of 8 related Canadian shannies which have very elongate bodies, large pectoral fins, and pelvic fins with 1 spine and 2–4 soft rays. It is distinguished by distribution, 60–67 dorsal fin spines, anal fin with 1 spine and 38–45 soft rays of equal length, and 15–17 pectoral fin rays. The upper jaw projects. Scales cover the body and the lateral line is complete. The caudal fin is rounded and the dorsal and anal fins are not joined to it. Light brown body with darker blotches and spots extending onto the lower flank. Head and pectoral fin yellowish. Dusky spot at pectoral fin base. The caudal fin is barred. Attains 36.5 cm.

Biology: An inshore species from 2 m down to 183 m, sometimes in water as cold as −1.6°C or as warm as 15.6°C. It may rest coiled like a snake. Food is crustaceans, worms and fish eggs. Clam siphons are ripped off. It may live as long as 17 years. It is eaten by **Atlantic cod** and by black guillemots. Spawning occurs in summer in seaweed in Greenland, but it may be later in the high Arctic. Eggs are large at 3 mm diameter, but few at 490 in each female.

slender fangjaw

Scientific name: *Gonostoma gracile*
   Günther, 1878
Family: **Bristlemouth**
Other common names: none
French name: gonostome élancé

Distribution: Found in the North Pacific Ocean including at Ocean Station Papa (50°N, 145°W).

Characters: This species is distinguished from its Pacific coast relatives by having SO photophores. Photophores: SO 1, ORB 1, OP

slender fangjaw

2, BR 9, IV 15, OA 11–14, VAV 3–5, AC 17–19, IC 35–39. The upper flank has 6 widely-spaced photophores. There is no adipose fin. The anal fin origin is well ahead of the dorsal fin origin. Dorsal fin rays 10–14, anal rays 26–29. Reaches 11.6 cm.

Biology: The Ocean Station Papa specimen was taken at less than 800 m.

slender fathead

Scientific name: *Cubiceps gracilis*
    (Lowe, 1843)
Family: **Ruff**
Other common names: none
French name: pompile élancé

Distribution: Found south of the Grand Bank in Atlantic Canada. Also known from the northeastern Atlantic Ocean and western Mediterranean Sea, possibly world-wide.

Characters: This species is distinguished from the related **Cape** and **fewray fatheads** by having broad knobby tooth patches on the vomer bone in the roof of the mouth, usually 3 anal fin spines and 32–34 vertebrae. Dorsal fin spines 9–11, followed by 1–2 spines and 20–22 soft rays. Anal fin soft rays 20–23. Pectoral fin rays 20–24. Upper procurrent (= inclined forward) caudal fin rays 8–9.

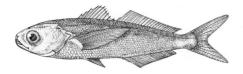

slender fathead

Lateral line scales 60–62. The colour in preservative is brown. Reaches 75 cm.

Biology: Strays are found as young fish at 50–100 m in Atlantic Canada. First discovered in 1979. Caught on longlines off Japan and used as food.

slender hatchetfish

Scientific name: *Argyropelecus affinis*
    Garman, 1899
Family: **Silver Hatchetfish**
Other common names: none
French name: hache d'argent élancée

Distribution: Found world-wide in warmer oceans and from Nova Scotia southwards in the western Atlantic Ocean.

Characters: The body is shaped like a hatchet, the eyes are telescopic and directed upwards, there are 12 abdominal light organs and there is a large blade anterior to the dorsal fin. In addition the lower light organs are in a nearly continuous row and the body profile below the dorsal blade is smooth and not raised. Colour is silvery on the flanks with a dark back. Preserved fish have dark spots on

slender hatchetfish

the flank, partially outlining muscle blocks. Light organs are silvery and outlined in black. Eyes are bright yellow in living fish. Reaches 7.2 cm standard length.

Biology: A single Canadian specimen was caught off the Scotian Shelf in 1979. This fish is found at 300–650 m, sometimes shallower. It does not migrate vertically for any great distance. Food includes various small crustaceans, salps and arrow worms. The yellow lens in the eye of this fish is unusual. It is probably used in the detection of longer wave light sources such as the yellowish-green emitted by predators. The photophores serve to obliterate the shadows formed by daylight and the fish's body.

slender lightfish

Scientific name: *Vinciguerria attenuata*
(Cocco, 1838)
Family: **Lightfish**
Other common names: none
French name: poisson étoilé svelte

Distribution: Tropical to temperate waters of all major oceans including Atlantic Canada.

Characters: This species is distinguished from its Canadian Atlantic relatives by having the end of the dorsal fin opposite or behind the anal fin origin, a photophore or light organ below the rear eye margin, 12–14 photophores over the anal fin and back to the tail, no pho-

slender lightfish

tophore at the tip of the chin, and 19–22 gill rakers. The anal and dorsal fin bases are about equal in length. The anal fin has 13–16 rays. The eyes are slightly tubular. The lower jaw tip, upper jaw margin and the fin rays lack pigment. Reaches 45 mm in standard length.

Biology: First caught on the Atlantic coast of Canada between Georges and Browns Banks in 1977 but also known off Sable Island Bank and in the mouth of the Laurentian Channel. Found at depths of 250–800 m by day and 100–500 m by night or even at the surface. This species is common in midwaters and an important food item for other fishes. Spawns in spring and early summer. This species and its relatives are named scientifically after Decio Vinciguerra, a nineteenth century Italian naturalist.

slender snipe eel

Scientific name: *Nemichthys scolopaceus*
Richardson, 1848
Family: **Snipe Eel**
Other common names: Atlantic snipe eel, threadfish
French name: avocette ruban

Distribution: Found in all temperate to tropical oceans including off both the Atlantic and Pacific coasts of Canada.

Characters: This species is distinguished from its Canadian relatives, the **carinate** and **closespine snipe eels**, by having a caudal fil-

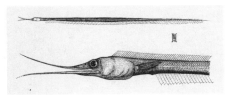

slender snipe eel

ament (a long, thin extension of the tail), 5 pores in each segment of the lateral line, 3 pore rows in the lateral line, and no sensory ridges on the head. The lateral line pore pattern looks like a "5" in dominoes. Teeth are fine, sharp and numerous. The anus lies below the pectoral fins. Over 750 vertebrae may be present. Both the dorsal and anal fins have over 320 rays. Overall colour black, dark-brown or grey, with darker brown speckles, belly often darker than back in young, a reversal of the usual pigment pattern. Reaches about 145 cm.

Biology: In Canada it is found from the west coast of Anticosti Island, Banquereau Bank off Nova Scotia, the Newfoundland Basin, and southward, as adults and leptocephalus larvae, and off British Columbia. It has been taken as shallow as 210 m south of LaHave and Sable Island banks and at 30 m off British Columbia. They are occasionally cast on shore by storms but it is usually in the depth range 457–3656 m. Leptocephalus larvae are found in shallower water at 90 m, but only over the deep ocean.

slender sole

Scientific name: *Eopsetta exilis*
(Jordan and Gilbert, 1880)
Family: **Righteye Flounder**
Other common names: slender flounder, rough sole
French name: plie mince

Distribution: Found from Alaska to Baja California including British Columbia.

Characters: This species is separated from its Pacific Canadian relatives by having a large, symmetrical mouth extending back to below the middle of the eye and with 2 rows of teeth in the upper jaw, a rounded caudal fin, a spine preceding the anal fin, and large, easily

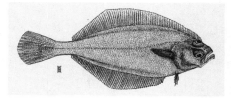

slender sole

detached scales. Dorsal fin rays 72–88, anal rays 57–66. Lateral line almost straight with 65–73 scales. Eyed side scales ctenoid, blind side scales ctenoid but cycloid on the central part under the dorsal fin. Eyed side pale brown with scale margins dark. Blind side pale orange to white. Dorsal and anal fins are dusky and pale on the margins. Reaches 35 cm.

Biology: This is a shallow water species which is common in British Columbia. Reported down to 800 m elsewhere. Food is various bottom invertebrates but it also takes crustaceans in midwater. About half the male population is mature at 14 cm, females at 16 cm. Spawning in southern British Columbia is probably in March and April. Its small size limits its commercial utilisation.

Slickhead Family

Scientific name: Alepocephalidae
French name: alépocéphales

Slickheads are deepsea fishes found in all oceans. There are about 75 species and 6 are reported from Canada, 4 on the Atlantic, 1 on the Pacific and 1 on the Arctic and Atlantic coasts.

These are dark-coloured fishes with anal and dorsal fins far back on the body near the tail, often weak teeth in a small mouth (fangs may be present or teeth may be absent altogether), no adipose fin and no swimbladder, many long gill rakers, no scales on the head (hence "slickhead" or "smoothhead"), but large scales on the body, sometimes absent and slippery skin over a flabby body. Light organs present in some under the skin, or on stalks or complexly arranged. Pectoral fins may be present or absent.

They are closely related to the **Tube-shoulder Family** and are sometimes united with them in a single family. However slickheads lack the shoulder organ of tubeshoulders. These fishes require further study and identifications are difficult. The family is a member of the **Smelt Order** and has been placed in the **Salmon Order**.

Some members of this family are only caught by research vessels, and rarely at that, while others, being larger, are occasionally taken by commercial deepsea trawlers.

Slickheads are found in the deep ocean often below 1000 m, but can be quite common. Eggs are large but do not float to the surface.

See **Atlantic gymnast**
     bigeye smoothhead
     dusky slickhead
     manyray smoothhead
     oarjaw wingmax
     threadfin slickhead

slim flounder

Scientific name: *Monolene antillarum*
    Norman, 1933
Family: **Lefteye Flounder**
Other common names: none
French name: cardeau svelte

Distribution: Found from Nova Scotia to Brazil.

Characters: This species is distinguished from other Canadian Atlantic adult **lefteye flounders** by having both pelvic fin bases short and the eyed side base on the belly midline, lateral line strongly arched over the eyed side pectoral fin and no blind side pec-

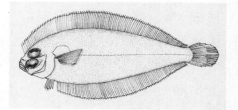

slim flounder

toral fin. This species and the **deepwater flounder** are difficult to distinguish and may be the same species. The slim flounder supposedly has a narrower body and a larger head, eye and pectoral fin. Dorsal fin rays 103–109, anal rays 81–89, eyed side pectoral rays 13–15, and lateral line scales 82–91. Lower arm gill rakers 8–9. Larvae have an elongated dorsal fin ray known as a tentacle. Eyed side colour is brown and pigmentation is generally similar to the **deepwater flounder**. Scale pockets are outlined in brown in preserved fish. Reaches 18 cm.

Biology: Known only from stray larvae caught in 1980 on and off the Scotian Shelf. Adults are found only as far north as North Carolina at depths of 150–550 m.

slim lightfish

Scientific name: *Ichthyococcus elongatus*
   Imai, 1941
Family: **Lightfish**
Other common names: none
French name: poisson étoilé élancé

Distribution: Northwest and northeast Pacific Ocean including British Columbia.

Characters: This lightfish is distinguished from the related **ovate lightfish** and other Canadian lightfishes by distribution, by the

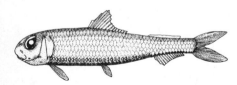

slim lightfish

SO photophore being present, gill rakers numbering 31–37, the anal fin origin being well behind the end of the dorsal fin and by the large, tubular and telescopic eye turned obliquely upwards. The body is terete. The adipose fin is long and low. A ventral adipose fin is absent. Dorsal fin rays 14–16, anal fin rays 14–17 and lateral line scales 40–44. Photophores: ORB 2, OP 3, BR 12–13, OA 30–32, IV 27, VAV 13–15, AC 13–15. Preserved fish are darkest along the ventral edge due to the black pigment lining the silvery photophores. It attains at least 12.5 cm in standard length.

Biology: Known from a single specimen caught near Vancouver Island at 350 m.

Adults and juveniles are caught at 150–650 m and there is no apparent vertical migration between day and night. Food is zooplankton.

slim sculpin

Scientific name: *Radulinus asprellus*
   Gilbert, 1890
Family: **Sculpin**
Other common names: darter sculpin
French name: chabot élancé

Distribution: Found from the Aleutian Islands to Baja California including British Columbia.

Characters: This species and its relative, the **darter sculpin**, are characterised by the dorsal body profile being straight, no scales

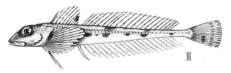

slim sculpin

below the lateral line on the midflank, the largest of 4 preopercular spines is simple, there is a fold of the branchiostegal membranes over the isthmus, and there are 3 soft pelvic fin rays. This species is distinguished from its relative by the snout length being equal to or less than the eye diameter and the nasal spines being short and stout. There is a long, thin anal papilla. First dorsal fin spines 8–11, second dorsal soft rays 20–23. Anal rays 21–25 and pectoral rays 17–20, the lower 10 free at the tips. Ctenoid scales run from between the eyes back above the lateral line to the middle of the soft dorsal fin level. There are 38–41 large, keeled lateral line scales. The back is olive-green to brown with orange blotches and 3–4 dark saddles. There are blotches along the lateral line. There is a dark bar from the eye antero-ventrally. The spiny dorsal fin has a dark spot on its rear edge. The dorsal, caudal and upper pectoral fins have red-brown bars on the rays. The anal fin edge is creamy white. Reputed to attain 15.2 cm.

Biology: Depth range is 18–290 m and rarely deeper but in British Columbia it is commonly taken by shrimp trawls at moderate depths on soft bottoms. It is believed to be a snail-puncher, making holes in snail shells to allow digestive enzymes better access to the snail tissues.

slim snailfish

Scientific name: *Rhinoliparis attenuatus*
    Burke, 1912
Family: **Snailfish**
Other common names: none
French name: limace svelte

Distribution: Found from the Bering Sea to California including British Columbia.

Characters: This species is identified by its lack of an adhesive disc and pelvic fins, and by having 9 barbels on the ventral sur-

slim snailfish

face of the snout. Teeth are in bands and are simple or trilobed. Branchiostegal rays 6. Nostrils single. The gill slit is above the pectoral fin or extends to the level of the first pectoral ray. The pectoral fin has a shallow notch with a lower lobe of about 5–6 rays with free tips. Dorsal fin rays about 68, anal rays about 60, pectoral rays 21–23 and caudal rays about 1–2. There are 9–12 pale pyloric caeca. The skin is mostly transparent, becoming dusky posteriorly. The muscles are tan. The stomach is pale. Mouth and gill cavities and peritoneum black. Attains 11 cm standard length.

Biology: Large specimens have been caught off southern Vancouver Island at 2189 m. This species has a depth range of 362–2189 m. It is extremely fragile and all specimens caught are damaged. Barbels, for example, are easily lost.

Slimehead Family

Scientific name: Trachichthyidae
French name: hoplites

Slimeheads or roughies are found in the Atlantic, Indian and Pacific oceans. There are about 33 species with 2 reported from Atlantic Canada.

These fishes have an obvious spine at the angle of the preopercle bone and on the posttemporal bone on the side of the head. The belly has a midline ridge formed from modified scales or scutes. Lateral line scales are enlarged also. Dorsal fin spines 3–8 and 9–19 soft rays. Anal fin with 2–3 spines and 8–12 soft rays. Pelvic fin with 1 spine and 6–8 soft rays. Scales may be thin and cycloid or thick and covered in spines. Some slimeheads are luminescent. The head has large mucous cavities covered by skin. Cavities are separated by bony crests. Jaw teeth are in small bands.

Slimeheads are related to the **Spinyfin** and **Ogrefish** families of the **Alfonsino Order**.

Most slimeheads are found in deep water from 100 to 1000 m. They feed on fish and crustaceans. Some species are quite abundant and are sold fresh, dried or salted. Some parts of a catch may be turned into fish meal or oil. They are caught by deep trawling or line trawling.

See **Darwin's slimehead**
    rosy soldierfish

slimy sculpin

Scientific name: *Cottus cognatus*
    Richardson, 1836
Family: **Sculpin**
Other common names: slimy muddler,
    Miller's thumb, northern sculpin,
    stargazer, big fin, cockatouch, Bear Lake
    bullhead, kanaiyok
French name: chabot visqueux

Distribution: Found from most of mainland Canada except coastal British Columbia, southern Alberta, eastern Labrador, Newfoundland, Nova Scotia and P.E.I. Also in eastern Siberia, Alaska, Washington, Great Lakes and upper Mississippi River basins and south to Virginia in the east.

Characters: This sculpin, and related species in the freshwater genus *Cottus*, are distinguished from the **deepwater sculpin** by the gill membrane being attached to the isthmus and the dorsal fins touching. It is separated from its relatives by having 2 pores on the tip of the chin, an incomplete lateral line, prickles only behind the pectoral fins, no palatine teeth, 3–4 pelvic rays, usually 3, and if present the fourth ray is less than two-thirds the length of the longest ray, and the last 2 dorsal and anal rays are usually well separated. Caudal peduncle length exceeds postorbital length. First dorsal fin spines

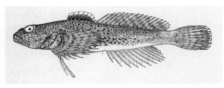

slimy sculpin

6–10, second dorsal rays 14–19, anal rays 10–14, and pectoral rays 12–16. The incomplete lateral line has 12–27 pores. There are 2 median, occipital pores. The male genital papilla is twice the length of that in females and is more triangular in shape.

Overall colour dark brown or grey-yellow, with dark mottles fading to a white belly. There may be 2–3 oblique saddles under the second dorsal fin and a caudal fin base bar. The lower flanks and under the pectoral fins may have orange patches. The first dorsal fin is dark at the base and clear at the margin, the margin being red to orange in spawning males. The pectoral fin has wide bars and other fins are thinly barred. The chin is not mottled but finely speckled. Males become darker in the spawning season.

Reaches 12.8 cm.

Biology: This species prefers cooler waters in the deep parts of lakes and in streams where the bottoms are gravel and rock. It may descend to 210 m in lakes but is commonest at 37–108 m while the **deepwater sculpin**, aptly named, was below these depths. It is the most numerous fish in the offshore benthos of Lake Ontario. In this lake, young slimy sculpin move from a shallow water habitat (less than 60 m) and a nocturnal feeding habit to deeper water (centred on 75 m) and continuous feeding as they mature. Shallow water sculpins are probably trying to avoid predators. In Lake Opeongo, Ontario slimy sculpins can be seen at night in 3–5 m of water resting on the bottom but during the day retreat to 30–35 m where it is almost completely dark. Preferred temperatures are about 9–14°C, lower than some related species.

Food is aquatic insects, crustaceans such as burrowing amphipods, and other bottom invertebrates. **Lake trout, burbot, northern pike, brook trout** and other fishes eat slimy sculpins.

In the Chandalar River, Alaska, life span is 7 years and most fish matured at 3–4 years. Growth is very slow compared to southern Canadian populations where life span is less, 5–6 years, and size of the oldest fish is larger (12.7 cm versus 10.4 cm). Slimy sculpins in large streams grow faster, have higher fecundity but are less numerous than those in small streams.

Spawning begins at 5–10°C when a male selects or excavates a site under a rock or root and courts a female. Males defend the nest site using a characteristic "barking" action against other males. The loser of this contest fades in colour and retreats. Eggs are deposited on the roof of the nest site when the male presses the female against the roof. The female leaves and the male guards the eggs. The male may have eggs from several females in the nest. In Ontario lakes males may be monogamous, polygynous where most males are bachelors and only large, old males successfully compete for limited nest sites and females, or intermediate between these two extremes. Males which are polygynous delay testis development until 5–6 years, a result of intense sexual selection. Each female produces up to 1400 eggs with a diameter in the water of up to 2.6 mm.

This sculpin has been used as bait for **brook trout**.

slimy snailfish

Scientific name: *Liparis mucosus* Ayres, 1855
Family: **Snailfish**
Other common names: none
French name: limace visqueuse

Distribution: Found from Alaska and British Columbia to Baja California.

Characters: This species is distinguished from its Pacific coast relatives by having an adhesive disc with its rear edge behind the level of the gill slit, 2 pairs of nostrils, gill slit partly in front of the pectoral fin down to rays 1–6, dorsal fin with a lobe at the front and 28–33 rays, anal rays 22–27 and pectoral rays

27–33. The lower pectoral lobe has thickened, finger-like rays. Teeth trilobed. Pyloric caeca about 48–70. The skin may have prickles.

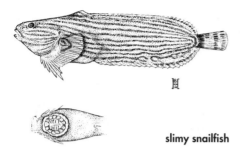

slimy snailfish

Colour varies markedly from a uniform red, pink, brown, olive or greenish-yellow to darkly striped or with a reticulate pattern. The dorsal and anal fins have a dark margin. The caudal fin base usually has a bar. The pectoral fin is dark brown. Lips are dark. Reaches 13 cm.

Biology: Apparently uncommon in Canada even though reported in depths less than 4 m down to 15 m. Not in tide pools.

slipskin snailfish

Scientific name: *Liparis fucensis*
Gilbert in Jordan and Starks, 1895
Family: **Snailfish**
Other common names: Juan de Fuca liparid
French name: limace de varech

Distribution: Found from the Bering Sea to California including British Columbia.

Characters: This species is distinguished from its Pacific coast relatives by having an adhesive disc with its rear edge behind the level of the gill slit, 2 pairs of nostrils, gill slit partly in front of the pectoral fin down to between rays 12–16, dorsal rays 33–35 in a slightly notched fin, anal rays 27–29 and pec-

toral rays 34–43. Lower lobe pectoral rays are thickened, elongate and finger-like. Teeth are trilobed and in bands. Pyloric caeca about 26–55. Overall colour olive to dark brown, often pinkish. Rarely the flanks are striped. Fins are irregularly banded. There may be an oblique light band on the caudal fin. Reaches 18 cm.

Biology: Common in Canada down to 388 m from near shore waters, over boulders, rocks, shells and sand with associated algae. Spawning takes place in late winter to late summer and up to 4800, 1.0 mm diameter pink, tan or orange eggs are laid and guarded by the male, sometimes in the empty shells of mussels or among worm tubes. Males may spawn with more than 1 female. Egg masses can be 2.5 by 2.5 by 0.6 cm. Larvae grow to a large size and develop a large space under the skin, "the cottoid bubblemorph," which may help to maintain buoyancy.

slipskin species

Scientific name: *Lycenchelys* sp.
Family: **Eelpout**
Other common names: none
French name: lycode

Distribution: Found off southern British Columbia.

Characters: This species has been recognised as new from preserved material. It has yet to be described scientifically.

smalldisk snailfish

Scientific name: *Careproctus gilberti*
Burke, 1912
Family: **Snailfish**
Other common names: small-disked liparid
French name: limace à petite ventouse

Distribution: Found from the Bering Sea to Oregon including British Columbia.

Characters: This snailfish is distinguished from its Canadian Pacific relatives by having a fleshy adhesive disc with its posterior margin anterior to the level of the gill opening, a single nostril, dorsal fin rays 49–55 and pyloric caeca pale, 10–12. The adhesive disc is very small. Anal fin rays 44–48, pectoral rays 30–33, and caudal rays 8–9. The pectoral fin has 2 lobes, the lower lobe rays being long and variably free of their mem-

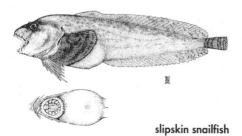

slipskin snailfish

brane. Teeth are in bands. The gill opening extends from above the pectoral fin down to about the 14th pectoral fin ray. Body colour cream to pink with scattered pigment spots. The dorsal and anal fin bases have denser patches of spots. The eyes are blue above

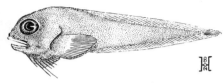

smalldisk snailfish

and silvery below. The mouth and gill cavities are somewhat darker than the body but are not black. Peritoneum pale or silvery. Stomach black. Reaches 11.7 cm.

Biology: Reported at depths of 187–886 m. Apparently nothing is known of its biology.

smalleye blacksmelt

Scientific name: *Bathylagus bericoides* (Borodin, 1929)
Family: **Deepsea Smelt**
Other common names: none
French name: garcette à petits yeux

Distribution: Found from tropical to temperate waters in all oceans. Off the coast of Nova Scotia where first reported in 1973.

Characters: The smalleye blacksmelt is distinguished from its Atlantic Canadian relatives by having a gill opening not extending half way up the side of the body and by hav-

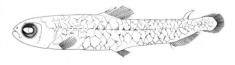

smalleye blacksmelt

ing about 50 lateral line scales and a small eye. Eye diameter can be divided into head length more than twice. Dorsal fin rays 10–11, anal rays 18–22 and pectoral rays 10–12. Scale pockets are in irregular rows, outlined with dark pigment and lined with purplish tissue. The fins and head are dusky. Attains 20 cm at least.

Biology: The Canadian specimens were caught at 183 m off the Grand Bank and this species is bathypelagic. Food is plankton.

smalleye cat shark

Scientific name: *Apristurus microps* (Gilchrist, 1922)
Family: **Cat Shark**
Other common names: none
French name: holbiche porc

Distribution: Found on the Grand Bank off Newfoundland and from between Iceland and Scotland and off the South African coast.

Characters: This cat shark is distinguished from its Atlantic coast relatives by lacking crests over the eyes, dorsal fins are about equal in size and by the space between the dorsal fins equal to, or slightly less than, the first dorsal fin base length. The inner margin of the pectoral fins is short, about a third of

smalleye cat shark

the pectoral bases. The eye is unusually small for a cat shark. The snout is thick. There is a crest of denticles on the upper margin of the dorsal fin. The denticles give the skin a fuzzy feel. Overall colour is dusky brown or grey-brown to purplish-black. Reaches at least 54 cm (adolescents); adult size is not known.

Biology: This species is known from only 10 specimens and the holotype from which it was described was discarded. It is poorly known and the 4 Newfoundland specimens were tentatively ascribed to this species. Smalleye cat sharks are bottom living at 1000–2000 m.

smalleye frostfish

Scientific name: *Benthodesmus tenuis* (Günther, 1877)
Family: **Cutlassfish**
Other common names: javelinfish, slender frostfish, sabre fleuret
French name: sabre d'argent à petits yeux

Distribution: Found in all oceans and on the Pacific and Atlantic coasts of Canada.

Characters: This species is distinguished from its Canadian relatives by a notch between the spiny and soft dorsal fin parts, the spiny part of the dorsal fin being about half as long as the soft part, no crest on the head from over the eye to the dorsal fin, and by dorsal fin spine counts which are higher than in the related **North Pacific frostfish** and **Simony's frostfish**. Total dorsal fin rays and spines 118–129. Dorsal spines 38–42, soft rays 78–88. Anal fin with 2 spines and 69–76 soft rays. Overall colour is silvery. Reaches 72.0 cm standard length, perhaps more.

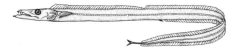

smalleye frostfish

Biology: First reported for the Pacific coast in 1986, a single specimen being caught by an angler near Victoria, although identity may be uncertain. A single specimen was caught on Browns Bank in the Atlantic in 1983 at a depth of 276–411 m. This species is benthopelagic at 200–850 m, with young mesopelagic.

smalleye squaretail

Scientific name: *Tetragonurus cuvieri* Risso, 1810
Family: **Squaretail**
Other common names: tétragonure à petits yeux
French name: tétragonure lilas

Distribution: Found in temperate areas of the Atlantic, Pacific and Indian oceans, including the northwest Grand Bank in Atlantic Canada, and from the Aleutian Islands south to Baja California including the coast of British Columbia in the Pacific.

Characters: This species is distinguished from the related **bigeye squaretail** by a higher scale count, 93–126 from the head to the origin of the caudal peduncle keels. First dorsal fin with 15–21 spines, second dorsal fin with 10–17 soft rays. Anal fin with 0–2 spines and 9–15 soft rays. The overall colour is dark brown to dark wine-red to almost black, with the head and tail base paler than the body. The fins are edged with black and are golden-yellow to greenish. The belly can be greenish

smalleye squaretail

with a silvery or golden caste. Young are greyish. Reaches 70 cm standard length.

Biology: Known from only 2 strays in Canadian waters, one of which was captured at 256–384 m. May be quite abundant elsewhere. Young fish may associate with jellyfish and with such salps or tunicates as *Salpa* and *Pyrosoma*, and feed on them and ctenophores (comb jellies) using their slicing teeth and scoop-like lower jaw. Adults are solitary and meso- to bathypelagic, but also feed on jellyfish and comb jellies, rising to the surface at night to do so. Spawning occurs in spring and summer. Often discovered inside the stomachs of captured **albacores**. Said to cause vomiting, diarrhoea, intense sore throat and limb pains when eaten, because of toxins from the jellyfish diet, but this is disputed.

smallfin snailfish

Scientific name: *Careproctus oregonensis* Stein, 1978
Family: **Snailfish**
Other common names: none
French name: limace à petites nageoires

Distribution: Found from British Columbia to Oregon.

Characters: This snailfish is distinguished from its Canadian Pacific relatives by having a fleshy adhesive disc with its posterior margin anterior to the level of the gill opening, a single nostril, dorsal fin rays 61–67 and

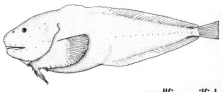

smallfin snailfish

pyloric caeca pale, 8–11. Anal fin rays 55–57, pectoral rays 19–23 and caudal rays 7–8. The pectoral fin has a deep notch with the upper lobe rays (10–13) usually shorter than those of the lower lobe (5–7). Overall colour is black or tan. The mouth, gill cavity and peritoneum are black. The stomach is pale. Reaches 15.3 cm standard length.

Biology: Reported from depths in the range 1900–2818 m. A specimen from off southern Vancouver Island was at 2532 m. Eggs may be as large as 5.6 mm but number only 3–5 in the ovary. Spawning may occur year-round.

smallmouth bass

Scientific name: *Micropterus dolomieu*
 Lacepède, 1802
Family: **Sunfish**
Other common names: northern smallmouth,
 black, brown, gold, green or Oswego bass;
 white, green or mountain trout; bronze-
 back, redeye, smallie, jumper
French name: achigan à petite bouche

Distribution: Found from southern Nova Scotia and New Brunswick, through south-western Québec, the southern half of Ontario including all the Great Lakes to southeast Manitoba. Also in central Saskatchewan, central Alberta, southeastern British Columbia and southern Vancouver Island. The original distribution was east-central North America so Maritime, Saskatchewan and B.C. populations are introduced. Widely introduced in North America, Europe, the former U.S.S.R. and even Africa.

Characters: This species is distinguished by having 67–81 lateral line scales, the upper jaw not reaching back beyond the eye and the pelvic fins are joined by a membrane. There are scales on the soft dorsal and anal fin bases. Dorsal fin spines 9–11, soft dorsal rays 12–15, anal fin with 3 spines and 10–12 soft rays. Pectoral rays 13–18.

The back and upper flank are dark brown, olive or green, the flanks are lighter, yellow-ish with some slaty areas and with a more golden colour, and the belly is cream to white, with some dusky pigment. Flanks have 8–16 thin bars which may only be weakly developed or broken up. The eye and snout have 3 dark bars radiating backwards. The eye is orange to red. Fins are dusky with some heavier black pigment along the rays. The pectoral fin is mostly transparent. Young have strong flank bars and a characteristic yellow to orange bar at the caudal fin base with a black bar on the fin and white to yellow fin tips. The fry are conspicuously jet black. Peritoneum silvery.

Attains 68.6 cm total length and 6.4 kg. The world, all-tackle angling record from Dale Hollow Lake, Kentucky in 1955 weighed 5.41 kg. The Canadian angling record from Birchbark Lake, Ontario, was caught by Andy Anderson in 1954 and weighed 4.47 kg.

smallmouth bass

Biology: Smallmouth bass are found in the clear shallows of lakes and slow rivers. They are often located near rocks and logs. They seem to prefer temperatures in the 20s°C, cooler than **largemouth bass**, and so retreat to deeper water in summer. They are inactive in winter.

Food is aquatic and terrestrial insects, crustaceans (particularly crayfish) and a wide variety of fishes. Frogs and fish eggs are also eaten. Crayfish are predominant in the diet of many bass populations but habitat and availability dictate the foods eaten. Various fishes and turtles eat the smaller bass.

Life span is 18 years. Females mature at 4–6 years and males at 3–5 years. Growth varies with latitude but also between populations within lakes such as Simcoe, Huron and Ontario and between oligotrophic Laurentide lakes and the richer, eutrophic waters of the Montréal plain.

Spawning occurs from May to July at about 12–24°C. The male excavates a nest up to 1.8 m across, but usually 60 cm, in quiet water at depths down to 6.1 m but usually about 1 m. The bottom is usually sand, gravel or rubble. Nest construction takes 4–48 hours usually and several may be built until one is deemed adequate. The bass positions itself head up in the water and lashes the tail to sweep debris from a site about twice its body length. The nest is usually close to a rock, log or rarely vegetation which afford some protection. Strong winds are particularly detrimental to nesting success. The nest site or its general area is returned to in subsequent years, up to 32% of spawners doing so in an Ontario river.

Males defend the nest by displays and nipping. A female approaches the shallows from deeper water and a male will attempt to drive her to the nest. She usually retreats and the process is repeated until the female gradually stays longer with the male. The female becomes mottled once she settles over the nest. The male may nudge and gently bite the female. A spawning pair swim about the nest for 25–45 seconds before entering it and settling on the bottom. The male remains vertical but the female inclines at an angle of 45° so their genital areas come into contact. Eggs and sperm are shed in about 4–10 seconds but the process is repeated over 2 hours. The spawning period at any one location usually lasts 6–18 days and most spawning takes place in the evening. Eggs are pale yellow to amber, 3.5 mm in maximum diameter and number up to 20,825 per female. The eggs adhere to stones in the nest. The male guards the eggs and school of young and fans the developing eggs. Schools of young fish disperse after 19–28 days and may be guarded this long, herded by the male. Females may spawn with other males and the male may spawn with at least 3 females.

Male bass may provide care for the eggs of **longnose gar** which may be shed at night when bass are inactive. While gar benefit from the bass guarding their eggs, the bass also benefits by having large, dispersed gar eggs in its nest which may be seized preferentially by predators dashing into the nest while the male is distracted. **Common shiners** may also spawn in bass nests.

This **bass** is a famous sport fish which has an extensive following and literature. It is one of the top 5 sport fishes in eastern Canada. Hooked fish fight strongly and leap,

"inch for inch and pound for pound, the gamest fish that swims" (Henshall, 1889). The flesh is white, flaky and excellent eating. It may be frozen easily for later eating.

• Most accessible July through October.
• Southern Ontario and Quebec, the Great Lakes and the St. Lawrence River watershed.
• Medium action spinning and baitcasting outfits used with eight- to 14–pound test line.
• 1/4– to 3/8–ounce crankbaits, hair and plastic bodied jigs, four- to six-inch long minnow-imitating lures, a variety of spinners and spinnerbaits and live **minnows**, crayfish, frogs, leeches and worms.

smallmouth flounder

Scientific name: *Etropus microstomus*
  (Gill, 1864)
Family: **Lefteye Flounder**
Other common names: none
French name: cardeau à petite bouche

Distribution: Found from Nova Scotia to the Caribbean Sea.

Characters: This species is distinguished from other Canadian Atlantic adult **lefteye flounders** by having both pelvic fin bases short and the eyed side base on the belly midline, the lateral line is not strongly arched over the eyed side pectoral fin, no caudal fin spots, jaws extending back to anterior edge of the lower eye, and body scales with small secondary scales in a single row at the base of each scale. Dorsal fin rays 67–83, anal rays 50–63, eyed side pectoral

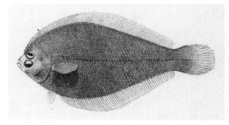

smallmouth flounder

rays 9–12, and lateral line scales 36–45. There are scales on the snout. Lower arm gill rakers 3–7, usually 6 or less. Larvae lack elongate dorsal fin rays. Eyed side brown to reddish-brown with dark colouring around the mouth and between the eyes. May be spotted or blotched. Reaches 15.2 cm.

Biology: Known only from stray larval specimens from Georges Bank caught in 1982. Adults occur only as far north as North Carolina, down to 340 m, but often inshore and entering estuaries. Maturity is reached at 5.0 cm standard length. Peak spawning is July–October but may occur year round. Larvae show eye migration at 10–12 mm standard length.

smallsail sculpin

Scientific name: *Nautichthys robustus*
    Peden, 1970
Family: **Sculpin**
Other common names: shortmast sculpin
French name: chabot à petite voile

Distribution: Found from the Aleutian Islands to Washington including British Columbia.

Characters: This sculpin and its relative, the **sailfin sculpin**, are distinguished from Pacific coast relatives by the steep rise of the

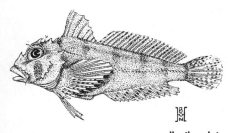

smallsail sculpin

back from the occiput to the dorsal fin origin, an oblique, black bar running from the eye downward on the side of the head, and the spiny dorsal fin has membranes to the end of the spines and is higher than the soft dorsal fin. This species is separated from its relative by having 19–21 second dorsal fin soft rays and a spiny dorsal fin height less than the width. Head spines are pointed and include nasal, postorbital, occipital, posttemporal and postocular. Preopercular spines number 4 and are blunt with the lower 2 reduced. First dorsal fin spines 7–9. Anal fin rays 14–16, pec-

toral rays 14–16 with the lower 8 rays finger-like and pelvic fin with 1 spine and 2–3 soft rays. Scales are strong prickles in fleshy papillae covering much of the head and body except the snout, lips and branchiostegal rays. Fins, except the pelvics, also bear scales on their rays. Lateral line pores 35–38. There is a large, branched cirrus on the eye, cirri on head spine tips, a large cirrus behind the postorbital spine, a large cirrus at the rear end of the upper jaw and 6 tubercle-like cirri along the suborbital margin. The body is pale brown with 4 saddles over the back and lighter on the belly. The caudal fin base has a dark bar. All fins are spotted and the spiny dorsal fin is dark. The black bar on the head runs through the cirrus over the eye. Reaches 6.4 cm.

Biology: A rare species found from 2 to 73 m on sand and rock bottoms.

smallscale lizardfish

Scientific name: *Synodus lucioceps*
    (Ayres, 1855)
Family: **Lizardfish**
Other common names: California lizardfish
French name: poisson-lézard à petites écailles

Distribution: Pacific coast of North America south to Mexico. First reported from Canada at Bamfield, Vancouver Island, in 1987 based on a single specimen.

Characters: Distinguished from other lizardfish by its colour. Dorsal fin rays 11–13, anal rays 12–14 and lateral line scales 63–67. The back is brown fading to a lighter colour on the belly. The pelvic fins and gill membranes are yellow. Attains 64 cm in length and 1.8 kg making it one of the largest lizardfishes.

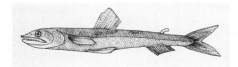

smallscale lizardfish

Biology: Found over mud or sand from 1.5–229 m, but more usual in 18–46 m. Larvae live in the open ocean near the surface many kilometres from the shore. It eats mostly fish and occasionally squid. Spawning occurs from June to August over sand. They may live 8–9 years.The smallscale lizardfish has been caught on baited hooks, spoons and plugs, but is poor eating.

smallscale mora

Scientific name: *Laemonema barbatula* Goode and Bean, 1883
Family: **Mora**
Other common names: none
French name: more à petites écailles

Distribution: Known from off the Bahamas and off Canada in the Atlantic Ocean.

Characters: This species is distinguished from its Canadian relatives on the Atlantic coast by its lack of a flattened snout and of a

smallscale mora

small, dark scaleless patch over a light organ in front of the anus, by having some small teeth on the head of the vomer bone in the roof of the mouth, and by having 2 rays in the pelvic fins. The first dorsal fin has 5 rays, the second 63. Anal fin rays are 59, anal fin not strongly indented. Scales in lateral line series are about 140. There is a chin barbel. The overall colour is brownish with dorsal and anal fins having narrow black margins. Reaches 33 cm standard length.

Biology: Only 4 Canadian specimens are known from off Browns Bank caught in 1981 at 159–388 m. They are a northern range extension for the species and are probably strays from the south.

Smelt Family

Scientific name: Osmeridae
French name: éperlans

Smelts are found in coastal sea waters and fresh waters near the coast of the Northern Hemisphere. Some populations are land-locked. There are about 11 species with 9 reported from Canada. Three species are found on the Pacific coast and its drainage, 2 species are on the Pacific coast, 1 is on the Pacific and western Arctic coast and drainages, 1 is on the Pacific, Arctic and Atlantic coasts, 1 is on the Atlantic coast and drainages and 1 is in fresh water of the Atlantic drainage. The Harrison/Pitt Lakes smelt may be a species distinct from the **longfin smelt**.

These small, silvery fishes have a single dorsal fin at midbody, an adipose fin, no pelvic axillary process (found in **Salmon Family** members), 8 pelvic fin rays and 19 principal caudal fin rays, forked tail, 6–10 branchiostegal rays, 0–11 pyloric caeca, a stomach sometimes with a blind sac, the last vertebra at the tail is turned up, teeth are on numerous mouth bones and are strong or weak, a mesocoracoid bone is present in the pectoral fin skeleton and the skull lacks the orbitosphenoid bone. Scales are cycloid and easily detached. Some smelts have a strong cucumber smell when fresh, the chemical being *trans*-2–*cis*-6–nonadienal. Its function is unknown.

Smelts are related to the **Salmon Family** and have been placed in the **Salmon Order**. They are members of the **Smelt Order**.

Breeding smelts can develop tubercles, modified scales and enlarged fins. Reproduction may occur in coastal waters or involve a migration into fresh water. Smelts are all carnivorous fishes. They are very numerous and so are important food fishes for commercially important species and are also used as bait by anglers. They are rich in oil and are excellent smoked for human consumption.

See **capelin**
    eulachon
    longfin smelt
    night smelt
    pond smelt
    pygmy smelt
    rainbow smelt
    surf smelt
    whitebait smelt

Smelt Order

The **argentines** or herring smelts, **deepsea smelts**, **pencil smelts**, **slickheads**, **smelts**, **spookfishes** or **barreleyes**, and **tubeshoulders** form the smelt order or Osmeriformes. There are 13 families and about 236 species world-wide with 7 families and 40 species in Canadian waters both fresh and marine.

The smelt order is characterised by the maxilla usually being included in the gape, an adipose fin may be present or absent, no radii (radiating lines) on the scales, and no orbitosphenoid and basisphenoid bones in the skull. Some members also have a complex organ in the epibranchial region, the crumenal organ, which is formed as a pair of pouches involving the last two gill arches and the anterior oesophagus. Members of this order were once placed within an expanded **Salmon Order**.

See **Argentine Family**
Deepsea Smelt Family
Pencil Smelt Family
Slickhead Family
Smelt Family
Spookfish Family
Tubeshoulder Family

smooth alligatorfish

Scientific name: *Anoplagonus inermis* (Günther, 1860)
Family: **Poacher**
Other common names: smooth poacher
French name: poisson-alligator lisse

Distribution: Found from Korea through the Bering Sea to British Columbia and northern California.

Characters: This species is unique in Pacific Canada in having only 1 dorsal fin. In addition the plates are all smooth and spineless. The dorsal fin has 5–6 soft rays and the anal fin 4–5 rays. The pectoral fin

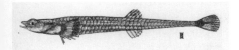

smooth alligatorfish

has 9–10 rays, the last 3 rays being finger-like. Lateral line pores 41–44. The head lacks cirri or spines. Gill membranes are not joined to the isthmus. The back is brown, becoming greyer below. A band extends from the snout to the pectoral fin base. The flanks are faintly barred and pigment on the pectoral and dorsal fins forms bars. There is a white band on the pectoral fin base. The caudal fin has 2 light patches. Originally

described from a single specimen caught off Vancouver Island, B.C. Reaches 15 cm.

Biology: Often found among rocks at 5–102 m and even areas covered with wood debris from logging. Diatoms, microscopic plants, may grow on the body of this poacher. Shrimp trawlers catch this species. Little else appears to be known of its biology.

smooth dogfish

Scientific name: *Mustelus canis* (Mitchill, 1815)
Family: **Hound Shark**
Other common names: dusky smooth-hound, smooth hound, émissole douce
French name: émissole

Distribution: Found from the Bay of Fundy in Atlantic Canada south to the Caribbean Sea. Also off southern Brazil and Argentina.

Characters: This species is distinguished by the anterior nasal flaps not reaching the mouth and not being barbel-like, by the sec-

smooth dogfish

ond dorsal fin being of comparable size to the first, the origin of the first dorsal fin is over or behind the pectoral fin inner margins, the ventral caudal lobe is short, teeth are broad, blunt, pavement-like and all alike, and the mouth is angular not arc-like. Teeth are replaced at the rate of 6 rows for every 10 cm of growth in total body length. The tail fin has a rounded lower lobe and the distance between the nostrils is 1 to 2 times nostril width. There is a conspicuous interdorsal ridge. Dermal denticles are spaced irregularly and have a single posterior point.

Overall colour is olive to slaty grey to brown above and lighter on the belly. No spots. Young have dusky tips to the dorsal and tail fins. The rear margin of the first dorsal fin is white in young fish. Capable of slowly changing colour to match the background. Reaches up to 152 cm but averages about 122 cm. The world, all-tackle angling record weighed 8.07 kg and was caught in Great Bay, New Jersey in 1988.

Biology: Canadian specimens were 1 caught in the St. Croix River estuary, N.B. in July 1913, on a longline, and 1 caught off Chance Harbour, Bay of Fundy, N.B. on 8 July 1977 by hook and line. This latter specimen was a female 106.5 cm long and gave birth to 3 live young shortly after capture while being transported to St. Andrews. This is a very common and active species of the U.S. coast, second only to the **spiny dogfish** in numbers. It is found in bays and harbours over sand and mud bottoms and down to 579 m. Occasionally it enters the lower reaches of rivers. Smooth dogfish migrate with the seasons moving northward towards Canada as the water warms up and south and offshore to a winter area when the water cools down.

Food is mostly large crustaceans such as crabs and lobsters but small fishes, snails, worms and garbage are also taken. It is most active at night when crustacean prey is also active. Crabs are attacked and shaken vigorously before being eaten.

They are viviparous with a yolk-sac placenta and a litter has 4 to 20 young measuring 32.8–39 cm. Mating occurs in midsummer and birth in early May to mid-July of the following year. Females mature at about 90 cm and males at about 82 cm. Maximum size is reached in the seventh or eighth year.

This species is eaten fresh or dried and salted. It is caught on bottom and floating longlines. It is an important competitor of humans for lobsters and crabs, one estimate for Buzzard's Bay, Massachusetts suggesting that 10,000 smooth dogfish ate 200,000 crabs and 60,000 lobsters each year in addition to large numbers of fish. Its numbers interfere with shrimp trawling operations. It is used as a laboratory animal for anatomy classes in schools and universities. Anglers can take this species on hook and line using squid or shrimp as bait.

smooth dreamer

Scientific name: *Chaenophryne melanorhabdus* Regan and Trewavas, 1932
Family: **Dreamer**
Other common names: none
French name: rêveur sombre

Distribution: Found world-wide and in the northeast Pacific Ocean including off British Columbia.

Characters: This species of deepsea **anglerfish** and its relative, the **can-opener smoothdream**, are distinguished by the lack of sphenotic spines, a slightly concave operculum posteriorly and high cancellous bones. The female smooth dreamer is separated from its relative by distribution, an esca or bait on the fishing apparatus with an unpaired anterior appendage and no medial appendages, and 16–17, rarely 18 pectoral fin rays. Overall colour is black except for unpigmented areas on the esca and in the mouth. Females reach 9.7 cm.

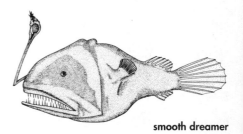

smooth dreamer

Biology: Known in Canada from only a single undamaged specimen taken off Cape Flattery. Most specimens of females are caught below 450 m down to at least 3000 m. Females use their fishing apparatus to catch fishes, cephalopods and crustaceans as described under **anglerfishes**.

smooth flounder

Scientific name: *Pleuronectes putnami* (Gill, 1864)
Family: **Righteye Flounder**
Other common names: blackback, eelback, foolfish, Christmas flounder, plaice
French name: plie lisse

Distribution: Possibly as far north as Frobisher Bay on southern Baffin Island and in Ungava Bay but certainly along the Labrador coast, throughout the Maritimes and south to Rhode Island.

Characters: This Atlantic species is characterised by a small, asymmetrical mouth, an almost straight lateral line over the pectoral fin, no pits on the blind side of the head, dorsal fin rays 48–58, and head between the eyes scaleless and smooth. Anal fin rays 35–41 and pectoral rays 10–11 on the eyed side. The

smooth flounder

dorsal and anal fins are longest at their centres giving an angular outline to the body. Males have ctenoid scales on the eyed side and ctenoid and cycloid scales on the blind side. Females have cycloid scales on both sides except for some ctenoid scales at the lateral line and upper and lower body margins. The eyed side is grey-brown to blackish with dark brown blotches and mottles. The blind side is white. The fins may be blotched or spotted with black. Attains 32.3 cm.

Biology: Smooth flounders are common in shallow waters on mud and silt bottoms down to 27 m, including estuaries where temperatures and salinities are variable. Food is worms, crustaceans such as crabs, and molluscs. Spawning occurs in late winter to spring. Eggs are up to 1.4 mm in diameter and do not float. This is not a commercially important species because of its small size but it is excellent eating.

smooth grenadier

Scientific name: *Nezumia aequalis*
(Günther, 1878)
Other common names: common Atlantic
grenadier
French name: grenadier lisse

Distribution: Found in the Atlantic Ocean and Mediterranean Sea and from the Davis Strait south to Brazil in the western Atlantic Ocean.

Characters: This species is distinguished from its Canadian Atlantic coast relatives by having second dorsal fin rays shorter than anal

rays, 7 branchiostegal rays, a small mouth which is strongly inferior, and 8–9, rarely 7, pelvic fin rays with the first ray elongated,. The first dorsal fin has 11–15, usually 12–13, rays, the first ray being serrated anteriorly. Pectoral rays number 15–23, usually 19–21. Body scales carry broad spinules which are lanceolate at the tip in small fish and shield-shaped in large fish. There is a "window" of the light organ on the belly between the pelvic fin bases. Overall colour is bluish to violet, the head is brownish, and the gill cover and lower body have silvery tones. The first dorsal fin is pale at the base and black at the tip. The pelvic fin is black but the longest ray is pale to white. Pectoral fins are dusky. The mouth cavity is greyish and the gill cavity black. Attains over 27 cm total length.

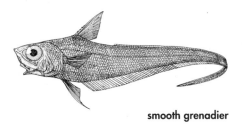

smooth grenadier

Biology: This species is found in a depth range of 200–2300 m, swimming over the sea floor. Food is benthic and pelagic items including crustaceans and worms. It is caught as a by-catch in offshore trawls and is used for fish meal and oil.

smooth hammerhead

Scientific name: *Sphyrna zygaena*
(Linnaeus, 1758)
Family: **Requiem Shark**
Other common names: shovelhead, shovel-
nose, common hammerhead, pantouflier
French name: requin-marteau commun

Distribution: From the Grand Bank, Bay of Fundy and southwestern Nova Scotia south to the Caribbean Sea. Also in Europe, California, the southern hemisphere and the Far East.

Characters: The only shark in Canadian waters with the distinctive hammer-shaped head. The nostrils are short, their widths 7 to 14 times in the internarial width, the posterior teeth are not expanded as crushers, the posterior margins of the hammer are arched, the rear tip of the first dorsal fin is well in

smooth hammerhead

front of the pelvic origin, teeth are only weakly serrated and have broad cusps, the anterior head margin is convex not straight, the anal base is about as large as the second dorsal base, the anal fin is deeply notched, and there is no median indentation (hence "smooth") on the anterior margin of the head although there are two notches on each side of the median. Dark olive or grey-brown above fading to white below. Dorsal and tail fins have dusky edges and tips and the undersides of the pectoral fin tips are dusky. Reaches about 4 m and about 408 kg although most fish are 3.0 m of less. Reputedly attains 6.56 m. The world, all-tackle angling record weighed 113 kg and was taken in the Azores in 1993.

Biology: This species is common in coastal waters entering bays and in the open ocean although not far from land. It is a very rare summer visitor to Canadian waters. Smooth hammerheads are usually close to the surface even when in the open ocean and the upper parts of fins may cut the surface of the water. Adults mature at 2.1–2.4 m and young at birth are 50–61 cm. Food includes squids, **herring, menhaden, mackerel**, small **sharks** including **hammerheads**, and **skates**, shrimps and crabs. They even eat **stingrays** and have been caught with their mouthparts heavily embedded with stings, apparently without effect. This species is viviparous with a yolk-sac placenta and there are 29–37 young per litter. This shark is common to abundant south of Canada and is often caught on pelagic long-lines, handlines and in pelagic and bottom trawls. It can be eaten fresh or dried and salted. The skin has been used for leather, the liver oil for vitamins, fins for soup, and the carcass for fish meal. Smooth hammerheads are dangerous to people. This species can be caught with trolled feathers, oily or bloody fish baits, or lures and puts up a strong fight.

smooth lumpfish

Scientific name: *Cyclopteropsis jordani* Soldatov, 1929
Family: **Lumpfish**
Other common names: none
French name: petite poule de mer douce

Distribution: Found at Baffin Island and in the Kara Sea.

Characters: This species is distinguished from its Arctic-Atlantic relatives by having the gill opening above the pectoral fin, about 5 large, blunt tubercles restricted to the compressed anterior half of the body, usually no supplemental pores above the lateral line, first dorsal fin rounded with rays unequal, and postorbital tubercle row present, extending onto the body. Dorsal fin spines 6, soft rays 12–13. Anal fin rays 10–12, pectoral rays 23–24. Each anterior tubercle has a few blunt prickles. First 2 tubercles of postorbital row obvious but rest weakly developed. A postbranchial row

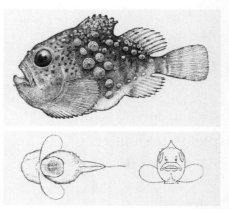

smooth lumpfish

runs from the gill opening arcing down posterior to 4 large tubercles of the circumpectoral row. A pair of tubercles is in front of the anal fin and between the dorsal fins. Young lack tubercles. Attains about 6.1 cm.

Biology: Known from few specimens so nothing is known of its biology.

smooth lumpsucker

Scientific name: *Aptocyclus ventricosus*
  (Pallas, 1770)
Family: **Lumpfish**
Other common names: none
French name: poule de mer ventrue

Distribution: Found from South Korea to northern British Columbia.

Characters: This species is distinguished from its Pacific coast relative, the **Pacific spiny lumpsucker**, by having a smooth skin.

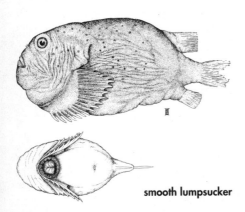

smooth lumpsucker

The gill opening is above the pectoral fin. One dorsal fin with 8–9 rays, anal rays 7–9 and pectoral rays 19–20. The male sucking disc is much larger than that of the female. Overall colour is brown to grey with dark spots on the head and back. The belly is grey. Breeding females are a conspicuous blue-black. Attains 39 cm in females and 36 cm in males.

Biology: Reported as deep as 1500 m but also inshore in shallow water. Some specimens are caught in midwaters. This species is eaten by sea lions and fur seals in Alaskan waters. Food is mainly jellyfish and comb jellies, occasionally free-swimming worms and crustaceans. In Japan, spawning occurs from February to April on a rocky sea bed at less than 10 m and a temperature of 3–6°C. Each female has up to 80,000 eggs with a diameter up to 2.4 mm. Males guard the eggs which are clumped together on the underside of a rock. This species is of minor commercial importance only in Japan.

smooth skate

Scientific name: *Malacoraja senta*
  (Garman, 1885)
Family: **Skate**
Other common names: smooth-tailed skate,
  prickly skate, raie lisse
French name: raie à queue de velours

Distribution: Found from off southern Labrador to the St. Lawrence River estuary and south to Georges Bank and to South Carolina.

Characters: This species is separated from its Canadian Atlantic relatives by having a rigid snout with its cartilaginous support thick and stiff, cartilaginous supports of the pectoral fin do not reach the snout tip, dorsal fins joined at the base, snout angle about 110°, large spines on body and tail midline becoming smaller posteriorly and indistinguishable from prickles. The upper disc is covered in prickles with bare patches on the shoulders and upper pelvics in adults. There are 10–15 large spines around the inner edge of the eye, 3–5 on each shoulder and males have several rows of alar spines. The underside is smooth with some prickles on the snout in mature fish. Teeth 38–40 series in the upper jaw, 36–38 in the lower jaw. Egg capsules are 5.6–6.9 cm by 3.5–3.9 cm and are dark brown. Horns are about 5 cm long. The upper disc is brown with many dark spots or blotches. The underside is white, sometimes with dusky spots at the

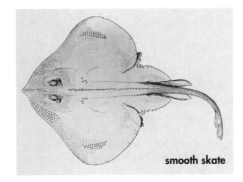

smooth skate

outer parts of the pectorals or one at the snout tip. The tail is white underneath, blotched dark or with the last third dark.

Young fish have 1–2 pale bars on the tail near its base. Reaches 61 cm.

Biology: This species is found on mud, clay, silt and sand bottoms from 27 to 914 m, most commonly below 73 m to 413 m. Temperature range is -1.3 to 13°C. Food is crustaceans such as decapods, euphausiids and mysids. Commercial catches are incidental to other species and this skate is used as fish meal and pet food.

smooth trunkfish

Scientific name: *Rhineosomus triqueter*
(Linnaeus, 1758)
Family: **Boxfish**
Other common names: coffre baquette
French name: coffre lisse

Distribution: Found from Brazil to Massachusetts and into Atlantic Canada.

Characters: The smooth trunkfish is distinguished from its relative, the **rough trunkfish**, by its lack of carapace spines. Pale yellow to grey with white spots. The plates are edged in black. The mouth, dorsal fin base and each end of the caudal peduncle are blackish. The caudal fin is tipped with white beyond a dusky band. The head sides are spotted yellow. Attains 30 cm.

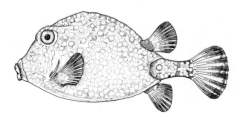

smooth trunkfish

Biology: First reported from off Nova Scotia in 1980, the northern limit of the species range. Usually associated with coral reefs down to about 50 m, feeding on worms, crabs, tunicates, sponges and shrimps. Spawning in the Caribbean probably peaks in January to March. It can be caught by hand and the fin movements involved in trying to evade capture produce a fluttering sound. It is sold fresh in the Caribbean and is caught mainly in traps but also with seines.

smoothbrow lampfish

Scientific name: *Taaningichthys bathyphilus*
(Tåning, 1928)
Family: **Lanternfish**
Other common names: spinelessbrow lampfish, lampe sans épine sourcilière
French name: lampe à front lisse

Distribution: Found in the Atlantic, Indian and Pacific oceans including off Atlantic Canada.

Characters: This species is distinguished from its Canadian Atlantic coast relatives by the large luminous glands, outlined with

smoothbrow lampfish

heavy, black pigment, on the upper and lower caudal peduncle and the pelvic fin origin in front of the dorsal fin origin, and from its close relative, the **lesser lampfish**, by photophore counts VO 3–5, AO 1–4 + 1–2, total 2–5, usually 4, and the Pol photophore lying behind the adipose fin base. No hook-like teeth near the tip of the lower jaw. Dorsal fin rays 11–14, anal rays 12–14, usually 13, and pectoral rays 12–14. The lower caudal peduncle gland is longer than the upper gland. There is a crescent of whitish tissue on the posterior half of the iris. Attains about 8 cm.

Biology: Reported from near the Flemish Cap in Canadian waters. A relatively uncommon species which is bathypelagic in some areas rather than mesopelagic like most lanternfishes. It apparently does not migrate vertically and is found usually below 800 m, rarely as shallow as 400 m. Females carrying large eggs are 5.7–6.1 cm long.

smoothcheek lanternfish

Scientific name: *Bolinichthys indicus*
(Nafpaktitis and Nafpaktitis, 1969)
Family: **Lanternfish**
Other common names: none
French name: lampe à joue lisse

Distribution: Found in the Indian and Atlantic oceans and off the Atlantic coast of Canada.

Characters: This species and its relatives, the **spinecheek** and **sidelight lanternfishes**, are distinguished from other Atlantic coast species by lacking photophores close to the dorsal body edge, the PLO photophore is well above the pectoral fin level, the second PVO photophore is not above the pectoral fin level, there are 3 Prc photophores, caudal luminous glands are a series of overlapping, scale-like structures without a black pigment border, the fourth PO photophore is highly elevated, there are 5 VO photophores, and a crescent of whitish tissue on the rear half of the iris. This species is separated from its relatives by having the VLO photophore at or just below the lateral line, patches of luminous tissue on top of the head and at the fin bases, 14–17 gill rakers, and no spine on the ventral preopercle. Dorsal fin rays 11–14, anal rays 12–14 and 12–14 pectoral rays. Total gill rakers 15–18. AO photophores 8–11. There are 2–4 scale-like infracaudal luminous structures. Reaches 4.5 cm.

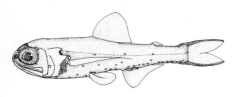

smoothcheek lanternfish

Biology: First recorded off Canada in 1988. This species is the most abundant lanternfish off Bermuda in winter. Reported from 425–900 m by day with a maximum abundance at 600–700 m and at 25–325 m by night with maximum abundance at 50–150 m. Daily migrations upward start 1–3 hours before sunset and last up to 3.5 hours. These small fish swim up to 800 m/hour. Day depths are attained within 1.5–2.0 hours after sunrise and take 2.0–2.5 hours. Sexual maturity is attained at 3.1 cm. Spawning starts in spring and peaks in early to late summer. Most fish die after spawning at about 1 year of age.

smoothchin mora

Scientific name: *Brosmiculus imberbis*
  Vaillant, 1888
Family: **Mora**
Other common names: beardless codling
French name: more imberbe

Distribution: Found off the Atlantic coast of Canada and at the Cape Verde Islands in the eastern Atlantic Ocean.

Characters: This species is distinguished from its Atlantic coast relatives by having a small, dark, scaleless patch on the belly in front of the anus covering a light organ, a rounded snout, and no chin barbel. There are

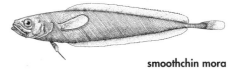

smoothchin mora

63–66 dorsal fin rays and 56–62 anal fin rays. The pelvic fin has 5 rays. Overall colour is dark with lighter areas on the head, the posterior part of the back and the caudal peduncle. Cheeks are silvery. The dorsal, anal and caudal fins are dark brown and the pectoral and pelvic fins are blackish. The inside of the mouth is darkly pigmented, in an anchor-shape. Reaches at least 15.9 cm total length.

Biology: Known from only a single Canadian specimen caught south of Sable Island Bank in 1983 at 201–276 m. This is a rare, deep sea species of which little is known.

smootheye poacher

Scientific name: *Xeneretmus leiops*
  Gilbert, 1915
Family: **Poacher**
Other common names: none
French name: agone à nageoire coupée

Distribution: Found from southeastern Alaska through British Columbia to southern California.

Characters: This poacher and the related **blacktip** and **bluespotted poachers** are distinguished by the absence of a pit on top of the head and by an exposed snout plate having a single, dorsally pointing spine. This species is identified by not having cheek plates, 1 cirrus at the rear of the upper jaw, the anal fin origin at or before the second

smootheye poacher

dorsal fin origin, and no spiny plates on the eyeball. First dorsal fin spines 6–7, second dorsal fin soft rays 6–8. Anal fin rays 5–8 and pectoral fin rays 13–15, with the lower 4 obviously finger-like and heavily swollen at their tips in some fish. Gill membranes are joined to the isthmus. Dusky olive above with a black snout tip. The dorsal fin is blotched black at the front and there is a black blotch below the eye. The belly is whitish. Reaches 24 cm.

Biology: Found on the bottom at 37 to 399 m.

smoothhead scorpionfish

Scientific name: *Scorpaena calcarata*
  Goode and Bean, 1882
Family: **Scorpionfish**
Other common names: none
French name: rascasse dénudée

Distribution: Found from Brazil to off Nova Scotia.

Characters: This species is distinguished from other Atlantic coast scorpionfishes by having 12 dorsal fin spines, lateral line complete, normal with tubed scales, the first preopercular spine longest, and 7–10, usually 9, soft dorsal fin rays. There are 18–21, usually 20, pectoral fin rays. The bone before the eye

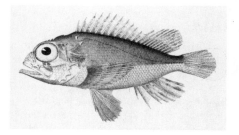

smoothhead scorpionfish

has 2 spines. There is a small cirrus above the eye. Scales are cycloid. Supraocular and postocular spines present. The body colour is reddish, fading to brown when dead. The axil of the pectoral fin is pale and the upper pectoral fin is dark. Reaches 13 cm.

Biology: Larvae and juveniles have been collected as strays from off the Scotian Shelf from 1977–1981 and are northern range extensions. Young are found at the shoreline and adults down to 90 m.

smoothhead sculpin

Scientific name: *Artedius lateralis*
  (Girard, 1854)
Family: **Sculpin**
Other common names: round-nosed sculpin, flathead sculpin
French name: chabot à tête lisse

Distribution: Found from the Bering Sea and the Gulf of Alaska to Baja California including British Columbia.

Characters: This species and its Pacific coast relatives, the **padded, Puget Sound,** and **scalyhead sculpins**, are distinguished by

smoothhead sculpin

having 2–3, mostly 3, pelvic fin soft rays, simple or branched uppermost preopercular spine but not antler-like, (except in the **padded sculpin**) and 3–16 scales in the rows above the lateral line. This species is separated from related species by lacking scales on the head and scale rows beyond the end of the soft dorsal fin. The nasal spine is blunt. There is only 1 preopercular spine with a blunt branch covered in skin. First dorsal fin spines 7–10, second dorsal fin rays 15–18. Anal rays 12–14, pectoral rays 14–16 with the lower 8 finger-like. There are 18–31 scale rows of 3–11 scales above the lateral line not touching the lateral line or the dorsal fins. Lateral line scales 35–36. Cirri are found in 3 cross rows on top of the head as filaments, in a row along the lateral line as far as the anterior third of the soft dorsal fin as flaps and filaments and in pairs, there is a small, branched nasal cirrus, 3 simple cirri at the end of the upper jaw, about 4 on the preopercle, occasionally 1 at the top of the gill opening and 1 near the top of the opercular flap. The back is olive green to dark brown with 6 dark saddles. Ventrally light green to cream. The lower body and head are spotted and blotched with light colour. Fins have dark bars except for the pelvic fins. Fins are duskier in breeding males. Reaches 14 cm.

Biology: This is a shallow water species found down to 13 m and is common in tide pools in British Columbia. Food is principally shrimps and such fishes as small **scorpionfishes**, **gunnels** and **shannies**. Spawning occurs in February when red, yellow or orange eggs are laid in masses among or under rocks.

snaggletooths

The snaggletooths (also known as bighead dragonfishes or star-eaters) comprise about 35 species which were once placed in their own family (Astronesthidae) but are now considered members of the **Barbeled Dragonfish Family**. Four species have been reported off the Atlantic and Arctic coasts of Canada. They are characterised by an elongate body, absence of gill rakers, a dorsal fin at the mid-point of the body and the absence of scales and scale-like markings. Pectoral and adipose fins are present and there is a chin barbel. Light organs lack a duct or lumen and are found in two rows on the lower flank. Smaller light organs are scattered over the head and body and there is one behind the eye. The name snaggletooth is derived from their fang-like teeth.

See **black snaggletooth**
     gem snaggletooth
     large-eye snaggletooth
     whitebearded snaggletooth

Snailfish Family

Scientific name: Liparidae (= Liparididae)
French name: limaces de mer

Snailfishes or sea snails are known mostly from northern cold and temperate waters and from the Antarctic. They may be world-wide in deep, cold waters. There are about 195 species with 37 reported from Canada, 23 on the Pacific coast, 7 on the Arctic-Atlantic coast, 5 on the Atlantic coast and 2 on the Arctic coast.

Snailfishes are easily recognised by their loose skin with jelly-like tissue underneath. This may aid in flotation for those species without a swimbladder. The skin lacks scales but may bear prickles in some species. The lateral line is absent. The body is often tadpole-shaped. The pelvic fins are modified into a thoracic sucking or adhesive disc in many species. A few, often pelagic, species lack pelvic fins. Dorsal and anal fins are long and often merge with the caudal fin.

Snailfish are sometimes classified with the **Lumpfish Family** species which also have the distinctive sucking disc. They are members of the **Mail-cheeked Order**. Snailfishes are difficult to identify and characters include pore counts and patterns, fin ray numbers, the gill slit position and size, teeth shape and rows, peritoneum (or body cavity lining) colour, body colour, disc form, and several others.

Snailfishes are found in tide-pools and offshore in moderately deep waters. Some are found at the incredible depth of 7588 m, an area known to oceanographers as the hadal zone for its supposed proximity to hell. Some deepsea species are pelagic. The adhesive, sucking disc is used to cling to rocks or algae. Food is crustaceans and other invertebrates, and rarely other fishes. Their eggs are adhesive and sometimes laid on or in other animals. Some species guard their eggs.

See **abyssal snailfish**
     Atlantic snailfish
     bigpored snailfish
     bigtail snailfish
     black seasnail
     blacksnout snailfish
     blacktail snailfish
     dusky snailfish
     gelatinous snailfish
     gulf snailfish
     kelp snailfish
     lobefin snailfish
     longfin snailfish

lowfin snailfish
marbled snailfish
pink snailfish
pouty snailfish
prickly snailfish
pygmy snailfish
ribbon snailfish
ringtail snailfish
scallop snailfish
Scotian snailfish
sea tadpole
showy snailfish
slim snailfish
slimy snailfish
slipskin snailfish
smalldisk snailfish
smallfin snailfish
spiny snailfish
spotted snailfish
swellhead snailfish
tadpole snailfish
threadfin snailfish
tidepool snailfish
toothless snailfish

Snake Eel Family

Scientific name: Ophichthidae
French name: serpents de mer

Snake eels are found along the coasts of tropical and warm temperate oceans, rarely in fresh water. There are about 250 species world-wide, of which 14 are found on Canada's Atlantic coast (one species is unidentified). They are also called worm eels, snapper eels or shrimp eels and are the most speciose eel family.

This family is characterised by the snake-like appearance of many species. They can be brightly coloured with bands and spots. The posterior nostril is within the upper lip or piercing the upper lip via a valve, the anterior nostril is tubular and widely separated from the posterior nostril, pectoral fins are present or absent, the tongue is not free but attached, various osteological characters are unique, and there are 15–49 branchiostegals which overlap below the head in the throat region to form a unique basket structure (or jugostegalia). Some species have a tail fin, while in others the fin is absent and the tip is hard and pointed to facilitate burrowing. There are no scales.

The family is a member of the **Eel Order** related to the **Cutthroat**, **Duckbill**, **Conger** and other families which have fused frontal bones in the skull.

Some snake eel species remain buried or hide in cracks in rocks and coral reefs, while others are often found in open water. They are often eaten by predators and may burrow out of the predator's gut only to die in the body cavity and become encased in tissue as a "mummy." These eels have strong teeth capable of wounding humans if carelessly handled. Prey is believed to be crustaceans and fishes. Almost all Canadian records for snake eels are of larvae which drifted north on the Gulf Stream. The larvae are leptocephali as in other eel families, and are leaf-like, elongate, transparent and gelatinous. They are characterised by 2 or more gut swellings or loops. Pigment is usually concentrated on these swellings or loops. Counts of myomeres or muscle blocks are often used in identification, with counts being related to various body parts including the nephros (kidney). These larvae are usually caught offshore in fine-meshed, scientific fishing trawls in midwaters. They are the most common eel larvae. The larvae transform into eel-shaped adults in 1–2 years and descend to the bottom. One adult specimen was found in the stomach lining of a **swordfish** and may well have been eaten outside Canadian waters but our scientists still claim it as a Canadian record! Adult snake eels are hard to catch because of their burrowing ability, both forwards and backwards, and the ease with which they wriggle through the smallest holes in nets.

See **academy eel**
  blotched snake eel
  broadnose worm eel
  horsehair eel
  key worm eel
  margined snake eel
  palespotted eel
  sharptail eel
  shrimp eel
  sooty eel
  speckled worm eel
  string eel
  striped sailfin eel

Snake Mackerel Family

Scientific name: Gempylidae
French name: escolars

Snake mackerels, escolars, oilfishes, gemfishes and sackfishes are found world-wide in warm waters. There are about 23 species with 4 recorded from Atlantic Canada.

The body shape and fin arrangements are characteristic. Several species resemble **tunas**. The body is oblong or elongate and compressed. The mouth is large with strong and often fang-like teeth. There are a series of small separated finlets behind the dorsal and anal fins in some species. The finlets are composed of a few rays. The first dorsal fin is long and spiny, and the second, excluding finlets, is shorter. Pelvic fins are reduced or absent. The caudal fin has a marked fork. Scales are absent, small or modified into prickles. Gill rakers are in the form of spiny tubercles although one normal raker is present at the angle of the gill arch.

Snake mackerels are related to the **Cutlassfish** and **Mackerel** families. The family is a member of the **Perch Order**.

These fishes are very fast predators of the open ocean. Some live in very deep water and most are found below 200 m, coming to the surface at night. They are occasionally caught by anglers, but are not usually eaten. Commercial fishing occurs for tasty species in Australasia and the Southern Hemisphere. In some species the flesh is oily and flabby and has a purgative effect. Sometimes they are stranded on ships at night, having leaped aboard, attracted by lights. Eggs and larvae are pelagic.

See **black snake mackerel**
 cone-chin
 escolar
 oilfish

snake prickleback

Scientific name: *Lumpenus sagitta*
 Wilimovsky, 1956
Family: **Shanny**
Other common names: Pacific snake
 prickleback, eel blenny
French name: lompénie élancée

Distribution: From northern California to the Bering Sea and Sea of Japan including British Columbia.

Characters: This species is 1 of 8 related Canadian shannies which have very elongate bodies, large pectoral fins and pelvic fins with 1 spine and 2–4 soft rays. It is distinguished by distribution, 1 anal fin spine

snake prickleback

before 45–50 soft rays, 64–72 dorsal fin spines and the pectoral fin without its lower rays extended and finger-like. Pectoral fin rays about 15–17. Scales are on the whole body and head except the cheek, and there is a straight lateral line. The back is a light green fading to a cream belly. The sides have midflank brown or green bars or streaks and upper flank spots and blotches. The lower flank is unmarked. The caudal fin has 5–9 bars and the dorsal fin is barred and spotted brown. The pectoral, pelvic and anal fins are pale. Reaches 51 cm.

Biology: Common down to 207 m as adults and off the Fraser River estuary as pelagic young. Adults have been caught by anglers using polychaete worms as bait.

snakeblenny

Scientific name: *Lumpenus lumpretaeformis*
 (Walbaum, 1792)
Family: **Shanny**
Other common names: serpent blenny,
 rock-eel, blennie-serpent
French name: lompénie-serpent

Distribution: Found in the eastern Arctic from Davis Strait and Baffin Island south to the Atlantic coast of Canada and on to Massachusetts. Also in the eastern north Atlantic Ocean.

Characters: This species is 1 of 8 related Canadian shannies which have very elongate bodies, large pectoral fins and pelvic fins with 1 spine and 2–4 soft rays. It is distinguished by distribution, dorsal fin spines 68–85, lower pectoral fin rays not prolonged and finger-like, and 1 spine and 47–62 soft rays in the anal fin. These fin ray counts tend to vary with area of capture with Newfoundland fish having more than Gulf of St. Lawrence fish. The pectoral fins have 14–15 rays. The caudal fin ends in a pointed tip. Scales cover the

snakeblenny

body and the lateral line is complete but indistinct. The body is pale brown with some bluish tinges and brown or greenish-yellow blotches. The belly is greenish-yellow. The dorsal fin has up to 18 oblique brown bars. The caudal fin is also barred with up to 8 present. The pelvic fins, anal fin tips and lower 8–9 pectoral rays are white. Reaches 48 cm.

Biology: Found over mud or hard bottoms, from the shallows down to 200 m, but not intertidally. In more northern waters off Greenland, it has been reported down to 333 m. It constructs a protective burrow in soft substrate taking 12–24 hours to excavate one. The burrow is usually Y-shaped and up to 73 cm long. Tail flexions are used to irrigate the burrow. Food is crustaceans, molluscs and small starfish. Spawning is probably in fall or winter and up to 1100 eggs may be deposited. Larvae are pelagic.

snakefish

Scientific name: *Trachinocephalus myops*
   (Forster in Bloch and Schneider, 1801)
Family: **Lizardfish**
Other common names: ground spearing
French name: poisson-lézard paille

Distribution: World-wide in warmer seas including Atlantic Canada.

Characters: The body has blue-grey and yellow stripes and a dusky spot behind the upper edge of the gill cover. There are usually 14–16 anal fin rays and, with the colour

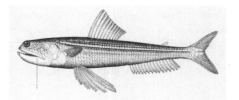

snakefish

pattern, this distinguishes it from the **red lizardfish**. Dorsal fin rays 11–14 and pectoral rays 11–13. Lateral line scales 53–61. Attains 40 cm.

Biology: First reported from Canada as post-larvae caught in 1976–1977 off Nova Scotia. Post-larvae are carried north to Canada on the warm Gulf Stream. Found as adults near reefs and on the continental shelf down to 387 m, but usually in 37–91 m. The snakefish burrows in sand or mud leaving only its eyes exposed.

snakehead eelpout

Scientific name: *Lycenchelys crotalina*
   (Gilbert, 1890)
Family: **Eelpout**
Other common names: no-tooth eelpout
French name: lycode-crotale

Distribution: Found from the Bering Sea to Baja California including British Columbia.

Characters: This species is distinguished from its Pacific coast relatives by having scales, a gill slit extending in front of the

snakehead eelpout

pectoral fin, pelvic fins present, a low body depth at the anal fin origin (2.3–8.3% of standard length), anterior suborbital pores parallel with the upper jaw, large pores around the mouth, and no teeth on the vomer bone in the roof of the mouth. The gill cover is scaled. There is a lateral line canal but it is indistinct. Dorsal fin rays 113–126, anal rays 99–110, and pectoral rays 14–17. Overall colour is a dark brownish-blue to purplish with dorsal, anal and pectoral fins and lower part of the head black. There are bright blue metallic lustres on the middle part of the pectoral fin rays and on fleshy folds of the head. The mouth and gill cavities are dark. Peritoneum blackish-brown. Attains 46.8 cm.

Biology: Depth range is 200–1829 m on mud bottoms. Canadian records off southern Vancouver Island and the Queen Charlotte Islands were at 908–1203 m. This eelpout is known to eat clams and worms.

Snapper Family

Scientific name: Lutjanidae
French name: vivaneaux

Snappers and fusiliers are found in warmer oceans world-wide, being most numerous in the tropics but extending to temperate regions. Rarely in fresh water. There are about 125 species of which only 2 are reported from Canada on the Atlantic coast.

These fishes resemble **sea basses** but usually have 1–2 large, canine teeth near the mouth tip on each side and the maxilla bone of the upper jaw fits into a slot under the pre-orbital bone on the side of the snout when the mouth is closed. The dorsal fin is single with 9–12 spines and 9–18 soft rays. The anal fin has 3 spines and 7–11 soft rays. Pectoral fins with 15–18 soft rays, pelvics with 1 spine and 5 branched rays inserted just behind the pectoral fin base. There may be a deep notch between the spiny and soft parts of the dorsal fin. There is no supramaxilla. Branchiostegal rays 7. The head has a typical snapper shape, long and triangular with a strongly sloping upper profile. Body scales are ctenoid and they extend onto the head except for areas on the snout, around the eye and on the lower jaw. There is usually a strong pelvic axillary process.

Snappers are placed near other **Perch Order** families such as **tripletails, drums** and **dolphins**.

Snappers are found near the bottom from shallows and reefs to over 800 m. Deeper reefs, areas around rock ledges and channels are favoured by adults. They are predators, feeding at night on other fishes and crustaceans. Young are most common in the shallow water of reefs, mangroves and seagrass beds which serve as nursery areas. Larger species live 20 years or more.

This family has a number of important food species but they may carry ciguatera poisoning, a tropical disease derived sporadically from the type of toxic, herbivorous fishes eaten. The herbivorous fishes derive the toxin in turn from dinoflagellates found on coral or benthic algae. Snappers are territorial and solitary and so are not usually caught in large quantities by trawlers but individually by fishermen using a variety of gear. About 28,000 tonnes were caught in the western Central Atlantic Ocean in 1983. They are a popular sport fish and are caught on hook and line and by spear fishing.

See **cubera snapper**
wenchman

Snipe Eel Family

Scientific name: Nemichthyidae
French name: avocettes

Snipe eels are found in deep waters of the Atlantic, Indian and Pacific oceans. There are about 9 species with 1 reported from the Pacific coast and 2 from both the Pacific and Atlantic coasts of Canada.

These eels (**Eel Order** members) are remarkable for their extremely elongate bodies, with over 750 vertebrae in some species, and the unusual jaws. The upper and lower jaws diverge and the upper is longer than the lower. The two jaws do not meet at the end except in ripe males (and probably, to some extent, females) which lose their teeth and undergo a shortening of the jaw. Ripe males and immature fish are so different in appearance that they were often described as different species. In addition to the changes in the male's jaws, the pectoral fins move posteriorly, the eyes enlarge, tubular anterior nostrils develop and the fish becomes darker.

The dorsal, anal and caudal fins are continuous. The end of the body is often lost in captured specimens because it is so thin and the vertebrae so weakly developed. The eye is large and pectoral fins are present. The anus is far forward, near the pectoral fins. There is no preopercle bone on the side of the head. There are no scales.

Snipe eels are related to the **Moray**, **Spaghetti Eel** and **Freshwater Eel** families of the **Eel Order** which all have the frontal bones on top of the head divided by a suture. "Snipe" is taken from the shore bird which has a similar beak.

Snipe eels are rarely caught inhabitants of deep midwaters down to 4300 m. Occasionally they are caught in **sablefish** traps in southern California. These unusual eels are believed to position themselves vertically, head up or down, in the water column and capture migrating shrimps by entangling their antennae in the diverging jaws. They may also make rapid sideways movements of the head to wedge a prey in the jaws. Some species have an extremely long tail filament. The lateral line extends along this filament which gives the fish better sensing ability. It may also give a larger echo to predators, which then avoid this apparently large fish. The larva of these eels is a leptocephalus, readily distinguished by its thin, elongate tail. The enlarged, tubular nostrils in males help locate females by smell at spawning time. Snipe eels probably spawn once and then die.

See **carinate snipe eel**
closespine snipe eel
slender snipe eel

Snipefish Family

Scientific name: Macroramphosidae
French name: bécasses de mer

Snipefishes or bellows fishes are found principally in the tropical and subtropical parts of the Atlantic, Indian and Pacific oceans. There are about 12 species with 1 reported from Atlantic Canada.

Their unique body form is unmistakeable. A deep, compressed body has a very elongate, narrow snout and the second dorsal spine is very long. There are long plates on the flanks, 4–8 dorsal fin spines and 10–19 dorsal soft rays. Scales bear sharp ridges and spines. The lateral line is present or absent.

Snipefish are related to the **Cornetfish** and **Pipefish** families in the **Stickleback Order**. The scientific name is from the Latin for long snout. Fossils are known from the Upper Cretaceous.

Young snipefish are pelagic while adults are found near the bottom at 50–150 m. They are usually found in schools. They can swim backwards or forwards with equal facility.

See **longspine snipefish**

snoutlet crotchfeeler

Scientific name: *Bathypterois dubius*
Vaillant, 1888
Family: **Tripodfish**
Other common names: spiderfish, notch
feelerfish
French name: cran-tactile à muselet

Distribution: Found mainly in the eastern North Atlantic Ocean, rarely in the Mediterranean Sea and off Atlantic Canada.

Characters: This species is separated from its Canadian relatives by having minute eyes, the upper 2 pectoral fin rays greatly elongated, the lowest pectoral ray not

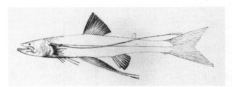

snoutlet crotchfeeler

enlarged and scales behind the lower pectoral base without strong spines. The gape is large. There is a notch at the lower base of the tail fin; its function is unknown. Dorsal fin rays 14–16, anal rays 8–10, pectoral rays 11–13 and pelvic rays 8. The two outermost pelvic rays and the lowest caudal fin ray are elongated. Lateral line scales 59–65. The head and body are black with scale pockets outlined in white. The caudal fin is black but other fins are dusky to transparent in preservative, possibly black when alive. Reaches 20.5 cm, perhaps 26 cm.

Biology: A single specimen is the only western North Atlantic record for this species. It was caught in a bottom trawl at 750–805 m in 1959 on the southwest slope of the Grand Bank. Elsewhere reported down to 1950 m. Food is planktonic and presumably bottom organisms. It is a hermaphrodite. The elongate fin rays are used as "stilts" to walk along the sea bottom without stirring up the fine mud deposits, and may also serve to find food by touch and taste.

snowflake hookear

Scientific name: *Artediellus uncinatus*
(Reinhardt, 1835)
Family: **Sculpin**
Other common names: Arctic hookear
sculpin, Arctic sculpin, crochet arctique
French name: hameçon neigeux

Distribution: Found from southeastern Baffin Island south to northern Nova Scotia off Cape Breton.

Characters: This sculpin and its Arctic-Atlantic relatives, the **Atlantic** and **rough hookears**, are distinguished by having the upper preopercular spine pointed and strongly hooked upwards, the margin of the first dorsal fin is often dark and both dorsal fins in males are spotted or barred. This species has 19–23 total caudal fin rays, cirri on the parietal region, 0–5 teeth on the vomer bone and 0–3 teeth on the palatine bone both in the roof of the mouth. First dorsal fin spines 7–8, second dorsal rays 10–14. Anal rays 10–12 and pectoral rays 19–24. Lateral line pores 20–30. The body is blotched or mottled with dark or pale brown or red. The dorsal fin is dark with white spots. White spots in rows may be found on the head, body, pectoral and caudal fins. The caudal fin has a basal blotch. Males have elongated first dorsal fin spines, free of the membrane at their tip and the first dorsal fin is larger than in females with prominent black-edged, white spots. Reaches 10.0 cm.

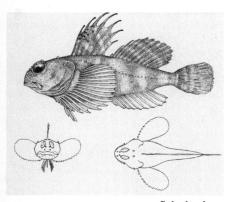

snowflake hookear

Biology: This sculpin is found on various bottom types at 13–350 m, usually less than 183 m. Food is assumed to be various invertebrates and spawning to take place in late summer. Eggs are orange and 3 mm in diameter. They may be spawned in clumps attached to hydroids. Egg numbers exceed 100. Mature females are found at only 4.0 cm total length. Life span is about 4 years.

snowy grouper

Scientific name: *Epinephelus niveatus*

(Valenciennes in Cuvier and Valenciennes, 1828)
Family: **Sea Bass**
Other common names: none
French name: mérou neigeux

Distribution: Found in both the western Atlantic and the eastern Pacific oceans including Nova Scotian waters.

Characters: There are about 95–104 scales along the flank which distinguishes this species from other Canadian sea basses.

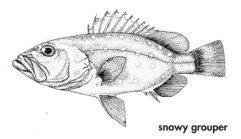

snowy grouper

Dorsal fin spines are 11, soft rays are 13–16, usually 14. Anal fin with 8–10, usually 9, soft rays. The posterior nostril is much larger than the anterior one. Overall colour is dark red to grey or chocolate brown, with pearly white spots arranged in rows most evident in young. Pelvic fins are black. Young fish have a black saddle in front of the yellow caudal fin but this is lost in adults. Reaches 104 cm fork length and 14 kg.

Biology: Canadian specimens are strays with only 4 fish being recorded from 1928 to 1981. The 1981 specimen was caught below 135 m by a Russian trawler and was a large adult, 104 cm to the tail fork. They are usually found at 240–484 m over rock, sand or mud bottoms or on wrecks and reefs. Food is principally pelagic fishes, with some squids and crabs. Life span is at least 25 years. Most females from Florida are mature by age 4–5. Snowy groupers are probably protogynous hermaphrodites, changing from female to male at some point in their life cycle. Larvae are pelagic. Headboats off the Carolinas caught 6482 kg of snowy groupers annually between 1972 and 1980 while off South Carolina commercial hook and line vessels caught 35,340 kg annually from 1976 to 1981.

snubnose eel

Scientific name: *Simenchelys parasiticus*
   Gill in Goode and Bean, 1879
Family: **Cutthroat Eel**
Other common names: slime-eel, snubnose
   parasitic eel, pugnose eel
French name: anguille à nez court

   Distribution: Found world-wide including
Atlantic Canada from south of Newfoundland.
   Characters: This eel is distinguished from
other family members in Canada by the blunt
head and the small, circular and terminal
mouth. Scales are deeply embedded in the
skin, elongate and arranged in a basket-
weave pattern. Juveniles lack scales. Pectoral
fins are present. Gill openings are small,

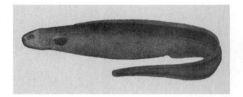

snubnose eel

oblique slits on the throat. Teeth are broad,
few in number and in a single row on the
jaws. Nostril pores are large and evident.
There are no teeth on the roof of the mouth.
Lateral line with 44 preanal pores and 2
prepectoral pores. Overall colour is grey to
grey-brown or dark brown with dark or
white fin margins. The lateral line is dark but
may be lighter than surrounding tissue in
preserved specimens. Reaches 61 cm.
   Biology: Reported from various banks
along the Canadian coast from St. Pierre to
LaHave banks and southward. Some specimens have been caught as deep as 3000 m or
as shallow as 100 m. Water temperatures are
about 4–7°C. The snubnose is parasitic on
other fishes, such as **halibut**, burrowing into
their flesh. The prey may have to be moribund
before the snubnose can successfully burrow.
This eel is probably also a scavenger on dead
fish and invertebrates. The snubnose's other
name, slime-eel, refers to the mucus produced
by the skin which literally drips off a captured
specimen. The unrelated **Hagfish Family** is

also a scavenger and has this slimy skin. Eggs
are pelagic and at least 2 mm in diameter.

snubnose eelpout

Scientific name: *Pachycara bulbiceps*
   (Garman, 1899)
Family: **Eelpout**
Other common names: none
French name: lycode camuse

   Distribution: Found in the North Atlantic
and North Pacific oceans. Off the Queen
Charlotte Islands in Canada.
   Characters: This species is separated from
its Pacific coast relatives by the lack of pelvic
fins, a large gill opening extending to the
lower edge of the pectoral fin base, terminal
mouth and blunt snout, robust body, scales
present on body, tail and up to three-quarters
of height of vertical fins and on pectoral base,
midlateral branch of the lateral line originating posterior to pectoral fin margin and running to tip of tail, usually 6 suborbital pores,
and firm flesh. There is a lower lateral line
from the head to the tail tip. Dorsal fin rays
104–114, anal rays 86–97 and pectoral rays
16–19. Vertebrae number 112–119. Overall
colour dark brown with head and pectoral fins
darker. Scales have brown pigmented skin
between them giving the preserved fish a fine,
light-speckled appearance. Belly and eyes
dark blue. Mouth and gill cavities pale to dark
brown. Reaches 52.5 cm standard length.

snubnose eelpout

   Biology: Reported in a depth range of
2400–4780 m over mud bottoms.

sockeye salmon

Scientific name: *Oncorhynchus nerka*
   (Walbaum, 1792)
Family: **Salmon**
Other common names: kokanee, kickininee,
   koke, little redfish, landlocked sockeye,
   Kennerly's salmon, silver trout, yank and
   kokani for the landlocked form; sockeye
   salmon, red salmon, blueback salmon for
   the sea run form

French name: saumon rouge

Distribution: Found from the Bering Strait south to Oregon including rivers draining to these coasts such as the Columbia and Fraser and Yukon but not the Canadian portion of the latter. Also landlocked in lakes. Also found on the Pacific coast of the Bering Sea and south to Japan. Widely introduced with varying success in North America including Alberta, Saskatchewan, Manitoba and Ontario and lakes Superior, Huron and Ontario.

Characters: This species is distinguished by having 120–150 lateral line scales, 11–18 principal anal fin rays, flanks and caudal fin without distinct black spots, long, slender gill rakers 28–44 and pyloric caeca 45–115. Dorsal fin principal rays 11–16, pectoral rays 11–21 and pelvic rays 9–11. Spawning males develop long, hooked jaws with enlarged teeth and a slight hump on the back before the dorsal fin but these features are not as marked as in some other Pacific salmons.

The back is steel- to green-blue with black speckles but no spots, flanks silvery and the belly silver to white. Fins are clear to dusky. Spawning males develop a bright red to reddish-grey back and flanks and a grey-red to grey belly. The flanks are usually darker red than the back. Dorsal, adipose and anal fins are red, and pectoral, pelvic and caudal fins green to blackish. The paired fins have red bases. The head is green to olive with a black snout and upper jaw and a white to grey lower jaw. Females are similar but the red is less intense. Some freshwater populations are green to yellow without the striking red. Young have 8–14 oval, widely-spaced parr marks, some centred across the lateral line. Light areas are greater than dark areas along the lateral line. Fins are clear, the back is blue-green and flanks silvery.

Reaches 53.3 cm as kokanee and 84.0 cm and 7.0 kg as sockeye. The world, all-tackle angling record for kokanee weighed 4.27 kg and was caught in Okanagan Lake, British Columbia on 18 June 1988 by Norm Kuhn. This fish is also recognized as the Canadian record. The sockeye record from the Kenai river, Alaska was caught in 1987 by Stan Roach and weighed 6.88 kg.

Biology: This **salmon** has both an anadromous form, living in the sea and migrating to fresh water to spawn (sockeye) and a landlocked form in lakes running up streams to spawn (kokanee). There are also populations

sockeye salmon

of sockeye which stay in fresh water but do not reproduce known as "residuals." Kokanee live in deeper lake waters in hot summers and in winter, and in spring and fall are widely distributed in lakes. They prefer temperatures in a 10–15°C range and move accordingly.

Food is crustacean plankton with some bottom invertebrates and surface insects in lakes. Young sockeye also feed on planktonic crustaceans during their lacustrine life. Sockeye disperse over the northeast Pacific Ocean to surface waters, migrating north in summer and south in winter. Young kokanee and sockeye are eaten by a wide variety of other fishes including a number of important sport fishes such as **rainbow, west-slope cutthroat** and **Dolly Varden trout, chars, coho salmon**, as well as **northern squawfish** and **prickly sculpin**. Seals and bears take some adult fish.

Kokanee usually live 4 years, spawning and dying at this age but some fish as young as 2 years or as old as 8 years may be found on spawning runs. Growth varies greatly between lakes with coastal lakes generally poorer than interior northern lakes in B.C.

Kokanee spawn from August to February, usually September–October in Kootenay Lake, B.C. at about 5–11°C. Most spawn in lake inlet streams but some spawn on gravel shores of lakes. Kokanee in Kootenay Lake, B.C. home to specific streams for spawning and there are at least 3 distinct stocks. Sockeye enter coastal waters and streams from May to October, early entrants having further to travel upstream to the spawning ground, being earlier spawners or spending up to 3–4 months in fresh water before spawning. Sockeye usually ascend streams with lakes in their drainage, passing through the lake to spawn in tributary streams. Some sockeye travel over 1000 km and use up to 96% of their fat and 53% of their protein reserves. Sockeye are 3–8 years old on the spawning run but are usually 4 years in the south and 5 years old in the north. Alternate years have dominant and subdominant runs, the latter being much less numerous.

Spawning occurs from July to December at 3–7°C. Female kokanee and sockeye excavate a redd in small gravel by lying on one side and lashing the tail up and down in streams but in lakes a vertical side-to-side sweep is used. The redd is about 10.2 cm deep and longer than the fish. A spawning pair enter the redd, gape, vibrate and shed eggs and sperm. Attendant or sneaky males rush in to spawn with the dominant and aggressive pair. The female dislodges gravel at the upstream end of the redd which washes down to cover the eggs. Females may excavate more than one redd and both sexes spawn with more than one partner. Both adults die after spawning within days or a few weeks although transplanted stocks may live through most of the winter and some B.C. kokanee will resume feeding after spawning. Up to 4300, orange-red and 5.0 mm diameter eggs are produced, number and size varying with the female size and stock. Eggs hatch several weeks to months later and fry emerge from the gravel in spring, usually April to June.

Sockeye may spend 1–4 years (mostly 1 year in B.C.) in fresh water before acquiring a silvery colouration and running to sea in spring when they are known as smolts. Both smolts and fry tend to move at night to avoid predators on their migrations. They may spend 1 to 4 years at sea feeding pelagically on zooplankton, particularly krill, squid and some fishes before returning to the stream in which they were born to spawn once and die.

Life history types in B.C. may change over time. In the Nass region a 1/4 life history type (1 year of freshwater growth and 4 years of sea growth) was about twice as numerous in 1982 as the 2/3 type which predominated in 1940. Fraser River stocks are always mostly of 1/3 type.

Homing to the stream of birth was proved by a classical 1931 experiment. All 365,265 yearling sockeye migrating to the sea from Cultus Lake, B.C. were marked by cutting off both pelvic fins. In the fall of 1933 when fish returned to the lake as adults they were overwhelmingly the marked fish, only 0.6% being strays from elsewhere.

Kokanee is an important sport fish, sockeye less so but both are caught by anglers on lures or hooks wrapped in red cotton. They will take worms, **salmon** eggs, maggots and artificial flies at the surface and can be attracted with cowbells. They are good fighters and the red, oily flesh is excellent smoked.

This is the most important Pacific **salmon**, caught by gill nets and purse seines and sometimes by trolling, in river mouths, nearshore areas and on the high seas. Most of the catch is canned (as "red salmon") because it has an oily, red flesh and fish are all similar in size and easy to process. In 1958, 12.04 million fish were caught in British Columbia, the Fraser River being the most important drainage. In 1990, 22 million sockeye returned to the Fraser River system, the largest run since 1913. About 8 of every 10 adults returning to spawn in the Fraser are caught by commercial, aboriginal and recreational fisheries. The Adams River, a Fraser tributary, has a run which is a major tourist attraction, attracting over 300,000 people in 1990. Commercial catches are carefully monitored to allow sufficient adults to reach spawning grounds and replenish the stock. Generally runs are declining because of dams and construction blocking or destroying spawning sites, chemical and thermal pollution and probably overfishing. A third of the world's largest population, of 30 million fish, failed to return to their Canadian breeding grounds on the Fraser River in 1994. Overfishing was blamed, but ecological factors, such as river and ocean warming, may be mostly responsible. The 1988 Canadian catch weighed 11,808 tonnes worth almost $82 million.

- Most accessible June through August.
- The waters of Vancouver Island and the Queen Charlotte Islands.
- Standard nine-and-one-half-foot salmon rods equipped with a mooching reel

used with eight- to 14–pound test line. Lighter spinner and baitcasting outfits can be used with eight- to 14–pound test line. Freshwater fishing include ultralight to light action spinning outfits used with six- to 10–pound test line.

• For saltwater, live **herring** or trolling with a cut-plug **herring**, for freshwater rivers and lakes, an assortment of 1/4– to 3/8–ounce flashy spoons, spinners and jigs.

soft eelpout

Scientific name: *Bothrocara molle* Bean, 1890
Family: **Eelpout**
Other common names: none
French name: lycode molle

Distribution: Found from Kamchatka to Mexico including British Columbia.

Characters: This species is distinguished from its Pacific relatives by lacking pelvic fins, having minute scales, oval eyes, a large gill opening extending to the throat, 8–10 small suborbital pores, 1 indistinct lateral line, gill rakers long and pointed, and eye diameter greater than snout length. Nape scales are present. The flesh is firm. There are numerous head pores and pits. Dorsal fin rays about 100–112, anal rays 89–101 and pectoral rays 13–14. Overall colour is light brown, translucent. Dorsal and anal fin margins are blue-black. The peritoneum is black and the mouth cavity light. Attains 25 cm.

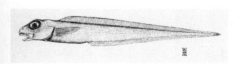

soft eelpout

Biology: Reported off the Queen Charlotte Islands at 1600 m, elsewhere at 577–2688 m.

soft-rayed fishes

This was a group of fishes distinguished from the **spiny-rayed fishes** by lacking, generally, true spines in the dorsal, anal and pelvic fins and on the opercular bones, among other characters. It was known scientifically as the Malacopterygii and included such orders as the **Herring, Carp, Eel** and **Gulper Eel**. This grouping is not in general use now but is still a convenient way of describing those lower fishes which lack spines.

soft sculpin

Scientific name: *Psychrolutes sigalutes* (Jordan and Starks, 1895)
Family: **Soft Sculpin**
Other common names: none
French name: chabot velouté

Distribution: Found from the Bering Sea to Washington including British Columbia.

Characters: This soft sculpin is distinguished from its Pacific coast relatives by having a continuous spiny and soft dorsal fin

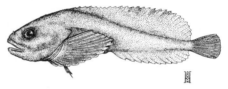

soft sculpin

with the spiny section buried in tissue, no preopercular spines, pectoral rays 14–18, the lower jaw projects and the anus is at the anal fin origin. The spiny dorsal fin tips protrude from the enveloping tissue. There are no cirri but papillae are found on the sides of the head and body. Total dorsal fin ray count 24–27. Anal fin rays 12–15. Overall colour is variable, usually translucent pink to grey or brown. The body and fins are spotted and blotched. The pectoral fin may be orange. The eye is orange. Reaches 8.3 cm.

Biology: Found usually on silt and rock bottoms and possibly in association with sponges, where it takes refuge. Captured at the surface and down to 225 m. This species is attracted to lights at night, especially when young and not yet a bottom dweller. This species is unique among fishes in having communal maternal nest care. Males guard a harem of females. The pelagic young, up to 4 cm long, are caught in April-May off the Fraser River mouth where they feed on plankton. Some young migrate into a surface current drift in Barkley Sound during the evening which has the effect of cancelling subsurface current drift. Larvae therefore stay near the adult habitat of boulders and cliffs. This sculpin is eaten by **lancetfish**.

Soft Sculpin Family

Scientific name: Psychrolutidae
French name: chabots veloutés

Soft sculpins, fatheads or tadpole sculpins are found in the Atlantic, Indian and Pacific oceans. There are about 29 species and in Canada there are 6 species on the Pacific coast and 2 species on the Arctic and Atlantic coasts.

They are characterised by scaleless bodies which may have plates covered in prickles, a loose skin which often covers dorsal and anal fin rays, a reduced lateral line with less than 21 pores, pelvic fins with 1 spine and 3 soft rays, the spiny dorsal fin is small and partly obscured by skin, dorsal fins usually continuous (not separated into spiny and soft parts as in the **Sculpin Family**) although the fin bases are nearly separate in some species, and various skeletal features such as 7 branchiostegal rays and narrow, bony arches on the cranium. There are two groups of soft sculpins: those with a rigid region between the eyes on top of the head and with spines, and those with a soft region on top of the head, no head spines and a tadpole-shaped body.

Soft sculpins are close relatives of the **Sculpin Family** and have been included in that family. Sculpins have 2–3 elongate postorbital bones. Soft sculpins only 1, or, if 2, then they are ring-like. They are members of the **Mail-cheeked Order**.

These fishes are benthic on soft bottoms and are found from shallow water down to 2800 m. They are rare in tropical waters and are best known from the North Atlantic and North Pacific oceans and off South Africa. Their food is both benthic and planktonic invertebrates and fishes. Their eggs sink and are quite large (2–4.5 mm in diameter). They have no commercial importance.

See **bartail sculpin**
blackfin sculpin
blob sculpin
pallid sculpin
polar sculpin
soft sculpin
spinyhead sculpin
tadpole sculpin

soft skate

Scientific name: *Malacoraja spinacidermis* (Barnard, 1923)
Family: **Skate**
Other common names: prickled ray, raie profonde
French name: raie molle

Distribution: Found in the North Atlantic Ocean including from off Baffin Island south to off Nova Scotia.

Characters: This species is separated from its Canadian Atlantic relatives by having a rigid snout with its cartilaginous support thick and stiff, cartilaginous supports of the pectoral fin do not reach the snout tip, dorsal

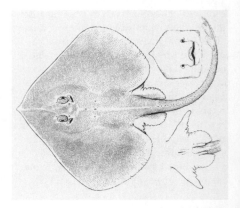

soft skate

fins joined at the base, snout angle 90° or greater, only small spines and prickles on the upper body and tail except for 1–2 thornlets in front of each eye and spiracle and 1–2 on each shoulder, and teeth in 54–63 rows in the upper jaw. Lower jaw teeth 54–64. Adults lose the upper disc thornlets. There are prickles on the front edge of the lower disc in adults and the rest of the underside is smooth. The underside of the tail is prickly. The upper disc is grey-brown. The underside has dark grey spots on the rear half of the pectoral fins, forming a dark fringe on the edge of the fin. The underside of the tail is grey. Adults may be almost entirely grey on the underside. Mouth corners, gill slits, pelvic axils and tail base are white. Reaches 70 cm.

Biology: Not commonly caught in Canadian waters and rare over its range with only about 15 specimens known. Depth range is 710–1568 m in Canada. Food is crustaceans.

soles

Soles are **flatfishes** of the **Righteye Flounder Family** and 14 species bear the name. Curiously, these species are all on the Pacific coast of Canada. Certain other species may also be called sole as an alternative common name — the **witch flounder** is known as the gray sole and the **winter flounder** as the lemon sole. Sole was originally used for a European species of the true soles (Soleidae), a family not found in Canada, but the term has come into general use for unrelated species. "Filet of sole" appears on menus and is used for any filleted flatfish. Sole is taken from the Latin for sandal, and refers to the flat shape of these fish.

See **butter sole**
    C-O sole
    curlfin sole
    deepsea sole
    Dover sole
    English sole
    flathead sole
    petrale sole
    rex sole
    rock sole
    roughscale sole
    sand sole
    slender sole
    yellowfin sole

sooty dragonfish

Scientific name: *Photonectes margarita*
    (Goode and Bean, 1895)
Family: **Barbeled Dragonfish**
Other common names: none
French name: dragon fuligineux

Distribution: Found in the western North Atlantic Ocean from off Nova Scotia south to the Caribbean Sea.

Characters: This species is distinguished from other Canadian Atlantic scaleless drag-

onfishes by having the anal and dorsal fin bases about the same length, pelvic fins low on the flank, no luminous organs (the preorbital and suborbital) before and below the eye, the lower jaw curved upwards, elongate

sooty dragonfish

and projecting beyond the snout, and only 1 pectoral fin ray which can be absent on one or both sides of the body. Dorsal fin rays 15–18, anal rays 19–24 and pelvic rays 7. The dorsal and anal fins are covered by thick, black skin except for their tips. The barbel is shorter to slightly longer than the head. Photophores between the pectoral and pelvic fin insertions number 30–35. Overall colour is velvety-black to a dark brownish-black. The postorbital luminous organ is rose-coloured in females and yellow in males. The bulb of the barbel is purple, photophore rows violet to purple and a luminous shoulder area pale blue. Reaches 36 cm in Canada, one of the largest known specimens.

Biology: Several specimens have been collected off the Scotian Shelf and southern Grand Bank in depths of 200–500 m. Elsewhere found from near surface waters down to about 2000 m.

sooty eel

Scientific name: *Bascanichthys bascanium*
    (Jordan, 1884)
Family: **Snake Eel**
Other common names: none
French name: serpenton charbonneux

Distribution: Found from the Scotian Shelf of Canada south to Puerto Rico and Mexico.

Characters: This species is distinguished as a larva by having the gut loops very low or absent except at liver lobes, dorsal fin origin anterior to myomere (muscle block) 20, total myomeres 174–194, the last 2 major vertical blood vessels 10–15 myomeres apart, 100–112 nephric myomeres and numerous pigment spots in the body wall ventral to the gut from the oesophagus to the anus. Preanal myomeres 101–114 and predorsal myomeres 11–18.

Adults have a hard, blunt, tail tip, the dorsal fin originates on the head, gill openings low on the body and crescent-shaped, and a minute

sooty eel

pectoral fin is present. Adults are dark overall, paling ventrally and with pale fins. Reaches 86 mm as a larva and 78.6 cm as an adult.

Biology: Known only from leptocephalus larvae in Canadian waters first reported in 1989. Adults are found from North Carolina southward on shallow sandy beaches but also as deep as 24 m. Adults actively seek worms, sipunculids and small crustaceans.

soupfin shark

Scientific name: *Galeorhinus galeus*
    (Linnaeus, 1758)
Family: **Hound Shark**
Other common names: tope shark, vitamin
    shark, school shark, oil shark, requin-hâ
French name: requin à grands ailerons

Distribution: From northern British Columbia to California and Mexico. Also in Europe and the southern hemisphere.

Characters: This species is distinguished by the anterior nasal flaps not reaching the mouth and not being barbel-like, absence of nasoral grooves, the second dorsal fin is less than half the area of the first dorsal fin and about the same size as the anal fin, and the ventral caudal lobe is very long, about half the length of the upper lobe. There are no

soupfin shark

keels on the caudal peduncle. The mouth is broadly arched. The labial groove is long but does not pass the front of the mouth. The eye is oval. Teeth are similar in both jaws, shaped like blades with an oblique cusp and 4–5 cus-

plets on the outer edge. Scales are small.

Overall colour is dark blue or brown to grey above, paling towards the belly. The anterior edges of the dorsal fins, tip of the tail fin and most of the pectoral fin are black. Young, less than 60 cm long, have a white edge to the pectoral fin.

Reaches over 2 m and 45 kg. Often referred to as *Galeorhinus zyopterus* Jordan and Gilbert, 1883, this species is regarded by some authors to be the same species as the tope (*G. galeus*) of Europe.

Biology: This species is known from the surf line down to 471 m but it is not an oceanic species. It is a strong-swimmer which shows a northerly migration in summer and a southerly migration in winter. Speeds of up to 56 km per day have been reported and an average speed of 16 km per day for 100 days. One fish travelled 1609 km from southern California to British Columbia in 22 months. Soupfins occur in small schools partially segregated by size and sex. Adult males tend to occur in deeper waters than adult females for example.

It feeds on whatever it encounters including **sardines, flounders, rockfishes, salmons, smelts, sauries, blue lanternfishes, cods, surf perches, sculpins** and many other fishes as well as squid, octopus, crabs, lobster, shrimps and worms.

Reproduction is ovoviviparous with 6 to 52 pups in a litter measuring about 35 cm at birth. Gestation lasts about 1 year. Males mature at about 120–170 cm and 8 years and females at about 130–185 cm and 11 years. This species may live up to 100 years! Mating occurs in spring and gestation lasts one year. Pups are dropped in shallow bays or estuaries and the females leave for offshore feeding grounds followed by the pups in late summer although some young may remain in the nursery area for two years.

This is an important commercial shark species. The flesh is excellent and is eaten fresh, fresh frozen, or dried and salted. The liver is rich in vitamin A and the fins are used to make shark fin soup. It is caught both on the bottom and pelagically with gill nets, longlines, drift nets, trawls and hook and line. A major fishery for these sharks based on their vitamin A content developed along the Pacific coast. In British Columbia they were caught with sunken gill nets off the west coast of Vancouver Island and in Hecate Strait, the catch peaking in 1944 with the livers valued at $300,641. Stocks and demand had declined by 1946. They are also a common sport fish taken on rod and reel with baits set on the bottom and put up a good fight although not considered a game fish by the International Game Fish Association. They have never been reported as attacking people but will snap when captured and so should be handled with care.

southern smoothtongue

Scientific name: *Bathylagus stilbius*
(Gilbert, 1890)
Family: **Deepsea Smelt**
Other common names: California
smoothtongue
French name: leuroglosse du sud

Distribution: Found from southern British Columbia to the Gulf of California.

Characters: This species has been confused with the **northern smoothtongue** but has fewer vertebrae and differences in larval

southern smoothtongue

pigment patterns. There are probably fewer scales in this species although this character has not been thoroughly investigated (scales are easily lost). Dorsal fin rays 9–10, anal rays 12–13, pectoral rays 8–9 and pelvic rays 8–9. Colour is silvery with a dusky back and fins. Reaches about 15 cm.

Biology: One of the commonest deepsea smelts, with 16,000 being caught in a four hour, midwater tow of a three metre trawl in California. Reported down to 254 m in Canada. Food is small crustaceans.

southseas lampfish

Scientific name: *Ceratoscopelus warmingi*
(Lütken, 1892)

Family: **Lanternfish**
Other common names: none
French name: lampe d'apparat des mers du sud

Distribution: Found in the Atlantic, Indian and Pacific oceans including off the Scotian Shelf in Atlantic Canada.

Characters: This species and its relative, the **horned lampfish**, are separated from other Atlantic species by lacking photophores

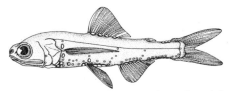

southseas lampfish

close to the dorsal body edge, the PLO photophore is well above the pectoral fin base level while the second PVO photophore is at or below the upper pectoral base level, there are 4 Prc, the first PO and two PVO photophores are not on a straight line, both males and females have caudal luminous glands composed of overlapping, scale-like structures without a black pigment border, and the fourth PO photophore is not elevated. It is distinguished from its relative by having 13–16 gill rakers and a series of scale-like, luminous glands between the pelvic fins and anus. Dorsal fin rays 13–15, anal rays 13–16 and pectoral rays 12–15. AO photophores 10–14. Vertebrae 35–38. Lateral line organs 38–39. Reaches 8.1 cm. This may be the same species as the **dogtooth lampfish**.

Biology: This species has a tropical-subtropical distribution and is carried north by the Gulf Stream. Its distribution overlaps that of the **horned lampfish**. Depth distribution is from the surface to 1550 m. There are concentrations at different levels according to season, time of day and locality as well as concentrations at several levels within each of the above. Migration rates are as high as 270 m/hour. The range of vertical migration is 700 m, one of the largest recorded for **lanternfishes**. Food is zooplankton but this lanternfish will feed on mats of diatoms, an exceptional case among its relatives. The gut in this fish is longer than related species and the ability to eat plant food is an advantage in the low-productivity oceanic environment. Life span is 1–2 years. Sexual maturity is attained at 5.5 cm. Spawning occurs from spring to fall, perhaps in winter, with a late spring peak.

Spaghetti Eel Family

Scientific name: Moringuidae
French name: anguilles spagetti

Spaghetti eels are marine, rarely freshwater, fishes of the Indo-Pacific and western Atlantic oceans. There are only about 12 species and 1 is reported from Atlantic Canada as a larva.

Also known as worm eels, these fish are extremely thin and elongate, lack scales, have a gill opening low on the flanks, dorsal and anal fins low and joined to the tail fin, posterior rounded nostrils near the eye not on the upper lips, pectoral fins absent or very small, have a lower jaw longer than the upper jaw, 9–10 branchiostegals, and the eyes small and overlain by skin. The eye enlarges in maturing males. The anus is located far posteriorly, behind the body midpoint. The heart is positioned posteriorly when compared to other eels.

The family is a member of the **Eel Order**. Spaghetti eels are common in sandy bottom areas both in tide pools and near reefs. They are burrowing eels, emerging at night, and so are seldom seen. Some are known to burrow head first.

See **ridged eel**

spark anglemouth

Scientific name: *Gonostoma bathyphilum*
      (Vaillant, 1888)
Family: **Bristlemouth**
Other common names: none
French name: gonostome étincelé

Distribution: Found in temperate to tropical waters in the North and South Atlantic Ocean including off the Atlantic coast of Canada.

Characters: This anglemouth is distinguished from its Atlantic coast relative, the **longtooth anglemouth**, by having 24–28 gill rakers, minute photophores or light organs, and a white, glandular mass in a fold of skin at the rear of the upper jaw. It is sepa-

rated from other Atlantic bristlemouths by lacking isthmus photophores, 14 or less branchiostegal rays, and the anus nearer to

spark anglemouth

the anal fin than the pelvic fin bases. Photophores: SO 1, ORB 1, OP 3, BR 9–11, IV 11–13, VAV 4–5, OA 14–16, AC 18–22, IC 32–38. Dorsal fin rays 11–15, anal rays 21–26 and pectoral rays 7–14. Overall colour is black. Ripe males have an excessively developed olfactory structure. Attains 20 cm for females and 15 cm for males.

Biology: Known from only 2 Canadian specimens taken on the south Grand Bank and northwest Flemish Cap in 1968 at 1025–1050 m. Also reported from the Greenland side of Davis Strait. Young and adults are found at 700–2700 m, depending on size. It is said to be more common below 2000 m than above this depth. There is no daily vertical migration. Sex reversal occurs at 50–100 mm standard length although some males are supermales and do not change to females. These supermales are the principal spawners and are mature at 10 cm or more. Females spawn first at 11–12 cm.

spatulate sculpin

Scientific name: *Icelus spatula*
      Gilbert and Burke, 1912
Family: **Sculpin**
Other common names: none
French name: icèle spatulée

Distribution: Found from the Bering Sea throughout the Canadian Arctic including Ellesmere Island in the north to Greenland and southward to Browns Bank in Atlantic Canada. Also on the Arctic coast of Eurasia.

Characters: This species and its relative, the **twohorn sculpin**, are distinguished from other Arctic-Atlantic sculpins by having a forked uppermost preopercular spine and row of spiny plates below the dorsal fins. It is separated from its relative by lacking spines below the lateral line pores and the lateral line is usually complete. There are 4 preopercular spines, the lower 3 directed downward. First dorsal fin spines 7–11, second dorsal fin soft rays 17–22. Anal fin with 13–18 rays. Pectoral rays 16–20. Lateral line scales 33–47. The head is covered with prickles. The male has a curved, spatulate genital papilla. Overall colour is brown to olive with darker saddles over the back or mottles. The belly is whitish. The first dorsal fin has 1–2 large blotches. The second dorsal fin is barred. The caudal and pectoral fins have thin bars. Reaches 14 cm standard length.

Biology: This sculpin is found from shallow water down to about 360 m over sand and mud at –1.85 to 7.8°C. It is common in

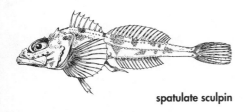

spatulate sculpin

Resolute Bay, N.W.T. Females grow larger than males. Males only reach 7.5 cm. Life span is 5 years. Food is crustaceans, worms and molluscs. Some planktonic food is taken by swimming up to 1 m off the bottom. Spawning occurs in August-September in the Bering Sea. Females carry up to 1500 eggs with diameters up to 2.5 mm.

spearfish remora

Scientific name: *Remora brachyptera*
    (Lowe, 1839)
Family: **Remora**
Other common names: swordfish sucker,
    grey marlinsucker
French name: rémora brun

Distribution: World-wide in warmer waters. From Brazil to Nova Scotia in the western Atlantic Ocean.

Characters: This remora is distinguished from its Canadian relatives by having a small disc with 14–18 laminae, rounded pectoral fins, a stout body, no stripes and 25–34 soft dorsal fin rays. Anal fin rays 22–34. The pectoral fin is flexible and has 23–27 rays. Dark brown or reddish-brown below, lighter

on the back, dorsal and anal fins pale in adults. Young have white-edged, dark dorsal and anal fins. Attains 30.4 cm.

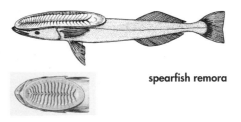

spearfish remora

Biology: This remora is found on **swordfish** and **marlins** primarily, but also on **ocean sunfish**, and in the gill cavities of these fishes and of **mantas** and **sharks**. This species is a stray off Nova Scotia but is the commonest Canadian Atlantic remora.

speckled dace

Scientific name: *Rhinichthys osculus*
    (Girard, 1856)
Family: **Carp**
Other common names: none
French name: naseux moucheté

Distribution: Found in the Kettle River system of the Columbia River basin in southeastern British Columbia south to the Colorado River system and California.

Characters: This species is distinguished by the premaxillae being protractile (lip separated by a groove from the snout), having 59–69 lateral line scales in Canada, lacking a barbel (present in some U.S. populations), mouth terminal, not overhung by snout, a dark brown peritoneum, and 5–6 branched anal rays. Dorsal fin branched rays 7–8, pec-

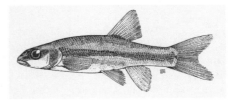

speckled dace

toral rays 13–14 and pelvic rays 8–9. The lateral line may end before the caudal fin base. Pharyngeal teeth 2,4–4,2 or 1,4–4,1.

Males have nuptial tubercles most evident on branched pectoral fin rays. The back and upper flanks are grey to grey-brown or olive with dark speckles. The lower flank and belly are yellowish to white. The midflank from the dorsal fin level to the tail base has a diffuse stripe ending in a spot. The lips, snout and lower fin bases may be orange-red. Young fish have a clearer stripe. Peritoneum brown and speckled. Reaches 5.5 cm in Canada, larger in the U.S.A., to at least 11.0 cm. This is a wide-ranging western **minnow** for which a number of subspecies have been described in response to its variability. The subspecific status of Canadian fish has not been determined.

Biology: In Canada this species is abundant in rocky habitats with moderately strong current, among stones at river edges, in shallows or under overhanging banks. Some young are found over sandy bottoms as well as rocks. Food is bottom invertebrates such as aquatic insects and some filamentous algae. Life span may be about 3 years with maturity attained at 2 years. Spawning takes place in July or later. Egg numbers reach 2000 and a diameter of about 1.3 mm. Used as a bait fish in the U.S.A. The Committee on the Status of Endangered Wildlife in Canada gave this species the status of "rare" in 1980.

speckled sanddab

Scientific name: *Citharichthys stigmaeus*
    Jordan and Gilbert, 1882
Family: **Lefteye Flounder**
Other common names: Catalina sand dab
French name: limande tachetée

Distribution: Found from southcentral Alaska to Baja California including British Columbia.

Characters: This species is separated from its only Pacific coast relative, the **Pacific sanddab**, by lacking a bony ridge over the lower eye and the lower eye diameter is about equal to snout length. The space between the eyes is flat to convex. Dorsal fin rays 75–97, anal rays 58–77. Caudal fin rounded. Gill rakers number 6–10 on the lower arch. Lateral line scales usually 52–58. Scales on both sides of the body are mostly ctenoid. The

eyed side is olive-brown to tan with fine dark speckles and spots and some larger blotches. The blind side is a dirty-white or cream. Young are grey to sand coloured with fine black speckles, almost translucent. Reaches 17 cm, but often 13 cm or less.

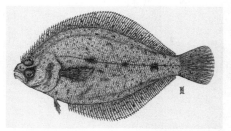

speckled sanddab

Biology: Common in shallow, sandy waters down to about 60 m, but reported down to 366 m. Food is crustaceans, worms and small fish. Life span is about 4 years. Spawning occurs from March to September in California. This small species is not commercially important in Canada. They are easy to catch with hand nets when SCUBA diving and can be maintained in a saltwater aquarium.

speckled worm eel

Scientific name: *Myrophis punctatus*
    Lütken, 1851
Family: **Snake Eel**
Other common names: none
French name: serpenton tacheté

Distribution: Found from Brazil and the west coast of Africa north to the Scotian Shelf and Georges Bank in Atlantic Canada.

Characters: Larvae are characterised by having 137–152 total myomeres (muscle blocks), 30–38 predorsal myomeres, star-shaped pigment on less than 55% of membranes between myomeres near the midline, and by lacking pigment spots under the skin just below the notochord on the tail. Nephric myomeres 53–60 and preanal myomeres

speckled worm eel

53–62. In adults, the dorsal fin origin is well in advance of the anal fin origin, about half way between the pectoral fin and the anus. The snout is pointed when viewed from above. The caudal fin is well-developed. The body is a uniform brown with the upper part bearing numerous small, brown or black spots. The iris is pale. Larvae are reported as 66–67 mm long in Canada. Adults attain 42.6 cm.

Biology: Known from Canada only as stray larvae (or leptocephali) taken at 100 m and first reported in 1988. It is one of the two most common snake eel larvae in the western North Atlantic. Adults are found in shallow water in bays and creeks, usually over soft mud. They may move in and out on flood and ebb tides each day. They are capable of regenerating lost tails.

spinecheek lanternfish

Scientific name: *Bolinichthys photothorax* (Parr, 1928)
Family: **Lanternfish**
Other common names: none
French name: lampe à joue épinée

Distribution: Found in the Atlantic, Indian and Pacific oceans. Off the coast of Nova Scotia in Canada.

Characters: This species and its relatives, the **smoothcheek** and **sidelight lanternfishes**, are distinguished from other Atlantic

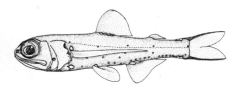

spinecheek lanternfish

coast species by lacking photophores close to the dorsal body edge, the PLO photophore is well above the pectoral fin level, the second PVO photophore is not above the pectoral fin level, there are 3 Prc photophores, caudal luminous glands are a series of overlapping, scale-like structures without a black pigment border, the fourth PO photophore is highly elevated, there are 5 VO photophores, and a crescent of whitish tissue on the rear half of the iris. This species is separated

from its relatives by having the VLO photophore at or just below the lateral line, patches of luminous tissue on top of the head and at the fin bases, 17–23, usually 18–20, gill rakers and a sharp, ventral preopercle spine. Dorsal fin rays 12–14, anal rays 13–15 and pectoral rays 12–16. AO photophores 9–11. Vertebrae 34–36. Supracaudal luminous gland with 2–3 scale-like structures and infracaudal with 2–4. Reaches 7.3 cm.

Biology: First reported from off the Scotian Shelf and off Sable Island Bank in 1988. In the Atlantic caught at 425–800 m by day and 40–500 m at night, most abundantly at 75 m. Specimens larger than 5.0 cm are not found above 125 m. This species is sexually mature at 5.0–6.0 cm.

spined pygmy shark

Scientific name: *Squaliolus laticaudus* Smith and Radcliffe, 1912
Family: **Sleeper Shark**
Other common names: dwarf shark, midwater shark
French name: squale nain

Distribution: Found world-wide usually in warmer waters but also including on the Atlantic coast of Canada, off the Scotian Shelf.

Characters: This is the only shark with a spine at the origin of the first dorsal fin (sometimes embedded in skin) but no second dorsal fin spine. Fin colour is also characteristic. Upper jaw teeth have small, narrow, smooth-edged cusps. Lower jaw teeth are larger and have a broad, blade-like form, interlock with adjacent teeth and have a cusp directed laterally. There are 22–23 upper jaw teeth and 16–21 lower jaw teeth. Denticles vary in size, are flat and have 4 points around a central depression. The belly has numerous photophores in the form of black dots. The flanks have fewer photophores and

spined pygmy shark

there are none on the back. Overall colour is dark brown to black or grey with the belly usually darkest. The mouth cavity is whitish and the fins have little or no pigment particularly on their margins. Reaches about 27 cm, the smallest known shark.

Biology: This shark is found over slopes at 200–500 m and down to at least 706 m. It migrates vertically, reaching shallower depths at night. The luminescent belly helps eliminate the shadow effect of downwelling light, rendering the shark less visible to predators from below. Food is squid, **lanternfishes**, **bristlemouths**, and **sawtailfishes**, presumably pursued on their vertical migrations. It is probably ovoviviparous with up to 12 eggs in each ovary. Males mature as small as 15 cm and females as small as 17 cm.

spinetail lanternfish

Scientific name: *Notoscopelus caudispinosus* (Johnson, 1863)
Family: **Lanternfish**
Other common names: none
French name: lanterne à queue épineuse

Distribution: Found in the warmer waters of the Atlantic, Indian and Pacific oceans including off Atlantic Canada.

Characters: This is 1 of 4 species characterised by stiff, spine-like rays at the upper and lower caudal fin bases, no large glands on the upper and lower caudal peduncle outlined by heavy black pigment, and a dorsal fin base longer than the anal fin base. It is

spinetail lanternfish

distinguished from its relatives (**Bolin's lanternfish**, **northern saillamp**, and **patchwork lanternfish**) by having only 13–15, usually 14, gill rakers. Dorsal fin rays are 24–27, usually 26, anal rays 19–21, usually 20, and pectoral rays 11–13, usually 12. Photophores: AO 6–8, usually 7, + 3–5, usually 4, total 10–12, usually 11. Adult males have a large luminous gland covering the top of the caudal peduncle divided into 6–8 seg-

ments. Reaches 13.6 cm, probably more.

Biology: Reported along the edge of the Scotian Shelf in Canada at 201–207 m in 1984. Off Bermuda, this species is found at 600–1150 m by day and at 20–100 m by night. Spawning probably occurs in autumn to winter in the western Atlantic Ocean.

spiny dogfish

Scientific name: *Squalus acanthias* Linnaeus, 1758
Family: **Dogfish Shark**
Other common names: dogfish, harbour halibut; grey-fish*, nursehound*, Folkestone beef*, flake*, rock-salmon*, huss*, (* = commercial names); piked or picked dogfish, spined dogfish, bonedogs, spurdog, mudshark, spikey jack, salmon shark, horned dogfish, sand shark, aiguillat
French name: aiguillat commun

Distribution: On the Atlantic coast from southwest Greenland and Labrador as far south as Cuba. Their extent along the Labrador coast appears to vary but they are rare north of Hamilton Inlet. They are found, rarely, as far north as Sarfanguaq, just north of the Arctic Circle in Greenland. In the Pacific they extend from the Bering Sea to Baja California and off Chile. They are also found in Europe.

Characters: The spines in the dorsal fins and the lack of an anal fin distinguish this species. The eye is oval and lacks the nictitating membrane. The spiracle is close behind the eye. The head is a little flattened and the snout is blunt. The mouth is ventral and the teeth small, each with a single cusp pointing sideways, so the inner edges of the teeth form a cutting edge across the mouth. The gill slits are short and low on the body in front of the pectoral fins. There is no subterminal notch on the tail fin.

Grey or brownish with a pale or white belly. There are some small white spots on the flanks which are particularly obvious in the young.

Pacific populations of the spiny dogfish were once considered to be a species distinct from those in the Atlantic Ocean, under the name *Squalus suckleyi*. The name "dog" fish may come from an animal unfit for human consumption but suitable for dogs and/or from the schools of dogfish which fishermen call "packs."

Up to about 130 cm and 9.1 kg for females and 96 cm and 3 kg for males. Reputedly attain 160 cm. The all-tackle, rod-caught record from Ireland weighed 7.14 kg, and was captured in 1989.

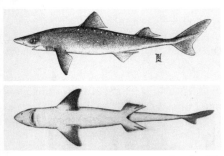

spiny dogfish

Biology: Spiny dogfish can be caught from the intertidal zone down to at least 900 m. They are reported 24 km upriver from the mouth of the St. John River, New Brunswick. Spiny dogfish arrive in Canadian inshore waters from the south off the Carolinas and Virginia each year on the Atlantic coast (June for Nova Scotia, July for the Gulf of St. Lawrence, and in August or early September for Labrador). They return south from mid-October to mid-November. Some fish may overwinter in deep holes and channels on St. Pierre Bank, the Laurentian Channel and bays on the south coast of Newfoundland but risk winter kill. They are mainly found at 3–15°C and in less than 360 m depths and will enter estuaries. Individuals tagged on both sides of the Atlantic have been recaptured on the other side and similar migrations are seen in the Pacific Ocean. A fish tagged near Fife Point, Queen Charlotte Islands was recaptured 1800 km away off Santa Cruz, California 171 days later. A dogfish was tagged on St. Pierre Bank off Newfoundland on 6 June 1963 and the tag was recovered in September 1974 when the dogfish was recaptured east of the Shetland Islands. When feeding or migrating large schools develop which are separated by sex and by size. Feeding "balls" of dogfish roil the water and create havoc among fish schools.

Food items include **herring, mackerel, eulachon, cod, pollock, salmon, ratfish, silver hake, capelin**, crustaceans such as crabs, krill and shrimps, comb jellies, jellyfish, worms and algae.

Young, or pups, are born offshore in late fall and winter and usually number 4–7, about 20–27 cm long. Maximum litter size is 25 pups but may be as low as 1. The females deliver young head first with a series of contractions similar to those in mammals. The young are released in midwater in British Columbia. The gestation period is 22–24 months, the longest for any vertebrate animal. Mating and fertilisation occur after the young are born. The fertilised eggs are enclosed in rubbery shells known as "candles." The shells dissolve after several months and the pups are free in the uterus to continue developing.

Males are mature at 6–14 years and females at 12–35 years but ages vary between populations. Individuals may live over 40 years, and possibly up to 100 years. Fully grown dogfish average 84–102 cm in length and weigh 3–5 kg.

Humans, larger sharks, some bony fishes such as **swordfish**, seals and killer whales eat this species. Spiny dogfish cause great damage to other fisheries by harrying and eating important food fishes and commercial crabs and by tangling and destroying nets. They take baits meant for **cod** and **haddock** and devour hooked or netted fish. Their numbers may cause suspension of fishing for desirable species and their name "locust of the sea" is well-deserved. Various suggestions have been advanced to protect fishing gear from "shark attack" including chemicals such as "Shark Chaser" (composed of copper acetate for its smell and black nigrosine dye to hide the gear), industrial surfactants, and the secretions from the Moses sole of the Red Sea. Other suggestions are more practicable such as shutting off the ship's engine just before setting nets (sharks are attracted to low frequency vibrations which may resemble struggling prey or predators feeding) and using dull rather than shiny, attractive hooks.

This is probably the most abundant shark and the only one which supports a fishery similar to those for bony fishes. It has the second greatest fish biomass in the Strait of Georgia after herring. Dogfish are sold for food in Europe but they have not met with the same favour in North America. Canadian catches are sold to Europe depending on the demand there. In the Atlantic the fishery is small and concentrated in south coast bays of Newfoundland. The Pacific fishery reached a peak in 1944 at 56,000 metric tons and the dogfish was the fourth most important species in Canada after Atlantic cod, lobster and herring. However, today few fishermen make even a part-time living from dogfish. The catch in the 1980s in British Columbia was about 2500 tonnes annually about half of which was landed in the U.S.A. The total Canadian catch in 1988 was 5065 tonnes. Spiny dogfish are taken in bottom trawls, on handlines and longlines and in gill nets. This is a slow growing species so it appears that the Canadian fishery will require careful management in the future.

They are a medium fat fish with a delicate white flesh which has a strong flavour. The food energy of 100 g of dogfish is 136 calories, twice that of cod. They must be processed quickly because of their urea content. They are not filleted but belly flaps are cut out, the fins removed and the body skinned. The belly flaps are exported to Germany where they are smoked as a delicacy for sale in beer gardens. The fins are frozen for the Orient shark fin soup trade and the body is sent to England where, known as rock salmon or flake, it forms part of English fish-n'-chips. Frozen dressed dogfish is sent from British Columbia to Japan and dogfish oil for sale to pharmaceutical and cosmetics industries in the U.S.A.

This species has been used extensively in immunology and biochemistry studies. The liver is used to make a houseplant fertiliser. Liver oil is use to make a fine grade of machine oil but the market for vitamin A from liver oil collapsed when the vitamin was synthesised in the laboratory. Spiny dogfish are also used extensively for teaching purposes in schools and universities.

Native peoples in British Columbia utilised this shark at least 4000 years ago. Spines were made into awls, the skin used to polish wood and the liver oil used in body paint, leather tanning and to waterproof wood. The oil was later used by Europeans in mine lamps in the Nanaimo area.

spiny dreamer

Scientific name: *Oneirodes thompsoni* (Schultz, 1934)
Family: **Dreamer**
Other common names: none
French name: queue-de-rêve épineuse

Distribution: Found in the North Pacific Ocean and Bering Sea and off the Queen Charlotte Islands.

Characters: This species of deepsea **anglerfish** is part of a group of dreamers including the **bulbous dreamer** on the Pacific coast. The females of this group are distinguished by having sphenotic spines, a deeply notched operculum posteriorly, a short and broad pectoral fin lobe, the tip of the lower jaw with a spine, the illicium or fishing rod emerging from between the frontal bones on the head, the dorsal edge of these bones being strongly curved, usually 4 anal fin rays and the caudal fin not covered by skin beyond the base. This species is distinguished from its relative on the Pacific coast by having an esca or bait with medial

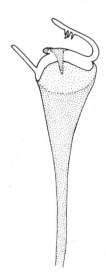

esca of spiny dreamer

appendages absent or minute. Dorsal fin rays 5–6 and pectoral fin rays 14–17. Overall colour black to dark brown with esca unpigmented in patches and the mouth cavity unpigmented. Females attain 12.8 cm.

Biology: Canadian specimens have been taken at less than 600 m but this species is reported down to 1630 m or more elsewhere. Females use the fishing apparatus to lure prey within reach.

spiny flounder

Scientific name: *Engyophrys senta* Ginsburg, 1933
Family: **Lefteye Flounder**
Other common names: none
French name: cardeau épineux

Distribution: Found from Nova Scotia south to Brazil.

Characters: This species is distinguished from other Canadian Atlantic adult **lefteye flounders** by having both pelvic fin bases

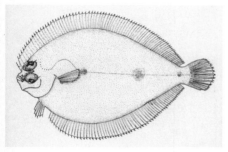

spiny flounder

short and the eyed side base on the belly midline, lateral line strongly arched over the eyed side pectoral fin, blind side pectoral fin present, spines on the ridge between the eyes, and tentacles on the eyes (lost in large males). Dorsal fin rays 74–83, anal rays 60–67, eyed side pectoral rays 8–10, and lateral line scales about 50. Lower arm gill rakers 4–7. Larvae have numerous fine spines on the head and a moderately long second dorsal fin ray. Eyed side brown with 3 blotches along the lateral line, 1 at the end of the arch, 1 at the front of the caudal peduncle and 1 in between. Blind side white in young and females but dusky in males with 3–7 dark diffuse bars on the anterior third of the body. Reaches 10 cm.

Biology: Known only from a stray larval specimen caught off the southern Scotian

Shelf in 1980. Adults only reach as far north as the Bahamas and are found at 37–183 m.

spiny-rayed fishes

The spiny-rayed fishes or Acanthopterygii are a group of fishes characterised by spiny rays at the front of the dorsal, anal and pelvic fins, a versatile and protrusible upper jaw, and by the arrangement of muscles in the gill arch region. Ctenoid scales are also characteristic, the pelvic fins are placed anteriorly on the body and the pectoral fins tend to be high on the flank. Since 60% of all living fishes fall within this group there is considerable variation in shape and form - some species have secondarily lost spines and scales for example. The term spiny-rayed fishes is often used to refer to "higher" fishes in contrast to the "lower" **soft-rayed fishes**. The Acanthopterygii are believed to be a natural group (a superorder) but the **soft-rayed fishes** is now used only as a convenient term. There are about 13 orders and 251 families in the spiny-rayed fishes world-wide, 12 orders and 102 families in Canada

See **Alfonsino Order**
Dory Order
Flatfish Order
Killifish Order
Mail-cheeked Order
Mullet Order
Needlefish Order
Perch Order
Pricklefish Order
Puffer Order
Silverside Order
Stickleback Order

spiny snailfish

Scientific name: *Acantholiparis opercularis* Gilbert and Burke, 1912
Family: **Snailfish**
Other common names: spinycheek liparid
French name: limace à joue épineuse

Distribution: Found from Kamchatka to Oregon including British Columbia.

Characters: This species is distinguished from other Canadian Pacific snailfishes by lacking the pelvic fins and adhesive disc, by having 6 branchiostegal rays, no barbels or papillae on the snout, and by having a laterally projecting opercular spine. There are no pyloric caeca. Teeth are in bands. Dorsal fin rays 45–52, anal rays 38–47, pectoral rays 20–26. The head and body are weakly pigmented except for black lips, fin margins and the belly area. The mouth and gill cavities, peritoneum and stomach are all dusky. Reaches 7.6 cm standard length.

spiny snailfish

Biology: Canadian records are from off southern Vancouver Island. Reported from 227 m down to 3609 m over its whole range. Ripe eggs number 1–6 in each female and may be almost 5 mm in diameter. Females mature at about 5.1 cm and spawning is believed to take place throughout the year.

spiny widejaw

Scientific name: *Synagrops spinosus*
Schultz, 1940
Family: **Temperate Ocean Bass**
Other common names: keelcheek bass
French name: gueulard épineux

Distribution: Found in the Atlantic Ocean off Nova Scotia, the Gulf of Mexico and Caribbean Sea and in the western Pacific Ocean.

Characters: This species is distinguished from its Atlantic coast relatives by having separate dorsal fins, by scale and fin ray counts and by having the anterior edge of the

spiny widejaw

pelvic spines serrated. First dorsal fin spines 9, second dorsal fin with 1 spine and 9 soft rays. Anal fin with 2 spines and 7–8 soft rays. Pectoral fin rays 15–18. Lateral line scales 29–32. Anterior scales of the lateral line and around the pectoral and pelvic fins are cycloid. The lateral line extends onto the caudal fin for only 1–2 pores. Gill rakers about 19. The anterior edge of the second spine of the first dorsal fin and the second spine of the anal fin are serrated. The lower jaw has 2 tooth rows in its middle section with the innermost row being 4–7 large, canines. Overall colour is brownish. The first dorsal fin margin is black. The mouth and gill cavities are blackish brown and the peritoneum is black or brown. Attains 12.2 cm standard length.

Biology: First caught between Georges and Browns Banks at 99 m in 1977, and off the Scotian Shelf in 1979 at 100–300 m as young specimens. Depth range is reported as 87–544 m.

spinycheek starsnout

Scientific name: *Bathyagonus infraspinatus* (Gilbert, 1904)
Family: **Poacher**
Other common names: none
French: astérothèque épineux

Distribution: Found from the Bering Sea to northern California including British Columbia.

Characters: This poacher is one of 4 related species called starsnouts (**bigeye, blackfin, gray** and **spinycheek starsnouts**)

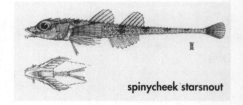

spinycheek starsnout

for an arrangement of 5 or more small spines at the tip of the snout on a moveable plate which form, supposedly, a star. Three spines point vertically and 2 laterally. The spinycheek starsnout is distinguished by having a small pit on the back of the head, plates in a single row or single pair in front of the pelvic fins, obvious spines on the bones beneath the eye, and the anal fin origin under the first dorsal fin. First dorsal fin spines are 5–8, second dorsal fin soft rays 5–7. The anal fin has 6–8 rays and the pectoral fin about 15, with the lower 5–6 rays obviously finger-like. There are 35–39 plates in the dorsal row. There are 2 large cirri at the rear of the upper jaw with several smaller cirri on the lower jaw. Gill membranes are joined to the isthmus. Olive-green to light brown on the back, paling ventrally. There are 5–6 saddles on the back and flanks. The dorsal, pectoral and caudal fins have narrow bars. Reaches 12.1 cm.

Biology: Habitat is the bottom at 18–183 m. Little appears to be known of biology for this species.

spinyfin

Scientific name: *Diretmus argenteus*
    Johnson, 1863
Family: **Spinyfin**
Other common names: none
French name: rayon épineux

Distribution: In the Atlantic and Pacific oceans but only off the Atlantic coast of Canada.

Characters: This species is characterised by a prepelvic ridge of scales and pelvic fins with a blade-like, anteriorly ridged spine and

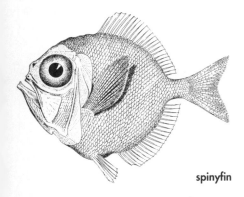

spinyfin

6 soft rays. Dorsal fin rays 25–29, anal rays 18–24 and pectoral rays 16–20. The anus is immediately in front of the anal fin. The opercular bones are striated. Overall colour is silvery with a darker blue-tinged back. The eye has a black rim. Fins are dark brown

and are black at their bases. Reaches about 40 cm although most individuals caught are much smaller.

Biology: Two specimens have been caught in Canada, 1 north of the Flemish Cap in 1956 at 640 m and 1 near Sable Island in 1971 at 475 m. Usually found between 300 and 1000 m when adult and 50 to 250 m when young, but may descend to 5000 m. Aspects of the biology are summarised in the family account.

Spinyfin Family

Scientific name: Diretmidae
French name: rayons épineux

Spinyfins are found in oceanic waters of the Atlantic, Indian and Pacific oceans. There are only 3 species in the family with 1 reported from Atlantic Canada.

These fishes lack a lateral line and the dorsal and anal fins lack spines. The pelvic fin has a laminar (blade-like) spine and 6 soft rays. Scales along the midline of the abdomen before the pelvic fins are formed into scutes giving the belly a sharp edge in some species, while others have normal scales. Body scales are ctenoid. The eyes are very large. Gill rakers are lathe-like. Jaw teeth are small.

Spinyfins are related to the **Ogrefish** and **Slimehead** families of the **Alfonsino Order**.

Adult spinyfins are found from medium to great depths (400 m or deeper) with young fish shallower. They probably migrate vertically. Food is plankton. The inner gill chamber wall of these fishes has clumps of epidermal glands which produce a secretion thought to be a defence mechanism against predators by producing a distasteful smell.

A combination of yellow eye lenses and a very sensitive ventral retina is thought to be a device to overcome the camouflage of mesopelagic animals. These animals use ventral light organs for countershading, matching the light from above to render them "invisible," rather than dark shadows against the daylight. Yellow lenses absorb short wavelength light and decrease the intensity of daylight and bioluminescence which peak in the blue part of the spectrum. Since some bioluminescence is of longer wavelength than blue daylight at depths where this fish is found, the effect may be to make the bioluminescent parts of the animals appear brighter than the daylight.

See **spinyfin**

spinyhead sculpin

Scientific name: *Dasycottus setiger*
Bean, 1890
Family: **Soft Sculpin**
Other common names: wooly sculpin, bullhead
French name: chabot à tête épineuse

Distribution: Found in the North Pacific Ocean from Japan to Washington including British Columbia.

Characters: This soft sculpin is distinguished from its Pacific coast relatives by having the spiny and soft rays in the dorsal fin the

spinyhead sculpin

same height, and clearly separated by a deep notch, large, upright spines on top of the head and a free fold to the gill membranes posteriorly over the isthmus. There are 4 preopercular spines, the 2 lowermost ones directed down or forwards and the upper 2 backward. There are 4 spines over the eyes. Cirri are large to small and numerous on the upper head and body, lateral line pores, tips of the dorsal fin spines, in a line on the caudal fin and on the eyeballs. There are prickly papillae in 1–2 interrupted rows below the dorsal fin. Dorsal fin spines 8–11, soft rays 13–16. Anal fin rays 12–16 and pectoral rays 23–26. Lateral line pores 13–16. Body colour is a pinkish-brown to grey. There are 5–6 dark saddles on the back and dark bars on all the fins except the pelvics. The belly is a brownish-white. Reaches 36 cm.

Biology: A moderately common species at 18–134 m on sand or silt bottoms among rocks. Feeds mainly on shrimps with some other crustaceans and fishes. Small rings of eggs are laid around hydroid or tubeworm stalks. Often caught by shrimp trawlers in the Strait of Georgia.

spinynose sculpin

Scientific name: *Asemichthys taylori*
Gilbert, 1912
Family: **Sculpin**
Other common names: Taylor's sculpin
French name: chabot à museau épineux

Distribution: Found in southeast Alaska, British Columbia and Washington.

Characters: This sculpin is distinguished by having 3 soft pelvic fin rays, the branchiostegal membranes united to form a free fold over the isthmus, 3 preopercular spines, the uppermost simple, scales in 1–4 rows above the lateral line, and 13–16 anal fin rays. The anal papilla is long. Nasal spine strong and recurved. First dorsal fin spines 9–11, second dorsal fin rays 14–16. Pectoral rays 16–18, fin long, and with lower 10–11 rays thickened. Lateral line scales 34–37 spiny, ridged plates. Scales are found on top of the head and around the eyes. Slender cirri are in an interrupted row on a level with the junction of the two dorsal fins below the lateral line canal. There is a short cirrus on the rear eye margin and a row of tiny spines on the upper front eyeball margin. The body is olive-brown above, paler below with 4 dark saddles across the back. The pectoral and caudal fins have narrow bars. Reaches 7.6 cm. This species was named for the Reverend G.W. Taylor, first director of the Biological Station at Nanaimo.

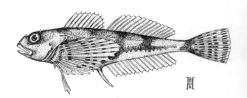

spinynose sculpin

Biology: This is a common sculpin in shallow water on shell bottoms near rocks, down to 50 m. Food is snails and clams exclusively, with up to 75% of the snail shells having holes punched in them using modifications of the vomer bone on the roof of the mouth.

spinytail skate

Scientific name: *Bathyraja spinicauda*
(Jensen, 1914)
Family: **Skate**
Other common names: spinetail ray
French name: raie à queue épineuse

Distribution: Found from Davis Strait and Labrador south to Georges Bank in the western Atlantic Ocean. Also around Greenland and in northwestern Europe and the Barents Sea.

Characters: This species is distinguished from its Canadian Atlantic relatives by having a soft and flabby snout with its cartilagi-

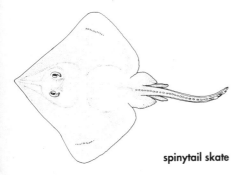

spinytail skate

nous support thin and flexible, cartilaginous supports of the pectoral fin reaching the snout tip, the upper disc surface lacks distinct spines except for a median row on the tail, and the lower surface of the disc is smooth and light coloured. There is a thorn between the dorsal fins. The tail midline has 21–26 thorns. There is a thorn between the dorsal fins. Upper jaw teeth 30–34, lower teeth 25–33. Egg cases are 13.7–14.2 cm long by 9.0–9.5 cm wide excluding the horns which are of disparate size at each end. The case has unique, numerous, close-set longitudinal ridges each with a single series of stiff rod-like structures, numbering about 30,000 on each side, which impart a velvety feel to the case. The upper disc surface is a light grey or pale brown. Lower surface whitish with grey margins, grey pelvic lobes and grey or brown blotches on the tail base. Reaches 172 cm.

Biology: Not commonly caught in Canadian waters, this species has a depth range of 120–800 m at temperatures below 7.5°C and down to –1.5°C. Food is various bottom invertebrates and also **capelin** and **thorny skates**. Development of the embryo in the egg case takes about 12 months.

splake

Male **brook trout** have been artificially crossed or bred with female **lake trout** producing a fertile hybrid known as a splake (from the older name for brook trout, *sp*eckled trout, and *lake* trout). Splake were first produced in the nineteenth century. They are also called wendigo, a name decided on by a contest sponsored by the Carling Conservation Club. The French name is moulac (from truite *mou*chettée and truite de *lac*). These hybrids have characters of both parents and are intermediate in appearance. One character used to distinguish the parents is the pyloric caeca, finger-like outgrowths of the stomach, which aid in digestion by producing enzymes. **Brook trout** have 23–55, **lake trout** 93–210 and splake 35–99. The tail fork is intermediate between the weak fork of the **brook trout** and the strong fork of the **lake trout**. The worm-track markings or vermiculations typical of **brook trout** are also found on splake. **Lake trout** have less pronounced vermiculations. Splake lack the red spots encircled by blue found on the flanks of **brook trout**, resembling **lake trout** in this character. Male breeding colours are similar to those in **brook trout** except the red belly is pinkish. The Canadian record for splake is a 9.39 kg. fish caught by Paul Thompson on Georgian Bay, Ontario, in May 1987.

Splake have been introduced to many waters in North America, particularly in Ontario, where they mature earlier than **lake trout**, before **lampreys** become a significant

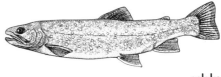

splake

scourge and yet occupy deep water and can take advantage of available food resources. They are less fecund than **lake trout** and therefore easier to control and manage and it was hoped that self-sustaining sport and commercial fisheries could be established to replace **lake trout** devastated by **sea lamprey** attacks. A second objective was to provide sport fishing in marginal inland lakes of northern Ontario. However they die earlier than the **lake trout** and are not now considered to be as successful as the parental **lake trout**. The Ontario Ministry of Natural Resources may discontinue plantings of splake in Georgian Bay and Lake Huron in the 1990s and replace them with **lake trout**. Splake may live at least 9 years, maturing at 3 years of age. They may reach 8.6 kg in weight. **Brook trout** spawn during the day, **lake trout** at night and the splake spawns during both the day and the night. Splake use sound during courtship. A click or thumps are used as threats when defending territory. Their food includes both plankton and bottom organisms such as insects.

splitnose rockfish

Scientific name: *Sebastes diploproa*
(Gilbert, 1890)
Family: **Scorpionfish**
Other common names: rosefish, lobe-jawed
rockfish, small red rockcod, red snapper,
bec-de-lièvre
French name: gueule-de-loup

Distribution: Found from southeast Alaska to Baja California including British Columbia.

Characters: This species is recognised by the 2 lobes at the tip of the upper jaw into which fits the central lower jaw lobe (hence "splitnose"). The eye is large, wider than the snout length. Dorsal fin spines 13, soft rays 11–14, usually 12 or 13. Anal fin soft rays 5–8, usually 7, second anal spine twice as thick as the third and about equal in length. Pectoral fin rays 17–19, usually 18. Gill rakers 32–37. Vertebrae 49. Lateral line pores 32–43, scale rows below the lateral line 53–57. Supraocular, coronal and nuchal head spines absent, tympanics occasionally absent, remainder strong and sharp. Overall colour rose-red to pink becoming silvery, pale pink or white on the belly. Sometimes darkly spotted or with a dark bar behind the pectoral fin but usually uniform pink. Mouth

and gill cavities rose. Peritoneum black. When captured by trawlers, the scales are knocked off, leaving white pockets rimmed by red. Reaches 46 cm.

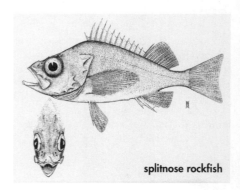

splitnose rockfish

Biology: Common offshore on soft bottoms at 91–579 m. Young fish are found in shallower water, often associated with floating kelp and become bottom dwellers after 1 year at a standard length of 40–45 mm. Food is principally krill with some salps and pteropods. Young are born in July in British Columbia, and a 37 cm female releases 255,000 fish. About half the population is mature at 26 cm for males and 27 cm for females in Canadian waters. Life span is estimated to be 80 years. Scorpionfish are difficult to age because the otoliths or "earstones" have crowded growth zones after 20 years when growth rate decreases. The decay of radioactive elements in ear-stones has been used to confirm the longevity of this species. Age structure of a population has important ramifications for managing commercial fisheries.

Spookfish Family

Scientific name: Opisthoproctidae
French name: revenants

Spookfishes or barreleyes are found in all temperate and tropical oceans. There are only about 15 species and 3 have been reported from the Pacific coast and 1 from the Atlantic coast of Canada.

Spookfishes have tubular eyes directed upwards or forwards. The dorsal fin is near the tail and an adipose fin is usually present.

Scales are large, cycloid and easily lost. Light organs may be present. The mouth is small, as are the teeth. Most species do not have a swimbladder. Both pectoral and pelvic fins can be high on the side of the body. The parietal bones do not meet in the midline. As their name indicates, they are weird in appearance including body form, which is best left to the figures to describe.

They are relatives of the **Deepsea Smelt** and **Argentine** families. The family is a member of the **Smelt Order** and has been placed in the **Salmon Order**.

These fishes are found in midwaters, usually deeper than 150 m. Eggs and larvae are pelagic. The upward or forward pointing telescopic eyes are said to enable spookfish to spot predators and prey above them. Tubular eyes appear to be more sensitive than normal ones and binocular vision enables spookfish to pinpoint their prey. Such unusual eyes may also serve to detect the distinctive light organ patterns of members of the same species, an important accomplishment when trying to find a mate in the murky depths.

Even more peculiar is the ability of some spookfish to harbour luminescent bacteria in a branch of the rectum. The light produced by these bacteria is spread over a flattened light organ on the belly, and this may play a part in species recognition by the tubular eyes.

See **barreleye**
　　binocular spookfish
　　javelin spookfish
　　winged spookfish

spoonhead sculpin

Scientific name: *Cottus ricei* (Nelson, 1876)
Family: **Sculpin**
Other common names: Rice's sculpin,
　　spoonhead muddler, cow-faced sculpin
French name: chabot à tête plate

Distribution: Found almost entirely in Canada from western Québec west through Ontario and all the Great Lakes to Manitoba, Saskatchewan, Alberta, northeastern British Columbia, down the Mackenzie River basin to the Arctic Ocean and in the southern N.W.T. South to northern Ohio and Montana.

Characters: This sculpin, and related species in the freshwater genus *Cottus*, are distinguished from the **deepwater sculpin** by the gill membrane being attached to the isthmus and the dorsal fins touching. It is separated from its relatives by having a complete lateral line without a downward bend on the caudal peduncle, the uppermost preopercular spine is long and has a marked upward curve and there is 1 pore at the chin tip. First dorsal fin spines 6–10, second dorsal rays 15–19, anal rays 11–16 (usually 12–13) and pectoral rays 14–16. There are 33–36 lateral line pores. The head is particularly flat, hence the name. Males have a short, triangular genital papilla. Young spoonheads have a dense covering of prickles.

Overall colour is light brown or olive-yellow to dark brown, with darker mottles and speckles. Northern fish are darker. The belly is white to yellowish. There may be 3 saddles under the second dorsal fin and 1 on the caudal peduncle, sometimes up to 4 other saddle-like marks. Fins have thin bars although the pelvic and anal fins are often clear. The chin may have a few speckles. Young fish have a bar at the caudal fin base. Males have a bright yellow edge to the first dorsal fin. Reaches 13.5 cm.

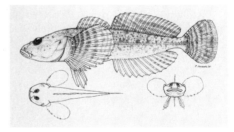

spoonhead sculpin

Biology: Spoonheads are known from small streams, especially in the north, in deep, turbid rivers and in lakes from shores down to 210 m but usually shallower at 50–90 m. It enters brackish waters in the estuaries of the St. Lawrence and Mackenzie rivers and James Bay. The dense covering of prickles in young protects them against abrasion in rocky areas. This sculpin, along with the **deepwater sculpin**, is an important indicator of glacial history. The distribution of these fishes is closely associated with the large, glacial lakes and postglacial marine inundations of the period 17,000 to 6000 years ago.

Food includes aquatic insects and crustaceans. **Lake trout, burbot, northern pike, yellow walleye, sauger** and **whitefish** eat this sculpin. Life span is 6 years.

Spawning occurs in late summer to fall in lakes although there is also evidence for May spawning in the Eastmain River, James Bay and May-July in the Great Lakes. Spawning may take place at 43 m in lakes, in lake shallows or on stream bottoms at 4–6°C. In shallow water, the male selects, and defends against other males, a site under a rock. The female is attracted by a courtship display to lay yellow or orange eggs in a mass on the undersurface of the rock. The male drives the female away. Males may spawn with at least 3 females. An egg mass may contain up to 1200 eggs. Males fan the eggs with their pectoral fins to clean and aerate them.

spotfin butterflyfish

Scientific name: *Chaetodon ocellatus*
　Bloch, 1787
Family: **Butterflyfish**
Other common names: none
French name: palhala

Distribution: From Nova Scotia south to the Caribbean Sea and Brazil, but specimens from New Jersey north are all strays from the south.

Characters: Colour is the most distinctive feature. Dorsal fin spines 12–14, soft rays 18–21. Anal fin spines 3, soft rays 15–17.

spotfin butterflyfish

Pectoral fin rays 14–16. Lateral line scales 33–40. The body is whitish on the flanks to a yellow or bronze above, with lips and fins yellowish. The dorsal, anal and caudal fins have a thin blue margin. There is a black bar margined with yellow from the nape through the eye to the bottom of the head. A yellow bar runs along the edge of the gill cover. There is a large dark spot on the base of the dorsal fin, partly spreading onto the adjacent back. Males have a small black spot at the edge of the soft dorsal fin. Young fish have a dark brown band from the dark spot at the dorsal fin base to the anal fin base. At night the large dark spot becomes very black, broad bands develop on the flank and the small black spot lightens. Reaches 20 cm.

Biology: The only Canadian specimens were collected in Musquodoboit Harbour, Nova Scotia in 1933 and Prospect Bay, N.S. in 1990 and were strays from warmer southern waters. This species rests in crevices at night. Found in shallow water in eelgrass beds, around coral and rocky reefs but also common at 40–80 m over sand. Often found in pairs or groups of 4–5.

spotfin dragonet

Scientific name: *Foetorepus agassizi*
　(Goode and Bean, 1888)
Family: **Dragonet**
Other common names: none
French name: callionyme à nageoire tachetée

Distribution: Found from Brazil north to off the Scotian Shelf and east of the LaHave Bank in Atlantic Canada.

Characters: This species can be distinguished from its relatives, the **spotted dragonet** and the **lancer dragonet**, by the preopercular spine having 2 barbs which are directed upward, and the second dorsal fin having 8 rays and the anal fin 7 rays. The first dorsal fin is about the same size as the second dorsal fin. There are 4 spines in the first dorsal fin and 20–23 pectoral fin rays. Males have the middle 2 rays of the caudal fin elongated and coloured bright yellow. Body orange-red. Fins have yellow markings. An eye-spot is found between dorsal spines 3–4. The anal fin has a black stripe bordered above and below by orange. Attains 16.5 cm.

spotfin dragonet

Biology: Known from only 3 adults in Canadian waters regarded as strays from the south. Caught at 105–220 m. Elsewhere reported down to 650 cm over sand and mud bottoms.

spotfin flounder

Scientific name: *Cyclopsetta fimbriata*
  (Goode and Bean, 1885)
Family: **Lefteye Flounder**
Other common names: none
French name: turbot à nageoires tachetées

Distribution: Found from Nova Scotia south to Guyana.

Characters: This species is distinguished from other Canadian Atlantic adult **lefteye flounders** by having both pelvic fin bases

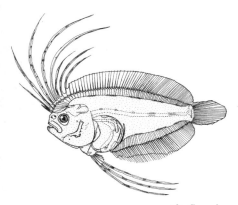

spotfin flounder

short and the eyed side base on the belly midline, the lateral line is not strongly arched over the eyed side pectoral fin, and there is a large black spot in the middle of the caudal fin and 3 smaller spots along its edge. Dorsal fin rays 78–87, anal rays 59–67, eyed side pectoral rays 11–12, and lateral line scales 65–75. Lower arm gill rakers 9–10. There are about 9 elongate dorsal fin rays in larvae. Eyed side brown. Two

large black spots are on the dorsal and anal fins. The end, and sometimes half, of the pectoral fin is blotched black. There is a large dark spot with a light central area in the middle of the caudal fin and sometimes 3 smaller spots on the rear margin. Blind side white. Reaches 38 cm.

Biology: Known only from a larval stray caught on Georges Bank in 1982. Adults are found only as far north as North Carolina, to depths of about 230 m. Adults feed on fishes and crustaceans and spawn in spring in the Gulf of Mexico. Life span is only 2.5 years.

spotfin flyingfish

Scientific name: *Cypselurus furcatus*
  (Mitchill, 1815)
Family: **Flyingfish**
Other common names: none
French name: exocet à nageoires tachetées

Distribution: Found from Nova Scotia south to southern South America and in the central Atlantic Ocean.

Characters: This species is distinguished from its Canadian relatives by having 2–5 more dorsal fin rays than anal fin rays, the anal fin origin lies under ray 3 or higher of the dorsal fin, by fin colour, and by having about 46 lateral line scales and the dorsal fin higher than long. Dorsal fin rays 12–14, usually 13, and anal rays 9–11, usually 10–11. The second pectoral fin ray is branched, ray count is 15–17. Young have 2 barbels even at 17 cm length. The back and upper flank are dark usually iridescent blue or green, the lower flank and belly silvery-grey. The dorsal fin is usually transparent except in young, where it has a dark margin. There may be

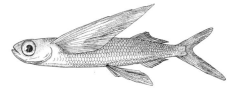

spotfin flyingfish

3–4 small spots in the dorsal and anal fins. The pectoral fin is dark deep-blue to black with a central, curving transparent or white area which is widest at the front of the fin. The pelvic fin has a dark margin and is black near the base. The anterior 2 pelvic rays are clear. The caudal fin is dusky. Young fish have dark bands on the belly, wider than the spaces between them. Reaches 36 cm.

Biology: Found in St. Margarets Bay, Nova Scotia in 1951 and 1968 with a third specimen caught off Nova Scotia in 1969 as strays from the south. This is an open ocean species which also enters bays and estuaries.

spotfin sculpin

Scientific name: *Icelinus tenuis* Gilbert, 1890
Family: **Sculpin**
Other common names: lesser filamented sculpin
French name: icéline à nageoires tachetées

Distribution: Found from northern British Columbia to Baja California.

Characters: The 5 Pacific coast members of the genus *Icelinus* are characterised by having 25 or more lateral line scales or

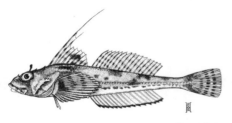

spotfin sculpin

pores, 2 pelvic fin soft rays, scales in 2 rows close to the dorsal fins and an antler-like preopercular spine. This species is separated from its relatives by the first 2 dorsal fin spines being elongate, the first the longer, and free of the membrane distally, 2 spines on the upper rear orbit, no nasal spine cirri and scale rows not reaching the end of the second dorsal fin base. The nasal spine is sharp and recurved. There are 4 preopercular spines, the uppermost with 3–5 dorsally directed spinules. First dorsal fin spines 9–11, second dorsal soft rays 16–19. Anal rays 13–17 and pectoral rays 15–17 with the lower 9 finger-like at their tips. There are 9–15 scales in each upper flank row. Lateral

line scales 38–42. There is a pair of flap-like cirri between the nasal spines and the nostril, a large branched cirrus over each eye, slender cirri on the head such as at the end of the upper jaw, and small cirri on the lateral line. The back and upper flank are brown with orange blotches and there are 4 dark saddles. The lower flank has dusky blotches. The belly is creamy white. The area between the gill opening and the pectoral base is silvery. The pectoral fin is yellowish. The dorsal, caudal and pectoral fins have brown bars and the anal fin has a dark margin. Males have a dark spot near the tip of the sixth dorsal fin spine. Reaches 14 cm.

Biology: Depth range is 33–373 m although Canadian records are only down to 128 m. Shrimp trawlers catch this species on sandy bottoms but it has also been caught in midwater by experimental fishery operations. It is not very common.

spotfin shiner

Scientific name: *Cyprinella spiloptera* (Cope in Günther, 1868)
Family: **Carp**
Other common names: silver-finned minnow, satin-finned minnow, blue minnow, steel-coloured shiner, lemonfin minnow
French name: méné bleu

Distribution: Found from Québec City west through the Great Lakes (but not in Lake Superior) and southern Ontario to North Dakota and south to Alabama and Oklahoma.

Characters: This species and its relatives in the genus *Notropis* (typical **shiners**) are separated from other family members by usually having 7 branched dorsal fin rays

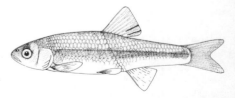

spotfin shiner

following thin unbranched rays, protractile premaxillaries (upper lip separated from the snout by a groove), no barbels, large lateral line scales (fewer than 50), and a simple, s-shaped gut. This species is separated from its relatives by the last 2–4 membranes of the dorsal fin having a black blotch. Dorsal fin branched rays usually 7, occasionally 6, anal fin branched rays 6–8, pectoral rays 12–16 and pelvic rays 7–9. Lateral line scales 34–41. Pharyngeal teeth 1,4–4,1 or 1,4–4,0. Males have large nuptial tubercles on top of the head back to the dorsal fin, on the snout and on the lower jaw in a single row. Small tubercles are present on posterior edges of scales, particularly over the anal fin, and on pectoral, pelvic, caudal and anal fin rays.

The back and flanks are silvery to bluish or olive and the belly white or silvery-white. Flank scales are outlined with pigment. There is a narrow, olive stripe on the rear half of the body positioned below the lateral line. There is a middorsal stripe passing on each side of the dorsal fin. Pectoral, pelvic and anal fins yellowish, especially in breeding males. Breeding males have an olive-yellow snout, steel-blue back, milky-white fin edges and the whole dorsal fin is blackened. Peritoneum silvery.

Formerly in the genus *Notropis*. Reaches 12.0 cm.

Biology: Spotfin shiners are usually found in rivers over sand and gravel but may also occur in lakes. It is said to be tolerant of turbidity, siltation, high temperatures (35°C) and pollution.

Food is aquatic and terrestrial insects, some plant material and even young fish. They eat eggs of their own species if these are deposited outside a crevice. Peak feeding occurred at 9 p.m. in a Michigan study. Life span is 5 years and both sexes mature at 1 year, sometimes at 2 years of age.

Spawning takes place from May to September in Wisconsin but each locality has a more restricted peak season. Up to 7474, 1.2 mm diameter, adhesive eggs are deposited on the undersurface of logs or roots, under log bark or in crevices. Males defend a spawning territory of 50 cm or more which includes a crevice. They have been seen dragging rivals away by a grip on the pelvic or anal fin when an erected fin display failed to drive away the other male. Each male may grab the other and

circle around at increasing speed until they are a blur in the water. Males make a "display pass" over crevices, swimming slowly and sometimes undulating or vibrating rapidly. Passes may occur up to 30 times before spawning. This usually attracts a female or the male may approach a school of females and hustle one toward the crevice. A male apparently presses a female against a log or crevice by positioning himself with his ventral surface touching her back, and both vibrate as eggs and sperm are shed. This can be repeated 2–3 times. When spawning on the undersurface of a log the male-female position is the same but they are upside down. Unusually for **minnows**, the male of this species makes purring noises during courtship which are believed to be recognition signals.

Spawning occurs fractionally, up to 12 times at intervals of 1–7 days. One female is reported to have laid 31 groups of eggs, each group having 10–97 eggs. Crevice spawning protects the eggs from predators, abrasion, smothering, displacement, and sunlight. Eggs laid in crevices have a better chance of being fertilised in the restricted space than those released into a current. Fractional spawning enables fecundity to be increased as not all eggs mature at the same time in a small body cavity. In addition, in crevice spawners a limited availability of crevices would restrict spawning activity unless crevices are used more than once. Fractional spawning also insures against loss of a generation to a sudden disaster.

spottail anglemouth

Scientific name: *Cyclothone braueri*
    Jespersen and Tåning, 1926
Family: **Bristlemouth**
Other common names: none
French name: cyclothone à queue tachetée

Distribution: Found in the Atlantic, Indian and Pacific oceans including off Atlantic Canada.

Characters: This species is distinguished from its Atlantic coast relatives by a lack of SO and isthmus photophores, OA photophores are present, gill rakers are 15–18, snout pigment is obvious only around the nostrils and 6–7 OA photophores. Photophores:

ORB 1, OP 2, BR 8–10, usually 9, IV 3 + 10, VAV 4, AC 13–15, IC 29–31. Scales are absent. Gill filaments are fused. Dorsal fin

spottail anglemouth

rays 12–15, anal rays 18–20. The body colour is off-white with some star-shaped pigment spots on the back. Less than 30 pigment spots on top of the head, often as few as 1–2. Reaches 3.9 cm.

Biology: About 6 specimens have been caught in 1977–1979 off the Scotian Shelf and in the Laurentian Channel, the first records for Canada reported in 1988. Adults are generally found at 200–900 m, but larvae are in 10–50 m. This is an abundant species and an important food for many predators in the midwaters of the ocean. Food is mainly copepods. The spawning season is April-October and eggs number 100–900 with a diameter of 0.5 mm. The number of eggs increases in higher latitudes.

spottail shiner

Scientific name: *Notropis hudsonius*
(Clinton, 1824)
Family: **Carp**
Other common names: spawneater, sucking carp
French name: queue à tache noire

Distribution: Found from southwestern Québec, most of Ontario, Manitoba, Saskatchewan, Alberta and Great Slave Lake tributaries and the Mackenzie River system. In the U.S.A. south to Georgia in the east, but absent south of the Great Lakes, and to Iowa and Missouri in the west.

Characters: This species and its relatives in the genus *Notropis* (typical **shiners**) are separated from other family members by usually having 7 branched dorsal fin rays following thin unbranched rays, protractile premaxillaries (upper lip separated from the snout by a groove), no barbels, large lateral line scales (fewer than 50), and a simple, s-

shaped gut. It is separated from its relatives by having 7 (rarely 6 or 8) anal fin branched rays, a subterminal mouth and a diffuse lateral stripe ending in a spot at the caudal fin base. Dorsal fin branched rays 7–8, pectoral rays 12–17 and pelvic rays 7–8. Lateral line scales 34–42. Pharyngeal teeth 2,4–4,2 with a wide range of variations, hooked at the tip. Breeding males have tubercles on the top of the head, up to 10 lining scales on the back, occasionally on the branchiostegal rays, and on pectoral fin rays 7–10.

The back is yellowish, pale green or olive and the belly silvery-white. The tail spot may be covered by the silvery flank colour but is obvious in young and dead fish. Fins are transparent. The lower caudal fin rays are whitish. Peritoneum silvery with scattered dark melanophores. Reaches 14.7 cm total length.

spottail shiner

Biology: Spottail shiners are found in large lakes and rivers with slow to moderate current. They may enter brackish water. The habitat bottom is sand, gravel, mud or silt and it has been caught as deep as 46 m. There is a movement into shallow water at night. In winter there is a retreat to deep water with individuals scattering. They can survive summer temperatures up to 35°C. They occur in dense schools, usually in shallow water, with larger fish below smaller fish. The tail spot is a recognition mark enabling other school members to recognise conspecifics and position themselves appropriately in the school. The spot may also resemble an eye to predators which strike at the wrong end and miss as the spottail darts away. A whole school of these eyes must be very confusing. The disappearance of these spots as the shiner attempts to escape will also trigger neighbouring members of the school to scatter.

Food includes plankton, aquatic and surface insects, molluscs, algae and eggs and fry of their own species. It is a very important food for all predatory fish found with them in Canada. Life span is 5 years. Males grow more slowly than females. Some fish mature at age 1 and all are mature at age 3.

Spawning occurs over sand in May to July in Canada, the timing depending on locality and its environmental conditions. It may be delayed until September in Wisconsin after a cold spring. In Iowa there are spawnings in May-June and in August. Yellow eggs number up to 8898 with a diameter of 1.0 mm. There are large spawning groups near stream mouths over gravel riffles or on sandy shoals.

This **shiner** has been used as a bait fish in Ontario and as a biomonitor fish to determine the distribution through time and space of organochlorine contaminations (PCBs, mirex, dioxin and others) in the Niagara River, Lake Erie and Lake St. Clair.

spotted dragonet

Scientific name: *Diplogrammus pauciradiatus*
 (Gill, 1865)
Family: **Dragonet**
Other common names: none
French name: dragonnet à trois épines

Distribution: From the Caribbean Sea north to off Browns Bank in Atlantic Canada.

Characters: This species can be distinguished from its relatives, the **spotfin dragonet** and the **lancer dragonet**, by the second dorsal fin having 6 rays and the anal fin 4 rays, and by the preopercular spine having 3 barbs on the upper side. The first dorsal fin has 4 spines. Pectoral fin rays number 16–19. There is a fleshy keel on the lower

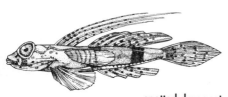

spotted dragonet

flank posteriorly running from the vent to the caudal fin. Males have a high first dorsal fin. Body mottled, overall tan, with reticulations ventrally in males. The keel bears a row of dark brown spots. The pelvic membrane has metallic centred dark rings. Attains 5 cm.

Biology: Canadian records are of a stray larva caught in 1977. Adults are found in seagrass beds and on sandy bottoms. They are sexually mature at 11–15 mm.

spotted gar

Scientific name: *Lepisosteus oculatus*
 (Winchell, 1864)
Family: **Gar**
Other common names: shortnose gar, billfish
French name: lépisosté tacheté

Distribution: Found in the Mississippi River and Great Lakes basins and Gulf of Mexico coastal rivers from Texas to Florida. In Canada known from Lake Erie, the Detroit River and Lake St. Clair.

Characters: This species is distinguished from its relative, the **longnose gar**, by the short, broad snout 6–8 times longer than mini-

spotted gar

mum width, 53–59 lateral line scales and spots on the head, body and fins. Gill rakers 15–24. Dorsal fin rays 6–9, anal rays 7–9, pectoral rays 9–13 and pelvic rays 5–6, usually 6. Young fish, less than 25 cm, have dorsal and ventral filaments on the caudal fin. The swimming young fish appears to be moved by a propeller as these filaments vibrate rapidly. Adults are brown with darker spots. Some fish are dark between the spots and appear black. Young fish (less than 15 cm) lack the heavy spotting and have a dark brown, broad stripe along the middle of the back, a dark midlateral stripe with a straight upper margin below a narrow reddish stripe and a chocolate-coloured belly. Reaches 111.8 cm and 13 kg. The world, all-tackle angling record weighed 3.96 kg and was caught in 1987 in the Tennessee River, Alabama.

Biology: This species is rarely encountered in Canada and its biology here has not been investigated. It is known from only 4 locations and 13 specimens collected since 1913. Food is fishes such as **yellow perch** and **Carp Family** members, taken usually in the morning. Females are larger and live longer than males, to at least 18 years. Males are mature at 2–3 years old, females at 3–4 years. Spawning occurs in spring in weedy, warm shallows. Eggs are poisonous although the flesh can be safely eaten. Young grow rapidly, at 2.1 mm per day. They have an adhesive disc on the snout which enables them to cling to vegetation. The Committee on the Status of Endangered Wildlife in Canada approved the status of "rare" for this gar in 1983.

spotted hake

Scientific name: *Urophycis regia*
    (Walbaum, 1792)
Family: **Cod**
Other common names: spotted codling,
    phycis tacheté
French name: merluche tachetée

Distribution: Found from the Scotian Shelf of Nova Scotia south to Florida and the eastern Gulf of Mexico.

Characters: This species and its relatives, the **longfin, red** and **white hakes**, are distinguished from other Arctic-Atlantic **cods** by having 2 dorsal and 1 anal fin, no snout barbels, pelvic fins with only 2, long, filamentous rays, and no canine teeth on the lower jaw and vomer bone in the roof of the mouth. The spotted hake is distinguished from its relatives by the pelvic fin filaments not reaching the end of the anal fin, no elongate dorsal fin ray, the lateral line has white spots and the first dorsal fin is black dorsally with a white edge. First dorsal fin rays 8–9,

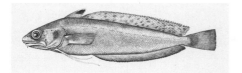

spotted hake

second dorsal rays 46–51, anal rays 43–49. Scales along flank 90–95. Overall colour is brownish. There are dark spots around the

eye and 2 dusky bars from the eye back to the pectoral fin. There is a white streak along the flank and the lateral line is alternately black and white. Reaches 40 cm

Biology: Uncommon in Canada with less than 10 records, such as off Halifax and near Sable Island. Found from near shore down to 420 m. Studies on this hake in North Carolina show a northward movement when temperatures warmed above 22°C. Food includes **gaspereau, menhaden, sand lances**, squid and crustaceans. Spawning takes place in winter. Estuaries in the U.S.A. are important nursery areas. Eggs are up to 0.8 mm in diameter. This hake has little commercial value.

spotted lanternfish

Scientific name: *Myctophum punctatum*
    Rafinesque, 1810
Family: **Lanternfish**
Other common names: none
French name: lanterne ponctuée

Distribution: Found in the North Atlantic Ocean and Mediterranean Sea. In Canada from off central Labrador throughout Atlantic waters even in the Gulf of St. Lawrence and coastal Newfoundland, south to Cape Hatteras.

Characters: This species and its Atlantic coast relatives, the **lunar, roughscale** and **metallic lanternfishes**, are distinguished by

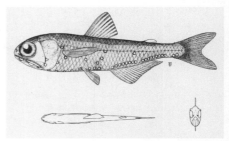

spotted lanternfish

lacking photophores near the dorsal body edge, the PLO photophore is above the upper pectoral fin base while the second PVO photophore is below this base, there are 2 Prc and 1 Pol photophores, the PVO photophores are not horizontal but inclined while the VO series is level, the SAO series is straight or almost so, and the first SAO is behind the third VO. This species is separated from its relatives by having 7–10 AOp photophores with 3–4 over the anal fin base. Dorsal fin rays 13–14, anal fin rays 20–22 and pectoral rays 13–14. Total gill rakers 22–27. AO photophores 14–18. Lateral line organs 43–44. Adult males have 1–4 overlapping scale-like structures edged narrowly with black in the supracaudal luminous gland. The gland begins developing at 3.5 cm. Adult females have 2–5 heart-shaped, overlapping patches in the infracaudal gland. The gland appears at 3.8–4.0 cm. Females may also have 1–2 supracaudal patches. Reaches 10.7 cm.

Biology: This species favours boreal and temperate waters and is a common Canadian species. Fish caught here are thought to be expatriates, specimens which do not breed in Canadian waters and which are all very large fish, with no post-larvae in the population. These expatriate fish show irregular and regressive growth in scales, otoliths and subopercles and caudal luminous glands are less developed than in other populations. These features suggest the fish are under stress and this is not their optimal habitat. However more recently juveniles have been caught in the expatriate area suggesting reproduction may occur. Differences in gland development may be owing to length at which maturity occurs in discrete populations. Depth range generally during the day is 100–1000 m, most abundantly at 700–800 m. At night from the surface to 800 m. This species is an important food for **cod** and **swordfish**. Maturity is attained at about 5.0 cm and fecundity is up to 12,968 eggs.

spotted ratfish

Scientific name: *Hydrolagus colliei*
   (Lay and Bennett, 1839)
Family: **Chimaera**
Other common names: rabbitfish, spookfish, elephant-fish, goatfish, water hare
French name: chimère d'Amérique

Distribution: Found from Alaska to Baja California including British Columbia.

Characters: This is the only chimaera on the Pacific coast of Canada and is easily recognised by the blunt, rabbit-like snout, scaleless, slippery skin, plate-like teeth and,

in males, the claspers on the head and pelvic fins. The upper jaw is divided in front revealing the nostrils. The first dorsal fin has 1 serrated spine and 10 soft rays. The second dorsal fin is connected to the first by a low fold of tissue which lacks rays. The second dorsal fin has a deep notch in the centre. Males have a spiny club on the head, the clasper, which folds into a depression. Clasping organs on each side of the vent are retractile and very sharp. The pelvic fin claspers are serrate. A lateral line is obvious and wavy on the flank, and extends onto the head. Overall colour is silvery or brownish with light spots on an iridescent green or golden background. The caudal and dorsal fins have a dark margin. The eye is emerald green. A general metallic sheen on the lower flank, bronze or silvery, is caused by platelets in the skin reflecting light. It was first caught off Monterey, California during the voyage of H.M.S. *Blossom* in the Pacific during 1825–1828. It is named for Mr. Collie, the ship's naturalist, who was first to dissect and describe it. Reaches 97 cm. *Hydrolagus* literally means "water rabbit", an illusion perhaps to the rounded snout and tooth plates reminiscent of a rabbit.

spotted ratfish

Biology: Abundant in Canada between 92 and 366 m, but also down to 913 m, and not uncommon in shallow water where its bizarre appearance as a fish with "legs" attracts comment. It should be handled with care as the clasping organs can inflict a nasty cut and the dorsal spine is venomous. This ratfish moves mostly with the aid of its large pectoral fins. Food includes clams, squids, echinoderms, crustaceans and fishes, detected by smell. Cannibalism may occur. Males grow more slowly than females. Respiration through the nostrils is as rapid as 100 per minute. Egg capsules are released throughout the year, but principally in late summer to early autumn. There is a courtship involving colour changes and a "dance." Egg capsules are brown and 12.5 cm long. The capsule takes 18–30 hours to be extruded and remains attached to the female by a filament for 4–6 days. Later, filaments attach the capsule to bottom items or the capsule is stuck vertically in the mud. Spotted ratfish are often seen by SCUBA divers. It is a nuisance to anglers and commercial fishermen, taking baits and clogging nets meant for more valuable species. The liver has been used to make a fine grade of machine oil. It is said to leave an unpleasant aftertaste when eaten.

spotted snailfish

Scientific name: *Liparis callyodon*
(Pallas, 1814)
Family: **Snailfish**
Other common names: Pallas's liparid
French name: limace tachetée

Distribution: Found from the Bering Sea to Oregon including British Columbia. Also in the Alaskan Beaufort Sea.

Characters: This species is distinguished from its Pacific coast relatives by having an adhesive disc with its rear edge behind the level of the gill slit, 2 pairs of nostrils, gill slit above the pectoral fin, or at most reaching the level of the first pectoral ray, dorsal fin with 2 lobes and no white bar across the caudal fin base. Dorsal fin rays 33–35, anal

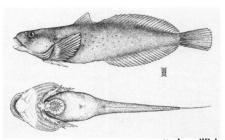

spotted snailfish

rays 25–27 and pectoral rays 28–31. Up to 7 lower pectoral rays are partly free of the membrane, elongate and they fold back onto

the rest of the fin. Teeth are trilobed and in bands. Pyloric caeca 42–66. The body and fins are olive-brown to olive, tawny, or purplish, and paler on the belly. The back and flanks have scattered, small, dark spots. Fin margins are black. Reaches 12.7 cm.

Biology: This species is common in tide pools, hiding under rocks. It eats mussels whole as well as crustaceans and snails. Egg masses contain up to 409 eggs with preserved diameters of 1.7 mm.

spotted sucker

Scientific name: *Minytrema melanops*
(Rafinesque, 1820)
Family: **Sucker**
Other common names: striped sucker, black sucker, sand sucker, speckled sucker, spotted redhorse, corncob sucker, winter sucker
French name: meunier tacheté

Distribution: Found in the southern and western basins of lakes Huron, Erie and St. Clair south to the Gulf of Mexico in the Mississippi River basin and east to Atlantic drainages of the U.S.A. Found in the basins of the Thames and Sydenham rivers, Lake St. Clair and Lake Erie off Point Pelee, in southern Ontario.

Characters: This species is identified by its short dorsal fin, lateral line being present but incomplete in places and not very obvious (absent in young), and the pigment pattern of about 8–12 horizontal flank rows of dark brown to black pupil-sized spots, one to each scale. The small mouth is overhung by the snout. The lips have fine plicae, and the lower lips meet at about a 90° angle and the cleft between them is incomplete. Dorsal fin rays 10–12, anal rays 7, pectoral rays about 16 and pelvic rays 9–10. Scales number 42–47 in the lateral line. Pharyngeal teeth are short, flat tipped and spaced widely on the arch. The gut is long with 4–5 coils. Males develop nuptial tubercles on the anal fin, caudal fin, on the snout top and head, including the lower surface, but sparse on the lower cheek. The back is dark green to brown, the flanks and side of the head copper to bronze-green sometimes silvery, and the belly is silvery to milky-white overlain by copper. Paired fins are dusky or white, other fins grey to olive. The pectoral fin can be orange. There is a dark blotch at the dorsal fin base. The lower caudal fin lobe has a black margin. Spawning males have a grey-brown midflank stripe bordered above by a greyish-pink stripe, an upper flank dark lavender stripe and the back has light lavender tinges. Flank spots are absent or weakly developed posteriorly in young fish. Peritoneum white. Reaches 51.0 cm.

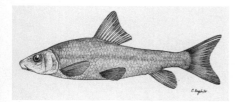

spotted sucker

Biology: This **sucker** is found in lakes, ponds and streams with firm sediments. It avoids turbid conditions and clay or silt bottoms according to some authors but others state that it can be found on soft sediments and slightly to heavily turbid water. It is sensitive to industrial pollution. Food is detritus and associated invertebrates including crustaceans and molluscs, and algae. Young fish feed on zooplankton but switch to bottom feeding at about 2.5 cm. Life span is about 8 years. Maturity is attained at age 3. Spawning takes place in the spring (May) at 12–19.5°C after a run up streams to shallow riffles. Males defend a territory against other males. Two or more males swim with any female entering the riffle, nudging her with their snouts. The female settles to the bottom with a male on each side, the males press against the rear part of her body, they quiver for 2–6 seconds and rise to the surface as eggs and milt are shed. Eggs are demersal and adhesive, 3.1 mm in diameter just before hatching. It is a good food fish (for a **sucker**) but is rarely eaten. Ontario catches were sold for agricultural purposes. This species was assigned the status of "rare" in 1983 by the Committee on the Status of Endangered Wildlife in Canada.

spotted wolffish

Scientific name: *Anarhichas minor* Olafsen, 1772
Family: **Wolffish**
Other common names: leopardfish, spotted codfish
French name: loup tacheté

Distribution: Found in the North Atlantic Ocean and adjacent Arctic waters. In Canada from the Davis Strait and Baffin Island, the Grand Bank and Scotian Shelf south to Massachusetts.

Characters: This wolffish is separated from its Arctic-Atlantic relatives in Canada by colour and by teeth on the palatine bones at the margins of the roof of the mouth extending beyond the vomer teeth in the centre of the mouth. Dorsal fin spines 74–80, anal rays 45–47, vertebrae 76–79. Caudal fin rays 20–23, usually 21. Colour is yellowish or pale olive to brown with small to large brown-black spots on the head, upper flank, dorsal and caudal fins. Young have 5–9 dark bands on the body. Reaches about 180 cm. The world, all-tackle angling record was caught in 1982 at Holsteinsborg, Greenland and weighed 23.35 kg.

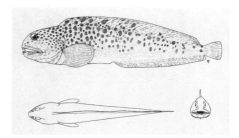

spotted wolffish

Biology: This species is found in deeper waters over mud or sand bottoms down to 600 m in Atlantic Canada, at temperatures below 5°C. Arctic populations elsewhere are known to be as shallow as 25 m. It does not school. Food includes various hard-shelled crustaceans, molluscs and most importantly echinoderms, but also some worms, algae, and fish, including those discarded from trawlers. **Cod** and **Greenland shark** are known to eat this wolffish. Spotted wolffish live to be 21 years.

Females are mature a year earlier than males at 48–62 cm in some populations and 75–80 cm in others, with all mature at sizes greater than 92 cm. Males mature at 53–71 cm. Spawning in the Newfoundland area is believed to take place in late autumn or early winter according to some authors or in summer in the Northwest Atlantic generally according to other authors. Up to 50,000 eggs of 6 mm diameter are laid in clumps on the sea bed. Larvae are pelagic and become bottom dwellers at 4–7 cm. This species is not part of a directed commercial fishery but is caught along with **Atlantic wolffish** and used as food. The skin is made into leather.

spotted wrymouth

Scientific name: *Cryptacanthodes maculatus*
   Storer, 1839
Family: **Wrymouth**
Other common names: ghostfish, bastard
   cusk, congo eel
French name: terrassier tacheté

Distribution: Found from southern Labrador to off New Jersey.

Characters: The eel-like body with a blunt head, eyes high on the head, very long, low, spiny dorsal fin confluent with the cau-

spotted wrymouth

dal and anal fins and the spotted body are characteristic. There are 73–77 spines in the dorsal fin and 45–50 anal fin rays. The caudal fin is pointed. No pelvic fins. Scales are absent and the lateral line is not evident. The body is brown or reddish-brown with 3 rows of dark brown to black spots irregularly aligned along the whole flank. The belly is grey-white. The dorsal fin is covered in spots and the caudal and anal fins are more lightly spotted. The top of the head, snout and lips have small black spots. Attains 91 cm.

Biology: Found in burrows in soft mud from the shallows to 110 m. The burrows may be dug to form a series of connecting tunnels about 3–8 cm below the surface, and up to 5 cm in diameter. There is a centrally-placed low mound with a broad, funnel-shaped depression which is the main entrance to the burrow system. Most branches open to the surface but some are blind. The fish emerge from the branches and the main entrance is probably the first point of entry into the mud. Waving motions of the body in the burrow maintain a flow of water and oxygen. Food is crustaceans and possibly fishes. Spawning probably occurs in winter or early spring. Some specimens are albinos.

spring cisco

Scientific name: *Coregonus* sp.
Family: **Salmon**
Other common names: none
French name: cisco de printemps

Distribution: Known only from Lac des Écorces, Québec, north of Ottawa.

Characters: This species is essentially the same as the **lake cisco** but has a shorter length, smaller head, deeper body, narrower and shorter caudal peduncle, and fewer gill

spring cisco

rakers (39–47, mean 42.7 compared to neighbouring **lake cisco** at 46–57, mean 50.5). Dorsal and anal fin rays and lateral line scale counts are smaller on average than in **lake cisco**. Pelvic fin ray counts are larger on average. Reaches 27.6 cm.

Biology: Most specimens have been caught at 20–30 m. This **cisco** prefers cold, deeper waters over a silt bottom. Food is plankton. Sexual maturity is attained at age 3. Life span is 11 years but few fish live beyond age 8. Spawning occurs in deep water (>20 m) in May and early June rather than in shallow areas in fall as in **lake cisco**. Spawning is at relatively high temperatures, up to 7°C. Eggs are 2.1 mm in diameter on average and fecundity is within the limits recorded for **lake cisco**. Larvae first appear at the end of July. Conditions in Lac des Écorces are deteriorating through eutrophication so this species is in danger. Spring spawning **cisco** are reproductively isolated from the fall spawning **lake cisco**. This is the definition of a species since the two forms never meet reproductively and have separate genetic histories. There are reports of other spring spawning **ciscoes** in Ontario which raise interesting questions on **cisco** evolution and speciation. The genus *Coregonus*, which includes **ciscoes** and **whitefishes** shows great variability in biology and anatomy which have yet to be satisfactorily explained and categorised (see also **Opeongo** and **Squanga whitefishes**). The spring cisco was assigned the status of "vulnerable" in 1992 by the Committee on the Status of Endangered Wildlife in Canada.

Squanga whitefish

Scientific name: *Coregonus* sp.
Family: **Salmon**
Other common names: none
French name: corégone de Squanga

Distribution: Known only from Dezadeash, Little Teslin, Teenah, Squanga and possibly Tatchun lakes in the Yukon. The latter 4 lakes are in the Yukon River basin and the first is in the Alsek River basin. A population in Hanson Lake was poisoned in 1963 for planting **rainbow trout**.

Characters: Squanga whitefish are very similar to **lake whitefish** but have more gill rakers (e.g. 30–37 in Dezadeash Lake for Squanga whitefish, 20–26 for **lake whitefish** although counts overlap in some of the

Squanga whitefish

lakes), longer and more closely spaced rakers, smaller heads and eyes (but larger in Little Teslin Lake Squanga whitefish), shorter fin origins and shorter fins. Body proportion differences vary between lakes within the Squanga whitefish, perhaps owing to differing environmental influences. Gill raker number differences are large enough to indicate genetic differences. There are also biochemical genetic differences. Gonads are similar in size although Squanga whitefish are smaller overall than **lake whitefish**. Males have highly developed tubercles on the head and body scales. Much of the difference between Squanga and **lake whitefish** in anatomy and biology is associated with plankton feeding. Biochemical data show that Squanga whitefish in these lakes have independent origins with at least 2 lineages and cannot be formally described as a distinct species. However they are unique populations and deserve protection and further study. Squanga is derived from the local Indian name for the fish. Usually up to about 28.0 cm fork length.

Biology: This **whitefish** is found near the surface in summer over deep water and near the bottom while **lake whitefish** are in shallows or near the bottom in deep water. Food is reflected in these distributions and in raker morphology being mostly crustacean zooplankton for Squanga whitefish and mostly bottom foods for **lake whitefish**. Potential fish predators are limited to **northern pike, lake** trout and burbot. Life span is 7 years for Squanga whitefish, 10 years for **lake whitefish**. Maturity is attained at ages 2–5 compared to age 6 for **lake whitefish**. Spawning occurs in inlet and outlet streams in November and December, apparently at a different time from **lake whitefish**. Spawning behaviour is unknown in detail. The Committee on the Status of Endangered Wildlife in Canada gave this species the status of "rare" in 1988.

square headlightfish

Scientific name: *Diaphus effulgens*
  (Goode and Bean, 1896)
Family: **Lanternfish**
Other common names: none
French name: lampe-de-tête carrée

Distribution: Found in the Atlantic, Indian and Pacific oceans off the Scotian Shelf and Flemish Cap in Atlantic Canada.

Characters: This species and its relatives, the **bouncer**, **eventooth**, **flashlight**, **straightcheek**, and **Taaning's headlightfishes** and

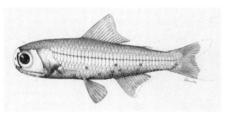

square headlightfish

the **doormat** and **slanteye parkinglightfishes**, are separated from other Atlantic coast lanternfishes by not having photophores near the dorsal body edge, the PLO photophore is well above the upper pectoral fin base level while the second PVO photophore is at or below this level, there are 4 Prc photophores, the PO and two PVO photophores form a straight, ascending line as do the first 3 VO photophores, supracaudal luminous glands are absent, and there is more than 1 pair of luminous head organs. This species is separated from its relatives by having the So photophore absent, vomer with a small, round to oval patch of teeth on each side, Dn photophore well-developed in a deep cup, directed forward and equal to or larger than

the nasal rosette, Dn photophore well above upper edge of eye, and total gill rakers 17–22. Dorsal fin rays 15–17, anal rays 14–16 and pectoral rays 11–13. AO photophores 10–12. Lateral line organs 36–37. Only the Dn "headlight" or photophore is present in fish up to 15.5 mm long, the Vn begins to develop at 16 mm and is large by 30 mm and the Ant begins to develop at 24–25 mm. Reaches at least 15.0 cm. The square headlightfish was described from a specimen taken out of the stomach of a **cod** caught on Browns Bank.

Biology: This species is subtropical and Canadian specimens are brought here by the Gulf Stream. Depth distribution in the Atlantic Ocean is 325–700 m by day, maximum abundance being 450–500 m and 40–250 by night, maximum abundance being 100 m. Larger fish, over 10.0 cm may not migrate. Life span is at least 2 years and a spawning peak occurs in late spring.

squarenose helmetfish

Scientific name: *Scopelogadus beani*
  (Günther, 1887)
Family: **Ridgehead**
Other common name: none
French name: heaume à nez carré

Distribution: Found in the Atlantic, southern Indian and western South Pacific oceans. Found off the Flemish Cap in Atlantic Canada.

Characters: This species, and the related **twospine bigscale**, are distinguished from other ridgeheads by having less than 17 scale rows from the nape to caudal fin base and no cheek scales. This species has more than 26 gill rakers usually. Dorsal fin with 2 spines and 10–11 soft rays. Anal fin with 1 spine and 7–9 rays. Pectoral rays 14–16. Overall colour is brownish. Attains 13.5 cm.

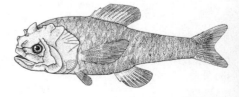

squarenose helmetfish

Biology: Fairly common in Atlantic Canada in experimental midwater trawls. Their occurrence in Canadian waters is associated with the Gulf Stream. Adults are usually found below 800 m while young may ascend to 150 m.

Squaretail Family

Scientific name: Tetragonuridae
French name: tétragonures

Squaretails are found in tropical to temperate waters world-wide. There are only 3 species.

There are 2 species in Atlantic Canada and 1 of these is also found on the Pacific coast.

The body in these fishes is more elongate than in related families. Pelvic fins are present. There are 2 dorsal fins with 10–21 short spines and 10–17 soft rays respectively. The second dorsal fin folds into a groove, as do the pelvic fins. The anal fin has 1 spine and 9–17 soft rays. There are 2 keels modified from scales on each side of the squarish caudal peduncle. The scales are unique. They are in curved rows and each scale is heavy, hard, strongly attached and bears fine ridges. The lower jaw is shovel-like with knife-like teeth and fits into the upper jaw. There are teeth on the roof of the mouth. There are 5–6 branchiostegal rays.

This family is related to the **Ruff**, **Driftfish**, **Sequinfish** and **Butterfish** families, all of which share toothed, sac-like outgrowths of the gut. If the gill cover is lifted, the sacs may be seen behind the last gill arch. Squaretails are sometimes placed in the **Butterfish Family**. The family is a member of the **Perch Order**.

Squaretails are believed to eat various jellyfishes and no other foods, using their peculiar mouth. They are oceanic with adults in deeper water and young near the surface associated with jellyfish. Squaretails may have poisonous flesh as a consequence of eating stinging jellyfish, but this has not been fully confirmed.

See **bigeye squaretail**
    smalleye squaretail

star-eye lightfish

Scientific name: *Pollichthys mauli*
    (Poll, 1953)

Family: **Lightfish**
Other common names: none
French name: cyclothone étoilée

Distribution: Tropical oceanic waters mainly but also in Atlantic Canada.

Characters: This species is distinguished from its Canadian Atlantic relatives by having the end of the dorsal fin opposite or

star-eye lightfish

behind the anal fin origin, a photophore or light organ below the rear eye margin and 18–21 photophores over the anal fin and back to the tail. There are 13–15 photophores over the anal fin. The anal fin is much longer than the dorsal fin, with 22–30 rays. The eyes are normal and the adipose fin has a short base. The back is dark and the flanks silvery. Reaches 6 cm in standard length.

Biology: First caught in Canadian waters on the Scotian Shelf in 1977. Juveniles and adults are found at 200–600 m rising to the upper 200 m at night. The first reported Canadian specimen was caught, unusually, at the surface during the day. Food is small crustaceans. Spawning occurs in summer.

stargazing seadevil

Scientific name: *Ceratias uranoscopus*
    Murray in Thomson, 1877
Family: **Seadevil**
Other common names: none
French name: pêcheur uranoscope

Distribution: Found world-wide including off Atlantic Canada.

Characters: This deepsea **anglerfish** is distinguished from its relatives the **twoclub**

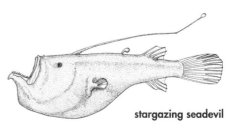

stargazing seadevil

angler and the **warted seadevil** by having 2 fleshy knobs on the back in front of the dorsal fin and no appendages on the end of the esca or bait. Vomer teeth on the roof of the mouth are absent. Females are black overall. The esca is dark except at the tip. Females attain 24 cm.

Biology: Collected from southeast of Nova Scotia in August 1913. Found between 95 and 4000 m but most specimens are collected in the 500–1000 m range.

starry blacksmelt

Scientific name: *Bathylagus compsus*
   Cohen, 1958
Family: **Deepsea Smelt**
Other common names: none
French name: garcette étoilée

Distribution: Found from the Scotian Shelf of Atlantic Canada south to Bermuda and the Bahamas.

Characters: This species is distinguished from its Atlantic Canadian relatives by having a gill opening extending at least half way up the side of the body and by having 19–21 anal fin rays. Lateral line scales about 40. Dorsal fin rays 10–11 and pectoral rays 9. Overall colour in preservative is a yellow-brown. The snout, operculum and around the eye are dark brown. Flanks, iris and operculum have a silvery sheen. The fins and abdomen of adults are reported to have luminous material. Reaches 9.4 cm standard length.

starry blacksmelt

Biology: Known in Canada from only 2 immature specimens caught off Georges Bank in 1982. Little is known of its biology but it appears to live nearer the surface in spring than in fall in Bermuda.

starry flounder

Scientific name: *Platichthys stellatus*
   (Pallas, 1787)
Family: **Righteye Flounder**

Other common names: flounder, grindstone, leatherjacket, emerywheel, nataaznak
French name: flet étoilé

Distribution: Found from Korea and Japan to California including British Columbia. Also on the Arctic coast to Bathurst Inlet, N.W.T. Enters fresh water.

Characters: This species is distinguished from related Canadian Pacific species by the very rough, stellate (star-shaped) scales on the eyed side and the distinctive 4–7 black bands on the dorsal, anal and caudal fins, separated

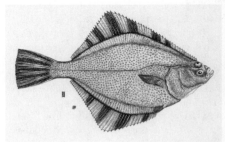

starry flounder

by white to orange bands. The mouth is small, asymmetrical and has most of the teeth on the blind side. Stellate scales are in bands along the dorsal and anal fin bases on the blind side, separated by cycloid scales, and scattered over the whole blind side. There is a slight arch to the lateral line which has 63–78 scales. Dorsal fin rays 52–68, anal fin with a strong, exposed spine and 36–51 rays. Caudal fin broadly rounded. Eyed side dark brown to almost black with vague blotches. Blind side white to cream and sometimes blotched. Reaches 91 cm and 9.1 kg.

Biology: Common in shallow waters in Canada but also descends below 375 m and enters rivers as far as 120 km from the mouth. This is the third most abundant species of fish on the Tuktoyaktuk Peninsula in Arctic waters. Food is crustaceans, such as shrimps and crabs, clams, worms and small fishes. Brittle stars are also eaten. Females grow larger and live longer than males. Maximum age may exceed 27 years. Males in California mature at age 2 and 30 cm, females at age 3 and 35 cm. Spawning occurs in February to April in Canada, June-

July in Arctic waters at 1.5–6.8°C. Eggs are a pale orange, pelagic and about 1.0 mm in diameter. Up to 11 million eggs may be spawned. Young become asymmetrical at 10.5 mm. Not very popular as a commercial item with about a metric tonne marketed annually in Canada. However this is a popular sport fish for anglers from wharves and along the coast. This species may have eyes and colour on either the right or left side. All Japanese starry flounders are "lefties," while in British Columbia about 60–70% are eyed and pigmented on the left side. The degree of sinistrality increases from south to north. The starry flounder often forms a hybrid with the **English sole** known as the hybrid sole or forkline sole. This hybrid is right eyed, has a short accessory lateral line, a nearly straight lateral line, ctenoid scales on both sides of the body but mixed with cycloid scales on the blind side, and weak bars on the dorsal and anal fins. It attains about 46 cm and is found on soft bottoms down to 660 m. Dorsal fin rays 68–76, anal fin preceded by a sharp, small spine and with 49–57 rays, lateral line scales 76–91.

starry skate

Scientific name: *Raja stellulata*
　(Jordan and Gilbert, 1880)
Family: **Skate**
Other common names: prickly skate
French name: raie du Pacifique

Distribution: Found from Alaska to Baja California including British Columbia.

Characters: This species is distinguished from Canadian Pacific relatives by having a rigid snout with its cartilaginous support thick and stiff, cartilaginous supports of the pectoral fin do not reach the snout tip, no enlarged snout tip thornlets or scapular (= shoulder) spines, pelvic fins deeply notched, and lateral tail thornlets present. There is a median row of thorns beginning behind the eyes. The shoulder area has large spines. There is a row of small spines on the inner eye margin. Both the upper and lower surface have strong, star-shaped prickles. The egg cases are 7–8.2 cm by 6.4–7 cm and have strong, longitudinal striations. Anterior horns are longer than posterior ones and have flattened tips. The ante-

rior margin is straight and the posterior margin is convex. Attachment fibres are few and limited to the bases of the anterior horns. Disc colour grey-brown to brown with many dark spots of various sizes. A weak eye-spot with a yellow centre surrounded by brown may be present on each pectoral fin. The undersurface is white. Reaches 76 cm.

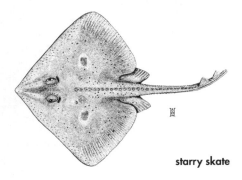

starry skate

Biology: Not uncommon in British Columbia. Depth range is 18–732 m.

stellate sculpin

Scientific name: *Myoxocephalus* sp.
Family: **Sculpin**
Other common names: none
French name: chabot étoilé

Distribution: Found in the Gulf of Alaska and British Columbia.

Characters: This species is a relative of the **great sculpin**. It is distinguished by having stellate scales above the lateral line. First

stellate sculpin

dorsal fin spines 8–10, usually 10, second dorsal rays 14–17, usually 16, anal rays reported as 10–12, usually 12, or 12–16, and pectoral rays 17–19. Scales above the lateral line are stellate and those below are spinate. Attains 25.5 cm.

Biology: Usually caught in deeper water than the **great sculpin** over mud, sand or rock at 1–21 m. First reported from British Columbia in 1977 but not yet described and named scientifically.

Stickleback Family

Scientific name: Gasterosteidae
French name: épinoches

Sticklebacks are found in coastal marine and fresh waters of the Northern Hemisphere. The number of species in the family is more than 7 with 5 named from Canada (but see below).

The family is characterised by 3–16 isolated spines in front of the soft dorsal fin, which has 6–14 rays, bony plates often present along the flank, the pelvic fin has 1 spine and 0–3 soft rays, caudal rays usually 12, slender caudal peduncle, small mouth with teeth, a swimbladder not connected to the gut, 3–4 branchiostegal rays, epipleural bones present, no postcleithrum bone in the pectoral girdle, and the circumorbital bone ring is not complete posteriorly.

Sticklebacks are members of the **Stickleback Order**. The number of species is uncertain and may not be readily explicable using the conventional, scientific naming system. The **threespine stickleback** as currently defined is a species complex containing populations which act as good species. This would require a major revisionary study given the great diversity shown by populations around the Northern Hemisphere. There is variation in colour, body form, maximum age (8 years as opposed to a usual 2–4 years), spine numbers and development, and plate numbers. These variations in anatomy are matched by variations in biology such as habitat, feeding and reproduction. In British Columbia, a centre for unusual sticklebacks, there is the **giant** Mayer Lake form, the unarmoured Boulton Lake form, the black Drizzle Lake form (all on the Queen Charlotte Islands), the **Enos** stickleback pair of Vancouver Island, and the Heisholt or **Texada** stickleback pairs of Paxton, Priest, Emily and Balkwill lakes on Texada Island and Hadley Lake on Lasqueti Island. The **white stickleback** is the only unusual Atlantic coast form to receive detailed attention.

Marine threespine sticklebacks are found in fossil deposits of about 10 million years ago and do not appear different from modern populations. Modern freshwater populations show a much greater range in variation.

This variation in behaviour, biology and in speciation has attracted extensive studies by scientists and makes these small fishes, which have no commercial value, particularly important. Some of the variation is owing to environmental factors while some has a genetic basis. Several books have been devoted to them and thousands of scientific studies. Sticklebacks make excellent aquarium fishes. Their reproductive behaviour is complex, involving courtship and nest building. Some populations are anadromous and enter fresh water to breed.

See **blackspotted stickleback**
brook stickleback
Enos stickleback
fourspine stickleback
giant stickleback
ninespine stickleback
Texada stickleback
threespine stickleback
white stickleback

Stickleback Order

The **sticklebacks**, sand eels, **tubesnouts**, **pipefishes**, seamoths, ghost pipefishes, **seahorses**, trumpetfishes, shrimpfishes, cometfishes and **snipefishes** form the Order Gasterosteiformes (= Thoracostei) with 11 families and at least 257 species in coastal marine and fresh waters of the Northern Hemisphere. There are 19 species in 5 families throughout Canadian fresh and salt waters.

They are characterised by a variety of body forms, often armoured with dermal plates, a single or no postcleithrum bone in the pectoral girdle, pelvic girdle not contacting the cleithrum bone of the pectoral girdle, supramaxillary, basisphenoid and orbitosphenoid bones absent, branchiostegal rays 1–5, and the mouth usually small.

The Stickleback Order may be restricted to the sticklebacks, tubesnouts and sand eels while others form a Pipefish Order.

These fishes are of no commercial importance but some have been studied extensively by scientists with regard to their puzzling evolutionary history and intriguing behaviour.

See **Cornetfish Family**
Pipefish Family
Snipefish Family
Stickleback Family
Tubesnout Family

Stingray Family

Scientific name: Dasyatidae (= Trygonidae)
French name: pastenagues

Stingrays, including whiprays, river stingrays, butterfly rays and round rays, are found in the warmer parts of the Atlantic, Indian and Pacific oceans and also in fresh water. There are about 70 species with 1 on the Atlantic coast, 1 on both the Atlantic and Pacific coasts of Canada and one other species thought to reach British Columbia, but not yet confirmed.

Stingrays lack a dorsal fin. The outer edge of the pectoral fins are continuous with the side of the head. The caudal fin may be present or absent and the tail long or short. Their name refers to 1 or more long serrated venomous spines on the tail. Spines are replaced if lost and there may be, rarely, 3–4 spines on the tail. Teeth are in bands.

Stingrays are related to the **Eagle Ray Family** in the **Ray Order**.

Stingrays are found mostly in coastal areas in shallow water. The spines are a defensive weapon against such predators as sharks. A stingray will whip its tail upwards and sidewards with some considerable force if disturbed, driving the spines into the attacker. Venom from glands along the spine is injected simultaneously. The spine can penetrate rubber boots and even the side of a wooden boat. There have been no fatalities associated with stingrays in Canada, but people elsewhere have died. The venom can cause the victim's heart to stop beating. Non-fatal envenomations are very painful. Stingrays are easily stepped on in the shallow, warm water of beaches, where they hide in the sand with only their eyes and spiracles showing. They are powerful swimmers when not hiding in the sand, but usually swim slowly by undulating the pectoral fins.

The bands of teeth are used to crush molluscs as food. They "jet" water at the sand to expose food items which also include crustaceans and worms. Commercially important clam and oyster beds may be damaged by stingrays. Stingrays give birth to up to 16 live young. Despite their spines, stingrays are good to eat but are not used commercially in any volume. The spines have been used as spear tips, daggers or awls in some parts of the world and are sold as souvenirs.

See **diamond stingray**
pelagic stingray
roughtail stingray

stonecat

Scientific name: *Noturus flavus*
Rafinesque, 1818
Family: **Bullhead Catfish**
Other common names: stone catfish, white cat, doogler, beetle-eye, mongrel bullhead, deepwater bullhead, little yellow cat
French name: barbotte des rapides

Distribution: Found in the Mississippi and Hudson river basins and the Great Lakes and Hudson Bay basins. In Canada in the southern Ontario basins of lakes Huron, Erie and Ontario and the upper St. Lawrence River basin of Ontario and Québec. It just enters Saskatchewan and Alberta in the Missouri River basin and in Manitoba is in the Assiniboine and Red River basins.

Characters: This species is identified by the posterior tip of the adipose fin not being free but attached to the back, pectoral spine nearly straight to moderately curved, with or without anterior teeth, posterior teeth present, not recurved, colour pattern dark without blotches or saddles on the body, premaxillary band of teeth with lateral processes

stonecat

extending backwards, and pectoral radials never fused. Dorsal fin soft rays 5–7, usually 6, anal rays 15–19, pelvic rays 8–10, usually

8, and pectoral soft rays 8–11, usually 10. There are 2 internasal pores. The head, back and upper flank are dark bluish-olive, blue-black, olive, slate-grey or yellow-brown fading to cream, white or grey on the belly. The dorsal fin has a grey blotch at its base. The adipose fin is dark with a pale edge. Fin margins are light to white. There is a light yellow spot behind the dorsal fin across the back and a light blotch on the nape. The caudal fin has a white blotch on its upper margin. Chin barbels are white and upper barbels grey. Reaches 31.2 cm and 0.5 kg.

Biology: The favoured habitat of this species is riffles of streams and lake margins with water movement by wave action. It tends to be a solitary species. Food is mainly larval insects such as mayflies, and crustaceans, particularly crayfish, with molluscs, small fishes and algae. Feeding probably takes place at night. Snakes and **smallmouth bass** are known to be successful predators despite the stinging pectoral fin spine. They may live 8–10 years. Females are mature at 4–5 years of age and males at 3 years. Spawning occurs in summer (June to August) at high water temperatures (27–29°C). A sticky mass of about 100–500 eggs is laid under stones and guarded by the male. Each female can produce up to 1205 yellow eggs of up to 4 mm diameter. A painful wound can be inflicted by the venomous pectoral spine. Stonecats have been used as bait for **bass** and **catfishes**.

stoplight loosejaw

Scientific name: *Malacosteus niger*
    Ayres, 1848
Family: **Barbeled Dragonfish**
Other common names: lightless loosejaw,
    black loosejaw, drague sans lampe
French name: drague rouge-verte

Distribution: Found in all tropical and subtropical oceans and even into the subarctic North Atlantic Ocean between Greenland and Iceland.

Characters: The absence of a barbel, poorly-developed light organs and only one pair of nostrils distinguishes this species from other loosejaws in Canada. The pectoral fin and suborbital light organ are present. There is a large, dark-red light organ under the eye and a smaller bright green one behind it. The diameter of this latter light organ is more than 25% the size of the eye. Other light organs are white or violet. The head and body are black. Size is to 24 cm, possibly as large as 30 cm. The **shortnose loosejaw** may not be a species distinct from the stoplight loosejaw.

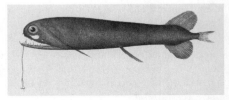

stoplight loosejaw

Biology: In Canada reported from Ocean Station Papa (50°N, 145°W) in the Pacific Ocean and at the south tip of the Grand Bank and the Flemish Cap area east of Newfoundland. Not uncommon compared with other loosejaws. This loosejaw has been caught at 915–1830 m depth, rarely at the surface. It is a bathypelagic species. The red fluorescent light emitted from the organ under the eye in ultraviolet light is rare among sea creatures, blue or green being more common. Only the **largeye**, and possibly the **shining loosejaw**, emit a similar light in Canadian waters.

stout beardfish

Scientific name: *Polymixia nobilis*
    Lowe, 1836
Family: **Beardfish**
Other common names: Atlantic beardfish,
    poisson à barbe
French name: gros barbudo

Distribution: Found in the Atlantic, Indian and Pacific oceans and possibly off Atlantic Canada.

Characters: This species is distinguished from its only Canadian relative, the **Caribbean beardfish**, by higher dorsal fin soft ray counts and lower gill raker counts. Dorsal fin with 4–6 spines and 30–38 (usually 36) soft rays. Anal fin with 3–4 spines and 15–18 soft rays. There are 45–61 lateral line scales (and 32–37 pores) with a further

2–3 on the caudal fin. Gill rakers 11–13 (usually 11–12). Overall colour is brownish grey to violet-brown above, silvery or

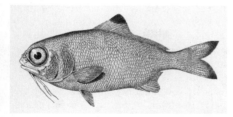

stout beardfish

golden-green below. The head has reddish tinges. There is a black blotch at the tip of the anterior dorsal fin and the tail fin is tipped black. The peritoneum is black. Reaches 40 cm.

Biology: A record of this species from Canada on the Grand Bank has been re-identified to the **Caribbean beardfish**. However this beardfish is reported from the Atlantic coast of the U.S.A. and may eventually be found in Canadian waters. Found on the bottom between 100 and 770 m, locally common in the eastern Atlantic Ocean.

stout blacksmelt

Scientific name: *Bathylagus milleri*
  Jordan and Gilbert, 1898
Family: **Deepsea Smelt**
Other common names: big-scaled blacksmelt
French name: grosse garcette

Distribution: Found from the western Pacific Ocean to southern California. In Canada known from the Queen Charlotte Sound region of British Columbia.

Characters: The stout blacksmelt is distinguished from other Pacific coast species

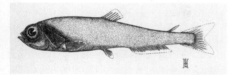

stout blacksmelt

of deepsea smelts by having 20–28 anal fin rays, 11–16 pectoral fin rays and 23–27 scale rows along the flank. Dorsal fin rays 6–9 and gill rakers 25–27. The skin is easily lost. It is dark brown to black in colour and reaches 16.6 cm standard length.

Biology: This species can be caught at the surface at night and down to 1420 m in the day. Food is assumed to be small crustaceans.

stout eelblenny

Scientific name: *Anisarchus medius*
  (Reinhardt, 1838)
Family: **Shanny**
Other common names: snake blenny,
  shalup-pau-gah
French name: lompénie naine

Distribution: Circumpolar, across Arctic Canada and as far south perhaps as Cape Breton Island, Nova Scotia in Atlantic Canada, but not in British Columbia.

Characters: This species is 1 of 8 related Canadian shannies which have very elongate bodies, large pectoral fins and pelvic fins

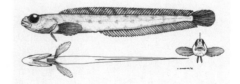

stout eelblenny

with 1 spine and 2–4 soft rays. It is distinguished by distribution, 58–63 dorsal fin spines, 40–43 soft anal fin rays with posterior rays longer and 13–15 pectoral fin rays. The upper jaw does not project. Scales cover the body but the lateral line is indistinct. The dorsal and anal fins are attached to the caudal fin. Overall colour is brown to yellowish with a few flank blotches. The dorsal fin has red oblique bars. The caudal fin has several bars. Reaches about 15.8 cm.

Biology: The record from Cape Breton Island was found in a cod stomach. The Strait of Belle Isle is the usual southern limit. Found on soft bottoms of sand and mud from 15 to 143 m at temperatures as low as -1°C and not much higher than 5°C. Food is crustaceans, worms and molluscs.

stout sand lance

Scientific name: *Ammodytes hexapterus*
    Pallas, 1814
Family: **Sand Lance**
Other common names: Pacific sand lance,
    American sand lance, Arctic sand lance,
    inshore sand lance, lant, needlefish,
    lançon d'Amérique, equille
French name: lançon gourdeau

Distribution: Found from Hudson Bay
and the Labrador coast south through Atlantic
Canada to Virginia. Also found from Japan to
California including the coast of British
Columbia and in the western Arctic in the
Beaufort Sea and southern Victoria Island.

Characters: This species is distinguished
from its only Canadian relative, the **northern
sand lance**, by having usually 51–62 dorsal

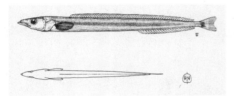

stout sand lance

fin rays, 23–34 anal rays and 60–75 vertebrae.
Overlaps occur in these counts and some fish
may be difficult to assign to species. However
Canadian inshore sand lances with deep bodies and low vertebral counts (mean 67.5) are
the stout sand lance. There are 106–126 plicae
or oblique, lateral skin folds.

Overall colour is silvery to silver-blue on
the sides with a white belly. The sides may
have a steel-blue iridescent stripe. The back
may be grey, olive, brown or blue-green.
Reaches 28 cm.

Biology: Unlike its relative, this species
can be found inshore in shallow waters but
also frequents offshore banks. Larger fish are
found offshore. Stout sand lances occur in
large schools containing millions of fish but
are also found as individuals buried in sand,
even between high and low tides with the
head occasionally protruding from the sand.
Clam diggers and anglers searching for bait
may see them. It is possible that this sand

lance, like a European relative, may stay
buried in sand for several weeks resting. At
Victoria, B.C. millions of sand lance have
been observed leaping a few centimetres out
of the water. A peregrine took one of these
fish from the water after about 15 attempts.

Food is principally copepod crustaceans
taken near the bottom or in the water column. Other crustaceans, snails and worms
are also eaten. Sand lances are eaten by
**Atlantic cod, haddock, pollock, rock sole,
starry flounder, yellowtail flounder, plaice,
great sculpin, whitespotted greenling, chinook** and **coho salmon**, and **halibut**, among
other fishes as well as whales and sea birds.
Humpback whale distribution in summer off
southern Nova Scotia in the Gulf of Maine is
directly related to the number of sand lances.
Porpoises and **flatfishes** are known to root
sand lances out of the sand and sand lances
often become stranded on beaches when trying to escape predators. Concentrations of
predators build up as the sand lance schools
burrow into sand for the night.

Spawning occurs inshore from October to
January. Up to 5196 eggs are laid with a
maximum diameter of 1.1 mm. This species
lives up to 9 years and may mature at the end
of the first year of life.

stout sawpalate

Scientific name: *Serrivomer beani* Gill and
    Ryder, 1883
Family: **Sawpalate**
Other common names: Bean's sawtoothed
    eel, thread eel, shortnosed snipe eel
French name: serrivomer trapu

Distribution: Found in the Atlantic and
Indian oceans and in Canada from the
Flemish Cap and Grand Bank southward.

Characters: This species is separated
from its Atlantic/Arctic Canadian relatives
by having 136–175 dorsal fin rays, 119–156
anal rays, 5–6 caudal rays, and 7 (rarely 8)
branchiostegal rays with the lower 5 having
an anterior process projecting beyond the
hyoid arch with which they articulate. The
characteristic, blade- or saw-shaped teeth on
the roof of the mouth number 50–100 and
are in 2 parallel and alternating lines.
Pectoral fin rays 6–7. Dorsal and anal fins

are delicate. The dorsal fin origin is behind the anal fin origin. The anal fin origin is about a head length behind the gill opening.

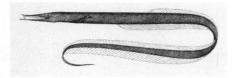

stout sawpalate

Vertebrae number variously 154–168 or 143–155, depending on the author. The anterior part of the body is subcircular in cross-section. Overall colour is iridescent brown to black and silvery-grey with the head black or blue-black but the skin is often lost or damaged in captured specimens. Reaches 78 cm.

Biology: Found at 475–1554 m in Canadian waters; elsewhere from 91–5998 m. They are apparently solitary and fast swimmers. Some have been observed in pairs or groups of 4–5. Leptocephali occur at 0–300 m, mostly between 50 and 70 m. Metamorphosis can be complete at 9.0 cm. Food is principally large shrimps, euphausiids and other crustaceans, along with small fishes. **Atlantic cod** are known to eat this sawpalate. Spawning off Bermuda occurs in late spring and summer. Leptocephalus larvae 17–33 mm long have been captured and adolescents in transition to adults can be about 96 mm or longer.

stout slipskin

Scientific name: *Lycodapus pachysoma*
    Peden and Anderson, 1978
Family: **Eelpout**
Other common names: none
French name: lycode trapue

Distribution: Found in Antarctica and Oregon to British Columbia.

Characters: This species is distinguished from its Pacific coast relatives by having the branchiostegal membranes free of the isth-

stout slipskin

mus posteriorly, gill rakers blunt and stout touching the adjacent raker only when depressed, gill opening extending above the upper base of the pectoral fin, and total vertebrae 75–78. The head is large and the body robust. Scales and pelvic fins are absent. The flesh is gelatinous. Dorsal fin rays 69–76, anal rays 58–65, pectoral rays 7–8, and teeth on vomer bone on the roof of the mouth 0–19. Preserved fish are translucent with muscles below the skin yellowish to pale brown. Mouth and gill cavities, jaws, peritoneum and stomach black. Reaches 16.1 cm standard length.

Biology: Reported from off Queen Charlotte Sound. Depth range is 2000–2195 m.

stout werewolf

Scientific name: *Melanocetus johnsoni*
    Günther, 1864
Family: **Werewolf**
Other common names: Johnson's black
    anglerfish, common blackdevil
French name: gros loup-garou

Distribution: Found in all temperate to tropical oceans including off Canada's Atlantic coast.

Characters: This deepsea **anglerfish** has a high dorsal fin ray count, 13–17, and few anal rays, 3–5. Pectoral fin rays 17–23. The skin is

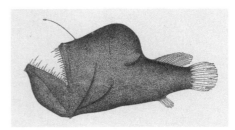

stout werewolf

thick. The esca or bait has a bulb which is slightly compressed and has an obvious posterior crest. Overall colour including the inside of the mouth is black. The esca has light patches. Males and juveniles have a concentration of pigment under the skin of the caudal peduncle. Females attain 18 cm.

Biology: Four specimens were caught off Newfoundland in 1968. This species may occur in relatively shallow water for a deepsea **anglerfish**, 100–2100 m. One stout werewolf was found to have eaten a **jewel lanternfish** nearly twice its own length. In the vast, dark, deep ocean **anglerfish** males locate mates by a chemical (pheromone) emitted by the female. Escal light patterns and filament shape may also help. This system works amazingly well and only one male stout werewolf of all the **anglerfish** species has been found attached to a female of the wrong species (a *Centrophryne spinulosa* of the family Centrophrynidae, not found in Canada).

straightcheek headlightfish

Scientific name: *Diaphus mollis*
  Tåning, 1928
Family: **Lanternfish**
Other common names: none
French name: lampe-de-tête joue-droite

Distribution: Found in the Atlantic, Indian and Pacific oceans and along the Scotian Shelf in Atlantic Canada.

Characters: This species and its relatives, the **bouncer**, **eventooth**, **flashlight**, **square** and **Taaning's headlightfishes** and the **doormat** and **slanteye parkinglightfishes**, are separated from other Atlantic coast

straightcheek headlightfish

lanternfishes by not having photophores near the dorsal body edge, the PLO photophore is well above the upper pectoral fin base level while the second PVO photophore is at or below this level, there are 4 Prc photophores, the PO and two PVO photophores form a straight, ascending line as do the first 3 VO photophores, supracaudal luminous glands are absent, and there is more than 1 pair of luminous head organs. This species is separated from its relatives by having the So photophore present, inner series of teeth on rear part of premaxillary obviously recurved,

vomer naked or with only a few, minute teeth, AOa 5 (rarely 6), first AOa in a line with other AOa photophores, and gill rakers 15–18 in the Atlantic Ocean. Dorsal fin rays 12–14, anal rays 12–14 and pectoral rays 9–12. AO photophores 8–10. Lateral line organs 34–35. Vertebrae 33. Adult males have a large patch of luminous tissue between the eye, nostril and upper jaw first appearing at a body length of 2.2–2.4 cm. The "headlights" or photophores at the front of the head are distinct at 11.5 mm. The Dn photophore is in a cup above the nostril. Reaches about 6.6 cm.

Biology: This species is common in subtropical to tropical waters and is carried to Canadian waters by the Gulf Stream. Depth distribution by day is 300–800 m and by night is surface waters to 225 m. Abundance depths vary with locality. Migration upward takes about 5 hours and downward 3.5 hours with respective speeds of 92 m/hour and 131 m/hour. Sexual maturity is attained at 3.0 cm. Spawning occurs from spring to fall, with a peak in late spring and early summer, at Bermuda. Only a few fish survive beyond 1 year of age.

streaklight tubeshoulder

Scientific name: *Holtbyrnia latifrons*
  Sazanov, 1976
Family: **Tubeshoulder**
Other common names: none
French name: circé à branchies longue

Distribution: Found in the eastern Pacific Ocean including off British Columbia.

Characters: This species is recognised by the family character of a tube projecting from the flank above the pectoral fin, by having an evident lateral line with enlarged scales and

streaklight tubeshoulder

by having scales on the head overlapping normally. In addition pelvic fin rays are 8–9, usually 9, and enlarged teeth or tusks are present on the maxillary bone of the upper jaw. It is distinguished from its relatives by having a light organ at the tip of the lower jaw and long gill filaments not united at their bases. Gill rakers are 25–30. Overall colour is dark with 2 patches of white tissue behind the eye. Reaches about 20 cm.

Biology: Usually found near coasts from 300 to about 1000 m.

striated argentine

Scientific name: *Argentina striata*
    Goode and Bean, 1895
Family: **Argentine**
Other common names: none
French name: argentine striée

Distribution: Found from Nova Scotia south to Brazil.

Characters: The pectoral fins are low on the side of the body and lateral line scales do not extend onto the tail fin. The eye is large

striated argentine

and scales are easily lost on capture. The striated argentine is distinguished from the **Atlantic argentine** by having 49–52 lateral line scales, scales without minute spines, 6 lower arm gill rakers and a dorsal fin origin behind the tip of the pectoral fins. There are 5 branchiostegal rays. Colour in preservative is brownish with traces of silvery pigmentation, darker above in a midlateral dark streak. The occiput is black. The swimbladder is not silvery. It reaches 20 cm.

Biology: Usually caught at depths of 95–365 m often over mud bottoms but little is known of the biology of this argentine.

string eel

Scientific name: *Gordiichthys leibyi*
    McCosker and Böhlke, 1984
Family: **Snake Eel**
Other common names: sooty eel
French name: serpenton de Leiby

Distribution: Found from Florida to the Scotian Shelf of Atlantic Canada.

Characters: This species is distinguished as a larva by having 167–175 total myomeres (muscle blocks), 101–106 nephric myomeres, dorsal fin origin anterior to myomere 21, often stellate melanophores along the middle

string eel

of the back, gut loops low and hard to detect, and the last two major vertical blood vessels widely separated. Preanal myomeres 102–107 and predorsal myomeres 13–18. Adults have a blunt tail tip with no caudal fin. The dorsal fin origin lies at the mid-point of the head. The mouth is small with weak jaws. The gill opening is low and crescentic. The head is rounded at the tip. No pectoral fins. Colour is yellow to tan with fins transparent. Adults attain 33.6 cm. Larvae attain 81 mm.

Biology: Known from Canada as a single, stray larva (or leptocephalus) taken at 195 m in 1981. Adults are quite rare and found in sand and mud.

striped anchovy

Scientific name: *Anchoa hepsetus*
    (Linnaeus, 1758)
Family: **Anchovy**
Other common names: broad-striped
    anchovy, anchois rayé
French name: piquitinga

Distribution: From Nova Scotia south to Uruguay.

Characters: This anchovy is distinguished from its Canadian relative on the Atlantic

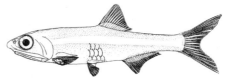

striped anchovy

coast, the **silver anchovy**, by having a long maxilla bone in the upper jaw ending in a pointed tip and by having more anal fin rays. Scales about 37–43 along the flank. There is no lateral line canal. Dorsal fin rays 14–17, anal rays 19–24 (usually 21–23), and pectoral rays 15–18. Lower gill rakers 18–25. Grey-green or greenish-blue on the back with dusky spots and a bright, narrow, silvery stripe along the side bordered above by a dark line. The head has yellowish tinges. Dorsal scales are outlined with pigment. The belly is white. Dorsal and caudal fins may be dusky. Reaches 15.3 cm.

Biology: Known only from 5 strays caught in the Bedford Basin, Nova Scotia, in 1931. Elsewhere an abundant, coastal species in shallow waters sometimes found as deep as 73 m. It can tolerate water saltier than the open ocean and water that is almost fresh. Spawning occurs in spring and summer and eggs hatch in 48 hours. Eggs are elliptical in shape, up to 1.6 mm long. It is an important food for many, larger commercial fishes and also seabirds. The striped anchovy is sold as food for humans.

striped bass

Scientific name: *Morone saxatilis*
(Walbaum, 1792)
Family: **Temperate Bass**
Other common names: rockfish, linesides, striper, sewer trout, greenhead, squid hound
French name: bar rayé

Distribution: Found from the St. Lawrence River and upper Gulf and the Maritimes south to Florida and the Gulf of Mexico. On the Pacific coast it is found from southern British Columbia to Mexico as an introduced species.

Characters: This species is distinguished from its relatives, the **white perch** and the **white bass**, by having usually 9–11 (range 7–13) soft anal rays, 4–9 dark flank stripes, dorsal fins separated, and the longest of 3 anal fin spines less than half the length of the longest soft ray. There are 2 separate patches of teeth on the base of the tongue. First dorsal fin spines 7–12, usually 9, second dorsal soft rays 8–14, usually 12, after 1 spine, and pectoral rays 13–19. Lateral line scales 50–72.

The back is olive-green inshore, more steel blue offshore, or black, the flanks silvery

and the belly white. There may be golden or brassy tints on the flank. Fins are dusky except the pelvics which are white. The anal fin is white posteriorly. Young fish, less than 8 cm, may have 6–10, dusky, flank bars.

Reaches 183 cm and 56.7 kg. The world, all-tackle angling record weighed 35.6 kg and was caught in 1982 at Atlantic City, New Jersey. The biggest one caught in Canada, in the Mira River, Nova Scotia by Gordon Strong, weighed 24.54 kg.

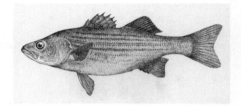

striped bass

Biology: This bass is found in schools in coastal waters in southern areas of Atlantic Canada, mostly in fresh waters in New Brunswick. The Gulf of St. Lawrence population was separated from the populations in the rest of Atlantic Canada, there being none in northern Gaspé. It is rare in British Columbia with 2 records (the northernmost in Barkley Sound), the result of the spread of bass introduced from New Jersey and elsewhere to California starting in 1879. Within 20 years, they had spread to Oregon. Temperatures above 18°C are necessary for successful spawning in the Annapolis River, Nova Scotia so it is unlikely to become established in British Columbia. Some populations are landlocked and never leave fresh waters. In Atlantic Canada some fish are summer visitors retreating south to winter in the U.S.A.

Food of adults in the sea is a wide variety of fishes, crustaceans including lobsters, and worms. In fresh waters food is small fishes such as **smelt, silversides, shads, gaspereau** and others. Small bass and larvae eat zooplankton, small crustaceans, insects, worms, and small fishes. Adults have few predators other than man but young bass are taken by various larger fishes including adults of their own species.

Maturity is attained at 2–7 years and life span is an estimated 31 years. Large fish, older than 11 years, are all females.

Spawning occured in May to July in the Gulf of St. Lawrence after a migration into a river. In the St. Lawrence River this migration started the preceding fall and the fish overwintered in the river but in other rivers the migration occurs in spring. A female is accompanied by up to 50 males. She rolls and quivers at the surface while males bump her with their snouts. This occasions much splashing known as "rock fights." Eggs and sperm are shed at this time. Water temperatures are usually in a range of about 14–24°C. Large females can contain over 40 million eggs of which about 10% are mature. Eggs are 1.5 mm in diameter. Females can spawn in subsequent years but not every year. The eggs are greenish to golden-green, semi-buoyant and float down river, hatching in 2–3 days. Estuaries serve as nursery areas.

This is an important sport and commercial fish on both coasts of the U.S.A. The Canadian populations are much less important, perhaps because numbers fluctuate widely. There have been small commercial catches in Nova Scotia and the St. Lawrence River and sport fisheries in the Bay of Fundy and near Sorel, Québec. The Shubenacadie River, N.S. and the St. John River, N.B. have both sport and commercial fisheries as do the estuaries of such Gulf of St. Lawrence rivers in New Brunswick as the Miramichi and Kouchibouguac. Canadian stocks show genetic differences from U.S. stocks and efforts to restore depleted Canadian stocks should bear this in mind to avoid genetic swamping of uniquely Canadian fish. The 1983 Canadian catch was 24 tonnes. Striped bass give a good fight on any type of artificial lure resembling the bait fish they are chasing. They can often be seen swirling or splashing at the surface. They have a white, flaky and tasty flesh.

- Most accessible July through October.
- The coastal waters and estuaries of the Maritimes and the mouth of the St. Lawrence River.
- Medium to heavy action baitcasting and spinning gear used with 14– to 20–pound test line.
- Large minnow-imitating plugs and a variety of 3/8–to one-ounce spoons and jigs and large, live or cut bait fish.

striped burrfish

Scientific name: *Chilomycterus schoepfi* (Walbaum, 1792)
Family: **Porcupinefish**
Other common names: swellfish, porcupinefish, rabbitfish, oysterfish
French name: atinga bariolé

Distribution: Found in the western Atlantic Ocean from Nova Scotia south to Brazil.

Characters: The beak-like jaws and the body covered with short, rigid, erect and flattened spines are characteristic. The spines have a triple root. The nostrils are at the end of a small tube. The dorsal and anal fins have 10–12 rays. The body is a yellowish-brown to green and has dark brown or black stripes. Ventrally the body is white to yellowish and even blackish. The belly is whitish with yellow or orange tinges. There are often large black patches at the dorsal and anal fin bases and behind the pectoral fins. Rarely albino burrfish are reported. Reaches 25 cm. The world, all-tackle angling record from Delaware Bay, New Jersey in 1989 weighed 0.63 kg.

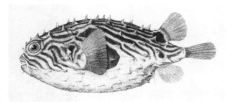

striped burrfish

Biology: Reported only once from Canada in deep water near Halifax in 1899 and so a rare stray from the south to Nova Scotia. In southern waters it is common in seagrass beds of bays and lagoons in summer, retreating to deeper water in winter. It has been seen to propel itself by a jet of water pushed from the gill openings. Food is hard-bodied invertebrates which are crushed by the beak. Small burrfish can be kept in aquaria.

striped kelpfish

Scientific name: *Gibbonsia metzi*
    Hubbs, 1927
Family: **Clinid**
Other common names: none
French name: clinide rayé

Distribution: From Baja California to British Columbia at Vancouver Island.

Characters: This species is distinguished from its relative, the **crevice kelpfish**, by having more than 175 scales (180–235) along the flank above the lateral line, 7–10, usually 8–9, dorsal fin soft rays and no flank spots. Dorsal fin soft rays are equally spaced. Gill membranes are joined but free of the isthmus. Dorsal fin with 34–37 spines before the few soft rays. Anal fin with 2 spines and 24–29 soft rays. Pectoral fin with about 11–13 rays and short, not reaching the anal fin. There are cirri at the dorsal fin spine tips, over each eye and over the nostrils. Red to brown with stripes and mottling, variable with the seaweed it is associated with. Attains 24 cm.

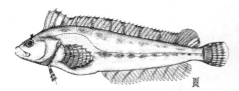

striped kelpfish

Biology: Found in shallow water (to 9.1 m) in tide pools and among kelp. The young hatch in spring and are pelagic before settling out into their bottom habitat. Females are usually larger than males.

striped mullet

Scientific name: *Mugil cephalus*
    Linnaeus, 1758
Family: **Mullet**
Other common names: grey mullet, jumping mullet, flathead mullet, sea mullet, river mullet
French name: mulet cabot

Distribution: World-wide in warm waters and from Nova Scotia to Brazil in the western Atlantic Ocean.

Characters: This mullet is distinguished from its only Canadian relative, the **white mullet**, by having the soft dorsal and anal fins unscaled, and flanks with 6–7 stripes. The second dorsal fin has 1 spine and 6–8

striped mullet

soft rays. Anal fin with 3 spines and 8 soft rays (young with 2 spines and 9 soft rays). Scales along midflank number 36–45. The back is brown, olive-green or bluish with silvery flanks and belly. Each scale has a dark spot which line up to give the impression of stripes. The pectoral fin base has a blue-black spot. Young are a bright, iridescent silver. Reaches 100 cm and 7 kg.

Biology: Known only from a juvenile caught in 1983, as a stray from the south, near Georges Bank. Earlier records are of the **white mullet**. This species forms large schools and is known to enter fresh waters. It descends to over 1300 m but can also be seen leaping out of the water. Food is microscopic algae and associated animals taken from the mud, sometimes plankton. Rarely, swarming marine worms are eaten rather than microscopic items, perhaps as an additional energy source prior to spawning. Striped mullet live about 16 years, with females attaining larger sizes than males. They are probably mature at about 3 years. Spawning occurs offshore in October to February with a peak in December, but fry move into inshore nursery areas. Eggs are pelagic and up to 1.08 mm in diameter. Juveniles can develop into either males or females, and hermaphrodites have been reported. This mullet is a very important sport and commercial fish outside Canadian waters, both wild and cultured.

striped sailfin eel

Scientific name: *Letharchus aliculatus*
    McCosker, 1974

Family: **Snake Eel**
Other common names: none
French name: serpenton rayé

Distribution: Found from the Scotian Shelf of Canada south to Brazil.

Characters: This species is distinguished as a larva by having 10 pronounced gut loops, the dorsal fin origin anterior to myomere (muscle block) 14, obvious, rounded patches of pigment in the body wall lateral to the gut loops, and no pigment on the dorsal oesophagus surface near the pectoral fin base. Total myomeres 153–163, preanal myomeres 100–109 and predorsal myomeres 7–11. Adults have a hard, pointed tail tip, the dorsal fin originates on the nape, the anal fin is absent and there is a light brown stripe along the body. Reaches 71 mm as larvae. Adults reach 25.8 cm total length and probably much larger.

striped sailfin eel

Biology: First reported from Canada in 1989 as leptocephalus larvae. Adults are known only from Bahia, Brazil where they are found in shallow tide pools.

striped seaperch

Scientific name: *Embiotoca lateralis*
  Agassiz, 1854
Family: **Surfperch**
Other common names: blue sea-perch,
  striped surfperch
French name: ditrème rayé

Distribution: From southeastern Alaska through British Columbia to Baja California.

Characters: This surfperch is distinguished from other Canadian species by having a frenum, 59–65 lateral line scales, a low spiny dorsal fin and a higher soft rayed dorsal fin, and about 15 blue stripes along the flanks. Dorsal fin spines 10–12, soft rays 23–26. Anal fin spines 3, soft rays 29–33. Pectoral fin rays 21–24. Caudal fin broadly forked. Overall colour is copper extending onto the fins with dark brown on the back. The flank has about

15 blue and orange to yellow stripes which are curved above the lateral line and horizontal below it. The head has blue spots and

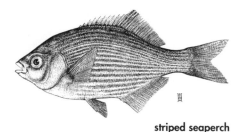

striped seaperch

lines. The caudal fin base is dark as are the anterior parts of the soft dorsal and anal fins. The upper lip is often black. Young fish are tinged orange. Reaches 38 cm.

Biology: Found on rocky coasts and in kelp beds, and around wharves and pilings. Occasionally in the surf on sand beaches near rocks. Descends to 21 m. Food is crustaceans such as amphipods, bryozoans, worms, mussels and herring eggs, which are browsed and "picked" selectively. Young are released in June–July and number up to 44. They are about 4–6 cm long. An important sport and commercial fish. Caught by anglers from rocks, piers and small boats and by spear fishermen.

striped searobin

Scientific name: *Prionotus evolans*
  (Linnaeus, 1766)
Family: **Searobin**
Other common names: northern striped
  gurnard, brown-winged searobin, grondin
  volant
French name: prionote strié

Distribution: From Nova Scotia to Florida.

Characters: This species is distinguished from its Canadian relatives by having scales rather than plates, 3 short, stout, lower, finger-like pectoral rays, no forked snout, by colour pattern, and by a long pectoral fin reaching back level with rays 9–10 of the second dorsal fin. The caudal fin is truncate or square posteriorly. First dorsal fin spines 9–11, usually 10, second dorsal fin rays 11–13. Anal fin rays 11–13. About 53 lateral line pores. Overall colour is reddish to olive-brown. The flank has 2 black or dusky stripes. There is a dark blotch between dorsal fin spines 4 and 5. The inner

striped searobin

surface of the pectoral fin is blackish and the outer orange to brown, with a pale edge. There are narrow brown bars on the finger-like pectoral rays. Reaches 45 cm. The world, all-tackle angling record weighed 1.55 kg and was caught in 1988 at Long Island, New York.

Biology: First caught in the Bay of Fundy in 1957 where it is a rare stray from southern waters, found from inshore to about 180 m. Food is mainly crustaceans and fishes. This searobin lives up to 9 years and males and females grow at the same rate. Half their growth occurs during the first 2 years of life. Growth slows when sexual maturity is attained in the third year of life. Spawning occurs from May to early July in the United States. Eggs number up to 218,000 with a maximum diameter of 1.25 mm. A commercial catch in the U.S.A., it is used for food, fish meal, bait, pet food and fertiliser.

striped shiner

Scientific name: *Luxilus chrysocephalus*
    Rafinesque, 1820
Family: **Carp**
Other common names: none
French name: méné rayé

Distribution: Found from southern tributaries of the Great Lakes south to Louisiana. Canadian records are from tributaries of lakes Huron, St. Clair and Erie, and the Niagara River and probably elsewhere in southwestern Ontario. Bait fish introductions have widened its distribution in southern Ontario.

Characters: This species and its relatives in the genus *Notropis* (typical **shiners**) are separated from other family members by usually having 7 branched dorsal fin rays follow-

ing thin unbranched rays, protractile premaxillaries (upper lip separated from the snout by a groove), no barbels, large lateral line scales (fewer than 50), and a simple, s-shaped gut. It is distinguished by having anal fin branched rays 7–10, usually 8, exposed part of anterior lateral line scales twice as high as wide, dorsal fin origin over or in front of pelvic fin insertion level, predorsal scale rows 12–19, usually 13–16 (counted from below dorsal fin origin to head, 3–6 scale rows up from the lateral line), the chin is pigmented anteriorly and the upper flank has dark stripes meeting in Vs behind the dorsal fin. Pectoral rays 14–16 and pelvic rays 8. Lateral line scales 36–42. Pharyngeal teeth strongly hooked, 2,4–4,2. Males have large nuptial tubercles on the snout, head and lower jaw, and smaller tubercles on the first dorsal fin ray, anterior pectoral fin rays and the nape.

The back is green, olive-blue to slate-blue, flanks are silvery-blue to silvery-green with some darkened scales and scales with dark crescents, and the belly is silvery-white. Upper flank scales are outlined with pigment in contrast to the closely related **common shiner**. A broad middorsal stripe is brown, grey, or slate-blue. Fins are clear. Breeding males develop a lead-blue to bright blue head and back, pink flanks and the distal third of the dorsal, caudal and anal fins become pink. Peritoneum brown to black.

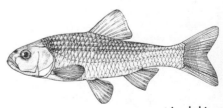

striped shiner

This species has long been confused with the **common shiner** with which it readily forms hybrids. It is separated on both morphological and biochemical evidence and the two species are thought to have diverged 2.2 million years ago, using the "molecular clock" analysis method for the biochemical data.

Formerly in the genus *Notropis*. Reaches 23.6 cm.

Biology: Striped shiners occur in clear rivers and streams, often in pools and associated with aquatic vegetation. They overwinter in larger, deeper rivers in contrast to **common shiners** and prefer warmer waters. Striped shiners are also thought to be more tolerant of turbidity and silt. Their biology is not well known since the species has been confused with the **common shiner**. Food is aquatic and terrestrial insects and various plant materials. Life span is at least 5 years with maturity attained at age 2. Spawning occurs from late April to June at water temperatures of 16°C or higher. Males defend a nest in a similar fashion to **common shiners**, but may use the nests of other species such as **hornyhead, river** and **creek chubs** and **central stonerollers** and forms hybrids with them and with other nest sharers such as **rosyface dace** and **redside dace**. A female is herded onto the nest site, the male curves around her so her head points upward, and eggs and sperm are shed. Eggs are 1.6 mm in diameter. Fewer than 50 orange eggs are shed during each spawning act.

stripetail rockfish

Scientific name: *Sebastes saxicola*
  (Gilbert, 1890)
Family: **Scorpionfish**
Other common names: olive-backed rockfish, popeye rockfish, bigeye rockfish
French name: sébaste à queue rayée

Distribution: Found from southeast Alaska to Baja California including British Columbia.

Characters: Colour pattern, head spines and 2 strong, sharp spines on the lower edge of the bone beneath the eye distinguish this species. Dorsal fin spines 13, soft rays 11–14, usually 12. Anal fin soft rays 5–8, usually 7, second anal spine twice as thick as third and longer. Pectoral fin rays 15–18, usually 16. Lateral line pores 35–43, scale rows below lateral line 43–53. Gill rakers 30–35. Vertebrae 26. The supraocular, coronal and sometimes nuchal spines are absent but the others are strong and sharp. There are 1–2 spines along the lower edge of the gill cover. Overall colour is pink with yellow or green tinges. The back has faint, dark saddles. The lower flank and belly are silvery-pink to

white. The tail fin has green streaks on the membranes but these are not always clear. Other fins are yellowish-pink. Peritoneum black. Reaches 39 cm.

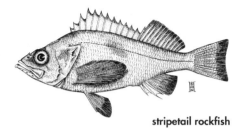

stripetail rockfish

Biology: A common species on soft bottoms at 46–421 m, usually in the deeper water below 180 m both inshore and offshore. Food is principally krill. Half the male population is mature before attaining 17 cm and for females 20 cm. Larger females produce 200,000 young in February in Canadian waters. Trawlers catch this species but it is not used commercially because of its small size, usually less than 30 cm.

stubraker slipskin

Scientific name: *Lycodapus parviceps*
  Gilbert, 1896
Family: **Eelpout**
Other common names: smallhead eelpout
French name: lycode à petite tête

Distribution: Found from the Bering Sea to British Columbia.

Characters: This species is distinguished from its Pacific coast relatives by having the branchiostegal membranes free of the isthmus posteriorly, gill rakers blunt and shorter than wide, and gill slit not extending above the pectoral fin base. Dorsal fin rays 94–98, anal rays 81–86, pectoral rays 8–9, total ver-

stubraker slipskin

tebrae 100–104, and teeth on vomer bone in the roof of the mouth 2–15. Scales and pelvic fins are absent. The flesh is gelatinous. Overall colour is a translucent creamy to silvery white. The muscles under the skin may be lightly or heavily spotted with pigment. Gill membranes and arch lightly pigmented. Lips and mouth and gill cavities pale. Peritoneum black. Reaches 11.6 cm standard length.

Biology: This species is pelagic but is usually caught in bottom trawls fishing at 81–457 m. Found around Vancouver Island.

Sturgeon Family

Scientific name: Acipenseridae
French name: esturgeons

Sturgeons are found in fresh and coastal waters around the Northern Hemisphere. There are 24 species with 5 occurring in Canada, 2 on the Pacific coast and its drainages, 2 on the Atlantic coast and its drainages and 1 on the Arctic and Atlantic coasts and their drainages.

These very large fishes are easily recognised by the 5 rows of bony scutes along the body, (1 dorsal, 2 lateral and 2 ventrolateral), 4 barbels in front of the mouth under an elongate snout, no teeth in adults, an upturned caudal fin skeleton (heterocercal) such that the upper tail lobe is larger than the lower, and various internal characters. The scutes may almost disappear in old sturgeons but are sharp and obvious in young. The skeleton is cartilaginous, there is a spiral intestinal valve, 1 branchiostegal ray, fin rays number more than the underlying basal bones which support them, no gular bones on the lower head surface and a large swimbladder. Canadian species have a spiracle, the mouth is transverse and gill membranes are joined to the isthmus. The unpaired fins have fulcra, or flat bony plates, distinct from the scutes, in front of them.

Sturgeons are related to the **Paddlefish Family** and are members of the **Sturgeon Order**.

This family contains the largest freshwater fishes including the European sturgeon reputed to attain over 9 m and 1451 kg. Their life span is reported to exceed 150 years although fish of great size are difficult to age accurately. Some species live entirely in fresh water while others are anadromous, spending some time in the sea but returning to fresh water to spawn. The barbels are highly sensitive and, as soon as they detect food, the tubular mouth protrudes to suck in the prey.

Sturgeon roe or eggs are known as caviar and form an expensive delicacy. The Caspian Sea basin in the former U.S.S.R. and Iran is the centre for caviar production. The eggs are stripped from the female by pressing on her belly or cut out of the dead fish. The unripe, greenish eggs are separated from the surrounding membranes, mixed with salt (which helps preserve them and incidentally turns them black), and canned. Up to an exceptional 180 kg of caviar can be taken from a large species of sturgeon. The flesh is also eaten, and is tasty when smoked. The total Canadian catch of sturgeons in 1988 was 53 tonnes.

Their migratory habits have made them victims of pollution and hydroelectric schemes and sturgeons are no longer as large nor as numerous as in the past. Slow growth makes them susceptible to overfishing. Hatcheries raise millions of sturgeons in Eurasia and North America in attempts to maintain stocks.

The swimbladders of sturgeons have been converted to isinglass, a transparent gelatin used in a variety of products including as a wine and beer clarifier and in jams and jellies. In the past, the scutes have been used as scrapers and steamboats on the American rivers trawled large numbers to extract their oil as fuel.

See **Atlantic sturgeon**
　　green sturgeon
　　lake sturgeon
　　shortnose sturgeon
　　white sturgeon

Sturgeon Order

Sturgeons and **paddlefishes** comprise the Order Acipenseriformes. There are 2 families with 25 species living in fresh and salt waters of the Northern Hemisphere. These are large fishes and include some of the largest fishes found in fresh water. Both families had Canadian representatives although one family is now extirpated in Canada. There are 5 species on the Atlantic and Pacific coasts and in fresh water.

These fishes are characterised by an elongate snout or rostrum with the toothless mouth underneath and with barbels on the lower snout surface, an upturned skeleton in the caudal fin with the upper caudal lobe longer than the lower (= heterocercal), a cartilage skeleton, only 1 branchiostegal ray, no gulars, shark-like fins with fin rays more numerous than the basals forming their internal ray skeleton, scales reduced and often forming 5 rows of bony plates or scutes, spiracles may be present, the operculum is the only gill cover bone, the gut is connected to the swimbladder by a duct, vertebrae without centra and a spiral valve in the intestine like that of **sharks**.

The cartilaginous skeleton was once thought to be primitive and indicate a close relationship to **sharks** and their relatives but it is a secondary development and these are **bony fishes**.

Fossils date back to Lower Jurassic times 170 million years ago and there are a number of extinct families. The 2 living families are survivors of early **ray-finned fishes**. These living and extinct families (sometimes grouped as Chondrostei) share such characters as the absence of myodomes in the skull, fusion of the premaxillae, maxillae and dermopalatine bones of the upper jaw region and an anterior palatoquadrate symphysis, i.e. this bone meets in the midline and does not articulate with the skull. All other **ray-finned fishes**, the **gars, bowfins** and true **bony fishes** are grouped as the Neopterygii.

Sea-living members enter fresh water to spawn. Some species are highly valued for their eggs which constitute caviar.

See **Paddlefish Family**
Sturgeon Family

sturgeon poacher

Scientific name: *Podothecus acipenserinus*
(Pallas in Tilesius, 1813)
Family: **Poacher**
Other common names: none
French name: agone-esturgeon

Distribution: Found from the Bering Sea to northern California including British Columbia. Also extends into Arctic waters adjacent to the Bering Sea.

Characters: This species is distinguished from other Canadian Pacific poachers by having a ventral mouth opening downwards and surrounded by clusters of cirri. There are 10 or more cirri at the rear of the upper jaw. The head and eye are comparatively large among poachers. The first dorsal fin has 6–10 spines, the second dorsal fin has 6–9 soft rays. The anal fin has 6–9 rays and the pectoral fin 16–19 with the lower 4–6 rays slightly finger-like. Lateral line pores 37–40. Spines are found on the snout, head over the eyes and back of the head. There are large spines on the anterior dorsal plates. Gill membranes are joined to the isthmus. Males have longer fins than females. The body is grey to brown above and yellow to orange below. The back has saddle marks extending onto the flanks. Plates are outlined by pigment. The cirri are bright yellow. There is an orange spot under the eye. The anal fin has a dark blotch on its posterior edge in adults. The caudal fin is yellowish. Males have black pelvic fin membranes, probably for signalling during reproduction. Attains 30.5 cm.

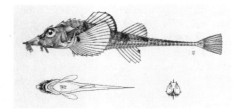

sturgeon poacher

Biology: Found at 2–475 m, often common on soft bottoms or around reefs. Food is chiefly crustaceans and worms, occasionally fish. These poachers have been observed swimming by means of an undulating movement of the pectoral fins. Maximum age is 11 years. Males are mature at 20 cm standard length. Spawning occurs in the spring, June in the southeastern Bering Sea. Trawlers often catch this species but it has no commercial value.

Sucker Family

Scientific name: Catostomidae
French name: meuniers

Suckers, redhorses, buffalofishes and carpsuckers are found in fresh waters of North America with 1 species in the Yangtse Kiang of China and 1 North American species also in northeastern Siberia. There are 68 species with 18 species and 1 subspecies in Canada. They are mostly small to medium-sized fishes with a maximum length of 1.0 m.

The family is characterised by the fleshy lips which are variously folded (plicae) or bumpy (papillae), the broad lower lip often has a cleft, the mouth is ventral, sucking and highly protrusible, no jaw teeth, pharyngeal or throat teeth in a single row of 16 or more teeth, up to as many as 190, which grind food against a horny pad at the base of the basioccipital bone as in the **Carp Family**, barbels and an adipose fin are absent, 10 or more dorsal fin rays, no fin spines, the anal fin is placed far back on the body, scales are cycloid, the upper jaw is bordered by the premaxilla and maxilla bones, there are y-shaped intermuscular bones, the swimbladder has 2–3 chambers and is connected to the gut, and pelvic fins are on the belly (abdominal). Suckers are tetraploids.

Suckers are members of the **Carp Order**. The redhorses (genus *Moxostoma*) are difficult to identify and require some practice. Fin ray counts used in identification are the principal, elongate rays. Rudimentary rays, usually 2–4, at the beginning of each fin are not included. Fossils date back to the Eocene.

Most suckers are bottom-feeders, grubbing through detritus for food by touch and taste. There are two basic body forms, a heavy, deep-bodied one and a more rounded, stream-lined form. The former are found in large slow rivers and lakes and the latter in faster streams. Young are often plankton feeders with mouths at the tip of the snout. The mouth migrates ventrally with growth and diet switches to bottom foods. Mollusc feeders have heavy, molar-shaped teeth while those feeding on aquatic insects and crustaceans have thin, sharp-edged teeth. Suckers have brightened colours during the spawning season and develop nuptial tubercles. Hybrids are common among suckers. They are not generally eaten in Canada but can be quite tasty, and are of only minor interest to anglers, perhaps unjustly so. However they are very important forage species, fed on by a variety of sport fishes.

See **bigmouth buffalo**
  black buffalo
  black redhorse
  bridgelip sucker
  copper redhorse
  golden redhorse
  greater redhorse
  Jasper longnose sucker
  lake chubsucker
  largescale sucker
  longnose sucker
  mountain sucker
  northern hog sucker
  quillback
  river redhorse
  shorthead redhorse
  silver redhorse
  spotted sucker
  white sucker

summer flounder

Scientific name: *Paralichthys dentatus*
  (Linnaeus, 1766)
Family: **Lefteye Flounder**
Other common names: none
French name: cardeau d'été

Distribution: Found from Nova Scotia to Florida.

Characters: This species is identified among its Canadian Atlantic relatives by the pelvic fin bases being short and not on the

summer flounder

midline of the belly, 5 large ocelli (or eye spots), 16–24 total gill rakers (13–18 lower arm) and small eyes. Dorsal fin rays 80–96, anal rays 60–75, eyed side pectoral rays 11–13 and lateral line scales 91–108. Scales are cycloid. Rare specimens may be reversed or "right-handed" with eyes and colour on the right side, and even retain colour on the blind side. Colour variable with the background from white to grey, olive, orange, pink, dark brown and almost black. There are numerous eye spots but 5 are prominent, 2 near the dorsal fin base, 2 opposite near the anal fin base and 1 in the middle on the lateral line. Reaches 1.23 m and 13.8 kg. The world, all-tackle angling record weighed 10.17 kg and was caught at Montauk, New York in 1975.

Biology: An uncommon species in Canadian waters with captures east of LaHave Bank, on the Scotian Shelf and in Passamaquoddy Bay. Reported down to 183 m but usually in shallow water. It has been reported from fresh water in the U.S.A. It may pursue fish up to the water surface and even leap out of the water for a moment, an unusual behaviour for a **flatfish**. Other food includes a variety of crustaceans and squid. Spawning occurs during an offshore migration in September to December north of Chesapeake Bay. Eggs are up to 1.1 mm in diameter and are pelagic. An important sport and commercial species in the U.S.A. Anglers catch this flounder by bottom fishing with bait from shore and from boats. The recreational fishery in the U.S.A. catches mostly 1–2 year old fish.

sun flashlightfish

Scientific name: *Electrona risso*
(Cocco, 1829)
Family: **Lanternfish**
Other common names: none
French name: lampion-soleil

Distribution: Found in the Pacific, Southern and Atlantic oceans. Mostly in the eastern Atlantic Ocean but occasionally in Canadian waters such as off the Flemish Cap.

Characters: This species is distinguished from its Atlantic coast relatives by lacking photophores close to the dorsal body edge, the PLO photophore is well below the upper pectoral fin base and is over the first PVO photophore, the mouth is terminal, and the PLO forms a triangle with the first and second PVO photophores. Dorsal fin rays 13–15, anal rays 18–20 and pectoral rays

13–17. Total gill rakers 26–30. Vertebrae 33–34. AO photophores 10–13. Males have a supracaudal or infracaudal luminous gland or both. Females usually have one of each or sometimes either one only. These glands develop at 4.0 cm. Reaches about 8.2 cm.

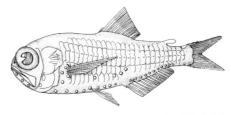

sun flashlightfish

Biology: Reported in the Atlantic to occur at 200–750 m by day. At 90–375 m and 400–700 m, centring on 200 and 500 m respectively, by night. Sexual maturity is attained at about 5.9 cm.

sunbeam lampfish

Scientific name: *Lampadena urophaos*
Paxton, 1963
Family: **Lanternfish**
Other common names: brightlight lanternfish
French name: lampe à rayon de soleil

Distribution: Found in the eastern Pacific Ocean from about Hawaii eastward and from British Columbia south to about 25°N. Also in the subtropical Atlantic Ocean.

Characters: This lanternfish is distinguished from its Pacific coast relatives by having 3 Prc photophores, the fourth PO

sunbeam lampfish

photophore is not elevated above the others, very large, undivided caudal luminous glands are present, and the procurrent caudal fin rays are spine-like. Dorsal fin rays 14–16, anal rays 13–14, pectoral rays 15–17 and vertebrae 35–38. Total gill rakers 13–18 and

AO photophores 7–9. Lateral line scales about 38. There is a strong, posteriorly directed pterotic spine. Reaches 23.7 cm.

Biology: First reported in 1985 based on a specimen taken at 60 m in 1958 from off Vancouver Island. Daytime depths in the Atlantic Ocean are 600–1000 m and night-time depths are 50–250 m. Life span is probably longer than 2 years. Spawning occurs in spring and summer and is prolonged, at least in Atlantic Ocean populations.

Sunfish Family

Scientific name: Centrarchidae
French name: crapets

Sunfishes, pygmy sunfishes, **basses, crappies** and their relatives are found only in North American fresh waters and have about 32 species. There are 12 species in Canada.

These fishes are characterised by continuous or notched spiny and soft dorsal fins, the spiny part lower than the soft part, 3 or more anal fin spines, thoracic pelvic fins, 5–7 branchiostegal rays, separate gill membranes, no suborbital shelf and a small, concealed or absent pseudobranch. Suborbital bones are present. The dentary and angular bones are penetrated by the head canal system. Body shape is elongate or compressed. Jaws and mouth cavity bones are variously armed with bands of teeth. There are also conical or molar-like throat or pharyngeal teeth. The swimbladder is not connected to the gut by a duct. Scales are ctenoid, occasionally cycloid.

Sunfishes are members of the **Perch Order**. Fossils date to the Eocene. The pygmy sunfishes (not in Canada) are smaller than 4 cm and are sometimes placed in their own family. Hybrids are common among sunfishes. Sunfishes are identified by body shape, and by fin ray and scale counts. One unique character used in identification is the "ear flap" or opercular flap, an extension of the upper, rear corner of the gill cover. This flap varies in shape and colour and the bony edge may be smooth or crenate. The bony edge is not the obvious rear margin of the flap, which is fleshy, but is an internal structure at varying distances anterior to the rear margin.

Sunfishes build nests, usually a shallow depression excavated by tail sweeps. The male guards the eggs and young. The sunfishes (genus *Lepomis*) make grunt-like sounds during courtship, an important method of mate recognition. The **basses** are important sport fishes and a number of sunfish species are used as experimental animals, being easy to maintain in aquaria. Colours of sunfishes rival those of tropical marine fishes and they are used in the aquarium trade. They have been introduced widely outside their natural range in North America and in other parts of the world.

See **black crappie**
   bluegill
   green sunfish
   largemouth bass
   longear sunfish
   orangespotted sunfish
   pumpkinseed
   redbreast sunfish
   rock bass
   smallmouth bass
   warmouth
   white crappie

surf smelt

Scientific name: *Hypomesus pretiosus*
   (Girard, 1855)
Family: **Smelt**
Other common names: silver smelt, day smelt
French name: éperlan argenté

Distribution: Found from the Gulf of Alaska to California including British Columbia.

Characters: This species and its relative, the **pond smelt**, are distinguished from other smelts by having 8–14 gill rakers on the upper arch, minute brush-like teeth on the

surf smelt

tongue, and an incomplete lateral line with usually 73 or fewer scales. This species has more pyloric caeca (4–7) than the **pond** smelt and the length of the adipose fin base is less than the eye diameter. The mouth is small and ends before the middle of the eye. Dorsal fin rays 8–11, anal rays 12–17 and pectoral rays 14–17. Total gill rakers 30–36. Scales in midlateral series 66–76. Adult males have tubercles on the scales and fin rays. The back is olive-green to brown or yellowish and the flanks and belly are silvery with a purplish iridescence. There is an iridescent stripe along the midflank (dark in preserved fish). Males develop golden tints at spawning. Peritoneum with pigment spots. Attains 30.5 cm but usually much smaller.

Biology: Found commonly in marine and brackish waters in Canada. Food includes various crustaceans, worms, comb jellies, larval fishes and insects. They are food for **salmon** and other fishes. Life span is at least 4 years and some fish mature at 1 year. Males predominate in catches while females are larger. Spawning occurs on quiet sandy beaches at high tide during the day. Eggs are adhesive and buried in sand. These smelt spawn over several days with females producing up to 29,950 eggs in each batch. There can be 3–5 spawnings per season. The spawning season is year round but peaks over summer. This smelt is of modest commercial importance in British Columbia where it is caught by gill nets and purse seines. The total Canadian catch varied from 0 to 4 tonnes over the period 1983–1988. Anglers catch this fish on smelt jigs, a series of shiny but bare hooks. It can be used as bait for other species. On the spawning run, surf smelt can be caught in buckets or by hand and are excellent fried in butter.

Surfperch Family

Scientific name: Embiotocidae
French name: ditrèmes

Surfperches, **seaperches** or viviparous perches, are found in the coastal waters of the North Pacific Ocean. There are about 24 species with 8 reported from British Columbia. A ninth species, the calico surfperch (*Amphistichus koelzi* Hubbs, 1933), has been found only 32 km south of the Canadian border, but has not yet been caught in British Columbia. It is distinguished from the related **redtail surfperch** by having a notch in the dorsal fin.

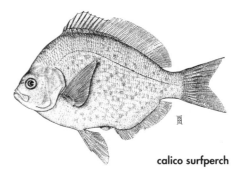

calico surfperch

Their body is compressed with a contiguous dorsal fin comprised of both spines (6–19) and soft rays (9–28). The anal fin has 3 spines followed by about 15–35 soft rays. The pelvic fin is thoracic and has 1 spine and 5 branched rays. The caudal fin is forked. Scales are cycloid and extend onto the head. A scaly sheath covers the dorsal fin base.

This family is a member of the **Perch Order**. An important character in identification is the presence or absence of the frenum, a connection between the lip and the lower jaw.

Surfperches are live-bearers, a rare phenomenon in marine fishes, and the female is impregnated by the male using a thickened part of the anterior anal fin. Actual fertilisation of eggs may occur months later. The embryos grow in the female ovary and obtain oxygen and food through the ovarian fluid. As the embryos grow they develop flap-like extensions to the dorsal and anal fins which aid in oxygen, and probably food, absorption. Each female releases about 3–30 young which are well-developed and almost sexually mature. Reproduction may follow shortly after birth in males.

Most species are marine and some live in the surf zone — hence the name. One species enters fresh water in California.

Surfperches have teeth in the throat and a complex series of muscles which allows them to feed in a highly specialised manner. Some species are oral-winnowers, i.e. they have the ability to sort and spit out material unsuitable as food. They select food after it is taken in the mouth. Non-winnower species select food before it is taken in. These are the picker-browsers which select food from algae and reefs, and the picker-crushers which select hard-shelled molluscs, crabs and brittle stars and crush them with massive, pavement-like throat teeth, spitting out some of the shell before swallowing.

These fish are often caught by anglers and some are fished commercially.

See **kelp perch**
 pile perch
 redtail surfperch
 shiner perch
 silver surfperch
 striped seaperch
 walleye surfperch
 white seaperch

Swallower Family

Scientific name: Saccopharyngidae
French name: avaleurs

Found in the Atlantic, Indian and Pacific oceans. There are about 10 species with 1 reported from the Atlantic coast of Canada.

Swallowers or whiptail gulpers are highly unusual, lacking various skeletal elements such as opercular bones, ribs and branchiostegal rays, and also scales, pelvic fins, pyloric caeca and a swimbladder. The caudal fin is absent or rudimentary. The eyes are tiny and placed far anterior. The gill openings are closer to the snout tip than the anus. The most obvious feature is the very large mouth and distensible pharynx which can take in very large fish. Jaws have curved teeth. There may be luminous grooves on the body and tail.

Swallowers are relatives of the **Gulper Family** and they all have a leptocephalus larva which relates them to the **eels** with which they are sometimes classified. The family is a member of the **Gulper Eel Order**.

These fishes are rarely seen and are known from less than 100 specimens.

See **taillight gulper**

swellhead snailfish

Scientific name: *Paraliparis cephalus*
 Gilbert, 1892
Family: **Snailfish**
Other common names: none

French name: limace à grosse tête

Distribution: Found from the Bering Sea south to Washington including British Columbia.

Characters: This snailfish is identified among its Canadian Pacific relatives by the lack of pelvic fins and an adhesive disc, by having 6 branchiostegal rays, no barbels or papillae on the snout and no laterally directed opercular spine, and an oblique mouth. There is a prominent knob at the tip of the lower jaw matched by a notch on the upper jaws. Teeth are in narrow bands. Dorsal fin rays 50–57, anal rays 44–51. Pectoral fin rays 14–16, with a deep notch separating an upper lobe of 8–10 rays from a lower lobe of 2–4 rays with notch rays short but well-developed. Pyloric caeca 6–10 and pale. The skin is transparent and there are scattered pigment spots on the pale body muscles. The mouth is pale. The mouth and gill cavities, peritoneum and stomach are black. Reaches 8.4 cm.

swellhead snailfish

Biology: This species inhabits the continental slope at 524–1384 m.

swordfish

Scientific name: *Xiphias gladius*
 Linnaeus, 1758
Family: **Swordfish**
Other common names: broadbill, albacore,
 billfish
French name: espadon

Distribution: World-wide and on the Atlantic and Pacific coasts of Canada.

Characters: The swordfish is distinguished by the long, pointed, flattened, sharp-edged, sword-like rostrum and by the absence of pelvic fins. Young swordfish have jaws of equal length. Scales are lost in adults and have spiny ridges in young. Jaw teeth disappear with growth. The adult caudal peduncle has a single, lateral keel on each side and both a dorsal and ventral notch. The adult dorsal fin is rigid but can be folded back in young. The first dorsal fin has 21–49 rays (widely different non-overlapping counts are given by different authors), the second dorsal 3–6 rays. First anal fin with 12–18 rays, second anal 3–4 rays. Young fish have continuous dorsal fins and continuous anal fins. Falcate pectoral fins have 16–18 rays.

Black, brownish or purplish above

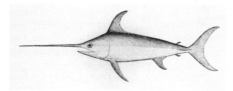

swordfish

becoming light brown below. The sword is black above, lighter below. The first dorsal fin membrane blackish brown, other fins brownish to brown-black.

Reaches 4.96 m and 675 kg. The world, all-tackle angling record from Chile in 1953 weighed 536.15 kg.

Biology: First reported from the Pacific coast of Canada in a gill net off Vancouver Island in 1984. Found from the northern tip of Newfoundland, the southern Gulf of St. Lawrence and southward in the Atlantic primarily entering Canadian waters in June-November. The swordfish is an offshore, pelagic species found mostly at 200–600 m but at the surface in temperate waters. Fish seen, and often harpooned, at the surface in Canadian waters are probably basking to avoid cold deeper waters. Swordfish often leap clear of the water in an effort to dislodge **remoras** and parasites. They are usually found at temperatures above 13°C but tolerate 5–27°C. They are migratory, but not in schools, between cooler waters for summer feeding and warmer waters for spawning and overwintering.

Food is pelagic fishes such as **tunas, dolphinfishes, flyingfishes, barracudas** as well as squids, but shallow water species such as **mackerels, herrings, sardines** and **sauries** and bottom and deepwater fishes such as **hakes, redfishes, lanternfishes** and others are also taken. Bottom fishes are digested

after a return to warmer surface waters. Some excellent museum specimens of deepsea fishes are from swordfish stomachs. The sword is used to kill prey by slashing as food items taken from swordfish stomachs bear slashes, often behind the head indicating an individual attack rather than a slashing attack on a school. Few fish, apart from **sharks**, attempt to eat the larger swordfish and even **sharks** do not always come off best as sword fragments have been found embedded in their bodies. However a 330 kg **mako** shark caught off the Bahamas had a whole 55 kg swordfish in its gut. Swordfish are known to attack boats and whales. Copper-covered boat hulls have been pierced and the sword broken off, leading inevitably to the death of the swordfish. A swordfish attacked the Woods Hole Oceanographic Institute's submersible *Alvin* at a depth of 605 m and its sword became wedged in a seam such that it could not break free. It is possible that many "attacks" are simply the inability of a swordfish, swimming at bursts of speed as fast as 100 km/h, to avoid boats.

Females are larger and live longer than males but are mature at 70 cm compared to 100 cm for males in the Atlantic Ocean. Few males exceed 200 cm and 120 kg and would be about 5–6 years old, indicative of a fast growth rate. Peak spawning is in April-September but occurs year round in the Caribbean Sea, Gulf of Mexico and off Florida. Spawning occurs in the upper 75 m at about 23°C and up to 5 million eggs with a diameter of 1.8 mm are produced.

This is a very valuable commercial species which is usually caught by longlines but may be harpooned or trolled. Important fisheries are on the Grand Bank and Georges Bank. The Canadian fishery ended in 1970 because mercury levels in swordfish were found to be 0.5 parts per million, the legal limit. At that time the fishery was 3620 tonnes worth $3,689,000. The limit was raised in the U.S.A. and Canada to 1.0 p.p.m. in 1979. Studies on old, museum-preserved specimens had shown that high levels of mercury were not simply a product of modern industrial pollution. However swordfish landed in Canada have to carry a "Danger to Health" label and only small amounts are offered for sale. Most Canadian caught sword-fish are transferred to U.S. vessels at sea. The Canadian catch in 1988 was 704 tonnes. The 1989 catch was worth about $5.2 million. It is excellent eating. Fish are sold fresh as steaks or frozen, canned or as "teriyaki." The world catch in 1982 was 40,321 tonnes. A major sport fishery using trolling or drifting bait lines exists along the U.S. coast from New York to Texas and in other parts of the world but not in Canada. It is one of the best sport-fish in the world.

Swordfish Family

Scientific name: Xiphiidae
French name: espadons

The swordfishes and the sailfishes, spearfishes and **marlins** (= **billfishes**) are found world-wide in temperate to tropical seas. There are only 12 species with 3 reported from Canadian waters.

These fishes are characterised by an elon-gate, rounded, pointed or depressed rostrum or "bill." Elongate, spike-like pelvic fins, embedded pointed and narrow scales and a lateral line are present in most species, absent in the swordfish. There are 1–2 keels on each side of the caudal peduncle. Jaws have file-like teeth, absent in adult swordfish. The dor-sal fin is very long and, in some species — the sailfishes (not in Canada) — very high. The swimbladder has many chambers. All species are streamlined with the first dorsal, first anal and pelvic fins folding into grooves.

Swordfish are in the **Perch Order**.

The bill is thrashed about in a school of fish to injure and stun them. Species with large fins will erect them to prevent encir-cled fish from escaping. Billfishes and swordfish are found offshore in open waters, as deep as 800 m or more. Females grow larger than males. These large fishes migrate long distances and are some of the speediest fish in the ocean. Young are pelagic. Billfishes experience wide temperature vari-ations as they pursue food in deep, cold and warm, surface waters. A mass of muscle attached to each eye keeps the brain warm so the whole body does not have to be heated to adapt to these temperature changes.

They are commercially important, partic-ularly to Japan, and are caught principally by longlining, but harpoons, drift nets, set nets and trolling are used. Larger fish are prepared as "*sashimi*" (sliced raw with soy sauce and green mustard) and "*sushi*" (sliced raw with green mustard on vinegar-boiled rice balls). However, they do have muscle mercury con-centrations higher than **tunas**. They are also extremely popular game fishes caught by trolling. There is no commercial fishery in Canada, but in the U.S.A. the sport requires boats and equipment which are rented to tourists. There is also a minor taxidermy industry mounting catches for display.

See **blue marlin**
swordfish
white marlin

T

Taaning's headlightfish

Scientific name: *Diaphus taaningi*
Norman, 1930
Family: **Lanternfish**
Other common names: none
French name: lampe-de-tête de Taaning

Distribution: Found in the Atlantic Ocean, Mediterranean and Caribbean seas, including the Scotian Shelf and off Georges Bank in Atlantic Canada.

Characters: This species and its relatives, the **bouncer, eventooth, flashlight, square,** and **straightcheek headlightfishes** and the

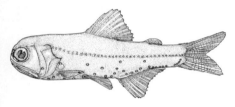

Taaning's headlightfish

doormat and **slanteye parkinglightfishes**, are separated from other Atlantic coast lanternfishes by not having photophores near the dorsal body edge, the PLO photophore is well above the upper pectoral fin base level while the second PVO photophore is at or below this level, there are 4 Prc photophores, the PO and two PVO photophores form a straight, ascending line as do the first 3 VO photophores, supracaudal luminous glands are absent, and there is more than 1 pair of luminous head organs. This species is separated from its relatives by having the So photophore absent, vomer with a small round to oval patch of teeth on each side, Dn photophore well developed in a deep cup, directed forward and about half the size of the nasal rosette, first SAO photophore above level of fifth VO photophore and pelvic fins reaching anal fin. Dorsal fin rays 13–15, anal rays 13–15 and pectoral rays 10–11. Total gill rakers 19–23. AO photophores 9–11. Lateral line organs 35–36. Adult males have an enlarged Vn photophore

extending down to the upper jaw. The "headlights" or photophores Dn and Vn are distinct at 1.9 cm body length. Reaches 7.0 cm.

Biology: This species is known as a pseudoceanic lanternfish, one that is found close to land. Depth distribution by day is 250–475 m and by night from the surface to 250 m, most abundantly at 100 m. Food is principally herbivorous zooplankton such as copepod crustaceans. Most feeding occurs in the early evening with the rest of the night occupied in digestion. Sexual maturity is reached at 4.0–5.0 cm.

tadpole madtom

Scientific name: *Noturus gyrinus*
(Mitchill, 1817)
Family: **Bullhead Catfish**
Other common names: tadpole stonecat, tadpole cat
French name: chat-fou brun

Distribution: Found in Atlantic coast drainages from New York to Florida, along the Gulf coast, in the Mississippi River basin and the southern Great Lakes basin. Absent from the mountains paralleling the Atlantic coast. In Canada found in southern Saskatchewan and Manitoba, the Quetico-Rainy River drainages of western Ontario which drain to Hudson Bay, tributaries of Lakes Huron, St. Clair, Erie and Ontario, and upper tributaries of the St. Lawrence River in Ontario and Quebec.

Characters: This species is identified by the posterior tip of the adipose fin not being free but attached to the back, pectoral spine

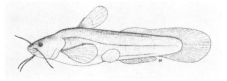

tadpole madtom

nearly straight to moderately curved, without teeth, colour pattern dark without blotches or saddles on the body, premaxillary band of teeth without lateral processes extending backwards, pectoral radials usually fused, pectoral soft rays usually 7, but a range of 5–10, pelvic rays usually 8 but range of 5–10, mouth terminal, typically 10 preoperculomandibular pores, and vertical fins without a black margin. Dorsal fin soft rays 4–7, usually 6, anal rays 12–18, usually 15. There are 2 internasal pores. Body shape resembles a tadpole, hence the name. The anterior rays of the caudal fin are more strongly developed than in any other madtom. The back and upper flank are olive-grey or brown to golden yellow, with the lower flank and belly light or with some pigmentation. Fins and barbels may be either darker or lighter than the adjacent body. The muscle segments of the body are darkly outlined and there is a dark line along the body axis. Breeding males are a dark chocolate brown or brownish-dusky. Attains 11.5 cm.

Biology: This madtom is found in quieter waters with slow current over mud bottoms with lots of vegetation, including streams and lakes down to 25 m. It is nocturnal and hides in holes, debris or vegetation during the day but is quite common. Food is various aquatic insects and crustaceans. Maximum age is 4 years. Males are larger and heavier than females in their fourth year of life. Some fish mature as early as 1 year and most by 2 years of age. Spawning occurs in summer (probably July in Canada) and eggs are laid in cavities or even tin cans. Eggs are yellow, up to 3.5 mm in diameter, but very variable in size, and are in an adhesive mass surrounded by a gelatinous envelope. Up to 150 eggs are found together, perhaps from more than 1 female. Clutches may be guarded by both male and female, or the male alone. Each female may contain up to 323 eggs but fecundity, like egg diameter, varies between populations. The pectoral spine is grooved and contains venomous tissue capable of inflicting a bad sting. This madtom has been used as bait for other fishes by anglers and is said to be excellent, despite the pectoral spine.

tadpole sculpin

Scientific name: *Psychrolutes paradoxus*
    Günther, 1861

Family: **Soft Sculpin**
Other common names: none
French name: chabot-têtard

Distribution: Found from Japan to the Bering Sea and south to Washington including British Columbia.

Characters: This soft sculpin is distinguished from its Pacific coast relatives by having a continuous spiny and soft dorsal fin with the spiny section buried in tissue, no preopercular spines, pectoral rays 19–23, usually 20–21, the upper jaw overhangs the lower, the anus is midway between the anal and pelvic fin bases, and 12–17 soft dorsal fin rays. There are no cirri but stout papillae are found on the head, body and part of the fins. Dorsal fin spines 10–12. Anal fin rays 10–14. Lateral line pores about 10. The body is brown to grey, white ventrally, with dark bars and mottling. The pectoral fin is orange to pink, or yellowish, with dark bars. The eye is blue. The caudal fin is barred. Reaches 6.4 cm.

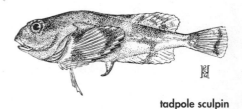

tadpole sculpin

Biology: Found at 9.1–220 m and locally common on soft and possibly rocky bottoms. It prefers cold water temperatures above freezing. May occur inshore in eelgrass or over mud. Eggs are up to 1.4 mm in diameter. Larvae are pelagic and are found off the Fraser River mouth in April-May, where they feed on plankton.

tadpole snailfish

Scientific name: *Nectoliparis pelagicus*
    Gilbert and Burke, 1912
Family: **Snailfish**
Other common names: tadpole liparid
French name: limace-têtard

Distribution: Found from Japan to southern California including British Columbia.

Characters: This snailfish is distinguished from its Canadian relatives on the Pacific coast by lacking pelvic fins modified into an adhesive disc, by having 5 branchiostegal rays and by the gill slit being below the uppermost

tadpole snailfish

pectoral fin ray. Minute teeth are in a single row in the lower jaw only. The anus is below the eyes and opens on a papilla facing forward into a trough running to the lower jaw. The anus is normal in fish smaller than 2.5 cm standard length. Dorsal fin rays 44–58, anal rays 40–53, pectoral rays 18–25 divided into 2 separated lobes with 3–5 lower lobe rays thickened and long. The gap between the lobes usually has rudimentary rays. There are 6–9 pale pyloric caeca. Overall colour is silvery under a transparent skin. Black pigment spots are present on the head and body, and are less developed on the dorsal, anal and caudal fins. The gill and mouth cavities are dark. Peritoneum and stomach black. Reaches 6.5 cm standard length.

Biology: Found from the surface down to 1000 m in British Columbia living pelagically, perhaps on the bottom. Elsewhere as deep as 3400 m.

taillight gulper

Scientific name: *Saccopharynx ampullaceus* (Harwood, 1827)
Family: **Swallower**
Other common names: none
French name: avaleur feu-arrière

Distribution: North Atlantic Ocean between 10° and 65°N, including Atlantic Canada.

Characters: The large mouth and the tiny eyes near the snout tip are characteristic. The

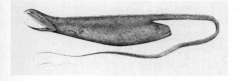

taillight gulper

gill openings are closer to the snout tip than to the anus in contrast to the related **pelican gulper**. Also the pectoral fins are well developed, jaw teeth are curved and the dorsal fin origin is well behind the head. The body and tail have filaments of varying length sticking out dorso-laterally. Black overall. Caudal organ with spots of luminescent tissue. Attains about 1.61 m total length, although much of this is the tail.

Biology: Found bathypelagically at 2000 m or more feeding on fish, some larger than itself. The leptocephalus larva occurs in shallower water. Sexually mature fish lose their teeth and their jaws shrink as bones resorb or disintegrate. Mature males develop greatly enlarged olfactory organs and the abdominal pouch is reduced, probably because feeding does not occur.

tail-light lanternfish

Scientific name: *Tarletonbeania taylori* Mead, 1953
Family: **Lanternfish**
Other common names: none
French name: lanterne feu-arrière

Distribution: Found in the North Pacific Ocean from Japan to British Columbia and southward. Also at Ocean Station Papa (50°N, 145°W).

Characters: This lanternfish is distinguished from its Pacific coast relatives by having only 1 Prc photophore and, in males,

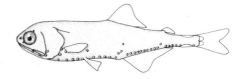

tail-light lanternfish

short, bulky luminous supracaudal and infracaudal glands. Females lack these glands and are difficult to distinguish from the related **blue lanternfish**. Identification is complicated further by hybridisation between the two species. Dorsal fin rays 12–14, anal rays 17–20, pectoral rays 11–16 and total vertebrae 40–42. AO photophores 14–18 and total gill rakers 14–18. Reaches about 7.1 cm.

Biology: Found at the surface where easily attracted by lights and, albeit confused with its relative, the commonest lanternfish at night off the British Columbia coast in the upper 20 m.

tan bristlemouth

Scientific name: *Cyclothone pallida* Brauer, 1902
Family: **Bristlemouth**
Other common names: none
French name: cyclothone pâle

Distribution: Found in the Atlantic, Indian and Pacific oceans including off the coast of British Columbia.

Characters: This species is separated from its Pacific coast relatives by lacking SO photophores, by having a basically light

tan bristlemouth

brown body with scales, a transparent area in front of the anal fin, usually 8, but sometimes 9 or 10, AO photophores, 21–27 gill rakers and all VAV photophores equally spaced. Gill filaments are not fused. Photophores: ORB 1, OP 2, BR 9–11, usually 10, IV 3 + 10, VAV 4–5, AC 14–16, IC 32–34. Dorsal fin rays 12–15, anal fin rays 16–19. Females reach 7.5 cm, but males only attain 4.8 cm standard length.

Biology: Found southwest of La Pérouse Bank in 1986, but also known from Ocean Station Papa (50°N, 145°W). This species is found at 400–1000 m, sometimes deeper, in the deep, mesopelagic zone of the ocean. Depth depends on age, season and latitude. There is no daily vertical migration. In Japan it spawns in spring and summer releasing about 1000–3000 eggs. It may spawn several times during its life. Males are mature at 3–4 years and 30–35 mm and females at 5–6 years at 40–45 mm standard length.

Tapirfish Family

Scientific name: Notacanthidae
French name: poissons-tapirs à épines

Tapirfishes, spiny tapirfishes or spiny eels are found world-wide in the deep sea in both the tropics and polar seas. There are 10 species, 1 on the Pacific coast, 2 on the Atlantic coast and 1 on the Arctic and Atlantic coasts of Canada.

They are characterised by having an elongate body, as in **eels** but pelvic fins are present (sometimes with 3 spine-like rays), a normal-sized mouth bearing teeth and up to 40 isolated spines on the back. There are 5–13 branchiostegal rays and a well-developed pectoral fin skeleton (degenerate in the backfin tapirfish). A true caudal fin is absent but the anal fin may regenerate around a broken off tail tip. Scales are small and cycloid and cover both the body and the head. Branchiostegal membranes are joined.

The **backfin tapirfish** has been placed in its own family, Lipogenyidae, since it differs in such features as the small, round, suctorial and toothless mouth structure and in having well-developed gill rakers. The Tapirfish Family is a member of the **Bonefish Order**, but has been placed in its own order. The term tapirfish refers to the swollen snout in allusion to the tropical mammals known as tapirs. The tapirfishes have also been called "spiny eels" but this is used for a family of tropical, freshwater fishes and is best avoided for these marine fishes which are not eels.

Tapirfishes are found at depths of 125–3500 m, sometimes in schools enabling commercial fishing off Japan for the **largescale tapirfish**. Their food is polychaetes, coelenterates and other items in and on the bottom. They feed by cropping and browsing. Some species have many more females than males in a population. Breeding males have darkened anterior nostrils. Some species have light organs. There are no oviducts and eggs are released into the abdominal cavity. They are laid through 2 abdominal pores near the anus. The young are a leptocephalus larva, often very large (1.84 m — the largest in the Animal Kingdom).

See **backfin tapirfish**
largescale tapirfish
longnose tapirfish
shortspine tapirfish

tarpon

Scientific name: *Megalops atlanticus*
  Valenciennes in Cuvier and Valenciennes, 1847
Family: **Tarpon**
Other common names: silverfish, silverking, tarpon argenté
French name: tarpon

Distribution: Found from Brazil to Nova Scotia in the western Atlantic Ocean, also in the eastern Atlantic Ocean.

Characters: The mouth is large and the lower jaw projects. There are 40–48 large scales in a complete lateral line. Scales have a crenulate, exposed margin. The last dorsal fin ray is elongated in fish larger than 10 cm. All these characters are distinct from the related **bonefish**. Dorsal fin rays 13–15, anal fin rays 19–25, pectoral fin rays 13–14. Leptocephali have less than 60 myomeres. Blue-grey back and silvery sides. Fins dusky. Attains 2.5 m and about 160 kg. The world, all-tackle angling record weighed 128.36 kg and was caught in 1956 at Lake Maracaibo, Venezuela.

tarpon

Biology: Rare in Atlantic Canada with less than 10 fish caught. Found in coastal areas even including fresh water. The young are leptocephalus larvae and migrate into estuaries. Tarpon can breath air, gulping it into a modified swimbladder via the duct connecting the gut and swimbladder. As a consequence they tolerate poor oxygen conditions in lagoons and mangrove swamps. Their principal food is schooling fishes but also includes crabs. They may live up to 50 years. Females are older and larger than males. Sexual maturity is attained at 100–120 cm. Spawning takes place from April to August and up to 12 million eggs are shed in open water. Leptocephali move into estuaries, rivers and lagoons. Too bony to be good eat-

ing, they are a superb angling fish eagerly sought after because of their rapid reaction, leaping and fighting ability. They have even reputedly broken the neck of an unlucky fisherman sitting in a boat! The large scales, up to 8 cm wide, have been made into jewellery. This species is threatened by man's alteration and pollution of the shallow coastal waters favoured by young fishes.

Tarpon Family

Scientific name: Megalopidae
French name: tarpons

Tarpons are tropical and subtropical marine fishes which may enter fresh water. There are 2 species with 1 entering Atlantic Canada.

These fishes are characterised by having the swimbladder lying against the skull unlike the related **Bonefish Family**. There is a well-developed gular plate on the throat. Branchiostegal rays are 23–27 and the maxilla has teeth in contrast to the **Bonefish Family**. The lateral line branches over the scale surface. Large specimens develop adipose tissue around the large eye. Pseudobranchiae are absent. A conus arteriosus is present. The swimbladder is joined to the gut by a duct. The larva is a leptocephalus as in **eels**.

Tarpons and the allied **Bonefish Family** have a fossil record extending back to the Upper Cretaceous, 135 million years ago, and are an ancient group of fishes. The gular plates were much more common in ancient fishes. Tarpons are members of the **Tarpon Order**.

See **tarpon**

Tarpon Order

Tarpons and tenpounders or ladyfishes (Elopiformes) are mainly tropical marine fishes and rarely have brackish and freshwater species. There is only 1 living genus with about 8 moderate-sized species. Six species may merely be variants of a single species. Canada has 1 species on the Atlantic coast.

They are characterised by having abdominal pelvic fins, a deep fork in the caudal fin and a primitive caudal fin skeleton, paired fins have a long, axillary scale, no fin spines, a single dorsal fin, cycloid, silvery scales, a compressed body, wide gill openings, mesocoracoid and postcleithral bones in the pectoral girdle, a duct connects the swimbladder to the gut, a median gular plate in the throat region, a large mouth framed by premaxilla and toothed maxilla bones, teeth on the tongue and roof of the mouth, branchiostegal rays, 23–36, and no sensory canal on the premaxilla. There is a ribbon-like or leptocephalus larva with a forked tail unlike that in **eels**. Only the closely related **Bonefish Order**, and the **Eel Order** have this kind of larva. The latter 2 orders are believed to be descendants of the tarpons. Fossils are known from the Lower Cretaceous. The **Bonefish Order** is sometimes included within the **Tarpon Order**.

See **Tarpon Family**

tautog

Scientific name: *Tautoga onitis*
(Linnaeus, 1758)
Family: **Wrasse**
Other common names: blackfish, whitechin,
black porgy, tog, Molly George, oyster-fish
French name: tautogue noir

Distribution: Found from southern New Brunswick and Nova Scotia to southern South Carolina.

Characters: This wrasse is distinguished from its only Canadian relative, the **cunner**, by having 16–17 dorsal fin spines, a blunt snout, and no scales on the lower half of the operculum. Dorsal fin soft rays 10–11, anal

tautog

fin with 3 spines and 7–8 soft rays. Lateral line scales number about 70.

Overall colour is dark brown, olive, dark grey or blackish, with a white chin and a white blotch on the flank in males. Large fish may be entirely black except for a white chin. Male

blotches and mottles are poorly developed except during spawning when they darken. Females and young are mottled dark grey or black on an olive, brown or grey background. Females develop intense barring from the anal fin origin posteriorly during the spawning season. Both males and females lose the bars and blotches and become a uniform dark brass colour just before mating is believed to occur. The name tautog is derived from a Narragansett Indian word for sheepshead.

Reaches 92.7 cm. The world, all-tackle angling record weighed 10.88 kg and was caught in 1987 at Wachapreague, Virginia.

Biology: Tautogs are found in rocky inshore areas and around artificial structures such as harbours, seawalls, pilings and wrecks. They may enter brackish water. They are often found in holes among rocks and become active with the rising tide and with daylight. Young are found in eelgrass beds. Food is shellfish particularly mussels, but also snails, and crustaceans, as well as a variety of other animals which are crushed by the powerful teeth. Tautog have been aged up to 22 years in the United States. They are probably mature at 3 years of age.

Spawning behaviour includes lip to lip contact of male and female with lateral wagging of the bodies. Females will heighten nuptial colouration to attract males but not when male attention is high. Spawning occurs in June-July. Eggs float and are 1 mm in diameter. Males maintain a territory and are very aggressive. Each male attempts to limit access to a female so pair spawning can result. His success depends on his place in a dominance hierarchy, the number of neighbouring males and the availability of shelter.

This is a popular food fish which had a sport fishery in the salty, estuarine Eel Brook Lake, Yarmouth County, Nova Scotia. About 2000 fish were caught in 1957 and about 450 in 1958. The fishery then failed, but some tautog are still resident there. Tautog bones are bluish in colour, a little disconcerting in a food fish, but of no harm. Tautog pass food back to the throat teeth to be crushed, causing several jerks to the angler's line. A sudden strike by the angler at the first twitch of the line is too early to catch this fish.

teardrop tubeshoulder

Scientific name: *Holtbyrnia macrops*
Maul, 1957
Family: **Tubeshoulder**
Other common names: bigeye searsiid
French name: circé-larme

Distribution: Reported from the Atlantic and Pacific oceans. The Canadian record is off Cape Flattery, Washington.

Characters: This species is recognised by the family character of a tube projecting from the flank above the pectoral fin, by having an evident lateral line with enlarged scales, and by having scales on the head overlapping normally, each scale overlapping the one behind. In addition pelvic fin

teardrop tubeshoulder

rays are 9 and enlarged teeth or tusks are present on the premaxillary bone of the upper jaw. It is distinguished from its relatives by having a light organ at least 1.5 organ diameters behind the lower jaw tip, short gill filaments united at the base and 27–29 gill rakers. Scales number 100–111 in lateral series. The colour is dark overall. There are two patches of white tissue behind the eye. Reaches about 20 cm.

Biology: Originally described from a specimen taken from the stomach of a **black scabbardfish** at Madeira. It has been caught at 300–1000 m during the day, and 100–120 m at night. Little else is known about this species.

teleosts

Teleosts or Teleostei are the *true* **bony fishes** comprising the majority of fishes found in Canada and the world. About 96% of all living fish species are teleosts and teleosts outnumber any other **vertebrate** group. Within the **ray-finned fishes**, only the **sturgeons, paddlefishes, gars** and **bowfins** are not regarded as true bony fishes. Teleost is used then as a general term for all the "higher" **fishes**. True bony fishes are defined by such

characters of the skeleton as mobile premaxillae, ural neural arches elongate and are termed uroneurals — they are part of the stiffening and supporting skeleton of the upper tail fin — and the hypurals are expanded making the tail fin externally symmetrical although internally asymmetrical (= homocercal), the basi-branchial toothplates are unpaired, complex changes in the arrangement of the ventral throat muscles which are used in controlling the pumping action of the branchiostegals during respiration, and the internal carotid foramen is enclosed in the parasphenoid bone. In addition the teleost level of evolution is characterised by intermuscular bones present, cycloid scales appear and enamel (or ganoin) is lost from them, fulcra (see **sturgeons**) are lost from the upper and lower caudal fin bases, there are 2 pairs of hypohyal bones, a supraoccipital bone, the prevomers fuse into a single vomer bone in the roof of the mouth, the number of bones in the lower jaw decreases, the vertebrae are more strongly ossified and the swimbladder becomes primarily a hydrostatic organ rather than a respiratory organ. Fossils date from the Middle of Late Triassic, about 220–200 million years ago.

There are 4 major groups (or Subdivisions) of teleosts, the Osteoglossomorpha (with 1 order, the **Bony-tongues** and about 217 species), the Elopomorpha (with 4 orders, the **Tarpons, Bonefishes, Eels** and **Gulper Eels** and about 800 species), the Clupeomorpha (with 1 living order, the **Herrings** and about 357 species) and the Euteleostei which contains 32 living orders, the bulk of living fishes with about 22,260 species (in Canada these are the orders **Carp, Catfish, Pike, Smelt, Salmon, Widemouth, Flagfin, Lanternfish, Opah, Beardfish, Trout-perch, Cusk-eel, Cod, Toadfish, Anglerfish, Mullet, Silverside, Needlefish, Killifish, Pricklefish, Alfonsino, Dory, Stickleback, Mail-cheeked, Perch, Flatfish,** and **Puffer**).

Temperate Bass Family

Scientific name: Moronidae
French name: bars

Temperate basses or "true" bass are medium to large fishes found in temperate marine, brackish and fresh waters of Atlantic

North America, Europe and north Africa. There are about 6 species with 3 occurring in Canada. They are found along the Atlantic coast, 1 in fresh water in Arctic and Atlantic drainages, 1 in brackish and fresh waters of the Atlantic and Arctic drainages and 1 on the Atlantic coast and its drainage with introduced populations in British Columbia.

These fishes are characterised by the possession of 2 rounded spines (rarely 3) on the opercle without a spine below the main spine, the lateral line is complete and extends onto the caudal fin, accessory lateral lines above and below the main one on the caudal fin, head canals are partly or wholly enclosed in bone, there is no pelvic axillary scale, the thoracic pelvic fin has 1 spine and 5 soft rays, there are 2–3, usually 3, anal fin spines, the caudal fin is usually forked, sexes are separated, a pseudobranch is present, a swimbladder is present and may have anterior and posterior extensions, 7 branchiostegal rays, jaws have numerous, strong teeth, the maxillary bone in the upper jaw is widened posteriorly, and scales are ctenoid.

Temperate basses are related to the **Sea Bass** and **Temperate Ocean Bass** families with which they were once classified, and to the **Perch Family**. The characters cited above are those of a generalised member of the **Perch Order**. Spawning in this family is random and there is no nest-building as in the superficially similar **Sunfish Family**. There is no hermaphroditism in contrast to the related **Sea Bass Family**. Several species are important food and sport fishes.

See **striped bass**
      white bass
      white perch

Temperate Ocean Bass Family

Scientific name: Acropomatidae
French name: macondes

Temperate ocean basses or lanternbellies are found in the Atlantic, Pacific and Indian oceans. There are about 40 species with 4 reported from Atlantic Canada.

This group of fishes is poorly defined. They are "oceanic" fishes, which are separated from the familiar freshwater **Temperate Bass Family** members for convenience.

There are 2 dorsal fins, the first with 7–10 spines and the second with 0–1 spines and 8–10 soft rays. The anal fin has 2–3 spines and 7–9 soft rays. There are 7 branchiostegal rays. Some species have light organs and the anus near the pelvic fin base.

See **blackmouth widejaw**
      recto
      spiny widejaw
      wreckfish

tench

Scientific name: *Tinca tinca*
      (Linnaeus, 1758)
Family: **Carp**
Other common names: none
French name: tanche

Distribution: Found across Eurasia and introduced to the Columbia River system of British Columbia in Christina, Tugulnuit and Osoyoos lakes. Also introduced to Washington State and other U.S. states, to Australia, New Zealand and elsewhere.

Characters: This species is distinguished from other minnows by possessing a barbel at each mouth corner and 87–120 (usually

tench

about 100) lateral line scales embedded in a thick and slimy skin. Pharyngeal teeth 5–4 or 5–5. Gill rakers 13. Dorsal fin branched rays 6–9, usually 8–9, anal rays 5–8, usually 6–7. The second pelvic ray is thickened in males. Overall colour is olive-green to dark green with dark fins. The flanks may have golden tinges. The eye is red. Reaches 63.5 cm and 7.0 kg. The world, all-tackle angling record weighed 4.64 kg and was caught in 1985 in Sweden. "Tench" is derived from the Latin tinca for this fish.

Biology: Tench are found in lakes and ponds or slow rivers and can enter brackish estuaries. They favour areas rich in aquatic plants which have muddy bottoms. Tench are reported to bury themselves in mud during severe winters, lying dormant until spring. Food is aquatic insects and molluscs. Life span is up to 30 years. Males mature at 9–10 cm and 3 years and females at 12 cm and 4 years. Spawning occurs in spring and early summer in weedy shallows. Green eggs are only 1.0 mm in diameter but are very numerous, about 124,850 per kg of body weight. Spawning occurs when water temperatures reach 18°C and the adhesive eggs attach to vegetation. This minnow has a thick and strongly muscled body which gives a powerful fight on the appropriate tackle in European waters. The lips are thick and do not tear easily. Bait includes worms and processed cheese. A golden (yellow to orange) variety is bred in Europe for ornamental ponds. It makes a good aquarium fish when small.

tenrayed loosejaw

Scientific name: *Aristostomias photodactylus* Beebe, 1933
Family: **Barbeled Dragonfish**
Other common names: none
French name: drague à dix rayons

Distribution: Reported only from off Bermuda and Atlantic Canada.

Characters: This species is distinguished from Canadian relatives by having a pectoral fin, a suborbital light organ, a barbel on the throat with a distinct bulb having 3 short filaments, 2 pairs of nostrils, light organs between the pectoral and pelvic fins evenly spaced (not in groups), and 10 pectoral fin rays. There is a patch of luminous tissue at the base of the pectoral fin. Head and body black. The suborbital light organ is scarlet and the postorbital organ greenish white. Attains 8.4 cm standard length.

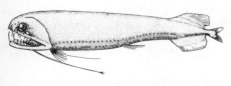

tenrayed loosejaw

Biology: Known from a single specimen in Canada caught in 1969 at 500 m off the Scotian Shelf. Descends to 1280 m. A very rare species.

tessellated darter

Scientific name: *Etheostoma olmstedi* Storer, 1842
Family: **Perch**
Other common names: none
French name: dard tesselé

Distribution: Found in Atlantic drainages from southeastern Ontario and southwestern Québec south to Georgia and Florida but not in Maritime Canada.

Characters: This darter is recognised by the small mouth not extending beyond the anterior eye margin, a smooth edge to the

tessellated darter

preopercle bone on the side of the head, an anal fin smaller than the soft dorsal fin, belly scaled or naked but no enlarged scales in midline, premaxillaries protractile, i.e. a deep groove separates the upper lip from the snout, 1 thin anal spine, 9–13, usually 11, pores in the preoperculomandibular canal (the head sensory canal running from the lower jaw onto the preopercle bone), and 10–17, usually 13 or more, dorsal fin soft rays. Usually confused with the **johnny darter** but has continuous infraorbital (under the eye) and supratemporal (over back of head) canals. Dorsal fin spines 5–11 (usually 8–10), anal fin usually with 1 spine in Canada and 5–11 (usually 7–9) soft rays. Lateral line scales 34–64. Scales on the nape, breast, belly and cheek vary from absent to fully scaled.

The back is yellowish to light green and has 6 dark brown saddles. The flank has 7–12, usually 8–11, brown w-, x-, or v-shaped marks. The belly is white. There is a bar below the eye and in front of the eye. The caudal fin has 4–9, usually 5–8, complete bars and the dorsal and pectoral fins are also barred. There is a faint spot at the caudal fin base. Breeding males develop 12–13 bands along the flank and lose the w-, x-, and v-shaped markings. Fin membranes become dark and the unpigmented rays stand out in contrast, the reverse of the non-breeding appearance. Breeding males have a blotch between the first 2 spines of the dorsal fin. Pelvic spine and ray tips form white knobs. The second dorsal fin is large and often reaches back to the caudal fin.

This species was long confused with the **johnny darter** and so little is known of its biology in Canada. Reaches 8.8 cm standard length.

Biology: This darter prefers larger rivers, but may also occur in streams and lakes, and is generally found over sand, mud or rock bottoms in slow to still water. It is occasionally found in brackish water and is tolerant of polluted water.

Food is crustaceans, insects, snails and algae taken mostly during the day.

Maximum age is between 3 and 4 years. All are mature at 2 years, and some at 1 year of age. Eggs are laid in clusters up to 7.5 cm wide on the underside of rocks in spring (April–June), when both sexes are upside down. The eggs are guarded and cleaned by the male. Up to 1435 eggs are laid with a diameter up to 1.6 mm. Eggs are laid in clutches of 19–324.

This darter is unique among fishes in that males clean and defend eggs which they did not fertilise. Large males are dominant over smaller males and defend the few rocks in a stream which can be used for spawning. However the dominant male will move from his original rock to others because they have more uncovered spawning area and attract females. Subordinate males take over the abandoned rock, clean the surface not yet used and also clean the dominant male's eggs. In effect the dominant male is exploiting the subordinate male's lack of access to spawning sites. The dominant male can spawn repeatedly at different sites but is assured of care of "his" eggs by the subordinate male.

The Committee on the Status of endangered Wildlife in Canada decided in 1993 not to designate a status for this species.

Texada stickleback

Scientific name: *Gasterosteus* sp.
Family: **Stickleback**
Other common names: none
French name: épinoche de Texada

Distribution: Found only in Paxton Lake, Texada Island in the Strait of Georgia, British Columbia.

Characters: This lake, as in Enos Lake (see **Enos stickleback**), has 2 forms of stickleback, a limnetic and a benthic one. The

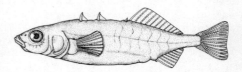

Texada stickleback

relation of either form to the widespread **threespine stickleback** is uncertain. The benthic form has a heavier body, wider mouth, less protruding eyes, no flank plates (compared to 9–14 in the limnetic form), no pelvic girdle or pelvic spines (present), and 11–21 gill rakers (18–25). These characters are adaptations to feeding on different foods, small plankton or large bottom-dwelling items. The more exposed limnetic form has armour plates and spines as protection against predators. There is evidence for gene exchange so the 2 forms are not completely isolated. Unusual populations such as this are important in studying the mechanism of speciation, forming a natural laboratory. This is only 1 of several unusual populations of sticklebacks in British Columbia, not all of which have been described (see as some other examples the **giant stickleback** and the **Enos stickleback**). Reaches 10.0 cm for benthics and usually not larger than 6.0 cm for limnetics.

Biology: The limnetic form is a schooling fish, non-aggressive and favours open waters under shade trees. The benthic form is solitary, aggressive and attracted to bottom cover. The limnetic feeds on zooplankton, mostly water-fleas, and the benthic form on large, bottom food items such as amphipods, midge larvae and ostracods. **Coho salmon** feed on these sticklebacks. Both forms spawn between April and early July. Benthic males build nests in cover and limnetics in open areas.

thornback sculpin

Scientific name: *Paricelinus hopliticus*
  Eigenmann and Eigenmann, 1889
Family: **Sculpin**
Other common names: none
French name: chabot à dos épineux

Distribution: Found from northern British Columbia to California.

Characters: This sculpin is uniquely characterised by a row of 32–36 scales on each side of the dorsal fin base bearing backward-pointing, sharp hooks. The nasal, postocular and 2 parietal spines on each side are strong, sharp and recurved. There are 3 preopercular spines, the middle being strongest, which are sharp, close together and directed backward. There are 2 small spines behind the eye followed by a strong posttemporal spine. There is a serrated ridge under the eye and a serrated ridge over the upper half of the eye and forming part of the head margin. The first dorsal fin has 12–13 spines and the second dorsal fin has 19–20 soft rays. Anal fin rays 23–24, pectoral rays 14–15 with the lower 6 rays finger-like, and the pelvic fin with 1 spine and 5 soft rays. Ctenoid scales have a spine embedded in a soft papilla. The scales extend from the whole body, except for areas under the pectoral and pelvic fins and along the anal fin base, onto the upper head as far forward as the nasal spines. Lateral line

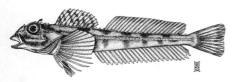

thornback sculpin

scales number about 43–44, are enlarged and have enlarged spines. There is a large postorbital cirrus and a flattened cirrus behind the

end of the upper jaw. Overall colour is olive-green with 4–6 brown bands. The flank below the lateral line has 7–8 purplish blotches. The lateral line bears yellow-brown flecks with blue spots below. The belly is light grey. The spiny dorsal fin has yellow-brown bars. Fin rays are brown. The pelvic fin tips are yellow. Reaches 20 cm.

Biology: Rare throughout its range and in British Columbia. First recorded from near Banks Island in Hecate Strait from a female caught in 1952. Also found in Queen Charlotte Sound and Kyuquot Sound. Usually on rock bottoms and from the surface down to 183 m.

thorny sculpin

Scientific name: *Icelus spiniger*
  Gilbert, 1896
Family: **Sculpin**
Other common names: none
French name: icéline épineuse

Distribution: Found from Japan to British Columbia.

Characters: This species is recognised by the 22–37 plate-like scales in a row from the nape to the caudal fin below the dorsal fin

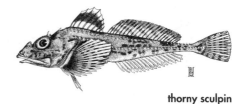

thorny sculpin

bases, each with a large, thorn-like spine, and a similar row below the lateral line canal. Lateral line scales 41–45, each with a central ridge. There are 2–17 axillary scales. There is a single cirrus above and behind the eye. The nasal spines are sharp and found on each side of the median snout bump. There are 4 preopercular spines, the uppermost branched. Spines over the eye are small and number 3 in a cluster. Occipital spines are strong and recurved. There are 2 spines on the ridge under the eye. First dorsal fin spines 8–10, second dorsal fin soft rays 19–23. Anal rays 15–19, pectoral rays 17–20 with lower tips free and pelvic fin with 3 soft rays. The body is brown fading ventrally. There are 4 dark saddles over the back. The flanks have dark brown splotches. The dorsal, caudal and pectoral fins have dark bands. The spiny dorsal fin has a brown to black spot near the posterior dorsal margin. Attains a reputed 28 cm, usually 19 cm or less.

Biology: This sculpin was recorded as a single specimen in 1971 from off the Queen Charlotte Islands, but this is in Alaskan waters. Several specimens were reported on in 1986 from Alice Arm and La Pérouse Bank and firmly place this species in Canadian waters. It is found at 25–770 m but most commonly at 100–200 m.

thorny skate

Scientific name: *Raja radiata*
   Donovan, 1807
Family: **Skate**
Other common names: Arctic thorny skate,
   starry skate, Atlantic prickly skate,
   raie radiée, qarlêk
French name: raie épineuse

Distribution: Found from Hudson Bay and Davis Strait throughout Atlantic Canada and south to South Carolina. Also in Europe.

Characters: This species is separated from its Canadian Atlantic relatives by having a

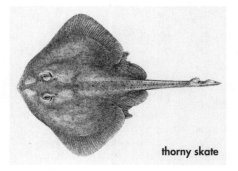

thorny skate

rigid snout with its cartilaginous support thick and stiff, cartilaginous supports of the pectoral fin do not reach the snout tip, dorsal fins usually not separate at the base (when separate with an intervening thorn), large thorns on the back but less than 10 on the tail behind the

level of the pelvic fin axils. The snout is blunt forming an angle of about 110–140°. Dorsal thorns number 11–20. Dorsal thorniness and relative size of thorns decrease with age. Mature males are particularly smooth. Higher numbers of dorsal thorns are found at lower temperatures while tooth-row counts are higher in warmer areas. Each shoulder has 2–3 thorns, the eye has 1 in front and 1 behind and there is 1 thorn at the inner side of the spiracle. Males have erectile, hooked, alar spines in 2–5 rows near the outer edge of the pectoral fin. Adults have spines on the underside of the snout. Upper jaw tooth row counts 27–49, lower jaw 26–49. The upper disc is grey-brown to brown and may have dark brown spots. There may be a white spot beside each eye, on each side opposite the nuchal region and on the posterior part of the disc. Underside white with brown or greyish blotches. There is a black spot at the tip of the tail. Reaches 109 cm. The world, all-tackle angling record was caught in Norway in 1982 and weighed 4.25 kg.

Biology: This is the most common skate in Atlantic Canada. It is found offshore at 18–996 m and –1.4 to 14°C, favouring lower temperatures of 2–5°C and 111–366 m depths, and on the Scotian Shelf from 37–108 m. Tagging experiments have shown that this species does not move far. Food changes with size with young fish (less than 40 cm) eating amphipod crustaceans or, in Passamaquoddy Bay, euphausiids, mysids and amphipods, later switching to worms and crabs, while the largest fish (70 cm or more) eat mainly fish. Fish include **sand lance** and **sculpins** but also offal and discarded fishes from trawlers are consumed. Even sea anemones are eaten and diet varies with area. Snow crabs, a commercially important species, are eaten off Cape Breton Island. Grey seals are known to eat thorny skates. Thorny skates live at least 20 years based on recaptures of tagged fish. Maturity in females may be attained at 40 cm but most are longer than this. Reproduction occurs year round and egg capsule size depends on female size, ranging from 4.2 to 9.6 cm by 2.5 to 7.7 cm, excluding the horns. Canadian catches are converted to fish meal but this is a table fish in Europe.

thorny tinselfish

Scientific name: *Grammicolepis brachiusculus*
Poey, 1873
Family: **Diamond Dory**
Other common names: none
French name: palissade à épines plates

Distribution: From Florida to Georges Bank and the Scotian Shelf in Atlantic Canada.

Characters: The very small mouth and the vertically elongate scales are characteristic. The body is deep and compressed. The first

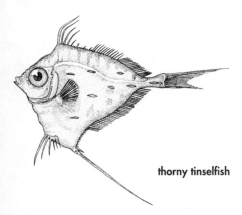

thorny tinselfish

dorsal and anal spines are elongated but often broken on capture. There are 5–7 dorsal fin spines and 32–33 soft rays and 2 anal fin spines followed by 33–34 soft rays. About 11–12 thorny scutes are widely scattered over the flanks, with their points directed posteriorly. Some scutes may be in pairs. The scutes distinguish this species from its relative, the **tinselfish**. The lateral line is arched anteriorly and follows a wavy course. Silvery with dark bars dorsally, best developed in young. Juveniles are also spotted on the flanks. Attains 38 cm.

Biology: Known from Canada by only 3 specimens taken in 1938, 1983 and 1985. Specimens were caught at 160–190 m.

threadfin sculpin

Scientific name: *Icelinus filamentosus*
Gilbert, 1890
Family: **Sculpin**
Other common names: filamented sculpin, long-rayed sculpin

French name: icéline filamenteuse

Distribution: Found from the Gulf of Alaska and northern British Columbia to California.

Characters: The 5 Pacific coast members of the genus *Icelinus* are characterised by having 25 or more lateral line scales or pores, 2 pelvic fin soft rays, scales in 2 rows close to the dorsal fins and an antler-like preopercular spine. This species is separated from its relatives by the first 2 dorsal fin spines being elongate and free of the membrane distally with the second the longest, the upper rear orbit lacks spines, a long flap-like cirrus at the nasal spine base and scale rows extending to the end of the soft dorsal fin. The frontal spine is weak but the parietal spine is well developed. There are 4 preopercular spines and the uppermost has 2 or more spinules pointing upward. First dorsal fin spines 9–12, second dorsal fin rays 15–18. Anal fin rays 13–16 and pectoral rays 16–18 the lower 8 finger-like at their tips. There are 27–33 scales in each of the upper flank rows. Lateral line scales 36–39. There are 2–6 scales in the pectoral fin axil. There is a large, dark, branched cirrus over the rear of the eye and a series of smaller cirri behind it. Other cirri are found on the upper jaw tip, preopercle, cheek and the lateral line and are white. The back is olive-green to light brown with 4 dark saddles. The belly is creamy yellow to light brown. The dorsal, caudal and pectoral fins are barred. The dorsal fin margin is black. The margin of the anal fin may be dusky. The area around the pectoral fin base is silvery. Males may have orange and red blotches. Attains about 30 cm.

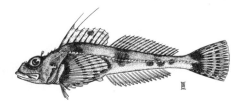

threadfin sculpin

Biology: Depth range is 18–800 m, but mostly caught at 50–300 m, and this species is not uncommon on sand or mud bottoms. Food is such crustaceans as shrimps and isopods.

threadfin slickhead

Scientific name: *Talismania bifurcata*
(Parr, 1951)
Family: **Slickhead**
Other common names: none
French name: alépocéphale filamenteux

Distribution: Found in the North Pacific Ocean including off British Columbia.

Characters: This species is distinguished by having teeth on the maxilla bone of the upper jaw, having the dorsal fin origin oppo-

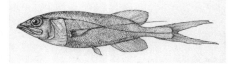

threadfin slickhead

site the anal fin origin, a black, wart-like spot near the base of the sixth dorsal fin ray (may be difficult to detect) and an elongate, uppermost pectoral ray. There are about 65–70 scales along the flank. Colour is dark overall and size attained is at least 20 cm.

Biology: Little is known but it is assumed to be similar in its biology to other slickheads.

threadfin snailfish

Scientific name: *Rhodichthys regina*
Collett, 1879
Family: **Snailfish**
Other common names: none
French name: limace à filaments

Distribution: North Atlantic Ocean and Baffin Bay.

Characters: This species is separated from other Arctic snailfishes by the lack of

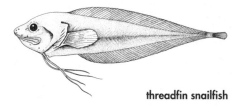

threadfin snailfish

an adhesive disc and pelvic fins, 2 pairs of nostrils, and the lower pectoral fin lobe

being comprised of 3 rays bound together as a filament which is longer than the head. The filament may split into 2 or 3 branches near its tip. The gap between the upper and lower lobes of the pectoral fin has rudimentary rays. Teeth are in bands. The gill opening is wide, extending from above the pectoral fin almost to the lower lobe. Dorsal fin rays 56–60, anal rays 54–57, and pectoral rays 16–17. The body is pink to bright red. Reaches 31 cm standard length.

Biology: This species is pelagic above or near soft mud bottoms at depths usually below 1500 m. Depth range is 1150–2341 m. At these depths in northern waters temperature is below 0°C. Spawning may occur through much of the year as ripe females have been caught from early summer to December. Eggs number 70 or more and are up to 7 mm in diameter.

threadtail conger

Scientific name: *Uroconger syringinus*
Ginsburg, 1954
Family: **Conger**
Other common names: none
French name: congre à queue élancée

Distribution: Found in the Gulf of Mexico and adjacent waters, the Gulf of Guinea, and off the Scotian Shelf of Atlantic Canada.

Characters: This species is distinguished as an adult from other Canadian Atlantic congers by having segmented dorsal and

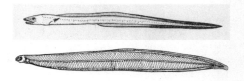

threadtail conger

anal fin rays, jaw teeth in rows without forming a cutting edge and vomer teeth in the roof of the mouth in a single row. The dorsal fin originates slightly to moderately behind the pectoral fin base. The pectoral fin lies at the upper angle of the gill opening. Sharp, slender teeth are in 2 rows anteriorly in the upper jaw and in 3 rows anteriorly in the lower jaw. Adults are yellowish, greyish or brown. Flanks with a row of irregularly arranged small dots. The tail and posterior parts of the dorsal and anal fins are black. Head and lower parts of the body with liliaceous tinges. Larvae are distinguished by having 216–227 total myomeres (muscle blocks) and the dorsal fin begins before the anus. A Canadian larval specimen was 12.2 cm long. Adults attain 41.6 cm.

Biology: The Canadian record is of a larval specimen caught in 1981. This species is poorly known.

threebeard rockling

Scientific name: *Gaidropsarus ensis* (Reinhardt, 1838)
Family: **Cod**
Other common names: Arctic threebeard rockling, threadfin rockling
French name: mustèle arctique à trois barbillons

Distribution: Found from Baffin Bay and Davis Strait south to Cape Hatteras.

Characters: This species and its relative, the **silver rockling**, are distinguished from other **cods** by having 2 dorsal and 1 anal

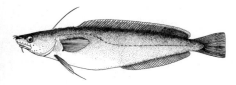

threebeard rockling

fins, the first ray in the first dorsal fin is elongate and the remaining rays are very short, and 2 snout barbels. This species is separated from its relative by having elongate gill rakers with teeth only on the middle part of each raker. Second dorsal fin rays 52–64, anal rays 40–48 and pectoral rays 20–27. Gill rakers 7–12 on the lower arch and 1 on the upper arch. The elongate dorsal ray is 14.0–20.3% of total body length. Adults are light chocolate brown or red overall with a blue-grey tinge over the faint red belly. Reaches 42 cm.

Biology: This rockling is commoner than its relative, especially off northern Labrador and Baffin Island. It is found down to 1569

m over mud at -0.2 to 2.5°C. Biology has not been studied.

threespine stickleback

Scientific name: *Gasterosteus aculeatus* Linnaeus, 1758
Family: **Stickleback**
Other common names: twospine, common, eastern, European or New York stickleback; banstickle, panstickle, pinfish, tiddler, kakilusuk, kakilaychok, katilautik, kakilishek
French name: épinoche à trois épines

Distribution: Found on the Hudson Bay and southern Baffin Island coasts and nearby fresh waters and south on the Atlantic coast and nearby fresh waters to Chesapeake Bay. Also inland to the Ottawa River and Lake Ontario. Introduced to Hasse Lake, Alberta and to lakes Huron and Michigan and possibly Lake Superior; also introduced as bait fish to various localities in southern Ontario. On the Pacific coast and nearby fresh waters from the Bering Strait of Alaska to California including British Columbia. Also in Europe and western Asia from the Arctic south to Syria and in the western Pacific Ocean south to Korea.

Characters: This species is distinguished by having usually 3 (range normally 2–4) dorsal fin spines, usually well-developed flank plates, 1 pelvic spine and 1 soft ray with a single cusp at the base, and colour. Second dorsal fin soft 7–14, anal fin with 1 spine and

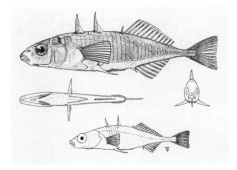

threespine stickleback

6–11 soft rays, and 8–11 pectoral rays. Flank plates may be restricted to the anterior body under the first 2 dorsal spines or continuous along the whole flank forming a keel on the caudal peduncle. Most marine populations have complete series of plates (up to 37) while freshwater populations may have a complete series, only a few anterior plates or both these extremes and intermediates.

Marine populations are more silvery on the flanks than freshwater ones which are more olive. Generally the back is green-brown, olive or grey to blue-black, flanks olive to silvery and the belly silvery-white. Fins are generally clear. Breeding males develop a red belly and throat, blue sides and have bright blue eyes. Some populations in the Queen Charlotte Islands have lost or reduced red throat and belly colour which may be related to diets deficient in carotenoids. Attains 10.2 cm.

This species is referred to as the "*Gasterosteus aculeatus* complex" because the fishes included under the scientific name include some forms which act as good species but have not yet been adequately defined. Some of these unusual forms, believed to be good species are described as the **Enos, giant** and **Texada sticklebacks**. There is also a stickleback in Nova Scotia marine waters which has unique male breeding colours, the **white stickleback**. A fully-plated marine form enters fresh water to spawn in the Little Campbell River, B.C. There it encounters a low-plated freshwater form. The 2 forms act as good species with a narrowly defined hybrid zone. Reproductive behaviour also differs. Freshwater males zig-zag more, glue more and bite less than marine males. However low and fully-plated forms co-exist in lakes and appear to be a single species.

Other Pacific coast populations variously have reduced or absent pelvic skeletons, plates, and dorsal fin spines, black rather than red breeding colours or are unusually large. Benthic forms have large, deep bodies, wide mouths and few, short gill rakers while limnetic forms have the opposite characters — both forms are found in Paxton Lake on Texada Island, B.C. Other characters, such as vertebral counts, show as much variation between localities from one river system in the Queen Charlotte Islands as in all of Europe. Rapid speciation rates are common in

these sticklebacks since the age of the lakes in which they live is about 9500 years. Local selection, related to predators in a fish poor environment and feeding environments, has resulted in a wide range of characters with a genetic basis.

Unarmoured populations of the threespine stickleback, which may be a distinct species, are reported from lakes on Graham Island in the Queen Charlotte Islands, B.C. They were given "rare" status in 1983 by the Committee on the Status of Endangered Wildlife in Canada. All the unusual populations of threespines in British Columbia should be protected as simple alterations of habitat or introduction of another fish species may upset the delicate balance which has led to their evolution.

Biology: These sticklebacks inhabit inshore coastal waters, lakes, ponds, rivers and streams. Marine and lake fish can be pelagic. Marine specimens have been caught 800 km offshore. Female fish in tidal marshes are most active during the day and are quiescent at night.

Food is various crustaceans, aquatic and terrestrial insects, snails, worms, fish eggs and fry including their own species, and a wide variety of other available organisms taken both on the bottom or pelagically. Females feed mostly in the early morning at Isle Verte, Québec. Females are important cannibals, forming raiding schools of up to 300 fish which overwhelm the nest-defending male. A male will divert the raiders by diving to the bottom and rooting in the mud away from his nest, as though feeding on the nest of another stickleback, by snout tapping on the bottom as though showing a nest to a female, or by swimming away high above the bottom on his side, silver flanks shimmering in the light, which leads the females away from his nest. A male may even pick up a dead stickleback or a discarded cigarette butt, bright underwater objects, and swim erratically away chased by the other sticklebacks which try to steal this attractive object. Some females known as courtship cannibals, not yet ready to spawn, mimic reproductive females and court males to gain access to eggs already in the nest on which they feed.

Many fishes and birds, and even snakes,

seals and small mammals, feed on stickle-backs despite their protective spines which are locked erect when they are disturbed. Spines and body plates are concentrated at the anterior end of the body and at the centre of mass. This is where most predators strike and even tail caught fish are manipulated so as to be swallowed head first incurring most injuries anteriorly. Loss of posterior plates may increase swimming ability and enable sticklebacks to escape predators where shelter is available or predators have similar swimming speed. Open waters and fast predators would encourage more plates.

A population in Boulton Lake on the Queen Charlotte Islands apparently lost or reduced its spines in adaptation to the grappling method of feeding by predatory dragonfly larvae. The dragonfly larvae have difficulty holding onto spineless sticklebacks. There are no other fish in the lake and predatory birds are few in number. Defensive spines are a disadvantage in this lake.

Maximum life span is a little over 3 years although some fish probably live only 1 year and a few months, dying after they spawn.

Spawning occurs from April to October, varying with locality over the wide range of this species. The male parental cycle at Isle Verte lasts 9–15 days with female interspawning intervals of 19 days. Males and females only complete one spawning here though laboratory studies show males capable of 5 reproductive cycles and females of producing a clutch of eggs every 3–4 days. Harsh physical conditions are probably the cause.

The male builds a barrel-shaped nest in shallow, sandy areas from plant fragments glued together on the bottom. The nest is in an open area but near vegetation. The nest has an opening at each end. The male has a complex courtship dance with zig-zag motions and a leading motion to the nest. A responsive female adopts a submissive head up position, which also reveals the egg-swollen belly. The male pokes his snout at the nest to indicate its position to the female, tipping his head sideways to display the bright red throat. The male jabs the female with his snout through the nest wall after she enters to stimulate egg release. He then fol-lows the female through the nest to fertilise the eggs and drives the female away. Some males steal eggs from a rival male and some eggs in a nest are fertilised by a "sneaker" male. The parenthood of eggs in nests, which determines these observations, was confirmed by DNA "fingerprinting."

In Crystal Lake, B.C. a female initiates courtship by "jumping" on the back of a male in open water, squirming and pressing against his erect dorsal spines. This courtship is not as conspicuous as zig-zag dancing and serves to avoid egg raids by large, bottom-feeding female schools. The male can search the surrounding water for raiders before leading the female down to his nest.

Several females may spawn in one nest which can contain up to 1026, yellowish 1.8 mm diameter eggs. Some females at Isle Verte have up to 838 eggs on average. The male guards and fans the eggs and guards the fry. Females often cannibalise eggs and the stress of defending against female attacks shortens male life span. Many males do not construct nests and many which do are unable to attract females. Nest cover and aggression are probably important factors in male success.

Threespines are more aggressive than **blackspotted sticklebacks** and will displace them. **Blackspotted sticklebacks** have a peak breeding later and breed closer to vegetation, probably in response to larger, aggressive relative.

Threespine sticklebacks have been studied extensively for the light they throw on speciation and evolution, and on fish behaviour.

threespot eelpout

Scientific name: *Lycodes rossi*
  Malmgren, 1864
Family: **Eelpout**
Other common names: none
French name: lycode à trois taches

Distribution: Found in the western Canadian Arctic in the Beaufort Sea east to Dease Strait south of Victoria Island. Also in the Kara Sea, Barents Sea and at Iceland.

Characters: This species is separated from its Canadian Arctic-Atlantic relatives by having small pelvic fins, a mouth under the snout, no large, nostril-like pores around the mouth, crests on the chin, lateral line single and on midflank, tail short (preanal dis-

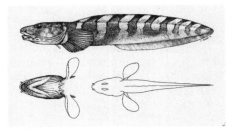

threespot eelpout

tance in the range 46–52% of total length), scales present on the body, pale peritoneum, gill opening not below pectoral fin base, 5–9 light non-reticulate, narrow bands which angle backward on the dorsal fin, pectoral fin rays usually 18–19, and vertebrae 98–99. Dorsal fin rays 91–97, anal rays 71–81 (each including half the continuous caudal fin rays). Pectoral fin rays 17–20. Overall colour is a light grey-brown. Scales are pale. Pectoral fin grey. Belly darker than the rest of the lower body. Attains 31 cm.

Biology: Reported from Canadian waters at 47–335 m and temperatures from –1.5 to 1.1°C on mud bottoms. Food is worms, clams and crustaceans.

thresher shark

Scientific name: *Alopias vulpinus*
    (Bonnaterre, 1788)
Family: **Thresher Shark**
Other common names: common thresher,
    thrasher, swiveltail, swingletail, fox shark,
    renard, renard de mer
French name: renard marin

Distribution: Found south from the Gulf of St. Lawrence and off eastern Newfoundland and from Goose Bay, British Columbia. In all warm seas world-wide.

Characters: The long tail is distinctive. In addition the head is strongly arched between the eyes and there is no distinct, deep groove on the nape above the gills. The eyes are small. Teeth are small, about 21 on each side of the lower jaw. The lateral teeth usually lack

outer cusplets and are triangular. The head is broad and the forehead strongly arched. The pectoral fins have narrow tips and are falcate. Scales have 3–5 low keels which end in marginal teeth.

The back is blue-grey to black or brown, the sides can be silvery, bluish or golden, and the belly white with a conspicuous white area over the pectoral fin bases. The dorsal, pectoral and pelvic fins are blackish and the tail, pectoral and pelvic fins sometimes have a white spot at the tip. The iris is black or green.

Possibly to 7.6 m and 450 kg. Accurately measured specimens to 5.7

thresher shark

Biology: This species is found in coastal waters and far from land in the open ocean from the surface down to 366 m. The young are often found in shallow bays and near beaches. It is an active shark and a strong swimmer which may leap. There is some segregation by sex according to depth and area. It is a summer visitor to Canadian waters from July to November and not common.

Food is mostly small, schooling fishes such as **mackerel, bluefish, menhaden, shad, herring, needlefish**, as well as squid, octopus, pelagic crustaceans and occasionally seabirds.

Threshers are ovoviviparous and there are 2–6 young in a litter. This species has uterine cannibalism. Gestation is about 9 months. Size at birth is 114–155 cm and 5–6 kg and males are adult at 319–333 cm, females at 376–390 cm, and ages of 5 and 7 years respectively. Maximum age is uncertain but theoretical calculations indicate this species may reach 50 years.

The flesh is excellent fresh, smoked or dried and salted. Fins are made into soup, the skin into leather, and the liver oil has been processed for vitamins. It is caught on long-lines, with bottom and surface anchored gill nets, and floating gill nets. It is often a nuisance to fishermen because it becomes entangled in nets and because it drives away more valuable fishes. Threshers can be caught on rod and reel although it may be tail hooked since it attempts to stun the live or dead fish bait. They are classed as gamefish and can be caught on trolled or drifted baits and lures although these must be small to match the mouth. They put up a good fight but tail hooked fish often tear free. Hooked threshers may leap out of the water.

Thresher Shark Family

Scientific name: Alopiidae
French name: renards marins

This family comprises only 3 species of sharks immediately recognisable by the long, curved upper lobe of the tail fin which is equal to the length of the head and body. There is only 1 species in Canada, found on both coasts.

Threshers are large heavy-bodied, active sharks found world-wide from tropical to cold-temperate waters. Thresher sharks are members of the **Mackerel Shark Order** and are related to the **Sand Tiger, Basking** and **Mackerel Shark** families.

There are no gill rakers or nictitating lower eyelids. Precaudal pits are present. The intestinal valve is a ring type. Teeth are small to moderately large and blade-like.

They are pelagic in shallow water and the open ocean. Their large tail fin is used in feeding. Schools of prey fishes and squids are crowded together by the long tail which is then used as a whip to stun and kill selected prey for easy capture. A pair of threshers may work together to herd a school of fish. They are not reported to attack people but there is an unconfirmed report from the Atlantic coast of the U.S. of a fisherman being decapitated by a blow from the tail of an adult thresher. There are also reports of boat attacks. The flesh of threshers is of high quality and is used fresh, frozen, smoked or dried and salted. It is also used in the shark fin soup trade and for vitamins from the liver. Floating longlines are used in commercial fisheries in the tropics. Some are caught as sport fishes on rod and line. The largest, all-tackle angling record for a thresher shark (species unidentified) weighed 363.8 kg and was caught in 1981 in New Zealand.

See **thresher shark**

tidepool sculpin

Scientific name: *Oligocottus maculosus* Girard, 1856
Family: **Sculpin**
Other common names: tidepool johnny
French name: chabot de bâche

Distribution: Found from possibly the Sea of Okhotsk and certainly the Gulf of Alaska to California including British Columbia.

Characters: This sculpin, and its relatives the **fluffy** and **saddleback sculpins**, are distinguished from other Pacific coast species by having 3 pelvic fin rays, the branchiostegal membranes form a fold over the isthmus, the upper preopercular spine is not antlerlike, scales are absent, the anal fin origin is below the end of the spiny dorsal fin and the anus is close to the anal fin. This species lacks body spines, the upper preopercular spine has 2–3 points, there is no nasal spine base cirrus and body cirri are single or paired and none lie above the lateral line. First dorsal fin spines 8–9, second dorsal rays 15–18, anal rays 11–14 and pectoral rays 12–15 with lower 6–7 finger-like. Lateral line pores 34–39. Cirri are found along the anterior half of the lateral line, on the top of the head from the rear of the eye to the occiput, 1–3 at the

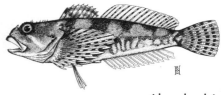

tidepool sculpin

end of the upper jaw along the edge of the preoperculum, upper rear operculum edge and near dorsal fin spine tips. Males have a slender anal papilla, which is usually curved forward, and enlarged anterior 3–4 anal rays.

Overall colour is red-brown, olive-green or reddish with a white to cream belly tinged green or blue. The back has 5 dark saddles. Fins are barred. The anterior base of the spiny dorsal fin has a black spot. Males develop an orange spot at the anterior tip of the spiny dorsal fin. Reaches 8.9 cm.

Biology: A common tide pool species which favours higher pools sheltered from surf. It can be caught by hand in a few centimetres of water. It is also common in lower tidepools and over sand in the largest tidepools. Up to 13.7 fish per sq m have been recorded at Helby Island, B.C. This sculpin tolerates extremes of temperature and salinity compared to other sculpins on the sea shore. It can respire in the air for several hours.

Food is crustaceans, molluscs, worms, small fishes and green and red algae. Great blue herons are efficient predators on these sculpins.

Females mature at 1 years and life span is at least 3 years, perhaps as much as 5 years, which is long for a small tide pool fish. Spawning begins in December and may last until June. Males clasp females with the pectoral fin placed in the notch between the dorsal fins. Puget Sound sculpins spawn twice each year. Green or red eggs are deposited on rocks, barnacles or mussels. Egg colour may relate to algal diet. They have an average diameter up to 1.3 mm.

Tidepool sculpins have a home pool to which they return if moved even over distances of 102 m and a time span of 6 months. Olfaction is the mechanism used in homing while vision is more important in maintaining position with respect to the sea bed during wave action while homing.

tidepool snailfish

Scientific name: *Liparis florae*
(Jordan and Starks, 1895)
Family: **Snailfish**
Other common names: shore liparid
French name: limace de bâche

Distribution: Found from the Bering Sea to California including British Columbia.

Characters: This species is distinguished from its Pacific coast relatives by having an adhesive disc with its rear edge behind the

level of the gill slit, 2 pairs of nostrils, gill slit partly in front of the pectoral fin down to between rays 3–5, dorsal fin with a lobe at

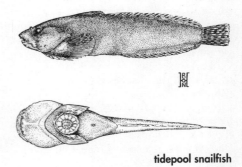

tidepool snailfish

the front and 31–33 rays, anal rays 25–27 and pectoral rays 29–33. The pectoral fin has a lower lobe partly folded underneath the upper lobe with rays separated from the membrane. Teeth are trilobed. Overall colour brown, olive-green, purplish or yellowish to red-brown. The flanks and fins are speckled. Flank spots are red. Reaches 18 cm.

Biology: Common in tide pools on exposed coasts over mud, sand, shell, rock, and rock walls and crevices with associated kelp and algae.

tiger rockfish

Scientific name: *Sebastes nigrocinctus*
Ayres, 1859
Family: **Scorpionfish**
Other common names: black-banded rockfish, banded rockfish, red rock cod
French name: sébaste-tigre

Distribution: Found from southeast Alaska to central California including British Columbia.

Characters: This species is recognised by its colour, the strongly concave space between the eyes on top of the head, the head spine arrangement and lateral line pore count. Dorsal fin spines 12–13, usually 13, soft rays 12–15, usually 14. Anal fin soft rays 6–7, usually 7, second anal spine at least twice as thick as third and about equal in length. Pectoral fin rays 18–20, usually 19. Gill rakers 27–32. Vertebrae 26. Lateral line pores 36–50, scale rows below lateral line 44–53. Head spines strong except supraocular is absent. Colour changes occur quickly in response to environmental changes. The ground colour is grey, pink or red with 5 black or dark red bars on the flanks and extending onto the dorsal fin. The eye has 2 black or red bars radiating downwards and back, 1 upwards and back and 1 towards the mouth. Young fish have black tips to the anal and pelvic fins. The peritoneum is white. Attains 61 cm. The world, all-tackle angling record weighed 2.22 kg and was caught in Depoe Bay, Oregon in 1993.

tiger rockfish

Biology: This is a solitary rockfish which aggressively defends a crevice or cave among rocks at 24–275 m. It may lie on its side in the crevice. Divers commonly see this fish in British Columbia. Food includes such items as shrimps, brittle stars and crabs which are probably picked from the bottom. Some fish are also eaten. Maximum age is an estimated 63 years. Spawning occurs in May after a fall mating in British Columbia. Juveniles are associated with floating seaweed. It is an important oriental market food fish because of its colour and flavour.

tiger shark

Scientific name: *Galeocerdo cuvier*
   (Péron and Le Sueur, 1822)
Family: **Requiem Shark**
Other common names: leopard shark
French name: requin tigre commun

Distribution: Circumtropical in temperate to tropical seas and from Atlantic Canada.

Characters: This species is distinguished from other Canadian requiem sharks by having upper labial furrows very long and extending nearly to the front of the eyes, by large spiracles being present and by strong keels on the caudal peduncle. Teeth have a cockscomb shape with oblique cusps and

tiger shark

strong serrations. The upper precaudal pit is transverse and crescent-shaped. There is a middorsal ridge.

There is a characteristic series of black bars (spots in young) along the upper flank but these fade in adults. The overall colour is blue-grey to brown-grey above and whitish or dirty yellow below.

Reputedly reaches 9.1 m but about 7.4 m and 3084 kg is probably the largest. The angling record is 807.4 kg and 422.91 cm caught on 14 June 1964 at Cherry Grove, South Carolina.

Biology: A specimen was caught on 15 July 1973 on the Scotian Shelf by a commercial longliner. Also recorded from the southern Scotian Shelf and northeastern tip of Georges Bank. This shark is a common species outside Canada in warm coastal and open waters from intertidal areas and the surface down to about 140 m. It may be found in estuaries and harbours. It is most active at night, retreating to deeper water during the day. Young tigers are more tolerant of light. Tiger sharks usually swim slowly but are capable of rapid movement when attacking prey or escaping danger.

This is the only ovoviviparous member of the family. A litter of 10–82 young, 51–85 cm long, is produced in April-June after a gestation of about 12–16 months. Males mature at 226–310 cm and females at 250–350 cm at ages of 4–6 years in southern waters but only at more than 10 years and 9 years respectively in the northwest Atlantic Ocean. They live at least 16 years and theoretically up to 50 years using growth curve projections. Growth is more rapid than in other requiem sharks.

Tiger sharks are both predators and scavengers, eating a wide variety of fishes including **sharks** and other **tiger sharks, stingrays, dolphins**, conches, whelks, crustaceans, jellyfish, octopi, tunicates, sea turtles, sea snakes, various sea birds including cormorants and pelicans, and strangely records of a yellow-billed cuckoo, a Bahama yellowthroat, and a mourning dove in one shark, and 2 wood thrushes in another shark. These unfortunate birds were unsuccessful migrants or had been blown out to sea. They have scavenged crocodiles, chickens, rats, pigs, cattle, sheep, dogs, donkeys, hyaenas, monkeys and humans. Some of these were taken alive, such as humans. Various inedible objects have also been recorded from their stomachs such as cans, bags, coal, wood, a rubber tire, seeds, cigarette packets, a bag of potatoes, a tom-tom, fabrics, feathers and small barrels. This is the most dangerous shark after the great white shark with many confirmed attacks on boats and swimmers, particularly around Florida in North America.

Tiger sharks are caught by longlines and in nets and used fresh, frozen, salted or smoked. The skin is made into leather, fins into soup and the liver is used for its vitamin A. It is a recognised sport fish. Caught by chumming and trolling whole fish or scraps. It often becomes hooked when it attacks fish being reeled in by anglers.

tilefish

Scientific name: *Lopholatilus chamaeleonticeps* Goode and Bean, 1879
Family: **Tilefish**
Other common names: great northern tilefish, blanquillo, rainbow tilefish, tile chameau
French name: tile

Distribution: Found from Nova Scotia to Surinam.

Characters: Tilefish are easily recognised by a triangular, greenish-yellow, fleshy tab on top of the head. There is also a small barbel-like structure at each lower jaw end. The dorsal fin has 7–8 spines and 14–15 soft rays. The anal fin has 1 spine and 13–15 soft rays. There are 66–75 lateral line scales. The jaws have canine teeth and bands of smaller teeth.

The back and upper flank are olive-green to bluish. The lower flank and belly are yellow or rosy. The belly midline is white. The upper head sides are blue with a rose flush. The upper flank is spotted yellow and the dorsal and anal fins have larger yellow spots. There are 8–9 yellow bands on the caudal fin but these may be broken up into spots and blotches. The anal fin is pink with blue to purple iridescent tinges. The pectoral fins are a pale brown with purple tints near the base. The pelvic fin spine is orange-yellow.

Reaches 130 cm and 30 kg.

tilefish

Biology: Found from Banquereau Bank, Nova Scotia southward including the Bay of Fundy. It is very common at temperatures between 8° and 17°C over clay, sand or mud bottoms at 80–540 m. Tilefish excavate burrows 4–5 m wide and 2–3 m deep which they enter head first and leave tail first. Burrows may be horizontal in clay outcrops of submarine canyons and known as "Pueblo Villages," under rocks and boulders or primarily funnel-shaped and vertical on the clay sea bed. There may be 1234 burrows per square kilometre.

Food is principally crustaceans (crabs) but includes such items as sea cucumbers, sea urchins, squids, worms and fishes. Crabs which live in tilefish burrows are part of their diet.

Males grow more rapidly than females after the first 4–5 years reaching 112 cm fork length at age 26, while females are 95 cm at age 35. They may live more than 40 years.

Females are mature at 8 years and spawning occurs from February to September. Large females contain 16 million eggs about 1.25 mm in diameter. Larvae are probably pelagic.

This species was first caught off New England in May, 1879, by a schooner fishing for **cod** and **hake**. The captain of the schooner found the fish so delicious he caught more and soon sold them. It looked as if a promising new fishery could be developed. However, in spring, 1882, there was a mass die-off of tilefish along the American coast, probably due to a sudden drop in temperature at the edge of the Gulf Stream caused by cold water from the Labrador Current. One estimate of the number of dead fish was over 1.5 billion; an area 40 × 275 km was covered with dead and dying large tilefish. It was calculated that at 10 lbs (4.5 kg) per fish, there would be 288 lbs (131 kg) for every man, woman and child in the United States! It was 10 years before any more tilefish were caught and the species, so recently discovered, was thought to be extinct. There is now a commercial longline fishery off the U.S. coast and tilefish are excellent fresh or smoked. There is also a sport fishery south of Cape Cod. The tilefish catch was worth U.S. $4.5 million in 1979 and 1980 when 3,700 tonnes were landed. Since tilefish are both slow-growing and long-lived they are easily over-exploited by relatively little fishing effort. The stocks require careful management if a consistent fishery is to be maintained.

Tilefish Family

Scientific name: Malacanthidae
(= Branchiostegidae)
French name: tiles

Tilefishes and sand tilefishes are found in the temperate to tropical waters of the Atlantic, Indian and Pacific oceans. There are 39 species with 2 species on the Atlantic and 1 on the Pacific coast of Canada. One Atlantic coast species has only been identified to the genus *Caulolatilus*, as it was a larva, and an account is not given.

These fishes have a long dorsal fin with 1–10 soft spines and 11–60 soft rays. The anal fin is long with 1–2 weak spines and 11–55 soft rays. The pelvic fin has 1–2 spines and 5 soft rays. The opercular spine is strong and sharp in many species. Scales are ctenoid on the body and mostly cycloid on the head. Larvae have elongate, serrate spines on the head and keeled scales and look so different from adults that they were originally described as distinct species.

Tilefish are in the **Perch Order**, related to the **Perch**, **Bluefish** and **Cobia** families.

These are fishes of relatively deep water (20–600 m) found over sand or rocky bottoms. Some species build large mounds of sand and rubble and burrows which other fishes and crabs use by building secondary burrows. Their excavations are extensive and have a marked effect on the shape, composition and stability of the seabed.

Some species are commercially important and some are sought by anglers using electric reels.

See **ocean whitefish**
tilefish

tinselfish

Scientific name: *Xenolepidichthys dalgleishi* Gilchrist, 1922
Family: **Diamond Dory**
Other common names: spotted tinselfish
French name: palissade

Distribution: Found in the Atlantic and Indo-West Pacific oceans including off the Atlantic coast of Canada.

Characters: The very small mouth and vertically elongate scales are characteristic. It is distinguished from its relative, the **thorny tin-**

tinselfish

selfish, by lacking thorny scutes on the body. The dorsal fin has 5–6 spines and 27–30 soft rays, the anal fin 2 spines and 27–29 soft rays. Dorsal and anal spines are elongate in young but easily break off. Colour is silvery-yellow with anterior pelvic rays and rear margin of the caudal fin black. Young have dark brown spots. Reaches about 12 cm standard length.

Biology: This species usually lives in deeper water, 90–885 m, but has been cast ashore by storms in South Africa. First reported from Canada in 1988 based on a single specimen from off Nova Scotia on the upper continental slope.

Tittmann's loosejaw

Scientific name: *Aristostomias tittmanni* Welsh, 1923
Family: **Barbeled Dragonfish**
Other common names: none
French name: drague de Tittmann

Distribution: Found in the North Atlantic Ocean including off Atlantic Canada. Also reported off Chile.

Characters: This species is distinguished from Canadian relatives by having a pectoral fin, a suborbital light organ, a barbel on the throat, 2 pairs of nostrils, light organs between the pectoral and pelvic fins in 5–6 groups or clusters, and 6–7 pectoral fin rays.

Tittmann's loosejaw

There is a distinct bulb at the tip of the barbel. Head and body black. Pale luminous spots are arranged in interrupted lines before and behind the eye. Luminous patches on the head are bluish. The barbel bulb is yellowish but the stem is whitish with minute black dots. Reaches 21.5 cm.

Biology: Two specimens have been caught off the Scotian Shelf in 1979 and 1982. They represent the northern range limit for this species.

Toadfish Family

Scientific name: Batrachoididae
French name: poissons-grenouilles

Found in the warmer parts of the Atlantic, Indian and Pacific oceans with 64 species, 1 of which is found along the Pacific coast of Canada.

Toadfishes have a large, flattened head and a long tapering body. The first dorsal fin is small with only 2–4 spines and the soft-rayed second dorsal fin is very long. The anal fin is spineless and long. The pelvic fins are jugular, i.e. on the throat ahead of the pectoral fins, and have 1 spine and 2–3 soft rays. There are 1–5 strong spines on the operculum. Most are scaleless. Many have barbels and skin flaps on the head. There may be a pit or pore behind the large, fan-shaped pectoral fin. Two or more lateral lines are present. There are only 3 pairs of gills.

Toadfishes are members of the **Toadfish Order**.

Some toadfishes can survive out of the water for several hours and also produce croaking, whistling and grunting noises with the swimbladder. Owners of boats anchored in harbours have had their sleep disturbed by grunting toadfishes. The midshipmen are the only fishes found in shallow water which have light-producing organs. Most toadfishes are found inshore, some enter freshwater or are found in deeper marine waters. They are sluggish but territorial and some have venomous spines in the dorsal fin and on the operculum giving a painful but not fatal sting. Some toadfish thrive in polluted water laying eggs in tin cans, old shoes and other debris.

See **plainfin midshipman**

Toadfish Order

Toadfishes or Batrachoidiformes (= Haplodoci) consist of a single family with about 69 species found world-wide in coastal marine waters with a few freshwater species. The largest species, the **plainfin midshipman**, reaches 38 cm and is found on the coast of British Columbia. The upper jaw has both premaxilla and maxilla bones. There are 6 branchiostegal rays, 4–5 pectoral radials and the upper hypural bones have an unusual articulation between the vertebra of the tail skeleton. Eyes are dorsal. There are no ribs, epiotic or intercalar bones and no pyloric caeca. The body is usually scaleless. There are 3 pairs of gills. Remaining characters of the order are covered in the family description.

The order is related to the **Anglerfish Order**. Fossils are known from the Miocene.

See **Toadfish Family**

tomcods

Tomcods are members of the marine **Cod Family** in the genus *Microgadus*. There are 2 Canadian species, the **Atlantic** and **Pacific tomcods**. The **Atlantic tomcod** will enter fresh water. Tomcod has been used in England for young **Atlantic cod** which the North American tomcods resemble.

Tonguefish Family

Scientific name: Cynoglossidae
French name: cynoglosses

Tonguefishes or tongue soles are found world-wide in warmer marine waters with some entering fresh water. There are about 110 species and 2 of these have been found in Atlantic Canada.

These **flatfishes** have sinistral eyes (on the left side). The dorsal and anal fins flow into a pointed caudal fin giving a tongue-shaped outline with the rounded head. The pectoral fins are absent except for a fine membrane in some. Usually only the left pelvic fin is developed and it may be joined with the anal fin. The eyes are small and close together. The mouth is asymmetrical being twisted to the eyed side of the body and it is usually arched. Many species lack a lateral line. Scales on the eyed side are ctenoid. The margin of the preopercle is covered by skin and scales.

Tonguefish are related to the Sole Family, which is not found in Canada. The tonguefishes are members of the **Flatfish Order**.

These are mostly shallow water fishes with bodies adapted for burrowing in sand or mud where their protective colouration makes them hard to see. They may descend to depths over 1100 m. They hunt for food at night aided by a strong sense of smell in fila-mentous tubercles on the blind, or underside, of the head. They are important food fishes in the Indian Ocean where a variety of species are common.

See **daubed tonguefish**
largescale tonguefish

toothed cod

Scientific name: *Arctogadus borisovi* Drjagin, 1932
Family: **Cod**
Other common names: East Siberian cod
French name: saïda barbu

Distribution: Found from northern Baffin Island and Ellef Ringnes Island west to the Beaufort Sea and the Kara Sea. Also on the northern and southern coasts of Greenland.

Characters: This species and its relative, the **polar cod**, are distinguished from other western Arctic **cods** by having the jaws about

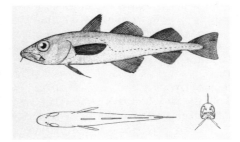

toothed cod

equal or the lower protrudes slightly, an emar-ginate to forked caudal fin, sensory head canals poreless or with few, very small pores, the lateral line is not continuous before the second dorsal fin, and the palatine bones in the roof of the mouth have strong teeth. This species is separated from its relative by the chin barbel length exceeding pupil diameter. First dorsal fin rays rarely 6, usually 9–14, second dorsal rays 16–23 and third dorsal rays 19–25. First anal fin rays 16–25 and second anal rays 16–25. Pectoral rays 16–23. Gill rakers 30–38. The back and upper flanks are dark olive, the lower flanks grey and the belly light grey with dark spots. Reaches 60 cm.

Biology: This species lives on or close to the sea floor usually at 17–40 m and may enter estuaries. It has also been caught far from shore under pack ice. Food includes amphipods. Spawning probably occurs in summer. Biology has not been studied and it is of little economic value.

toothless snailfish

Scientific name: *Paraliparis paucidens*
 Stein, 1978
Family: **Snailfish**
Other common names: none
French name: limace édentée

Distribution: Found from off the Queen Charlotte Islands to Oregon.

Characters: This snailfish is identified among its Canadian Pacific relatives by the lack of pelvic fins and an adhesive disc, by having 6 branchiostegal rays, no barbels or papillae on the snout and no laterally directed opercular spine, horizontal mouth, and 4–5 tiny canines in a single row on the upper jaw such that teeth appear to be absent. Teeth may be completely absent. There is an unusual, cartilaginous rod on each side of the lower jaw which may enable the gape to be larger or support the sides of the mouth. Dorsal fin rays 58–60, anal fin rays 53–54. Pectoral rays 19–24, in 2 lobes of 10–18 and 3–4 rays with short rays bridging the gap. Pale pyloric caeca number 5–8. The skin is dark brown with the head darkest. The mouth and gill cavities are dusky or black. The peritoneum is dark brown or black. The stomach is pale. Reaches 16.4 cm.

toothless snailfish

Biology: Found between 1536–2275 m and first reported from Canada off the Queen Charlotte Islands in 1979.

toothnose lampfish

Scientific name: *Lampadena speculigera*
 Goode and Bean, 1896
Family: **Lanternfish**
Other common names: mirror lanternfish

French name: lampe à nez denté

Distribution: Found in the Atlantic, Indian and Pacific oceans including off Atlantic Canada, mostly in temperate waters.

Characters: This species is distinguished from its Canadian Atlantic coast relatives by the large luminous glands, outlined with heavy, black pigment, on the upper and lower caudal peduncle and the pelvic fin origin under the front of the dorsal fin, and from its close relative, the **highfourthpo lampfish** by the light organ PO4 not being elevated and above light organ PO3. Dorsal fin rays 13–15, usually 14, anal fin rays 13–15, usually 14, and pectoral rays 13–16, usually 14. Photophores: PO 5–6, usually 5, VO 4–6, usually 5, AO 5–7 + 2–5, total 7–12 but usually 10. Attains 15.3 cm.

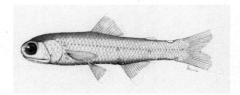

toothnose lampfish

Biology: Common in Canadian waters off Newfoundland and Nova Scotia. In the Atlantic Ocean found at 475–950 m during the day with maximum abundance at 800 m and at 60–750 m during the night with a maximum abundance at 100 m. Eaten by **swordfish** in Canada.

toothy dreamer

Scientific name: *Dolopichthys pullatus*
 (Regan and Trewavas, 1932)
Family: **Dreamer**
Other common names: toothful dreamer
French name: rêveur très-denté

Distribution: Found in all oceans including off the Atlantic coast of Canada.

Characters: This deepsea **anglerfish** and its relative, the **shorthorn dreamer**, are distinguished as females by having the dorsal edge of the frontal bones on the head nearly straight, sphenotic spines present and a deeply notched operculum posteriorly. The pectoral lobe is short and broad. The lower jaw has a well-developed spine at its tip. The illicium or fishing rod originates in front of

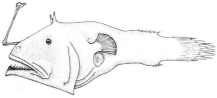

toothy dreamer

the sphenotic spines. Males have 8–10 denticles on the lower jaw and 10–11 olfactory lamellae. The toothy dreamer has 4–14 teeth on the vomer bone in the roof of the mouth and the lower jaw has more than 130 teeth in specimens larger than 60 mm, more than 115 in specimens 25–60 mm, up to nearly 600. There are 5–8 dorsal fin rays, 4–6 anal fin rays and 17–22 pectoral fin rays. Overall colour dark brown to black with the esca or bait having unpigmented areas. Females reach 11.5 cm standard length.

Biology: Only a single specimen has been caught in Canadian waters on the northwest slope of the Grand Bank in 1968, a northern record for the species. As in other **anglerfishes** the fishing apparatus is used to entice prey close enough to be gulped down.

toplights lanternfish

Scientific name: *Lampanyctus photonotus* Parr, 1928
Family: **Lanternfish**
Other common names: none
French name: lanterne de Noël

Distribution: Found in the Atlantic and Pacific oceans including off the Scotian Shelf in Atlantic Canada.

Characters: This species and 7 relatives in the genus *Lampanyctus* are separated from other Atlantic species by lacking major photophores close to the dorsal body edge, the PLO photophore is well above the pectoral fin base level while the second PVO photophore is at or below the upper pectoral base level, there are 4 Prc, the first PO and two PVO photophores are not on a straight line, both males and females have caudal luminous glands composed of overlapping, scale-like structures without a black pigment border, the fourth PO photophore is highly elevated, there are no luminous, scale-like structures on the belly between the pelvic fin bases or these bases and the anus, there are 4 VO photophores and the SAO series is strongly angled. This species is distinguished from its relatives by having 13–15 gill rakers, pectoral fins extending back beyond pelvic fin bases, 2 cheek photophores, no luminous tissue at the adipose fin base and 37–38 lateral line organs. The infracaudal luminous gland covers the entire underside of the caudal peduncle length and the Prc and AOp photophores are separate. Dorsal fin rays 12–15, anal rays 16–18 and pectoral rays 11–14. AO photophores 11–14. Adult males have a supracaudal luminous gland with 7–8 scale-like segments while females have only 3–5 segments. Reaches 8.5 cm.

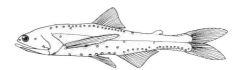

toplights lanternfish

Biology: This is a subtropical to tropical species but it is common in temperate areas. Depth distribution is 600–1100 m by day, and 40–250 m and 850–900 m by night with a maximum at 100–150 m near Bermuda. There are seasonal and age depth peaks also. However some fish may be caught down to 1550 m (if they are not contaminants from previous tows). Downward migration rates of up to 260 m/hour have been calculated. Sexual maturity is attained at 5.0–6.0 cm and there is a spring or early summer spawning peak. Life span is probably 2 years.

topsmelt

Scientific name: *Atherinops affinis* (Ayres, 1860)
Family: **Silverside**
Other common names: none
French name: capucette barrée

Distribution: Found from Vancouver Island south to Baja California.

Characters: The only member of its family in Pacific Canada, topsmelt have characteristic forked teeth in a single row. The first

topsmelt

dorsal fin has 5–9 spines and is separated by 5–8 scales from the second dorsal fin which has 1 spine and 8–14 soft rays. The anal fin origin is below the first dorsal fin and has 1 spine and 19–25 soft rays. There are 13–18 pectoral fin rays. Lateral line scales number 52–68. The back is blue-grey to green, the belly silvery and the flank has a bright silver stripe. Attains 36.8 cm.

Biology: Topsmelt are found in surface schools in inshore waters such as bays, kelp beds and rocky areas. Food is plankton. Life span is about 7 years. Females grow faster than males. Maturity is attained at 2 years by some fish and most spawn at 3 years. Spawning takes place from late May to early July in Oregon and eggs adhere to kelp or eelgrass. Egg size is about 1.7 mm. In Baja California, topsmelt are known to have a cleaning symbiosis with gray whales, picking at parasitic barnacles and eating whale lice. They are caught in California both by sport fishermen on hook and line and commercially using encircling nets.

torrent sculpin

Scientific name: *Cottus rhotheus*
    (Smith, 1882)
Family: **Sculpin**
Other common names: none
French name: chabot de torrent

Distribution: Found only in British Columbia in Canada in the Columbia and Fraser river systems. Also in Washington, Oregon, Idaho and Montana.

Characters: This sculpin, and related species in the freshwater genus *Cottus*, are distinguished from the **deepwater sculpin** by the gill membrane being attached to the isth-

mus and the dorsal fins touching. It is separated from its relatives by having 2 pores at the tip of the chin, a complete lateral line with a downward bend on the obviously narrow caudal peduncle, and prickles on the flanks and back. First dorsal fin spines 7–9, second dorsal rays 15–17, anal rays 11–13, and pectoral rays 15–18. Prickles may only be found in a patch behind the pectoral fin in some fish. Each prickle base is serrated. Overall colour brown to grey-brown with 2–3 dark saddles sloping forward under the second dorsal fin. The belly is white. The chin has mottles. Fins have bands or thin bars. Spawning males develop a thickened first dorsal fin with an orange margin. Reaches 15.5 cm.

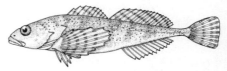

torrent sculpin

Biology: Recorded mainly in rocky streams in riffles and rarely pools, but also on beach areas of large lakes. Larger torrent sculpins eat mostly fish such as **redside shiners** and small **northern squawfish**, with some **coho salmon** fry particularly on moonless nights. Young fish eat crustaceans and insects. Life span is at least 4 years and maturity is attained at age 2. Spawning probably occurs in April–June. Eggs number up to 448.

transparent hatchetfish

Scientific name: *Sternoptyx diaphana*
    Hermann, 1781
Family: **Silver Hatchetfish**
Other common names: none
French name: hache d'argent diaphane

Distribution: World-wide in tropical to temperate waters. Found off the Atlantic coast of Canada from the Grand Bank southward.

Characters: The body is shaped like a hatchet, there are 10 abdominal light organs but only 3 at the anal fin, the eyes are normal and the first anal fin support is enlarged supporting a transparent membrane above the anal fin rays. This species differs from its relative, the **highlight hatchetfish**, in having a low supra-anal light organ and gill raker tooth plates without spines. Darkly pigmented on the back, but overall a bright silvery colour with light organs outlined in black. Reaches 5.5 cm standard length.

transparent hatchetfish

Biology: Found between 300–1200 m, usually 500–800 m or 700–1000 m depending on locality, and does not migrate vertically. May be found as deep as 3082 m in the Atlantic Ocean and occasionally dying specimens have been found at the surface. Food is small crustaceans and fishes. In areas overlain by cooler water masses, such as the northwest Atlantic, fewer and larger food items are taken compared to other areas. This species has light organs in the roof of the mouth which may be used to attract prey, but light is also guided towards the eye and may be used to modify the output of light by the external light organs so the fish merges with the background illumination. Breeding occurs year round and the adults die after spawning and a one-year life cycle.

triangle-light dragon

Scientific name: *Trigonolampa miriceps* Regan and Trewavas, 1930
Family: **Barbeled Dragonfish**
Other common names: threelight dragon, dragon trois-lampes
French name: dragon à lampe triangulaire

Distribution: Found in the Atlantic and Southern oceans including from off Georges Bank.
Characters: This barbeled dragonfish is distinguished from Canadian Atlantic relatives by having the dorsal and anal fin bases about the same length, pelvic fins low on the flank, no obvious luminous organs (the preorbital and suborbital) before or below the eye, 3–7 pectoral fin rays of about equal length, lower jaw not curved upward or projecting, 21–26 photophores between the pectoral and pelvic fin insertions and luminous tissue in patches, spots and stripes on the side of the head behind the postorbital organ. The pectoral rays have lumps of luminous tissue. The barbel has a small bulb at the tip with a single filament and is shorter than the head. Dorsal fin rays 17–20, anal rays 16–19 and pelvic rays 3–7. Overall colour is black. There may be 1–2 pale lines on the flanks extending back as far as the dorsal and anal fin. Reaches 32 cm.

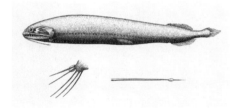

triangle-light dragon

Biology: The Canadian record is of a specimen taken from the stomach of a harpooned **swordfish** in 1922. It is believed to occur off Nova Scotia generally.

triggerfishes

Triggerfishes are members of the **Leatherjacket Family** and there are 3 Canadian species on the Atlantic coast (**gray**, **ocean** and **queen triggerfishes**). The first dorsal fin spine can be locked upright and is released by a "trigger" mechanism formed from the small second dorsal fin spine.

tripletail

Scientific name: *Lobotes surinamensis* (Bloch, 1790)
Family: **Tripletail**
Other common names: jumping cod
French name: croupia roche

Distribution: Found from Argentina to Nova Scotia as well as world-wide.

Characters: The elongate dorsal and anal fins giving the appearance of 3 tails is characteristic. The nape is very concave. The preopercle is strongly serrated. There are 11–12 dorsal fin spines and 14–16 soft rays. The

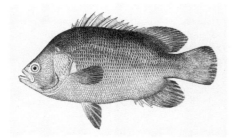

tripletail

anal fin has 3 spines and 11–12 soft rays. There are 37–45 scales along the flank. The soft dorsal, anal and caudal fins are covered with scales. The overall colour is brown, bronze to tan, often mottled and blotched. Some may be pale green or yellow. Silvery on the belly. Fins are mostly black except the pectoral, which is pale yellow. There is a pale olive basal band on the caudal fin. The cheek has a broad, brown bar from the eye to below the preopercle. Young have spots at the bases of the dorsal and anal fins. Attains 1.1 m. The world, all-tackle angling record weighed 19.2 kg and was caught in South Africa in 1989.

Biology: First reported for Canada from St. Margarets Bay, Nova Scotia in 1985. Often found in coastal waters entering muddy creeks and harbours. They may be seen lying on their side at the surface. May jump wildly when netted. Little is known of its biology but the flesh is very tasty. Food is fishes such as **menhaden** and crustaceans. Spawning occurs in mid-summer. Young float in seaweed and drift long distances. Life span is estimated to be 7–10 years.

Tripletail Family

Scientific name: Lobotidae
French name: croupias roches

Tripletails are found in warmer waters both marine and fresh world-wide. There are about 4 species, with 1 species reported from Atlantic Canada.

The name tripletail is derived from the elongate, rounded, posterior lobes of the dorsal and anal fins which makes the tail appear to be triple. Jaw teeth are small and pointed and there are no teeth on the roof of the mouth. In adults the head is small in relation to the deep, compressed body. Scales are ctenoid and cover the head except the jaws and before the eye. There are 6 branchiostegal rays.

This family is a member of the **Perch Order**.

Young may float on their sides in a curved position and are then camouflaged as floating leaves.

See **tripletail**

tripletwig smoothgill

Scientific name: *Eustomias fissibarbis*
(Pappenheim, 1914)
Family: **Barbeled Dagonfish**
Other common names: none
French name: triorné

Distribution: Found in the North Atlantic Ocean including from off the Scotian Shelf south to the Caribbean Sea.

Characters: This species is distinguished from its Canadian Atlantic relatives by the anal fin base being longer than the dorsal fin base, the anal fin origin being well in advance of the dorsal fin origin, and 2 pec-

tripletwig smoothgill

toral fin rays about equal in length. The upper jaw is slender and protrusible. No teeth on the gill rakers. A single branch from the stem of the chin barbel has 3 ornate, secondary branches. Dorsal fin rays 22–26, anal rays 36–41, pelvic rays 7. Photophores between the pectoral and pelvic fin insertions number 27–29. Overall colour is black. Reaches 13.0 cm.

Biology: Only a single specimen has been found in Canada (in 1980) southeast of Point Tupper, Nova Scotia, between 85 and 260 m.

Tripodfish Family

Scientific name: Ipnopidae
French name: cran-tactiles

The tripodfishes or spiderfishes are found in the Atlantic, Pacific and Indian oceans. There are about 29 species with 2 reported from the Atlantic coast of Canada.

They have minute eyes or a large, dorsal eye which lacks a lens, no pseudobranch and no pyloric caeca, a large mouth, and in some very elongate pectoral, pelvic and caudal fin rays. They are members of the **Flagfin Order**.

The tripod fishes live over a sea floor of ooze or fine sand. Their elongate pelvic fins and lower tail lobe raise them above this. It has been suggested that the fin rays serve as tactile or taste organs but it seems probable that their purpose is to prevent disturbance of the fine sediment on the sea floor. The large pectoral fins are raised over the head and, since they are rich in nerve endings, may well serve to detect food items drifting past in the current. There can be as many as 88 tripod fish per square kilometre off the Bahamas, an unusually common frequency for a deepsea fish.

See **roughscale wirewing**
  snoutlet crotchfeeler

trout-perch

Scientific name: *Percopsis omiscomaycus*
  (Walbaum in Artedi, 1792)
Family: **Trout-Perch**
Other common names: silver chub, sand roller
French name: omisco

Distribution: Found in central and northern North America. In Canada it occurs from western Québec, including around James Bay, throughout Ontario, Manitoba and Alberta, but only in northeastern British Columbia, and in the eastern Yukon and the Northwest Territories.

Characters: The combination of weakly ctenoid scales, an adipose fin, weak spines in the dorsal, anal and pelvic fins, and the pelvic fin base under the pectoral fin is unique. Pyloric caeca number 7–14, arranged in 2 rows on each side of the intestine. Dorsal fin with 2 weak spines, 9–12 soft rays. Anal fin with 1 weak spine and 5–8 soft rays. Pelvic fin with 1 weak spine and 7–9 soft rays. Pectoral fin rays 12–15. Scales 41–60 in a complete lateral line.

Background colour is silvery with 5 rows of black spots. There are 9–12 spots on the back midline, 7–12 weak spots on the upper flank and 8–13 obvious spots or blotches along the midflank. The back may have a purplish tinge or be yellowish, brownish or greyish. Large cavities on the cheek and lower jaw are silvery-white. The body is often translucent and the internal body cavity lining can be seen through the skin. Reaches 20 cm.

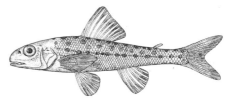

trout-perch

Biology: Trout-perch favour deeper water of lakes (down to 60 m) but enter streams to spawn in the east. In western Canada they may be found in shallow streams.

Food includes aquatic insects, crustaceans and fish, perhaps taken mostly at night during an inshore migration. Trout-perch are an important food for **northern pike, yellow walleye, burbot, lake trout, brook trout, sauger, yellow perch** and **drum**. Often the only evidence of trout-perch in predator stomachs is the pyloric caeca, which produce, and are therefore resistant to, digestive enzymes.

Males live to 3, and occasionally to 4, years in Lake Champlain with females living to 6 years. Maximum age elsewhere is reported as 8 years but maturity can be reached at 1 year. Females are larger than males.

Spawning occurs in streams or over sand and gravel in lake shallows. Most southern Canadian populations are believed to migrate to spawn in streams in May and then return to lakes. Lake spawning may run from May to August. In the north, ripe males and females have been caught in June and July. Egg diameters are up to 1.85 mm and egg numbers to 1825. Eggs are heavier than water and stick to the bottom.

Occasionally used as bait but otherwise not of direct, commercial importance. One important function of this species may be as a nutrient transporter. **Lake trout** are confined to cool depths of lakes and cannot feed in the food-rich but warm shallows. However trout-perch feed in the shallows at night and return to deep water for the day where they fall prey to the **lake trout**.

Trout-perch Family

Scientific name: Percopsidae
French name: perches-truites

The trout-perch family contains only 2 species in temperate North American fresh waters, 1 of which is found in Canada, the other, the sand roller, being restricted to the Columbia River drainage in the U.S.A.

The name derives from their anatomy, which contains characters of both the trout or salmon-like fishes and the perch-like fishes (see **Salmon** and **Perch** orders). These characters are detailed in the account of the **Trout-perch Order**. They include an adipose fin, weakly ctenoid scales, a scaleless head, weak spines at the origins of the dorsal, anal and pelvic fins, and 7–8 pelvic soft rays. The alveolar premaxillary process is broadly arched. Biology is summarised in the species account. Eocene fossils were more speciose than living members.

See **trout-perch**

Trout-perch Order

The trout-perches and their relatives form the Order Percopsiformes, comprising 3 families of small fishes with 9 species found only in North America. One family, the **Trout-perch Family**, extends into Canada while the others (pirate-perch and cavefishes) are found only in the fresh waters of the eastern and southern United States. The pirate-perch is unusual in that the anus is between the gill membranes under the throat in adults. It is found in U.S. drainages of Lakes Ontario, Erie and Huron, and may eventually be captured on the Canadian side. The cavefish family includes both surface species with functional eyes and others which are sightless and live in caves in limestone areas. These fishes are of no economic importance, but the adaptations of some species to underground life fascinate scientists. Fossil relatives of this order date back to the Cretaceous, 100–65 million years ago.

This order is characterised by the single dorsal and anal fins having 1–4 weak anterior spines, pelvic fins when present lying behind the pectoral fin base and having 3–8 soft rays, the pelvic girdle when present attached to the pectoral girdle, the upper jaw is bordered by the premaxillae bones and is non-protractile, the swimbladder is not connected by a duct to the gut, scales are often ctenoid but can be cycloid, the ectopterygoid and palatine bones in the roof of the mouth have teeth, some species have an adipose fin, there are 6 branchiostegal rays, 16 branched caudal fin rays, and certain skull bones are absent, such as the orbitosphenoid, basisphenoid and the suborbital shelf. These characters place this order intermediate between more primitive salmon-like fish (see **Salmon Order**) and the more advanced **spiny-rayed fishes**.

See **Trout-perch Family**

trouts

Trouts are members of the **Salmon Family**. There are 7 species bearing this name in Canada, the **brook, brown, bull, cutthroat, golden, lake**, and **rainbow trouts**.

The **brown trout** is introduced from Europe and is most closely related to the **Atlantic salmon** among Canadian fishes. The **bull trout**, **Brook trout**, and **lake trout** are in the same genus, *Salvelinus*, as the various **char** species and the remaining 3 species are related to the Pacific coast members of the genus *Oncorhynchus* which has been applied in various ways to members of the **Salmon Family**. The familiar "brook trout" and "lake trout" of eastern North America are called chars by scientists here because they are in the char genus *Salvelinus*. Common names often do not reflect the scientific understanding of relationships. Even the unrelated **smallmouth bass** has been referred to as white or mountain trout. Trout comes from the Greek for "gnawer."

trunkfishes

Trunkfishes are members of the **Boxfish Family** represented by 2 species in Atlantic Canada, the **rough** and the **smooth trunkfish**. They are named for the bony carapace which encases them like a box or trunk.

tubenose goby

Scientific name: *Proterorhinus marmoratus*
(Pallas, 1814)
Family: **Goby**
Other common names: mottled Black Sea goby
French name: gobie à nez tubulaire

Distribution: Naturally found in the Black, Caspian and Aral seas and tributary rivers including the Danube River in Austria, and in rivers of the northern Aegean Sea. A specimen was caught in the St. Clair River on the Michigan side. Not yet reported from Canada.

Characters: This is one of only two goby species reported from the Great Lakes basin and is easily recognised by the tube-like ante-

tubenose goby

rior nostrils which hang over the upper lip. First dorsal fin spines 6–7, second dorsal fin with 1 spine and 14–20 soft rays, anal fin with 1 spine and 11–17 soft rays. Scales 36–48 along the flank. Overall colour brown-grey to yellow-grey with spots or about 5 irregular, oblique bars on the flank. The lateral snout has a dark spot with a white, rear margin. The base of the caudal fin has a triangular black spot edged with white spots. Males are darker than females. Fins may be clear or speckled and the dorsal fin usually has oblique, thin bars. Reaches 11.5 cm.

Biology: A small specimen was caught in 1990 on a power plant, water-filtering screen in Michigan. It was probably transported to North America in the ballast of a ship. The species may become established if adults were also transported and rapidly spread

through the Great Lakes. The effects of such an introduction are unknown and potentially dangerous to fishes and other organisms. The goby, as with other introduced species, may carry parasites and diseases, compete for food with native species, eat eggs of other fishes, and compete for living space. In Europe and Asia, this goby lives in fresh and slightly brackish, shallow waters of rivers and estuaries. It is found under rocks and in weedy areas feeding on crustaceans and insects. Maturity is reached at 1 year. Spawning occurs in late spring and summer and eggs, 2.5 by 1.3 mm, are laid under shells and stones.

tubenose poacher

Scientific name: *Pallasina barbata aix*
Starks, 1896
Family: **Poacher**
Other common names: tubesnout poacher
French name: agone barbu

Distribution: Found from Japan, through the Bering Sea to central California. Another subspecies is found in the North Pacific Ocean.

Characters: This species is identified by its elongate shape and the barbel on the lower jaw, projecting forwards. Spines are reduced or absent. There are no cirri at the rear of the upper jaw. The first dorsal fin has 6–9 spines and the second dorsal fin 6–8 soft rays. The anal fin has 10–14 rays and the pectoral fin 10–13 rays, none finger-like. Lateral line pores 45–46. Gill membranes are not joined to the isthmus. The body is grey or brown with fine black dots, which extend onto the dorsal and pectoral fins. The lower part of the head is white. The belly is yellowish. It is named for Petrus Simon Pallas, whose descriptions of Pacific sea life are amongst the earliest scientific accounts. Attains 14 cm.

tubenose poacher

Biology: This species is often found in seaweed intertidally and down to at least 55 m, possibly 128 m. It may stay in shallow waters through the winter or migrate to deeper water.

Tubeshoulder Family

Scientific name: Platytroctidae (= Searsiidae)
French name: circés

Tubeshoulders are deepsea fishes found in all temperate to tropical oceans. There are about 37 species, with 7 reported from Canada, all but 2 on the Pacific coast.

These fishes are unique in having a special sac under the cleithrum (the large bone supporting the pectoral fin). This shoulder organ is a black-lined pit and produces a luminous fluid which reaches the outside by means of a tube visible above the pectoral fin. Many species also have light organs, particularly on the belly, where they are not in rows. The dorsal fin is over the anal fin at the rear of the body. There is a canal system under the skin connected to scale pockets by pores.

This family is closely related to the **Slickhead Family** and has been combined with it in a single family. Many of the more obvious characters like fin ray and scale counts overlap between species and these fishes can be difficult to identify. Identifications and distributions of some species are suspect in literature records for Canada. Tubeshoulders are members of the **Smelt Order**.

Adults are found mostly at depths of 250–900 m, with some species below 1000 m, and are only seen by scientists. The shoulder organ, with its backward pointing tube, acts as a mechanism to confuse predators by a squirt of shining liquid, rather like the ink cloud of octopus and cuttlefish. The sudden blinding cloud of blue-green points of light enables the tubeshoulder to escape into the darkness.

> See **hippo combchin**
> **Innes' tubeshoulder**
> **longsnout manypitshoulder**
> **pitted tubeshoulder**
> **shining tubeshoulder**
> **streaklight tubeshoulder**
> **teardrop tubeshoulder**

tube-snout

Scientific name: *Aulorhynchus flavidus*
  Gill, 1861

Family: **Tube-snout**
Other common names: tubenose, needlefish
French name: trompe

Distribution: Found from southeastern Alaska to Baja California including British Columbia.

Characters: The elongate shape and numerous short, free spines before a soft dorsal fin are characteristic. The snout is a tube with a tiny mouth at the tip. The lower jaw is flattened and protrudes. Dorsal fin spines 23–27, soft rays 9–11. Anal fin with 1 small but broad spine and 9–10 soft rays. Pectoral fin rays 10. There are 52–57 scutes along the flank. There are no ribs. The upper part of the body is brownish with green or yellow tinges, and has dark bars. The body may be light olive-green and transparent with short, light streaks in the flesh. The lower part of the body and the belly are white. A dark stripe through the eye on the head may extend onto the flank. The area behind the head is silvery below the dark stripe. The tip of the lower jaw is dark. Breeding males have bright red pelvic fins and a phosphorescent snout. Attains about 18.8 cm.

tube-snout

Biology: Found in schools in kelp beds, over sand, in eelgrass and in rocky areas, and around docks and pilings. They range from the surface down to 30 m. Their swimming movements are jerky as they use the pectoral fins. Food is minute crustaceans, worms and larval fish. They may live to 9 years although it has been suggested that the entire life-cycle takes only 1 year.

Spawning occurs in April and eggs hatch in May in Canadian waters. The orange eggs are large (2 mm), sticky and are laid around kelp stems, adhering to each other but not the kelp. The kelp is tied so that the growing tips point downwards thus forming a nest. Thread-like secretions from the male urogenital area are used to tie down the kelp. The male guards the eggs and as many as 10 clusters of eggs from different females will be under his care. Curiously, the egg masses (13–33 mm across) are above the nest rather than in it. Nests are usually deeper than 10 m and there can be up to 10 on a single kelp stem. If a nest is lost, a new one is built. These fish have been used in aquaria but are very susceptible to shock. They are an important food for other fishes because of their large numbers. Tube-snouts can be eaten floured and fried whole in butter.

Tube-snout Family

Scientific name: Aulorhynchidae
French name: trompes

Tube-snouts or tubenoses are marine fishes of the North Pacific Ocean with only 2 species in the family, 1 of which is found in British Columbia.

These fishes have elongate bodies with body scutes along the side and 23–27 short, separate spines before a short, soft dorsal fin. The pelvic fin has 1 spine and 4 soft rays and the caudal fin 13 rays. There are 4 branchiostegal rays. There is a ring of bones completely encircling the orbit.

Tube-snouts are relatives of the **Stickleback Family** in the **Stickleback Order**, and share with them the presence of isolated spines on the back, lateral scutes and the nest-building habit.

These are common inshore fishes and have been reported to occur in schools numbering millions of fish. They are slow swimmers but can make rapid lunges to seize prey. They swim backwards or forwards slowly, using the pectoral fins.

The tube-snout does not migrate and has a very short larval life. It has been suggested that dispersal occurs when egg masses are torn off the delicate plants, favoured for laying by females, during stormy weather.

See **tube-snout**

tunas

Tunas are members of the **Mackerel Family**. Species in Canadian waters are the **bigeye, bluefin, bullet, skipjack** and **yellowfin tunas**. Other large members of the family have also been called tunas in addition to their accepted common names. Tuna is

derived from the Greek and Latin name for these fishes and is a Spanish-American word.

turbots

Turbots are **flatfishes** usually with a deep body. The name has been used interchangeably for some **sole** species, such as the **C-O sole** and the **curlfin sole**. It is also used in French for the **spotfin flounder** (turbot à nageoires tachetées) and the **windowpane** (turbot de sable), and for the **Lefteye Flounder Family**. The **Greenland halibut** is known commercially as turbot or Greenland turbot. The **arrowtooth flounder** of British Columbia is often referred to as turbot by fishermen. The word turbot is derived from the Latin for top or spindle in reference to its shape.

twinpored eel

Scientific name: *Xenomystax atrarius*
    Gilbert, 1891
Family: **Pike Conger**
Other common name: none
French name: anguille à pores jumelées

Distribution: Found from Chile to off Vancouver Island.

Characters: The wide, crescentic gill opening and fang-like teeth on the roof of the mouth are characteristic. There are 11–14 pectoral fin rays and the pectoral fins are well-developed. The pelvic fins are absent. There are no scales but there is an obvious lateral line. The upper jaw is deeply grooved dividing the teeth into two rows. There are no gill rakers. Colour is mostly black or brownish. The pectoral fin tips are whitish. Head pores and the lateral line are white. Attains 66.9 cm standard length.

twinpored eel

Biology: Rare in Canadian waters and first caught in 1970. Found at about 450 m.

twoclub angler

Scientific name: *Ceratias holboelli*
    Krøyer, 1845

Family: Seadevil
Other common names: northern seadevil,
   giant seadevil, deepsea angler
French name: pêcheur à deux massettes

   Distribution: Found world-wide including
off Atlantic Canada.

   Characters: This deepsea **anglerfish** is distinguished from its relatives, the **warted
seadevil** and the **stargazing seadevil**, by hav-

twoclub angler

ing 2 fleshy, club-shaped knobs on the back in
front of the dorsal fin, and by the esca or bait
having 1 main filament, branched or not.
There is no spine on the anterior margin of the
subopercle. Mature males develop rough skin
and become slender but immature ones have
loose skin and are rounded. Overall colour of
females is black with colourless spines
appearing as white in contrast. Males have an
unpigmented body. Females reach 1.45 m,
large for a deepsea anglerfish, with parasitic
males reaching 15 cm.

   Biology: Occasionally enters shallow
waters and was originally discovered in 1844
stranded on a beach in Greenland by the
Dane Lt. Commander C. Holbøll. Most specimens are caught between 400 and 2000 m,
but they may be found as shallow as 150 m
and as deep as 3400 m. Maturity may be
attained at 5 years for females. May contain
nearly 5 million immature eggs. Whales are
known to eat this large seadevil.

twohorn barbelthroat

Scientific name: *Linophryne bicornis*
   Parr, 1927
Family: **Leftvent**
Other common names: none
French name: gorge bicornue à barbe

   Distribution: Found in the northwest

Atlantic Ocean, including off Newfoundland,
and the Indian Ocean.

   Characters: Females of this species of
deepsea **anglerfish** are distinguished by having an esca or bait with a short filament on
each side of the bulb tip. The barbel is undivided at its base. Its tip has 2 short branches
each with several internal and stalked photophores and 3–4 long filaments also with
internal photophores. The filaments are often
longer than the main barbel stem. Males
have pointed sphenotic spines. Overall
female colour is black with parts of the esca
unpigmented. Females reach 24.1 cm and
males 3.0 cm.

twohorn barbelthroat

   Biology: Known from Canadian waters
by a single specimen caught on the bottom at
620–660 m. Elsewhere down to 1272 m.
Females attract prey items close to the mouth
using the fishing apparatus.

twohorn sculpin

Scientific name: *Icelus bicornis*
   (Reinhardt, 1840)
Family: **Sculpin**
Other common names: none
French name: icèle à deux cornes

   Distribution: Found from the Beaufort
Sea to Greenland across the Arctic including
northern Ellesmere Island and south to the
southern Scotian Shelf in Atlantic Canada.
Also on the Arctic coast of Eurasia.

   Characters: This species and its relative,
the **spatulate sculpin**, are distinguished from

other Arctic-Atlantic sculpins by having a forked uppermost preopercular spine and row of spiny plates below the dorsal fins. It is

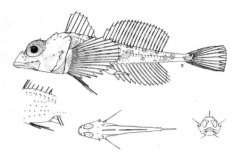

twohorn sculpin

separated from its relative by having lateral line plates with spines above and below the pores and a lateral line often ending on the caudal peduncle. There are 4 preopercular spines, the lower 3 directed downward. First dorsal fin spines 7–10, second dorsal with 17–23 soft rays. Anal fin with 12–17 soft rays. Pectoral rays 15–19. Lateral line scales 23–43. The male has a long, cylindrical, genital papilla. Overall colour yellowish-brown with darker spots and blotches dorsally. White on the belly. There is a dark spot at the pectoral fin base. The caudal, second dorsal and pectoral fins are thinly barred. Reaches 13 cm standard length.

Biology: Twohorn sculpins are found at –1.8 to 8.8°C from shallow water to 560 m on sand or rock bottoms or in algae. In the Canadian Arctic it is in shallower water than in warmer, southern, Atlantic waters. Food is worms and crustaceans. Up to 91 species of food items are recorded for Arctic Canadian populations, amphipods being the most important. Females are larger than males which reach a maximum size of about 7.0 cm. Females mature at 4 years of age at 6 cm. In northern waters spawning occurs in August to October and females have up to 700 eggs with a diameter of 3.1 mm.

twoline eelpout

Scientific name: *Bothrocara brunneum* (Bean, 1891)
Family: **Eelpout**
Other common names: none

French name: lycode à deux lignes

Distribution: Found from the Okhotsk Sea to Baja California including British Columbia.

Characters: This species is distinguished from its Pacific relatives by lacking pelvic fins, having minute scales, oval eyes, a large gill opening extending to the throat, 2 lateral lines, one high on the flank from the head to above the anus, the other beginning on mid-flank above the anus and running almost to the end of the body, gill rakers short and stout, and eye diameter less than snout length. Nape scales are present. The flesh is firm. Dorsal fin rays 100–112, anal rays 89–100 and pectoral rays 14–17. Dorsal and anal fins are enclosed in gelatinous tissue anteriorly. Head pores large. Overall colour light grey or brown, translucent. Dorsal and anal fins with blue or black margins, almost transparent at the base. Peritoneum black. Mouth cavity light. Attains 66 cm.

twoline eelpout

Biology: Canadian specimens have been caught off La Pérouse Bank, near southern Vancouver Island, at 550–582 m, elsewhere at 25–1829 m on mud or sand-mud bottoms. This is a not uncommon eelpout often caught in bottom trawls and **sablefish** traps.

twospine bigscale

Scientific name: *Scopelogadus mizolepis bispinosus* (Gilbert, 1915)
Family: **Ridgehead**
Other common name: soft melamphid
French name: heaume à deux épines

Distribution: This particular subspecies is found in the eastern Pacific Ocean including off British Columbia.

Characters: This species, and the related **squarenose helmetfish**, are distinguished from other ridgeheads by having less than 17 scale rows from the nape to the caudal fin base and no cheek scales. The supramaxillary bone of the upper jaw is absent. This species has less than 25 gill rakers usually. Rakers are elongate flaps with 2 medial rows

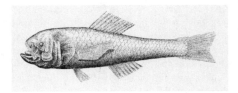

twospine bigscale

of teeth. Dorsal fin with 2 spines and 10–12 soft rays. Anal fin with 1 spine and 7–9 soft rays. Pectoral fin rays 13–15. Overall brownish to black in colour. Gill and mouth cavities very dark. Attains 10.2 cm.

Biology: Rarely caught in Canadian waters. Adults are known only up to 400–500 m while post-larvae may ascend to about 50 m. Maximum depth is 1464 m.

twospot cardinalfish

Scientific name: *Apogon pseudomaculatus* Longley, 1932
Family: **Cardinalfish**
Other common names: none
French name: apogon à deux taches

Distribution: Found from Nova Scotia south to Brazil.

Characters: This species is distinguished from its adult relative, the **flamefish**, by hav-

ing a round black spot on the upper part of the caudal peduncle rather than a saddle, and 14–16 scales around the caudal peduncle. Gill rakers on the lower limb of the arch 12–14, usually 13. Lateral line scales 24. Pectoral fin rays 11–13. Overall colour is red, with a black blotch on the operculum and heavy, black spots below the soft dorsal fin and on the upper caudal peduncle. The second dorsal, anal and caudal fins are black tipped. Reaches 10.5 cm.

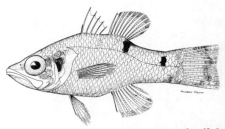

twospot cardinalfish

Biology: Records from the Scotian Bank are of larval strays from warmer waters to the south where it is more common in deeper water than its relative, but is also found around harbours. Several specimens have been caught from 1977–1982. Fish brooding eggs have been caught in June-August and larval fish in Nova Scotia were caught from July to September. This is the most widely distributed **cardinalfish** in the Atlantic Ocean.

U

Umatilla dace

Scientific name: *Rhinichthys umatilla*
(Gilbert and Evermann, 1894)
Family: **Carp**
Other common names: none
French name: naseux d'Umatilla

Distribution: Found in the Columbia River system of southern British Columbia and adjacent U.S. states.

Characters: This species is distinguished by possession of a short, rounded barbel at each mouth corner lying mostly in the lip groove (in contrast to the **leopard dace**), the upper lip separated from the snout by a

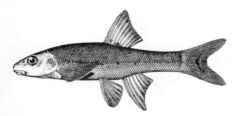

Umatilla dace

groove, an inferior mouth where the snout projects beyond the upper lip, and 55–72 lateral line pores and 29–40 scales around the caudal peduncle. The pelvic fins may have weakly developed fleshy stays connecting the fins to the body. The body is robust and scales are difficult to detect in living fish. The back and upper head are dark, flanks mostly creamy, with some irregular dark spotting. Breeding males develop orange to red pelvic fins. The peritoneum is specked but may by brown or silvery-white. Reaches about 12 cm.

Biology: This species prefers somewhat faster current than **leopard dace** in clear, large rivers with cobbles and stones for cover. It has a restricted distribution in Canada and is not very common. Some Canadian populations may depend on "immigrants" from the United States. Food is derived from algae and associated animals covering stones and possibly various invertebrates found under stones. Life span is not known but probably

exceeds 2 years. Spawning is also unrecorded but is probably in spring and summer. The Committee on the Status of Endangered Wildlife in Canada accorded a status of "rare" to this species in 1988.

upmouth hugo

Scientific name: *Hygophum taaningi*
Bekker, 1965
Family: **Lanternfish**
Other common names: none
French name: hugo bécot

Distribution: Found in the Atlantic Ocean and Gulf of Mexico. Off the coast of Nova Scotia in Canada.

Characters: This species and its relatives, the **highvelo** and **longnose hugos**, are distinguished from other Atlantic coast lanternfishes by having no photophores close to the dorsal body edge, the PLO photophore is well above the pectoral fin level, the second PVO photophore is below the upper end of the pectoral fin base, there are 2 Prc photophores, the PVO photophores are inclined, not horizontal, while the VO photophores are horizontal, and there are 2 Pol photophores. This species is separated from its relatives by the second Prc photophore being at or close to the lateral line and the VLO photophore being midway between the lateral line and the pelvic fin base. Dorsal fin rays 12–14, anal rays 17–23 and pectoral rays 13–14. Total gill rakers 16–21. AO photophores 9–13. These characters vary with distribution and particular populations in a limited area

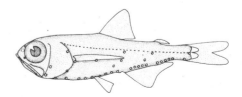

upmouth hugo

will have a narrower range of counts. Lateral line organs 37. Adult males have a large supracaudal luminous gland which first develops at 2.3 cm. Adult females have 2–4 elongate, small patches, sometimes merging into 1 patch, forming an infracaudal luminous gland also developing in fish 2.3 cm. long. Reaches 6.1 cm.

Biology: Known only from a single specimen taken south of Sable Island Bank off Nova Scotia and reported in 1969. Identifi-cation of this specimen needs confirmation. Depth distribution in the Atlantic Ocean is 475–1000 m by day and near surface to 250 m and 650–1250 m at night. Night captures are mostly at 20–100 m and deeper fish are all juveniles which apparently do not migrate. This species is sexually mature at 4.0 cm.

V

Vanhoeffen's whipnose

Scientific name: *Gigantactis vanhoeffeni*
  (Brauer, 1902)
Family: **Whipnose**
Other common names: none
French name: tact géant de Vanhoeffen

Distribution: Found world-wide including off the Scotian Shelf of Atlantic Canada.

Characters: Females of this deepsea **anglerfish** have lower jaw teeth and only 5–7 dorsal fin rays which distinguishes it from its Canadian relative, the **longtail whipnose**. The fishing apparatus is relatively short. The esca or bait has a black, spiny extension at its tip. The esca is whitish, tuberculate and covered in fine spines in small specimens. Males are unknown. Females reach 34 cm.

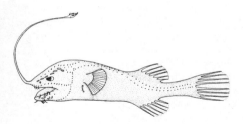

Vanhoeffen's whipnose

Biology: The Canadian record is of a single specimen taken east of the Banquereau Bank in 1984 at a depth of 1015–1116 m. This whipnose is usually caught between 700 and 1300 m, and perhaps as deep as 5300 m.

veiled anglemouth

Scientific name: *Cyclothone microdon*
  (Günther, 1878)
Family: **Bristlemouth**
Other common names: small-eyed lantern fish
French name: cyclothone à petites dents

Distribution: Found in the Atlantic, Indian and Pacific oceans including off Atlantic and eastern Arctic Canada from Baffin Bay and Davis Strait southward.

Characters: This species is distinguished from its Atlantic coast relatives by a lack of SO and isthmus photophores, OA pho-

veiled anglemouth

tophores are present, gill rakers are 19–22, the snout is pigmented diffusely and the branchiostegal membranes are uniformly pigmented. Gill rakers are visible in the open mouth. Photophores: ORB 1, OP 2, BR 9–11, IV 2–3 + 10, VAV 4–5, AC 13–15, OA 8–9, IC 31–33. Photophores are edged in black. Scales are present, about 27–31 or more along the lateral line. Gill filaments are fused. Dorsal fin rays 12–15, anal rays 16–20, pectoral rays 8–10. Overall colour is brown to brown-black or jet-black with dense, star-shaped pigment cells on the head, body and fins. Females reach 7.6 cm but males only reach 4.9 cm.

Biology: Widely distributed off eastern Canada including as shallow as 201 m in the Laurentian Channel. Adults and young are found at 200–2700 m but precise depth varies with age, season and latitude. Some individuals have been caught down to 5301 m off Bermuda. Larvae are in the upper 50 m. There is no daily vertical migration. This is an extremely abundant species found in large, midwater schools. Over 82% of all fishes from the deep-sea in the Atlantic Ocean are this species and nearly 55% in the Pacific Ocean. It is a major food item for many other fish species. Food is mainly copepods. In this species sex reversal occurs at 22–42 mm standard length. Spawning occurs in the summer and autumn with each female producing up to 10,000 eggs with a diameter of 0.5 mm. The number of eggs increases in higher latitudes.

velvet whalefish

Scientific name: *Barbourisia rufa*
(Parr, 1945)
Family: **Whalefish**
Other common names: none
French name: poisson-baleine velouté

Distribution: Found in the Atlantic, Pacific and Indian oceans, including the Labrador Shelf and on the Grand Bank in Atlantic Canada.

Characters: This is the only family member and more information is given under **Whalefish Family**. Dorsal fin rays 19-22, anal fin rays 15-18, pectoral fin rays 13-14 and pelvic fin with 6 rays. Lateral line pores 28-33. The teeth are minute and form felt-like patches. Overall colour is orange-red or brick-red. Gill cavity dark brown or black. Mouth interior white. Peritoneum black. Attains 38 cm.

velvet whalefish

Biology: Rare and so little is known of its biology. Known from only 2 specimens in Canada caught in 1976 and 1982 at depths of 800-850 m and 1250 m.

vermilion rockfish

Scientific name: *Sebastes miniatus*
(Jordan and Gilbert, 1880)
Family: **Scorpionfish**
Other common names: red snapper, red rock cod, rasher, genuine red
French name: sébaste vermillon

Distribution: Found from southeast Alaska and the Queen Charlotte Islands south to Baja California.

Characters: This species is distinguished from its Canadian relatives by the unique colour and by having scales on the jaw bones. The rear edge of the anal fin slopes back-wards. Dorsal fin spines 13, soft rays 13-15, usually 14. Anal fin soft rays 6-8, usually 7, second anal spine only slightly thicker than the third, usually shorter in length except in young when about equal. Pectoral fin rays 16-

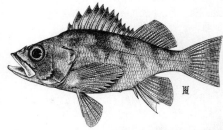

vermilion rockfish

18, usually 18. Gill rakers 35-43. Vertebrae 26. Lateral line pores 40-48, scale rows below the lateral line 45-48. Coronal head spines absent, nuchals usually absent. The overall colour is vermilion or dark red with grey mottling on the flanks and paler on the belly. The mouth is red. Three weak orange stripes radiate from the eye. Larger fish have weak, dark mottling on the head and back. Deep-water specimens are the most red; those in shallow water are brownish. Young fish have dark edges to the fins and are more mottled on the flanks. Peritoneum silvery-white. Reaches 91 cm and 6.8 kg. The world, all-tackle angling record weighed 4.3 kg and was caught in Depoc Bay, Oregon in 1989.

Biology: Found on rocky reefs and guy-ots from the shallows down to 350 m as adults with young in shallow water only. Food is octopi, squids, crustaceans and small fishes such as **anchovies** and **lanternfishes**. Precocious females mature at 3 years and half the population is mature at 6 years. Life span is at least 22 years. Females release up to 1.6 million young in winter. Sport fisher-men take this species on baited hooks fished from boats, or by spearing. Young can be caught from piers. Said to be good eating when fresh but not when frozen.

vertebrates

Vertebrates (Vertebrata or Craniata) are characterised chiefly by the presence of ver-tebrae and a cranium or skull. All **fishes** are vertebrates along with amphibians, reptiles, birds and mammals. **Fishes** are the dominant group of vertebrates having first appeared 480 million years ago and still outnumbering other vertebrates in numbers of species.

The Vertebrata are a subphylum of the Phylum Chordata (**chordates**). Phyla are the principal, classificatory subdivisions of the Animal Kingdom. There are several other subphyla within the **chordates** including the urochordates or seasquirts, the hemichordates or acorn worms, the fossil calcichordates and the cephalochordates or lancelets. Only the lancelets are fish-like as adults, looking rather like the ammocoetes of **lampreys**. Lancelets are usually included in fish books but have not been reported from Canada. The lancelets have been suggested to be closest to the ancestral form of the vertebrates.

Additional characters of the vertebrates in contrast to the lancelets are the notochord never extending in front of the brain, cartilage or bone is present, there is a brain, the heart has chambers, red blood cells are usually present, the epidermis has several cell layers, and only the **lampreys** have an endostyle (a ciliated groove which traps food in mucus), the rest having thyroid glands.

viperfishes

Viperfishes are found in all oceans including Arctic and Atlantic waters. There are 3 species in Canada which in some classifications would be grouped in their own family (Chauliodontidae). They are members of the **Barbeled Dragonfish Family**. These deepsea fishes are characterised by having a

dorsal fin close to the head and in advance of the pelvic fins, typical hexagonal areas or "scales" along the flank, very large fang-like

viperfish

teeth on both upper and lower jaws (which give these fishes their name for a supposed resemblance to a snake), and adipose fins behind the dorsal and in front of the anal fin. The scales are easily lost or dissolved in preservative but the hexagonal pattern remains distinctively on the flank.

See **Dana viperfish**
manylight viperfish
Pacific viperfish

W

walleye pollock

Scientific name: *Theragra chalcogramma*
  (Pallas, 1814)
Family: **Cod**
Other common names: pollock, whiting,
  bigeye, Pacific pollock, Alaska pollock,
  bugeye, scrapcod, lieu d'Alaska
French name: goberge de l'Alaska

Distribution: Found from Korea to
California including British Columbia. Also
in the Chukchi Sea.

Characters: This species is distinguished
from other Pacific coast **cods** by having 3
dorsal and 2 anal fins, no or a minute barbel
and the lower jaw projects. The first anal fin
origin lies under the space between the first

walleye pollock

and second dorsal fins. First dorsal fin rays
10–13, second dorsal rays 12–18 and third
dorsal rays 14–20. First anal fin rays 15–22,
second anal rays 15–21. Pectoral fin rays
18–21. Gill rakers 34–40.

The back and upper flank are olive-green
to brown often with blotches and mottles.
The flanks are silvery, the belly whitish and
fins are dusky to black except for the pale
anal fin. Young fish have 2–3 yellow stripes
along the flank. Reaches 91 cm.

Biology: Walleye pollock occur from the
surface down to 975 m, but usually at less
than 300 m, mainly in midwater. It is a common species in Canadian waters. Young pollock may associate with jellyfish but avoid
the tentacles. They probably derive some
protection from predators by this association
but this may merely be the common habit of
many fish species to gather around floating
objects in the open ocean. The latter view is
supported by the observation that, when
threatened from above, the pollock dive into

deeper water rather than taking refuge in the
jellyfish tentacles.

Food is crustaceans, **sand lances, Pacific
hake, Pacific herring, deepsea smelts**, and
some **salmons**. Seals, porpoises and various
fishes and sea birds eat walleye pollock.
Lamprey scars may occur on up to 10% of
Canadian pollock.

Life span is 17 years. Maturity is attained
at 3–4 years and half the population is
mature at 39.6 cm for males and 41.4 cm for
females both at age 4 in Dixon Entrance but
28.9 cm and 32.8 cm both at age 3 in the
Strait of Georgia.

Spawning occurs in March–May in
Canadian waters although in the Bering Sea it
occurs year round. Depth of spawning may be
between 46 and 360 m. Eggs are pelagic and
1.8 mm in diameter. They are shed in batches
at intervals of 1–2 days over several weeks. A
female may contain up to 15 million eggs.

Walleye pollock may be used as mink
food. In Japan the roe is highly prized and
Canadian pollock entered this market in
1978. Pollock stocks in North America have
recently (1976) become important as human
food. In 1979 3385 tonnes were landed in
Canada. The total Canadian catch in 1985
was 1700 tonnes but only 460 tonnes in
1988. In 1987 a world total of 6.7 million
tonnes were caught making it the most abundant, endemic fish caught by man in the
North Pacific Ocean. It contributes 8% to the
world catch of all fishes and 41% of all **cods**,
outranking even the **Atlantic cod** at 2.05
million tonnes. Anglers occasionally catch
this species but it is not sought after.

walleye surfperch

Scientific name: *Hyperprosopon argenteum*
  Gibbons, 1854
Family: **Surfperch**
Other common names: none
French name: ditrème-vairon

Distribution: From Vancouver Island to
Baja California.

Characters: This surfperch is distinguished
from other Canadian species by having the

pelvic fins black-tipped, no small scales along the posterior half of the anal fin base, no frenum and 68–73 lateral line scales with 5–7

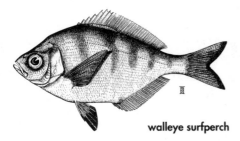

walleye surfperch

on the tail. Dorsal fin spines 7–11, soft rays 25–29. Anal fin spines 3, soft rays 30–35. Pectoral fin rays 25–28. The eye is very large. The back is dark blue, the flanks and belly silvery. There are faint dusky, golden or pink bars. The margins of the caudal, pelvic and anal fins are dusky to black. Males are darker when breeding and the anal fin is more angular. Females have a dark anal fin when breeding. Reaches 30 cm.

Biology: Found on sandy beaches and around piers and down to 18 m often in large schools. Food is small crustaceans. The young number 5–12 and are born in spring after a gestation of 5–6 months at about 3.8–4.0 cm in length. Males drive away other males when courting. A commercially important species in California. Often caught by anglers in southern California where 200,000 or more are taken each year.

walleyes

Walleyes are members of the **Perch Family** with a single species of that name. However 2 subspecies have been recognised, the **blue walleye** or **blue pike** of the Atlantic drainages, now extinct, and the familiar sport fish called **yellow walleye**. Walleyes are named for the large, staring eyes.

warbonnets

Warbonnets are members of the **Shanny Family** belonging to the genus *Chirolophis*. The species are the **Atlantic, decorated, matcheek** and **mosshead warbonnets** with the last 3 species being found on Canada's Pacific coast. They are named for the charac-

teristic fleshy tabs or cirri on the head in allusion to an Indian headdress.

warmouth

Scientific name: *Lepomis gulosus*
　(Cuvier in Cuvier and Valenciennes, 1829)
Family: **Sunfish**
Other common names: goggle-eye, black sunfish, wide-mouthed sunfish, stump-knocker, mud bass, wood bass, weed bass, bigmouth, perch-mouth bream, yawnmouth perch, jugmouth, Indian fish
French name: crapet sac-à-lait

Distribution: Found in Rondeau Provincial Park and Point Pelee National Park, Lake Erie, Ontario. In the U.S.A. from Maryland to Wisconsin and in the south from Mexico to Florida. Introduced elsewhere, including California.

Characters: This species is distinguished by having 3 anal fin spines, 9–11, usually 10 dorsal fin spines, 35–48 lateral line scales, teeth present on the tongue, ectopterygoid and entopterygoid, a supramaxilla bone longer than the greatest width of the maxilla, and 3–5 dark, reddish-brown bars radiating back from the eye. Dorsal fin soft rays 9–11, anal soft rays 8–10.

Overall body colour is olive-brown fading to light brown or yellow on the belly. The back may have a purplish tinge. There are 5–11 dark purplish-brown bars on the flank

warmouth

or stripes formed of dark dots along the scale rows. The iris is red or reddish-brown. Dorsal, anal and caudal fins are dark and mottled with spots in irregular, parallel lines. Pelvic fins are white-edged. Breeding males are bright yellow, the eyes are bright red and there is a bright orange spot at the base of the last 3 dorsal rays.

Sometimes placed in the genus *Chaenobryttus*. Reaches 28.7 cm. The world, all-tackle angling record from the Yellow River, Florida in 1985 weighed 1.1 kg.

Biology: First collected in Canada in 1966 and reported in 1979. It is found in lakes, ponds, ditches and slow streams with mud, sand or gravel bottoms. The water is often muddy or turbid and has dense vegetation or tree stumps. Low oxygen concentrations are tolerated.

Food is aquatic insects, crustaceans and fishes. Peak feeding period is early morning. The large mouth and fast movements enable it to snap up fishes by sight.

Life span is 8 years. Maturity can be attained as early as age 1 and 7.9 cm. Spawning takes place from May to August, peaking in June, in Illinois as water temperatures approach 21.5°C. Nest sites are chosen near a root, rock or vegetation clump on silt or other bottoms with some silt. The nest is 10–15 cm wide and is cleared by a male using sweeping motions of his tail while hanging head up in the water. The nest is defended by the male who approaches intruders with his mouth open and opercles spread. The breeding colour appears at this time. The intruder is scared away by nips or pressure waves made by the tail fin. The male directs a female to the nest by a similar aggressive behaviour and colour display. The colour change takes 5–10 seconds.

Once in the nest, the 2 fish circle each other with the female inclined to one side beneath the male. She gapes 3–4 times, bangs into the male and sheds about 20 eggs. It is assumed the bang against the male stimulates sperm release. A female can have up to 63,200, 1.0 mm diameter eggs. The male guards the fry for 5–6 days until they leave the nest and shelter in weeds.

In the U.S.A. this **sunfish** is a sport fish taken on live or artificial baits including flies.

warted seadevil

Scientific name: *Cryptosaras couesi*
   Gill, 1883
Family: **Seadevil**
Other common names: triplewart seadevil

French name: pêcheur à trèfle

Distribution: Found world-wide including off Atlantic Canada.

Characters: This deepsea **anglerfish** is distinguished from its relatives, the **twoclub angler** and the **stargazing seadevil**, by having 3 fleshy knobs on the back in front of the dorsal fin, a central large one and 2 smaller, lateral ones. There is an obvious spine on the anterior margin of the subopercle. The esca or bait has a single filament. Males have a large pair of anterior denticles on the lower jaw followed by a smaller pair. They are parasitic.

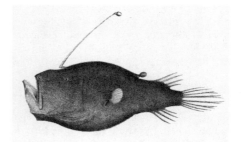

warted seadevil

Males have pigment on the operculum, back and caudal peduncle. Females are black with a white illicium and a black esca. Females reach 46 cm and the parasitic male 7.3 cm.

Biology: The commonest collected deepsea **anglerfish**. It is found between 75 and 4000 m although mostly caught in the 500–1250 m range. One female has been found with 3 parasitic males attached. Females as small as 15.5 mm may have a 9.8 mm attached male, a precocious sexual parasitism. Perhaps the attachment of the male stimulates early ovary development. This **anglerfish** is capable of luminescent countershading with the head directed upwards towards the light source. The luminescence comes from the skin and one fish was able to match overhead light in a fish tank so that it practically disappeared from view, an efficient means of avoiding predators.

warty poacher

Scientific name: *Occella verrucosa*
   (Lockington, 1880)
Family: **Poacher**

Other common names: none

French name: agone verruqueux

Distribution: Found from Alaska to central California including British Columbia.

Characters: This species is related to the **pixie poacher** but is distinguished by having usually 10–12 (range 7–12) anal rays and

warty poacher

13–15 pectoral fin rays. In addition the nasal spine is absent or very blunt and the anus is nearer the pelvic fin base than the anal fin origin. There are no spiny plates on the breast. The mouth is turned upwards in a flattened head. Breast plates are knobby. First dorsal fin with 7–9 spines, second dorsal fin with 6–9 soft rays. Pelvic fins extend to the anal fin in males. There is a cirrus at the rear end of the upper jaw. Gill membranes are not joined to the isthmus. The overall body colour is dark grey or brown becoming lighter ventrally. There may be 6 or more saddles on the back and flanks. Both dorsal fins have a dark edge and the spiny dorsal fin is barred. The pectoral fin has thin lines on the rays forming bands and an orange spot in the centre. Males have a pelvic fin with orange and black pigmentation. Reaches 20 cm.

Biology: Habitat is a soft bottom at 18 to 274 m.

Waryfish Family

Scientific name: Notosudidae
   (= Scopelosauridae)

French name: guetteurs

Widely found, although not common, from subarctic to subantarctic waters. There are 19 species with 3 reported from Canada.

Waryfish or paperbone fishes are small to medium-sized fishes from surface layers to the bottom in oceanic waters. Their snout is spatulate and they have large, oval eyes. Their body shape is like that of a **Barracudina Family** member. Waryfish lack a

swimbladder and light organs. Scales are large, cycloid and easily detached. An adipose fin is present over the anal fin. Anal fin rays are 16–21 and the dorsal fin is at the middle of the body. They are unique among their relatives in that their larvae have teeth on the maxillary bone. Adults lose their teeth and gill rakers at maturity.

Waryfish are related to the **Greeneye** and **Pearleye** families in the **Flagfin Order**.

They are very active and dart from a hovering position to catch such food items as zooplankton, crustaceans and small fishes. They can easily dodge trawls. Waryfish migrate from the bottom in the day to the mesopelagic zone at night. They are only likely to be seen by scientists. Young waryfish live higher in the water column than adults but even adults may be in the upper 200 m. However some descend below 1000 m. Waryfish are hermaphrodites. Some species are known to migrate long distances over the ocean in search of food.

See **blackfin waryfish**
      Maul's waryfish
      scaly waryfish

wattled eelpout

Scientific name: *Lycodes palearis*
   Gilbert, 1896

Family: **Eelpout**

Other common names: none

French name: lycode tressée

Distribution: Found from the Sea of Japan to the Chukchi Sea and the Alaskan Beaufort Sea, and south to Oregon including British Columbia.

Characters: This species is distinguished from its Pacific coast relatives by having prominent ridges on the ventral surface of the

wattled eelpout

lower jaw known as "mental crests", the pectoral fin has a rounded outline, the eye is smaller than snout length, mouth and gill cavities and peritoneum are not black, and pelvic fins are small (length enters 1.5 times into eye diameter). Pelvic fins are present and there are no mucous pores on the jaws. There are teeth on the vomer and palatine bones on the roof of the mouth. The flesh is firm. Dorsal fin rays 94–106, anal rays 81–90, and pectoral rays about 17. The lateral line is indistinct. Vertebrae number 106–114. Overall body colour is grey, light brown to blue-black. There is usually a black spot on the front of the dorsal fin and the dorsal and anal fins have dark margins. Pelvic fins are pale. The peritoneum is creamy-white to pink. Young have white flank bars with the second bar in front of the dorsal fin. Reaches 51 cm.

Biology: Depth range is 25–925 m over mud or sand. Food is clams and shrimps. Spawning occurs in winter near Canadian waters. Eggs are up to 7 mm in diameter.

weakfish

Scientific name: *Cynoscion regalis*
(Bloch and Schneider, 1801)
Family: **Drum**
Other common names: sea trout, gray trout, gray weakfish, squeteague
French name: acoupa royal

Distribution: Found from Nova Scotia south to Florida.

Characters: This drum is separated from its Canadian Atlantic relative, the **black drum**, by dorsal and anal fin ray counts.

weakfish

First dorsal fin with 10 spines, second dorsal fin with 1 spine and 24–29 soft rays. Anal fin with 2 slender spines and 10–13, usually 12, soft rays. The lower jaw protrudes and lacks barbels. The back is a dark olive-green to bluish. Flanks are iridescent green, bluish, golden or even purplish. The upper flank has black to green or bronze spots arranged in irregular, diagonal lines. Lower flank and

belly silvery to white. Fins are yellowish, the dorsal fins duskier than the others. Reaches 1.2 m. The world, all-tackle angling record was caught in 1984 at Long Island, New York and weighed 8.67 kg.

Biology: Summer strays have been reported from the Minas and Cumberland basins in the Bay of Fundy and off Nova Scotia. Found in shore waters over sand in schools, wintering in deeper water down to 100 m. Food is crustaceans, worms, molluscs and a wide variety of small fish. They are said to be voracious feeders, concentrating more on fish as they become larger. Both sexes mature at 2–3 years of age and in some populations most yearlings are mature. Life span exceeds 12 years. Spawning occurs from March to October in U.S. waters. Eggs are pelagic, number up to 1,725,920 in 4 year old fish and are up to 1.1 mm in diameter. Females may spawn more than once in a year. Young weakfish use low salinity estuaries as nursery areas. This is an important commercial species and is used for "surimi" in Japan. It is an appreciated sport fish in the U.S. although hooks tear easily from the mouth (hence "weakfish").

weed shiner

Scientific name: *Notropis texanus*
(Girard, 1856)
Family: **Carp**
Other common names: Richardson shiner, northern weed shiner
French name: méné diamant

Distribution: Found in Great Falls Dam, Winnipeg River, Manitoba in Canada and in the Mississippi River and Gulf coast basins in the U.S.A.

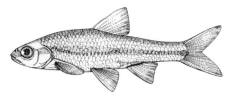

weed shiner

Characters: This species and its relatives in the genus *Notropis* (typical **shiners**) are separated from other family members by usually having 7 branched dorsal fin rays following thin unbranched rays, protractile premaxillaries (upper lip separated from the snout by a groove), no barbels, large lateral line scales (fewer than 50), and a simple, s-shaped gut. It is distinguished from the only other species in Manitoba with a lateral stripe along the flank, across the head and onto the snout by having 2,4–4,2 hooked pharyngeal teeth (rarely 1,4–4,2; 1,4–4,1; 0,4–4,2), branched anal fin rays 5–7 with a strong mode at 6, a caudal fin base spot distinct from the lateral stripe, lateral stripe not a zigzag and on the lip but not the chin, the lower jaw is included in the upper jaw, upper jaw not reaching beyond the snout tip, and the gape reaches the anterior eye margin. Lateral line scales 31–39. The breast anterior to the pectoral fins is scaleless. Pectoral rays 12–14 and pelvic rays 8. Breeding males have large tubercles on the head, snout, lower jaw tip and pectoral fin rays. Tubercles on the body are restricted to the anterior half on and above lateral line scales. The back is olive-yellow to olive-green with the scales outlined by black pigment. The flanks are silvery. The belly is silvery-white. The lateral stripe is dark and has a light area above it where scales are not dark edged. There is a middorsal stripe ending at the dorsal fin with an expanded patch. The posterior 3–4 anal fin rays are outlined with black pigment in some populations. Peritoneum silvery with melanophores. Breeding males become rosy pink, orange or amber on the body and have rosy fins. Reaches 8.6 cm.

Biology: Weed shiners prefer, appropriately, quiet weedy areas of clear lakes and large rivers and streams; however they are not restricted to weedy areas. They were first reported from Canada in 1988. They occur in schools in the lower-middle part of the water column. Food is filamentous algae and associated organisms. Life span exceeds 3 years. Spawning in the U.S.A. occurs from February to September, depending on area. In Wisconsin the spawning season is late June to July. A female may have up to 420 maturing yellow eggs.

wenchman

Scientific name: *Pristipomoides aquilonaris*
(Goode and Bean, 1896)

Family: **Snapper**
Other common names: none
French name: colas vorace

Distribution: Found from Nova Scotia south to Brazil.

Characters: This species is distinguished from the **cubera snapper**, its only Canadian relative, by having no scales on the dorsal and anal fins and the last ray of the dorsal and anal fins is longer than adjacent rays.

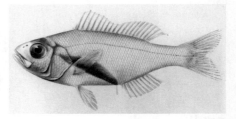

wenchman

Dorsal fin spines 10, soft rays 10–11, usually 11. Anal fin spines 3, soft rays 7–8, usually 8. Pectoral rays 14–17, usually 15–16. Lateral line scales 48–53. The body, head and fins are a uniform pink to pale lavender except the outer edge of the spiny dorsal fin and of the caudal fin which is yellow to orange. The belly is silvery. The iris is dark. Reaches 30 cm. The English common name is of uncertain origin. It may be an allusion to an angler's reel or winch.

Biology: Known from a single specimen caught in 1978 on the southern edge of the Scotian Shelf as a stray from the south. This is a northern record and this species is only common from Florida southward. The wenchman is an abundant species found from 24 to 366 m or more. Juveniles taken from the stomachs of predators over deep water may have been carried out to sea by currents with no chance of reaching suitable habitat for further growth. Food is mostly small fishes. It has been sold fresh and is caught by beam trawls, and also longlines and handlines.

Werewolf Family

Scientific name: Melanocetidae
French name: loups-garous

Werewolves, blackdevil anglerfishes or devil-anglers are found in all temperate to tropical oceans. There are only 5 species with 1 reported from Atlantic Canada.

These deepsea fishes have 12–17 dorsal fin rays and 3–5 anal fin rays which distinguishes them from related families. Females do not have filaments on the esca or bulb of the fishing apparatus. Females reach 18 cm. Males are non-parasitic dwarfs reaching 4.3 cm, have spiny skin, 2–3 transverse series and a median snout series of denticular teeth on the upper jaw, and a median and 2 lateral groups of denticular teeth on the lower jaw. These teeth are all fused at the base.

Werewolves are related to the **Fanfin**, **Seadevil**, **Whipnose**, **Leftvent**, **Dreamer**, **Wolftrap** and **Footballfish** families, which all lack pelvic fins, scales and a pseudobranch, have bones at the front of the head (frontals) which are not united, have the lower pharyngeal bones reduced and toothless, and have 8–9 caudal fin rays. They are identified on the basis of escal characters which require some expertise to understand. Escae are often lost or damaged. The family is a member of the **Anglerfish Order**.

Werewolves are found from depths as shallow as 100 m down to over 3000 m.

See **stout werewolf**

western brook lamprey

Scientific name: *Lampetra richardsoni*
   Vladykov and Follett, 1965
Family: **Lamprey**
Other common names: none
French name: lamproie de l'ouest

Distribution: Found from British Columbia south to Oregon, and possibly from Alaska to California.

Characteristics: There are 57–68 myomeres. The bar below the mouth has 6–10 blunt cusps and teeth are generally blunt. This lamprey is distinguished from other Canadian species by having 2 dorsal fins, 2 cusps on the bar above the mouth, 3 weak teeth on each side of the mouth, usually bicuspid but some may be unicuspid or tricuspid, and no sharp teeth on the tongue. Adults are brown, olive or black, pale ventrally. Fins are olive-green and translucent.

Ammocoetes have most of the head region and the tail pigmented. Attains 16.3 cm as an adult, probably larger.

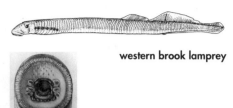

western brook lamprey

disc view

Biology: This is a non-parasitic species which lives solely in fresh water. A parasitic form called *L. richardsoni* var. *marifuga* Beamish and Withler, 1986 is found on Vancouver Island. Its biology and morphology are intermediate between the non-parasitic western brook lamprey and the parasitic **river lamprey**. Spawning occurs from late April to early July and nests are only about 10–13 cm long. They are constructed by body movements and only rarely is gravel carried by the mouth. Up to 12 lampreys may use a nest and the nest may be re-used by other groups. Eggs number up to 3700, measure 1.1 mm, and are slightly oval. Ammocoetes live 3–6 years and are very common in suitable habitats, up to 170 individuals per square metre. They may "rest" for a year before transforming to an adult in August to November, overwintering without feeding to spawn the following spring. This species has been used as bait for **white sturgeon**.

west-slope cutthroat trout

Scientific name: *Oncorhynchus clarki lewisi*
   Suckley, 1874
Family: **Salmon**
Other common names: red-throated trout, lake trout, short tailed trout, native trout, black-spotted trout, Montana blackspot, Yellowstone cutthroat trout
French name: truite fardée du flanc de l'ouest

Distribution: Found in western Alberta and southeastern British Columbia. Also introduced into Saskatchewan, Manitoba, Ontario and Québec but perhaps not established. In the U.S.A. south to Montana (and New Mexico as various subspecies). Introduced elsewhere in the U.S.A.

Characters: This subspecies is one of two in Canada, the other being the **coastal cutthroat trout** (q.v. for characters separating cutthroats from other **Salmon Family** mem-

west-slope cutthroat trout

bers). There is much overlap in their characters and they are difficult to identify. Distribution is perhaps the simplest means of separating the two subspecies, the west-slope cutthroat being found inland, separated by a distinct gap. Dorsal fin with 8–11 principal rays, pectoral rays 12–15 and pelvic rays 9–10. Lateral line scales 116–240 and pyloric caeca 24–60.

Colour is very variable and is complicated by the introduction of **coastal cutthroat trout**. Hybrids with **rainbow** and **golden trout** further complicate colour patterns and identifications. The body has a yellow-green to olive back and red on the head sides, anterior flank and belly. The red may be present year round or develop in the breeding season. The flanks are sparsely spotted as are the dorsal, adipose and caudal fins. Flank spots below the lateral line are more numerous posteriorly (cf. **coastal cutthroat trout**). The flanks may have a narrow pink stripe. The roof of the mouth is whitish in spawning males. Young are the same colour as **coastal cutthroat trout**.

Pure stocks are probably rare in Canada because of introductions from other areas and hybridisation with other **trouts** such as **rainbow trout**. Yellowstone cutthroat trout, another subspecies (*O. c. bouvieri* (Bendire in Jordan and Gilbert, 1881)) are reported from Alberta where they are introduced to Taylor Lake in the Bow River drainage. Formerly in the genus *Salmo*.

Reaches 99.0 cm. The world, all-tackle record for a "cutthroat trout" weighed 18.59 kg and was caught in Pyramid Lake, Nevada in 1925.

Biology: This subspecies is found in lakes and streams up to over 2440 m, favouring headwaters and small tributaries. Some stream populations are permanent residents, others being spawning fish on a migration from a lake.

Food is aquatic and terrestrial insects, crustaceans, frogs, small fishes and their eggs. Fish eaten include **trout, sculpins, carps** and **sticklebacks**.

Maximum life span is about 10 years. Males mature earlier than females, as early as 2 years compared to as late as 6 years. Most fish spawn at 2–4 years. In Alberta fish are larger and faster growing in the larger streams and growth is generally faster in warmer water. There are also differences in growth between lake and stream dwelling fish, depending in part on the time spent in streams compared to lake residency.

Spawning takes place in spring when water temperatures reach 10°C, June–July in Sheep River, Alberta, May–June in the Flathead River of British Columbia, Alberta and Montana. Small gravel streams are favoured. The female excavates a redd by lying on her flank and lashing her tail. Redds are about 30 cm across and 10–13 cm deep. Males court females with nudges and by quivering. The female lies in the redd with head and tail bent up, the male joins her, they gape, vibrate and release eggs and sperm. The fertilised eggs fall between the gravel. The female dislodges gravel at the upstream rim of the redd to cover the eggs with up to 20 cm of gravel. The spawning pair may have other males sneaking in to shed sperm. Females may dig more than 1 redd and both sexes spawn with more than 1 other fish. Each female may have 2000 or more orange-red, adhesive eggs of 5.1 mm maximum diameter. The red cut throat may be used in aggressive displays. Beach and shoal spawning occurs in some lakes. Fry emerge from the gravel in July-August and stay in streams for up to 4 years before migrating to a lake. Repeat spawning occurs in subsequent years and about 18% of a run is fish which have spawned before. About 7% of the run is non-spawners and 75% are first spawners.

This is an important sport fish caught on flies, spoons and live bait although it does not leap as much as some **salmons**. The flesh is orange-red and best when smoked, fried or baked.

western silvery minnow

Scientific name: *Hybognathus argyritus*
Girard, 1856
Family: **Carp**
Other common names: none
French name: méné d'argent de l'ouest

Distribution: Found from the South Saskatchewan and Milk rivers of Alberta and Manitoba and south in the Missouri River basin and the Mississippi River to the Ohio River mouth.

Characters: This species resembles the **shiners** (genus *Notropis*) but has an elongate intestine which has coils on the right, and a subterminal mouth. It is distinguished from its relative, the **brassy minnow**, by its falcate dorsal fin, silvery colour and 12 or less radii on adult scales and from the **eastern silvery minnow** by distribution. Eye diameter is less than mouth width. Dorsal fin branched rays 7, anal branched rays 7. Lateral line scales 36–40. Pharyngeal teeth 4–4. The back is dusky brown, brownish-yellow to olive with silvery flanks and a white belly. There is a slaty, middorsal stripe along the back. There may be dusky spots along the midflank. Peritoneum dusky black. Reaches 17.3 cm. This species was formerly regarded as the same as the **eastern silvery minnow** and

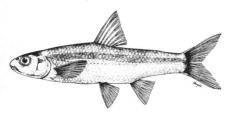

western silvery minnow

both were combined with the central or Mississippi silvery minnow (not in Canada) under the name *Hybognathus nuchalis*.

Biology: This **minnow** is found in large, silty and turbid streams where there are backwaters or current is slow. Food is probably bottom ooze and algae. Sexual maturity is attained after 1 year and life span is 4 years. The spawning season is May to August and up to 7000 eggs are produced. This minnow has been used as a bait fish in the U.S.A.

westnorat dreamtail

Scientific name: *Oneirodes macrosteus*
Pietsch, 1974
Family: **Dreamer**
Other common names: none
French name: queue-de-rêve atnorouest

Distribution: Known only from off Newfoundland, Iceland and Bermuda.

Characters: This species of deepsea **anglerfish** is part of a group of dreamers including the **cosmopolitan** and the **forefour**

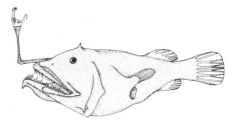

westnorat dreamtail

dreamtails on the Atlantic coast. The females of this group are distinguished by having sphenotic spines, a deeply notched operculum posteriorly, a short and broad pectoral fin lobe, the tip of the lower jaw with a spine, the illicium or fishing rod emerging from between the frontal bones on the head, the dorsal edge of these bones being strongly curved, usually 4 anal fin rays and the caudal fin not covered by skin beyond the base. Females of this species are distinguished from Canadian Atlantic relatives by having an esca or bait without medial appendages and a single pair of anterolateral appendages. Dorsal fin rays 6 and pectoral rays 15–17. Overall colour is black except the esca is unpigmented in parts. Females reach 20.6 cm total length.

Biology: Three specimens were caught off the Grand Bank in 1968 and used as the basis for the description of this species. Females use the fishing apparatus to entice prey within reach.

whale shark

Scientific name: *Rhincodon typus*
  Smith, 1828
Family: **Whale Shark**
Other common names: none
French name: requin baleine

Distribution: A specimen is reported from off the Scotian Shelf of Atlantic Canada. World-wide in warmer seas.

Characters: Huge size, terminal mouth, 3 ridges on the back and upper flank, spots and very large gill slits identify this species. Adults

whale shark

have over 300 rows of minute, hooked teeth and young have over 100 rows. Only the first 10–15 rows are functional. There is a short lobe on the nostrils. The eye is minute. The caudal peduncle has strong lateral keels and an upper precaudal pit. The gill slits have a unique filter mechanism with interconnecting transverse lamellae supporting soft spongy masses. These masses form a sieve with openings only 1–2 by 2–3 mm. Overall colour is dark grey, reddish or greenish-brown on the back and white to yellowish below. Pale yellowish to whitish spots, bars and stripes evident. The lips, mouth and tongue are whitish and the oesophagus black. Reaches 12.1 m, based on an accurately measured specimen, possibly 21 m. A specimen 11.58 m long weighed an estimated 12,088 kg.

Biology: Usually seen near the surface, inshore and often in schools but also found offshore and perhaps down to 600 m. It swims slowly and is mostly harmless, allowing itself to be touched and even ridden by divers. The whale shark will swim to divers out of an apparent curiosity. Food is crustaceans, squids and small fishes (and some large fish too) strained from the water. Feeding may occur vertically with the head near the surface. The body is lowered to suck water and food into the cavernous mouth and then the head is raised out of the water to drain excess water from the gill slits. Suction contrasts with the basking shark which must swim through plankton to extract food. Eggs are laid in large horny cases. One measured 30 cm by 14 cm and 9 cm thick and the embryo was 36 cm long. This case may have been aborted prematurely and the whale shark could be ovoviviparous. Females have up to 16 egg cases and the smallest, free-living young are 55–56 cm long.

Whale Shark Family

Scientific name: Rhincodontidae
French name: requins baleines

This family contains only 1 species found world-wide in warm seas. It has the distinction of being the largest fish. There are 3 ridges on the back and there are pale spots and bars on the body. The head is broad, flattened and, unusual in sharks, the mouth is near the tip of the head. The gill slits are long but less than those of the basking shark, which lacks spots.

The Whale Shark Family is a member of the **Carpet Shark Order**.

There are accounts of this shark attacking boats in South Africa when anglers were retrieving large fish. The sharp denticles can lacerate skin and a blow from the huge tail can stun or even kill a swimmer. It has been harpooned and used as food or for oil in various parts of the world.

Biology is covered in the species account.
See **whale shark**

Whalefish Family

Scientific name: Barbourisiidae
French name: poissons-baleines

The whalefish or red whalefish family is found scattered through the warmer oceans, for example in the Gulf of Mexico, off South Africa and in the western North Pacific Ocean. Also found in Atlantic Canada. There is only one species, which is quite rare.

The scales are tiny and each bears a central spine in contrast to other whalefishes. Pelvic fins are present, with 6 rays.

This whalefish is related to the **Flabby Whalefish** and **Redmouth Whalefish** families in the **Pricklefish Order**. All are characterised by a whale-shaped body, very large mouth and a distensible stomach. The dorsal and anal fins are opposite each other near the rear of the body. There is no swimbladder. The typical orange-brown colour of these fishes is probably derived from their crustacean food, and serves as camouflage. They can eat fish as large as themselves because of their distensible stomach.

See **velvet whalefish**

whalehead dreamer

Scientific name: *Lophodolus acanthognathus* Regan, 1925
Family: **Dreamer**
Other common names: none
French name: faune rêveur fer-de-lance

Distribution: Found in all oceans including off Newfoundland.
Characters: This deepsea **anglerfish** is distinguished as a female from related family members by having the dorsal profile of the frontal bones of the head concave. The sphenotic and symphysial spines are strong. The illicium or fishing rod is short and the esca

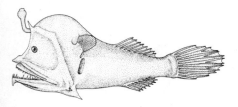

whalehead dreamer

or bait relatively long. Lower jaw teeth may number up to 280. Dorsal fin rays 5–7, anal fin rays 4–6, and pectoral fin rays 17–21.

Males have not yet been discovered. Overall colour dark brown to black with parts of the esca unpigmented and silvery-white. The mouth cavity is unpigmented. Females reach 7.9 cm.

Biology: Only caught by scientific fishing expeditions but probably not uncommon below 650 m. Descends below 1500 m. Females use the fishing apparatus to attract prey close enough to be seized.

whalesucker

Scientific name: *Remora australis* (Bennett, 1840)
Family: **Remora**
Other common names: none
French name: rémora austral

Distribution: World-wide in warmer waters and on the Pacific coast of Canada.
Characters: This remora is distinguished from its Canadian relatives by having 24–28 laminae in a very large disc, about half its

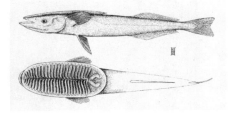

whalesucker

head and body length, a stout body and no stripes. The edge of each lamina has a band of rounded spines. There are 20–27 dorsal fin rays, 20–26 anal fin rays and 21–24 pectoral fin rays. Dark brown, grey, violet, black or bluish overall but darkest ventrally. The dorsal and anal fins have a narrow white margin. Attains 76 cm.

Biology: This remora is found attached only to whales and porpoises. Blue whales are favoured as hosts because they feed on the large plankton eaten by this **remora**. Whalesuckers may also eat whale parasites, fragments of sloughed off skin and even faeces.

Whipnose Family

Scientific name: Gigantactinidae
French name: tacts géants

Found world-wide in the deep ocean with about 20 species of which 2 occur in Atlantic Canada.

Whipnose females have an elongate body, slender head and elongate caudal peduncle, with the fishing apparatus at least as long as the body. The upper jaw extends somewhat beyond the lower jaw. The dorsal fin has 3–10 rays and the anal fin 3–8 rays. The skin spines are minute or obvious. Males are free-living and have well-developed nostrils, minute eyes, but no teeth in the jaws although there are 3–4 upper and 3–5 lower denticular teeth outside the jaws. There are no sphenotic spines in males or females. Larvae have pectoral fins about half the standard length of the fish.

Whipnoses are related to the **Fanfin**, **Seadevil**, **Leftvent**, **Dreamer**, **Wolftrap**, **Footballfish** and **Werewolf** families, which all lack pelvic fins, scales and a pseudobranch, have bones at the front of the head (frontals) which are not united, have the lower pharyngeal bones reduced and toothless, and have 8–9 caudal fin rays. They are distinguished by details of the esca or bait and fin rays counts. This family is a member of the **Anglerfish Order**.

These fishes are predators on other midwater fishes, cephalopods and various crustaceans and coelenterates. *Gigantactis* is Latin for "giant touching structure" and refers to the long fishing apparatus. The illicium may be whipped back and forth but it can be held steady while a vibration is passed to the esca or bait, making it attractive to prey. Whipnoses with a long fishing apparatus must make a strong lunge to catch their food, aided perhaps by their elongate, streamlined body and strong tail fin. The lower jaws are connected by an elastic ligament and can be rotated outwards. The long, hooked teeth can then be used to grasp the prey which is taken into the mouth by a rapid, inward twist of the lower jaws. Each lower jaw can be used alternately to push the prey down the throat. A sucking action to take in prey as found in other **anglerfishes** is not found in whipnoses. They occur generally between 1000 and 2500 m.

See **longtail whipnose**
    Vanhoeffen's whipnose

white barracudina

Scientific name: *Notolepis rissoi kroeyeri* (Lütken, 1892)
Family: **Barracudina**
Other common names: sandeel
French name: lussion blanc

Distribution: This subspecies is found only in the North Atlantic Ocean and adjacent Arctic waters. In Canada reported from Davis Strait southward through the Maritimes to Georgia.

Characters: This species is distinguished from its Canadian relatives by the pectoral fins being shorter than the anal fin base,

white barracudina

smooth-edged lower jaw teeth, body scales (but easily lost), pelvic fin origin behind the dorsal fin origin, many anal fin rays, and an Arctic-Atlantic distribution. This subspecies has smaller teeth then its Pacific coast relative and there are, on average, more vertebrae and anal fin rays. Dorsal fin rays 8–11, anal rays 30–34, pectoral rays 11–13 and pelvic rays 9. Lateral line scales 61–70. Vertebrae 80–85. Overall colour is silvery with a dark, upper flank stripe. Peritoneum black. Reaches 30 cm. The nominate subspecies is found world-wide.

Biology: It is found mostly between 200 and 1000 m but as shallow as 64 m. It is one of the better known barracudinas because it enters shallow waters in the north, sometimes dying from cold and being cast up on shore. It is a midwater species, occurring in small schools or individually, with young in shallower water than adults. Food is small fishes and crustaceans such as shrimps. An important food species for **Atlantic cod, ogac, pollock, swordfish, redfishes** and seals. Peak spawning is thought to occur in May but larval stages indicate that January-September is the season.

white bass

Scientific name: *Morone chrysops*
  (Rafinesque, 1820)
Family: **Temperate Bass**
Other common names: silver bass, white
  lake bass, striper, streaker, sand bass,
  barfish, gray bass, striped lake bass,
  black-striped bass
French name: bar blanc

Distribution: Found from the lower St.
Lawrence River west through the Great
Lakes and southern Ontario to Lake Huron
in Canada and to South Dakota in the U.S.A.
Also in the Red River and Lake Winnipeg,
Manitoba. In the south it reaches the Gulf of
Mexico.

Characters: This species is distinguished
from its relatives, the **striped bass** and **white
perch**, by having 11–13 anal fin soft rays,
4–12 dark flank stripes, and the longest of 3
anal fin spines is half the length or more of
the soft rays. The tongue has small teeth at
its base in 2 patches which are close together
and appear as a single patch, and the dorsal
fins are close but separate. First dorsal fin
spines 9, second dorsal fin with 1 spine and
12–15 branched rays. Pectoral fin rays
15–17. Lateral line scales 50–60. Overall silvery with dark green or blue-grey back and a
milky-white to yellowish belly. There may
be a golden tinge to the lower flank. The eye
is yellowish. The lower flank stripes may be
broken up irregularly. The pectoral and
pelvic fins are milky-white or clear and other
fins are dusky. Reaches 46 cm. The world

white bass

record sport fish weighed 3.09 kg and was
caught in Lake Orange, Virginia in 1989.
The Canadian angling record taken in 1990

by Stan Zadel from Pickering, Lake Ontario
weighed 1.37 kg.

Biology: White bass prefer clear waters
and are schooling fishes of surface waters in
large lakes and rivers. Food is crustaceans,
insects and fishes with larger white bass eating mostly the latter. Some populations of
adults eat predominately zooplankton. Fish
eaten include **yellow perch, bluegills, carp,
black crappies, gizzard shad** and various
minnows. Most feeding occurs in early
morning and late afternoon. Life span is at
least 10 years and maturity is reached at 2–3
years for males and 3–4 years for females.
White bass near Québec in the St. Lawrence
River grow more slowly than those elsewhere in Canada and the U.S.A. as they are
at the northern limit of their distribution.
Spawning occurs in the May-June in Canada
after schools enter estuaries and rivers or
inshore shoals at 13–16°C. Peak spawning
occurs at 17–23°C. Eggs and sperm are
released near the surface or in midwater and
sink to become attached to rocks, gravel or
vegetation. Eggs are about 1.0 mm in diameter and number up to 994,000. Spawning
occurs by day and night. Young fish spawn
later than older fish. White bass are an
important sport fish in the U.S.A., less so in
Canada. The fatty, red meat is usually
removed from the side of fillets to leave only
white meat for consumption. As much as
1,185,370 kg has been caught commercially
in Lake Erie in 1965.

- Most accessible June through August.

- The Great Lakes watershed.

- Ultralight to light action spinning gear
  used with four- to six-pound test line.

- 1/8– to 1/4–ounce spoons, a variety of
  small spinners, small minnow-imitating
  plugs, small crankbaits and a variety of
  1/8– to 1/4–ounce hair and plastic body
  jigs. The best bait, small live **minnows**
  and worms fished near bottom or under
  a float.

white bristlemouth

Scientific name: *Cyclothone alba*
  Brauer, 1906
Family: **Bristlemouth**

Other common names: albino anglemouth

French name: cyclothone blanche

Distribution: Found in the Atlantic, Indian and Pacific Oceans including off Atlantic Canada.

Characters: This species is distinguished from its Atlantic coast relatives by a lack of SO and isthmus photophores, OA pho-

white bristlemouth

tophores are present, gill rakers are 13–14, and snout pigment is absent or faint. Photophores: ORB 1, OP 2, BR 8–9, IV 3 + 10, VAV 3–4, AC 12, OA 6, IC 27–30. Scales are absent. Gill filaments are fused. Dorsal fin rays 12–15, anal rays 17–20. The body colour is an off-white. The branchiostegals have streaks of pigment basal to the BR photophores, along the inner free edge and over the rays. No pigment spots on top of the head. Reaches about 4.0 cm.

Biology: About 8 larval specimens have been caught along the Scotian shelf in 1977 at 59–556 m, the first records for Canada reported in 1980. Found usually at 300–600 m as adults and young, but as deep as 3000 m. There is no daily vertical migration. Males are smaller than females. In Japan, spawning occurs mainly in late spring and summer with 198–659 eggs being released at the end of the life span. Many fish mature at 1 year and all are mature at 2 years.

white crappie

Scientific name: *Pomoxis annularis* Rafinesque, 1818

Family: **Sunfish**

Other common names: silver, white, strawberry or calico bass; silver, pale, timber or ringed crappie; newlight, bachelor, campbellite, tinmouth, papermouth; bridge, speckled, or white perch; shad, John Demon, goggle-eye, slab, gold ring, sac-à-lait, crapet

French name: marigane blanche

Distribution: Found in the Great Lakes drainage of southern Ontario including western Lake Ontario, Lake Erie, Lake St. Clair and Lake Huron and in the Red River basin of Manitoba. In the U.S.A. south to Florida and Texas and widely introduced elsewhere.

Characters: This species is characterised by having 6, rarely 7, 5 or 4, dorsal fin spines, an anal fin base longer than that of the dorsal fins, and 5–10 black, double bars on the upper back and flank. Second dorsal fin soft rays 12–16, anal fin with 5–7 spines and 16–19 soft rays, and pectoral rays about 13. Lateral line scales 34–46. Gill rakers 22–24 on the lower arch.

Overall colour is silvery-white with the back brown, dark olive or dark green, flanks silvery and belly silvery-white. There is a dark opercle spot. The eye is yellow or green. The dorsal, anal and caudal fins have black vermiculations or "worm tracks" or have rows of black spots. Pectoral fins are yellowish but transparent and pelvic fins white and opaque but are usually colourless in small fish. Breeding males are dark black on the head, lower jaw and breast. Peritoneum silvery. Hybrids with **black crappie** are known. The French word crapet may derive from crêpe for the pancake shape of this fish.

white crappie

Reaches 53.3 cm. The world, all-tackle angling record from Enid Dam, Mississippi in 1957 weighed 2.35 kg. The Canadian angling record from Kratz Pond, Ontario on January 11,1995 was caught by Joe Rapattoni and weighed 1.02 kg.

Biology: White crappies are found in ponds, lakes, streams and slower rivers where vegetation and debris are common. Old Christmas trees are sunk in reservoirs to enhance crappie habitat. White crappies toler-ate turbid and silted conditions better than **black crappie**.

Food is plankton when young, switching to aquatic insects, crustaceans and small fishes when adult including their own species. Most feeding occurs at dusk and dawn but also occurs more often during the day than in **black crappie**.

Life span is up to 13 years, although most only live 5 years, with maturity attained at 1–3 years. Some populations become stunted in small water bodies. Growth is slower in Canada than in the southern U.S.A. Females grow faster than males at the older age groups.

Spawning occurs at 14–23°C, peaking at 16–20°C, in the spring. The male clears an area in shallow water in vegetated areas or under overhanging banks. Eggs may be deposited on tree roots and other vegetation. Females may assist in clearing the nest. Nests are up to 30 cm cross and up to 35 nests can be found in the same area, at 0.5–0.6 m apart. A female will spawn with several males. Each spawning act lasts from 2–5 seconds. The female positions herself alongside the male after circling the nest several times. The pair touch flanks after a few seconds and then move forward and upward, quivering their bodies, the female coming to lie under the male so as to push him upward in a curve. Eggs and sperm are shed as the male presses against the female in the curve motion. Repeat spawning occurs at intervals as short as 30 seconds or as long as 2 hours. Up to 50 spawning acts occur in one period of 145 minutes. Most spawning is between 8 a.m. and 4 p.m. Eggs are adhesive, colourless and 0.9 mm in diameter. A female may contain up to 496,000 mature eggs. The male guards and fans the eggs using his pectoral fins. The fry are also guarded.

This is an important sport fish in the U.S.A. caught on hooks using minnows or artificial baits, flies and by retrieving artificial lures. The flesh is white, soft and flaky. It is too uncommon in Canada to be regularly pursued.

white croaker

Scientific name: *Genyonemus lineatus* (Ayres, 1855)

Family: **Drum**
Other common names: king-fish
French name: tambour rayé

Distribution: Found from Baja California to British Columbia.

Characters: This drum is separated from its Canadian Pacific relatives by first dorsal fin and anal fin ray counts. First dorsal fin spines 12–16, usually 13–14, second dorsal fin with 1 spine and 18–25 soft rays. Anal fin

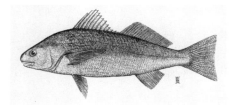

white croaker

with 2 spines and 10–12 soft rays. Lateral line scales 52–54. The lower jaw has very small barbels. Overall colour is silver with brassy tinges and small black spots. The scale rows have vague wavy lines. The belly is whitish. The first dorsal fin is dusky. The second dorsal, caudal and anal fins are whitish to yellow-ish. The caudal fin has a dark margin. The pectoral fin axil (inside base) has a black spot. The peritoneum is whitish. Reaches 41 cm.

Biology: First caught in Barkley Sound in 1945 with a second specimen trawled in Swanson Channel at 55 m in 1983. This species is found in schools inshore but may descend to 183 m. Food is a variety of inver-tebrates. Fish are mature at 13–15 cm after only 1 year in some fish or as old as 4 years for others in California. Life span is 12 years. The spawning season is throughout the year with a peak in late winter. Eggs average 0.85 mm in diameter. This croaker is a batch spawner, shedding eggs 18–24 times a season with a batch numbering up to 37,200 eggs. The white croaker is an impor-tant sport and commercial fish in California.

white hake

Scientific name: *Urophycis musicki* Cohen and Lavenberg, 1984
Family: **Cod Family**

Other common names: mud hake, ling, Boston hake, black hake, red hake, squirrel hake, codling, steakfish, lingue
French name: merluche blanche

Distribution: Found from southern Labrador to Florida and occasionally to Iceland.

Characters: This species and its relatives, the **longfin, spotted** and **red hakes**, are separated from other Canadian Arctic-Atlantic

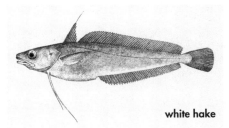

white hake

cods by having 2 dorsal fins, 1 anal fin, no snout barbels, pelvic fins with only 2 long, filamentous rays, and no canine teeth on the lower jaw and vomer bone in the roof of the mouth. The white hake is distinguished from its relatives by the pelvic fin filaments not reaching the end of the anal fin, the third ray in the first dorsal fin is an elongate filament, 2 gill rakers on the upper arm of the gill arch and 119–148 lateral line scales (11–15 scales between the first dorsal fin and lateral line). First dorsal fin rays 9–11, second dorsal rays 50–58. Anal fin with 41–52 rays and pectoral with 15–17 rays. The chin barbel is small.

Overall colour grey, olive, purplish or reddish-brown fading to dusky white or yellowish on belly. The dorsal and anal fins have black margins. Pelvic fins are white to yellow. The lateral line is pale. There may be a dusky blotch on the opercle.

Attains 135 cm and 22.3 kg. The world, all-tackle angling record weighed 20.97 kg and was caught in 1986 in Perkins Cove, Maine.

Biology: This hake is found over mud and silt bottoms usually at 190–1000 m on the continental shelf and slope and in deeper channels. White hake are found over a wide range of temperatures, 0–15°C. On the Scotian Shelf preferred depth range is

146–364 m and preferred temperature range 5–9°C. Young fish can be found in water only a metre deep but they hide in sand with only the head showing. Hake move to deeper water as they grow.

Life span is over 10 years, with, in the southern Gulf of St. Lawrence, males maturing at 37–44 cm and females at 40–54 cm which are then 3–5 years old. Maturity size has decreased in recent years. Growth is rapid, a "get big quick" strategy achieved by delaying maturity. Small fish entering the benthic world have to compete in an environment dominated by big fish. Rapid growth is one answer. Prolonged spawning can take advantage of varying environmental conditions and avoids overloading nursery areas with millions of hungry young fish.

Food is principally **Atlantic herring**, other **Cod Family** members, **mackerel, argentines** and other fishes. Crustaceans are also taken. White hake are cannibals.

Spawning has been reported from winter to summer, varying with locality. Some mature fish can be caught year round. Spawning may be a prolonged process rather than restricted to a short period at any one locality. White hake however are known to spawn in late summer in the southern Gulf of St. Lawrence and on the Scotian Shelf, and in early spring along the Scotian Shelf slopes and Georges Bank. Eggs are pelagic, 0.8 mm in diameter and number up to 15 million.

White hake are often caught as a by-catch in other commercial fisheries although some foreign vessels fish specifically for this species. Catches on the Grand Bank may be up to 9000 tonnes. The total Canadian catch in 1988 was 12,530 tonnes. The flesh is white, flaky and tasty and is sold as fresh or frozen fillets. The liver is processed for oil.

white marlin

Scientific name: *Tetrapterus albidus* Poey, 1860
Family: **Swordfish**
Other common names: none
French name: makaire blanc

Distribution: Found in the Atlantic Ocean including from Nova Scotia southward to Brazil.

Characters: The white marlin is distinguished from its relative, the **blue marlin**, by having the first dorsal fin tip rounded,

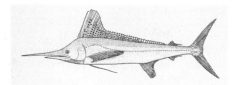

white marlin

first dorsal fin height equal to or greater than body depth and a compressed body. There is a distinct rise in the nape region between the eye and the dorsal fin. First dorsal fin rays 38–46, usually 40–43, second dorsal rays 5–7. First anal fin rays 12–18, second anal rays 5–7. Body scales are embedded and have 1 acute spine. The lateral line is a single canal. Young have high dorsal and anal fins. The back is blue-green to blue-grey, or blue-black. The flanks are silvery white with brown markings and the belly is silvery-white. The flanks may have about 15 whitish stripes. The first dorsal and first anal fins have many dark spots. Reaches 3.3 m. The all-tackle world record is a fish weighing 82.5 kg taken off Brazil in 1979.

Biology: Rare summer strays have been caught on the Scotian Shelf, not confirmed by preserved specimens, off Halifax on Sable Island Bank and off Glace Bay. Confirmed records exist for Georges Bank. It is a blue water, open ocean species favouring temperatures over 22°C. It is known to migrate long distances. Small schools of 5–12 fish have been seen. Food includes many pelagic fish species and crustaceans, but squids are particularly important. The food is stunned or killed by hitting or spearing with the bill. Not all food is captured in this way as some stomach contents are unmarked. Females grow larger than males. Spawning takes place in the summer in subtropical waters but little is known about it. The world catch in 1982 was 131 tonnes, much less than related species. They are caught by handline, longline and rod and reel. The flesh is excellent and is sold locally or frozen in Japan.

white mullet

Scientific name: *Mugil curema* Valenciennes in Cuvier and Valenciennes, 1836
Family: **Mullet**
Other common names: silver mullet, mulet blanc
French name: muge curema

Distribution: Found from Nova Scotia south to Brazil in the western Atlantic Ocean. Also in the eastern Atlantic and Pacific oceans.

Characters: This mullet is distinguished from its only Canadian relative, the **striped mullet**, by having scales extending onto the soft dorsal and anal fins and no flank stripes. Anal fin with 3 spines and 9–10 soft rays (young with 2 spines and 10–11 soft rays). Scales along midflank number 35–40. Exposed scale surfaces are covered with minute secondary scales. The back is dark olive, tinted blue, and silvery on the flank. The head usually has 2 yellow or bronze blotches on the side. There is a blue-black blotch at the pectoral fin base. The anal and pelvic fins are pale or yellowish. The caudal fin has a dusky margin with some yellow at the base of the fin. Said to reach 91 cm, although most specimens are smaller.

white mullet

Biology: Found in inshore waters off Halifax and Lunenburg counties, Nova Scotia, where it has long been confused with the **striped mullet**. The specimens are all juveniles, strays from the south. It is a schooling fish with young found at beaches and in lagoons, surviving temperatures over 30°C. This mullet is reported from fresh water in Florida. They may "stand on their heads" to feed on detritus leaving conical depressions in the sea bed. Spawning in the southern U.S.A. occurs at sea from late March until September with a peak in April-June. Eggs are pelagic and up to 0.86 mm in diameter. The young spend several weeks out at sea in the Gulf Stream before moving inshore. In the Caribbean it is caught with gill nets, beach seines and cast nets and is marketed fresh and salted. The roe is eaten in Venezuela.

white perch

Scientific name: *Morone americana*
    (Gmelin, 1789)
Family: **Temperate Bass**
Other common names: sea perch, silver perch,
    narrow-mouthed bass, bluenose perch,
    gray perch
French name: baret

Distribution: Found in brackish waters from New Brunswick, P.E.I. and Nova Scotia south to South Carolina. Also in the upper St. Lawrence River and lakes Ontario and rarely Erie.

Characters: This species is distinguished from its relatives, the **white** and **striped basses**, by having the dorsal fins joined by a membrane at the base, 8–10, usually 9, soft

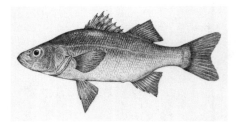

white perch

anal fin rays, the second and third anal fin spines are about the same length, no lateral stripes and no teeth on the tongue base. First dorsal fin spines usually 9, range 8–11, second dorsal fin with 1 spine and 10–13 branched rays, and pectoral with 10–18 rays. Lateral line scales 44–53.

The back is olive to dark grey or green-grey, or almost black, the flanks are silvery-green and the belly silvery-white. There may be faint flank stripes in young fish. Fins are dusky. The pelvic and anal fins may have a pinkish tint. Spawning adults have a bluish or lavender sheen on the head and lower jaw.

Reaches 58 cm and 2.72 kg. The world all-tackle angling record weighed 2.15 kg

and was caught in 1949 in Messalonskee Lake, Maine.

Biology: Coastal populations may be in brackish waters of river mouths or in lakes near the sea. Sea run populations are not common in Canadian waters where temperatures are lower than the favoured minimum of 24°C for summer months. In fresh waters white perch enter surface waters at night and retreat to deeper water for the day.

Food in fresh water is insect larvae and fishes, such as **yellow perch, johnny darters, smelt**, young **eels**, fish eggs, and other **white perch**, with small amounts of molluscs and worms.

Life span is 17 years although most fish in a population are 5–7 years old. Growth rates vary with latitude, the availability of food and temperature regime. Some populations become so numerous in respect to food supply that individuals are stunted. Such populations often affect other species, such as **yellow perch** in the Bay of Quinte, Ontario, which decrease in abundance and growth rate. Maturity is attained at 3 years of age on average.

Spawning occurs in May to June at 11–24°C, peaking at 18–20°C. Eggs are released in 2–3 spawnings over 1–2 weeks. Eggs and sperm are shed in shallow water as the large school of perch swim about.

There are up to 321,000 eggs per female and each egg is 0.8 mm before fertilisation. The adhesive eggs become attached to plants and rocks. There are significant commercial fisheries in the Chesapeake Bay but the only Canadian fisheries are in the Bay of Quinte, Lake Ontario and in Lake Erie. White perch are a sport fish in the Maritimes, caught easily on worms, minnows, spoons, wet flies and streamers. The flesh is white, flaky and very tasty.

white seabass

Scientific name: *Atractoscion nobilis*
    (Ayres, 1860)
Family: **Drum**
Other common names: croaker
French name: acoupa blanc

Distribution: Found from Baja California to southeastern Alaska including British Columbia.

Characters: This drum is separated from its Canadian Pacific relatives by first dorsal fin and anal fin ray counts. First dorsal fin with 9–10 spines, second dorsal fin with 1 spine and 20–23 soft rays. Anal fin with 2 spines and 8–9, usually 8, soft rays. Lateral line scales 75–87. There are no chin barbels. The snout and chin pores are minute. The belly has a raised central ridge. The back is a metallic blue to coppery. The body has small, dark speckles. Flanks are silvery fading to whitish. The pectoral fin axil (inside base) has a dusky blotch. The inner surface of the pelvic fins is dusky. The peritoneum is grey-white. Young fish less than 60 cm long have 3–6 dusky bars over the back and on the sides and dusky yellow fins. Reaches 1.8 m and 41 kg. The world, all-tackle angling record weighed 37.98 kg and was caught in 1953 in Mexico.

white seabass

Biology: An uncommon species in Canadian waters, reported from Toba Inlet, Juan de Fuca Strait and the west coast of Vancouver Island. Usually found in schools over rocks down to 122 m, in kelp and the surf zone. Young fish enter bays. There is a northward migration in spring and a return south in fall. Food is mainly fishes but includes squid and crustaceans. More males mature at a smaller size than females, but all fish of both sexes are mature at 75 cm. Some females spawn at 3 years and all by 4 years of age. Life span exceeds 20 years. Spawning occurs in March to August in Californian kelp beds. This species is an excellent food and sport fish in California.

white seaperch

Scientific name: *Phanerodon furcatus* Girard, 1854
Family: **Surfperch**
Other common names: white surfperch
French name: ditrème fourchu

Distribution: Found from Vancouver Island south to Baja California.

Characters: This surfperch is distinguished from other Canadian species by having a frenum, a low spinous dorsal fin which

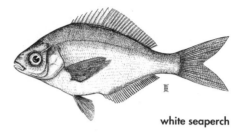

white seaperch

becomes gradually longer and smoothly joins the soft dorsal fin, and 56–67 lateral line scales with 5–7 on the tail. Dorsal fin spines 9–11, soft rays 20–26. Anal fin with 3 spines and 29–34 soft rays. Pectoral fin with 20–21 soft rays. The caudal fin is deeply forked. The back is olive, silvery or bluish, the flanks and belly silvery or with yellow or rose tinges. There is a black line at the rear part of the dorsal fin. Fins usually yellow. Pelvic fins may be white. The caudal fin has a dusky margin and the anal fin occasionally has a dark spot anteriorly. Reaches 34 cm.

Biology: Found in quiet water of bays and offshore near rocks but also near harbour structures. Uncommon in Canada. Caught down to 43 m. Food is principally isopod and gammarid crustaceans but also bryozoans attached to kelp. This food is "picked" from the bottom or off the kelp. This surfperch is also a "cleaner" of other fishes, pecking parasites off them. Females grow faster than males and reach 7 years of age. The main spawning season in California is October-December. Females have 3–11 embryos which are born in May-July. The most important species commercially in California.

white stickleback

Scientific name: *Gasterosteus* sp.
Family: **Stickleback**
Other common names: none
French name: épinoche blanche

Distribution: Found only in Nova Scotia on the eastern Atlantic coast around Cape

Breton Island and the shores of Georges Bay on the Gulf of St. Lawrence.

Characters: This species resembles the **threespine stickleback** but is smaller than threespines caught with it and body depth is significantly less. Meristic and other morphometric characters show a variation between this species and the **threespine stickleback** which is encompassed within the **threespine stickleback** and cannot be used to separate the 2 species. Biochemical differences could not be demonstrated using starch gel electrophoresis. The most obvious difference is the male breeding colour which is visible 20 m or more away. Dorsal fin soft

white stickleback

rays 10–13, anal soft rays 7–11 and pectoral rays 9–10, usually 10. Lateral plates 30–35 and total gill rakers 19–26.

Males have an overall breeding colour which is an iridescent white. The back and upper flank is white-green changing to an amber or rose belly. The iris is whitish-blue and the throat is pink or red. This overall white is lost within 90 seconds when the male is disturbed and he becomes drab green or olive-brown with grey bars and a silver belly. Females resemble this drab male colouration. Reaches 48.5 mm.

Biology: White sticklebacks are found in clear, still brackish or marine waters with mud bottoms and dense filamentous algae. Spawning occurs where predator numbers are low. The startling white male colour may serve to warn those predators which are present that this fish is difficult to catch. This difficulty is caused by the habit of the white stickleback of diving into the filamentous algae when frightened. The algae both hides the fish and could entangle a predator. Sexual selection through female choice and competition between males would also favour enhanced white colouration. Males

are whitest when courting females, when fighting other males or other sticklebacks or when building or tending the nest.

The nest is composed of filamentous algal strands which are glued together by kidney secretions. Nests are above the bottom on the algal mass in contrast to the open bottom nesting habit of **threespine sticklebacks**. Some white stickleback nests are concealed in the algae. Within 15 minutes of spawning, the male removes the eggs from the nest with his mouth and spreads them out over the algae. The eggs are then abandoned and males can court another female ("male emancipation!"). The dispersed eggs in the algae are presumably less susceptible to predators than eggs concentrated in a nest, even one defended by a male, or increased opportunities for further mating offset any dispersed egg loss.

Laboratory and field studies show that white females respond little to courtship by threespine males and females of both species break off courtship when shown the "wrong" nest type by the male of the other species.

white sturgeon

Scientific name: *Acipenser transmontanus* Richardson, 1836
Family: **Sturgeon**
Other common names: Pacific sturgeon, Oregon sturgeon, Columbia sturgeon, Sacramento sturgeon
French name: esturgeon blanc

Distribution: Found from the Gulf of Alaska to California including British Columbia, particularly in the Fraser and Columbia rivers.

Characters: This species is distinguished from its Pacific coast relative, the **green sturgeon**, by having 38–48 lateral scutes or shields along the midflank, a grey-white colour and barbels nearer the snout tip than the mouth. Dorsal fin rays 44–48, anal rays 28–31. Dorsal scute row 11–14 and ventral row 9–12. Scutes are absent behind the dorsal and anal fins. Gill rakers 34–36.

Overall colour is grey, olive or brownish fading to pale grey or white. The belly is white. The flanks have small white spots. Scutes are lighter than the adjacent body. The internal organs of the abdomen are blackish.

Reaches 6.1 m, the largest Canadian and North American freshwater fish. The largest sturgeon by weight, reputedly over 900 kg,

white sturgeon

was taken near Mission, B.C. The world, all-tackle angling record weighed 212.28 kg and was caught in 1983 at Benicia, California.

Biology: The white sturgeon is commoner in rivers and lakes than its relative, the **green sturgeon**, and may remain there throughout its life. Small sturgeon migrate up rivers to feed and adults enter deeper water. Small sturgeon move downstream during late winter and early spring. Anadromous white sturgeon spend most of their life at sea and may travel over 1000 km during this time but marine occurrence is poorly documented for Canada.

Food includes fishes such as **eulachon, sculpins, sticklebacks, lampreys, northern squawfish, salmon**, young **sturgeon** and various crustaceans and molluscs. Adults also scavenge and have been found to contain onions, wheat, birds and a house cat. Some of the fish eaten, such as **eulachon, lampreys** and **salmon**, may be scavenged from post-spawning mortalities. **Pacific lamprey** may be found attached to white sturgeon. Large sturgeon have been seen to leap out of the water.

Large females grow faster than large males, after about 20 years of age. Males mature at 11–22 years and females at 11–34 years. Life span has been estimated at 82 years and may exceed 100 years.

Spawning occurs in spring to early summer at 9–17°C over rocks in fast water. Females spawn at intervals of 2–11 years. The brown eggs number over 4 million in larger fish.

This species has been used commercially for its flesh, caviar, spinal marrow for use in Chinese soups, and in production of isinglass from the swimbladder. The Fraser River catch in 1897 was 516,514 kg but fluctuated widely and fell to an average of 16,798 kg in 1901. The fishery is susceptible to rapid decline because the fish have a long life span and slow growth and are easily overexploited. Catches in recent years are estimated at 12–30 tonnes, perhaps up to 40 tonnes. Most sturgeon are caught incidentally in **salmon** nets although a few are taken with handlines. There is a sport fishery in the Fraser River system using dead forage fish and worms. The Committee on the Status of Endangered Wildlife in Canada approved a "vulnerable" status for this species in 1990.

• Most accessible May through August.
• The large coastal rivers in British Columbia.
• Heavy action baitcasting outfits used with 20– to 40–pound test line and heavier Penn rod and reel outfits loaded with 40– to 50–pound test line.
• Cut pieces of **lamprey**, shrimp and pieces of dead forage fish and worms. These are normally fished on the bottom.

white sucker

Scientific name: *Catostomus commersoni* (Lacepède, 1803)
Family: **Sucker**
Other common names: common brook, coarse scaled, fine scaled, June, eastern, mud, slender, grey or black sucker, black whitehorse, mullet, carp
French name: meunier noir

Distribution: Found across Canada; absent only from Newfoundland, P.E.I., Gaspé, the margins of Labrador, the N.W.T. (except for the prairie border area and the Great Slave and Mackenzie River basins), absent from most of the Yukon and from southern and western British Columbia. In the U.S.A. south to Georgia and New Mexico.

white sucker

Characters: This species is recognised by having 53–85 (usually 58–68) scales in a complete lateral line, 8–11 scales between the dorsal fin origin and lateral line, 9–14 principal dorsal fin rays, a completely cleft lower lip which is wider than deep, and no membrane connecting the pelvic fins to the body. Principal anal rays 6–8, pectoral rays 15–18 and pelvic rays 10–11. Gill rakers 20–27. The numerous pharyngeal teeth are comb-like except the lower 5 which have wide crowns. Males have large nuptial tubercles on the anal fin, lower caudal fin and the caudal peduncle. Smaller tubercles are found on the head and belly, number 1–3 on the rear margin of back and upper flank scales and line the rays of the dorsal and pelvic fins.

The back and upper flanks are grey, dusky olive, brassy, brown or almost black, flanks are greenish-yellow to brassy and the lower flank and belly are creamy to white. Scales on the upper flank and back are outlined with pigment. The anal fin is white and other fins are dusky. Pectoral, pelvic and anal fins may have an orange tinge and the pectoral and pelvic fins may have a white leading edge. Spawning fish are more golden on the flank and darker on the back. Males have a pink to scarlet or blackish lateral stripe, which is cream-coloured in Saskatchewan and absent west of the Rocky Mountains. Young fish have 3–4 obvious blotches along the flank. Peritoneum pale.

Reaches 76.0 cm total length, and reputedly 17.5 kg. The world, all-tackle angling record weighed 2.94 kg and was caught in the Rainy River, Minnesota in 1984. Hybrids with the **largescale sucker** and the **longnose sucker** are reported for Canada.

Biology: White suckers are found in shallows of lakes, but may descend to about 50 m, and in tributary rivers and streams. These suckers are very tolerant of polluted waters.

Food is aquatic insects, crustaceans, molluscs and sometimes eggs of other fishes although they are not now considered to be a major predator on sport fishes. Water fleas are often a major diet component. Young suckers feed on plankton until about 1.8 cm long when the mouth moves to a ventral position and bottom feeding is adopted. Most feeding occurs at dawn and dusk. These suckers are very numerous and an important food for a wide variety of sport and other fishes, birds and even bears. **Sea lampreys** invading Lake Huron caused a loss of larger fish in the population.

Maximum life span is about 25 years. Pectoral fin ray sections are used in aging white suckers as scales give underestimates of age. Annual mortality in the Laurentides, Québec is 90% for 7 year old and older fish. Females grow faster, live longer and are larger than males. Sexual maturity is reached at 2–9 years, varying with locality across Canada and sex (males mature 1 year younger than females; in Saskatchewan males matured at 6–7, and females at 6–9; in Alberta at 2 and 3 years respectively, although first spawning was at 5 and 6 years). A dwarf or stunted population near Chicoutimi, Québec matured at 2–3 years and had an 8 year life span. Dwarf populations are known to co-exist with normal sized suckers but in one case at least these are large females and small males, the size difference compounded by a higher rate of male mortality.

Spawning occurs in May to July in Canada after a migration into gravelly streams or lake margins at 10°C or warmer. Lake spawners may clean the gravel before spawning. Males arrive on the spawning ground 2–3 days before females. Most eggs are shed at night with much splashing in the shallow water of riffles. Each female is pressed against by 1–10 males, using their tuberculate anal and caudal fins. The dorsal fin is held erect, pectoral fins are spread, the tail lashes the water and the head is shaken. Usually the female is flanked by a male on each side. Spawning only takes 1.5–4 seconds but occurs 6–40 times an hour and the season lasts about 2 weeks. Each female can carry up to 139,000 yellow eggs with a diameter up to 3.0 mm. There is an estimated spawning mortality of 16–47% depending on the population and its predators. Females do not spawn every year but the frequency of spawning increases with age. Males are 3 times as likely to spawn in a given year than females. Nuptial tubercles are lost shortly after spawning. A hermaphrodite white sucker has been reported from Alberta, the first record of this condition in the **Sucker Family**.

This sucker has white, flaky flesh and is quite tasty. It has been marketed with other suckers as "mullet" but has never formed a major fishery. The spring spawning run offers an opportunity for dip-netting and considerable numbers are eaten locally across Canada. White suckers are not fished for but can provide good sport taken on light tackle using various baits. Young white suckers are sold as bait in Canada for **smallmouth** and **largemouth bass, northern pike** and **muskellunge**. In the U.S.A. they are reared artificially and in both Canada and the U.S.A. are used for feeding hatchery sport fishes. In the past, Canadian farmers pitch-forked wagon-loads of suckers out of streams to use as pig food.

- Most accessible May through July.
- The Great Lakes watershed.
- Medium action spinning and baitcasting outfits used with 10– to 14–pound test.
- Worms fished on the bottom.

whitebait

The **Atlantic silverside** of the **Silverside Family** may be referred to as whitebait. The term has been generally applied, in many parts of the world, to small, white or silvery fishes used as food or bait.

whitebait smelt

Scientific name: *Allosmerus elongatus*
  (Ayres, 1854)
Family: **Smelt**
Other common names: none
French name: éperlan blanchaille

Distribution: Found from British Columbia to California.
Characters: This species is distinguished from other smelts by having 9–13 upper arch gill rakers (total 33–41), conical to large canine teeth on the tongue, a large canine

whitebait smelt

tooth on the roof of the mouth, 0–1 pyloric caeca, and the eye diameter is longer than 80% of the caudal peduncle depth. Dorsal fin rays 9–12, anal rays 13–17 and pectoral rays 11–14. Scales along flank 62–68, lateral line scales about 20. Males develop elongate, midflank scales and tubercles on head, scales and fin rays. Overall colour is a translucent pale green or greenish-grey with a silvery stripe along the flank. The peritoneum is light with pigment spots. Reaches 22.9 cm.

Biology: First caught in the Strait of Juan de Fuca in 1969 at 70 m. Since reported also at the northern end of Vancouver Island. One specimen from Pine Island, Queen Charlotte Islands was taken from nesting Rhinocerus Aukelets. Spawning occurs in the ocean on sand banks and translucent larvae have a long developmental period until about 7.6 cm long. This species has been used as food and bait in California.

whitebarred prickleback

Scientific name: *Poroclinus rothrocki*
  Bean, 1890
Family: **Shanny**
Other common names: white-barred blenny
French name: lompénie à barres blanches

Distribution: Found from southern California to the Bering Sea including British Columbia.
Characters: This species is 1 of 8 related Canadian shannies which have very elongate bodies, large pectoral fins and pelvic fins

whitebarred prickleback

with 1 spine and 2–4 soft rays. It is distinguished by distribution, 3 anal fin spines, a short snout and 9–12 white bars edged in black or brown on the upper flank. Dorsal spines number 57–67, anal soft rays 40–44 and pectoral fin rays about 13–15. Scales cover the body and head and the lateral line runs along midflank. The caudal fin is longer than in most shannies, and is bluntly rounded. The body is light brown, paler on the belly. Attains 25 cm.

Biology: Found between 46–128 m, but little else is known. It is said to hide under shells and stones in captivity.

whitebearded snaggletooth

Scientific name: *Astronesthes leucopogon*
    Regan and Trewavas, 1929
Family: **Barbeled Dragonfish**
Other common names: none
French name: dragon-saumons à barbe blanche

Distribution: Found in both the North and South Atlantic oceans and off Atlantic Canada.

Characters: This species is separated from its Canadian relatives by having comb-like teeth on the maxillary bone of the upper

whitebearded snaggletooth

jaw which slant rearwards, a ventral adipose fin, 43–47 light organs in the ventral row, the ventral row forming a u-shaped bend at the pectoral fin level, 17 anal fin rays, and a barbel without a swelling at the tip. Overall colour is black. The barbel is creamy in small preserved fish. There is a pale, luminous patch anterior to the eye, 2 patches over the pectoral fin, a long patch below the pelvic fins and a long patch in midflank anterior to the anal fin origin. Small fish may have irregular luminous patches on the flank from the gill opening to the pelvic fin origin. Attains about 12 cm.

Biology: Found off the Scotian Shelf and near the Flemish Cap.

whitefishes

Whitefishes are members of the **Salmon Family** belonging to the genera *Coregonus* and *Prosopium*. The word is also used for the subfamily which also includes **ciscoes** and the **inconnu**. Recent studies advocate placing whitefishes and their relatives as a family,

Coregonidae, distinct from the **Salmon Family**. They are retained here as a subfamily as the new classification is not yet generally accepted. The subfamily is one of 3 within the **Salmon Family** the other 2 being the **graylings** and the **chars, salmons** and **trouts**. There is also the unrelated **ocean whitefish**, a member of the **Tilefish Family**. Young **capelin** of the **Smelt Family** are known as whitefish in Newfoundland and Labrador. Whitefish has been applied generally to fishes with a white, silvery or light colour, unmarked by spots or other decoration.

See **Acadian whitefish**
    broad whitefish
    lake whitefish
    mountain whitefish
    Opeongo whitefish
    pygmy whitefish
    round whitefish
    Squanga whitefish

whitespotted greenling

Scientific name: *Hexagrammos stelleri*
    Tilesius, 1810
Family: **Greenling**
Other common names: rock trout, tommy cod,
    kelp cod
French name: sourcil à taches blanches

Distribution: From northern California to Japan including British Columbia.

Characters: Dorsal fin with 20–25 spines and 18–24 soft rays. Anal fin with 20–25 rays and no spines. Scales are ctenoid on the body and top of the head, cycloid on the side of the head. The 5 lateral lines run along the body from the back of the head close to the dorsal

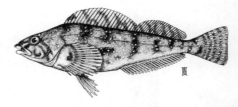

whitespotted greenling

fin ending below the spiny part, on the upper flank from head to tail, from the tip of the gill opening to the tail, from the gill opening below the pectoral fin to a point above the pelvic fin, and from the isthmus to behind the pelvic fins branching to pass on each side of the anal fin to reach the tail. This species is distinguished from other Canadian greenlings by having 5 lateral lines, no cirrus between the eye and dorsal fin origin, a small cirrus over the eye about half the eye diameter in length and the first lateral line not extending beyond the spines in the dorsal fin. Overall colour is light brown to green, or tinged pale red, characteristically spotted white and with several bars or blotches. The anal fin is yellowish. Rows of spots forming bars on all fins except the pelvics. Males have darkened fins and bodies when spawning and a noticeable black blotch on the anterior dorsal fin. Attains 48 cm.

Biology: A coastal species associated with rocky shores and eelgrass down to about 50 m but perhaps to 475 m. Often found around jetties and wharves. Food is crustaceans, worms and small fishes when adult and plankton when larvae. Spawning occurs in April according to some, late summer-winter depending on latitude according to other authors. The eggs are blue and number up to 5,200, with a diameter of 2.5 mm, in each mass. The eggs in a mass may be from several females. Males guard the eggs, which are deposited in rock crevices or among the branches of red algae. Males are aggressive enough to bite the face masks of inquisitive divers. The flesh is edible and this greenling is easily caught on baited hook and line.

whitings

Whitings are members of the **Cod Family** with 1 species in Canada, the **blue whiting** of the Atlantic coast. The **Pacific hake**, of the related **Hake Family**, is marketed as the Pacific whiting in the U.S.A. Both the **Pacific tomcod** and the **walleye pollock** are called whiting by British Columbian fishermen. The name has been generally applied to fishes with pearly-white flesh and white or light body colouration.

Widemouth Order

The widemouths, **barbeled dragonfishes, bristlemouths, silver hatchetfishes, lightfishes, viperfishes, scaled dragonfishes,** **snaggletooths, scaleless dragonfishes, loosejaws** and blackdragons or **sawtailfishes** are members of the Order Stomiiformes. There are 4 families with about 320 species usually found in the deeper waters of cold to temperate and tropical oceans world-wide. All 4 families have Canadian representatives with 62 species.

These mostly small fishes are characterised by luminescent organs, known as photophores, arranged in series along the body and with a unique structure. Some species have a chin barbel with a complex anatomy. The large gape of the mouth is bordered by premaxilla and maxilla bones in the upper jaw, teeth are bristly or fang-like and usually hinged anteriorly, scales are cycloid and easily detached or absent, some species have dorsal and ventral adipose fins, pectoral, dorsal and adipose fins may be absent, there are no fin spines, pelvic fin rays 4–9, retractor dorsalis muscles present (muscles associated with the pharyngeal jaws playing an important role in swallowing food), a rostral cartilage, the exoccipital bone of the skull forms part of the cranial condyle, the morphology of the adductor mandibulae muscle is unique, branchiostegal rays 5–24, some of which articulate with the ventral hypohyal bones, and colour mostly dark brown to black or silvery.

The Widemouth Order is considered to be the most primitive member of a group of fishes, the Neoteleostei or neoteleosts, linked by features of the pharyngeal jaw apparatus such as the presence of a retractor dorsalis muscle. This group includes most **bony fishes** except **Herring, Eel** and other related lower orders. Widemouths are related to the **Salmon Order**. The **loosejaws, sawtailfishes, scaleless dragonfishes, snaggletooths** and **viperfishes** were formerly each in a distinct family.

These fishes are a major part of the midwater fauna in the open ocean. Their interesting biology and unusual anatomy is summarised in the family accounts.

See **Barbeled Dragonfish**
 Bristlemouth Family
 Lightfish Family
 Silver Hatchetfish Family

wideside alfonsin

Scientific name: *Beryx decadactylus*
  Cuvier in Cuvier and Valenciennes, 1829
Family: **Alfonsino**
Other common names: Alfonsin a Casta
  Larga, red bream, beryx
French name: béryx large

Distribution: World-wide. Found south of Nova Scotia.

Characters: Distinguished from the **narrowside alfonsin** by having many more pyloric caeca (74–100), a lower scale count

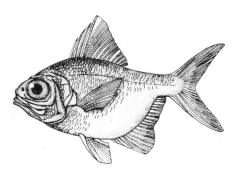

wideside alfonsin

(61–73 total, 56–61 excluding those on the caudal fin), more dorsal fin soft rays (16–20), and a deeper body. The dorsal fin spines number 3, the anal fin has 4 spines and 25–29 soft rays. There are 22–24 gill rakers. The eyes are very large, about two-fifths of head length. This fish is bright red on the upper parts of the head and body including the fins, the iris of the eye and the inner edges of the jaws. The flanks and belly have silvery to yellowish tinges with a few yellow-red flank stripes. The peritoneum is purplish. Size up to about 61 cm in one source, usually cited as up to 40 cm standard length.

Biology: Two specimens were caught south of Nova Scotia without further information and are northern records for the western Atlantic Ocean. A deep water fish found mostly from 300–600 m but occasionally shallower and down to 1000 m. Feeds on shrimps, fish and squid. This fish is used for food in Madeira and Japan.

widow rockfish

Scientific name: *Sebastes entomelas*
  (Jordan and Gilbert, 1880)
Family: **Scorpionfish**
Other common names: brown bomber,
  soft brown, widow rockcod
French name: veuve

Distribution: Found from southeast Alaska to Baja California including British Columbia.

Characters: This species is distinguished by having a convex space between the eyes on top of the head, weak or absent spines, scale counts and colour. Dorsal fin spines 13, soft rays 14–16, usually 15. Anal fin soft rays 7–10, usually 8, second anal spine little thicker than the third and shorter. Pectoral rays 17–19, usually 18, 8–10 unbranched. Gill rakers 34–47. Vertebrae 26–27. Lateral line pores 52–60, scale rows below lateral line 58–66. Head spines are absent although weak nasals, preoculars or parietals may be seen in adults. Greyish-black, dusky or a brassy brown or golden with yellowish mottling on the back and upper flank. A large, light blotch is often found below the spiny dorsal fin on the upper flank. Belly whitish or grey with red tinges. The operculum and suboperculum each have a single dark spot. A bar extends down and back from the eye. Fins are dusky to black, especially on the fin membranes. The anal fin has a blotchy white bar near its edge. The peritoneum is black or silver-grey with black dots. Young fish have orange streaks on the body. Attains 59 cm.

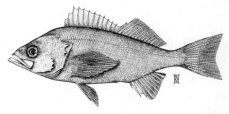

widow rockfish

Biology: First recorded from British Columbia in 1965. Found in schools over rocky banks at about 24 to 549 m when adult and in shallower water when young. Adults are known to school in midwater at night.

Food is pelagic crustaceans, fish such as **northern lanternfish**, salps, octopi and jellyfish. Half the population is mature at 37 cm for males and 38 cm for females in Canadian waters. Maximum age approaches an estimated 60 years. Young are born in April in British Columbia, and a 50.8 cm female can produce 900,000 young. Often caught on hook and line by **salmon** fishermen who consider them a nuisance. Widow rockfish are taken by commercial trawlers and filleted for sale with other **rockfishes**.

windowpane

Scientific name: *Scophthalmus aquosus*
(Mitchill, 1815)
Family: **Lefteye Flounder**
Other common names: sand flounder, brill, spotted flounder, sand dab, turbot, sundial, New York plaice
French name: turbot de sable

Distribution: Found from the southern Gulf of St. Lawrence and southern Newfoundland south to Florida.

Characters: This species is uniquely characterised among Atlantic coast **lefteye flounders** by both pelvic fin bases being very

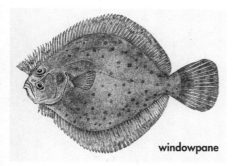

windowpane

long, extending from near the vent and anal fin origin to the urohyal bone and the body being both very deep and thin (hence "windowpane"). The anterior 10 or more rays of the dorsal fin are free of the membrane and fringe-like. Dorsal fin rays 63–73, anal rays 46–55, eyed side pectoral rays 9–12, usually 11, and lateral line scales 85–102. Scales are cycloid. Lower arm gill rakers 22–26. Eyed side translucent brown to olive-green, red-

dish or grey, with small black dots and some orange dots. Fins are darkly mottled and spotted. Blind side white, occasionally blotched. Reaches 45.7 cm.

Biology: Common in Canadian waters on sand bottoms but also found on mud. At 55–73 m on Georges Bank but also inshore. Food is primarily fish when adult such as **hake, herring, pollock, smelt, sand lance, tomcod,** and **striped bass**. Crustaceans such as shrimp are also important. Windowpanes are mature at 23–25 cm and 3–4 years old. Life span exceeds 7 years. Spawning in Canada is in late spring and early summer and the floating eggs are up to 2 mm in diameter. The thin body makes filleting difficult and this species is usually processed into fish meal.

winged barracudina

Scientific name: *Sudis hyalina*
Rafinesque, 1810
Family: **Barracudina**
Other common names: none
French name: lussion ailé

Distribution: Found in the Atlantic Ocean and Mediterranean Sea. In Canada from off Nova Scotia.

Characters: This species is distinguished from its Canadian relatives by the very long pectoral fins, longer than the anal fin base, and by having large, fixed lower jaw teeth with serrated edges. Dorsal fin with 12–16 rays, anal fin 21–24 rays, pectoral fins 13–15 rays and pelvic fins 9 rays. Lateral line scales 59–77. Vertebrae 59–60. Scales are absent except in the lateral line and on the preoperculum. Lateral line scales have 4–7 pores above and below their midline. Overall colour is a silvery-pink, or light with a dark dorsal band. Adults may be black. Peritoneum black. Probably reaches more than 100 cm.

winged barracudina

Biology: A single specimen has been caught off Georges Bank in 1977 at about 100 m. Elsewhere descends to 700 m or more. Individuals are still juveniles at 40 cm, the largest specimen caught, and maximum length is an estimate.

winged hake

Scientific name: *Macruronus brachycolus*
(Holt and Byrne, 1906)
Family: **Hake**
Other common names: none
French name: merlu ailé

Distribution: Found in the western North Atlantic Ocean including off Canada and from off Ireland and Madeira in the eastern Atlantic Ocean.

Characters: This hake is distinguished from its Atlantic coast relatives, the **silver** and **offshore hakes**, by the small caudal fin confluent with the dorsal and anal fins. The jaws are large with 1–2 large sharp fangs in each jaw among smaller teeth. There are about 4 teeth on each side of the vomer bone in the roof of the mouth. The first dorsal fin has 9–11 rays with the second ray spiny. Pectoral fin rays 13–14. There are 27 short pyloric caeca. This species is placed in a distinct family, Macruronidae, by one author based on tooth arrangement and osteological characters. Attains 23.7 cm.

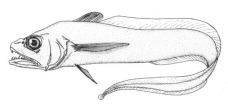

winged hake

Biology: Known only from two specimens caught south of LaHave Bank in 1978 at 995 m and south of Sable Island Bank at 997 m. This is a rare species found on the slope of the continental shelf. Biology is unknown.

winged spookfish

Scientific name: *Dolichopteryx* sp.
Family: **Spookfish**
Other common names: none

French name: revenant ailé

Distribution: Caught at Ocean Station Papa (50°N, 145°W) and in the Gulf of Alaska.

Characters: This species is distinguished from other spookfish by the elongate rounded body, few vertebrae, teeth on the roof of the mouth in 2 or more rows, and

winged spookfish

eyes lacking accessory corneal bodies. The body and head are encased in a gelatinous covering. The pelvic and pectoral fins are dark and the body yellowish in alcohol. When fresh, this fish was transparent with the blood-rich gill region pinkish-red. Size to 15.4 cm.

Biology: A very rare species, as yet undescribed and known only from a few specimens housed in museums.

winter flounder

Scientific name: *Pleuronectes americanus*
Walbaum, 1792
Family: **Righteye Flounder**
Other common names: blackback, flounder, sole, mud dab, rough flounder, black flounder, dab, lemon sole, Georges Bank flounder, carrelet
French name: plie rouge

Distribution: Found from central Labrador, throughout Atlantic Canada and south to Georgia.

Characters: This Atlantic species is characterised by a small, asymmetrical mouth, an almost straight lateral line over the pectoral fin, no pits on the blind side of the head, dorsal fin rays 59–76, and head between the eyes scaled and rough. Anal fin rays 44–58 and pectoral rays 10–11 with 5–7 branched. Scales number 78–100 in the lateral line. Gill rakers on the lower arch number 7–8. Eyed side scales are ctenoid and blind side scales are cycloid at body centre but ctenoid around the dorsal, ventral and anterior body margins.

Eyed side reddish-brown, olive-green or dark grey to blackish, variably spotted, mottled and blotched. Blind side white but may be yellowish on the caudal peduncle and the body margins blue tinged. Rarely the blind side may be partly pigmented ("black bellies"). The dorsal and anal fins are pink, reddish or yellowish on the eyed side. Also placed in the genus *Pseudopleuronectes* Reaches 63.5 cm and 3.6 kg. The world, all-tackle angling record weighed 1.9 kg and was caught in 1989 at Perkins Cove, Maine.

winter flounder

Biology: Winter flounders are found from tide pools down to 273 m but are usually in water shallower than about 37 m. On the Scotian Shelf preferred depth range is 37–90 m and temperature range 6–9°C. They become stranded in tide pools as they move inshore to feed with the rising tide. Older fish are found in deeper water. They also enter fresh water. They are found on both mud and hard bottoms. They may retreat offshore for the winter in Canada and return inshore to spawn in spring and for feeding. In the U.S.A. they enter shallower waters in winter, hence their name. In Canada they are very tolerant of cold conditions but leave shallows to avoid turbulence and ice scouring.

Food is taken during the day and actively sought visually. Food items include worms, molluscs, crustaceans, coelenterates, some algae and **capelin** eggs. Clam siphons are bitten off. Winter flounders are an important food for various fishes, seals and such birds as ospreys, blue herons and cormorants.

Growth varies with locality and is slower in the north. Males mature at about 20 cm and females at about 25 cm, both at 3–4 years of age, but this varies with area and with fishing pressure. Females grow 20–35% faster than males. Maximum age exceeds 13 years. Spawning also varies with locality and is later in the north, usually from March to June in Canada.

Winter flounder males and females swim in tight, clockwise circles with the vent outward, releasing the sex products for about 10 seconds before resting on the bottom. Up to 3.3 million eggs are shed, each with a diameter of about 1 mm. The eggs are adhesive and sink to the sea bed, sometimes in clumps. The typical flatfish shape is attained after 2.5–3.5 months.

Winter flounder were aptly named. They possess special proteins in the blood which act as anti-freeze, depressing the freezing point about 0.5°C, enabling them to live in cold, coastal waters where ice forms in winter. The anti-freeze proteins block the entry of external ice crystals through the skin and membranes. This anti-freeze develops each winter in November when water temperatures around Newfoundland are 4–6°C and disappears in May when temperatures begin to rise above 0°C. Survival at −1.4°C is facilitated by the flounders burying themselves 12–15 cm in the sediment where temperatures are 0.1– 0.4°C. In the southern Gulf of St. Lawrence they move into brackish, estuarine waters to overwinter as this water is warmer than the sea. They do not feed during this period.

This flounder is important commercially on a regional basis and is caught by otter trawls and flounder drags offshore and by a variety of means inshore including shut-off seines, fyke nets, weirs, smelt traps and on hook and line and by spearing. Catches are usually incidental to other fisheries. The Canadian catch in 1988 was 3449 tonnes and was 6449 tonnes in 1986. The flesh is excellent and is sold fresh or frozen as fillets of "sole," "lemon sole" or flounder. Anglers catch this flounder in estuaries and near-shore waters.

winter skate

Scientific name: *Raja ocellata*
  Mitchill, 1814
Family: **Skate**
Other common names: big skate, eyed skate, spotted skate
French name: raie tachetée

Distribution: Found from the Gulf of St. Lawrence and southern Newfoundland south to North Carolina.

Characters: This species is separated from its Canadian Atlantic relatives by having a rigid snout with its cartilaginous support

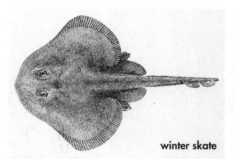

winter skate

thick and stiff, cartilaginous supports of the pectoral fin do not reach the snout tip, dorsal fins joined at the base, snout angle 130° or greater, no distinct row of large spines on body and tail midline except in young, and teeth rows in upper jaw 63–110 when adult (over 50 cm) and 44–55 when young (up to 16 cm). Thorns decrease in number with growth. There are 2–3 irregular rows on each side of the disc and tail midline, and patches of thorns on the shoulders and around the eyes. Males have 4–6 irregular rows of alar spines. The underside is smooth except for a few snout spines. The egg case is green-brown to olive-brown and measures 5.5–8.6 cm by 3.5–5.2 cm excluding horns. The end with the shorter horns is weakly concave, the other end straight or weakly convex with a

ragged edge. The upper disc is light brown, spotted black with 1–4 eyespots posteriorly. Eyespots may be obscure in preserved fish. There is a white area on each side of the snout. The underside is white, sometimes blotched brown on the posterior disc and on the tail. Attains 109 cm.

Biology: A common skate in Atlantic Canada on sand or gravel bottoms usually in shallow water but sometimes as deep as 371 m. Temperature range is –1.2 to 19°C with lower temperatures preferred, 5–9°C on the Scotian Shelf for example. Winter skates, as their name suggests, enter shallow waters, such as Passamaquoddy Bay, in December and leave after March. Food is principally amphipods and worms but also includes fishes, clams and other crustaceans. **Sand lance** is the most important fish species in the diet but **butterfish, cunners** and others are eaten. This skate prefers infauna, animals found within sediments, as opposed to the **little skate**, with which it occurs, which feeds on epifauna, animals on the sea bed. **Sharks, skates** and grey seals eat the winter skate. All winter skate are mature at 78 cm although some mature at 50 cm. Egg cases are deposited year round in New England and in summer to autumn off Nova Scotia. Commercial catches are incidental to other species and are used as fish meal and for pet food.

witch flounder

Scientific name: *Glyptocephalus cynoglossus* (Linnaeus, 1758)
Family: **Righteye Flounder**
Other common names: greysole, Craig fluke, pole flounder, pale flounder, white sole, flet
French name: plie grise

Distribution: Found from southern Labrador off Hamilton Inlet and on Hamilton Bank south to North Carolina. Also in Europe.

Characters: This Atlantic species is characterised by a small, asymmetrical mouth, a nearly straight lateral line over the pectoral fin, about 12 mucous pits on the blind side of the head and a black tip to the eyed side pectoral fin in adults. Dorsal fin rays 95–120, anal rays 85–102 and pectoral rays 9–13.

Scales are mostly cycloid and number 110–140 along the flank above the lateral line. Gill rakers 6–9 on the lower arm.

Eyed side a grey-brown to reddish and blind side grey-white with small dark spots. Bars may be formed on the eyed side but it is usually thickly speckled with black dots. The dorsal and anal fins may bear spots. The eyed side pectoral fin is dark or dusky. The blind side may be about as dark as the eyed side in rare specimens.

Attains 78.1 cm and about 5 kg.

witch flounder

Biology: Found offshore at 18–1569 m and -1 to 13°C on clay, mud and mud-sand, favouring channels and holes in winter. Different age-classes may prefer different depths and temperatures although this is difficult to assess. Certainly adults only concentrate in the winter and this is when the commercial fishery catches them. The largest catches in Canadian waters are taken at 2–6°C and 185–366 m.

Food is worms, crustaceans, snails, clams, brittle stars and small fishes.

Reaches about 38 years and grows slowly. Females live longer than males and grow larger and faster. Growth is faster in warmer waters for both sexes. About half the male population around Newfoundland is mature at 25–30 cm and 4.2–6.0 years (all are mature at 10 years) and half the females at 40–50 cm and 8.4–10.2 years (most are mature at 12 years).

Spawning occurs from March to September in deep channels. Up to 450,000, sometimes more, floating eggs of 1.45 mm are laid. After about a year in the plankton, the young settle to the bottom.

A commercially important species taken incidentally in otter trawls, seines and gill nets while fishing for other species. They are generally associated with **golden redfish**. Commercial fishing has reduced the size of individuals in the catch and most average 45 cm and 0.7 kg. Annual catch was 12,891 tonnes in 1988 for Canada but may have been as high as 50,000 tonnes. The largest catches are made in the Labrador-North Grand Bank area. The flesh is white and tasty. It is sold as sole fillets either fresh or frozen. This flounder is also sought after by anglers.

wolf-eel

Scientific name: *Anarrhichthys ocellatus* Ayres, 1855
Family: **Wolffish**
Other common names: Pacific wolf-eel
French name: loup ocellé

Distribution: Found from Japan to Baja California including the coast of British Columbia.

Characters: This is the only Pacific coast wolffish and is characterised by its elongate shape, large canine and molar teeth in the mouth, no pelvic fins and the eyespots on the body. Scales are buried in the skin. The dorsal fin has 218–250 spines, the anal 180–233 rays and the pectoral about 19–20 rays. Vertebrae number 221–251. Overall colour is a silver-grey, brown or dark green, even orange in young fish. White lines, like grey-black scratches, cover the head and body. The most distinctive feature is the large, round black spots surrounded by a light halo which cover the body and dorsal fin. The anal and caudal fins are light, becoming mottled in large fish. Females are darker than males. Reaches 2.4 m and 18.4 kg.

wolf-eel

Biology: Reported from shallow and surface waters down to 226 m in British Columbia. One wolf-eel was tagged off Doyle Island, B.C. and recaptured off Willapa Bay, Washington having travelled 593 km at a speed of almost 1 km/day. Food is a variety of hard-shelled bottom animals but fish may be eaten too. Young wolf-eels are pelagic and do not develop a crushing adult dentition until 50–60 cm long. The male and female coil around the whitish egg mass until it hatches. The parents rotate the egg mass using their muscular body coils. This apparently aids hatching but other reports indicate that the egg mass is rotated by the adults to ensure adequate oxygen supplies. The eggs stick to a rock surface in a cave or crevice and there may be up to 7000 in each egg mass. This species is occasionally caught by angling and by spear fishing. In some waters, such as off West Vancouver, wolf-eels have been eliminated by spear fishermen. Wolf-eels can be trained by divers to accept hand-proffered food held in front of their den, but the powerful jaws and teeth are quite dangerous. Some Indian tribes restricted consumption of this fish to medicine men as it supposedly increased their healing abilities.

wolf eelpout

Scientific name: *Lycenchelys verrilli*
  (Goode and Bean, 1877)
Family: **Eelpout**
Other common names: none
French name: lycode à tête longue

Distribution: Found from off southern Newfoundland south to North Carolina.

Characters: This species is separated from its Canadian relatives by having short pelvic fins, a mouth under the snout, large

wolf eelpout

pores around the mouth, no crests on the chin, no bony plates along the dorsal and anal fin bases, and by colour pattern. The snout of this species is very long. Scales are embedded. Dorsal fin rays about 92, anal rays about 88, and vertebrae 109. Overall colour is a pale grey-brown. The flank has 8–10 dark brown blotches, large and rounded anteriorly and bar-like posteriorly. The belly is pearly-white. The anterior, tubular nostril is dark. Reaches 25 cm.

Biology: Depth range is 46–1097 m and not uncommon in Canadian waters although it is poorly known.

Wolffish Family

Scientific name: Anarhichadidae
French name: poissons-loups

Wolffishes or sea catfishes are found in the North Atlantic, North Pacific and Arctic oceans. There are 9 species in the family, with 3 on the Arctic/Atlantic coast, 1 on the Arctic coast and 1 on the Pacific coast of Canada.

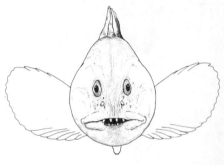

Bering wolffish

These fishes have large heads with strong, protruding, anterior canine teeth and large, molar teeth posteriorly.

The body scales are minute and cycloid, or absent. There is no lateral line. The dorsal fin contains only flexible spines. The long dorsal and anal fins may be confluent with the tail. The pectoral fins are large and fan-shaped but pelvic fins are absent. Gill openings are only on the flank.

Wolffishes are members of the **Perch Order** related to **Gunnel, Quillfish, Wrymouth** and **Prowfish** families among others. Colour pattern is used to identify species.

These fishes are found in cold coastal waters feeding on molluscs, crustaceans, sea urchins and starfish. They are usually on rocky bottoms with a territory based on a crevice, hole or cave. Males and females guard the eggs which are deposited in a clump by the females. They are commercially important and are caught by trawlers. The total Canadian catch in 1988 was 2278 tonnes but was as high as 6037 tonnes in 1983. The skin is used to make a leather. Wolffishes must be handled very carefully as their strong jaws and teeth can inflict a nasty wound. Wolffish are aggressive and attack with a hissing sound.

See **Atlantic wolffish**
Bering wolffish
northern wolfish
spotted wolffish
wolf-eel

Wolftrap Family

Scientific name: Thaumatichthyidae
French name: pièges-à-loup

Wolftraps are found in the Atlantic and Pacific oceans where there are about 6 species with 1 recorded from Atlantic Canada.

Females are easily distinguished from other deepsea **anglerfishes** by the upper jaw being much longer than the lower. A wide, elastic membrane lines the two sides of the upper jaw. The upper part of the operculum has 2 or more branches. There are numerous teeth which protrude and give these fishes a bizarre appearance. The esca or bait on the fishing apparatus has 1–3 denticles. Males and larvae have not yet been caught.

Wolftraps are related to the **Fanfin**, **Seadevil**, **Whipnose**, **Leftvent**, **Dreamer**, **Footballfish** and **Werewolf** families, which all lack pelvic fins, scales and a pseudobranch, have bones at the front of the head (frontals) which are not united, have the lower pharyngeal bones reduced and toothless, and have 8–9 caudal fin rays. The family is a member of the **Anglerfish Order**.

These fishes live as deep as 2500 m. Mature males are probably not parasitic. Prey is seized with the protruding teeth rather than sucked into the mouth as with other **anglerfishes**.

See **grapnel compleat-angler**

Wrasse Family

Scientific name: Labridae
French name: labres

Wrasses are found world-wide in warmer seas and there are about 500 species, making it the second largest marine family after the **Goby Family**. There are only 2 Canadian species on the Atlantic coast. An unidentified, southern species of this family has been reported on the Scotian Shelf.

Wrasses are often recognised by having protruding canine or incisor teeth which make them appear bucktoothed. Lips are usually thick. There is a long dorsal fin with 8–21 spines followed by 6–21 soft rays. The anal fin usually has 3 spines (range 2–6) and 7–18 soft rays. The pelvic fins have 1 spine and 5 soft rays. Scales are cycloid and often large but some species have over 100 small scales in the lateral line. The lateral line may be complete or interrupted. In life they characteristically swim jerkily, using their pectoral fins and the rear of the fish drags behind as if paralysed.

Wrasse are members of the **Perch Order**. The word wrasse is derived from a Cornish word for this kind of fish.

Wrasses are more usually associated with the coral reefs of the tropics, but a few species are adapted to cold, northern waters. They are widely variable in size, body shape and colour. A single species may show various colour phases during growth and between sexes which have led them to be described as distinct species. Some species bury themselves in sand at night, to sleep on their sides. Sleeping wrasse in aquaria have shown rapid eye movements (REM), and perhaps dream as humans do! One species secretes a mucous capsule around itself to ensure an uninterrupted night's sleep. Certain species are "cleaners," picking parasites off large predatory fish at a recognised cleaning station without being devoured, while others use their incisor teeth like forceps to snip fins and pull eyes out of other fishes. Some wrasse are known to change sex from female to male as they age (protogynous hermaphrodites). The terminal male, or supermale, as he is known, establishes a territory and keeps a harem of females.

Wrasse live about coral reefs, rocks and among seaweed. Most wrasses feed on hardshelled invertebrates, which are crushed with pharyngeal or throat teeth. Large wrasse are good food fish, but they are not fished on a commercial scale, since most live alone. Smaller species are popular marine aquarium fish.

See **cunner**
  tautog

wreckfish

Scientific name: *Polyprion americanus*
  (Schneider in Bloch and Schneider, 1801)
Family: **Temperate Ocean Bass**
Other common names: shern, sherny, stone
  bass, wreck bass
French name: cernier

Distribution: Found from the Grand Bank south to Argentina in the western Atlantic Ocean. Common in Europe and also in the Indian Ocean and off New Zealand.

Characters: This species is distinguished from its Atlantic coast relatives by the dorsal fins being close together and by the high lat-

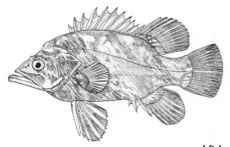

wreckfish

eral line scale count. Dorsal fin with 10–12 spines and 11–12 soft rays, anal fin with 2–3 spines and 8–10 soft rays and pectoral fin with 17–18 rays. Scales are strongly ctenoid and number 90–114 in the lateral line. The dorsal, anal and caudal fins have high scaly sheaths. Overall colour is brown, brownish-red, bluish-grey or blackish-brown. The belly is grey-white to yellowish. Dorsal and anal fins blue-black. Pelvic fins with white rays but blue-black membranes and a white margin to the fin. The caudal fin has a white margin. Young are mottled and marbled. Attains 2.1 m. The world, all-tackle angling record from the Azores Islands weighed 48.5 kg and was caught in 1985.

Biology: Occasionally caught in Atlantic Canada with an early report in about 1880 from the Grand Bank. As the name suggests it is often found under floating pieces of wreckage or seaweed when young. There are instances of young wreckfish entering a floating crate when small enough to fit through the bars and becoming trapped there as they grow too big to escape. Adults are found over rock or mud-sand bottoms at 40–450 m, usually at 100–200 m but sometimes as deep as 1000 m. Sometimes enters rivers. Young are found in small groups but adults are solitary. Food is crustaceans, molluscs and fishes. Wreckage often attracts other fishes for shelter which are then stalked and eaten by the wreckfish. Spawning occurs January to July in the Mediterranean Sea. Eggs are 1.4 mm in diameter. It is a food fish in Europe.

Wrymouth Family

Scientific name: Cryptacanthodidae
French name: terrassiers

Wrymouths are found in the North Pacific Ocean and the northwest Atlantic Ocean. There are only 4 species with 2 reported on Canada's Pacific coast and 1 on the Atlantic coast.

They have a very elongate body, no pelvic fins (but a pelvic girdle), small pectoral fins, a large and very oblique mouth with the lower jaw the longest, a poorly developed lateral line, and a long spiny dorsal fin originating near the head and joined (as is the anal fin) with the caudal fin. The head is broad and flat. The eyes are near the top of the head. The lower jaw and side of the head have mucous pits. They are members of the **Perch Order**.

They are close relatives of the **Shanny Family** and have been classified with them as one family.

These are shallow water fishes which may burrow in soft bottoms to form a network of tunnels.

See **dwarf wrymouth**
  giant wrymouth
  spotted wrymouth

Y

Y-prickleback

Scientific name: *Allolumpenus hypochromus*
Hubbs and Schultz, 1932
Family: **Shanny**
Other common names: Y-blenny, lompénie
i-grec
French name: stichée-Y

Distribution: Found from California,
although records are uncertain, British
Columbia including Browning Entrance in
the Queen Charlotte Islands.

Characters: This species is most closely
related to the **bluebarred prickleback**. It is
distinguished by having about 44–50 dorsal
fin spines, 1 anal fin spine and about 30–31
soft rays, and by colour. Scales are over the

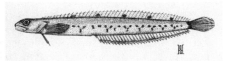

Y-prickleback

whole body but are not on the head. The lateral line canal is absent. The gill membranes
are joined and attached to the isthmus. The
jaw has a pair of large canine teeth at the
front. In preservative this species is a light
brown with about 5 dark spots at the dorsal
fin base and spots on the lower flank arranged
in a letter "y" shape. There is a black spot at
the upper and lower caudal fin base. Reaches
7.6 cm.

Biology: This species was recommended
for official status as "rare" in Canada by the
Committee on the Status of Endangered
Wildlife in Canada but no status designation
was given as of 1991. It is found down from
30–100 m over rock and sand. A poorly
known species which deserves further inves-
tigation into its biology.

yellow bristlemouth

Scientific name: *Cyclothone pacifica*
Mukhacheva, 1964
Family: **Bristlemouth**
Other common names: veiled anglemouth

French name: cyclothone jaune

Distribution: Found in the northern
Pacific Ocean including off the whole coast
of British Columbia.

Characters: The yellow bristlemouth is
separated from other Pacific coast bristlemouths by lacking SO photophores, by hav-

yellow bristlemouth

ing a basically dark brown to black body
with scales, no transparent area in front of
the anal fin, 9 OA photophores and the anus
is midway between the pelvic fin base and
the anal fin origin. Gill filaments are not
fused. Photophores: ORB 1, OP 2, BR 8–10,
IV 12–14, VAV 5, AC 14–16, usually 15.
Dorsal fin rays 12–14, anal rays 17–20.
Reaches 7.6 cm.

Biology: Found off northwestern British
Columbia at 100–1190 m, off Cape Flattery,
and at Ocean Station Papa (50°N, 145°W) at
500–1000 m.

yellow bullhead

Scientific name: *Ameiurus natalis*
(Le Sueur, 1819)
Family: **Bullhead Catfish**
Other common names: northern yellow
bullhead, yellow catfish, creek cat,
white whiskered bullhead, greaser,
polliwog, yellowbelly bullhead, butterball,
buttercat, paper skin, slick bullhead,
Mississippi bullhead
French name: barbotte jaune

Distribution: Found in southern Ontario
from the St. Lawrence River basin west
through lakes Ontario, Erie, St. Clair and
southern Huron to North Dakota and south to
the Gulf of Mexico.

Characters: This species is identified by
the posterior tip of the adipose fin being free
of the back, the caudal fin is not deeply

forked, mouth corner barbels are about twice as long as nostril barbels, there is no bony ridge between the head and the dorsal fin, the

yellow bullhead

anal fin touches the caudal fin when pressed to the body, chin barbels are yellow to white or pinkish, and upper barbels are yellow to grey. Dorsal fin soft rays 6, total anal rays 24–28, pelvic rays 8 and pectoral rays 7–8. The barbs on the dorsal fin spine are very weak. The pectoral spine has strong barbs in young fish but these do not grow with the fish and are weak in large fish. Gill rakers 12–15. The back and top of the head are olive-brown to blackish, sometimes grey or even yellow, the flanks are yellowish without mottles and the belly is yellow to white. Fins are brown or olive to dusky with the thicker bases darker. The anal fin may have a central stripe. The adipose fin tip may be pale. Young fish are jet black above and white below with white chin barbels. Formerly in the genus *Ictalurus*. Reaches 46.5 cm. The world, all-tackle angling record weighed 1.92 kg and was caught in 1984 in Mormon Lake, Arizona.

Biology: Yellow bullheads are found in still or slow waters of lakes, ponds and rivers where there is a lot of vegetation. They may be found in slow riffles. They are tolerant of some pollution compared to **black** and **brown bullheads**. These bullheads are active at night, scavenging for crustaceans, insects, molluscs and fishes. Older fish specialise on crayfish and fish in Lake Opinicon, Ontario. Young fish travel in large schools feeding generally on whatever is available. Life span is 6–7 years with maturity attained at 2–3 years. Spawning occurs in May to July after both sexes construct a nest. The nest is an open depression on a stream bed, a short burrow in a stream bank

or under a rock or log, or a deserted muskrat burrow. Eggs are cream, adhesive, up to 3.0 mm in diameter and laid in batches of up to 700. A female may contain up to 7000 eggs. The male guards the nest and the young until they reach 51 mm. The flesh of this species is white and tasty and it is caught by anglers using baited hooks in the U.S.A.

yellow perch

Scientific name: *Perca flavescens*
  (Mitchill, 1814)
Family: **Perch**
Other common names: lake perch, American perch, raccoon perch, coontail, ring perch, striped perch, redfin perch, convict, yellow ned, jack perch
French name: perchaude

Distribution: Found from Nova Scotia except Cape Breton Island, through New Brunswick, southwest Quebec, Ontario and Manitoba including the Hudson Bay lowlands, Saskatchewan, Alberta and north to Great Slave Lake. Present in southern Columbia River drainages of British Columbia from the spread of specimens introduced to Washington. In the U.S.A. south to Missouri and to South Carolina east of the Appalachians. Widely introduced outside this natural range.

Characters: The most distinctive feature of the perch is the 5–10 wide black bands on the flank although these may be faint in some populations. In addition the mouth is large

yellow perch

with the upper jaw extending back to the middle of the eye or further, the preopercle bone on the side of the head is serrated at its angle, and there are only 6–9, usually 7–8, soft rays in the anal fin. Lower jaw teeth are small and none are canines. First dorsal fin spines 11–15, second dorsal fin with 1–2 spines and 12–16 soft rays. There are 2 anal fin spines. Pectoral rays 13–15. The space between the pelvic fin bases is less than 1 base width. Ctenoid scales number 50–70 in the lateral line. Cheeks are scaled. There are 3 short, thick, pyloric caeca.

The back and sides are green, olive or yellow-brown fading ventrally to grey or white. The flanks may be a rich golden yellow. The eye is yellow or green. The spiny dorsal fin is yellowish to green with a black margin and often with black on the membranes anteriorly and posteriorly. Other fins are usually yellowish but the pectoral and pelvic fins may be more orange. The pelvic fins may be silvery. Fin membranes may be clear to cloudy and usually not coloured. Breeding males have orange to bright red lower fins and colours generally are more intense.

Reaches 53.3 cm. The world, all-tackle angling record from Bordentown, New Jersey in 1865 weighed 1.91 kg. The Canadian angling record from Moose Lake, Alberta, was caught by R. Hancheruk in 1983 and weighed 1.35 kg.

Biology: Perch are found in lakes, ponds and rivers where there is some vegetation, clear open water and low turbidity. They may enter brackish water or be found in saline prairie lakes up to concentrations of 13‰ or about one-third seawater. Preferred temperatures are in the 20–24°C range. pH as low as 4.4 is tolerated. Depth range is down to 46 m but they are mostly found in water shallower than about 9 m. Their distribution in the southern U.S.A. is limited by the 31°C summer isotherm. They travel in schools of up to 200 fish, daily and seasonally for spawning and feeding and in response to temperatures. Schools of young perch may be mixed in with schools of **spottail shiners** swimming near the surface. Predators such as the larger **perch**, **northern pike** and **yellow walleye** swim below the mixed school and are 10 times more likely to take a **shiner** than a perch. They rest at night on the lake or river bottom and, unlike **walleyes** and **sauger**, are most active during the day. Schooling by adult, predatory perch

reduces the chances of a prey fish to escape - it may encounter another school member. Yellow perch are active under winter ice.

Food changes with age but is principally insects and other invertebrates, and fishes including all life stages. Peak feeding occurs at sunrise and sunset. Perch may hunt in packs which improves the chance of capturing active prey. They are food for many other fishes and birds but also compete with such sport fishes as **trout** and **bass**. Perch are a major food of **walleye**.

Some populations of perch comprise stunted fish because of their strong appetite, high rate of reproduction, competition for food and such factors as predators and available space. Stunting is often a feature of small lakes while the best growth occurs in large water systems. A stunted population has been known from Lac Hertel, Québec for over 20 years yet when young perch were grown under optimal conditions in the laboratory, their growth was comparable to normal populations. Perch biomass in small lakes and ponds without other species can reach 215 kg/ha but in lakes with other species it is usually under 65 kg/ha.

Spawning occurs usually from mid-April to May but may be as late as July. There is a spawning migration upriver or onto lake shallows and spawning occurs at temperatures of 5.6–19.0°C. Fish return to the same spawning ground in subsequent years. Males arrive earlier and stay longer than females on the spawning grounds. Spawning takes place during the night and early morning hours over vegetation, roots or fallen trees or over sand and gravel. Each female is attended by a double line of males, numbering up to 25! The first 2 males keep their noses pushing the female's belly and the remaining males follow as the female pursues a curved course. The female lays up to 210,000 eggs of 3.5 mm diameter in a twisted, gelatinous, transparent string up to 2.1 m long and 10.2 cm wide. The string has a central tube and holes to afford oxygen circulation and is folded in convolutions like an accordion. The egg mass adheres to vegetation and is often twisted around it during a spiral clockwise movement by the female.

Females grow faster than males and reach a larger final size. Males are usually mature at 2–3 years at females at 2–4 years but this varies with latitude as does growth. Some one-year-old males are mature in Lake Erie. In Québec it takes 4–5 years minimum to produce fish of a harvestable size (18–20 cm). Maximum age may be about 21 years although 13 years is a more usual figure in the literature. Perch in rivers of James Bay have a slower growth rate and shorter maximum length but longer life span than perch from southern Québec.

Yellow perch are important commercially, as sport fish and are used in schools and universities to typify a fish for anatomy classes. Anglers take this species in both summer and winter and enjoy its white, flaky flesh. Bait is usually **minnows**, worms or cut fish and perch can be caught on small plugs, spoons and even flies. Commercial fisheries centre on the Great Lakes where pollution and overfishing have taken their toll. A catch of 32.7 million kg was made in the Great Lakes in 1934 but catches have been as low as 4% of this figure. The total Canadian catch in 1988 was 6400 tonnes. Unbreaded perch fillets sold for as much at $17.50/kg in the mid-1980s and demand exceeded supply.

- Most accessible April through August.
- The Great Lakes watershed and the western end of the St. Lawrence River.
- Ultralight to light action spinning outfits used with four-to six-pound test line.
- The best lures, 1/8–to 1/4–ounce spoons, a variety of small spinners, small minnow-imitating pugs, small crankbaits and a variety of 1/8–to 1/4–ounce hair and plastic bodied jigs. The best bait, small live **minnows** and worms fished near the bottom or under a float.

yellow walleye

Scientific name: *Stizostedion vitreum vitreum*
    (Mitchill, 1818)
Family: **Perch**
Other common names: various combinations of yellow, walleye, pickerel and pike; dory, gray pike, green pike, jack salmon, glass eye, marble eye

French name: doré

Distribution: Found from western Quebec, throughout Ontario, Manitoba, Saskatchewan and Alberta and north to the mouth of the Mackenzie River including Great Bear and Great Slave lakes and extreme northeastern British Columbia, and southward to the Gulf of Mexico in Alabama. Also introduced outside native range.

Characters: This is 1 of 2 subspecies of **walleye**. The **blue walleye** was the other species in Canada. Anglers often call the

yellow walleye

walleye "pickerel" but the word pickerel should be confined to members of the unrelated **Pike Family**. The yellow walleye has a large mouth with the upper jaw extending back to the rear edge of the eye, the preopercle bone on the side of the head is serrated at its outer angle, there are 10–14 soft rays in the anal fin after 2–3 spines, 2 canine teeth are present at the lower jaw tip, there is a large, black blotch at the rear base of the spiny dorsal fin and 5–8 saddles on the back. First dorsal fin spines 11–16, second dorsal fin with 1–2 spines and 17–22 soft rays, and pectoral rays 13–16. Lateral line scales 80–108. There are 3 pyloric caeca attached to, and as long as, the stomach.

Overall colour has brassy tones and is dark green, olive-brown or yellow with gold flecks on the sides. The belly is white to yellowish. The lower lobe tip in the caudal fin and the anal fin tip are white. Males have a more pronounced white lower lobe to the caudal fin. The spiny dorsal fin membranes are not spotted but dusky. The second dorsal and caudal fins are speckled in rows. Pelvic fins are yellowish to orangish. Pectoral fins have a dark, basal blotch. The peritoneum is white. The eyes are silvery from reflections of the tapetum lucidum and the cornea is milky (hence "walleye"). Young fish often have 4–14 bars on the flank, particularly in clear water. Grey-blue walleyes or "hards" in Lake Erie have a bluish mucus and are not the **blue walleye**.

Reaches 1.04 m. The world, all-tackle angling record weighed 11.34 kg and was caught in 1960 in Old Hickory Lake, Tennessee. The Canadian record is a 10.10 kg. fish caught by Patrick Noonan in the Niagara River in May 1993.

Biology: Walleye favour both turbid and clear lakes but the very sensitive eyes limits their activity in clear water. They rest on the bottom during the day in clear waters. Nevertheless they prefer less turbid conditions than **sauger**. Large streams and rivers which are turbid or have deep, sheltered pools, weed beds or fallen trees, also harbour walleye. A temperature range of 0–30°C is tolerated although 20–23°C is preferred. They are active in winter and swim in schools often associated with other sport fish such as **northern pike, yellow perch, muskellunge** and **smallmouth bass**. Water depth preferred is moderate, down to about 21 m, usually shallower. There are morning and evening migrations into shallow or surface waters to feed.

Food when adult is a wide variety of available fishes but young can be cannibals if other food is not available. Young walleye are of the same size in a school and attempts at cannibalism may have peculiar results. A chain of up to 4 walleye may happen when successive fish try to ingest the tail of the one ahead. The end of the chain will eventually digest the tail in its mouth and reject the rest. Young feed on invertebrates and even adults will take mostly mayflies and chironomids when these are emerging. **Northern pike** are the most important walleye predator.

Growth varies with latitude and northern populations may be only half the length of southern ones at the end of their first growing season. Northern populations may live 26 years and southern ones up to 12 years. Males are usually mature at 2–4 years and about 28 cm while females are usually mature at 3–6 years and about 36 cm or more. However maturity of females is governed by tempera-

ture — in the southern U.S.A. it is attained at 2 years but only at 10 years in the N.W.T. Females grow more rapidly than males. Some fish have been recorded as moving 160 km, but this movement is unusual apart from regular spawning migrations. Spawning occurs in early April in southern Ontario to June or later in the north usually after ice break up at 2.2–15.6°C. Some populations spawn under the ice in lakes. Males arrive on the rocky or gravel spawning ground first.

Spawning takes place at night in groups of up to 2 females and 6 males. There is some spawning behaviour with chases, pushing and fin erection before the group swims rapidly into shallow water where the females roll on their sides and release their eggs at the surface. Eggs number up to 615,000, are up to 2.1 mm in diameter and fall into crevices between rocks.

The walleye is the most economically important fish in Canadian fresh waters. It is both a commercial and sport fish with firm white or pinkish flesh. Anglers catch it in both summer and winter using live **minnows** or artificial lures and drifting and trolling techniques. The best fishing is at dusk or dawn, during the night or on cloudy days. The peak commercial catch in 1956 weighed 9.5 million kg and was worth $3.1 million. Pollution and overfishing, particularly in Lake Erie, has greatly reduced this resource. Mercury contamination of walleyes in Lake Erie was discovered in 1970 and led to closure of commercial fisheries. The stock has recovered dramatically indicating overfishing was the main cause of stock decline. The total Canadian catch was an estimated 8153 tonnes in 1988 and was worth $28 million.

- Most accessible May through September.
- Manitoba, Saskatchewan, Lake Erie, the eastern basin of Lake Ontario and the western end of the St. Lawrence River in Quebec.
- Medium action spinning and baitcasting outfits used with six- to 12–pound test line.
- Trolled or cast minnow-imitating plugs from three to five inches in length, a variety of crankbaits and spinners as

well as a wide assortment of 1/4– to 3/8–ounce hair and plastic body jigs. The best bait is worms, live **minnows** and leeches fished near the bottom. A spinner and worm or jig and **minnow** combination are favourites.

yelloweye rockfish

Scientific name: *Sebastes ruberrimus* (Cramer, 1895)

Family: **Scorpionfish**

Other common names: red snapper, turkey-red rockfish, pot belly, rasphead, goldeneye rockfish

French name: sébaste aux yeux jaunes

Distribution: Found from the Gulf of Alaska to Baja California including British Columbia.

Characters: Colour, gill raker count and head spines identify this species. Dorsal fin spines 13, soft rays 13–16, usually 15. Anal

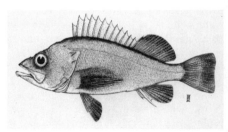

yelloweye rockfish

soft rays 5–8, usually 7, second spine twice as thick as third, about equal. Pectoral fin rays 18–20, usually 19. Lateral line pores 39–46, scale rows below lateral line 45–50. Gill rakers short, rough and club-shaped, 25–30. Vertebrae 26. Head spines are strong and form a ridge over the eye. The nuchal and coronal spines may be absent. The eye is a characteristic bright yellow. Overall colour is orange-yellow or scarlet-pink with pink tinges. Fins are pink, usually with black tips. The head in the largest fish is mottled with black. Younger fish, up to 30 cm, are orange to reddish or a rich, dark red with some dark markings outlining scales. There is a white stripe along the lateral line and a shorter stripe underneath it. The upper stripe merges with a pale bar crossing the base of the tail fin. The pectoral, anal

and caudal fins have black on them. The margin of the dorsal, anal and caudal fins is white in young fish. The peritoneum is white with black dots. Reaches 91 cm. There are two world, all-tackle angling records and both weighed 10.43 kg, both were caught at Langara Island, British Columbia, one on 27 August 1992 by Mike K. Ackert and one on 2 June 1993 by Bob Alverts.

Biology: Commonly found on rocky reefs at 41–550 m in Canada. In the Strait of Georgia submersible observations show this species to be common at 41–100 m in complex rock habitats. Young are found as shallow as 20 m. Food is crustaceans, fishes and even the eggs of such species as **lingcod**. Life span is over an estimated 90 years. Females reach 50% maturity at 50–52 cm and males at 52–60 cm with an age range of 15–20 years for both sexes. Young are born principally in May in Canada and up to 2.9 million are released. They are caught on baited hooks and make good fillets. A variety of fishing gear captures this species which is the most important shallow water bottom fish in southeast Alaska. It is marketed as Pacific red snapper.

yellowfin bass

Scientific name: *Anthias nicholsi* Firth, 1933

Family: **Sea Bass**

Other common names: saffron bass

French name: barbier ligne-en-palier

Distribution: Found from the Caribbean Sea north to Virginia and on the Scotian Shelf in Atlantic Canada.

Characters: This species is one of the streamer basses, so-called because the dorsal and caudal fins often have 1 or more filamentous rays. Colour, scale count, and caudal filaments in adults distinguishes this species from the other streamer bass species, the **red barbier**. The caudal fin in this species is not filamentous but has rounded lobes, the upper one being slightly longer than the lower. Filaments on the dorsal fin are short tabs. There are 29–33 lateral line scales. Dorsal fin spines are 10, soft rays 14–15. Anal fin soft rays are 7, after 3 spines. The head and body are pale red to orange-red. The flanks have

3–4 yellow stripes and the 2 central ones extend onto the head. The dorsal and anal fins are bright yellow. The caudal fin is white

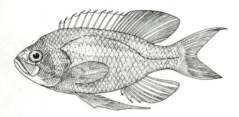

yellowfin bass

with a pink margin. The pelvic fin is yellow with a red outer edge. A deep blue blotch is on the back below the spiny dorsal fin. Attains 25 cm.

Biology: Found as both larval and adult strays in Canada. First reported in 1981 from an adult specimen taken at 190 m by Japanese squid fishermen. Submersible operations off South Carolina show that this fish aggregates above the bottom.

yellowfin sole

Scientific name: *Pleuronectes asper*
    (Pallas, 1814)
Family: **Righteye Flounder**
Other common names: muddab
French name: limande à nageoires jaunes

Distribution: Found from Korea and Japan, the Bering and Chukchi seas south to British Columbia.

yellowfin sole

Characters: This species is distinguished from its Canadian Pacific relatives by having a strongly arched lateral line over the pec-

toral fin but no accessory lateral line. Scales are ctenoid on both sides of the body and extend onto dorsal, anal and caudal fin rays. Lateral line scales 73–90. Mouth small, asymmetrical and with teeth mainly on lower side. Dorsal fin rays 61–77, anal fin preceded by a sharp spine and with 48–58 rays. Caudal fin truncate with rounded edges. Eyed side light or dark brown to olive, sometimes spotted gold, with darker mottles. Dark line at the dorsal and anal fin bases and faint dark bars on these fins which may have a yellowish tinge. Blind side white with yellow fins. Reaches 50 cm standard length.

Biology: Barkley Sound is the southern limit of this species. Found in shallow waters, usually less than 92 m, but reported down to 183 m. Food is worms, molluscs, hydroids and brittle stars. Males are mature at 20 cm and 4–5 years and females at 23–24 cm and 6–7 years in Asian waters. Maximum age is at least 13 years. Egg production exceeds 1 million. This species is not common enough in Canadian waters to support a commercial fishery.

yellowfin tuna

Scientific name: *Thunnus albacares*
    (Bonnaterre, 1788)
Family: **Mackerel**
Other common names: Allison's tunny,
    autumn albacore, thon albacore
French name: albacore à nageoires jaunes

Distribution: Found world-wide in warmer waters. In the western Atlantic Ocean from Nova Scotia south to Brazil. Also reported off the coast of British Columbia.

Characters: This species is separated (as adults greater than 120 cm long) from its relatives on both coasts by the greatly elongated second dorsal and anal fins. Dorsal fins are separated by a distance less than snout length, gill rakers are 26–35 and first dorsal fin spines 11–14. The ventral surface of the liver lacks the striations found in **albacore** and **bigeye tuna**. The second dorsal fin has 13–16 rays followed by 8–10 finlets. Anal fin rays 12–15 followed by 7–10 finlets. Pectoral rays 33–36. The back is dark blue fading to a silvery-grey below. Some fish have a yellow to golden flank stripe.

Belly with about 20 vertical lines of light spots. Dorsal and anal fins yellow. Dorsal and anal finlets bright yellow with thin black

yellowfin tuna

margins. Young have white bars and spots on the belly. Reaches 209 cm fork length and 204 kg. The world, all-tackle angling record weighed 176.35 kg and was caught off Mexico in 1977.

Biology: Reported first from 3 specimens caught in 1957 southeast of Cape Sable, N.S. with occasional reports since then. The British Columbia record was first reported in 1990 but has not been documented in detail. This is a pelagic, oceanic species found from surface to mid-level waters at 18–31°C. It is found in schools by size. Larger fish school with dolphins and porpoises but the reasons for this are unknown. Sometimes found associated with floating weed and debris, various hypotheses have been advanced to explain this association. The fish use the floating objects as shade, protection from predators, to lay eggs on, as a source of associated food organisms and as a cleaning station where other fishes pick parasites from pelagic fishes. Food includes various fishes, squid and crustaceans. Some fish mature at 1 year at 50–60 cm fork length but others do not mature until a length of 120 cm. Life span is about 5 years. Spawning occurs year round with peaks in different areas at different times. This is a commercially important species caught with longlines, by pole-fishing and with purse seines, mainly in the tropical Pacific and Indian oceans. The world catch in 1981 was 526,340 tonnes. The Canadian catch in 1988 was 30 tonnes. The meat is light coloured and is sold frozen or canned. It is one of the most important tunas commercially and is a famous game fish.

yellowmouth rockfish

Scientific name: *Sebastes reedi*
  (Westrheim and Tsuyuki, 1967)
Family: **Scorpionfish**
Other common names: none
French name: sébaste à bouche jaune

Distribution: Found from Alaska to California including British Columbia.

Characters: This species is characterised by yellow and black blotches inside a pinkish mouth. Dorsal fin spines 13, soft rays 13–15, usually 14. Anal fin soft rays 7–8, usually 7, second spine thicker than third and almost equal. Pectoral fin rays 18–20, usually 19, unbranched rays 7–13. Gill rakers 30–36. Vertebrae 26. Lateral line pores 47–55, scale rows below lateral line 57–67. Coronal and nuchal head spines are absent, other spines moderate to weak. There are strong spines on the lower gill cover edge. The body colour is red-orange, with yellow-orange tinges. The belly is white. There are 3–5 faint saddles on the back. The jaws are red. The lateral line is pink. Peritoneum silvery-grey with black dots. Smaller fish are red with black mottles. Reaches 58 cm.

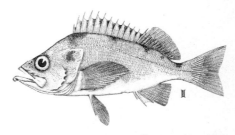

yellowmouth rockfish

Biology: The scientific name is from the *G. B. Reed*, a Fisheries Research Board of Canada vessel. Found on rough bottoms at 141–366 m. This rough habitat prevents easy commercial exploitation. Young are born in May in British Columbia. Half the population is mature at 37 cm for males and 38 cm for females. A maximum age of over 70 is estimated. Catches of this species are usually small but larger aggregations do occur off southwest and northwest Vancouver Island and northwest of the Queen Charlotte Islands.

yellowtail

Scientific name: *Seriola lalandi dorsalis*
(Gill, 1863)
Family: **Jack**
Other common names: California yellowtail,
yellowtail amberjack, giant yellowtail
French name: sériole à queue jaune

Distribution: World-wide in warmer waters
and from British Columbia to Chile in the
eastern Pacific Ocean.

Characters: This jack is distinguished from
its Canadian Pacific coast relatives by lacking
scutes (enlarged scales) in the lateral line and

yellowtail

by having a yellow stripe along the flank. The
caudal peduncle is grooved above and below.
First dorsal fin spines usually 7 (range 4–7),
the first very small and embedded in flesh in
adults; second dorsal fin with 1 spine and
30–39 soft rays. Anal fin with 3 spines and
19–23 soft rays. Overall colour is silvery with
a blue, olive or brown back and yellowish
fins. There is a dusky yellow stripe along the
flank. An oblique, dark band passes through
the eye to the snout. Young fish less than 13
cm have flank bars. Reaches 1.93 m and over
58 kg but usually less than 10 kg. The world,
all-tackle angling record was caught in 1987
in Mexico and weighed 35.38 kg.

Biology: Probably a regular summertime
visitor to waters off British Columbia. First
reported in 1980 from between Dundas and
Zayas islands near the Alaskan border but also
known from waters off Vancouver Island. This
is a schooling species in California around
islands, close to shore and over banks offshore
down to about 69 m. Yellowtails live at least
12 years but many are mature at 2 years of age
and all at 3 years. Larger females produce over
1 million eggs during the summer months.
Food includes various fishes, pelagic crustaceans and squids. Sea lions are known to eat
yellowtails. Yellowtails are "cleaner" fish,
removing parasites attached to sharks without
being threatened or eaten by the shark. These
fishes are important for sport in southern
California and in 1959 457,000 yellowtails
were caught by party boats. Fish are caught by
trolling, on live bait and by spearfishing. There
is a commercial fishery in Mexico and yellowtails are excellent fresh or smoked.

yellowtail flounder

Scientific name: *Pleuronectes ferrugineus*
(Storer, 1839)
Family: **Righteye Flounder**
Other common names: rusty dab, rusty
flounder, sole, mud dab, sand dab, sériole
French name: limande à queue jaune

Distribution: Found from the Strait of
Belle Isle in southern Labrador, the western
and southern coasts of Newfoundland, Gulf
of St. Lawrence, Grand Bank and south to
Chesapeake Bay.

Characters: This Atlantic species is characterised by a small, asymmetrical mouth,
and a strong bend or arch to the lateral line
over the pectoral fin. The head has a concave
upper margin. Dorsal fin rays 73–91, anal
rays 51–68 and pectoral rays 10. There is a
forward-pointing, short spine in front of the
anal fin. Gill rakers are long and number
10–12 on the lower arch. Scales are ctenoid
on the eyed side and cycloid on the blind

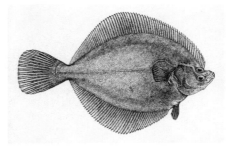

yellowtail flounder

side. Lateral line scales 88–100. The eyed
side is reddish-brown to olive-green with
rusty spots of various sizes. Blind side white
with yellow on the caudal peduncle and the

edges of the caudal, dorsal and anal fins. Attains 64 cm.

Biology: This flounder is common on sand and mud bottoms of offshore banks at 36–91 m but depth range is 9–364 m. Temperatures in the range 2–6°C are favoured on the Scotian Shelf. Yellowtails retreat to deeper water in winter. Food is worms, crustaceans, shellfish and some smaller fishes such as **sand lances** and **capelin**. Much of the diet on Georges Bank is a few amphipod and worm species selected because of their suitable size and availability. Spawning occurs in May–July in Canada, earlier in the U.S.A. As many as 4.57 million floating eggs are produced with a diameter of 0.9 mm when fertilised. Growth is moderately fast for a **flatfish** with a maximum age of 14 years. Fish in warmer waters in Canada mature at younger ages than those in colder waters. Yellowtails are abundant on the Grand Bank where most of the commercial catch is 6–8 years old and 37–43 cm long. They are sought there with otter trawls but many are taken in the Canadian plaice fishery. The catch in 1972 was 39,000 tonnes but the take has decreased dramatically because of overfishing. They are also caught on the Scotian Shelf. The total Canadian catch in 1988 was 7001 tonnes and in 1987 15,096 tonnes. This species is an important food fish, fresh or frozen, and much of the catch is exported.

yellowtail rockfish

Scientific name: *Sebastes flavidus*
(Ayres, 1863)
Family: **Scorpionfish**
Other common names: green snapper,
yellowtail rockcod
French name: sébaste à queue jaune

Distribution: Found from Alaska to California including British Columbia.

Characters: This species is characterised by a convex space between the eyes on top of the head, head spines weak to absent, an obvious knob at the tip of the lower jaw, colour, and the vertical posterior edge to the anal fin. Dorsal fin spines 12–13, usually 13, soft rays 14–16, usually 14. Anal fin soft rays 7–9, usually 8, second anal spine not much thicker than third and shorter. Pectoral

fin rays 17–19, usually 18. Gill rakers 33–39. Vertebrae 26. Lateral line pores 49–60, scale rows below lateral line 55–60. Only weak nasal spines are present. Overall colour is brown, olive-green or dark grey mottled with orange-brown. There are light patches on the upper flank. The gill cover has yellow patches. Scales have reddish-brown speckles. The belly is white. Fins are a dusky green with yellow or red tinges. The caudal fin is dirty yellow. The lower pectoral fin rays are tinged pink. Young fish are speckled brown with a black blotch on the rear of the caudal fin. The peritoneum is silvery-white in adults and speckled black in young. Reaches 66 cm. The world, all-tackle angling record was caught at Cape Flattery, Washington in 1988 and weighed 2.51 kg.

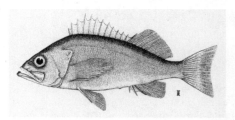

yellowtail rockfish

Biology: Common in pelagic schools usually at 24–46 m or 91–183 but ranging from surface down to 550 m. It can swim quickly, especially up and down in the water column. Individuals may hide in rock crevices and, if displaced, can return to their home even after 3 months have elapsed and from a distance of 22 km. Food is pelagic crustaceans, salps, squids, and fish such as the **northern lanternfish, poachers, hakes** and **flatfishes**. Feeding occurs mainly at night or in the early morning, related to the diurnal movements of prey. Half the population is mature at 40 cm for males and 42 cm for females. Life span is estimated to be over 60 years. Young are born in March and females about 50 cm produce 633,000. An annoyance to salmon anglers but good sport on light tackle using lures such as surface poppers or bait. They can be caught from piers. A commercial catch of "greenies", as they are also known, is caught by trawling and longlining and is sold fresh or frozen as fillets.

Z

Zugmayer's pearleye

Scientific name: *Benthalbella infans*
   Zugmayer, 1911
Family: **Pearleye**
Other common names: none
French name: oeil-perlé de Zugmayer

Distribution: Found in all warmer oceans and south of Nova Scotian waters. Rare in the western North Atlantic Ocean.

Characters: This pearleye is separated from its Atlantic coast relative, the **black-belly pearleye**, by the lack of flank stripes,

Zugmayer's pearleye

and from other pearleyes by fin ray counts. Dorsal fin rays 8–10, usually 9, anal rays 19–25 and pectoral rays 24–29. Lateral line scales 53–59. Overall colour is a dull brown with scale pockets outlined with a slightly darker pigmentation. All fins are pigmented. The four light organs on the belly are lemon-yellow in adults and emit a blue-green light. There is a dense, black stripe between the last 2 light organs on the belly. The light organs are unusual in that they are derived from muscle tissue. The peritoneum is black. Reaches 13.8 cm.

Biology: Known from a single larval specimen first reported in 1988 as a northern range extension. They may descend as deep as 1800 m and even larvae are usually caught below 300 m. Occasionally adults are caught in the upper 200 m but are usually below 500 m. This species is the only Canadian pearleye to be bioluminescent. Food includes squid and fishes. It is an hermaphrodite with both eggs and sperm maturing simultaneously. About 2300 eggs are produced. The rarity of adults is compensated for by the hermaphroditism.

Acknowledgments

The writing of this book would not have been possible without the forbearance of my family, Sylvie and Nicholas, during many weekends and evening hours when I was lost to them.

A work of this nature requires extensive resources in materials on which to base the text. Dr. Don E. McAllister, Curator of Fishes from 1958 to 1986 in the Canadian Museum of Nature selflessly built up not only the fish collections but also its associated data bases including illustrations and colour slides, counts and measurements, books and an indexed collection of reprints on Canadian ichthyology. His efforts in this regard and his continuing encouragement made this book a lighter task. Don also taught me to plough ahead regardless of the petty irritations of administrative life.

The staff in the Ichthyology Section at the museum carried the load of daily work in their usual efficient fashion. My thanks to Jadwiga Frank, Sylvie Laframboise, Alison Murray and Michèle Steigerwald for allowing me to bury myself in my office.

Henry Waszczuk and Italo Labignan of Canadian Sportfishing Productions have contributed doubly. They share their expert sportfishing knowledge in the points found under the gamefish entries. And second, their marketing ability allowed this project to be actually realized after spending two years on the shelf — thanks, Henry and Italo.

Dr. Claude B. Renaud proved to be a masterly committee man, pacifying and coordinating various groups involved in planning and executing the move of both Ichthyology and Herpetology to new quarters. Without his intercession the writing of this book could not have been completed on time. Claude also enlivened breaks by his stories replete with those gesticulations so foreign to the English soul but beloved of the Latin races. His advice on interpersonal relationships was ignored but proved a great tension reliever.

As a hunt-and-peck typist I owe a debt of gratitude to Alison Murray who converted my oft illegible scribbles into a real manuscript. Elemae Lashley and Michèle Steigerwald also typed sections of text.

The staff of the Canadian Museum of Nature library did yeoman service in searching out books and papers and let out only a mild protest when my requests occupied 80% of their budget. Several thousand reprint request forms were filled out by the summer students of 1990, Andrew Cooper, Kelly Gannon, Ian Jones and Marc-André Olivier, who were kept to their task by Alison Murray.

Dr. Francis Cook, formerly Curator of Herpetology at the Canadian Museum of Nature, made an invaluable though intangible contribution to this book in many discussions on organisation, both personal and bureaucratic, and on a general philosophy of life.

Many people contributed to the text in a variety of ways, directing me to sources of information or of illustrations. It is not possible to list them all here but I would like to thank my father-in-law, M. Paul Pharand, for information on that quintessential Canadian fish, the fur-bearing trout.

The line illustrations of fishes were taken from a number of sources. The Ichthyology Section houses several hundred drawings by C. H. Douglas made from fishes in the collection. His patience in transforming battered specimens to scientifically accurate drawings, even of the dreaded flatfishes, is much appreciated. A further selection of drawings were loaned by the Division of Fishes, Department of Vertebrate Zoology, National Museum of Natural History, Washington through the kind help of Susan Jewett. Three hatchetfish species were taken from illustrations used by S. H. Wietzman and some drawings were from W. Gosline. Susan Laurie-Bourque cheerfully drew several hundred more for this book from a diverse array of sources. Her artistic talents and speed at producing the illustrations made the goal of illustrating all the fishes attainable. Various people gave permission for their drawings to be used as templates for re-drawing including, in no particular order, D. G. Smith, National Museum of Natural History, Washington, B. G. Nafpaktitis, University of Southern California, Los Angeles, A. Peden, Royal B.C. Museum, Victoria, E. Bertelsen, Zoologisk Museum, Copenhagen, E. B. Böhlke, Academy of Natural Sciences, Philadelphia, B. B. Collette, National Museum of Natural History, Washington, I. Nakamura, Kyoto University, Japan, D. Stein, NOAA, Silver Spring, Maryland, K. W. Able, Rutgers College, New Jersey, J. W. Orr, University of Washington, Washington, J. J. Govoni, NOAA, Beaufort, North Carolina, M. M. Leiby, Florida Department of Natural Resources, St. Petersburg, Florida, K. E. Carpenter and K. Richmond, FAO, Rome, J. E. McCosker, Steinhart Aquarium, San Francisco, California, J. T. Williams, National Museum of Natural History, Washington, D.C. M. Hénault, Ministère du Loisir, de la Chasse et de la Pêche, Mont-Laurier, Québec provided the slide of the spring cisco and D. Bodaly, Freshwater Institute, Department of Fisheries and Oceans, Winnipeg a slide of the Squanga whitefish.

The colour photographs were taken by several photographers and institutions and their permission to use this material is gratefully acknowledged. These were A. Peden, Royal B.C. Museum, Victoria, Bernard P. Hanby, Vancouver, British Columbia, D. Methven, Memorial University of Newfoundland, St. John's, St. Andrews Biological Station, Department of Fisheries and Oceans, New Brunswick (with thanks to F. Cunningham), the Freshwater Institute, Department of Fisheries and Oceans, Winnipeg, Manitoba (with thanks to J. Johnson), James M. Haynes, Department of Biological Sciences, State University of New York, College at Brockport, New York, L. Bernatchez, then of the Department of Zoology, University of Guelph, Ontario, T. Hurlbut, Department of Fisheries and Oceans, Moncton, New Brunswick, E. Snucins, Laurentian University, Sudbury, Ontario, S. Muldal, Kingston, Ontario, R. Semple, Waverly, Nova Scotia, G. Power, University of Waterloo, Ontario, R. John Gibson, Fisheries and Oceans, St. John's, Newfoundland and the slide collection of the Canadian Museum of Nature.

The staff of the Publishing Division, Canadian Museum of Nature, Bonnie Livingstone, Helen Meubus and Dawn Arnold, carried the load of managing this project, sparing me the details of contracts and budgets. They shepherded me through the publishing process so efficiently that few bleats of authorial protest were heard from me.

Bibliography

There is an immense literature on fishes, much of it highly technical and found in scientific journals. The books listed below are a small selection relevant to Canada.

Bernatchez, L. and M. Giroux. 1991. *Guide des poissons d'eau douce du Québec.* Broquet, La Prairie. xxiv + 304 pp.

Boschung, H. T., J. D. Williams, D. W. Gotshall, D. K. Caldwell and M. C. Caldwell. 1983. *The Audubon Society Field Guide to North American Fishes, Whales, and Dolphins.* Alfred A. Knopf, New York. 848 pp.

Coad, B. W. 1992. *Guide to the Marine Sport Fishes of Atlantic Canada and New England.* University of Toronto Press, Toronto. xiii + 307 pp. (also available in French as *Guide des poissons marins de pêche sportive de l'Atlantique canadien et de la Nouvelle-Angleterre.* Broquet, La Prairie. xii + 400 pp.).

Eschmeyer, W. N. and E. S. Herald. 1983. *A Field Guide to Pacific Coast Fishes of North America from the Gulf of Alaska to Baja California.* Houghton Mifflin Company, Boston (Peterson Field Guide Series 28). xii + 336 pp.

Fedoruk, A. N. 1971. *Freshwater Fishes of Manitoba: Checklist and Keys.* Department of Mines, Resources and Environmental Management, Manitoba. 130 pp.

Hart, J. L. 1973. *Pacific Fishes of Canada.*

Bulletin of the Fisheries Research Board of Canada, 180:ix + 740 pp.

Hubbs, C. L. and K. F. Lagler. 1964. *Fishes of the Great Lakes Region.* The University of Michigan Press, Ann Arbor. xv + 213 pp.

International Game Fish Association. 1990. *World Record Game Fishes.* International Game Fish Association, Fort Lauderdale, Florida. 336 pp.

Lee, D. S., C. R. Gilbert, C. H. Hocutt, R. E. Jenkins, D. E. McAllister and J. R. Stauffer. 1980. *Atlas of North American Freshwater Fishes.* North Carolina State Museum of Natural History, Raleigh. x + 854 pp.

McAllister, D. E. 1990. *A List of the Fishes of Canada/Liste des Poissons du Canada.* Syllogeus, Ottawa, 64:1-310.

McAllister, D. E. and B. W. Coad. 1974. *Fishes of Canada's National Capital Region/Poissons de la région de la capitale du Canada.* Fisheries Research Board of Canada, Miscellaneous Special Publication, 24:1-200.

McAllister, D. E. and E. J. Crossman. 1973. *A Guide to the Freshwater Sport Fishes of Canada.* National Museum of Natural Sciences, Natural History Series, 1:xi + 89 pp.

McAllister, D. E., V. Legendre and J. G. Hunter. 1987. *Liste des noms inuktitut (esquimaux), français, anglais et scien-tifiques des poissons marins du Canada Arctique/List of Inuktitut (Eskimo), French, English and scientific names of marine fishes of Arctic Canada.* Canadian Manuscript Report of Fisheries and Aquatic Sciences, 1932:v + 106 pp.

McPhail, J. D. and C. C. Lindsey. 1970. *Freshwater Fishes of Northwestern Canada and Alaska.* Bulletin of the Fisheries Research Board of Canada, 173:1-381.

Nelson, J. S. 1994. *Fishes of the World.* 3rd Edition. John Wiley and Sons, New York. xvii + 600 pp.

Nelson, J. S. and M. J. Paetz. 1992. *The Fishes of Alberta.* 2nd Edition. University of Alberta and University of Calgary Presses. xxvi + 437 pp.

Page, L. M. and B. M. Burr. 1991. *A Field Guide to Freshwater Fishes North America North of Mexico.* Houghton Mifflin Company, Boston (Peterson Field Guide Series 42). xii + 432 pp.

Robins, C. R., R. M. Bailey, C. E. Bond, J. R. Brooker, E. A. Lachner, R. N. Lea, and W. B. Scott. 1991. *Common and Scientific Names of Fishes from the United States and Canada.* Fifth Edition. American Fisheries Society Special Publication, 20:1-183.

Robins, C. R. and G. C. Ray. 1986. *A Field Guide to the Atlantic Coast Fishes of North America.* Houghton Mifflin Company, Boston (Peterson Field Guide Series 32). xi + 354 pp.

Scott, W. B. and E. J. Crossman. 1973. *Freshwater Fishes of Canada.* Bulletin of the Fisheries Research Board of Canada, 184:xi + 966 pp. (1979 reprint with sup-plements).

Scott, W. B. and M. G. Scott. 1988. *Atlantic Fishes of Canada.* Canadian Bulletin of Fisheries and Aquatic Sciences, 219:xxx + 731 pp.

Glossary of Technical Terms

A

abbreviate heterocercal
a type of tail or caudal fin where the vertebrae extend only a short distance into the upper fin lobe. The upper fin lobe is longer than the lower lobe. Found in the **Gar** and **Bowfin** families for example.

abdominal
pertaining to the abdomen. The pelvic fins have an abdominal fin position when found on the abdomen and remote from the pectoral fins.

abdominal cavity
the part of the body containing the viscera or guts, liver, ovaries, testes, kidneys, etc.

abdominal pores
external openings near the vent communicating with the abdominal cavity (see **Bonefish Order**). Also present in **hagfishes, lampreys** and **sharks.**

abyssal plain
the ocean floor below 3660 metres.

AC
a series of ventro-lateral photophores extending between a vertical at the anal fin origin and the end on the caudal peduncle. The AC row may begin posterior to the anal fin origin if it is offset from other ventro-lateral photophores.

accessory lateral line
a branch of the lateral line in certain **flatfishes** originating at the head and extending along the upper flank near the base of the dorsal fin.

accessory male
a male fish which attempts to fertilise eggs of a breeding female at the expense of a dominant male.

acrodin
tissue forming a cap on teeth found in **rayfinned fishes.**

adductor mandibulae

muscles which act to close the mouth.

adenohypophysis
part of the pituitary organ of the lower brain involved in hormone control.

adhesive disc
a sucker; found on the head of **Remora Family** members and modified from dorsal fin rays, or on the belly of, e.g., **Goby** and **Snailfish Family** members and modified from the pelvic fins.

adhesive head gland
an organ near the mouth of larvae used to attach larvae to the substrate. Found in members of the **Sturgeon, Gar** and **Pike** families for example. Sometimes called an adhesive disc.

adipose eyelid
transparent membranes over the anterior and posterior parts of the eye, e.g. in **Bonefish, Herring, Mackerel**, and **Mullet** families.

adipose fin
a small, tab-like fin on the back behind the dorsal fin. It is fleshy and lacks rays and spines. See also ventral adipose fin.

aestivate
the ability to remain dormant in the dry season. See **bowfin** and **Bowfin Family**.

aglomerular kidney
lacking glomeruli, capillaries which filter water and waste from the bloodstream. Found in some members of the **Stickleback Order.**

alar spines
see alar thorns.

alar thorns
large spines near the tips of the upper surface of the pectoral fins of male **Skate Family** members.

alarm substance
a chemical released from specialised skin cells in members of the **Carp Order** when the fish is injured. The chemical stimulates

the fright reaction, and warns other fishes of the presence of predators.

alevin
a newly-hatched fish with a yolk-sac. The young fish develops directly into a juvenile without going through post-larval stages, e.g. members of the **Salmon Family.**

all-female species
the production and survival of a clone by gynogenesis, e.g. in the **northern redbelly dace** and **Livebearer Family.**

alveolar
pitted, honeycomb-like.

ambicoloration
pigmentation on both the eyed and blind sides of **flatfishes** which normally have only the upper (or eyed side) pigmented.

ammocoete
the larval stage of **lampreys** characterised by the absence of teeth, disc and eyes, and presence of an oral hood.

ampullae of Lorenzini
jelly-filled canals on the snout and head of **sharks** and **rays** which are involved in electroreception.

anadromous
said of fishes which spawn in fresh water but spend part of their life in the sea, e.g. **Salmon Family** members. The opposite is catadromous.

anaerobic
without oxygen.

anal fin
the fin behind the vent on the lower, rear part of the body. There may be two anal fins in some fishes.

anal papilla
a fleshy protuberance before the anal fin through which the end of the intestine passes. Well-developed in some members of the **Sculpin Family.**

angular
a bone forming the posterior part of the lower jaw.

ankylosed
fusion of bones, e.g. of teeth to the jaw bones.

annual fish
a fish species which lives out its life as an adult in less than one year, e.g. certain non-Canadian members of the **Killifish Order.** Adults spawn in the rainy season, die, and only the eggs survive the dry season buried in mud to hatch in the next rainy season.

Ant
a photophore at the antero-dorsal margin of the orbit.

anterior
in front of; towards the front (opposite of posterior).

anus
the posterior opening of the digestive system through which faeces are voided.

AO
the anal photophores, a series of light organs above the anal fin base and along the lower caudal peduncle.

AOa
anterior photophores in the AO row, above the anal fin base.

AOp
posterior photophores in the AO row, on the caudal peduncle.

area temporalis
an area of high resolution in the retina of the eye, e.g. see **Herring Family.**

articular process
a projection of the upper border of the premaxilla acting as a fulcrum for the protrusion of the maxilla.

attendant male
a male which is not the member of the spawning pair; often a sneaky male.

auditory capsule
the skeleton about the ear; also called the otic capsule.

auditory region
the area around the ear.

autopalatine
a bone on the roof of the mouth, one on each side of the vomer. Also called palatine.

axil
the angle between the upper side of the pectoral or pelvic fins and the body.

axillary scale
a scale found at the base or axil of the pectoral or pelvic fins. It may serve to streamline the fin.

B

bar seine
nets used to close off a small cove so that fish can be taken out with a small seine.

barb
another term for spinules, e.g. in the **Sculpin Family.**

barbel
    a thin, fleshy appendage near the mouth used for touch or taste senses.

basal
    a bone in the body supporting the posterior rays at the end of a dorsal or anal fin.

basibranchial
    median bones at the base of the gill arches.

basihyal
    the anterior and median bone of the basi-branchial series joining the hyoid arch branches and forming the tongue skeleton in **teleosts.**

basioccipital
    a deep median bone at the posterior end of the parasphenoid on the underside of the skull. The first vertebra articulates with the basioccipital.

basisphenoid
    a deep skull bone which lies above the parasphenoid and medial to the pterosphe-noids, forming part of the floor of the neu-rocranium.

batch spawner
    a fish which sheds eggs more than once through a spawning season rather than within a short period (= fractional spawner, q.v.).

Batesian mimicry
    the condition where a rare species closely resembles a common and distasteful species and thus escapes being eaten as it deceives predators.

bathypelagic
    pertaining to deep midwaters between 1000 and 6000 metres.

benthic
    bottom dwelling.

benthopelagic
    pertaining to fishes which swim just above the sea bed.

beryciform foramen
    an opening in the ceratohyal of uncertain function.

bicuspid
    teeth having two points or cusps.

bill
    see rostrum.

bioluminescence
    the production of light by living organisms using a chemical reaction.

biomass
    the weight of living material in a given area, sample, or for a given species.

blade
    the anterior dorsal fin rays fused into a blade-like structure in members of the **Silver Hatchetfish Family**.

bone
    a hard supporting tissue made up of cells, fibres, and calcium and phosphate salts, c.f. cartilage.

bottom trawl
    a net shaped like a bag which is dragged along the sea bed.

BR
    photophores along the lower jaw or on the branchiostegal rays.

branchial
    relating to the gills.

branchial basket
    a network skeleton in **Lamprey Order** and **Chimaera Order** members supporting the gill region.

branchiostegal membrane
    the membrane below the operculum which helps enclose the gill chamber. This membrane is separate when the two sides are not joined to each other or the isthmus beneath the head. It is united and free from the isthmus when both sides are joined with each other and have a narrow or wide margin posteriorly which is unattached to the isthmus. It is joined when both sides fuse to the isthmus without a free posterior margin.

branchiostegal rays
    the curved, strut-like skeletal supports for the branchiostegal membranes.

breast
    the area anterior to the abdomen on the ventral surface of the fish.

breeding tubercles
    epidermal structures, often keratinised, on the head, body and fins which function to maintain contact between sexes during spawning, to defend territory and nests against the same and other species, to stimulate females during courtship and possibly for sex and species recognition. The tubercles develop during the spawning season and are shed afterwards. They are found in **Salmon, Carp** and **Perch Order** members. Also called nuptial tubercles.

brood pouch
    a groove supplied with blood vessels and formed by skin flaps on the underside of the tail in male **Pipefish Family** members. The eggs develop in the brood pouch. Also called marsupium.

buckler
a bony shield or scute.

bulb
the rounded swelling forming the main body of the esca or bait at the end of the illicium or fishing rod in members of the **Anglerfish Order.**

bulla
a bony projection or swelling of the skull.

by-catch
fishes caught incidental to a fishery for a commercially important species.

C

cancellous
spongy, porous or reticulate bone, e.g. in **anglerfishes.**

canine teeth
large, pointed teeth; usually few in number.

cannibalism
eating members of one's own species.

carapace
a bony shield covering the back as in members of the **Boxfish Family.**

cardioid scales
scales with notches on the posterior margin, e.g. in members of the **Pike Family.**

cartilage
a flexible supporting tissue made up of cells and fibres but low in calcium and phosphate salts. Also known as gristle, c.f. bone.

caruncle
fleshy knob.

catadromous
said of fish which spawn in the sea but spend most of their life in fresh water, e.g. the **American eel.**

caudal fin
the tail fin. See also abbreviate heterocercal, diphycercal, gephyrocercal, heterocercal, homocercal and hypocercal.

caudal peduncle
the part of the body between the end of the anal fin and the base of the tail fin; the tail stem.

centrum (pl. centra)
the central body of each vertebra.

cephalic fin
a flap-like, fleshy appendage of the pectoral fin found on each side of the mouth in the **manta.**

ceratobranchial
a long, deep bone of the middle part of the gill arches between the epibranchials and hypobranchials. It may bear pharyngeal teeth. There are usually 5 pairs of ceratobranchials.

ceratohyal
a deep bone of the hyoid arch between the hypohyal and the epihyal.

ceratotrichia
part of the fin skeleton in **cartilaginous fishes.** Used to make shark fin soup.

characters
structures and other features like colour used to distinguish and describe species, families, orders, etc.

cheek
the area between the eye and the preoperculum.

chest
the anterior part of the ventral surface of a fish just behind the head.

chum (chumming)
cut up fish or meat mixed with blood and garbage and used to attract fishes, such as **sharks,** to a fishing area (the act of spreading chum in the water).

ciguatera
a form of poisoning from eating fish which may have consumed a poisonous alga. The fish are usually tropical, marine fishes. A particularly dangerous poisoning because of its unpredictable occurrence; a given fish species may be safe to eat one year and not the next, safe on one side of an island but not the other. Mortality is high.

circadian
pertaining to a daily and rhythmic biological cycle.

circuli (sing. circulus)
the concentric rings on the scales.

circumorbital bone
one of a series of dermal bones around the eye.

cirrus (pl. cirri)
fringe-like, fleshy appendages.

claspers
finger-like extensions of the pelvic fins of male **sharks** and **rays** used to deliver sperm to the female but not for holding as the name suggests. Also called myxopterygia.

class
the group above order and below phylum in classification.

clavicular spine
a spine in the shoulder region.

clavus
a rudder-like lobe at the end of the body in
the **Mola Family.**

cleaner
a fish which picks dead tissue and parasites
off other fishes. Cleaner fish may establish a
cleaning station and have a particular behaviour which clues other fishes into their function and prevents them from being eaten.

cleithral head spine
see head spines.

cleithrum
the main, dermal, L-shaped bone of the pectoral girdle.

cloaca
the vestibule into which empty the urogenital and digestive systems and which opens
to the exterior, usually in front of the anal
fin.

clone
a group of descendants of the same genetic
constitution; see gynogenesis.

club cells
specialised, club-shaped cells in the epidermis which produce, e.g., pheromones in
members of the **Carp Order.**

cod trap
a pound net designed to capture cod.

coelom
abdominal cavity or body cavity containing
the guts, gonads, kidneys, etc.

commensal
a member of one species living in close
association with a member of a different
species, benefiting one but not harming the
other, or benefiting both.

"complex"
a convenient term used to recognise a group
of closely related species which have not
yet been adequately distinguished by scientists.

compressed
flattened from side to side. The opposite is
depressed.

condyle
the articulating surface of a bone.

contact organ
dermal bony outgrowths from a fin ray or
scale margin in males; used in tactile contact with females during spawning, e.g. in
the **mummichog.**

continental shelf
the gently sloping and shallow waters near
the coast where most fisheries occur.

continental slope
the steep slope connecting the ocean basins
with the shallow continental shelf waters.
Also called the continental rise.

conus arteriosus
a part of the heart structure.

coprolite
fossil faecal matter.

coronal head spine
see head spines.

corselet
enlarged scales behind the pectoral fin in
members of the **Mackerel Family.**

cottoid bubblemorph
a large space under the skin in larvae of the
Snailfish Family; it may help to maintain
buoyancy.

counter-current heat exchanger
the mechanism of blood vessels where heat
is exchanged between those vessels going
to the skin and gills with those vessels
going to the deep body tissues.

countershading
the typical pigmentation pattern of fishes,
dark above and light below. The effect is to
obscure the image of the fish to predators
by blending with the dark sea floor when
viewed from above, the light sky when
viewed from below, and with the general
diffused pattern of light when viewed from
the side.

cranium
the skull.

crenate
scalloped.

crenulate
minutely scalloped.

crest
a ridge, usually on the middle of the top of
the head.

crumenal organ
an organ of the epibranchial region which is
formed as a pair of pouches involving the
last two gill arches and the anterior oesophagus found in some members of the **Smelt
Order.**

ctenoid scale
a scale with small spines or ctenii on the
posterior part giving the fish a rough feel-
ing; found mainly in **spiny-rayed fishes.**

cusp
point as on a tooth or spine.

cusplet
a small or secondary cusp; also a denticle.

cycloid scale
  a smooth-edged scale without spines; found mainly in **soft-rayed fishes**.

D

Danish seine
  a seine which is hauled to a stationary vessel, the towing ropes disturbing clouds of mud which help herd the fish into the net.

. deciduous
  easily detached.

demersal
  living on or near the bottom.

dentary
  the dermal bone on each side forming much of the lower jaw.

denticle
  a small scale in the skin; also called placoid scale or dermal denticle. Sometimes used for cusplet.

denticular teeth
  specialised teeth which may lie outside the mouth on the snout and lower jaw in male **anglerfishes** and which are used to attach to the female.

depressed
  flattened from top to bottom, e.g. **Skate Family** members. The opposite is compressed.

dermal bone
  any of the superficial bones overlying the deeper skull bones. They arise directly from connective tissue rather than from cartilage.

dermal folds
  flaps distinct from the pectoral fin on the side of the head in the **Pacific angel shark**.

dermopalatine
  a dermal bone overlying the autopalatines, e.g. in members of the **Sturgeon Order**.

diel vertical migration
  a daily vertical migration.

dimethyl sulphide
  a harmless chemical contaminant of **Atlantic mackerel**, derived from eating pelagic snails. It gives an odour of petroleum products.

dip-net
  a fine- or large-meshed, rounded or square net on the end of a pole.

diphycercal
  a tail fin which is both internally and externally symmetrical, e.g. in **longnose chimaera**.

directed fishery
  a commercial effort aimed at catching a certain species.

disc
  the circular body of **rays;** the area surrounding the mouth of **lampreys.** See also adhesive disc.

distal
  away from the centre of the body or point of attachment.

diurnal
  pertaining to a day; daily.

Dn
  a photophore above and in front of the eye and above the olfactory capsule.

dominant
  used to describe a male fish which is the chief spawner and which endeavours to exclude other males from the spawning act.

dorsal
  of or pertaining to the back.

dorsal fins
  the fins on the midline of the back. There may be up to three of these.

DNA
  deoxyribonucleic acid, the chemical basis of heredity.

drift fishing
  using a series of gill nets which are allowed to drift in the open ocean.

duct
  any tube-like structure.

E

ear flap
  the fleshy and bony extension of the postero-dorsal tip of the operculum in members of the **Sunfish Family**.

ectopterygoid
  a deep dermal bone in the roof of the mouth.

egg case
  the keratinous egg shell of **sharks** and **rays.**

egg raft
  a supporting structure of various shapes and dimensions which carries eggs, e.g in the **sargassumfish**.

electro-shocker
  a device generating an electrical current used to paralyse or kill fish and facilitate their capture.

electrophoresis
  the movement and separation of chemicals in a fluid medium under electrical stimulation. Used to determine the chemical content of fishes and other organisms and

thereby to distinguish and relate them.

elver
young, transparent but round **eels.**

emarginate
having a slightly concave edge; often used to describe a shallowly forked tail fin.

endopterygoid
a paired dermal bone articulating with the palatine and ectopterygoid.

endostyle
a groove lined with cilia on the ventral pharynx wall, producing mucus to gather food particles, e.g. in the ammocoete larva of **lampreys.**

entopterygoid
see endopterygoid.

epibranchial
a deep bone on the upper part of each of the gill arches below the pharyngobranchial bone and above the ceratobranchial bone.

epifauna
organisms on the sea bed.

epihyal
a deep bone at the upper end of the hyoid arch below the interhyal, joining the hyomandibular and symplectic.

epineural
a thin, elongate bone in the muscles of the back, sloping backwards from the neural arch and spine.

epiotic bone
a bone forming the upper part of the otic or auditory capsule.

epipelagic
living in surface waters, down to about 200 metres.

epipleural intermuscular bone
one of a series of bones found inbetween the upper and lower muscle masses of the body, e.g in the **Bony-tongue Order.**

epural
an elongate bone, detached from other elements of the caudal fin skeleton, which supports the upper fin rays.

esca
the structure on the end of the illicium in the **Anglerfish Order.** It serves as a lure and may be worm-like, fish-like or luminous.

eutrophic
a highly productive, shallow, plant-fringed lake which usually has low oxygen levels in deeper water because of vegetation decay. Eutrophication is a natural aging process of lakes but becomes accelerated when man-made chemicals such as phosphates are introduced from farming runoff and sewage.

exoccipital
one of a pair of deep bones at the rear end of the cranium beside the opening for the connection of the brain and spinal cord.

exocrine pancreas
a well-defined organ which secretes enzymes into the digestive tract by means of a duct.

exotic species
a species not native to the habitat where it has become established. Exotics are usually from a completely different fauna and may carry diseases and parasites which native fish have no resistance to, be major predators on native species, or compete for habitat and food.

expatriate
a fish which has been removed from its usual habitat, e.g. by a current, to an environment where it cannot reproduce.

eye spot
a pigmentation pattern resembling an eye; often functions to distract or confuse predators. Also called an ocellus.

F

falcate
sickle-shaped.

family
a group of closely related genera.

fang
a long, sharp tooth.

fatty eyelid
adipose eyelid.

filter feeder
a fish that obtains small particles of food by filtering them out of the water, usually with numerous, elongate and fine gill rakers.

fin rays
cartilaginous or bony rod-like supports of fins.

finfold
the median body wall folds in members of the **Hagfish Family** and also the supposed origin of paired fins in other fishes.

fingerling
an immature fish, less than one year old.

finlets
small fins on the caudal peduncle; notably in members of the **Mackerel Family.**

fins
> see also under adipose, anal, caudal, dorsal, pectoral, pelvic, and ventral adipose fins. Fins are flap-like external organs used in steering, balance, propulsion and behaviour. They are composed of fatty tissue (hence adipose) or of rays separated by membranes. The rays may be stiffened into spines or flexible and branched, when they are known as soft rays. Median fins include the dorsal, adipose, caudal and anal fins while paired fins are the pectoral and pelvic fins.

fishing apparatus
> a mechanism for attracting prey close to the mouth in members of the **Anglerfish Order** formed from dorsal fin spines modified into a fishing rod (illicium) with a lure (esca) at the tip.

fish meal
> ground-up fish used as fertiliser or as an ingredient in foods.

flexion
> a stage in larval development which is often accompanied by rapid fin ray development, change in body shape, ability to move and a change in feeding method.

fontanelle
> a gap between bones in the skull closed by a membrane, e.g. in certain members of the **Sucker Family**.

foramen (pl. foramina)
> a small opening.

fork length
> the distance from the anteriormost tip of the body to the innermost part of the fork of the tail fin. Abbreviated as FL.

fractional spawning
> release of eggs at intervals, usually over several days or weeks. This allows more, smaller and immature eggs to be carried in a limited abdominal cavity space as the intervals enable the smaller eggs time to mature; and once shed, eggs mature at different times and thus may avoid complete loss of a season's spawning to predators (= batch spawner).

frenum
> the tissue joining the lip to the tip of the jaw, e.g. in certain members of the **Carp Family** on the upper jaw and in certain members of the **Surfperch Family** on the lower jaw. A frenum prevents the jaw from being projected outwards.

fright reaction
> wriggling, darting and other movements of **Carp Order** members in response to scenting alarm substance released from injured skin of their own or a related species. These movements serve to warn of or confuse a predator.

frontal
> a superficial, paired dermal bone on top of the skull above the eyes.

fulcral spine or fulcrum
> unsegmented, unbranched rays in front of the dorsal, anal, and caudal fins found in **sturgeons, gars, bowfin** and **tapirfishes.**

fyke net
> a bag-shaped fish trap with funnels which direct the fish into successive compartments. Fish are deflected towards the mouth of the bag by nets set obliquely on either side of the mouth.

G

ganoid scale
> a scale with a thick outer layer of ganoine, an enamel-like substance, and an inner bony layer. Often rhomboidal in shape, e.g. in the **Gar** and **Bowfin** families.

gas bladder
> a sac in the upper part of the body cavity of bony fishes containing a mixture of gases and often used to adjust the vertical position of a fish in the water by varying the gas content. Also called swimbladder.

genital palp or papilla
> a small fleshy projection behind the anus through which eggs and sperm pass, e.g. in the **brook silverside**, members of the **Sculpin Family**.

genus (pl. genera)
> the category below family. Each genus may contain several species which are more closely related to one another than to species in other genera. The genus is the first word (always capitalised) of the scientific name.

gephyrocercal fin
> a symmetrical tail fin where the original fin has been lost, e.g. in the **Mola Family**.

gill arches
> the skeletal support of the gill filaments and gill rakers.

gill cover
> the operculum, the bones and tissues covering the gills on the side of the head.

gill filaments
the blood-infused structures of the gills which take up oxygen from the water and give off waste carbon dioxide.

gill membrane
the tissue forming the lower wall of the gill chamber, supported by the branchiostegal rays. Usually called the branchiostegal membrane.

gill net
a net which is hung in the water like a curtain and which catches fish by entangling them around the gills when the head is pushed through.

gill opening
the single opening on the side of the head which allows inhaled water to exit after passing over the gills.

gill pouch
the internal chambers containing the gills in, e.g., **hagfishes.**

gill rakers
bony projections on the inner side of the gill which strain or retain food from inhaled water. Counts of gill rakers are used to identify some fishes, the count being of the upper arm rakers, lower arm rakers or total rakers.

gill slits
the series of openings on the head of **sharks** and **rays** which allow inhaled water to exit after passing over the gills.

glacial relict
a relict isolated by events associated with one of the glacial periods when much of Canada was ice-covered and fishless.

glass eel
see elver.

gonopodium
specialised rays at the front of the anal fin of males used to transfer sperm to the female, e.g. in the **mosquitofish** and **kelp perch.**

grilse
immature members of the **Salmon Family** returning to spawn for the first time.

gular plate
a dermal bone between the lower jaws on the underside of the head, e.g. in the **bowfin.**

guyot
a flat-topped seamount or submarine mountain.

gynogenesis
production of only female young. Eggs in the female are stimulated to develop by sperm from a male of the same or a closely related species but the male makes no genetic contribution, e.g. in the **Livebearer Family** and the **northern redbelly dace.**

gyre
in fisheries science used for a circular current.

H

hadal zone
pertaining to that part of the ocean below 6000 metres (referring to its proximity to hell).

haemal spine
a spine extending downwards from the posterior or caudal vertebrae.

handline
a line with baited hooks on short side lines usually laid on the bottom and set and hauled by hand.

head canals
the extension of the lateral line system on the head. The canals open to the surface through pores and contain neuromasts. The canals may be lost and the neuromasts are exposed.

head clasper
a spiny, knob-like structure in male members of the **Chimaera Order** used to grasp females during copulation.

head crest
a raised ridge on the head, e.g. in **pricklebacks.**

head flaps
see cephalic fins.

head gland
see adhesive head gland.

head spines
spines on the head of **Scorpionfish Family** members—they are illustrated in the Introduction. They are, from anterior to posterior over the top of the head on each side, the nasal, preocular, supraocular, postocular, tympanic, coronal (medial to the tympanic and postocular spines), parietal, and nuchal. Opercular spines are at the postero-dorsal corner of the operculum, preopercular spines line the posterior margin of the preopercula, and the cleithral, supracheithral and postcleithral spines are just above the opercular spines on the side of the head.

heat-exchanger
see counter-current heat exchanger.

hepatic float
the oil-rich liver of **sharks** which functions to give buoyancy.

hermaphrodite
having both ovarian and testicular tissue in one individual, i.e. both female and male reproductive organs. Eggs and sperm are not necessarily produced simultaneously.

heterocercal
a type of tail fin where the vertebral column turns upwards into the upper lobe which is usually longer than the lower lobe.

hibernium
an area or group of fishes for overwintering.

histamine
a chemical which can develop in the flesh of **Mackerel Family** members when these are left too long in the sun. It imparts a peppery taste and serves to warn of inedibility.

histology
the study of tissues.

holostyly
a type of jaw suspension where the upper jaw is fused to the skull, e.g. in the **Chimaera Order**.

homocercal
a type of tail fin where the vertebrae turn upwards but which is symmetrical when viewed externally.

hoop net
a fyke net mounted on hoops which help support the netting.

horny capsule
an egg case as in the **Skate Family**.

hyoid arch
the series of bones between the jaws and gill arches comprising the hyomandibular, symplectic, interhyal, epihyal, ceratohyal, and branchiostegal rays.

hyoid barbel
a barbel which hangs down from the hyoid region of the throat in members of the **Leftvent Family**.

hyomandibular
a deep, paired bone forming part of the hyoid arch.

hypocercal
a type of tail fin where the lower lobe is longer and contains the vertebrae. It is asymmetrical both internally and externally.

hypocoracoid
the coracoid, a bone in the pectoral girdle.

hypohyal
a deep bone in the hyoid arch.

hypural
a flattened bone at the base of the caudal fin supporting the fin rays.

I

IC
the entire, ventral row of photophores running from the anterior end of the isthmus to the posteriormost photophore on the caudal peduncle.

illicium
a modified spine of the first dorsal fin in members of the **Anglerfish Order** used as a mobile fishing rod to lure prey near the mouth.

included
contained, as in the lower jaw is included when the upper jaw extends over it.

infauna
organisms found in sea bed sediment.

inferior
below or ventral, often used in referring to the mouth being positioned on the lower surface of the head.

infracaudal luminous gland
a long, median and ventral gland on the caudal peduncle of some **Lanternfish Family** members.

infraoral lamina
a plate bearing teeth just below the mouth in members of the **Lamprey Family**.

infraorbital
one of a series of dermal bones below the eye, associated with the infraorbital canal.

infraorbital canal
the head canal running from behind the upper lip and below and behind the eye.

inquiline
an animal that lives in another animal.

insertion
the posterior end of a fin at a point closest to the body (opposite of origin).

interarcual cartilage
cartilage connecting the epibranchial bone of the first gill arch to the infrapharyngobranchial bone of the second gill arch.

intercalar
a bone forming the posterior wall of the otic or auditory capsule.

interhyal
a deep bone of the hyoid arch, joining the hyomandibular to the epihyal.

intermuscular bone
one of a series of bones lying between the muscle masses.

internal fertilisation
the deposition of sperm within the female by the male. Most fishes shed eggs and sperm to the outside so fertilisation is usually external.

internarial
between the nostrils.

internasal pores
pores between the nostrils, e.g. in the **northern madtom**.

interopercle
a dermal bone of the lower gill cover below the preoperculum and anterior to the suboperculum.

interorbital septum
a thin sheet of bone or cartilage lying vertically under the midline of the skull, separating the eyes.

intestinal valve
a fold in the intestine which increases surface area for processing food without lengthening the intestine. Found in sharks and sturgeons, for example. See also ring, scroll and spiral intestinal valves.

introgression
the spread of inherited characters between species by hybridisation.

intromittent fertilisation
internal fertilisation where the male deposits sperm in the female using a specialised structure such as the gonopodium.

isinglass
a transparent gelatin extracted from fish swimbladders. Used as a clarifier of wine and beer and in jams and jellies.

isocercal
see diphycercal.

isotherm
a line on a map connecting points of equal temperature.

isthmus
tissue between the gill openings on the lower surface of the head.

IV
a row of ventral photophores running from the anterior end of the isthmus to the origin of the pelvic fin.

J

jigger
a jig for fishing. Jigs are weighted hooks or hooked lures of various kinds which are jerked up and down in the water to attract and catch fish. Also an apparatus for setting gill nets under ice which bounces the end of the net from an entry hole to another hole a net's distance away.

jugal pitline
a character of **ray-finned fishes** where the jugal (or second suborbital bone) sensory canal is absent and represented by pitlines only.

jugostegalia
basket-like structure supporting the branchial chamber formed from numerous branchiostegal rays, e.g. in the **Snake Eel Family**.

jugular
of or pertaining to the throat region. Position of the pelvic fins when they lie in front of the pectoral fins on the throat.

K

keel
a ridge, often on the sides of the caudal peduncle or belly midline.

kelt
a member of the **Salmon Family** which has recently spawned; usually used for **Atlantic salmon.**

kinethmoid
correct term for the rostral bone, a median bone found in the antero-dorsal part of the ethmoidal region (between the nostrils) involved in jaw protrusion.

kype
the hooked and lengthened lower jaw in male **Salmon Family** members.

L

labial
pertaining to the lip, e.g. the labial furrow is a fold behind the mouth corner which provides slack skin for jaw protrusion in **sharks.**

lachrymal
the first and largest infraorbital bone, extending in front and below the anterior part of the orbit.

lamellae
a layer or thin plate, e.g. in the sucking disc on the head of **Remora Family** members.

laminae
lamellae.

laminar
blade-like.

lamphedrin
an anticoagulant fluid secreted by a gland in members of the **Lamprey Family**.

lampricide
a poison used to kill **lampreys.**

lanceolate
spear-shaped.

land-locked
living in waters shut off from the sea, or in waters with access to the sea though the fish are non-migrating populations.

larvae
young after hatching, usually different in appearance to the parents.

lateral
relating to the side or flanks.

lateral ethmoid
a paired deep bone in front of the orbit.

lateral line
a sense organ in a pored tube along the side of the body which detects movement, low frequency vibrations and temperature changes. The lateral line extends onto the head in a series of head canals.

lateral line organs
horseshoe-shaped structures left on the flank of **Lanternfish Family** members when the scales become detached. A lateral line organ count is often used in place of a scale count because scales are very deciduous in this family.

lateral line pores
openings of the lateral line organ along the side of the body. The lateral line may be completely pored from head to tail or interrupted.

lateral line scales
scales along the lateral line, a count of which is often used to identify species.

lateral series scales
a count of scales along the flank when the lateral line is absent or incompletely pored.

length
see fork, standard and total length.

lepidotrichia
fin rays, including spines.

leptocephali (sing. leptocephalus)
the transparent, leaf-like, compressed larvae of **Eel Order** members and their relatives.

lift-net
a net used to remove fishes from a ship or from a larger net.

light organ
structures producing light by a chemical reaction or by means of light-producing bacteria, e.g. in the **Lanternfish Family**.

limnetic
living in lakes between the surface and the bottom region.

littoral
shore waters, down to 200 metres in the sea or to the limit of rooted vegetation in lakes.

longline
a line up to several kilometres long with baited hooks at intervals. The longline may be anchored or may drift free, its position marked by a float or floats.

luciferase
an enzyme used in speeding up the production of light in bioluminescence.

lumen
the cavity of any organ, duct or sac.

lunate
crescent-shaped.

M

malar spines
spines found close to the edge of the disk in some male **Skate Family** members.

mandible
the lower jaw.

mandibular pores
pores of the head canal system on the undersurface of the lower jaw.

marsupium
a groove supplied with blood vessels and formed by skin flaps on the underside of the tail in male **Pipefish Family** members. The eggs develop in the marsupium. Also called brood pouch.

maxilla
a paired, dermal bone forming part of the upper jaw.

medial
towards the vertical plane running through the middle of the body.

median fins
the dorsal, adipose, caudal and anal fins. Also called vertical fins.

melanophore
a black chromatophore or dermal pigment cell. Expansion and contraction of pigment within the cell effects the darkness or lightness of the body structure.

mental crest
a crest on the chin, e.g. in the **bigfin eelpout.**

meristic character
    a countable character which is serially
    repeated, e.g. fin rays, vertebrae, scales.
mermaid's purse
    an egg case of **sharks** and **rays.**
mesethmoid
    the ethmoid, a deep bone anterior to the
    orbit between the olfactory capsules.
mesocoracoid
    a paired bone of the pectoral girdle.
mesopelagic
    pertaining to the poorly lighted midwaters
    between 200 and 1000 metres.
mesopterygoid
    see endopterygoid.
metamorphosis
    a marked change in the appearance and
    structure as between a leaf-like larval **eel**
    and the elongate, rounded adult.
metapterygium
    the posterior and innermost basal cartilage
    in the paired fins, modified into claspers in
    male **sharks** and **rays.**
metapterygoid
    a deep, paired bone forming part of the
    palatoquadrate.
mitochondrial DNA (mt DNA)
    a form of DNA, the chemical basis of
    heredity, found in the mitochondria (or
    energy producing structures within cells)
    and used to identify and relate fish species.
molariform
    large, flat, crushing or grinding teeth.
morphometric character
    a character based on measurement.
mouthbrooder
    see oral brooder.
Müllerian mimicry
    the condition where unpalatable species
    resemble each other, and are recognised and
    avoided by predators. The chance of being
    damaged by an uneducated predator is
    reduced by more than one species having
    the same appearance.
myelin
    white, fatty material covering nerves.
myodome
    a cavity in the skull where muscles insert,
    e.g. eye muscles.
myomere
    a lateral body segment muscle.
myoseptum (pl. myosepta)
    the tissue separating muscle blocks.
myxosporean or myxosporidian

protozoans which are parasites of cavities
and tissues of fishes, rendering them unsuitable for market.

N

nape
    the area behind the back and top of the
    head.
nasal
    a paired dermal bone usually enclosing the
    nostrils.
nasal capsule
    the structures enclosing the nostrils.
nasal head spine
    see head spines.
nasal lamellae
    flaps of tissue in the nostril.
nasal rosette
    the lamellae and associated elements of the
    nostril.
nasohypophysial opening
    an opening allowing water into the olfac-
    tory organ of **lampreys** and **hagfishes.**
    Found on top of the head in **lampreys** and
    in front of the head in **hagfishes.**
nephric myomeres
    in **eel** leptocephali, the number of
    myomeres or muscle blocks anterior to the
    end of the kidney is a diagnostic character.
nephros
    the kidney in leptocephali.
neural spine
    the spine on top of the vertebral neural arch
    which itself encloses the spinal cord.
neurocranium
    the part of the skull surrounding the brain;
    includes the olfactory (smell), optic (sight)
    and otic (auditory or hearing) capsules.
neuromast
    a sensory cell which detects motion or
    vibrations. The cell has a sensitive hair-like
    structure embedded in a gelatinous capsule.
    Neuromasts are enclosed in canals (e.g. lat-
    eral line), freely exposed or sunk in a pit on
    the skin surface, or in the inner ear.
neurotoxin
    a nerve toxin.
nictitating eyelid
    a membrane which covers the eye, an eye-
    lid, found particularly in **sharks.**
nocturnal
    pertaining to the night.

notochord
> a rod structure composed of a sheath enclosing tightly-packed cells. It lies below the nerve cord and may act as a skeletal support, e.g. in members of the **Hagfish Order.**

nuchal head spine
> see head spines.

nuchal thorns
> strong spines on the nape region in members of the **Skate Family**.

nuptial tubercles
> epidermal structures, often keratinised, on the head, body and fins which function to maintain contact between sexes during spawning, to defend territory and nests against the same and other species, to stimulate females during courtship and possibly for sex and species recognition. The tubercles develop during the spawning season and are shed afterwards. They are found in **Salmon, Carp** and **Perch Order** members. Also called breeding tubercles.

O

OA
> the upper, ventro-lateral row of photophores running above the ventral series from just behind the operculum to above the anal fin.

occipital
> a median bone on the surface of the back of the head.

occiput
> the rear end of the head.

oceanic
> pertaining to the sea, especially when depths exceed 200 metres, i.e. offshore.

ocellus (pl. ocelli)
> an eye spot, a dark mark surrounded by a lighter halo.

olfactory bulb
> a large organ of smell, e.g. in **sharks.**

oligotrophic
> a lake with low productivity, little shore vegetation, a deep and narrow basin, clear water and no shortage of oxygen.

OP
> photophores on the gill cover, one near the anterior base of the preopercle, one in front of the anterior part of the subopercle, and one antero-dorsally to the operculum.

opercle
> the principal dermal bone of the gill cover.

opercular flap
> see ear flap; also the fleshy edge of the whole gill cover.

opercular head spine
> see head spines.

opercular opening
> see gill opening.

opercular pumping
> sucking or blowing water through the mouth by means of lifting the operculum to create a suction mechanism. Used by some fishes to aerate their eggs.

operculum
> the main bone of the gill cover.

opisthocoelus
> vertebrae which have the centra concave posteriorly and convex anteriorly, e.g. in the **Gar Family**.

oral brooder
> a fish which broods or protects the young by taking them into the mouth.

oral hood
> lip extensions in the form of a scoop leading to the mouth in larval **lampreys.**

ORB
> photophores near the eye; one antero-ventral to the eye is called the suborbital (or preorbital) and one postero-ventrally is called the postorbital.

orbit
> the skull cavity which contains the eye; also used for the eye itself.

orbitosphenoid
> a deep, median or paired bone lying under the frontal bone.

order
> a group of closely related families.

oreosoma
> the young of members of the **Oreo Family**, having scutes or horny protuberances in a leathery skin, and thus unlike the adult.

origin
> the anterior end of the base of a fin.

osmoregulation
> maintenance of a proper balance of salts and water within an organism.

ostracitoxin
> a toxin secreted by members of the **Boxfish Family**. It affects blood cells and is not easily destroyed by heat.

otolith
> ear stones, small calcium carbonate structures lying in the inner ear of fishes. Used to detect changes in motion and gravity by

stimulation of sensory nerve cells as the fish moves.

otter trawl
a towed net which strains fish out of the water. Named for the otter boards on the tow ropes which serve to keep the mouth of the net open.

outlier male
a male **pink salmon** which is smaller than the dominant male, is coloured like a female, and maintains a position to one side of a spawning pair; in this fashion it is able to deposit sperm since the dominant male does not chase it away.

oviduct
a tube used to carry eggs away from the ovary.

oviparous
laying eggs from which the young hatch later.

ovipositor
a tubular extension of the female genital opening used to facilitate egg deposition.

ovoviviparous
eggs develop and hatch in the mother but do not feed at maternal expense. There may be some exchange of food and gases between the mother and embryo but there is no well-developed placental connection. Young are born as miniature, free-swimming adults, e.g. in **sharks.**

P

paired fins
the pectoral and pelvic fins. Other fins are called the vertical or median fins.

palate
the roof of the mouth.

palatine
one of a pair of bones on the roof of the mouth lateral to the vomer, often bearing teeth.

palatoquadrate
the functional upper jaw of **cartilaginous fishes** and the embryonic upper jaw of other **vertebrates.**

papilla
a fleshy protuberance.

parasitic males
small male members of the **Anglerfish Order** which live attached to the much larger female. Much of the body is degenerate and depends on the female blood supply for food. Gonads are well-developed.

parasphenoid
the median dermal bone running along the base of the skull behind the vomer.

parietal
a dermal paired bone covering the auditory region of the skull.

parietal head spine
see head spines.

parr
a young **Salmon Family** member before it migrates to the sea, having dark, almost oval blotches along the side.

parr marks
round to oval or pear-shaped dark blotches on the side of young **Salmon Family** members.

pearl tubercles
see nuptial tubercles.

pectoral fins
the paired fins on the side of the body just behind the gill opening or head.

pectoral girdle
the cartilage and bones supporting the pelvic fins and attaching them to the skeleton.

pectoral propterygium
the outer or anteriormost basal cartilage in the paired fins.

pectoral radials
bony or cartilaginous supports for the pectoral fin.

pelagic
living in open water above the bottom.

pelagic trawl
a net shaped like a bag which is dragged through open waters above the bottom.

pelvic fins
the paired fins on the belly. They may be abdominal (remote from the pectoral fins on the belly), thoracic (on the chest) or jugular (on the throat).

penis
male copulatory organ, e.g. in the **Livebearing Brotula Family**.

perianal organ
an organ near or surrounding the anus, e.g. in the **Greeneye Family.**

peritoneum (or peritoneal membrane)
a membrane covering the coelom and the organs within. It may be black, silvery, speckled or some other colour and is often used as a distinguishing character.

pH
a measure of the concentration of hydrogen

ions in a solution; pH 7.0 is neutral, lower values are acidic and higher values alkaline. Acid rain decreases the natural pH of rivers and lakes.

pharyngeal mill
molar teeth in the pharyngeal region used to crush shellfish, e.g. in the **Porgy Family**.

pharyngeal teeth
teeth on the pharyngeal bones. These may be a dorsal and ventral pair, or pairs laterally opposed to each other and working against a horny pad on the basioccipital bone, e.g in members of the **Carp** and **Sucker** families. Dorsal pharyngeal teeth are on the fourth pharyngobranchials and the lower on the fifth ceratobranchials. In **carps** and **suckers** the teeth are on the fifth ceratobranchials.

pharyngeal tooth formula
a means of expressing the number and arrangement of pharyngeal teeth used particularly in identifying members of the **Carp Family,** e.g. 2,5-4,1 means 2 outer, left row teeth, 5 inner, left row teeth, 4 inner, right row teeth and 1 outer, right row tooth. There may be one to three rows of teeth on each side, e.g. 5-5 or 1,3,4-4,3,1.

pharyngobranchial
the deep bone at the top of the gill arch, which may bear teeth and occur on arches 1 to 4.

pharynx
the part of the intestine between the mouth and the oesophagus.

pheromone
a chemical secreted by an organism which affects the behaviour of others of the same species.

photocytes
light-producing cells.

photophore
a light producing organ. There are various abbreviations for photophore positions, the arrangement of which and counts of photophores are used in identification - see AC, Ant, AO, AOa, AOp, BR, Dn, IC, IV, OA, OP, ORB, PLO, PO, Pol, Prc, PVO, SAO, So, SO, VAV, Vn, and VO and the illustrations in the Introduction.

physoclist
fish having no connection between the gut and gas bladder.

physostome
fish having a tube connecting the gut and gas bladder.

phytoplankton
plant members of the plankton.

pineal eye
a median, eye-like structure on the top of the head in members of the **Lamprey Family**. It develops from the pineal organ.

pineal organ
a light-sensitive part of the brain which influences behaviour and the melanophores.

placoid scale
thorn-shaped scales of **sharks** and **rays**; also called denticles. They consist of a spine and a rhomboidal basal plate.

plankton
small animals and plants living above the bottom in the water column. Fish eggs and larvae are often members of the plankton. Zooplankton are animal plankton and phytoplankton are plant plankton.

plates
any flattened structure, usually an external armament in certain fishes.

pleural rib
ribs lying just outside but close to the abdominal cavity.

plicae
small skin folds, e.g. in the lips of **suckers.**

PLO
a photophore above the base of the pectoral fin.

PO
a row of photophores on the breast in front of the pelvic fin.

Pol
one or more ventro-lateral photophores above the AO series which itself lies along the base of the anal fin.

polygynous
mating of one male with 2 or more females.

population
a local group of individuals which form a potentially interbreeding community.

post
behind; often used in measurements for identification, e.g. post-branchial - behind the gill region.

postcleithrum
a bone of the pectoral girdle behind the cleithrum.

posterior
behind; opposite of anterior.

postglacial lake
  a lake formed after a glaciation from melting ice; it often provides a route for fish migrations.

post-larva
  a larval fish after the yolk is absorbed when the structure is still unlike the juvenile. Post-larvae were often described as species distinct from the adult and these names are now used to describe the post-larval form, e.g. see oreosoma and tholichthys.

postocular head spine
  see head spines.

postorbital
  behind the orbit. Also refers to a bone in the series around the eye.

posttemporal
  a dermal bone connecting the pectoral girdle to the epiotic bone of the skull.

pot
  portable traps which fish enter through a small opening and from which they cannot readily escape.

pound net
  nets or fences set in streams or along the coast to direct fish into a holding container for easy removal.

Prc
  photophores on the lower half of the caudal peduncle at the caudal fin base.

pre
  before, anterior. Often used in measurements for identification, e.g. predorsal length.

preanal myomeres
  a count of the number of myomeres or muscle blocks before the anal fin in **eel** leptocephali. The count includes the myomere over the anus.

precaudal pit
  the notch on the caudal peduncle just anterior to the tail fin. Also called caudal pit.

predorsal
  before the dorsal fin. Also bones located between the head and dorsal fin above the vertebral column.

predorsal myomeres
  a count of the number of myomeres or muscle blocks before the dorsal fin in **eel** leptocephali. The count includes the myomere under the dorsal fin origin.

premaxilla
  a paired dermal bone at the anterior end of the upper jaw, often toothed.

prenasal
  an anterior dermal bone near the snout tip.

preocular head spine
  see head spines.

preopercular head spine
  see head spines.

preoperculomandibular canal
  the head canal running along the preoperculum and the lower jaw or mandible.

preoperculum
  an L-shaped dermal bone on the side of the head behind and below the eye and in front of the gill cover.

preorbital
  before the orbit. Also the first bone of the infraorbital series; the lachrymal.

preorbital spine
  a spine on the lachrymal bone.

prepectoral pores
  a count of pores before the pectoral fin used in identification of members of the **Eel Order**.

preural vertebra
  vertebra anterior to those vertebrae bearing hypurals.

prevomer
  a median or paired dermal bone in the roof of the mouth, often toothed. Also called vomer.

priapium
  a clasping and copulatory organ modified partly from the pelvic fins and found under the head in some exotic members of the **Silverside Order**.

pristane
  a hydrocarbon chemical in the liver oil of **sharks** used in manufacturing machine lubricants and skin softeners.

procurrent
  inclined forward.

pronephros
  a type of kidney with one pair of tubules for each body segment. Found in the anterior part of the abdominal cavity of **hagfishes,** some **teleosts** and embryos of other fishes.

prootic
  the anterior deep bone of the otic or auditory capsule.

protandrous hermaphrodite
  an individual which has initially testicular tissue then ovarian tissue (male becomes female).

protogynous hermaphrodite
  an individual which initially has ovarian tis-

sue then testicular tissue (female becomes male).

protractile
capable of being retracted.

protrusible
capable of being thrust out.

pseudobranch
a small gill on the inside of the gill cover. Also called the hemibranch or pseudo-branchia.

pseudocaudal fin
see gephyrocercal fin.

pterosphenoid
the paired deep bone over the skull and lying under the frontal.

pterotic
the paired deep bone and the dermal bone over it forming the lateral part of the skull between the parietal and hyomandibular bones. It also contacts the semicircular canals.

pterygiophore
the skeletal base of the fins inside the body.

pup
embryonic or young **shark.**

purse seine
a seine used to encircle a school of fish in open water. It is set at speed from a large, powered vessel and the other end of the net is held by a small boat.

PVO
photophores below the pectoral fin and above the PO series.

pyloric caeca
finger-like blind sacs attached to the junction of the stomach and the intestine which serve to aid in digestion.

Q

quadrate
a paired deep bone forming part of the palatoquadrate and acting as a pivot for the jaw suspension.

quincunx
an arrangement of five objects in a square with one in the middle.

R

r-selection
a life history strategy characterised by early maturity, rapid growth, large numbers of young produced at an early age, small body size, high mortality and short life span. This

strategy is an adaptation to an unpredictable environment such as that found in the Arctic.

radius (pl. radii)
grooves radiating out from the centre of a scale.

ram ventilation
the extraction of oxygen during the passage of water over the gills owing to motion through the water rather than active, muscular pumping. Used by the **sharksucker** when hitching a ride.

rays
dermal, rod-like and bilaterally paired supports of the fins. They are usually flexible, branched and segmented (soft rays) but ray may also be used to include the stiff, unbranched, unsegmented spines. Some soft rays are inflexible and resemble true spines. Rudimentary rays are short, unbranched and unsegmented rays found at the origin of fins. Ray counts (usually omitting rudimentary rays) are used in identification. Soft ray counts are usually given in the scientific literature as Arabic numerals and spines as Roman numerals.

recessus lateralis
a chamber of the neurocranium where the infraorbital and preopercular head canals meet; a characteristic of members of the **Herring Order**.

recruitment
the new members and/or the numbers of fishes born in a given year.

recurved
curved upwards.

redd
a nest made by **Salmon Family** members. Gravel is excavated by motions of the tail fin of the female to form a hollow for the eggs, which are then covered over by more gravel.

refugium (pl. refugia)
an isolated locality often surrounded by a different climate or habitat; often a centre for relicts.

relict
survivor of a nearly extinct group or a species surviving widely separated from its relatives.

residuals
members of a generally anadromous species which do not migrate but remain in fresh water and do not spawn, e.g. in **sockeye salmon**.

reticulate
having the appearance or form of a network.
retractor dorsalis
muscles associated with the pharyngeal jaws and used in swallowing food.
retrorse
turned backwards.
ring intestinal valve
an intestinal valve with a radius lower than that of the gut so the valve is internally open and some food can pass through without coming in contact with the valve.
rods
elongate, rod-shaped cells in the eye sensitive to dim light.
rostral bar
an anterior extension of the skull in some members of the **Skate Family**.
rostral cartilage
an element in the olfactory region skeleton.
rostrum
a snout-like extension of the head, e.g. in members of the **Electric Ray, Sturgeon, Paddlefish** and **Swordfish** families.

S

saddle
pigmentation straddling the back in the form of a saddle.
sagittal otolith
the largest otolith.
SAO
a sloping, ventro-lateral row of photophores above the anal fin origin.
sashimi
thin slices of raw fish, usually with soy sauce and green mustard; a Japanese delicacy.
satellite
a small male fish which mimics a female and attempts to sneak a spawning opportunity by darting in on an adult spawning pair, e.g. in **pumpkinseeds.**
satellite species
the condition found in **lampreys** where a non-parasitic species is believed to have evolved from most parasitic species, forming a series of species pairs.
scales
see cycloid, ctenoid and placoid scales. Scales form an overlapping protective covering to the body and sometimes to the head and fins.

scapular thorns
thorns on the shoulder region (each side of the anterior midline of the body) in members of the **Skate Family**.
scapulo-coracoid
a region of the pectoral girdle skeleton in **ray-finned fishes**.
Schreckstoff
see alarm substance.
scientific name
the name in Latin of an animal or plant used by scientists. It consists of two words, the genus name and the species or trivial name, e.g. *Squalus acanthias*, the spiny dogfish. Convention demands that this name be underlined, italicised, in bold face or in some other fashion distinguished from the rest of the printed text.
scroll intestinal valve
an intestinal valve where the valve is very long and rather like a scroll of paper inserted along the length of the intestine.
scute
a bony plate as in **Sturgeon Family** members or a modified scale with a sharp or blunt ridge as in **Herring Family** or **Jack Family** members.
sea run
said of fishes which enter the ocean, usually for feeding.
secretory granulocyte
a type of blood cell of unknown function found in the **bigmouth** and **black buffalos**.
segmented rays
fin rays which are divided into segments along their length.
seine
a net with floats at the top and weights at the bottom used to catch fish by encircling them.
semicircular ear canal
fluid-filled canals embedded in the cranium and concerned with balance and hearing. **Jawed fishes** have 3 canals, **lampreys** have 2 (lacking a horizontal canal) and **hagfishes** have only one canal.
setline
a line of baited hooks laid out on the sea floor.
shagreen
a rough sandpaper-like surface; also used to refer to the skin of **sharks** which has been treated by filing down and painting or varnishing to produce a form of leather.
shoulder girdle
see pectoral girdle.

shoulder organ
a black-lined pit or sac under the cleithrum in members of the **Tubeshoulder Family** which is connected to the exterior by a tube visible above the pectoral fin. The sac produces a luminous fluid which can be discharged to confuse predators.

shut-off seine
a seine used to enclose a bay or area of water.

sinus
a space in the tissues of an organism, usually a blood cavity, e.g. see **Hagfish Family**.

slime pore
one of a long series of pores along the flank of **hagfishes** which produce large amounts of slime used in defense or in suffocating other fishes.

smolt
a young **Salmon Family** member migrating to the sea recognised by the silvery pigment which hides the parr marks on the flank.

sneak-spawner
see sneaky male.

sneaky male
a small, non-dominant male fish which attempts to fertilise eggs by darting suddenly onto the nest site (= sneaker).

So
a photophore below the middle of the eye and above the upper jaw.

SO
a photophore near the tip of the lower jaw.

sonic scattering
see sound scattering layer.

sound scattering layer
any layer or object which scatters sound in water. Sonar devices can be used to detect fish schools by recording sound scattering layers.

sp.
abbreviation for species, usually used in the sense of the specific or trivial part of the scientific name to indicate an undescribed species, e.g. *Gasterosteus* sp. (see **Enos stickleback, giant stickleback, Texada stickleback, white stickleback**).

species
the scientific name of an animal or plant which represents a group of populations of interbreeding or potentially interbreeding individuals which are reproductively isolated from other groups.

species name
the trivial name; combined with the genus name it forms the scientific name unique to a species.

sperm packet
a mass of sperm transferred from the male to the female by a gonopodium of the **Livebearer Family**.

spermatogonia
precursors of sperm.

spermatozoa
the flagellated male gamete or sperm.

sphenotic spines
a spine borne on the bone separating the orbital and otic regions of the skull at the back of the head in members of the **Anglerfish Order**.

spine
a stiff, pointed and sharp process on the head or supporting a fin.

spinule
small spine.

spiracle
a small cleft between the eye and gill slits in **sharks** and **rays. Rays** use it to inhale water.

spiral intestinal valve
an intestinal valve with a spiral or helical fold . Often used as a general term to include ring and scroll intestinal valves.

squalene
a low specific gravity hydrocarbon found in the liver of some **sharks** and used in cosmetics, lipsticks, hair-setting preparations, moisturisers and lubricants for fine machinery.

standard length
the distance from the anterior tip of the body to the end of the hypural bones or the vertebral column. This posterior point can be found by flexing the caudal fin laterally. Standard length is the usual scientific measurement of body length in fishes. Abbreviated to SL.

stay
a fleshy, or cartilaginous or bony supporting strut.

stern chasers
luminous glands on the upper and lower surfaces of the caudal peduncle in members of the **Lanternfish Family**. They are believed to help distract predators which strike at this attractive region and are confused when the lights are extinguished and the **lanternfish** darts away.

stock
> a distinct population or quantity of fish in a given area. Also to add fish or eggs to an area to increase the population.

striae
> fine lines or ridges.

stylophthalmoid
> the larvae of **Lanternfish Family** members, characterised by eyes on stalks.

subocular shelf
> a bony plate which extends inwards from the bones of the infraorbital series.

suboperculum
> the dermal bone lying below the operculum in the gill cover on the side of the head.

suborbital
> below the eye.

suborbital stay
> the bone running across the cheek from the eye to the preopercle; characterises members of the **Mail-cheeked Order**.

subspecies
> a geographic group of local populations differing from, and isolated from, other such groups. The groups do not usually meet but can interbreed if they do unlike most species. The subspecies is the third Latinised word in the scientific name.

subterminal
> before the end and ventral. Often refers to the mouth position in fishes.

summerkill
> the death of fishes in enclosed water bodies during summer owing to oxygen depletion and/or toxic algal blooms.

superfetation
> the development of several broods within the ovary at the same time. This is facilitated by storing sperm, e.g. in the **Livebearer Family**.

supermale
> a male which does not change sex and is the principal spawner, e.g. see **spark anglemouth.**

supracaudal luminous gland
> a long, median and dorsal gland on the caudal peduncle of some **Lanternfish Family** members.

supracleithral head spine
> see head spines.

supracleithrum
> the dermal bone above the cleithrum and below the posttemporal.

supramaxilla
> the dermal bone on the upper, rear end of the maxilla.

supraoccipital
> the deep median bone on the posterior dorsal skull surface forming the upper rim of the opening for the spinal column from the skull.

supraocular head spine
> see head spines.

supraoral lamina
> a plate bearing teeth above the mouth in members of the **Lamprey Family**.

supraorbital photophore
> a light organ on the postero-dorsal margin of the orbit in the **Lanternfish Family.** Abbreviated as SuO.

supraorbital pores
> openings over the eyes on the top of the head.

supratemporal canal
> the head canal across the rear of the head connecting the lateral lines.

sushi
> thin slices of raw fish, usually with green mustard and vinegar-boiled rice; a Japanese delicacy.

swimbladder
> see gas bladder.

symphysis
> cartilaginous joint where two bones are united, e.g. the two halves of the lower jaw.

symplectic
> a paired deep bone lying between the quadrate and the metapterygoid bones.

synchronous hermaphrodite
> having both ovarian and testicular tissue present in one individual at the same time.

T

tabular bones
> often small and thin dermal bones on the nape or above the opercular membrane related to the supratemporal sensory canal.

TAC
> total allowable catch, the weight of fish of a given species or type caught by commercial fishing in any year. The TAC is set by the Canadian government in an effort to manage the resource.

tagging
> attachment of numbered and addressed labels or tags, usually of plastic or metal, to

a live fish which is then released and hopefully recaptured at a later date. Used to estimate growth and movement.

tail fin
the fin at the end of the body. Also called
the caudal fin.

tail rings
the dermal plates in members of the
Pipefish Family forming a series of rings
enclosing the body; tail rings run from the
first behind the anus (it usually carries the
anal fin), trunk rings run from the ring bearing the pectoral fin to the ring with the
anus.

tapetum lucidum
a reflecting layer behind the retina of the
eye which ensures extra stimulation of the
retina for better vision. Makes the eyes
shine.

temporal pore canal
the head canal over the temporal region.

temporal region
the head just behind the eyes.

tentacle
a short, fleshy appendage.

tenuis larva
a larval member of the **Pearlfish Family**
which follows the stage having a vexillum.
It is characterised by having no vexillum,
by a long, cylindrical and transparent body
and by a small head. The tenuis is free-living at first but soon occupies the body cavity of a sea cucumber.

terminal
at the end. Said of the mouth when it is at
the tip of the body rather than ventral or
subterminal.

terminal male
supermale, the dominant male, e.g. seen in
members of the **Wrasse Family**.

terminus
the end.

tetraploid
having a chromosome complement of 4n,
twice the usual number of most organisms.

thalasso
pertaining to the sea.

thermocline
a zone of rapid temperature change with
warm water above and cold water below.

tholichthys
a postlarval stage in **Butterflyfish Family**
members. It has large bony plates on the head
and body which are lost with maturation.

thoracic
pertaining to the thorax, the area anterior to
the abdomen. Said of the pelvic fins when
they are under the pectoral fins.

thorn
a sharp, often curved, prickle or spine.

thornlet
a small thorn.

throat
the anterior ventral surface of the fish,
under the head.

throat teeth
see pharyngeal teeth.

tooth plate
a flattened structure bearing teeth or a type
of tooth which is the form of a flattened
plate, e.g. in **chimaeras** and **hagfishes**.

total length
the greatest length of a fish from the anterior tip of the head to the tip of the tail.
Abbreviated as TL.

toxin
a poisonous chemical secreted by an organism.

trap net
see pound net.

trawl
a net shaped like a bag which is dragged by
a boat to scoop up fish.

tricuspid
teeth having three points or cusps.

trimethylamine oxide
a non-toxic product made from toxic
ammonia and used by **sharks** to keep the
body fluid concentration high to prevent
loss of water to the sea.

triploid
an abnormal chromosome complement,
three times the number in gametes. The
usual complement in a species is twice that
in gametes, e.g. see **grass carp**.

trivial name
the species name; combined with the genus
name it forms the scientific name unique to
a species.

trolling
trailing a fishing line behind a moving boat.

truncate
square-cut; said of the tail fin when it has a
straight edge.

trunk rings
see tail rings.

tubercles
a small projection from a surface.

tubules
elements of the kidneys of fishes.
tusk
enlarged tooth.
tympanic head spine
see head spines.
tympanum
an area of enlarged scales behind the gill
opening in some members of the
Leatherjacket Family. This area can be
vibrated to produce sound.
type subspecies
the original populations described as a new
species are also the type subspecies and
bear the species name as the subspecies
name also, e.g. *Sarda chiliensis lineolata* is
the subspecies of **Pacific bonito** found in
Canadian waters; the species (and therefore
the type subspecies, *Sarda chiliensis chilen-
sis*) was described from off South America.
A subspecies distinct from the original
species requires a new, subspecific name,
the third Latinised word in a scientific
name.

U

uncinate
hooked at the tip.
unculi
horny projections arising from single cells.
underslung jaw
subterminal mouth or jaw.
underyearling
a fish less than one year of age.
unicuspid
teeth having a single point or cusp.
unsegmented rays
a soft ray, usually small, without segments
and found at the beginning of a fin.
ural centrum
the central body of the vertebrae which
carry hypurals.
urea
a waste product of metabolism excreted via
the kidneys but also found in **shark** blood
to maintain osmotic balance.
urodermal
paired, thin dermal bones at the rear of the
caudal fin skeleton.
urogenital region
the area of the abdomen near the urinary
and genital openings.

uroneural
one of paired elongate bones projecting
from the lateral surfaces of the urostyle.
urostyle
the upturned rear tip of the vertebral column, formed of fused vertebrae.
uterine cannibalism
the condition in some **sharks** where the
embryos feed on eggs and smaller siblings
inside the mother.

V

VAV
a ventro-lateral row of photophores running
from the pelvic fin insertion to the anal fin
origin.
veil
a large mucous sheet containing eggs.
velar tentacles
tentacles at the junction of the pharynx and
oesophagus in **lampreys,** probably used to
deflect large food particles from the
branchial region.
venom
the poison secreted by a gland.
vent
the posterior opening of the intestine, gonads
and kidney ducts in front of the anal fin.
ventral
of or pertaining to the lower body.
ventral adipose fin
a fin before the anal fin on the belly.
ventral fin fold
the lower finfold.
ventral photophores
a row of light organs along the abdomen on
each side of the midline.
vermiculations
worm-track markings.
vertebra
a segment of the spinal column composed
of a central body, the centrum, with a neural
arch and spine above and a haemal arch and
spine below.
vertical migration
the upward and downward movement of
fish in a lake or the ocean. Movement is
usually into surface waters at night to feed
and into deeper waters to avoid predators
during the day.
vexillum
a long dorsal appendage of the dorsal fin in
larvae of **Pearlfish Family** members.

visceral clefts
>the jaw, hyoid and gill arches.

vitreous body
>the liquid filling the eye.

viviparous
>giving birth to free-swimming young.

VLO
>a photophore on the flank above the pelvic fin.

Vn
>a photophore in front of the eye and below the olfactory capsule.

VO
>a row of photophores on the abdomen behind the pelvic fin and before the anal fin.

vomer
>a dermal bone in the middle of the roof of the mouth.

W

Weberian apparatus
>four bones and associated tissues connecting the gas bladder to the inner ear and conveying pressure changes and sound, e.g. in the **Carp Order**.

Weberian ossicles
>the four bones derived from vertebrae in the Weberian apparatus.

weir
>nets or fences set in streams or along the coast to direct fish into a holding container for easy capture. Some weirs take advantage of the falling tide to trap fish.

window
>a clear area, e.g. in species with a light organ a patch of skin without scales such as in the **lamp grenadier** or **marlin-spike**.

wings
>the enlarged, wing-like pectoral fins of **Skate Family** members.

Y

year class
>fish in a population born in the same year.

yearling
>a fish in its second year of life.

yolk-sac
>a sac containing yolk used for nourishment in larval fish.

yolk-sac placenta
>the yolk-sac helps in formation of a placenta which allows a connection of the embryo to the mother for nourishment.

young-of-the-year
>a fish less than one year old.

Z

zooplankton
>animal members of the plankton.

Cross Reference
of Scientific and Common Names

This index lists common names of fishes, in English and French, which are not the principal name used for the species in the Encyclopaedia. Some of these names have a wide use as an alternative name and the index serves to locate the appropriate account under the name used here. An example is the **brook trout** which is still commonly referred to as the speckled trout. Other names have a more local usage, e.g. caplin for **capelan** in Newfoundland, and the index then serves to place local knowledge in a national and international context. Also included are the scientific names of fishes and their families as these are often used, even in popular works, to ensure accuracy; common names are widely misapplied and can be very confusing, e.g. see under **basses**.

Usually there is a direct equivalence of names, the speckled trout is the same fish as the **brook trout** for example, but additionally some species or families not found in Canada are mentioned in accounts to place Canadian fishes in a world context and these names are indexed too. The reader should check the main Encyclopaedia account referred to.

The Introduction gives a classification of Canadian fishes in two tables and this is not indexed here. It should be referred to for the arrangement of classes, orders and families.

The Introduction also contains a list of exotic species released into Canadian waters. Some of these exotics have not established reproducing populations and do not have separate accounts in this book. They are all indexed here.

"fish" = Atlantic cod
a na = brook trout
aanaaksiiq = broad whitefish
aanaatlik = broad trout
aanak = brook trout
aaqaksaaq = Bering wolffish
abbot = monkfish
Abudefduf saxatilis = sergeant major
abyssal grenadier = russet grenadier
abyssal liparid = abyssal snailfish
abyssal skate = chocolate skate
Acanthodii = bony fishes
Acantholiparis opercularis = spiny snailfish
Acantholumpenus mackayi = black-line prickleback
Acanthopterygii = spiny-rayed fishes
Acentronura dendritica = pipehorse
achigan à grande bouche = large-mouth bass
achigan à petite bouche = small-mouth bass
achigan de mer = cunner
Acipenser brevirostrum = shortnose sturgeon
Acipenser fulvescens = lake sturgeon
Acipenser medirostris = green sturgeon
Acipenser oxyrhynchus = Atlantic sturgeon
Acipenser transmontanus = white sturgeon
Acipenseridae = Sturgeon Family

Acipenseriformes = Sturgeon Order
acoupa blanc = white seabass
acoupa royal = weakfish
Acrocheilus alutaceus = chiselmouth
Actinopterygii = bony fishes
Actinopterygii = fishes
Actinopterygii = ray-finned fishes
African jewelfish = jewelfish
Agassiz' smoothhead = dusky slick-head
Agnatha = jawless fishes
agone à dorsale noire = blacktip poacher
agone à dos denté = sawback poacher
agone à nageoire coupée = smooth-eye poacher
agone à poitrine épineuse = prickle-breast poacher
agone à quatre cornes = fourbeard rockling
agone à trois épines = bluespotted poacher
agone atlantique = Atlantic poacher
agone barbu = tubenose poacher
agone de varech = kelp poacher
agone foncé = northern spearnose poacher
agone pygmée = pygmy poacher
agone verruqueux = warty poacher
agone-esturgeon = sturgeon poacher
agones = Poacher Family
Agonidae = Poacher Family

Agonomalus mozinoi = kelp poacher
Agonopsis emmelane = northern spearnose poacher
Agonopsis vulsa = northern spearnose poacher
Agonus acipenserinus = sturgeon poacher
Agonus decagonus = Atlantic poacher
Ahlia egmontis = key worm eel
aiglefin = haddock
aigles de mer = Eagle Ray Family
aiguillat = spiny dogfish
aiguillat commun = spiny dogfish
aiguillat noir = black dogfish
aiguille de mer = Atlantic saury
Alaska blackcod = sablefish
Alaska blackfish = Introduction
Alaska cod = Pacific cod
Alaska pollock = walleye pollock
Alaskan ronquil = bluefin searcher
albacore = swordfish
albacore à nageoires jaunes = yellowfin tuna
Albatrossia pectoralis = pectoral rattail
albino anglemouth = white bristlemouth
Albula vulpes = bonefish
Albulidae = Bonefish Family
Albuliformes = Bonefish Order
Aldrovandia phalacra = bald halosaur

Alepisauridae = Lancetfish Family
Alepisaurus brevirostris = shortnose lancetfish
Alepisaurus ferox = longnose lancetfish
alépocéphale à grands yeux = bigeye smoothhead
alépocéphale filamenteux = threadfin slickhead
alépocèphale multirai = manyray smoothhead
alépocéphale obscur = dusky slick-head
alépocéphales = Slickhead Family
Alepocephalidae = Slickhead Family
Alepocephalus agassizi = dusky slickhead
Alepocephalus bairdi = manyray smoothhead
alewife = gaspereau
Alfonsin a Casta = narrowside alfonsin
Alfonsin a Casta Larga = wideside alfonsin
Alfonsin de Costa = narrowside alfonsin
algae eaters = Carp Order
alligatorfishes = Poacher Family
Allison's tunny = yellowfin tuna
allmouth = monkfish
Allocyttus folletti = oxeye oreo
Allolumpenus hypochromus = Y-prickleback

Allosmerus elongatus = whitebait smelt
Allotriognathi = Opah Order
Alopias vulpinus = thresher shark
Alopiidae = Thresher Shark family
Alosa aestivalis = blueback herring
Alosa pseudoharengus = gaspereau
Alosa sapidissima = American shad
alose à gésier = gizzard shad
alose d'été = blueback herring
alose savoureuse = American shad
alose tyran = Atlantic menhaden
alpine char = Arctic char
Alutera schoepfi = orange filefish
Alutera scripta = scrawled filefish
alutère écrit = scrawled filefish
alutère orangé = orange filefish
amagiak = capelin
amber jack = banded rudderfish
Ambloplites rupestris = rock bass
Ameiurus = Bullhead Catfish Family
Ameiurus melas = black bullhead
Ameiurus natalis = yellow bullhead
Ameiurus nebulosus = brown bullhead
American angler = monkfish
American bream = golden shiner
American burbot = burbot
American chub = fallfish
American conger eel = conger eel
American grayling = Arctic grayling
American perch = yellow perch
American plaice = Canadian plaice
American roach = golden shiner
American sand lance = stout sand lance
American smelt = rainbow smelt
Amia = Bowfin Family
Amia calva = bowfin
Amiidae = Bowfin Family
Amiiformes = Bowfin Order
Ammocrypta pellucida = eastern sand darter
Ammodytes americanus = Sand Lance Family
Ammodytes dubius = northern sand lance
Ammodytes hexapterus = Sand Lance Family
Ammodytes hexapterus = stout sand lance
Ammodytidae = Sand Lance Family
Amphistichus koelzi = Surfperch Family
Amphistichus rhodoterus = redtail surfperch
an-ark-hlirk = broad whitefish
âna = brook trout
Anabantidae = Introduction
Anacanthini = Cod Order
anadleq = lake whitefish
anâdlerk = lake whitefish
anah'lih' = broad whitefish
anahik = lake whitefish
anaklek = broad whitefish
anakleq = brook trout
Anarchias similis = pygmy moray
Anarchias yoshiae = pygmy moray
Anarhichadidae = Wolffish Family
Anarhichas denticulatus = northern wolffish
Anarhichas lupus = Atlantic wolffish

Anarhichas minor = spotted wolffish
Anarhichas orientalis = Bering wolffish
Anarrhichthys ocellatus = wolf-eel
Anchoa hepsetus = striped anchovy
anchois = Anchovy Family
anchois argenté = silver anchovy
anchois du Pacifique = northern anchovy
anchois gris = silver anchovy
anchois rayé = striped anchovy
anchoveta = Anchovy Family
anchoveta = Atlantic herring
ange de mer du Pacifique = Pacific angel shark
anges de mer = Angel Shark Family
anglemouths = Bristlemouth Family
anglerfishes = Frogfish Family
Anguilla anguilla = Freshwater Eel Family
Anguilla rostrata = American eel
anguille à col = neckeel
anguille à nez court = snubnose eel
anguille à pores jumelées = twin-pored eel
anguille argentée = American eel
anguille d'Amérique = American eel
anguille égorgée bécue = slatjaw cutthroat eel
anguille égorgée brune = brown cutthroat eel
anguille enfaitée = ridged eel
anguilles à col = Neckeel Family
anguilles d'eau douce = Freshwater Eel Family
anguilles égorgées = Cutthroat Eel Family
anguilles spagetti = Spaghetti Eel Family
Anguillidae = Freshwater Eel Family
Anguilliformes = Eel Order
aniaq = Arctic char
Anisarchus medius = stout eelblenny
anokik = brook trout
Anoplagonus inermis = smooth alligatorfish
Anoplarchus insignis = slender cockscomb
Anoplarchus purpurescens = high cockscomb
Anoplogaster cornuta = fangtooth
Anoplogastridae = Ogrefish Family
Anoplopoma fimbria = sablefish
Anoplopomatidae = Sablefish Family
Anotopteridae = Daggertooth Family
Anotopterus pharao = daggertooth
antennaire ocellé = ocellated frogfish
antennaires = Frogfish Family
Antennariidae = Frogfish Family
Antennarius ocellatus = ocellated frogfish
Anthias nicholsi = yellowfin bass
Antigonia combatia = shortspine boarfish
Antimora microlepis = Pacific flatnose
Antimora rostrata = blue antimora
antimore à petites écailles = Pacific flatnose
antimore bleu = blue antimora
anuk = brook trout

Apeltes quadracus = fourspine stickleback
aphanope charbon = black scabbardfish
Aphanopus carbo = black scabbardfish
Aphanopus intermedius = Cutlassfish Family
Aplodinotus grunniens = freshwater drum
Apodichthys flavidus = penpoint gunnel
Apodichthys fucorum = rockweed gunnel
apogon à deux taches = twospot cardinalfish
apogon flamboyant = flamefish
Apogon maculatus = flamefish
Apogon pseudomaculatus = twospot cardinalfish
Apogonidae = Cardinalfish Family
apogons = Cardinalfish Family
Appaluchion = flathead catfish
Apristurus brunneus = brown cat shark
Apristurus laurussoni = Iceland cat shark
Apristurus manis = ghost cat shark
Apristurus microps = smalleye cat shark
Apristurus profundorum = deepsea cat shark
Apristurus riveri = broadgill cat shark
Apterichtus ansp = academy eel
Aptocyclus ventricosus = smooth lumpsucker
Archosargus probatocephalus = sheepshead
Arctic cod = polar cod
Arctic Greenland cod = polar cod
Arctic hookear sculpin = snowflake hookear
Arctic rainbow smelt = rainbow smelt
Arctic rockling = silver rockling
Arctic salmon = Arctic char
Arctic sand lance = northern sand lance
Arctic sand lance = stout sand lance
Arctic sculpin = polar sculpin
Arctic sculpin = snowflake hookear
Arctic sea poacher = Arctic alligatorfish
Arctic skate = darkbelly skate
Arctic thorny skate = thorny skate
Arctic threebeard rockling = threebeard rockling
Arctic tomcod = Arctic cod
arctic trout = Arctic grayling
Arctic wolffish = northern wolffish
Arctogadus borisovi = toothed cod
Arctogadus glacialis = polar cod
Argentina silus = Atlantic argentine
Argentina striata = striated argentine
argentine à gorge bleue = bluethroat argentine
argentine oubliée = forgotten argentine
argentine striée = striated argentine
argentines = Argentine Family
Argentinidae = Argentine Family

Argyropelecus aculeatus = longspine silver hatchetfish
Argyropelecus affinis = slender silver hatchetfish
Argyropelecus gigas = greater silver hatchetfish
Argyropelecus hemigymnus = short silver hatchetfish
Argyropelecus lychnus = silvery hatchetfish
Argyropelecus sladeni = lowcrest hatchetfish
Ariomma bondi = silver-rag
Ariommatidae = Sequinfish Family
ariommatids = Sequinfish Family
ariomme grise = silver-rag
Ariosoma balearicum = bandtooth conger
Aristostomias lunifer = crescent loosejaw
Aristostomias photodactylus = ten-rayed loosejaw
Aristostomias polydactylus = Pleiades loosejaw
Aristostomias scintillans = shining loosejaw
Aristostomias tittmanni = Tittmann's loosejaw
armed bullhead = Arctic alligatorfish
armored searobins = Searobin Family
arnaqsleq = lake cisco
arrow dragonfish = longfin dragonfish
arrow-pikes = Barracuda Family
arrowfish = longfin dragonfish
arrowtooth halibut = arrowtooth flounder
Artediellus atlanticus = Atlantic hookear
Artediellus scaber = rough hookear
Artediellus uncinatus = snowflake hookear
Artedius fenestralis = padded sculpin
Artedius harringtoni = scalyhead sculpin
Artedius lateralis = smoothhead sculpin
Ascelichthys rhodorus = rosylip sculpin
Asemichthys taylori = spinynose sculpin
Asian cherry salmon = Salmon Family
aspidophore = Atlantic alligatorfish
Aspidophoroides monopterygius = Atlantic alligatorfish
Aspidophoroides olriki = Arctic alligatorfish
assiette atlantique = Atlantic moonfish
Asterotheca alascanus = gray starsnout
astérothèque à cinq épines = bigeye starsnout
astérothèque à nageoires noires = blackfin starsnout
astérothèque épineux = spinycheek starsnout
astérothèque gris = gray starsnout
Astronesthes gemmifer = gem snaggletooth

Astronesthes leucopogon = white-bearded snaggletooth
Astronesthes niger = black snaggle-tooth
Astronesthidae = Barbeled Dragonfish Family
Astronesthinae = snaggletooths
astronotus = Cichlid Family
astronotus = Introduction
astronotus = oscar
Astronotus ocellatus = Cichlid Family
Astronotus ocellatus = Introduction
Atheresthes evermanni = Asiatic arrowtooth flounder
Atheresthes stomias = arrowtooth flounder
Atherinidae = Silverside Family
Atheriniformes = Silverside Order
Atherinops affinis = topsmelt
atinga bariolé = striped burrfish
atingas = Porcupinefish Family
Atlantic beardfish = stout beardfish
Atlantic bigeye = bigeye
Atlantic blue marlin = blue marlin
Atlantic croaker = Drum Family
Atlantic eel = American eel
Atlantic electric ray = Atlantic torpedo
Atlantic footballfish = lightlamp footballfish
Atlantic fourline = fourline snake-blenny
Atlantic lancet fish = longnose lancetfish
Atlantic manta = manta
Atlantic prickly skate = thorny skate
Atlantic rainbow smelt = rainbow smelt
Atlantic round herring = round herring
Atlantic sea poacher = Atlantic poacher
Atlantic shad = American shad
Atlantic silver hatchetfish = longspine silver hatchetfish
Atlantic smelt = rainbow smelt
Atlantic snipe eel = slender snipe eel
Atlantic whitefish = Acadian white-fish
Atractoscion nobilis = white seabass
Aulopiformes = Flagfin Order
Aulorhynchidae = Tube-snout Family
Aulorhynchus flavidus = tube-snout
aurin chaîne = chain pearlfish
aurins = Pearlfish Family
aurora char = aurora trout
aurora pout = aurora unernak
autumn albacore = yellowfin tuna
autumn salmon = chum salmon
autumn salmon = pink salmon
auxide = bullet tuna
Auxis rochei = bullet tuna
avaleur feu-arrière = taillight gulper
avaleurs = Swallower Family
avocet snipe eel = closespine snipe eel
avocette carênée = carinate snipe eel
avocette immature = closespine snipe eel
avocette ruban = slender snipe eel

avocettes = Snipe Eel Family
Avocettina gilli = closespine snipe eel
Avocettina infans = closespine snipe eel
bachelor = white crappie
bachelor perch = black crappie
Back's grayling = Arctic grayling
Baird's smooth-head = manyray smoothhead
baitstealer = cunner
Bajacalifornia megalops = bigeye smoothhead
Bajacalifornia michaelsarsi = oarjaw wingmax
balaou = Atlantic saury
balaou japonais = Pacific saury
balaous = Saury Family
balarin = bluefish
balbo sabertooth = pink sabertooth
Balearic conger = bandtooth conger
baliste capri = gray triggerfish
baliste gris = gray triggerfish
baliste océanique = ocean triggerfish
baliste royal = queen triggerfish
baliste vieille = queen triggerfish
balistes = Leatherjacket Family
Balistes capriscus = gray triggerfish
Balistes vetula = queen triggerfish
Balistidae = Leatherjacket Family
balloonfish = northern puffer
balourou = ballyhoo
balourous = Halfbeak Family
bamboosharks = Carpet Shark Order
bananafish = bonefish
banane de mer = bonefish
bananes de mer = Bonefish Family
band-shaped blenny = penpoint gunnel
banded darter = rainbow darter
banded pickerel = redfin pickerel
banded rockfish = tiger rockfish
bandeye sculpin = longfin sculpin
bandit = redbanded rockfish
banklick bass = black crappie
banstickle = threespine stickleback
bar blanc = white bass
bar rayé = striped bass
barbel = mummichog
barbelled houndsharks = Ground Shark Family
barber pole = redbanded rockfish
barbier ligne-en-palier = yellowfin bass
barbier rouge = red barbier
barbotte brune = brown bullhead
barbotte des rapides = stonecat
barbotte jaune = yellow bullhead
barbotte noire = black bullhead
barbottes = Bullhead Catfish Family
Barbourisia rufa = velvet whalefish
Barbourisiidae = Whalefish Family
barbudo des Caraïbes = Caribbean beardfish
barbudos = Beardfish Family
barbue à tête plate = flathead catfish
barbue de rivière = channel catfish
baret = white perch
barfish = black crappie
barfish = white bass
barracuda argenté = Pacific barracuda

barracuda du nord = northern sennet
barracudas = Barracuda Family
barred fantail darter = fantail darter
barred minnow = banded killifish
barred muskellunge = muskellunge
barreleyes = Smelt Order
barreleyes = Spookfish Family
barrelfish = Cornish blackfish
bars = Temperate Bass Family
Bascanichthys bascanium = sooty eel
bashaw = flathead catfish
bastard buffalo = black buffalo
bastard cusk = spotted wrymouth
bastard halibut = arrowtooth flounder
bastard halibut = Greenland halibut
Bathophilus flemingi = highfin dragonfish
Bathophilus vaillanti = bronze-green flagfin
Bathyagonus alascanus = gray starsnout
Bathyagonus infraspinatus = spiny-cheek starsnout
Bathyagonus nigripinnis = blackfin starsnout
Bathyagonus pentacanthus = bigeye starsnout
Bathyclupea argentea = silver deep-herring
Bathyclupeidae = Deepherring Family
Bathylagidae = Deepsea Smelt Family
Bathylagus bericoides = smalleye blacksmelt
Bathylagus compsus = starry blacksmelt
Bathylagus euryops = goitre blacksmelt
Bathylagus greyae = Grey's smooth-tongue
Bathylagus milleri = stout blacksmelt
Bathylagus ochotensis = popeye blacksmelt
Bathylagus pacificus = slender blacksmelt
Bathylagus schmidti = northern smoothtongue
Bathylagus stilbius = southern smoothtongue
Bathylychnops exilis = javelin spook-fish
Bathymaster caeruleofasciatus = bluefin searcher
Bathymaster signatus = blue-eyed searcher
Bathymasteridae = Ronquil Family
Bathypterois dubius = snoutlet crotchfeeler
Bathypterois quadrifilis = roughscale wirewing
Bathyraja = Skate Family
Bathyraja abyssicola = abyssal skate
Bathyraja interrupta = sandpaper skate
Bathyraja richardsoni = deepwater skate
Bathyraja sp. = skate species
Bathyraja spinicauda = spinytail skate
Bathyraja trachura = roughtail skate
Bathysaurus agassizi = ferocious

lizardfish
Bathysaurus ferox = ferocious lizard-fish
Bathytroctes michaelsarsi = oarjaw wingmax
Batrachoididae = Toadfish Family
Batrachoidiformes = Toadfish Order
baudroie d'Amérique = monkfish
baudroies = Goosefish Family
bay shark = dusky shark
bayeur rouge = redeye gaper
beaked redfish = Acadian redfish
beaked redfish = deepwater redfish
Bean's sawtoothed eel = stout saw-palate
Bear Lake bullhead = slimy sculpin
Bear Lake herring = lake cisco
beardless codling = smoothchin mora
beau gueulard = blackmouth wide-jaw
beauclaire soleil = bigeye
beaumaris shark = porbeagle
beaverfish = bowfin
bec-de-lièvre = cutlips minnow
bec-de-lièvre = splitnose rockfish
bécasse de mer = longspine snipefish
bécasses de mer = Snipefish Family
beetle-eye = stonecat
Bellingham sole = butter sole
Bellota michaelsarsia = oarjaw wingmax
bellows fishes = Snipefish Family
bellowsfish = northern puffer
bellyfish = monkfish
Beloniformes = Needlefish Order
belted blenny = ribbon prickleback
belted bonito = Atlantic bonito
belted bonito = Pacific bonito
bengal = cunner
Benthalbella dentata = northern pearleye
Benthalbella infans = Zugmayer's pearleye
Benthalbella linguidens = longfin pearleye
Benthodesmus elongatus = Cutlassfish Family
Benthodesmus pacificus = North Pacific frostfish
Benthodesmus simonyi = Simony's frostfish
Benthodesmus tenuis = smalleye frostfish
Benthosema glaciale = glacier lanternfish
Benthosema suborbitale = eyelight lanternfish
bentnose rabbitfish = longnose chimaera
bergall = cunner
Bering skate = sandpaper skate
Berycidae = Alfonsino Family
Beryciformes = Alfonsino Order
béryx = Alfonsino Family
beryx = wideside alfonsin
béryx allongé = narrowside alfonsin
Beryx decadactylus = wideside alfonsin
béryx large = wideside alfonsin
Beryx splendens = narrowside alfon-sin
Beryx splendens = Introduction
Betta splendens = Introduction

big fin = slimy sculpin
big skate = winter skate
big-eared sunfish = longear sunfish
big-eye = least cisco
big-eyed rockfish = sharpchin rockfish
big-finned eel-pout = bigfin eelpout
big-headed darter = river darter
big-jawed sucker = river redhorse
big-scaled blacksmelt = stout blacksmelt
big-toothed redhorse = river redhorse
bigeye = walleye pollock
bigeye cigarfish = fewray fathead
bigeye lanternfish = bigeye flashlightfish
bigeye poacher = bigeye starsnout
bigeye rockfish = stripetail rockfish
bigeye searsiid = teardrop tubeshoulder
bighead dragonfishes = snaggletooths
bighead sucker = northern hog sucker
bigjawed sucker = black redhorse
bigmouth = warmouth
bigmouth bass = largemouth bass
bigscale sucker = shorthead redhorse
bigscales = Ridgehead Family
billfish = Atlantic saury
billfish = longnose gar
billfish = spotted gar
billfish = swordfish
billy gar = longnose gar
bitterhead = black crappie
bitterhead = golden shiner
bitterling = Introduction
black bass = black rockfish
black bass = black sea bass
black bass = blue rockfish
black bass = largemouth bass
black bass = smallmouth bass
black belly = blueback herring
black blenny = black prickleback
black catfish = black bullhead
black cod = pollock
black dragonfish = ribbon sawtailfish
black dragonfishes = Barbeled Dragonfish Family
black eel = American eel
black eel = rock prickleback
black flounder = winter flounder
black gemfish = cone-chin
black grenadier = rock grenadier
black hake = white hake
black halibut = Greenland halibut
black jack = kitefin shark
black loosejaw = stoplight loosejaw
black mullet = black redhorse
black perch = black sea bass
black perch = green sunfish
black pilot = barrelfish
black pilotfish = black ruff
black porgy = tautog
black rockcod = black rockfish
black rockcod = blue rockfish
black salmon = Atlantic salmon
black salmon = cobia
black saw-toothed eel = short-tooth sawpalate
black sculpin = shorthorn sculpin
black shark = kitefin shark

black skate = roughtail skate
black skate = sandpaper skate
black snapper = black rockfish
black star-eater = black snaggletooth
black stickleback = brook stickleback
black sturgeon = lake sturgeon
black sucker = longnose sucker
black sucker = northern hog sucker
black sucker = spotted sucker
black sucker = white sucker
black sunfish = warmouth
black whitehorse = white sucker
black-and-white prickleback = blue-barred prickleback
black-back tullibee = blackfin cisco
black-banded rockfish = tiger rockfish
black-bellied eel-pout = blackbelly eelpout
black-chain pike = chain pickerel
black-fin tullibee = blackfin cisco
black-finned eelpout = black eelpout
black-Harry = black sea bass
black-mouthed alfonsin = rosy soldierfish
black-sided minnow = blacknose shiner
black-spotted trout = coastal cutthroat trout
black-spotted trout = west-slope cutthroat trout
black-striped bass = white bass
black-striped minnow = blackchin shiner
black-tailed liparid = blacktail snailfish
black-will = black sea bass
blackback = Canadian plaice
blackback = smooth flounder
blackback = winter flounder
blackback minnow = blackstripe topminnow
blackbelly skate = darkbelly skate
blackblotched rockfish = darkblotched rockfish
blackcod = sablefish
blackdevil anglerfishes = Werewolf Family
blackdragons = sawtailfishes
blackdragons = Widemouth Order
blackear bream = bluegill
blackeared pondfish = redbreast sunfish
blackears = longear sunfish
blackfin poacher = blackfin starsnout
blackfish = black ruff
blackfish = black sea bass
blackfish = bowfin
blackfish = tautog
blackhead minnow = fathead minnow
blackjaw = chinook salmon
blackline snipe eel = closespine snipe eel
blackmouth = chinook salmon
blackmouth bass = blackmouth widejaw
blackmouth eelpout = black eelpout
blackmouth rockfish = darkblotched rockfish
blacknose dace = blacknose shiner

blackrag = bluefin driftfish
blacksmelts = Deepsea Smelt Family
blackspot chub = creek chub
blackspot grenadier = longnose grenadier
blacktail netdevil = greatbarbelthroat
blackthroated rockfish = rougheye rockfish
blacktip rockfish = rougheye rockfish
blanquillo = tilefish
blennie fouisseuse = graveldiver
blennie plume = feather blenny
blennie-serpent = snakeblenny
blennies = Combtooth Blenny Family
blennies fouisseuses = Graveldiver Family
Blenniidae = Combtooth Blenny Family
Blepsias bilobus = crested sculpin
Blepsias cirrhosus = silverspotted sculpin
blind sharks = Carpet Shark Order
blister back = pollock
bloat = bloater
bloater = Atlantic bonito
bloater = Atlantic herring
blob = mottled sculpin
blood sucker = northern brook lamprey
bloodsucker = chestnut lamprey
bloody stickleback = fourspine stickleback
bloody sunfish = longear sunfish
blue and green sunfish = green sunfish
blue and orange sunfish = longear sunfish
blue bass = green sunfish
blue bream = bluegill
blue buffalo = bigmouth buffalo
blue buffalo = black buffalo
blue channel cat = channel catfish
blue cod = lingcod
blue cod = sablefish
blue darter = rainbow darter
blue dog = blue shark
blue dog = porbeagle
blue fulton = channel catfish
blue garnet = cabezon
blue hake = blue antimora
blue halibut = Greenland halibut
blue lump = lumpfish
blue mako = porbeagle
blue minnow = spotfin shiner
blue mouth = blackbelly rosefish
blue perch = blue rockfish
blue perch = cunner
blue pickerel = sauger
blue pike = blue walleye
blue pike = sauger
blue pike-perch = sauger
blue pointer = great white shark
blue pointer = shortfin mako
blue rooter = black buffalo
blue sea-perch = striped seaperch
blue sucker = black redhorse
blue sucker = central stoneroller
blue sunfish = bluefish
blue sunfish = bluegill
blue whaler = blue shark

blue-spotted sunfish = green sunfish
blueback = coho salmon
blueback = lake cisco
blueback mulhaden = blueback herring
blueback salmon = sockeye salmon
blueback shad = blueback herring
blueback trout = Arctic char
blueback tullibee = lake cisco
bluebacks = Ridgehead Family
bluebottle fish = man-of-war fish
bluefin = blackfin cisco
bluefin = shortjaw cisco
bluefish = Arctic grayling
bluefish = black sea bass
bluefish = blue rockfish
bluefish = cunner
bluefish = kelp greenling
bluegill bream = bluegill
bluemouth sunfish = bluegill
bluenose perch = white perch
bluenosed chub = bluntnose minnow
bluespot goby = blackeye goby
blunt-nosed minnow = blacknose shiner
bluntnose = Atlantic moonfish
bluntnose sixgill shark = sixgill shark
bluntsnout smooth-head = Atlantic gymnast
boarfishes = Armorhead Family
bocaccio = bocaccio
bodieron = kelp greenling
bolina = brown rockfish
Bolinichthys indicus = smoothcheek lanternfish
Bolinichthys photothorax = spinecheek lanternfish
Bolinichthys supralateralis = sidelight lanternfish
Bonapartia pedaliota = bonaparte
bone jack = Atlantic bonito
bone shark = basking shark
bone-dogs = spiny dogfish
bonite à dos rayé = Atlantic bonito
bonite du Pacifique = Pacific bonito
bonito shark = porbeagle
bonito shark = shortfin mako
bonitou = bullet tuna
bonnet à joues touffues = matcheek warbonnet
bony sturgeon = lake sturgeon
bonypike = longnose gar
boregat = kelp greenling
Boreogadus saida = Arctic cod
Borostomias antarcticus = large-eye snaggletooth
Boston bluefish = pollock
Boston eel = American eel
Boston hake = white hake
Boston mackerel = Atlantic bonito
Boston mackerel = Atlantic mackerel
Bothidae = Lefteye Flounder Family
Bothragonus swani = rockhead
Bothrocara brunneum = twoline eelpout
Bothrocara molle = soft eelpout
Bothrocara pusillum = Alaska eelpout
Bothrocara remigerum = longsnout eelpout
Bothus ocellatus = eyed flounder
bottlefish = lake chub

bottlenose = shortnose sturgeon
bouche coupante = chiselmouth
bourse émeri = fringed filefish
bourse orange = orange filefish
bouvière = Introduction
boxhead = northern hog sucker
Brachyistius frenatus = kelp perch
bracketed blenny = crescent gunnel
Brama brama = Atlantic pomfret
Brama japonica = Pacific pomfret
Brama rayi = Atlantic pomfret
bramble sharks = Dogfish Shark
Order
Bramidae = Pomfret Family
branch herring = gaspereau
branch perch = green sunfish
Branchiostegidae = Tilefish Family
bras-de-rêve menton-uni = plainchin
dreamarm
bratan = Atlantic salmon
bream = bluefish
bream = bluegill
bream = golden shiner
bream = green sunfish
bream = pumpkinseed
breams = Pomfret Family
Breviraja marklei = Markle's ray
Brevoortia tyrannus = Atlantic menhaden
bridge perch = white crappie
brightlight lanternfish = sunbeam
lanternfish
brill = petrale sole
brill = windowpane
brilliant sunfish = longear sunfish
brindled stone cat = brindled madtom
brit = Atlantic herring
broad mullet = quillback
broad-headed catfish = northern
wolffish
broad-striped anchovy = striped
anchovy
broadbill = swordfish
broadfin sole = rock sole
broadnose sevengill shark = sevengill shark
brochet d'Amérique = redfin pickerel
brochet maillé = chain pickerel
brochet vermiculé = grass pickerel
brochets = Pike Family
bronze eel = American eel
bronze minnow = finescale dace
bronzeback = smallmouth bass
brook char = brook trout
brook chub = creek chub
brook lamprey = American brook
lamprey
brook lamprey = silver lamprey
brook minnow = blacknose dace
brook mullet = shorthead redhorse
brookie = brook trout
brosme = cusk
Brosme brosme = cusk
Brosmiculus imberbis = smoothchin
mora
Brosmophycis marginata = red brotula
brown bass = smallmouth bass
brown bomber = bocaccio
brown bomber = widow rockfish
brown buffalo = bigmouth buffalo
brown catfish = black bullhead

brown catfish = brown bullhead
brown lamprey = chestnut lamprey
brown rockcod = brown rockfish
brown rockfish = quillback rockfish
brown rudderfish = medusafish
brown ruff = Cornish blackfish
brown sea-perch = kelp perch
brown shark = brown cat shark
brown shark = sandbar shark
brown trout = Introduction
brown-winged searobin = striped
searobin
brownback whitefish = pygmy
whitefish
brownie = brown trout
Bryozoichthys marjorius = pearly
prickleback
Bryx dunckeri = pugnose pipefish
bubbler = freshwater drum
buckeye shiner = emerald shiner
buffalo à grande bouche = bigmouth
buffalo
buffalo back = lake whitefish
buffalo cod = lingcod
buffalo noir = black buffalo
buffalo sunfish = green sunfish
buffalo trunkfish = rough trunkfish
buffalofishes = Sucker Family
bugeye = walleye pollock
bugfish = Atlantic menhaden
bughead = Atlantic menhaden
buglemouth = black buffalo
buglemouth bass = common carp
bugler = black buffalo
bulb-fish = bulbous dreamer
bull char = Dolly Varden
bull-headed catfish = northern wolffish
bull-rout = shorthorn sculpin
bulldog pickerel = redfin pickerel
bullet mackerel bullet tuna
bulleye = chub mackerel
bullhead = blackfin sculpin
bullhead = longhorn sculpin
bullhead = spinyhead sculpin
bullhead buffalo = bigmouth buffalo
bullhead minnow = bluntnose minnow
bullheads = Sculpin Family
bullmouth buffalo = bigmouth buffalo
bullnose buffalo = bigmouth buffalo
bullpout = brown bullhead
buoy keg = rougheye rockfish
buoy keg = shortraker rockfish
buoy tender = black buffalo
burrfishes = Porcupinefish Family
burrowing blenny = graveldiver
butter bass = black crappie
butterball = yellow bullhead
buttercat = yellow bullhead
butterfish = golden shiner
butterfish = rock gunnel
butterfly rays = Stingray Family
Bythitidae = Livebearing Brotula
Family
C-O turbot = C-O sole
cabezon = Pacific staghorn sculpin
cabio = cobia
Caelorinchus caelorhincus = longnose grenadier
Caelorinchus caelorhincus carmina-

tus = longnose grenadier
Calcichordata = chordates
calicagère blanche = Bermuda chub
calico bass = black crappie
calico bass = white crappie
calico salmon = chum salmon
calico surfperch = Surfperch Family
California anchovy = northern
anchovy
California barracuda = Pacific bar-
racuda
California bonito = Pacific bonito
California flashlightfish = penlight
fish
California golden trout = golden
trout
California grenadier = lamp
grenadier
California grunion = Silverside
Order
California hake = Pacific hake
California herring = Pacific herring
California lizardfish = smallscale
lizardfish
California pilchard = Pacific sardine
California pompano = Pacific pom-
pano
California rattail = lamp grenadier
California smoothtongue = southern
smoothtongue
California sole = English sole
California turbot = curlfin sole
California yellowtail = yellowtail
Californian anchoveta = northern
anchovy
Callechelys muraena = blotched
snake eel
callionyme à nageoire tachetée =
spotfin dragonet
Callionymidae = Dragonet Family
Callionymus agassizi = spotfin drag-
onet
Callionymus pauciradiatus = spotted
dragonet
Campbell sucker = Salish sucker
campbellite = white crappie
Campostoma anomalum = central
stoneroller
camus = lake sturgeon
Canada pike = northern pike
Canadian eelpout = polar eelpout
candiru = Catfish Order
candlefish = eulachon
candlefish = sablefish
Canthidermis sufflamen = ocean triggerfish
Cape cigarfish = Cape fathead
Cape sole = petrale sole
capelan = capelin
capelin = Atlantic silverside
caplin = capelin
Caproidae = Boarfish Family
capucette = Atlantic silverside
capucette barrée = topsmelt
capucettes = Silverside Family
Carangidae = Jack Family
carangue coubali = blue runner
carangue crevallée = crevalle jack
carangue jaune = blue runner
carangue symétrique = jack mackerel
carangues = Jack Family
Caranx crysos = blue runner

Caranx hippos = crevalle jack
Carapidae = Pearlfish Family
carapids = Pearlfish Family
Carassius auratus = goldfish
Carassius auratus = Introduction
Carcharhinidae = Requiem Shark
Family
Carcharhiniformes = Ground Shark
Order
Carcharhinus falciformis = silky
shark
Carcharhinus longimanus = ocean
whitetip shark
Carcharhinus obscurus = dusky
shark
Carcharhinus plumbeus = sandbar
shark
Carcharias taurus = sand tiger
Carchariidae = Sand Tiger Family
Carcharodon carcharias = great
white shark
cardeau à petite bouche = smallmouth flounder
cardeau à quatre ocelles = fourspot
flounder
cardeau d'été = summer flounder
cardeau de profondeurs = deepwater
flounder
cardeau épineux = spiny flounder
cardeau frangé = fringed flounder
cardeau svelte = slim flounder
Careproctus gilberti = smalldisk
snailfish
Careproctus longipinnis = longfin
snailfish
Careproctus melanurus = blacktail
snailfish
Careproctus oregonensis = smallfin
snailfish
Careproctus ovigerum = abyssal
snailfish
Careproctus ranulus = Scotian snailfish
Careproctus reinhardti = sea tadpole
cariste = manefish
cariste de Groenland = Greenland
manefish
caristes = Manefish Family
Caristiidae = Manefish family
Caristius groenlandicus = Greenland
manefish
Caristius macrops = manefish
carp = white sucker
Carp Family = Introduction
carpe = common carp
carpe = Introduction
carpe de roseau = grass carp
carpe de roseau = Introduction
carpes = Carp Family
Carpiodes cyprinus = quillback
carpsucker = quillback
carpsuckers = Sucker Family
carrelet = winter flounder
Caspian round goby = round goby
castagnole fauchoir = bigscale pomfret
castagnole mince = Pacific pomfret
castagnole rugueuse = rough pomfret
castagnoles = Pomfret Family
castor oil fish = oilfish
Catalina sand dab = speckled
sanddab

catalufa = bigeye
catalufas = Bigeye Family
catfish = Atlantic wolffish
Catostomidae = Sucker Family
Catostomus catostomus = longnose sucker
Catostomus catostomus lacustris = Jasper longnose sucker
Catostomus columbianus = bridgelip sucker
Catostomus commersoni = white sucker
Catostomus macrocheilus = largescale sucker
Catostomus platyrhynchus = mountain sucker
Catostomus sp. = Salish sucker
Caulolatilus = Tilefish Family
Caulolatilus princeps = ocean whitefish
Caulophryne jordani = fanfin
Caulophrynidae = Fanfin Family
cavally = crevalle jack
cavalo féroce = longnose lancetfish
cavalo ocellé = shortnose lancetfish
cavalos = Lancetfish Family
cavefishes = Trout-perch Order
Cayuga minnow = blacknose shiner
central johnny darter = johnny darter
central redfin pickerel = grass pickerel
central silvery minnow = eastern silvery minnow
central silvery minnow = western silvery minnow
Centrarchidae = Sunfish Family
Centrobranchus nigroocellatus = sickle-ear slimlantern
Centrolophidae = Ruff Family
Centrolophus britannicus = Cornish blackfish
Centrolophus medusophagus = Cornish blackfish
Centrolophus niger = black ruff
Centrophryne spinulosa = stout werewolf
Centrophrynidae = stout werewolf
Centropristis striata = black sea bass
Centroscyllium fabricii = black dogfish
Centroscymnus coelolepis = Portuguese shark
Cephalaspidomorphi = fishes
Cephalaspidomorphi = hagfishes
Cephalaspidomorphi = lampreys
Cephalochordata = chordates
Ceratias holboelli = twoclub angler
Ceratias uranoscopus = stargazing seadevil
Ceratiidae = Seadevil Family
Ceratoscopelus = lampfishes
Ceratoscopelus maderensis = horned lampfish
Ceratoscopelus townsendi = dogtooth lampfish
Ceratoscopelus warmingi = southseas lampfish
cernier = wreckfish
Cetomimidae = Flabby Whalefish Family
Cetorhinidae = Basking Shark Family

Cetorhinus maximus = basking shark
chaboisseau à dix-huit épines = longhorn sculpin
chaboisseau à épines courtes = shorthorn sculpin
chaboisseau à quatre cornes = fourhorn sculpin
chaboisseau arctique = Arctic sculpin
chaboisseau bronzé = grubby
chabot à dos épineux = thornback sculpin
chabot à dos rugueux = roughback sculpin
chabot à grande voile = sailfin sculpin
chabot à joue écailleuse = Puget Sound sculpin
chabot à lèvres roses = rosylip sculpin
chabot à longues nageoires = longfin sculpin
chabot à museau épineux = spinynose sculpin
chabot à nageoires noires = blackfin sculpin
chabot à nez pointu = sharpnose sculpin
chabot à petite voile = smallsail sculpin
chabot à queue barrée = bartail sculpin
chabot à taches argentées = silverspotted sculpin
chabot à tête courte = shorthead sculpin
chabot à tête écailleuse = scalyhead sculpin
chabot à tête épineuse = spinyhead sculpin
chabot à tête lisse = smoothhead sculpin
chabot à tête moussue = mosshead sculpin
chabot à tête plate = spoonhead sculpin
chabot armé = Pacific staghorn sculpin
chabot bilobé = crested sculpin
chabot calico = calico sculpin
chabot casqué = armorhead sculpin
chabot côtier = coastrange sculpin
chabot de bâche = tidepool sculpin
chabot de leister = leister sculpin
chabot de profondeur = deepwater sculpin
chabot de torrent = torrent sculpin
chabot élancé = slim sculpin
chabot emmenoté = manacled sculpin
chabot étoilé = stellate sculpin
chabot grogneur = grunt sculpin
chabot maculé = blob sculpin
chabot mantelé = saddleback sculpin
chabot marbré = cabezon
chabot pelucheux = fluffy sculpin
chabot piquant = prickly sculpin
chabot rembourré = padded sculpin
chabot tacheté = mottled sculpin
chabot trilobé brun = brown Irish lord
chabot trilobé rouge = red Irish lord
chabot velouté = soft sculpin

chabot visqueux = slimy sculpin
chabot-bison = buffalo sculpin
chabot-dard = darter sculpin
chabot-têtard = tadpole sculpin
chabots = Sculpin Family
chabots veloutés = Soft Sculpin Family
Chaenobryttus = warmouth
Chaenophryne longiceps = canopener smoothdream
Chaenophryne melanorhabdus = smooth dreamer
Chaetodon = Butterflyfish Family
Chaetodon ocellatus = spotfin butterflyfish
Chaetodontidae = Butterflyfish Family
chain dogfish = chain cat shark
chain-sided sunfish = bluegill
Chalinura brevibarbis = shortbeard grenadier
channel mimic shiner = mimic shiner
channel pickerel = northern pike
channel rockcod = shortspine thornyhead
Characidae = Introduction
Characin Family = Introduction
characins = Carp Order
charbonnier = lake sturgeon
charr = chars
chat = haddock
chat-fou brun = tadpole madtom
chat-fou du nord = northern madtom
chat-fou livré = margined madtom
chat-fou tacheté = brindled madtom
chatauqua = muskellunge
chatte de l'est = golden shiner
chauffet soleil = sergeant major
chauliode de Dana = Dana viperfish
chauliode féroce = Pacific viperfish
chauliode très-lumineux = manylight viperfish
Chauliodontidae = Barbeled Dragonfish Family
Chauliodontidae = viperfishes
Chauliodus = Pacific viperfish
Chauliodus danae = Dana viperfish
Chauliodus macouni = Pacific viperfish
Chauliodus sloani = manylight viperfish
Chaunacidae = Sea Toad Family
Chaunax nuttingi = redeye gaper
Chaunax stigmaeus = redeye gaper
chauve-souris atlantique = Atlantic batfish
chercheur aux yeux bleus = blueeyed searcher
cherry bellies = Atlantic halibut
cherry bream = longear sunfish
cherry salmon = Introduction
chèvre impériale = blackbelly rosefish

chimère à nez mou = knifenose chimera
chimère à nez rigide = longnose chimaera
chimère à petits yeux = deepwater chimaera
chimère d'Amérique = spotted ratfish
chimère d'Haeckel = Haeckel's chimaera
chimère de profondeurs = deepwater chimaera
chimère-couteau = knifenose chimaera
chimère-spatule = longnose chimaera
chimères = Chimaera Family
chimères à long nez = Longnose Chimaera Family
chinchard frappeur = rough scad
Chinese sole = Dover sole
Chirolophis = warbonnets
Chirolophis ascanii = Atlantic warbonnet
Chirolophis decoratus = decorated warbonnet
Chirolophis nugator = mosshead warbonnet
Chirolophis tarsodes = matcheek warbonnet
Chirostomias pliopterus = flexfin dragonfish
chirus = kelp greenling
Chitonotus pugetensis = roughback sculpin
chivin = fallfish
Chlamydoselachus anguineus = Cow Shark Order
Chlorophthalmidae = Greeneye Family
Chlorophthalmus = Greeneye Family
Chlorophthalmus agassizi = shortnose greeneye
chogset = cunner
chogy = cunner
Chondrichthyes = cartilaginous fishes
Chondrichthyes = fishes
Chondrichthyes = jawed fishes
Chondrichthyes = sharks
Chondrostei = ray-finned fishes
Chondrostei = Sturgeon Order
chopper = black buffalo
chopper = bluefish
choquemort = mummichog
Chordata = chordates
Chordata = vertebrates
choupique = bowfin
Christmas flounder = smooth flounder
Chrosomus eos = northern redbelly dace
Chrosomus neogaeus = finescale dace
chub = golden shiner
chub = kiyi
chub = mummichog
chub minnow = lake chub
chub salmon = chinook salmon
chucklehead = black buffalo
chucklehead = black bullhead
chucklehead = channel catfish
Cichlasoma managuense = Cichlid

phin
coryphènes = Dolphin Family
Coryphopterus nicholsi = blackeye goby
cotte arctique = polar sculpin
cotte blême = pallid sculpin
cotte polaire = polar sculpin
Cottidae = Sculpin Family
cottonfish = bowfin
Cottunculus microps = polar sculpin
Cottunculus thomsoni = pallid sculpin
Cottus aleuticus = coastrange sculpin
Cottus asper = prickly sculpin
Cottus asper asper = prickly sculpin
Cottus asper parvus = prickly sculpin
Cottus bairdi = mottled sculpin
Cottus cognatus = slimy sculpin
Cottus confusus = shorthead sculpin
Cottus rhotheus = torrent sculpin
Cottus ricei = spoonhead sculpin
Couch's whiting = blue whiting
Couesius plumbeus = lake chub
couette = quillback
Coulter's whitefish = pygmy whitefish
cow bass = largemouth bass
cow-faced sculpin = spoonhead sculpin
cowfishes = Boxfish Family
cowfishes = Puffer Order
cownose rays = Eagle Ray Family
crabeater = cobia
Craig fluke = witch flounder
crampfish = Atlantic torpedo
crampon bariolé = northern clingfish
crampon de varech = kelp clingfish
crampons = Clingfish Family
cran-tactile à muselet = snoutlet crotchfeeler
cran-tactile losange = roughscale wirewing
cran-tactiles = Tripodfish Family
Craniata = vertebrates
crapaud de mer = polar sculpin
crapaud de mer à courtes épines = shorthorn sculpin
crapauds de mer = Sea Toad Family
crapet = white crappie
crapet à longues oreilles = longear sunfish
crapet arlequin = bluegill
crapet de roche = rock bass
crapet menu = orangespotted sunfish
crapet rouge = redbreast sunfish
crapet sac-à-lait = warmouth
crapet vert = green sunfish
crapet-soleil = pumpkinseed
crapets = Sunfish Family
crayon d'argent = brook silverside
creek cat = brown bullhead
creek cat = yellow bullhead
creek chub = lake chub
creek shiner = common shiner
creek sunfish = green sunfish
creek sunfish = longear sunfish
crested bigscale = crested ridgehead
crested blenny = high cockscomb
crested chub = river chub
crested goby = blackeye goby
crestfishes = Opah Order

crête-de-coq mince = slender cockscomb
crête-de-coq pourpre = high cockscomb
croaker = white seabass
croakers = Drum Family
crochet arctique = snowflake hookear
crocodile sharks = Mackerel Shark Order
crocus = freshwater drum
cross whitefish = round whitefish
croupia roche = tripletail
croupias roches = Tripletail Family
Cryptacanthodes aleutensis = dwarf wrymouth
Cryptacanthodes giganteus = giant wrymouth
Cryptacanthodes maculatus = spotted wrymouth
Cryptacanthodidae = Wrymouth Family
Cryptosaras couesi = warted seadevil
cryptous broad shiner = butterfly
Ctenopharyngodon idella = grass carp
Ctenopharyngodon idella = Introduction
Cuban snapper = cubera snapper
Cubiceps capensis = Cape fathead
Cubiceps gracilis = slender fathead
Cubiceps pauciradiatus = fewray fathead
cuckoo fish = northern searobin
Culaea inconstans = brook stickleback
cultus cod = lingcod
curlfin turbot = curlfin sole
current buffalo = black buffalo
cuttus cod = lingcod
Cyclopsetta fimbriata = spotfin flounder
Cyclopteridae = Lumpfish Family
Cyclopteropsis jordani = smooth lumpfish
Cyclopteropsis macalpini = Arctic lumpsucker
Cyclopterus lumpus = lumpfish
cyclothone à petites dents = veiled anglemouth
cyclothone à queue tachetée = spottail anglemouth
Cyclothone alba = white bristlemouth
cyclothone blanche = white bristlemouth
Cyclothone braueri = spottail anglemouth
cyclothone camuse = bluntnose bristlemouth
cyclothone étoilée = star-eye lightfish
cyclothone jaune = yellow bristlemouth
cyclothone matelot = sailor lightfish
Cyclothone microdon = veiled anglemouth
cyclothone mince = slender bristlemouth
Cyclothone pacifica = yellow bristlemouth

cyclothone pâle = tan bristlemouth
Cyclothone pallida = tan bristlemouth
cyclothone prétentieuse = showy bristlemouth
Cyclothone pseudopallida = slender bristlemouth
cyclothone ruban = ribbon bristlemouth
Cyclothone signata = showy bristlemouth
cyclothones = Bristlemouth Family
Cymatogaster aggregata = shiner perch
cynoglosses = Tonguefish Family
Cynoglossidae = Tonguefish Family
Cynoscion nobilis = white seabass
Cynoscion regalis = weakfish
cypress trout = bowfin
cyprin doré = goldfish
cyprin doré = Introduction
Cyprinella spiloptera = spotfin shiner
Cyprinidae = Carp Family
Cyprinidae = Introduction
Cypriniformes = Carp Order
Cyprinodontiformes = Killifish Order
Cyprinus carpio = common carp
Cyprinus carpio = Introduction
Cypselurus furcatus = spotfin flyingfish
Cypselurus melanurus = Atlantic flyingfish
Cyttopsis roseus = red dory
dab = winter flounder
dace = common shiner
dace = golden shiner
dactyloptère = flying gurnard
dactyloptères = Flying Gurnard Family
Dactylopteridae = Flying Gurnard Family
Dactylopterus volitans = flying gurnard
daddy sculpin = shorthorn sculpin
Dalatias licha = kitefin shark
Dalatiidae = Sleeper Shark Family
dallia = Introduction
Dallia pectoralis = Introduction
Dallia pectoralis = Mudminnow Family
Damalichthys vacca = pile perch
danaphe = bottlelight
Danaphos oculatus = bottlelight
dard à ventre jaune = Iowa darter
dard arc-en-ciel = rainbow darter
dard barré = fantail darter
dard d'herbe = Iowa darter
dard de rivière = river darter
dard de sable = eastern sand darter
dard gris = channel darter
dard noir = blackside darter
dard tesselé = tesselated darter
dard vert = greenside darter
dark dusky rockfish = dusky rockfish
darkfin sculpin = bartail sculpin
darkie charlie = kitefin shark
darktail lamprey = Alaskan lamprey
darter sculpin = slim sculpin
Dasyatidae = Stingray Family
Dasyatis brevis = diamond stingray

Dasyatis centroura = roughtail stingray
Dasyatis violacea = pelagic stingray
Dasycottus setiger = spinyhead sculpin
day smelt = surf smelt
décaptère faux-maquereau = mackerel scad
Decapterus macarellus = mackerel scad
Decapterus punctatus = round scad
Decapterus tabl = redtail scad
decorated blenny = decorated warbonnet
decorated prickleback = decorated warbonnet
deep-pitted sea-poacher = rockhead
deep-sea lizardfish = ferocious lizardfish
deep-water scratchtail = rosethorn rockfish
deepsea angler = twoclub angler
deepsea cods = Mora Family
deepsea eels = Sawpalate Family
deepsea skate = abyssal skate
deepwater blob = deepwater sculpin
deepwater buffalo = black buffalo
deepwater bullhead = stonecat
deepwater catshark = deepsea catshark
deepwater chub = deepwater cisco
deepwater ray = chocolate skate
demi-bec africain = silverstripe halfbeak
demi-bec brésilien = ballyhoo
demi-lune = halfmoon
demoiselles = Damselfish Family
Denny's liparid = marbled snailfish
denticle herrings = Herring Order
dents-de-rêve = dreamteeth
dents-de-sabre rose = pink sabertooth
Derepodichthys alepidotus = cuskpout
Derichthyidae = Neckeel Family
Derichthys serpentinus = neckeel
devil rays = Eagle Ray Family
devil rays = Ray Order
devil-anglers = Werewolf Family
diable de mer = monkfish
Diaphus = headlightfishes
Diaphus dumerili = flashlight headlightfish
Diaphus effulgens = square headlightfish
Diaphus metopoclampus = bouncer headlightfish
Diaphus mollis = straightcheek headlightfish
Diaphus perspicillatus = eventooth headlightfish
Diaphus rafinesquii = doormat parkinglightfish
Diaphus taaningi = Taaning's headlightfish
Diaphus termophilus = slanteye parkinglightfish
Diaphus theta = California headlightfish
Dibranchus atlanticus = Atlantic batfish
Dicrolene intronigra = blackgut tendrilfin

Digby chick = Atlantic herring
Diodon holocanthus = balloonfish
diodon tacheté = balloonfish
Diodontidae = Porcupinefish Family
Diogenichthys atlanticus = longfin lanternfish
Diplogrammus pauciradiatus = spotted dragonet
Diplophos taenia = ribbon bristlemouth
Diretmidae = Spinyfin Family
Diretmus argenteus = spinyfin
diskfishes = Remora Family
ditrème argenté = silver surfperch
ditrème fourchu = white seaperch
ditrème rayé = striped seaperch
ditrème rosé = redtail surfperch
ditrème-vairon = walleye surfperch
ditrèmes = Surfperch Family
dix-bards à épines courtes = short-spine tenplate
dog salmon = chum salmon
dog salmon = pink salmon
dogface sturgeon = lake sturgeon
dogfish = bowfin
dogfish = burbot
dogfish = central mudminnow
dogfish = spiny dogfish
dogfish shark = sand tiger
Dolichopteryx binocularis = binocular spookfish
Dolichopteryx sp. = winged spookfish
dollardee = bluegill
dollarfish = Atlantic moonfish
dollarfish = butterfish
Dolly Varden char = Dolly Varden
Dololepis gigantea = giant wrymouth
Dolopichthys allector = shorthorn dreamer
Dolopichthys pullatus = toothy dreamer
dolphinfishes = Dolphin Family
donzelle à grands yeux = mooneye cusk-eel
donzelle d'Agassiz = Agassiz' cusk-eel
donzelle fauve = fawn cusk-eel
donzelle géante = giant cusk-eel
donzelle rouge = red brotula
donzelles = Cusk-eel Family
donzelles vivipares = Livebearing Brotula Family
doogler = stonecat
dorade = common dolphin
dorado = common dolphin
doré = yellow walleye
doré bleu = blue walleye
doré noir = sauger
Dorosoma cepedianum = gizzard shad
dory = yellow walleye
doughbelly = central stoneroller
doux-rêve ouvre-boîte = can-opener smoothdream
dragon à haute nageoire = highfin dragonfish
dragon à lampe triangulaire = triangle-light dragon
dragon à longues nageoires = longfin dragonfish

dragon à nageoires ployées = flexfin dragonfish
dragon barbu = bearded dragonfish
dragon fuligineux = sooty dragonfish
dragon japonais = pitgum lanternfish
Dragon Lake whitefish = Salmon Family
dragon trois-lampes = triangle-light dragon
dragon vert = shortbarbel dragonfish
dragon-boa = boa dragonfish
dragon-saumon à grands yeux = large-eye snaggletooth
dragon-saumon noir = black snaggletooth
dragon-saumon précieux = gem snaggletooth
dragon-saumons à barbe blanche = whitebearded snaggletooth
dragonnet à trois épines = spotted dragonet
dragonnet de Baird = lancer dragonet
dragonnets = Dragonet Family
dragons à barbillon = Barbeled Dragonfish Family
drague à dix rayons = tenrayed loosejaw
drague à grande gueule = bigmouth loosejaw
drague à nez court = shortnose loosejaw
drague de Tittmann = Tittmann's loosejaw
drague grands-yeux = largeye
drague lunée = crescent loosejaw
drague Pléiades = Pleiades loosejaw
drague rouge-verte = stoplight loosejaw
drague sans lampe = stoplight loosejaw
drague scintillante = shining loosejaw
drum = quillback
drummers = Sea Chub Family
duck-billed pike = chain pickerel
duckbill cat = paddlefish
duckbill oceanic eel = duckbill eel
dusky sea-perch = pile perch
dusky smooth-hound = smooth dogfish
dwarf shark = spined pygmy shark
dwarf sunfish = orangespotted sunfish
eared blacksmelt = popeye blacksmelt
East Siberian cod = toothed cod
Easter herring = Pacific herring
eastern banded killifish = banded killifish
eastern blacknose dace = blacknose dace
eastern brook trout = brook trout
eastern golden shiner = golden shiner
eastern mosquitofish = mosquitofish
eastern Pacific bonito = Pacific bonito
eastern pickerel = chain pickerel
eastern quillback = quillback
eastern redhorse = shorthead redhorse
eastern river chub = river chub
eastern shiner = common shiner

eastern stickleback = threespine stickleback
eastern sucker = white sucker
eastern whitefish = lake whitefish
Echeneidae = Remora Family
Echeneididae = Remora Family
Echeneis naucrates = sharksucker
Echinodermata = chordates
Echiodon dawsoni = chain pearlfish
Echiostoma barbatum = bearded dragonfish
Ectreposebastes imus = scaly hedgehogfish
Edriolychnus schmidti = Schmidt's leftvent
eel blenny = snake prickleback
eelback = smooth flounder
eelpout = burbot
eelpout = ocean pout
églefin = haddock
ekaluk = Arctic char
electric catfishes = Catfish Order
Electrona risso = sun flashlightfish
Eleginus gracilis = saffron cod
elephant fishes = Chimaera Order
elephant-fish = spotted ratfish
elephantfishes = Bony-tongue Order
elephantfishes = Mooneye Family
elf = bluefish
Elopiformes = Tarpon Order
Elopomorpha = teleosts
Embassichthys bathybius = deepsea sole
Embiotoca lateralis = striped seaperch
Embiotocidae = Surfperch Family
Embryx crotalina = snakehead eelpout
emerywheel = starry flounder
émissole = smooth dogfish
émissole douce = smooth dogfish
émissoles = Hound Shark Family
Enchelyopus cimbrius = fourbeard rockling
English sole = petrale sole
Engraulidae = Anchovy Family
Engraulis eurystole = silver anchovy
Engraulis mordax = northern anchovy
Engyophrys senta = spiny flounder
Enophrys bison = buffalo sculpin
Enophrys lucasi = leister sculpin
Enos Lake stickleback = Enos stickleback
Eopsetta exilis = slender sole
Eopsetta jordani = petrale sole
épaule-criblée long nez = longsnout manypitsshoulder
éperlan arc-en-ciel = rainbow smelt
éperlan argenté = surf smelt
éperlan blanchaille = whitebait smelt
éperlan d'hiver = longfin smelt
éperlan du nord = rainbow smelt
éperlan nain = pygmy smelt
éperlan nocturne = night smelt
éperlans = Smelt Family
Epigonidae = Greateye Family
Epigonus denticulatus = greateye
Epinephelus niveatus = snowy grouper
épingle = emerald shiner

épinoche à cinq épines = brook stickleback
épinoche à neuf épines = ninespine stickleback
épinoche à quatre épines = fourspine stickleback
épinoche à trois épines = threespine stickleback
épinoche blanche = white stickleback
épinoche d'Enos = Enos stickleback
épinoche de Texada = Texada stickleback
épinoche géante = giant stickleback
épinoche tachetée = blackspotted stickleback
épinoches = Stickleback Family
Eptatretus deani = black hagfish
Eptatretus stouti = Pacific hagfish
eqaludjuaq = Greenland shark
eqalukjuaq = Greenland shark
equaluaq = Arctic cod
equille = stout sand lance
Eretmophoridae = Mora Family
Erilepis zonifer = skilfish
Erimystax x-punctatus = gravel chub
Erimyzon sucetta = lake chubsucker
Errex zachirus = rex sole
escaille = Atlantic sturgeon
escargot = Atlantic sturgeon
escargot maillé = lake sturgeon
escolar = escolar
escolars = Snake Mackerel Family
escolier long nez = cone-chin
escolier noir = escolar
Eskimo tarpon = inconnu
Esmark's eelpout = greater eelpout
Esocae = Pike Order
Esocidae = Pike Family
Esociformes = Pike Order
Esox americanus americanus = redfin pickerel
Esox americanus vermiculatus = grass pickerel
Esox lucius = northern pike
Esox masquinongy = muskellunge
Esox niger = chain pickerel
espadon = swordfish
espadons = Swordfish Family
Estreita = narrowside alfonsin
esturgeon à museau court = shortnose sturgeon
esturgeon blanc = white sturgeon
esturgeon de lac = lake sturgeon
esturgeon jaune = lake sturgeon
esturgeon noir = Atlantic sturgeon
esturgeon vert = green sturgeon
esturgeons = Sturgeon Family
étendard vert-bronzé = bronze-green flagfin
Etheostoma blennioides = greenside darter
Etheostoma caeruleum = rainbow darter
Etheostoma exile = Iowa darter
Etheostoma flabellare = fantail darter
Etheostoma microperca = least darter
Etheostoma nigrum = johnny darter
Etheostoma olmstedi = tesselated darter
Etheostoma pellucidum = eastern sand darter
Etmopterus princeps = rough sagre

Etropus crossotus = fringed flounder
Etropus microstomus = smallmouth flounder
Etrumeus teres = round herring
Eugomphodus taurus = sand tiger
eulakane = eulachon
Eumesogrammus praecisus = fourline snakeblenny
Eumicrotremus andriashevi = Newfoundland spiny lumpsucker
Eumicrotremus derjugini = leatherfin lumpsucker
Eumicrotremus orbis = Pacific spiny lumpsucker
Eumicrotremus spinosus = Atlantic spiny lumpsucker
Eumicrotremus terraenovae = Newfoundland spiny lumpsucker
European brown trout = brown trout
European carp = common carp
European char = Arctic char
European eel = American eel
European eel = Freshwater Eel Family
European flounder = Introduction
European houting = Salmon Family
European stickleback = threespine stickleback
Eurypharyngidae = Gulper Family
Eurypharynx pelecanoides = pelican gulper
Eustomias fissibarbis = tripletwig smoothgill
Euteleostei = teleosts
Euthynnus alletteratus = little tunny
Euthynnus pelamis = skipjack tuna
Evermanellidae = Sabertooth Fish Family
Evermannella balbo = pink sabertooth
exocet à frange blanche = fourwing flyingfish
exocet à nageoires noires = blackwing flyingfish
exocet à nageoires tachetées = spotfin flyingfish
exocet aile noire = blackwing flyingfish
exocet atlantique = Atlantic flyingfish
exocet hirondelle = fourwing flyingfish
exocets = Flyingfish Family
Exocoetidae = Flyingfish Family
Exocoetus vinciguerrae = blackwing flyingfish
Exoglossum maxillingua = cutlips minnow
expatrié rétropinne = rearfin expatriate
eye-picker = cutlips minnow
eyed skate = winter skate
fair maid = scup
false brotulas = Cusk-eel Order
false catsharks = Ground Shark Order
false seascorpion = Arctic sculpin
fan-tailed ragfish = ragfish
fanfre = pilotfish
fanfre noir = black sea bass
fanged viperfish = Pacific viperfish
fangtooth lanternfish = dogtooth

lampfish
fangtooths = Alfonsino Order
Far Eastern navaga = saffron cod
fat back = Atlantic menhaden
fat lake trout = lake trout
fat-head chub = bluntnose minnow
fat-priest fish = skilfish
fatheads = Soft Sculpin Family
fathom fish = eulachon
faune rêveur fer-de-lance = whalehead dreamer
fausse limande pâté = channel flounder
faux flétan = Canadian plaice
faux-trigle armé = moustache sculpin
faux-trigle aux grands yeux = bigeye sculpin
faux-trigle bardé = ribbed sculpin
faux-trigle épineux = roughspine sculpin
featherbacks = Bony-tongue Order
federation pickerel = chain pickerel
feu-arrière à joue courte = shortcheek tail-light
feu-follet à platine courte = shortplate will-o'-the-wisp
fiddler = channel catfish
fierasfers Pearlfish Family
filamented grenadier = filamented rattail
filamented sculpin = threadfin sculpin
finback catsharks = Ground Shark Order
fine scaled sucker = white sucker
finescale antimora = Pacific flatnose
finescale codling = Pacific flatnose
finescale goby = bay goby
finescale mullet = black redhorse
finescale redhorse = black redhorse
finescale sucker = longnose sucker
fishing frog = monkfish
fistulaire tabac = bluespotted cornetfish
fistulaires = Cornetfish Family
Fistularia tabacaria = bluespotted cornetfish
Fistulariidae = Cornetfish Family
five-banded damselfish = sergeant major
five-spined stickleback = brook stickleback
fjord cod = ogac
flake = spiny dogfish
flatbelly = flathead catfish
flatfish = pumpkinseed
flathead clingfish = northern clingfish
flathead mullet = striped mullet
flathead sculpin = smoothhead sculpin
flatnose cod = blue antimora
flatnose codling = blue antimora
flatnose cods = Mora Family
flet = witch flounder
flet d'Europe = European flounder
flet d'Europe = Introduction
flet étoilé = starry flounder
flétan atlantique = Atlantic halibut
flétan du Groenland = Greenland halibut
flétan du Pacifique = Pacific halibut

flétan noir = Greenland halibut
Florida gar = Introduction
flotsamfish = bluefin driftfish
flotsamfishes = Driftfish Family
flounder = Canadian plaice
flounder = starry flounder
flounder = winter flounder
flutemouths = Cornetfish Family
flying toad = northern searobin
Foetorepus agassizi = spotfin dragonet
Folkestone beef = spiny dogfish
fondule barré = banded killifish
fondule rayé = blackstripe topminnow
fondules = Killifish Family
foolfish = smooth flounder
football atlantique = lightlamp football fish
football de Maul = Maul's football fish
football fine-lampe = lightlamp football fish
forkbarbel netdevil = forkbarbelthroat
forktail greenling = Atka mackerel
forktail perch = pile perch
forktail trout = lake trout
fouette-queue = quillfish
fouette-queues = Quillfish Family
fouille-roche = logperch
four-eyed fishes = Killifish Order
four-horned sea scorpion = fourhorn sculpin
four-spined sculpin = fourhorn sculpin
fourbarbel netdevil = fourbarbelthroat
fox shark = thresher shark
French sole = arrowtooth flounder
freshwater angelfish = Cichlid Family
freshwater angelfish = Introduction
freshwater butterflyfish = Bony-tongue Order
freshwater butterflyfishes = Mooneye Family
freshwater catfishes = Bullhead Catfish Family
freshwater cod = burbot
freshwater cusk = burbot
freshwater eel = burbot
freshwater herring = Bering cisco
freshwater herring = lake cisco
freshwater herring = mooneye
freshwater killy = banded killifish
freshwater mummichog = banded killifish
freshwater sculpin = mottled sculpin
freshwater smelt = rainbow smelt
freshwater stingrays = Ray Order
freshwater sturgeon = lake sturgeon
friar = brook silverside
frilled shark = Cow Shark Family
frilled shark = Cow Shark Order
fringe sole = sand sole
fringe-finned fishes = bony fishes
fringed greenling = rock greenling
frost fish = round whitefish
frostfish = Atlantic tomcod
frostfish = rainbow smelt
frostfish = silver hake

frostfishes = Cutlassfish Family
fucus blenny = rockweed gunnel
Fundulidae = Killifish Family
Fundulus diaphanus = banded killifish
Fundulus diaphanus diaphanus = banded killifish
Fundulus diaphanus menona = banded killifish
Fundulus heteroclitus = mummichog
Fundulus heteroclitus macrolepidotus = mummichog
Fundulus notatus = blackstripe topminnow
furfish = fur-bearing trout
fusiliers = Snapper Family
Gadidae = Cod Family
Gadiformes = Cod Order
Gadus macrocephalus = Pacific cod
Gadus morhua = Atlantic cod
Gadus ogac = ogac
Gaidropsarus argentatus = silver rockling
Gaidropsarus ensis = threebeard rockling
Galeocerdo cuvier = tiger shark
Galeorhinus galeus = soupfin shark
Galeorhinus zyopterus = soupfin shark
Gambusia affinis = Introduction
Gambusia affinis = mosquitofish
Gambusia holbrooki = mosquitofish
gambusie = Introduction
gambusie = mosquitofish
gapers = Sea Toad Family
Gar Family = Introduction
garcette à oreilles = popeye blacksmelt
garcette à petits yeux = smalleye blacksmelt
garcette de Grey = Grey's smoothtongue
garcette élancée = slender blacksmelt
garcette étoilée = starry blacksmelt
garcette-goître = goitre blacksmelt
garcettes = Deepsea Smelt Family
gardon rouge = Introduction
gardon rouge = rudd
garguncle = rock bass
garpike = longnose gar
gaspareau = gaspereau
gaspareau = blueback herring
gaspergou = freshwater drum
Gasterosteus aculeatus complex = threespine stickleback
Gasterosteidae = Stickleback Family
Gasterosteiformes = Stickleback Order
Gasterosteus aculeatus = threespine stickleback
Gasterosteus sp. = Enos stickleback
Gasterosteus sp. = giant stickleback
Gasterosteus sp. = Texada stickleback
Gasterosteus sp. = white stickleback
Gasterosteus wheatlandi = blackspotted stickleback
gator = northern pike
gatte = American shad
gelatinous seasnail = gelatinous snailfish
gemfishes = Snake Mackerel Family

Gempylidae = Snake Mackerel Family

genuine red = vermilion rockfish

Genyonemus lineatus = white croaker

Georges Bank flounder = winter flounder

Gephyroberyx darwini = Darwin's slimehead

German bass = common carp

German brown trout = brown trout

German carp = common carp

germon = albacore

ghost pipefishes = Stickleback Order

ghost sharks = Chimaera Order

ghostfish = spotted wrymouth

giant devil ray = manta

giant grenadier = pectoral rattail

giant halibut = Atlantic halibut

giant marbled sculpin = cabezon

giant pygmy whitefish = Salmon Family

giant seabass = skilfish

giant seadevil = twoclub angler

giant tuna = bluefin tuna

giant yellowtail = yellowtail

gibber = haddock

Gibbonsia metzi = striped kelpfish

Gibbonsia montereyensis = crevice snailfish

Gigantactinidae = Whipnose Family

Gigantactis = Whipnose Family

Gigantactis longicirra = longtail whipnose

Gigantactis vanhoeffeni = Vanhoeffen's whipnose

Gilbert's minnow = bigmouth shiner

gizzard fish = lake whitefish

glass eye = yellow walleye

glassfish = brook silverside

globe-headed sculpin = mosshead sculpin

globefish = northern puffer

glut herring = blueback herring

glut herring = gaspereau

Glyptocephalus cynoglossus = witch flounder

Glyptocephalus zachirus = rex sole

Gnathostomata = jawed fishes

Gnathostomata = jawless fishes

gnomefishes = Bluefish Family

goatfish = spotted ratfish

goberge = pollock

goberge de l'Alaska = walleye pollock

gobie à nez tubulaire = Introduction

gobie à nez tubulaire = tubenose goby

gobie arrondie = Introduction

gobie arrondie = round goby

gobie aux yeux noirs = blackeye goby

gobie de baie = bay goby

gobie-flèche = arrow goby

gobies = Goby Family

Gobiesocidae = Clingfish Family

Gobiesox maeandricus = northern clingfish

Gobiidae = Goby Family

Gobiidae = Introduction

goblin sharks = Mackerel Shark Order

Goby Family = Introduction

goggle eye = rock bass

goggle eye jack = bigeye scad

goggle-eye = green sunfish

goggle-eye = warmouth

goggle-eye = white crappie

gold bass = smallmouth bass

gold ring = white crappie

golden carp = goldfish

golden mullet = golden redhorse

golden shad = gaspereau

golden sucker = golden redhorse

golden trout = Arctic char

golden trout = Introduction

golden trout = rainbow trout

goldeneye rockfish = yelloweye rockfish

goldfish = golden shiner

goldfish = Introduction

Gonichthys cocco = linestop lanternfish

Gonostoma bathyphilum = spark anglemouth

Gonostoma elongatum = longtooth anglemouth

Gonostoma gracile = slender fangjaw

Gonostomatidae = Bristlemouth Family

gonostome à grandes dents = longtooth anglemouth

gonostome élancé = slender fangjaw

gonostome étincelé = spark anglemouth

gonostome nu = longtooth anglemouth

goo = freshwater drum

google-eyed scad = bigeye scad

goosefish = monkfish

gopher rock cod = quillback rockfish

Gordiichthys irretitus = horsehair eel

Gordiichthys leibyi = string eel

gorge à barbe fourchue = forkbarbelthroat

gorge à grande barbe = greatbarbelthroat

gorge à quatre barbes = fourbarbelthroat

gorge bicornue à barbe = twohorn barbelthroat

goujon = flathead catfish

gourami bleu = Introduction

Gourami Family = Introduction

gourdhead buffalo = bigmouth buffalo

gourdseed buffalo = bigmouth buffalo

Grammicolepididae = Diamond Dory Family

Grammicolepis brachiusculus = thorny tinselfish

grand avaleur = black swallower

grand brochet = northern pike

grand chaboisseau = great sculpin

grand corégone = lake whitefish

grand requin blanc = great white shark

grand tambour = black drum

grande argentine = Atlantic argentine

grande castagnole = Atlantic pomfret

grande hache d'argent = greater silver hatchetfish

grande lamproie marine = sea lamprey

grande lingue = European ling

grande lycode = greater eelpout

grande raie = barndoor skate

grande raie = broad skate

grande sériole = greater amberjack

grandgousier pélican = pelican gulper

grandgousiers = Gulper Family

grands avaleurs = Black Swallower Family

grands yeux = emerald shiner

grands yeux = Greateye Family

grands-yeux = greateye

granny cat = flathead catfish

grass bass = black crappie

grass carp = Introduction

grass minnow = brassy minnow

grass pickerel = chain pickerel

grass pickerel = redfin pickerel

grass pike = chain pickerel

grass pike = grass pickerel

grass pike = northern pike

gravelier = gravel chub

gray bass = white bass

gray cod = Pacific cod

gray perch = freshwater drum

gray perch = white perch

gray pike = yellow walleye

gray sculpin = longhorn sculpin

gray trout = weakfish

gray weakfish = weakfish

Gray's cutthroat eel = slatjaw cutthroat eel

grayback = banded killifish

grayback tullibee = lake cisco

grayling = Atlantic salmon

grayling = mountain whitefish

greased chub = central stoneroller

greaser = shortnose cisco

greaser = yellow bullhead

great albacore = bluefin tuna

great blue shark = blue shark

Great Lake catfish = channel catfish

Great Lakes fourhorn sculpin = deepwater sculpin

Great Lakes longear = longear sunfish

Great Lakes longnose dace = longnose dace

Great Lakes muskellunge = muskellunge

Great Lakes pike = northern pike

Great Lakes sturgeon = lake sturgeon

Great Lakes trout = lake trout

Great Lakes whitefish = lake whitefish

great lanternshark = rough sagre

great muskellunge = muskellunge

great northern pike = northern pike

great northern tilefish = tilefish

greater argentine = Atlantic argentine

greater redhorse = river redhorse

greater silver smelt = Atlantic argentine

greater yellowtail = greater amberjack

greedigut = monkfish

green bass = largemouth bass

green bass = smallmouth bass

green cod = lingcod

green cod = pollock

green eel = American eel

green ocean pout = fish doctor

green perch = green sunfish

green pike = chain pickerel

green pike = yellow walleye

green smelt = Atlantic silverside

green snapper = yellowtail rockfish

green swordtail = Introduction

green swordtail = Livebearer Family

green trout = largemouth bass

green trout = smallmouth bass

Green's liparid = lobefin snailfish

green-eye = northern searobin

greenhead = striped bass

Greenland argentine = large-eye argentine

Greenland char = Arctic char

Greenland cod = ogac

Greenland sand lance = northern sand lance

Greenland sculpin = shorthorn sculpin

Greenland snailfish = kelp snailfish

Greenland turbot = Greenland halibut

greenling sea trout = kelp greenling

grémille = Introduction

grémille = ruffe

grenadier à barbe courte = shortbeard grenadier

grenadier à barbillon court = carapine grenadier

grenadier à écailles minces = ghostly grenadier

grenadier à écailles rudes = roughscale grenadier

grenadier à long nez = longnose grenadier

grenadier barbu = bearded rattail

grenadier berglax = roughhead grenadier

grenadier cendré = popeye

grenadier de Grand Banc = marlinspike

grenadier de Günther = Günther's grenadier

grenadier de profondeur = russet grenadier

grenadier de roche = rock grenadier

grenadier filamenté = filamented rattail

grenadier lisse = smooth grenadier

grenadier pectoral = pectoral rattail

grenadier raton = longnose grenadier

grenadier roux = russet grenadier

grenadier scie = American straptail grenadier

grenadier-lampe = lamp grenadier

grenadier-scie = roughnose grenadier

grenadiers = Grenadier Family

grey herring = gaspereau

grey marlinsucker = spearfish remora

grey mullet = striped mullet

grey mullets = Mullet Family

grey pickerel = sauger

grey pike = sauger

grey pike-perch = sauger

grey reef shark = silky shark

grey shark = Greenland shark

grey sucker = white sucker

grey trout = lake trout

humpback = lake whitefish
humpback = pink salmon
huss = spiny dogfish
Hybognathus argyritus = western silvery minnow
Hybognathus hankinsoni = brassy minnow
Hybognathus nuchalis = eastern silvery minnow
Hybognathus nuchalis = western silvery minnow
Hybognathus regius = eastern silvery minnow
Hybopsis gracilis = flathead chub
Hybopsis storeriana = silver chub
Hybopsis x-punctata = gravel chub
Hydrolagus affinis = deepwater chimaera
Hydrolagus colliei = spotted ratfish
Hygophum benoiti = longnose hugo
Hygophum hygomi = highvelo hugo
Hygophum taaningi = upmouth hugo
Hypentelium nigricans = northern hog sucker
Hyperoglyphe perciformis = barrelfish
Hyperprosopon argenteum = walleye surfperch
Hyperprosopon ellipticum = silver surfperch
Hypomesus olidus = pond smelt
Hypomesus pretiosus = surf smelt
Hyporhamphus unifasciatus = silverstripe halfbeak
Hypsagonus quadricornis = fourhorn poacher
Hypsoblennius hentz = feather blenny
i ha luk = brook trout
Icatalurus natalis = yellow bullhead
icefish = rainbow smelt
icèle à deux cornes = twohorn sculpin
icèle spatulée = spatulate sculpin
icéline à grandes yeux = fringed sculpin
icéline à nageoires tachetées = spotfin sculpin
icéline boréale = northern sculpin
icéline épineuse = thorny sculpin
icéline filamenteuse = threadfin sculpin
icéline obscure = dusky sculpin
Icelinus = threadfin sculpin
Icelinus borealis = northern sculpin
Icelinus burchami = dusky sculpin
Icelinus filamentosus = threadfin sculpin
Icelinus fimbriatus = fringed sculpin
Icelinus tenuis = spotfin sculpin
Icelus bicornis = twohorn sculpin
Icelus spatula = spatulate sculpin
Icelus spiniger = thorny sculpin
Ichthyococcus elongatus = slim lightfish
Ichthyococcus ovatus = ovate lightfish
Ichthyomyzon castaneus = chestnut lamprey
Ichthyomyzon fossor = northern brook lamprey
Ichthyomyzon unicuspis = silver lam-

prey
Icichthys lockingtoni = medusafish
Icosteidae = Ragfish Family
Icosteus aenigmaticus = ragfish
Ictaluridae = Bullhead Catfish Family
Ictalurus = yellow bullhead
Ictalurus melas = black bullhead
Ictalurus nebulosus = brown bullhead
Ictalurus punctatus = channel catfish
Ictiobus cyprinellus = bigmouth buffalo
Ictiobus niger = black buffalo
idiacanthus ruban = ribbon sawtailfish
Idiacanthidae = Barbeled Dragonfish Family
Idiacanthidae = sawtailfishes
Idiacanthus fasciola = ribbon sawtailfish
idiotfish = longspine thornyhead
idiotfish = shortspine thornyhead
idlûlukak = northern pike
ihok = lake trout
ihok = northern pike
iituuq = Pacific herring
ilkalupik = Arctic char
iloraq = Arctic char
ilortoq = lake trout
Ilyophis brunneus = brown cutthroat eel
Indian chub = hornyhead chub
Indian fish = warmouth
ingminniset = roughhead grenadier
inland char = bull trout
inland whitefish = lake whitefish
inquiline snailfish = scallop snailfish
inshore sand lance = stout sand lance
Ipnopidae = Tripodfish Family
iqalujjuaq = Greenland shark
iqaluk tasirsiutik = brook trout
iqalukuak = Greenland shark
iqluq = lake trout
ironsides = scup
isok = lake trout
Isopsetta isolepis = butter sole
Isurus oxyrinchus = shortfin mako
Isurus paucus = longfin mako
isuuq = lake trout
isuuqiq = lake trout
isuuraaryok = lake trout
itok = Arctic cod
ivatarak = Arctic char
ivitaruk = lake trout
jack = chain pickerel
jack = muskellunge
jack = northern pike
jack perch = yellow perch
jack salmon = sauger
jack salmon = yellow walleye
jack shad = gizzard shad
jackfish = logperch
jaguar guapote = Cichlid Family
jaguar guapote = Introduction
javelinfish = daggertooth
javelinfish = smalleye frostfish
jelly-cat = northern wolffish
Jensen's skate = shorttail skate
jerker = hornyhead chub
Jerusalem haddock = opah
jewel cichlid = jewelfish
jewel-head = freshwater drum

jewelfish = Introduction
jikuktok = lake whitefish
John Demon = white crappie
Johnny cat = flathead catfish
johnny cod = chilipepper
Johnson's black anglerfish = stout werewolf
Jordan's sucker = mountain sucker
Jordania zonope = longfin sculpin
Juan de Fuca liparid = slipskin snailfish
jugmouth = warmouth
julienne = European ling
jumbo = haddock
jumper = smallmouth bass
jumper bass = largemouth bass
jumping cod = tripletail
jumping mullet = striped mullet
June sucker = white sucker
kakidlautidlik = ninespine stickleback
kakilahaq = ninespine stickleback
kakilasak = ninespine stickleback
kakilaychok = threespine stickleback
kakilishek = ninespine stickleback
kakilishek = threespine stickleback
kakilusuk = ninespine stickleback
kakilusuk = threespine stickleback
kakiva = ninespine stickleback
kakiviartût = lake whitefish
kakiviatktok = lake whitefish
kaktak = Arctic cisco
kaloarpok = Arctic char
Kamchatka flounder = Asiatic arrowtooth flounder
Kamloops trout = rainbow trout
kanaiyok = slimy sculpin
kanayuk = Arctic sculpin
kanayuk = fourhorn sculpin
kapihilik = lake whitefish
kapahilik = least cisco
kapisilik = Arctic cisco
kapisilik = lake cisco
kapisilik = round whitefish
katilautik = threespine stickleback
Katsuwonus pelamis = skipjack tuna
Kaup's deepsea eel = slatjaw cutthroat eel
kaviselik = lake cisco
kavisilâq = Pacific herring
kavisilik = Atlantic salmon
kavisilik = lake whitefish
keelcheek bass = spiny widejaw
keki-yuak-tuk = lake whitefish
kelp cod = whitespotted greenling
kelp sea-perch = kelp perch
kelpfishes = Clinid Family
Kennebec salmon = Atlantic salmon
Kennerly's salmon = sockeye salmon
Kern River trout = golden trout
keta = chum salmon
kewlook powak = Arctic grayling
kicker = black buffalo
kickininee = sockeye salmon
kikiyuk = northern pike
king carp = common carp
king salmon = chinook salmon
king-fish = white croaker
kingfish = opah
kipper = Atlantic herring
kivvy = pumpkinseed
knife-teeth eels = Pike Conger

Family
knifefishes = Bony-tongue Order
knifefishes = Carp Order
knifefishes = Mooneye Family
ko le le kuk = capelin
kokanee = sockeye salmon
kokani = sockeye salmon
koke = sockeye salmon
koupjhaun-ohuk = fish doctor
kraaktak = Arctic cisco
kraaktak = least cisco
krolleliprark = Pacific herring
Krøyer's barracudina = duckbill barracudina
Krøyer's lanternfish = northern saillamp
kugsaunak = banded gunnel
kugsaunak = fish doctor
kyack = blueback herring
kyack = gaspereau
kyphose des Bermudes = Bermuda chub
kyphoses = Sea Chub Family
Kyphosidae = Sea Chub Family
Kyphosus sectatrix = Bermuda chub
Labichthys carinatus = carinate snipe eel
Labidesthes sicculus = brook silverside
Labrador herring = Atlantic herring
Labrador redfish = Acadian redfish
Labrador whitefish = lake whitefish
labres = Wrasse Family
Labridae = Wrasse Family
Lactophrys trigonus = rough trunkfish
Lactophrys triqueter = smooth trunkfish
lady cat = channel catfish
ladyfish = bonefish
ladyfishes = Bonefish Family
ladyfishes = Tarpon Order
Laemonema barbatula = smallscale mora
lafayette = butterfish
Lagocephalus lagocephalus = oceanic puffer
laimargue atlantique = Greenland shark
laimargue dormeur = Pacific sleeper shark
laimargue du Pacifique = Pacific sleeper shark
laimargues = Sleeper Shark Family
lake Atlantic salmon = Atlantic salmon
lake bass = largemouth bass
lake buffalo = bigmouth buffalo
lake char = lake trout
lake catfish = channel catfish
lake drum = freshwater drum
lake herring = Bering cisco
lake herring = lake cisco
lake herring = lake whitefish
lake herring = least cisco
lake herrings = ciscoes
lake lamprey = sea lamprey
Lake Michigan shiner = emerald shiner
lake minnow = round whitefish
lake perch = yellow perch
lake pickerel = chain pickerel

lake quillback = quillback
lake sculpin = deepwater sculpin
lake sculpin = mottled sculpin
lake shad = gizzard shad
lake shiner = emerald shiner
lake silverside = emerald shiner
lake smelt = rainbow smelt
Lake Superior longjaw = shortjaw cisco
lake trout = west-slope cutthroat trout
laker = lake trout
Lamna ditropis = salmon shark
Lamna nasus = porbeagle
Lamnidae = Mackerel Shark Family
lamnies = Mackerel Shark Family
Lamniformes = Mackerel Shark Order
Lampadena = lampfishes
Lampadena luminosa = highfourthpo lampfish
Lampadena speculigera = toothnose lampfish
Lampadena urophaos = sunbeam lampfish
Lampanyctus = toplights lanternfish
Lampanyctus alatus = lesser beacon-lamp
Lampanyctus ater = shortwing lanternfish
Lampanyctus crocodilus = jewel lanternfish
Lampanyctus festivus = seven-aoa platelamp
Lampanyctus intricarius = diamond-cheek lanternfish
Lampanyctus jordani = brokenline lanternfish
Lampanyctus macdonaldi = rakery lanternfish
Lampanyctus photonotus = toplights lanternfish
Lampanyctus pusillus = shortplate will-o'-the-wisp
Lampanyctus regalis = pinpoint lanternfish
Lampanyctus ritteri = broadfin lanternfish
lampe à feux latéraux = sidelight lanternfish
lampe à front lisse = smoothbrow lampfish
lampe à grandes nageoires = broadfin lanternfish
lampe à haut-po-quatre = high-fourthpo lampfish
lampe à joue épinée = spinecheek lanternfish
lampe à joue lisse = smoothcheek lanternfish
lampe à nez denté = toothnose lamp-fish
lampe à rayon de soleil = sunbeam lampfish
lampe à sourcils lumineux = dog-tooth lampfish
lampe cornée = horned lampfish
lampe d'apparat des mers du sud = southseas lampfish
lampe royale = pinpoint lanternfish
lampe sans épine sourcilière = smoothbrow lampfish

lampe-de-plongée de la Méditerranée = Mediterranean divinglamp
lampe-de-plongée des Caraïbes = Caribbean divinglamp
lampe-de-tête à taches blanches = California headlightfish
lampe-de-tête carrée = square head-lightfish
lampe-de-tête de casseur = bouncer headlightfish
lampe-de-tête de Taaning = Taaning's headlightfish
lampe-de-tête joue-droite = straightcheek headlightfish
lampe-de-tête lampion = flashlight headlightfish
lampe-de-tête unidentée = eventooth headlightfish
lampe-platine à sept-aoa = seven-aoa platelamp
lampe-veilleuse oeil-penché = slant-eye parkinglightfish
lampe-veilleuse paillasson = doormat parkinglightfish
lampe-voilière du nord = northern saillamp
lampe-voilière sao-en-coin = patch-work lanternfish
lamper eel = sea lamprey
Lampetra alaskense = Alaskan lam-prey
Lampetra appendix = American brook lamprey
Lampetra ayresi = river lamprey
Lampetra japonica = Arctic lamprey
Lampetra lamotteni = American brook lamprey
Lampetra macrostoma = lake lam-prey
Lampetra richardsoni = western brook lamprey
Lampetra richardsoni var. *marifuga* = western brook lamprey
Lampetra tridentata = Pacific lam-prey
Lampetra wilderi = American brook lamprey
lampion-soleil = sun flashlightfish
lamplighter = black crappie
lamprey eel = sea lamprey
Lampridae = Opah Family
Lamprididae = Opah Family
Lampridiformes = Opah Order
Lampriformes = Opah Order
Lampris guttatus = opah
Lampris regius = opah
lamproie à grand disque = lake lam-prey
lamproie à queue noire = river lam-prey
lamproie arctique = Arctic lamprey
lamproie argentée = silver lamprey
lamproie brun = chestnut lamprey
lamproie d'Alaska = Alaskan lam-prey
lamproie de l'est = American brook lamprey
lamproie de l'ouest = western brook lamprey
lamproie du nord = northern brook lamprey
lamproie du Pacifique = Pacific lam-

prey
lamproies = Lamprey Family
lançon d'Amérique = stout sand lance
lançon du nord = northern sand lance
lançon gourdeau = stout sand lance
lançons = Sand Lance Family
landlocked salmon = Atlantic salmon
landlocked salmon = lake trout
landlocked sockeye = sockeye salmon
lant = stout sand lance
lanternbellies = Temperate Ocean Bass Family
lanterne à grandes écailles = glow-ingfish
lanterne à joue pailletée = diamond-cheek lanternfish
lanterne à ligne brisée = brokenline lanternfish
lanterne à longues nageoires = longfin lanternfish
lanterne à pectorale courte = short-wing lanternfish
lanterne à queue épineuse = spinetail lanternfish
lanterne bleu = blue lanternfish
lanterne boute-ligne = linestop lanternfish
lanterne de Bolin = Bolin's lantern-fish
lanterne de Noël = toplights lantern-fish
lanterne du nord = northern lantern-fish
lanterne feu-arrière = tail-light lanternfish
lanterne feu-avant = eyelight lantern-fish
lanterne glaciaire = glacier lantern-fish
lanterne grenat = garnet lanternfish
lanterne japonaise = Japanese lanternfish
lanterne lunaire = lunar lanternfish
lanterne ponctuée = spotted lantern-fish
lanterne rude du nord = metallic lanternfish
lanterne rugueuse = roughscale lanternfish
lanterne-bouée râtelière = rakery lanternfish
lanterne-de-coin nord-atlantique = North Atlantic cornerlantern
lanterne-fine oreille-faucille = sickle-ear slimlantern
lanterne-joyau = jewel lanternfish
lanterne-lézard écaillée = scaly wary-fish
lanternes à grandes nageoires = bigfin lanternfish
lanterneyes = Alfonsino Order
laquaiche argentée = mooneye
laquaiche aux yeux d'or = goldeye
laquaiches = Mooneye Family
large sleeper = Greenland shark
largenoses = Opah Order
largescale lanternfish = North Atlantic cornerlantern
Lasiognathus beebei = grapnel com-pleat-angler

laughing jack = ocean pout
launces = lances
launces = Sand Lance Family
lauretta = Bering cisco
lavaret = European houting
lavaret = Introduction
lavaret = Salmon Family
lawyer = bowfin
lawyer = burbot
leather carp = common carp
leather ear = redbreast sunfish
leatherback = finescale dace
leatherjacket = starry flounder
leefish = rainbow smelt
lemon sole = English sole
lemon sole = winter flounder
lemonfin minnow = spotfin shiner
lemonfish = cobia
leopard cod = lingcod
leopard muskellunge = muskellunge
leopard shark = tiger shark
leopardfish = spotted wolffish
lépidion à grands yeux = largeye lep-idion
Lepidion eques = largeye lepidion
Lepidocybium flavobrunneum = escolar
Lepidogobius lepidus = bay goby
Lepidophanes guentheri = short-cheek tail-light
Lepidopsetta bilineata = rock sole
Lepidopus altifrons = crested scab-bardfish
lépisosté osseux = longnose gar
lépisosté tacheté = spotted gar
Lepisosteidae = Gar Family
Lepisosteidae = Introduction
Lepisosteiformes = Gar Order
lépisostés = Gar Family
Lepisosteus oculatus = spotted gar
Lepisosteus osseus = longnose gar
Lepisosteus platyrhincus = Introduction
lepisuk = lumpfish
Lepomis = Sunfish Family
Lepomis auritus = redbreast sunfish
Lepomis cyanellus = green sunfish
Lepomis gibbosus = pumpkinseed
Lepomis gulosus = warmouth
Lepomis humilis = orangespotted sunfish
Lepomis macrochirus = bluegill
Lepomis megalotis = longear sunfish
Lepophidium profundorum = fawn cusk-eel
Leptacanthichthys gracilispinis = plainchin dreamarm
Leptagonus decagonus = Atlantic poacher
Leptoclinus maculatus = daubed shanny
Leptocottus armatus = Pacific staghorn sculpin
lesser filamented sculpin = spotfin sculpin
lesser halibut = Greenland halibut
Lestidiops elongatum = slender bar-racudina
Lestidiops jayakari = pale lathfish
Lestidiops ringens = slender barracu-dina
Letharchus aliculatus = striped sail-

fin eel
Leucichthys = ciscoes
leuroglosse de sud = southern smoothtongue
leuroglosse luisant = northern smoothtongue
Leuroglossus schmidti = northern smoothtongue
Leuroglossus stilbius = southern smoothtongue
liberty trout = brown trout
lieu d'Alaska = walleye pollock
lieu noire = pollock
light-back tullibee = shortjaw cisco
lightcheek eelpout = saddled eelpout
lightfishes = Bristlemouth Family
lightless loosejaw = stoplight loosejaw
limace à filaments = threadfin snailfish
limace à front large = bigpored snailfish
limace à grosse tête = swellhead snailfish
limace à joue épineuse = spiny snailfish
limace à longues nageoires = longfin snailfish
limace à museau noir = blacksnout snailfish
limace à nageoire lobée = lobefin snailfish
limace à petite ventouse = smalldisk snailfish
limace à petites nageoires = smallfin snailfish
limace à petits yeux = marbled snailfish
limace à queue noire = blacktail snailfish
limace à tête trouée = bigscale snailfish
limace acadienne = Scotian snailfish
limace annelée = ringtail snailfish
limace ardente = lowfin snailfish
limace atlantique = Atlantic snailfish
limace de bâche = tidepool snailfish
limace de Cohen = gulf snailfish
limace de profondeur = abyssal snailfish
limace de varech = slipskin snailfish
limace des laminaires = kelp snailfish
limace des pétoncles = scallop snailfish
limace édentée = toothless snailfish
limace épineuse = prickly snailfish
limace gélatineuse = gelatinous snailfish
limace marbrée = dusky snailfish
limace naine = pygmy snailfish
limace noire = black seasnail
limace pote = pouty snailfish
limace prétentieuse = showy snailfish
limace rosâtre = pink snailfish
limace svelte = slim snailfish
limace tachetée = spotted snailfish
limace visqueuse = slimy snailfish
limace-ruban = ribbon snailfish
limace-têtard = tadpole snailfish
limaces de mer = Snailfish Family

Limanda aspera = yellowfin sole
Limanda ferruginea = yellowtail flounder
Limanda proboscidea = longhead dab
limande à nageoires jaunes = yellowfin sole
limande à queue jaune = yellowtail flounder
limande carline = longhead dab
limande cornée = horned whiff
limande sordide = Pacific sanddab
limande tachetée = speckled sanddab
lime à grande tête = planehead filefish
lime frangée = fringed filefish
limes = Filefish Family
line side = largemouth bass
linesides = striped bass
ling = blue ling
ling = burbot
ling = cobia
ling = red hake
ling = white hake
lingue = white hake
lingue bleue = blue ling
Linophryne = Leftvent Family
Linophryne algibarbata = fourbarbelthroat
Linophryne bicornis = twohorn barbelthroat
Linophryne coronata = greatbarbelthroat
Linophryne lucifer = forkbarbelthroat
Linophrynidae = Leftvent Family
Lionurus carapinus = carapine grenadier
Liopsetta glacialis = Arctic flounder
Liopsetta putnmai = smooth flounder
Liparidae = Snailfish Family
Liparididae = Snailfish Family
Liparis atlanticus = Atlantic snailfish
Liparis callyodon = spotted snailfish
Liparis coheni = gulf snailfish
Liparis cyclopus = ribbon snailfish
Liparis cyclostigma = dusky snailfish
Liparis dennyi = marbled snailfish
Liparis fabricii = gelatinous snailfish
Liparis florae = tidepool snailfish
Liparis fucensis = slipskin snailfish
Liparis gibbus = dusky snailfish
Liparis greeni = lobefin snailfish
Liparis herschelinus = kelp snailfish
Liparis inquilinus = scallop snailfish
Liparis koefedi = gelatinous snailfish
Liparis mucosus = slimy snailfish
Liparis pulchellus = showy snailfish
Liparis rutteri = ringtail snailfish
Liparis tunicatus = kelp snailfish
Lipariscus nanus = pygmy snailfish
Lipogenys gilli = backfin tapirfish
listao = skipjack tuna
little dragon sculpin = silverspotted sculpin
little pickerel = grass pickerel
little redeye = green sunfish
little redfish = sockeye salmon
little sculpin = grubby
little sturgeon = shortnose sturgeon
little sucker = cutlips minnow
little tuna = little tunny
little yellow cat = stonecat

Livebearer Family = Introduction
loaches = Carp Order
lobe-finned fishes = bony fishes
lobe-finned fishes = fishes
lobe-jawed rockfish = splitnose rockfish
Lobianchia dofleini = Mediterranean divinglamp
Lobianchia gemellari = Caribbean divinglamp
Lobotes surinamensis = tripletail
Lobotidae = Tripletail Family
Loch Leven trout = brown trout
loche = Atlantic tomcod
loche = burbot
lodde = capelin
logfish = barrelfish
logfish = green sunfish
lompe = lumpfish
lompénie à barres blanches = whitebarred prickleback
lompénie à barres bleues = bluebarred prickleback
lompénie de Fabricius = slender eelblenny
lompénie de roche = rock prickleback
lompénie élancée = snake prickleback
lompénie élancée = slender eelblenny
lompénie i-grec = Y-prickleback
lompénie naine = stout eelblenny
lompénie noire = black prickleback
lompénie ruban = ribbon prickleback
lompénie tachetée = daubed shanny
lompénie-serpent = snakeblenny
long rough dab = Canadian plaice
long-finned bream = bigscale pomfret
long-finned sucker = quillback
long-finned tuna = albacore
long-jaw flounder = arrowtooth flounder
long-rayed sculpin = threadfin sculpin
long-snouted blenny = longsnout prickleback
long-spined sculpin = longhorn sculpin
longear bream = redbreast sunfish
longfin cod = Pacific flatnose
longfin sole = rex sole
longfinned cod = blue antimora
longjaw = shortjaw cisco
longjaw chub = longjaw cisco
longjaw rockfish = Pacific ocean perch
longneck eels = Neckeel Family
longnose eel = slatjaw cutthroat eel
longsnout lancetfish = longnose lancetfish
longspine channel rockfish = longspine thornyhead
longspine greenling = longspine combfish
Lophiidae = Goosefish Family
Lophiiformes = Anglerfish Order
Lophius americanus = monkfish
Lophodolus acanthognathus = whalehead dreamer
Lopholatilus chamaeleonticeps =

tilefish
loquette d'Amérique = ocean pout
Loricariidae = Introduction
Lota lota = burbot
lotte = burbot
lotte = monkfish
lotte de rivière = burbot
loup à tête large = northern wolffish
loup atlantique = Atlantic wolffish
loup de Béring = Bering wolffish
loup ocellé = wolf-eel
loup tacheté = spotted wolffish
loups-garous = Werewolf Family
louvereau = louvar
louvereaux = Louvar Family
lowbelly bullhead = black bullhead
Lumpenella longirostris = longsnout prickleback
Lumpenus fabricii = slender eelblenny
Lumpenus lumpretaeformis = snakeblenny
Lumpenus maculatus = daubed shanny
Lumpenus medius = stout eelblenny
Lumpenus sagitta = snake prickleback
lumpsucker = lumpfish
lunge = muskellunge
lungfishes = bony fishes
lungfishes = ray-finned fishes
lush = burbot
lussion à bec de canard = duckbill barracudina
lussion à menton = sharpchin barracudina
lussion ailé = winged barracudina
lussion blanc = ribbon barracudina
lussion blanc = white barracudina
lussion long = slender barracudina
lussions = Barracudina Family
lutin = pixie poacher
Lutjanidae = Snapper Family
Lutjanus cyanopterus = cubera snapper
Luvaridae = Louvar Family
Luvarus imperialis = louvar
Luxilus chrysocephalus = striped shiner
Luxilus cornutus = common shiner
lycaspine à chevrons = chevron scutepout
Lycenchelys albus = Labrador wolf eel
Lycenchelys crotalina = snakehead eelpout
Lycenchelys jordani = shortjaw eelpout
Lycenchelys kolthoffi = checkered wolf eel
Lycenchelys labradorensis = Labrador wolf eel
Lycenchelys paxillus = common wolf eel
Lycenchelys sp. = slipskin species
Lycenchelys verrilli = wolf eelpout
Lycodapus endemoscotus = deepwater slipskin
Lycodapus fierasfer = blackmouth slipskin
Lycodapus grossidens = blackmouth slipskin

Lycodapus mandibularis = pallid slipskin
Lycodapus pachysoma = stout slipskin
Lycodapus parviceps = stubraker slipskin
lycode = slipskin species
lycode à arc = archer eelpout
lycode à carreaux = checker eelpout
lycode à courtes nageoires = shortfin eelpout
lycode à deux lignes = twoline eelpout
lycode à grandes nageoires = bigfin eelpout
lycode à long nez = longsnout eelpout
lycode à longues branchiospines = pallid slipskin
lycode à nuque écaillée = scaled-nape eelpout
lycode à nuque nue = naked-nape eelpout
lycode à oeil ovale = Alaska eelpout
lycode à oreilles = longear eelpout
lycode à petite tête = stubraker slipskin
lycode à selles = saddled eelpout
lycode à tête longue = wolf eelpout
lycode à trois taches = threespot eelpout
lycode à ventre noir = blackbelly eelpout
lycode abyssale = deepwater slipskin
lycode arctique = Arctic eelpout
lycode atlantique = Atlantic eelpout
lycode camuse = snubnose eelpout
lycode commune = common wolf eel
lycode d'Adolf = Adolf's eelpout
lycode d'Esmark = greater eelpout
lycode de Jordan = shortjaw eelpout
lycode de Laval = Laval eelpout
lycode de Terre-Neuve = Newfoundland eelpout
lycode de Vahl = checker eelpout
lycode du Labrador = Labrador wolf eel
lycode du Labrador = Laval eelpout
lycode flasque = looseskin eelpout
lycode glaciale = glacial eelpout
lycode molle = soft eelpout
lycode nacrée = blackmouth slipskin
lycode noire = black eelpout
lycode pâle = pale eelpout
lycode plume = shulupaoluk
lycode polaire = polar eelpout
lycode quadrillée = checkered wolf eel
lycode sourcillier = eyebrow eelpout
lycode trapue = stout slipskin
lycode tressée = wattled eelpout
lycode-crotale = snakehead eelpout
lycode-donzelle = cuskpout
lycodes = Eelpout Family
Lycodes adolfi = Adolf's eelpout
Lycodes atlanticus = Atlantic eelpout
Lycodes brevipes = shortfin eelpout
Lycodes cortezianus = bigfin eelpout
Lycodes diapterus = black eelpout
Lycodes esmarki = greater eelpout
Lycodes frigidus = glacial eelpout
Lycodes jugoricus = shulupaoluk

Lycodes lavalaei = Laval eelpout
Lycodes mucosus = saddled eelpout
Lycodes palearis = wattled eelpout
Lycodes pallidus = pale eelpout
Lycodes perspicillus = eyebrow eelpout
Lycodes polaris = polar eelpout
Lycodes reticulatus = Arctic eelpout
Lycodes rossi = threespot eelpout
Lycodes sagittarius = archer eelpout
Lycodes seminudus = longear eelpout
Lycodes terraenovae = Newfoundland eelpout
Lycodes vahli = checker eelpout
Lycodonus mirabilis = chevron scutepout
Lycodopsis pacifica = blackbelly eelpout
Lyopsetta exilis = slender sole
Lythrurus umbratilis = redfin shiner
Macdonaldia rostrata = shortspine tapirfish
Mackenzie herring = least cisco
mackerel shark = porbeagle
mackerel shark = salmon shark
mackerel shark = shortfin mako
mackereljack = jack mackerel
mackinaw trout = lake trout
macondes = Temperate Ocean Bass Family
Macrhybopsis storeriana = silver chub
Macropinna microstoma = barreleye
Macrorhamphosidae = Snipefish Family
Macrorhamphosus scolopax = longspine snipefish
Macrouridae = Grenadier Family
Macrourus berglax = roughhead grenadier
Macrozoarces americanus = ocean pout
Macrurocyttidae = Eyefish Family
Macruronus brachycolus = winged hake
mafou = cobia
mahi mahi = common dolphin
maiden = scup
mailed sculpin = bigeye sculpin
mailed sculpin = moustache sculpin
Makaira nigricans = blue marlin
makaire blanc = white marlin
makaire bleu = blue marlin
mako à nageoires courtes = shortfin mako
mako shark = shortfin mako
Malacanthidae = Tilefish Family
malachigan = freshwater drum
Malacocephalus occidentalis = American straptail grenadier
Malacocottus kincaidi = blackfin sculpin
Malacocottus zonurus = bartail sculpin
Malacopterygii = soft-rayed fishes
Malacoraja senta = smooth skate
Malacoraja spinacidermis = soft skate
Malacosteidae = Barbeled Dragonfish Family
Malacosteidae = loosejaws
Malacosteus danae = shortnose

loosejaw
Malacosteus danae = stoplight loosejaw
Malacosteus niger = shortnose loosejaw
Malacosteus niger = stoplight loosejaw
malarmat à dix aiguillons = armored searobin
Mallotus villosus = capelin
malthe atlantique = Atlantic batfish
malthes = Batfish Family
mammose = shortnose sturgeon
mammy = central stoneroller
man-iktoe = Atlantic spiny lumpsucker
maneater shark = great white shark
mangeur d'homme = great white shark
mangeurs d'hommes = Requiem Shark Family
Manitou darter = logperch
manta atlantique = manta
Manta birostris = manta
Manta hamiltoni = manta
mantas = Eagle Ray Family
mante = manta
many-spined stickleback = ninespine stickleback
maquereau blanc = chub mackerel
maquereau bleu = Atlantic mackerel
maquereau d'Atka = Atka mackerel
maquereau espanol = chub mackerel
maquereaux = Mackerel Family
maraîche = porbeagle
marble eye = yellow walleye
marbled bullhead = brown bullhead
Margariscus margarita = pearl dace
Margrethia obtusirostrata = bluntnose bristlemouth
marguerite perlée = pearlsides
maria = burbot
marigane blanche = white crappie
marigane noire = black crappie
marine mink = skilfish
marine piranha = bluefish
marlins = billfishes
marsh pickerel = northern pike
Marston trout = Arctic char
maskinongé = muskellunge
maskinongo = muskellunge
Mason perch = black crappie
mattie = Atlantic herring
Maulisia argipalla = pitted tubeshoulder
Maurolicus muelleri = pearlsides
maxailé aviron = oarjaw wingmax
Maynea bulbiceps = snubnose eelpout
medakas = Needlefish Order
Medialuna californiensis = halfmoon
Mediterranean slimehead = rosy soldierfish
medium red salmon = coho salmon
medusafishes = Ruff Family
mégalope rouge = red eyefish
mégalopes = Eyefish Family
Megalopidae = Tarpon Family
Megalops atlanticus = tarpon
megamouth sharks = Mackerel Shark Order
Melamphaeidae = Ridgehead Family

Melamphaes lugubris = highsnout ridgehead
Melamphaes microps = numerous helmetfish
Melamphaes suborbitalis = shortspine helmetfish
Melanocetidae = Werewolf Family
Melanocetus johnsoni = stout werewolf
Melanogrammus aeglefinus = haddock
Melanonidae = Arrowtail Family
Melanonus zugmayeri = arrowtail
Melanostigma atlanticum = Atlantic soft pout
Melanostigma pammelas = Pacific soft pout
Melanostomias bartonbeani = bluenose rearfin
Melanostomias spilorhynchus = bluenose rearfin
Melanostomias valdiviae = flatbarbel rearfin
Melanostomiidae = Barbeled Dragonfish Family
Melanostomiidae = scaleless dragonfishes
melgrim = Pacific sanddab
méné à grande bouche = bigmouth shiner
méné à grandes écailles = silver chub
méné à nageoires rouges = common shiner
méné à tête plate = flathead chub
méné bâton = river chub
méné bleu = eastern silvery minnow
méné bleu = spotfin shiner
méné camus = pugnose shiner
méné d'argent de l'est = eastern silvery minnow
méné d'argent de l'ouest = western silvery minnow
méné d'herbe = bridle shiner
méné d'ombre = redfin shiner
méné de lac = lake chub
méné de rivière = river shiner
méné deux-barres = peamouth
méné diamant = weed shiner
méné émeraude = emerald shiner
méné fantôme = ghost shiner
méné laiton = brassy minnow
méné long = redside dace
méné paille = sand shiner
méné pâle = mimic shiner
méné plat = golden shiner
méné rayé = striped shiner
méné rose = redside shiner
méné-miroir = silver shiner
menhaden tyran = Atlantic menhaden
Menidia menidia = Atlantic silverside
Menominee whitefish = round whitefish
ménomini de montagnes = mountain whitefish
ménomini pygmée = pygmy whitefish
ménomini rond = round whitefish
menona killifish = banded killifish
menton noir = blackchin shiner
menton-peigne tocson = hippo combchin

menton-pointu = cone-chin
mentons noirs = Blackchin Family
merlan = pollock
merlan bleu = blue whiting
merlan-noir = pollock
merlu ailé = winged hake
merlu argenté = silver hake
merlu argenté du large = offshore hake
merlu blanc = offshore hake
merlu du Pacifique = Pacific hake
Merlucciidae = Hake Family
Merluccius albidus = offshore hake
Merluccius bilinearis = silver hake
Merluccius productus = Pacific hake
merluche à longues nageoires = longfin hake
merluche blanche = white hake
merluche écureuil = red hake
merluche rouge = red hake
merluche tachetée = spotted hake
merlus = Hake Family
mérou neigeux = snowy grouper
mérou noir = black sea bass
metallic codling = brown peeper
methy = burbot
meunier à grandes écailles = largescale sucker
meunier à tête carrée = northern hog sucker
meunier de Campbell = Salish sucker
meunier de Jasper = Jasper longnose sucker
meunier de l'ouest = bridgelip sucker
meunier des montagnes = mountain sucker
meunier des Salish = Salish sucker
meunier noir = white sucker
meunier rouge = longnose sucker
meunier tacheté = spotted sucker
meuniers = Sucker Family
Michael Sars smooth-head = oarjaw wingmax
Michigan brook lamprey = northern brook lamprey
microbecs = Pencilsmelt Family
Microgadus = tomcods
Microgadus proximus = Pacific tomcod
Microgadus tomcod = Atlantic tomcod
Microlophichthys microlophus = dreamteeth
Micromesistius poutassou = blue whiting
Micropogonias undulatus = Drum Family
Micropterus dolomieu = smallmouth bass
Micropterus salmoides = largemouth bass
Microstomatidae = Pencilsmelt Family
Microstomus pacificus = Dover sole
midshipman = plainfin midshipman
midwater eelpout = Pacific soft pout
midwater shark = spined pygmy shark
mikiapic kapisilik = glacier lanternfish
Miller's thumb = mottled sculpin
Miller's thumb = slimy sculpin

millstone = ocean sunfish
milugiak = longnose sucker
miluiak = longnose sucker
miluqiaq = longnose sucker
Milwaukee shiner = emerald shiner
minister = brown bullhead
Minytrema melanops = spotted sucker
mirror carp = common carp
mirror lanternfish = toothnose lanternfish
Mississippi bullhead = yellow bullhead
Mississippi cat = flathead catfish
Mississippi mudminnow = central mudminnow
Mississippi silvery minnow = western silvery minnow
Mississippi stoneroller = central stoneroller
mock halibut = Greenland halibut
mohawk = fallfish
moiva = capelin
Mola mola = ocean sunfish
môle commun = ocean sunfish
môles = Mola Family
Molidae = Mola Family
mollasse atlantique = Atlantic soft pout
mollasse noire = Pacific soft pout
molliénésie à voilure = Introduction
molliénésie à voilure = sailfin molly
Mollienisia = sailfin molly
molligut = monkfish
Molly George = tautog
Molva dypterygia = blue ling
Molva molva = European ling
molykite = monkfish
Monacanthidae = Filefish Family
Monacanthus ciliatus = fringed filefish
Monacanthus hispidus = planehead filefish
mongrel buffalo = black buffalo
mongrel bullhead = stonecat
monkfishes = Goosefish Family
Monolene antillarum = slim flounder
Monolene sessilicauda = deepwater flounder
Monomitopus agassizi = Agassiz's cusk-eel
Montana blackspot = west-slope cutthroat trout
mooneye = kiyi
mooneye cisco = blackfin cisco
moonfish = black crappie
moonfish = lookdown
moonfish = ocean sunfish
moonfish = opah
Moose Lake minnow = lake chub
more à petites écailles = smallscale mora
more délicat = dainty mora
more imberbe = smoothchin mora
more noir = arrowtail
mores = Mora Family
mores noirs = Arrowtail Family
Morgan cat = flathead catfish
morid cods = Mora Family
Moridae = Mora Family
Moringuidae = Spaghetti Eel Family
Morone americana = white perch

Morone chrysops = white bass
Morone saxatilis = striped bass
Moronidae = Temperate Bass Family
morue arctique = polar cod
morue bariolée = skilfish
morue boréale = saffron cod
morue charbonnière = sablefish
morue commune = Atlantic cod
morue de l'Atlantique = Atlantic cod
morue de roche = ogac
morue du Pacifique = Pacific cod
morue franche = Atlantic cod
morue ogac = ogac
morue-lingue = lingcod
morues = Cod Family
morues noires = Sablefish Family
mosquitofish = Introduction
mossback bass = largemouth bass
mossbunker = Atlantic menhaden
mosshead prickleback = mosshead warbonnet
mossy sculpin = calico sculpin
motelle à quatre barbillons = fourbeard rockling
mother-of-eels = burbot
mother-of-eels = ocean pout
mottled Black Sea goby = tubenose goby
mottled gunnel = banded gunnel
mottled sanddab = Pacific sanddab
mottled turbot = C-O sole
moulac = splake
mountain char = Arctic char
mountain char = bull trout
mountain trout = brook trout
mountain trout = lake trout
mountain trout = smallmouth bass
Moxostoma = redhorses
Moxostoma = Sucker Family
Moxostoma anisurum = silver redhorse
Moxostoma carinatum = river redhorse
Moxostoma duquesnei = black redhorse
Moxostoma erythrurum = golden redhorse
Moxostoma hubbsi = copper redhorse
Moxostoma macrolepidotum = shorthead redhorse
Moxostoma valenciennesi = greater redhorse
mud bass = largemouth bass
mud bass = warmouth
mud buffalo = bigmouth buffalo
mud cat = brown bullhead
mud cat = flathead catfish
mud chub = creek chub
mud dab = winter flounder
mud dab = yellowtail flounder
mud dabbler = mummichog
mud hake = white hake
mud pickerel = chain pickerel
mud pickerel = grass pickerel
mud pickerel = redfin pickerel
mud pike = bowfin
mud pike = grass pickerel
mud shad = gizzard shad
mud shark = sixgill shark
mud sucker = northern hog sucker
mud sucker = white sucker

mud trout = brook trout
mud-fish = monkfish
mud-perch = fourspine stickleback
mud-pouch = fourspine stickleback
mudcat = black bullhead
mudcat = brown bullhead
muddab = yellowfin sole
muddler = mottled sculpin
muddy arrowtooth eel = brown cutthroat eel
muddy flounder = C-O sole
mudfish = bowfin
mudfish = central mudminnow
Mudminnow Family = Introduction
mudpuppy = central mudminnow
mudshark = spiny dogfish
muffle-jaw = mottled sculpin
muge curema = white mullet
muges = Mullet Family
Mugil cephalus = striped mullet
Mugil curema = white mullet
Mugilidae = Mullet Family
Mugiliformes = Mullet Order
mulet à cornes = creek chub
mulet blanc = white mullet
mulet cabot = striped mullet
mulet perlé = pearl dace
mulhaden = gaspereau
Müller's pearlsides = pearlsides
mullet = white sucker
Mullidae = Goatfish Family
Mullus auratus = red goatfish
multipore searsid = longsnout manypitshoulder
mummy = mummichog
Muraenesocidae = Pike Conger Family
Muraenidae = Moray Family
murène = moray species
murène pygmée = pygmy moray
murène verte = green moray
murènes = Moray Family
Murray's longsnout grenadier = roughnose grenadier
museau noir = blacknose shiner
muskie = muskellunge
Muskoka minnow = blacknose shiner
musky = muskellunge
musso atlantique = Atlantic moonfish
musso panache = lookdown
mustèle arctique à trois barbillons = threebeard rockling
mustèle argentée = silver rockling
Mustelus canis = smooth dogfish
muttonfish = ocean pout
Myctophidae = Lanternfish Family
Myctophiformes = Lanternfish Order
Myctophum affine = metallic lanternfish
Myctophum asperum = roughscale lanternfish
Myctophum punctatum = spotted lanternfish
Myctophum selenops = lunar lanternfish
Myliobatidae = Eagle Ray Family
Myliobatididae = Eagle Ray Family
Mylocheilus caurinus = peamouth
Myoxocephalus aenaeus = grubby
Myoxocephalus octodecemspinosus = longhorn sculpin
Myoxocephalus polyacantho-

cephalus = great sculpin
Myoxocephalus quadricornis = fourhorn sculpin
Myoxocephalus scorpioides = Arctic sculpin
Myoxocephalus scorpius = shorthorn sculpin
Myoxocephalus scorpius groenlandicus = shorthorn sculpin
Myoxocephalus sp. = stellate sculpin
Myoxocephalus thompsoni = deepwater sculpin
Myrichthys breviceps = sharptail eel
Myrophis platyrhynchus = broadnose worm eel
Myrophis punctatus = speckled worm eel
myxine brune = Pacific hagfish
myxine du nord = Atlantic hagfish
Myxine glutinosa = Atlantic hagfish
Myxine limosa = Atlantic hagfish
myxine noire = black hagfish
myxines = Hagfish Family
Myxini = fishes
Myxini = hagfishes
Myxinidae = Hagfish Family
Myxiniformes = Hagfish Order
nachtrieb dace = pearl dace
nageoire-éventail = fanfin
nageoire-frangée = blackgut tendrilfin
nageoires-éventails = Fanfin Family
nageoires-reculées à barbillon aplati = flatbarbel rearfin
nageoires-reculées nez-bleu = bluenose rearfin
näluarryuk = lake trout
namaycush = lake trout
nannilik = longnose sucker
Nansenia candida = bluethroat argentine
Nansenia groenlandica = large-eyed argentine
Nansenia oblita = forgotten argentine
narrow-mouthed bass = white perch
narrowneck eel = neckeel
narrownecked oceanic eel = neckeel
naseus de rapides = longnose dace
naseus de rapides de Banff = Banff longnose dace
naseus léopard = leopard dace
naseux moucheté = speckled dace
naseux noir = blacknose dace
naseux Nooky = Nooky dace
nat-ah-nuh = Greenland halibut
nataaznak = starry flounder
natarnak = Greenland halibut
nätarrnaq = burbot
native trout = brook trout
native trout = west-slope cutthroat trout
naucrate = sharksucker
Naucrates ductor = pilotfish
nauktoq = lake trout
Nautichthys oculofasciatus = sailfin sculpin
Nautichthys robustus = smallsail sculpin
navaja jaune = saffron cod
Nealotus tripes = black snake mackerel

Nectoliparis pelagicus = tadpole snailfish
nee-fitz-shak = kelp snailfish
needle-tooth halibut = arrowtooth flounder
needlefish = Atlantic saury
needlefish = stout sand lance
needlefish = tube-snout
needlenose = longnose gar
Nematonurus armatus = russet grenadier
Nemichthyidae = Snipe Eel Family
Nemichthys scolopaceus = slender snipe eel
Neoconger mucronatus = ridged eel
Neogobius melanostomus = Introduction
Neogobius melanostomus = round goby
Neopterygii = ray-finned fishes
Neopterygii =Sturgeon Order
Neoscopelidae = Blackchin Family
Neoscopelus macrolepidotus = glowingfish
Neoteleostei = Widemouth Order
Nesiarchus nasutus = cone-chin
nesso = duckbill eel
Nessorhamphus ingolfianus = duckbill eel
net-eater shark = silky shark
netdevil anglerfishes = Leftvent Family
nettârnak = burbot
New England hake = silver hake
New World minnow = finescale dace
New York plaice = windowpane
New York stickleback = threespine stickleback
Newfoundland eelpout = Laval eelpout
Newfoundland turbot = Greenland halibut
newlight = white crappie
Nezumia = lamp grenadier
Nezumia aequalis = smooth grenadier
Nezumia bairdi = marlin-spike
Nezumia stelgidolepis = lamp grenadier
nibblers = Sea Chub Family
nipi-sak = kelp snailfish
nipisa = lumpfish
nipishah = kelp snailfish
nipper = cunner
no-tooth eelpout = snakehead eelpout
Nocomis biguttatus = hornyhead chub
Nocomis micropogon = river chub
Nomeidae = Driftfish Family
Nomeus gronovii = man-of-war fish
Nooksack dace = Nooky dace
Nooky longnose dace = Nooky dace
Normichthys operosus = longsnout manypitshoulder
North Atlantic codling = largeye lepidion
North Atlantic flounder = European flounder
northern alligatorfish = Atlantic poacher
northern blacknose shiner = blacknose shiner

northern bluefin tuna = bluefin tuna
northern bluegill sunfish = bluegill
northern brown bullhead = brown bullhead
northern catfish = channel catfish
northern chub = lake chub
northern cod = Atlantic cod
northern cutthroat eel = slatjaw cutthroat eel
northern dace = peamouth
northern dace = pearl dace
northern fathead minnow = fathead minnow
northern hagfish = Atlantic hagfish
northern lamprey = Arctic lamprey
northern lamprey = chestnut lamprey
northern lamprey = silver lamprey
northern largemouth bass = largemouth bass
northern least darter = least darter
northern longear = longear sunfish
northern longnose gar = longnose gar
northern mailed fish = longnose gar
northern minnow = pearl dace
northern mooneye = goldeye
northern mountain sucker = mountain sucker
northern pearl dace = pearl dace
northern porgy = scup
northern redhorse = shorthead redhorse
northern sculpin = Arctic sculpin
northern sculpin = slimy sculpin
northern sea horse = grunt sculpin
northern seadevil = twoclub angler
northern smallmouth bass = smallmouth bass
northern striped gurnard = striped searobin
northern sucker = longnose sucker
northern weed shiner = weed shiner
northern yellow bullhead = yellow bullhead
Notacanthiformes = Tapirfish Family
Notacanthus chemnitzi = largescale tapirfish
Notacanthus nasus = largescale tapirfish
notch feelerfish = snoutlet crotchfeeler
Notemigonus crysoleucas = golden shiner
Notolepis rissoi = ribbon barracudina
Notolepis rissoi kroeyeri = white barracudina
Notolychnus valdiviae = fourtoplamps
Notorhynchus cepedianus = sevengill shark
Notorhynchus maculatus sevengill shark
Notoscopelus bolini = Bolin's lanternfish
Notoscopelus caudispinosus = spinetail lanternfish
Notoscopelus japonicus = Japanese lanternfish
Notoscopelus kroeyeri = northern saillamp
Notoscopelus resplendens = patchwork lanternfish
Notosudidae = Waryfish Family

Notropis = brassy minnow
Notropis = eastern silvery minnow
Notropis = shiners
Notropis = western silvery minnow
Notropis anogenus = pugnose shiner
Notropis atherinoides = emerald shiner
Notropis bifrenatus = bridle shiner
Notropis blennius = river shiner
Notropis buchanani = ghost shiner
Notropis chrysocephalus = striped shiner
Notropis cornutus = common shiner
Notropis dorsalis = bigmouth shiner
Notropis emiliae = pugnose minnow
Notropis heterodon = blackchin shiner
Notropis heterolepis = blacknose shiner
Notropis hudsonius = spottail shiner
Notropis ludibundus = sand shiner
Notropis photogenis = silver shiner
Notropis rubellus = rosyface shiner
Notropis spilopterus = spotfin shiner
Notropis stramineus = sand shiner
Notropis texanus = weed shiner
Notropis umbratilis = redfin shiner
Notropis volucellus = mimic shiner
Noturus flavus = stonecat
Noturus gyrinus = tadpole madtom
Noturus insignis = margined madtom
Noturus miurus = brindled madtom
Noturus stigmosus = northern madtom
nulilighuk = capelin
numbfish = Atlantic torpedo
nurse fish = basking shark
nurse shark = sand tiger
nurse sharks = Carpet Shark Order
nursehound = spiny dogfish
nutidilik = Arctic char
Nybelin's sculpin = bigeye sculpin
oarfish = Opah Order
oarfish = paddlefish
oarfishes = Opah Order
Occella impi = pixie poacher
Occella verrucosa = warty poacher
ocean perch = Acadian redfish
ocean perch = deepwater redfish
ocean perch = golden redfish
ocean whitefish = Atlantic wolffish
ocean wolffish = Atlantic wolffish
oceanic bonito = skipjack tuna
oceanic eels = Neckeel Family
oceanic whitetip shark = ocean whitetip shark
Odontaspididae = Sand Tiger Family
Odontaspis taurus = sand tiger
Odontopyxis trispinosa = pygmy poacher
oeil-perlé à longues nageoires = longfin pearleye
oeil-perlé à ventre noir = blackbelly pearleye
oeil-perlé de Zugmayer = Zugmayer's pearleye
oeil-perlé du nord = northern pearleye
oeil-vert à long nez = longnose greeneye
oeil-vert camus = shortnose greeneye
offshore sand lance = northern sand

lance
ogac = ogac
ogac = Atlantic cod
ogak = saffron cod
ogaq = Arctic cod
ôgark = Arctic cod
ogavik = saffron cod
Ogcocephalidae = Batfish Family
ogre = fangtooth
ogrefish = fangtooth
ogres = Ogrefish Family
Ohio muskellunge = muskellunge
oil shark = soupfin shark
oilfish = eulachon
oilfishes = Snake Mackerel Family
okeugnak = round whitefish
old wench = queen triggerfish
old wife = Atlantic menhaden
old wife = queen triggerfish
Oligocottus maculosus = tidepool sculpin
Oligocottus rimensis = saddleback sculpin
Oligocottus snyderi = fluffy sculpin
olive-backed rockfish = stripetail rockfish
omble à tête plate = bull trout
omble chevalier = Arctic char
omble de fontaine = brook trout
omble de fontaine aurora = aurora trout
ombre arctique = Arctic grayling
omisco = trout-perch
Omosudidae = Halterfish Family
Omosudis lowei = halterfish
Oncorhynchus = trouts
Oncorhynchus aguabonito = golden trout
Oncorhynchus aguabonito = Introduction
Oncorhynchus clarki bouvieri = west-slope cutthroat trout
Oncorhynchus clarki clarki = coastal cutthroat trout
Oncorhynchus clarki lewisi = west-slope cutthroat trout
Oncorhynchus gorbuscha = pink salmon
Oncorhynchus keta = chum salmon
Oncorhynchus kisutch = coho salmon
Oncorhynchus masou = Introduction
Oncorhynchus masou = Salmon Family
Oncorhynchus mykiss = rainbow trout
Oncorhynchus mykiss = Salmon Family
Oncorhynchus mykiss gairdneri = rainbow trout
Oncorhynchus mykiss irideus = rainbow trout
Oncorhynchus nerka = sockeye salmon
Oncorhynchus tshawytscha = chinook salmon
Oneirodes bulbosus = bulbous dreamer
Oneirodes epithales = nightmare dreamer
Oneirodes eschrichti = cosmopolitan

dreamtail
Oneirodes macrosteus = westnorat dreamtail
Oneirodes schmidti = forefour dreamtail
Oneirodes thompsoni = spiny dreamer
Oneirodidae = Dreamer Family
onion-eye = roughhead grenadier
ooligan = eulachon
ooze eel = brown cutthroat eel
opa = opah
opah = opah
opahs = Opah Family
Opelousas cat = flathead catfish
Ophichthidae = Snake Eel Family
Ophichthus cruentifer = margined snake eel
Ophichthus gomesi = shrimp eel
Ophichthus puncticeps = palespotted eel
Ophidiidae = Cusk-eel Family
Ophidiiformes = Cusk-eel Order
Ophidion selenops = mooneye cusk-eel
Ophiodon elongatus = lingcod
Opisthoproctidae = Spookfish Family
Opostomias mitsuii = pitgum lanternfish
Opsopoeodus emiliae = pugnose minnow
Oquassa trout = Arctic char
orange rockfish = canary rockfish
orange-spotted rockfish = quillback rockfish
orangespot = orangespotted sunfish
orbe étoilé = oceanic puffer
Orectolobiformes = Carpet Shark Order
Oregon sturgeon = white sturgeon
oréo occulé = oxyeye oreo
oréos = Oreo Family
Oreosomatidae = Oreo Family
ornamented blenny = mosshead warbonnet
oscar = Cichlid Family
oscar = Introduction
Osmeridae = Smelt Family
Osmeriformes = Smelt Order
Osmerus mordax = rainbow smelt
Osmerus mordax dentex = rainbow smelt
Osmerus spectrum = pygmy smelt
Ostariophysi = Carp Order
Osteichthyes = bony fishes
Osteodiscus cascadiae = bigtail snailfish
Osteoglossiformes = Bony-tongue Order
Osteoglossomorpha = teleosts
Ostraciidae = Boxfish Family
Ostraciontidae = Boxfish Family
ostracoderms = jawless fish
osungnak = round whitefish
Oswego bass = black crappie
Oswego bass = largemouth bass
Oswego bass = smallmouth bass
ouananiche = Atlantic salmon
ouitouche = fallfish
ovac = Arctic cod

ovak = Atlantic cod
Oxylebius pictus = painted greenling
oyster-fish = tautog
oysterfish = striped burrfish
Pachycara bulbiceps = snubnose eelpout
Pachycara gymninium = naked-nape eelpout
Pachycara lepinium = scaled-nape eelpout
Pachystomias microdon = largeye
Pacific anchovy = northern anchovy
Pacific barndoor skate = big skate
Pacific blacksmelt = slender blacksmelt
Pacific brook char = Dolly Varden
Pacific butterfish = Pacific pompano
Pacific capelin = capelin
Pacific great skate = big skate
Pacific grenadier = roughscale grenadier
Pacific mackerel = chub mackerel
Pacific pollock = walleye pollock
Pacific river lamprey = Arctic lamprey
Pacific sand lance = stout sand lance
Pacific smelt = longfin smelt
Pacific snake prickleback = snake prickleback
Pacific sturgeon = white sturgeon
Pacific trout = rainbow trout
Pacific whiting = Pacific hake
Pacific wolf-eel = wolf-eel
pacu = Introduction
paddle-cock = lumpfish
pailona = Portuguese shark
pailona commun = Portuguese shark
pale crappie = white crappie
pale eelpout = pallid slipskin
pale flounder = witch flounder
pale sunfish = bluegill
pale-back tullibee = shortjaw cisco
palegold searsid = pitted tubeshoulder
palhala = spotfin butterflyfish
palhalas = Butterflyfish Family
Palinurichthys perciformis = barrelfish
palissade = tinselfish
palissade à épines plates = thorny tinselfish
Pallas's liparid = spotted snailfish
Pallasina barbata aix = tubenose poacher
pallid eelpout = pallid slipskin
palomino trout = rainbow trout
Panaque nigrolineatus = Introduction
panstickle = threespine stickleback
pantouflier = smooth hammerhead
paper bass = yellow bullhead
paperbone fishes = Waryfish Family
papermouth = black crappie
papermouth = white crappie
Parabassogigas grandis = giant cusk-eel
Paradiplogrammus bairdi = lancer dragonet
paradoxical stalkeye = Barbeled Dragonfish Family
paradoxical stalkeye = sawtailfishes

Paralepidae = Barracudina Family
Paralepis atlantica = duckbill barracudina
Paralepis brevis = duckbill barracudina
Paralepis coregonoides borealis = sharpchin barracudina
Paralichthys dentatus = summer flounder
Paralichthys oblongus = fourspot flounder
Paraliparis bathybius = black seasnail
Paraliparis calidus = lowfin snailfish
Paraliparis cephalus = swellhead snailfish
Paraliparis copei = blacksnout snailfish
Paraliparis deani = prickly snailfish
Paraliparis garmani = pouty snailfish
Paraliparis latifrons = bigpored snailfish
Paraliparis paucidens = toothless snailfish
Paraliparis rosaceus = pink snailfish
Parasudis truculenta = longnose greeneye
parfait-pêcheur à grappin = grapnel compleat-angler
Paricelinus hoplicitcus = thornback sculpin
Parmaturus manis = ghost cat shark
Parophrys vetula = English sole
pastenague à deux queues = diamond stingray
pastenague à queue épineuse = roughtail stingray
pastenague violette = pelagic stingray
pastenagues = Stingray Family
patchwork lampfish = patchwork lanternfish
patudo = bigeye tuna
pavement-toothed redhorse = river redhorse
peamouth chub = peamouth
peau bleue = blue shark
pêcheur à deux massettes = twoclub angler
pêcheur à trèfle = warted seadevil
pêcheur uranoscope = stargazing seadevil
pelagic basslet = recto
pelagic cods = Arrowtail Family
pélamide = Atlantic bonito
pèlerin = basking shark
pèlerins = Basking Shark Family
pelican = Atlantic sturgeon
pelican = China rockfish
pelican eel = pelican gulper
pen-point blenny = penpoint gunnel
pencil cardinal = greateye
Pentacerotidae = Armorhead Family
Peprilus simillimus = Pacific pompano
Peprilus triacanthus = butterfish
Perca flavescens = yellow perch
Perch Family = Introduction
perch-mouth bream = warmouth
perchaude = yellow perch

perche de pilotis = pile perch
perche de varech = kelp perch
perche-méné = shiner perch
perches = Perch Family
perches-truites = Trout-perch Family
Percichthyidae = Temperate Bass Family
Percidae = Introduction
Percidae = Perch Family
Perciformes = Perch Order
Percina = Perch Family
Percina caprodes = logperch
Percina copelandi = channel darter
Percina maculata = blackside darter
Percina shumardi = river darter
Percopsidae = Trout-perch Family
Percopsiformes = Trout-perch Order
Percopsis omiscomaycus = trout-perch
Peristedion miniatum = armored searobin
petit dard = least darter
petit poisson-lampe = lesser lampfish
petit requin-taupe = longfin mako
petit-bec = pugnose minnow
petite lampe-bouée = lesser beacon-lamp
petite laquaiche = golden shiner
petite limace de mer = sea tadpole
petite morue = Atlantic tomcod
petite poule de mer arctique = leatherfin lumpsucker
petite poule de mer atlantique = Atlantic spiny lumpsucker
petite poule de mer de MacAlpine = Arctic lumpsucker
petite poule de mer douce = smooth lumpfish
petite poule de mer ronde = Pacific spiny lumpsucker
petite poule de Terre-Neuve = Newfoundland spiny lumpsucker
Petromyzon marinus = sea lamprey
Petromyzontidae = Lamprey Family
Petromyzontiformes = Lamprey Order
Phanerodon furcatus = white seaperch
phantom = bonefish
phantom bristlemouth = slender bristlemouth
pharaon = daggertooth
pharaons = Daggertooth Family
Pholidae = Gunnel Family
Pholis clemensi = longfin gunnel
Pholis fasciata = banded gunnel
Pholis gunnellus = rock gunnel
Pholis laeta = crescent gunnel
Pholis ornata = saddleback gunnel
Pholis schultzi = red gunnel
Photichthyidae = Lightfish Family
Photonectes margarita = sooty dragonfish
Photostomias guernei = bigmouth loosejaw
Phoxinus eos = northern redbelly dace
Phoxinus neogaeus = finescale dace
phycis tacheté = spotted hake
physalier = man-of-war fish
physaliers = Driftfish Family

physicule fauve = brown peeper
Physiculus fulvus = brown peeper
Phytichthys chirus = ribbon prickleback
pi-kok-tok = lake whitefish
picked dogfish = spiny dogfish
pickerel = northern pike
pickerel = yellow walleye
pickering = sauger
picquerelle = chain pickerel
pieded cat = flathead catfish
pièges-à-loup = Wolftrap Family
pigfish = northern searobin
pighead prickleback = blackline prickleback
pike-perches = Perch Family
piked dogfish = spiny dogfish
pikuktuuq = lake whitefish
pilchard = Pacific sardine
pilchard = sardines
pilchards = Herring Family
pile surfperch = pile perch
pilot = ogac
pilot fish = round whitefish
pilot sucker = sharksucker
pilotfish = banded rudderfish
pilotin tacheté = plainfin midshipman
Pimephales notatus = bluntnose minnow
Pimephales promelas = fathead minnow
pimpled lumpsucker = Atlantic spiny lumpsucker
pimpled lumpsucker = Newfoundland spiny lumpsucker
pin sucker = lake chubsucker
pin-nose gar = longnose gar
pinecones = Alfonsino Order
pinfish = brook stickleback
pinfish = fourspine stickleback
pinfish = ninespine stickleback
pinfish = threespine stickleback
ping pong = haddock
pinger = haddock
pinkster = shortnose sturgeon
pinpoint lampfish = pinpoint lanternfish
piquitinga = striped anchovy
pirarucú = Bony-tongue Order
pirate-perch = Trout-perch Order
pirkroartitak = Pacific herring
pitgum dragonfish = pitgum lanternfish
pithead poacher = rockhead
Pitt Lake smelt = Smelt Family
Pittsburgh sucker = black redhorse
placoderms = jawed fish
plaice = smooth flounder
plain anchovy = northern anchovy
plains carpsucker = quillback
plains mountain sucker = mountain sucker
plaintail = oilfish
Platichthys flesus = European flounder
Platichthys flesus = Introduction
Platichthys stellatus = starry flounder
Platygobio gracilis = flathead chub
Platytroctidae = Tubeshoulder Family

Plectognathi = Puffer Order
Plectrobranchus evides = bluebarred prickleback
Pleurogrammus monopterygius = Atka mackerel
Pleuronectes americanus = winter flounder
Pleuronectes asper = yellowfin sole
Pleuronectes bilineatus = rock sole
Pleuronectes ferrugineus = yellowtail flounder
Pleuronectes glacialis = Arctic flounder
Pleuronectes isolepis = butter sole
Pleuronectes proboscideus = longhead dab
Pleuronectes putnami = smooth flounder
Pleuronectes vetulus = English sole
Pleuronectidae = Introduction
Pleuronectidae = Righteye Flounder Family
Pleuronectiformes = Flatfish Order
Pleuronichthys coenosus = C-O sole
Pleuronichthys decurrens = curlfin sole
Pleurotremata = sharks
plie à écailles régulières = butter sole
plie à grande bouche = arrowtooth flounder
plie à nageoire frangée = sash flounder
plie à nageoires frisées = curlfin sole
plie à points noirs = sand sole
plie à tête plate = flathead sole
plie arctique = Arctic flounder
plie asiatique à dents crochues = Asiatic arrowtooth flounder
plie canadienne = Canadian plaice
plie carrelée = anglefin whiff
plie de Béring = Bering flounder
plie de Californie = petrale sole
plie de profondeur = deepsea sole
plie du Gulf Stream = Gulf Stream flounder
plie grise = witch flounder
plie lisse = smooth flounder
plie mince = slender sole
plie oculée = eyed flounder
plie rouge = winter flounder
plie rugueuse = roughscale sole
plie vaseuse = C-O sole
plies = Righteye Flounder Family
plumose sculpin = scalyhead sculpin
pocheteau long-nez = longnose skate
pocheteau noir = longnose skate
Podothecus acipenserinus = sturgeon poacher
Poecilia latipinna = Introduction
Poecilia latipinna = sailfin molly
Poecilia reticulata = Introduction
Poecilia reticulata = Livebearer Family
poecilies = Livebearer Family
Poeciliidae = Introduction
Poeciliidae = Livebearer Family
Pogonias cromis = black drum
pogy = Atlantic menhaden
poinsetta = greenstriped rockfish
pointed-nose sole = English sole
poisson à barbe = stout beardfish

poisson à licou = halterfish
poisson bleu = Arctic grayling
poisson constellation atlantique = Atlantic constellation fish
poisson de marais = bowfin
poisson de Nöel = Atlantic tomcod
poisson de St. Pierre = haddock
poisson des chenaux = Atlantic tomcod
poisson étoilé de Power = highseas lightfish
poisson étoilé élancé = slim lightfish
poisson étoilé océanique = oceanic lightfish
poisson étoilé oval = ovate lightfish
poisson étoilé svelte = slender lightfish
poisson lune = opah
poisson pailletés = Sequinfish Family
poisson pilote = pilotfish
poisson sabre crénelé = crested scabbardfish
poisson sabre ganse = Simony's frostfish
poisson sabre nord-pacifique = North Pacific frostfish
poisson-alligator arctique = Arctic alligatorfish
poisson-alligator atlantique = Atlantic alligatorfish
poisson-alligator lisse = smooth alligatorfish
poisson-baleine diable = redmouth whalefish
poisson-baleine flasque = flabby whalefish
poisson-baleine velouté = velvet whalefish
poisson-castor = bowfin
poisson-éventail atlantique = Atlantic fanfish
poisson-latte pâle = pale lathfish
poisson-lézard à petites écailles = smallscale lizardfish
poisson-lézard féroce = ferocious lizardfish
poisson-lézard paille = snakefish
poisson-lézard rouge = red lizardfish
poisson-montre = rosy soldierfish
poisson-pêcheur = monkfish
poissons à licou = Halterfish Family
poissons dents-de-sabre = Sabertooth Fish Family
poissons étoilés = Lightfish Family
poissons-baleines = Whalefish Family
poissons-baleines diables = Redmouth Whalefish Family
poissons-baleines flasques = Flabby Whalefish Family
poissons-castors = Bowfin Family
poissons-football = Footballfish Family
poissons-grenouilles = Toadfish Family
poissons-heaumes = Ridgehead Family
poissons-lanternes = Lanternfish Family
poissons-lézards = Lizardfish Family

poissons-loups = Wolffish Family
poissons-palissades = Diamond Dory Family
poissons-pêcheurs = Seadevil Family
poissons-tapirs à épines = Tapirfish Family
polar cod = Arctic cod
pole flounder = witch flounder
polka-dot snailfish = dusky snailfish
Pollachius virens = pollock
Pollichthys mauli = star-eye lightfish
polliwog = black bullhead
polliwog = yellow bullhead
pollock = walleye pollock
Polyacanthonotus challengeri = longnose tapirfish
Polyacanthonotus rissoanus = short-spine tapirfish
Polyipnus asteroides = shortspine tenplate
Polymetme corythaeola = sailor lightfish
Polymixia lowei = Caribbean beardfish
Polymixia nobilis = stout beardfish
Polymixiidae = Beardfish Family
Polymixiiformes = Beardfish Order
Polyodon spathula = paddlefish
Polyodontidae = Paddlefish Family
Polyprion americanus = wreckfish
Pomacentridae = Damselfish Family
Pomatomidae = Bluefish Family
Pomatomus saltatrix = bluefish
pomfret = Pacific pomfret
Pomoxis annularis = white crappie
Pomoxis nigromaculatus = black crappie
pompano du Pacifique = Pacific pompano
pompanos = Jack Family
pompile à nageoires bleues = bluefin driftfish
pompile brun = Cornish blackfish
pompile d'Amérique = barrelfish
pompile du Cap = Cape fathead
pompile élancé = slender fathead
pompile noir = black ruff
pompile paucirayonné = fewray fathead
pompiles = Ruff Family
pond perch = green sunfish
pond perch = pumpkinseed
poor minnow = river shiner
pop = Pacific ocean perch
pope = ruffe
popeye rockfish = stripetail rockfish
popeye sole = C-O sole
porcupinefish = striped burrfish
pore-gauche de Schmidt = Schmidt's leftvent
pores-gauches = Leftvent Family
porgy = pile perch
porgy = redtail surfperch
porgy = scup
porgy = silver surfperch
Porichthys notatus = plainfin midshipman
Poroclinus rothrocki = whitebarred prickleback
Poromitra capito = bull rhinofish
Poromitra crassiceps = crested

ridgehead
Poromitra megalops = largeye rhinofish
Portuguese dogfish = Portuguese shark
pot belly = yelloweye rockfish
potbelly = blacknose dace
pottlebelly = blacknose dace
poulamon atlantique = Atlantic tomcod
poulamon du Pacifique = Pacific tomcod
poule de l'eau = lumpfish
poule de mer = flying gurnard
poule de mer ventrue = smooth lumpsucker
poules de mer = Lumpfish Family
poutassou = blue whiting
pouty snailfish = pouty snailfish
prairie buffalo = black buffalo
priacanthe oeil-de-taureau = bulleye
priacanthe sablé = bigeye
priacanthe-crapet = short bigeye
priacanthes = Bigeye Family
Priacanthidae = Bigeye Family
Priacanthus arenatus = bigeye
prickled ray = soft skate
prickly bullhead = prickly sculpin
prickly liparid = prickly snailfish
prickly sculpin = saddleback sculpin
prickly skate = smooth skate
prickly skate = starry skate
priest-fish = blue rockfish
priestfish = skilfish
Prionace glauca = blue shark
prionote du nord = northern searobin
prionote strié = striped searobin
Prionotus carolinus = northern searobin
Prionotus evolans = striped searobin
Pristigenys alta = short bigeye
Pristipomoides aquilonaris = wenchman
Prosopium = whitefishes
Prosopium coulteri = pygmy whitefish
Prosopium cylindraceum = round whitefish
Prosopium sp. = Salmon Family
Prosopium williamsoni = mountain whitefish
Proterorhinus marmoratus = Introduction
Proterorhinus marmoratus = tubenose goby
Protomyctophum arcticum = Arctic telescope
Protomyctophum crockeri = penlight fish
Protomyctophum thompsoni = bigeye flashlightfish
psène maculé = silver driftfish
Psenes maculatus = silver driftfish
Psenes pellucidus = bluefin driftfish
Psettichthys melanostictus = sand sole
Pseudopentaceros pectoralis = longfin armorhead
Pseudophichthys splendens = purplemouthed conger
Pseudopleuronectes americanus =

winter flounder
Psychrolutes paradoxus = tadpole sculpin
Psychrolutes phrictus = blob sculpin
Psychrolutes sigalutes = soft sculpin
Psychrolutidae = Soft Sculpin Family
Pteraspidomorphi = hagfishes
Pterophyllum scalare = Cichlid Family
Pterophyllum scalare = Introduction
Pterycombus brama = Atlantic fanfish
Ptilichthyidae = Quillfish Family
Ptilichthys goodei = quillfish
Ptychocheilus oregonensis = northern squawfish
puff-belly = sea raven
Puget Sound smelt = longfin smelt
pugfish = grunt sculpin
pugnose buffalo = bigmouth buffalo
pugnose eel = snubnose eel
pumpkinseed = butterfish
pumpkinseed buffalo = black buffalo
Pungitius occidentalis = ninespine stickleback
Pungitius pungitius = ninespine stickleback
punky = pumpkinseed
pupfishes = Killifish Order
pygmy shark = Sleeper Shark Family
pygmy sunfish = orangespotted sunfish
pygmy sunfishes = Sunfish Family
Pylodictis olivaris = flathead catfish
pyramodontines = Cusk-eel Order
qanirkuutuk = shorthorn sculpin
qarlêk = thorny skate
qelaluqaq = lake whitefish
qualla = chum salmon
quatre-lampes-hautes = fourtoplamps
quatre-lignes atlantique = fourline snakeblenny
Québec red trout = Arctic char
queue à tache noire = spottail shiner
queue d'épée = green swordtail
queue d'épée = Introduction
queue d'épée = Livebearer Family
queue de voile = guppy
queue de voile = Introduction
queue de voile = Livebearer Family
queue-de-rat d'Amérique = American straptail grenadier
queue-de-rêve atnorouest = westnorat dreamtail
queue-de-rêve bulbeuse = bulbous dreamer
queue-de-rêve cosmopolite = cosmopolitan dreamtail
queue-de-rêve épineuse = spiny dreamer
queue-de-rêve quatravant = forefour dreamtail
quinnat = chinook salmon
quiver = pumpkinseed
qulilirraq = capelin
rabbitfish = deepwater chimaera
rabbitfish = spotted ratfish
rabbitfish = striped burrfish
rabbitfishes = Longnose Chimaera Family

raccoon perch = yellow perch
racehorse chub = central stoneroller
Rachycentridae = Cobia Family
Rachycentron canadum = cobia
Radulinus asprellus = slim sculpin
Radulinus boleoides = darter sculpin
raie = skate species
raie à queue courte = shorttail skate
raie à queue de velours = smooth skate
raie à queue épineuse = spinytail skate
raie à queue rude = roughtail skate
raie abyssale = abyssal skate
raie arctique = darkbelly skate
raie bathyale = chocolate skate
raie biocellée = big skate
raie boréale = darkbelly skate
raie chocolat = chocolate skate
raie de Bigelow = Bigelow's skate
raie de Markle = Markle's ray
raie de profondeur = abyssal skate
raie de profondeurs = deepwater skate
raie du Pacifique = starry skate
raie épineuse = thorny skate
raie hérisson = little skate
raie large = broad skate
raie linon = linen skate
raie lisse = smooth skate
raie molle = soft skate
raie profonde = soft skate
raie radiée = thorny skate
raie ronde = round skate
raie rugueuse = sandpaper skate
raie tachetée = winter skate
raie voile = linen skate
raies = Skate Family
rainbow chub = finescale dace
rainbow tilefish = tilefish
rainbowfishes = Silverside Order
Raja = Skate Family
Raja abyssicola = abyssal skate
Raja badia = broad skate
Raja bathyphila = chocolate skate
Raja bigelowi = Bigelow's skate
Raja binoculata = big skate
Raja erinacea = little skate
Raja fyllae = round skate
Raja hyperborea = darkbelly skate
Raja interrupta = sandpaper skate
Raja jenseni = shorttail skate
Raja kincaidii = sandpaper skate
Raja laevis = barndoor skate
Raja lintea = linen skate
Raja mollis = soft skate
Raja ocellata = winter skate
Raja radiata = thorny skate
Raja rhina = longnose skate
Raja richardsoni = deepwater skate
Raja senta = smooth skate
Raja sp. = skate species
Raja spinacidermis = soft skate
Raja spinicauda = spinytail skate
Raja stellulata = starry skate
Rajidae = Skate Family
Rajiformes = Ray Order
rameur = ocean whitetip shark
rape = monkfish
rascasse dénudée = smoothhead scorpionfish

raseux-de-terre = johnny darter
rasher = vermilion rockfish
rasphead = yelloweye rockfish
ratfish = deepwater chimaera
ratfishes = Chimaera Family
rattlesnake pike = sauger
Ray's bream = Atlantic pomfret
rayon épineux = spinyfin
rayons épineux = Spinyfin Family
razorback = black crappie
recto = recto
red bream = blackbelly rosefish
red bream = wideside alfonsin
red brim = redbreast sunfish
red brotulid = red brotula
red cat = brown bullhead
red cichlid = jewelfish
red devil = dwarf wrymouth
red hake = white hake
red lump = lumpfish
red mullets = Goatfish Family
red perch = longear sunfish
red perch = redbreast sunfish
Red River bass = freshwater drum
red rock cod = tiger rockfish
red rock cod = vermilion rockfish
red rock trout = rock greenling
red salmon = sockeye salmon
red sculpin = red Irish lord
red sculpin = sea raven
red snapper = canary rockfish
red snapper = splitnose rockfish
red snapper = vermilion rockfish
red snapper = yelloweye rockfish
red sturgeon = lake sturgeon
red sucker = longnose sucker
red sucker = shorthead redhorse
red whalefish family = Whalefish
Family
red-bellied bream = longear sunfish
red-bellied bream = redbreast sunfish
red-bellied dace = northern redbelly
dace
red-eye round herring = round herring
red-finned pike = redfin pickerel
red-headed bream = redbreast sunfish
red-sided darter = Iowa darter
red-sided shiner = redside dace
red-sided sucker = longnose sucker
red-spotted Rocky Mountain trout =
Dolly Varden
red-throated trout = coastal cutthroat
trout
red-throated trout = west-slope cutthroat trout
redband trout = rainbow trout
redeye = rock bass
redeye = smallmouth bass
redeyed sunfish = longear sunfish
redfin = shorthead redhorse
redfin dace = blacknose dace
redfin perch = yellow perch
redfin redhorse = river redhorse
redfin shiner = common shiner
redfish = Acadian redfish
redfish = deepwater redfish
redfish = golden redfish
redmouth buffalo = bigmouth buffalo
redsides = rainbow trout

redspotted sunfish = orangespotted
sunfish
redspotted trout = brook trout
redtail chub = hornyhead chub
redtail seaperch = redtail surfperch
reefer = black buffalo
Regalecus glesne = Opah Order
Reighard's chub = shortnose cisco
Reighard's cisco = shortnose cisco
Reinhardtius hippoglossoides =
Greenland halibut
remora = black remora
rémora austral = whalesucker
Remora australis = whalesucker
Remora brachyptera = spearfish
remora
rémora brun = spearfish remora
rémora noir = black remora
Remora remora = black remora
rémoras = Remora Family
renard = thresher shark
renard de mer = thresher shark
renard marin = thresher shark
renards marins = Thresher Shark
Family
réquiem de sable = dusky shark
réquiem océanique = ocean whitetip
shark
réquiem plombe = sandbar shark
requin à grands ailerons = soupfin
shark
requin à longues nageoires = ocean
whitetip shark
requin à nez pointu = Atlantic sharpnose shark
requin à sept branchies = sevengill
shark
requin aiguille gussi = Atlantic
sharpnose shark
requin baleine = whale shark
requin bleu = blue shark
requin dormeur = Greenland shark
requin gris = sandbar shark
requin grisé = sixgill shark
requin griset = sixgill shark
requin lézard = Cow Shark Order
requin obscur = dusky shark
requin océanique = ocean whitetip
shark
requin sable tacheté = sand tiger
requin sombre = dusky shark
requin soyeux = silky shark
requin tigre commun = tiger shark
requin-hâ = soupfin shark
requin-marteau commun = smooth
hammerhead
requin-taupe saumon = salmon shark
requin-taureau = sand tiger
requins baleines = Whale Shark
Family
requins-taureau = Sand Tiger Family
reticulated pickerel = chain pickerel
revenant à yeux télescopiques =
binocular spookfish
revenant ailé = winged spookfish
revenant javeline = javelin spookfish
revenants = Spookfish Family
rêveur à petites cornes = shorthorn
dreamer
rêveur cauchemar = nightmare
dreamer

rêveur piquant = prickly dreamer
rêveur sombre = smooth dreamer
rêveur très-denté = toothy dreamer
rêveurs = Dreamer Family
Rhacochilus vacca = pile perch
Rhamphocottus richardsoni = grunt
sculpin
Rhectogramma sherboni = recto
Rhincodon typus = whale shark
Rhincodontidae = Whale Shark
Family
Rhineosomus triqueter = smooth
trunkfish
Rhinichthys = northern hog sucker
Rhinichthys atratulus = blacknose
dace
Rhinichthys cataractae = longnose
dace
Rhinichthys cataractae = Nooky
dace
Rhinichthys cataractae smithi =
Banff longnose dace
Rhinichthys falcatus = leopard dace
Rhinichthys meleagris = blacknose
dace
Rhinichthys osculus = speckled dace
Rhinichthys sp. = Nooky dace
Rhinichthys umatilla = Umatilla dace
rhino à grands yeux = largeye rhi-
nofish
rhino à petits yeux = crested ridge-
head
rhino boeuf = bull rhinofish
Rhinochimaera atlantica = knifenose
chimaera
Rhinochimaeridae = Longnose
Chimaera Family
Rhinoliparis attenuatus = slim snail-
fish
Rhinonemus cimbrius = fourbeard
rockling
Rhizoprionodon terraenovae =
Atlantic sharpnose shark
Rhodeus sericeus = Introduction
Rhodichthys regina = threadfin snail-
fish
ribbed sculpin = bigeye sculpin
ribbonfishes = Opah Order
Rice's sculpin = spoonhead sculpin
ricefield slick = green sunfish
ricefishes = Needlefish Order
Richardson shiner = weed shiner
Richardson's sculpin = grunt sculpin
Richardson's skate = deepwater skate
Richardsonius balteatus = redside
shiner
riffle sucker = northern hog sucker
Righteye Flounder Family =
Introduction
Rimicola muscarum = kelp clingfish
ring perch = yellow perch
ring-tailed liparid = ringtail snailfish
ringed crappie = white crappie
river bass = largemouth bass
river chub = hornyhead chub
river drum = freshwater drum
river herring = blueback herring
river herring = gaspereau
river mullet = river redhorse
river mullet = striped mullet
river pike = chain pickerel

river pike = sauger
river snapper = black bullhead
river stingrays = Ray Order
river stingrays = Stingray Family
river sucker = shorthead redhorse
river whitefish = mooneye
rivulines = Killifish Order
roach = bluefish
roach = bluegill
roach = golden shiner
roach = pumpkinseed
robin = redbreast sunfish
rock bass = black sea bass
rock bass = green sunfish
rock blenny = rock prickleback
rock cod = Atlantic cod
rock cod = dusky rockfish
rock cod = ogac
rock cod = Puget Sound rockfish
rock cod = redstripe rockfish
rock eel = rock gunnel
rock eel = rock prickleback
rock flounder = rock sole
rock salmon = Atlantic wolffish
rock salmon = bluefish
rock salmon = bocaccio
rock salmon = pollock
rock salmon = silvergray rockfish
rock sturgeon = lake sturgeon
rock trout = kelp greenling
rock trout = whitespotted greenling
rock-eel = snakeblenny
rock-salmon = spiny dogfish
rockcods = Sea Bass Family
rockfish = logperch
rockfish = striped bass
rockspear = red lizardfish
rockweed blenny = rockweed gunnel
Rocky Mountain whitefish = mountain whitefish
roi-des-saumons = king-of-the-
salmon
rondeau mouton = sheepshead
Rondelia loricata = redmouth
whalefish
Rondeletiidae = Redmouth
Whalefish Family
ronquille à nageoires bleues =
bluefin searcher
ronquille du nord = northern ronquil
ronquilles = Ronquil Family
Ronquilus jordani = northern ronquil
rosefish = Acadian redfish
rosefish = deepwater redfish
rosefish = golden redfish
rosefish = splitnose rockfish
rotgut minnow = central stoneroller
rouget doré = red goatfish
rough dab = Canadian plaice
rough fish = rosy soldierfish
rough flounder = winter flounder
rough scad = jack mackerel
rough sharks = Dogfish Shark Order
rough sole = slender sole
rough-head = common shiner
roughback sole = rock sole
roughies = Alfonsino Order
roughies = Slimehead Family
roughnosed chub = fallfish
roule-caillou = central stoneroller
round buffalo = black buffalo

round goby = Introduction
round ray = round skate
round rays = Stingray Family
round sunfish = pumpkinseed
round-headed sculpin = mosshead sculpin
round-nosed sculpin = smoothhead sculpin
round-nosed sole = petrale sole
round-nosed whitefish = broad whitefish
roundhead buffalo = bigmouth buffalo
roundnose grenadier = rock grenadier
roundnoser = shortnose sturgeon
roussette = brown cat shark
roussette d'Islande = Iceland cat shark
roussette de profondeur = deepsea cat shark
roussette maille = chain cat shark
roussettes = Cat Shark Family
router = black buffalo
rouvet = oilfish
royal panaque = Introduction
rubber nose = lake sturgeon
rubber sole = Dover sole
rubbertail = green sunfish
rudd = Introduction
rudder fish = black ruff
rudderfish = barrelfish
rudderfishes = Sea Chub Family
ruddy sturgeon = lake sturgeon
ruff = ruffe
ruffe = Introduction
runner = cobia
Ruscarius meanyi = Puget Sound sculpin
Russian cat = flathead catfish
rusty dab = yellowtail flounder
rusty flounder = yellowtail flounder
Ruvettus pretiosus = oilfish
saama = Atlantic salmon
saamakutaak = Atlantic salmon
sabre d'argent à petits yeux = smalleye frostfish
sabre fleuret = smalleye frostfish
sabre noir = black scabbardfish
sac-à-lait = white crappie
Saccopharyngidae = Swallower Family
Saccopharyngiformes = Gulper Eel Order
Saccopharynx ampullaceus = taillight gulper
sackfishes = Snake Mackerel Family
Sacramento cat = brown bullhead
Sacramento smelt = longfin smelt
Sacramento sturgeon = white sturgeon
saddled blenny = saddleback gunnel
saddled grenadier = longnose grenadier
saffron bass = yellowfin bass
Sagamichthys abei = shining tubeshoulder
sagre rude = rough sagre
saïda barbu = toothed cod
saïda franc = Arctic cod
saïda imberbe = polar cod

sailbackfishes = Scorpionfish Family
sailfin arctic grayling = Arctic grayling
sailfin dory = buckler dory
sailfin molly = Introduction
sailfish = basking shark
sailfishes = billfishes
sailfishes = Swordfish Family
sailor-fish = sailfin sculpin
sailray = linen skate
saithe = pollock
Salmo aguabonito = golden trout
Salmo clarki = coastal cutthroat trout
Salmo clarki = west-slope cutthroat trout
Salmo gairdneri = rainbow trout
Salmo gairdneri = Salmon Family
Salmo salar = Atlantic salmon
Salmo trutta = brown trout
Salmo trutta = Introduction
Salmon Family = Introduction
salmon grouper = bocaccio
salmon shark = porbeagle
salmon shark = spiny dogfish
salmon trout = lake trout
salmon-herring = Arctic cisco
salmon-trout = Dolly Varden
Salmonidae = Introduction
Salmonidae = Salmon Family
Salmoniformes = Salmon Order
salter = brook trout
saltmarsh killifish = mummichog
saltwater minnow = mummichog
saltwater smelt = rainbow smelt
salvation fish = eulachon
Salvelinus = chars
Salvelinus = trouts
Salvelinus alpinus = Arctic char
Salvelinus aureolus = Arctic char
Salvelinus confluentus = bull trout
Salvelinus fontinalis = brook trout
Salvelinus fontinalis timagamiensis = aurora trout
Salvelinus malma = Dolly Varden
Salvelinus marstoni = Arctic char
Salvelinus namaycush = lake trout
Salvelinus oquassa = Arctic char
sâma = Atlantic salmon
sand bass = green sunfish
sand bass = white bass
sand dab = Canadian plaice
sand dab = windowpane
sand dab = yellowtail flounder
sand devils = Angel Shark Family
sand devils = Angel Shark Order
sand eels = Sand Lance Family
sand eels = Stickleback Order
sand flounder = sand sole
sand flounder = windowpane
sand herring = lake cisco
sand ling = burbot
sand pickerel = sauger
sand pike = sauger
sand pike-perch = sauger
sand roller = trout-perch
sand shark = spiny dogfish
sand smelt = Atlantic silverside
sand smelts = Silverside Family
sand sucker = spotted sucker
sandeel = white barracudina
sanglier à courtes épines = shortspine

boarfish
sangliers = Boarfish Family
Sarcopterygii = bony fishes
Sarcopterygii = fishes
Sarda chiliensis lineolata = Pacific bonito
Sarda sarda = Atlantic bonito
sardine = Atlantic herring
sardine du Pacifique = Pacific sardine
Sardinops sagax caeruleus = Pacific sardine
sargassier = sargassumfish
Sarritor frenatus = sawback poacher
Saskatchewan dace = flathead chub
satin-finned minnow = spotfin shiner
saugeye = sauger
Sault whitefish = Acadian whitefish
Sault whitefish = lake whitefish
saumon coho = coho salmon
saumon d'eau douce = Atlantic salmon
saumon de l'Atlantique = Atlantic salmon
saumon kéta = chum salmon
saumon quinnat = chinook salmon
saumon rose = pink salmon
saumon rouge = sockeye salmon
saumons = Salmon Family
saurel = Atlantic saury
saurel = jack mackerel
saurel maxécus = rough scad
saury = Atlantic saury
sauvagesse du nord = northern squawfish
saw-cheeked fish = Cornish blackfish
sawbelly = gaspereau
sawbelly = gizzard shad
sawfishes = Ray Order
sawtooth eels = Sawpalate Family
scabbardfishes = Cutlassfish Family
scalaire = Cichlid Family
scalaire = freshwater angelfish
scalaire = Introduction
scaled blennies = Clinid Family
scaled dragonfishes = Barbeled Dragonfish Family
scaled lancet fish = sharpchin barracudina
scaled ling = bowfin
scaleless black dragonfishes = Barbeled Dragonfish Family
scaleless black dragonfishes = scaleless dragonfishes
scaly dragonfishes = Barbeled Dragonfish Family
scaly dragonfishes = scaled dragonfishes
scaly paperbone = scaly waryfish
scalyfin sole = butter sole
Scardinius erythrophthalmus = Introduction
Scardinius erythrophthalmus = rudd
school shark = soupfin shark
Schuylkill cat = brown bullhead
Sciaenidae = Drum Family
scissorbill = longnose gar
Scomber colias = chub mackerel
Scomber japonicus = chub mackerel =

Scomber scombrus = Atlantic mackerel
Scomberesocidae = Saury Family
Scomberesox saurus = Atlantic saury
Scomberomorus cavalla = king mackerel
Scomberomorus maculatus = Atlantic Spanish mackerel
Scombridae = Mackerel Family
Scopelarchidae = Pearleye Family
Scopelarchus analis = blackbelly pearleye
Scopeloberyx opisthopterus = rearfin expatriate
Scopelogadus beani = squarenose helmetfish
Scopelogadus mizolepis bispinosus = twospine bigscale
Scopelosauridae = Waryfish Family
Scopelosaurus harryi = scaly waryfish
Scopelosaurus lepidus = blackfin waryfish
Scopelosaurus mauli = Maul's waryfish
Scophthalmus aquosus = windowpane
Scorpaena calcarata = smoothhead scorpionfish
Scorpaenichthys marmoratus = cabezon
Scorpaenidae = Scorpionfish Family
Scorpaeniformes = Mail-cheeked Order
scorpènes = Scorpionfish Family
scorpionfish = deepwater sculpin
scourfish = oilfish
scrapcod = walleye pollock
scratch belly = sea raven
scribbled leatherjacket = scrawled filefish
scrod = Atlantic cod
scrod = cusk
scrod = haddock
Scyliorhinidae = Cat Shark Family
Scyliorhinus retifer = chain cat shark
Scytalina cerdale = graveldiver
Scytalinidae = Graveldiver Family
scythe fishes = Ribbonfish Family
sea bream = scup
sea catfishes = Wolffish Family
sea cock = lumpfish
sea devil = monkfish
sea drum = black drum
sea eel = conger eel
sea hen = lumpfish
sea hen = sea raven
sea herring = Atlantic herring
sea lamprey = Pacific lamprey
sea mullet = striped mullet
sea owl = lumpfish
sea perch = cunner
sea perch = white perch
sea poacher = Atlantic alligatorfish
sea sculpin = sea raven
sea smelt = rainbow smelt
sea snails = Snailfish Family
sea squab = northern puffer
sea sturgeon = Atlantic sturgeon
sea trout = Arctic char
sea trout = brook trout

shovelnose = dusky shark
shovelnose = smooth hammerhead
shovelnose cat = flathead catfish
shovelnose pike = northern pike
shovelnose shark = sand tiger
shovelnose shark = sixgill shark
shovelnose whitefish = inconnu
shrimp eels = Snake Eel Family
shrimpfishes = Stickleback Order
shulukpaoluk = burbot
si-airryuk = inconnu
Siamese fightingfish = Introduction
sid = Atlantic herring
sierak = inconnu
sigguayaq = lake trout
sigouine à longue nageoire = longfin gunnel
sigouine de roche = rock gunnel
sigouine de varech = rockweed gunnel
sigouine jaunâtre = penpoint gunnel
sigouine lunée = crescent gunnel
sigouine mantelée = saddleback gunnel
sigouine rouge = red gunnel
sigouine rubanée = banded gunnel
sigouines = Gunnel Family
Siluriformes = Catfish Order
silver bass = black crappie
silver bass = freshwater drum
silver bass = white bass
silver bass = white crappie
silver char = Arctic char
silver chub = fallfish
silver chub = trout-perch
silver crappie = white crappie
silver eel = American eel
silver gambusia = mosquitofish
silver ghost = bonefish
silver hatchetfish = longspine silver hatchetfish
silver lamprey = chestnut lamprey
silver mullet = silver redhorse
silver mullet = white mullet
silver perch = pile perch
silver perch = white perch
silver salmon = coho salmon
silver shiner = common shiner
silver smelt = surf smelt
silver spot = silverspotted sculpin
silver trout = rainbow trout
silver trout = sockeye salmon
silver-finned minnow = spotfin shiner
silver-rag driftfish = silver-rag
silverfish = tarpon
silverking = tarpon
silverside = common shiner
silversides = coho salmon
silvery carp = quillback
silvery chub = creek chub
silvery grey minnow = leopard dace
Simenchelys parasiticus = snubnose eel
singing fish = plainfin midshipman
siolik = northern pike
siscowet = lake trout
siuktuuk = lake trout
siun = northern pike
siuryuktuuq = saffron cod
six-spined stickleback = brook stick-leback
sjulik = northern pike
skadlin = Atlantic herring
Skidegate sole = butter sole
skilfish = sablefish
skipjack = Atlantic bonito
skipjack = Atlantic saury
skipjack = common shiner
skipjack = butterfish
skipjack = brook silverside
skipjack = gizzard shad
skipjack = Pacific bonito
skipjack = rosyface shiner
skipjack = silverstripe halfbeak
skipper = Atlantic saury
slab = black crappie
slab = white crappie
sleeper shark = Greenland shark
sleeper sharks = Dogfish Shark Order
slender alphonsino = narrowside alfonsin
slender beryx = narrowside alfonsin
slender clingfish = kelp clingfish
slender codling = dainty mora
slender flounder = slender sole
slender frostfish = smalleye frostfish
slender rockfish = pygmy rockfish
slender rockfish = shortbelly rockfish
slender sucker = white sucker
slick = black bullhead
slick bullhead = yellow bullhead
slicker = blacknose dace
slim rockfish = shortbelly rockfish
slime eel = Atlantic hagfish
slime sole = Dover sole
slime-eel = snubnose eel
slimy muddler = slimy sculpin
slinker = northern pike
slippery flounder = Dover sole
Sloane's viperfish = manylight viperfish
slob = brook trout
slough buffalo = bigmouth buffalo
slough pickerel = grass pickerel
small black brook lamprey = American brook lamprey
small red rockcod = splitnose rockfish
small-disked liparid = smalldisk snailfish
small-eyed lantern fish = veiled anglemouth
small-eyed lanternfish = pinpoint lanternfish
small-mouthed minnow = pugnose minnow
smalleyed rabbitfish = deepwater chimaera
smallfin lanternfish = northern lanternfish
smallhead eelpout = stubraker slipskin
smallheaded mullet = golden redhorse
smallie = smallmouth bass
smallmouth smelt = pond smelt
smallmouth spiny eel = shortspine tapirfish
smooth hound = smooth dogfish
smooth hounds = Hound Shark Family
smooth poacher = smooth alligatorfish
smooth-spined rattail = roughhead grenadier
smooth-tailed skate = smooth skate
smoothback = lake sturgeon
smoothhounds = Ground Shark Order
smoothscale rattail = russet grenadier
smoothtongues = Deepsea Smelt Family
snake = chain pickerel
snake = northern pike
snake blenny = stout eelblenny
snakeblenny = fourline snakeblenny
snakefish = American eel
snapper = bluefish
snapper blue = bluefish
snapper eels = Snake Eel Family
snapper haddock = haddock
snapping mackerel = bluefish
snig = Atlantic tomcod
snubnose parasitic eel = snubnose eel
snubnosed spiny eel = largescale tapirfish
sobaco = ocean triggerfish
soft brown = widow rockfish
soft flounder = Pacific sanddab
soft melamphid = twospine bigscale
soft shell sturgeon = shortnose sturgeon
softnosed skates = Skate Family
soldier darter = rainbow darter
soldierfishes = Alfonsino Order
sole = Canadian plaice
sole = winter flounder
sole = yellowtail flounder
sole à grandes écailles = largescale tonguefish
sole à petite bouche = Dover sole
sole américaine = rex sole
sole anglaise = English sole
sole de Pacifique = rock sole
sole tachetée = daubed tonguefish
Solomon Gundy = Atlantic herring
Somniosus microcephalus = Greenland shark
Somniosus pacificus = Pacific sleeper shark
sooty eel = string eel
sourcil à longues épines = longspine combfish
sourcil à taches blanches = whitespotted greenling
sourcil à tête pointue = painted greenling
sourcil de roche = rock greenling
sourcil de varech = kelp greenling
sourcil masqué = masked greenling
sourcils = Greenling Family
spaced snipe eel = closespine snipe eel
spadefish = paddlefish
Spanish mackerel = chub mackerel
Spanish mackerels = Mackerel Family
spare doré = scup
spare tête-de-mouton = sheepshead
spares = Porgy Family
Sparidae = Porgy Family
spatulaire = paddlefish
spatules = Paddlefish Family
spawneater = spottail shiner
spearfishes = billfishes
spearfishes = Swordfish Family
speck = brook trout
speckled bass = black crappie
speckled cat = bowfin
speckled cat = brown bullhead
speckled perch = white crappie
speckled rockfish = quillback rockfish
speckled sea trout = kelp greenling
speckled sucker = spotted sucker
speckled trout = brook trout
specks = black crappie
Spectrunculus grandis = giant cuskeel
sperling = Atlantic herring
sperling = Atlantic silverside
sphéroïde du nord = northern puffer
sphéroïde trogne = blunthead puffer
sphéroïdes = Puffer Family
Sphoeroides maculatus = northern puffer
Sphoeroides pachygaster = blunthead puffer
Sphyraena argentea = Pacific barracuda
Sphyraena borealis = northern sennet
Sphyraenidae = Barracuda Family
Sphyrna zygaena = smooth hammerhead
Sphyrnidae = hammerhead sharks
spiderfish = snoutlet crotchfeeler
spikefishes = Puffer Order
spikey jack = spiny dogfish
spined dogfish = spiny dogfish
spineless cat = burbot
spinelessbrow lampfish = smoothbrow lampfish
spinetail ray = spinetail ray
Spiniphryne gladisfenae = prickly dreamer
spiny eel = largescale tapirfish
spiny eel = longnose tapirfish
spiny eel = shortspine tapirfish
spiny eelblenny = blackline prickleback
spiny eels = Tapirfish Family
spiny puffer = balloonfish
spiny puffers = Porcupinefish Family
spiny puffers = Puffer Order
spiny sharks = bony fishes
spiny sharks = jawed fishes
spiny tapirfishes = Tapirfish Family
spinycheek liparid = spiny snailfish
spinycheek rockfish = shortspine thornyhead
Spirinchus starksi = night smelt
Spirinchus thaleichthys = longfin smelt
spirling = rainbow smelt
splitfins = Killifish Order
splittail perch = pile perch
spookfish = spotted ratfish
spoonbill cat = paddlefish
spoonbill eel = duckbill eel
spoonhead = mottled sculpin
spoonhead muddler = spoonhead sculpin

spot flounder = C-O sole
spot-tail = bowfin
spotfin pike = sauger
spotted catfish = channel catfish
spotted chub = gravel chub
spotted codfish = spotted wolffish
spotted codling = spotted hake
spotted cow shark = sevengill shark
spotted flounder = sand sole
spotted flounder = windowpane
spotted gambusia = mosquitofish
spotted Irish lord = red Irish lord
spotted kelpfish = crevice kelpfish
spotted muskellunge = muskellunge
spotted opah = opah
spotted ragfish = ragfish
spotted ragged-tooth shark = sand tiger
spotted redhorse = spotted sucker
spotted seaweed blenny = feather blenny
spotted skate = winter skate
spotted snakeblenny = Arctic shanny
spotted tinselfish = tinselfish
spotted trout = brown trout
spotted trout = sauger
spreau = gaspereau
spring herring = gaspereau
spring salmon = chinook salmon
springfish = mottled sculpin
spurdog = spiny dogfish
squale liche = kitefin shark
squale nain = spined pygmy shark
Squalidae = Dogfish Shark Family
Squaliformes = Dogfish Shark Order
Squaliolus laticaudus = spined pygmy shark
Squalus acanthias = spiny dogfish
Squalus suckleyi = spiny dogfish
square-tail = brook trout
squaremouth = chiselmouth
Squatina californica = Pacific angel shark
Squatinidae = Angel Shark Family
Squatiniformes = Angel Shark Order
squeteague = weakfish
squid hound = striped bass
squirrel hake = red hake
squirrel hake = white hake
squirrelfishes = Alfonsino Order
staghorn sculpin = Pacific staghorn sculpin
stalkeyes = sawtailfishes
star-eaters = snaggletooths
starfish = butterfish
stargazer = slimy sculpin
starry skate = thorny skate
steakfish = white hake
steamer rockfish = shortbelly rockfish
steel-backed chub = central stoneroller
steelcoloured shiner = spotfin shiner
steelhead trout = rainbow trout
stelgidolepis = lamp grenadier
Stellerina xyosterna = pricklebreast poacher
Stenobrachius leucopsarus = northern lanternfish
Stenobrachius nannochir = garnet lanternfish

Stenodus leucichthys = inconnu
Stenotomus chrysops = scup
Stephanoberyciformes = Pricklefish Order
Stephanolepis hispidus = planehead filefish
Sternoptychidae = Silver Hatchetfish Family
Sternoptyx diaphana = transparent hatchetfish
Sternoptyx pseudobscura = highlight hatchetfish
Stichaeidae = Shanny Family
Stichaeus punctatus = Arctic shanny
stichée à long nez = longsnout prickleback
stichée arctique = Arctic shanny
stichée perlée = pearly prickleback
stichée-Y = Y-prickleback
stichées = Shanny Family
stingaree = roughtail stingray
stinger = black bullhead
stink shad = gizzard shad
stinker = C-O sole
Stizostedion canadense = sauger
Stizostedion vitreum glaucum = blue walleye
Stizostedion vitreum vitreum = yellow walleye
Stomias boa ferox = boa dragonfish
Stomias brevibarbatus = shortbarbel dragonfish
Stomias ferox = boa dragonfish
Stomiidae = Barbeled Dragonfish Family
Stomiidae = scaled dragonfishes
Stomiiformes = Widemouth Order
stone bass = wreckfish
stone catfish = stonecat
stone lugger = central stoneroller
stone sturgeon = lake sturgeon
stone sucker = sea lamprey
stonefishes = Scorpionfish Family
stonelugger = northern hog sucker
stoneroller = northern hog sucker
stonetoter = northern hog sucker
Storer's chub = silver chub
straightline dragonfish = large-eye snaggletooth
straightnose rabbitfish = knifenose chimera
straw bass = black crappie
straw bass = largemouth bass
straw-coloured minnow = river shiner
straw-coloured minnow = sand shiner
strawberry bass = black crappie
strawberry bass = bluegill
strawberry bass = white crappie
strawberry rockfish = greenstriped rockfish
streaker = white bass
stream shooter = longnose dace
streamer basses = Sea Bass Family
striped bonito = skipjack tuna
striped dace = blacknose dace
striped fantail darter = fantail darter
striped lake bass = white bass
striped perch = yellow perch
striped rockfish = greenstriped rock-

fish
striped sucker = spotted sucker
striped surfperch = striped seaperch
striped wolffish = Atlantic wolffish
striper = striped bass
striper = white bass
stromatée à fossettes = butterfish
stromatée-méduse = medusafish
stromatées = Butterfish Family
Stromateidae = Butterfish Family
stubnose buffalo = bigmouth buffalo
stump-knocker = warmouth
sturgeon sucker = longnose sucker
Stylophthalmus paradoxus = sawtailfishes
Stylophthalmus paradoxus = Barbeled Dragonfish Family
sucet de lac = lake chubsucker
suceur ballot = river redhorse
suceur blanc = silver redhorse
suceur cuivré = copper redhorse
suceur doré = golden redhorse
suceur jaune = greater redhorse
suceur noir = black redhorse
suceur rouge = shorthead redhorse
suckerfish = sharksucker
Suckermouth Catfish Family = Introduction
sucking carp = spottail shiner
Sudis hyalina = winged barracudina
sugar toad = northern puffer
sulukpaugaq = Arctic grayling
sulukpauvak = Arctic grayling
sulupavak = Arctic eelpout
summer herring = blueback herring
sun bass = pumpkinseed
sun perch = bluegill
Sunapee trout = Arctic char
sundial = windowpane
sunfish = bluefish
sunfish = golden shiner
sunfish = orange filefish
sunfishes = Mola Family
sunny = pumpkinseed
sunperch = green sunfish
sunperch = redbreast sunfish
surmulets = Goatfish Family
surmullet = red goatfish
surmullets = Goatfish Family
sweet sucker = lake chubsucker
swellfish = northern puffer
swellfish = striped burrfish
swelltoad = northern puffer
swingletail = thresher shark
swiveltail = thresher shark
swordfish sucker = spearfish remora
swordtail eel = largescale tapirfish
Syacium micrurum = channel flounder
Symbolophorus californiensis = bigfin lanternfish
Symbolophorus veranyi = North Atlantic cornerlantern
Symphurus minor = largescale tonguefish
Symphurus pterospilotus = daubed tonguefish
Synagrops bellus = blackmouth widejaw
Synagrops spinosus = spiny widejaw
Synaphobranchidae = Cutthroat Eel

Family
Synaphobranchus kaupi = slatjaw cutthroat eel
Synchirus gilli = manacled sculpin
syngnathe à lignes grises = bay pipefish
syngnathe bouledogue = bull pipefish
syngnathe brun = northern pipefish
syngnathe camus = pugnose pipefish
syngnathe dendritique = pipehorse
syngnathe sargassier = sargassum pipefish
Syngnathidae = Pipefish Family
Syngnathus fuscus = northern pipefish
Syngnathus griseolineatus = bay pipefish
Syngnathus leptorhynchus = bay pipefish
Syngnathus pelagicus = sargassum pipefish
Syngnathus springeri = bull pipefish
Synodontidae = Lizardfish Family
Synodus lucioceps = smallscale lizardfish
Synodus synodus = red lizardfish
Taaningichthys = lampfishes
Taaningichthys bathyphilus = smoothbrow lampfish
Taaningichthys minimus = lesser lampfish
tacks = Atlantic mackerel
tact géant à queue filamenteuse = longtail whipnose
tact géant de Vanhoeffen = Vanhoeffen's whipnose
Tactostoma macropus = longfin dragonfish
tacts géants = Whipnose Family
tadpole cat = tadpole madtom
tadpole liparid = tadpole snailfish
tadpole sculpins = Soft Sculpin Family
tadpole stonecat = tadpole madtom
tailor = bluefish
Talismania bifurcata = threadfin slickhead
tallow-mouth minnow = central stoneroller
tally-wag = black sea bass
tambour rayé = white croaker
tambour royal = queenfish
tambours = Drum Family
tanche = cunner
tanche = Introduction
tanche = tench
tanche-tautogue = cunner
tansy = banded gunnel
tansy = rock gunnel
tapetails = Opah Order
tapir à dorsale = backfin tapirfish
tapir à grandes écailles = largescale tapirfish
tapir à nez long = longnose tapirfish
tapir à petites épines = shortspine tapirfish
taque = lake trout
Taractes asper = rough pomfret
Taractichthys longipinnis = bigscale pomfret

Taranetzella lyoderma = looseskin eelpout
Tarletonbeania crenularis = blue lanternfish
Tarletonbeania taylori = tail-light lanternfish
tarpon = tarpon
tarpon argenté = tarpon
tarpons = Tarpon Family
tassard royal = king mackerel
tassel-finned fishes = bony fishes
tassergal = bluefish
tassergals = Bluefish Family
taupe bleu = shortfin mako
taupe de Pacifique = salmon shark
taupe longue aile = longfin mako
Tautoga onitis = tautog
Tautogolabrus adspersus = cunner
tautogue noir = tautog
Taylor's sculpin = spinynose sculpin
tchulupa = Arctic grayling
Teleostei = Bowfin Family
Teleostei = teleosts
Teleostomi = bony fishes
télescope à grands yeux = bigeye flashlightfish
télescope arctique = Arctic telescope
télescope californien = penlight fish
tench = Introduction
tenpounders = Tarpon Order
tenspine stickleback = ninespine stickleback
terrassier à six lignes = blackline prickleback
terrassier géant = giant wrymouth
terrassier nain = dwarf wrymouth
terrassier tacheté = spotted wry-mouth
terrassiers = Wrymouth Family
tête à taches rouges = hornyhead chub
tête rose = rosyface shiner
tête-casquée à longues nageoires = longfin armorhead
tête-de-boule = fathead minnow
tête-de-roche = rockhead
têtes casquées = Armorhead Family
tétraponure à petits yeux = smalleye squaretail
tétragonure gris = bigeye squaretail
tétragonure lilas = smalleye square-tail
tétragonures = Squaretail Family
Tetragonuridae = Squaretail Family
Tetragonurus atlanticus = bigeye squaretail
Tetragonurus cuvieri = smalleye squaretail
Tetraodon = Puffer Family
Tetraodontidae = Puffer Family
Tetraodontiformes = Puffer Order
Tetrapterus albidus = white marlin
Texas gambusia = mosquitofish
tezra = broad whitefish
Thaleichthys pacificus = eulachon
Thaumatichthyidae = Wolftrap Family
thazard atlantique = Atlantic Spanish mackerel
thazard barré = king mackerel
thazard tacheté = Atlantic Spanish

mackerel
Theragra chalcogramma = walleye pollock
Theta lanternfish = California head-lightfish
thon albacore = yellowfin tuna
thon obèse = bigeye tuna
thon rouge = bluefin tuna
thon ventru = bigeye tuna
thonine à ventre rayé = skipjack tuna
thonine commune = little tunny
Thoracostei = Stickleback Order
thornbacks = Ray Order
thrasher = thresher shark
thread eel = longfin sawpalate
thread eel = stout sawpalate
thread eels = Sawpalate Family
threadfin rockling = threebeard rock-ling
threadfish = slender snipe eel
three-eyed haddock = fur-bearing trout
three-eyed haddock = haddock
three-toothed lamprey = Pacific lam-prey
threelight dragon = triangle-light dragon
threespot gourami = Introduction
thunder-pumper = freshwater drum
Thunnus alalunga = albacore
Thunnus albacares = yellowfin tuna
Thunnus obesus = bigeye tuna
Thunnus thynnus = bluefin tuna
Thunnus thynnus orientalis = bluefin tuna
Thymallus arcticus = Arctic grayling
Thyrsitops violaceus = cone-chin
tiddler = threespine stickleback
tidepool johnny = tidepool sculpin
tierak = inconnu
tiger muskellunge = muskellunge
tiktabek = burbot
tiktalerk = inconnu
tile = tilefish
tile chameau = tilefish
tile océanique = ocean whitefish
tiles = Tilefish Family
timber crappie = white crappie
Tinca tinca = Introduction
Tinca tinca = tench
tinker = Atlantic mackerel
tinmouth = black crappie
tinmouth = white crappie
tinselfishes = Diamond Dory Family
tiny burnstickle = ninespine stickle-back
tissy = banded gunnel
tissy = rock gunnel
titaliq = burbot
tittimeg = Arctic grayling
tivaqiq = Arctic sculpin
tizareh = broad whitefish
toad sculpin = sea raven
toadfish = longhorn sculpin
toadfishes = Frogfish Family
toadfishes = Puffer Family
toados = Puffer Family
tobacco box = little skate
tobacco box = pumpkinseed
tobacco box = redbreast sunfish
tobacco pipefish = bluespotted cor-

netfish
tobaccobox = longear sunfish
tobiefish = Pacific sandfish
tobies = Puffer Family
toby = oceanic puffer
tog = tautog
togue = lake trout
tomcod = Pacific tomcod
tommy cod = kelp greenling
tommy cod = whitespotted greenling
tommycod = Atlantic tomcod
tommycod = creek chub
tongue soles = Tonguefish Family
tooth-carps = Killifish Order
toothed herring = goldeye
toothed herring = mooneye
toothful dreamer = toothy dreamer
tope = soupfin shark
tope shark = soupfin shark
topes = Hound Shark Family
topminnow = banded killifish
topminnows = Killifish Family
topminnows = Killifish Order
topwater = brook silverside
torchon mou = ragfish
torchons = Ragfish Family
toro = crevalle jack
Torpedinidae = Electric Ray Family
Torpedo californica = Pacific electric ray
Torpedo nobiliana = Atlantic torpedo
torpille du Pacifique = Pacific elec-tric ray
torpille noire = Atlantic torpedo
torpilles = Electric Ray Family
torske = cusk
touladi = lake trout
toupet décoré = decorated warbonnet
toupet élégant = mosshead warbon-net
toupet marbré = Atlantic warbonnet
Trachichthyidae = Slimehead Family
Trachinocephalus myops = snakefish
Trachipteridae = Ribbonfish Family
Trachipterus altivelus = king-of-the-salmon
Trachurus lathami = rough scad
Trachurus symmetricus = jack mack-erel
trachyptères = Ribbonfish Family
Trachyrhynchus murrayi = rough-nose grenadier
trevallies = Jack Family
Triakidae = Hound Shark Family
trichiures = Cutlassfish Family
Trichiuridae = Cutlassfish Family
Trichodon trichodon = Pacific sand-fish
trichodonte = Pacific sandfish
trichodontes = Sandfish Family
Trichodontidae = Sandfish Family
Trichogaster trichopterus = Introduction
Trichopsetta orbisulcus = sash floun-der
tricorne arctique = Arctic staghorn sculpin
tridentate lamprey = Pacific lamprey
triggerfishes = Leatherjacket Family
trigles = Searobin Family
Triglidae = Searobin Family

Triglops macellus = roughspine sculpin
Triglops murrayi = moustache sculpin
Triglops nybelini = bigeye sculpin
Triglops pingeli = ribbed sculpin
Trigonolampa miriceps = triangle-light dragon
triorné = tripletwig smoothgill
triplespines = Puffer Order
triplewart seadevil = warted seadevil
trompe = tube-snout
trompes = Tube-snout Family
trout pickerel = redfin pickerel
true bass = Temperate Bass Family
true cod = Pacific cod
true soles = soles
truite arc-en-ciel = rainbow trout
truite brune = brown trout
truite brune = Introduction
truite de mer = brook trout
truite dorée = golden trout
truite dorée = Introduction
truite fardée côtière = coastal cut-throat trout
truite fardée du flanc de l'ouest = west-slope cutthroat trout
truite grise = lake trout
truite mouchetée = brook trout
trumpet buffalo = bigmouth buffalo
trumpet fish = longspine snipefish
trumpetfishes = Stickleback Order
trunkfish = ocean sunfish
Trygonidae = Stingray Family
tube-eyes = Opah Order
tubenose = tube-snout
tubenose goby = Introduction
tubenoses = Tube-snout Family
tubesnout poacher = tubenose poacher
Tuffy minnow = fathead minnow
tullibee = Bering cisco
tullibee = lake cisco
tunnies = Mackerel Family
tunny = bluefin tuna
turbot = arrowtooth flounder
turbot = Greenland halibut
turbot = orange filefish
turbot = windowpane
turbot à nageoires tachetées = spotfin flounder
turbot de sable = windowpane
turbots = Lefteye Flounder Family
turkey-red rockfish = yelloweye rockfish
tusk = cusk
two-lined dab = rock sole
twospine stickleback = threespine stickleback
twospined stickleback = blackspotted stickleback
tyee = chinook salmon
ulvaire deux-lignes = radiated shanny
Ulvaria subbifurcata = radiated shanny
Umbra limi = central mudminnow
umbre de vase = central mudminnow
umbrellamouth gulper = pelican gulper
umbres de vase = Mudminnow